SECOND EDITION

Exploring Lifespan Development

Laura E. Berk
Illinois State University

Allyn & Bacon

Boston • Columbus • Indianapolis • New York • San Francisco • Upper Saddle River
Amsterdam • Cape Town • Dubai • London • Madrid • Milan • Munich • Paris • Montreal • Toronto
Delhi • Mexico City • Sao Paulo • Sydney • Hong Kong • Seoul • Singapore • Taipei • Tokyo

Dedication

In loving memory of my parents,
Sofie Lentschner Eisenberg and Philip Vernon Eisenberg

Editor in Chief: Jessica Mosher
Managing Editor: Tom Pauken
Supplements Editor: Sara Harris
Development Editor: Richard Wilcox
Editorial Assistants: Paige Clunie, Amelia Benner
Senior Marketing Manager: Wendy Albert
Senior Production Project Manager: Donna Simons
Manufacturing Buyer: Debbie Rossi
Cover Administrator: Joel Gendron
Interior Designer: Carol Somberg
Photo Researcher: Sarah Evertson—ImageQuest
Electronic Composition: TexTech, Inc.
Copyeditor: Margaret Pinette
References Editor: William Heckman
Proofreader: Beyond Words Proofreading

Library of Congress Cataloging-in-Publication Data
Berk, Laura E.
   Exploring lifespan development / Laura E. Berk. — 2nd ed.
      p.   cm.
   Includes bibliographical references and index.
   ISBN-13: 978-0-205-74859-4 (alk. paper)
   ISBN-10: 0-205-74859-7 (alk. paper)
   1. Developmental psychology—Textbooks.   I. Title
   BF713.B466   2010
   155—dc22
                                         2009053080

10 9 8 7 6 5 4 3   CKV   14 13 12 11 10

Allyn & Bacon
is an imprint of

PEARSON

www.pearsonhighered.com

ISBN-10: 0-205-74859-7
ISBN-13: 978-0-205-74859-4

Milestones Photo Credits
(credit sequence keyed to top-to-bottom placement of photos)

Page 212: column 1: © Ariel Skelly/Getty Images/Blend Images; column 2: © Marcus Mok/Getty Images/Asia Images; column 3: © Myrleen Ferguson Cate/PhotoEdit. **Page 213:** column 1: © Ellen B. Senisi Photography; column 2: © Geri Engberg/The Image Works; column 3: © Laura Dwight/CORBIS.

Page 286: column 1: © Don Smetzer/PhotoEdit; column 2: © John-Francis Bourke/zefa/CORBIS; column 3: © Bill Aron/PhotoEdit. **Page 287:** column 1 top: © Retna/Index Stock/photolibrary; column 1 bottom: Peter Hvizdak/The Image Works; column 2: © David Madison/Getty Images/Photographer's Choice; column 3 top: Ellen B. Senisi/The Image Works; column 3 bottom: Brand X Pictures/Jupiter Images/Getty Images.

Page 358: column 1 top: © Dennis MacDonald/PhotoEdit; column 1 bottom: © David Young-Wolff/ Getty Images/Photographer's Choice; column 3 top: Nancy R. Cohen/ Getty Images/Digital Vision; column 3 bottom: © David Young-Wolff/ Getty Images/Photographer's Choice. **Page 359:** column 1: © CP Photo/Paul Chiasson; column 2 top: Toronto Star/First Light; column 2 bottom: © David Young-Wolff/PhotoEdit; column 3 top: © Gideon Mendel/Corbis; column 3 bottom: © Thomas Downs/Lonely Planet Images.

Page 428: column 1: © Catherine Wessel/Corbis; column 2: © Kayte M. Deioma/PhotoEdit; column 3 top: © Rudy von Briel/PhotoEdit; column 3 bottom: © Steve Skjold/Alamy. **Page 429:** column 1: © Leland Bobbé/Corbis; column 2 top: © Journal Courier/Clayton Stalter/The Image Works; column 2 bottom: © Don Smelzer/Getty Images/Stone; column 3: © Ariel Skelley/Corbis.

Page 498: column 1: © Jacksonville Journal/Clayton Stalter/The Image Works; column 2 top: © Bob Daemmrich/The Image Works; column 2 bottom: © Zefa RF/Alamy; column 3 top: © moodboard/Alamy; column 3 bottom: © David Young Wolff/PhotoEdit. **Page 499:** column 1: © Jim Craigmyle/Corbis; column 2 top: © David Young-Wolff/Getty Images/Photographer's Choice; column 2 bottom: Jose Luis Pelaez, Inc./Blend Images/Getty Images; column 3 top: © Ariel Skelley/Getty Images/Blend Images; column 3 bottom: Jim Craigmyle/Corbis.

Page 560: column 1 top: © Jon Feingersh/Getty Images/Blend Images; column 1 bottom: © Golden Pixels LLC/Alamy; column 2: © Image Source/photolibrary; column 3 top: © Paul A. Souders/CORBIS; column 3 bottom: © Elyse Lewin/Getty Images/Photographer's Choice. **Page 561:** column 1 top: © Blend images RF/photolibrary; column 1 bottom: © Lee Snider/The Image Works; column 2 top: © Blend Images RF/photolibrary; column 2 bottom: © Jonathan Nourok/PhotoEdit; column 3 top: © Design Pics Inc./photolibrary; column 3 middle: © Creatas/photolibrary; column 3 bottom: © David Young-Wolff/PhotoEdit.

Page 636: column 1 top: © Choups/Alamy; column 1 bottom: © Corbis; column 2 top: © Johnny Crawford/The Image Works; column 2 bottom: AP Images/Greg Baker; column 3 top: © Jon Feingersh/Getty Images/Blend Images; column 3 bottom: © Dennis MacDonald/Alamy. **Page 637:** column 1 top: © Studio Zanello/Ken Chernus Photography/Getty Images; column 1 bottom: © Hill Street Studios/Getty Images/Blend Images; column 2 top: Jacobs Stock Photography/Getty Images/Digital Vision; column 2 bottom: © John Birdsall/The Image Works; column 3 top: Damon Higgins/Palm Beach Post/ZUMA Press; column 3 bottom: © Mike Kemp/Getty Images.

About the Author

Laura E. Berk is a distinguished professor of psychology at Illinois State University, where she has taught human development to both undergraduate and graduate students for more than three decades. She received her bachelor's degree in psychology from the University of California, Berkeley, and her master's and doctoral degrees in child development and educational psychology from the University of Chicago. She has been a visiting scholar at Cornell University, UCLA, Stanford University, and the University of South Australia.

Berk has published widely on the effects of school environments on children's development, the development of private speech, and most recently the role of make-believe play in development. Her research has been funded by the U.S. Office of Education and the National Institute of Child Health and Human Development. It has appeared in many prominent journals, including *Child Development, Developmental Psychology, Merrill-Palmer Quarterly, Journal of Abnormal Child Psychology, Development and Psychopathology,* and *Early Childhood Research Quarterly.* Her empirical studies have attracted the attention of the general public, leading to contributions to *Psychology Today* and *Scientific American.* She has also been featured on National Public Radio's *Morning Edition* and in *Parents Magazine, Wondertime,* and *Reader's Digest.*

Berk has served as a research editor for *Young Children* and a consulting editor for *Early Childhood Research Quarterly.* Currently, she is an associate editor for the *Journal of Cognitive Education and Psychology.* She is a frequent contributor to edited volumes on early childhood development, having recently authored chapters on the importance of parenting, on make-believe play and self-regulation, and on the kindergarten child. She has also written the chapter on development for *The Many Faces of Psychological Research in the Twenty-First Century* (Society for the Teaching of Psychology); the article on social development for *The Child: An Encyclopedic Companion;* the article on Vygotsky for the *Encyclopedia of Cognitive Science;* and the chapter on storytelling as a teaching strategy for *Voices of Experience: Memorable Talks from the National Institute on the Teaching of Psychology* (Association for Psychological Science).

Berk's books include *Private Speech: From Social Interaction to Self-Regulation; Scaffolding Children's Learning: Vygotsky and Early Childhood Education; Landscapes of Development: An Anthology of Readings;* and *A Mandate for Playful Learning in Preschool: Presenting the Evidence.* In addition to *Development Through the Lifespan,* she is author of the best-selling texts *Child Development* and *Infants, Children, and Adolescents,* published by Allyn and Bacon. Her book for parents and teachers is *Awakening Children's Minds: How Parents and Teachers Can Make a Difference.*

Berk is active in work for children's causes. In addition to service in her home community, she is a member of the national board of directors and chair of the central region advisory board of Jumpstart, a nonprofit organization that provides literacy intervention to thousands of low-income preschoolers across the United States, using college and university students as interveners. Berk is a fellow of the American Psychological Association, Division 7: Developmental Psychology.

Features at a Glance

Contents

CHAPTER **6**

Emotional and Social Development in Infancy and Toddlerhood   **140**

Milestones
Development in Infancy and Toddlerhood   *162*

CHAPTER **10**

Emotional and Social Development in Middle Childhood   **256**

CHAPTER **16**

Emotional and Social Development in Middle Adulthood   **418**

CHAPTER **17**

Physical and Cognitive Development in Late Adulthood   **442**

Preface for Instructors

I wrote *Exploring Lifespan Development* with the goal of retaining all the vital features of *Development Through the Lifespan* while providing students with a clear, efficient read of the most important concepts and empirical findings in the field of lifespan development. The text has been refashioned with an exceptionally strong emphasis on applications. Classic, contemporary, and cutting-edge theories and research are made accessible to students in a manageable and relevant way with a wealth of content and teaching tools designed to underscore the following current trends:

- *Diverse pathways of change are highlighted.* Investigators have reached a broad consensus that variations in biological makeup and everyday tasks lead to wide individual differences in paths of change and resulting competencies. This text pays attention to variability in development and to recent theories—ecological, sociocultural, dynamic systems, and the lifespan perspective—that attempt to explain it. Multicultural and cross-cultural findings, including international comparisons, are presented throughout the text. Biology and Environment and Cultural Influences boxes also accentuate the theme of diversity in development.

- *The complex, bidirectional relationship between biology and environment is addressed.* Accumulating evidence on development of the brain, motor skills, cognitive and language competencies, temperament and personality, and developmental problems underscores the way biological factors emerge in, are modified by, and share power with experience. Interconnections between biology and environment are revisited throughout the text narrative and in the Biology and Environment boxes.

- *A rich body of interdisciplinary research is included.* The move toward viewing thoughts, feelings, and behavior as an integrated whole, affected by a wide array of influences in biology, social context, and culture, has motivated developmental researchers to strengthen their ties with other fields of psychology and with other disciplines. Topics and findings throughout the text reflect the contributions of educational psychology, social psychology, health psychology, clinical psychology, neuropsychology, biology, pediatrics, geriatrics, sociology, anthropology, social welfare, and other fields.

- *Links among theory, research, and applications permeate each chapter.* As researchers intensify their efforts to generate findings relevant to real-life situations, I consider many social policy issues and sound theory- and research-based applications. Further applications are provided in the Applying What We Know tables, which give students concrete ways of building bridges between their learning and the real world.

- The role of active student learning is made explicit. A new **TAKE A MOMENT...** feature, built into the chapter narrative, asks students to think deeply and critically or to engage in an exercise or application as they read. Ask Yourself questions at the end of each major section promote three approaches to engaging actively with the subject matter—*Review, Apply,* and *Reflect.* The *Reflect* questions help make the study of lifespan development personally meaningful by encouraging students to take a well-reasoned stand on important issues and to relate theory and research to their own lives. In addition, highlighting of key terms within the text narrative reinforces student learning in context.

Text Philosophy

The basic approach of this book has been shaped by my own professional and personal history as a teacher, researcher, and parent. It consists of seven philosophical ingredients that I regard as essential for students to emerge from a course with a thorough understanding of lifespan development. Each theme is woven into every chapter:

1. **An understanding of major theories in the field and the strengths and shortcomings of each.** The first chapter begins by emphasizing that only knowledge of multiple theories can do justice to the richness of human development. As I take up each age period and domain of development, I present a variety of theoretical perspectives, indicate how each highlights previously overlooked aspects of development, and discuss research that evaluates it. Consideration of contrasting theories also serves as the context for an even-handed analysis of many controversial issues.

2. **A grasp of the lifespan perspective as an integrative approach to development.** I introduce the lifespan perspective as an organizing framework in the first chapter and refer to and illustrate its assumptions—development as lifelong, multidimensional, multidirectional, plastic, and embedded in multiple contexts—throughout the text. By emphasizing the lifespan perspective, I aim to help students construct an overall vision of development from conception to death.

3. **Knowledge of both the sequence of human development and the processes that underlie it.** Students are provided with a discussion of the organized sequence of development along with processes of change. An understanding of process—how complex combinations of biological and

environmental events produce development—has been the focus of most recent research. Accordingly, the text reflects this emphasis. But new information about the timetable of change has also emerged. In many ways, the very young and the old have proved to be far more competent than they were believed to be in the past. In addition, many milestones of adult development, such as finishing formal education, entering a career, getting married, having children, and retiring, have become less predictable. Current evidence on the sequence and timing of development, along with its implications for process, is presented for all periods of the lifespan.

4. **An appreciation of the impact of context and culture on human development.** A wealth of research indicates that people live in rich physical and social contexts that affect all domains of development. Throughout the book, students travel to distant parts of the world as I review a growing body of cross-cultural evidence. The text narrative also discusses many findings on socioeconomically and ethnically diverse people within the United States. Furthermore, the impact of historical time period and cohort membership receives continuous attention. In this vein, gender issues—the distinctive but continually evolving experiences, roles, and life paths of males and females—are granted substantial emphasis. Besides highlighting the effects of immediate settings, such as family, neighborhood, and school, I make a concerted effort to underscore the influence of larger social structures—societal values, laws, and government programs—on lifelong well-being.

5. **An understanding of the joint contributions of biology and environment to development.** The field recognizes more powerfully than ever before the combined roles of hereditary/constitutional and environmental factors—that these influences on development join in complex ways and cannot be separated in a simple manner. Numerous examples of how biological dispositions can be maintained as well as transformed by social contexts are presented throughout the book.

6. **A sense of the interdependency of all domains of development—physical, cognitive, emotional, and social.** Every chapter emphasizes an integrated approach to human development. I show how physical, cognitive, emotional, and social development are interwoven. Within the text narrative, students are referred to other sections of the book to deepen their grasp of relationships among various aspects of change.

7. **An appreciation of the interrelatedness of theory, research, and applications.** Throughout this book, I emphasize that theories of human development and the research stimulated by them provide the foundation for sound, effective practices with children, adolescents, and adults. The links among theory, research, and applications are reinforced by an organizational format in which theory and research are presented first, followed by practical implications. In addition, a current focus in the field—harnessing knowledge of human development to shape social policies that support human needs throughout the lifespan—is reflected in every chapter. The text addresses the current condition of children, adolescents, and adults in the United States and elsewhere in the world and shows how theory and research have combined with public interest to spark successful interventions. Many important applied topics are considered, such as family planning, infant mortality, maternal employment and child care, teenage pregnancy and parenthood, domestic violence, exercise and adult health, lifelong learning, grandparents rearing grandchildren, caring for elders with dementia, adjustment to retirement, and palliative care for the dying.

Text Organization

I have chosen a chronological organization for *Exploring Lifespan Development*. The book begins with an introductory chapter that describes the scientific history of the field, influential theories, and research strategies. It is followed by two chapters on the foundations of development. Chapter 2 combines an overview of biological and environmental contexts into a single, integrated discussion of these multifaceted influences on development. Chapter 3 is devoted to prenatal development, birth, and the newborn baby. With this foundation, students are ready to look closely at seven major age periods: infancy and toddlerhood (Chapters 4, 5, and 6), early childhood (Chapters 7 and 8), middle childhood (Chapters 9 and 10), adolescence (Chapters 11 and 12), early adulthood (Chapters 13 and 14), middle adulthood (Chapters 15 and 16), and late adulthood (Chapters 17 and 18). Topical chapters within each chronological division cover physical development, cognitive development, and emotional and social development. The book concludes with a chapter on death, dying, and bereavement (Chapter 19).

The chronological approach assists students in thoroughly understanding each age period. It also eases the task of integrating the various domains of development because each is discussed in close proximity. At the same time, a chronologically organized book requires that theories covering several age periods be presented piecemeal. This creates a challenge for students, who must link the various parts together. To assist with this task, I frequently remind students of important earlier achievements before discussing new developments, referring back to related sections with page references. Also, chapters or sections devoted to the same topic (for example, cognitive development) are similarly organized, making it easier for students to draw connections across age periods and construct an overall view of developmental change.

New Coverage in the Second Edition

Lifespan development is a fascinating and ever-changing field of study, with constantly emerging new discoveries and refinements in existing knowledge. The second edition represents this burgeoning contemporary literature, with over 1,700 new citations. Cutting-edge topics throughout the text underscore the book's major themes. Here is a sampling:

CHAPTER 1: New Lifespan Vista box on the baby-boom generation, illustrating history-graded influences (cohort effects) on the life course • Developmental cognitive neuroscience as a new area of investigation • New examples of research using systematic observation, structured interviews, ethnography, correlational research, and field experiments

CHAPTER 2: Updated Social Issues box on the pros and cons of reproductive technologies • Updated section on development of adopted children • Enhanced attention to the impact of poverty on development • Updated research on neighborhood influences on physical and mental health of children and adults • Updated section on public policies and human development, including current statistics on the condition of children, families, and the aged in the United States compared with other Western nations • Updated Lifespan Vista box on worldwide education of girls and its transforming impact on current and future generations • New examples of environmental influences on gene expression

CHAPTER 3: Updated research on fetal sensory and behavioral capacities • Updated consideration of a wide range of teratogens • Inclusion of the new designation for harmful effects of prenatal alcohol exposure—fetal alcohol spectrum disorder • New evidence on the long-term consequences of emotional stress during pregnancy • New findings on older maternal age and prenatal and birth complications • Updated discussion of preterm and low-birth-weight infants, including long-term developmental outcomes in very-low-birth-weight babies • Expanded Social Issues box on health care and other policies for parents and newborn babies, including cross-national infant mortality rates and the importance of generous parental leave

CHAPTER 4: Updated introduction to major methods of assessing brain functioning, including NIROT • New research on children adopted from Romanian orphanages, bearing on the question of whether infancy is a sensitive period of development • Updated Cultural Influences box on cultural variation in infant sleeping arrangements • Updated section on breastfeeding • Expanded and updated section on newborn imitation, including the role of mirror neurons

• New dynamic systems research on development of walking and reaching • New findings on development of infant speech perception, including infants' statistical learning capacity • New Biology and Environment box on "tuning in" to familiar speech, faces, and music during the second half of the first year, suggesting a sensitive period for culture-specific learning • Expanded and updated section on intermodal perception

CHAPTER 5: New research on deferred imitation in toddlerhood • New evidence on young infants' understanding of object permanence, including brain-wave findings • New research on development of categorization in toddlerhood, including the animate—inanimate distinction • Updated findings on quality of child care in the United States, with consequences for cognitive and language development • New evidence on the relationship between language comprehension and production in toddlers, with implications for early language progress

CHAPTER 6: Revised and updated Lifespan Vista box on parental depression and child development, with expanded treatment of the impact of paternal depression • New research on parenting and early development of emotional self-regulation • Expanded treatment of infants' developing understanding of others' emotions • New research on the self-regulatory dimension of temperament—effortful control—and consequences for children's cognitive and social competence • New findings on attachment difficulties of children adopted from deprived institutions, including neurophysiological evidence • New research on the joint contributions of infant characteristics and parental sensitivity to attachment security • Expanded section on fathers' involvement with infants, including cultural variations • Updated Social Issues box on the influence of child-care quality and long child-care hours on attachment and later development, including cross-cultural evidence • Updated section on development of self-recognition and self-awareness, with new research on cultural variations • New evidence on joint contributions of temperament and parenting to toddlers' developing capacity to delay gratification

CHAPTER 7: Updated consideration of advances in brain development in early childhood, with emphasis on the hippocampus • Updated statistics and research on childhood immunizations • New findings on the contribution of child temperament, parenting practices, and societal conditions to unintentional injury in early childhood • Updated research on development of attention, highlighting gains in inhibition • Enhanced discussion of the development of autobiographical memory, including the influence of the parent–child relationship • Updated Biology and Environment box on "mindblindness" and autism • New findings on gains in academic and social skills associated with

Montessori preschool education • Updated discussion of educational media, including effects of television and computers on cognitive and academic learning • Expanded and updated research on the diverse strategies preschoolers use to figure out word meanings

CHAPTER 8: New evidence on the contribution of attachment to parent–child narratives about emotions and, thus, to emotional understanding • Updated consideration of emotional self-regulation in early childhood • Enhanced Cultural Influences box on ethnic differences in the consequences of physical punishment • New evidence on the importance of social skills and friendships in fostering children's successful transition to school • Updated discussion of gender schema theory, noting individual differences among children in gender-schematic processing • New findings on the harmful impact of parental psychological control on children's adjustment • Expanded consideration of ethnic variations in child-rearing beliefs and practices • Updated consideration of consequences of child maltreatment, including new evidence on central nervous system damage • Research on Healthy Families America, an early intervention program aimed at reducing child maltreatment

CHAPTER 9: Revised and updated section on overweight and obesity, including rapid increase in developing nations • Updated statistics on physical activity and fitness among U.S. school-age children • New Social Issues box on physical, cognitive, and social benefits of school recess • Revised and updated Biology and Environment box on children with attention-deficit hyperactivity disorder • Expanded treatment of cultural influences on mathematical development, with special attention to Asian nations • Updated Social Issues box on high-stakes testing • Updated research on bilingual development

CHAPTER 10: Enhanced attention to cultural variations in self-concept, with special attention to Asian versus U.S. comparisons • New research on the impact of gender-stereotyped expectations on school-age children's self-esteem • Updated research on parenting practices and children's achievement-related attributions, including the influence of cultural values on likelihood of developing learned helplessness • Updated evidence on school-age children's grasp of individual rights • Updated findings on development of gender identity in middle childhood, with implications for emotional adjustment • Expanded attention to the role of fathers in children's development, with special attention to blended families and dual-career families • New evidence on the impact of self-care and after-school programs on school-age children's adjustment

CHAPTER 11: Updated findings on adolescent physical activity and sports participation, including gender differences

and consequences for development • Updated research on adolescent brain development • New findings on implications of pubertal timing for psychological adjustment in adolescence and adulthood, including ethnic variations • Updated evidence on factors that contribute to anorexia nervosa and treatment outcomes • Discussion of the Internet as a hazardous "sex educator" • New evidence on the long-term consequences of adolescent parenthood and on prevention and intervention strategies • New Lifespan Vista box on intergenerational continuity in adolescent parenthood • New findings on the influence of schooling on development of propositional thought • Expanded and updated research on adolescent decision making • New research on the impact of school transitions on adolescent adjustment • New research on ethnic variations in peer support for school achievement

CHAPTER 12: New research on identity statuses, cognitive styles, and adjustment • Updated Cultural Influences box on identity development among ethnic minority youths • Expanded evaluation of Kohlberg's stages, including issues raised by a pragmatic approach to moral development • Enhanced consideration of factors that promote moral self-relevance, including a just and civil school climate • Updated section on parenting and adolescent autonomy • Inclusion of the impact of acculturative stress on adjustment of ethnic minority teenagers • New findings on Internet friendships and adjustment • Updated section on dating • New findings on adolescent suicide, including high suicide rates among Native-American youths • Evaluations of zero tolerance policies in schools, including their failure to reduce youth misconduct

CHAPTER 13: Updated discussion of theories of biological aging • New Biology and Environment box on telomere length as a marker of the impact of life circumstances on biological aging • Updated evidence on causes and consequences of overweight and obesity in adulthood • New findings on the contribution of physical activity to psychological well-being and cognitive functioning • Updated discussion of SES variations in adult health • Consideration of continued development of the cerebral cortex in early adulthood, including experience-dependent brain growth • Updated findings on factors that foster development of epistemic cognition • New evidence on the role of parents and teachers in vocational choice

CHAPTER 14: Expanded section on emerging adulthood, including new evidence on identity development, cultural influences, and cultural variations • New Cultural Influences box addressing the controversy over whether emerging adulthood really is a distinct period of development • Enhanced consideration of cultural influences on the experience of love • Updated Social Issues box on partner abuse • Updated research on factors contributing to relationship satisfaction among heterosexual and gay and lesbian couples • New findings on factors influencing successful transition to parenthood • Updated evidence on life satisfaction of never-married single people and childless couples • New findings on cohabitation and durability of relationships • New evidence on career development and workplace challenges faced by women and ethnic minority young adults

CHAPTER 15: Updated evidence on risks of hormone therapy to reduce physical discomforts of menopause • New findings on women's psychological reactions to menopause • Updated consideration of lifestyle changes that can reduce cancer incidence and deaths • New findings on prevalence of osteoporosis, including ethnic variations • Updated discussion of the contribution of processing speed to diverse cognitive changes in older adults • Updated consideration of memory changes during midlife • New research on returning students, with special attention to factors influencing women's adjustment • Revised and updated Biology and Environment box on anti-aging effects of dietary calorie restriction, including physiological processes that mediate its impact on longevity

CHAPTER 16: Inclusion of the Midlife Development in the United States (MIDUS) survey findings on emotional and social development • Expanded discussion of the midlife experience of the baby-boom generation • Enhanced attention to factors contributing to generativity, including the role of fatherhood for men • New research on "turning points" at midlife • Updated Biology and Environment box on contributions to midlife psychological well-being • New findings on gender identity, including androgyny among middle-aged baby boomers • Expanded discussion of factors contributing to involved grandparenting and satisfaction with the grandparent role • Updated Lifespan Vista box on grandparents rearing grandchildren—the "skipped generation" family • New research on middle-aged adults' relationships with their aging parents, including cultural variations • Updated findings on caring for aging parents • New evidence on challenges faced by women in advancing to high-level managerial positions in the workplace

CHAPTER 17: Inclusion of international comparisons in healthy life expectancy • New research on brain development, including neurological changes that enable elders to compensate for declines in central nervous system function-

ing • Updated findings on risk and protective factors associated with various aspects of physical aging • Expanded and updated discussion of stereotypes of aging and their impact on elders' well-being • New evidence on the impact of nutrition and exercise on health status in late adulthood • New survey findings on sexual activity in late adulthood • Updated evidence on genetic and environmental contributions to arthritis • New evidence on genetic and environmental risks for Alzheimer's and on protective factors • Updated Social Issues box on interventions for caregivers of elders with dementia • Expanded consideration of benefits of assisted living • Enhanced attention to elders' use of selective optimization with compensation in adapting to cognitive changes • Updated research on everyday problem solving in late adulthood • New findings on the impact of cognitive training on older adults' long-term health and mental functioning

CHAPTER 18: New Lifespan Vista box on the Third Age as a new phase of late adulthood spanning the years 65 to 79—a time of new goal setting and high life satisfaction • New research on late-life personality development, with emphasis on elders' resilience • Updated findings on the interrelationship between physical and mental health in late adulthood • Expanded consideration of the role of social support in elders' psychological well-being • Enhanced discussion of the importance of aging in place, with special attention to high-quality assisted living and THE GREEN HOUSE® nursing home model • Expanded attention to cultural variations in elders' social networks, including implications for psychological well-being • New evidence on elders' relationships with adult children • Updated research on elder abuse • Enhanced discussion of variations in the retirement process • New evidence on elders' contribution to society through volunteering • Discussion of factors that contribute to optimal aging

CHAPTER 19: New evidence on factors affecting death anxiety, including religiosity and gender • New section on the experience of dying in nursing homes • Updated statistics on prevalence of hospice in the United States, along with information on its affordability • Updated cross-national evidence on religiosity and attitudes toward voluntary active euthanasia • Revised and updated discussion of assisted suicide, including attitudes of U.S. doctors • New research supporting the dual-process model of coping with loss • Updated evidence on the course of bereavement after death of a spouse

Pedagogical Features

Maintaining a highly accessible writing style—one that is lucid and engaging without being simplistic—continues to be one of my major goals. I frequently converse with students, encouraging them to relate what they read to their own lives. In doing so, I hope to make the study of human development involving and pleasurable.

Stories and Vignettes About Real People. To help students construct a clear image of development and to enliven the text narrative, each chronological age division is unified by case examples woven throughout that set of chapters. For example, the middle childhood section highlights the experiences and concerns of 10-year-old Joey; 8-year-old Lizzie; their divorced parents, Rena and Drake; and their classmates. In the chapters on late adulthood, students get to know Walt and Ruth, a vibrant retired couple, along with Walt's older brother Dick and his wife Goldie and Ruth's sister Ida, a victim of Alzheimer's disease. Besides a set of main characters who bring unity to each age period, many additional vignettes offer vivid examples of development and diversity among children, adolescents, and adults.

Chapter Introductions and End-of-Chapter Summaries. To provide a helpful preview, I include an outline and overview of chapter content in each chapter introduction. Concise end-of-chapter summaries, organized according to the major divisions of each chapter and highlighting important terms, remind students of key points in the text discussion. Review questions are included in the summaries to encourage active study.

Ask Yourself Questions. Active engagement with the subject matter is also supported by study questions at the end of each major section. Three types of questions prompt students to think about human development in diverse ways: *Review* questions help students recall and comprehend information they have just read; *Apply* questions encourage the application of knowledge to controversial issues and problems faced by children, adolescents, adults, and professionals who work with them; and *Reflect* questions help make the study of human development personally meaningful by asking students to reflect on their own development and life experiences. Each question is answered on the text's MyDevelopmentLab website.

Take a Moment... This new active-learning feature, built into the text narrative, asks students to "take a moment" to think about an important point, integrate information on human development, or engage in an exercise or an application to clarify a challenging concept. ***TAKE A MOMENT...*** highlights and reinforces the text's strength in conversing with and actively engaging the student in learning and in inspiring critical thinking.

Four types of thematic boxes accentuate the philosophical themes of this book:

A Lifespan Vista boxes are devoted to topics that have long-term implications for development or involve intergenerational issues. Examples include: *The Baby Boomers Reshape the Life Course; Like Parent, Like Child: Intergenerational Continuity in Adolescent Parenthood; Childhood Attachment Patterns and Adult Romantic Relationships;* and *The New Old Age.*

Social Issues boxes discuss the impact of social conditions on children, adolescents, and adults and emphasize the need for sensitive social policies to ensure their well-being—for example, *School Recess—A Time to Play, a Time to Learn; High-Stakes Testing; Gay, Lesbian, and Bisexual Youths: Coming Out to Oneself and Others; Masculinity at Work: Men Who Choose Nontraditional Careers;* and *Interventions for Caregivers of Elders with Dementia.*

Cultural Influences boxes have been expanded and updated to deepen attention to culture threaded throughout the text. They highlight both cross-cultural and multicultural variations in human development—for example, *Immigrant Youths: Amazing Adaptation; Cultural Variation in Infant Sleeping Arrangements; Children in Village and Tribal Cultures Observe and Participate in Adult Work; Is Emerging Adulthood Really a Distinct Period of Development?;* and *Cultural Variations in Mourning Behavior.*

Biology and Environment boxes highlight the growing attention to the complex, bidirectional relationship between biology and environment during development. Examples include *"Tuning In" to Familiar Speech, Faces, and Music: A Sensitive Period for Culture-Specific Learning; "Mindblindness" and Autism; Bullies and Their Victims; Telomere Length: A New Marker of the Impact of Life Circumstances on Biological Aging; Anti-Aging Effects of Dietary Calorie Restriction;* and *What Factors Promote Psychological Well-Being in Midlife?*

Applying What We Know Tables. To accentuate the link between theory and research and applications, Applying What We Know tables provide easily accessible practical advice on the importance of caring for oneself and others throughout the lifespan. The tables also speak directly to students as parents or future parents and to those pursuing child- and family-related careers or areas of study, such as teaching, health care, counseling, or social work. They include: *Do's and Don'ts of a Healthy Pregnancy, Signs of Developmentally Appropriate Infant and Toddler Child Care, Using Positive Discipline, Helping Children Adjust to Their Parents' Divorce, Communicating with Adolescents About Sexual Issues, Resources That Foster Resilience in Emerging Adulthood, Relieving the Stress of Caring for an Aging Parent,* and *Fostering Adaptation to Widowhood in Late Adulthood.*

Milestones Tables. A Milestones table appears at the end of each age division of the text. These tables summarize major physical, cognitive, language, emotional, and social attainments, providing a convenient aid for reviewing the chronology of lifespan development.

Enhanced Art and Photo Program. A revised art style presents concepts and research findings with clarity and attractiveness, thereby greatly aiding student understanding and retention. Each photo has been carefully selected to portray human development and to represent the diversity of people in the United States and around the world.

In-Text Key Terms with Definitions, End-of-Chapter Term List, and End-of-Book Glossary. Mastery of terms that make up the central vocabulary of the field is promoted through in-text highlighting of key terms and concept definitions, which encourages students to review the terminology of the field in greater depth by rereading related information. Key terms also appear in an end-of-chapter page-referenced list of important terms and concepts and an end-of-book page-referenced glossary.

Acknowledgments

The dedicated contributions of many individuals helped make this book a reality. An impressive cast of reviewers provided many helpful suggestions, constructive criticisms, and enthusiasm for the organization and content of the text. I am grateful to each one of them.

Reviewers for the Second Edition

Cheryl Anagnopoulos, Black Hills State University
Toni Bisconti, University of Akron
Tracie Blumentritt, University of Wisconsin–La Crosse
Lou de la Cruz, Sheridan Institute
Karen Fingerman, Purdue University
Beth Fauth, Utah State University
Bert Hayslip, University of North Texas
Bob Heller, Athabasca University
Dale Lund, California State University, San Bernardino
David Mitchell, Kennesaw State University
Julie Patrick, West Virginia University
Aurora Sherman, Oregon State University
Carey Sherman, University of Michigan
David Shwalb, Southeastern Louisiana University
Jacqui Smith, University of Michigan
Bruce Thompson, University of Southern Maine
Laura Thompson, New Mexico State University
Paul Wink, Wellesley College

Reviewers for the First Edition

Gerald Adams, University of Guelph
Jackie Adamson, S.D. School of Mines and Technology
Cheryl Anagnopoulos, Black Hills State University
Sherry Beaumont, University of Northern British Columbia
Kimberly Blair, University of Pittsburgh
Tracie L. Blumentritt, University of Wisconsin–La Crosse
Lanthan Camblin, University of Cincinnati
Byron Egeland, University of Minnesota
Karen Fingerman, Purdue University
Laurie Gottlieb, McGill University
Dan Grangaard, Austin Community College
Marlene Groomes, Miami Dade College
Laura Gruntmeir, Redlands Community College
Deb Hollister, Valencia Community College
Hui-Chin Hsu, University of Georgia
Marita Kloseck, University of Western Ontario
Karen Kopera-Frye, University of Nevada, Reno
Valerie Kuhlmeier, Queens University
Deanna Kuhn, Teachers College, Columbia University
Dale Lund, University of Utah
Ashley Maynard, University of Hawaii
Kate McLean, University of Toronto at Mississauga
Carol Miller, Anne Arundel Community College
Ulrich Mueller, University of Victoria
Marion Perlmutter, University of Michigan
Dolores Pushkar, Concordia University
David Shwalb, Southeastern Louisiana University

Judi Smetana, University of Rochester
JoNell Strough, West Virginia University
Mojisola Tiamiyu, University of Toledo
Ruth Tincoff, Harvard University
Laura Thompson, New Mexico State University

An outstanding editorial staff in my home community contributed greatly to the entire project. Sara Harris, Supplements Editor, coordinated the preparation of the teaching ancillaries and wrote major sections of the Instructor's Resource Manual, bringing to these tasks great depth of knowledge, impressive writing skill, enthusiasm, and imagination. Claire Christensen, Editorial Assistant, spent countless hours searching, gathering, and organizing scholarly literature; writing portions of the Study Guide; designing highly creative MyDevelopmentLab simulations; and contributing to the Explorations in Lifespan Development video segments and video guide. With Claire's departure for doctoral study, Amelia Benner capably assisted with completion of these tasks.

I have been fortunate to collaborate with a highly effective editorial team at Pearson Education. It has been a great pleasure to work once again with Tom Pauken, Managing Editor, who oversaw the preparation of the third edition of *Development Through the Lifespan* and who returned to edit both its fifth edition and this second edition of *Exploring Lifespan Development*. His careful review of manuscript, keen organizational skills, responsive day-to-day communication, insightful suggestions, astute problem solving, interest in the subject matter, and thoughtfulness have greatly enhanced the quality of the text and made its preparation especially enjoyable and rewarding. Judy Ashkenaz and Pam Barter, Development Editors, carefully reviewed and commented on each chapter, helping to ensure that every thought and concept would be clearly expressed and well-developed. My appreciation, also, to Jessica Mosher, Editor in Chief of Psychology, for reorganizing the management of my projects to enable the focused work that is vital for precise, inspired writing and timely manuscript preparation.

The supplements package benefited from the talents and diligence of several other individuals. Kimberly Michaud prepared a superb Test Bank, and Heather Heinrich authored the excellent MyDevelopmentLab assessments. Diana Murphy designed and wrote a highly attractive PowerPoint presentation, and Judy Ashkenaz authored the informative biographies of major figures in the field and Careers in Lifespan Development, which appear in MyDevelopmentLab. Maria Henneberry and Phil Vandiver of Contemporary Visuals in Bloomington, IL, prepared an extraordinarily artistic and inspiring set of new video segments covering diverse topics in lifespan development.

Donna Simons, Senior Production Project Manager, coordinated the complex production tasks that resulted in an exquisitely beautiful second edition. I am grateful for her keen aesthetic sense, attention to detail, flexibility, efficiency, and thoughtfulness. I thank Sarah Evertson for obtaining the exceptional photographs that so aptly illustrate the text narrative. I am also grateful for Susan Messer's fine contributions to the photo specifications and captions. Margaret Pinette, Bill Heckman, and Beyond Words Proofreading provided outstanding copyediting and proofreading.

Wendy Albert, Executive Marketing Manager, prepared the beautiful print ads and informative e-mails to the field about *Exploring Lifespan Development,* Second Edition. She has also ensured that accurate and clear information reached Pearson Education's sales force and that the needs of prospective and current adopters were met.

A final word of gratitude goes to my family, whose love, patience, and understanding have enabled me to be wife, mother, teacher, researcher, and text author at the same time. My sons, David and Peter, grew up with my texts, passing from childhood to adolescence and then to adulthood as successive editions were written. David has a special connection with the books' subject matter as an elementary school teacher, and Peter is now an experienced attorney and recently married to his vivacious, talented, and caring Melissa. All three continue to enrich my understanding through reflections on events and progress in their own lives. My husband, Ken, willingly made room for yet another time-consuming endeavor in our life together and communicated his belief in its importance in a great many unspoken, caring ways.

—Laura E. Berk

Supplementary Materials

Instructor Supplements

A variety of teaching tools are available to assist instructors in organizing lectures, planning demonstrations and examinations, and ensuring student comprehension.

- **MyDevelopmentLab.** This interactive and instructive multimedia resource can be used as a supplement to a classroom course or to completely administer an online course. Prepared in collaboration with Laura Berk, MyDevelopmentLab includes a variety of assessments that enable continuous evaluation of students' learning. Extensive video footage, multimedia simulations, biographies of major figures in the field, and interactive activities that are unique to *Exploring Lifespan Development* are also included. A new feature, "Careers in Lifespan Development," explains how studying human development is essential for a wide range of career paths. The power of MyDevelopmentLab lies in its design as an all-inclusive teaching and learning tool. For a sampling of its rich content, contact your Pearson representative or visit *www.mydevelopmentlab.com.*

- **Instructor's Resource Manual (IRM).** This thoroughly revised IRM can be used by first-time or experienced instructors to enrich classroom experiences. Each chapter includes a Chapter-at-a-Glance grid, Brief Chapter Summary, Learning Objectives, detailed Lecture Outline, Lecture Enhancements, Learning Activities, Ask Yourself questions with answers, Suggested Readings, a list of transparencies, PowerPoint Presentation, and Media Materials list.

- **Test Bank.** The Test Bank contains over 1,500 multiple-choice questions, each of which is page-referenced to chapter content and classified by type (factual, applied, or conceptual). Each chapter also includes a selection of essay questions and sample answers.

- **Computerized Test Bank.** This computerized version of the Test Bank, in easy-to-use MyTest format, lets you prepare tests for printing as well as for network and online testing. It has full editing capability. Test items are also available in CourseCompass, Blackboard, and WebCT formats.

- **PowerPoint Presentation.** The PowerPoint presentation contains illustrations and outlines of key topics for each chapter of the text.

- **"Explorations in Lifespan Development" DVD and Guide.** This new DVD is over three hours in length and contains more than 50 four- to ten-minute narrated segments, illustrating the many theories, concepts, and milestones of human development. New additions include Reproductive Technology, High-Quality Child Care, Civic Engagement in Early Adulthood, Transition to Parenthood, Caring for an Elder with Alzheimer's Disease, Late-Life Creativity, and Hospice. "Explorations in Lifespan Development" DVD and DVD Guide are available to instructors who adopt the text and to students as a free supplement when packaged with the text. The DVD Guide helps students use the DVD in conjunction with the textbook, deepening their understanding and applying what they have learned to everyday life.

Student Supplements

Beyond the study aids found in the textbook, Pearson offers a number of supplements for students:

- **MyDevelopmentLab.** See "Instructor Supplements" above.

- **Study Guide with Practice Tests.** This helpful study guide offers Chapter Summaries, Learning Objectives, Study Questions, Suggested Readings, Crossword Puzzles for mastering important terms, and two multiple-choice Practice Tests per chapter.

- **Milestones Study Cards.** These colorfully illustrated study cards outline key developmental attainments. They assist students in integrating the various domains of development and constructing a vision of the whole developing person.

A Personal Note to Students

My more than 30 years of teaching human development have brought me in contact with thousands of students like you—students with diverse college majors, future goals, interests, and needs. Some are affiliated with my own department, psychology, but many come from other related fields—education, sociology, anthropology, family studies, social service, nursing, and biology, to name just a few. Each semester, my students' aspirations have proved to be as varied as their fields of study. Many look toward careers in applied work—counseling, caregiving, nursing, social work, school psychology, and program administration. Some plan to teach, and a few want to do research. And almost all arrive with a deep curiosity about how they themselves developed into the complex adults they are today.

My goal in preparing this second edition of *Exploring Lifespan Development* is to provide students with a clear, efficient read of the most important concepts and empirical findings in the field, while also offering a wide variety of research-based practical applications. To achieve these objectives, I have grounded this book in a carefully selected body of classic and current theory and research. In addition, the text highlights the lifespan perspective on development and the interacting contributions of biology and environment to the developing person. It also illustrates commonalities and differences among ethnic groups and cultures and discusses the broader social contexts in which we develop. A unique pedagogical program will assist you in mastering information, integrating various aspects of development, critically examining controversial issues, applying what you have learned, and relating the information to your own life.

I hope that learning about human development will be as rewarding for you as I have found it over the years. I would like to know what you think about this book. I welcome your comments; please feel free to send them to me at Department of Psychology, Box 4620, Illinois State University, Normal, IL 61790, or in care of the publisher, who will forward them to me.

—Laura E. Berk

Legend for Photos Accompanying Sofie's Story   Sofie's story is told in Chapters 1 and 19, from her birth to her death. The photos that appear at the beginning of Chapter 1 follow her through her lifespan and include family members of two succeeding generations.

Page 1
1. Sophie, age 18, at her high school graduation in 1926.
2. Sofie as a baby, with her mother in 1908.
3. Sofie, age 6, with her brother, age 8, in 1914.
4. Sofie's German passport.
5. Sofie, age 60, and daughter Laura on Laura's wedding day in 1968.
6. Sofie and Phil in 1968, less than two years before Sofie died.
7. Sofie's grandsons, David and Peter, ages 5 and 2, children of Laura and Ken.
8. Laura, Ken, and sons Peter and David, ages 10 and 13, on the occasion of David's Bar Mitzvah in 1985.
9. Ken and sons David and Peter as young adults, in 2005.
10. Peter and Melissa on their wedding day in 2007.

Page 2
Top: Sofie, age 61, and her first grandchild, Ellen, in October 1969, less than three months before Sofie died.
Bottom: Sofie and Phil in their midthirties, during World War II, when they became engaged.

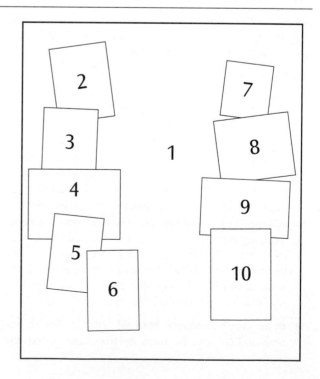

History, Theory, and Research Strategies

PHOTOS COURTESY OF LAURA E. BERK

This photo essay chronicles the life course and family legacy of Sofie Lentschner. It begins in 1908 with Sofie's infancy and concludes in 2007, 37 years after Sofie's death, with the marriage of her young adult grandson, Peter, to Melissa. For a description of each photo, see the legend on page xxiv.

1

Sofie Lentschner was born in 1908, the second child of Jewish parents who made their home in Leipzig, Germany, a city of thriving commerce and cultural vitality. Her father was a successful businessman and community leader, her mother a socialite well-known for her charm, beauty, and hospitality. As a baby, Sofie displayed the determination and persistence that would be sustained throughout her life. She sat for long periods inspecting small objects with her eyes and hands. As soon as Sofie could crawl, she steadfastly pulled herself up to finger the keys of the piano in the parlor and marveled at the tinkling sounds.

COURTESY OF LAURA E. BERK

By the time Sofie entered elementary school, she was an introspective child, often ill at ease at the festive parties that girls of her family's social standing were expected to attend. She immersed herself in her schoolwork, especially in mastering foreign languages. Twice a week, she took piano lessons from the finest teacher in Leipzig. By the time Sofie graduated from high school, she spoke English and French fluently and had become an accomplished pianist. Whereas most German girls of her time married by age 20, Sofie postponed serious courtship in favor of entering the university.

Sofie wanted marriage as well as education, but her plans were thwarted by the political turbulence of her times. When Hitler rose to power in the early 1930s, Sofie's father, fearing for the safety of his wife and children, moved the

COURTESY OF LAURA E. BERK

family to Belgium. Conditions for Jews in Europe quickly worsened. The Nazis plundered Sofie's family home and confiscated her father's business. By the end of the 1930s, Sofie had lost contact with all but a handful of her aunts, uncles, cousins, and childhood friends, many of whom (she later learned) were herded into cattle cars and transported to Nazi death camps. In 1939, as anti-Jewish laws and atrocities intensified, Sofie's family fled to the United States.

As Sofie turned 30, her parents, convinced that she would never marry and would need a career for financial security, agreed to support her return to school. Sofie earned two master's degrees, one in music and the other in librarianship. Then, on a blind date, she met Philip, a U.S. army officer. Philip's calm, gentle nature complemented Sofie's intensity and worldliness. Within six months they married. During the next four years, two daughters and a son were born. Soon Sofie's father became ill, his health shattered by the strain of uprooting his family and losing his home and business. After months of being bedridden, he died of heart failure.

When World War II ended, Philip left the army and opened a small men's clothing store. Sofie divided her time between caring for the children and helping Philip in the store. Now in her forties, she was a devoted mother, but few women her age were still rearing young children. As Philip struggled with the business, he spent longer hours at work, and Sofie often felt lonely. She rarely touched the piano, which brought back painful memories of youthful life plans shattered by war. Sofie's sense of isolation and lack of fulfillment frequently left her short-tempered. Late at night, she and Philip could be heard arguing.

As Sofie's children grew older, she returned to school again, this time to earn a teaching credential. Finally, at age 50, she launched a career. For the next decade, she taught German and French to high school students and English to newly arrived immigrants. Besides easing her family's financial difficulties, she felt a gratifying sense of accomplishment and creativity. These years were among the most energetic and satisfying of Sofie's life. She had an unending enthusiasm for teaching—for transmitting her facility with language, her firsthand knowledge of the consequences of hatred and oppression, and her practical understanding of how to adapt to life in a new land. She watched her children, whose young lives were free of the trauma of war, adopt many of her values and commitments and begin their marital and vocational lives at the expected time.

Sofie approached age 60 with an optimistic outlook. Released from the financial burden of paying for their children's college education, she and Philip looked forward to greater leisure. Their affection and respect for each other deepened. Once again, Sofie began to play the piano. But this period of contentment was short-lived.

One morning, Sofie felt a hard lump under her arm. Several days later, her doctor diagnosed cancer. Sofie's spirited disposition and capacity to adapt to radical life changes helped her meet the illness head on, defining it as an enemy to be fought and overcome. As a result, she lived five more years. Despite the exhaustion of chemotherapy, Sofie maintained a full schedule of teaching duties and continued to visit and run errands for her elderly mother. But as she weakened physically, she no longer had the stamina to meet her classes. Bedridden for the last few weeks, she slipped quietly into death with Philip at her side. The funeral chapel overflowed with hundreds of Sofie's students. She had granted each a memorable image of a woman of courage and caring.

One of Sofie's three children, Laura, is the author of this book. Married a year before Sofie died, Laura and her husband, Ken, often think of Sofie's message, spoken privately to them on the eve of their wedding day: "I learned from my own life and marriage that you must build a life together but also a life apart. You must grant each other the time, space, and support to forge your own identities, your own ways of expressing yourselves and giving to others. The most important ingredient of your relationship must be respect."

Laura and Ken settled in a small midwestern city, near Illinois State University, where they have served on the faculty for many years—Laura in the Department of Psychology, Ken in the Department of Mathematics. They have two sons, David and Peter, who carry Sofie's legacy forward. David shares his grandmother's penchant for teaching; he is a second-grade teacher. Peter, a lawyer, shares his grandmother's love of music, and his wife Melissa—much like Sofie—is both a talented linguist and a musician.

Sofie's story raises a wealth of fascinating issues about human life histories:

- What determines the features that Sofie shares with others and those that make her unique—in physical characteristics, mental capacities, interests, and behaviors?
- What led Sofie to retain the same persistent, determined disposition throughout her life but to change in other essential ways?
- How do historical and cultural conditions—for Sofie, the persecution that destroyed her childhood home, caused the death of family members and friends, and led her family to flee to the United States—affect well-being throughout life?
- How does the timing of events—for example, Sofie's early exposure to foreign languages and her delayed entry into marriage, parenthood, and career—affect development?

- What factors—both personal and environmental—led Sofie to die sooner than expected?

These are central questions addressed by **developmental science**, a field of study devoted to understanding constancy and change throughout the lifespan (Lerner, 2006). Great diversity characterizes the interests and concerns of investigators who study development. But all share a single goal: to identify those factors that influence consistencies and transformations in people from conception to death.

A Scientific, Applied, and Interdisciplinary Field

The questions just listed are not merely of scientific interest. Each has *applied*, or practical, importance as well. Research about development has also been stimulated by social pressures to improve people's lives. For example, the beginning of public education in the early twentieth century led to a demand for knowledge about what and how to teach children of different ages. The interest of the medical profession in improving people's health required an understanding of physical development, nutrition, and disease. The social service profession's desire to treat emotional problems and to help people adjust to major life events required information about personality and social development. And parents have continually sought expert advice about child-rearing practices and experiences that would promote their children's well-being.

Our large storehouse of information about development is *interdisciplinary*. It has grown through the combined efforts of people from many fields of study. Because of the need for solutions to everyday problems at all ages, researchers from psychology, sociology, anthropology, biology, and neuroscience have joined forces in research with professionals from education, family studies, medicine, public health, and social service, to name just a few. Together, they have created the field as it exists today—a body of knowledge that is not just scientifically important but also relevant and useful.

Basic Issues

Speculations about how people grow and change have existed for centuries. As they combined with research, they inspired the construction of *theories* of development. A **theory** is an orderly, integrated set of statements that describes, explains, and predicts behavior. For example, a good theory of infant–caregiver attachment would (1) *describe* the behaviors of babies of 6 to 8 months of age as they seek the affection and comfort of a familiar adult, (2) *explain* how and why infants develop this strong desire to bond with a caregiver, and (3) *predict* the consequences of this emotional bond for future relationships.

Theories are vital tools for two reasons. First, they provide organizing frameworks for our observations of people, *guiding and giving meaning* to what we see. Second, theories that are verified by research provide a sound basis for practical action. Once a theory helps us *understand* development, we are in a much better position to know *how to improve* the welfare and treatment of children and adults.

As we will see, theories are influenced by the cultural values and belief systems of their times. But theories differ from mere opinion or belief: A theory's continued existence depends on *scientific verification*. Every theory must be tested using a fair set of research procedures agreed on by the scientific community, and findings must endure, or be replicated, over time.

The field of developmental science contains many theories about what people are like and how they change. Humans are complex beings; they change physically, mentally, emotionally, and socially. And investigators do not always agree on the meaning of what they see. But the existence of many theories helps advance knowledge as researchers try to support, contradict, and integrate these different points of view.

This chapter introduces you to major theories of human development and research strategies used to test them. Although there are many theories, we can easily organize them by looking at the stand they take on three basic issues: (1) Is the course of development continuous or discontinuous? (2) Does one course of development characterize all people, or are there many possible courses? (3) Are genetic or environmental factors more important in influencing development?

Continuous or Discontinuous Development?

How can we best describe the differences in capacities among infants, children, adolescents, and adults? As Figure 1.1 illustrates, major theories recognize two possibilities.

One view holds that infants and preschoolers respond to the world in much the same way as adults do. The difference between the immature and mature being is simply one of *amount or complexity*. For example, when Sofie was a baby, her perception of a piano melody, memory for past events, and ability to categorize objects may have been much like our own. Perhaps her only limitation was that she could not perform these skills with as much information and precision as we can. If this is so, then changes in her thinking must be **continuous**—a process of gradually augmenting the same types of skills that were there to begin with.

According to a second view, infants and children have *unique ways of thinking, feeling, and behaving,* ones quite different from adults'. If so, then development is **discontinuous**—a process in which new ways of understanding and responding to the world emerge at specific times. From this perspective, Sofie could not yet perceive, remember, and categorize experiences as a mature person can. Rather, she moved through a series of developmental steps, each of which has unique features, until she reached the highest level of functioning.

Theories that accept the discontinuous perspective regard development as taking place in **stages**—*qualitative* changes in thinking, feeling, and behaving that characterize specific periods of development. In stage theories, development is like climbing a staircase, with each step corresponding to a more mature, reorganized way of functioning. The stage concept also assumes that people undergo periods of rapid transformation as they step up from one stage to the next. In other words, change is fairly sudden rather than gradual and ongoing.

One Course of Development or Many?

Stage theorists assume that people everywhere follow the same sequence of development. Yet children and adults live in distinct **contexts**—unique combinations of personal and environmental circumstances that can result in different paths of change. For

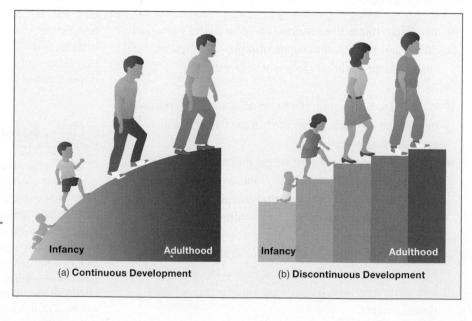

■ **FIGURE 1.1** ■ **Is development continuous or discontinuous?** (a) Some theorists believe that development is a smooth, continuous process. Individuals gradually add more of the same types of skills. (b) Other theorists think that development takes place in discontinuous stages. People change rapidly as they step up to a new level and then change very little for a while. With each new step, the person interprets and responds to the world in a qualitatively different way.

Infancy   **Adulthood**

(a) Continuous Development

Infancy   **Adulthood**

(b) Discontinuous Development

example, a shy individual who fears social encounters develops in very different contexts from those of an outgoing agemate who readily seeks out other people (Kagan & Fox, 2006). Children and adults in non-Western village societies have experiences that differ sharply from those of people in large Western cities, which result in markedly different intellectual capacities, social skills, and feelings about the self and others (Shweder et al., 2006).

As you will see, contemporary theorists regard the contexts that shape development as many-layered and complex. On the personal side, they include heredity and biological makeup. On the environmental side, they include home, school, and neighborhood as well as circumstances more remote from everyday life—community resources, societal values, and historical time period. Finally, researchers have become increasingly conscious of cultural diversity in development.

Relative Influence of Nature and Nurture?

In addition to describing the course of human development, each theory takes a stand on a major question about its underlying causes: Are genetic or environmental factors more important? This is the age-old **nature–nurture controversy.** By *nature,* we mean inborn biological givens—the hereditary information we receive from our parents at the moment of conception. By *nurture,* we mean the complex forces of the physical and social world that influence our biological makeup and psychological experiences before and after birth.

Although all theories grant at least some role to both nature and nurture, they vary in emphasis. A theory's position affects how it explains individual differences. Theorists who emphasize *stability*—that individuals who are high or low in a characteristic (such as verbal ability, anxiety, or sociability) will remain so at later ages—typically stress the importance of *heredity.* If they regard environment as important, they usually point to *early experiences* as establishing a lifelong pattern of behavior. Powerful negative events in the first few years, they argue, cannot be fully overcome by later, more positive ones (Bowlby, 1980; Johnson, 2000; Sroufe, 2005). Other theorists, taking a more optimistic view, emphasize *plasticity*—that *change* is possible and even likely if new experiences support it (Greenspan & Shanker, 2004; Lester, Masten, & McEwen, 2006).

The Lifespan Perspective: A Balanced Point of View

So far, we have discussed basic issues of human development in terms of extremes—solutions favoring one side or the other. But as we trace the unfolding of the field, you will see that positions have softened. Today, some theorists believe that both continuous and discontinuous changes occur. Many acknowledge that development has both universal features and features unique to each individual and his or her contexts. And

Since the 1960s, researchers have moved from focusing only on child development to investigating development over the entire life course. These hikers, all in their seventies, continue to change physically, mentally, and socially. They convey the health, vitality, and life satisfaction of many contemporary older adults.

a growing number regard heredity and environment as inseparably interwoven, each affecting the potential of the other to modify the child's traits and capacities (Gottlieb, Wahlsten, & Lickliter, 2006; Lerner, 2006; Rutter, 2007).

These balanced visions owe much to the expansion of research from a nearly exclusive focus on the first two decades to include adulthood. In the first half of the twentieth century, it was widely assumed that development stopped at adolescence. Adulthood was viewed as a plateau and aging as a period of decline. The changing character of the North American population awakened researchers to the idea that gains in functioning are lifelong.

Because of improvements in nutrition, sanitation, and medical knowledge, *average life expectancy* (the number of years an individual born in a particular year can expect to live) gained more in the twentieth century than in the preceding five thousand years. In 1900, life expectancy was just under age 50; today, it is 78.1 years in the United States and even higher in most other industrialized nations, including neighboring Canada. Life expectancy continues to increase; in the United States, it is predicted to reach 84 years in 2050 (U.S. Census Bureau, 2009a, 2009b).

Older adults are not only more numerous but also healthier and more active. Challenging the earlier stereotype of the withering person, they have contributed to a profound shift in our view of human change. Increasingly, researchers are envisioning *development as a dynamic system*—a perpetually ongoing process, extending from conception to death, that is molded by a complex network of biological, psychological, and social influences (Lerner, Theokas, & Bobek, 2005). A leading dynamic systems approach is the **lifespan perspective.** Four assumptions make up this broader view: that development is (1) lifelong,

■ **TABLE 1.1** ■ *Major Periods of Human Development*

PERIOD	APPROXIMATE AGE RANGE	BRIEF DESCRIPTION
Prenatal	Conception to birth	The one-celled organism transforms into a human baby with remarkable capacities to adjust to life outside the womb.
Infancy and toddlerhood	Birth–2 years	Dramatic changes in the body and brain support the emergence of a wide array of motor, perceptual, and intellectual capacities and first intimate ties to others.
Early childhood	2–6 years	During the "play years," motor skills are refined, thought and language expand at an astounding pace, a sense of morality is evident, and children establish ties with peers.
Middle childhood	6–11 years	The school years are marked by improved athletic abilities; more logical thought processes; mastery of basic literacy skills; advances in self-understanding; morality, and friendship; and the beginnings of peer-group membership.
Adolescence	11–18 years	Puberty leads to an adult-sized body and sexual maturity. Thought becomes abstract and idealistic and school achievement more serious. Adolescents focus on defining personal values and goals and establishing autonomy from the family.
Early adulthood	18–40 years	Most young people leave home, complete their education, and begin full-time work. Major concerns are developing a career, forming an intimate partnership, and marrying, rearing children, or establishing other lifestyles.
Middle adulthood	40–65 years	Many people are at the height of their careers and attain leadership positions. They must also help their children begin independent lives and their parents adapt to aging. They become more aware of their own mortality.
Late adulthood	65 years–death	People adjust to retirement, to decreased physical strength and health, and often to the death of a spouse. They reflect on the meaning of their lives.

(2) multidimensional and multidirectional, (3) highly plastic, and (4) affected by multiple interacting forces (Baltes, Lindenberger, & Staudinger, 2006; Smith & Baltes, 1999; Staudinger & Lindenberger, 2003).

Development Is Lifelong

According to the lifespan perspective, no single age period is supreme in its impact on the life course. Rather, events occurring during each major period, summarized in Table 1.1, can have equally powerful effects on future change. Within each period, change occurs in three broad domains: *physical, cognitive,* and *emotional/social,* which we separate for convenience of discussion (see Figure 1.2 for a description of each). Yet, as you already know from the first part of this chapter, these domains overlap and interact.

Development Is Multidimensional and Multidirectional

Think back to Sofie's life and how she continually faced new demands and opportunities. From a lifespan perspective, the chal-

lenges and adjustments of development are *multidimensional*—affected by an intricate blend of biological, psychological, and social forces.

Lifespan development is also *multidirectional:* At every period, development is a joint expression of growth and decline. When Sofie mastered languages and music as a school-age child, she gave up refining other skills. Later, when she chose to become a teacher, she let go of other career options. Although gains are especially evident early in life, and losses during the final years, people of all ages can improve current skills and develop new ones (Freund & Baltes, 2000). Most older adults, for example, devise compensatory techniques for dealing with their increasing memory failures, such as relying more on external aids like calendars and lists.

Besides being multidirectional over time, change is multidirectional within each domain of development. Although some qualities of Sofie's cognitive functioning (such as memory) probably declined in her mature years, her knowledge of both English and French grew throughout her life. And she also developed new forms of thinking—for example, expertise in practical matters, a quality of reasoning called *wisdom.* Recall Sofie's wise advice to Laura and Ken on the eve of their wedding

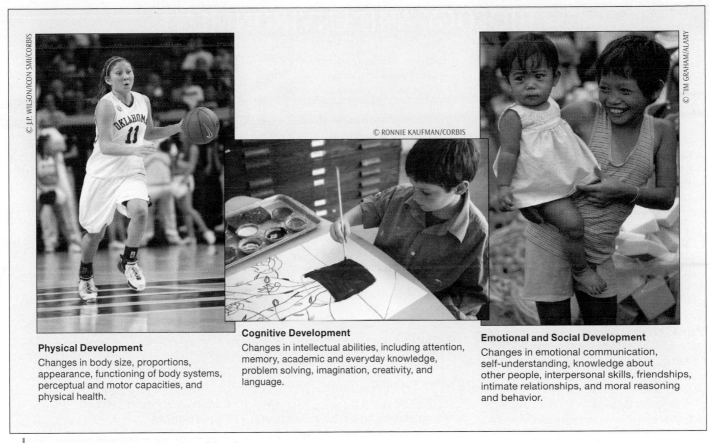

Physical Development

Changes in body size, proportions, appearance, functioning of body systems, perceptual and motor capacities, and physical health.

Cognitive Development

Changes in intellectual abilities, including attention, memory, academic and everyday knowledge, problem solving, imagination, creativity, and language.

Emotional and Social Development

Changes in emotional communication, self-understanding, knowledge about other people, interpersonal skills, friendships, intimate relationships, and moral reasoning and behavior.

■ **FIGURE 1.2** ■ **Major domains of development.**
The three domains are not really distinct. Rather, they overlap and interact.

day. Notice how the lifespan perspective includes both continuous and discontinuous change.

Development Is Plastic

Lifespan researchers emphasize that development is plastic at all ages. Consider Sofie's social reserve in childhood and her decision to study rather than marry as a young adult. As new opportunities arose, Sofie moved easily into marriage and childbearing in her thirties. And although parenthood and financial difficulties posed challenges to Sofie's and Philip's happiness, their relationship gradually became richer and more fulfilling. In Chapter 17, we will see that intellectual performance also remains flexible with advancing age. Elderly people respond to special training with substantial (but not unlimited) gains in a wide variety of mental abilities (Willis et al., 2006).

Evidence on plasticity reveals that aging is not an eventual "shipwreck," as has often been assumed. Instead, the metaphor of a "butterfly"—of metamorphosis and continued potential—provides a more accurate picture of lifespan change (Lemme, 2006). Still, development gradually becomes less plastic, as both capacity and opportunity for change are reduced. And plasticity varies across individuals. Some children and adults experience

more diverse life circumstances. Also, as the Biology and Environment box on page 8 indicates, some adapt more easily than others to changing conditions.

Development Is Influenced by Multiple, Interacting Forces

According to the lifespan perspective, *development is influenced by multiple forces:* biological, historical, social, and cultural. Although these wide-ranging influences can be organized into three categories, they work together, combining in unique ways to fashion each life course.

■ **AGE-GRADED INFLUENCES.** Events that are strongly related to age and therefore fairly predictable in when they occur and how long they last are called **age-graded influences.** For example, most individuals walk shortly after their first birthday, acquire their native language during the preschool years, reach puberty around age 12 to 14, and (for women) experience menopause in their late forties or early fifties. These milestones are influenced by biology, but social customs—such as starting school around age 6, getting a driver's license at age 16, and entering college around age 18—can create age-graded influences as well.

■ BIOLOGY AND ENVIRONMENT ■

Resilience

John and his best friend, Gary, grew up in a rundown, crime-ridden, inner-city neighborhood. By age 10, each had experienced years of family conflict followed by parental divorce. Reared from then on in mother-headed households, John and Gary rarely saw their fathers. Both dropped out of high school and were in and out of trouble with the police.

Then John's and Gary's paths diverged. By age 30, John had fathered two children with women he never married, had spent time in prison, was unemployed, and drank alcohol heavily. In contrast, Gary had returned to finish high school, had studied auto mechanics at a community college, and had become manager of a gas station and repair shop. Married with two children, he had saved his earnings and bought a home. He was happy, healthy, and well-adapted to life.

A wealth of evidence shows that environmental risks—poverty, negative family interactions and parental divorce, job loss, mental illness, and drug abuse—predispose children to future problems (Masten & Gewirtz, 2006; Sameroff, 2006). Why did Gary "beat the odds" and come through unscathed?

New evidence on **resilience**—the ability to adapt effectively in the face of threats to development—is receiving increased attention as investigators look for ways to protect young people from the damaging effects of stressful life conditions (Masten & Powell, 2003). This interest has been inspired by several long-term studies on the relationship of life stressors in childhood to competence and adjustment in adolescence and adulthood (Fergusson & Horwood, 2003; Garmezy, 1993; Masten et al., 1995; Werner & Smith, 2001). In each study, some individuals were shielded from negative outcomes, whereas others had lasting problems. Four broad factors offered protection from the damaging effects of stressful life events.

Personal Characteristics

A child's biologically endowed characteristics can reduce exposure to risk or lead to experiences that compensate for early stressful events. High intelligence and socially valued talents (in music or athletics, for example) increase the chances that a child will have rewarding experiences in school and in the community that offset the impact of a stress-

ful home life. Temperament is particularly powerful. Children who have easygoing, sociable dispositions and who can readily inhibit negative emotions and impulses tend to have an optimistic outlook on life and a special capacity to adapt to change—qualities that elicit positive responses from others. In contrast, emotionally reactive and irritable children often tax the patience of people around them (Mathiesen & Prior, 2006; Wong et al., 2006). For example, both John and Gary moved several times during their childhoods. Each time, John became anxious and angry, whereas Gary looked forward to making new friends.

A Warm Parental Relationship

A close relationship with at least one parent who provides warmth, appropriately high expectations, monitoring of the child's activities, and an organized home environment fosters resilience (Masten & Shaffer, 2006). But this factor (as well as the next one) is not independent of children's personal characteristics. Children who are relaxed, socially responsive, and able to deal with change are easier to rear and more likely to enjoy positive relationships with parents and other people. At the same time, some children may develop more attractive dispositions as a result of parental warmth and attention (Conger & Conger, 2002; Gulotta, 2008).

Social Support Outside the Immediate Family

The most consistent asset of resilient children is a strong bond to a competent, caring adult. For children who do not have a close bond with either parent, a grandparent, aunt, uncle, or teacher who forms a special relationship with the child can promote resilience (Masten & Reed, 2002). Gary received support in adolescence from his grandfather, who listened to Gary's concerns and helped him solve problems. Associations with rule-abiding peers who value school achievement are also linked to resilience. But children who have positive relationships with adults are far more likely to establish these supportive peer ties.

This boy's special relationship with his grandmother promotes resilience. By providing social support, she helps him cope with stress and solve problems constructively.

Community Resources and Opportunities

Community supports—good schools, convenient and affordable health care and social services, libraries, and recreation centers—foster both parents' and children's well-being. In addition, engaging in extracurricular activities at school and in religious youth groups, scouting, and other organizations teaches important social skills, such as cooperation, leadership, and contributing to others' welfare. As participants acquire these competencies, they gain in self-reliance, self-esteem, and community commitment (Benson et al., 2006). As a student, Gary volunteered for Habitat for Humanity, joining a team building affordable housing in low-income neighborhoods. Community involvement offered Gary opportunities to form meaningful relationships, which further strengthened his resilience.

Research on resilience highlights the complex connections between heredity and environment. Armed with positive characteristics, which stem from innate endowment, favorable rearing experiences, or both, children and adolescents take action to reduce stressful situations. But when many risks pile up, they are increasingly difficult to overcome (Luthar, 2006). To inoculate children against the negative effects of risk, interventions must not only reduce risks but also enhance children's protective relationships at home, in school, and in the community.

■ **HISTORY-GRADED INFLUENCES.** Development is also profoundly affected by forces unique to a historical era. Examples include epidemics, wars, and periods of economic prosperity or depression; technological advances, such as the introduction of television, computers, and the Internet; and changes in cultural values, such as attitudes toward women and ethnic minorities. These **history-graded influences** explain why people born around the same time—called a *cohort*—tend to be alike in ways that set them apart from people born at other times.

Consider the *baby boomers,* a term used to describe people born between 1946 and 1964, the post–World War II period during which birth rates soared in most Western nations. The population increase was especially sharp in the United States: By 1960, the prewar birth rate had nearly doubled, yielding the largest population increase in the nation's history. The sheer size of the baby boom generation made it a powerful social force from the time its members became young adults; today, the baby boomers are redefining our view of middle age (see the Lifespan Vista box on page 10).

■ **NONNORMATIVE INFLUENCES.** Age-graded and history-graded influences are *normative*—meaning typical, or average—because each affects large numbers of people. **Nonnormative influences** are events that are irregular: They happen to just one person or a few people and do not follow a predictable timetable. Nonnormative influences that had a major impact on the direction of Sofie's life were piano lessons in childhood with an inspiring teacher; a blind date with Philip; delayed marriage, parenthood, and career entry; and a battle with cancer.

Nonnormative influences have become more powerful and age-graded influences less so in contemporary adult development. Compared with Sofie's era, much greater diversity exists today in the ages at which people finish their education, enter careers, get married, have children, and retire. Indeed, Sofie's "off-time" accomplishments would have been less unusual had

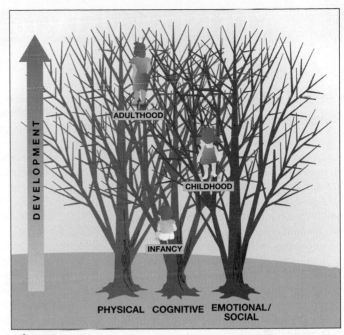

■ **FIGURE 1.3** ■ **The lifespan view of development.** Rather than envisioning a single line of stagewise or continuous change (see Figure 1.1 on page 4), lifespan theorists conceive of development as more like tree branches extending in diverse directions. Many potential pathways are possible, depending on the contexts that influence the individual's life course. Each branch in this treelike image represents a possible skill within one of the major domains of development. The crossing of the branches signifies that the domains—physical, cognitive, emotional, and social—are interrelated.

she been born a generation or two later! Notice that instead of a single line of development, the lifespan perspective emphasizes many potential pathways and outcomes—an image more like fibers extending in diverse directions (see Figure 1.3). Now let's turn to the scientific foundations of the field as a prelude to major theories that address various aspects of change.

© DANIEL RODRIGUEZ/ISTOCKPHOTO

For this 16-year-old, getting a driver's license is a major life transition, offering new privileges and responsibilities. In industrialized nations, starting to drive independently is an age-graded influence—one that occurs at about the same age for most young people.

ASK YOURSELF

》 REVIEW
Distinguish among age-graded, history-graded, and nonnormative influences on lifespan development. Cite an example of each in Sofie's story.

》 APPLY
Anna, a high school counselor, has devised a program that integrates classroom learning with vocational training to help adolescents at risk for school dropout stay in school. What is Anna's position on *stability versus plasticity* in development? Explain.

》 REFLECT
Describe an aspect of your development that differs from a parent's or a grandparent's when he or she was your age. Using influences highlighted by the lifespan perspective, explain this difference in development.

■ A LIFESPAN VISTA: Looking Forward, Looking Back ■

The Baby Boomers Reshape the Life Course

From 1946 to 1964, 92 percent of all American women of childbearing age gave birth, averaging almost four children each—a new baby every 8 seconds (Croker, 2007). This splurge of births, which extended for nearly two decades, yielded a unique generation often credited with changing the world. Today, the baby boomers—comprising more than 80 million middle-aged adults—make up nearly 30 percent of the U.S. population (U.S. Census Bureau, 2009b).

Several interrelated factors sparked the post–World War II baby boom. Many people who had postponed marriage and parenthood throughout the Great Depression of the 1930s started families in the 1940s, once the economy had improved. With the end of World War II, returning GIs and their wives also began to have children. As these two cohorts focused on childbearing, they gave birth to babies who under other circumstances would have been spaced out over 10 to 15 years. And as economic growth and prosperity accelerated in the 1950s, making larger families affordable, more people married at younger ages and had several children closely spaced, which led the baby boom to persist into the 1960s (Stewart & Malley, 2004). Finally, after a war, the desire to make babies generally strengthens. Besides replacing massive loss of life, new births signify hope—a belief that "human life will continue" (Croker, 2007, p. 9).

Compared with the previous generation, many more young baby boomers were economically privileged. They were also the recipients of deep investment by their parents, who—having undergone the deprivations of depression and war—often ranked children as the most enduring benefit of their adult lives. These factors may have engendered optimism, confidence, even a sense of entitlement (Elder, Nguyen, & Caspi, 1985). At the same time, their huge numbers—evident in overflowing school classrooms—may have sparked in boomers an intense struggle for individual recognition. By the time the boomers reached early adulthood, this constellation of traits led critics to label them a narcissistic, indulged, "me" generation.

From the mid-1960s to the early 1970s, the "leading-edge" baby boomers (born in the late 1940s and early 1950s) entered colleges and universities in record numbers, becoming better educated than any previous generation. This cohort—self-focused, socially aware, and in search of distinction—broke away from their parents' family- and marriage-centered lifestyles. Starting in the mid-sixties, marriage rates declined, age of first marriage rose, and divorce rates increased. And the baby boomers responded to the turbulence of those times—the assassination of President Kennedy in 1963, the Vietnam War, and growing racial tensions—by mobilizing around the antiwar, civil rights, and women's movements, yielding a generation of student activists.

By the time the "trailing-edge" boomers (born in the late 1950s and early 1960s) came of age, these movements had left an enduring mark. Even as they turned toward family life and career development, the boomers' collective identity continued to emphasize search for personal meaning, self-expression, and social responsibility. By midlife, the generation had produced an unusually large number of socially concerned writers, teachers, filmmakers, and labor and community organizers, as well as innovative musicians and artists (Cole & Stewart, 1996; Dickstein, 1992). And a multitude of ordinary citizens worked to advance social causes.

In addition, as baby-boom women entered the labor market and struggled for career advancement and equal pay, their self-confidence grew, and they paved the way for the next generation: On average, younger women attained this same level of self-confidence at a much earlier age (Stewart & Ostrove, 1998; Twenge, 1997, 2001). And as baby boom activists pressed for gender and racial equality, they influenced the direction of national policy. The 1960s saw laws passed that banned discrimination in employment practices, in racial access to public accommodations, and in sale or rental of housing. By the 1970s, progress in civil rights served as the springboard for the gay and lesbian rights movement.

Today, the baby boomers are the largest generation ever to enter middle age, and they are healthier, better educated, and financially better off than any previous midlife cohort (Whitbourne & Willis, 2006). Their sense of self-empowerment and innovativeness is bringing new vitality to this period of the lifespan, including efforts to increase the personal meaningfulness of their vocational lives and to deepen their lifelong engagement with social causes. Yet another concern of

Actor George Clooney, born in 1961, is one of the "trailing edge" baby boomers. Like many in his cohort, he has an unusually strong sense of social responsibility. He is cofounder of Not On Our Watch, an organization that focuses on ending atrocities around the world. Here he visits a refugee camp in Darfur, Sudan, where hundreds of thousands have been slaughtered and millions displaced during years of civil war.

baby-boom midlifers is an intense desire to control the physical changes of aging (Lachman & Firth, 2004). Far more than their predecessors, they resist growing old, as indicated by their interest in a wide array of anti-aging products and procedures—from cosmetics to Botox to plastic surgery—that are now a multi-billion-dollar U.S. industry. Nevertheless, it is important to keep in mind that the baby boomers—though advantaged as a generation—are diverse in health status and sense of control over their lives, with those higher in education and income considerably better off.

What lies ahead as this gigantic population bulge approaches late adulthood? Most analysts focus on societal burdens, such as rising social security and health-care costs. At the same time, as the boomers continue to build on the foundation laid in middle age, they could become "our only increasing natural resource" (Freedman, 1999). After retirement, they will have more time to care about others—and more relevant experience and years left to do so—than any previous generation. Policies and programs aimed at recruiting older adults into volunteer and service roles may be one of the most effective ways to "channel good will into good deeds," combat social ills, and enhance development during all periods of life.

Scientific Beginnings

Scientific study of human development dates back to the late nineteenth and early twentieth centuries. Early observations of human change were soon followed by improved methods and theories, contributing to the firm foundation on which the field rests today.

Darwin: Forefather of Scientific Child Study

British naturalist Charles Darwin (1809–1882) observed the infinite variation among plant and animal species. He saw that within a species, no two individuals are exactly alike. From these observations, he constructed his famous *theory of evolution.*

The theory emphasized two related principles: *natural selection* and *survival of the fittest.* Darwin explained that certain species survive in particular environments because they have characteristics that fit with, or are adapted to, their surroundings. Other species die off because they are less well-suited to their environments. Individuals within a species who best meet the environment's survival requirements live long enough to reproduce and pass their more beneficial characteristics to future generations. Darwin's (1859/1936) emphasis on the adaptive value of physical characteristics and behavior found its way into important developmental theories.

During his explorations, Darwin discovered that early prenatal growth is strikingly similar in many species. Other scientists concluded from Darwin's observations that the development of the human child follows the same general plan as the evolution of the human species. Although this belief eventually proved inaccurate, efforts to chart parallels between child growth and human evolution prompted researchers to make careful observations of all aspects of children's behavior. As a result, scientific child study was born.

The Normative Period

G. Stanley Hall (1844–1924), one of the most influential American psychologists of the early twentieth century, is regarded as the founder of the child study movement (Cairns & Cairns, 2006). He also wrote one of the few books of his time on aging, foreshadowing lifespan research. Inspired by Darwin's work, Hall and his well-known student Arnold Gesell (1880–1961) devised theories based on evolutionary ideas. They regarded development as a *maturational process*—a genetically determined series of events that unfold automatically, much like a flower (Gesell, 1933; Hall, 1904).

Hall and Gesell are remembered less for their one-sided theories than for their intensive efforts to describe all aspects of development. This launched the **normative approach**, in which measures of behavior are taken on large numbers of individuals, and age-related averages are computed to represent typical development. Using this procedure, Hall constructed elaborate questionnaires asking children of different ages almost everything they could tell about themselves—interests, fears, imaginary playmates, dreams, friendships, everyday knowledge, and more. Through careful observations and parent interviews, Gesell collected detailed normative information on infants' and children's motor achievements, social behaviors, and personality characteristics. Gesell was also among the first to make knowledge about child development meaningful to parents. His books, along with Benjamin Spock's *Baby and Child Care,* became central to a rapidly expanding child-rearing advice literature for parents.

The Mental Testing Movement

While Hall and Gesell were developing their theories and methods in the United States, French psychologist Alfred Binet (1857–1911) was also taking a normative approach, but for a different reason. In the early 1900s, Binet and his colleague Theodore Simon were asked by Paris school officials to find a

Darwin's theory of evolution emphasizes the adaptive value of physical characteristics and behavior. Affection and care in families are adaptive throughout the lifespan, promoting survival and psychological well-being. Here, a son helps his father adjust to using a walker.

© LISA F YOUNG/ALAMY

way to identify children with learning problems for placement in special classes. To address this practical educational concern, they constructed the first successful intelligence test.

In 1916, at Stanford University, Binet's test was adapted for use with English-speaking children. Since then, the English version has been known as the *Stanford-Binet Intelligence Scale.* Besides providing a score that successfully predicted school achievement, the Binet test sparked tremendous interest in individual differences in development. Intelligence tests moved quickly to the forefront of the nature–nurture controversy.

Mid-Twentieth-Century Theories

In the mid-twentieth century, the study of human development expanded into a legitimate discipline. As it attracted increasing interest, a variety of theories emerged, each of which still has followers today.

The Psychoanalytic Perspective

In the 1930s and 1940s, as more people sought help from professionals to deal with emotional difficulties, a new question had to be addressed: How and why do people become the way they are? To treat psychological problems, psychiatrists and social workers turned to an approach to personality development that emphasizes each individual's unique life history.

According to the **psychoanalytic perspective,** people move through a series of stages in which they confront conflicts between biological drives and social expectations. How these conflicts are resolved determines the person's ability to learn, to get along with others, and to cope with anxiety. Among the many individuals who contributed to the psychoanalytic perspective, two were especially influential: Sigmund Freud, founder of the psychoanalytic movement, and Erik Erikson.

■ **FREUD'S THEORY.**   Freud (1856–1939), a Viennese physician, sought a cure for emotionally troubled adults by having them talk freely about painful events of their childhoods. On the basis of these recollections, he examined the unconscious motivations of his patients and constructed his **psychosexual theory,** which emphasizes that how parents manage their child's sexual and aggressive drives in the first few years is crucial for healthy personality development.

In Freud's theory, three parts of the personality—id, ego, and superego—become integrated during five stages, summarized in Table 1.2. The *id,* the largest portion of the mind, is the source of basic biological needs and desires. The *ego,* the conscious, rational part of personality, emerges in early infancy to redirect the id's impulses into acceptable behaviors.

Between 3 and 6 years of age, the *superego,* or conscience, develops through interactions with parents, who insist that children conform to the values of society. Now the ego faces the increasingly complex task of reconciling the demands of the

id, the external world, and conscience (Freud, 1923/1974). According to Freud, relations established among the id, ego, and superego during the preschool years determine the individual's basic personality.

Freud (1938/1973) believed that during childhood sexual impulses shift their focus from the oral to the anal to the genital regions of the body. In each stage, parents walk a fine line between permitting too much or too little gratification of their child's basic needs. If parents strike an appropriate balance, then children grow into well-adjusted adults with the capacity for mature sexuality and investment in family life.

Freud's theory was the first to stress the influence of the early parent–child relationship on development. But his perspective was eventually criticized. First, it overemphasized the influence of sexual feelings in development. Second, because it was based on the problems of sexually repressed, well-to-do adults in nineteenth-century Viennese society, it did not apply in other cultures. Finally, Freud had not studied children directly.

■ **ERIKSON'S THEORY.**   Several of Freud's followers took what was useful from his theory and improved on his vision. The most important of these neo-Freudians is Erik Erikson (1902–1994). In his **psychosocial theory,** Erikson emphasized that in addition to mediating between id impulses and superego demands, the ego makes a positive contribution to development, acquiring attitudes and skills at each stage that make the individual an active, contributing member of society. A basic psychological conflict, which is resolved along a continuum from positive to negative, determines healthy or maladaptive

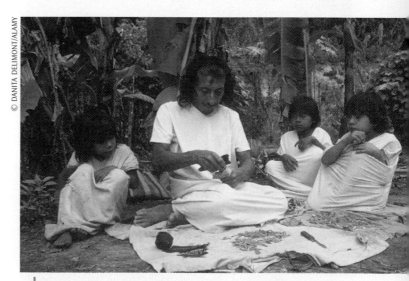

Children of the Lacandon Mayan people of southern Mexico look on as their father makes souvenir arrows similar to those of their ancestors. The Lacandon—descendants of hunter-gatherers and subsistence farmers who lived in isolation for hundreds of years—teach their children many ancient skills and traditions, including tool making and agricultural techniques. As Erikson recognized, these child-rearing practices can be understood only in relation to the Lacandon's distinct culture.

■ **TABLE 1.2** ■ *Freud's Psychosexual Stages*

PSYCHOSEXUAL STAGE	PERIOD OF DEVELOPMENT	DESCRIPTION
Oral	Birth–1 year	The new ego directs the baby's sucking activities toward breast or bottle. If oral needs are not met appropriately, the individual may develop such habits as thumb sucking, fingernail biting, and pencil chewing in childhood and overeating and smoking in later life.
Anal	1–3 years	Toddlers and preschoolers enjoy holding and releasing urine and feces. Toilet training becomes a major issue between parent and child. If parents insist that children be trained before they are ready, or if they make too few demands, conflicts about anal control may appear in the form of extreme orderliness and cleanliness or messiness and disorder.
Phallic	3–6 years	As preschoolers take pleasure in genital stimulation, Freud's Oedipus conflict for boys and Electra conflict for girls arise: Children feel a sexual desire for the other-sex parent. To avoid punishment, they give up this desire and adopt the same-sex parent's characteristics and values. As a result, the superego is formed, and children feel guilty each time they violate its standards.
Latency	6–11 years	Sexual instincts die down, and the superego develops further. The child acquires new social values from adults and same-sex peers outside the family.
Genital	Adolescence	With puberty, the sexual impulses of the phallic stage reappear. If development has been successful during earlier stages, it leads to marriage, mature sexuality, and the birth and rearing of children. This stage extends through adulthood.

outcomes at each stage. As Table 1.3 on page 14 shows, Erikson's first five stages parallel Freud's stages, but Erikson added three adult stages.

Unlike Freud, Erikson pointed out that normal development must be understood in relation to each culture's life situation. For example, in the 1940s, he observed that Yurok Indians of the northwest coast of the United States deprived babies of breastfeeding for the first 10 days after birth and instead fed them a thin soup. At age 6 months, infants were abruptly weaned—an experience that, from our cultural vantage point, might seem cruel. But Erikson explained that the Yurok lived in a world in which salmon filled the river just once a year, a circumstance requiring considerable self-restraint for survival.

■ **CONTRIBUTIONS AND LIMITATIONS OF THE PSYCHO-ANALYTIC PERSPECTIVE.** A special strength of the psychoanalytic perspective is its emphasis on understanding the individual's unique life history. Consistent with this view, psychoanalytic theorists accept the *clinical,* or *case study, method,* which synthesizes information from a variety of sources into a detailed picture of the personality of a single person. The psychoanalytic approach has also inspired a wealth of research on many aspects of emotional and social development, including infant–caregiver attachment, aggression, sibling relationships, child-rearing practices, morality, gender roles, and adolescent identity.

Despite its contributions, the psychoanalytic perspective is no longer in the mainstream of human development research. Psychoanalytic theorists may have become isolated from the rest

of the field because they were so strongly committed to the clinical approach that they failed to consider other methods. In addition, many psychoanalytic ideas, such as psychosexual stages and ego functioning, are so vague that they are difficult or impossible to test empirically (Crain, 2005; Thomas, 2005). Nevertheless, Erikson's broad outline of lifespan change captures the essence of personality development during each major period of the life course, so we will return to it in later chapters.

Behaviorism and Social Learning Theory

As the psychoanalytic perspective gained in prominence, the study of development was also influenced by a very different perspective. According to **behaviorism**, directly observable events—stimuli and responses—are the appropriate focus of study. North American behaviorism began in the early twentieth century with the work of psychologist John Watson (1878–1958), who wanted to create an objective science of psychology.

■ **TRADITIONAL BEHAVIORISM.** Watson was inspired by Russian physiologist Ivan Pavlov's studies of animal learning. Pavlov knew that dogs release saliva as an innate reflex when they are given food. But he noticed that his dogs were salivating before they tasted any food—when they saw the trainer who usually fed them. The dogs, Pavlov reasoned, must have learned to associate a neutral stimulus (the trainer) with another stimulus (food) that produces a reflexive response (salivation).

■ **TABLE 1.3** ■ *Erikson's Psychosocial Stages, with Corresponding Psychosexual Stages Indicated*

PSYCHOSOCIAL STAGE	PERIOD OF DEVELOPMENT	DESCRIPTION	
Basic trust versus mistrust (Oral)	Birth–1 year	From warm, responsive care, infants gain a sense of trust, or confidence, that the world is good. Mistrust occurs when infants have to wait too long for comfort and are handled harshly.	
Autonomy versus shame and doubt (Anal)	1–3 years	Using new mental and motor skills, children want to choose and decide for themselves. Parents can foster autonomy by permitting reasonable free choice and not forcing or shaming the child.	
Initiative versus guilt (Phallic)	3–6 years	Through make-believe play, children explore the kind of person they can become. Initiative—a sense of ambition and responsibility—develops when parents support their child's new sense of purpose. When parents demand too much self-control, they induce excessive guilt.	**Erik Erikson**
Industry versus inferiority (Latency)	6–11 years	At school, children develop the capacity to work and cooperate with others. Inferiority develops when negative experiences at home, at school, or with peers lead to feelings of incompetence.	
Identity versus role confusion (Genital)	Adolescence	The adolescent tries to answer the questions, Who am I, and what is my place in society? By exploring values and vocational goals, the young person forms a personal identity. The negative outcome is confusion about future adult roles.	
Intimacy versus isolation	Early adulthood	Young people work on establishing intimate ties to others. Because of earlier disappointments, some individuals cannot form close relationships and remain isolated.	
Generativity versus stagnation	Middle adulthood	Middle-aged adults contribute to the next generation through child rearing, caring for other people, or productive work. The person who fails in these ways feels an absence of meaningful accomplishment.	
Integrity versus despair	Late adulthood	Elders reflect on the kind of person they have been. Integrity results from feeling that life was worth living as it happened. Those who are dissatisfied with their lives fear death.	

Because of this association, the neutral stimulus alone could bring about a response resembling the reflex. Eager to test this idea, Pavlov successfully taught dogs to salivate at the sound of a bell by pairing it with the presentation of food. He had discovered *classical conditioning.*

Watson wanted to find out if classical conditioning could be applied to children's behavior. In a historic experiment, he taught Albert, an 11-month-old infant, to fear a neutral stimulus—a soft white rat—by presenting it several times with a sharp, loud sound, which naturally scared the baby. Little Albert, who at first had reached out eagerly to touch the furry rat, began to cry and turn his head away when he caught sight of it (Watson & Raynor, 1920). Watson concluded that environment is the supreme force in development and that adults can mold children's behavior by carefully controlling stimulus–response associations. He viewed development as a continuous process, consisting of a gradual increase with age in the number and strength of these associations.

Another form of behaviorism was American psychologist B. F. Skinner's (1904–1990) *operant conditioning theory.*

According to Skinner, the frequency of a behavior can be increased by following it with a wide variety of *reinforcers,* such as food, praise, or a friendly smile. It can also be decreased through *punishment,* such as disapproval or withdrawal of privileges. We will consider these conditioning techniques further in Chapter 4.

■ **SOCIAL LEARNING THEORY.** Psychologists wondered whether behaviorism might offer a more direct and effective explanation of the development of social behavior than the less precise concepts of psychoanalytic theory. This sparked approaches that built on the principles of conditioning, offering expanded views of how children and adults acquire new responses.

Several kinds of **social learning theory** emerged. The most influential, devised by American psychologist Albert Bandura (1925–), emphasizes *modeling,* also known as *imitation* or *observational learning,* as a powerful source of development. The baby who claps her hands after her mother does so and the child who angrily hits a playmate in the same way that he has

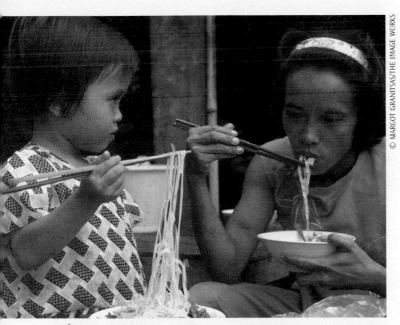

© MARGOT GRANITSAS/THE IMAGE WORKS

Social learning theory recognizes that children acquire many skills through modeling. By observing and imitating her mother, this Vietnamese preschooler learns to use chopsticks.

been punished at home are displaying observational learning. In his early work, Bandura found that diverse factors affect children's motivation to imitate: their own history of reinforcement or punishment for the behavior, the promise of future reinforcement or punishment, and even observing the model being reinforced or punished.

Bandura's work continues to influence much research on social development. But today his theory stresses the importance of *cognition*, or thinking. In fact, the most recent revision of Bandura's (1992, 2001) theory places such strong emphasis on how we think about ourselves and other people that he calls it a *social-cognitive* rather than a social learning approach.

In Bandura's revised view, children gradually become more selective in what they imitate. From watching others engage in self-praise and self-blame and through feedback about the worth of their own actions, children develop *personal standards* for behavior and *a sense of self-efficacy*—the belief that their own abilities and characteristics will help them succeed. These cognitions guide responses in particular situations (Bandura, 1999, 2001). For example, imagine a parent who often remarks, "I'm glad I kept working on that task, even though it was hard," and who encourages persistence by saying, "I know you can do a good job on that homework!" Soon the child starts to view herself as hardworking and high-achieving and selects people with these characteristics as models. In this way, as individuals acquire attitudes, values, and convictions about themselves, they control their own learning and behavior.

■ **CONTRIBUTIONS AND LIMITATIONS OF BEHAVIORISM AND SOCIAL LEARNING THEORY.** Behaviorism and social learning theory have been helpful in treating adjustment prob-

lems. **Behavior modification** consists of procedures that combine conditioning and modeling to eliminate undesirable behaviors and increase desirable responses. It has been used to relieve difficulties in children and adults, ranging from poor time management and unwanted habits to serious problems, such as language delays and persistent aggression (Conyers et al., 2004; Martin & Pear, 2007).

Nevertheless, many theorists believe that behaviorism and social learning theory offer too narrow a view of important environmental influences, which extend beyond immediate reinforcement, punishment, and modeled behaviors to people's rich physical and social worlds. Behaviorism and social learning theory have also been criticized for underestimating people's contributions to their own development. Bandura, in emphasizing cognition, is unique among theorists whose work grew out of the behaviorist tradition in granting children and adults an active role in their own learning.

Piaget's Cognitive-Developmental Theory

If one individual has influenced research on child development more than any other, it is Swiss cognitive theorist Jean Piaget (1896–1980). North American investigators did not grant Piaget's work much attention until the 1960s, mainly because Piaget's ideas were at odds with behaviorism, which dominated North American psychology in the mid-twentieth century (Cairns & Cairns, 2006). Piaget did not believe that children's learning depends on reinforcers, such as rewards from adults. According to his **cognitive-developmental theory,** children actively construct knowledge as they manipulate and explore their world.

■ **PIAGET'S STAGES.** Piaget's view of development was greatly influenced by his early training in biology. Central to his theory is the biological concept of *adaptation* (Piaget, 1971). Just as structures of the body are adapted to fit with the environment, so structures of the mind develop to better fit with, or represent, the external world. In infancy and early childhood, Piaget claimed, children's understanding is different from adults'. For example, he believed that young babies do not realize that an object hidden from view continues to exist. He also concluded that preschoolers' thinking is full of faulty logic. For example, children younger than age 7 commonly say that the amount of a liquid changes when it is poured into a different-shaped container. According to Piaget, children eventually revise these incorrect ideas in their ongoing efforts to achieve an *equilibrium*, or balance, between internal structures and information they encounter in their everyday worlds.

In Piaget's theory, as the brain develops and children's experiences expand, they move through four broad stages, each characterized by qualitatively distinct ways of thinking. Table 1.4 on page 16 provides a brief description of Piaget's stages.

Piaget devised special methods for investigating how children think. Early in his career, he carefully observed his three infant children and presented them with everyday problems,

■ **TABLE 1.4** ■ *Piaget's Stages of Cognitive Development*

STAGE	PERIOD OF DEVELOPMENT	DESCRIPTION	
Sensorimotor	Birth–2 years	Infants "think" by acting on the world with their eyes, ears, hands, and mouth. As a result, they invent ways of solving sensorimotor problems, such as pulling a lever to hear the sound of a music box, finding hidden toys, and putting objects into and taking them out of containers.	
Preoperational	2–7 years	Preschool children use symbols to represent their earlier sensorimotor discoveries. Development of language and make-believe play takes place. However, thinking lacks the logic of the two remaining stages.	
Concrete operational	7–11 years	Children's reasoning becomes logical. School-age children understand that a certain amount of lemonade or play dough remains the same even after its appearance changes. They also organize objects into hierarchies of classes and subclasses. However, children think in a logical, organized fashion only when dealing with concrete information they can perceive directly.	
Formal operational	11 years on	The capacity for abstract, systematic thinking enables adolescents, when faced with a problem, to start with a hypothesis, deduce testable inferences, and isolate and combine variables to see which inferences are confirmed. Adolescents can also evaluate the logic of verbal statements without referring to real-world circumstances.	**Jean Piaget**

such as an attractive object that could be grasped, mouthed, kicked, or searched for. From their responses, Piaget derived his ideas about cognitive changes during the first two years. To study childhood and adolescent thought, Piaget adapted the clinical method of psychoanalysis, conducting open-ended *clinical interviews* in which a child's initial response to a task served as the basis for Piaget's next question.

■ **CONTRIBUTIONS AND LIMITATIONS OF PIAGET'S THEORY.** Piaget convinced the field that children are active learners whose minds consist of rich structures of knowledge. Besides investigating children's understanding of the physical world, Piaget explored their reasoning about the social world. His stages have sparked a wealth of research on children's conceptions of themselves, other people, and human relationships. In practical terms, Piaget's theory encouraged the development of educational philosophies and programs that emphasize discovery learning and direct contact with the environment.

Despite Piaget's overwhelming contributions, his theory has been challenged. Research indicates that Piaget underestimated the competencies of infants and preschoolers. When young children are given tasks scaled down in difficulty and relevant to their everyday experiences, their understanding appears closer to that of the older child and adult than Piaget assumed. Furthermore, many studies show that children's performance on Piagetian problems can be improved with training—findings that call into question Piaget's assumption that discovery learning rather than adult teaching is the best way to foster development (Siegler & Svetina, 2006). Critics also point out that Piaget's stagewise account pays insufficient attention to social and cultural influences on development. Finally, some lifespan theorists disagree with Piaget's conclusion that no

In Piaget's operational stage, school-age children think in an organized, logical fashion about concrete objects. This 6-year-old girl and 7-year-old boy understand that the amount of milk remains the same after being poured into a differently shaped container, even though its appearance changes.

major cognitive changes occur after adolescence. Several have proposed important transformations in adulthood (Labouvie-Vief, 2003; Moshman, 2005; Perry, 1970/1998).

ASK YOURSELF

≫ REVIEW

What aspect of behaviorism made it attractive to critics of the psychoanalytic perspective? How did Piaget's theory respond to a major limitation of behaviorism?

≫ APPLY

A 4-year-old becomes frightened of the dark and refuses to go to sleep at night. How would a psychoanalyst and a behaviorist differ in their views of how this problem developed?

≫ REFLECT

Find out whether your parents read child-rearing advice books when you were growing up. What questions most concerned them? Do you think the concerns of today's parents differ from those of your parents' generation? Explain.

Recent Theoretical Perspectives

New ways of understanding development are constantly emerging—questioning, building on, and enhancing earlier theories. Today, a burst of fresh approaches is broadening our understanding.

Information Processing

In the 1970s and 1980s, researchers turned to the field of cognitive psychology for ways to understand the development of thinking. The design of digital computers that use mathematically specified steps to solve problems suggested to psychologists that the human mind might also be viewed as a symbol-manipulating system through which information flows—a perspective called **information processing** (Munakata, 2006). From the time information is presented to the senses at *input* until it emerges as a behavioral response at *output,* information is actively coded, transformed, and organized.

■ **CONCERN WITH RIGOR AND PRECISION.** Information-processing researchers often use flowcharts to map the precise steps individuals use to solve problems and complete tasks, much like the plans devised by programmers to get computers to perform a series of "mental operations" (Siegler & Alibali, 2005). To see the usefulness of this approach, let's look at an example.

In a study of problem solving, a researcher asked school-age children to build a bridge of blocks across a "river" too wide for any single block to span (Thornton, 1999). Whereas older children easily built successful bridges, only one 5-year-old did. Careful tracking of her efforts revealed that she repeatedly tried unsuccessful strategies, such as pushing two planks together and pressing down on their ends to hold them in place. But eventually, her experimentation triggered the idea of using blocks as counterweights, as shown in Figure 1.4. Her mistaken procedures helped her understand why the counterweight approach worked.

Some information-processing models, like the one just considered, track children's mastery of one or a few tasks. Others

■ **FIGURE 1.4** ■ **Information-processing flowchart showing the steps that a 5-year-old used to solve a bridge-building problem.** Her task was to use blocks varying in size, shape, and weight, some of which were planklike, to construct a bridge across a "river" (painted on a floor mat) too wide for any single block to span. The child discovered how to counterweight and balance the bridge. The arrows reveal that, even after building a successful counterweight, she returned to earlier, unsuccessful strategies, which seemed to help her understand why the counterweight approach worked. (Adapted from Thornton, 1999.)

describe the human cognitive system as a whole (Atkinson & Shiffrin, 1968; Lockhart & Craik, 1990). These general models are used as guides for asking questions about broad changes in thinking: Does a child's ability to solve problems become more organized and "planful" with age? Are declines in memory during old age evident on all types of tasks or only some?

Like Piaget's cognitive-developmental theory, the information-processing approach regards people as active, sense-making beings (Halford, 2005). But unlike Piaget's theory, it does not divide development into stages. Rather, the thought processes studied—perception, attention, memory, planning, categorization of information, and comprehension of written and spoken prose—are regarded as similar at all ages but present to a lesser or greater extent. Therefore, the view of development is one of continuous change.

A great strength of the information-processing approach is its commitment to rigorous research methods. Because it has provided precise accounts of how children and adults tackle many cognitive tasks, its findings have important implications for education (Blumenfeld, Marx, & Harris, 2006). But information processing has fallen short in some respects. It has been better at analyzing thinking into its components than at putting them back together into a comprehensive theory. And it virtually ignores aspects of cognition that are not linear and logical, such as imagination and creativity (Birney et al., 2005).

■ **DEVELOPMENTAL COGNITIVE NEUROSCIENCE.** Over the past two decades, information-processing research has expanded to include a new area of investigation called **developmental cognitive neuroscience.** It brings together researchers from psychology, biology, neuroscience, and medicine to study the relationship between changes in the brain and the developing person's cognitive processing and behavior patterns. Improved methods for analyzing brain activity while children and adults perform various tasks have greatly enhanced knowledge of relationships between brain functioning, cognitive capacities, and behavior (Johnson, 2005; Westermann et al., 2007).

Although much remains to be discovered, developmental cognitive neuroscience is already transforming our understanding of development by tackling questions like these: How do specific experiences influence the growth and organization of the child's brain? What neurological changes are related to declines in speed of thinking, memory, and other aspects of cognitive processing in old age?

During the first five years, the brain is highly plastic—especially open to growth as a result of experience. But it retains considerable plasticity throughout life. Neuroscientists are identifying the types of experiences that support or undermine brain development at various ages. They are also discovering the brain-based origins of many learning and behavior disorders and contributing to the design of effective interventions (Munakata, Casey, & Diamond, 2004).

An advantage of having many theories is that they encourage researchers to attend to previously neglected dimensions of people's lives. The final three perspectives we will discuss focus

on *contexts* for development. The first of these views emphasizes that the development of many capacities is influenced by our long evolutionary history.

Ethology and Evolutionary Developmental Psychology

Ethology is concerned with the adaptive, or survival, value of behavior and its evolutionary history. Its roots can be traced to the work of Darwin. Two European zoologists, Konrad Lorenz and Niko Tinbergen, laid its modern foundations. Watching diverse animal species in their natural habitats, Lorenz and Tinbergen observed behavior patterns that promote survival. The best known of these is *imprinting,* the early following behavior of certain baby birds, such as geese, that ensures that the young will stay close to the mother and be fed and protected from danger. Imprinting takes place during an early, restricted period of development. If the mother goose is absent during this time but an object resembling her in important features is present, young goslings may imprint on it instead (Lorenz, 1952).

Observations of imprinting led to a major concept in human development: the *critical period.* It refers to a limited time span during which the individual is biologically prepared to acquire certain adaptive behaviors but needs the support of a stimulating environment. Many researchers have investigated whether complex cognitive and social behaviors must be learned during certain time periods. For example, if children are deprived of adequate physical and social stimulation during their early years, will their intelligence be impaired? If language is not mastered in early childhood, is the capacity to acquire it reduced?

Ethology focuses on the adaptive, or survival, value of behavior and on similarities between human behavior and that of other species, especially our primate relatives. Observing this mother cuddling her 8-day-old infant helps us understand the human–infant caregiver relationship.

In later chapters, we will see that the term *sensitive period* applies better to human development than the strict notion of a critical period (Bornstein, 1989). A **sensitive period** is a time that is optimal for certain capacities to emerge and in which the individual is especially responsive to environmental influences. However, its boundaries are less well-defined than those of a critical period. Development can occur later, but it is harder to induce.

Inspired by observations of imprinting, British psychoanalyst John Bowlby (1969) applied ethological theory to the understanding of the human infant–caregiver relationship. He argued that infant smiling, babbling, grasping, and crying are built-in social signals that encourage the caregiver to approach, care for, and interact with the baby. By keeping the parent near, these behaviors help ensure that the infant will be fed, protected from danger, and provided with stimulation and affection necessary for healthy growth. The development of attachment in humans is a lengthy process that leads the baby to form a deep affectionate tie with the caregiver (Thompson, 2006). Bowlby believed that this bond has lifelong consequences for human relationships. In later chapters, we will consider research that evaluates this assumption.

Recently, researchers have extended this effort in a new area of research called **evolutionary developmental psychology.** It seeks to understand the adaptive value of specieswide cognitive, emotional, and social competencies as those competencies change with age (Geary, 2006b). Evolutionary developmental psychologists ask questions like these: What role does the newborn's visual preference for facelike stimuli play in survival? Does it support older infants' capacity to distinguish familiar caregivers from unfamiliar people? Why do children play in gender-segregated groups? What do they learn from such play that might lead to adult gender-typed behaviors, such as male dominance and female investment in caregiving?

As these examples suggest, evolutionary psychologists are not just concerned with the biological basis of development. They recognize that humans' large brains and extended childhood resulted from the need to master an increasingly complex environment, so they are also interested in learning (Bjorklund & Blasi, 2005). And they realize that today's lifestyles differ so radically from those of our evolutionary ancestors that certain evolved behaviors (such as life-threatening risk taking in adolescents and male-to-male violence) are no longer adaptive (Blasi & Bjorklund, 2003). By clarifying the origins and development of such behaviors, evolutionary developmental psychology may help spark effective interventions.

Vygotsky's Sociocultural Theory

The field of human development has recently seen a dramatic increase in studies addressing the cultural context of people's lives. Investigations that make comparisons across cultures, and between ethnic groups within cultures, provide insight into whether developmental pathways apply to all people or are limited to particular environmental conditions.

Today, much research is examining the relationship of *culturally specific beliefs and practices* to development. The contributions of Russian psychologist Lev Vygotsky (1896–1934) have played a major role in this trend. Vygotsky's (1934/1987) perspective, called **sociocultural theory,** focuses on how *culture*— the values, beliefs, customs, and skills of a social group—is transmitted to the next generation. According to Vygotsky, *social interaction*—in particular, cooperative dialogues with more knowledgeable members of society—is necessary for children to acquire the ways of thinking and behaving that make up a community's culture (Rowe & Wertsch, 2002). Vygotsky believed that as adults and more expert peers help children master culturally meaningful activities, the communication between them becomes part of children's thinking. As children internalize the essential features of these dialogues, they can use the language within them to guide their own thought and actions and to acquire new skills (Berk & Harris, 2003; Winsler, Fernyhough, & Montero, 2009).

In Vygotsky's theory, children undergo certain stagewise changes. For example, when they acquire language, their ability to participate in dialogues with others is greatly enhanced, and mastery of culturally valued competencies surges forward. When children enter school, they spend much time discussing language, literacy, and other academic concepts—experiences that encourage them to reflect on their own thinking (Bodrova &

With her mother's guidance, this Navajo child learns to use a vertical weaving loom. According to Vygotsky's sociocultural theory, social interaction between children and more knowledgeable members of their culture leads to ways of thinking and behaving essential for success in that culture.

Leong, 2007; Kozulin, 2003). As a result, they gain dramatically in reasoning and problem solving.

Although most research inspired by Vygotsky's theory focuses on children, his ideas apply to people of any age. A central theme is that cultures select tasks for their members, and social interaction surrounding those tasks leads to competencies essential for success in a particular culture. For example, in industrialized nations, teachers help people learn to read, drive a car, or use a computer. Among the Zinacanteco Indians of southern Mexico, adult experts guide young girls as they master complicated weaving techniques (Greenfield, 2004).

Research stimulated by Vygotsky's theory reveals that people in every culture develop unique strengths. But Vygotsky's emphasis on social experiences led him to neglect the biological side of development. Although he recognized the importance of heredity and brain growth, he said little about their role in cognitive change.

Ecological Systems Theory

Urie Bronfenbrenner (1917–2005) is responsible for an approach that has moved to the forefront of the field because it offers the most differentiated and complete account of contextual influences on development. **Ecological systems theory** views the person as developing within a complex *system* of relationships affected by multiple levels of the surrounding environment. Because the child's biologically influenced dispositions join with environmental forces to mold development, Bronfenbrenner characterized his perspective as a *bioecological model* (Bronfenbrenner & Morris, 2006).

Bronfenbrenner envisioned the environment as a series of nested structures, including but also extending beyond the home, school, neighborhood, and workplace settings in which people spend their everyday lives (see Figure 1.5). Each layer of the environment is viewed as having a powerful impact on development.

■ **THE MICROSYSTEM.**   The innermost level of the environment, the **microsystem,** consists of activities and interaction patterns in the person's immediate surroundings. Bronfenbrenner emphasized that to understand development at this level, we must keep in mind that all relationships are *bidirectional*. For example, adults affect children's behavior, but children's biologically and socially influenced characteristics—their physical attributes, personalities, and capacities—also affect adults' behavior. A friendly, attentive child is likely to evoke positive, patient reactions from parents, whereas an irritable or distractible child is more likely to receive impatience, restriction, and punishment (Crockenberg & Leerkes, 2003).

Third parties—other individuals in the microsystem—also affect the quality of any two-person relationship. If they are supportive, interaction is enhanced. For example, when parents encourage each other in their child-rearing roles, each engages in more effective parenting (Caldera & Lindsey, 2006).

■ **THE MESOSYSTEM.**   The second level of Bronfenbrenner's model, the **mesosystem,** encompasses connections between microsystems. For example, a child's academic progress depends not just on activities that take place in classrooms but also on parent involvement in school life and on the extent to which

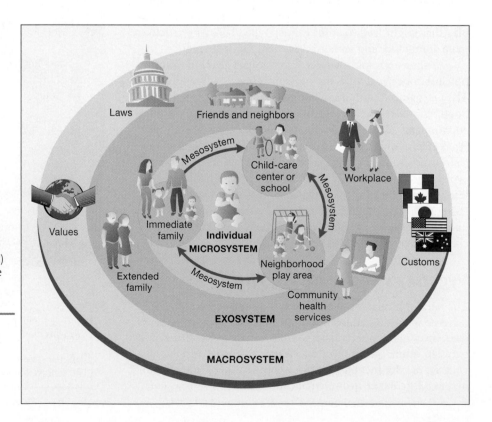

■ **FIGURE 1.5** ■ **Structure of the environment in ecological systems theory.** The *microsystem* concerns relations between the developing person and the immediate environment; the *mesosystem,* connections among immediate settings; the *exosystem,* social settings that affect but do not contain the developing person; and the *macrosystem,* the values, laws, customs, and resources of the culture that affect activities and interactions at all inner layers. The *chronosystem* (not pictured) is not a specific context. Instead, it refers to the dynamic, ever-changing nature of the person's environment.

In ecological systems theory, development occurs within a complex system of relationships affected by multiple levels of the environment. This father says good-bye to his daughter at the start of the school day. The girl's experiences at school (microsystem) and the father's experiences at work (exosystem) affect the father–daughter relationship.

academic learning is carried over into the home (Gershoff & Aber, 2006). Among adults, how well a person functions as spouse and parent at home is affected by relationships in the workplace, and vice versa (Gottfried, Gottfried, & Bathurst, 2002).

■ **THE EXOSYSTEM.** The **exosystem** consists of social settings that do not contain the developing person but nevertheless affect experiences in immediate settings. These can be formal organizations, such as the board of directors in the individual's workplace, religious institution, or community health and welfare services. Flexible work schedules, paid maternity and paternity leave, and sick leave for parents whose children are ill are examples of ways that work settings can help parents rear children and, indirectly, enhance the development of both adult and child. Exosystem supports can also be informal. Children are affected by their parents' social networks—friends and extended-family members who provide advice, companionship, and even financial assistance.

■ **THE MACROSYSTEM.** The outermost level of Bronfenbrenner's model, the **macrosystem,** consists of cultural values, laws, customs, and resources. The priority that the macrosystem gives to the needs of children and adults affects the support they receive at inner levels of the environment. For example, in countries that set high standards for child care and workplace benefits for employed parents, children are more likely to have favorable experiences in their immediate settings. And governments that provide a generous pension plan for retirees support the well-being of the elderly.

■ **A DYNAMIC, EVER-CHANGING SYSTEM.** The environment is not a static force that affects people in a uniform way. Instead, it is ever-changing. Whenever individuals alter the

roles or settings in their lives, the breadth of their microsystems changes. These shifts in contexts—or *ecological transitions,* as Bronfenbrenner called them—are often important turning points in development. Starting school, entering the workforce, marrying, becoming a parent, getting divorced, moving, and retiring are examples.

Bronfenbrenner called the temporal dimension of his model the **chronosystem** (the prefix *chrono* means "time"). Life changes can be imposed externally or can arise from within the person, since individuals shape many of their own settings and experiences. How they do so depends on their age; their physical, intellectual, and personality characteristics; and their environmental opportunities. Therefore, in ecological systems theory, people are both products and producers of their environments: The person and the environment form a network of interdependent effects.

ASK YOURSELF

» REVIEW
Explain how each recent theoretical perspective regards children and adults as active contributors to their own development.

» APPLY
Mario wants to find out precisely how children of different ages recall stories. Anna is interested in how adult–child communication in different cultures influences children's storytelling. Which theoretical perspective has Mario probably chosen? How about Anna? Explain.

» REFLECT
To illustrate the chronosystem in ecological systems theory, select an important event from your childhood, such as a class with an inspiring teacher or parental divorce. How did the event affect you? How might its impact have differed had you been five years younger? How about five years older?

Comparing Theories

In the preceding sections, we reviewed major theoretical perspectives in human development research. They differ in many respects.

First, they focus on different domains of development. Some, such as the psychoanalytic perspective and ethology, emphasize emotional and social development. Others, such as Piaget's cognitive-developmental theory, information processing, and Vygotsky's sociocultural theory, stress changes in thinking. The remaining approaches—behaviorism, social learning theory, evolutionary developmental psychology, ecological systems theory, and the lifespan perspective—discuss many aspects of human functioning.

Second, every theory contains a point of view about development. ***TAKE A MOMENT...*** As we conclude our review of theoretical perspectives, identify the stand each theory takes on the controversial issues presented at the beginning of this chapter. Then check your analysis against Table 1.5 on page 22.

■ **TABLE 1.5** ■ *Stances of Major Theories on Basic Issues in Human Development*

THEORY	CONTINUOUS OR DISCONTINUOUS DEVELOPMENT?	ONE COURSE OF DEVELOPMENT OR MANY?	RELATIVE INFLUENCE OF NATURE AND NURTURE?
Psychoanalytic perspective	*Discontinuous:* Psychosexual and psychosocial development takes place in stages.	*One course:* Stages are assumed to be universal.	*Both nature and nurture:* Innate impulses are channeled and controlled through child-rearing experiences. *Early experiences* set the course of later development.
Behaviorism and social learning theory	*Continuous:* Development involves an increase in learned behaviors.	*Many possible courses:* Behaviors reinforced and modeled may vary from person to person.	*Emphasis on nurture:* Development is the result of conditioning and modeling. *Both early and later experiences* are important.
Piaget's cognitive-developmental theory	*Discontinuous:* Cognitive development takes place in stages.	*One course:* Stages are assumed to be universal.	*Both nature and nurture:* Development occurs as the brain grows and children exercise their innate drive to discover reality in a generally stimulating environment. *Both early and later experiences* are important.
Information processing	*Continuous:* Children and adults change gradually in perception, attention, memory, and problem-solving skills.	*One course:* Changes studied characterize most or all children and adults.	*Both nature and nurture:* Children and adults are active, sense-making beings who modify their thinking as the brain grows and they confront new environmental demands. *Both early and later experiences* are important.
Ethology and evolutionary developmental psychology	*Both continuous and discontinuous:* Children and adults gradually develop a wider range of adaptive behaviors. Sensitive periods occur in which qualitatively distinct capacities emerge fairly suddenly.	*One course:* Adaptive behaviors and sensitive periods apply to all members of a species.	*Both nature and nurture:* Evolution and heredity influence behavior, and learning lends greater flexibility and adaptiveness to it. In sensitive periods, *early experiences* set the course of later development.
Vygotsky's sociocultural theory	*Both continuous and discontinuous:* Language development and schooling lead to stagewise changes. Dialogues with more expert members of society also lead to continuous changes that vary from culture to culture.	*Many possible courses:* Socially mediated changes in thought and behavior vary from culture to culture.	*Both nature and nurture:* Heredity, brain growth, and dialogues with more expert members of society jointly contribute to development. *Both early and later experiences* are important.
Ecological systems theory	*Not specified.*	*Many possible courses:* Biological dispositions join with environmental forces at multiple levels to mold development in unique ways.	*Both nature and nurture:* The individual's characteristics and the reactions of others affect each other in a bidirectional fashion. *Both early and later experiences* are important.
Lifespan perspective	*Both continuous and discontinuous:* Continuous gains and declines and discontinuous, stagewise emergence of new skills occur.	*Many possible courses:* Development is influenced by multiple, interacting biological, psychological, and social forces, many of which vary from person to person, leading to diverse pathways of change.	*Both nature and nurture:* Development is multidimensional, affected by an intricate blend of hereditary and environmental factors. Emphasizes plasticity at all ages. *Both early and later experiences* are important.

Studying Development

In every science, research is usually based on a *hypothesis*—a prediction about behavior drawn from a theory. Theories and hypotheses, however, merely initiate the many activities that result in sound evidence on human development.

Conducting research according to scientifically accepted procedures involves many steps and choices. Investigators must decide which participants, and how many, to include. Then they must figure out what the participants will be asked to do and when, where, and how many times each will be seen. Finally, they must examine and draw conclusions from their data.

In the following sections, we look at research strategies commonly used to study human development. We begin with *methods of gathering information*—the specific activities of participants, such as taking tests, answering questionnaires, responding to interviews, or being observed. Then we turn to *research designs*—overall plans for research studies that permit the best possible test of the investigator's hypothesis. Finally, we discuss ethical issues involved in doing research with human participants.

Common Research Methods

How does a researcher choose a basic approach to gathering information? Common methods include systematic observation, self-reports (such as questionnaires and interviews), clinical or case studies of a single individual, and ethnographies of the life circumstances of a specific group of people. Table 1.6 summarizes the strengths and limitations of each of these methods.

■ **SYSTEMATIC OBSERVATION.** Observations of behavior can be made in different ways. One approach is to go into the field, or natural environment, and record the behavior of interest—a method called **naturalistic observation.**

A study of preschoolers' responses to their peers' distress provides a good example (Farver & Branstetter, 1994). Observing 3- and 4-year-olds in child-care centers, the researchers recorded each instance of crying and the reactions of nearby children—whether they ignored, watched, commented on the child's unhappiness, scolded or teased, or shared, helped, or expressed sympathy. Caregiver behaviors—explaining why a child was crying, mediating conflict, or offering comfort—were noted to see if adult sensitivity was related to children's caring responses. A strong relationship emerged. The great strength of naturalistic observation is that investigators can see directly the everyday behaviors they hope to explain.

■ TABLE 1.6 ■ *Strengths and Limitations of Common Research Methods*

METHOD	DESCRIPTION	STRENGTHS	LIMITATIONS
SYSTEMATIC OBSERVATION			
Naturalistic observation	Observation of behavior in natural contexts	Reflects participants' everyday lives.	Cannot control conditions under which participants are observed.
Structured observation	Observation of behavior in a laboratory, where conditions are the same for all participants	Grants each participant an equal opportunity to display the behavior of interest.	May not yield observations typical of participants' behavior in everyday life.
SELF-REPORTS			
Clinical interview	Flexible interviewing procedure in which the investigator obtains a complete account of the participant's thoughts	Comes as close as possible to the way participants think in everyday life. Great breadth and depth of information can be obtained in a short time.	May not result in accurate reporting of information. Flexible procedure makes comparing individuals' responses difficult.
Structured interview, questionnaires, and tests	Self-report instruments in which each participant is asked the same questions in the same way	Permits comparisons of participants' responses and efficient data collection. Researchers can specify answer alternatives that participants might not think of in an open-ended interview.	Does not yield the same depth of information as a clinical interview. Responses are still subject to inaccurate reporting.
CLINICAL, OR CASE STUDY, METHOD			
	A full picture of one individual's psychological functioning, obtained by combining interviews, observations, and test scores	Provides rich, descriptive insights into factors that affect development.	May be biased by researchers' theoretical preferences. Findings cannot be applied to individuals other than the participant.
ETHNOGRAPHY			
	Participant observation of a culture or distinct social group; by making extensive field notes, the researcher tries to capture the culture's unique values and social processes	Provides a more complete description than can be derived from a single observational visit, interview, or questionnaire.	May be biased by researchers' values and theoretical preferences. Findings cannot be applied to individuals and settings other than the ones studied.

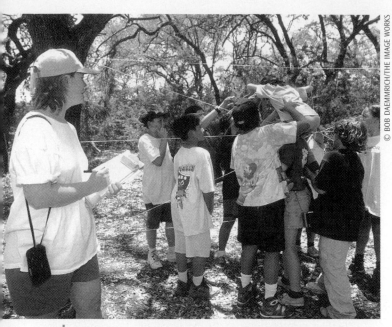

© BOB DAEMMRICH/THE IMAGE WORKS

In naturalistic observation, the researcher goes into the field and records the behavior of interest. Here, the researcher observes children at a summer camp. She may be focusing on their playmate choices, cooperation, helpfulness, or conflicts.

Naturalistic observation also has a major limitation: Not all individuals have the same opportunity to display a particular behavior in everyday life. In the study just described, some children might have witnessed a child crying more often than others or been exposed to more cues for positive social responses from caregivers. For these reasons, they might have displayed more compassion.

Researchers commonly deal with this difficulty by making **structured observations,** in which the investigator sets up a laboratory situation that evokes the behavior of interest so that every participant has an equal opportunity to display the response. In one study, 2-year-olds' emotional reactions to harm that they thought they had caused were observed by asking them to take care of a rag doll that had been modified so its leg would fall off when the child picked it up. Researchers recorded children's facial expressions of sadness, efforts to help the doll, and body tension—responses indicating worry, remorse, and a desire to make amends for the mishap. In addition, mothers were asked to engage in brief conversations about emotions with their children (Garner, 2003). Toddlers whose mothers more often explained the causes and consequences of emotion were more likely to express concern for the injured doll.

Systematic observation provides invaluable information on how children and adults actually behave, but it tells us little about the reasoning behind their responses. For that information, researchers must turn to self-report techniques.

■ **SELF-REPORTS.** Self-reports ask research participants to provide information on their perceptions, thoughts, abilities, feelings, attitudes, beliefs, and past experiences. They range from relatively unstructured interviews to highly structured interviews, questionnaires, and tests.

In a **clinical interview,** researchers use a flexible, conversational style to probe for the participant's point of view. In the following example, Piaget questioned a 5-year-old child about his understanding of dreams:

Where does the dream come from?—I think you sleep so well that you dream.—*Does it come from us or from outside?*—From outside.—*When you are in bed and you dream, where is the dream?*—In my bed, under the blanket. I don't really know. If it was in my stomach, the bones would be in the way and I shouldn't see it.—*Is the dream there when you sleep?*—Yes, it is in the bed beside me. (Piaget, 1926/1930, pp. 97–98)

Although a researcher conducting clinical interviews with more than one participant would typically ask the same first question to establish a common task, individualized prompts are used to provide a fuller picture of each person's reasoning (Ginsburg, 1997).

The clinical interview has two major strengths. First, it permits people to display their thoughts in terms that are as close as possible to the way they think in everyday life. Second, the clinical interview can provide a large amount of information in a fairly brief period. For example, in an hour-long session, we can obtain a wide range of information on child rearing from a parent or on life circumstances from an elder—much more than we could capture by observing for the same amount of time.

A major limitation of the clinical interview has to do with accuracy. Some participants, wishing to please the interviewer, may make up answers that do not represent their actual thinking. When asked about past events, some may have trouble recalling exactly what happened. And because the clinical interview depends on verbal ability and expressiveness, it may underestimate the capacities of individuals who have difficulty putting their thoughts into words.

The clinical interview has also been criticized because of its flexibility. When questions are phrased differently for each participant, responses may reflect the manner of interviewing rather than real differences in the way people think about a topic. **Structured interviews** (including tests and questionnaires), in which each participant is asked the same set of questions in the same way, eliminate this problem. But structured interviews do not yield the same depth of information as clinical interviews. And they can still be affected by the problem of inaccurate reporting.

■ **THE CLINICAL, OR CASE STUDY, METHOD.** An outgrowth of psychoanalytic theory, the **clinical, or case study, method** brings together a wide range of information on one person, including interviews, observations, and sometimes test scores. The aim is to obtain as complete a picture as possible of that individual's psychological functioning and the experiences that led up to it.

The clinical method is well-suited to studying the development of certain types of individuals who are few in number but

Using the clinical, or case study, method, this researcher combines interviews with the mother and observations and testing of the child to construct an in-depth picture of one child's psychological functioning.

vary widely in characteristics. For example, the method has been used to find out what contributes to the accomplishments of *prodigies*—extremely gifted children who attain adult competence in a field before age 10. Consider Adam, a boy who read, wrote, and composed musical pieces before he was out of diapers. Clinical research indicates that such children rarely realize their extraordinary potential without nurturing, committed parents and exceptional teachers who guide and encourage the child's special gift (Goldsmith, 2000; Moran & Gardner, 2006).

The clinical method yields richly detailed case narratives that offer valuable insights into the many factors influencing development. Nevertheless, like all other methods, it has drawbacks. Because information often is collected unsystematically and subjectively, researchers' theoretical preferences may bias their observations and interpretations. In addition, investigators cannot assume that their conclusions apply, or generalize, to anyone other than the person studied (Stanovich, 2007). Even when patterns emerge across several cases, it is wise to confirm these with other research strategies.

■ **METHODS FOR STUDYING CULTURE.** To study the impact of culture, researchers adjust the methods just considered or tap procedures specially devised for cross-cultural and multicultural research (Triandis, 2007). Which approach investigators choose depends on their research goals.

Sometimes researchers are interested in characteristics that are believed to be universal but that vary in degree from one society to the next: Are parents warmer or more directive in some cultures than others? How strong are gender stereotypes in different nations? In each instance, several cultural groups will be compared, and all participants must be questioned or observed in the same way. Therefore, researchers draw on the self-report and observational procedures we have already considered, adapting them through translation so they can be understood in each cultural context.

At other times, researchers want to uncover the *cultural meanings* of children's and adults' behaviors by becoming as familiar as possible with their way of life. To achieve this goal, investigators rely on a method borrowed from the field of anthropology—**ethnography**. Like the clinical method, ethnographic research is a descriptive, qualitative technique. But instead of aiming to understand a single individual, it is directed toward understanding a culture or a distinct social group through *participant observation*. Typically, the researcher spends months, and sometimes years, in the cultural community, participating in its daily life. Extensive field notes are gathered, consisting of a mix of observations, self-reports from members of the culture, and careful interpretations by the investigator (Miller, Hengst, & Wang, 2003; Shweder et al., 2006). Later, these notes are put together into a description of the community that tries to capture its unique values and social processes.

In some ethnographies, investigators look at many aspects of experience, as one team of researchers did in describing what it is like to grow up in a small American town. Others focus on one or a few settings and issues—for example, barriers to effective parent–school communication in a Mexican-American community or African-Caribbean adults' reactions to a diagnosis of high blood pressure, signaling elevated risk for heart disease (Higginbottom, 2006; Peshkin, 1997; Valdés, 1998). Researchers

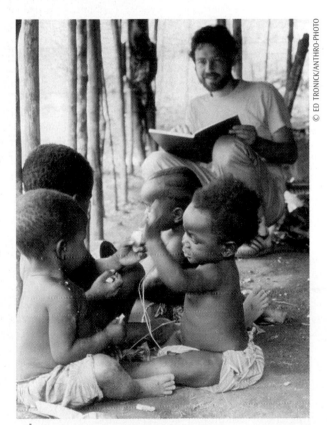

This Western ethnographer spent months living among the Efe people of the Republic of Congo. Here he observes young children sharing food. The Efe value and encourage cooperation and generosity at an early age.

■ CULTURAL INFLUENCES ■

Immigrant Youths: Amazing Adaptation

Over the past several decades, a rising tide of immigrants has come to North America, fleeing war and persecution in their homelands or seeking better life chances. Today, one-fifth of the U.S. youth population have foreign-born parents; nearly one-third of these youths are foreign-born themselves, mostly from Asia and Latin America (Suarez-Orozco, Todorova, & Qin, 2006).

How well are immigrant youths adapting to their new country? To find out, researchers use multiple research methods, including academic testing, questionnaires assessing psychological adjustment, and in-depth ethnographies.

Academic Achievement and Adjustment

Although educators and laypeople often assume that the transition to a new country has a negative impact on psychological well-being, evidence reveals that children of immigrant parents adapt amazingly well. Students who are first-generation (foreign-born) and second-generation (American-born, with immigrant parents) often achieve in school as well as or better than students of native-born parents (Fuligni, 2004; Saucier et al., 2002).

Findings on psychological adjustment are similar. Compared with their agemates, adolescents from immigrant families are less likely to commit delinquent and violent acts, to use drugs and alcohol, or to have early sex. They are also less likely to be obese or to have missed school because of illness. And they feel as positively about themselves as young people with native-born parents. These successes do not depend on having extensive time to adjust to a new way of life. Recently arrived high school students do as well in school and report just as favorable self-esteem as those who came at younger ages (Fuligni, 1998; Saucier et al., 2002).

These outcomes are strongest for Chinese, Filipino, Japanese, Korean, and East Indian youths (Fuligni, 2004; Louie, 2001; Portes & Rumbaut, 2005). And a minority of young people—especially of certain ethnicities, including Cambodians and Laotians—deviate from these favorable patterns, showing high rates of school dropout, delinquency, teenage parenthood, and drug use (Zhou & Xiong, 2005). Variations in parental economic resources and education contribute to these trends. Still, even youths from ethnic groups that face considerable financial hardship (such as Mexican and Vietnamese) are successful (Fuligni & Yoshikawa, 2003). Factors other than income are responsible.

Family and Community Influences

Ethnographies reveal that immigrant parents view education as the surest way to improve life chances and underscore the importance of trying hard (Goldenberg et al., 2001; Louie, 2001). They remind their children that, because educational opportunities were not available in their native countries, they themselves are often limited to menial jobs.

Adolescents from immigrant families internalize their parents' valuing of education, endorsing it more strongly than agemates with native-born parents (Asakawa, 2001; Fuligni, 2004). Because minority ethnicities usually stress allegiance to family and community over individual goals, first- and second-generation young people feel a strong sense of obligation to their parents. They view school success as both their own and their parents' success and as a way to repay parents for the hardships they have endured (Bacallao & Smokowski, 2007; Fuligni, Yip, & Tseng, 2002). Both family relationships and school achievement protect these youths from delinquency, early pregnancy and drug use, and other risky behaviors.

Immigrant parents of successful youths typically develop close ties to an ethnic community, which exerts additional control through a high consensus on values and constant monitoring of young people's activities. As one 16-year-old straight-A student remarked, "My parents know pretty much all the kids in the neighborhood. . . . Everybody here knows everybody else. It's hard to get away with much" (Zhou & Bankston, 1998, p. 93).

The experiences of well-adjusted immigrant youths are not problem-free. Chinese adolescents who had arrived in the United States within the previous year described their adjustment as very difficult because they were not proficient in English and, as a result, found many everyday tasks challenging and felt socially isolated (Yeh et al., 2008). Young immigrants also encounter racial and ethnic prejudices and experience tensions between family values and the new culture—challenges we will take up in Chapter 12. In the long term, however, family and community cohesion, supervision, and high expectations promote favorable outcomes.

© JEFF GREENBERG/ALAMY

In Miami, Florida, Asian-American girls participate in the Hong Kong Dragon Boat Race Festival. Cultural values that foster allegiance to family and community promote high achievement and protect many immigrant youths from involvement in risky behaviors.

---

may supplement traditional self-report and observational methods with ethnography if they suspect that unique meanings underlie cultural differences, as the Cultural Influences box above reveals.

Ethnographers strive to minimize their own influence on the culture they are studying by becoming part of it. Never-

theless, as with clinical studies, investigators' cultural values and theoretical commitments sometimes lead them to observe selectively or misinterpret what they see. In addition, the findings of ethnographic studies cannot be assumed to generalize beyond the people and settings in which the research was conducted.

ASK YOURSELF

>> REVIEW

Why might a researcher choose structured observation over naturalistic observation? How about the reverse?

>> APPLY

A researcher wants to study the thoughts and feelings of parents on active duty in the military and those of their school-age and adolescent children. Which method should she use? Explain.

>> REFLECT

Reread the description of nonnormative influences on page 9, and cite an example from your own life. Which method would be best-suited to studying the impact of such an event on development?

General Research Designs

In deciding on a research design, investigators choose a way of setting up a study that permits them to test their hypotheses with the greatest certainty possible. Two main types of designs are used in all research on human behavior: *correlational* and *experimental*.

■ **CORRELATIONAL DESIGN.** In a **correlational design,** researchers gather information on individuals, generally in natural life circumstances, without altering their experiences. Then they look at relationships between participants' characteristics and their behavior or development. Suppose we want to answer the following question: Do parents' styles of interacting with children have any bearing on children's intelligence? In this and many other instances, the conditions of interest are difficult or impossible to arrange and control and must be studied as they currently exist.

Correlational studies have one major limitation: We cannot infer cause and effect. For example, if we were to find that parental interaction is related to children's intelligence, we would not know whether parents' behavior actually *causes* intellectual differences among children. In fact, the opposite is possible: The behaviors of highly intelligent children may be so attractive that they cause parents to interact more favorably. Or a third variable that we did not even consider, such as the amount of noise and distraction in the home, may cause changes in both parental interaction and children's intelligence.

In correlational studies and in other types of research designs, investigators often examine relationships by using a **correlation coefficient**—a number that describes how two measures, or variables, are associated with each other. We will encounter the correlation coefficient in discussing research findings throughout this book, so let's look at what it is and how it is interpreted. A correlation coefficient can range in value from +1.00 to –1.00. The *magnitude, or size, of the number* shows the *strength of the relationship.* A zero correlation indicates no relationship; the closer the value is to +1.00 or –1.00, the stronger the relationship. For instance, a correlation of –.78 is high, –.52 is

moderate, and –.18 is low. Note, however, that correlations of +.52 and –.52 are equally strong. The *sign of the number* (+ or –) refers to the *direction of the relationship.* A positive sign (+) means that as one variable *increases,* the other also *increases.* A negative sign (–) indicates that as one variable *increases,* the other *decreases.*

Let's look at some examples of how a correlation coefficient works. One researcher reported a +.55 correlation between a measure of maternal language stimulation and the size of children's vocabularies at 2 years of age (Hoff, 2003). This is a moderate correlation, which indicates that mothers who spoke more to their toddlers had children who were more advanced in language development. In two other studies, maternal sensitivity was modestly associated with children's cooperativeness in consistent ways. First, maternal warmth during play correlated positively with 2-year-olds' willingness to comply with their mother's directive to clean up toys, at +.34 (Feldman & Klein, 2003). Second, the extent to which mothers spoke harshly, interrupted, and controlled their 4-year-olds' play correlated negatively with children's compliance, at –.31 for boys and –.42 for girls (Smith et al., 2004).

TAKE A MOMENT... Are you tempted to conclude from these correlations that the maternal behaviors influenced children's responses? Although the researchers suspected this was so, they

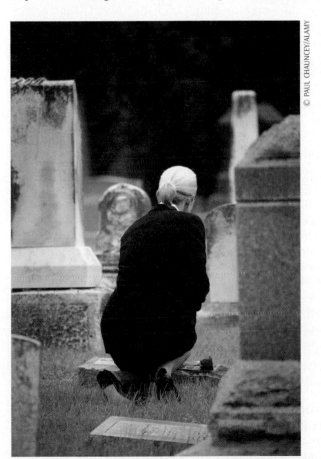

© PAUL CHAUNCEY/ALAMY

Does the death of a spouse in old age affect the surviving partner's physical health and psychological well-being? A correlational design can be used to answer this question, but it does not permit researchers to determine the precise cause of their findings.

could not be sure of cause and effect. Can you think of other possible explanations? Finding a relationship in a correlational study does suggest that tracking down its cause—using a more powerful experimental strategy, if possible—would be worthwhile.

■ **EXPERIMENTAL DESIGN.** An **experimental design** permits inferences about cause and effect because researchers use an evenhanded procedure to assign people to two or more treatment conditions. In an experiment, the events and behaviors of interest are divided into two types, independent and dependent variables. The **independent variable** is the one the investigator expects to cause changes in another variable. The **dependent variable** is the one the investigator expects to be influenced by the independent variable. Cause-and-effect relationships can be detected because the researcher directly *controls* or *manipulates* changes in the independent variable by exposing participants to the treatment conditions. Then the researcher compares their performance on measures of the dependent variable.

In one *laboratory experiment*, investigators explored the impact of adults' angry interactions on children's adjustment (El-Sheikh, Cummings, & Reiter, 1996). They hypothesized that the way angry encounters end (independent variable) affects children's emotional reactions (dependent variable). Four- and 5-year-olds were brought to a laboratory one at a time, accompanied by their mothers. One group was exposed to an *unresolved-anger treatment,* in which two adult actors entered the room and argued but did not work out their disagreements. The other group witnessed a *resolved-anger treatment,* in which the adults ended their disputes by apologizing and compromising. When witnessing a follow-up adult conflict, children in the resolved-anger treatment showed less distress, as measured by fewer anxious facial expressions, less freezing in place, and less seeking of closeness to their mothers. The experiment revealed that anger resolution can reduce the stressful impact of adult conflict on children.

In experimental studies, investigators must control for participants' characteristics that could reduce the accuracy of their findings. In the study just described, if a greater number of children from homes high in parental conflict ended up in the unresolved-anger treatment, we could not tell what produced the results—the independent variable or the children's backgrounds. To protect against this problem, researchers engage in **random assignment** of participants to treatment conditions. By using an unbiased procedure, such as drawing numbers out of a hat or flipping a coin, investigators increase the chances that participants' characteristics will be equally distributed across treatment groups.

■ **MODIFIED EXPERIMENTAL DESIGNS: FIELD AND NATURAL EXPERIMENTS.** Most experiments are conducted in laboratories, where researchers can achieve the maximum possible control over treatment conditions. But, as we have already indicated, findings obtained in laboratories may not always apply to everyday situations. In *field experiments,* investigators assign participants randomly to treatment conditions in natural settings. In the experiment just described, we can conclude that the emotional climate established by adults affects children's behavior in the laboratory. But does it also do so in daily life? To answer this question, researchers might have caregivers deliberately act differently—in a nurturing way versus blandly—with two groups of children in a child-care center.

When researchers cannot randomly assign participants and manipulate conditions in the real world, they can sometimes compromise by conducting *natural, or quasi-, experiments* comparing treatments that already exist, such as different family environments, schools, workplaces, or retirement villages. These studies differ from correlational research only in that groups of participants are carefully chosen to ensure that their characteristics are as much alike as possible. In this way, investigators do their best to rule out alternative explanations for their treatment effects. But, despite these efforts, natural experiments cannot achieve the precision and rigor of true experimental research.

Table 1.7 summarizes the strengths and limitations of correlational and experimental designs. It also includes an overview of designs for studying development, to which we turn next.

Designs for Studying Development

Scientists interested in human development require information about the way research participants change over time. To answer questions about development, they must extend correlational and experimental approaches to include measurements at different ages, using longitudinal and cross-sectional designs.

■ **THE LONGITUDINAL DESIGN.** In a **longitudinal design,** participants are studied repeatedly, and changes are noted as they get older. The time spanned may be relatively short (a few months to several years) or very long (a decade or even a lifetime). The longitudinal approach has two major strengths. First, because it tracks the performance of each person over time, researchers can identify common patterns as well as individual differences in development. Second, longitudinal studies permit investigators to examine relationships between early and later events and behaviors. Let's illustrate these ideas.

A group of researchers wondered whether children who display extreme personality styles—either angry and explosive or shy and withdrawn—retain the same dispositions when they become adults. In addition, the researchers wanted to know what kinds of experiences promote stability or change in personality and what consequences explosiveness and shyness have for long-term adjustment. To answer these questions, the researchers delved into the archives of the Guidance Study, a well-known longitudinal investigation initiated in 1928 at the University of California, Berkeley, and continued for several decades (Caspi, Elder, & Bem, 1987, 1988).

Results revealed that the two personality styles were moderately stable. Between ages 8 and 30, a good number of individuals remained the same, whereas others changed substantially. When stability did occur, it appeared to be due to a "snowballing effect," in which children evoked responses from adults and peers that acted to maintain their dispositions. Explosive youngsters were likely to be treated with anger, whereas shy children were apt to

■ **TABLE 1.7** ■ *Strengths and Limitations of Research Designs*

DESIGN	DESCRIPTION	STRENGTHS	LIMITATIONS
GENERAL			
Correlational	The investigator obtains information on participants without altering their experiences.	Permits study of relationships between variables.	Does not permit inferences about cause-and-effect relationships.
Experimental	Through random assignment of participants to treatment conditions, the investigator manipulates an independent variable and examines its effect on a dependent variable. Can be conducted in the laboratory or the natural environment.	Permits inferences about cause-and-effect relationships.	When conducted in the laboratory, findings may not generalize to the real world. In *field experiments,* control over the treatment is usually weaker than in the laboratory. In *natural,* or *quasi-, experiments,* lack of random assignment substantially reduces the precision of research.
DEVELOPMENTAL			
Longitudinal	The investigator studies the same group of participants repeatedly at different ages.	Permits study of common patterns and individual differences in development and relationships between early and later events and behaviors.	Age-related changes may be distorted because of participant dropout, practice effects, and cohort effects.
Cross-sectional	The investigator studies groups of participants differing in age at the same point in time.	More efficient than the longitudinal design. Not plagued by such problems as participant dropout and practice effects.	Does not permit study of individual developmental trends. Age differences may be distorted because of cohort effects.
Sequential	The investigator conducts several similar cross-sectional or longitudinal studies (called sequences) at varying times.	When the design includes longitudinal sequences, permits both longitudinal and cross-sectional comparisons. Also reveals cohort effects. Permits tracking of age-related changes more efficiently than the longitudinal design.	May have the same problems as longitudinal and cross-sectional strategies, but the design itself helps identify difficulties.

be ignored. As a result, explosive children came to view others as hostile, while shy children regarded them as unfriendly (Caspi & Roberts, 2001). Together, these factors led explosive children to sustain or increase their unruliness and shy children to continue to withdraw—patterns that tended to persist into adulthood and to negatively affect adjustment to marriage, parenting, and work life. Shy women, however, were an exception. Because a withdrawn, unassertive style was socially acceptable for females at that time, they showed no special adjustment problems.

■ **PROBLEMS IN CONDUCTING LONGITUDINAL RESEARCH.** Despite their strengths, longitudinal investigations pose a number of problems. For example, participants may move away or drop out of the research for other reasons. This biases the sample so that it no longer represents the population to whom researchers would like to generalize their findings. Also, from repeated study, people may become more aware of their own thoughts, feelings, and actions and revise them in ways that have little to do with age-related change. In addition, they may become "test-wise." Their performance may improve as a result of *practice effects*—better test-taking skills and increased famil-

iarity with the test—not because of factors commonly associated with development.

The most widely discussed threat to longitudinal findings is **cohort effects** (see page 9): Individuals born in the same time period are influenced by a particular set of historical and cultural conditions. Results based on one cohort may not apply to people developing at other times. For example, unlike the findings on female shyness described in the preceding section, which were gathered in the 1950s, today's shy young women tend to be poorly adjusted—a difference that may be due to changes in gender roles in Western societies. Shy adults, whether male or female, feel more anxious, depressed, and lonely and may do less well in educational and career attainment than their agemates (Caspi et al., 2003; Mounts et al., 2006). Similarly, a longitudinal study of lifespan development would probably result in quite different findings if it were carried out around the time of World War II or in the first decade of the twenty-first century.

■ **THE CROSS-SECTIONAL DESIGN.** The length of time it takes for many behaviors to change, even in limited longitudinal

AP IMAGES/PABLO MARTINEZ MONSIVAIS

Cohort effects are particular historical and cultural conditions that affect individuals born in the same time period. Young people who witnessed this victory celebration—Barack and Michelle Obama and their two daughters standing before a jubilant crowd in Chicago's Grant Park the night of the 2008 presidential election—came away with a new sense of what is possible for members of America's ethnic minorities.

studies, has led researchers to turn toward a more efficient strategy. In the **cross-sectional design,** groups of people differing in age are studied at the same point in time. Because participants are measured only once, researchers need not be concerned about such difficulties as participant dropout or practice effects.

A study in which students in grades 3, 6, 9, and 12 filled out a questionnaire about their sibling relationships provides a good illustration (Buhrmester & Furman, 1990). Findings revealed that feelings of sibling companionship declined during adolescence. The researchers speculated that as adolescents move from psychological dependence on the family to greater involvement with peers, they may have less time and motional need to invest in siblings. As we will see in Chapter 12, subsequent research has confirmed this age-related trend.

■ **PROBLEMS IN CONDUCTING CROSS-SECTIONAL RESEARCH.** Despite its convenience, cross-sectional research does not provide evidence about development at the level at which it actually occurs: the individual. For example, in the cross-sectional study of sibling relationships just discussed, comparisons are limited to age-group averages. We cannot tell if important individual differences exist. Indeed, longitudinal findings reveal that adolescents vary considerably in the changing quality of their sibling relationships. Although many become more distant, others become more supportive and intimate, and still others more rivalrous and antagonistic (Branje et al., 2004; Kim et al., 2006; Whiteman & Loken, 2006).

Cross-sectional studies—especially those that cover a wide age span—have another problem. Like longitudinal research, they can be threatened by cohort effects. For example, compar-

isons of 10-year-old cohorts, 20-year-old cohorts, and 30-year-old cohorts—groups born and reared in different years—may not really represent age-related changes. Instead, they may reflect unique experiences associated with the historical period in which the age groups were growing up.

■ **IMPROVING DEVELOPMENTAL DESIGNS.** Researchers have devised ways of building on the strengths and minimizing the weaknesses of longitudinal and cross-sectional approaches. Several modified developmental designs have resulted.

Sequential Designs. To overcome some of the limitations of traditional developmental designs, investigators sometimes use **sequential designs,** in which they conduct several similar cross-sectional or longitudinal studies (called *sequences*) at varying times. As the illustration in Figure 1.6 reveals, some sequential designs combine longitudinal and cross-sectional strategies, an approach that has two advantages:

■ We can find out whether cohort effects are operating by comparing participants of the same age who were born in different years. In the example in Figure 1.6, we can compare the three longitudinal samples at ages 20, 30, and 40. If they do not differ, we can rule out cohort effects.

■ We can make longitudinal and cross-sectional comparisons. If outcomes are similar in both, then we can be especially confident about our findings.

In a study that used the design in Figure 1.6, researchers wanted to find out whether adult personality development progresses as Erikson's psychosocial theory predicts (Whitbourne et al., 1992). Questionnaires measuring Erikson's stages were given to three cohorts of 20-year-olds, each born a decade apart. The cohorts were reassessed at ten-year intervals. Consistent with Erikson's theory, longitudinal and cross-sectional gains in identity and intimacy occurred between ages 20 and 30—a trend unaffected by historical time period. But a powerful cohort effect emerged for consolidation of the sense of industry: At age 20, Cohort 1 scored substantially below Cohorts 2 and 3. Notice that members of Cohort 1 reached age 20 in the mid-1960s. As college students, they were part of an era of political protest that reflected disenchantment with the work ethic. Once out of college, they caught up with the other cohorts in industry. Followed up in 2001 at age 54, Cohort 1 showed a decline in focus on identity issues and a gain in ego integrity—trends expected to continue as they reach their sixties and seventies (Sneed, Whitbourne, & Culang, 2006). Future tracking of Cohorts 2 and 3 will reveal whether they, too, follow this Erikson-predicted psychosocial path.

By uncovering cohort effects, sequential designs help explain diversity in development. Yet to date only a small number of sequential studies have been conducted.

Combining Experimental and Developmental Designs. Perhaps you noticed that all the examples of longitudinal and cross-sectional research we have considered permit only correlational, not causal, inferences. Sometimes researchers can ex-

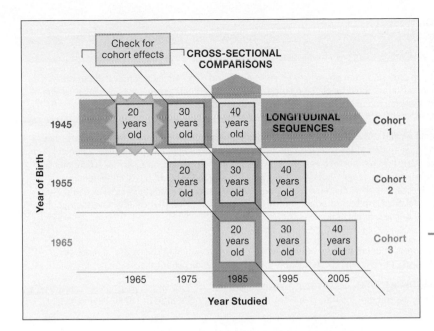

■ **FIGURE 1.6** ■ **Example of a sequential design.**
Three cohorts, born in 1945 (blue), 1955 (pink), and 1965 (green), are followed longitudinally from 20 to 40 years of age. The design permits the researcher to check for cohort effects by comparing people of the same age who were born in different years. In a study that used this design, the 20-year-olds in Cohort 1 differed substantially from the 20-year-olds in Cohorts 2 and 3, indicating powerful history-graded influences. This design also permits longitudinal and cross-sectional comparisons. Similar findings lend additional confidence in the results.

plore the causal link between experiences and development by experimentally manipulating the experiences. If, as a result, development improves, then we have strong evidence for a causal association. Today, research that combines an experimental strategy with either a longitudinal or a cross-sectional approach is increasingly common.

ASK YOURSELF

≫ **REVIEW**
Explain how cohort effects can affect the findings of both longitudinal and cross-sectional studies. How do sequential designs reveal cohort effects?

≫ **APPLY**
A researcher compares older adults with chronic heart disease to those with no major health problems and finds that the first group scores lower on mental tests. Can the researcher conclude that heart disease causes a decline in intellectual functioning in late adulthood? Explain.

≫ **REFLECT**
Suppose a researcher asks you to enroll your baby in a ten-year longitudinal study. What factors would lead you to agree and stay involved? Do your answers shed light on why longitudinal studies often have biased samples?

Ethics in Lifespan Research

Research into human behavior creates ethical issues because, unfortunately, the quest for scientific knowledge can sometimes exploit people. For this reason, special guidelines for research have been developed by the federal government, by funding agencies, and by research-oriented associations, such as the American Psychological Association (2002) and the Society for Research in Child Development (2007). Table 1.8 on page 32 presents a summary of basic research rights drawn from these guidelines. **TAKE A MOMENT...** After examining them, read about the following research situations, each of which poses a serious ethical dilemma. What precautions do you think should be taken in each instance?

■ In a study of moral development, an investigator wants to assess children's ability to resist temptation by videotaping their behavior without their knowledge. She promises 7-year-olds a prize for solving difficult puzzles but tells them not to look at a classmate's correct solutions, which are deliberately placed at the back of the room. Informing children ahead of time that cheating is being studied or that their behavior is being monitored will destroy the purpose of the study.

■ A researcher wants to study the impact of mild daily exercise on the physical and mental health of elderly patients in nursing homes. He consults each resident's doctor to make sure that the exercise routine will not be harmful. But when he seeks the residents' consent, he finds that many do not comprehend the purpose of the research. And some appear to agree simply to relieve feelings of isolation and loneliness.

As these examples indicate, when children or the aged take part in research, the ethical concerns are especially complex. Immaturity makes it difficult or impossible for children to evaluate for themselves what participation in research will mean. And because mental impairment rises with very advanced age, some older adults cannot make voluntary and informed choices. The life circumstances of others make them unusually vulnerable to pressure for participation (Kim et al., 2004; Society for Research in Child Development, 2007).

The ultimate responsibility for the ethical integrity of research lies with the investigator. But researchers are advised—and often required—to seek advice from others. Committees for this purpose, called *institutional review boards (IRBs)*, exist

■ **TABLE 1.8** ■ *Rights of Research Participants*

RESEARCH RIGHT	DESCRIPTION
Protection from harm	Participants have the right to be protected from physical or psychological harm in research. If in doubt about the harmful effects of research, investigators should seek the opinion of others. When harm seems possible, investigators should find other means for obtaining the desired information or abandon the research.
Informed consent	All participants, including children and the elderly, have the right to have explained to them, in language appropriate to their level of understanding, all aspects of the research that may affect their willingness to participate. When children are participants, informed consent of parents as well as of others who act on the child's behalf (such as school officials) should be obtained, preferably in writing. Older adults who are cognitively impaired should be asked to appoint a surrogate decision maker. If they cannot do so, then someone should be named by an institutional review board (IRB) after careful consultation with relatives and professionals who know the person well. All participants have the right to discontinue participation in the research at any time.
Privacy	Participants have the right to concealment of their identity on all information collected in the course of research. They also have this right with respect to written reports and any informal discussions about the research.
Knowledge of results	Participants have the right to be informed of the results of research in language that is appropriate to their level of understanding.
Beneficial treatments	If experimental treatments believed to be beneficial are under investigation, participants in control groups have the right to alternative beneficial treatments if they are available.

Sources: American Psychological Association, 2002; Society for Research in Child Development, 2007.

in colleges, universities, and other institutions. If there are any risks to participants' safety and welfare that the research does not justify, then the IRB always favors the participants' interests.

The ethical principle of *informed consent* requires special interpretation when participants cannot fully appreciate the research goals and activities. Parental consent is meant to protect the safety of children, whose ability to decide is not yet mature. But as soon as children are old enough to appreciate the purpose of the research, and certainly by age 7, their own informed consent should be obtained in addition to parental consent. Around this age, changes in children's thinking permit them to better understand simple scientific principles and the needs of others. Researchers should respect and enhance these new capacities by giving school-age children a full explanation of research activities in language they can understand (Fisher, 1993). Extra care must be taken when telling children that the information they provide will be kept confidential and that they can end their participation at any time. Even adolescents may not understand, and sometimes do not believe, these promises (Bruzzese & Fisher, 2003; Ondrusek et al., 1998).

Most older adults require no more than the usual informed-consent procedures. Yet many investigators set upper age limits in studies relevant to the elderly, thereby excluding the oldest adults (Bayer & Tadd, 2000). The elderly should not be stereotyped as incompetent to decide about their own participation or to engage in research activities. Nevertheless, extra measures, such as the appointment of a surrogate decision maker to safeguard the elder's welfare, must be taken to protect those who are cognitively impaired or chronically ill.

Finally, all ethical guidelines advise that special precautions be taken in the use of deception and concealment, as occurs when researchers observe people from behind one-way mirrors, give them false feedback about their performance, or do not tell

Older adults should not be arbitrarily excluded from research. Most require only the typical informed-consent procedures, and their participation brings both personal and scientific benefits. For elders who are cognitively impaired—like this man with Alzheimer's disease—informed consent may not be possible without the assistance of a surrogate decision maker.

them the truth about the real purpose of the research. When these kinds of procedures are used, *debriefing,* in which the investigator provides a full account and justification of the activities, occurs after the research session is over. But young children often lack the cognitive skills to understand the reasons for deceptive procedures, and despite explanations, even older children may leave the research situation with their trust in adults

undermined. Ethical standards permit deception if investigators satisfy IRBs that a study's potential benefits to society are great enough to justify infringing on participants' right to informed consent and risking other harm (Fisher, 2005). Nevertheless, because deception may have serious emotional consequences for some youngsters, many experts in research ethics believe that investigators should use it only if the risk of harm is minimal.

Summary

A Scientific, Applied, and Interdisciplinary Field

What is developmental science, and what factors stimulated expansion of the field?

➤ **Developmental science** is an interdisciplinary field devoted to understanding human constancy and change throughout the lifespan. Research on human development has been stimulated by both scientific curiosity and social pressures to improve people's lives.

Basic Issues

Identify three basic issues on which theories of human development take a stand.

➤ Each **theory** of human development takes a stand on three basic issues: (1) development as a **continuous** process or a series of **discontinuous stages;** (2) one course of development characterizing all individuals, or many possible courses, depending on **contexts;** and (3) development determined primarily by genetic or environmental factors, and either stable or open to change.

The Lifespan Perspective: A Balanced Point of View

Describe the lifespan perspective on development.

➤ The **lifespan perspective** recognizes great complexity in the factors that contribute to human change. In this view, development is lifelong, multidimensional (affected by biological, psychological, and social forces), multidirectional (an expression of both growth and decline), and plastic (open to change through new experiences).

➤ Furthermore, in the lifespan perspective, three categories of influences shape the life course: (1) **age-graded influences,** which are predictable in timing and duration; (2) **history-graded influences,** unique to a particular historical era; and (3) **nonnormative influences,** which are unique to one or a few individuals.

Scientific Beginnings

Describe the major early influences on the scientific study of development.

➤ Darwin's theory of evolution influenced important developmental theories and inspired scientific child study. In the early twentieth century, Hall and Gesell introduced the **normative approach,** which produced a large body of descriptive facts about development.

➤ Binet and Simon constructed the first successful intelligence test, which sparked interest in individual differences in development and led to a heated **controversy over nature versus nurture.**

Mid-Twentieth-Century Theories

What theories influenced human development research in the mid-twentieth century?

➤ In the 1930s and 1940s, psychiatrists and social workers turned to the **psychoanalytic perspective** for help in treating people's emotional problems. In Freud's **psychosexual theory,** the individual moves through five stages, during which three portions of the personality—id, ego, and superego—become integrated. Erikson's **psychosocial theory** expands Freud's theory by emphasizing the development of culturally relevant attitudes and skills and the lifespan nature of development.

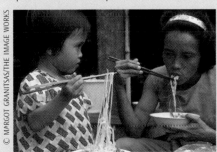
© MARGOT GRANITSAS/THE IMAGE WORKS

➤ As the psychoanalytic perspective gained in prominence, **behaviorism** and **social learning theory** emerged, emphasizing principles of conditioning and modeling and practical procedures of **behavior modification.**

➤ In contrast to behaviorism, Piaget's **cognitive-developmental theory** emphasizes children's active role in constructing knowledge as they manipulate and explore their world. According to Piaget, children move through four stages, from the baby's sensorimotor action patterns to the adolescent's capacity for abstract, systematic thinking.

Recent Theoretical Perspectives

Describe recent theoretical perspectives on human development.

➤ **Information processing** views the mind as a complex, symbol-manipulating system and development as undergoing continuous change. This approach strives for precise accounts of how children and adults solve problems and complete tasks.

➤ Researchers in **developmental cognitive neuroscience** study the relationship between changes in the brain and the development of cognitive processing and behavior patterns. They are identifying the types of experiences that support or undermine brain development at various ages and the brain-based origins of learning and behavior disorders.

➤ Three contemporary perspectives emphasize contexts of development. **Ethology,** which stresses the adaptive value and evolutionary history of behavior, inspired the **sensitive period** concept. In **evolutionary developmental psychology,** which extends this emphasis, researchers seek to understand the adaptiveness of specieswide competencies as they change with age.

➤ Vygotsky's **sociocultural theory,** which focuses on how culture is transmitted from one generation to the next through social interaction, views cognitive development as a socially mediated process. Through cooperative dialogues with more expert members of society, children acquire culturally relevant knowledge and skills.

>> **Ecological systems theory** views the individual as developing within a complex system of relationships affected by multiple, nested layers of the surrounding environment—**microsystem, mesosystem, exosystem,** and **macrosystem.** The **chronosystem** represents the dynamic, ever-changing nature of individuals and their experiences.

© ELLEN B. SENISI

Comparing Theories

Identify the stand taken by each major theory on the three basic issues of human development.

>> Theories vary in their focus on different domains of development and in their stand on three basic issues: whether development is continuous or discontinuous, whether there is one course of development or many, and whether nature or nurture is more influential. (For a full summary, see Table 1.5 on page 22.)

Studying Development

Describe methods commonly used in research on human development.

>> **Naturalistic observations,** gathered in everyday environments, permit researchers to see directly the everyday behaviors they hope to explain. In contrast, **structured observations,** which take place in laboratories, give every participant an equal opportunity to display the behavior of interest.

>> Self-report methods can be flexible and open-ended, as in the **clinical interview.** Alternative methods include **structured interviews,** tests, and questionnaires in which each participant is asked the same set of questions in the same way. Investigators use the **clinical,** or **case study, method** to gain an in-depth understanding of a single individual.

>> To understand the unique values and social processes of a culture or distinct social group, researchers rely on **ethnography,** engaging in participant observation.

Distinguish between correlational and experimental research designs, noting the strengths and limitations of each.

>> The **correlational design** examines relationships between variables as they occur but does not permit inferences about cause and effect. The **correlation coefficient** is often used to measure the association between variables.

>> An **experimental design** permits cause-and-effect inferences. Researchers manipulate an **independent variable** and determine its effect on a **dependent variable. Random assignment** to treatment conditions reduces the chances that participant characteristics will affect the accuracy of experimental findings.

>> Experiments conducted in laboratories permit a high degree of control, but findings may not apply to everyday life. Field and natural, or quasi-, experiments compare treatments in natural environments. These approaches, however, are less rigorous than laboratory experiments.

Describe designs for studying development, noting the strengths and limitations of each.

>> The **longitudinal design** permits researchers to identify common patterns and individual differences in development and to examine relationships between early and later events and behaviors. Longitudinal research poses several

problems, including participant dropout that biases the sample, practice effects, and **cohort effects.**

>> The **cross-sectional design** is an efficient way to study age-related trends, but it is limited to comparisons of age-group averages. Cross-sectional studies, especially those that cover a wide age span, are also vulnerable to cohort effects.

>> To overcome some limitations of these designs, investigators sometimes use **sequential designs,** in which they conduct several similar cross-sectional or longitudinal studies at varying times. When researchers combine experimental and developmental designs, they can examine causal influences on development.

Ethics in Lifespan Research

What special ethical concerns arise in research on human development?

>> Research creates ethical issues because the quest for scientific knowledge has the potential to exploit people. The ethical principle of informed consent requires special safeguards for children and for elderly people who are cognitively impaired or chronically ill. The use of deception in research with children is especially risky because it may undermine their basic faith in the trustworthiness of adults.

© DAVID YOUNG-WOLFF/PHOTOEDIT

Important Terms and Concepts

Biological and Environmental Foundations

© RYAN MCVAY/GETTY IMAGES

A complex blend of genetic and environmental influences leads members of this three-generation family of Mexico to be both alike and different in physical characteristics and behavior.

"It's a girl!" announces the doctor, holding up the squalling baby as her parents gaze with amazement at their miraculous creation.

"A girl! We've named her Sarah!" exclaims the proud father to eager relatives waiting for news of their new family member.

As we join these parents in thinking about how this wondrous being came into existence and imagining her future, we are struck by many questions. How could this baby, equipped with everything necessary for life outside the womb, have developed from the union of two tiny cells? What ensures that Sarah will, in due time, roll over, walk, talk, make friends, learn, imagine, and create—just like other typical children born before her? Why is she a girl and not a boy, dark-haired rather than blond, calm and cuddly instead of wiry and energetic? What difference will it make that Sarah is given a name and place in one family, community, nation, and culture rather than another?

© ARIEL SKELLEY/BLEND IMAGES/JUPITERIMAGES

To answer these questions, this chapter takes a close look at the foundations of development: heredity and environment. Because nature has prepared us for survival, all humans have features in common. Yet each of us is also unique. *TAKE A MOMENT...* Think about several of your friends, and jot down the most obvious physical and behavioral similarities between them and their parents. Did you find that one person shows combined features of both parents, another resembles just one parent, whereas a third is not like either parent? These directly observable characteristics are called **phenotypes.** They depend in part on the individual's **genotype**—the complex blend of genetic information that determines our species and influences all our unique characteristics. Yet phenotypes are also affected by each person's lifelong history of experiences.

We begin our discussion at the moment of conception, an event that establishes the hereditary makeup of the new individual. First we review basic genetic principles that help explain similarities and differences among us in appearance and behavior. Then we turn to aspects of the environment that play powerful roles throughout the lifespan. Finally, we consider how nature and nurture *work together* to shape the course of development.

Genetic Foundations

Each of us is made up of trillions of units called *cells*. Within every cell (except red blood cells) is a control center, or *nucleus*, containing rodlike structures called **chromosomes**, which store and transmit genetic information. Human chromosomes come in 23 matching pairs (an exception is the XY pair in males, which we will discuss shortly). Each member of a pair corresponds to the other in size, shape, and genetic functions, with one chromosome inherited from the mother and the other from the father (see Figure 2.1).

The Genetic Code

Chromosomes are made up of a chemical substance called **deoxyribonucleic acid,** or **DNA.** As Figure 2.2 shows, DNA is a long, double-stranded molecule that looks like a twisted ladder. Each rung of the ladder consists of a specific pair of chemical

■ **FIGURE 2.1** ■ **A karyotype, or photograph, of human chromosomes.** The 46 chromosomes shown on the left were isolated from a human cell, stained, greatly magnified, and arranged in pairs according to decreasing size of the upper "arm" of each chromosome. The twenty-third pair, XY, reveals that the cell donor is a male. In a female, this pair would be XX. (Photo © CNRI/Science Photo Library/Photo Researchers, Inc.)

Cytoplasm

Nucleus

Chromosomes

■ **FIGURE 2.2** ■ **DNA's ladderlike structure.** This figure shows that the pairings of bases across the rungs of the ladder are very specific: Adenine (A) always appears with thymine (T), and cytosine (C) always appears with guanine (G). Here, the DNA ladder duplicates by splitting down the middle of its ladder rungs. Each free base picks up a new complementary partner from the area surrounding the cell nucleus.

substances called *bases,* joined together between the two sides. It is this sequence of bases that provides genetic instructions. A **gene** is a segment of DNA along the length of the chromosome. Genes can be of different lengths—perhaps 100 to several thousand ladder rungs long. An estimated 20,000 to 25,000 genes lie along the human chromosomes (International Human Genome Sequencing Consortium, 2004).

A unique feature of DNA is that it can duplicate itself through a process called **mitosis.** This special ability permits the one-celled fertilized ovum to develop into a complex human being composed of a great many cells. Refer again to Figure 2.2, and you will see that during mitosis, the chromosomes copy themselves. As a result, each new body cell contains the same number of chromosomes and the identical genetic information.

Genes accomplish their task by sending instructions for making a rich assortment of proteins to the *cytoplasm,* the area surrounding the cell nucleus. Proteins, which trigger chemical reactions throughout the body, are the biological foundation on which our characteristics are built. How do humans, with far fewer genes than scientists once thought, develop into such complex beings? The answer lies in the proteins our genes make, which break up and reassemble in staggering variety— about 10 to 20 million altogether. Within the cell, a wide range of environmental factors modify gene expression (Lashley, 2007). So even at this microscopic level, biological events are the result of *both* genetic and nongenetic forces.

The Sex Cells

New individuals are created when two special cells called **gametes,** or sex cells—the sperm and ovum—combine. A gamete contains only 23 chromosomes, half as many as a regular body cell. Gametes are formed through a cell division process called **meiosis,** which halves the number of chromosomes normally present in body cells. When sperm and ovum unite at conception, the resulting cell, called a **zygote,** will again have 46 chromosomes.

In meiosis, the chromosomes pair up and exchange segments, so that genes from one are replaced by genes from another. Then chance determines which member of each pair will gather with others and end up in the same gamete. These events make the likelihood extremely low—about 1 in 700 trillion—that nontwin siblings will be genetically identical (Gould & Keeton, 1996). The genetic variability produced by meiosis is adaptive: It increases the chances that at least some members of a species will cope with ever-changing environments and survive.

In the male, four sperm are produced when meiosis is complete. Also, the cells from which sperm arise are produced continuously throughout life, so a healthy man can father a child at any age after sexual maturity. In the female, meiosis results in just one ovum. In addition, the female is born with all her ova in her ovaries and can bear children for only three to four decades. Still, there are plenty of female sex cells: About 350 to 450 will mature during a woman's childbearing years (Moore & Persaud, 2008).

Boy or Girl?

Return to Figure 2.1 and note that 22 of the 23 pairs of chromosomes are matching pairs, called **autosomes.** The twenty-third pair consists of **sex chromosomes.** In females, this pair is called XX; in males, it is called XY. The X is a relatively large chromosome, whereas the Y is short and carries little genetic material. When gametes form in males, the X and Y chromosomes separate into different sperm cells. The gametes that form in females all carry an X chromosome. Therefore, the sex of the new organism is determined by whether an X-bearing or a Y-bearing sperm fertilizes the ovum.

Multiple Offspring

Ruth and Peter, a couple I know well, tried for several years to have a child, without success. When Ruth reached age 33, her doctor prescribed a fertility drug, and twins—Jeannie and

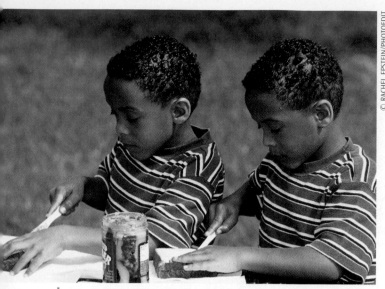

© RACHEL EPSTEIN/PHOTOEDIT

These identical, or monozygotic, twins were created when a duplicating zygote separated into two clusters of cells, and two individuals with the same genetic makeup developed. Identical twins look alike and tend to resemble each other in a variety of psychological characteristics.

Jason—were born. Jeannie and Jason are **fraternal,** or **dizygotic, twins,** the most common type of multiple birth, resulting from the release and fertilization of two ova. Genetically, they are no more alike than ordinary siblings. Older maternal age, fertility drugs, and in vitro fertilization (to be discussed shortly) are major causes of the dramatic rise in fraternal twinning and other multiple births in industrialized nations over the past several decades (Machin, 2005; Russell et al., 2003). Currently, fraternal twins account for 1 in about every 60 births in the United States (U.S. Department of Health and Human Services, 2008b).

Twins can also be created when a zygote that has started to duplicate separates into two clusters of cells that develop into two individuals. These are called **identical,** or **monozygotic, twins** because they have the same genetic makeup. The frequency of identical twins is the same around the world—is about 1 in every 330 births (Hall, 2003). Animal research has uncovered environmental influences that prompt this type of twinning, including temperature changes, variation in oxygen levels, and late fertilization of the ovum. In a minority of cases, identical twinning runs in families, suggesting a genetic influence (Lashley, 2007).

During their early years, children of single births often are healthier and develop more rapidly than twins. Jeannie and Jason, like most twins, were born several weeks early and required special care in the hospital. When the twins came home, Ruth and Peter had to divide time between them. Perhaps because neither baby received as much attention as the average single infant, each walked and talked several months later than average, although both caught up by middle childhood (Lytton & Gallagher, 2002). Parental energies are further strained by triplets, whose early development is slower than that of twins (Feldman, Eidelman, & Rotenberg, 2004).

Patterns of Genetic Inheritance

Jeannie has her parents' dark, straight hair; Jason is curly-haired and blond. Patterns of genetic inheritance—the way genes from each parent interact—explain these outcomes. Recall that, except for the XY pair in males, all chromosomes come in corresponding pairs. Two forms of each gene occur at the same place on the chromosomes, one inherited from the mother and one from the father. Each form of a gene is called an **allele.** If the alleles from both parents are alike, the child is **homozygous** and will display the inherited trait. If the alleles differ, then the child is **heterozygous,** and relationships between the alleles determine the trait that will appear.

■ **DOMINANT–RECESSIVE INHERITANCE.** In many heterozygous pairings, **dominant–recessive inheritance** occurs: Only one allele affects the child's characteristics. It is called *dominant;* the second allele, which has no effect, is called *recessive.* Some human characteristics that follow the rules of dominant–recessive inheritance are listed in Table 2.1. Hair color is an example. The allele for dark hair is dominant (we can represent it with a capital *D*), whereas the one for blond hair is recessive (symbolized by a lowercase *b*). A child who inherits a homozygous pair of dominant alleles *(DD)* and a child who inherits a heterozygous pair *(Db)* will both be dark-haired, even though their genotypes differ. Blond hair (like Jason's) can result only from having two recessive alleles *(bb).* Still, heterozygous

■ **TABLE 2.1** ■ *Examples of Dominant and Recessive Characteristics*

DOMINANT	RECESSIVE
Dark hair	Blond hair
Normal hair	Pattern baldness
Curly hair	Straight hair
Nonred hair	Red hair
Facial dimples	No dimples
Normal hearing	Some forms of deafness
Normal vision	Nearsightedness
Farsightedness	Normal vision
Normal vision	Congenital eye cataracts
Normally pigmented skin	Albinism
Double-jointedness	Normal joints
Type A blood	Type O blood
Type B blood	Type O blood
Rh-positive blood	Rh-negative blood

Note: Many normal characteristics that were previously thought to result from dominant–recessive inheritance, such as eye color, are now regarded as due to multiple genes. For the characteristics listed here, most experts agree that the simple dominant–recessive relationship holds.

Source: McKusick, 2007.

individuals with just one recessive allele *(Db)* can pass that trait to their children. Therefore, they are called **carriers** of the trait.

Many disabilities and diseases are the product of recessive alleles. One of the most frequently occurring is *phenylketonuria,* or *PKU,* which affects the way the body breaks down proteins contained in many foods. Infants born with two recessive alleles lack an enzyme that converts one of the basic amino acids that make up proteins (phenylalanine) into a byproduct essential for body functioning (tyrosine). Without this enzyme, phenylalanine quickly builds to toxic levels that damage the central nervous system, causing permanent mental retardation.

Despite its potentially damaging effects, PKU illustrates that inheriting unfavorable genes does not always lead to an untreatable condition. All U.S. states require that each newborn be given a blood test for PKU. If the disease is found, doctors place the baby on a diet low in phenylalanine. Children who receive this treatment still show mild deficits in memory, planning, decision making, and problem solving, because even small amounts of phenylalanine interfere with brain functioning (Anderson et al., 2007; Channon, Mockler, & Lee, 2005; Christ et al., 2006). But as long as dietary treatment begins early and continues, children with PKU usually attain an average level of intelligence and have a normal lifespan.

In dominant–recessive inheritance, if we know the genetic makeup of the parents, we can predict the percentage of children in a family who are likely to display or carry a trait. Figure 2.3 illustrates this for PKU. Notice that for a child to inherit the condition, each parent must have a recessive allele.

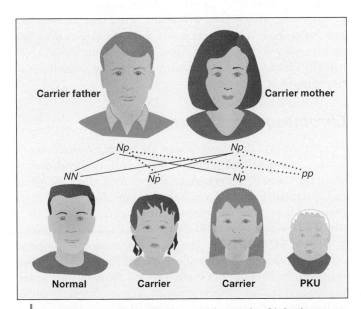

■ **FIGURE 2.3** ■ **Dominant–recessive mode of inheritance, as illustrated by PKU.** When both parents are heterozygous carriers of the recessive gene *(p),* we can predict that 25 percent of their offspring are likely to be normal *(NN),* 50 percent are likely to be carriers *(Np),* and 25 percent are likely to inherit the disorder *(pp).* Notice that the PKU-affected child, in contrast to his siblings, has light hair. The recessive gene for PKU affects more than one trait. It also leads to fair coloring.

■ **INCOMPLETE DOMINANCE.** In some heterozygous circumstances, the dominant–recessive relationship does not hold completely. Instead, we see **incomplete dominance,** a pattern of inheritance in which both alleles are expressed, resulting in a combined trait, or one that is intermediate between the two.

The *sickle cell trait,* a heterozygous condition present in many black Africans, provides an example. *Sickle cell anemia* occurs in full form when a child inherits two recessive genes. They cause the usually round red blood cells to become sickle (crescent-moon) shaped, especially under low-oxygen conditions. The sickled cells clog the blood vessels and block the flow of blood, causing intense pain, swelling, and tissue damage. Despite medical advances that today allow 85 percent of affected children to survive to adulthood, North Americans with sickle cell anemia have an average life expectancy of only 55 years (Driscoll, 2007). Heterozygous individuals are protected from the disease under most circumstances. However, when they experience oxygen deprivation—for example, at high altitudes or after intense physical exercise—the single recessive allele asserts itself, and a temporary, mild form of the illness occurs.

■ **X-LINKED INHERITANCE.** Males and females have an equal chance of inheriting recessive disorders carried on the autosomes. But when a harmful allele is carried on the X chromosome, **X-linked inheritance** applies. Males are more likely to be affected because their sex chromosomes do not match. In females, any recessive allele on one X chromosome has a good chance of being suppressed by a dominant allele on the other X. But the Y chromosome is only about one-third as long and therefore lacks many corresponding genes to override those on the X. A well-known example is *hemophilia,* a disorder in which the blood fails to clot normally. Figure 2.4 on page 40 shows its greater likelihood of inheritance by male children whose mothers carry the abnormal allele.

Besides X-linked disorders, many sex differences reveal the male to be at a disadvantage. Rates of miscarriage, infant and childhood deaths, birth defects, learning disabilities, behavior disorders, and mental retardation all are higher for boys (Butler & Meaney, 2005). It is possible that these sex differences can be traced to the genetic code. The female, with two X chromosomes, benefits from a greater variety of genes. Nature, however, seems to have adjusted for the male's disadvantage. Worldwide, about 106 boys are born for every 100 girls, and an even greater number of males are conceived (United Nations, 2006b).

■ **GENOMIC IMPRINTING.** More than 1,000 human characteristics follow the rules of dominant–recessive and incomplete-dominance inheritance (McKusick, 2007). In these cases, whichever parent contributes a gene to the new individual, the gene responds in the same way. Geneticists, however, have identified exceptions. In **genomic imprinting,** alleles are *imprinted,* or chemically *marked,* so that one pair member (either the mother's or the father's) is activated, regardless of its makeup. The imprint is often temporary; it may be erased in the next

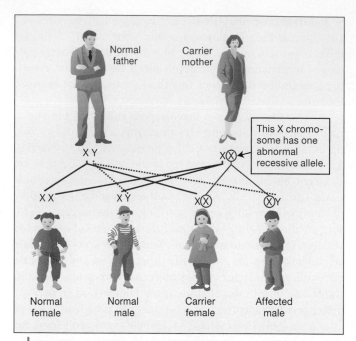

Normal father   Carrier mother

This X chromosome has one abnormal recessive allele.

X Y   X (X)

X X   X Y   X(X)   (X)Y

Normal female   Normal male   Carrier female   Affected male

■ **FIGURE 2.4** ■ **X-linked inheritance.** In the example shown here, the allele on the father's X chromosome is normal. The mother has one normal and one abnormal recessive allele on her X chromosomes. By looking at the possible combinations of the parents' alleles, we can predict that 50 percent of these parents' male children are likely to have the disorder and 50 percent of their female children are likely to be carriers of it.

generation, and it may not occur in all individuals (Everman & Cassidy, 2000).

Imprinting helps us understand certain puzzling genetic patterns. For example, children are more likely to develop diabetes if their father, rather than their mother, suffers from it. And people with asthma tend to have mothers, not fathers, with the illness. Genomic imprinting can also operate on the sex chromosomes, as *fragile X syndrome*—the most common inherited cause of mental retardation—reveals. In this disorder, which affects about 1 in 2,000 males and 1 in 4,000 females, an abnormal repetition of a sequence of DNA bases occurs on the X chromosome, damaging a particular gene. The defective gene at the fragile site is expressed only when it is passed from mother to child (Reiss & Dant, 2003).

■ **MUTATION.** Although less than 3 percent of pregnancies result in the birth of a baby with a hereditary abnormality, these children account for about 20 percent of infant deaths and contribute substantially to lifelong impaired physical and mental functioning (U.S. Department of Health and Human Services, 2008b). How are harmful genes created in the first place? The answer is **mutation,** a sudden change in a segment of DNA. A mutation may affect only one or two genes, or it may involve many genes, as in the chromosomal disorders we will discuss shortly. Some mutations occur spontaneously, by chance. Others are caused by hazardous environmental agents.

Ionizing (high-energy) radiation is an established cause of mutation. Women who receive repeated doses before conception

are more likely to miscarry or to give birth to children with hereditary defects. The incidence of genetic abnormalities, such as physical malformations and childhood cancer, is also higher in children whose fathers are repeatedly exposed to radiation in their occupation.

The examples just given illustrate *germline mutation,* which takes place in the cells that give rise to gametes. When the affected individual mates, the defective DNA is passed on to the next generation. In a second type, called *somatic mutation,* normal body cells mutate, an event that can occur at any time of life. The DNA defect appears in every cell derived from the affected body cell, eventually becoming widespread enough to cause disease or disability. Many cancers originate this way. Other diseases, such as epilepsy and heart disease, are also believed to be due to somatic mutation (Gottlieb, Beitel, & Trifiro, 2001; Steinlein, 2004).

Somatic mutation shows that each of us does not have a single, permanent genotype. Rather, the genetic makeup of each cell can change over time. Somatic mutation increases with age, raising the possibility that it contributes to the age-related rise in disease and to the aging process itself (Salvioli et al., 2008).

■ **POLYGENIC INHERITANCE.** So far, we have discussed patterns of inheritance in which people either do or do not display a trait. These cut-and-dried individual differences are much easier to trace to their genetic origins than are characteristics that vary on a continuum among people, such as height, weight, intelligence, and personality. These traits are due to **polygenic inheritance,** in which many genes influence the characteristic in question. Polygenic inheritance is complex, and much about it is still unknown. In the final section of this chapter, we will discuss how researchers infer the influence of heredity on human attributes when they do not know the precise patterns of inheritance.

Chromosomal Abnormalities

Abnormalities of the chromosomes are another major cause of serious developmental problems. Most chromosomal defects result from mistakes occurring during meiosis, when the ovum and sperm are formed. A chromosome pair does not separate properly, or part of a chromosome breaks off.

■ **DOWN SYNDROME.** The most common chromosomal disorder, occurring in 1 out of every 1,000 live births, is *Down syndrome.* In 95 percent of cases, it results from a failure of the twenty-first pair of chromosomes to separate during meiosis, so the new individual inherits three of these chromosomes rather than the normal two. In other, less frequent forms, an extra broken piece of a twenty-first chromosome is attached to another chromosome (called *translocation* pattern). Or an error occurs during the early stages of mitosis, causing some but not all body cells to have the defective chromosomal makeup (called *mosaic* pattern) (Saitta & Zackai, 2005). Because the mosaic type involves less genetic material, symptoms may be less extreme.

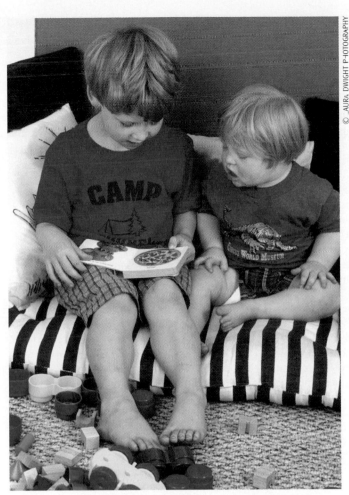

The boy on the right has facial features typical of children with Down syndrome. Despite his impaired intellectual development, he is doing well because he is growing up in a stimulating home where he is loved and accepted by family members, including his older brother.

The consequences of Down syndrome include mental retardation, memory and speech problems, limited vocabulary, and slow motor development. Affected individuals also have distinct physical features—a short, stocky build, a flattened face, a protruding tongue, almond-shaped eyes, and (in 50 percent of cases) an unusual crease running across the palm of the hand. Infants with Down syndrome are often born with eye cataracts, hearing loss, and heart and intestinal defects. Because of medical advances, many individuals with Down syndrome survive into their fifties and a few into their sixties to eighties (Roizen & Patterson, 2003).

The risk of bearing a Down syndrome baby rises dramatically with maternal age, from 1 in 1,900 births at age 20, to 1 in 300 at age 35, to 1 in 30 at age 45 (Halliday et al., 1995; Meyers et al., 1997). Why is this so? Geneticists believe that the ova weaken over time. As a result, chromosomes do not separate properly as they complete the process of meiosis at conception. But in about 5 to 10 percent of cases, the extra genetic material originates with the father (Dzurova & Pikhart, 2005; Fisch et al., 2003; Sherman et al., 2005).

■ **ABNORMALITIES OF THE SEX CHROMOSOMES.** Other disorders of the autosomes usually disrupt development so severely that miscarriage occurs. When such babies are born, they rarely survive beyond early childhood. In contrast, abnormalities of the sex chromosomes—generally involving an extra X or Y chromosome or the absence of one X in females—usually lead to fewer problems.

A variety of myths about individuals with sex chromosome disorders have been discredited by research. For example, males with *XYY syndrome* are not necessarily more aggressive and antisocial than XY males. And most children with sex chromosome disorders are not mentally retarded but, instead, have specific intellectual deficits. Verbal difficulties—for example, with reading and vocabulary—are common among girls with *triple X syndrome* and boys with *Klinefelter syndrome*, both of whom inherit an extra X chromosome. In contrast, girls with *Turner syndrome,* who are missing an X, have trouble with spatial relationships—for example, drawing pictures, telling right from left, following travel directions, and noticing changes in facial expressions (Kesler, 2007; Lawrence et al., 2003; Simpson et al., 2003). Brain-imaging research confirms that adding to or subtracting from the usual number of X chromosomes alters the development of certain brain structures, yielding particular intellectual deficits (Cutter et al., 2006; Itti et al., 2006).

ASK YOURSELF

>> **REVIEW**
Explain the genetic origins of PKU and Down syndrome. Cite evidence that both heredity and environment contribute to the development of individuals with these disorders.

>> **APPLY**
Gilbert's genetic makeup is homozygous for dark hair. Jan's is homozygous for blond hair. What color is Gilbert's hair? How about Jan's? What proportion of their children are likely to be dark-haired? Explain.

>> **REFLECT**
Select a genetic disorder discussed in the preceding sections, and imagine that you were the parent of a child with that disorder. What factors, within and beyond the family, could help you support your child's development?

Reproductive Choices

Two years after they married, Ted and Marianne gave birth to their first child. Kendra appeared to be a healthy infant, but by 4 months her growth slowed, and she was diagnosed with Tay-Sachs disease, a degenerative disease of the central nervous system caused by inheritance of two recessive alleles. When Kendra died at 2 years of age, Ted and Marianne were devastated. Although they did not want to bring another infant into the world who would endure such suffering, they badly wanted to have a child.

SOCIAL ISSUES

The Pros and Cons of Reproductive Technologies

Some couples decide not to risk pregnancy because of a history of genetic disease. Many others—in fact, one-sixth of all couples who try to conceive—discover that they are infertile. And some never-married adults and gay and lesbian partners want to bear children. Today, increasing numbers of individuals are turning to alternative methods of conception—technologies that have become the subject of heated debate.

Donor Insemination and In Vitro Fertilization

For several decades, *donor insemination*—injection of sperm from an anonymous man into a woman—has been used to overcome male reproductive difficulties. In recent years, it has also permitted women without a male partner to become pregnant. Donor insemination is 70 to 80 percent successful, resulting in about 40,000 deliveries and 52,000 newborn babies in the United States each year (Wright et al., 2008).

In vitro fertilization is another reproductive technology that has become increasingly common. About 1 percent of all children in developed countries—about 40,000 babies in the United States—are conceived through this technique annually (Jackson, Gibson, & Wu, 2004). A woman is given hormones that stimulate the ripening of several ova, which are removed surgically and placed in a dish of nutrients, to

which sperm are added. Once an ovum is fertilized and begins to duplicate into several cells, it is injected into the mother's uterus.

By mixing and matching gametes, pregnancies can be brought about when either or both partners have a reproductive problem. Usually, in vitro fertilization is used to treat women whose fallopian tubes are permanently damaged. But a recently developed technique permits a single sperm to be injected directly into an ovum, thereby overcoming most male fertility problems. And a "sex sorter" method helps ensure that couples who carry X-linked diseases (which usually affect males) have a daughter.

Although donor insemination and in vitro fertilization have many benefits, serious questions have arisen about their use. Most U.S. states have few legal guidelines for these procedures. As a result, donors are not always screened for genetic or sexually transmitted diseases. Furthermore, in many countries (including the United States and Canada), doctors are not required to keep records of donor characteristics (Richards, 2004). Canada does retain a file on donor identities, permitting contact only in cases of serious disease, where knowledge of the child's genetic background might have medical value (Bioethics Consultative Committee, 2003).

Another concern is that about 50 percent of in vitro procedures result in multiple births. Most are twins, but 9 percent are triplets and higher-order multiples. Consequently, among in vitro babies, the rate of low birth weight is

nearly three times as high as in the general population (Wright et al., 2008). Risk of major birth defects also doubles because of many factors, including drugs used to induce ripening of ova and delays in fertilizing the ova outside the womb (Machin, 2005).

Surrogate Motherhood

An even more controversial form of medically assisted conception is *surrogate motherhood*. Typically in this procedure, sperm from a man whose wife is infertile are used to inseminate a woman, called a surrogate, who is paid a fee for her childbearing services. In return, the surrogate agrees to turn the baby over to the man (who is the natural father). The child is then adopted by his wife.

Although most of these arrangements proceed smoothly, those that end up in court highlight serious risks for all concerned. In one case, both parties rejected the infant with severe disabilities who resulted from the pregnancy. In several others, the surrogate mother wanted to keep the baby, or the couple changed their mind during the pregnancy. These children came into the world in the midst of conflict that threatened to last for years. Furthermore, because surrogacy favors the wealthy as contractors for infants and the less economically advantaged as surrogates, it may promote exploitation of financially needy women.

New Reproductive Frontiers

Reproductive technologies are evolving faster than societies can weigh the ethics of these

---

In the past, many couples with genetic disorders in their families chose not to bear a child at all rather than risk the birth of an abnormal baby. Today, genetic counseling and prenatal diagnosis help people make informed decisions about conceiving, carrying a pregnancy to term, or adopting a child.

Genetic Counseling and Prenatal Diagnosis

Genetic counseling is a communication process designed to help couples understand genetic principles, genetic testing, and prevention of genetic disorders; assess their chances of giving birth to a baby with a hereditary disorder; and choose the best course of action in view of risks and family goals (Resta et al., 2006). Individuals likely to seek counseling are those who have

had difficulties bearing children or who know that genetic problems exist in their families. In addition, women who delay childbearing are candidates because after age 35, the overall rate of chromosomal abnormalities rises sharply, from 1 in every 190 to as many as 1 in every 20 pregnancies at age 43 (Wille et al., 2004).

If a family history of mental retardation, physical defects, or inherited diseases exists, the genetic counselor interviews the couple and prepares a *pedigree*, a picture of the family tree in which affected relatives are identified. The pedigree is used to estimate the likelihood of an abnormal child, using the genetic principles discussed earlier in this chapter. For many disorders, blood tests or genetic analyses can reveal whether the parent is a carrier of the harmful gene.

When all the relevant information is in, the genetic counselor helps people consider appropriate options. These include procedures. Doctors have used donor ova from younger women in combination with in vitro fertilization to help postmenopausal women become pregnant. Most recipients are in their forties, but several women in their fifties and sixties have given birth. These cases raise questions about bringing children into the world whose parents may not live to see them reach adulthood.

Among other reproductive options, at donor banks, customers can select ova or sperm on the basis of physical characteristics and even IQ. And scientists are devising ways to alter the DNA of human ova, sperm, and embryos to protect against hereditary disorders—techniques that could be used to engineer other desired characteristics. Many worry that these practices are a dangerous step toward selective breeding through "designer babies"—controlling offspring characteristics by manipulating genetic makeup.

Furthermore, scientists have successfully cloned (made multiple copies of) fertilized ova in sheep, cattle, and monkeys, and they are working on ways to do so in humans. By providing extra ova for injection, cloning might improve the success rate of in vitro fertilization. But it also opens the possibility of mass-producing genetically identical people. Therefore, it is widely condemned.

Although reproductive technologies permit many barren couples to rear healthy newborn babies, laws are needed to regulate such practices. In the case of surrogate motherhood, the ethical problems are so complex that

Fertility drugs and in vitro fertilization often lead to multiple fetuses. Although these sextuplets are healthy, reproductive technologies can pose grave ethical dilemmas. When two or more fetuses fill the womb, pregnancy complications may be so severe that doctors recommend aborting one or more to save the others.

AP IMAGES/THE HOLLAND SENTINEL, DENNIS R. J. GEPPERT

18 U.S. states have sharply restricted the practice. Australia, Canada, and many European nations have banned it (Chen, 2003; McGee, 1997). Denmark, France, and Great Britain have prohibited in vitro fertilization for women past menopause (Bioethics Consultative Committee, 2003). At present,

nothing is known about the psychological consequences of being a product of these procedures. Research on how such children grow up, including later-appearing medical conditions and knowledge and feelings about their origins, is important for weighing the pros and cons of these techniques.

taking a chance and conceiving, choosing from among a variety of reproductive technologies (see the Social Issues box above), or adopting a child.

If couples who might bear an abnormal child decide to conceive, several **prenatal diagnostic methods**—medical procedures that permit detection of problems before birth—are available (see Table 2.2 on page 44). Women of advanced maternal age are prime candidates for *amniocentesis* or *chorionic villus sampling*. Except for *maternal blood analysis*, however, prenatal diagnosis should not be used routinely because other methods pose some risk of injury to the developing organism.

Prenatal diagnosis has led to advances in fetal medicine. For example, by inserting a needle into the uterus, doctors can administer drugs to the fetus. Surgery has been performed to repair such problems as heart, lung, and diaphragm malformations, urinary tract obstructions, and neural defects (Kunisaki & Jennings,

2008). Fetuses with blood disorders have been given blood transfusions. And those with immune deficiencies have received bone marrow transplants that succeeded in creating a normally functioning immune system (Williams, 2006). Nevertheless, decisions to use these techniques are difficult because they frequently result in complications, the most common being premature labor and miscarriage (Flake, 2003).

Advances in *genetic engineering* also offer hope for correcting hereditary defects. As part of the Human Genome Project—an ambitious international research program—thousands of genes have been identified, including those involved in hundreds of diseases (National Institutes of Health, 2008). As a result, new treatments are being explored, such as *gene therapy*—correcting genetic abnormalities by delivering DNA carrying a functional gene to the cells. In recent experiments, gene therapy relieved symptoms in patients with severe immune system dysfunction,

■ **TABLE 2.2** ■ *Prenatal Diagnostic Methods*

METHOD	DESCRIPTION
Amniocentesis	The most widely used technique. A hollow needle is inserted through the abdominal wall to obtain a sample of fluid in the uterus. Cells are examined for genetic defects. Can be performed by the 14th week after conception; 1 to 2 more weeks are required for test results. Small risk of miscarriage.
Chorionic villus sampling	Can be used if results are needed very early in pregnancy. A thin tube is inserted into the uterus through the vagina, or a hollow needle is inserted through the abdominal wall. A small plug of tissue is removed from the end of one or more chorionic villi, the hairlike projections on the membrane surrounding the developing organism. Cells are examined for genetic defects. Can be performed at 9 weeks after conception; results are available within 24 hours. Entails a slightly greater risk of miscarriage than amniocentesis and is also associated with a small risk of limb deformities.
Fetoscopy	A small tube with a light source is inserted into the uterus to inspect the fetus for defects of the limbs and face. Also allows a sample of fetal blood to be obtained, permitting diagnosis of such disorders as hemophilia and sickle cell anemia, as well as neural defects (see below). Usually performed between 15 and 18 weeks after conception but can be done as early as 5 weeks. Entails some risk of miscarriage.
Ultrasound	High-frequency sound waves are beamed at the uterus; their reflection is translated into a picture on a video screen that reveals the size, shape, and placement of the fetus. Permits assessment of fetal age, detection of multiple pregnancies, and identification of gross physical defects. Also used to guide amniocentesis, chorionic villus sampling, and fetoscopy. When used five or more times, increases the risk of low birth weight.
Maternal blood analysis	By the second month of pregnancy, some of the developing organism's cells enter the maternal bloodstream. An elevated level of alpha-fetoprotein may indicate kidney disease, abnormal closure of the esophagus, or neural tube defects, such as anencephaly (absence of most of the brain) and spina bifida (bulging of the spinal cord from the spinal column). Isolated cells can be examined for genetic defects.
Preimplantation genetic diagnosis	After in vitro fertilization and duplication of the zygote into a cluster of cells, one or two cells are removed and examined for hereditary defects. Only if that sample is normal is the fertilized ovum implanted.

Sources: Bianchi, 2005; Kumar & O'Brien, 2004; Moore & Persaud, 2008; Sermon, Van Steirteghem, & Liebaers, 2004.

© JOEY MCLEISTER/MCT/LANDOV

This mother sings while delivering medication through a nebulizer to her 2-year-old daughter, who has cystic fibrosis. The girl also wears a vest for a twice-daily treatment that pounds her chest to clear her lungs of thick mucus. In the future, such children may benefit from the discovery of gene-based treatments for hereditary disorders.

though a few experienced serious side effects (Anson & Fletcher, 2007). In another approach, called *proteomics*, scientists modify gene-specified proteins involved in disease (Bradshaw & Burlingame, 2005). But genetic treatments are still some distance away for most single-gene defects—and far off for diseases involving multiple genes that combine in complex ways with each other and the environment.

Adoption

Adults who are infertile, who are likely to pass along a genetic disorder, or who are older and single but want a family are turning to adoption in increasing numbers. Because the availability of healthy babies has declined (fewer young unwed mothers give up their babies than in the past), more people in North America and Western Europe are adopting from other countries or accepting children who are past infancy or who have known developmental problems (Schweiger & O'Brien, 2005).

Adopted children and adolescents have more learning and emotional difficulties than other children, a difference that increases with the child's age at time of adoption (Brodzinsky &

Pinderhughes, 2002; Nickman et al., 2005; van IJzendoorn, Juffer, & Poelhuis, 2005). There are many possible reasons for adoptees' more problematic childhoods. The biological mother may have been unable to care for the child because of problems believed to be partly genetic, such as alcoholism or severe depression, and may have passed this tendency to her offspring. Or perhaps she experienced stress, poor diet, or inadequate medical care during pregnancy—factors that can affect the child. Furthermore, children adopted after infancy often have a preadoptive history of conflict-ridden family relationships, including neglect and abuse, or deprived institutional rearing. Finally, adoptive parents and children, who are genetically unrelated, are less alike in intelligence and personality than are biological relatives—differences that may threaten family harmony.

Despite these risks, most adopted children fare well, and those with preexisting problems usually make rapid progress (Bimmel et al., 2003; Johnson, 2002). In a study of internationally adopted children in the Netherlands, sensitive maternal care and secure attachment in infancy predicted cognitive and social competence at age 7 (Stams, Juffer, & van IJzendoorn, 2002).

International adoptees fare much better in development than birth siblings or institutionalized agemates who stay behind. By middle childhood, those who were adopted in infancy have mental test scores resembling those of their nonbiological siblings and school classmates, although they tend to achieve less well in school, to have more learning problems that require special treatment, and to be slightly delayed in language skills (van IJzendoorn, Juffer, & Poelhuis, 2005). Children adopted at older ages develop feelings of trust and affection for their adoptive parents as they come to feel loved and supported by them (Veríssimo & Salvaterra, 2006).

By adolescence, adoptees' lives are often complicated by unresolved curiosity about their roots. Some have difficulty accepting the possibility that they may never know their birth parents. Others worry about what they would do if their birth parents suddenly reappeared. Although these concerns are common, most adoptees appear well-adjusted as adults. And as long as their parents took steps to help them learn about their heritage, young people adopted into a different ethnic group or culture generally develop identities that are healthy blends of their birth and rearing backgrounds (Nickman et al., 2005; Thomas & Tessler, 2007).

As we conclude our discussion of reproductive choices, perhaps you are wondering how things turned out for Ted and Marianne. Through genetic counseling, Marianne discovered a history of Tay-Sachs disease on her mother's side of the family. Ted had a distant cousin who died of the disorder. The genetic counselor explained that the chances of giving birth to another affected baby were 1 in 4. Ted and Marianne took the risk. Their son Douglas, now 12, is a carrier of the recessive allele but is a normal, healthy boy. In time, Ted and Marianne will explain to Douglas the importance of genetic counseling and testing before he has children of his own.

ASK YOURSELF

>> **REVIEW**

Why is genetic counseling called a *communication process*? Who should seek it?

>> **APPLY**

Suppose that you must counsel a couple considering in vitro fertilization using the wife's ova and sperm from an anonymous man to overcome the husband's infertility. What medical and ethical risks would you raise?

>> **REFLECT**

Imagine that you are a woman who is a carrier of fragile X syndrome but who wants to have children. Would you become pregnant, adopt, use a surrogate mother, or give up your desire for parenthood? If you became pregnant, would you seek prenatal diagnosis? Explain your decisions.

Environmental Contexts for Development

Just as complex as genetic inheritance is the surrounding environment—a many-layered set of influences that combine to help or hinder physical and psychological well-being. **TAKE A MOMENT...** Think about your childhood and adult life, and jot down a brief description of events and people that influenced your development. Do the items on your list mostly involve your family? This emphasis is not surprising, since the family is the first and longest-lasting context for development. Other influences that make the top ten are friends, neighbors, school, workplace, and community and religious organizations.

Return to Bronfenbrenner's ecological systems theory, discussed in Chapter 1. It emphasizes that environments extending beyond the *microsystem*—the immediate settings just mentioned—powerfully affect development. Indeed, my students rarely mention one important context. Its impact is so pervasive that we seldom stop to think about it in our daily lives. This is the *macrosystem,* or broad social climate of society—its values and programs that support and protect human development. In the following sections, we take up these various contexts. Because they affect every age and aspect of change, we will return to them in later chapters. For now, our discussion emphasizes that environments, as well as heredity, can enhance or create risks for development.

The Family

In power and breadth of influence, no other context equals the family. The family creates unique bonds among people. Attachments to parents and siblings usually last a lifetime and serve as models for relationships in the wider world of neighborhood, school, and community. Within the family, children learn the language, skills, and social and moral values of their culture. Warm, gratifying family ties predict physical and psychological health throughout development. In contrast, isolation or alienation from the family is often associated with developmental problems (Deković & Buist, 2005; Parke & Buriel, 2006).

Contemporary researchers view the family as a *social system* (Bronfenbrenner & Morris, 2006; Lerner et al., 2002). Recall from ecological systems theory that *bidirectional influences* exist in which the behaviors of each family member affect those of others. Indeed, the very term *system* implies a network of interdependent relationships. These system influences operate both directly and indirectly.

■ **DIRECT INFLUENCES.** *TAKE A MOMENT...* The next time you have a chance to observe family members interacting, watch carefully. You are likely to see that kind, patient communication evokes cooperative, harmonious responses, whereas harshness and impatience engender angry, resistive behavior. Each of these reactions, in turn, forges a new link in the interactive chain. In the first instance, a positive message tends to follow; in the second, a negative or avoidant one is likely.

These observations fit with a wealth of research on the family system. Many studies show that when parents' requests are firm but made with warmth and affection, children tend to comply willingly, leading their parents to be warm and gentle in the future. In contrast, children whose parents discipline with harshness and impatience are likely to refuse and rebel. And because children's misbehavior is stressful for parents, they may increase their use of punishment, which results in more

unruliness by the child (Stormshak et al., 2000; Whiteside-Mansell et al., 2003). This principle also applies to other family relationships, such as siblings and marital partners. In each case, the behavior of one family member helps sustain a form of interaction in the other that either promotes or undermines psychological well-being.

■ **INDIRECT INFLUENCES.** The impact of family relationships on development becomes even more complicated when we consider that interaction between any two members is affected by others present in the setting. Bronfenbrenner calls these indirect influences the effect of *third parties*.

Third parties can serve as supports for or barriers to development. For example, parents with a warm, considerate marital relationship praise and stimulate their children more. In contrast, parents whose marriage is tense and hostile tend to be less responsive to their children's needs and more likely to criticize, express anger, and punish (McHale et al., 2002b). Children chronically exposed to angry, unresolved parental conflict have serious emotional problems (Harold et al., 2004). These include both *internalizing difficulties* (especially among girls), such as feeling worried and afraid and trying to repair their parents' relationship, and *externalizing difficulties* (especially among boys), including verbal and physical aggression (Davies & Lindsay, 2004). These child problems can further disrupt parents' marital relationship.

■ **ADAPTING TO CHANGE.** Think back to the *chronosystem* in Bronfenbrenner's theory (see page 21 in Chapter 1). The interplay of forces within the family is dynamic and ever-changing. Important events, such as the birth of a baby or the addition to the household of an ill elderly parent, create challenges that modify existing relationships. The way such events affect family interaction depends on the support other family members provide and on the developmental status of each participant. For example, the arrival of a new baby prompts very different reactions in a toddler than in a school-age child. And caring for an elderly parent is more stressful for a middle-aged adult still rearing young children than for an adult of the same age with no child-rearing responsibilities.

Historical time period also contributes to a dynamic family system. In recent decades, a declining birth rate, a high divorce rate, and expansion of women's roles have led to a smaller family size. This, combined with a longer lifespan, means that more generations are alive, with fewer members in the youngest ones, leading to a "top-heavy" family structure. Young people today are more likely to have older relatives than at any time in history— a circumstance that can be enriching as well as a source of tension.

Despite these variations, some general patterns in family functioning do exist. In the United States and other Western nations, one important source of these consistencies is socioeconomic status.

© ATEF HASSAN/REUTERS/CORBIS

An Iraqi family shares a morning meal before a dawn-to-dusk fast during the Muslim Holy month of Ramadan. The family is a complex system of interdependent relationships in which each person's behavior influences the behavior of others, both directly and indirectly.

Socioeconomic Status and Family Functioning

People in industrialized nations are stratified on the basis of what they do at work and how much they earn for doing it—factors that determine their social position and economic well-being. Researchers assess a family's standing on this continuum through an index called **socioeconomic status (SES),** which combines three related, but not completely overlapping, variables: (1) years of education and (2) the prestige of one's job and the skill it requires, both of which measure social status; and (3) income, which measures economic status. As SES rises and falls, people face changing circumstances that profoundly affect family functioning.

SES affects the timing and duration of phases of the family life cycle. People who work in skilled and semiskilled manual occupations (for example, construction workers and custodians) tend to marry and have children earlier as well as give birth to more children than people in professional and technical occupations. The two groups also differ in values and expectations. For example, when asked about personal qualities they desire for their children, lower-SES parents tend to emphasize external characteristics, such as obedience, politeness, and cleanliness. In contrast, higher-SES parents emphasize psychological traits, such as curiosity, happiness, and cognitive and social maturity (Duncan & Magnuson, 2003; Hoff, Laursen, & Tardif, 2002).

These differences are reflected in family interaction. Parents higher in SES talk to, read to, and otherwise stimulate their infants and preschoolers more. When their children are older, higher-SES parents use more warmth, explanations, and verbal praise. Commands ("You do that because I told you to"), criticism, and physical punishment all occur more often in low-SES households (Bradley & Corwyn, 2003).

Education contributes substantially to these variations in child rearing. Higher-SES parents' interest in providing verbal stimulation and nurturing inner traits is supported by years of schooling, during which they learned to think about abstract, subjective ideas. In diverse cultures around the world, as the Lifespan Vista box on page 48 makes clear, education of women in particular fosters patterns of thinking that greatly improve quality of life, for both parents and children.

Because of limited education and low social status, many lower-SES parents feel a sense of powerlessness in their relationships beyond the home. At work, for example, they must obey rules of others in positions of authority. When they get home, their parent–child interaction seems to duplicate these experiences—but now they are in authority. Higher levels of stress combined with a stronger belief in the value of physical punishment contribute to low-SES parents' greater use of coercive discipline (Conger & Donnellan, 2007; Pinderhughes et al., 2000). Higher-SES parents, in contrast, typically have more control over their own lives. At work, they are used to making independent decisions and convincing others of their point of view. At home, they teach these skills to their children (Greenberger, O'Neil, & Nagel, 1994).

Affluence

Despite advanced education and great material wealth, affluent parents—those in highly prestigious, well-paying occupations—often fail to engage in family interaction and parenting that promote favorable development. In several studies, researchers tracked the adjustment of youths growing up in wealthy suburbs (Luthar & Latendresse, 2005). By seventh grade, many showed serious problems that worsened in high school. Their school grades were poor, and they were more likely to engage in alcohol and drug use and to report high levels of anxiety and depression than low-SES youths (Luthar & Becker, 2002).

Why are so many affluent youths troubled? Compared to their better-adjusted counterparts, poorly adjusted affluent young people report less emotional closeness and supervision from their parents, who lead professionally and socially demanding lives. As a group, wealthy parents are nearly as physically and emotionally unavailable to their youngsters as parents coping with serious financial strain. At the same time, these parents often make excessive demands for achievement (Luthar & Becker, 2002). Adolescents whose parents value their accomplishments more than their character are more likely to have academic and emotional problems.

Poverty

When families slip into poverty, development is seriously threatened. Consider the case of Zinnia Mae, who grew up in a close-knit black community located in a small southeastern American city (Heath, 1990). As unemployment struck and citizens moved away, 16-year-old Zinnia Mae caught a ride to Atlanta. Two years later, she was the mother of a daughter and twin boys, living in public housing.

Zinnia Mae worried constantly about scraping together enough money to put food on the table, freeing herself from a cycle of rising debt, and finding the twins' father, who had stopped sending money. The children's play space was limited to a mattress on the living room floor. Toys consisted of spoons and food cartons, a rubber ball, and a few plastic cars. At the researcher's request, Zinnia Mae agreed to tape record her interactions with her children. Cut off from family and community ties and overwhelmed by financial strain and feelings of helplessness, she found herself unable to join in activities with her children. In 500 hours of tape, she started a conversation with them only 18 times.

Today, about 13 percent—40 million Americans—live in poverty. Those hit hardest are parents under age 25 with young children and elderly people who live alone. Poverty is also magnified among ethnic minorities and women. For example, 19 percent of U.S. children are poor, a rate that climbs to 30 percent for Hispanic children, 32 percent for Native-American children, and 34 percent for African-American children. For single mothers with preschool children and elderly women on their own, the poverty rate is nearly 50 percent (DeNavas-Walt, Proctor, & Smith, 2009).

■ A LIFESPAN VISTA: Looking Forward, Looking Back ■

Worldwide Education of Girls: Transforming Current and Future Generations

When a new school opened in the Egyptian village of Beni Shara'an, Ahmen, an illiterate shopkeeper, immediately enrolled his 8-year-old daughter Rawia (Bellamy, 2004, p. 19). Until that day, Rawia had divided her days between back-breaking farming and confinement to her home.

Before long, Rawia's advancing language, literacy, and reasoning skills transformed her family's quality of life. "My store accounts were in a mess, but soon Rawia started straightening out the books," Ahmen recalled. She also began helping her older sister learn to read and write. In addition, Rawia began to envision a better life for herself. "When I grow up," she told her father, "I want to be a doctor. Or maybe a teacher."

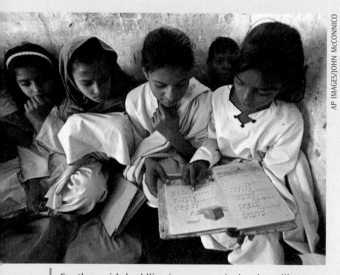

For these girls huddling in an open-air class in a village in Pakistan, attending school will dramatically improve their life opportunities and their nation's welfare. In both developed and developing nations, educating girls leads to gains in family income and relationships that carry over to improved health, education, and economic well-being in the next generation.

Over the past century, the percentage of children in the developing world who go to school has increased from a small minority of boys to a majority of all children in most regions. Still, some 73 million children, most of them poverty-stricken girls, do not start elementary school, and more than 200 million, again mostly girls, do not go to secondary school (UNICEF, 2006).

Although schooling is vital for all children, educating girls has an especially powerful impact on the welfare of families, societies, and future generations. The diverse benefits of girls' schooling largely accrue in two ways: (1) through enhanced verbal skills—reading, writing, and oral communication; and (2) through empowerment—a growing desire to improve their life conditions (LeVine, LeVine, & Schnell, 2001).

Family Health

Education gives people the communicative skills and confidence to seek health services and to benefit from public health information. As a result, years of schooling strongly predict women's preventive health behavior: prenatal visits, child immunizations, healthy diet, and sanitary practices (LeVine et al., 2004; Peña, Wall, & Person, 2000). In addition, because educated women have more life opportunities, they are more likely to take advantage of family planning services, delay marriage and childbearing, and have more widely spaced and fewer children (Stromquist, 2007). All these practices are linked to increased maternal and child survival and family health.

AP IMAGES/JOHN McCONNICO

Family Relationships and Parenting

In developed and developing nations alike, the empowerment that springs from educa-tion leads to more equitable husband–wife relationships and a reduction in harsh disciplining of children (LeVine et al., 1991; LeVine, LeVine, & Schnell, 2001). Also, educated mothers engage in more verbal stimulation and teaching of literacy skills to their children, which fosters success in school, higher educational attainment, reduced crime rates, and economic gains in the next generation. Regions of the world that have invested more in girls' education, such as southeast Asia and Latin America, tend to have higher levels of economic development (King & Mason, 2001).

Donor nations and international organizations are increasingly coming to the same conclusion: The education of girls is the most effective means of combating the most profound, global threats to human development: poverty, maternal and child mortality, and disease (Bellamy, 2004; Herz, 2004). Rawia got the chance to go to school because of an Egyptian national initiative, which led to the establishment of several thousand one-classroom schools in rural areas with the poorest record in educating girls. Because of cultural beliefs about gender roles or reluctance to give up a daughter's work at home, parents sometimes resist. But the largest barrier is that many countries continue to charge parents a fee for each child enrolled in school, often amounting to nearly one-third of the income of poverty-stricken families. Under these conditions, parents—if they send any children—tend to send only sons.

In 2003, Kenya eliminated fees for primary school. Immediately, enrollments of both boys and girls surged—by more than 30 percent. Uganda followed suit, increasing its primary school enrollment by 70 percent (Alter, 2008; RESULTS, 2006). When governments abolish enrollment fees, provide information about the benefits of education for girls, and create employment possibilities for women, the overwhelming majority of parents—including the very poor—choose to send their daughters to school, and some make great sacrifices to do so.

As we will see later, inadequate government programs to meet family needs are responsible for these disheartening statistics. The poverty rate is higher among children than any other age group. And of all Western nations, the United States has the highest percentage of extremely poor children. Nearly 8 percent of U.S. children live in deep poverty (at less than half the poverty threshold, the income level judged necessary for a minimum living standard). The earlier poverty begins, the

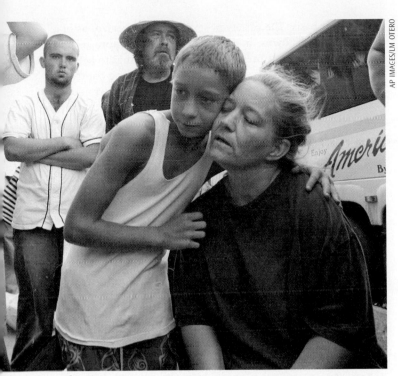

A boy hugs his mother as they wait to board a bus that will take them away from Galveston, Texas, following Hurricane Ike, which in 2008 left a massive path of destruction on the island. For low-income families, dislocation caused by a natural disaster is especially likely to result in long-term homelessness, impoverishment, and emotional stress.

deeper it is, and the longer it lasts, the more devastating are its effects. Children of poverty are more likely than other children to suffer from lifelong poor physical health, persistent deficits in cognitive development and academic achievement, high school dropout, mental illness, and antisocial behavior (Aber, Jones, & Raver, 2007; Ryan, Fauth, & Brooks-Gunn, 2006).

The constant stressors that accompany poverty weaken the family system. Poor families have many daily hassles—loss of welfare and unemployment payments, the car breaking down, something stolen from the house, to name just a few. When daily crises arise, family members become depressed, irritable, and distracted, and hostile interactions increase (Conger & Donnellan, 2007; Evans, 2006).

Beyond the Family: Neighborhoods, Towns, and Cities

As the concepts of *mesosystem* and *exosystem* in ecological systems theory make clear, connections between family and community are vital for psychological well-being. From our discussion of poverty, perhaps you can see why: In poverty-stricken urban areas, community life is usually disrupted. Families move often, parks and playgrounds are in disarray, and community centers providing organized activities do not exist. Family violence, child abuse and neglect, children's problem

behavior, youth antisocial activity, and adult criminal behavior are especially high (Brody et al., 2003; Kohen et al., 2002). In contrast, strong family ties to the surrounding social context—as indicated by frequent contact with friends and relatives and regular church, synagogue, or mosque attendance—reduce family stress and enhance adjustment (Boardman, 2004; Leventhal & Brooks-Gunn, 2003).

■ **NEIGHBORHOODS.** Communities offer resources and social ties that play an important part in children's development. In several studies, low-SES families were randomly assigned vouchers to move out of public housing into neighborhoods varying widely in affluence. Compared with their peers who remained in poverty-stricken areas, children and youths who moved into low-poverty neighborhoods showed substantially better physical and mental health and school achievement (Goering, 2003; Leventhal & Brooks-Gunn, 2003).

Neighborhood resources have a greater impact on economically disadvantaged than well-to-do young people. Higher-SES families can afford to reach beyond the streets near their homes, transporting their children to lessons and entertainment and, if necessary, to better-quality schools. In low-income communities, well-planned youth programs offering art, music, sports, and other lessons and activities predict favorable child and adolescent development, including increased self-confidence, school achievement, and educational aspirations (Barnes et al., 2007).

The Better Beginnings, Better Futures Project of Ontario, Canada, is a government-sponsored set of pilot programs aimed at preventing the dire consequences of neighborhood poverty (Gershoff & Aber, 2006). The most successful of these efforts provided children with in-class and summer enrichment activities. Project staff also visited each child's parents regularly, encouraging their involvement in the child's school and neighborhood life (Peters, 2005; Peters, Petrunka, & Arnold, 2003). An evaluation after four years revealed gains in neighborhood satisfaction, family functioning, effective parenting, and children's reading skills, along with a reduction in emotional and behavior problems.

As these outcomes suggest, neighborhoods also affect adults' well-being. An employed parent who can rely on a neighbor to assist her school-age child in her absence gains the peace of mind essential for productive work. In low-SES areas with high resident stability and social cohesion, where neighbors help and look after one another, adults report less stress, which in turn predicts substantially better physical health (Boardman, 2004; Feldman & Steptoe, 2004).

During late adulthood, neighborhoods become increasingly important because people spend more time at home. Despite the availability of planned housing for elders, about 90 percent remain in regular housing, usually in the same neighborhood where they lived during their working lives (U.S. Census Bureau, 2009b). In the absence of nearby family members, the elderly mention neighbors and nearby friends as resources they rely on most for physical and social support (Hooyman & Kiyak, 2008).

AP IMAGES/MUSCATINE JOURNAL, CONNIE STREET

At a block party in an inner-city neighborhood, children participate in a doughnut-eating contest while their parents look on with amusement. According to the social systems perspective, ties to the community are essential for families to function at their best.

■ **TOWNS AND CITIES.**   Neighborhoods are embedded in towns and cities, which also mold children's and adults' daily lives. In rural areas and small towns, children and youths are more likely to be given important work tasks—caring for livestock, operating the snowplow, or playing in the town band. They usually perform these tasks alongside adults, who instill in them a sense of responsibility and teach them practical and social skills needed to sustain their community. Compared with large urban areas, small towns also offer stronger connections between settings that influence children's lives. For example, because most citizens know one another and schools serve as centers of community life, contact between teachers and parents occurs often—an important factor in promoting children's academic achievement (Hill & Taylor, 2004).

Adults in small towns participate in more civic groups and are more likely to occupy positions of leadership because a greater proportion of residents are needed to meet community needs (Elder & Conger, 2000). In late adulthood, people residing in small towns and suburbs have neighbors who are more willing to provide assistance. As a result, they form a greater number of warm relationships with nonrelatives.

Of course, small-town residents cannot visit museums, go to professional baseball games, or attend orchestra concerts on a regular basis. The variety of settings is not as great as in a large city. Small towns, however, are safer and more secure. Responsible adults are present in almost all settings to keep an eye on children. And the elderly feel safer—a strong contributor to how satisfied they are with their place of residence (Parmelee & Lawton, 1990; Shields et al., 2002).

The Cultural Context

Our discussion in Chapter 1 emphasized that human development can be fully understood only when viewed in its larger cultural context. In the following sections, we expand on this theme by taking up the role of the *macrosystem* in development. First, we discuss ways that cultural values and practices affect environmental contexts for development. Second, we consider how healthy development depends on laws and government programs that shield people from harm and foster their well-being.

■ **CULTURAL VALUES AND PRACTICES.**   Cultures shape family interaction and community settings beyond the home—in short, all aspects of daily life. Many of us remain blind to aspects of our own cultural heritage until we see them in relation to the practices of others.

TAKE A MOMENT... Consider the question, Who should be responsible for rearing young children? How would you answer it? Here are some typical responses from my students: "If parents decide to have a baby, then they should be ready to care for it." "Most people are not happy about others intruding into family life." These statements reflect a widely held opinion in the United States—that the care and rearing of children, and paying for that care, are the duty of parents, and only parents. This view has a long history—one in which independence, self-reliance, and the privacy of family life emerged as central American values (Halfon & McLearn, 2002). It is one reason, among others, that the public has been slow to endorse government-supported benefits for all families, such as high-quality child care and paid employment leave for meeting family needs. And it has also contributed to the large number of U.S. families who remain poor, even though family members are employed (Gruendel & Aber, 2007; Pohl, 2002; UNICEF, 2005).

Although the culture as a whole may value independence and privacy, not all citizens share the same values. Some belong to **subcultures**—groups of people with beliefs and customs that differ from those of the larger culture. Many ethnic minority groups in the United States have cooperative family structures, which help protect their members from the harmful effects of poverty. For example, the African-American tradition of **extended-family households,** in which three or more generations live together, is a vital feature of black family life that has enabled its members to survive, despite a long history of prejudice and economic deprivation. Grandparents play meaningful roles in guiding younger generations; adolescents and adults with educational, employment, marital, or child-rearing difficulties receive assistance and emotional support; and caregiving is enhanced for children and the elderly. Active, involved extended families also characterize other minorities, such as Asian, Native-American, and Hispanic subcultures (Becker et al., 2003; Harwood et al., 2002).

Our discussion so far reflects a broad dimension on which cultures and subcultures differ: the extent to which *collectivism* versus *individualism* is emphasized. In **collectivist societies,** people define themselves as part of a group and stress group goals over individual goals. In **individualistic societies,** people think of themselves as separate entities and are largely concerned with their own personal needs (Triandis, 1995, 2005). As these definitions suggest, the two cultural patterns are associated with two distinct views of the self. Collectivist societies value an *interdependent self,* which stresses social harmony, obligations and responsibility to others, and collaborative endeavors. In contrast, individualistic societies value an *independent self,* which emphasizes personal exploration, discovery, and achievement and individual choice in relationships. Both interdependence and independence are part of the makeup of every person (Greenfield et al., 2003; Tamis-LeMonda et al., 2008). But societies vary greatly in the extent to which they emphasize each alternative.

■ **PUBLIC POLICIES AND LIFESPAN DEVELOPMENT.** When widespread social problems arise, such as poverty, homelessness, hunger, and disease, nations attempt to solve them through **public policies**—laws and government programs designed to improve current conditions. In the United States, public policies safeguarding children have lagged behind policies for the elderly. And both sets of policies have been slow to emerge relative to other industrialized nations.

Policies for Children, Youths, and Families. We have already seen that although many U.S. children fare well, a large number grow up in environments that threaten their development. As Table 2.3 reveals, the United States does not rank well on any key measure of children's health and well-being.

The problems of children and youths extend beyond the indicators in the table. For example, approximately 10 percent of U.S. children—most of them in low-income families—have no health insurance (DeNavas-Walt, Proctor, & Smith, 2009). Furthermore, the United States has been slow to move toward national standards and funding for child care. Affordable care is in short supply, and much of it is substandard in quality (Lamb & Ahnert, 2006; Muenchow & Marsland, 2007). In families affected by divorce, weak enforcement of child support payments heightens poverty in mother-headed households. And by ages 18 to 20, about 11 percent of U.S. adolescents have not yet earned a high school diploma (U.S. Department of Education, 2009).

Why have attempts to help children and youths been difficult to realize in the United States? Cultural values of self-reliance and privacy have made government hesitant to become involved in family matters. Furthermore, good social programs are expensive, and they must compete for a fair share of a country's economic resources. Children can easily remain unrecognized in this process because they cannot vote or speak out to protect their own interests (Ripple & Zigler, 2003). Instead, they must rely on the goodwill of others to become an important government priority.

■ **TABLE 2.3** ■ *How Does the United States Compare to Other Nations on Indicators of Children's Health and Well-Being?*

INDICATOR	U.S. RANK[a]	SOME COUNTRIES THE UNITED STATES TRAILS
Childhood poverty (among 25 industrialized nations considered)	25th	Canada, Czech Republic, Germany, Norway, Sweden, Poland, Spain[b]
Infant deaths in the first year of life (worldwide)	28th	Canada, Hong Kong, Ireland, Singapore, Spain
Teenage birth rate (among 28 industrialized nations considered)	28th	Australia, Canada, Czech Republic, Denmark, Hungary, Iceland, Poland, Slovak Republic
Public expenditures on education as percentage of gross domestic product[b] (among 22 industrialized nations considered)	12th	Belgium, France, Iceland, New Zealand, Portugal, Spain, Sweden
Public expenditures on health as a percentage of gross domestic product (among 22 industrialized nations considered)	16th	Austria, Australia, Canada, France, Hungary, Iceland, Switzerland, New Zealand

[a]1 = highest, or best, rank.

[b]Gross domestic product is the value of all goods and services produced by a nation during a specified time period. It provides an overall measure of a nation's wealth.

Sources: Canada Campaign 2000, 2007; OECD, 2006, 2008a; UNICEF, 2005; U.S. Census Bureau, 2009a; U.S. Department of Education, 2009.

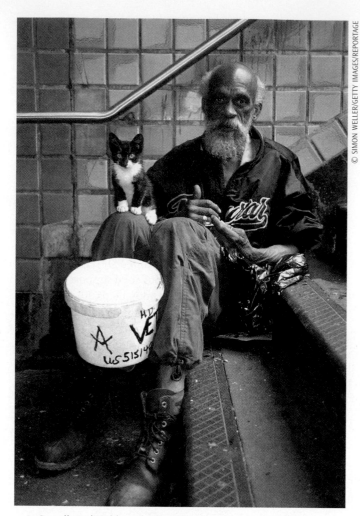

© SIMON WELLER/GETTY IMAGES/REPORTAGE

Overall, senior citizens in the United States are better off economically than are children. But many older adults—especially ethnic minorities, women, and those living alone—are poverty-stricken.

Policies for the Elderly. Until well into the twentieth century, the United States had few policies in place to protect its aging population. For example, Social Security benefits were not awarded until the late 1930s. Yet most Western nations had social security systems in place a decade or more earlier (Karger & Stoesz, 2008). In the 1960s, U.S. federal spending on programs for the elderly expanded rapidly. Medicare, a national health insurance program for older people, was initiated. But it requires participants to pay part of those costs, leaving about half of elderly health spending to be covered by supplemental private insurance, government health insurance for the poor, or out-of-pocket payments (U.S. Department of Health and Human Services, 2008j).

Social Security and Medicare consume 96 percent of the U.S. federal budget for the elderly; only 4 percent is devoted to other programs. Consequently, U.S. programs for the aged have been criticized for neglecting social services (Hooyman & Kiyak, 2008). To meet this need, 660 Area Agencies on Aging

have been established at regional and local levels to assess community needs and offer communal and home-delivered meals, self-care education, elder abuse prevention, and a wide range of other social services. But limited funding means that the Area Agencies help far too few people in need.

As noted earlier, many senior citizens—especially women, ethnic minorities, and those living alone—remain in dire economic straits. Although all Americans age 65 and older are guaranteed a minimum income, the guaranteed amount is below the poverty line—the amount judged necessary for bare subsistence by the federal government. Furthermore, Social Security benefits are rarely adequate as a sole source of retirement income. Therefore, U.S. elders are more likely than other age groups to be among the "near poor" (Greenberg, 2007).

Nevertheless, the U.S. aging population is financially much better off now than in the past. Today, the elderly are a large, powerful, well-organized constituency, far more likely than children or low-income families to attract the support of politicians. As a result, the number of aging poor has declined from 1 out of 3 people in 1960 to 1 out of 10 in the early twenty-first century (U.S. Census Bureau, 2009b). Still, as Figure 2.5 shows,

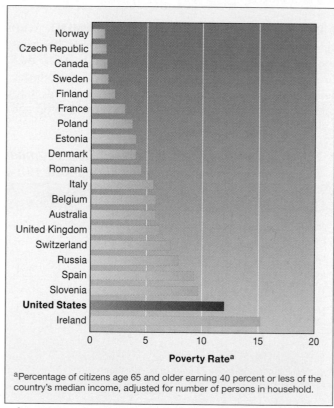

[a]Percentage of citizens age 65 and older earning 40 percent or less of the country's median income, adjusted for number of persons in household.

■ **FIGURE 2.5** ■ **Percentage of elderly living in poverty in twenty industrialized nations.** Among the countries listed, the United States has the highest rate of elderly living in poverty. Public expenditures on social security and other income guarantees for senior citizens are far greater in the highly ranked nations than in the United States. (Adapted from Luxembourg Income Study, 2008.)

the elderly in the United States are less well-off than those in many other Western nations.

■ **LOOKING TOWARD THE FUTURE.** Despite the worrisome state of many children, families, and aging citizens, efforts are being made to improve their condition. Growing awareness of the gap between what we know and what we do to better people's lives has led experts in human development to join with concerned citizens as advocates for more effective policies. As a result, several influential interest groups devoted to the well-being of children or the elderly have emerged.

In the United States, the Children's Defense Fund (CDF)—a private, nonprofit organization founded by Marian Wright Edelman in 1973—engages in research, public education, legal action, drafting of legislation, congressional testimony, and community organizing. To learn more about the Children's Defense Fund, visit its website at *www.childrensdefense.org.*

Nearly half of Americans over age 50, both retired and employed, are members of AARP (originally known as the American Association of Retired Persons). Founded by Ethel Percy Andrus in 1958, AARP has a large and energetic lobbying staff that works for increased government benefits of all kinds for the aged. A description of AARP and its activities can be found at *www.aarp.org.*

Besides strong advocacy, public policies that enhance human development depend on policy-relevant research that documents needs and evaluates programs to spark improvements. Today, more researchers are collaborating with community and government agencies to enhance the social relevance of their investigations. They are also doing a better job of disseminating their findings to the public through television documentaries, newspaper stories, magazine articles, websites, and direct reports to government officials. As a result, they are helping to create a sense of immediacy about the condition of children, families, and the aged that is necessary to spur a society into action.

ASK YOURSELF

>> **REVIEW**
Links between family and community foster development throughout the lifespan. Cite several examples from our discussion that support this idea.

>> **APPLY**
Check your local newspaper or one or two national news magazines to see how often articles on the condition of children, families, and the aged appear. Why is it important for researchers to communicate with the general public about the well-being of these sectors of the population?

>> **REFLECT**
Review the discussion of cultural values and practices on pages 50–51. Under what circumstances do you believe government should become involved in family life?

Policy-relevant research helps child advocates make the case for expanding programs like this summer day camp for Boston inner-city children. Schools coordinate with community centers to combine academic and athletic activities. Here, children participate in a science experiment, followed by gym time. They spend the summer exercising both their minds and their bodies.

Understanding the Relationship Between Heredity and Environment

So far we have discussed a wide variety of genetic and environmental influences, each of which has the power to alter the course of development. Yet people who are born into the same family (and who therefore share genes and environments) are often quite different in characteristics. We also know that some individuals are affected more than others by their homes, neighborhoods, and communities. How do scientists explain the impact of heredity and environment when they seem to work in so many different ways?

Although scientists are making progress in identifying the multiple variations in DNA sequences associated with such complex traits as intelligence and personality, so far these genetic markers explain only a small amount of variation in human behavior, and a minority of cases of most psychological disorders (Plomin, 2005; Plomin et al., 2003). For the most part, scientists are still limited to investigating the impact of genes on complex characteristics indirectly.

Some believe that it is useful and possible to answer the question of *how much each factor contributes* to differences among people. A growing consensus, however, regards that question as unanswerable. These investigators believe that genetic and environmental influences are inseparable (Gottlieb, Wahlsten, & Lickliter, 2006). The important question, they maintain, is *how nature and nurture work together*. Let's consider each position in turn.

The Question, "How Much?"

To infer the role of heredity in complex human characteristics, researchers use special methods, the most common being the *heritability estimate*. Let's look closely at the information this procedure yields, along with its limitations.

■ **HERITABILITY.** **Heritability estimates** measure the extent to which individual differences in complex traits in a specific population are due to genetic factors. We will take a brief look at heritability findings on intelligence and personality here and will return to them in later chapters, when we consider these topics in greater detail. Heritability estimates are obtained from **kinship studies,** which compare the characteristics of family members. The most common type of kinship study compares identical twins, who share all their genes, with

fraternal twins, who, on average, share only half. If people who are genetically more alike are also more similar in intelligence and personality, then the researcher assumes that heredity plays an important role.

Kinship studies of intelligence provide some of the most controversial findings in the field of human development. Some experts claim a strong genetic influence, whereas others believe that heredity is barely involved. Currently, most kinship findings support a moderate role for heredity. When many twin studies are examined, correlations between the scores of identical twins are consistently higher than those of fraternal twins. In a summary of more than 10,000 twin pairs, the correlation for intelligence was .86 for identical twins and .60 for fraternal twins (Plomin & Spinath, 2004).

Researchers use a complex statistical procedure to compare these correlations, arriving at a heritability estimate ranging from 0 to 1.00. The value for intelligence is about .50 for child and adolescent twin samples in Western industrialized nations. This suggests that differences in genetic makeup explain half the variation in intelligence. However, heritability increases in adulthood, with some estimates as high as .80. As we will see later, one explanation is that, compared to children, adults exert greater personal control over their intellectual experiences—for example, how much time they spend reading or solving challenging problems (McClearn et al., 1997; McGue & Christensen, 2002).

Heritability research also reveals that genetic factors are important in personality. For frequently studied traits, such as sociability, anxiety, agreeableness, and activity level, heritability estimates obtained on child, adolescent, and young adult twin samples are moderate, in the .40s and .50s (Bouchard, 2004; Rothbart & Bates, 2006). Moderate heritabilities have also been reported for psychological disorders of depression and antisocial behavior, with schizophrenia yielding high heritability, around .80 (Bouchard, 2004). Unlike intelligence, however, heritability of personality does not increase over the lifespan (Loehlin et al., 2005).

■ **LIMITATIONS OF HERITABILITY.** Serious questions have been raised about the accuracy of heritability estimates, which depends on the extent to which the twin pairs studied reflect genetic and environmental variation in the population. Within a population in which all people have very similar home, school, and community experiences, individual differences in intelligence and personality would be largely genetic, and heritability estimates would be close to 1.00. Conversely, the more environments vary, the more likely they are to account for individ-

Adriana and Tamara, identical twins born in Mexico, were separated at birth and adopted into different homes in the New York City area. They were unaware of each other until a mutual acquaintance noted resemblances between them. At age 20, when they decided to meet, they discovered many similarities: Both like the same clothing styles, were B students, and love to dance. The study of identical twins reared apart reveals that heredity contributes to many personality characteristics. But not all separated twins match up as well as this pair, and generalizing from twin evidence to the broader population is controversial.

© JACQUIE HEMMERDINGER/THE NEW YORK TIMES/REDUX PICTURES

ual differences, yielding lower heritability estimates. In twin studies, most twin pairs are reared together under highly similar conditions. Even when separated twins are available for study, social service agencies have often placed them in advantaged homes that are alike in many ways (Rutter et al., 2001). Because the environments of most twin pairs are less diverse than those of the general population, heritability estimates are likely to exaggerate the role of heredity.

Heritability estimates are controversial measures because they can easily be misapplied. For example, high heritabilities have been used to suggest that ethnic differences in intelligence, such as the poorer performance of black children compared to white children, have a genetic basis (Jensen, 1969, 1998, 2001; Rushton & Jensen, 2005, 2006). Yet this line of reasoning is widely regarded as incorrect. Heritabilities computed on mostly white twin samples do not tell us what is responsible for test score differences between ethnic groups. We have already seen that large economic and cultural differences are involved. In Chapter 9, we will discuss research indicating that when black children are adopted into economically advantaged homes at an early age, their scores are well above average and substantially higher than those of children growing up in impoverished families.

Perhaps the most serious criticism of heritability estimates has to do with their limited usefulness. Though interesting, these statistics give us no precise information on how intelligence and personality develop or how children might respond to environments designed to help them develop as far as possible (Rutter, 2002). Indeed, the heritability of children's intelligence increases as parental education and income increase—that is, as children grow up in conditions that allow them to make the most of their genetic endowment. In disadvantaged environments, children are prevented from realizing their potential. Consequently, enhancing their experiences through interventions—such as increasing parent education and income and providing high-quality preschool or child care—has a greater impact on development (Bronfenbrenner & Morris, 2006; Turkheimer et al., 2003).

The Question, "How?"

Today, most researchers view development as the result of a dynamic interplay between heredity and environment. How do nature and nurture work together? Several concepts shed light on this question.

■ **REACTION RANGE.** The first of these ideas is **range of reaction,** each person's unique, genetically determined response to the environment (Gottesman, 1963). Let's explore this idea in Figure 2.6. Reaction range can apply to any characteristic; here it is illustrated for intelligence. Notice that when environments vary from extremely unstimulating to highly enriched, Ben's intelligence increases steadily, Linda's rises sharply and

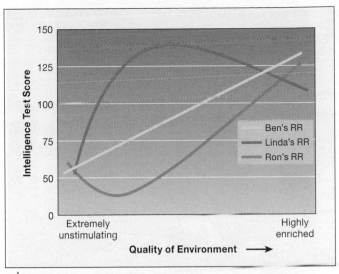

■ **FIGURE 2.6** ■ **Intellectual ranges of reaction (RR) for three children in environments that vary from extremely unstimulating to highly enriched.** Each child, because of his or her genetic makeup, responds differently to changes in quality of the environment. Ben's intelligence test score increases steadily, Linda's rises sharply and then falls off, and Ron's begins to increase only after the environment becomes modestly stimulating. (Adapted from Wahlsten, 1994.)

then falls off, and Ron's begins to increase only after the environment becomes modestly stimulating.

Reaction range highlights two important points. First, it shows that because each of us has a unique genetic makeup, we respond differently to the same environment. Notice in Figure 2.6 how a poor environment results in similarly low scores for all three individuals. But when the environment provides an intermediate level of stimulation, Linda is by far the best-performing child. And in a highly enriched environment, Ben does best, followed by Ron, both of whom now outperform Linda. Second, sometimes different genetic–environmental combinations can make two people look the same! For example, if Linda is reared in a minimally stimulating environment, her score will be about 100—average for people in general. Ben and Ron can also obtain this score, but to do so, they must grow up in a fairly enriched home. In sum, range of reaction reveals that unique blends of heredity and environment lead to both similarities and differences in behavior (Gottlieb, Wahlsten, & Lickliter, 2006).

■ **GENETIC–ENVIRONMENTAL CORRELATION.** A major problem in trying to separate heredity and environment is that they are often correlated (Plomin et al., 2001; Scarr & McCartney, 1983). According to the concept of **genetic–environmental correlation,** our genes influence the environments to which we are exposed. The way this happens changes with age.

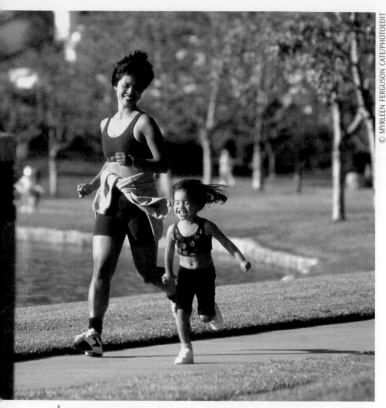

This mother shares her love of running with her daughter. In addition, her child may have inherited her mother's athletic ability. When heredity and environment are correlated, they jointly foster the same capacities, and the influence of one cannot be separated from the influence of the other.

Passive and Evocative Correlation. At younger ages, two types of genetic–environmental correlation are common. The first is called *passive* correlation because the child has no control over it. Early on, parents provide environments influenced by their own heredity. For example, parents who are good athletes emphasize outdoor activities and enroll their children in swimming and gymnastics. Besides being exposed to an "athletic environment," the children may have inherited their parents' athletic ability. As a result, they are likely to become good athletes for both genetic and environmental reasons.

The second type of genetic–environmental correlation is *evocative.* Children evoke responses that are influenced by the child's heredity, and these responses strengthen the child's original style. For example, an active, friendly baby is likely to receive more social stimulation than a passive, quiet infant. And a cooperative, attentive child probably receives more patient interactions from parents than a distractible child. In support of this idea, the less genetically alike siblings are, the more their parents treat them differently, in both warmth and negativity. Thus, parents' treatment of identical twins is highly similar, whereas their treatment of fraternal twins and nontwin biological siblings is only moderately so. And little resemblance exists in parents' warm and negative interactions with unrelated stepsiblings (Reiss, 2003).

Active Correlation. At older ages, *active* genetic–environmental correlation becomes common. As children extend their experiences beyond the immediate family and are given the freedom to make more choices, they actively seek environments that fit with their genetic tendencies. The well-coordinated, muscular child spends more time at after-school sports, the musically talented youngster joins the school orchestra and practices his violin, and the intellectually curious child is a familiar patron at her local library.

This tendency to actively choose environments that complement our heredity is called **niche-picking** (Scarr & McCartney, 1983). Infants and young children cannot do much niche-picking because adults select environments for them. In contrast, older children, adolescents, and adults are increasingly in charge of their environments. The niche-picking idea explains why pairs of identical twins reared apart during childhood and later reunited may find, to their surprise, that they have similar hobbies, food preferences, and vocations—a trend that is especially marked when twins' environmental opportunities are similar (Plomin, 1994). And niche-picking sheds light on why identical twins, compared to fraternal twins and other adults, select more similar spouses and best friends—in height, weight, personality, political attitudes, and other characteristics (Rushton & Bons, 2005).

The influence of heredity and environment is not constant but changes over time. With age, genetic factors may become more important in influencing the environments we experience and choose for ourselves.

■ ENVIRONMENTAL INFLUENCES ON GENE EXPRESSION.

Notice how, in the concepts just considered, heredity is granted priority. In range of reaction, it *limits* individual responsiveness to varying environments. Similarly, some theorists regard genetic–environmental correlation as entirely driven by genetics (Harris, 1998; Rowe, 1994). They believe that children's genetic makeup causes them to receive, evoke, or seek experiences that actualize their inborn tendencies.

Others argue that heredity does not dictate children's experiences or development in a rigid way. In a large Finnish adoption study, children of schizophrenic mothers reared by healthy adoptive parents showed little mental illness—no more than a control group with healthy biological and adoptive parents. In contrast, schizophrenia and other psychological impairments piled up in adoptees whose biological and adoptive parents were both disturbed (Tienari et al., 2003; Tienari, Wahlberg, & Wynne, 2006).

As these findings suggest, parents and other caring adults can provide children with experiences that modify the expression of heredity. For example, in a study that tracked the development of 5-year-old identical twins, pair members tended to resemble each other in level of aggression. And the

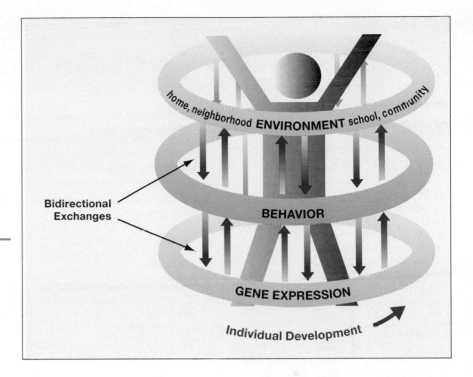

■ **FIGURE 2.7** ■ **The epigenetic framework.**
Development takes place through ongoing, bidirectional exchanges between heredity and all levels of the environment. Genes affect behavior and experiences. Experiences and behavior also affect gene expression. (Adapted from Gottlieb, 2007.)

more aggression they displayed, the more maternal anger and criticism they received (a genetic–environmental correlation). Nevertheless, some mothers treated their twins differently. When followed up at age 7, twins who had been targets of more maternal negativity engaged in even more antisocial behavior. In contrast, their better-treated, genetically identical counterparts showed a reduction in disruptive acts (Caspi et al., 2004). Good parenting protected them from a spiraling, antisocial course of development.

Accumulating evidence reveals that the relationship between heredity and environment is not a one-way street, from genes to environment to behavior. Rather, like other system influences considered in this and the previous chapter, it is *bidirectional:* Genes affect people's behavior and experiences, but their experiences and behavior also affect gene expression (Gottlieb, 2000, 2003; Rutter, 2006; Ryff & Singer, 2005).

Researchers call this view of the relationship between heredity and environment the *epigenetic framework* (Gottlieb, 1998, 2007). It is depicted in Figure 2.7. **Epigenesis** means development resulting from ongoing, bidirectional exchanges between heredity and all levels of the environment. To illustrate, providing a baby with a healthy diet increases brain growth, leading to new connections between nerve cells, which transform gene expression. This opens the door to new gene–environment exchanges—for example, advanced exploration of objects and interaction with caregivers, which further enhance brain growth and gene expression. These ongoing, bidirectional influences foster cognitive and social development. In contrast, harmful environments can dampen gene expression,

at times so profoundly that later experiences can do little to change characteristics (such as intelligence and personality) that were flexible to begin with.

The concept of epigenesis reminds us that development is best understood as a series of complex exchanges between nature and nurture. Although people cannot be changed in any way we might desire, environments can modify genetic influences. The success of any attempt to improve development depends on the characteristics we want to change, the genetic makeup of the individual, and the type and timing of our intervention.

ASK YOURSELF

» REVIEW
What is epigenesis, and how does it differ from range of reaction and genetic–environmental correlation? Provide an example of epigenesis.

» APPLY
Bianca's parents are accomplished musicians. At age 4, Bianca began taking piano lessons. By age 10, she was accompanying the school choir. At age 14, she asked if she could attend a special music high school. Explain how genetic–environmental correlation promoted Bianca's talent.

» REFLECT
What aspects of your own development—for example, interests, hobbies, college major, or vocational choice—are probably due to niche-picking? Explain.

Summary

Genetic Foundations

What are genes, and how are they transmitted from one generation to the next?

>> Each individual's **phenotype,** or directly observable characteristics, is a product of both **genotype** and environment. **Chromosomes,** rodlike structures within the cell nucleus, contain our hereditary endowment. Along their length are **genes,** segments of **deoxyribonucleic acid (DNA)** that send instructions for making a rich assortment of proteins to the cell's cytoplasm—a process that influences our development and characteristics.

>> **Gametes,** or sex cells, result from a process of cell division called **meiosis,** in which each individual receives a unique set of genes from each parent. Once sperm and ovum unite, the resulting **zygote** starts to develop into a complex human being through cell duplication, or **mitosis.**

>> If the fertilizing sperm carries an X chromosome, the child will be a girl; if it contains a Y chromosome, a boy. **Fraternal,** or **dizygotic, twins** result when two ova are released from the mother's ovaries and each is fertilized. **Identical,** or **monozygotic, twins** develop when a zygote divides in two during the early stages of cell duplication.

Describe various patterns of genetic inheritance.

>> Traits controlled by single genes follow **dominant–recessive** and **incomplete-dominance** patterns of inheritance. **Homozygous** individuals have two identical **alleles,** or forms of a gene. **Heterozygous** individuals, with one dominant and one recessive allele, are **carriers** of the recessive trait.

>> **X-linked inheritance** applies when recessive disorders are carried on the X chromosome and, therefore, are more likely to affect males. In **genomic imprinting,** one parent's gene is activated, regardless of its makeup.

>> Unfavorable genes arise from **mutation,** which can occur spontaneously or be caused by hazardous environmental agents. Germline mutation affects the cells that give rise to gametes; somatic mutation can occur in body cells at any time of life.

>> **Polygenic inheritance** of human traits, such as intelligence and personality, is influenced by many genes. For such characteristics, scientists must study the influence of heredity indirectly.

Describe major chromosomal abnormalities, and explain how they occur.

>> Most chromosomal abnormalities are due to errors in meiosis. The most common, Down syndrome, results in physical defects and mental retardation. Disorders of the **sex chromosomes** are generally milder than defects of the **autosomes.**

Reproductive Choices

What procedures can assist prospective parents in having healthy children?

>> **Genetic counseling** helps couples at risk for giving birth to children with genetic abnormalities decide whether or not to conceive. **Prenatal diagnostic methods** permit early detection of genetic problems.

>> Reproductive technologies such as donor insemination, in vitro fertilization, surrogate motherhood, and postmenopausal-assisted childbirth permit many individuals to become parents who otherwise would not, but they raise serious legal and ethical concerns.

>> Many parents who cannot conceive or who are at high risk of transmitting a genetic disorder decide to adopt. Although adopted children have more learning and emotional problems than children in general, most fare well in the long run. Warm, sensitive parenting predicts favorable development.

Environmental Contexts for Development

Describe family functioning as a social system along with aspects of the environment that support family well-being and development.

>> Human development takes place within a complex, many-layered environment. The first and foremost context for development is the family, a dynamic system characterized by bidirectional influences, in which each family member's behaviors affect those of others. Both direct and indirect influences operate within the family system, which must continually adjust to new events and changes in its members.

>> **Socioeconomic status (SES)** profoundly affects family functioning. Higher-SES families tend to be smaller, to emphasize psychological traits, and to engage in warm, verbally stimulating interaction with children. Lower-SES families often stress external characteristics and use more commands, criticism, and physical punishment. Many affluent parents are physically and emotionally unavailable, thereby impairing their children's adjustment. Poverty and homelessness can seriously undermine development.

>> Connections between family and community are vital for psychological well-being. Stable, socially cohesive neighborhoods in which residents have access to enrichment activities and social support promote favorable development in both children and adults.

>> The values and practices of cultures and **subcultures** affect all aspects of daily life. **Extended-family households,** which are common among ethnic minorities, help protect family members from negative effects of poverty and other stressful life conditions.

>> In our complex world, favorable development depends on **public policies.** Factors promoting effective social programs include cultural values emphasizing **collectivism** over **individualism,** a nation's economic resources, and the presence of organizations and individuals that work to improve quality of life.

Understanding the Relationship Between Heredity and Environment

Explain the various ways heredity and environment may combine to influence complex traits.

>> Researchers use **kinship studies** to compute **heritability estimates,** which show that genetic factors influence such traits as intelligence and personality. However, the accuracy and usefulness of heritability estimates have been challenged.

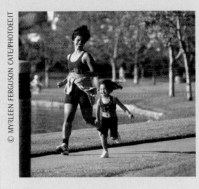

© MYRLEEN FERGUSON CATE/PHOTOEDIT

>> **Range of reaction, genetic–environmental correlation,** and **niche-picking** describe how genes affect the environments to which people are exposed. **Epigenesis** reminds us that development is best understood as a series of complex exchanges between nature and nurture that change over the lifespan.

Important Terms and Concepts

allele (p. 38)
autosomes (p. 37)
carrier (p. 39)
chromosomes (p. 36)
collectivist societies (p. 51)
deoxyribonucleic acid (DNA) (p. 36)
dominant–recessive inheritance (p. 38)
epigenesis (p. 57)
extended-family household (p. 50)
fraternal, or dizygotic, twins (p. 38)
gametes (p. 37)
gene (p. 37)

genetic counseling (p. 42)
genetic–environmental correlation (p. 55)
genomic imprinting (p. 39)
genotype (p. 36)
heritability estimate (p. 54)
heterozygous (p. 38)
homozygous (p. 38)
identical, or monozygotic, twins (p. 38)
incomplete dominance (p. 39)
individualistic societies (p. 51)
kinship studies (p. 54)
meiosis (p. 37)

mitosis (p. 37)
mutation (p. 40)
niche-picking (p. 56)
phenotype (p. 36)
polygenic inheritance (p. 40)
prenatal diagnostic methods (p. 43)
public policies (p. 51)
range of reaction (p. 55)
sex chromosomes (p. 37)
socioeconomic status (SES) (p. 47)
subculture (p. 50)
X-linked inheritance (p. 39)
zygote (p. 37)

CHAPTER 3

Prenatal Development, Birth, and the Newborn Baby

© BLEND IMAGES/ALAMY

As these parents share an intimate moment with their children, they convey a sense of delight in their growing family and help their older daughter welcome the new baby.

When I met Yolanda and Jay one fall in my child de-velopment class, Yolanda was just two months pregnant. After months of wondering if the time in their lives was right, they had decided to have a baby. Both were full of questions: "How does the baby grow before birth?" "When is each organ formed?" "Has its heart begun to beat?" "Can it hear, feel, or sense our presence?"

Yolanda and Jay wanted to do everything possible to make sure their baby would be born healthy. At first, they believed that the uterus completely shielded the developing organism from any dangers in the environment, but after browsing through several pregnancy books, Yolanda and Jay realized they were wrong. Yolanda started to wonder about her diet and whether she should keep up her daily aerobics routine. And she asked me whether an aspirin for a headache, a glass of wine at dinner, or a few cups of coffee during study hours might be harmful.

In this chapter, we answer Yolanda and Jay's questions, along with many more that scientists have asked about the events before birth. First, we trace prenatal development, paying special attention to environmental supports for healthy growth, as well as damaging influences that threaten the child's health and survival. Next, we turn to the events of childbirth, including the choices available to women in in-dustrialized nations about where and how to give birth.

Yolanda and Jay's son Joshua was strong, alert, and healthy at birth. But the birth process does not always go smoothly. We will consider the pros and cons of medical in-terventions, such as pain-relieving drugs and surgical deliver-ies, designed to ease a difficult birth and protect the health of mother and baby. Our discussion also addresses the devel-opment of infants born underweight or too early, before the prenatal period is complete. We conclude with the remark-able capacities of newborns.

Prenatal Development

The sperm and ovum that unite to form the new individual are uniquely suited for the task of reproduction. The ovum is a tiny sphere, measuring $1/175$ inch in diameter—the size of the period at the end of this sentence. But in its

microscopic world, it is a giant—the largest cell in the human body, making it a perfect target for the much smaller sperm, which measure only $1/500$ inch.

Conception

About once every 28 days, in the middle of a woman's menstrual cycle, an ovum bursts from one of her *ovaries,* two walnut-sized organs located deep inside her abdomen, and is drawn into one of two *fallopian tubes*—long, thin structures that lead to the hollow, soft-lined uterus (see Figure 3.1). While the ovum is traveling, the spot on the ovary from which it was released, now called the *corpus luteum,* secretes hormones that prepare the lin-ing of the uterus to receive a fertilized ovum. If pregnancy does not occur, the corpus luteum shrinks, and the lining of the uterus is discarded two weeks later with menstruation.

The male produces sperm in vast numbers—an average of 300 million a day—in the *testes,* two glands located in the *scrotum,* sacs that lie just behind the penis. Each sperm devel-ops a tail that permits it to swim long distances upstream in the female reproductive tract, through the *cervix* (opening of the uterus) and into the fallopian tube, where fertilization usually takes place. The journey is difficult: Only 300 to 500 reach their destination. Sperm live for up to six days and can lie in wait for the ovum, which survives for only one day after being released into the fallopian tube. However, most conceptions result from intercourse occurring during a three-day period—on the day of ovulation or during the two days preceding it (Wilcox, Weinberg, & Baird, 1995).

With conception, the story of prenatal development begins to unfold. The vast changes that take place during the 38 weeks of pregnancy are usually divided into three phases: (1) the

In this photo taken with the aid of a powerful microscope, sperm have completed their journey up the female reproductive tract and are beginning to penetrate the surface of the enormous-looking ovum, the largest cell in the human body. When one sperm success-fully fertilizes the ovum, the resulting zygote begins to duplicate.

■ FIGURE 3.1 ■ Female reproductive organs, showing fertilization, early cell duplication, and implantation. (From *Before We Are Born,* 6th ed. by K. L. Moore and T. V. N. Persaud, p. 87. Copyright © 2003, reprinted with permission from Elsevier, Inc.)

① Zygote
Fallopian tube
② Blastocyst
Fertilization
Maturing ova
③ Implantation
Ovulation
Ovary
Mature ovum
Uterus
Cervix
Embryonic disk
Trophoblast
Soft uterine lining
Vagina

① Zygote
As the zygote moves down the fallopian tube, it duplicates, at first slowly and then more rapidly.

② Blastocyst
By the fourth day it forms a hollow, fluid-filled ball, called a blastocyst. The inner cells, called the embryonic disk, will become the new organism. The outer cells, or trophoblast, will provide protective covering.

③ Implantation
At the end of the first week, the blastocyst begins to implant in the uterine lining.

period of the zygote, (2) the period of the embryo, and (3) the period of the fetus. As we consider each, refer to Table 3.1, which summarizes milestones of prenatal development.

Period of the Zygote

The period of the zygote lasts about two weeks, from fertilization until the tiny mass of cells drifts down and out of the fallopian tube and attaches itself to the wall of the uterus. The zygote's first cell duplication is long and drawn out; it is not complete until about 30 hours after conception. Gradually, new cells are added at a faster rate. By the fourth day, 60 to 70 cells exist that form a hollow, fluid-filled ball called a *blastocyst* (refer again to Figure 3.1). The cells on the inside, called the *embryonic disk,* will become the new organism; the outer ring of cells, termed the *trophoblast,* will become the structures that provide protective covering and nourishment.

■ IMPLANTATION. Between the seventh and ninth days, **implantation** occurs: The blastocyst burrows deep into the uterine lining. Surrounded by the woman's nourishing blood, it starts to grow in earnest. At first, the trophoblast (protective outer layer) multiplies fastest. It forms a membrane, called the **amnion,** that encloses the developing organism in *amniotic fluid,* which helps keep the temperature of the prenatal world constant and provides a cushion against any jolts caused by the woman's movements. A *yolk sac* emerges that produces blood cells until the liver, spleen, and bone marrow are mature enough to take over this function (Moore & Persaud, 2008).

As many as 30 percent of zygotes do not survive these first two weeks. In some, the sperm and ovum do not join properly. In others, cell duplication never begins. By preventing implantation in these cases, nature eliminates most prenatal abnormalities (Sadler, 2006).

Period of the zygote: seventh to ninth day. The fertilized ovum duplicates rapidly, forming a hollow ball of cells, or blastocyst, by the fourth day after fertilization. Here the blastocyst, magnified thousands of times, burrows into the uterine lining between the seventh and ninth day.

© LENNART NILSSON, A CHILD IS BORN/BONNIERS

■ **TABLE 3.1** ■ *Milestones of Prenatal Development*

TRIMESTER	PERIOD	WEEKS	LENGTH AND WEIGHT	MAJOR EVENTS
First	Zygote	1		The one-celled zygote multiplies and forms a blastocyst.
		2		The blastocyst burrows into the uterine lining. Structures that feed and protect the developing organism begin to form—*amnion, chorion, yolk sac, placenta,* and *umbilical cord.*
	Embryo	3–4	¼ inch (6 mm)	A primitive brain and spinal cord appear. Heart, muscles, ribs, backbone, and digestive tract begin to develop.
		5–8	1 inch (2.5 cm); ½ ounce (4 g)	Many external body structures (face, arms, legs, toes, fingers) and internal organs form. The sense of touch begins to develop, and the embryo can move.
	Fetus	9–12	3 inches (7.6 cm); less than 1 ounce (28 g)	Rapid increase in size begins. Nervous system, organs, and muscles become organized and connected, and new behavioral capacities (kicking, thumb sucking, mouth opening, and rehearsal of breathing) appear. External genitals are well-formed, and the fetus's sex is evident.
Second		13–24	12 inches (30 cm); 1.8 pounds (820 g)	The fetus continues to enlarge rapidly. In the middle of this period, fetal movements can be felt by the mother. Vernix and lanugo keep the fetus's skin from chapping in the amniotic fluid. Most of the brain's neurons are present by 24 weeks. Eyes are sensitive to light, and the fetus reacts to sound.
Third		25–38	20 inches (50 cm); 7.5 pounds (3,400 g)	The fetus has a chance of survival if born during this time. Size increases. Lungs mature. Rapid brain development causes sensory and behavioral capacities to expand. In the middle of this period, a layer of fat is added under the skin. Antibodies are transmitted from mother to fetus to protect against disease. Most fetuses rotate into an upside-down position in preparation for birth.

Source: Moore & Persaud, 2008.

Photos (from top to bottom): © Claude Cortier/Photo Researchers, Inc.; © G. Moscoso/Photo Researchers, Inc.; © John Watney/Photo Researchers, Inc.; © James Stevenson/Photo Researchers, Inc.; © Lennart Nilsson, *A Child Is Born*/Bonniers.

■ **THE PLACENTA AND UMBILICAL CORD.** By the end of the second week, cells of the trophoblast form another protective membrane—the **chorion,** which surrounds the amnion. From the chorion, tiny hairlike *villi,* or blood vessels, emerge.[1] As these villi burrow into the uterine wall, the placenta starts to develop. By bringing the embryo's and mother's blood close together but preventing them from mixing directly, the **placenta** permits food and oxygen to reach the organism and waste products to be carried away.

The placenta is connected to the developing organism by the **umbilical cord.** It contains one large vein that delivers blood loaded with nutrients and two arteries that remove waste products. The force of blood flowing through the cord keeps it firm, so it seldom tangles while the embryo, like a space-walking astronaut, floats freely in its fluid-filled chamber (Moore & Persaud, 2008).

[1]Recall from Table 2.2 on page 44 that *chorionic villus sampling* is the prenatal diagnostic method that can be performed earliest, at nine weeks after conception.

Period of the Embryo

The period of the **embryo** lasts from implantation through the eighth week of pregnancy. During these brief six weeks, the groundwork is laid for all body structures and organs.

■ **LAST HALF OF THE FIRST MONTH.** In the first week of this period, the embryonic disk forms three layers of cells: (1) the *ectoderm,* which will become the nervous system and skin; (2) the *mesoderm,* from which will develop the muscles, skeleton, circulatory system, and other internal organs; and (3) the *endoderm,* which will become the digestive system, lungs, urinary tract, and glands. These three layers give rise to all parts of the body.

At first, the nervous system develops fastest. The ectoderm folds over to form the **neural tube,** which will become the spinal cord and brain. At 3½ weeks, production of *neurons* (nerve cells that store and transmit information) begins deep inside the neural tube at an astounding pace—more than 250,000 per minute. Once formed, neurons travel along tiny threads to their permanent locations, where they will form the major parts of the brain (Nelson, Thomas, & de Haan, 2006).

Meanwhile, the heart begins to pump blood, and the muscles, backbone, ribs, and digestive tract appear. At the end of the first month, the embryo—only ¼ inch long—consists of millions of organized groups of cells with specific functions.

■ **THE SECOND MONTH.** In the second month, growth continues rapidly. The eyes, ears, nose, jaw, and neck form. Tiny buds become arms, legs, fingers, and toes. Internal organs are more distinct: The intestines grow, the heart develops separate

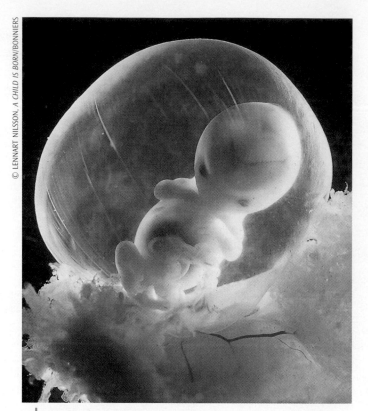

© LENNART NILSSON, *A CHILD IS BORN*/BONNIERS

Period of the embryo: seventh week. The embryo's posture is more upright. Body structures—eyes, nose, arms, legs, and internal organs—are more distinct. An embryo of this age responds to touch. It can also move, although at less than one inch long and one ounce in weight, it is still too tiny to be felt by the mother.

chambers, and the liver and spleen take over production of blood cells so that the yolk sac is no longer needed. Now 1 inch long and ½ ounce in weight, the embryo can sense its world. It responds to touch, particularly in the mouth area and on the soles of the feet. And it can move, although its tiny flutters are still too light to be felt by the mother (Moore & Persaud, 2008).

Period of the Fetus

The period of the **fetus,** from the ninth week to the end of pregnancy, is the longest prenatal period. During this "growth and finishing" phase, the organism increases rapidly in size.

■ **THE THIRD MONTH.** In the third month, the organs, muscles, and nervous system start to become organized and connected. When the brain signals, the fetus kicks, bends its arms, opens its mouth, and even sucks its thumb. The tiny lungs expand and contract in an early rehearsal of breathing movements. By the twelfth week, the external genitals are well-formed, and the sex of the fetus can be detected with ultrasound (Sadler, 2006). Other finishing touches appear, such as fingernails, tooth buds, and eyelids that open and close. The heartbeat can now be heard through a stethoscope.

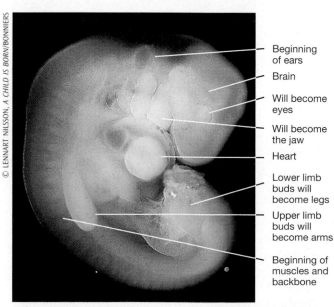

© LENNART NILSSON, *A CHILD IS BORN*/BONNIERS

- Beginning of ears
- Brain
- Will become eyes
- Will become the jaw
- Heart
- Lower limb buds will become legs
- Upper limb buds will become arms
- Beginning of muscles and backbone

Period of the embryo: fourth week. This 4-week-old embryo is only ¼-inch long, but many body structures have already begun to form. The primitive tail will disappear by the end of the embryonic period.

Prenatal development is sometimes divided into **trimesters,** or three equal time periods. At the end of the third month, the *first trimester* is complete.

■ **THE SECOND TRIMESTER.**   By the middle of the second trimester, between 17 and 20 weeks, the new being has grown large enough that the mother can feel its movements. A white, cheeselike substance called **vernix** protects its skin from chapping during the long months spent bathing in the amniotic fluid. White, downy hair called **lanugo** also appears over the entire body, helping the vernix stick to the skin.

At the end of the second trimester, many organs are well-developed, and most of the brain's billions of neurons are in place. However, *glial cells,* which support and feed the neurons, continue to increase at a rapid rate throughout pregnancy, as well as after birth. Consequently, brain weight increases tenfold from the twentieth week until birth (Roelfsema et al., 2004).

Brain growth means new behavioral capacities. The 20-week-old fetus can be stimulated or irritated by sounds. And if a doctor looks inside the uterus using fetoscopy (see Table 2.2 on page 44), fetuses try to shield their eyes from the light with their hands, indicating that sight has begun to emerge (Moore & Persaud, 2008). Still, a fetus born at this time cannot survive. Its

lungs are immature, and the brain cannot yet control breathing and body temperature.

■ **THE THIRD TRIMESTER.**   During the final trimester, a fetus born early has a chance for survival. The point at which the fetus can first survive, called the **age of viability,** occurs sometime between 22 and 26 weeks (Moore & Persaud, 2008). A baby born between the seventh and eighth month, however, usually needs oxygen assistance to breathe because tiny air sacs in the lungs are not yet ready to inflate and exchange carbon dioxide for oxygen.

The brain continues to make great strides. The *cerebral cortex,* the seat of human intelligence, enlarges. As neurological organization improves, the fetus spends more time awake—about 11 percent at 28 weeks, a figure that rises to 16 percent just before birth (DiPietro et al., 1996). Between 30 and 34 weeks, fetuses show rhythmic alternations between sleep and wakefulness that gradually increase in organization (Rivkees, 2003). Around this time, synchrony between fetal heart rate and motor activity peaks: A rise in heart rate is usually followed within five seconds by a burst of motor activity (DiPietro et al., 2006). These are clear signs that coordinated neural networks are beginning to form in the brain. The fetus also shows signs of developing temperament. In one study, more active fetuses

Period of the fetus: eleventh week. The organism grows rapidly. At 11 weeks, the brain and muscles are better connected. The fetus can kick, bend its arms, open and close its hands and mouth, and suck its thumb. Notice the yolk sac, which shrinks as pregnancy advances. The internal organs have taken over its function of producing blood cells.

Period of the fetus: twenty-second week. This fetus is almost a foot long and weighs slightly more than one pound. Its movements can be felt easily by the mother and by other family members who place a hand on her abdomen. The fetus has reached the age of viability. If born, it has a slim chance of surviving.

© LENNART NILSSON, *A CHILD IS BORN*/BONNIERS

© LENNART NILSSON, *A CHILD IS BORN*/BONNIERS

during the third trimester became 1-year-olds who could better handle frustration and 2-year-olds who were less fearful, in that they more readily interacted with toys and with an unfamiliar adult in a laboratory (DiPietro et al., 2002). Perhaps fetal activity is an indicator of healthy neurological development.

The third trimester brings greater responsiveness to stimulation. As we will see later when we discuss newborn capacities, fetuses acquire taste and odor preferences from bathing in and swallowing amniotic fluid. Between 23 and 30 weeks, connections form between the cerebral cortex and brain regions involved in pain sensitivity. By this time, painkillers should be used in any surgical procedures performed on a fetus (Lee et al., 2005).

Within the next six weeks, fetuses distinguish the tone and rhythm of different voices and sounds. They show systematic heart rate changes to a male versus a female speaker, to the mother's voice versus a stranger's, and to a simple familiar melody versus an unfamiliar melody (Granier-Deferre et al., 2003; Huotilainen et al., 2005; Kisilevsky et al., 2003; Lecanuet et al., 1993).

In the final three months, the fetus gains more than 5 pounds and grows 7 inches. In the eighth month, a layer of fat is added to assist with temperature regulation. The fetus also receives antibodies from the mother's blood that protect against illnesses, since the newborn's own immune system will not work well until several months after birth. In the last weeks, most fetuses assume an upside-down position.

© LENNART NILSSON, *A CHILD IS BORN*/BONNIERS

Period of the fetus: thirty-sixth week. This fetus fills the uterus. To support its need for nourishment, the umbilical cord and placenta have grown large. Notice the vernix (cheeselike substance) on the skin, which protects it from chapping. The fetus has accumulated a layer of fat to assist with temperature regulation after birth. In two more weeks, it will be full-term.

ASK YOURSELF

>> **REVIEW**

Why is the period of the embryo regarded as the most dramatic prenatal period? Why is the fetal period called the "growth and finishing" phase?

>> **REVIEW**

How is brain development related to fetal capacities and behavior?

>> **APPLY**

Amy, two months pregnant, wonders how the embryo is being fed and what parts of the body have formed. "I don't look pregnant yet, so does that mean not much development has occurred?" she asks. How would you respond to Amy?

Prenatal Environmental Influences

Although the prenatal environment is far more constant than the world outside the womb, many factors can affect the embryo and fetus. Yolanda and Jay learned that parents—and society as a whole—can do a great deal to create a safe environment for development before birth.

Teratogens

Teratogen refers to any environmental agent that causes damage during the prenatal period. The harm done by teratogens is not always simple and straightforward. It depends on the following factors:

- *Dose.* Larger doses over longer time periods usually have more negative effects.

- *Heredity.* The genetic makeup of the mother and the developing organism plays an important role. Some individuals are better able than others to withstand harmful environments.

- *Other negative influences.* The presence of several negative factors at once, such as additional teratogens, poor nutrition, and lack of medical care, can worsen the impact of a harmful agent.

- *Age.* The effects of teratogens vary with the age of the organism at time of exposure. To understand this last idea, think of the *sensitive period* concept introduced in Chapter 1. A sensitive period is a limited time span in which a part of the body or a behavior is biologically prepared to develop rapidly and is especially sensitive to its surroundings. If the environment is harmful, then damage occurs, and recovery is difficult and sometimes impossible.

Figure 3.2 summarizes prenatal sensitive periods. In the *period of the zygote*, before implantation, teratogens rarely have any impact. If they do, the tiny mass of cells is usually so damaged

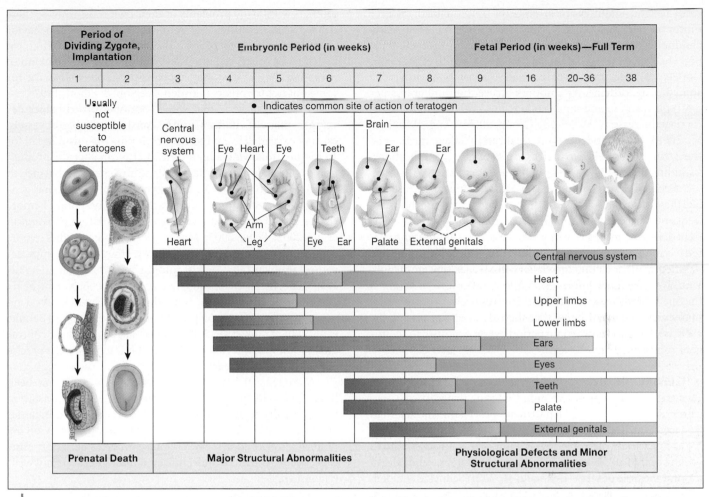

Period of Dividing Zygote, Implantation		Embryonic Period (in weeks)						Fetal Period (in weeks)—Full Term			
1	2	3	4	5	6	7	8	9	16	20–36	38

■ FIGURE 3.2 ■ Sensitive periods in prenatal development. Blue horizontal bars indicate highly sensitive periods. Green horizontal bars indicate periods that are somewhat less sensitive. (Adapted from *Before We Are Born,* 7th ed., by K. L. Moore and T. V. N. Persaud, p. 313. Copyright © 2008, reprinted with permission from Elsevier, Inc.)

that it dies. The *embryonic period* is the time when serious defects are most likely to occur because the foundations for all body parts are being laid down. During the *fetal period,* teratogenic damage is usually minor. However, organs such as the brain, ears, eyes, teeth, and genitals can still be strongly affected.

■ **PRESCRIPTION AND NONPRESCRIPTION DRUGS.** In the early 1960s, the world learned a tragic lesson about drugs and prenatal development. At that time, a sedative called *thalidomide* was widely available in Canada, Europe, and South America. When taken by mothers four to six weeks after conception, thalidomide produced gross deformities of the embryo's arms and legs and, less frequently, damage to the ears, heart, kidneys, and genitals. About 7,000 infants worldwide were affected (Moore & Persaud, 2008). As these children grew older, many scored below average in intelligence. Perhaps the drug damaged the central nervous system directly, or the rearing conditions of these severely deformed youngsters impaired their intellectual development.

Another medication, a synthetic hormone called *diethylstilbestrol (DES),* was widely prescribed between 1945 and 1970

to prevent miscarriages. As daughters of these mothers reached adolescence and young adulthood, they showed unusually high rates of cancer of the vagina, malformations of the uterus, and infertility. Similarly, young men were at increased risk of genital abnormalities and cancer of the testes (Hammes & Laitman, 2003; Palmer et al., 2001).

Currently, the most widely used, potent teratogen is a vitamin A derivative called *Accutane,* used to treat severe acne (also known by the generic name *isotretinoin*). Hundreds of thousands of women of childbearing age in industrialized nations take it. Exposure during the first trimester results in eye, ear, skull, brain, heart, and immune system abnormalities (Honein, Paulozzi, & Erickson, 2001). Accutane's packaging warns users to avoid pregnancy by using two methods of birth control, but many women do not heed this advice (Garcia-Bournissen et al., 2008).

Indeed, any drug with a molecule small enough to penetrate the placental barrier can enter the embryonic or fetal bloodstream. Yet many pregnant women continue to take over-the-counter medications without consulting their doctors. Several studies suggest that regular aspirin use is linked to low birth weight, infant death around the time of birth, poorer motor development, and lower intelligence scores in early childhood, although other research fails to confirm these findings (Barr et al., 1990; Kozer et al., 2003; Streissguth et al., 1987). Coffee, tea, cola, and cocoa contain another frequently consumed drug, caffeine. As amounts exceed 100 milligrams per day (equivalent to one cup of coffee), low birth weight and miscarriage increase (CARE Study Group, 2008; Weng, Odouli, & Li, 2008). And antidepressant medication taken during the third trimester is linked to increased risk of birth complications, including respiratory distress (Oberlander et al., 2006).

Because children's lives are involved, we must take findings like these seriously. At the same time, we cannot be sure that these frequently used drugs actually cause the problems just mentioned. Often mothers take more than one drug. If the embryo or fetus is injured, it is hard to tell which drug might be responsible or whether other factors correlated with drug taking are at fault. Until we have more information, the safest course of action is the one Yolanda took: Avoid these drugs entirely. Unfortunately, many women do not know that they are pregnant during the early weeks of the embryonic period, when exposure to teratogens can be of greatest threat.

■ **ILLEGAL DRUGS.** Nearly 4 percent of U.S. pregnant women use highly addictive mood-altering drugs, such as cocaine and heroin (U.S. Department of Health and Human Services, 2007d). Babies born to users of these drugs are at risk for a wide variety of problems, including prematurity, low birth weight, physical defects, breathing difficulties, and death around the time of birth (Behnke et al., 2001; Schuetze & Eiden, 2006; Walker, Rosenberg, & Balaban-Gil, 1999). In addition, these infants are born drug-addicted. They are often feverish and irritable, and their cries are abnormally shrill—a common symptom among stressed newborns (Bauer et al., 2005). When

This 3-day-old infant, who was born many weeks before his due date and is underweight, breathes with the aid of a respirator. Prematurity and low birth weight can result from a variety of environmental influences during pregnancy, including maternal drug use and cigarette smoking.

mothers with many problems of their own must care for these babies, who are difficult to calm, cuddle, and feed, behavior problems are likely to persist. After infancy, some children get better, while others remain jittery and inattentive. The kind of parenting they receive may explain why problems persist for some but not for others (Cosden, Peerson, & Elliott, 1997).

Evidence suggests that some cocaine-exposed babies develop lasting difficulties. Cocaine constricts the blood vessels, causing oxygen delivered to the developing organism to fall for 15 minutes following a high dose. It also can alter the production and functioning of neurons and the chemical balance in the fetus's brain. These effects may contribute to eye, bone, genital, urinary tract, kidney, and heart deformities; brain hemorrhages and seizures; and severe growth retardation (Covington et al., 2002; Feng, 2005; Mayes, 1999). Some studies report perceptual, motor, attention, memory, language, and impulse-control problems that persist into the preschool years (Dennis et al., 2006; Lester et al., 2003; Linares et al., 2006; Noland et al., 2005; Singer et al., 2004). But other investigations reveal no major negative effects of prenatal cocaine exposure (Behnke et al., 2006; Frank et al., 2005; Hurt et al., 2005). These contradictory findings indicate how difficult it is to isolate the precise damage caused by illegal drugs.

Marijuana, the most widely used illegal drug, has been linked to low birth weight and smaller head size (a measure of brain growth); to attention, memory, and academic difficulties and to depression in childhood; and to poorer problem-solving performance in adolescence (Goldschmidt et al., 2004; Gray et al., 2005). As with cocaine, however, these effects are not well-established.

■ **TOBACCO.** Although smoking has declined in Western nations, an estimated 17 percent of U.S. women smoke during their pregnancies (U.S. Department of Health and Human Services, 2007d). The best-known prenatal effect of smoking is low birth weight. But the likelihood of other serious consequences, such as miscarriage, prematurity, impaired heart rate and breathing during sleep, infant death, and asthma and cancer later in childhood, also increases (Franco et al., 2000; Jaakkola & Gissler, 2004). The more cigarettes a mother smokes, the greater the chances that her baby will be affected. If a pregnant woman stops smoking at any time, even during the last trimester, she reduces the likelihood that her infant will be born underweight and suffer from future problems (Klesges et al., 2001).

Newborns of smoking mothers also display slight behavioral abnormalities. They are less attentive to sounds, display more muscle tension, are more excitable when touched and visually stimulated, and more often have colic (persistent crying) (Law et al., 2003; Sondergaard et al., 2002). Some studies report that prenatally exposed children and adolescents have shorter attention spans, poorer memories, lower mental test scores, and more behavior problems (Fried, Watkinson, & Gray, 2003; Huizink & Mulder, 2006; Nigg & Breslau, 2007; Thapar et al., 2003). However, other factors closely associated with smoking, such as lower maternal education and income levels, may contribute to these outcomes (Huijbregts et al., 2006).

© CHET GORDON/THE IMAGE WORKS

How does smoking harm the fetus? Nicotine, the addictive substance in tobacco, constricts blood vessels, lessens blood flow to the uterus, and causes the placenta to grow abnormally. This reduces the transfer of nutrients, so the fetus gains weight poorly. Also, nicotine raises the concentration of carbon monoxide in the bloodstreams of both mother and fetus. Because carbon monoxide displaces oxygen from red blood cells, it can damage the central nervous system and slow body growth.

From one-third to one-half of nonsmoking pregnant women are "passive smokers" because their husbands, relatives, or co-workers use cigarettes. Passive smoking is also related to low birth weight, infant death, childhood respiratory illnesses, and possible long-term impairments in attention and learning (Hanke, Sobala, & Kalinka, 2004; Makin, Fried, & Watkinson, 1991; Pattenden et al., 2006). Clearly, expectant mothers should avoid smoke-filled environments.

Left photo: This toddler's mother drank heavily during pregnancy. Her widely spaced eyes, thin upper lip, and short eyelid openings are typical of fetal alcohol syndrome (FAS). *Right photo:* This 11-year-old girl also has the facial abnormalities of FAS and shows the slow physical growth that accompanies the disorder.

■ **ALCOHOL.** In his moving book *The Broken Cord,* Michael Dorris (1989), a Dartmouth College anthropology professor, described what it was like to rear his adopted son Abel (called Adam in the book), whose biological mother drank heavily throughout pregnancy and died of alcohol poisoning shortly after his birth. A Sioux Indian, Abel was born with **fetal alcohol spectrum disorder (FASD),** a term encompassing a range of physical, mental, and behavioral outcomes caused by prenatal alcohol exposure. Children with FASD are given one of three diagnoses, which vary in severity:

1. **Fetal alcohol syndrome (FAS),** distinguished by (a) slow physical growth, (b) a pattern of three facial abnormalities (short eyelid openings, a thin upper lip, and a smooth or flattened philtrum, or indentation running from the bottom of the nose to the center of the upper lip), and (c) brain injury, evident in a small head and impairment in at least three areas of functioning—for example, memory, language and communication, attention span and activity level (overactivity), planning and reasoning, motor coordination, or social skills. Other defects—of the eyes, ears, nose, throat, heart, genitals, urinary tract, or immune system— may also be present. Abel was diagnosed as having FAS. As is typical for this disorder, his mother drank heavily throughout pregnancy.

2. **Partial fetal alcohol syndrome (p-FAS),** characterized by (a) two of the three facial abnormalities just mentioned and (b) brain injury, again evident in at least three areas of impaired functioning. Mothers of children with p-FAS generally drank alcohol in smaller quantities, and children's defects vary with the timing and length of alcohol exposure. Furthermore, recent evidence suggests that paternal alcohol use around the time of conception may induce genetic alterations, thereby contributing to symptoms (Abel, 2004).

3. **Alcohol-related neurodevelopmental disorder (ARND),** in which at least three areas of mental functioning are impaired, despite typical physical growth and absence of facial abnormalities. Again, prenatal alcohol exposure, though confirmed, is less pervasive than in FAS (Chudley et al., 2005; Loock et al., 2005).

Even when provided with enriched diets, FAS babies fail to catch up in physical size during childhood. Mental impairment associated with all three FASD diagnoses is also permanent: In his teens and twenties, Abel had trouble concentrating and keeping a routine job, and he suffered from poor judgment. For example, he would buy something and not wait for change or wander off in the middle of a task. He died at age 23, after being hit by a car. The more alcohol a pregnant woman consumes, the poorer the child's motor coordination and intelligence and achievement test scores and the greater the likelihood of antisocial behavior and other mental health problems in adolescence (Burden, Jacobson, & Jacobson, 2005; Mattson, Calarco, & Lang, 2006; Streissguth et al., 2004).

Alcohol produces its devastating effects by interfering with the production and migration of neurons in the primitive neural tube. Brain-imaging research reveals reduced brain size, damage to many brain structures, and abnormalities in brain functioning, including transferring messages from one part of the brain to another (Riley, McGee, & Sowell, 2004; Spadoni et al., 2007). Also, the body uses large quantities of oxygen to metabolize alcohol. A pregnant woman's heavy drinking draws away oxygen that the developing organism needs for cell growth.

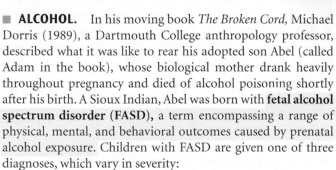

About 25 percent of U.S. mothers report drinking at some time during their pregnancies. As with heroin and cocaine, alcohol abuse is higher in poverty-stricken women. On some Native-American reservations, the incidence of FAS is as high as 10 to 20 percent (Szlemko, Wood, & Thurman, 2006; U.S. Department of Health and Human Services, 2007d). Even mild drinking, less than one drink per day, is associated with reduced head size and body growth among children followed into adolescence (Jacobson et al., 2004; Martinez-Frias et al., 2004). Therefore, expectant mothers should avoid alcohol entirely.

■ **RADIATION.** Defects due to ionizing radiation were tragically apparent in children born to pregnant women who survived the bombing of Hiroshima and Nagasaki during World War II. Similar abnormalities surfaced in the nine months following the 1986 Chernobyl, Ukraine, nuclear power plant accident. After each disaster, the incidence of miscarriage and babies born with underdeveloped brains, physical deformities, and slow physical growth rose dramatically (Hoffmann, 2001; Schull, 2003).

Even when a radiation-exposed baby seems normal, problems may appear later. For example, low-level radiation, resulting from industrial leakage or medical X-rays, can increase the risk of childhood cancer (Fattibene et al., 1999). In middle childhood, prenatally exposed Chernobyl children had abnormal brain-wave activity, lower intelligence test scores, and rates of language and emotional disorders two to three times greater than those of nonexposed Russian children (Loganovskaja & Loganovsky, 1999; Loganovsky et al., 2008).

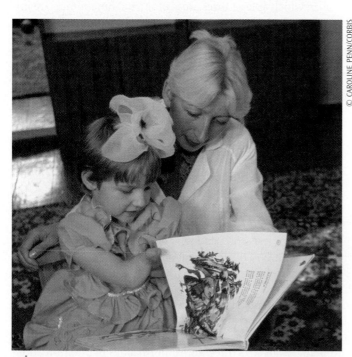

This child's deformities are linked to radiation exposure during the Chernobyl nuclear power plant disaster of 1986. Her mother was just a few weeks pregnant at that time. She is also at risk for low intelligence and language and emotional disorders.

■ **ENVIRONMENTAL POLLUTION.** In industrialized nations, an astounding number of potentially dangerous chemicals are released into the environment. In the United States, more than 75,000 are in common use. When 10 newborns were randomly selected from U.S. hospitals for analysis of umbilical cord blood, researchers uncovered a startling array of contaminants—287 in all! They concluded that many babies are "born polluted" by chemicals that not only impair prenatal development but increase the chances of life-threatening diseases and health problems later on (Houlihan et al., 2005).

Pregnant women are wise to avoid eating long-lived predatory fish, such as swordfish, albacore tuna, and shark, which are heavily contaminated with mercury. High levels of prenatal mercury exposure disrupt production and migration of neurons, causing widespread brain damage (Clarkson, Magos, & Myers, 2003; Hubbs-Tait et al., 2005).

For many years, *polychlorinated biphenyls (PCBs)* were used to insulate electrical equipment until research showed that they entered waterways and the food supply. Prenatal exposure to high levels of PCBs results in low birth weight, skin deformities, brain-wave abnormalities, and delayed cognitive development (Chen & Hsu, 1994; Chen et al., 1994). Even at low levels, PCBs are linked to reduced birth weight, smaller head size, persisting attention and memory difficulties, and lower intelligence test scores in childhood (Jacobson & Jacobson, 2003; Stewart et al., 2000; Walkowiak et al., 2001).

Another teratogen, *lead,* is present in paint flaking off the walls of old buildings and in certain materials used in industrial occupations. High levels of prenatal lead exposure are related to prematurity, low birth weight, brain damage, and a wide variety of physical defects. Babies with low-level exposure show slightly poorer mental and motor development (Bellinger, 2005).

Finally, prenatal exposure to *dioxins*—toxic compounds resulting from incineration—is linked to brain, immune system, and thyroid damage in babies. It is also associated with an increased incidence of breast and uterine cancers in women, perhaps through altering hormone levels (ten Tusscher & Koppe, 2004). Furthermore, even tiny amounts of dioxin in the paternal bloodstream cause a dramatic change in sex ratio of offspring: Affected men father nearly twice as many girls as boys (Ishihara et al., 2007). Dioxin seems to impair the fertility of Y-bearing sperm prior to conception.

■ **INFECTIOUS DISEASE.** Most infectious diseases seem to have no prenatal impact. Nevertheless, a few cause extensive damage.

In the mid-1960s, a worldwide epidemic of *rubella* (three-day, or German, measles) led to the birth of more than 20,000 North American babies with serious defects. Consistent with the sensitive-period concept, over 50 percent of infants whose mothers become ill during the embryonic period show eye cataracts; deafness; heart, genital, urinary, and intestinal abnormalities; and mental retardation (Eberhart-Phillips, Frederick, & Baron, 1993). Infection during the fetal period is less harmful, but low birth weight, hearing loss, and bone defects may still occur. And the brain abnormalities resulting from prenatal rubella increase the risk of severe mental illness in adulthood (Brown, 2006). Routine vaccination in infancy and childhood has made new rubella outbreaks unlikely in industrialized nations (Hyde et al., 2006). But an estimated 100,000 cases of prenatal infection occur annually in developing countries with weak or absent immunization programs (Robinson et al., 2006).

The *human immunodeficiency virus (HIV)*, which can lead to *acquired immune deficiency syndrome (AIDS),* a disease that destroys the immune system, has infected increasing numbers of women over the past two decades. In developing countries, where 95 percent of new infections occur, more than half affect women. In South Africa, for example, one-fourth of all pregnant women are HIV-positive (Kasmauski & Jaret, 2003; Quinn & Overbaugh, 2005). HIV-infected expectant mothers pass the deadly virus to the developing organism 20 to 30 percent of the time.

AIDS progresses rapidly in infants, with most becoming ill by age 6 months and surviving only five to eight months after the appearance of symptoms (O'Rahilly & Müller, 2001). The antiviral drug zidovudine (ZDV) reduces prenatal AIDS transmission by as much as 95 percent, but it is not widely available in impoverished regions of the world (United Nations, 2006b).

The developing organism is especially sensitive to the family of herpes viruses, for which no vaccine or treatment exists. Among these, *cytomegalovirus* (the most frequent prenatal infection, transmitted through respiratory or sexual contact) and *herpes simplex 2* (which is sexually transmitted) are especially dangerous. In both, the virus invades the mother's genital tract, infecting babies either during pregnancy or at birth.

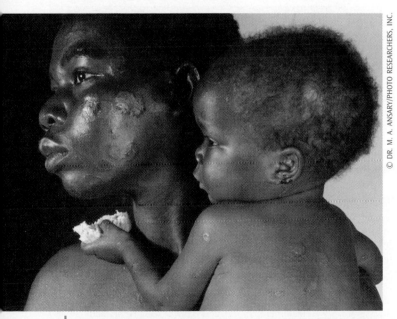

© DR. M. A. ANSARY/PHOTO RESEARCHERS, INC.

This South African mother and infant, who are suffering from AIDS, both have extensive ringworm skin rashes. Their weakened immune systems make normally harmless infections life threatening. Because AIDS progresses rapidly in infants, the baby may live only a few months.

Toxoplasmosis, caused by a parasite found in many animals, can affect pregnant women who eat raw or undercooked meat or who come in contact with the feces of infected cats. If it strikes during the first trimester, it is likely to cause eye and brain damage. Later infection is linked to mild visual and cognitive impairments (Jones, Lopez, & Wilson, 2003). Expectant mothers can avoid toxoplasmosis by making sure that the meat they eat is well-cooked, having pet cats checked for the disease, and turning over the care of litter boxes to other family members.

Other Maternal Factors

Besides avoiding teratogens, expectant parents can support the development of the embryo and fetus in other ways. In the following sections, we examine nutrition, emotional stress, blood type, age, and previous births.

■ **NUTRITION.** During the prenatal period, when children are growing more rapidly than at any other time, they depend totally on the mother for nutrients. A healthy diet that results in a weight gain of 25 to 30 pounds (10 to 13.5 kilograms) helps ensure the health of mother and baby.

Prenatal malnutrition can cause serious damage to the central nervous system. The poorer the mother's diet, the greater the loss in brain weight, especially if malnutrition occurred during the last trimester. During that time, the brain is increasing rapidly in size, and a maternal diet high in all the basic nutrients is necessary for it to reach its full potential (Morgane et al., 1993). An inadequate diet during pregnancy can also distort the structure of other organs, including the liver, kidneys, pancreas, and cardiovascular system, resulting in lifelong health problems (Barker, 2002; Fowden, Giussani, & Forhead, 2005; Roseboom, de Rooij, & Painter, 2006).

Many studies show that providing pregnant women with adequate food has a substantial impact on the health of their newborn babies. Vitamin–mineral enrichment is particularly crucial. For example, taking a folic acid supplement around the time of conception reduces by more than 70 percent abnormalities of the neural tube, such as *anencephaly* and *spina bifida* (see Table 2.2 on page 44) (MCR Vitamin Study Research Group, 1991; Scholl, Heidiger, & Belsky, 1996). U.S. government guidelines recommend that all women of childbearing age consume 0.4 milligrams of folic acid per day. For women who have previously had a pregnancy affected by a neural tube defect, the recommended amount is 4 to 5 milligrams (dosage must be carefully monitored, as excessive intake can be harmful) (American Academy of Pediatrics, 2006). Currently, bread, flour, rice, pasta, and other grain products are being fortified with folic acid.

When poor nutrition persists throughout pregnancy, infants usually require more than dietary improvement. Successful interventions must also break the cycle of apathetic mother–baby interactions. Some do so by teaching parents how to interact effectively with their infants, while others focus on stimulating infants to promote active engagement with their physical and social surroundings (Grantham-McGregor et al., 1994; Grantham-McGregor, Schofield, & Powell, 1987).

Although prenatal malnutrition is highest in developing countries, women and children in the industrialized world are also affected. The U.S. Special Supplemental Food Program for Women, Infants, and Children (WIC), which provides food packages to low-income pregnant women, reaches about 90 percent of those who qualify. But many who need nutrition intervention are not eligible for WIC.

■ **EMOTIONAL STRESS.** When women experience severe emotional stress during pregnancy, their babies are at risk for a wide variety of difficulties, including miscarriage, prematurity, low birth weight, respiratory and digestive illnesses, sleep disturbances, and irritability during the first three years (Field et al., 2007; Mulder et al., 2002; Wadhwa, Sandman, & Garite, 2001). Intense maternal anxiety is also related to several commonly occurring physical defects, such as cleft lip and palate, heart deformities, and pyloric stenosis (tightening of the infant's stomach outlet, which often must be treated surgically) (Carmichael & Shaw, 2000).

How can maternal stress affect the fetus? ***TAKE A MOMENT...*** To understand this process, list the changes you sensed in your own body the last time you were under stress. When we experience fear and anxiety, stimulant hormones released into our bloodstream cause us to be "poised for action." Large amounts of blood are sent to parts of the body involved in the defensive response—the brain, the heart, and the muscles in the arms, legs, and trunk. Blood flow to other organs, including the uterus, is reduced, depriving the fetus of a full supply of oxygen and nutrients.

Stress hormones also cross the placenta, causing a dramatic rise in fetal heart rate (Monk et al., 2000, 2004). They also may permanently alter fetal neurological functioning, thereby heightening stress reactivity in later life (Monk et al., 2003). In one study, researchers identified mothers who had been directly exposed to the September 11, 2001, World Trade Center collapse during their pregnancies. At age 9 months, their babies were tested for saliva concentrations of *cortisol,* a hormone involved in regulating the stress response. Infants whose mothers had reacted to the disaster with severe anxiety had abnormally low cortisol levels, a symptom of reduced physiological capacity to manage stress (Yehuda et al., 2005). Consistent with this finding, maternal emotional stress during pregnancy predicts anxiety, short attention span, anger, aggression, and overactivity among preschool and school-age children, above and beyond the impact of other risk factors (de Weerth & Buitelaar, 2005; Gutteling et al., 2006; Van den Bergh, 2004).

But stress-related prenatal complications are greatly reduced when mothers have partners, other family members, and friends who offer social support (Federenko & Wadhwa, 2004). The link between social support and positive pregnancy outcomes is particularly strong for low-income women, who often lead highly stressful daily lives (Hoffman & Hatch, 1996).

■ **RH FACTOR INCOMPATIBILITY.** When the inherited blood types of mother and fetus differ, serious problems sometimes result. The most common cause of these difficulties is **Rh factor incompatibility.** When the mother is Rh-negative (lacks the Rh blood protein) and the father is Rh-positive (has the protein), the baby may inherit the father's Rh-positive blood type. If even a little of a fetus's Rh-positive blood crosses the placenta into the Rh-negative mother's bloodstream, she begins to form antibodies to the foreign Rh protein. If these enter the fetus's system, they destroy red blood cells, reducing the oxygen supply to organs and tissues. Miscarriage, mental retardation, heart damage, and infant death can occur.

It takes time for the mother to produce Rh antibodies, so firstborn children are rarely affected. The danger increases with each additional pregnancy. Fortunately, Rh incompatibility can be prevented in most cases. After the birth of each Rh-positive baby, Rh-negative mothers are routinely given a vaccine to prevent the buildup of antibodies.

■ **MATERNAL AGE.** In Chapter 2, we noted that women who delay childbearing until their thirties or forties face increased risk of infertility, miscarriage, and babies born with chromosomal defects. Are other pregnancy complications more common among older mothers? Research consistently indicates that healthy women in their thirties have about the same rates of prenatal and birth complications as those in their twenties (Bianco et al., 1996; Dildy et al., 1996; Prysak, Lorenz, & Kisly, 1995). Thereafter, as Figure 3.3 reveals, complication rates increase, with a sharp rise among women age 50 to 55—an age at which because of menopause (end of menstruation) and

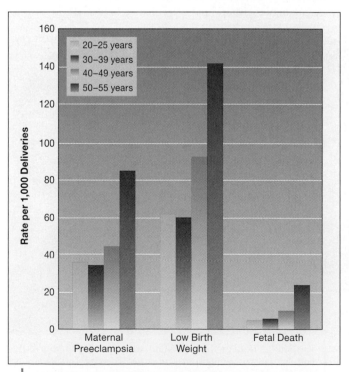

■ **FIGURE 3.3** ■ **Relationship of maternal age to prenatal and birth complications.** Complications increase after age 40, with a sharp rise between 50 and 55 years. See page 73 for a description of preeclampsia. (Adapted from Salihu et al., 2003.)

Applying What We Know

Do's and Don'ts for a Healthy Pregnancy

Do	Don't
Do make sure that you have been vaccinated against infectious diseases that are dangerous to the embryo and fetus, such as rubella, before you get pregnant. Most vaccinations are not safe during pregnancy.	Don't take any drugs without consulting your doctor.
Do see a doctor as soon as you suspect that you are pregnant, and continue to get regular medical checkups throughout pregnancy.	Don't smoke. If you are a smoker, cut down or, better yet, quit. Avoid secondhand smoke. If other members of your family are smokers, ask them to quit or to smoke outside.
Do eat a well-balanced diet and take vitamin–mineral supplements, as prescribed by your doctor, both prior to and during pregnancy. Gain 25 to 30 pounds gradually.	Don't drink alcohol from the time you decide to get pregnant.
Do obtain literature from your doctor, library, or bookstore about prenatal development. Ask your doctor about anything that concerns you.	Don't engage in activities that might expose your embryo or fetus to environmental hazards, such as radiation or pollutants.
Do keep physically fit through mild exercise. If possible, join an exercise class for expectant mothers.	Don't engage in activities that might expose your embryo or fetus to harmful infectious diseases, such as toxoplasmosis.
Do avoid emotional stress. If you are a single expectant mother, find a relative or friend on whom you can count for emotional support.	Don't choose pregnancy as a time to go on a diet.
Do get plenty of rest. An overtired mother is at risk for complications.	Don't gain too much weight during pregnancy. A very large weight gain is associated with complications.
Do enroll in a prenatal and childbirth education class with your partner or other companion. When you know what to expect, the nine months before birth can be one of the most joyful times of life.	

aging reproductive organs, few women can conceive naturally (Salihu et al., 2003).

In the case of teenage mothers, does physical immaturity cause prenatal complications? Infants born to teenagers have a higher rate of problems, but not directly because of maternal age. Most pregnant teenagers come from low-income backgrounds, where stress, poor nutrition, and health problems are common. Also, many are afraid to seek medical care or, in the United States, do not have access to care because they lack health insurance (U.S. Department of Health and Human Services, 2008f).

The Importance of Prenatal Health Care

Yolanda had her first prenatal appointment three weeks after missing her menstrual period. After that, she visited the doctor's office once a month until she was seven months pregnant, then twice during the eighth month, increasing her visits to once a week when birth grew near. The doctor kept track of her general health, her weight gain, and the capacity of her uterus and cervix to support the fetus. The fetus's growth was also carefully monitored.

Yolanda's pregnancy, like most others, was free of complications. But unexpected difficulties can arise, especially if mothers have health problems. For example, women with diabetes need careful monitoring. Extra sugar in the diabetic mother's blood-

stream causes the fetus to grow larger than average, making pregnancy and birth problems more common. Another complication, experienced by 5 to 10 percent of pregnant women, is *preeclampsia* (sometimes called *toxemia*), in which blood pressure increases sharply and the face, hands, and feet swell in the last half of pregnancy. If untreated, preeclampsia can cause convulsions in the mother and fetal death. Usually, hospitalization, bed rest, and drugs can lower blood pressure to a safe level (Vidaeff, Carroll, & Ramin, 2005). If not, the baby must be delivered at once.

Unfortunately, 16 percent of pregnant women in the United States wait until after the first trimester to seek prenatal care, and 4 percent receive none at all. Why do these mothers delay going to the doctor? One reason is a lack of health insurance. Although the poorest of these mothers are eligible for government-sponsored health services, many low-income women do not qualify.

Besides financial hardship, *situational barriers* (difficulty finding a doctor, getting an appointment, and arranging transportation) and *personal barriers* (psychological stress and the demands of taking care of other young children) prevent many mothers from seeking prenatal care. Clearly, public education about the importance of early and sustained prenatal care is badly needed. Refer to Applying What We Know above, which lists "do's and don'ts" for a healthy pregnancy, based on our discussion of the prenatal environment.

© CHAD EHLERS/ALAMY

During a routine prenatal visit, a doctor uses ultrasound to evaluate the development of this expectant mother's 5-month-old fetus. All pregnant women should receive regular prenatal care to protect their own health as well as the health of their babies.

ASK YOURSELF

>> **REVIEW**
Why is it difficult to determine the prenatal effects of many environmental agents, such as drugs and pollution?

>> **APPLY**
Nora, pregnant for the first time, believes that a few cigarettes and a glass of wine a day won't be harmful. Provide Nora with research-based reasons for not smoking or drinking.

>> **REFLECT**
If you had to choose five environmental influences to publicize in a campaign aimed at promoting healthy prenatal development, which ones would you choose, and why?

Childbirth

Yolanda and Jay agreed to return the following spring to share their experiences with my next class. Two-week-old Joshua came along as well. Their story revealed that the birth of a baby is one of the most dramatic and emotional events in human experience. Yolanda explained:

By morning, we knew I was in labor. It was Thursday, so we went in for my usual weekly appointment. The doctor said, yes, the baby was on the way, but it would be a while. He told us to go home and relax and come to the hospital in three or four hours. We checked in at three in the afternoon; Joshua arrived at two o'clock the next morning. When, finally, I was ready to deliver, it went quickly; a half hour or so and some good hard pushes, and there he was! His face was red and puffy, and his head was misshapen, but I thought, "Our son! I can't believe he's really here."

Jay was also elated by Joshua's birth. "I wanted to support Yolanda and to experience as much as I could. It was awesome,

indescribable," he said, holding Joshua and kissing him gently. In the following sections, we explore the experience of childbirth, from both the parents' and the baby's point of view.

The Stages of Childbirth

It is not surprising that childbirth is often referred to as labor. It is the hardest physical work a woman may ever do. A complex series of hormonal changes between mother and fetus initiates the process, which naturally divides into three stages:

1. *Dilation and effacement of the cervix.* This is the longest stage of labor, lasting an average of 12 to 14 hours with a first birth and 4 to 6 hours with later births. Contractions of the uterus gradually become more frequent and powerful, causing the cervix, or uterine opening, to widen and thin to nothing, forming a clear channel from the uterus into the birth canal, or vagina (see Figure 3.4a and b).
2. *Delivery of the baby.* This stage is much shorter, lasting about 50 minutes for a first birth and 20 minutes with later births. Strong contractions of the uterus continue, but the mother also feels a natural urge to squeeze and push with her abdominal muscles. As she does so with each contraction, she forces the baby down and out (see Figure 3.4c and d).
3. *Delivery of the placenta.* Labor comes to an end with a few final contractions and pushes. These cause the placenta to separate from the wall of the uterus and be delivered in about 5 to 10 minutes.

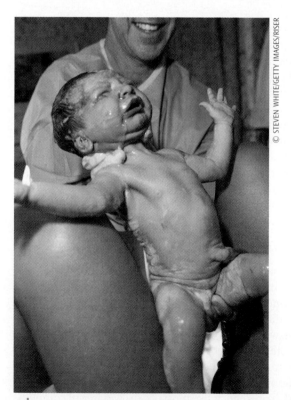

© STEVEN WHITE/GETTY IMAGES/RISER

To accommodate the well-developed brain, a newborn's head is large in relation to the trunk and legs. This newborn's body readily turns pink as he takes his first few breaths.

Stage 1

(a) Dilation and Effacement of the Cervix
Contractions of the uterus cause dilation and effacement of the cervix.

(b) Transition
Transition is reached when the frequency and strength of the contractions are at their peak and the cervix opens completely.

Stage 2

(c) Pushing
With each contraction, the mother pushes, forcing the baby down the birth canal, and the head appears.

(d) Birth of the Baby
Near the end of Stage 2, the shoulders emerge, followed quickly by the rest of the baby's body.

■ **FIGURE 3.4** ■ **A Normal Birth.** The first two stages of labor are depicted. In the third stage, the placenta is delivered.

The Baby's Adaptation to Labor and Delivery

At first glance, labor and delivery seem like a dangerous ordeal for the baby. The strong contractions exposed Joshua's head to a great deal of pressure, and they squeezed the placenta and the umbilical cord, temporarily reducing Joshua's supply of oxygen.

Fortunately, healthy babies are well-equipped to withstand these traumas. The force of the contractions causes the infant to produce high levels of stress hormones. But in contrast to high maternal stress levels during pregnancy, which can endanger the baby, the infant's production of stress hormones during childbirth is adaptive. It helps the baby withstand oxygen deprivation by sending a rich supply of blood to the brain and heart (Gluckman, Sizonenko, & Bassett, 1999). In addition, stress hormones prepare the baby to breathe by causing the lungs to absorb any remaining fluid. Finally, stress hormones arouse the infant into alertness (Lagercrantz & Slotkin, 1986). Joshua was born wide awake, ready to interact with the surrounding world.

Assessing the Newborn's Physical Condition: The Apgar Scale

Infants who have difficulty making the transition to life outside the uterus require special help at once. To assess the newborn's physical condition quickly, doctors and nurses use the **Apgar Scale.** As Table 3.2 on page 76 shows, a rating of 0, 1, or 2 on each of five characteristics is made at 1 minute and again at 5 minutes after birth. A combined Apgar score of 7 or better indicates that the infant is in good physical condition. If the score is between 4 and 6, the baby needs assistance in establishing breathing and other vital signs. If the score is 3 or below, the infant is in serious danger and requires emergency medical attention. Two Apgar ratings are given because some babies have trouble adjusting at first but do quite well after a few minutes (Apgar, 1953).

Approaches to Childbirth

Childbirth practices, like other aspects of family life, are molded by the society of which mother and baby are a part. In many village and tribal cultures, expectant mothers are well-acquainted with the childbirth process, having witnessed it many times. They also know that they will be assisted. Among the Mayans of the Yucatán, for example, the mother leans against a woman called the "head helper," who supports her weight and breathes with her during each contraction (Jordan, 1993).

In Western nations, childbirth has changed dramatically over the centuries. Before the late 1800s, birth usually took

■ **TABLE 3.2** ■ *The Apgar Scale*

| Sign | RATING | | |
	0	1	2
Heart rate	No heartbeat	Under 100 beats per minute	100 to 140 beats per minute
Respiratory effort	No breathing for 60 seconds	Irregular, shallow breathing	Strong breathing and crying
Reflex irritability (sneezing, coughing, and grimacing)	No response	Weak reflexive response	Strong reflexive response
Muscle tone	Completely limp	Weak movements of arms and legs	Strong movements of arms and legs
Color[a]	Blue body, arms, and legs	Body pink with blue arms and legs	Body, arms, and legs completely pink

[a]The skin tone of nonwhite babies makes it difficult to apply the "pink" color criterion. However, newborns of all races can be rated for pinkish glow resulting from the flow of oxygen through body tissues.

Source: Apgar, 1953.

place at home and was a family-centered event. The industrial revolution brought greater crowding to cities, along with new health problems. As a result, childbirth moved from home to the hospital, where the health of mothers and babies could be protected. Once doctors assumed responsibility for childbirth, women's knowledge of it declined, and relatives and friends no longer participated (Borst, 1995).

By the 1950s and 1960s, women had begun to question the medical procedures that had come to be used routinely during

In a hospital birth center in New Zealand, the father and a close family friend coached and supported this Maori mother during labor and delivery. New Zealand places no limitations on the number of people parents can invite to attend a birth.

labor and delivery. Many felt that use of strong drugs and delivery instruments had robbed them of a precious experience and were often neither necessary nor safe for the baby. Gradually, a natural childbirth movement arose in Europe and spread to North America. Its purpose was to make hospital birth as comfortable and rewarding for mothers as possible. Today, most hospitals offer birth centers that are family-centered and home-like and that encourage early contact between parents and baby.

Natural, or Prepared, Childbirth

Yolanda and Jay chose **natural,** or **prepared, childbirth**—a group of techniques aimed at reducing pain and medical intervention and making childbirth as rewarding an experience as possible. Although many natural childbirth programs exist, most draw on methods developed by Grantly Dick-Read (1959) in England and Fernand Lamaze (1958) in France. These physicians recognized that cultural attitudes had taught women to fear the birth experience. An anxious, frightened woman in labor tenses muscles, turning the mild pain that sometimes accompanies strong contractions into intense pain.

In a typical natural childbirth program, the expectant mother and a companion (a partner, relative, or friend) participate in three activities:

■ *Classes.* Yolanda and Jay attended a series of classes in which they learned about the anatomy and physiology of labor and delivery. Knowledge about the birth process reduces a mother's fear.

■ *Relaxation and breathing techniques.* During each class, Yolanda practiced breathing exercises aimed at counteracting the pain of uterine contractions.

■ *Labor coach.* Jay learned how to help Yolanda during childbirth by reminding her to relax and breathe, supporting her body, and offering encouragement and affection.

Social support, in which a companion stays with the mother throughout labor and delivery, talking to her, holding her hand, and rubbing her back to promote relaxation, is an important part of the success of natural childbirth techniques. It is associated with shorter labors, fewer birth complications, higher newborn Apgar scores, and more positive maternal interaction with infants in the days after birth (Kennell et al., 1991; Sauls, 2002; Sosa et al., 1980).

Home Delivery

Home birth has always been popular in certain industrialized nations, such as England, the Netherlands, and Sweden. The number of North American women choosing to have their babies at home increased during the 1970s and 1980s but remains small, at about 1 percent (Studelska, 2006). Although some home births are attended by doctors, many more are handled by certified *nurse–midwives,* who have degrees in nursing and additional training in childbirth management.

Is it just as safe to give birth at home as in a hospital? For healthy women who are assisted by a well-trained doctor or midwife, it seems so because complications rarely occur (Fullerton, Navarro, & Young, 2007; Johnson & Daviss, 2005). However, if attendants are not carefully trained and prepared to handle emergencies, the rate of infant death is high (Mehlmadrona & Madrona, 1997). When mothers are at risk for any kind of complication, the appropriate place for labor and delivery is the hospital, where life-saving treatment is available.

This midwife checks the baby's heartbeat minutes after he was born at home. As long as a woman is healthy and has a well-trained doctor or midwife, home birth is as safe as hospital birth.

Medical Interventions

Four-year-old Melinda walks with a halting, lumbering gait and has difficulty keeping her balance. She has *cerebral palsy,* a general term for a variety of impairments in muscle coordination caused by brain damage before, during, or just after birth. For about 10 percent of these children, including Melinda, brain damage was caused by **anoxia,** or inadequate oxygen supply, during labor and delivery (Anslow, 1998; Bracci, Perrone, & Buonocore, 2006). Her mother got pregnant accidentally, was frightened and alone, and arrived at the hospital at the last minute. Melinda was in **breech position,** turned so that the buttocks or feet would be delivered first, and the umbilical cord was wrapped around her neck. Had her mother come to the hospital earlier, doctors could have monitored Melinda's condition and delivered her surgically as soon as squeezing of the umbilical cord led to distress, thereby reducing the damage or preventing it entirely.

In cases like Melinda's, medical interventions are clearly justified. But in others, they can interfere with delivery and even pose new risks. In the following sections, we examine some commonly used medical procedures during childbirth.

Fetal Monitoring

Fetal monitors are electronic instruments that track the baby's heart rate during labor. An abnormal heartbeat may indicate that the baby is in distress due to anoxia and needs to be delivered immediately. Continuous fetal monitoring, which is required in most U.S. hospitals, is used in over 80 percent of American births (Natale & Dodman, 2003). The most popular type of monitor is strapped across the mother's abdomen throughout labor. A second, more accurate method involves threading a recording device through the cervix and placing it directly under the baby's scalp.

Fetal monitoring is a safe medical procedure that has saved the lives of many babies in high-risk situations. But in healthy pregnancies, it does not reduce the already low rates of infant brain damage and death (Priddy, 2004). Furthermore, most infants have some heartbeat irregularities during labor, so critics worry that fetal monitors identify many babies as in danger who, in fact, are not. Monitoring is linked to an increase in the number of cesarean (surgical) deliveries, which we will discuss shortly (Thacker & Stroup, 2003).

Still, fetal monitors will probably continue to be used routinely in the United States, even though they are not necessary in most cases. Doctors fear that they will be sued for malpractice if an infant dies or is born with problems and they cannot show that they did everything possible to protect the baby.

Labor and Delivery Medication

Some form of medication is used in more than 80 percent of U.S. births (Althaus & Wax, 2005). *Analgesics,* drugs used to relieve pain, may be given in mild doses during labor to help a mother relax. *Anesthetics* are a stronger type of painkiller that blocks sensation. Currently, the most common approach to controlling pain during labor is *epidural analgesia,* in which a regional pain-relieving drug is delivered continuously through a catheter into a small space in the lower spine, numbing the pelvic region. Because the mother retains the capacity to feel the pressure of the contractions and to move her trunk and legs, she is able to push during the second stage of labor.

Although pain-relieving drugs help women cope with childbirth and enable doctors to perform essential medical interventions, they also can cause problems. Epidural analgesia, for example, weakens uterine contractions. As a result, labor is prolonged, and the chances of cesarean (surgical) delivery increase (Klein, 2006). And because drugs rapidly cross the placenta, exposed newborns tend to be sleepy and withdrawn, to suck poorly during feedings, and to be irritable when awake (Caton et al., 2002; Eltzschig, Lieberman, & Camann, 2003).

Cesarean Delivery

A **cesarean delivery** is a surgical birth; the doctor makes an incision in the mother's abdomen and lifts the baby out of the uterus. Forty years ago, cesarean delivery was rare. Since then, cesarean rates have climbed internationally, reaching 16 percent in Finland, 20 percent in New Zealand, 22 percent in Australia, 26 percent in Canada, and 30 percent in the United States (Betrán et al., 2007; Society of Obstetricians and Gynaecologists, 2008; U.S. Department of Health and Human Services, 2008f).

Cesareans have always been warranted by medical emergencies and in breech births, in which the baby risks head injury or anoxia (as in Melinda's case). But these factors do not explain the worldwide rise in cesarean deliveries. Instead, medical control over childbirth is largely responsible. Because many needless cesareans are performed, pregnant women should ask questions about the procedure before choosing a doctor. Although the operation itself is safe, mother and baby require more time for recovery. Anesthetic may have crossed the placenta, making cesarean newborns sleepy and unresponsive and at increased risk for breathing difficulties (McDonagh, Osterweil, & Guise, 2005).

ASK YOURSELF

>> **REVIEW**
Describe the features and benefits of natural childbirth. What aspect contributes greatly to favorable outcomes, and why?

>> **APPLY**
How might use of epidural analgesia negatively affect the parent–newborn relationship? Does your answer illustrate bidirectional influences between parent and child, emphasized in ecological systems theory? Explain.

>> **REFLECT**
If you were an expectant parent, would you choose home birth? Why or why not?

Preterm and Low-Birth-Weight Infants

The average newborn weighs 7½ pounds (3,400 grams). Birth weight is the best available predictor of infant survival and healthy development. Many newborns who weigh less than 3½ pounds (1,500 grams) experience difficulties that are not overcome, an effect that becomes stronger as length of pregnancy and birth weight decrease (Bolisetty et al., 2006; Dombrowski, Noonan, & Martin, 2007). Frequent illness, inattention, overactivity, sensory impairments, poor motor coordination, language delays, low intelligence test scores, deficits in school learning, and emotional and behavior problems are some of the difficulties that persist through childhood and adolescence and into adulthood (Bayless, 2007; Grunau, Whitfield, & Fay, 2004; Hultman et al., 2007; Lefebvre, Mazurier, & Tessier, 2005).

About 1 in 13 American infants is born underweight. Although the problem is common among twins (see Chapter 2) and can strike unexpectedly, it is highest among poverty-stricken women (U.S. Department of Health and Human Services, 2007a). These mothers, as noted earlier, are more likely to be undernourished and to be exposed to other harmful environmental influences. In addition, they often do not receive adequate prenatal care.

Preterm versus Small-for-Date Infants

Despite many obstacles to healthy development, most low-birth-weight infants go on to lead normal lives. About half of those born at 23 to 24 weeks' gestation and weighing only a couple of pounds at birth have no disability. To better understand why some babies do better than others, researchers divide them into two groups. **Preterm** infants are those born several weeks or more before their due date. Although they are small, their weight may still be appropriate, based on time spent in the uterus. **Small-for-date** babies are below their expected weight considering length of the pregnancy. Some small-for-date infants are actually full-term. Others are preterm infants who are especially underweight.

Of the two types of babies, small-for-date infants usually have more serious problems. During the first year, they are more likely to die, catch infections, and show evidence of brain damage. By middle childhood, they have lower intelligence test scores, are less attentive, achieve less well in school, and are socially immature (Hediger et al., 2002; O'Keefe et al., 2003). Small-for-date infants probably experienced inadequate nutrition before birth. Perhaps their mothers did not eat properly, the placenta did not function normally, or the babies themselves had defects that prevented them from growing as they should.

Even among preterm newborns whose weight is appropriate for length of pregnancy, just seven more days—from 34 to 35 weeks—greatly reduces rates of illness, costly medical procedures, and lengthy hospital stays (Gladstone & Katz, 2004). And despite being low-risk for disabilities, a substantial number of 34-week preterms are below average in physical growth and mildly to moderately delayed in cognitive development in early and middle childhood (de Haan et al., 2000; Pietz et al., 2004). Yet doctors often induce births several weeks preterm, under the misconception that these babies are developmentally "mature."

Consequences for Caregiving

The appearance and behavior of preterm babies—scrawny and thin-skinned, sleepy and unresponsive, irritable when briefly awake—can lead parents to be less sensitive in caring for them. Compared with full-term infants, preterm babies—especially those who are very ill at birth—are less often held close, touched, and talked to gently (Feldman, 2007). When they are born to isolated, poverty-stricken mothers who cannot provide good nutrition, health care, and parenting, the likelihood of unfavorable outcomes increases. In contrast, parents with stable life circumstances and social supports usually can overcome the stresses of caring for a preterm infant. In these cases, even sick preterm babies have a good chance of catching up in development by middle childhood (Ment et al., 2003).

These findings suggest that how well preterm infants develop has a great deal to do with the parent–child relationship. Consequently, interventions directed at supporting both sides of this tie are more likely to help these infants recover.

Interventions for Preterm Infants

A preterm baby is cared for in a special Plexiglas-enclosed bed called an *isolette*. Temperature is carefully controlled because these babies cannot yet regulate their own body temperature effectively. To help protect the baby from infection, air is filtered before it enters the isolette. Infants born more than six weeks early commonly have a disorder called *respiratory distress syndrome*. Their tiny lungs are so poorly developed that the air sacs collapse, causing serious breathing difficulties. When a preterm infant breathes with the aid of a respirator, is fed through a stomach tube, and receives medication through an intravenous needle, the isolette can be very isolating indeed!

■ **SPECIAL INFANT STIMULATION.** In proper doses, certain kinds of stimulation can help fragile preterm infants develop. In some intensive care nurseries, preterm babies rock in suspended hammocks or are exposed to an attractive mobile or a tape recording of a heartbeat, soft music, or the mother's voice. These experiences promote faster weight gain, more predictable sleep patterns, and greater alertness (Arnon et al., 2006; Marshall-Baker, Lickliter, & Cooper, 1998; Standley, 1998).

Touch is especially important. In baby animals, touching the skin releases brain chemicals that support physical growth—effects believed to occur in humans as well. When preterm infants were massaged several times each day in the hospital, they gained weight faster and, at the end of the first year, were advanced in mental and motor development over preterm babies not given this stimulation (Field, 2001; Field, Hernandez-Reif, & Freedman, 2004).

In developing countries where hospitalization is not always possible, skin-to-skin "kangaroo care" is the most readily

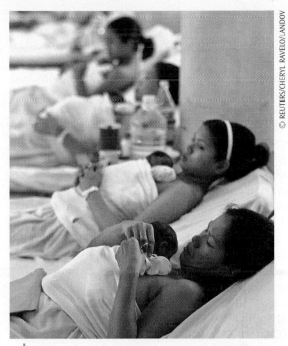

New mothers in a hospital ward in the Philippines practice skin-to-skin "kangaroo care," which is widely used in developing countries to promote the survival and recovery of preterm babies. Because of its many physical and psychological benefits, kangaroo care has spread to western nations, where it supplements hospital intensive care.

available intervention for promoting the survival and recovery of preterm babies. It involves placing the infant in a vertical position between the mother's breasts or next to the father's chest (under the parent's clothing) so the parent's body functions as a human incubator. Kangaroo skin-to-skin contact fosters improved oxygenation of the baby's body, temperature regulation, sleep, feeding, and infant survival (Feldman & Eidelman, 2003). Mothers and fathers practicing kangaroo care feel more confident about caring for their fragile babies and interact more sensitively and affectionately with them (Dodd, 2005; Feldman et al., 2002, 2003). Together, these factors may explain why preterm babies given many hours of kangaroo care in their early weeks, compared to those given little or no such care, score higher on measures of mental and motor development during the first year (Charpak, Ruiz-Peláez, & Figueroa, 2005; Tessier et al., 2003). Because of its diverse benefits, more than 80 percent of North American nurseries now offer kangaroo care to preterm newborns (Field et al., 2006).

■ **TRAINING PARENTS IN INFANT CAREGIVING SKILLS.** Interventions that support parents of preterm infants generally teach them about the infant's characteristics and promote caregiving skills. For parents with adequate economic and personal resources to care for a preterm infant, just a few sessions of coaching in recognizing and responding to the baby's needs are linked to steady gains in mental test performance that, after several years, resemble those of full-term children (Achenbach et al., 1990).

When preterm infants live in stressed, low-income households, long-term, intensive intervention is necessary. In the Infant Health and Development Program, preterm babies born into poverty received a comprehensive intervention that combined medical follow-up, weekly parent training sessions, and cognitively stimulating child care from 1 through 3 years of age. More than four times as many intervention children as controls (39 versus 9 percent) were within normal range in intelligence, psychological adjustment, and physical growth (Bradley et al., 1994). In addition, mothers in the intervention group were more affectionate and more often encouraged play and cognitive mastery in their children—one reason their 3-year-olds may have been developing so favorably (McCarton, 1998). At ages 5 and 8, children who had attended the child-care program regularly—for more than 350 days over the three-year period—continued to show better intellectual functioning. In contrast, children who attended only sporadically gained little or even lost ground (Hill, Brooks-Gunn, & Waldfogel, 2003).

■ **VERY LOW BIRTH WEIGHT, ENVIRONMENTAL ADVANTAGES, AND LONG-TERM OUTCOMES.** Although very-low-birth-weight babies often have lasting problems, in a Canadian study, participants who had weighed between 1 and 2.2 pounds (500 to 1,000 grams) at birth were doing well as young adults (Saigal et al., 2006). At 22 to 25 years of age, they resembled normal-birth-weight individuals in educational attainment, rates of marriage and parenthood, and (for those who had no neurological or sensory impairments) employment status. Researchers believe that home, school, and societal advantages combine to explain these excellent outcomes (Hack & Klein, 2006). Most participants were reared in two-parent middle-SES homes, attended good schools where they received special services, and benefited from Canada's government-sponsored, universal health-care system.

But even the best environments cannot "fix" the serious biological risks associated with being born severely underweight. An even better course of action would be to prevent this serious threat to infant survival and development. The high rate of underweight babies in the United States—one of the worst in the industrialized world—could be greatly reduced by improving the health and social conditions described in the Social Issues box on the following pages.

Birth Complications, Parenting, and Resilience

In the preceding sections, we considered a variety of birth complications. Can any general principles help us understand how infants who survive a traumatic birth are likely to develop? A landmark study carried out in Hawaii provides answers to this question.

In 1955, Emmy Werner and Ruth Smith began to follow nearly 700 infants on the island of Kauai who had experienced mild, moderate, or severe birth complications. Each was

matched on SES and ethnicity with a healthy newborn (Werner & Smith, 1982). Findings revealed that the likelihood of long-term difficulties increased if birth trauma was severe. But among mildly to moderately stressed children, those growing up in stable families did almost as well on measures of intelligence and psychological adjustment as those with no birth problems. Children exposed to poverty, family disorganization, and mentally ill parents often developed serious learning difficulties, behavior problems, and emotional disturbance.

The Kauai study tells us that as long as birth injuries are not overwhelming, a supportive home environment can restore children's growth. But the most intriguing cases in this study were the handful of exceptions. A few children with both fairly serious birth complications and troubled family environments grew into competent, well-adjusted adults. Werner and Smith found that these children relied on factors outside the family and within themselves to overcome stress. Some had attractive personalities that drew positive responses from relatives, neighbors, and peers. In other instances, a grandparent, aunt, uncle, or babysitter provided the needed emotional support (Werner, 1989, 2001; Werner & Smith, 1992).

Do these outcomes remind you of the characteristics of resilient children, discussed in Chapter 1? The Kauai study and other similar investigations reveal that the impact of early biological risks often wanes as children's personal characteristics and social experiences contribute increasingly to their functioning (Resnick et al., 1999). In sum, when the overall balance of life events tips toward the favorable side, children with serious birth problems can develop successfully.

ASK YOURSELF

REVIEW
Sensitive care can help preterm infants recover, but they are less likely than full-term newborns to receive such care. Explain why.

APPLY
List factors discussed in this chapter that increase the chances that an infant will be born underweight. How many of these factors could be prevented by better health care for expectant mothers?

REFLECT
Many people question the use of extraordinary medical measures to save extremely low-birth-weight babies because of their high risk of developing serious physical, cognitive, and emotional problems. Do you agree or disagree? Explain.

The Newborn Baby's Capacities

Newborn infants have a remarkable set of capacities that are crucial for survival and for evoking adult attention and care. In relating to their physical and social worlds, babies are active from the very start.

SOCIAL ISSUES

A Cross-National Perspective on Health Care and Other Policies for Parents and Newborn Babies

Infant mortality—the number of deaths in the first year of life per 1,000 live births—is an index used around the world to assess the overall health of a nation's children. The United States has the most up-to-date health-care technology in the world, but it has made less progress in reducing infant deaths than many other countries. Over the past three decades, it has slipped in the international rankings, from seventh in the 1950s to twenty-sixth in 2008. Members of America's poor ethnic minorities are at greatest risk. African-American and Native-American babies are twice as likely as white infants to die in the first year of life (U.S. Census Bureau, 2009a, 2009b).

Neonatal mortality, the rate of death within the first month of life, accounts for 67 percent of the U.S. infant death rate. Two factors are largely responsible. The first is serious physical defects, most of which cannot be prevented. The percentage of babies born with physical defects is about the same in all ethnic and income groups. The second leading cause of neonatal mortality is low birth weight, which is largely preventable. African-American and Native-American babies are more than twice as likely as white infants to be born early and underweight (U.S. Census Bureau, 2009b).

Widespread poverty and weak health-care programs for mothers and young children are largely responsible for these trends. Each country in Figure 3.5 that outranks the United States in infant survival provides all its citizens with government-sponsored health-care benefits. And each takes extra steps to make sure that pregnant mothers and babies have access to good nutrition, high-quality medical care, and social and economic supports that promote effective parenting.

For example, all Western European nations guarantee women a certain number of prenatal visits at very low or no cost. After a baby is born, a health professional routinely visits the home to provide counseling about infant care and to arrange continuing medical services. Paid, job-protected employment leave is another vital societal intervention for new parents. Canadian mothers are eligible for 15 weeks' maternity leave at 55 percent of prior earnings (up to a maximum of $413 per week), and Canadian mothers or fathers can take an additional year of parental leave at the same rate in certain cases—for example, when a child is ill following birth or adoption. Paid leave is widely available in other industrialized nations as well. Sweden has the most generous parental leave program in the world. Mothers can begin maternity leave 60 days prior to expected delivery, extending it to six weeks after birth; fathers are granted two weeks of birth leave. In addition, either parent

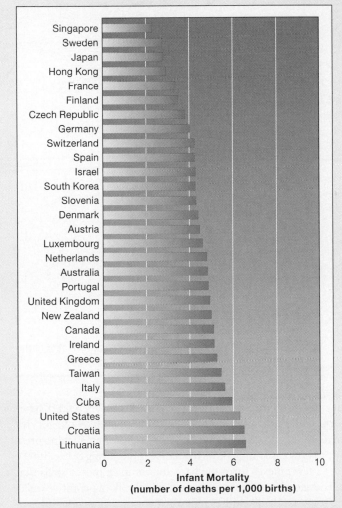

Infant Mortality (number of deaths per 1,000 births)

■ **FIGURE 3.5** ■ **Infant mortality in 30 nations.** Despite its advanced health-care technology, the United States ranks poorly. It is twenty-eighth in the world, with a death rate of 6.6 infants per 1,000 births. (Adapted from U.S. Census Bureau, 2009a.)

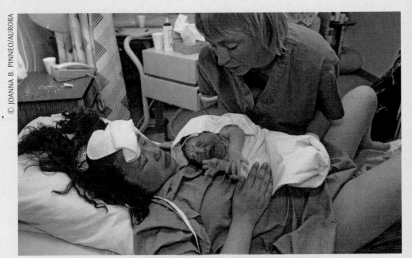

© JOANNA B. PINNEO/AURORA

This Inuit mother, from Baffin Island in northernmost Canada, experienced pregnancy complications and had to be flown 190 miles to deliver her son. Limited access to health care and social services in remote areas compromises the future of many Inuit newborns.

(continued on page 82)

can take full leave until the child reaches age 18 months at 80 percent of prior earnings, followed by an additional three months at a modest flat rate. Each parent is also entitled to another 18 months of unpaid leave (OECD, 2006; Waldfogel, 2001).

Yet in the United States, the federal government mandates *only 12 weeks of unpaid leave* for employees in businesses with at least 50 workers. Most women, however, work in smaller businesses, and even those who work in large enough companies may be unable to afford to take unpaid leave (Hewlett, 2003). And because of financial pressures, many new

mothers who are eligible for unpaid work leave take far less than 12 weeks, while new fathers tend to take little or none at all (OECD, 2006). In 2002, California became the first state to guarantee a mother or father paid leave—up to six weeks at half salary, regardless of the size of the company.

Nevertheless, six weeks of childbirth leave (the norm in the United States) is not enough. When a family is stressed by a baby's arrival, leaves of six weeks or less are linked to increased maternal anxiety, depression, marital dissatisfaction, sense of role overload (conflict between work and family

responsibilities), and negative interactions with the baby. A longer leave (12 weeks or more) predicts favorable maternal mental health, supportive marital interaction, and sensitive caregiving (Feldman, Sussman, & Zigler, 2004; Hyde et al., 2001).

In countries with low infant mortality rates, expectant parents need not wonder how they will get health care and other resources to support their baby's development. The powerful impact of universal, high-quality health care, generous parental leave, and other social services on maternal and infant well-being provides strong justification for these policies.

Newborn Reflexes

A **reflex** is an inborn, automatic response to a particular form of stimulation. Reflexes are the newborn baby's most obvious organized patterns of behavior. When Jay let Joshua's head drop slightly, Joshua reacted with the *Moro (or "embracing") reflex,* flinging his arms wide and bringing them back toward his body. As Yolanda stroked Joshua's cheek, he turned his head in her direction—a response called the *rooting reflex.* When she put her finger in Joshua's palm, he grabbed on tightly, in the *palmar grasp reflex.*

Some reflexes have survival value. In our evolutionary past when infants were carried about all day, the Moro reflex helped a baby who lost support to embrace and, along with the grasp reflex, regain its hold on the mother's body. The rooting reflex helps a breastfed baby find the mother's nipple. Babies display it only when hungry and touched by another person, not when

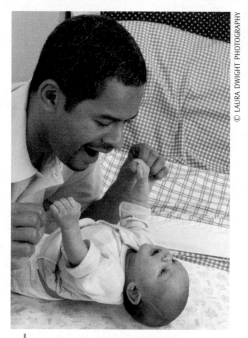

The palmar grasp reflex is so strong during the first week after birth that many infants can use it to support their entire weight.

In the Moro reflex, loss of support or a sudden loud sound causes this baby to arch her back, extend her arms outward, and then bring them in toward her body.

they touch themselves (Rochat & Hespos, 1997). And if newborns could not suck, our species would be unlikely to survive for a single generation! At birth, babies adjust their sucking pressure to how easily milk flows from the nipple (Craig & Lee, 1999).

A few reflexes form the basis for complex motor skills that will develop later. The stepping reflex looks like a primitive walking response. Unlike other reflexes, it appears in a wide range of situations—with the newborn's body in a sideways or upside-down orientation, with feet touching walls or ceilings, and even with legs dangling in the air (Adolph & Berger, 2006). When stepping is exercised regularly, babies are likely to walk several weeks earlier than if stepping is not practiced (Zelazo et al., 1993).

However, there is no special need for infants to practice the stepping reflex because all normal babies walk in due time.

Reflexes help parents and infants establish gratifying interaction. A baby who searches for and successfully finds the nipple, sucks easily during feedings, and grasps when the hand is touched encourages parents to respond lovingly. Caregivers can also make use of reflexes in comforting the baby. For example, on short trips with Joshua to the grocery store, Yolanda brought along a pacifier. If he became fussy, sucking helped quiet him until she could feed, change, or hold him.

Most newborn reflexes disappear during the first six months, due to a gradual increase in voluntary control over behavior as the cerebral cortex develops. Pediatricians test reflexes carefully because responses that are weak or absent, overly rigid or exaggerated, or evident beyond the time when they should normally disappear can signal brain damage (Schott & Rossor, 2003).

Newborn States

Throughout the day and night, newborn infants move in and out of five **states of arousal,** or degrees of sleep and wakefulness, described in Table 3.3. Much to the relief of their fatigued parents, newborns spend the greatest amount of time asleep—about 16 to 18 hours a day. However, striking individual differences in daily rhythms exist that affect parents' attitudes toward and interaction with the baby. A few newborns sleep for long periods, increasing the energy their well-rested parents have for sensitive, responsive care. Other babies cry a great deal, and their parents must exert great effort to soothe them. If these parents do not succeed, they may feel anxious, less competent, and less positively toward their infant. Babies who spend more time alert probably receive more social stimulation and opportunities to explore and, therefore, may have a slight advantage in mental development (Gertner et al., 2002; Smart & Hiscock, 2007).

Of the states listed in Table 3.3, the two extremes—sleep and crying—have been of greatest interest to researchers. Each tells us something about normal and abnormal early development.

■ **SLEEP.** Observing Joshua as he slept, Yolanda and Jay wondered why his eyelids and body twitched and his rate of breathing varied. Sleep is made up of at least two states. During irregular, or **rapid-eye-movement (REM), sleep,** brain-wave activity is remarkably similar to that of the waking state. The eyes dart beneath the lids; heart rate, blood pressure, and breathing are uneven; and slight body movements occur. In contrast, during regular, or **non-rapid-eye-movement (NREM) sleep,** the body is almost motionless, and heart rate, breathing, and brain-wave activity are slow and even.

Like children and adults, newborns alternate between REM and NREM sleep, but they spend far more time in the REM state than they ever will again. REM sleep accounts for 50 percent of a newborn baby's sleep time. By 3 to 5 years, it has declined to an adultlike level of 20 percent (Louis et al., 1997). The stimulation of REM sleep is vital for growth of the central nervous system. Young infants seem to have a special need for this stimulation because they spend little time in an alert state, when they can get input from the environment. The percentage of REM sleep is especially great in the fetus and in preterm babies, who are even less able than full-term newborns to take advantage of external stimulation (de Weerd & van den Bossche, 2003; DiPietro et al., 1996).

Because normal newborn sleep behavior is organized and patterned, observations of sleep states can help identify central nervous system abnormalities. In infants who are brain-damaged or who have experienced birth trauma, disturbed REM–NREM sleep cycles are often present. Babies with poor sleep organization are likely to be behaviorally disorganized and, therefore, to have difficulty learning and evoking caregiver interactions that enhance their development. In the preschool

■ **TABLE 3.3** ■ *Infant States of Arousal*

STATE	DESCRIPTION	DAILY DURATION IN NEWBORN
Regular sleep	The infant is at full rest and shows little or no body activity. The eyelids are closed, no eye movements occur, the face is relaxed, and breathing is slow and regular.	8–9 hours
Irregular sleep	Gentle limb movements, occasional stirring, and facial grimacing occur. Although the eyelids are closed, occasional rapid eye movements can be seen beneath them. Breathing is irregular.	8–9 hours
Drowsiness	The infant is either falling asleep or waking up. Body is less active than in irregular sleep but more active than in regular sleep. The eyes open and close; when open, they have a glazed look. Breathing is even but somewhat faster than in regular sleep.	Varies
Quiet alertness	The infant's body is relatively inactive, with eyes open and attentive. Breathing is even.	2–3 hours
Waking activity and crying	The infant shows frequent bursts of uncoordinated body activity. Breathing is very irregular. Face may be relaxed or tense and wrinkled. Crying may occur.	1–4 hours

Source: Wolff, 1966.

years, they show delayed motor, cognitive, and language development (Feldman, 2006; Holditch-Davis, Belyea, & Edwards, 2005). And the brain-functioning problems that underlie newborn sleep irregularities may culminate in sudden infant death syndrome, a major cause of infant mortality (see the Biology and Environment box on the following page).

■ **CRYING.**   Crying is the first way that babies communicate, letting parents know they need food, comfort, or stimulation. The baby's cry is a complex stimulus that varies in intensity, from a whimper to a message of all-out distress (Gustafson, Wood, & Green, 2000). But most of the time, the nature of the cry, combined with the experiences leading up to it, helps guide parents toward its cause.

Young infants usually cry because of physical needs, most commonly hunger, but babies may also cry in response to temperature change when undressed, a sudden noise, or a painful stimulus. Newborns (as well as older babies) often cry at the sound of another crying baby (Dondi, Simion, & Caltran, 1999). Some researchers believe that this response reflects an inborn capacity to react to the suffering of others. Furthermore, crying typically increases during the early weeks, peaks at about six weeks, and then declines. Because this trend appears in many cultures with vastly different infant care practices, researchers believe that normal readjustments of the central nervous system underlie it (Barr, 2001).

Soothing Crying Infants.   Although parents do not always interpret their baby's cry correctly, their accuracy improves with experience (Thompson & Leger, 1999). Fortunately, there are many ways to soothe a crying baby when feeding and diaper changing do not work. The technique Western parents usually try first, lifting the baby to the shoulder and rocking or

These Quechua women, who live in the cold, high-altitude desert regions of Peru, dress their young babies in layers of clothing and blankets that cover the head and body. In addition to reducing crying and promoting sleep, swaddling helps babies conserve energy for early growth in the harsh Peruvian highlands.

walking, is the most effective. Another common soothing method is swaddling—wrapping the baby snugly in a blanket. The Quechua, who live in the cold, high-altitude desert regions of Peru, dress young babies in layers of clothing and blankets that cover the head and body. The result—a warm pouch placed on the mother's back that moves rhythmically as she walks—reduces crying and promotes sleep. It also allows the baby to conserve energy for early growth in the harsh Peruvian highlands (Tronick, Thomas, & Daltabuit, 1994).

In many tribal and village societies and non-Western developed nations, infants spend most of the day and night in close physical contact with their caregivers. Among the !Kung of the desert regions of Botswana, Africa, mothers sling their young babies on their hips, so infants can see their surroundings and nurse at will. Japanese mothers and babies also spend much time in close body contact (Small, 1998). Infants in these cultures show shorter bouts of crying than their North American counterparts (Barr, 2001).

Abnormal Crying.   Like reflexes and sleep patterns, the infant's cry offers a clue to central nervous system distress. The cries of brain-damaged babies and those who have experienced prenatal and birth complications are often shrill, piercing, and shorter in duration than those of healthy infants (Green, Irwin, & Gustafson, 2000). Even newborns with a fairly common problem—*colic*, or persistent crying—tend to have high-pitched, harsh-sounding cries (Zeskind & Barr, 1997). Although the cause of colic is unknown, certain newborns, who react especially strongly to unpleasant stimuli, are susceptible.

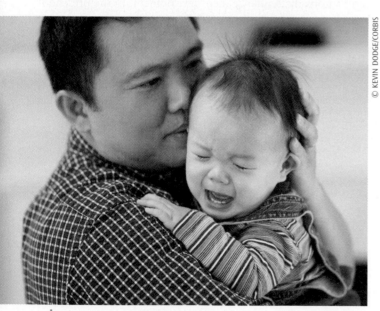

To soothe his crying infant, this father holds his baby upright against his gently moving body. Besides encouraging infants to stop crying, this technique causes them to become quietly alert.

▪ BIOLOGY AND ENVIRONMENT ▪

The Mysterious Tragedy of Sudden Infant Death Syndrome

Millie awoke with a start one morning and looked at the clock. It was 7:30, and Sasha had missed both her night waking and her early morning feeding. Wondering if she was all right, Millie and her husband Stuart tiptoed into the room. Sasha lay still, curled up under her blanket. She had died silently during her sleep.

Sasha was a victim of **sudden infant death syndrome (SIDS),** the unexpected death, usually during the night, of an infant under 1 year of age that remains unexplained after thorough investigation. In industrialized nations, SIDS is the leading cause of infant mortality between 1 and 12 months, accounting for about 20 percent of these deaths in the United States (Mathews & MacDorman, 2008).

Although the precise cause of SIDS is not known, its victims usually show physical problems from the beginning. Early medical records of SIDS babies reveal higher rates of prematurity and low birth weight, poor Apgar scores, and limp muscle tone. Abnormal heart rate and respiration and disturbances in sleep–wake activity and in REM–NREM cycles while asleep are also involved (Cornwell & Feigenbaum, 2006; Kato et al., 2003). At the time of death, many SIDS babies have a mild respiratory infection (Samuels, 2003). This seems to increase the chances of respiratory failure in an already vulnerable baby.

One hypothesis about the cause of SIDS is that impaired brain functioning prevents these infants from learning how to respond when their survival is threatened—for example, when respiration is suddenly interrupted. Between 2 and 4 months, when SIDS is most likely to occur, reflexes decline and are replaced by voluntary, learned responses. Respiratory and muscular weaknesses may stop SIDS babies from acquiring behaviors that replace defensive reflexes (Lipsitt, 2003). As a result, when breath-

ing difficulties occur during sleep, infants do not wake up, shift their position, or cry out for help. Instead, they simply give in to oxygen deprivation and death. In support of this interpretation, autopsies reveal that SIDS babies, more often than other infants, show abnormalities in brain centers controlling breathing (Paterson et al., 2006).

In an effort to reduce the occurrence of SIDS, researchers are studying environmental factors related to it. Babies exposed to cigarette smoke both during and after pregnancy are twice as likely as nonexposed infants to die of SIDS (Anderson, Johnson, & Batal, 2005; Shah, Sullivan, & Carter, 2006). Prenatal abuse of drugs that depress central nervous system functioning (opiates and barbiturates) increases the risk of SIDS as much as fifteenfold (Hunt & Hauck, 2006). SIDS babies are also more likely to sleep on their stomachs than on their backs and often are wrapped very warmly in clothing and blankets (Hauck et al., 2003).

Researchers suspect that nicotine, depressant drugs, excessive body warmth, and respiratory infection all lead to physiological stress, which disrupts the normal sleep pattern. When sleep-deprived infants experience a sleep "rebound," they sleep more deeply, which results in loss of muscle tone in the airway passages. In at-risk babies, the airway may collapse, and the infant may fail to arouse sufficiently to reestablish breathing (Simpson, 2001). In other cases, healthy babies sleeping face down on soft bedding may die from continually breathing their own exhaled breath.

Quitting smoking, changing an infant's sleeping position, and removing a few bedclothes can reduce the incidence of SIDS. Public education campaigns that encourage parents to put their infants down on their backs have cut the incidence of SIDS in half in many Western nations (Byard & Krous, 2003).

Public education campaigns encouraging parents to put their infants down on their backs to sleep have helped reduce the incidence of SIDS by half in many Western nations.

Another protective measure is pacifier use: Sleeping babies who suck arouse more easily in response to breathing and heart-rate irregularities (Li et al., 2006).

When SIDS does occur, surviving family members require a great deal of help to overcome a sudden and unexpected death. As Millie commented six months after Sasha's death, "It's the worst crisis we've ever been through. What's helped us most are the comforting words of others who've experienced the same tragedy."

Colic generally subsides between 3 and 6 months (Barr et al., 2005; St James-Roberts et al., 2003).

Most parents try to respond to a crying baby with extra care and attention, but sometimes the cry is so unpleasant and persistent that parents become frustrated and angry. Preterm

and ill babies are more likely to be abused by highly stressed parents, who frequently mention a high-pitched, grating cry as one factor that caused them to lose control (St James-Roberts, 2007; Zeskind & Lester, 2001). We will discuss a host of additional influences on child abuse in Chapter 8.

Sensory Capacities

On his visit to my class, Joshua looked wide-eyed at my bright pink blouse and turned to the sound of his mother's voice. During feedings, he lets Yolanda know through his sucking rhythm that he prefers the taste of breast milk to a bottle of plain water. In the following sections, we explore the newborn's responsiveness to touch, taste, smell, sound, and visual stimulation.

■ **TOUCH.**   In our discussion of preterm infants, we saw that touch helps stimulate early physical growth. As we will see in Chapter 6, it is vital for emotional development as well. Therefore, it is not surprising that sensitivity to touch is well-developed at birth. The newborn responds to touch, especially around the mouth, on the palms, and on the soles of the feet. During the prenatal period, these areas, along with the genitals, are the first to become sensitive to touch (Humphrey, 1978; Streri, 2005).

At birth, infants are highly sensitive to pain. If male newborns are circumcised, anesthetic is sometimes not used because of the risk of giving drugs to a very young infant. Babies often respond with a high-pitched, stressful cry and a dramatic rise in heart rate, blood pressure, palm sweating, pupil dilation, and muscle tension (Lehr et al., 2007; Warnock & Sandrin, 2004). Brain-imaging research suggests that because of central nervous system immaturity, preterm and male babies feel the pain of a medical injection especially intensely (Bartocci et al., 2006).

Recent research establishing the safety of certain local anesthetics for newborns promises to ease the pain of these procedures. Offering a nipple that delivers a sugar solution is also helpful in reducing crying and discomfort, and combining the sweet liquid with gentle holding by the parent lessens pain even more. Research on infant mammals indicates that physical touch releases *endorphins*—painkilling chemicals in the brain (Axelin, Salanterä, & Lehtonen, 2006; Gormally et al., 2001).

■ **TASTE AND SMELL.**   Newborns can distinguish several basic tastes. Like adults, they relax their facial muscles in response to sweetness, purse their lips when the taste is sour, and show a distinct archlike mouth opening when it is bitter (Steiner, 1979; Steiner et al., 2001). These reactions are important for survival: The food that best supports the infant's early growth is the sweet-tasting milk of the mother's breast. Not until 4 months do babies prefer a salty taste to plain water, a change that may prepare them to accept solid foods (Mennella & Beauchamp, 1998).

As with taste, certain odor preferences are present at birth. The smell of bananas or chocolate causes a relaxed, pleasant facial expression, whereas the odor of rotten eggs makes the infant frown (Steiner, 1979). During pregnancy, the amniotic fluid is rich in tastes and smells that vary with the mother's diet—early experiences that influence newborns' preferences. In a study carried out in the Alsatian region of France, where anise is frequently used to flavor foods, researchers tested new-

Similar to women in the Zambian culture, this mother of the El Molo people of northern Kenya carries her baby all day, providing close physical contact, a rich variety of stimulation, and ready feeding.

borns for their reaction to the anise odor (Schaal, Marlier, & Soussignan, 2000). The mothers of some babies had regularly consumed anise during the last two weeks of pregnancy; the other mothers had never consumed it. When presented with the anise odor on the day of birth, the babies of non-anise-consuming mothers were far more likely to turn away with a negative facial expression (see Figure 3.6). These different reactions were still apparent four days later, even though all mothers had refrained from consuming anise during this time.

In many mammals, the sense of smell plays an important role in feeding and in protecting the young from predators by helping mothers and babies identify each other. Although smell is less well-developed in humans, traces of its survival value remain. If one breast is washed to remove its natural scent, most newborns grasp the unwashed breast, indicating that they are guided by smell (Varendi & Porter, 2001). At 4 days of age, breastfed babies prefer the smell of their own mother's breast to that of an unfamiliar lactating mother (Cernoch & Porter, 1985). And both breast- and bottle-fed 3- to 4-day-olds orient more and display more mouthing to the smell of unfamiliar

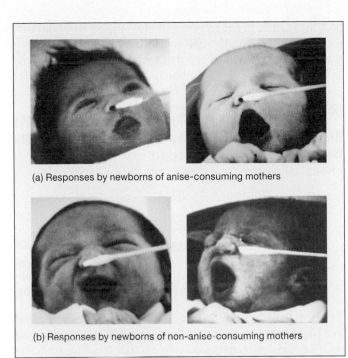

(a) Responses by newborns of anise-consuming mothers

(b) Responses by newborns of non-anise-consuming mothers

■ **FIGURE 3.6** ■ **Examples of facial expressions of newborns exposed to the odor of anise whose mothers' diets differed in anise-flavored foods during late pregnancy.** (a) Babies of anise-consuming mothers spent more time turning toward the odor and sucking, licking, and chewing. (b) Babies of non-anise-consuming mothers more often turned away with a negative facial expression. (From B. Schaal, L. Marlier, & R. Soussignan, 2000, "Human Foetuses Learn Odours from Their Pregnant Mother's Diet," *Chemical Senses, 25,* p. 731. Reprinted by permission of Benoist Schaal.)

human milk than to formula milk, indicating that (even without prior exposure) the odor of human milk is more attractive to newborns (Marlier & Schaal, 2005). Newborns' dual attraction to the odor of their mother and to that of breast milk helps them locate an appropriate food source and, in the process, begin to distinguish their caregiver from other people.

■ **HEARING.** Newborn infants can hear a wide variety of sounds, and their sensitivity improves greatly over the first few months (Saffran, Werker, & Werner, 2006). At birth, infants prefer complex sounds, such as noises and voices, to pure tones. And babies only a few days old can tell the difference between a few sound patterns—a series of tones arranged in ascending versus descending order, utterances with two versus three syllables, the stress patterns of words, such as *ma*-ma versus ma-*ma,* and happy-sounding speech as opposed to speech with negative or neutral emotional qualities (Mastropieri & Turkewitz, 1999; Sansavini, Bertoncini, & Giovanelli, 1997; Trehub, 2001).

Young infants listen longer to human speech than structurally similar nonspeech sounds (Vouloumanos & Werker, 2004). And they make fine-grained distinctions among many speech sounds. Indeed, researchers have found only a few speech sounds in human languages that newborns cannot discriminate (Saffran, Werker, & Werner, 2006). These capacities reveal that the baby is marvelously prepared for the awesome task of acquiring language.

Immediately after birth, infants will suck more on a nipple to hear a recording of their mother's voice than that of an unfamiliar woman and to hear their native language as opposed to a foreign language—preferences that may have developed from hearing the muffled sounds of the mother's voice before birth (Moon, Cooper, & Fifer, 1993; Spence & DeCasper, 1987).

■ **VISION.** Vision is the least-developed of the newborn baby's senses. Visual structures in both the eye and the brain are not yet fully formed. For example, cells in the *retina,* a membrane lining the inside of the eye that captures light and transforms it into messages that are sent to the brain, are not as mature or densely packed as they will be in several months. The optic nerve that relays these messages, and the visual centers in the brain that receive them, will not be adultlike for several years. And the muscles of the *lens,* which permit us to adjust our visual focus to varying distances, are weak (Kellman & Arterberry, 2006).

As a result, newborns cannot focus their eyes well, and **visual acuity,** or fineness of discrimination, is limited. At birth, infants perceive objects at a distance of 20 feet about as clearly as adults do at 600 feet (Slater, 2001). In addition, unlike adults (who see nearby objects most clearly), newborn babies see unclearly across a wide range of distances (Banks, 1980; Hainline, 1998). Images such as the parent's face, even from close up, look blurred. Nevertheless, newborns prefer to look at simple, facelike stimuli over patterns with scrambled facial features (Mondloch et al., 1999). And they gaze more at colored rather than gray stimuli, although they are not yet good at discriminating colors (Adams & Courage, 1998; Kellman & Arterberry, 2006). Despite limited vision and slow, imprecise eye movements, newborns actively explore their visual world by scanning it for interesting sights and tracking moving objects.

ASK YOURSELF

≫ **REVIEW**
What functions does REM sleep serve in young infants? Can sleep tell us anything about the health of the newborn's central nervous system? Explain.

≫ **APPLY**
How do the diverse capacities of newborn babies contribute to their first social relationships? Provide as many examples as you can.

≫ **REFLECT**
Are newborns more competent than you thought they were before you read this chapter? Which of their capacities most surprised you?

Adjusting to the New Family Unit

Nature helps prepare expectant mothers and fathers for their new role. Toward the end of pregnancy, mothers begin producing the hormone oxytocin, which stimulates uterine contractions; causes the breasts to "let down" milk; induces a calm, relaxed mood; and promotes responsiveness to the baby (Russell, Douglas, & Ingram, 2001). And in several studies, first-time fathers enrolled in prenatal classes showed hormonal changes around the time of birth—specifically, slight increases in *prolactin* (a hormone that stimulates milk production in females) and *estrogens* (sex hormones produced in larger quantities in females) and a drop in *androgens* (sex hormones produced in larger quantities in males). In animal and human research, these changes are associated with positive emotional reactions to infants (Storey et al., 2000; Wynne-Edwards, 2001).

Although birth-related hormones can facilitate caregiving, their release and effects may depend on experiences, such as a positive couple relationship and paternal close contact with the pregnant mother. Furthermore, humans can parent effectively without experiencing birth-related hormonal changes, as successful adoption reveals. And as we have seen, a great many factors—from family functioning to social policies—are involved in good infant care.

Indeed, the early weeks after the baby's arrival are full of profound challenges. The mother needs to recuperate from childbirth. If she is breastfeeding, energies must be devoted to working out this intimate relationship. The father needs to support the mother in her recovery and become a part of this new threesome. At times, he may feel ambivalent about the baby, who constantly demands and gets the mother's attention. And as we will see in Chapter 6, siblings—especially those who are young and firstborn—understandably feel displaced. They sometimes react with jealousy and anger.

While all this is going on, the tiny infant demands to be fed, changed, and comforted at odd times of the day and night. The family schedule becomes irregular and uncertain. Yolanda spoke candidly about the changes she and Jay experienced:

> When we brought Joshua home, he seemed so small and helpless, and we worried about whether we would be able to take proper care of him. It took us 20 minutes to change the first diaper! I rarely feel rested because I'm up two to four times every night, and I spend a good part of my waking hours trying to anticipate Joshua's rhythms and needs. If Jay weren't so willing to help by holding and walking Joshua, I think I'd find it much harder.

How long does this time of adjustment to parenthood last? In Chapter 14, we will see that when marital relationships are positive, social support is available, and families have sufficient income, the stress caused by the birth of a baby remains manageable. Nevertheless, as one pair of counselors who have worked with many new parents pointed out, "As long as children are dependent on their parents, those parents find themselves preoccupied with thoughts of their children. This does not keep them from enjoying other aspects of their lives, but it does mean that they never return to being quite the same people they were before they became parents" (Colman & Colman, 1991, p. 198).

Summary

Prenatal Development

List the three phases of prenatal development, and describe the major milestones of each.

>> The period of the zygote lasts about two weeks, from fertilization until **implantation** of the blastocyst in the uterine lining. During this time, structures that will support prenatal growth begin to form, including the **placenta** and the **umbilical cord.**

>> The period of the **embryo** lasts from two to eight weeks, during which the foundations for all body structures are laid down. In the first week of this period, the **neural tube** forms, and the nervous system starts to develop.

Other organs follow and grow rapidly. At the end of this phase, the embryo responds to touch and can move.

>> The period of the **fetus,** lasting until the end of pregnancy, involves dramatic increase in body size and completion of physical structures. At the end of the second **trimester,** most of the brain's neurons are in place. At the beginning of the third trimester, between 22 and 26 weeks, the fetus reaches the **age of viability.** The brain continues to develop rapidly, and new sensory and behavioral capacities emerge. The lungs gradually mature, the fetus fills the uterus, and birth is near.

Prenatal Environmental Influences

What are teratogens, and what factors influence their impact?

>> **Teratogens** are environmental agents that cause damage during the prenatal period. Their impact varies with the amount and length of exposure, the genetic makeup of mother and fetus, the presence or absence of other harmful agents, and the age of the organism at time of exposure. The developing organism is especially vulnerable during the embryonic period.

List agents that are known or suspected teratogens, and discuss evidence supporting the harmful impact of each.

≫ Currently, the most widely used potent teratogen is Accutane, a drug used to treat acne. The prenatal impact of many other commonly used medications, such as aspirin and caffeine, is hard to separate from other factors correlated with drug taking. Babies whose mothers used heroin, methadone, or cocaine during pregnancy are at risk for a wide variety of problems, including prematurity, low birth weight, physical defects, and breathing difficulties around the time of birth.

≫ Infants of parents who use tobacco are often born underweight and may have attention, learning, and behavior problems in childhood. Maternal alcohol consumption can lead to **fetal alcohol spectrum disorder (FASD). Fetal alcohol syndrome (FAS)** involves slow physical growth, facial abnormalities, and impairment in mental functioning. Milder forms—**partial fetal alcohol syndrome (p-FAS)** and **alcohol-related neurodevelopmental disorder (ARND)**—affect children whose mothers consumed smaller quantities of alcohol.

≫ Prenatal exposure to high levels of radiation, mercury, PCBs, lead, and dioxins leads to physical malformations and severe brain damage. Low-level exposure has also been linked to diverse impairments, including lower intelligence test scores and, in the case of radiation, language and emotional disorders.

≫ Among infectious diseases, rubella (German measles) causes a wide variety of abnormalities. Babies with prenatally transmitted HIV rapidly develop AIDS, leading to rapid physical decline and early death. Cytomegalovirus, herpes simplex 2, and toxoplasmosis can also be devastating to the fetus.

© DR. M. A. ANSARY/PHOTO RESEARCHERS, INC.

Describe the impact of other maternal factors on prenatal development.

≫ When the mother's diet is inadequate, low birth weight and damage to the brain and other organs are major concerns. A folic acid supplement greatly reduces neural tube abnormalities.

≫ Severe emotional stress is linked to many pregnancy complications, although its impact can be reduced by providing the mother with emotional support. **Rh factor incompatibility**—an Rh-negative mother carrying an Rh-positive fetus—can lead to oxygen deprivation, brain and heart damage, and infant death.

≫ Aside from the risk of chromosomal abnormalities in older women, maternal age through the thirties is not a major cause of prenatal problems. Poor health and environmental risks associated with poverty are the strongest predictors of pregnancy complications.

© CHAD EHLERS/ALAMY

Why is early and regular health care vital during the prenatal period?

≫ Unexpected difficulties, such as preeclampsia, can arise, especially when mothers have health problems to begin with. Yet many U.S. low-income women lack health insurance or experience situational barriers that prevent them from seeking prenatal care.

Childbirth

Describe the stages of childbirth and the baby's adaptation to labor and delivery.

≫ In the first stage of childbirth, contractions widen and thin the cervix. In the second stage, the mother feels an urge to push the baby through the birth canal. In the final stage, the placenta is delivered.

≫ During labor, infants produce high levels of stress hormones, which help them withstand oxygen deprivation, clear the lungs for breathing, and arouse them into alertness at birth. The **Apgar Scale** assesses the baby's physical condition at birth.

Approaches to Childbirth

Describe natural childbirth and home delivery, noting any benefits and concerns associated with each.

≫ **Natural, or prepared, childbirth** involves classes in which prospective parents learn about labor and delivery, relaxation and breathing techniques to counteract pain, and coaching during childbirth. Social support, a vital part of natural childbirth, is linked to fewer birth complications and shorter labors. Home birth is safe for healthy mothers who are assisted by a well-trained doctor or midwife, but mothers at risk for any kind of complication are safer giving birth in a hospital.

Medical Interventions

List common medical interventions during childbirth, circumstances that justify their use, and any dangers associated with each.

≫ When pregnancy and birth complications make **anoxia** likely, **fetal monitors** help save the lives of many babies. However, when used routinely, they may identify infants as in danger who, in fact, are not.

≫ Medication to relieve pain is necessary in complicated deliveries. When given in large doses, it may prolong labor and produce a depressed state in the newborn that affects the early mother–infant relationship.

≫ **Cesarean deliveries** are justified in cases of medical emergency and serious maternal illness and sometimes when babies are in **breech position.** Many unnecessary cesareans are performed, especially in the United States.

Preterm and Low-Birth-Weight Infants

Describe risks associated with preterm birth and low birth weight, along with effective interventions.

≫ Low birth weight, a major cause of neonatal and **infant mortality** and wide-ranging developmental problems, is most common in infants born to poverty-stricken women. Compared with **preterm infants,** whose weight is appropriate for time spent in the uterus, **small-for-date infants** usually have longer-lasting difficulties.

≫ Some interventions provide special stimulation in the intensive care nursery. Others teach parents how to care for and interact with their babies. Preterm infants in stressed, low-income households need long-term, intensive intervention.

Birth Complications, Parenting, and Resilience

What factors predict positive outcomes in infants who survive a traumatic birth?

>> When infants experience birth trauma, a supportive home environment can help restore their growth. Even infants with fairly serious birth complications can recover with the help of favorable experiences with parents, relatives, neighbors, and peers.

The Newborn Baby's Capacities

Describe the newborn baby's reflexes and states of arousal, including sleep characteristics and ways to soothe a crying baby.

>> **Reflexes** are the newborn baby's most obvious organized patterns of behavior. Some have survival value, others provide the foundation for voluntary motor skills, and still others contribute to early social relationships.

© LAURA DWIGHT PHOTOGRAPHY

>> Although newborns move in and out of five different **states of arousal,** they spend most of their time asleep. Sleep consists of at least two states, **rapid-eye-movement (REM) sleep** and **non-rapid-eye-movement (NREM) sleep.** Newborns spend more time in REM sleep than they will at any later age. This state provides stimulation essential for central nervous system development.

© KEVIN DODGE/CORBIS

>> A crying baby stimulates strong feelings of discomfort in nearby adults. The intensity of the cry and the experiences that led up to it help parents identify what is wrong. Once feeding and diaper changing have been tried, the most effective soothing technique is lifting the baby to the shoulder and rocking and walking.

Describe the newborn baby's sensory capacities.

>> The senses of touch, taste, smell, and sound are well-developed at birth. Newborns are sensitive to pain, prefer sweet tastes and smells, and orient toward the odor of their own mother's lactating breast. Already they can distinguish a few sound patterns as well as almost all speech sounds. They are especially responsive to high-pitched, expressive voices; their own mother's voice; and speech in their native tongue.

>> Vision is the least mature of the newborn's senses. At birth, focusing ability and **visual acuity** are limited. Nevertheless, newborns actively explore their visual world, scanning it for interesting sights and tracking moving objects.

Adjusting to the New Family Unit

Describe typical changes in the family after the birth of a new baby.

>> The new baby's arrival is exciting but stressful, as the mother recuperates from childbirth and the family schedule becomes irregular and uncertain. When parents are sensitive to each other's needs, adjustment problems are usually temporary, and the transition to parenthood goes well.

Important Terms and Concepts

age of viability (p. 65)
alcohol-related neurodevelopmental disorder (ARND) (p. 69)
amnion (p. 62)
anoxia (p. 77)
Apgar Scale (p. 75)
breech position (p. 77)
cesarean delivery (p. 78)
chorion (p. 63)
embryo (p. 64)
fetal alcohol spectrum disorder (FASD) (p. 69)
fetal alcohol syndrome (FAS) (p. 69)

fetal monitors (p. 77)
fetus (p. 64)
implantation (p. 62)
infant mortality (p. 81)
lanugo (p. 65)
natural, or prepared, childbirth (p. 76)
neural tube (p. 64)
non-rapid-eye-movement (NREM) sleep (p. 83)
partial fetal alcohol syndrome (p-FAS) (p. 69)
placenta (p. 63)
preterm infants (p. 78)
rapid-eye-movement (REM) sleep (p. 83)

reflex (p. 82)
Rh factor incompatibility (p. 72)
small-for-date infants (p. 78)
states of arousal (p. 83)
sudden infant death syndrome (SIDS) (p. 85)
teratogen (p. 66)
trimesters (p. 65)
umbilical cord (p. 63)
vernix (p. 65)
visual acuity (p. 87)

Physical Development in Infancy and Toddlerhood

CHAPTER 4

© SARAH MONTE/GETTY IMAGES/WESTEND61

Babies acquire new motor skills by building on previously acquired capacities. Eager to explore his world, this baby has just about mastered the art of crawling. Once he can fully move on his own, he will make dramatic strides in understanding his surroundings.

On a brilliant June morning, 16-month-old Caitlin emerged from her front door, ready for the short drive to the child-care home where she spent her weekdays while her mother, Carolyn, and her father, David, worked. Clutching a teddy bear in one hand and her mother's arm with the other, Caitlin descended the steps. "One! Two! Threeee!" Carolyn counted as she helped Caitlin down. "How much she's changed," Carolyn thought to herself, looking at the child who, not long ago, had been a newborn. With her first steps, Caitlin had passed from *infancy* to *toddlerhood*—a period spanning the second year of life. At first, Caitlin did, indeed, "toddle" awkwardly, rocking from side to side and frequently tipping over. But her face reflected the thrill of conquering a new skill.

As they walked toward the car, Carolyn and Caitlin spotted 3-year-old Eli and his father, Kevin, in the neighboring yard. Eli dashed toward them, waving a bright yellow envelope. Carolyn bent down to open the envelope and took out a card. It read, "Announcing the arrival of Grace Ann. Born: Cambodia. Age: 16 months." Carolyn turned to Kevin and Eli. "That's wonderful news! When can we see her?"

COURTESY OF LAURA E. BERK

"Let's wait a few days," Kevin suggested. "Monica's taken Grace to the doctor this morning. She's underweight and malnourished." Kevin described Monica's first night with Grace in a hotel room in Phnom Penh. Grace lay on the bed, withdrawn and fearful. Eventually she fell asleep, clutching crackers in both hands.

Carolyn felt Caitlin's impatient tug at her sleeve. Off they drove to child care, where Vanessa had just dropped off her 18-month-old son, Timmy. Within moments, Caitlin and Timmy were in the sandbox, shoveling sand into plastic cups and buckets with the help of their caregiver, Ginette.

A few weeks later, Grace joined Caitlin and Timmy at Ginette's child-care home. Although still tiny and unable to crawl or walk, she had grown taller and heavier, and her sad, vacant gaze had given way to an alert expression, a ready smile, and an enthusiastic desire to imitate and explore. When Caitlin headed for the sandbox, Grace stretched out her arms, asking Ginette to carry her there, too. Soon Grace was pulling herself up at every opportunity. Finally, at age 18 months, she walked!

This chapter traces physical growth during the first two years—one of the most remarkable and busiest times of development. We will see how rapid changes in the infant's body and brain support learning, motor skills, and perceptual capacities. Caitlin, Grace, and Timmy will join us along the way to illustrate individual differences and environmental influences on physical development.

Body Growth

TAKE A MOMENT... The next time you're walking in your neighborhood or at the mall, observe the contrast between the capabilities of infants and those of toddlers. One reason for the vast changes in what children can do over the first two years is that their bodies change enormously—faster than at any other time after birth.

Changes in Body Size and Muscle–Fat Makeup

By the end of the first year, a typical infant's height is about 32 inches—more than 50 percent greater than at birth. By 2 years, it is nearly 75 percent greater (36 inches). Similarly, by 5 months of age, birth weight has doubled, to about 15 pounds. At 1 year it has tripled, to 22 pounds, and at 2 years it has quadrupled, to about 30 pounds. Figure 4.1 illustrates this dramatic increase in body size.

One of the most obvious changes in infants' appearance is their transformation into round, plump babies by the middle of the first year. This early rise in "baby fat," which peaks at about 9 months, helps the small infant maintain a constant body temperature. In the second year, most toddlers slim down, a trend that continues into middle childhood (Fomon & Nelson, 2002). In contrast, muscle tissue increases very slowly during infancy and will not reach a peak until adolescence. Babies are not very muscular; their strength and physical coordination are limited.

Individual and Group Differences

In infancy, girls are slightly shorter and lighter than boys, with a higher ratio of fat to muscle. These small sex differences persist throughout early and middle childhood and are greatly magnified at adolescence. Ethnic differences in body size are apparent as well. Grace was below the *growth norms* (height and weight averages for children her age). Early malnutrition contributed, but even after substantial catch-up Grace—as is typical for Asian children—remained below North American norms. In contrast, Timmy is slightly above average, as African-American children tend to be (Bogin, 2001).

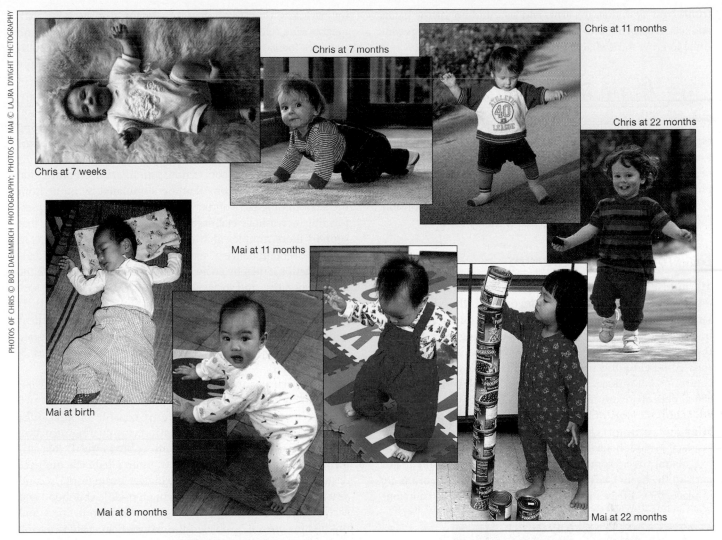

Chris at 7 weeks

Chris at 7 months

Chris at 11 months

Chris at 22 months

Mai at birth

Mai at 11 months

Mai at 8 months

Mai at 22 months

■ **FIGURE 4.1** ■ **Body growth during the first two years.** These photos depict the dramatic changes in body size and proportions during infancy and toddlerhood in two individuals—a boy, Chris, and a girl, Mai. In the first year, the head is quite large in proportion to the rest of the body, and height and weight gain are especially rapid. During the second year, the lower portion of the body catches up. Notice, also, how both children added "baby fat" in the early months of life and then slimmed down, a trend that continues into middle childhood.

Children of the same age also differ in *rate* of physical growth; some progress more rapidly than others. The best way of estimating a child's physical maturity is to use *skeletal age,* a measure of bone development. It is determined by X-raying the long bones of the body to see the extent to which soft, pliable cartilage has hardened into bone, a gradual process that is completed in adolescence. When skeletal ages are examined, African-American children tend to be slightly ahead of Caucasian children at all ages, and girls are considerably ahead of boys (Tanner, Healy, & Cameron, 2001). Girls' greater physical maturity may contribute to their greater resistance to harmful environmental influences. As noted in Chapter 2, girls experience fewer developmental problems and have lower infant and childhood mortality rates.

Changes in Body Proportions

As the child's overall size increases, different parts of the body grow at different rates. Two growth patterns describe these changes. The first is the **cephalocaudal trend**—from the Latin for "head to tail." During the prenatal period, the head develops more rapidly than the lower part of the body. At birth, the head takes up one-fourth of total body length, the legs only one-third. Notice how, in Figure 4.1, the lower portion of the body catches up. By age 2, the head accounts for only one-fifth and the legs for nearly one-half of body length.

In the second pattern, the **proximodistal trend,** growth proceeds, literally, from "near to far"—from the center of the body outward. In the prenatal period, the head, chest, and trunk grow first, then the arms and legs, and finally the hands and feet. During infancy and childhood, the arms and legs continue to grow somewhat ahead of the hands and feet.

Brain Development

At birth, the brain is nearer to its adult size than any other physical structure, and it continues to develop at an astounding pace throughout infancy and toddlerhood. We can best understand brain growth by looking at it from two vantage points: (1) the microscopic level of individual brain cells and (2) the larger level of the cerebral cortex, which is responsible for the highly developed intelligence of our species.

Development of Neurons

The human brain has 100 to 200 billion **neurons,** or nerve cells that store and transmit information, many of which have thousands of direct connections with other neurons. Unlike other body cells, neurons are not tightly packed together. Between them are **synapses**—tiny gaps where fibers from different neurons come close together but do not touch (see Figure 4.2). Neurons send messages to one another by releasing chemicals called **neurotransmitters,** which cross the synapse.

The basic story of brain growth concerns how neurons develop and form this elaborate communication system. In the prenatal period, neurons are produced in the embryo's primitive neural tube. From there, they migrate to form the major parts of the brain (see page 64 in Chapter 3). Once neurons are in place, they differentiate, establishing their unique functions

■ **FIGURE 4.2** ■ **Neurons and their connective fibers.** This photograph of several neurons, taken with the aid of a powerful microscope, shows the elaborate synaptic connections that form with neighboring cells.

by extending their fibers to form synaptic connections with neighboring cells. During the first two years, neural fibers and synapses increase at an astounding pace (Huttenlocher, 2002; Moore & Persaud, 2008). Because developing neurons require space for these connective structures, a surprising aspect of brain growth is that as synapses form, many surrounding neurons die—20 to 80 percent, depending on the brain region (de Haan & Johnson, 2003; Stiles, 2001). Fortunately, during the prenatal period, the neural tube produces far more neurons than the brain will ever need.

As neurons form connections, *stimulation* becomes vital to their survival. Neurons that are stimulated by input from the surrounding environment continue to establish synapses, forming increasingly elaborate systems of communication that support more complex abilities. At first, stimulation results in massive overabundance of synapses, many of which serve identical functions, thereby ensuring that the child will acquire the motor, cognitive, and social skills that our species needs to survive. Neurons that are seldom stimulated soon lose their synapses, in a process called **synaptic pruning** that returns neurons not needed at the moment to an uncommitted state so they can support future development (Nelson, Thomas, & de Haan, 2006).

If few neurons are produced after the prenatal period, what causes the dramatic increase in brain size during the first two years? About half the brain's volume consists of **glial cells,** which are responsible for **myelination,** the coating of neural fibers with an insulating fatty sheath (called *myelin*) that improves the efficiency of message transfer. Glial cells multiply dramatically from the end of pregnancy through the second year of life, a process that slows through middle childhood and accelerates again in adolescence. Gains in neural fibers and myelination are responsible for the extraordinary gain in overall size of the brain—from nearly 30 percent of its adult weight at birth to 70 percent by age 2 (Johnson, 2005; Thatcher et al., 1996).

Brain development can be compared to molding a "living sculpture." After neurons and synapses are overproduced, cell death and synaptic pruning sculpt away excess building material to form the mature brain—a process jointly influenced by genetically programmed events and the child's experiences. The resulting sculpture is a set of interconnected regions, each with specific functions—much like countries on a globe that communicate with one another (Johnston et al., 2001).

Neurophysiological Methods

This "geography" of the brain permits researchers to study its developing organization and the activity of its regions. To do so, scientists use *neurophysiological methods* (see Table 4.1).

For example, *EEG brain-wave patterns* can be examined for stability and organization—signs of mature cortical functioning. As the individual processes a stimulus, *ERPs* detect the general location of brain-wave activity in the cerebral cortex—a method often used to study preverbal infants' responsiveness to various stimuli and the impact of experience on specialization of cortical regions (DeBoer, Scott, & Nelson, 2007).

■ **TABLE 4.1** ■ *Methods for Measuring Brain Functioning*

METHOD	DESCRIPTION
Electroencephalogram (EEG)	Electrodes, usually embedded in a head cap, are attached to the scalp with conductive gel to record electrical brain-wave activity in the brain's outer layers—the cerebral cortex.
Event-related potentials (ERPs)	Using the EEG, the frequency and amplitude of brain waves in response to particular stimuli (such as a picture, music, or speech) are recorded in the cerebral cortex. Enables identification of general regions of stimulus-induced activity.
Functional magnetic resonance imaging (fMRI)	While the person lies inside a tunnel-shaped apparatus that creates a magnetic field, a scanner magnetically detects increased blood flow and oxygen metabolism in areas of the brain as the individual processes particular stimuli. The result is a computerized moving picture of activity anywhere in the brain (not just its outer layers).
Positron emission tomography (PET)	After injection or inhalation of a radioactive substance, the person lies inside an apparatus with a scanner that emits fine streams of X-rays, which detect increased blood flow and oxygen metabolism in areas of the brain as the person processes particular stimuli. As with fMRI, the result is a computerized image of activity anywhere in the brain.
Near-Infrared Optical Topography (NIROT)	Using thin, flexible optical fibers attached to the scalp through a head cap, infrared (invisible) light is beamed at the brain; its absorption by areas of the cerebral cortex varies with changes in blood flow and oxygen metabolism as the individual processes particular stimuli. The result is a computerized moving picture of active areas in the cerebral cortex. Unlike fMRI and PET, NIROT is appropriate for infants and young children, who can move within limited range during testing.

Neuroimaging techniques, which yield detailed, three-dimensional computerized pictures of the entire brain and its active areas, provide the most precise information about which brain regions are specialized for certain capacities. The most promising of these methods is fMRI. Unlike PET, fMRI does not depend on X-ray photography. Rather, when an individual is exposed to a stimulus, fMRI detects changes in blood flow and oxygen metabolism magnetically, yielding a colorful, moving picture of parts of the brain used to process information or perform an activity (see Figure 4.3a and b).

Because PET and fMRI require the participant to lie as motionless as possible in an enclosed space, they are not suitable for infants and young children (Nelson, Thomas, & de Haan, 2006). A neuroimaging technique that works well in infancy and early childhood is NIROT. Because the apparatus consists only of optical fibers attached to the scalp using a head cap, a baby can sit on the parent's lap and move during testing—as Figure 4.3c illustrates (Meek, 2002; Taga et al., 2003). Unlike PET and fMRI, which map activity changes throughout the brain, NIROT is limited to examining the functioning of the cerebral cortex.

Development of the Cerebral Cortex

The **cerebral cortex** surrounds the rest of the brain, resembling half of a shelled walnut. It is the largest, most complex brain structure—accounting for 85 percent of the brain's weight and containing the greatest number of neurons and synapses. Because it is also the last brain structure to stop growing, it is

■ **FIGURE 4.3** ■ **Functional magnetic resonance imaging (fMRI) and NIROT.** (a) This 6-year-old is part of a study that uses fMRI to find out how his brain processes light and motion. (b) The fMRI image shows which areas of the child's brain are active while he views changing visual stimuli. (c) Here, NIROT is used to investigate a 2-month-old's response to a visual stimulus. During testing, the baby can move freely within a limited range. (Photo (c) from G. Taga, K. Asakawa, A. Maki, Y. Konishi, & H. Koizumi, 2003, "Brain Imaging in Awake Infants by Near-Infrared Optical Topography," *Proceedings of the National Academy of Sciences, 100,* p. 10723. Reprinted by permission.)

sensitive to environmental influences for a much longer period than any other part of the brain.

■ **REGIONS OF THE CORTEX.**   Figure 4.4 shows specific functions of regions of the cerebral cortex. The order in which cortical regions develop corresponds to the order in which various capacities emerge in the infant and growing child. For example, a burst of synaptic growth occurs in the auditory and visual cortexes and in areas responsible for body movement over the first year—a period of dramatic gains in auditory and visual perception and mastery of motor skills (Johnson, 2005). Language areas are especially active from late infancy through the preschool years, when language development flourishes (Pujol et al., 2006; Thompson, 2000).

The cortical regions with the most extended period of development are the *frontal lobes,* which are responsible for thought—in particular, consciousness, inhibition of impulses, integration of information, and use of memory, reasoning, planning, and problem-solving strategies. From age 2 months on, the frontal lobes function more effectively. But they undergo especially rapid myelination and formation and pruning of synapses during the preschool and school years, followed by another period of accelerated growth in adolescence, when the frontal lobes reach an adult level of synapses (Nelson, 2002; Nelson, Thomas, & de Haan, 2006; Sowell et al., 2002).

■ **LATERALIZATION AND PLASTICITY OF THE CORTEX.**
The cerebral cortex has two *hemispheres,* or sides, that differ in their functions. Some tasks are done mostly by the left hemisphere, others by the right. For example, each hemisphere receives sensory information from the side of the body opposite to it and controls only that side.[1] For most of us, the left hemisphere is largely responsible for verbal abilities (such as spoken and written language) and positive emotion (such as joy). The right hemisphere handles spatial abilities (judging distances, reading maps, and recognizing geometric shapes) and negative emotion (such as distress) (Banish & Heller, 1998; Nelson & Bosquet, 2000). In left-handed people, this pattern may be reversed—or, more commonly, the cerebral cortex may be less clearly specialized than in right-handers.

Why does this specialization of the two hemispheres, called **lateralization,** occur? Studies using fMRI reveal that the left hemisphere is better at processing information in a sequential, analytic (piece-by-piece) way, a good approach for dealing with communicative information—both verbal (language) and emotional (a joyful smile). In contrast, the right hemisphere is specialized for processing information in a holistic, integrative manner, ideal for making sense of spatial information and regulating negative emotion. A lateralized brain is certainly adaptive (Rogers, 2000). It permits a wider array of functions to be

---

[1]The eyes are an exception. Messages from the right half of each retina go to the right hemisphere; messages from the left half of each retina go to the left hemisphere. Thus, visual information from *both* eyes is received by *both* hemispheres.

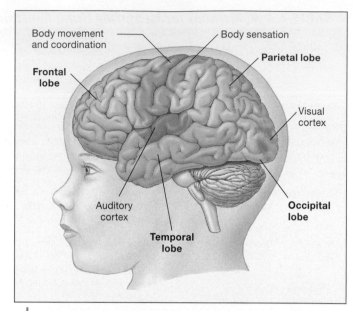

■ **FIGURE 4.4** ■ **The left side of the human brain, showing the cerebral cortex.** The cortex is divided into different lobes, each containing a variety of regions with specific functions. Some major regions are labeled here.

carried out effectively than if both sides processed information in the same way.

Researchers study the timing of brain lateralization to learn more about **brain plasticity.** A highly *plastic* cerebral cortex, in which many areas are not yet committed to specific functions, has a high capacity for learning. And if a part of the cortex is damaged, other parts can take over tasks it would have handled. But once the hemispheres lateralize, damage to a specific region means that the abilities it controls cannot be recovered as fully or as easily as earlier.

At birth, the hemispheres have already begun to specialize. Most newborns show greater ERP brain-wave activity in the left hemisphere while listening to speech sounds or displaying a positive state of arousal. In contrast, the right hemisphere reacts more strongly to nonspeech sounds and to stimuli (such as a sour-tasting fluid) that evoke a negative reaction (Davidson, 1994; Fox & Davidson, 1986).

Nevertheless, research on brain-damaged children and adults offers dramatic evidence for substantial plasticity in the young brain. Among preschoolers with brain injuries sustained in the first year of life, deficits in language and spatial abilities were milder than those observed in brain-injured adults (Akshoomoff et al., 2002; Stiles et al., 2005). As the children gained perceptual, motor, and cognitive experiences, other stimulated cortical structures compensated for the damaged areas, regardless of the site of injury. Still, mild deficits in complex skills, such as reading, math, and telling stories, were evident in the school years—the price these children pay for massive brain reorganization. When healthy brain regions take over the functions of damaged areas, multiple tasks must be done by a smaller-than-usual volume of brain tissue, so the brain processes information less quickly and accurately than it would if it were intact (Huttenlocher, 2002).

Another illustration of how early experience greatly influences brain organization comes from studies of deaf adults who, as infants and children, learned sign language (a spatial skill). Compared with hearing adults, these individuals depend more on the right hemisphere for language processing (Neville & Bavelier, 2002). Also, toddlers who are advanced in language development show greater left-hemispheric specialization for language than their more slowly developing agemates (Luna et al., 2001; Mills et al., 2005). Apparently, the very process of acquiring language and other skills promotes lateralization.

In sum, the brain is more plastic during the first few years than it will ever be again. An overabundance of synaptic connections supports brain plasticity and, therefore, young children's ability to learn, which is fundamental to their survival.

Sensitive Periods in Brain Development

Animal studies confirm that early, extreme sensory deprivation results in permanent brain damage and loss of functions—findings that verify the existence of sensitive periods in brain development. For example, early, varied visual experiences must occur for the brain's visual centers to develop normally. If a 1-month-old kitten is deprived of light for just three or four days, these areas of the brain degenerate. If the kitten is kept in the dark during the fourth week of life and beyond, damage is severe and permanent (Crair, Gillespie, & Stryker, 1998). And the general quality of the early environment affects overall brain growth. When animals reared from birth in physically and socially stimulating surroundings are compared with those reared in isolation, the brains of the stimulated animals show much denser synaptic connections (Greenough & Black, 1992).

■ **HUMAN EVIDENCE: VICTIMS OF DEPRIVED EARLY ENVIRONMENTS.** For ethical reasons, we cannot deliberately deprive some infants of normal rearing experiences and observe the impact on their brains and competencies. Instead, we must turn to natural experiments, in which children were victims of deprived early environments that were later rectified. Such studies are consistent with the animal evidence just described.

In one investigation, researchers followed the progress of a large sample of children transferred between birth and 3½ years from extremely deprived Romanian orphanages to adoptive families in Great Britain (Beckett et al., 2006; O'Connor et al., 2000; Rutter et al., 1998, 2004). On arrival, most were impaired in all domains of development. By the preschool years, catch-up in physical size was dramatic. Cognitive catch-up, assessed at ages 6 and 11, was impressive for children adopted before 6 months, who attained average mental test scores and performed as well as a comparison group of early-adopted British-born children. But Romanian children who had been institutionalized for more than the first six months showed persisting intellectual deficits. And most had serious mental health problems, such as inattention, overactivity, and unruly behavior, that

are seldom seen in children adopted before 6 months of age (Kreppner et al., 2007).

Additional evidence shows that the chronic stress of early, deprived orphanage rearing disrupts the brain's capacity to manage stress, with long-term physical and psychological consequences. In another investigation, researchers followed children who had spent their first eight months or more in Romanian institutions and were then adopted into Canadian homes (Gunnar et al., 2001; Gunnar & Cheatham, 2003). Compared with agemates adopted shortly after birth, these children showed extreme stress reactivity, as indicated by high concentrations of the stress hormone *cortisol* in their saliva—a physiological response linked to persistent illness and learning and behavior problems.

In other investigations, orphanage children displayed abnormally low cortisol—a blunted stress response that may be the central nervous system's adaptation to earlier, frequent cortisol elevations (Carlson & Earls, 1997; Gunnar & Vasquez, 2001). Extremely low cortisol interferes with release of growth hormone (GH) and, thus, can stunt physical growth.

© ANDREW HOLBROOKE/CORBIS

These children, in an orphanage in Romania, receive very little adult contact or stimulation. The longer they remain in this barren environment, the more they will withdraw and wither, displaying profound impairments in all domains of development.

■ **APPROPRIATE STIMULATION.** Unlike the orphanage children just described, Grace, whom Monica and Kevin had adopted in Cambodia at 16 months of age, showed favorable progress. Two years earlier, they had adopted Grace's older brother, Eli. When Eli was 2 years old, Monica and Kevin sent a letter and a photo of Eli to his biological mother, describing a bright, happy child. The next day, the Cambodian mother tearfully asked an adoption agency to send her baby daughter to join Eli and his American family.

Although Grace's early environment was very depleted, her biological mother's loving care—holding tenderly, speaking softly, and breastfeeding—may have prevented irreversible damage to her brain. Besides offering gentle, appropriate stimulation, sensitive adult care helps normalize cortisol production in both typically developing and emotionally traumatized infants and young children (Gunnar & Quevedo, 2007; Tarullo & Gunnar, 2006).

In addition to impoverished environments, ones that overwhelm children with expectations beyond their current capacities interfere with the brain's potential. In recent years, expensive early learning centers have sprung up, in which infants are trained with letter and number flash cards and slightly older toddlers are given a full curriculum of reading, math, science, art, music, gym, and more. There is no evidence that these programs yield smarter, better "superbabies" (Hirsh-Pasek & Golinkoff, 2003). To the contrary, trying to prime infants with stimulation for which they are not ready can cause them to withdraw, thereby threatening their interest in learning and creating conditions much like stimulus deprivation!

How, then, can we characterize appropriate stimulation during the early years? To answer this question, researchers distinguish between two types of brain development. The first, **experience-expectant brain growth,** refers to the young brain's rapidly developing organization, which depends on ordinary experiences—opportunities to see and touch objects, to hear language and other sounds, and to move about and explore the environment. As a result of millions of years of evolution, the brains of all infants, toddlers, and young children expect to encounter these experiences and, if they do, grow normally. The second type of brain development, **experience-dependent brain growth,** consists of additional growth and refinement of established brain structures as a result of specific learning experiences that occur throughout our lives, varying widely across individuals and cultures (Greenough & Black, 1992). Reading and writing, playing computer games, and practicing the violin are examples. The brain of a violinist differs in certain ways from the brain of a poet because each has exercised different brain regions for a long time (Thompson & Nelson, 2001).

Experience-expectant brain growth occurs early and naturally, as caregivers offer babies and preschoolers age-appropriate play materials and engage them in enjoyable daily routines—a shared meal, a game of peekaboo, a bath before bed, or a picture book to talk about. The resulting growth provides the foundation for later-occurring experience-dependent development (Huttenlocher, 2002; Shonkoff & Phillips, 2001). No evidence exists for a sensitive period in the first few years of life for mastering skills that depend on extensive training, such as reading, musical performance, or gymnastics (Bruer, 1999). To the contrary, rushing early learning harms the brain by overwhelming its neural circuits, thereby reducing the brain's sensitivity to the everyday experiences it needs for a healthy start in life.

Changing States of Arousal

Rapid brain growth means that the organization of sleep and wakefulness changes substantially between birth and age 2, and fussiness and crying also decline. The newborn baby takes round-the-clock naps totaling about 16 to 18 hours (Davis, Parker & Montgomery, 2004). Total sleep time declines slowly; the average 2-year-old still needs 12 to 13 hours. But the sleep–wake pattern increasingly conforms to a night–day schedule. Most 6- to 9-month-olds take two daytime naps; by 18 months, children generally need only one nap. Between ages 3 and 5, napping subsides (Iglowstein et al., 2003).

These changing arousal patterns are due to brain development, but they are also affected by the social environment. In

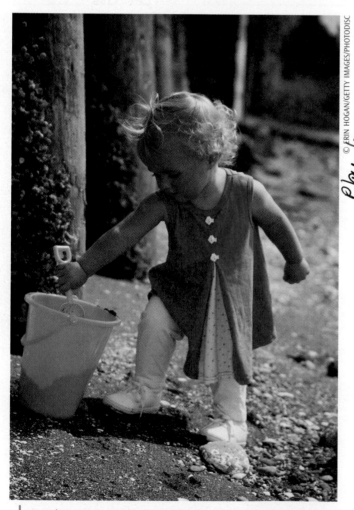

© ERIN HOGAN/GETTY IMAGES/PHOTODISC

Experience-expectant brain growth takes place naturally, through ordinary, stimulating experiences. This toddler, focused on shoveling pebbles into her bucket at the beach, enjoys the type of activity that is best for promoting brain development in the early years.

■ CULTURAL INFLUENCES ■

Cultural Variation in Infant Sleeping Arrangements

For decades, North American child-rearing advice from experts has strongly encouraged the nighttime separation of baby from parent. For example, the most recent edition of Benjamin Spock's *Baby and Child Care* recommends that infants be moved into their own room by 3 months of age, explaining, "By 6 months, a child who regularly sleeps in her parents' room may become dependent on this arrangement" (Spock & Needlman, 2004, p. 60).

Yet parent–infant "cosleeping" is the norm for approximately 90 percent of the world's population, in cultures as diverse as the Japanese, the rural Guatemalan Maya, the Inuit of Canada, and the !Kung of Botswana. Japanese and Korean children usually lie next to their mothers in infancy and early childhood (Takahashi, 1990; Yang & Hahn, 2002). Among the Maya, mother–infant cosleeping is interrupted only by the birth of a new baby, when the older child is moved next to the father or to another bed in the same room (Morelli et al., 1992). Cosleeping is also common in some American subcultures, including African-American families and Appalachian families of eastern Kentucky (Abbott, 1992; Brenner et al., 2003).

Cultural values—specifically, collectivism versus individualism (see Chapter 2)—strongly influence infant sleeping arrangements. In one study, researchers interviewed Guatemalan Mayan mothers and American middle-SES mothers about their sleeping practices. Mayan mothers stressed a collectivist perspective, explaining that cosleeping helps build a close parent–child bond, which children need to learn the ways of people around them. In contrast, American mothers took an individualistic perspective, mentioning the importance of instilling early independence, preventing bad habits, and protecting their own privacy (Morelli et al., 1992).

Over the past 15 years, cosleeping has increased dramatically in Western nations, perhaps because more mothers are breastfeeding. Today, the rate of bedsharing among U.S. mothers of young babies may be as high as 50 percent (Buswell & Spatz, 2007; Willinger et al., 2003). Research suggests that cosleeping evolved to protect infants' survival and health. During the night, cosleeping babies breastfeed three times as long as infants who sleep alone. Because infants arouse to nurse more often when sleeping next to their mothers, some researchers believe that cosleeping may actually help safeguard babies at risk for sudden infant death syndrome (SIDS) (see page 85 in Chapter 3). SIDS is rare in Asian cultures where cosleeping is widespread, including Cambodia, China, Japan, Korea, Thailand, and Vietnam (McKenna, 2002; McKenna & McDade, 2005).

Infant sleeping practices affect other aspects of family life. For example, Mayan babies doze off in the midst of ongoing family activities and are carried to bed by their mothers. In contrast, for many North American parents, bedtime involves an elaborate ritual that takes a good part of the evening. Perhaps bedtime struggles, so common in Western homes but rare elsewhere in the world, are related to the stress young children feel when they are required to fall asleep without assistance (Latz, Wolf, & Lozoff, 1999).

Critics warn that cosleeping children will develop emotional problems, especially excessive dependency. Yet a longitudinal study following children from birth through age 18 showed that young people who had bedshared in the early years were no different from others in any aspect of adjustment (Okami, Weisner, & Olmstead, 2002). Another concern is that infants might become trapped under the parent's body or in soft covers and suffocate. Parents who are obese or who use alcohol, tobacco, or illegal drugs do pose a serious risk to their sleeping babies, as does the use of quilts and comforters or an overly soft mattress (Willinger et al., 2003).

But with appropriate precautions, parents and infants can cosleep safely (McKenna & Volpe, 2007). In cultures where cosleeping is widespread, parents and infants usually sleep with light covering on hard surfaces, such as firm mattresses, floor mats, and wooden planks, or infants sleep in a cradle or hammock next to the parents' bed (McKenna, 2001, 2002). And when sharing the same bed, infants typically lie on their back or side facing the mother—positions that promote frequent, easy communication between parent and baby and arousal if breathing is threatened.

© STEPHEN L. RAYMER/NATIONAL GEOGRAPHIC IMAGE COLLECTION

This Cambodian father and child sleep together—a practice common in their culture and around the globe. The family sleeps on hard wooden surfaces, which protect cosleeping children from entrapment in soft bedding.

Western nations, many parents try to get their babies to sleep through the night around 4 months of age by offering an evening feeding before putting them down in a separate, quiet room. In this way, they push young infants to the limits of their neurological capacities. Not until the middle of the first year is the secretion of *melatonin*, a hormone within the brain that promotes drowsiness, much greater at night than during the day (Sadeh, 1997).

As the Cultural Influences box above reveals, isolating infants to promote sleep is rare elsewhere in the world. When babies sleep with their parents, their average sleep period remains constant at three hours from 1 to 8 months of age. Only at the end of the first year, as REM sleep (the state that usually prompts waking) declines, do infants move in the direction of an adultlike sleep–waking schedule (Ficca et al., 1999).

Influences on Early Physical Growth

Physical growth, like other aspects of development, results from the continuous and complex interplay between genetic and environmental factors. Heredity, nutrition, and emotional well-being all affect early physical growth.

Heredity

Because identical twins are much more alike in body size than fraternal twins, we know that heredity is important in physical growth (Estourgie-van Burk et al., 2006). When diet and health are adequate, height and rate of physical growth are largely determined by heredity. In fact, as long as negative environmental influences such as poor nutrition and illness are not severe, children and adolescents typically show *catch-up growth*—a return to a genetically influenced growth path once conditions improve. Still, the brain, the heart, the digestive system, and many other internal organs may be permanently compromised (Hales & Ozanne, 2003).

Genetic makeup also affects body weight: The weights of adopted children correlate more strongly with those of their biological than of their adoptive parents (Sørensen, Holst, & Stunkard, 1998). At the same time, environment—in particular, nutrition—plays a vital role.

Nutrition

Nutrition is especially crucial for development in the first two years because the baby's brain and body are growing so rapidly. Pound for pound, an infant's energy needs are twice those of an adult. Twenty-five percent of infants' total caloric intake is devoted to growth, and babies need extra calories to keep rapidly developing organs functioning properly (Trahms & Pipes, 1997).

■ **BREASTFEEDING VERSUS BOTTLE-FEEDING.** Babies need not only enough food but the right kind of food. In early infancy, breastfeeding is ideally suited to their needs, and bottled formulas try to imitate it. Applying What We Know on the following page summarizes major nutritional and health advantages of breastfeeding.

Because of these benefits, breastfed babies in poverty-stricken regions are much less likely to be malnourished and 6 to 14 times more likely to survive the first year of life. The World Health Organization (2008b) recommends breastfeeding until age 2 years, with solid foods added at 6 months—practices that, if widely followed, would save the lives of more than a million infants annually. Even breastfeeding for just a few weeks offers some protection against respiratory and intestinal infections, which are devastating to young children in developing countries (Bellamy, 2005).

Yet many mothers in the developing world give their babies commercial formula or low-grade nutrients, such as rice water or highly diluted cow or goat milk, in place of breast milk. Contamination of these foods as a result of poor sanitation is common and often leads to illness and infant death. The United Nations has encouraged all hospitals and maternity units in

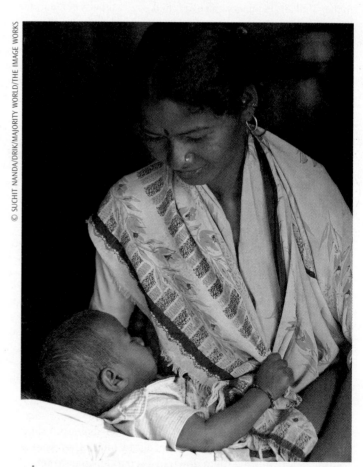

© SUCHIT NANDA/DRIK/MAJORITY WORLD/THE IMAGE WORKS

Breastfeeding is especially important in developing countries, where infants are at risk for malnutrition and early death due to widespread poverty. This baby from a village in India is likely to grow normally during the first year because his mother decided to breastfeed.

Applying What We Know

Reasons to Breastfeed

Nutritional and Health Advantages	Explanation
Provides the correct balance of fat and protein	Compared with the milk of other mammals, human milk is higher in fat and lower in protein. This balance, as well as the unique proteins and fats contained in human milk, is ideal for a rapidly myelinating nervous system.
Ensures nutritional completeness	A mother who breastfeeds need not add other foods to her infant's diet until the baby is 6 months old. The milks of all mammals are low in iron, but the iron contained in breast milk is much more easily absorbed by the baby's system. Consequently, bottle-fed infants need iron-fortified formula.
Helps ensure healthy physical growth	In the first few months, breastfed infants add weight and length slightly faster than bottle-fed infants, who catch up by the end of the first year. One-year-old breastfed babies are leaner (have a higher percentage of muscle to fat), a growth pattern that may help prevent later overweight and obesity.
Protects against many diseases	Breastfeeding transfers antibodies and other infection-fighting agents from mother to child and enhances functioning of the immune system. As a result, compared with bottle-fed infants, breastfed babies have far fewer allergic reactions and respiratory and intestinal illnesses. Breast milk also has anti-inflammatory effects, which ease the severity of illness symptoms. U.S. infant mortality rates are reduced by 21 percent in breastfed infants.

Sources: American Academy of Pediatrics, 2005; Buescher, 2001; Kramer et al., 2003; Weyermann, Rothenbacher, & Brenner, 2006.

developing countries to promote breastfeeding as long as mothers do not have viral or bacterial infections (such as HIV or tuberculosis) that can be transmitted to the baby.

Partly as a result of the natural childbirth movement, breastfeeding has become more common in industrialized nations, especially among well-educated women. Today, 74 percent of American mothers breastfeed, but nearly two-thirds of them of stop after a few months (U.S. Department of Health and Human Services, 2008c). Not surprisingly, mothers who return to work sooner wean their babies from the breast earlier (Kimbro, 2006). But mothers who cannot be with their infants all the time can still combine breast- and bottle-feeding. The U.S. Department of Health and Human Services advises exclusive breastfeeding for the first 6 months and inclusion of breast milk in the baby's diet until at least 1 year.

Women who do not breastfeed sometimes worry that they are depriving their baby of an experience essential for healthy psychological development. Yet breastfed and bottle-fed children in industrialized nations do not differ in emotional adjustment (Fergusson & Woodward, 1999). Some studies report a slight advantage in intelligence test performance for children and adolescents who were breastfed, after controlling for many factors. Most, however, find no cognitive benefits (Der, Batty, & Deary, 2006).

As babies transition to solid foods, a nutritious diet is crucial for healthy growth. Yet interviews with more than 3,000 U.S. parents of 4- to 24-month-olds revealed that many routinely served them french fries, pizza, candy, sugary fruit drinks, and soda. On average, infants consumed 20 percent and toddlers 30 percent more calories than they needed. At the same time, one-third ate no fruits or vegetables (Briefel et al., 2004). Recent evidence indicates a strengthening relationship between rapid weight gain in the first two years and later obesity (Botton et al., 2008; Chomtho et al., 2008).

Malnutrition

In developing countries and war-torn areas where food resources are limited, malnutrition is widespread. About one-third of the world's children under age 5 are affected (Bellamy, 2005; Pronczuk & Surdu, 2008). The 9 percent who are severely malnourished suffer from two dietary diseases. **Marasmus** is a wasted condition of the body caused by a diet low in all essential nutrients. It usually appears in the first year when a baby's mother is too malnourished to produce enough breast milk and bottle-feeding is also inadequate. Her starving baby becomes painfully thin and is in danger of dying. **Kwashiorkor** is caused by an unbalanced diet very low in protein. The disease usually strikes after weaning, between 1 and 3 years of age. It is common in regions where children get just enough calories from starchy foods, but little protein. The child's body responds by breaking down its own protein reserves, which causes swelling of the abdomen and limbs, hair loss, skin rash, and irritable, listless behavior.

Children who survive these extreme forms of malnutrition grow to be smaller in all body dimensions and suffer from lasting damage to the brain, heart, liver, and other organs (Müller & Krawinkel, 2005). When their diets get better, they tend to gain excessive weight (Branca & Ferrari, 2002; Martins et al., 2004). A malnourished body protects itself by establishing a low basal metabolism rate, which may endure after nutrition improves. Also, malnutrition may disrupt appetite control centers in the brain, causing the child to overeat when food becomes plentiful.

Learning and behavior are also seriously affected. One long-term study of marasmic children revealed that an improved diet did not result in catch-up in head size, suggesting permanent loss in brain weight (Stoch et al., 1982). And animal evidence reveals that a deficient diet alters the production of neurotransmitters in the brain—an effect that can disrupt all

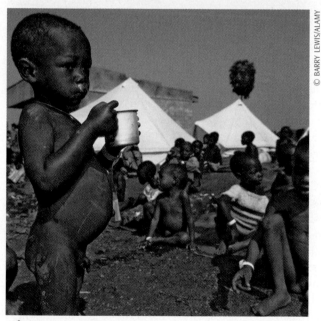

Top photo: This baby of Niger, Africa, has marasmus, a wasted condition caused by a diet low in all essential nutrients. *Bottom photo:* The swollen abdomen of this toddler, who lives in a Rwandan refugee camp, is a symptom of kwashiorkor, which results from a diet very low in protein. If they survive, these children are likely to suffer stunted growth, damage to vital organs, and lasting intellectual and emotional impairments.

aspects of development (Haller, 2005). These children score low on intelligence tests, show poor fine-motor coordination, and have difficulty paying attention (Galler et al., 1990; Liu et al., 2003). They also display a more intense stress response to fear-arousing situations, perhaps caused by the constant, gnawing pain of hunger (Fernald & Grantham-McGregor, 1998).

Inadequate nutrition is not confined to developing countries. Because government-supported supplementary food programs do not reach all families in need, an estimated 17 percent of U.S. children suffer from *food insecurity*—uncertain access to enough food for a healthy, active life. Food insecurity is especially high among single-parent and low-income ethnic minority families (U.S. Census Bureau, 2008). Although few of these children have marasmus or kwashiorkor, their physical growth and ability to learn are still affected.

Emotional Well-Being

We may not think of affection and stimulation as necessary for healthy physical growth, but they are just as vital as food. **Nonorganic failure to thrive,** a growth disorder resulting from lack of parental love, is usually present by 18 months of age. Infants who have it show all the signs of marasmus—their bodies look wasted, and they are withdrawn and apathetic. But no organic (or biological) cause for the baby's failure to grow can be found (Black, 2005).

Lana, an observant nurse at a public health clinic, became concerned about 8-month-old Melanie, who was 3 pounds lighter than she had been at her last checkup. Lana noted that Melanie kept her eyes on nearby adults, anxiously watching their every move, rarely smiling, and avoiding her mother's gaze (Steward, 2001). During feeding, diaper changing, and play, Melanie's mother sometimes acted cold and distant, at other times impatient and hostile (Hagekull, Bohlin, & Rydell, 1997). Often an unhappy marriage and parental psychological disturbance contribute to these serious caregiving problems (Drotar, Pallotta, & Eckerle, 1994; Duniz et al., 1996). Sometimes the baby is irritable and displays abnormal feeding behaviors, such as poor sucking or vomiting—circumstances that stress the parent–child relationship further (Linscheid, Budd, & Rasnake, 2005).

In Melanie's case, her alcoholic father was out of work, and her parents argued constantly. Melanie's mother had little energy to meet Melanie's psychological needs. When treated early, by helping parents or placing the baby in a caring foster home, failure-to-thrive infants show quick catch-up growth. But if the disorder is not corrected in infancy, most of these children remain small and show lasting cognitive and emotional difficulties (Drewett, Corbett, & Wright, 2006; Dykman et al., 2001).

ASK YOURSELF

>> **REVIEW**
Explain why breastfeeding can have lifelong consequences for the development of babies born in poverty-stricken regions of the world.

>> **APPLY**
Ten-month-old Shaun is below average in height and painfully thin. He has one of two serious growth disorders. Name them, and indicate what clues you would look for to tell which one Shaun has.

>> **REFLECT**
Imagine that you are the parent of a newborn baby. Describe feeding practices you would use, and ones you would avoid, to prevent overweight and obesity.

Learning Capacities

Learning refers to changes in behavior as the result of experience. Babies are capable of two basic forms of learning, which were introduced in Chapter 1: classical and operant conditioning. They also learn through their natural preference for novel stimulation. Finally, shortly after birth, babies learn by observing others; they can imitate the facial expressions and gestures of adults.

Classical Conditioning

Newborn reflexes, discussed in Chapter 3, make **classical conditioning** possible in the young infant. In this form of learning, a neutral stimulus is paired with a stimulus that leads to a reflexive response. Once the baby's nervous system makes the connection between the two stimuli, the neutral stimulus produces the behavior by itself. Classical conditioning helps infants recognize which events usually occur together in the everyday world, so they can anticipate what is about to happen next. As a result, the environment becomes more orderly and predictable. Let's take a closer look at the steps of classical conditioning.

As Carolyn settled down in the rocking chair to nurse Caitlin, she often stroked her baby's forehead. Soon Carolyn noticed that each time she did this, Caitlin made sucking movements.

Caitlin had been classically conditioned. Here is how it happened (see Figure 4.5):

1. Before learning takes place, an **unconditioned stimulus (UCS)** must consistently produce a reflexive, or **unconditioned, response (UCR)**. In Caitlin's case, sweet breast milk (UCS) resulted in sucking (UCR).
2. To produce learning, a *neutral stimulus* that does not lead to the reflex is presented just before, or at about the same time as, the UCS. Carolyn stroked Caitlin's forehead as each nursing period began. The stroking (neutral stimulus) was paired with the taste of milk (UCS).
3. If learning has occurred, the neutral stimulus by itself produces a response similar to the reflexive response. The neutral stimulus is then called a **conditioned stimulus (CS)**, and the response it elicits is called a **conditioned response (CR)**. We know that Caitlin has been classically conditioned because stroking her forehead outside the feeding situation (CS) results in sucking (CR).

If the CS is presented alone enough times, without being paired with the UCS, the CR will no longer occur, an outcome called *extinction*. In other words, if Carolyn repeatedly strokes Caitlin's forehead without feeding her, Caitlin will gradually stop sucking in response to stroking.

Young infants can be classically conditioned most easily when the association between two stimuli has survival value.

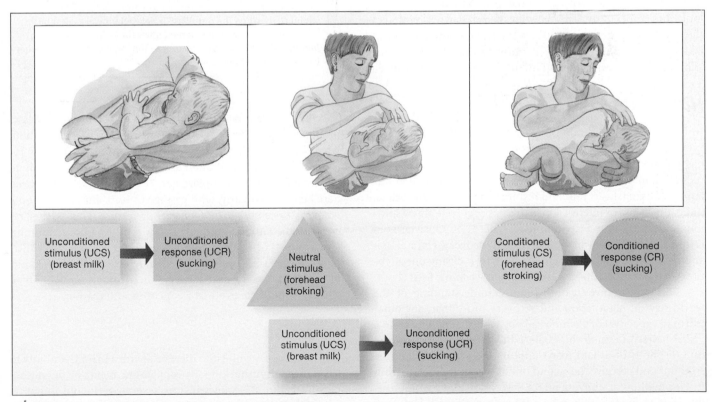

■ **FIGURE 4.5** ■ **The steps of classical conditioning.** This example shows how Caitlin's mother classically conditioned her to make sucking movements by stroking her forehead at the beginning of feedings.

Learning which stimuli regularly accompany feeding improves the infant's ability to get food and survive (Blass, Ganchrow, & Steiner, 1984). In contrast, some responses, such as fear, are very difficult to classically condition in young babies. Until infants have the motor skills to escape unpleasant events, they have no biological need to form these associations.

Operant Conditioning

In classical conditioning, babies build expectations about stimulus events in the environment, but their behavior does not influence the stimuli that occur. In **operant conditioning,** infants act, or *operate,* on the environment, and stimuli that follow their behavior change the probability that the behavior will occur again. A stimulus that increases the occurrence of a response is called a **reinforcer.** For example, sweet liquid *reinforces* the sucking response in newborns. Removing a desirable stimulus or presenting an unpleasant one to decrease the occurrence of a response is called **punishment.** A sour-tasting fluid *punishes* newborns' sucking response, causing them to purse their lips and stop sucking entirely.

Many stimuli besides food can also serve as reinforcers of infant behavior. For example, newborns will suck faster on a nipple when their rate of sucking produces interesting sights and sounds, making operant conditioning a powerful tool for finding out what stimuli babies can perceive and which ones they prefer. Operant conditioning also plays a vital role in the formation of social relationships. As the baby gazes into the adult's eyes, the adult looks and smiles back, and then the infant looks and smiles again. The behavior of each partner reinforces the other, so both continue their pleasurable interaction. In Chapter 6, we will see that this contingent responsiveness contributes to the development of infant–caregiver attachment.

Habituation

At birth, the human brain is set up to be attracted to novelty. Infants tend to respond more strongly to a new element that has entered their environment. **Habituation** refers to a gradual reduction in the strength of a response due to repetitive stimulation. Looking, heart rate, and respiration rate may all decline, indicating a loss of interest. Once this has occurred, a new stimulus—a change in the environment—causes responsiveness to return to a high level, an increase called **recovery.** Habituation and recovery promote efficient learning by focusing our attention on those aspects of the environment we know least about.

Researchers investigating infants' understanding of the world rely on habituation and recovery more than any other learning capacity. For example, a baby who first *habituates* to a visual pattern (a photo of a baby) and then *recovers* to a new one (a photo of a bald man) appears to remember the first stimulus and perceive the second one as new and different from it. This method of studying infant perception and cognition, illustrated in Figure 4.6, can be used with newborns, including preterm infants.

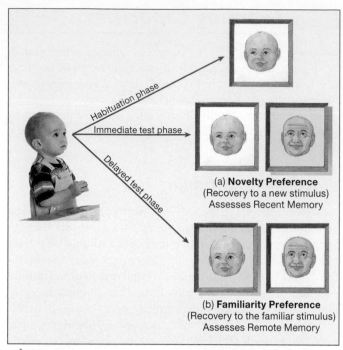

(a) Novelty Preference
(Recovery to a new stimulus)
Assesses Recent Memory

(b) Familiarity Preference
(Recovery to the familiar stimulus)
Assesses Remote Memory

■ **FIGURE 4.6** ■ **Using habituation to study infant memory and knowledge.** In the habituation phase, infants view a photo of a baby until their looking declines. In the test phase, infants are again shown the baby photo, but this time it appears alongside a photo of a bald-headed man. (a) When the test phase occurs soon after the habituation phase (within minutes, hours, or days, depending on the age of the infants), participants who remember the baby face and distinguish it from the man's face show a *novelty preference*; they recover to (spend more time looking at) the new stimulus. (b) When the test phase is delayed for weeks or months, participants who continue to remember the baby face shift to a *familiarity preference*; they recover to the familiar baby face rather than to the novel man's face.

Recovery to a new stimulus, or *novelty preference,* assesses infants' *recent memory.* **TAKE A MOMENT...** Think about what happens when you return to a place you have not seen for a long time. Instead of attending to novelty, you are likely to focus on aspects that are familiar: "I recognize that. I've been here before!" Similarly, with passage of time, infants *shift from a novelty preference to a familiarity preference.* That is, they recover to the familiar stimulus rather than to a novel stimulus (see Figure 4.6) (Bahrick & Pickens, 1995; Courage & Howe, 1998). By focusing on that shift, researchers can also use habituation to assess *remote memory,* or memory for stimuli to which infants were exposed weeks or months earlier.

Imitation

Newborn babies come into the world with a primitive ability to learn through **imitation**—by copying the behavior of another person. Figure 4.7 shows infants several weeks old imitating adult facial expressions (Meltzoff & Moore, 1977). The newborn's capacity to imitate extends to certain gestures, such as head movements, and has been demonstrated in many ethnic groups and cultures (Meltzoff & Kuhl, 1994; Nagy et al., 2005). As the figure reveals, even newborn chimpanzees, our closest primate relatives, imitate some facial expressions (Myowa-Yamakoshi et al., 2004).

Although newborns' capacity to imitate is widely accepted, a few studies have failed to reproduce the findings (see, for example, Anisfeld et al., 2001). And because newborn mouth and tongue movements occur with increased frequency to

■ **FIGURE 4.7** ■ **Imitation by human and chimpanzee newborns.** The human infants in the middle row imitating (left) tongue protrusion and (right) mouth opening are 2 to 3 weeks old. The chimpanzee imitating both facial expressions is 2 weeks old. (From A. N. Meltzoff & M. K. Moore, 1977, "Imitation of Facial and Manual Gestures by Human Neonates," *Science, 198,* p. 75; and M. Myowa-Yamakoshi et al., 2004, "Imitation in Neonatal Chimpanzees (Pan Troglodytes)," *Developmental Science, 7,* p. 440. Copyright © 1977 by AAAS, copyright 2004 by Blackwell Publishing. Reprinted by permission.)

almost any arousing change in stimulation (such as lively music or flashing lights), some researchers argue that certain newborn "imitative" responses are actually mouthing—a common early exploratory response to interesting stimuli (Jones, 2006). Others claim that newborns imitate a variety of facial expressions and head movements with effort and determination, even after short delays—when the adult is no longer demonstrating the behavior (Hayne, 2002; Meltzoff & Moore, 1999).

According to Andrew Meltzoff, newborns imitate much as older children and adults do—by actively trying to match body movements they *see* with ones they *feel* themselves make (Meltzoff, 2007). Scientists have identified specialized cells in motor areas of the cerebral cortex in primates—called **mirror neurons**—that underlie this capacity (Rizzolatti & Craighero, 2004). Mirror neurons fire identically when a primate sees or hears an action and when it carries out that action on its own. Human adults have especially elaborate systems of mirror neurons, which enable us to observe another's behavior (such as smiling or throwing a ball) while simulating the behavior in our own brain. Mirror neurons are believed to be the biological basis of a variety of interrelated, complex social abilities, including imitation, empathic sharing of emotions, and understanding others' intentions (Iocaboni et al., 2005; Schulte-Ruther et al., 2007).

Still, Meltzoff and Moore's view of newborn imitation as a flexible, voluntary capacity remains controversial. Mirror neurons, although possibly functional at birth, undergo an extended period of development (Bertenthal & Longo, 2007; Lepage & Théoret, 2007). Similarly, as we will see in Chapter 5, the capacity to imitate expands greatly over the first two years. But however limited it is at birth, imitation is a powerful means of learning. Using imitation, infants explore their social world and get to know people by matching their behavioral states. As babies notice similarities between their own and others' actions, they learn about themselves. And by tapping into infants' ability to imitate, adults can get infants to express desirable behaviors. Finally, caregivers take great pleasure in a baby who imitates, which helps get the parent–infant relationship off to a good start.

ASK YOURSELF

>> **REVIEW**
Provide an example of classical conditioning, of operant conditioning, and of habituation/recovery in young infants. Why is each type of learning useful?

>> **APPLY**
Nine-month-old Byron has a toy with large, colored push buttons on it. Each time he pushes a button, he hears a nursery tune. Which learning capacity is the toy's manufacturer taking advantage of? What can Byron's play with the toy reveal about his perception of sound patterns?

Motor Development

Carolyn, Monica, and Vanessa each kept a baby book, filled with proud notations about when their children first reached for objects, sat by themselves, and walked alone. Parents are understandably excited about these new motor skills, which allow babies to master the environment in new ways. For example, reaching permits babies to find out about objects by acting on them. Sitting upright gives infants a new perspective on the world. And when infants can move on their own, exploration multiplies.

Babies' motor achievements have a powerful effect on their social relationships. When Caitlin crawled at 7½ months, Carolyn and David began to restrict her movements. When she walked three days after her first birthday, the first "testing of wills" occurred (Biringen et al., 1995). Despite her mother's warnings, she sometimes pulled items from shelves that were off limits. "Don't do that!" Carolyn would say firmly while redirecting Caitlin's attention. At the same time, newly walking babies more actively attend to and initiate social interaction (Clearfield, Obsborn, & Mullen, 2008). Caitlin frequently toddled over to her parents to express a greeting or hold out a picture book to look at. And Caitlin's delight as she worked on new motor skills triggered pleasurable reactions in others, which encouraged her efforts. Motor, social, cognitive, and language competencies developed together and supported one another.

The Sequence of Motor Development

Gross-motor development refers to control over actions that help infants get around in the environment, such as crawling, standing, and walking. *Fine-motor development* has to do with smaller movements, such as reaching and grasping. Table 4.2 shows the average age at which North American infants and toddlers achieve a variety of gross- and fine-motor skills. It also presents the age ranges during which most babies accomplish each skill, indicating large individual differences in *rate* of motor progress. We would be concerned about a child's development only if many motor skills were seriously delayed.

Children acquire motor skills in highly individual ways. Many influences—both internal and external to the child—support the vast gains in motor competences of the first two years.

Motor Skills as Dynamic Systems

According to **dynamic systems theory of motor development,** mastery of motor skills involves acquiring increasingly complex

■ **TABLE 4.2** ■ *Gross- and Fine-Motor Development in the First Two Years*

MOTOR SKILL	AVERAGE AGE ACHIEVED	AGE RANGE IN WHICH 90 PERCENT OF INFANTS ACHIEVE THE SKILL
When held upright, holds head erect and steady	6 weeks	3 weeks–4 months
When prone, lifts self by arms	2 months	3 weeks–4 months
Rolls from side to back	2 months	3 weeks–5 months
Grasps cube	3 months, 3 weeks	2–7 months
Rolls from back to side	4½ months	2–7 months
Sits alone	7 months	5–9 months
Crawls	7 months	5–11 months
Pulls to stand	8 months	5–12 months
Plays pat-a-cake	9 months, 3 weeks	7–15 months
Stands alone	11 months	9–16 months
Walks alone	11 months, 3 weeks	9–17 months
Builds tower of two cubes	11 months, 3 weeks	10–19 months
Scribbles vigorously	14 months	10–21 months
Walks up stairs with help	16 months	12–23 months
Jumps in place	23 months, 2 weeks	17–30 months
Walks on tiptoe	25 months	16–30 months

Sources: Bayley, 1969, 1993, 2005.

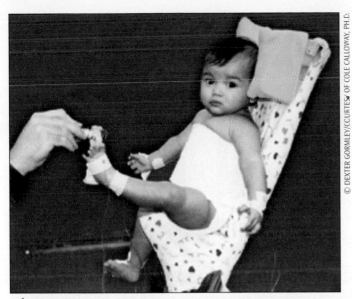

■ FIGURE 4.8 ■ Reaching "feet first." When sounding toys were held in front of babies' hands and feet, they reached with their feet as early as 8 weeks of age, a month or more before they reached with their hands—a clear violation of the cephalocaudal pattern. This 2½-month-old skillfully explores an object with her foot.

systems of action. When motor skills work as a *system,* separate abilities blend together, each cooperating with others to produce more effective ways of exploring and controlling the environment. For example, control of the head and upper chest combine into sitting with support. Kicking, rocking on all fours, and reaching combine to become crawling. And standing, stepping, and improved upright postural control unite into walking (Adolph & Berger, 2006; Thelen, 1989).

Each new skill is a joint product of four factors: (1) central nervous system development, (2) the body's movement capacities, (3) the goals the child has in mind, and (4) environmental supports for the skill. Change in any element makes the system less stable, and the child starts to explore and select new, more effective motor patterns.

When a skill is first acquired, infants must refine it. For example, in learning to walk, toddlers practice six or more hours a day, traveling the length of 29 football fields! Gradually their small, unsteady steps change to a longer stride, their feet move closer together, their toes point to the front, and their legs become symmetrically coordinated (Adolph, Vereijken, & Shrout, 2003). As movements are repeated thousands of times, they promote new connections in the brain that govern motor patterns.

■ DYNAMIC MOTOR SYSTEMS IN ACTION. To find out how babies acquire motor capacities, some studies have tracked their first attempts at a skill until it became smooth and effortless. In one investigation, researchers held sounding toys alternately in front of infants' hands and feet, from the time they showed interest until they engaged in well-coordinated reaching and grasping (Galloway & Thelen, 2004). As Figure 4.8 shows, the infants violated the cephalocaudal trend (reaching with hands before feet), long believed to characterize the sequence of

motor development. Instead, the babies first reached for the toys with their feet—as early as 8 weeks of age, at least a month before reaching with their hands!

Why did babies reach "feet first"? Because the hip joint constrains the legs to move less freely than the shoulder constrains the arms, infants could more easily control their leg movements. Consequently, foot reaching required far less practice than hand reaching. As these findings confirm, rather than following a strict cephalocaudal pattern, the order in which motor skills develop depends on the anatomy of the body part being used, the surrounding environment, and the baby's efforts.

■ CULTURAL VARIATIONS IN MOTOR DEVELOPMENT. Cultural variations in infant-rearing practices also affect motor development. *TAKE A MOMENT...* Take a quick survey of several parents you know: Should sitting, crawling, and walking be deliberately encouraged? Answers vary widely from culture to culture. Japanese mothers and mothers from rural India, for example, believe such efforts are unnecessary (Seymour, 1999). Among the Zinacanteco Indians of Southern Mexico, rapid motor progress is actively discouraged. Babies who walk before they know enough to keep away from cooking fires and weaving looms are viewed as dangerous to themselves and disruptive to others (Greenfield, 1992).

In contrast, among the Kipsigis of Kenya, babies hold their heads up, sit alone, and walk considerably earlier than North American infants. Kipsigi parents deliberately teach these motor skills. In the first few months, babies are seated in holes

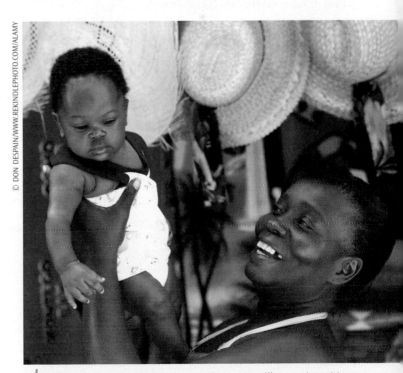

The West Indians of Jamaica use a formal handling routine with their babies, believing that exercise helps infants grow up strong, healthy, and physically attractive. This mother "walks" her baby up her body—an exercise that contributes to earlier mastery of independent walking.

Prereaching — Newborn

Reaching with ulnar grasp — 3–4 months

Transfer object from hand to hand — 4–5 months

Pincer grasp — 9 months

■ **FIGURE 4.9** ■ **Some milestones of reaching.** The average age at which each skill is attained is given. (Ages from Bayley, 1969; Rochat, 1989.)

dug in the ground, with rolled blankets used to keep them upright. Walking is promoted by frequently bouncing babies on their feet (Super, 1981).

By decreasing exposure to "tummy time," the current Western practice of having babies sleep on their backs to protect them from SIDS (see page 85 in Chapter 3) delays gross-motor milestones of rolling, sitting, and crawling (Majnemer & Barr, 2005). Regularly exposing infants to the tummy-lying position during waking hours prevents these delays.

Fine-Motor Development: Reaching and Grasping

Of all motor skills, reaching may play the greatest role in infant cognitive development. By grasping things, turning them over, and seeing what happens when they are released, infants learn a great deal about the sights, sounds, and feel of objects.

Reaching and grasping, like many other motor skills, start out as gross, diffuse activity and move toward mastery of fine movements. Figure 4.9 illustrates some milestones of reaching over the first nine months. Newborns make poorly coordinated swipes, called *prereaching*, toward an object in front of them, but because of poor arm and hand control, they rarely contact the object. Like newborn reflexes, prereaching drops out around 7 weeks of age. Yet these early behaviors suggest that babies are biologically prepared to coordinate hand with eye in the act of exploring (von Hofsten, 2004).

Around 3 to 4 months, as infants develop the necessary eye, head, and shoulder control, reaching reappears and gradually improves in accuracy (Bhat, Heathcock, & Galloway, 2005; Spencer et al., 2000). By 5 to 6 months, infants reach for an object in a room that has been darkened during the reach by switching off the lights (McCarty & Ashmead, 1999). Early on, vision is freed from the basic act of reaching so it can focus on more complex adjustments. During the next few months,

infants become better at reaching with just one arm (rather than both) and reaching for moving objects (Fagard & Pezé, 1997; Wentworth, Benson, & Haith, 2000).

Once infants can reach, they modify their grasp. The newborn's grasp reflex is replaced by the *ulnar grasp*, a clumsy motion in which the fingers close against the palm. Still, even 3-month-olds adjust their grasp to the size and shape of an object—a capacity that improves over the first year (Witherington, 2005). Around 4 to 5 months, when infants begin to sit up, they coordinate both hands in exploring objects (Rochat & Goubet, 1995). By the end of the first year, infants use the thumb and index finger opposably in a well-coordinated *pincer grasp*. Then the ability to manipulate objects greatly expands. The 1-year-old can pick up raisins and blades of grass, turn knobs, and open and close small boxes.

Finally, the capacity to reach for and manipulate an object increases infants' attention to the way an adult reaches for and plays with that particular object (Hauf, Aschersleben, & Prinz, 2007). As a result, babies broaden their understanding of others' behaviors and—as they watch what others do—of the range of actions that can be performed on various objects.

ASK YOURSELF

>> **REVIEW**
Cite evidence that motor development is a joint product of biological, psychological, and environmental factors.

>> **APPLY**
List everyday experiences that support mastery of reaching, grasping, sitting, and crawling. Why should caregivers place young infants in a variety of waking-time body positions?

>> **REFLECT**
Do you favor early, systematic training of infants in motor skills such as crawling, walking, and stair climbing? Why or why not?

Perceptual Development

In Chapter 3, you learned that the senses of touch, taste, smell, and hearing—but not vision—are remarkably well-developed at birth. Now let's turn to a related question: How does perception change over the first year? Our discussion will address hearing and vision, the focus of almost all research. Recall that in Chapter 3, we used the word *sensation* to talk about these capacities. It suggests a fairly passive process—what the baby's receptors detect when exposed to stimulation. Now we use the word *perception,* which is active: When we perceive, we organize and interpret what we see. As we review the perceptual achievements of infancy, you may find it hard to tell where perception leaves off and thinking begins.

Hearing

On Timmy's first birthday, Vanessa bought several CDs of nursery songs, and she turned one on each afternoon at naptime. Soon Timmy let her know his favorite tune. If she put on "Twinkle, Twinkle," he stood up in his crib and whimpered until she replaced it with "Jack and Jill." Timmy's behavior illustrates the greatest change in hearing over the first year: Babies organize sounds into increasingly complex patterns.

Between 4 and 7 months, infants display a sense of musical phrasing: They prefer Mozart minuets with pauses between phrases to those with awkward breaks (Krumhansl & Jusczyk, 1990). Around 6 to 7 months, they can distinguish musical tunes on the basis of variations in rhythmic patterns, including beat structure (duple or triple) and accent structure (emphasis on the first note of every beat unit or at other positions) (Hannon & Johnson, 2004). And by the end of the first year, infants recognize the same melody when it is played in different keys (Trehub, 2001). As we will see next, 6- to 12-month-olds make comparable discriminations in human speech.

■ **SPEECH PERCEPTION.** *Newborn → Infancy* Recall from Chapter 3 that newborns can distinguish nearly all sounds in human languages and that they prefer listening to human speech, especially their native tongue. As they listen to people talking, they learn to focus on meaningful sound variations. ERP brain-wave recordings reveal that around 5 months, babies become sensitive to syllable stress patterns in their own language (Weber et al., 2004). Between 6 and 8 months, they start to "screen out" sounds not used in their native tongue (Anderson, Morgan, & White, 2003; Polka & Werker, 1994). As the Biology and Environment box on page 110 explains, this increased responsiveness to native-language sounds is part of a general "tuning" process in the second half of the first year—a possible sensitive period in which infants acquire a range of perceptual skills for picking up socially important information.

Soon after, infants focus on larger speech segments. They recognize familiar words in spoken passages and listen longer to speech with clear clause and phrase boundaries (Jusczyk &

Hohne, 1997; Soderstrom et al., 2003). Around 7 to 9 months, infants extend this sensitivity to speech structure to individual words. They begin to divide the speech stream into wordlike units (Jusczyk, 2002; Saffran, Werker, & Werner, 2006).

How do infants make such rapid progress in perceiving the structure of language? Research shows that they have an impressive **statistical learning capacity.** By analyzing the speech stream for patterns—repeatedly occurring sequences of sounds—they acquire a stock of speech structures for which they will later learn meanings, long before they start to talk around age 12 months. For example, when presented with controlled sequences of nonsense syllables, babies listen for statistical regularities: They locate words by distinguishing syllables that often occur together (indicating they belong to the same word) from syllables that seldom occur together (indicating a word boundary) (Saffran, Aslin, & Newport, 1996; Saffran & Thiessen, 2003).

Once infants locate words, they focus on the words and, around 7 to 8 months, identify regular syllable-stress patterns—for example, in English and Dutch, that the onset of a strong syllable (*hap*-py, *rab*-bit) often signals a new word (Saffran & Thiessen, 2007). By 10 months, babies can detect words that start with weak syllables, such as "sur*prise*" (Jusczyk, 2001).

Clearly, babies have a powerful ability to extract patterns from complex, continuous speech. Some researchers believe that infants are innately equipped with a general statistical learning capacity for detecting structure in the environment, which they also apply to visual stimulation (Kirkham, Slemmer, & Johnson, 2002).

Vision

For exploring the environment, humans depend on vision more than any other sense. Although at first a baby's visual world is fragmented, it undergoes extraordinary changes during the first 7 to 8 months.

Visual development is supported by rapid maturation of the eye and visual centers in the cerebral cortex. Around 2 months, infants can focus on objects about as well as adults can, and their color vision is adultlike by 4 months (Kellman & Arterberry, 2006). *Visual acuity* (fineness of discrimination) improves steadily, reaching a near-adult level of about 20/20 by 6 months (Slater, 2001). Scanning the environment and tracking moving objects also improve over the first half-year as infants better control their eye movements and build an organized perceptual world (Johnson, Slemmer, & Amso, 2004).

As babies explore their visual field, they figure out the characteristics of objects and how they are arranged in space. To understand how they do so, let's examine the development of depth and pattern perception.

■ **DEPTH PERCEPTION.** *Depth perception* is the ability to judge the distance of objects from one another and from ourselves. It is important for understanding the layout of the environment and for guiding motor activity.

▪ BIOLOGY AND ENVIRONMENT ▪

"Tuning In" to Familiar Speech, Faces, and Music: A Sensitive Period for Culture-Specific Learning

To share experiences with members of their family and community, babies must become skilled at making perceptual discriminations that are meaningful in their culture. As we have seen, at first babies are sensitive to virtually all speech sounds, but around 6 months, they narrow their focus to the language they hear and will soon learn.

The ability to perceive faces shows a similar path of development. After habituating to one member of each pair of faces in Figure 4.10, 6-month-olds were shown the familiar and the novel face side by side. For both pairs, they recovered to (looked longer at) the novel face, indicating that they could discriminate individual faces of both humans and monkeys equally well (Pascalis, de Haan, & Nelson, 2002). But at 9 months, infants no longer showed a novelty preference when viewing the monkey pair. Like adults, they could distinguish only the human faces.

This developmental trend appears again in musical rhythm perception. Western adults are accustomed to the even-beat pattern of Western music—repetition of the same rhythmic structure in every measure of a tune—and easily notice rhythmic changes that disrupt this familiar beat. But present them with music that does not follow this typical Western rhythmic form—Baltic folk tunes, for example—and they fail to pick up on rhythmic-pattern deviations. Six-month-olds, however, can detect such disruptions in both Western and non-Western melodies. But by 12 months, after added exposure to Western music, babies are no longer aware of deviations from foreign musical rhythms, although their sensitivity to Western rhythmic structure remains unchanged (Hannon & Trehub, 2005b).

Several weeks of regular interaction with a foreign-language speaker and of daily opportunities to listen to non-Western music fully restore 12-month-olds' sensitivity to wide-ranging speech sounds and music rhythms (Hannon & Trehub, 2005a; Kuhl, Tsao, & Liu, 2003). Adults given similar extensive experiences, by contrast, show little improvement in perceptual sensitivity.

Taken together, these findings suggest a heightened capacity—or sensitive period—in the second half of the first year, when babies are biologically prepared to "zero in" on socially meaningful perceptual distinctions. Notice how, between 6 and 12 months, learning is especially rapid across several domains (speech, faces, and music) and is easily modified by experience. This suggests a broad neurological change—perhaps a special time of brain development in which babies analyze everyday stimulation of all kinds similarly, in ways that prepare them to participate in their cultural community.

■ FIGURE 4.10 ■ Discrimination of human and monkey faces. Which of these pairs is easiest for you to tell apart? After habituating to one of the photos in each pair, infants were shown the familiar and the novel face side-by-side. For both pairs, 6-month-olds recovered to (looked longer at) the novel face, indicating that they could discriminate human and monkey faces equally well. By 12 months, babies lost their ability to distinguish the monkey faces. Like adults, they showed a novelty preference only to human stimuli. (From O. Pascalis et al., 2002, "Is Face Processing Species-Specific During the First Year of Life?" *Science, 296,* p. 1322. Reprinted with permission from AAAS.)

Figure 4.11 shows the *visual cliff,* designed by Eleanor Gibson and Richard Walk (1960) and used in the earliest studies of depth perception. It consists of a Plexiglas-covered table with a platform at the center, a "shallow" side with a checkerboard pattern just under the glass, and a "deep" side with a checkerboard several feet below the glass. The researchers found that crawling babies readily crossed the shallow side, but most reacted with fear to the deep side. They concluded that around the time infants crawl, most distinguish deep and shallow surfaces and avoid drop-offs.

Visual cliff findings show that crawling and avoidance of drop-offs are linked but not how they are related or when depth perception first appears. Recent research has looked at babies' ability to detect specific depth cues, using methods that do not require that they crawl.

Motion is the first depth cue to which infants are sensitive. Babies 3 to 4 weeks old blink their eyes defensively when an object moves toward their face as if it is going to hit (Nánez & Yonas, 1994). *Binocular depth cues* arise because our two eyes have slightly different views of the visual field. Sensitivity to

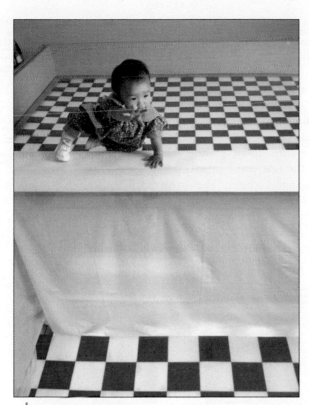

■ **FIGURE 4.11** ■ **The visual cliff.** Plexiglas covers the deep and shallow sides. By refusing to cross the deep side and showing a preference for the shallow side, this infant demonstrates the ability to perceive depth.

binocular cues emerges between 2 and 3 months and improves rapidly over the first year (Brown & Miracle, 2003). Finally, around 6 to 7 months, babies become sensitive to *pictorial* depth cues, the ones artists use to make a painting look three-dimensional. Examples include receding lines that create the illusion of perspective, changes in texture (nearby textures are more detailed than faraway ones), and overlapping objects (an object partially hidden by another object is perceived to be more distant) (Sen, Yonas, & Knill, 2001; Yonas, Elieff, & Arterberry, 2002).

Why does perception of depth cues emerge in the order just described? Researchers speculate that motor development is involved. For example, control of the head during the early weeks of life may help babies notice motion and binocular cues. Around the middle of the first year, the ability to turn, poke, and feel the surface of objects may promote perception of pictorial cues (Bushnell & Boudreau, 1993). And as we will see next, one aspect of motor progress—independent movement—plays a vital role in refinement of depth perception.

■ **INDEPENDENT MOVEMENT AND DEPTH PERCEPTION.** At 6 months, Timmy started crawling. "He's fearless!" exclaimed Vanessa. "If I put him down in the middle of our bed, he crawls right over the edge. The same thing's happened by the stairs." Will Timmy become more wary of the side of the bed

and the staircase as he becomes a more experienced crawler? Research suggests that he will. From extensive everyday experience, babies gradually figure out how to use depth cues in each body position (sitting, crawling, then walking) to detect the danger of falling (Adolph, 2000, 2002; Joh & Adolph, 2006). For example, infants with more crawling experience (regardless of when they start to crawl) are far more likely to refuse to cross the deep side of the visual cliff (Campos et al., 2000).

Independent movement promotes other aspects of three-dimensional understanding. Seasoned crawlers are better than their inexperienced agemates at remembering object locations and finding hidden objects (Campos et al., 2000). Why does crawling make such a difference? **TAKE A MOMENT...** Compare your own experience of the environment when you are driven from one place to another as opposed to walking or driving yourself. When you move on your own, you are much more aware of landmarks and routes of travel, and you take more careful note of what things look like from different points of view. The same is true for infants.

■ **PATTERN AND FACE PERCEPTION.** Even newborns prefer to look at patterned rather than plain stimuli (Fantz, 1961). But because of their poor vision, very young babies cannot resolve the features in complex patterns, so they prefer, for example, to look at a checkerboard with large, bold squares than one with many small squares. Around 2 months of age, when detection of fine-grained detail has improved, infants spend more time looking at the more complex checkerboard (Gwiazda & Birch, 2001). With age, they prefer increasingly intricate patterns.

In the early weeks of life, infants respond to the separate parts of a pattern, staring at single, high-contrast features (Hunnius & Geuze, 2004a, 2004b). In exploring drawings of human faces, for example, 1-month-olds often limit themselves to the edges of the stimulus and focus on the hairline or chin. At 2 to 3 months, when vision improves and infants can better control their scanning, they thoroughly explore a pattern's internal features (Bronson, 1994).

But babies' inspection of a stimulus varies with pattern characteristics. When exposed to dynamic stimuli, such as the mother's nodding, smiling face, even 6-week-olds fixate more on internal features (the mouth and eyes) than on edges. Nevertheless, thorough scanning of a dynamic stimulus emerges later—after 4 months of age (Hunnius & Geuze, 2004b). Exploring patterns with moving stimuli is more demanding than exploring static patterns.

Once babies can take in all aspects of a pattern, they integrate the parts into a unified whole. Gradually, they become so good at detecting pattern organization that they even perceive subjective boundaries that are not really present. For example, 9-month-olds look much longer at an organized series of moving lights that resembles a human being walking than at upside-down or scrambled versions (Bertenthal, 1993). At 12 months, infants can detect familiar objects represented by incomplete drawings, even when as much as two-thirds of the drawing is

■ FIGURE 4.12 ■ Subjective boundaries in visual patterns. What does this image, missing two-thirds of its outline, look like to you? By 12 months, infants detect the image of a motorcycle. After habituating to the incomplete motorcycle image, they were shown an intact motorcycle figure paired with a novel form. Twelve-month-olds recovered to (looked longer at) the novel figure, indicating that they recognized the motorcycle pattern on the basis of very little visual information. (Adapted from Rose, Jankowski, & Senior, 1997.)

missing (see Figure 4.12) (Rose, Jankowski, & Senior, 1997). As these findings reveal, infants' increasing knowledge of objects and actions supports pattern perception.

The tendency to search for structure in a patterned stimulus also applies to face perception. Newborns prefer to look at photos and simplified drawings with facial features arranged naturally (upright) rather than unnaturally (upside-down or sideways) (see Figure 4.13a) (Cassia, Turati, & Simion, 2004; Mondloch et al., 1999). They also track a facial pattern moving across their visual field farther than they track other stimuli (Johnson, 1999). Some researchers claim that these behaviors reflect a built-in capacity to orient toward members of one's own species, just as many newborn animals do (Johnson, 2001; Slater & Quinn, 2001). Others assert that newborns prefer any stimulus in which the most salient elements are arranged horizontally in the upper part of a pattern—like the "eyes" in Figure 4.13b (Turati, 2004). Another conjecture is that newborns are exposed to faces more often than to other stimuli—early experiences that might quickly "wire" the brain to detect faces (Nelson, 2001).

Although newborns respond to a general facelike structure, they cannot discriminate a complex facial pattern from other, equally complex patterns (see Figure 4.13c). But from repeated exposures to their mother's face, they quickly learn to prefer her face to that of an unfamiliar woman, although they are sensitive only to its broad outlines. Around 2 months, when they can combine pattern elements into an organized whole, babies prefer a complex drawing of the human face to other equally complex stimulus arrangements (Dannemiller & Stephens, 1988). They also prefer their mother's detailed facial features to those of another woman (Bartrip, Morton, & de Schonen, 2001).

Early experience influences other aspects of face processing, yielding group biases at a tender age. As early as 3 months,

infants prefer and more easily discriminate among female faces than among male faces, probably because they typically spend more time with female adults. And 3-month-olds exposed mostly to members of their own race prefer and more easily detect differences among faces of that race (Bar-Haim et al., 2006; Kelly et al., 2007). In contrast, babies who have frequent contact with members of other races show no own-race face preference.

Around 5 months—and strengthening over the second half of the first year—infants perceive emotional expressions as meaningful wholes. They treat positive faces (happy and surprised) as different from negative ones (sad and fearful) (Bornstein & Arterberry, 2003; Ludemann, 1991). As babies recognize and respond to the expressive behavior of others, face perception supports their earliest social relationships.

(a)

(b)

(c)

■ FIGURE 4.13 ■ Early face perception. Newborns prefer to look at the upright photo of a face (a) and the simple pattern resembling a face (b) over the upside-down versions. (c) When the complex drawing of a face on the left and the equally complex, scrambled version on the right are moved across newborns' visual field, they follow the face longer. But if the two stimuli are stationary, infants show no preference for the face until around 2 months of age. (From Cassia, Turati, & Simion, 2004; Johnson, 1999; Mondloch et al., 1999.)

Intermodal Perception

Our world provides rich, continuous *intermodal stimulation*—simultaneous input from more than one modality, or sensory system. In **intermodal perception,** we make sense of these running streams of light, sound, tactile, odor, and taste information by perceiving them as unified wholes.

Babies perceive input from different sensory systems in a unified way by detecting *amodal sensory properties*—information that overlaps two or more sensory systems. Consider the sight and sound of a bouncing ball or the face and voice of a speaking person. In each event, visual and auditory information occur simultaneously and with the same rate, rhythm, duration, and intensity.

Even newborns are impressive perceivers of amodal properties. After touching an object (such as a cylinder) placed in their palms, they recognize it visually, distinguishing it from a different-shaped object (Sann & Streri, 2007). And they require just one exposure to learn the association between the sight and sound of a toy, such as a rhythmically jangling rattle (Morrongiello, Fenwick, & Chance, 1998). Within the first half-year, infants master a remarkable range of intermodal relationships. For example, 3- and 4-month-olds can link the age of a voice (child versus adult) and its emotional tone (happy or angry) with the appropriate face of a person (Bahrick, Netto, & Hernandez-Reif, 1998; Walker-Andrews, 1997). Between 4 and 6 months, infants can perceive and remember the unique face–voice pairings of unfamiliar adults (Bahrick, Hernandez-Reif, & Flom, 2005). By 8 months, they can match voices and faces on the basis of gender (Patterson & Werker, 2002).

How does intermodal perception develop so quickly? Young infants seem biologically primed to focus on amodal information. Their detection of amodal relations—for example, the common tempo and rhythm in sights and sounds—precedes and seems to provide the basis for detecting more specific intermodal matches, such as the relation between a particular person's face and the sound of her voice or between an object and its verbal label (Bahrick, Hernandez-Reif, & Flom, 2005).

Intermodal sensitivity is crucial for perceptual development. In the first few months, when much stimulation is unfamiliar and confusing, it enables babies to notice meaningful correlations between sensory inputs and rapidly make sense of their surroundings (Bahrick, Lickliter, & Flom, 2004). And as the examples just reviewed suggest, intermodal perception also facilitates social and language processing.

Finally, early parent–infant interaction presents the baby with a rich context—consisting of many concurrent sights, sounds, touches, and smells—for expanding intermodal knowledge (Lickliter & Bahrick, 2000). Intermodal perception is a fundamental ability that fosters all aspects of psychological development.

Understanding Perceptual Development

Now that we have reviewed the development of infant perceptual capacities, how can we put together this diverse array of

Within the first half-year, infants master a remarkable range of intermodal relationships. This 3-month-old, assisted by her mother, quickly picks up associations between the sights, sounds, and feel of toys.

amazing achievements? Widely accepted answers come from the work of Eleanor and James Gibson. According to the Gibsons' **differentiation theory,** infants actively search for *invariant features* of the environment—those that remain stable—in a constantly changing perceptual world. In pattern perception, for example, young babies—confronted with a confusing mass of stimulation—search for features that stand out and also orient toward faces. Soon they explore internal features, noticing *stable relationships* among them. As a result, they detect patterns, such as complex designs and faces. The development of intermodal perception also reflects this principle. Babies seek out invariant relationships—first, amodal properties, such as common rate and rhythm in a voice and face, and later, more detailed associations, such as unique voice–face matches.

The Gibsons described their theory as *differentiation* (where "differentiate" means "analyze" or "break down") because over time, the baby detects finer and finer invariant features among stimuli. Thus, one way of understanding perceptual development is to think of it as a built-in tendency to search for order and consistency—a capacity that becomes increasingly fine-tuned with age (Gibson, 1970; Gibson, 1979).

Acting on the environment is vital in perceptual differentiation. ***TAKE A MOMENT...*** Think back to the links between motor milestones and perceptual development discussed in this chapter. Infants constantly look for ways in which the environment affords opportunities for action (Gibson, 2000, 2003). By exploring their surroundings, they figure out which things can be grasped, squeezed, bounced, or stroked and when a surface is safe to cross or presents a risk of falling (Adolph & Eppler, 1998, 1999). And from handling objects, they become more aware of a variety of observable object properties (Perone et al., 2008). As a result, they differentiate the world in new ways and act more competently.

As we conclude this chapter, it is only fair to note that some researchers believe that babies do more than make sense of experience by searching for invariant features and action possibilities: They also *impose meaning on* what they perceive, constructing categories of objects and events in the surrounding environment. We have seen the glimmerings of this *cognitive* point of view in this chapter. For example, older babies *interpret* a familiar face as a source of pleasure and affection and a pattern of blinking lights as a moving human being. This cognitive perspective also has merit in understanding the achievements of infancy. In fact, many researchers combine these two positions, regarding infant development as proceeding from a perceptual to a cognitive emphasis over the first year of life.

ASK YOURSELF

>> **REVIEW**

Using examples, explain why intermodal perception is vital for infants' developing understanding of their physical and social worlds.

>> **APPLY**

At 8 months, Ben has just begun to crawl. Can his parents trust him to avoid going headfirst down a steep staircase? Explain.

>> **REFLECT**

Are young infants more competent than you believed before you read this chapter? List the capacities that most surprised you.

Summary

Body Growth

Describe major changes in body growth over the first two years.

>> Changes in height and weight are rapid during the first two years. In the first nine months, body fat is laid down quickly, while muscle development is slow and gradual. Skeletal age is the best way to estimate a child's physical maturity. Body proportions change as growth follows **cephalocaudal** and **proximodistal trends.**

Brain Development

Describe brain development during infancy and toddlerhood, including appropriate stimulation to support the brain's potential.

>> Early in development, the brain grows faster than any other organ. Once **neurons** are in place, they rapidly form **synapses.** To communicate, neurons release **neurotransmitters,** which cross synapses. To make room for new synaptic connections, many surrounding neurons die. Neurons that are seldom stimulated lose their synapses in a process called **synaptic pruning. Glial cells,** responsible for **myelination,** multiply rapidly into the second year, contributing to large gains in brain weight.

>> The **cerebral cortex** is the largest, most complex brain structure and the last to stop growing. The hemispheres of the cerebral cortex specialize, a process called **lateralization.** In the first few years of life, there is high **brain plasticity,** with many areas not yet committed to specific functions.

>> Stimulation of the brain is essential during periods in which it is growing most rapidly. Early, **experience-expectant brain growth** depends on ordinary experiences. No evidence exists for a sensitive period in the first few years for **experience-dependent brain growth,** which relies on specific learning experiences. In fact, environments that overwhelm children with inappropriately advanced expectations can undermine the brain's potential.

© ERIN HOGAN/GETTY IMAGES/PHOTODISC

How does the organization of sleep and wakefulness change over the first two years?

>> Infants' changing arousal patterns are affected by brain growth, but the social environment also plays a role. Periods of sleep and wakefulness increasingly conform to a night–day schedule. Parents in Western nations try to get their babies to sleep through the night much earlier than parents throughout most of the world, who are more likely to sleep with their babies.

Influences on Early Physical Growth

Cite evidence that heredity, nutrition, and affection and stimulation contribute to early physical growth.

>> Twin and adoption studies reveal the contribution of heredity to body size and rate of physical growth.

>> Breast milk is ideally suited to infants' growth needs. Breastfeeding protects against disease and prevents malnutrition and infant death in poverty-stricken areas of the world. Breast- and bottle-fed babies do not differ in emotional adjustment, and cognitive benefits of breastfeeding are inconclusive.

>> **Marasmus** and **kwashiorkor** are dietary diseases caused by malnutrition that affect many children in developing countries and, if prolonged, can permanently stunt body growth and brain development. **Nonorganic failure to thrive,** which occurs in infants who lack affection and stimulation, illustrates the importance of these factors in normal physical growth.

Learning Capacities

Describe infant learning capacities, the conditions under which they occur, and the unique value of each.

>> **Classical conditioning** is based on the infant's ability to associate events that usually occur together in the everyday world. Infants can be classically conditioned most easily when the pairing of an **unconditioned stimulus (UCS)**

and a **conditioned stimulus (CS)** has survival value—for example, learning which stimuli regularly accompany feeding.

» In **operant conditioning,** infants act on their environment and their behavior is followed by either **reinforcers,** which increase the occurrence of a preceding behavior, or **punishment,** which either removes a desirable stimulus or presents an unpleasant one to decrease the occurrence of a response. In young infants, interesting sights and sounds and pleasurable caregiver interaction serve as effective reinforcers.

» **Habituation** and **recovery** reveal that at birth, babies are attracted to novelty. Novelty preference (recovery to a novel stimulus) assesses recent memory, whereas familiarity preference (recovery to the familiar stimulus) assesses remote memory.

» Newborns have a primitive ability to imitate adults' facial expressions and gestures. **Imitation** is a powerful means of learning and contributes to the parent–infant bond, though whether it is a voluntary capacity in newborns remains controversial.

Motor Development

Describe the general course of motor development during the first two years, along with factors that influence it.

» According to **dynamic systems theory of motor development,** children acquire new motor skills by combining existing skills into increasingly complex systems of action. Each new skill is a joint product of central nervous system development, movement possibilities of the body, the child's goals, and environmental supports for the skill. Cultural values and child-rearing customs also contribute to motor development.

» During the first year, infants perfect reaching and grasping. Reaching gradually becomes more accurate and flexible, and the clumsy ulnar grasp is transformed into a refined pincer grasp.

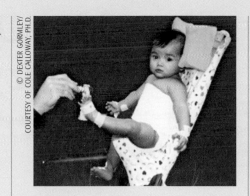

COURTESY OF COLE CALLOWAY, PH.D.
© DEXTER GORMLEY/

Perceptual Development

What changes in hearing, depth and pattern perception, and intermodal perception take place during infancy?

» Infants organize sounds into increasingly complex patterns and, in the middle of the first year, become more sensitive to the sounds of their own language. They have an impressive **statistical learning capacity,** which enables them to detect regular sound patterns for which they will later learn meanings.

» Rapid maturation of the eye and visual centers in the brain supports gains in focusing, color discrimination, and visual acuity during the first half-year. The ability to scan the environment and track moving objects also improves.

» Research on depth perception reveals that responsiveness to motion cues develops first, followed by sensitivity to binocular and then to pictorial cues. Experience in crawling enhances depth perception and other aspects of three-dimensional understanding.

» At first, babies stare at single, high-contrast features and often focus on the edges of a pattern. At 2 to 3 months, they explore a pattern's internal features and start to detect pattern organization. Over time, they discriminate increasingly complex, meaningful patterns.

» Newborns prefer to look at and track simple, facelike stimuli. Around 2 months, infants prefer a drawing of the human face to other stimulus arrangements and their mother's detailed facial features to those of another woman. In the second half-year, they perceive emotional expressions as meaningful wholes.

» From the start, infants are capable of **intermodal perception.** Detection of amodal relations (such as common rhythm) precedes and may provide a basis for detecting other intermodal matches.

© LAURA DWIGHT PHOTOGRAPHY

Explain differentiation theory of perceptual development.

» According to **differentiation theory,** perceptual development is a matter of detecting invariant features in a constantly changing perceptual world. Acting on the world plays a major role in perceptual differentiation. According to a more cognitive view, at an early age, infants impose meaning on what they perceive. Many researchers combine these two ideas.

Important Terms and Concepts

CHAPTER 5

Cognitive Development in Infancy and Toddlerhood

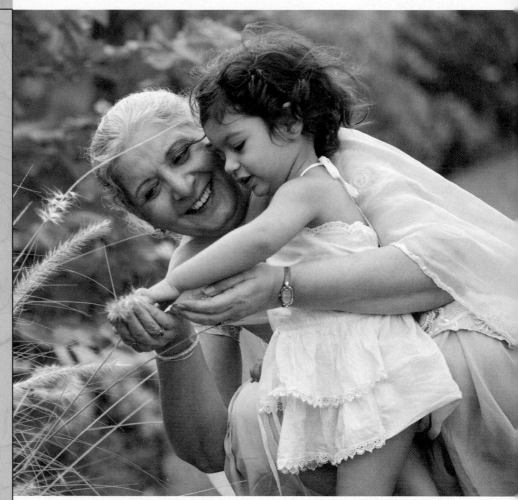

© KEN SEET/CORBIS

This grandmother shares her grandchild's curiosity and delight in discovery. With the sensitive support of caring adults, infants' and toddlers' cognition and language develop rapidly.

When Caitlin, Grace, and Timmy, each nearly 18 months old, gathered at Ginette's child-care home, the playroom was alive with activity. Grace dropped shapes through holes in a plastic box that Ginette adjusted so the harder ones would fall smoothly into place. Once a few shapes were inside, Grace grabbed the box and shook it, squealing with delight as the lid fell open and the shapes scattered around her. The clatter attracted Timmy, who picked up a shape, carried it to the railing at the top of the basement steps, and dropped it overboard, then followed with a teddy bear, a ball, his shoe, and a spoon.

As the toddlers experimented, I could see the beginnings of spoken language—a whole new way of influencing the world. "All gone baw!" Caitlin exclaimed as Timmy tossed the ball down the basement steps. Later that day, Grace revealed that she could use words and gestures to pretend. "Night-night," she said, putting her head down and closing her eyes.

Over the first two years, the small, reflexive newborn baby becomes a self-assertive, purposeful being who solves simple problems and starts to master the most amazing human ability: language. Parents wonder, How does all this happen so quickly? This question has also captivated researchers, yielding a wealth of findings along with vigorous debate over how to explain the astonishing pace of infant and toddler cognition.

In this chapter, we take up three perspectives on early cognitive development: Piaget's *cognitive-developmental theory, information processing,* and Vygotsky's *sociocultural theory.* We also consider the usefulness of tests that measure early intellectual progress. Finally, we look at the beginnings of language. We will see how toddlers' first words build on cognitive achievements and how, very soon, new words and expressions greatly increase the speed and flexibility of thinking.

Piaget's Cognitive-Developmental Theory

Swiss theorist Jean Piaget inspired a vision of children as busy, motivated explorers whose thinking develops as they act directly on the environment. According to Piaget, all aspects of cognition develop in an integrated fashion, changing in a similar way at about the same time as children move through four stages between infancy and adolescence.

Piaget's first stage, the **sensorimotor stage,** spans the first two years of life. Piaget believed that infants and toddlers "think" with their eyes, ears, hands, and other sensorimotor equipment. They cannot yet carry out many activities inside their heads. But by the end of toddlerhood, children can solve practical, everyday problems and represent their experiences in speech, gesture, and play.

Piaget's Ideas About Cognitive Change

According to Piaget, specific psychological structures—organized ways of making sense of experience called **schemes**—change with age. First schemes are sensorimotor action patterns. For example, at 6 months, Timmy dropped objects in a fairly rigid way, simply letting go of a rattle and watching with interest. By 18 months, his "dropping scheme" had become deliberate and creative. In tossing objects down the basement stairs, he threw some in the air, bounced others off walls, released some gently and others forcefully. Soon, instead of just acting on objects, he will show evidence of thinking before he acts, marking the transition from sensorimotor to preoperational thought.

In Piaget's theory, two processes, *adaptation* and *organization,* account for changes in schemes.

■ **ADAPTATION.** *TAKE A MOMENT...* The next time you have a chance, notice how infants and toddlers tirelessly repeat actions that lead to interesting effects. **Adaptation** involves building schemes through direct interaction with the environment. It consists of two complementary activities, *assimilation* and *accommodation.* During **assimilation,** we use our current schemes to interpret the external world. For example, when Timmy dropped objects, he was assimilating them to his sensorimotor "dropping scheme." In **accommodation,** we create new schemes or adjust old ones after noticing that our current ways of thinking do not capture the environment completely. When Timmy dropped objects in different ways, he modified his dropping scheme to take account of the varied properties of objects.

According to Piaget, the balance between assimilation and accommodation varies over time. When children are not changing much, they assimilate more than they accommodate. Piaget called this a state of cognitive *equilibrium,* implying a steady, comfortable condition. During rapid cognitive change, however, children are in a state of *disequilibrium,* or cognitive discomfort. Realizing that new information does not match their current schemes, they shift from assimilation toward accommodation. After modifying their schemes, they move back toward assimilation, exercising their newly changed structures until they are ready to be modified again.

Each time this back-and-forth movement between equilibrium and disequilibrium occurs, more effective schemes are produced. Because the times of greatest accommodation are the earliest ones, the sensorimotor stage is Piaget's most complex period of development.

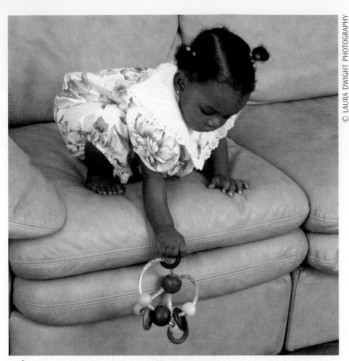

In Piaget's theory, first schemes are motor action patterns. As this 11-month-old repeatedly experiments with her "dropping scheme," her dropping behavior will become more deliberate and varied.

■ **ORGANIZATION.** Schemes also change through **organization,** a process that takes place internally. Once children form new schemes, they rearrange them, linking them with other schemes to create a strongly interconnected cognitive system. For example, eventually Timmy will relate "dropping" to "throwing" and to "nearness" and "farness." According to Piaget, schemes truly reach equilibrium when they become part of a broad network of structures that can be jointly applied to the surrounding world (Piaget, 1936/1952).

In the following sections, we will first describe infant development as Piaget saw it, noting research that supports his observations. Then we will consider evidence demonstrating that, in some ways, babies' cognitive competence is more advanced than Piaget believed.

The Sensorimotor Stage

The difference between the newborn baby and the 2-year-old child is so vast that Piaget divided the sensorimotor stage into six substages, summarized in Table 5.1. Piaget based this sequence on a very small sample: his own three children. He observed his son and two daughters carefully and also presented them with everyday problems (such as hidden objects) that helped reveal their understanding of the world.

According to Piaget, newborns know so little about the world that they cannot purposefully explore it. The **circular reaction** provides a special means of adapting their first schemes. It involves stumbling onto a new experience caused by the baby's own motor activity. The reaction is "circular" because, as the infant tries to repeat the event again and again, a sensorimotor response that first occurred by chance becomes strengthened into a new scheme. Consider Caitlin, who at age 2 months accidentally made a smacking noise after a feeding. Intrigued, she tried to repeat the sound until she became expert at smacking her lips. Infants' difficulty inhibiting new and interesting behaviors may underlie the circular reaction. This immaturity in inhibition seems to be adaptive, ensuring that new skills will not be interrupted before they strengthen (Carey & Markman, 1999). Piaget considered revisions in the circular reaction so important that, as Table 5.1 shows, he named the sensorimotor substages after them.

■ **REPEATING CHANCE BEHAVIORS.** In Substage 1, babies are reflexive beings who suck, grasp, and look in much the same way, no matter what experiences they encounter. Around 1 month, as they enter Substage 2, infants start to gain voluntary control over their actions through the *primary circular reaction,* by repeating chance behaviors largely motivated by basic needs. This leads to some simple motor habits, such as

■ **TABLE 5.1** ■ *Summary of Piaget's Sensorimotor Stage*

SENSORIMOTOR SUBSTAGE	TYPICAL ADAPTIVE BEHAVIORS
1. Reflexive schemes (birth–1 month)	Newborn reflexes (see Chapter 3, page 82)
2. Primary circular reactions (1–4 months)	Simple motor habits centered around the infant's own body; limited anticipation of events
3. Secondary circular reactions (4–8 months)	Actions aimed at repeating interesting effects in the surrounding world; imitation of familiar behaviors
4. Coordination of secondary circular reactions (8–12 months)	Intentional, or goal-directed, behavior; ability to find a hidden object in the first location in which it is hidden (object permanence); improved anticipation of events; imitation of behaviors slightly different from those the infant usually performs
5. Tertiary circular reactions (12–18 months)	Exploration of the properties of objects by acting on them in novel ways; imitation of novel behaviors; ability to search in several locations for a hidden object (accurate A–B search)
6. Mental representation (18 months–2 years)	Internal depictions of objects and events, as indicated by sudden solutions to problems; ability to find an object that has been moved while out of sight (invisible displacement); deferred imitation; and make-believe play

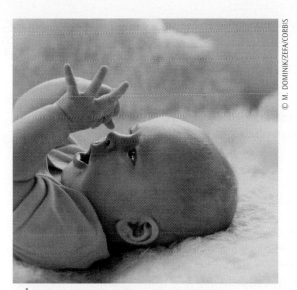

This 3-month-old sees his hands touch, open, and close. He tries to repeat these movements, in a primary circular reaction that helps him gain voluntary control over his behavior.

sucking their fists or thumbs. Babies also begin to vary their behavior in response to environmental demands. For example, they open their mouths differently for a nipple than for a spoon. And they start to anticipate events. At 3 months, when Timmy awoke from his nap, he cried out with hunger. As soon as Vanessa entered the room, he stopped crying. He knew that feeding time was near.

During Substage 3, from 4 to 8 months, infants sit up and reach for and manipulate objects. These motor achievements strengthen the *secondary circular reaction*, through which babies try to repeat interesting events in the surrounding environment that are caused by their own actions. For example, 4-month-old Caitlin accidentally knocked a toy hung in front of her, producing a fascinating swinging motion. Over the next three days, Caitlin tried to repeat this effect, gradually forming a new "hitting" scheme.

■ **INTENTIONAL BEHAVIOR.** In Substage 4, 8- to 12-month-olds combine schemes into new, more complex action sequences. As a result, actions that lead to new schemes no longer have a hit-or-miss quality—*accidentally* bringing the thumb to the mouth or *happening* to hit the toy. Instead, infants engage in **intentional,** or **goal-directed, behavior,** coordinating schemes deliberately to solve simple problems. Consider Piaget's famous object-hiding task, in which he shows the baby a toy and then hides it behind his hand or under a cover. Infants of this substage can find the object by coordinating two schemes—"pushing" aside the obstacle and "grasping" the toy. Retrieving hidden objects reveals that infants have begun to master **object permanence,** the understanding that objects continue to exist when out of sight. But awareness of object permanence is not yet complete. Babies still make the *A-not-B search error:* If they reach several times for an object at a first hiding place *(A),* then see it moved to a second *(B),* they still search for it in the first hiding place *(A).*

Infants of Substage 4, who can better anticipate events, sometimes use their capacity for intentional behavior to try to change those events. At 10 months, Timmy crawled after Vanessa when she put on her coat, whimpering to keep her from leaving. Also, babies can now imitate behaviors slightly different from those they usually perform. After watching someone else, they try to stir with a spoon or push a toy car. Again, they draw on intentional behavior, purposefully modifying schemes to fit an observed action (Piaget, 1945/1951).

In Substage 5, from 12 to 18 months, the *tertiary circular reaction,* in which toddlers repeat behaviors with variation, emerges. Recall how Timmy dropped objects over the basement steps, trying first one action, then another. Because they approach the world in this deliberately exploratory way, 12- to 18-month-olds become better problem solvers. According to Piaget, this capacity to experiment leads toddlers to look for a hidden toy in several locations, displaying an accurate A–B search. Their more flexible action patterns also permit them to imitate many more behaviors.

■ **MENTAL REPRESENTATION.** Substage 6 brings the ability to create **mental representations**—internal depictions of information that the mind can manipulate. Our most powerful mental representations are of two kinds: (1) *images,* or mental pictures of objects, people, and spaces; and (2) *concepts,* or categories in which similar objects or events are grouped together. We can use a mental image to retrace our steps when we've misplaced something or to imitate someone's behavior long after we've observed it. And by thinking in concepts and labeling them (for example, "ball" for all rounded, movable

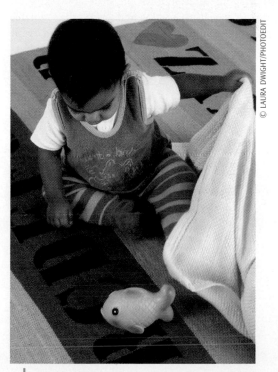

The capacity to search for and find hidden objects between 8 and 12 months of age marks a major advance in cognitive development.

objects used in play), we can organize our diverse experiences into more manageable units.

Representation enables older toddlers to solve advanced object permanence problems involving *invisible displacement*—finding a toy moved while out of sight, such as into a small box while under a cover. It also permits **deferred imitation**—the ability to remember and copy the behavior of models who are not present. And it makes possible **make-believe play,** in which children act out everyday and imaginary activities. As the sensorimotor stage draws to a close, mental symbols have become major instruments of thinking.

Follow-Up Research on Infant Cognitive Development

Many studies suggest that infants display a wide array of understandings earlier than Piaget believed. Recall the operant conditioning research reviewed in Chapter 4, in which newborns sucked vigorously on a nipple to gain access to interesting sights and sounds. This behavior, which closely resembles Piaget's secondary circular reaction, shows that infants explore and control the external world long before 4 to 8 months. In fact, they do so as soon as they are born.

To discover what young infants know about hidden objects and other aspects of physical reality, researchers often use the **violation-of-expectation method.** They may *habituate* babies to a physical event (expose them to the event until their looking declines) to familiarize them with a situation in which their knowledge will be tested. Or they may simply show babies an *expected event* (one that follows physical laws) and an *unexpected event* (a variation of the first event that violates physical laws). Heightened attention to the unexpected event suggests that the infant is "surprised" by a deviation from phys-ical reality and, therefore, is aware of that aspect of the physical world.

■ **OBJECT PERMANENCE.** In a series of studies using the violation-of-expectation method, Renée Baillargeon and her collaborators claimed to have found evidence for object permanence in the first few months of life (Aguiar & Baillargeon, 1999, 2002; Baillargeon, 2004; Wang, Baillargeon, & Paterson, 2005). One of Baillargeon's studies is illustrated and explained in Figure 5.1.

Critics argue that the violation-of-expectation method indicates only a perceptual preference for novelty or, at best, implicit (nonconscious) detection of physical events—not the full-blown understanding that was Piaget's focus in requiring infants to search for hidden objects (Bremner & Mareschal, 2004; Hood, 2004; Munakata, 2001). But another type of looking behavior suggests that young infants are aware that objects persist when out of view. Four- and 5-month-olds will track a ball's path of movement as it disappears and reappears from behind a barrier, even gazing ahead to where they expect it to emerge (Bertenthal, Longo, & Kenny, 2007; Rosander & von Hofsten, 2004). With age, babies are more likely to fixate on the predicted place of the ball's reappearance and wait for it—evidence of an increasingly secure grasp of object permanence.

In related research, investigators recorded 6-month-old's ERP brain-wave activity as the babies watched two events on a computer screen. In one, a black square moved until it covered an object, then moved away to reveal the object (object permanence). In the other, as a black square began to move across an object, the object disintegrated (object disappearance) (Kaufman, Csibra, & Johnson, 2005). Only while watching the first event did infants show a particular brain-wave pattern in the right temporal lobe—the same pattern adults exhibit when told to sustain a mental image of an object.

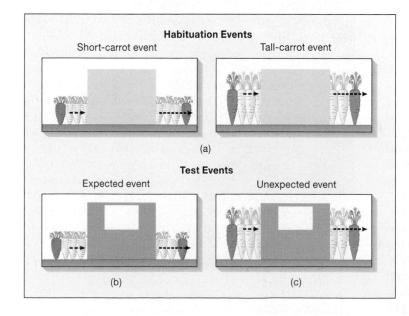

■ **FIGURE 5.1** ■ **Testing young infants for understanding of object permanence using the violation-of-expectation method.** (a) First, infants were habituated to two events: a short carrot and a tall carrot moving behind a yellow screen, on alternate trials. Next, the researchers presented two test events. The color of the screen was changed to help infants notice its window. (b) In the *expected event,* the carrot shorter than the window's lower edge moved behind the blue screen and reappeared on the other side. (c) In the *unexpected event,* the carrot taller than the window's lower edge moved behind the screen and did not appear in the window, but then emerged intact on the other side. Infants as young as 2½ to 3½ months recovered to (looked longer at) the *unexpected event,* suggesting that they had some understanding of object permanence. (From R. Baillargeon & J. DeVos, 1991, "Object Permanence in Young Infants: Further Evidence," *Child Development, 62,* p. 1230. © The Society for Research in Child Development. Adapted with permission.)

Once 8- to 12-month-olds actively search for hidden objects, they make the *A-not-B* search error. Some research suggests that after finding the object several times at *A*, they do not attend closely when it is hidden at *B* (its most recent location) (Ruffman & Langman, 2002). A more comprehensive explanation is that a *dynamic system* of factors—having built a habit of reaching toward *A*, continuing to look at *A*, having the hiding place at *B* appear similar to the one at *A*, and maintaining a constant body posture—increases the chances that the baby will make the *A-not-B* search error. Disrupting any one of these factors increases 10-month-olds' accurate searching at *B* (Thelen et al., 2001).

In sum, mastery of object permanence is a gradual achievement: Babies' understanding becomes increasingly complex with age (Cohen & Cashon, 2006). Success at object search tasks coincides with rapid development of the frontal lobes of the cerebral cortex (Bell, 1998). Also crucial are a wide variety of experiences perceiving, acting on, and remembering objects.

■ **MENTAL REPRESENTATION.** In Piaget's theory, infants lead purely sensorimotor lives, unable to mentally represent experience until about 18 months of age. Yet 8-month-olds' ability to recall the location of a hidden object after delays of more than a minute, and 14-month-olds' recall after delays of a day or more, indicate that babies construct mental representations of objects and their whereabouts (McDonough, 1999; Moore & Meltzoff, 2004). And in studies of deferred imitation and problem solving, representational thought is evident even earlier.

Deferred Imitation. Piaget studied deferred imitation by noting when his three children demonstrated it in their everyday behavior. But laboratory research suggests that it is present at 6 weeks of age! Infants who watched an unfamiliar adult's facial expression imitated it when exposed to the same adult the next day (Meltzoff & Moore, 1994). As motor capacities improve, infants copy actions with objects. In one study, an adult showed 6- and 9-month-olds a novel series of actions with a puppet: taking its glove off, shaking the glove to ring a bell inside, and replacing the glove. When tested a day later, infants who had seen the novel actions were far more likely to display them (see Figure 5.2 on page 122) (Barr, Marrott, & Rovee-Collier, 2003).

Between 12 and 18 months, toddlers use deferred imitation to enrich their range of sensorimotor schemes. They retain modeled behaviors for at least several months, copy the actions of peers as well as adults, and imitate across a change in context—for example, enact at home a behavior learned at child care or on TV (Barr & Hayne, 1999; Hayne, Boniface, & Barr, 2000; Klein & Meltzoff, 1999). Over the second year, toddlers also gain in ability to imitate an adult's action on toys in the order in which those actions occurred (Bauer, 2002, 2006). And when toddlers imitate in correct sequence, they remember more modeled behaviors (Knopf, Kraus, & Kressley-Mba, 2006).

Toddlers even imitate rationally, by inferring others' intentions! Fourteen-month-olds are more likely to imitate purposeful than accidental behaviors (Carpenter, Akhtar, & Tomasello,

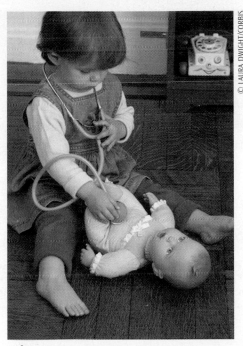

As this 18-month-old reenacts a procedure she herself has experienced, she demonstrates her capacity for deferred imitation. She can retain modeled behaviors for at least several months and imitate across situational changes—from the doctor's office to home.

1998). If 12-month-olds see an adult perform an unusual action for fun (making a toy dog enter a miniature house by jumping through the chimney, even though its door is wide open), they copy the behavior. But if the adult engages in the odd behavior because she *must* (making the dog go through the chimney only after trying to use the door and finding it locked), 12-month-olds typically imitate the more efficient action (putting the dog through the door) (Schwier et al., 2006).

Around 18 months, toddlers can imitate actions an adult *tries* to produce, even if these are not fully realized (Meltzoff, 1995). On one occasion, Ginette attempted to pour some raisins into a bag but missed, spilling them onto the counter. A moment later, Grace began dropping the raisins into the bag, indicating that she had inferred Ginette's goal (Falck-Ytter, Gredebäck, & von Hofsten, 2006).

Problem Solving. As Piaget indicated, around 7 to 8 months, infants develop intentional action sequences, which they use to solve simple problems, such as pulling on a cloth to obtain a toy resting on its far end (Willatts, 1999). Soon after, infants' representational skills permit more effective problem solving than Piaget's theory suggests.

By 10 to 12 months, infants can *solve problems by analogy*—apply a solution strategy from one problem to other relevant problems. In one study, 12-month-olds who were repeatedly presented with a spoon in the same orientation (handle to one side) readily adapted their motor actions when the spoon was presented with the handle to the other side, successfully transporting food to their mouths (McCarty & Keen, 2005). With

■ **FIGURE 5.2** ■ **Testing infants for deferred imitation.** After researchers performed a novel series of actions with a puppet, this 6-month-old imitated the actions a day later—at left, removing the glove; at right, shaking the glove to ring a bell inside. During the second half-year, gains in recall are evident in deferred imitation of others' behaviors over longer delays.

age, children become better at reasoning by analogy, applying relevant strategies across increasingly dissimilar situations (Goswami, 1996). But even in the first year, infants have some ability to move beyond trial-and-error experimentation, represent solutions mentally, and use them in new contexts.

Evaluation of the Sensorimotor Stage

Table 5.2 summarizes the remarkable cognitive attainments we have just considered. ***TAKE A MOMENT...*** Compare this table with the description of Piaget's account of sensorimotor substages in Table 5.1 on page 118. You will see that infants anticipate events, actively search for hidden objects, master the A–B object search, flexibly vary their sensorimotor schemes, and engage in make-believe play within Piaget's time frame. Yet other capacities—including secondary circular reactions, understanding of object properties, first signs of object permanence, deferred imitation, and problem solving by analogy—emerge earlier than Piaget expected.

These findings show that the cognitive attainments of infancy do not develop together in the neat, stepwise fashion that Piaget assumed. They also reveal that infants comprehend a great deal before they are capable of the motor behaviors that Piaget believed led to those understandings. How can we account for babies' amazing cognitive accomplishments?

■ **ALTERNATIVE EXPLANATIONS.** Unlike Piaget, who thought young babies constructed all mental representations out of sensorimotor activity, most researchers now believe that infants have some built-in cognitive equipment for making sense of experience. But intense disagreement exists over the extent of this initial understanding. Researchers who lack confidence in the violation-of-expectation method argue that babies' cognitive starting point is limited (Campos et al., 2008; Cohen & Cashon, 2006; Kagan, 2008). For example, some believe that

newborns begin life with a set of biases for attending to certain information and with general-purpose learning procedures, such as powerful techniques for analyzing complex perceptual information. Together, these capacities enable infants to construct a wide variety of schemes (Bahrick, Lickliter, & Flom, 2004; Mandler, 2004; Quinn, 2008).

Others, convinced by violation-of-expectation findings, believe that infants start out with impressive understandings. According to this **core knowledge perspective,** babies are born with a set of innate knowledge systems, or *core domains of thought*. Each of these prewired understandings permits a ready grasp of new, related information and therefore supports early, rapid development (Carey & Markman, 1999; Leslie, 2004; Spelke, 2004; Spelke & Kinzler, 2007). Core knowledge theorists argue that infants could not make sense of the complex stimulation around them without having been genetically "set up" in the course of evolution to comprehend its crucial aspects.

Researchers have conducted many studies of infants' *physical knowledge,* including object permanence, object solidity (that one object cannot move through another), and gravity (that an object will fall without support). Violation-of-expectation findings suggest that in the first few months, infants have some awareness of all these basic object properties and quickly build on this knowledge (Baillargeon, 2004; Hespos & Baillargeon, 2001; Luo & Baillargeon, 2005; Spelke, 2000). Core knowledge theorists also assume that an inherited foundation of *linguistic knowledge* enables swift language acquisition in early childhood—a possibility we will consider later in this chapter. Further, these theorists argue, infants' early orientation toward people initiates rapid development of *psychological knowledge*—in particular, understanding of mental states, such as intentions, emotions, desires, and beliefs.

Researchers have even examined infants' *numerical knowledge!* In the best-known study, 5-month-olds saw a screen cover a single toy animal, then watched a hand place a second toy

■ **TABLE 5.2** ■ *Some Cognitive Attainments of Infancy and Toddlerhood*

AGE	COGNITIVE ATTAINMENTS
Birth–1 month	Secondary circular reactions using limited motor skills, such as sucking a nipple to gain access to interesting sights and sounds
1–4 months	Possible awareness of object permanence, object solidity, and gravity, as suggested by violation-of-expectation findings; deferred imitation of an adult's facial expression over a short delay (one day)
4–8 months	Improved knowledge of object properties and of basic numerical knowledge, as suggested by violation-of-expectation findings; deferred imitation of an adult's novel actions on objects over a short delay (one day)
8–12 months	Ability to search for a hidden object when covered by a cloth; ability to solve simple problems by analogy to a previous problem
12–18 months	Ability to search for a hidden object when a hand deposits it under a cloth and when it is moved from one location to another (accurate A–B search). Deferred imitation of an adult's novel actions on an object over a long delay (at least several months) and across a change in situation (from child care to home, from TV to everyday life); rational imitation, taking into account the model's intentions
18 months–2 years	Deferred imitation of actions an adult tries to produce, again indicating a capacity to infer others' intentions; imitation of everyday behaviors in make-believe play

TAKE A MOMENT... Which of the capacities listed in the table indicate that mental representation emerges earlier than Piaget believed?

behind the screen. Finally, the screen was removed to reveal either one or two toys. Infants looked longer at the unexpected, one-toy display, indicating that they kept track of the two objects and were able to add one object to another (Wynn, Bloom, & Chiang, 2002). Findings like these suggest that babies can discriminate quantities up to three and use that knowledge to perform simple arithmetic—both addition and subtraction (in which two objects are covered and one object is removed) (Kobayashi et al., 2004; Kobayashi, Hiraki, & Hasegawa, 2005).

But babies' numerical capacities are controversial—not evident in all studies (Langer, Gillette, & Arriaga, 2003; Wakeley, Rivera, & Langer, 2000). Critics also note that claims for number concepts in infants are surprising, given that before 14 to 16 months, toddlers have difficulty with less-than and greater-than relationships between small sets. And not until the preschool years do children add and subtract small sets correctly.

The core knowledge perspective, while emphasizing native endowment, acknowledges that experience is essential for children to extend this initial knowledge. But so far, it has said little about which experiences are most important in each core domain of thought and how those experiences advance children's thinking. Despite these limitations, core knowledge research has sharpened the field's focus on clarifying the starting point of human cognition and on carefully tracking the changes that build on it.

■ **PIAGET'S LEGACY.** Current research on infant cognition yields broad agreement on two issues: First, many cognitive changes of infancy are not abrupt and stagelike but gradual and continuous (Bjorklund, 2004). Second, rather than developing together, various aspects of infant cognition change unevenly because of the challenges posed by different types of tasks and infants' varying experience with them. These ideas serve as the basis for another major approach to cognitive development—*information processing.*

Before turning to this alternative point of view, let's recognize Piaget's enormous contributions. Piaget's work inspired a wealth of research on infant cognition, including studies that challenged his theory. His observations also have been of great practical value. Teachers and caregivers continue to look to the sensorimotor stage for guidelines on how to create developmentally appropriate environments for infants and toddlers.

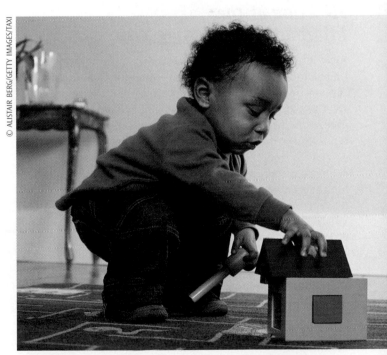

© ALISTAIR BERG/GETTY IMAGES/TAXI

Did this toddler acquire the knowledge to build a block tower by repeatedly acting on objects, as Piaget assumed? Or did he begin life with innate physical knowledge that enables him to understand objects and their relationships quickly, with little hands-on exploration?

ASK YOURSELF

>> **REVIEW**

Using the text discussion on pages 120–122, construct an age-related list of infant and toddler cognitive attainments. Which ones are consistent with Piaget's sensorimotor stage? Which develop earlier than Piaget anticipated?

>> **APPLY**

Several times, after her father hid a teething biscuit under a red cup, 12-month-old Mimi retrieved it easily. Then Mimi's father hid the biscuit under a nearby yellow cup. Why did Mimi persist in searching for it under the red cup?

>> **REFLECT**

Which explanation of infants' cognitive competencies do you prefer, and why?

Information Processing

Recall from Chapter 1 that the information-processing approach frequently relies on computerlike flowcharts to describe the human cognitive system. Information-processing theorists are not satisfied with general concepts, such as assimilation and accommodation, to describe how children think. Instead, they want to know exactly what individuals of different ages do when faced with a task or problem (Birney et al., 2005; Halford, 2002).

Structure of the Information-Processing System

Most information-processing researchers assume that we hold information in three parts of the mental system for processing: *the sensory register; working,* or *short-term, memory;* and *long-term memory* (see Figure 5.3). As information flows through each, we can use **mental strategies** to operate on and transform it, increasing the chances that we will retain information, use it efficiently, and think flexibly, adapting the information to changing circumstances. To understand this more clearly, let's look at each aspect of the mental system.

First, information enters the **sensory register,** where sights and sounds are represented directly and stored briefly. ***TAKE A MOMENT...*** Look around you, and then close your eyes. An image of what you saw persists for a few seconds, but then it decays, or disappears, unless you use mental strategies to preserve it. For example, by *attending to* some information more carefully than to other information, you increase the chances that it will transfer to the next step of the information-processing system.

In the second part of the mind, **working,** or **short-term, memory,** we actively apply mental strategies as we "work" on a limited amount of information. For example, if you are studying this book effectively, you are taking notes, repeating information to yourself, or grouping pieces of information together, thereby reducing the number of pieces you must attend to and making room in working memory for more.

To manage its complex activities, a special part of working memory—called the **central executive**—directs the flow of information. It decides what to attend to, coordinates incoming information with information already in the system, and selects, applies, and monitors strategies (Baddeley, 1993, 2000; Pressley & Hilden, 2006). The central executive is the conscious, reflective part of our mental system. It works closely with working memory to direct such activities as comprehension, reasoning, and problem solving.

The longer we hold information in working memory, the more likely it will transfer to the third, and largest, storage area—**long-term memory,** our permanent knowledge base, which is unlimited. In fact, we store so much in long-term memory that *retrieval*—getting information back from the system—can be problematic. To aid retrieval, we apply strategies, just as we do in working memory. Information in long-term memory is *categorized* according to a master plan based on content, much like a library shelving system that allows us to retrieve items easily by following the same network of associations used to store them.

Information-processing researchers believe that the basic structure of the mental system remains similar throughout life. But the *capacity* of the system—the amount of information that can be retained and processed at once—and the speed with which it can be processed increases, making more complex forms of thinking possible with age (Case, 1998; Kail, 2003). Gains in information-processing capacity are due in part to brain development and in part to improvements in strategies—such as attending to information and categorizing it effectively—that are already developing in the first two years of life.

Attention

Recall from Chapter 4 that at 2 to 3 months of age, infants explore objects and patterns more thoroughly. Besides attending to more aspects of the environment, infants gradually take in information more quickly. Preterm and newborn babies require a long time to habituate and recover to novel visual stimuli—about 3 or 4 minutes. But by 4 or 5 months, infants require as little as 5 to 10 seconds to take in a complex visual stimulus and recognize it as different from a previous one (Rose, Feldman, & Janowski, 2001; Slater et al., 1996).

One reason for young babies' long habituation times is that they have difficulty disengaging their attention from interesting stimuli (Colombo, 2002). The ability to shift attention from one stimulus to another is just as important as attending to a stimulus. By 4 months, infants' attention becomes more flexible (Posner & Rothbart, 2007).

During the first year, infants attend to novel and eye-catching events. With the transition to toddlerhood, children become increasingly capable of intentional behavior (refer back to Piaget's Substage 4). Consequently, attraction to novelty declines (but does not disappear) and *sustained attention* improves. A toddler who engages even in simple goal-directed behavior, such as stacking blocks or putting them in a container, must sustain attention to reach the goal. As plans and activities become more complex, so does the duration of attention (Ruff & Capozzoli, 2003).

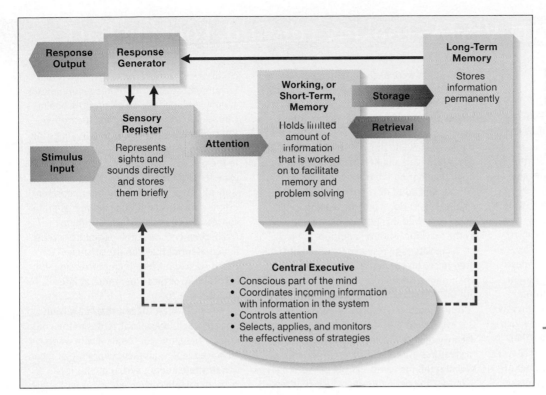

■ **FIGURE 5.3** ■ **Model of the human information-processing system.** Information flows through three parts of the mental system: the *sensory register*, *working*, or *short-term, memory*; and *long-term memory*. In each, mental strategies can be used to manipulate information, increasing the efficiency and flexibility of thinking and the chances that information will be retained. The *central executive* is the conscious, reflective part of working memory. It coordinates incoming information already in the system, decides what to attend to, and oversees the use of strategies.

Memory

Operant conditioning and habituation provide windows into early memory. Both methods show that retention of visual events increases dramatically over infancy and toddlerhood.

Using operant conditioning, researchers study infant memory by teaching 2- to 6-month-olds to move a mobile by kicking a foot tied to it with a long cord. Three-month-olds still remember how to activate the mobile one week after training. By 6 months, memory increases to two weeks (Rovee-Collier, 1999; Rovee-Collier & Bhatt, 1993). Even after 3- to 6-month-olds forget an operant response, they need only a brief prompt—an adult who shakes the mobile—to reinstate the memory (Hildreth & Rovee-Collier, 2002). And when 6-month-olds are given a chance to reactivate the response themselves for just a couple of minutes, their memory not only returns but extends dramatically, to about 17 weeks (Hildreth, Sweeney, & Rovee-Collier, 2003). Perhaps permitting the baby to generate the previously learned behavior strengthens memory because it reexposes the child to more aspects of the original learning situation.

Habituation/recovery research shows that infants learn and retain a wide variety of information just by watching objects and events, sometimes for much longer time spans than in operant conditioning studies. Babies are especially attentive to the movements of objects and people. In one investigation, 5½-month-olds remembered a woman's captivating action (such as blowing bubbles or brushing hair) seven weeks later, as indicated by a *familiarity preference* (see page 104 in Chapter 4) (Bahrick, Gogate, & Ruiz, 2002). The babies were so attentive to the woman's action that they did not remember her face, even when tested 1 minute later for a *novelty preference*.

So far, we have discussed only **recognition**—noticing when a stimulus is identical or similar to one previously experienced. It is the simplest form of memory: All babies have to do is indicate (by kicking or looking) that a new stimulus is identical or similar to a previous one. **Recall** is more challenging because it involves remembering something not present. But by the end of the first year, infants are capable of recall, as indicated by their ability to find hidden objects and to imitate others' actions long after observing the behavior (see pages 120–121).

Long-term recall depends on connections among multiple regions of the cerebral cortex, especially with the frontal lobes. During the second year, these neural circuits start to increase rapidly (Bauer et al., 2006; Nelson, Thomas, & de Haan, 2006). Yet older children and adults no longer recall their earliest experiences—a puzzling find discussed in the Lifespan Vista box on page 126.

Categorization

Categorization—grouping similar objects and events into a single representation—helps infants make sense of experience. It reduces the enormous amount of new information they encounter so they can learn and remember (Cohen, 2003; Oakes & Madole, 2003).

Some creative variations of operant conditioning research with mobiles have been used to investigate infant categorization. One such study, of 3-month-olds, is described and illustrated in Figure 5.5. Similar investigations reveal that in the first few months, babies categorize stimuli on the basis of shape, size, color, and other physical properties (Wasserman & Rovee-Collier, 2001). By 6 months of age, they can categorize on the basis of two

■ A LIFESPAN VISTA: Looking Forward, Looking Back ■

Infantile Amnesia

If toddlers remember many aspects of their everyday lives, how do we explain **infantile amnesia**—that most of us cannot retrieve events that happened to us before age 3? The reason we forget cannot be merely the passage of time because we can recall many personally meaningful one-time events from both the recent and the distant past: the day a sibling was born, a birthday party, or a move to a new house—recollections known as **autobiographical memory.**

Several explanations of infantile amnesia exist. One theory credits brain development, suggesting that vital changes in the frontal lobes of the cerebral cortex may pave the way for an *explicit* memory system—one in which children remember deliberately rather than *implicitly,* without conscious awareness (Boyer & Diamond, 1992). But a growing number of researchers argue that even young infants remember consciously: Their memory processing is not fundamentally different from that of children and adults (Bauer, 2006; Rovee-Collier & Barr, 2001).

Another conjecture is that older children and adults often use verbal means for storing information, whereas infants' and toddlers' memory processing is largely nonverbal—an incompatibility that may prevent long-term retention of early experiences. To test this idea, researchers sent two adults to the homes of 2- to 4-year-olds with an unusual toy that

the children were likely to remember: The Magic Shrinking Machine, shown in Figure 5.4. One adult showed the child how, after inserting an object in an opening on top of the machine and turning a crank that activated flashing lights and musical sounds, the child could retrieve a smaller, identical object from behind a door on the front of the machine. (The second adult discreetly dropped the smaller object down a chute leading to the door.) The child was encouraged to participate as the machine "shrank" additional objects.

A day later, the researchers tested the children to see how well they recalled the event. Their nonverbal memory—based on acting out the "shrinking" event and recognizing the "shrunken" objects in photos—was excellent. But even when they had the vocabulary, children younger than age 3 had trouble describing features of the "shrinking" experience. Verbal recall increased sharply between ages 3 and 4—the period during which children "scramble over the amnesia barrier" (Simcock & Hayne, 2003, p. 813). In a second study, preschoolers could not translate their nonverbal memory for the game into language six months to one year later, when their language had improved dramatically. Their verbal reports were "frozen in time," reflecting their limited language skill at the time they played the game (Simcock & Hayne, 2002).

These findings help us reconcile infants' and toddlers' remarkable memory skills with infantile amnesia. During the first few years,

children remember largely with nonverbal techniques, such as visual images and motor actions. As language develops, preschoolers can use it to refer to preverbal memories. But their ability to do so is fragile, requiring strong contextual cues, such as direct exposure to the physical setting of the to-be-recalled experience (Morris & Baker-Ward, 2007). Only after age 3 do children often represent events verbally and participate in elaborate conversations with adults about them. As children encode autobiographical events in verbal form, they can use language-based cues to retrieve them, increasing the accessibility of these memories at later ages (Hayne, 2004).

Other findings suggest that the advent of a clear self-image contributes to the end of infantile amnesia. Toddlers who were advanced in development of a sense of self demonstrated better verbal memories a year later while conversing about past events with their mothers (Harley & Reese, 1999). Very likely, both biology and social experience contribute to the decline of infantile amnesia. Brain development and adult–child interaction may jointly foster self-awareness, language, and improved memory, which enable children to talk with adults about significant past experiences (Bauer, 2007). As a result, preschoolers begin to construct a long-lasting autobiographical narrative of their lives and enter into the history of their family and community.

(a)

(b)

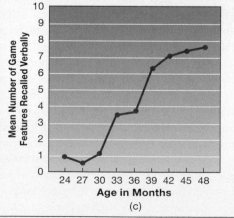

(c)

■ **FIGURE 5.4** ■ **The Magic Shrinking Machine, used to test young children's verbal and nonverbal memory of an unusual event.** After being shown how the machine worked, the child participated in selecting objects from a polka-dot bag, dropping them into the top of the machine (a) and turning a crank, which produced a "shrunken" object (b). When tested the next day, 2- to 4-year-olds' nonverbal memory for the event was excellent. But below 36 months, verbal recall was poor, based on the number of features recalled about the game during an open-ended interview (c). Recall improved between 36 and 48 months, the period during which infantile amnesia subsides. (From G. Simcock & H. Hayne, 2003, "Age-Related Changes in Verbal and Nonverbal Memory During Early Childhood," *Developmental Psychology, 39,* pp. 807, 809. Copyright © 2003 by the American Psychological Association. Reprinted with permission of the American Psychological Association.) *Photos:* Ross Coombes/Courtesy of Harlene Hayne.

correlated features—for example, the shape and color of the alphabet letter (Bhatt et al., 2004). This ability to categorize using clusters of features prepares babies for acquiring many complex everyday categories.

Habituation has also been used to study infant categorization. Researchers show babies a series of pictures belonging to one category and then see whether they recover to (look longer at) a picture that does not belong to the category. Findings reveal that 6- to 12-month-olds structure objects into an impressive array of meaningful categories—food items, furniture, animals, plants, vehicles, kitchen utensils, and spatial location ("above" and "below," "on" and "in") (Casasola, Cohen, & Chiarello, 2003; Mandler & McDonough, 1998; Oakes, Coppage, & Dingel, 1997). Besides organizing the physical world, infants of this age categorize their emotional and social worlds. Their looking responses reveal that they sort people and their voices by gender and age, have begun to distinguish emotional

expressions, and can separate people's natural movements from other motions (see Chapter 4, pages 111, 112, and 113).

Compared with habituation/recovery, toddlers' play behaviors better reveal the meanings they attach to categories. After watching an adult give a toy dog a drink from a cup, 14-month-olds shown a rabbit and a motorcycle usually offer the drink only to the rabbit (Mandler & McDonough, 1998). They clearly understand that certain actions are appropriate for some categories of items (animals) but not others (vehicles). By the end of the second year, toddlers' grasp of the animate–inanimate distinction expands. Nonlinear motions are typical of animates (a person or a dog jumping), linear motions of inanimates (a car or a table pushed along a surface). At 22 months, toddlers imitate a nonlinear motion only with toys in the animate category (a cat but not a bed) (Rakison, 2005, 2006). They seem to grasp that whereas animates are self-propelled and, therefore, have varied paths of movement, inanimates move only when acted on, in highly restricted ways.

Notice in the findings just reviewed that babies' earliest categories are *perceptual*—based on similar overall appearance. But from the second half-year on, more categories are *conceptual*—based on common functions or behaviors (Cohen, 2003; Mandler, 2004; Quinn, 2008). How does this perceptual-to-conceptual shift occur? Although researchers disagree on whether it requires a new approach to analyzing experience, all acknowledge that exploration of objects and expanding knowledge of the world contribute greatly (Mandler, 2004; Oakes & Madole, 2003). In addition, language both builds on and facilitates categorization. Adult labeling of objects ("This one's a car, and that one's a bicycle") helps toddlers refine their categories (Gelman & Kalish, 2006).

Evaluation of Information-Processing Findings

The information-processing perspective underscores the continuity of human thinking from infancy into adult life. In attending to the environment, remembering everyday events, and categorizing objects, Caitlin, Grace, and Timmy think in ways that are remarkably similar to our own, though their mental processing is far from proficient. Findings on infant memory and categorization join other evidence that challenges Piaget's view of early cognitive development. If 3-month-olds can remember events for as long as three months and can categorize stimuli, then they must have some ability to represent their experiences.

Information-processing research has contributed greatly to our view of young babies as sophisticated cognitive beings. But its central strength—analyzing cognition into its components, such as perception, attention, and memory—is also its greatest drawback. Information processing has had difficulty putting these components back together into a broad, comprehensive theory.

One approach to overcoming this weakness has been to combine Piaget's theory with the information-processing approach, an effort we will explore in Chapter 9. A more recent

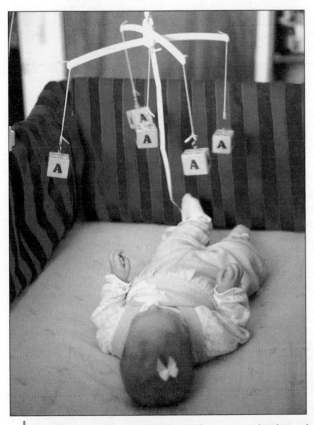

■ **FIGURE 5.5** ■ **Investigating infant categorization using operant conditioning.** Three-month-olds were taught to kick to move a mobile that was made of small blocks, all with the letter *A* on them. After a delay, kicking returned to a high level only if the babies were shown a mobile whose elements were labeled with the same form (the letter *A*). If the form was changed (from *A*s to *2*s), infants no longer kicked vigorously. While making the mobile move, the babies had grouped together its features. They associated the kicking response with the category *A* and, at later testing, distinguished it from the category *2*. (Bhatt, Rovee-Collier, & Weiner, 1994; Hayne, Rovee-Collier, & Perris, 1987.)

handwritten notes: fine motor → toy patty speter wheels on bus → movement _learning peek-a-boo - object permanen

trend has been the application of a *dynamic systems view*. Researchers analyze each cognitive attainment to see how it results from a complex system of prior accomplishments and the child's current goals (Spencer & Perone, 2008; Thelen & Smith, 2006). Once these ideas are fully tested, they may move the field closer to a more powerful view of how the minds of infants and children develop.

The Social Context of Early Cognitive Development

Recall the description at the beginning of this chapter of Grace dropping shapes into a container. Notice that she learns about the toy with Ginette's support. According to Vygotsky's sociocultural theory, complex mental activities have their origins in social interaction (Bodrova & Leong, 2007; Rogoff, 2003). Through joint activities with more mature members of their society, children master activities and think in ways that have meaning in their culture.

A special Vygotskian concept explains how this happens. The **zone of proximal** (or potential) **development** refers to a range of tasks that the child cannot yet handle alone but can do with the help of more skilled partners. To understand this idea, think about how a sensitive adult (such as Ginette) introduces a child to a new activity. The adult picks a task that the child can master but that is challenging enough that the child cannot do it alone. As the adult guides and supports, the child joins in the interaction and picks up mental strategies. As her competence increases, the adult steps back, permitting the child to take more responsibility for the task.

A study by Barbara Rogoff and her collaborators (1984) illustrates this process. Placing a jack-in-the-box nearby, the researchers watched how several adults played with Rogoff's son and daughter over the first two years. In the early months, the adults tried to focus the baby's attention by working the toy and, as the bunny popped out, saying something like "My, what happened?" By the end of the first year, when the baby's cognitive and motor skills had improved, interaction centered on how to use the toy. The adults guided the baby's hand in turning the crank and putting the bunny back in the box. During the second year, the adults helped from a distance, using gestures and verbal prompts, such as making a turning motion with the hand near the crank. Research indicates that this fine-tuned support is related to advanced play, language, and problem solving in toddlerhood and early childhood (Bornstein et al., 1992; Charman et al., 2001; Tamis-LeMonda & Bornstein, 1989).

As early as the first year, cultural variations in social experiences affect mental strategies. In the jack-in-the-box example, adults and children focused their attention on a single activity— a strategy common in Western middle-SES infant and toddler play. In contrast, Guatemalan Mayan babies often attend to several events at once. For example, one 12-month-old skillfully put objects in a jar while also watching a passing truck and blowing a toy whistle (Chavajay & Rogoff, 1999). Processing

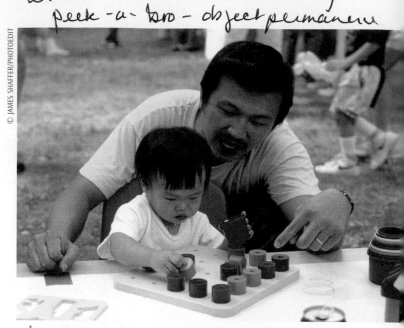

© JAMES SHAFFER/PHOTOEDIT

Using simple words and gestures, this father brings a challenging task within his toddler's zone of proximal development. By adjusting his communication to suit the child's needs, the father transfers mental strategies to the child and promotes learning.

several competing events simultaneously may be vital in cultures where children learn largely through keen observation of others' ongoing activities. Mexican children from low-SES families continue to display this style of attention well into middle childhood (Correa-Chavez, Rogoff, & Mejía-Arauz, 2005).

Earlier we saw how infants and toddlers create new schemes by acting on the physical world (Piaget) and how certain skills become better developed as children represent their experiences more efficiently and meaningfully (information processing). Vygotsky adds a third dimension to our understanding by emphasizing that many aspects of cognitive development are socially mediated. The Cultural Influences box on the following page presents additional evidence for this idea, and we will see even more in the next section.

ASK YOURSELF

›› REVIEW
Cite evidence that categorization becomes less perceptual and more conceptual with age. How can adults foster toddlers' categorization?

›› APPLY
Timmy's mother stood behind him, helping him throw a large ball into a box. As his skill improved, she stepped back, letting him try on his own. Using Vygotsky's ideas, explain how Timmy's mother is supporting his cognitive development.

›› REFLECT
Describe your earliest autobiographical memory. How old were you when the event occurred? Do your responses fit with research on infantile amnesia?

■ CULTURAL INFLUENCES ■

Social Origins of Make-Believe Play

One of the activities my husband, Ken, used to do with our two sons when they were young was to bake pineapple upside-down cake, a favorite treat. One Sunday afternoon as 4-year-old David stirred the cake batter, Ken poured some into a small bowl for 21-month-old Peter and handed him a spoon.

"Here's how you do it, Petey," instructed David, with a superior air. Peter watched as David stirred, then tried to copy his motion. When it was time to pour the batter, Ken helped Peter hold and tip the small bowl.

"Time to bake it," said Ken.

"Bake it, bake it," repeated Peter, watching Ken slip the pan into the oven.

Several hours later, we observed one of Peter's earliest instances of make-believe play. He got his pail from the sandbox and, after filling it with a handful of sand, carried it into the kitchen and put it down on the floor in front of the oven. "Bake it, bake it," Peter called to Ken. Together, father and son placed the pretend cake in the oven.

Vygotsky believed that society provides children with opportunities to represent culturally meaningful activities in play. Make-believe, he claimed, is first learned under the guidance of experts (Berk, Mann, & Ogan, 2006). In the example just described, Peter extended his capacity to represent daily events when Ken drew him into the baking task and helped him act it out in play.

Current evidence supports the idea that early make-believe is the combined result of children's readiness to engage in it and social experiences that promote it. In a study of U.S. middle-SES toddlers, 75 to 80 percent of make-believe involved mother–child interaction (Haight & Miller, 1993). At 12 months, almost all play episodes were initiated by mothers, but by the end of the second year, half of pretend episodes were initiated by each.

During make-believe, mothers offer toddlers a rich array of cues that they are pretending— looking and smiling at the child more, making more exaggerated movements, and using more "we" talk (acknowledging that pretending is a joint endeavor) than they do during the same real-life event (Lillard, 2007). When adults participate, toddlers' make-believe is more elaborate (Keren et al., 2005). And the more parents pretend with their toddlers, the more time their children devote to make-believe.

But in some cultures, such as those of Indonesia and Mexico, where extended-family households and sibling caregiving are common, make-believe is more frequent and more complex with older siblings than with mothers. As early as age 3 to 4, children provide rich, challenging stimulation to their younger brothers and sisters, take these teaching responsibilities seriously, and, with age, become better at them (Zukow-Goldring, 2002). In a study of Zinacanteco Indian children of southern Mexico, by age 8, sibling teachers were highly skilled at showing

In cultures where sibling caregiving is common, make-believe play is more frequent and complex with older siblings than with mothers. These Kenyan brothers pretend with sand and rocks— "toys" that are plentiful in their surroundings. The older boy easily engages his toddler sibling, teaching him how to play.

2-year-olds how to play at everyday tasks, such as washing and cooking. They often guided toddlers verbally and physically and provided feedback (Maynard, 2002).

As we will see in Chapter 7, make-believe is a major means through which children extend their cognitive skills and learn about important activities in their culture. Vygotsky's theory, and the findings that support it, tell us that providing a stimulating physical environment is not enough to promote early cognitive development. In addition, toddlers must be invited and encouraged by more skilled members of their culture to participate in the social world around them.

Individual Differences in Early Mental Development

Because of Grace's deprived early environment, Kevin and Monica had a psychologist give her one of many tests available for assessing mental development in infants and toddlers. Worried about Timmy's progress, Vanessa also arranged for him to be tested. At age 22 months, he had only a handful of words in his vocabulary, played in a less mature way than Caitlin and Grace, and seemed restless and overactive.

The cognitive theories we have just discussed try to explain the *process* of development—how children's thinking changes. Mental tests, in contrast, focus on cognitive *products*. Their goal is to measure behaviors that reflect development and to arrive at scores that *predict* future performance, such as later intelligence and school achievement.

Infant and Toddler Intelligence Tests

Accurately measuring infants' intelligence is a challenge because babies cannot answer questions or follow directions. As a result, most infant tests emphasize perceptual and motor responses. But new tests are being developed that also tap early language, cognition, and social behavior. One commonly used test, the *Bayley Scales of Infant and Toddler Development,* is suitable for children between 1 month and 3½ years. The most recent edition, the Bayley-III, has three main subtests: (1) the Cognitive Scale, which includes such items as attention to familiar and unfamiliar objects, looking for a fallen object, and pretend play; (2) the Language Scale, which assesses understanding and expression of language—for example, recognition of objects and people, following simple directions, and naming objects and pictures; and (3) the Motor Scale, which includes gross and fine motor skills, such as grasping, sitting, stacking blocks, and climbing stairs (Bayley, 2005).

Two additional Bayley-III scales depend on parental report: (4) the Social-Emotional Scale, which asks caregivers about such behaviors as ease of calming, social responsiveness, and imitation in play; and (5) the Adaptive Behavior Scale, which asks about adaptation to the demands of daily life, including communication, self-control, following rules, and getting along with others.

■ **COMPUTING INTELLIGENCE TEST SCORES.** Intelligence tests for infants, children, and adults are scored in much the same way—by computing an **intelligence quotient (IQ),** which indicates the extent to which the raw score (number of items passed) deviates from the typical performance of same-age individuals. To make this comparison possible, test designers

engage in **standardization**—giving the test to a large, representative sample and using the results as the *standard* for interpreting scores.

Within the standardization sample, performances at each age level form a **normal distribution** in which most scores cluster around the mean, or average, with progressively fewer falling toward the extremes (see Figure 5.6). This *bell-shaped* distribution results whenever researchers measure individual differences in large samples. When intelligence tests are standardized, the mean IQ is set at 100. An individual's IQ is higher or lower than 100 by an amount that reflects how much his or her test performance deviates from the standardization-sample mean. In this way, the IQ indicates whether the individual is ahead, behind, or on time (average) in mental development in relation to others of the same age. The IQs of 96 percent of individuals fall between 70 and 130; only a few achieve higher or lower scores.

■ **PREDICTING LATER PERFORMANCE FROM INFANT TESTS.** Despite careful construction, infant tests—including previous editions of the Bayley—predict later intelligence poorly. Because infants and toddlers easily become distracted, fatigued, or bored during testing, their scores often do not reflect their true abilities. And infant perceptual and motor items differ from the tasks given to older children, which increasingly emphasize verbal, conceptual, and problem-solving skills. In contrast, the Bayley-III Cognitive and Language Scales, which better dovetail with childhood tests, are good predictors of preschool mental test performance (Albers & Grieve, 2007).

Most infant tests are better at making long-term predictions for extremely low-scoring babies. Today, they are largely used for *screening*—helping to identify for further observation and intervention babies who are likely to have developmental problems.

As an alternative to infant tests, some researchers have turned to information-processing measures, such as habituation, to assess early mental progress. Their findings show that speed of habituation and recovery to novel visual stimuli are among the best available infant predictors of IQ from early childhood through early adulthood (Fagan, Holland, & Wheeler, 2007; Kavsek, 2004; McCall & Carriger, 1993). These measures assess memory as well as quickness and flexibility of thinking, which underlie intelligent behavior at all ages (Colombo, 1995; Rose & Feldman, 1997). The consistency of these findings has prompted designers of the Bayley-III to include items that tap such cognitive skills as habituation/recovery, problem-solving, and categorization.

Early Environment and Mental Development

In Chapter 2, we indicated that intelligence is a complex blend of hereditary and environmental influences. Many studies have examined the relationship of environmental factors to early

© PHOTO BY STEPHEN AUSMUS, USDA/ARS

A trained examiner administers the Bayley Scales of Infant Development to a 1-year-old sitting in her mother's lap. Compared with earlier editions, the Bayley-III Cognitive and Language Scales better predict preschool mental test performance.

■ **FIGURE 5.6** ■ **Normal distribution of intelligence test scores.** To determine what percentage of same-age individuals in the population a person with a certain IQ outperformed, add the figures to the left of that IQ score. For example, an 8-year-old child with an IQ of 115 scored better than 84 percent of the population of 8-year-olds.

mental test scores. As we consider this evidence, you will encounter findings that highlight the role of heredity as well.

■ **HOME ENVIRONMENT.** The **Home Observation for Measurement of the Environment (HOME)** is a checklist for gathering information about the quality of children's home lives through observation and parental interview (Caldwell & Bradley, 1994). Factors measured by HOME during the first three years include an organized, stimulating physical setting and parental affection, involvement, and encouragement. Regardless of SES and ethnicity, each predicts better language and IQ scores in toddlerhood and early childhood (Fuligni, Han, & Brooks-Gunn, 2004; Linver, Martin, & Brooks-Gunn, 2004; Tamis-LeMonda et al., 2004). The extent to which parents talk to infants and toddlers is particularly important. It contributes strongly to early language progress, which, in turn, predicts intelligence and academic achievement in elementary school (Hart & Risley, 1995).

Yet we must interpret these correlational findings cautiously. Parents who are genetically more intelligent may provide better experiences while also giving birth to genetically brighter children, who evoke more stimulation from their parents. Research supports this hypothesis, which refers to *genetic–environmental correlation* (see Chapter 2, page 55) (Saudino & Plomin, 1997). But heredity does not account for the entire association between home environment and mental test scores. Family living conditions—both HOME scores and affluence of the surrounding neighborhood—continue to predict children's IQ beyond the contribution of parental IQ and education (Chase-Lansdale et al., 1997; Klebanov et al., 1998).

How can the research summarized so far help us understand Vanessa's concern about Timmy's development? Ben, the psychologist who tested Timmy, found that he scored only slightly below average. Ben talked with Vanessa about her child-rearing practices and watched her play with Timmy. A single

parent who worked long hours, Vanessa had little energy for Timmy at the end of the day. Ben also noticed that Vanessa, anxious about Timmy's progress, tended to pressure him, dampening his active behavior and bombarding him with directions: "That's enough ball play. Stack these blocks."

Ben explained that when parents are intrusive in these ways, infants and toddlers are likely to be distractible, play immaturely, and do poorly on mental tests (Bono & Stifter, 2003; Stilson & Harding, 1997). He coached Vanessa in how to interact sensitively with Timmy, while also assuring her that warm, responsive parenting is a much better indicator of how children will do later than an early mental test score.

■ **INFANT AND TODDLER CHILD CARE.** Today, more than 60 percent of U.S. mothers with a child under age 2 are employed (U.S. Census Bureau, 2009b). Child care for infants and toddlers has become common, and its quality has a major impact on mental development. Infants and young children exposed to poor-quality child care—whether they come from middle-class or from low-SES homes—score lower on measures of cognitive and social skills (Hausfather et al., 1997; NICHD Early Child Care Research Network, 2000b, 2001, 2003, 2006). In contrast, good child care can reduce the negative impact of a

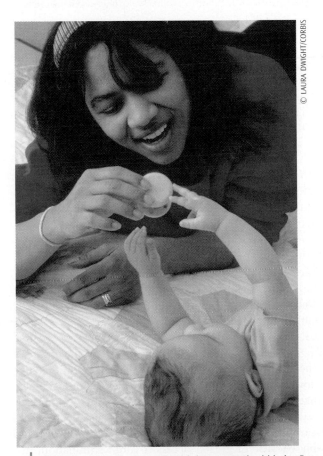

A mother plays affectionately with her 5-month-old baby. Parental warmth, attention, and verbal communication in infancy predict better language and IQ scores in toddlerhood and early childhood.

Applying What We Know

Signs of Developmentally Appropriate Infant and Toddler Child Care

Program Characteristics	Signs of Quality
Physical setting	Indoor environment is clean, in good repair, well-lit, well-ventilated, and not overcrowded. Fenced outdoor play space is available.
Toys and equipment	Play materials are appropriate for infants and toddlers and are stored on low shelves within easy reach. Cribs, highchairs, infant seats, and child-sized tables and chairs are available. Outdoor equipment includes small riding toys, swings, slide, and sandbox.
Caregiver–child ratio	In child-care centers, caregiver–child ratio is no greater than one to three for infants and one to six for toddlers. Group size (number of children in one room) is no greater than six infants with two caregivers and 12 toddlers with two caregivers. In family child care, caregiver is responsible for no more than six children; within this group, no more than two are infants and toddlers.
Daily activities	Daily schedule includes times for active play, quiet play, naps, snacks, and meals. Atmosphere is warm and supportive, and children are never left unsupervised.
Interactions among adults and children	Caregivers respond promptly to infants' and toddlers' distress; hold, talk to, sing to, and read to them; and interact with them in a manner that respects the individual child's interests and tolerance for stimulation. Staffing is consistent, so infants and toddlers can form relationships with particular caregivers.
Caregiver qualifications	Caregivers have some training in child development, first aid, and safety.
Relationships with parents	Parents are welcome anytime. Caregivers talk frequently with parents about children's behavior and development.
Licensing and accreditation	Child-care setting, whether a center or a home, is licensed by the state. In the United States, voluntary accreditation by the National Academy of Early Childhood Programs *(www.naeyc.org/accreditation)* or the National Association for Family Child Care *(www.nafcc.org)* is evidence of an especially high-quality program.

Sources: Copple & Bredekamp, 2009.

stressed, poverty-stricken home life, and it sustains the benefits of growing up in an economically advantaged family (Lamb & Ahnert, 2006; McCartney et al., 2007; NICHD Early Child Care Research Network, 2003).

TAKE A MOMENT... Visit several child-care settings, and take notes on what you see. Unlike most European countries and Australia and New Zealand, where child care is nationally regulated and funded to ensure its quality, U.S. child care is cause for concern. Standards are set by the states and vary widely. In studies of U.S. child care, only 20 to 25 percent of child-care centers and family child-care homes provided infants and toddlers with sufficiently positive, stimulating experiences to promote healthy psychological development (NICHD Early Childhood Research Network, 2000a, 2004).

U.S. settings providing the very worst care tend to serve middle-SES families. These parents are especially likely to place their children in for-profit centers, where quality tends to be lowest. Low-SES children more often attend publicly subsidized, nonprofit centers, which have smaller group sizes and better teacher–child ratios (Lamb & Ahnert, 2006). Still, child-care quality for low-SES children varies widely. And probably because of greater access to adult stimulation, infants and toddlers in high-quality family child care score higher than those in center care in cognitive and language development (NICHD Early Child Care Research Network, 2000b).

See Applying What We Know above for signs of high-quality care for infants and toddlers, based on standards for **developmentally appropriate practice.** These standards, devised by the U.S. National Association for the Education of Young Children, specify program characteristics that serve young children's developmental and individual needs, based on both current research and expert consensus.

© ELLEN B. SENISI PHOTOGRAPHY

High-quality child care, with a generous caregiver–infant ratio, well-trained caregivers, and developmentally appropriate activities, can be especially beneficial to children from low-SES homes.

Child care in the United States is affected by a macrosystem of individualistic values and weak government regulation and funding. Recognizing that child care is in a state of crisis, the U.S. federal government and some states have allocated additional funds to subsidize it, especially for low-income families. Though far from meeting the need, this increase in resources has had a positive impact on child care quality and accessibility (Children's Defense Fund, 2008).

Good child care is a cost-effective means of protecting children's well-being. And much like the programs we are about to consider, it can serve as effective early intervention for children whose development is at risk.

Early Intervention for At-Risk Infants and Toddlers

Children living in poverty are likely to show gradual declines in intelligence test scores and to achieve poorly when they reach school age (Bradley et al., 2001; Gutman, Sameroff, & Cole, 2003). These problems are largely due to stressful home environments that undermine children's ability to learn and that increase their likelihood of remaining poor throughout their lives (McLoyd, Aikens, & Burton, 2006). A variety of intervention programs have been developed to break this tragic cycle of poverty. Although most begin in the preschool years, a few start during infancy and continue through early childhood.

In center-based interventions, children attend an organized child-care or preschool program where they receive educational, nutritional, and health services, and their parents receive child-rearing and other social-service supports. In home-based interventions, a skilled adult visits the home and works with parents, teaching them how to stimulate young children's development. In most programs of either type, participating children score higher than untreated controls on mental tests by age 2. The earlier intervention begins, the longer it lasts, and the greater its scope and intensity, the better participants' cognitive and academic performance is throughout childhood and adolescence (Brooks-Gunn, 2004; Ramey, Ramey, & Lanzi, 2006).

The Carolina Abecedarian Project illustrates these favorable outcomes. In the 1970s, more than 100 infants from poverty-stricken families, ranging in age from 3 weeks to 3 months, were randomly assigned to either a treatment group or a control group. Treatment infants were enrolled in full-time, year-round child care through the preschool years. There they received stimulation aimed at promoting motor, cognitive, language, and social skills and, after age 3, literacy and math concepts. Special emphasis was placed on rich, responsive adult–child verbal communication. All children received nutrition and health services; the primary difference between treatment and control groups was the intensive child-care experience.

As Figure 5.7 shows, by 12 months, the IQs of the two groups diverged. Treatment children sustained their advantage until last tested—at age 21. In addition, throughout their school years, treatment youths achieved considerably better in reading and math. These gains translated into more years of schooling completed, higher rates of college enrollment and

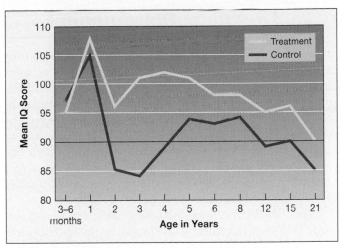

■ **FIGURE 5.7** ■ **IQ scores of treatment and control children from infancy to 21 years in the Carolina Abecedarian Project.** At 1 year, treatment children outperformed controls, an advantage consistently maintained through age 21. The IQ scores of both groups declined gradually during childhood and adolescence, probably due to the damaging impact of poverty on mental development. (Adapted from Campbell et al., 2001.)

employment in skilled jobs, and lower rates of drug use and adolescent parenthood (Campbell et al., 2001, 2002; Ramey & Ramey, 1999).

Without early intervention, many children born into economically disadvantaged families will not reach their potential. Recognition of this reality led the U.S. Congress to provide limited funding for intervention directed at infants and toddlers at risk for developmental problems. *Early Head Start*, begun in 1995, currently has 700 sites serving 65,000 low-income families. A recent evaluation, conducted when children reached age 3, showed that intervention led to warmer, more stimulating parenting, a reduction in harsh discipline, gains in cognitive and language development, and lessening of child aggression (Love et al., 2005; Love, Chazan-Cohen, & Raikes, 2007). The strongest effects occurred at sites offering a mix of center- and home-based services. Though not yet plentiful enough to meet the need, such programs are a promising beginning.

ASK YOURSELF

≫ REVIEW
Using what you learned about brain development in Chapter 4, explain why it is best to initiate intervention for poverty-stricken children in the first two years rather than later.

≫ APPLY
Fifteen-month-old Jocy's IQ is 115. His mother wants to know exactly what this means and what she should do to support his mental development. How would you respond?

≫ REFLECT
Suppose you were seeking a child-care setting for your baby. What would you want it to be like, and why?

Language Development

Improvements in perception and cognition during infancy pave the way for an extraordinary human achievement—language. In Chapter 4, we saw that by the second half of the first year, infants make dramatic progress in distinguishing the basic sounds of their language and in segmenting the flow of speech into word and phrase units. They also start to comprehend some words and, around 12 months, say their first word. Between 1½ and 2 years, toddlers combine two words (MacWhinney, 2005). By age 6, children have a vocabulary of about 10,000 words and speak in elaborate sentences.

How do infants and toddlers make such remarkable progress in launching these skills? To address this question, let's examine several prominent theories of language development.

Theories of Language Development

In the 1950s, researchers did not take seriously the idea that very young children might be able to figure out important properties of language. As a result, the first two theories of how children acquire language were extreme views. One, *behaviorism*, regards language development as entirely due to environmental influences. The second, *nativism*, assumes that children are "prewired" to master the intricate rules of their language.

■ **THE BEHAVIORIST PERSPECTIVE.** Behaviorist B. F. Skinner (1957) proposed that language, like any other behavior, is acquired through *operant conditioning* (see Chapter 4, page 104). As the baby makes sounds, parents reinforce those that are most like words with smiles, hugs, and speech in return. Some behaviorists believe that children rely on *imitation* to rapidly acquire complex utterances, such as whole phrases and sentences (Moerk, 2000). Imitation can combine with reinforcement to promote language, as when a parent coaxes, "Say, 'I want a cookie,'" and delivers praise and a treat after the toddler responds, "Wanna cookie!"

Although reinforcement and imitation contribute to early language development, they are best viewed as supporting rather than fully explaining it. "It's amazing how creative Caitlin is with language," Carolyn remarked one day. "She combines words in ways she's never heard before, like 'needle it' when she wants me to sew up her teddy bear and 'allgone outside' when she has to come in." Carolyn's observations are accurate: Young children create many novel utterances that are not reinforced by or copied from others (Owens, 2005).

■ **THE NATIVIST PERSPECTIVE.** Linguist Noam Chomsky (1957) proposed a nativist theory that regards the young child's amazing language skill as etched into the structure of the human brain. Focusing on grammar, Chomsky reasoned that the rules of sentence organization are too complex to be directly taught to or discovered by even a cognitively adept young child. Rather, he argued, all children have a **language acquisition device (LAD),** an innate system that contains a *universal grammar,* or set of rules common to all languages. It enables children, no matter which language they hear, to understand and speak in a rule-oriented fashion as soon as they pick up enough words.

Are children biologically primed to acquire language? Recall from Chapter 4 that newborn babies are remarkably sensitive to speech sounds. And children the world over reach major language milestones in a similar sequence (Gleitman & Newport, 1996).

Furthermore, evidence that childhood is a *sensitive period* for language acquisition is consistent with Chomsky's idea of a biologically based language program. Researchers have examined the language competence of deaf adults who acquired their first language—American Sign Language (ASL), a gestural system used by the deaf—at different ages. The late learners, whose parents chose to educate them through speech and lip-reading, did not acquire spoken language because of their profound deafness. Consistent with the sensitive period notion, those who learned ASL in adolescence or adulthood never became as proficient as those who learned in childhood (Mayberry, 1994; Newport, 1991; Singleton & Newport, 2004).

But challenges to Chomsky's theory suggest that it, too, provides only a partial account of language development. First, researchers have had great difficulty identifying the single system of grammar that Chomsky believes underlies all languages (Maratsos, 1998; Tomasello, 2003, 2005). Second, children's progress in mastering many sentence constructions is gradual, with errors along the way, indicating more learning and discovery than Chomsky assumed (Tomasello, 2003, 2006).

■ **THE INTERACTIONIST PERSPECTIVE.** Recent ideas about language development emphasize *interactions* between inner capacities and environmental influences. One type of interactionist theory applies the information-processing perspective to language development. A second type emphasizes social interaction.

Some information-processing theorists assume that children make sense of their complex language environments by applying powerful cognitive capacities of a general kind (Bates, 2004; Elman, 2001; Munakata, 2006). These theorists note that brain regions housing language also govern similar perceptual and cognitive abilities, such as the capacity to analyze musical and visual patterns (Koelsch et al., 2002; Saygin et al., 2004).

Other theorists blend this information-processing view with Chomsky's nativist perspective. They agree that infants are amazing analyzers of speech and other information. But, they argue, these capacities probably are not sufficient to account for mastery of higher-level aspects of language, such as intricate grammatical structures (Newport & Aslin, 2000). They also point out that grammatical competence may depend more on specific brain structures than the other components of language. When 2- to 2½-year-olds and adults listened to short sentences—some grammatically correct, others with phrase-structure violations—both groups showed similarly distinct ERP brain-wave patterns for each sentence type in the left frontal and temporal lobes of the cerebral cortex (Oberecker &

Friederici, 2006; Oberecker, Friedrich, & Friederici, 2005). This suggests that 2-year-olds process sentence structures using the same neural system as adults do.

Still other interactionists emphasize that children's social skills are central to language development. In this social-interactionist view, an active child strives to communicate, cuing caregivers to provide appropriate language experiences, which help the child relate the content and structure of language to its social meanings (Bohannon & Bonvillian, 2009). Among social interactionists, disagreement continues over whether or not children are equipped with specialized language abilities (Lidz, 2007; Shatz, 2007; Tomasello, 2006). Nevertheless, as we chart the course of language development, we will encounter much support for their central premise—that children's social competencies and language experiences greatly affect their progress.

Getting Ready to Talk

Before babies say their first word, they make impressive progress toward understanding and speaking their native tongue. They listen attentively to human speech, and they make speechlike sounds. As adults, we can hardly help but respond.

■ **COOING AND BABBLING.** Around 2 months, babies begin to make vowel-like noises, called **cooing** because of their pleasant "oo" quality. Gradually, consonants are added, and around 6 months, **babbling** appears, in which infants repeat consonant–vowel combinations in long strings, such as "bababababa" or "nanananana."

Babies everywhere (even those who are deaf) start babbling at about the same age and produce a similar range of early sounds. But for babbling to develop further, infants must be able to hear human speech. In hearing-impaired babies, these speechlike sounds are greatly delayed. And a deaf infant not exposed to sign language will stop babbling entirely (Oller, 2000).

As infants listen to spoken language, babbling expands to include a broader range of sounds. Around 7 months, it includes many sounds common in spoken languages. By 10 months, it reflects the sound and intonation patterns of infants' language community, some of which are transferred to their first words (Boysson-Bardies & Vihman, 1991).

Deaf infants exposed to sign language from birth and hearing babies of deaf, signing parents produce babblelike hand motions with the rhythmic patterns of natural sign languages (Petitto et al., 2001, 2004; Petitto & Marentette, 1991). This sensitivity to language rhythm—evident in both spoken and signed babbling—supports both discovery and production of meaningful language units.

■ **BECOMING A COMMUNICATOR.** At birth, infants are prepared for some aspects of conversational behavior. For example, they initiate interaction through eye contact and terminate it by looking away. By 3 to 4 months, infants start to gaze in the same direction adults are looking, a skill that becomes more accurate at 10 to 11 months, as babies realize that others'

Infants communicate from the very beginning of life, as seen in this interchange between a father and his baby. How will this child accomplish the impressive task of becoming a fluent speaker of his native language within just a few years? Theorists disagree sharply on answers to this question.

focus provides information about their communicative intentions (Brooks & Meltzoff, 2005). Adults also follow the baby's line of vision and comment on what the infant sees. This **joint attention,** in which the child attends to the same object or event as the caregiver, contributes greatly to early language development. Infants and toddlers who often experience it sustain attention longer, comprehend more language, produce meaningful gestures and words earlier, and show faster vocabulary development (Carpenter, Nagell, & Tomasello, 1998; Flom & Pick, 2003; Silvén, 2001).

Between 4 and 6 months, interactions between caregivers and babies begin to include *give-and-take,* as in pat-a-cake and peekaboo games. At first, the parent starts the game, and the baby is an amused observer. By 12 months, babies participate actively, practicing the turn-taking pattern of conversation. Infants' play maturity and vocalizations during games predict advanced language progress in the second year (Rome-Flanders & Cronk, 1995).

At the end of the first year, babies extend their joint attention and social interaction skills. They use *preverbal gestures* to influence others' behavior (Liszkowski et al., 2004). For example, while looking at her mother, Caitlin held up a toy to show it and pointed to the cupboard when she wanted a cookie. Carolyn responded to these gestures and also labeled them ("Oh, you want a cookie!"). In this way, toddlers learn that using language leads to desired results. Soon they integrate words with gestures, using the gesture to expand their verbal message, as in pointing to a toy while saying "give" (Capirci et al., 2005). The earlier toddlers form word–gesture combinations, the sooner they produce two-word utterances at the end of the second year (Özçaliskan & Goldin-Meadow, 2005).

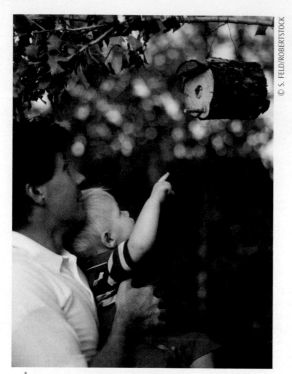

This baby uses a preverbal gesture to draw his father's attention to the birdhouse. His father's verbal response promotes the baby's transition to spoken language.

First Words

In the second half of the first year, infants begin to understand word meanings. When 6-month-olds listened to the word "Mommy" or "Daddy" while looking at side-by-side videos of their parents, they looked longer at the video of the named parent (Tincoff & Jusczyk, 1999). First spoken words, around 1 year, build on the sensorimotor foundations Piaget described and on categories children form during their first two years. Usually they refer to important people ("Mama," "Dada"), animals ("doggie," "kitty,"), objects that move ("car," "ball,"), foods ("milk," "apple"), familiar actions ("bye-bye," "more"), or outcomes of familiar actions ("wet," "hot") (Hart, 2004; Nelson, 1973).

When toddlers first learn words, they often apply them too narrowly, an error called **underextension.** At 16 months, Caitlin used "bear" only to refer to the worn and tattered bear she carried nearly constantly. As vocabulary expands, a more common error is **overextension**—applying a word to a wider collection of objects and events than is appropriate. For example, Grace used "car" for buses, trains, trucks, and fire engines. Toddlers' overextensions reflect their sensitivity to categories (MacWhinney, 2005). They apply a new word to a group of similar experiences, often overextending deliberately because they have difficulty recalling or have not acquired a suitable word.

Overextensions illustrate another important feature of language development: the distinction between language *production* (the words children use) and language *comprehension* (the words they understand). At all ages, comprehension develops ahead of production. Still, the two capacities are related. The speed and accuracy of toddlers' comprehension of spoken language increase dramatically over the second year. And toddlers who are faster and more accurate in comprehension tend to show more rapid growth in words understood and produced (Fernald, Perfors, & Marchman, 2006). Quick comprehension frees space in working memory for picking up new words and for the more demanding task of using them to communicate.

The Two-Word Utterance Phase

Young toddlers add to their spoken vocabularies at a rate of one to three words per week. Because gains in word production between 18 and 24 months are so impressive (one or two words per day), many researchers concluded that toddlers undergo a *spurt in vocabulary*—a transition from a slower to a faster learning phase. But recent evidence indicates that most children show a steady, continuous increase in rate of word learning that continues through the preschool years (Ganger & Brent, 2004).

Once toddlers produce about 200 words, they start to combine two words: "Mommy shoe," "go car," "more cookie." These two-word utterances are called **telegraphic speech** because, like a telegram, they focus on high-content words, omitting smaller, less important ones. Children the world over use them to express an impressive variety of meanings.

Two-word speech consists largely of simple formulas ("more + X," "eat + X"), with different words inserted in the X position. Rather than following grammatical rules, toddlers' word-order regularities are usually copies of adult word pairings, as when the parent says, "How about *more sandwich?*" (Tomasello, 2006).

Individual and Cultural Differences

Although, on average, children produce their first word around their first birthday, the range is large, from 8 to 18 months—variation due to a complex blend of genetic and environmental influences. Earlier we saw that Timmy's spoken language was delayed, in part because of Vanessa's tense, directive communication with him. But Timmy is also a boy, and many studies show that girls are slightly ahead of boys in early vocabulary growth (Fenson et al., 1994). The most common explanation is girls' faster rate of physical maturation, believed to promote earlier development of the left cerebral hemisphere.

Temperament matters, too. Shy toddlers often wait until they understand a great deal before trying to speak. Once they do speak, their vocabularies increase rapidly, although they remain slightly behind their agemates (Spere et al., 2004). Temperamentally negative toddlers also acquire language more slowly because their high emotional reactivity diverts them from processing linguistic information (Salley & Dixon, 2007).

Also, the more words caregivers use, the more children learn (Weizman & Snow, 2001). Mothers talk much more to toddler-age girls than to boys, and parents converse less often with shy than with sociable children (Leaper, Anderson, & Sanders, 1998; Patterson & Fisher, 2002). Because low SES children receive less parental verbal stimulation (both conversation and book reading), their vocabularies are, on average, only one-fourth as large as their higher-SES agemates' at kindergarten age (Hoff, 2004; Lee & Burkam, 2002).

Young children have distinct styles of early language learning. Caitlin and Grace, like most toddlers, used a **referential style**; their vocabularies consisted mainly of words that refer to objects. A smaller number of toddlers use an **expressive style**; compared with referential children, they produce many more social formulas and pronouns ("thank you," "done," "I want it"). These styles reflect early ideas about the functions of language. Grace, for example, thought words were for naming things. In contrast, expressive-style children believe words are for talking about people's feelings and needs. The vocabularies of referential-style toddlers grow faster because all languages contain many more object labels than social phrases (Bates et al., 1994).

What accounts for a toddler's language style? Rapidly developing referential-style children eagerly imitate their parents' frequent naming of objects, and their parents imitate back—a strategy that supports swift vocabulary growth by helping children remember new labels (Masur & Rodemaker, 1999). Expressive-style children tend to be highly sociable, and their parents more often use verbal routines ("How are you?" "It's no trouble") that support social relationships (Goldfield, 1987).

The two language styles are also linked to culture. Whereas object words are common in the vocabularies of English-speaking toddlers, words for social routines are more numerous among Chinese, Japanese, and Korean toddlers. Mothers' speech reflects this difference: Asian mothers, perhaps because of a cultural emphasis on group membership, teach social routines as soon as their children begin to speak (Choi & Gopnik, 1995; Fernald & Morikawa, 1993; Tardif, Gelman, & Xu, 1999).

Supporting Early Language Development

Consistent with the interactionist view, a rich social environment builds on young children's natural readiness to acquire language. Adults in many cultures speak to young children in **child-directed speech (CDS),** a form of communication made up of short sentences with high-pitched, exaggerated expression, clear pronunciation, distinct pauses between speech segments, and repetition of new words in a variety of contexts ("See the ball," "The ball bounced!") (Fernald et al., 1989;

O'Neill et al., 2005). Deaf parents use a similar style of communication when signing to their deaf babies (Masataka, 1996). CDS builds on several communicative strategies we have already considered: joint attention, turn-taking, and caregivers' sensitivity to toddlers' preverbal gestures. In this example, Carolyn uses CDS with 18-month old Caitlin:

Caitlin: "Go car."

Carolyn: "Yes, time to go in the car. Where's your jacket?"

Caitlin: [Looks around, walks to the closet.] "Dacket!" [Points to her jacket.]

Carolyn: "There's that jacket! [She helps Caitlin into the jacket.] Now, say bye-bye to Grace and Timmy."

Caitlin: "Bye-bye, G-ace. Bye-bye, Te-te."

Carolyn: "Where's your bear?"

Caitlin: [Looks around.]

Carolyn: [Pointing.] "See? Go get the bear. By the sofa."

From birth on, infants prefer CDS over other adult talk, and by 5 months they are more emotionally responsive to it (Aslin, Jusczyk, & Pisoni, 1998). Parents constantly fine-tune the length and content of their utterances to fit their children's needs—adjustments that foster word learning and enable toddlers to join in (Cameron-Faulkner, Lieven, & Tomasello, 2003; Fernald & Hurtado, 2006). As we saw earlier, parent–toddler conversation—especially reading and talking about picture books—strongly predicts language development and academic success during the school years.

Do social experiences that promote language development remind you of those that strengthen cognitive development in general? CDS and parent–child conversation create a *zone of proximal development* in which children's language skills expand. In the next chapter, we will see that sensitivity to children's needs and capacities supports their emotional and social development as well.

ASK YOURSELF

≫ REVIEW

Describe evidence that supports the social interactionist perspective on language development.

≫ APPLY

Fran frequently corrects her 17-month-old son Jeremy's attempts to talk and—fearing that he won't use words—refuses to respond to his gestures. How might Fran be contributing to Jeremy's slow language progress?

≫ REFLECT

Find an opportunity to speak to an infant or toddler. How did your manner of speaking differ from the way you typically speak to an adult? What features of your speech are likely to promote early language development?

Summary

Piaget's Cognitive-Developmental Theory

According to Piaget, how do schemes change over the course of development?

>> By acting on the environment, children move through four stages in which psychological structures, or **schemes,** achieve a better fit with external reality.

>> Schemes change in two ways: through **adaptation,** which is made up of two complementary activities—**assimilation** and **accommodation**—and through **organization.**

Describe the major cognitive achievements of the sensorimotor stage.

>> In the **sensorimotor stage,** the **circular reaction** provides a means of adapting first schemes, and the newborn's reflexes are transformed into the flexible action patterns of the older infant. Around 8 months, infants develop **intentional,** or **goal-directed, behavior** and begin to understand **object permanence.** Between 18 and 24 months, **mental representation** is evident in sudden solutions to sensorimotor problems, mastery of object permanence problems involving invisible displacement, **deferred imitation,** and **make-believe play.**

What does follow-up research reveal about the accuracy of Piaget's sensorimotor stage?

>> Many studies suggest that infants display certain understandings earlier than Piaget believed. Some awareness of object permanence, as revealed by the **violation-of-expectation method** and object-tracking research, may be evident in the first few months. In addition, young infants display deferred imitation and analogical problem solving, which suggests that they are capable of mental representation.

>> Today, researchers believe that newborns have more built-in equipment for making sense of their world than Piaget assumed. According to the **core knowledge perspective,** infants begin life with core domains of thought that support early, rapid cognitive development. Although findings on early, ready-made knowledge are mixed, there is broad agreement that many cognitive changes are continuous rather than stagelike and that cognition develops unevenly rather than in an integrated fashion.

Information Processing

Describe the information-processing view of cognitive development.

>> Information-processing researchers regard development as gradual and continuous and study many aspects of thinking. Most assume that we hold information in three parts of the system, the **sensory register; working,** or **short-term, memory;** and **long-term memory.** As information flows through the system, **mental strategies** operate on it so that it can be retained and used efficiently. To manage the complex activities of working memory, the **central executive** directs the flow of information.

What changes in attention, memory, and categorization take place during the first two years?

>> With age, infants attend to more aspects of the environment and take information in more quickly. In the second year, attention to novelty declines and sustained attention improves.

>> Young infants are capable of **recognition** memory. By the end of the first year, they can **recall** past events.

>> During the first year, infants group stimuli into increasingly complex categories, and categorization shifts from a *perceptual* to a *conceptual* basis.

Describe contributions and limitations of the information-processing approach to our understanding of early cognitive development.

>> Information-processing findings challenge Piaget's view of babies as purely sensorimotor beings who cannot mentally represent experiences. But information processing has not yet provided a broad, comprehensive theory of children's thinking.

The Social Context of Early Cognitive Development

How does Vygotsky's concept of the zone of proximal development expand our understanding of early cognitive development?

>> Vygotsky believed that infants master tasks within the **zone of proximal development**—that is, tasks just ahead of their current capacities—through the support and guidance of more skilled partners. As early as the first year, cultural variations in social experiences affect mental strategies.

Individual Differences in Early Mental Development

Describe the mental testing approach and the extent to which infant tests predict later performance.

>> The mental testing approach measures intellectual development in an effort to predict future performance. Scores are arrived at by computing an **intelligence quotient (IQ),** which compares an individual's test performance with that of a **standardization** sample of same-age individuals.

>> Most infant tests, which consist largely of perceptual and motor responses, predict later intelligence poorly. Speed of habituation and recovery to visual stimuli are better predictors of future performance.

Discuss environmental influences on early mental development, including home, child care, and early intervention for at-risk infants and toddlers.

>> An organized, stimulating home environment and parental encouragement, involvement, and affection repeatedly predict early mental test scores. Although the home environment–IQ relationship is partly due to heredity, family living conditions also affect mental development.

>> Quality of infant and toddler child care has a major impact on mental development. Standards for **developmentally appropriate practice** specify program characteristics that meet young children's developmental needs.

>> Intensive intervention beginning in infancy and extending through early childhood can prevent the declines in intelligence and poor academic performance seen in many poverty-stricken children.

Language Development

Describe theories of language development, and indicate how much emphasis each places on innate abilities and environmental influences.

>> According to the *behaviorist* perspective, parents train children in language skills through operant conditioning and imitation. Behaviorism, however, has difficulty accounting for children's novel utterances.

>> In contrast, Chomsky's *nativist* view regards children as naturally endowed with a **language acquisition device (LAD)**. Although evidence that mastery of a complex language system is unique to humans and that childhood is a *sensitive period* for language acquisition is supportive, Chomsky's theory provides only a partial account of language development.

>> Recent theories suggest that language development results from *interactions* between inner capacities and environmental influences. Some interactionists apply the information-processing perspective to language development. Others emphasize children's social skills and language experiences.

© LWA-SHARIE KENNEDY/ZEFA/CORBIS

Describe major language milestones in the first two years, individual differences, and ways adults can support early language development.

>> Infants begin **cooing** at 2 months and **babbling** at about 6 months. Around 10 to 11 months, their skill at establishing **joint attention** improves. Adults can encourage language progress by responding to infants' coos and babbles, establishing joint attention and labeling what babies see, playing turn-taking games, and acknowledging infants' preverbal gestures.

>> In the second half of the first year, infants begin to understand word meanings. At the end of the first year, they use *preverbal gestures,* such as pointing, to influence others' behavior.

>> Around 12 months, toddlers say their first word. Young children often make errors of **underextension** and **overextension**. Rate of word learning increases steadily, and once vocabulary reaches about 200 words, two-word utterances called **telegraphic speech** appear. At all ages, language *comprehension* is ahead of *production*.

>> Girls show faster language progress than boys, and reserved, cautious toddlers may wait before trying to speak. Most toddlers use a **referential style** of language learning; their early words consist largely of names for objects. A few use an **expressive style,** in which pronouns and social formulas are common and vocabulary grows more slowly.

>> Adults in many cultures speak to young children in **child-directed speech (CDS),** a simplified form of language that is well-suited to their learning needs. Conversation between parent and toddler is one of the best predictors of early language development and academic success during the school years.

Important Terms and Concepts

accommodation (p. 117)
adaptation (p. 117)
assimilation (p. 117)
autobiographical memory (p. 126)
babbling (p. 135)
central executive (p. 124)
child-directed speech (CDS) (p. 137)
circular reaction (p. 118)
cooing (p. 135)
core knowledge perspective (p. 122)
deferred imitation (p. 120)
developmentally appropriate practice (p. 132)
expressive style of language learning (p. 137)

Home Observation for Measurement of the Environment (HOME) (p. 131)
infantile amnesia (p. 126)
intelligence quotient (IQ) (p. 130)
intentional, or goal-directed, behavior (p. 119)
joint attention (p. 135)
language acquisition device (LAD) (p. 134)
long-term memory (p. 124)
make-believe play (p. 120)
mental representation (p. 119)
mental strategies (p. 124)
normal distribution (p. 130)
object permanence (p. 119)
organization (p. 118)

overextension (p. 136)
recall (p. 125)
recognition (p. 125)
referential style of language learning (p. 137)
scheme (p. 117)
sensorimotor stage (p. 117)
sensory register (p. 124)
standardization (p. 130)
telegraphic speech (p. 136)
underextension (p. 136)
violation-of-expectation method (p. 120)
working, or short-term, memory (p. 124)
zone of proximal development (p. 128)

CHAPTER 6

Emotional and Social Development in Infancy and Toddlerhood

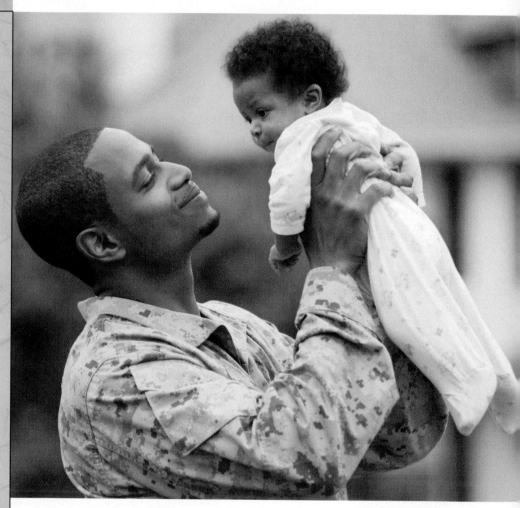

© BLEND IMAGES/SUPERSTOCK

*Separations—a fact of life in military families—
are highly stressful, especially during wartime.
Nevertheless, the time this father takes to build
a strong, affectionate bond with his baby will engender
feelings of security in the child—a vital foundation
for all aspects of early development.*

As Caitlin reached 8 months of age, her parents noticed that she had become more fearful. One evening, when Carolyn and David left her with a babysitter, she wailed as they headed for the door—an experience she had accepted easily a few weeks earlier. Caitlin and Timmy's caregiver Ginette also observed an increasing wariness of strangers. At the mail carrier's knock at the door, they clung to Ginette's legs, reaching out to be picked up.

At the same time, each baby seemed more willful. Removing an object from the hand produced little response at 5 months. But at 8 months, when Timmy's mother, Vanessa, took away a table knife he had managed to reach, he burst into angry screams and could not be consoled or distracted.

All Monica and Kevin knew about Grace's first year was that she had been deeply loved by her destitute, homeless mother. Separation from her had left Grace in shock. At first she was extremely sad, turning away when Monica or Kevin picked her up. But as Grace's new parents held her close, spoke gently, and satisfied her craving for food, Grace returned their affection. Two weeks after her arrival, her despondency gave way to a sunny, easygoing disposition. As her second birthday approached, she pointed to herself, exclaiming "Gwace!" and laid claim to treasured possessions: "Gwace's teddy bear!"

Taken together, the children's reactions reflect two related aspects of personality development during the first two years: close ties to others and a sense of self. We begin with Erikson's psychosocial theory, which provides an overview of infant and toddler personality development. Then, as we chart the course of emotional development, we will discover why fear and anger became more apparent in Caitlin's and Timmy's range of emotions by the end of the first year. Our attention then turns to the origins and developmental consequences of individual differences in temperament.

Next, we take up attachment to the caregiver, the child's first affectionate tie. We will see how the feelings of security that grow out of this important bond support the child's sense of independence and expanding social relationships. Finally, we consider how cognitive advances combine with social experiences to foster early self-development and the beginnings of self-control in the second year.

Erikson's Theory of Infant and Toddler Personality

Our discussion in Chapter 1 revealed that psychoanalytic theory is no longer in the mainstream of human development research. But one of its lasting contributions is its ability to capture the essence of personality during each period of development. Recall that Sigmund Freud believed that psychological health and maladjustment could be traced to the early years—in particular, to the quality of the child's relationships with parents. Although Freud came to be heavily criticized, the basic outlines of his theory were elaborated in several subsequent theories. The most influential is Erik Erikson's *psychosocial theory*, also introduced in Chapter 1.

Basic Trust versus Mistrust

Erikson accepted Freud's emphasis on the importance of the parent–infant relationship during feeding, but he expanded and enriched Freud's view. A healthy outcome during infancy, Erikson believed, depends on the *quality* of caregiving: relieving discomfort promptly and sensitively, waiting patiently until the baby has had enough milk, and weaning when the infant shows less interest in breast or bottle.

Erikson recognized that many factors affect parental responsiveness—feelings of personal happiness, current life conditions (for example, additional young children in the family), and culturally valued child-rearing practices. But when the *balance of care* is sympathetic and loving, the psychological conflict of the first year—**basic trust versus mistrust**—is resolved on the positive side. The trusting infant expects the world to be good and gratifying, so he feels confident about venturing out and exploring it. The mistrustful baby cannot count on the kindness and compassion of others, so she protects herself by withdrawing from people and things around her.

Autonomy versus Shame and Doubt

With the transition to toddlerhood, Freud viewed the parents' manner of toilet training as decisive for psychological health. But in Erikson's view, toilet training is only one of many influential experiences. The familiar refrains of newly walking, talking toddlers—"No!" "Do it myself!"—reveal a period of budding selfhood. The conflict of **autonomy versus shame and doubt** is resolved favorably when parents provide young children with suitable guidance and reasonable choices. A self-confident, secure 2-year-old has parents who do not criticize or attack him when he fails at new skills—using the toilet, eating with a spoon, or putting away toys. And they meet his assertions of independence with tolerance and understanding—for example, by giving him an extra five minutes to finish his play before leaving for the grocery store. In contrast, when parents are over- or undercontrolling, the outcome is a child who feels forced and shamed or who doubts his ability to control his impulses and act competently on his own.

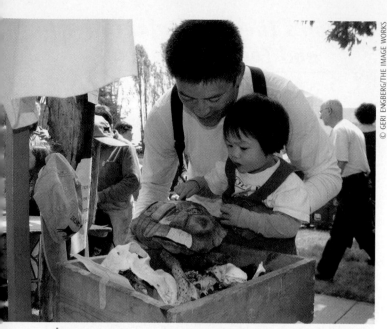

At a community Earth Day festival, this father gently encourages his 1-year-old daughter as she examines a strange object—a turtle shell. The more sensitive he is in this and other situations, the more likely she is to view the world as good and gratifying and to confidently explore it.

In sum, basic trust and autonomy grow out of warm, sensitive parenting and reasonable expectations for impulse control starting in the second year. If children emerge from the first few years without sufficient trust in caregivers and without a healthy sense of individuality, the seeds are sown for adjustment problems.

Emotional Development

Researchers have conducted careful observations to find out how babies convey their emotions and interpret those of others. They have discovered that emotions play powerful roles in organizing the attainments that Erikson regarded as so important: social relationships, exploration of the environment, and discovery of the self (Halle, 2003; Saarni et al., 2006).

Development of Basic Emotions

Basic emotions—happiness, interest, surprise, fear, anger, sadness, and disgust—are universal in humans and other primates and have a long evolutionary history of promoting survival. Do newborns express basic emotions? Although signs of some emotions are present, babies' earliest emotional life consists of little more than two global arousal states: attraction to pleasant stimulation and withdrawal from unpleasant stimulation (Camras et al., 2003; Fox, 1991). Only gradually do emotions become clear, well-organized signals.

According to one view, sensitive, contingent caregiver communication, in which parents selectively mirror aspects of the baby's diffuse emotional behavior, helps infants construct emotional expressions that closely resemble those of adults (Gergely & Watson, 1999). Around 6 months, face, voice, and posture form organized patterns that vary meaningfully with environmental events. For example, Caitlin typically responded to her parents' playful interaction with a joyful face, pleasant babbling, and a relaxed posture, as if to say, "This is fun!" In contrast, an unresponsive parent often evokes a sad face, fussy vocalizations, and a drooping body (sending the message, "I'm despondent") or an angry face, crying, and "pick-me-up" gestures (as if to say, "Change this unpleasant event!") (Weinberg & Tronick, 1994; Yale et al., 1999).

Four basic emotions—happiness, anger, sadness, and fear—have received the most research attention. Let's see how they develop.

■ **HAPPINESS.** Happiness—expressed first in blissful smiles and later through exuberant laughter—contributes to many aspects of development. When infants achieve new skills, they smile and laugh, displaying delight in motor and cognitive mastery. As the smile encourages caregivers to be affectionate and stimulating, the baby smiles even more (Aksan & Kochanska, 2004). Happiness binds parent and baby into a warm, supportive relationship that fosters the infant's developing competences.

During the early weeks, newborn babies smile when full, during REM sleep, and in response to gentle stroking of the skin and the mother's soft voice. By the end of the first month, infants smile at dynamic, eye-catching sights, such as a bright object jumping suddenly across their field of vision. Between 6 and 10 weeks, the parent's communication evokes a broad grin called the **social smile** (Lavelli & Fogel, 2005; Sroufe & Waters, 1976). These changes in smiling parallel the development of infant perceptual capacities—in particular, babies' increasing sensitivity to visual patterns, including the human face (see Chapter 4).

Laughter, which appears around 3 to 4 months, reflects faster processing of information than smiling. As with smiling, the first laughs occur in response to very active stimuli, such as the parent saying playfully, "I'm gonna get you!" and kissing the baby's tummy. As infants understand more about their world, they laugh at events with subtler elements of surprise, such as a silent game of peekaboo (Sroufe & Wunsch, 1972). Around the middle of the first year, infants smile and laugh more when interacting with familiar people, a preference that strengthens the parent–child bond. Between 8 and 10 months, the smile becomes a deliberate social signal: Infants interrupt their play with an interesting toy to relay their delight to an attentive adult (Venezia et al., 2004).

■ **ANGER AND SADNESS.** Newborn babies respond with generalized distress to a variety of unpleasant experiences, including hunger, changes in body temperature, and too much or too little stimulation. From 4 to 6 months into the second year, angry expressions increase in frequency and intensity. Older infants react with anger in a wider range of situations—when an object is taken away, the caregiver leaves for a brief time, they are put down for a nap, or they cannot control an expected outcome—for example, a toy that previously produced interesting sounds but no longer does so (Camras et al., 1992; Stenberg & Campos, 1990; Sullivan & Lewis, 2003).

Cognitive and motor development contribute to this rise in angry reactions. As infants become capable of intentional behavior (see Chapter 5), they want to control their own actions. They are also more persistent about obtaining desired objects (Mascolo & Fischer, 2007). Furthermore, older infants are better at identifying who caused them pain or removed a toy. The rise in anger is also adaptive. New motor capacities enable an angry infant to defend herself or overcome an obstacle (Izard & Ackerman, 2000).

Although expressions of sadness also occur in response to pain, removal of an object, and brief separations, they are less frequent than anger (Alessandri, Sullivan, & Lewis, 1990; Izard, Hembree, & Huebner, 1987). But when caregiver–infant communication is seriously disrupted, infant sadness is common— a condition that impairs all aspects of development (see the Lifespan Vista box on page 144).

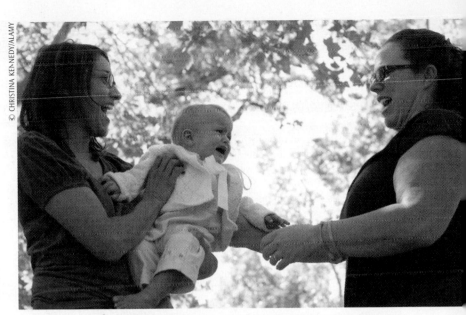

When an unfamiliar adult attempts to hold her, an 8-month-old makes it clear that she prefers her mother! Fear rises during the second half of the first year. Its most frequent expression is stranger anxiety.

■ **FEAR.**   Like anger, fear rises during the second half of the first year. Older infants often hesitate before playing with a new toy, and newly crawling infants soon show fear of heights (see Chapter 4). But the most frequent expression of fear is to unfamiliar adults, a response called **stranger anxiety.** Many infants and toddlers are quite wary of strangers, although the reaction varies with the infant's temperament (some babies are generally more fearful), past experiences with strangers, and the current situation (Thompson & Limber, 1991). When an unfamiliar adult picks up the infant, stranger anxiety is likely. But if the adult sits still or acts warmly and playfully and a parent is nearby, infants often show positive and curious behavior (Horner, 1980).

Infant-rearing practices can modify stranger anxiety, as cross-cultural research reveals. Among the Efe hunters and gatherers of Congo, West Africa, where the maternal death rate is high, infant survival is safeguarded by a collective caregiving system in which, starting at birth, Efe babies are passed from one adult to another. Consequently, Efe infants show little stranger anxiety (Tronick, Morelli, & Ivey, 1992).

The rise in fear after age 6 months keeps newly mobile babies' enthusiasm for exploration in check. Once wariness develops, babies use the familiar caregiver as a **secure base,** or point from which to explore, venturing into the environment and then returning for emotional support. As part of this adaptive system, encounters with strangers lead to two conflicting tendencies: approach (indicated by interest and friendliness) and avoidance (indicated by fear). The infant's behavior is a balance between the two.

As toddlers discriminate more effectively between threatening and nonthreatening people and situations, stranger anxiety and other fears of the first two years decline. Fear also wanes as toddlers acquire more strategies for coping with it, as you will see when we discuss emotional self-regulation.

Understanding and Responding to the Emotions of Others

Infants' emotional expressions are closely tied to their ability to interpret the emotional cues of others. We have seen that in the first few months, babies match the feeling tone of the caregiver in face-to-face communication. Perhaps infants respond in kind to others' emotions through a fairly automatic process of *emotional contagion*—feeling happy or sad when they sense these emotions in others (Stern, 1985). Alternatively, they may acquire these emotional contingencies through operant conditioning—learning that a smile generally triggers pleasurable feedback and that distress prompts a comforting response (Saarni et al., 2006).

Around 3 to 4 months, infants become sensitive to the structure and timing of face-to-face interactions. When they gaze, smile, or vocalize, they now expect their social partner to respond in kind (Markova & Legerstee, 2006; Rochat, Striano, & Blatt, 2002). According to some researchers, out of this early imitative communication, infants start to view others as "like me"—an awareness believed to lay the foundation for understanding others' thoughts and feelings (Gergely & Watson, 1996; Meltzoff, 2007).

From 5 months on, infants perceive facial expressions as organized patterns and can match the emotion in a voice with the appropriate face of a speaking person (see Chapter 4). As skill at establishing joint attention improves, infants realize that an emotional expression not only has meaning but is also a meaningful reaction to a specific object or event (Moses et al., 2001; Tomasello, 1999).

■ A LIFESPAN VISTA: Looking Forward, Looking Back ■

Parental Depression and Children's Development

About 8 to 10 percent of women experience chronic depression—mild to severe feelings of sadness and withdrawal that continue for months or years. Sometimes, depression emerges or strengthens after childbirth and fails to subside. Julia experienced this type—called *postpartum depression*.

Although less recognized and studied, fathers, too, experience chronic depression. About 3 to 5 percent of fathers report symptoms after the birth of a child (Madsen & Juhl, 2007; Spector, 2006). Parental depression can interfere with effective parenting and seriously impair children's development. Genetic makeup increases the risk of depressive illness, but social and cultural factors are also involved.

Maternal Depression

During Julia's pregnancy, her husband, Kyle, showed so little interest in the baby that Julia worried that having a child might be a mistake. Shortly after Lucy was born, Julia's mood plunged. She became anxious and weepy, overwhelmed by Lucy's needs, and angry at loss of control over her own schedule. When Julia approached Kyle about her own fatigue and his unwillingness to help with the baby, he snapped that she was overreacting.

Julia's depressed mood quickly affected her baby. The more extreme the depression and the greater the number of stressors in a mother's life (such as marital discord, little or no social support, and poverty), the more the parent–child relationship suffers (Simpson et al., 2003). Julia rarely smiled at, comforted, or talked to Lucy, who responded to her mother's sad, vacant gaze by turning away, crying, and often looking sad or angry herself (Herrera, Reissland, & Shepherd, 2004; Stanley, Murray, & Stein, 2004). By age 6 months, Lucy showed symptoms common in babies of depressed mothers—delays in development, an

irritable mood, and attachment difficulties (Cornish et al., 2005; McMahon et al., 2006).

Depressed mothers view their infants more negatively than independent observers do (Forman et al., 2007). And they use inconsistent discipline—sometimes lax, at other times too forceful. As we will see in later chapters, children who experience these maladaptive parenting practices often have serious adjustment problems. Some withdraw into a depressed mood themselves; others become impulsive and aggressive.

In several studies, children of depressed mothers showed atypical EEG brain-wave patterns—reduced activation of the left hemisphere (which governs positive emotion) and increased activation of the right hemisphere (which governs negative emotion). These alterations, a sign of difficulty controlling negative emotional arousal, are associated with increased behavior problems (Dawson et al., 2003; Jones, Field, & Davalos, 2000).

Paternal Depression

Paternal depression is also linked to dissatisfaction with marriage and family life after childbirth and to other life stressors, including job loss and divorce (Bielawska-Batorowicz & Kossakowska-Petrycka, 2006). Persistent paternal depression strongly predicts child behavior problems—especially overactivity, defiance, and aggression in boys (Ramchandani et al., 2005).

Paternal depression is linked to frequent father–child conflict as children grow older (Kane & Garber, 2004). Over time, children subjected to parental negativity develop a pessimistic worldview—one in which they lack self-confidence and perceive their parents and other people as threatening. Children who constantly feel endangered are especially likely to become overly aroused in stressful

This depressed mother appears completely uninterested in her infant. If her disengagement continues, the baby is likely to become negative and irritable, eventually withdraw, and develop serious emotional and behavioral problems.

© RICHARD NEWTON/ALAMY

situations, easily losing control in the face of cognitive and social challenges (Cummings & Davies, 1994).

Interventions

Early treatment is vital to prevent parental depression from interfering with the parent–child relationship. Julia's doctor referred her to a therapist, who helped Julia and Kyle with their marital problems. At times, antidepressant medication is prescribed.

In addition to alleviating parental depression, therapy that encourages depressed mothers to revise their negative views of their babies and to engage in emotionally positive, responsive caregiving is vital for reducing young children's attachment and other developmental problems (Forman et al., 2007). When a depressed parent does not respond easily to treatment, a warm relationship with the other parent or another caregiver can safeguard children's development (Mezulis, Hyde, & Clark, 2004).

Once these understandings are in place, beginning at 8 to 10 months, infants engage in **social referencing**—actively seeking emotional information from a trusted person in an uncertain situation (Mumme et al., 2007). Many studies show that the caregiver's emotional expression (happy, angry, or fearful) influences whether a 1-year-old will be wary of strangers, play

with an unfamiliar toy, or cross the deep side of the visual cliff (see page 111 in Chapter 4) (Repacholi, 1998; Stenberg, 2003; Striano & Rochat, 2000).

Parents can take advantage of social referencing to teach their baby how to react to many everyday events. And around the middle of the second year, as toddlers begin to appreciate that others' emotional reactions may differ from their own, social referencing allows them to compare their own and others' assessments of events. In one study, an adult showed 14- and 18-month-olds broccoli and crackers and acted delighted with one food but disgusted with the other. When asked to share the food, 18-month-olds gave the adult whichever food she appeared to like, regardless of their own preferences (Repacholi & Gopnik, 1997).

In sum, social referencing helps young children move beyond simply reacting to others' emotional messages. They use those signals to guide their own actions and to find out about others' intentions and preferences.

Emergence of Self-Conscious Emotions

Besides basic emotions, humans are capable of a second, higher-order set of feelings, including guilt, shame, embarrassment, envy, and pride. These are called **self-conscious emotions** because each involves injury to or enhancement of our sense of self. We feel guilt when we have harmed someone and want to correct the wrongdoing. When we are ashamed or embarrassed, we have negative feelings about our behavior, and we want to retreat so others will no longer notice our failings. In contrast, pride reflects delight in the self's achievements, and we are inclined to tell others what we have accomplished (Saarni et al., 2006).

Self-conscious emotions appear at the end of the second year, as 18- to 24-month-olds become firmly aware of the self as a separate, unique individual. Toddlers show shame and embarrassment by lowering their eyes, hanging their heads, and hiding their faces with their hands. They show guiltlike reactions, too: One 22-month-old returned a toy she had grabbed and patted her upset playmate. Pride also emerges around this time, and envy by age 3 (Barrett, 2005; Garner, 2003; Lewis et al., 1989).

Besides self-awareness, self-conscious emotions require an additional ingredient: adult instruction in when to feel proud, ashamed, or guilty. Situations in which adults encourage these feelings vary from culture to culture. In Western individualistic nations, most children are taught to feel pride in personal achievement. But in collectivist cultures such as China and Japan, calling attention to individual success evokes embarrassment and self-effacement. And violating cultural standards by failing to show concern for others—a parent, a teacher, or an employer—sparks intense shame (Akimoto & Sanbonmatsu, 1999; Lewis, 1992).

Beginnings of Emotional Self-Regulation

Besides expressing a wider range of emotions, infants and toddlers begin to manage their emotional experiences. **Emotional self-regulation** refers to the strategies we use to adjust our emotional state to a comfortable level of intensity so we can accomplish our goals (Thompson & Goodvin, 2007).

When you remind yourself that an anxiety-provoking event will be over soon, suppress your anger at a friend's behavior, or decide not to see a scary horror film, you are engaging in emotional self-regulation.

Emotional self-regulation requires voluntary, effortful management of emotions, a capacity that improves gradually, as a result of development of the cerebral cortex and the assistance of caregivers (Rothbart, Posner, & Kieras, 2006). A good start in regulating emotion during the first two years contributes greatly to autonomy and mastery of cognitive and social skills (Eisenberg et al., 2004; Lawson & Ruff, 2004).

In the early months, infants are easily overwhelmed by intense emotion. They depend on the soothing interventions of caregivers—lifting the distressed baby to the shoulder, rocking, and talking softly. Rapid development of the frontal lobes of the cerebral cortex increases the baby's tolerance for stimulation. Between 2 and 4 months, caregivers build on this capacity by initiating face-to-face play and attention to objects. In these interactions, parents arouse pleasure in the baby while adjusting the pace of their behavior so the infant does not become distressed. As a result, the baby's tolerance for stimulation increases further (Kopp & Neufeld, 2003). By 4 to 6 months, the ability to shift attention away from unpleasant events helps infants control emotion (Crockenberg & Leerkes, 2003). At the end of the first year, crawling and walking enable infants to regulate feelings by approaching or retreating from various situations.

Infants whose parents "read" and respond contingently and sympathetically to their emotional cues tend to be less fussy, to express more pleasurable emotion, to be more interested in

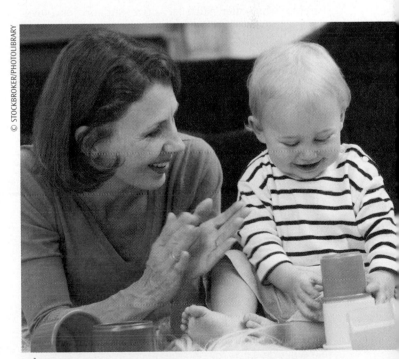

A mother applauds her toddler's success at tower-building. To experience self-conscious emotions, such as pride, babies need self-awareness as well as adult instruction.

© STOCKBROKER/PHOTOLIBRARY

exploration, and to be easier to soothe (Crockenberg & Leerkes, 2004; Volling et al., 2002). In contrast, parents who respond impatiently or angrily or who wait to intervene until the infant has become extremely agitated reinforce the baby's rapid rise to intense distress. Consequently, brain structures that buffer stress may fail to develop properly, resulting in an anxious, reactive child with a reduced capacity for regulating emotion (Feldman, 2007; Little & Carter, 2005).

Caregivers also provide lessons in socially approved ways of expressing feelings. From the first few months, parents encourage infants to suppress negative emotion by imitating their expressions of interest, happiness, and surprise more often than their expressions of anger and sadness. Boys get more of this training than girls, in part because boys have a harder time regulating negative emotion (Else-Quest et al., 2006; Malatesta et al., 1986). As a result, the well-known sex difference—females as emotionally expressive and males as emotionally controlled—is promoted at a tender age.

Toward the end of the second year, a vocabulary for talking about feelings—"happy," "scary," "yucky"—develops rapidly (Bretherton et al., 1986). But toddlers are not yet good at using language to manage their emotions. Temper tantrums tend to occur when an adult rejects their demands, particularly when toddlers are fatigued or hungry (Mascolo & Fischer, 2007). When parents are emotionally sympathetic but set limits (by not giving in to tantrums), distract the child from prohibited activities by offering alternatives, and later suggest better ways to handle adult refusals, children acquire more effective anger-regulation strategies and social skills during the preschool years (Laible & Thompson, 2002; Lecuyer & Houck, 2006).

Parents who offer such sensitive support encourage toddlers to describe their internal states. Then, when 2-year-olds feel distressed, they can guide caregivers in helping them. For example, while listening to a story about monsters, Grace whimpered, "Mommy, scary." Monica put the book down and gave Grace a comforting hug.

ASK YOURSELF

>> **REVIEW**
Why do many infants show stranger anxiety in the second half of the first year? What factors can increase or decrease wariness of strangers?

>> **APPLY**
At age 14 months, Reggie built a block tower and gleefully knocked it down. But at age 2, he called to his mother and pointed proudly to his tall block tower. What explains this change in Reggie's emotional behavior?

>> **REFLECT**
How do you typically manage negative emotion? How might your early experiences have influenced your style of emotional self-regulation?

Temperament and Development

When we describe one person as cheerful and "upbeat," another as active and energetic, and still others as calm, cautious, or prone to anger, we are referring to **temperament**— early-appearing, stable individual differences in reactivity and self-regulation. *Reactivity* refers to quickness and intensity of emotional arousal, attention, and motor activity. *Self-regulation,* as we have seen, refers to strategies that modify that reactivity (Rothbart & Bates, 2006). The psychological traits that make up temperament are believed to form the cornerstone of the adult personality.

In 1956, Alexander Thomas and Stella Chess initiated the New York Longitudinal Study, a groundbreaking investigation of the development of temperament that followed 141 children from early infancy well into adulthood. Results showed that temperament can increase a child's chances of experiencing psychological problems or, alternatively, protect a child from the negative effects of a highly stressful home life. At the same time, Thomas and Chess (1977) discovered that parenting practices can modify children's temperaments considerably.

These findings stimulated a growing body of research on temperament. Let's begin with the structure, or makeup, of temperament and how it is measured.

The Structure of Temperament

Thomas and Chess's nine dimensions, listed in Table 6.1, served as the first influential model of temperament. When detailed descriptions of infants' and children's behavior obtained from parent interviews were rated on these dimensions, certain characteristics clustered together, yielding three types of children:

- The **easy child** (40 percent of the sample) quickly establishes regular routines in infancy, is generally cheerful, and adapts easily to new experiences.

- The **difficult child** (10 percent of the sample) is irregular in daily routines, is slow to accept new experiences, and tends to react negatively and intensely.

- The **slow-to-warm-up child** (15 percent of the sample) is inactive, shows mild, low-key reactions to environmental stimuli, is negative in mood, and adjusts slowly to new experiences.

Note that 35 percent of the children did not fit any of these categories. Instead, they showed unique blends of temperamental characteristics.

Difficult children are at high risk for adjustment problems— both anxious withdrawal and aggressive behavior in early and middle childhood (Bates, Wachs, & Emde, 1994; Ramos et al., 2005; Thomas, Chess, & Birch, 1968). Although slow-to-warm-up children present fewer problems, they tend to show excessive fearfulness and slow, constricted behavior in the late preschool

■ **TABLE 6.1** ■ *Two Models of Temperament*

THOMAS AND CHESS		ROTHBART	
DIMENSION	**DESCRIPTION**	**DIMENSION**	**DESCRIPTION**
Activity level	Ratio of active periods to inactive ones	**REACTIVITY**	
Rhythmicity	Regularity of body functions, such as sleep, wakefulness, hunger, and excretion	Activity level	Level of gross motor activity
Distractibility	Degree to which stimulation from the environment alters behavior—for example, whether crying stops when a toy is offered	Attention span/ persistence	Duration of orienting or interest
Approach/withdrawal	Response to a new object, food, or person	Fearful distress	Wariness and distress in response to intense or novel stimuli, including time to adjust to new situations
Adaptability	Ease with which child adapts to changes in the environment, such as sleeping or eating in a new place	Irritable distress	Extent of fussing, crying, and distress when desires are frustrated
Attention span and persistence	Amount of time devoted to an activity, such as watching a mobile or playing with a toy	Positive affect	Frequency of expression of happiness and pleasure
Intensity of reaction	Energy level of response, such as laughing, crying, talking, or gross motor activity	**SELF-REGULATION**	
Threshold of responsiveness	Intensity of stimulation required to evoke a response	Effortful control	Capacity to voluntarily suppress a dominant, reactive response in order to plan and execute a more adaptive response
Quality of mood	Amount of friendly, joyful behavior as opposed to unpleasant, unfriendly behavior		

Sources: Left: Thomas & Chess, 1977; Right: Rothbart, Ahadi, & Evans, 2000; Rothbart & Mauro, 1990.

and school years, when they are expected to respond actively and quickly in classrooms and peer groups (Chess & Thomas, 1984; Schmitz et al., 1999).

Table 6.1 also shows a second model of temperament, devised by Mary Rothbart, that is more concise than that of Thomas and Chess (Rothbart, Ahadi, & Evans, 2000; Rothbart & Mauro, 1990). According to Rothbart, individuals differ not just in their reactivity on each dimension, but also in the self-regulatory dimension of temperament, **effortful control**—the capacity to voluntarily suppress a dominant response in order to plan and execute a more adaptive response (Rothbart, 2003; Rothbart & Bates, 2006). Variations in effortful control are evident in how effectively a child can focus and shift attention, inhibit impulses, and manage negative emotion.

Measuring Temperament

Temperament is often assessed through interviews or questionnaires given to parents. Behavior ratings by pediatricians, teachers, and others familiar with the child and laboratory observations by researchers have also been used. Parental reports are convenient and take advantage of parents' depth of knowledge about their child (Gartstein & Rothbart, 2003). Although information from parents has been criticized as biased, parental reports are moderately related to researchers' observations of children's behavior (Mangelsdorf, Schoppe, & Buur, 2000).

Observations by researchers avoid the subjectivity of parental reports but can lead to other inaccuracies. In homes, observers find it hard to capture rare but important events, such as infants' response to frustration. And in an unfamiliar lab, fearful children who calmly avoid certain experiences at home may become too upset to complete the session (Wachs & Bates, 2001). Still, researchers can better control children's experiences in the lab. And they can conveniently combine observations of behavior with physiological measures to gain insight into the biological bases of temperament.

Most physiological research has focused on children who fall at opposite extremes of the positive-affect and fearful-distress dimensions of temperament (refer again to Table 6.1): **inhibited, or shy, children,** who react negatively to and withdraw from novel stimuli, and **uninhibited, or sociable, children,** who display positive emotion to and approach novel stimuli. As the Biology and Environment box on page 148 reveals, biologically based reactivity differentiates children with inhibited and uninhibited temperaments.

Stability of Temperament

Young children who score low or high on dimensions of temperament tend to respond similarly when assessed again several months to a few years later and, occasionally, even into the adult years (Caspi et al., 2003; Kochanska & Knaack, 2003; Komsi et al., 2006; Majdandžić & van den Boom, 2007).

■ BIOLOGY AND ENVIRONMENT ■

Development of Shyness and Sociability

Two 4-month-old babies, Larry and Mitch, visited the laboratory of Jerome Kagan, who observed their reactions to various unfamiliar experiences. When exposed to new sights and sounds, such as a moving mobile decorated with colorful toys, Larry moved his arms and legs with agitation and cried. Mitch remained relaxed and quiet, smiling and cooing.

As toddlers, Larry and Mitch returned to the lab, where they experienced procedures designed to induce uncertainty. Electrodes were placed on their bodies and blood pressure cuffs on their arms to measure heart rate; toy robots, animals, and puppets moved before their eyes; and unfamiliar people behaved in unexpected ways. While Larry whimpered and quickly withdrew, Mitch watched with interest, laughed, and approached the toys and strangers.

On a third visit, at age 4½, Larry barely talked or smiled during an interview with an unfamiliar adult. In contrast, Mitch expressed pleasure at each new activity. In a playroom with two unfamiliar peers, Larry pulled back and watched, while Mitch made friends quickly.

In longitudinal research on several hundred Caucasian children, Kagan found that about 20 percent of 4-month-old babies were, like Larry, easily upset by novelty; 40 percent, like Mitch, were comfortable, even delighted, with new experiences. About 20 to 30 percent of these groups retained their temperamental styles as they grew older (Kagan, 2003; Kagan & Saudino, 2001; Kagan et al., 2007). But most children's dispositions became less extreme over time. Biological makeup and child-rearing experiences jointly influenced stability and change in temperament.

Physiological Correlates of Shyness and Sociability

Individual differences in arousal of the *amygdala,* an inner brain structure that controls avoidance reactions, contribute to these contrasting temperaments. fMRI research reveals that in shy, inhibited children, novel stimuli easily excite the amygdala and its connections to the cerebral cortex and the sympathetic nervous system, which prepares the body to act in the face of threat. In sociable, uninhibited children, the same level of stimulation evokes minimal neural excitation (Kagan & Fox, 2006). And the two emotional styles are distinguished by additional physiological responses mediated by the amygdala:

- *Heart rate.* From the first few weeks of life, the heart rates of shy children are consistently higher than those of sociable children, and they speed up further in response to unfamiliar events (Schmidt et al., 2007; Snidman et al., 1995).
- *Cortisol.* Saliva concentrations of the stress hormone cortisol tend to be higher, and to rise more in response to a stressful event, in shy than in sociable children (Schmidt et al., 1997, 1999; Zimmermann & Stansbury, 2004).
- *Pupil dilation, blood pressure, and skin surface temperature.* Compared with sociable children, shy children show greater pupil dilation, rise in blood pressure, and cooling of the fingertips when faced with novelty (Kagan et al., 1999, 2007).
- *EEG brain-wave activity in the cerebral cortex.* Inhibited children also show greater generalized activation of the cerebral cortex, an indicator of high emotional arousal and monitoring of new situations for potential threats (Henderson et al., 2004).

Child-Rearing Practices

According to Kagan, extremely shy or sociable children inherit a physiology that biases them toward a particular temperamental style. Yet experience, too, has a powerful impact. Warm, supportive parenting reduces shy infants' and preschoolers' intense physiological reaction to novelty, whereas cold, intrusive parenting heightens anxiety (Rubin, Burgess, & Hastings, 2002). And if parents protect infants who dislike novelty from minor stresses, they make it harder for the child to overcome an urge to retreat. Parents who make appropriate demands for their baby to approach new experiences help the child overcome fear (Rubin et al., 1997).

When inhibition persists, it leads to excessive cautiousness, low self-esteem, and loneliness and, in adolescence, increases the risk of severe anxiety, especially social phobia—intense fear of being humiliated in social situations (Kagan & Fox, 2006). To acquire effective social skills, inhibited children need parenting tailored to their temperaments—a theme we will encounter again in this and later chapters.

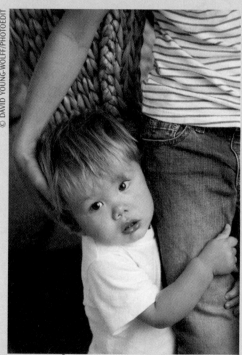

© DAVID YOUNG-WOLFF/PHOTOEDIT

A strong physiological response to unfamiliar situations prompts this toddler to cling to his older sister. With patient but insistent encouragement, the family can help the child overcome the urge to retreat.

However, the overall stability of temperament is only low to moderate.

A major reason is that temperament itself develops with age. To illustrate, let's look at irritability. Recall from Chapter 3 that the early months are a period of fussing and crying for most babies. As infants can better regulate their attention and emotions, many who initially seemed irritable become calm and content. Furthermore, toddlers with irritable temperaments who experience patient, supportive parenting are better at managing their reactivity (Warren & Simmens, 2005).

These findings help us understand why long-term prediction from early temperament is best achieved after age 3, when styles of responding are better established (Roberts & DelVecchio, 2000). In line with this idea, between ages 2½ and 3, children improve substantially on tasks requiring effortful control, such as waiting for a reward and selectively attending to one stimulus while ignoring competing stimuli (Kochanska, Murray, & Harlan, 2000; Li-Grining, 2007). Researchers believe that around this time, areas in the frontal lobes involved in suppressing impulses develop rapidly (Rothbart & Bates, 2006).

Nevertheless, the ease with which children manage their reactivity depends on the type and strength of the reactive emotion. Preschoolers who were highly fearful as toddlers score slightly better than their agemates in effortful control. In contrast, angry, irritable toddlers tend to be less effective at effortful control at later ages (Kochanska & Knaack, 2003; Kochanska, Murray, & Harlan, 2000).

In sum, the low to moderate stability of temperament makes sense when we consider that many factors affect the persistence of a temperamental style, including the development of biological systems on which temperament is based, the child's capacity for effortful control, the success of her efforts, and rearing experiences. With these ideas in mind, let's turn to genetic and environmental contributions to temperament and personality.

Genetic Influences

Research indicates that identical twins are more similar than fraternal twins across a wide range of temperamental and personality traits (Bouchard, 2004; Bouchard & Loehlin, 2001; Caspi & Shiner, 2006; Goldsmith, Pollak, & Davidson, 2008). In Chapter 2, we noted that heritability estimates suggest a moderate role for heredity in personality: On average, half of individual differences have been attributed to differences in genetic makeup.

Consistent ethnic and sex differences in early temperament exist, again implying a role for heredity. Compared with North American Caucasian infants, Japanese and Chinese babies tend to be less active, irritable, and vocal, more easily soothed when upset, and better at quieting themselves (Kagan et al., 1994; Lewis, Ramsay, & Kawakami, 1993). From an early age, boys are more active and daring, more irritable when frustrated, and slightly more impulsive—factors that contribute to boys' higher injury rates throughout childhood and adolescence. And girls' large advantage in effortful control undoubtedly contributes to their greater compliance, better school performance, and lower incidence of behavior problems (Eisenberg et al., 2004; Else-Quest et al., 2006).

Environmental Influences

Environment also has a powerful influence on temperament. For example, we have seen in earlier chapters that persistent nutritional and emotional deprivation profoundly alters temperament, resulting in maladaptive emotional reactivity. Other research shows that heredity and environment often combine to influence temperament, since a child's approach to the world affects the experiences to which she is exposed. To see how this works, let's take a second look at ethnic and sex differences in temperament.

Japanese mothers usually say that babies come into the world as independent beings who must learn to rely on their mothers through close physical contact. North American mothers typically believe just the opposite—that they must wean babies away from dependency toward autonomy. Consistent with these beliefs, Asian mothers interact gently, soothingly, and gesturally with their babies, whereas Caucasian mothers use a more active, stimulating, verbal approach (Rothbaum et al., 2000a). These differences enhance early ethnic variations in temperament.

A similar process seems to contribute to sex differences in temperament. Parents rate their newborn sons as larger, better coordinated, more alert, and stronger and their newborn daughters as softer, weaker, and more delicate and awkward (Stern & Karraker, 1989; Vogel et al., 1991). These gender-stereotyped beliefs influence parents' treatment of infants and toddlers. Parents more often encourage their young sons to be physically active and their daughters to seek help and physical closeness (Ruble, Martin, & Berenbaum, 2006).

In families with several children, an additional influence is at work. **TAKE A MOMENT...** Ask several parents to describe each of their children's personalities. You will see that they often look for differences between siblings: "She's a lot more active," "He's more sociable," "She's far more persistent." As a result, parents often view siblings (including identical twins) as more distinct than other observers do (Saudino, 2003). Parents' tendency to emphasize each child's unique qualities affects their child-rearing practices. In an investigation of identical-twin toddlers, mothers' differential treatment predicted differences in psychological adjustment. The twin who received more warmth and less harshness was more positive in mood and social behavior (Deater-Deckard et al., 2001).

Besides different experiences within the family, siblings have distinct experiences with teachers, peers, and others in their community that affect personality development. And in middle childhood and adolescence, they often seek ways to differ from one another. In adulthood, both identical and fraternal twins tend to become increasingly dissimilar (Loehlin & Martin, 2001; McCartney, Harris, & Bernieri, 1990). In sum, temperament and personality can be understood only in terms of complex interdependencies between genetic and environmental factors.

Temperament and Child Rearing: The Goodness-of-Fit Model

If a child's disposition interferes with learning or getting along with others, adults must gently but consistently counteract the child's maladaptive style. Thomas and Chess (1977) proposed a **goodness-of-fit model** to describe how temperament and environment together can produce favorable outcomes. Goodness of fit involves creating child-rearing environments that recognize each child's temperament while encouraging more adaptive functioning.

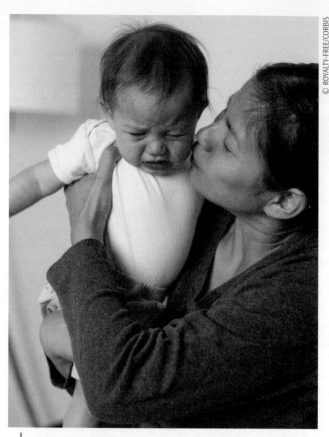

"Goodness-of-fit" describes the interaction between a child's biologically based temperament and the child-rearing environment. This mother's calm, soothing response to her baby's fussiness will help the child regulate intense emotions and develop more adaptive responses to frustration.

Difficult children frequently experience parenting that fits poorly with their dispositions. By the second year, their parents often resort to angry, punitive discipline, which causes the child to react with defiance and disobedience and parents to become increasingly stressed (Paulussen-Hoogeboom et al., 2007). As a result, they continue their coercive tactics and also discipline inconsistently, at times rewarding the child's noncompliance by giving in to it—practices that sustain the child's irritable, conflict-ridden style (Calkins, 2002). In contrast, when parents are positive and sensitive, difficultness declines by age 2 or 3 (Feldman, Greenbaum, & Yirmiya, 1999; Raikes et al., 2007).

An effective match between rearing conditions and child temperament is best accomplished early, before unfavorable temperament–environment relationships produce maladjustment. Both difficult and shy children benefit from warm, accepting parenting that makes firm but reasonable demands for mastering new experiences. With reserved, inactive toddlers, highly stimulating parental behavior—encouraging, questioning, and pointing out objects—fosters exploration. Yet for highly active babies, this approach is too directive, dampening their play and curiosity (Miceli et al., 1998).

The goodness-of-fit model reminds us that infants have unique dispositions that adults must accept. But parents can turn an environment that exaggerates a child's problems into one that builds on the child's strengths. As we will see, goodness of fit is also at the heart of infant–caregiver attachment. This first intimate relationship grows out of interaction between parent and baby, to which the emotional styles of both partners contribute.

ASK YOURSELF

》 REVIEW
How do genetic and environmental factors work together to influence temperament? Cite several examples from research.

》 APPLY
Mandy and Jeff are parents of 2-year-old inhibited Sam and 3-year-old difficult Maria. Explain the importance of effortful control to Mandy and Jeff, and suggest ways they can strengthen it in each of their children.

》 REFLECT
How would you describe your temperament as a young child? Do you think your temperament has remained stable, or has it changed? What factors might be involved?

Development of Attachment

Attachment is the strong affectionate tie we have with special people in our lives that leads us to feel pleasure when we interact with them and to be comforted by their nearness in times of stress. By the second half of the first year, infants have become attached to familiar people who have responded to their needs. **TAKE A MOMENT...** Watch how babies of this age single out their parents for special attention. When the mother enters the room, the baby breaks into a broad, friendly smile. When she picks him up, he snuggles against her. When he feels anxious or afraid, he crawls into her lap and clings closely.

Attachment has been the subject of intense theoretical debate. Turn back to Erikson's theory at the beginning of this chapter, and notice how the *psychoanalytic perspective* regards feeding as the primary context in which caregivers and babies build this emotional bond. *Behaviorism,* too, emphasizes the importance of feeding, but for different reasons. According to a well-known behaviorist explanation, infants learn to prefer the mother's soft caresses, warm smiles, and tender words of comfort because these events are paired with tension relief as she satisfies the baby's hunger.

Although feeding is an important context for building a close relationship, attachment does not depend on hunger satisfaction. In the 1950s, a famous experiment showed that rhesus monkeys reared with terry-cloth and wire-mesh "surrogate mothers" clung to the soft terry-cloth substitute, even though the wire-mesh "mother" held the bottle and infants had to climb onto it to be fed (Harlow & Zimmerman, 1959). Human infants, too, become attached to family members who seldom feed them, including fathers, siblings, and grandparents. And

Baby monkeys reared with "surrogate mothers" preferred to cling to a soft terry-cloth "mother" over a wire-mesh "mother" that held a bottle. These findings contradict both psychoanalytic and behaviorist views of feeding as central to building infant–caregiver attachment.

toddlers in Western cultures who sleep alone and experience frequent daytime separations from their parents sometimes develop strong emotional ties to cuddly objects, such as blankets and teddy bears, that have never played a role in infant feeding!

Ethological Theory of Attachment

Today, **ethological theory of attachment,** which recognizes the infant's emotional tie to the caregiver as an evolved response that promotes survival, is the most widely accepted view. John Bowlby (1969), who first applied this idea to the infant–caregiver bond, was inspired by Konrad Lorenz's studies of imprinting (see Chapter 1). Bowlby believed that the human infant, like the young of other animal species, is endowed with a set of built-in behaviors that help keep the parent nearby to protect the infant from danger and to provide support for exploring and mastering the environment (Waters & Cummings, 2000).

The infant's relationship with the parent begins as a set of innate signals that call the adult to the baby's side. Over time, a true affectionate bond develops, supported by new cognitive and emotional capacities as well as by a history of warm, sensitive care. Attachment develops in four phases:

1. *Preattachment phase* (birth to 6 weeks). Built-in signals—grasping, smiling, crying, and gazing into the adult's eyes—help bring newborn babies into close contact with other humans, who comfort them.

2. *"Attachment-in-the-making" phase* (6 weeks to 6–8 months). During this phase, infants respond differently to a familiar caregiver than to a stranger. For example, at 4 months, Timmy smiled, laughed, and babbled more freely when interacting with his mother and quieted more quickly when she picked him up. As infants learn that their own actions affect the behavior of those around them, they begin to develop a *sense of trust*—the expectation that the caregiver will respond when signaled—but they still do not protest when separated from her.

3. *"Clear-cut" attachment phase* (6–8 months to 18 months–2 years). Babies display **separation anxiety,** becoming upset when their trusted caregiver leaves. Like stranger anxiety (see page 143), separation anxiety does not always occur; it depends on infant temperament and the current situation. But in many cultures, separation anxiety increases between 6 and 15 months. Besides protesting the parent's departure, older infants and toddlers approach, follow, and climb on her in preference to others. And they use the familiar caregiver as a secure base from which to explore.

4. *Formation of a reciprocal relationship* (18 months–2 years and on). Rapid growth in representation and language permits toddlers to understand some of the factors that influence the parent's coming and going and to predict her return. As a result, separation protest declines. Now children negotiate with the caregiver to alter her goals. At age 2, Caitlin asked Carolyn and David to read a story before leaving her with a babysitter. The extra time with her parents, along with a better understanding of when they would be back ("right after you go to sleep"), helped Caitlin withstand her parents' absence.

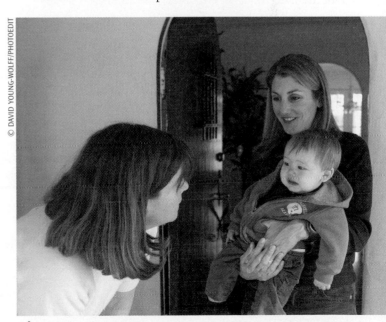

Separation anxiety increases as clear-cut infant–caregiver attachment develops. But the occurrence of separation anxiety depends on infant temperament, context, and adult behavior. Here, the child's distress at his mother's departure will probably be short-lived because his caregiver is supportive and sensitive.

According to Bowlby (1980), out of their experiences during these four phases, children construct an enduring affectionate tie to the caregiver that they can use as a secure base in the parents' absence. This image serves as an **internal working model,** or set of expectations about the availability of attachment figures and their likelihood of providing support during times of stress. The internal working model becomes a vital part of personality, serving as a guide for all future close relationships (Bretherton & Munholland, 1999). With cognitive development and continuing experiences in close relationships, the internal working model expands into a more complex representation. Children revise it as they interact with parents and form other bonds with adults, siblings, and friends.

Measuring the Security of Attachment

Although virtually all family-reared babies become attached to a familiar caregiver, the quality of this relationship varies. A widely used laboratory procedure for assessing attachment quality between 1 and 2 years of age is the **Strange Situation.** Designed by Mary Ainsworth, it takes the baby through eight short episodes in which brief separations from and reunions with the parent occur in an unfamiliar playroom (see Table 6.2).

Observing infants' responses to these episodes, researchers have identified a secure attachment pattern and three patterns of insecurity (Ainsworth et al., 1978; Barnett & Vondra, 1999; Main & Solomon, 1990; Thompson, 2006). **TAKE A MOMENT...** From the description at the beginning of this chapter, which pattern do you think Grace displayed after adjusting to her adoptive family?

- **Secure attachment.** These infants use the parent as a secure base. When separated, they may or may not cry, but if they do, it is because the parent is absent and they prefer her to the stranger. When the parent returns, they actively seek contact, and their crying is reduced immediately.

About 60 percent of North American infants in middle-SES families show this pattern. (In low-SES families, a smaller proportion of babies are secure, with higher proportions falling into the insecure patterns.)

- **Avoidant attachment.** These infants seem unresponsive to the parent when she is present. When she leaves, they usually are not distressed, and they react to the stranger in much the same way as to the parent. During reunion, they avoid or are slow to greet the parent, and when picked up, they often fail to cling. About 15 percent of North American infants in middle-SES families show this pattern.

- **Resistant attachment.** Before separation, these infants seek closeness to the parent and often fail to explore. When the parent leaves, they are usually distressed, and on her return they combine clinginess with angry, resistive behavior, sometimes hitting and pushing. Many continue to cry after being picked up and cannot be comforted easily. About 10 percent of North American infants in middle-SES families show this pattern.

- **Disorganized/disoriented attachment.** This pattern reflects the greatest insecurity. At reunion, these infants show confused, contradictory behaviors—for example, looking away while the parent is holding them or approaching the parent with flat, depressed emotion. About 15 percent of North American infants in middle-SES families show this pattern.

An alternative method, the **Attachment Q-Sort,** suitable for children between 1 and 4 years, depends on home observation (Waters et al., 1995). Either the parent or a highly trained observer sorts 90 behaviors ("Child greets mother with a big smile when she enters the room," "If mother moves very far, child follows along") into nine categories ranging from highly descriptive to not at all descriptive of the child. Then a score, ranging from high to low in security, is computed. The Q-Sort responses of expert observers correspond well with babies'

■ **TABLE 6.2** ■ *Episodes in the Strange Situation*

EPISODE	EVENTS	ATTACHMENT BEHAVIOR OBSERVED
1	Researcher introduces parent and baby to playroom and then leaves.	
2	Parent is seated while baby plays with toys.	Parent as a secure base
3	Stranger enters, is seated, and talks to parent.	Reaction to unfamiliar adult
4	Parent leaves room. Stranger responds to baby and offers comfort if baby is upset.	Separation anxiety
5	Parent returns, greets baby, and offers comfort if necessary. Stranger leaves room.	Reaction to reunion
6	Parent leaves room.	Separation anxiety
7	Stranger enters room and offers comfort.	Ability to be soothed by stranger
8	Parent returns, greets baby, offers comfort if necessary, and tries to reinterest baby in toys.	Reaction to reunion

Note: Episode 1 lasts about 30 seconds; each of the remaining episodes lasts about 3 minutes. Separation episodes are cut short if the baby becomes very upset. Reunion episodes are extended if the baby needs more time to calm down and return to play.
Source: Ainsworth et al., 1978.

secure-base behavior in the Strange Situation, but parents' Q-Sorts do not (van IJzendoorn et al., 2004). Parents of insecure children, especially, may have difficulty accurately reporting their child's attachment behaviors.

Stability of Attachment

Research on the stability of attachment patterns between 1 and 2 years of age yields a wide range of findings (Thompson, 2000, 2006). Quality of attachment is usually secure and stable for middle-SES babies experiencing favorable life conditions. And infants who move from insecurity to security typically have well-adjusted mothers with positive family and friendship ties. Perhaps many became parents before they were psychologically ready but, with social support, grew into the role. In contrast, in low-SES families with many daily stresses and little social support, attachment generally moves away from security or changes from one insecure pattern to another (Belsky et al., 1996; Fish, 2004; Vondra, Hommerding, & Shaw, 1999; Vondra et al., 2001).

These findings indicate that securely attached babies more often maintain their attachment status than insecure babies. The exception is disorganized/disoriented attachment, an insecure pattern that is as stable as attachment security: Nearly 70 percent retain this classification over time (Hesse & Main, 2000; Weinfield, Whaley, & Egeland, 2004). As you will soon see, many disorganized/disoriented babies experience extremely negative caregiving, which may disrupt emotional self-regulation so severely that confused, ambivalent feelings toward parents persist.

Cultural Variations

Cross-cultural evidence indicates that attachment patterns may have to be interpreted differently in certain cultures. For example, as Figure 6.1 reveals, German infants show considerably more avoidant attachment than American babies do. But German parents value independence and encourage their infants to be nonclingy (Grossmann et al., 1985). In contrast, a

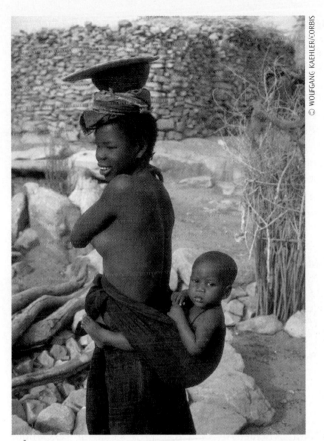

Among the Dogon people of Mali, Africa, mothers stay close to their babies and respond promptly and gently to infant distress. Dogon mothers are almost never overly stimulating or intrusive—practices linked to avoidant attachment. And none of their infants were avoidantly attached to their mothers.

study of infants of the Dogon people of Mali, Africa, revealed that none showed avoidant attachment to their mothers (True, Pisani, & Oumar, 2001). Even when grandmothers are primary caregivers (as they are with firstborn sons), Dogon mothers remain available, holding their babies close and nursing promptly in response to hunger and distress.

Japanese infants, as well, rarely show avoidant attachment. Rather, many are resistantly attached, but this reaction may not represent true insecurity. Japanese mothers seldom leave their babies in others' care, so the Strange Situation is probably unusually stressful for them (Takahashi, 1990). Also, Japanese parents view the infant attention seeking that is part of resistant attachment as a normal indicator of infant dependency (Rothbaum et al., 2000b). Despite such cultural variations, the secure pattern is still the most common attachment quality in all societies studied (van IJzendoorn & Sagi, 1999).

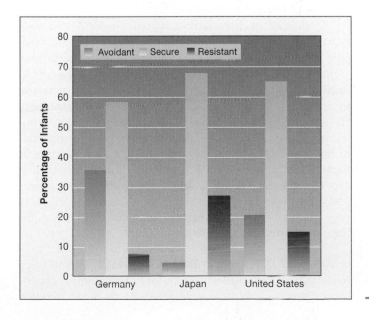

■ **FIGURE 6.1** ■ **A cross-cultural comparison of infants' reactions in the Strange Situation.** A high percentage of German babies seem avoidantly attached, whereas a substantial number of Japanese infants appear resistantly attached. These responses are probably due to cultural differences in values and child-rearing practices. (Adapted from van IJzendoorn & Kroonenberg, 1988.)

Factors That Affect Attachment Security

What factors might influence attachment security? Researchers have looked closely at four important influences: (1) opportunity to establish a close relationship, (2) quality of caregiving, (3) the baby's characteristics, and (4) family context.

■ **OPPORTUNITY FOR ATTACHMENT.** In a longitudinal study, researchers followed the development of infants in an institution with a good caregiver–child ratio and a rich selection of books and toys. However, staff turnover was so rapid that the average child had 50 caregivers by age 4½ and no opportunity to establish an affectionate tie with one or a few adults. Many of these children became "late adoptees" who were placed in homes after age 4. Most developed deep ties with their adoptive parents, indicating that a first attachment bond can develop as late as 4 to 6 years of age (Hodges & Tizard, 1989; Tizard & Rees, 1975). But these children were more likely to display attachment difficulties, including an excessive desire for adult attention, "overfriendliness" to unfamiliar adults and peers, and failure to check back with the parent in anxiety-arousing situations.

Adopted children who spent their first 6 to 8 months or more in deprived Romanian orphanages often display these same difficulties (O'Connor et al., 2003). Symptoms are associated with wide-ranging mental health problems in middle childhood, including cognitive impairments, peer rejection, inattention and hyperactivity, and disruptive behavior (O'Connor et al., 2003; Rutter et al., 2007). Furthermore, as early as 7 months, Romanian orphanage children show reduced ERP brain waves in response to facial expressions of emotion and have trouble discriminating such expressions—outcomes that suggest disrupted formation of neural structures involved in "reading" emotions (Parker et al., 2005). Taken together, the evidence indicates that fully normal development depends on establishing close ties with caregivers early in life.

■ **QUALITY OF CAREGIVING.** Dozens of studies report that **sensitive caregiving**—responding promptly, consistently, and appropriately to infants and holding them tenderly and carefully—is moderately related to attachment security in diverse cultures and SES groups (De Wolff & van IJzendoorn, 1997; Posada et al., 2004; van IJzendoorn et al., 2004). In contrast, insecurely attached infants tend to have mothers who engage in less physical contact, handle them awkwardly or "routinely," and are resentful and rejecting, particularly in response to infant distress (Isabella, 1993; McElwain & Booth-LaForce, 2006; Pederson & Moran, 1996).

Cultures, however, vary in their view of sensitivity toward infants. Among the Gusii people of Kenya, for example, mothers rarely cuddle, hug, or interact playfully with their babies, although they are very responsive to their infants' needs. Yet most Gusii infants appear securely attached (LeVine et al., 1994). This suggests that security depends on attentive caregiving, not necessarily on frequent physical affection or face-to-face interaction. Puerto Rican mothers, who highly value obedience and socially appropriate behavior, often physically direct and limit their babies' actions—a caregiving style linked to attachment security in Puerto Rican culture. Yet in many Western cultures, such physical control predicts insecurity (Carlson & Harwood, 2003).

Compared with securely attached infants, avoidant babies tend to receive overstimulating, intrusive care. By avoiding the mother, these infants try to escape from overwhelming interaction. Resistant infants often experience inconsistent care. Their mothers are unresponsive to infant signals. Yet when the baby begins to explore, these mothers interfere. As a result, the baby is overly dependent as well as angry at the mother's lack of involvement (Cassidy & Berlin, 1994; Isabella & Belsky, 1991).

Highly inadequate caregiving is a powerful predictor of disruptions in attachment. Child abuse and neglect are associated with all three forms of attachment insecurity. Among maltreated infants, disorganized/disoriented attachment is especially high (van IJzendoorn, Schuengel, & Bakermans-Kranenburg, 1999). Persistently depressed mothers, mothers with very low marital satisfaction, and parents suffering from a traumatic event, such as loss of a loved one, also tend to promote the uncertain behaviors of this pattern (Campbell et al., 2004; Moss et al., 2005; van IJzendoorn, 1995). Some of these mothers display frightening, contradictory, and unpleasant behaviors—looking scared, teasing the baby, holding the baby stiffly at a distance, or seeking reassurance from the upset child (Goldberg et al., 2003; Madigan, Moran, & Pederson, 2006).

■ **INFANT CHARACTERISTICS.** Because attachment is the result of a *relationship* between two partners, infant characteristics affect how easily it is established. For example, babies whose temperament is emotionally reactive and difficult are more likely to develop later insecure attachments (Kagan & Fox, 2006; van IJzendoorn et al., 2004). However, caregiving is also involved. In a study extending from birth to age 2, difficult infants more often had highly anxious mothers—a combination that, by the second year, often resulted in a "disharmonious relationship" characterized by both maternal insensitivity and attachment insecurity (Symons, 2001).

Overall, infant characteristics are only weakly related to attachment quality because *many* child attributes can lead to secure attachment as long as the caregiver behaves sensitively (Seifer & Schiller, 1995). Interventions that teach parents to interact with difficult-to-care-for infants are highly successful in enhancing both sensitive care and attachment security (Bakermans-Kranenburg, van IJzendoorn, & Juffer, 2003). But when parents' capacity is strained—by their own personalities or by stressful living conditions, such as a failing marriage or financial difficulties—then infants with illnesses, disabilities, and difficult temperaments are at high risk for attachment problems. Child care—as the Social Issues box on the following page indicates—is yet another context with consequences for the infant–parent attachment relationship.

■ **PARENTS' INTERNAL WORKING MODELS.** Parents bring to the family context their own history of attachment experiences, from which they construct internal working models that

▁ SOCIAL ISSUES ▁

Does Child Care in Infancy Threaten Attachment Security and Later Adjustment?

Research suggests that infants placed in full-time child care before 12 months of age are more likely than infants who remain at home to display insecure attachment—especially avoidance—in the Strange Situation (Belsky, 2001, 2005). Does this mean that infants who experience daily separations from their employed parents and early placement in child care are at risk for developmental problems? Not necessarily. The relationship between child care and emotional well-being depends on both family and child-care experiences.

Family Circumstances

We have seen that family conditions affect attachment security. For many employed women, handling two full-time jobs—work and motherhood—is stressful. Some, especially those who receive little help from the child's father, may respond less sensitively to their babies (Stifter, Coulehan, & Fish, 1993). Other employed parents probably value and encourage their infants' independence. Or their babies may be unfazed by the Strange Situation because they are used to separating from their parents. In these cases, avoidance in the Strange Situation may represent healthy autonomy, not insecurity (Clarke-Stewart, Althusen, & Goosens, 2001).

Quality and Extent of Child Care

Long periods spent in poor-quality child care may contribute to a higher rate of insecure attachment. In the U.S. National Institute of Child Health and Human Development (NICHD) Study of Early Child Care—the largest longitudinal study to date, including more than 1,300 infants and their families—child care alone did not contribute to attachment

insecurity. But when babies were exposed to combined home and child-care risk factors—insensitive caregiving at home along with insensitive caregiving in child care, long hours in child care, or more than one child-care arrangement—the rate of insecurity increased. Overall, mother–child interaction was more favorable when children attended higher-quality child care and also spent fewer hours in child care (NICHD Early Child Care Research Network, 1997, 1999).

Furthermore, when these children reached age 3, a history of higher-quality child care predicted better social skills (NICHD Early Child Care Research Network, 2002b). However, at age 4½ to 5, children averaging more than 30 child-care hours per week displayed more behavior problems, especially defiance, disobedience, and aggression (NICHD Early Child Care Research Network, 2003, 2006). This does not necessarily mean that child care causes behavior problems. Rather, heavy exposure to substandard care, which is widespread in the United States, may promote these difficulties. In Australia, infants enrolled full-time in government-funded, high-quality child care have a higher rate of secure attachment than infants informally cared for by relatives, friends, or babysitters (Love et al., 2003). And in the Canadian province of Quebec, time in high-quality child care is associated with fewer behavior problems (Palacio-Quintin, 2000).

Conclusions

The evidence just reviewed suggests that some infants may be at risk for attachment insecurity and adjustment problems due to inadequate child care, long hours in child care, and maternal pressures of full-time employment and parenthood. But it is inappropriate to use these findings to justify a reduction in

At the end of her day in child care, an 11-month-old eagerly greets her mother. High-quality child care and fewer hours in child care are associated with attachment security.

child-care services. When family incomes are limited or mothers who want to work are forced to stay at home, children's emotional security is not promoted.

Instead, it makes sense to educate parents about child-care quality, to increase its availability, and to provide paid employment leave so parents can limit child-care hours. Return to Chapter 5, page 132, to review signs of developmentally appropriate child care for infants and toddlers. When caregiver–child ratios are generous, group sizes are small, and caregivers are educated about child development, caregivers' interactions are more positive and children develop more favorably (McCartney et al., 2007; NICHD Early Child Care Research Network, 2000b, 2002a, 2006).

---

they apply to the bonds they establish with their babies. Monica, who recalled her mother as tense and preoccupied, expressed regret that they had not had a closer relationship. Is her image of parenthood likely to affect Grace's attachment security?

To assess parents' internal working models, researchers have asked them to evaluate childhood memories of attachment experiences (Main & Goldwyn, 1998). Parents who discuss their

childhoods with objectivity and balance, regardless of whether they were positive or negative, tend to have securely attached infants. In contrast, parents who either dismiss the importance of early relationships or described them in angry, confused ways usually have insecurely attached babies (Slade et al., 1999; van IJzendoorn, 1995). And parents of disorganized/disoriented infants often express extremely negative feelings—either hostile or fearful—about their early attachment bonds, while also viewing themselves as "bad" and deserving of unkind treatment (Lyons-Ruth et al., 2005).

But internal working models are *reconstructed memories* affected by many factors, including relationship experiences over the life course, personality, and current life satisfaction. Longitudinal research shows that negative life events can weaken the link between an individual's attachment security in infancy and a secure internal working model in adulthood. And insecurely attached babies who become adults with insecure internal working models often have lives that, based on self-reports in adulthood, are filled with family crises (Waters et al., 2000; Weinfield, Sroufe, & Egeland, 2000).

In sum, early rearing experiences do not destine us to become sensitive or insensitive parents. Rather, the way we *view* our childhoods—our ability to come to terms with negative events and to integrate new information into our working models is much more influential in how we rear our children than the actual history of care we received.

Multiple Attachments

Babies develop attachments to a variety of familiar people— not just mothers but also fathers, siblings, grandparents, and professional caregivers. Although Bowlby (1969) acknowledged the existence of multiple attachments, he believed that infants are predisposed to direct their attachment behaviors to a single special person, especially when they are distressed. Consistent with this view, when anxious or unhappy, most babies prefer to be comforted by their mother. But this preference declines over the second year. And when babies are not distressed, they approach, vocalize to, and smile at both parents equally (Bornstein, 2006; Parke, 2002).

■ **FATHERS.**   Fathers' sensitive caregiving with infants, like mothers', predicts attachment security (van IJzendoorn et al., 2004). But in many cultures—Australia, Canada, India, Israel, Italy, Japan, and the United States—mothers and fathers tend to interact differently with babies. Mothers devote more time to physical care and expressing affection, fathers to playful interaction (Roopnarine et al., 1990).

Mothers and fathers also play differently. Mothers more often provide toys, talk to infants, and gently play conventional games like pat-a-cake. In contrast, fathers—especially with their infant sons—tend to engage in highly arousing physical play with bursts of excitement (Feldman, 2003). Through this stimulating, surprising play style, perhaps fathers teach children how to approach unfamiliar situations, such as play with peers (Paquette, 2004).

In cultures such as Japan, where long work hours prevent most fathers from sharing in infant caregiving, play is a vital context in which fathers build secure attachments (Hewlett, 2004; Shwalb et al., 2004). In many Western nations, however, a strict division of parental roles—mother as caregiver, father as playmate—has changed over the past several decades in response to

women's workforce participation. Recent surveys indicate that in dual-earner families, U.S. fathers devote 85 percent as much time as mothers do to children—on average, about 3½ hours per day (Pleck & Masciadrelli, 2004; Sandberg & Hofferth, 2001). Paternal time availability to children is fairly similar across SES and ethnic groups, with one exception: Hispanic fathers spend more time engaged, probably because of the particularly high value that Hispanic cultures place on family involvement (Cabrera & Garcia-Coll, 2004; Parke et al., 2004a).

A warm marital relationship supports both parents' involvement with babies, but it is especially important for fathers (Lamb & Lewis, 2004). And in studies carried out in many societies and ethnic groups, fathers' affectionate care of young children predicted later cognitive, emotional, and social competence as strongly, and occasionally more strongly, than did mothers' (Rohner & Veneziano, 2001; Veneziano, 2003).

■ **SIBLINGS.**   Despite declines in family size, 80 percent of North American and European children grow up with at least one sibling (Dunn, 2004). The arrival of a new baby is a difficult experience for most preschoolers, who—realizing that they must now share their parents' attention and affection—often become demanding, clingy, and deliberately naughty for a time. Attachment security also declines, especially for children over age 2 (old enough to feel threatened and displaced) and for those with mothers under stress (Baydar, Greek, & Brooks-Gunn, 1997; Teti et al., 1996).

The arrival of a baby brother or sister is a difficult experience for most preschoolers. Maternal warmth toward both children assures the older sibling of continuing parental love, models affectionate caring, and is related to positive sibling interaction.

Yet resentment is only one feature of a rich emotional relationship that starts to build between siblings after a baby's birth. Older children also show affection and concern when the infant cries. By the end of the first year, babies typically spend much time with older siblings and are comforted by the presence of a preschool-age brother or sister during short parental absences. And in the second year, toddlers often imitate and join in play with older siblings (Barr & Hayne, 2003).

Nevertheless, individual differences in sibling relationships emerge early. Temperament plays an important role. For example, conflict is greater when one sibling is emotionally intense or highly active (Brody, Stoneman, & McCoy, 1994; Dunn, 1994). And maternal warmth toward both children is related to positive sibling interaction and to preschoolers' support of a distressed younger sibling (Volling, 2001; Volling & Belsky, 1992). In contrast, maternal harshness and lack of involvement are linked to antagonistic sibling relationships (Howe, Aquan-Assee, & Bukowski, 2001). Finally, a good marriage is correlated with older preschool siblings' capacity to cope adaptively with jealousy and conflict (Volling, McElwain, & Miller, 2002). Perhaps good communication between parents serves as a model of effective problem solving. It may also foster a generally happy family environment, giving children less reason to feel jealous.

Attachment and Later Development

According to psychoanalytic and ethological theories, the inner feelings of affection and security that result from a healthy attachment relationship support all aspects of psychological development. Yet contrary evidence exists. In longitudinal research, secure infants sometimes developed into more competent children and adolescents than did their insecure counterparts, but not always (Lewis, 1997; McCartney et al., 2004; Schneider, Atkinson, & Tardif, 2001; Stams, Juffer, & van IJzendoorn, 2002).

What accounts for this inconsistency? Mounting evidence indicates that *continuity of caregiving* determines whether attachment security is linked to later development (Lamb et al., 1985; Thompson, 2006). Parents who respond sensitively not just in infancy but also during later years promote many aspects of development: a more confident self-concept, more advanced understanding of others' perspectives, more favorable relationships with teachers and peers, a stronger sense of moral responsibility, and higher motivation to achieve in school (Repacholi & Trapolini, 2004; Thompson, Easterbrooks, & Padilla-Walker, 2003). In contrast, children of parents who react insensitively over a long period are at risk for a wide array of developmental difficulties.

In sum, a secure attachment in infancy launches the parent–child relationship on a positive path. But the effects of early attachment security depend on the quality of the baby's future relationships. A child who experiences tender care in infancy but lacks sympathetic ties later is at risk for problems. In contrast, a child whose parental caregiving improves or who has other compensating ties outside the immediate family is likely to display *resilience*, or recovery from adversity (Belsky & Fearon, 2002).

ASK YOURSELF

» REVIEW

What factors explain stability in attachment pattern for some children and change for others? Are these factors also involved in the link between attachment in infancy and later development? Explain.

» APPLY

Explain how the caregiving experiences of securely attached infants promote development of emotional self-regulation, described on pages 145–146.

» REFLECT

How would you characterize your internal working model? What factors, in addition to your relationship with your parents, might have influenced it?

Self-Development During the First Two Years

Infancy is a rich formative period for the development of physical and social understanding. In Chapter 5, you learned that infants develop an appreciation of the permanence of objects. And in this chapter, we have seen that over the first year, infants recognize and respond appropriately to others' emotions and distinguish familiar from unfamiliar people. That both objects and people achieve an independent, stable existence for the infant implies that knowledge of the self as a separate, permanent entity is also emerging.

Self-Awareness

After Caitlin's bath, Carolyn often held her in front of the bathroom mirror. As early as the first few months, Caitlin smiled and returned friendly behaviors to her image. At what age did she realize that the charming baby gazing and grinning back was herself?

■ **BEGINNINGS OF SELF-AWARENESS.** Infants' remarkable capacity for *intermodal perception* (see page 113 in Chapter 4) supports the beginnings of self-awareness (Rochat, 2003). As they feel their own touch, feel and watch their limbs move, and feel and hear themselves cry, babies experience intermodal matches that differentiate their own body from surrounding bodies and objects.

Over the first few months, infants distinguish their own visual image from other stimuli. When shown two side-by-side video images of their kicking legs, one from their own perspective (camera behind the baby) and one from an observer's perspective (camera in front of the baby), 3-month-olds looked longer at the unfamiliar, observer's view (Rochat, 1998). By 4 months, infants look and smile more at video images of others than at video images of themselves, indicating that they treat another person (as opposed to the self) as a social partner (Rochat & Striano, 2002).

■ **SELF-RECOGNITION.**   During the second year, toddlers become consciously aware of the self's physical features. In several studies, 9- to 28-month-olds were placed in front of a mirror. Then, under the pretext of wiping the baby's face, each mother rubbed red dye on her child's nose or forehead. Around 20 months, toddlers began to rub their strange-looking noses, indicating awareness of their unique appearance (Bard et al., 2006; Lewis & Brooks-Gunn, 1979). Around age 2, **self-recognition**—identification of the self as a physically unique being—is well-established. Children point to themselves in photos and refer to themselves by name or with a personal pronoun ("I" or "me").

According to many theorists, self-awareness develops as infants and toddlers increasingly realize that their own actions cause objects and people to react in predictable ways (Harter, 1998). In support of this idea, babies whose parents respond sensitively to their signals and encourage exploration tend to be advanced in self-development (Pipp, Easterbrooks, & Harmon, 1992). As infants act on the environment, they notice effects that help them sort out self, other people, and objects (Nadel, Prepin, & Okanda, 2005; Rochat, 2001). For example, batting a mobile and seeing it swing in a pattern different from the infant's own actions informs the baby about the relation between self and physical world. Smiling and vocalizing at a caregiver who smiles and vocalizes back helps clarify the relation between self and social world. These experiences help infants build an image of the self as separate from, but vitally connected to, external reality.

Cultural variations exist in early self-development. Urban German and Greek toddlers attain mirror self-recognition earlier than toddlers of the Nso people of Cameroon, a collectivist rural farming society that highly values social harmony and responsibility to others (Keller et al., 2004, 2005). Compared to their German and Greek counterparts, Nso mothers engage in less face-to-face communication and object stimulation and more body contact and physical stimulation of their babies. German and Greek practices reflect a *distal parenting style* common in cultures that emphasize independence; the Nso practice a *proximal parenting style* typical in cultures that promote interdependence. In line with these differences, Nso proximal parenting predicts later attainment of self-recognition but earlier emergence of toddlers' compliance with adult requests (see Figure 6.2).

■ **SELF-AWARENESS AND EARLY EMOTIONAL AND SOCIAL DEVELOPMENT.**   Recall that self-conscious emotions depend on a strengthening sense of self. Self-awareness also leads to first efforts to appreciate others' perspectives. Toddlers show the beginnings of **empathy**—the ability to understand another's emotional state and *feel with* that person, or respond emotionally in a similar way. For example, they start to give to

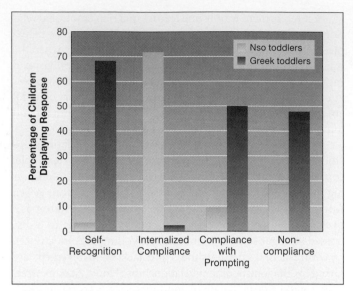

■ **FIGURE 6.2** ■ **Self-recognition and compliance among Nso and Greek toddlers.** At 18 and 20 months, toddlers were tested for mirror self-recognition and for compliance (they were told not to open a transparent container with an attractive food). Among Greek toddlers, whose culture values independence, many more had attained self-recognition. But Nso toddlers, reared in an interdependent culture, were greatly advanced in compliance. The majority displayed internalized compliance (following directions without prompting), whereas Greek toddlers either needed reminders or did not comply. (Adapted from Keller et al., 2004.)

others what they themselves find comforting—a hug, a reassuring comment, or a favorite doll or blanket (Hoffman, 2000). At the same time, toddlers demonstrate clearer awareness of how to upset others. One 18-month-old heard her mother talking to another adult about an older sibling: "Anny is really frightened of spiders" (Dunn, 1989, p. 107). The innocent-looking toddler ran to the bedroom, returned with a toy spider, and pushed it in front of Anny's face!

Categorizing the Self

Because language permits children to represent the self more clearly, it greatly enhances self-awareness from the second year on. Between 18 and 30 months, children develop a **categorical self** as they classify themselves and others on the basis of age ("baby," "boy," or "man"), sex ("boy" or "girl"), physical characteristics ("big," "strong"), and even goodness versus badness ("I a good girl," "Tommy mean!") (Stipek, Gralinski, & Kopp, 1990). Toddlers use their limited understanding of these social categories to organize their own behavior. For example, as early as 18 months, they select and play in a more involved way with toys that are stereotyped for their own gender—dolls and tea sets for girls, trucks and cars for boys. Parents then encourage these preferences by responding positively when toddlers display them (Ruble, Martin, & Berenbaum, 2006). As we will see in Chapter 8, gender-typed behavior increases dramatically in early childhood.

Self-Control

Self-awareness also contributes to strengthening of *effortful control* (see page 147). To behave in a self-controlled fashion, children must have some ability to think of themselves as separate, autonomous beings who can direct their own actions. And they must have the representational and memory capacities to recall a caregiver's directive ("Caitlin, don't touch that light socket!") and apply it to their own behavior.

As these capacities emerge between 12 and 18 months, toddlers first become capable of **compliance.** They show clear awareness of caregivers' wishes and expectations and can obey simple requests and commands. And as every parent knows, they can also decide to assert their autonomy and do just the opposite! But for most, opposition is far less common than compliance with an eager, willing spirit, which suggests that the child is beginning to adopt the adult's directives as his own (Kochanska, Murray, & Harlan, 2000). Compliance quickly leads to toddlers' first consciencelike verbalizations—for example, correcting the self by saying "No, can't" before touching a delicate object or jumping on the sofa.

Researchers often study the early emergence of self-control by giving children tasks that, like the situations just mentioned, require **delay of gratification**—waiting for an appropriate time and place to engage in a tempting act. Between ages 1½ and 3, children show an increasing capacity to wait before eating a treat, opening a present, or playing with a toy (Vaughn, Kopp, & Krakow, 1984). Children who are advanced in development of attention and language tend to be better at delaying gratification—findings that help explain why girls are typically more self-controlled than boys (Else-Quest et al., 2006). Some toddlers already use verbal and other attention-diverting techniques—talking to themselves, singing, or looking away—to keep from engaging in prohibited acts.

Like effortful control in general, young children's capacity to delay gratification is influenced by both biologically based temperament and quality of caregiving (Kochanska & Aksan, 2006; Kochanska & Knaack, 2003). Inhibited children find it easier to wait than angry, irritable children do. But toddlers who experience parental warmth and gentle encouragement are more likely to be cooperative and to resist temptation. Parenting that encourages and models patient, nonimpulsive behavior is particularly important for temperamentally reactive babies. In one study, anger-prone 7-month-olds with gentle, responsive mothers became eagerly compliant 15-month-olds, whereas angry infants with insensitive mothers developed into uncooperative toddlers (Kochanska, Aksan, & Carlson, 2005).

As self-control improves, parents gradually expand the rules they expect toddlers to follow, from safety and respect for property and people to family routines, manners, and responsibility for simple chores (Gralinski & Kopp, 1993). Still, toddlers' control over their own actions depends on constant parental oversight and reminders. Several prompts ("Remember, we're going to go in just a minute") and gentle insistence were usually necessary to get Caitlin to stop playing so that she and her parents could go on an errand. Applying What We Know on page 160 summarizes ways to help toddlers develop compliance and self-control.

As the second year of life drew to a close, Carolyn, Monica, and Vanessa were delighted at their children's readiness to learn the rules of social life. As we will see in Chapter 8, advances in cognition and language, along with parental warmth and reasonable maturity demands, lead preschoolers to make tremendous strides in this area.

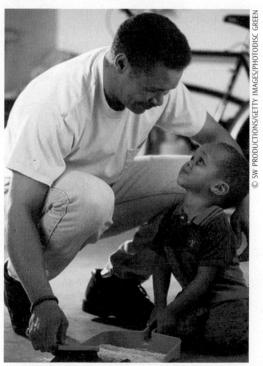

© SW PRODUCTIONS/GETTY IMAGES/PHOTODISC GREEN

This father is encouraging compliance and the beginnings of self-control. The toddler joins in the task with a willing spirit, which suggests he is adopting the adult's directive as his own.

ASK YOURSELF

≫ **REVIEW**
Why is insisting that infants comply with parental directives inappropriate? What competencies are necessary for the emergence of compliance and self-control?

≫ **APPLY**
Len, a caregiver of 1- and 2-year-olds, wonders whether toddlers recognize themselves. List signs of self-recognition in the second year that Len can observe.

Applying What We Know

Helping Toddlers Develop Compliance and Self-Control

Suggestion	Rationale
Respond to the toddler with sensitivity and encouragement.	Toddlers whose parents are sensitive and supportive are more compliant and self-controlled.
Provide advance notice when the toddler must stop an enjoyable activity.	Toddlers find it more difficult to stop a pleasant activity already under way than to wait before engaging in a desired action.
Offer many prompts and reminders.	Toddlers' ability to remember and comply with rules is limited; they need continuous adult oversight.
Respond to self-controlled behavior with verbal and physical approval.	Praise and hugs reinforce appropriate behavior, increasing its likelihood of occurring again.
Encourage sustained attention (see Chapter 5, page 124).	Development of attention is related to self-control. Children who can shift attention from a captivating stimulus and focus on a less attractive alternative are better at controlling their impulses.
Support language development (see Chapter 5, page 137).	In the second year, children begin to use language to remind themselves of adult expectations and to delay gratification.
Gradually increase rules in accord with the toddler's developing capacities.	As cognition and language improve, toddlers can follow more rules related to safety, respect for people and property, family routines, manners, and simple chores.

Summary

Erikson's Theory of Infant and Toddler Personality

According to Erikson's psychosocial theory, how do infants and toddlers resolve the psychological conflicts of the first two years?

>> Warm, responsive caregiving leads infants to resolve the psychological conflict of **basic trust versus mistrust** on the positive side. During toddlerhood, **autonomy versus shame and doubt** is resolved favorably when parents provide appropriate guidance and reasonable choices.

Emotional Development

Describe changes in happiness, anger, and fear over the first year, noting the adaptive function of each.

>> During the first half-year, **basic emotions** gradually become clear, well-organized signals. The **social smile** appears between 6 and 10 weeks, laughter around 3 to 4 months. Happiness strengthens the parent–child bond and both reflects and supports physical and cognitive mastery.

>> Anger and fear, especially in the form of **stranger anxiety,** increase in the second half-year. Newly mobile babies use the familiar caregiver as a **secure base** from which to explore. Sadness is common when caregiver–infant communication is seriously disrupted.

Summarize changes during the first two years in understanding others' emotions, expression of self-conscious emotions, and emotional self-regulation.

>> As infants' ability to detect the meaning of emotional expressions improves over the first year, **social referencing** appears; in uncertain situations, 8- to -10-month-olds begin actively seeking emotional information from caregivers. By the middle of the second year, infants appreciate that others' emotional reactions may differ from their own.

>> During toddlerhood, self-awareness and adult instruction provide the foundation for **self-conscious emotions. Emotional self-regulation** emerges as the frontal lobes of the cerebral cortex develop and as caregivers sensitively assist infants in adjusting their emotional reactions. In the second year, growth in representation and language leads to more effective ways of regulating emotion.

Temperament and Development

What is temperament, and how is it measured?

>> Children differ greatly in **temperament—** early-appearing, stable individual differences in reactivity and self-regulation. Thomas and Chess's New York Longitudinal Study identified three patterns of temperament: the **easy child, the difficult child,** and the **slow-to-warm-up child.** Another model of temperament, devised by Mary Rothbart, includes **effortful control,** the ability to regulate one's reactivity.

>> Temperament is assessed using parental reports, behavior ratings by others familiar with the child, and laboratory observations. Most physiological research has focused on distinguishing **inhibited,** or **shy, children** from **uninhibited,** or **sociable, children.**

>> Stability of temperament is generally low to moderate. Temperament has a genetic foundation, but child rearing and cultural beliefs and practices have much to do with maintaining or changing it. In the **goodness-of-fit model,** parenting practices that create a good fit with the child's temperament help children achieve more adaptive functioning.

Development of Attachment

Describe the development of attachment during the first two years.

>> The most widely accepted perspective on development of **attachment** is **ethological theory,** which recognizes the infant's emotional tie to the caregiver as an evolved response that promotes survival. In early infancy, a set of built-in behaviors encourages the parent to remain close to the baby.

>> Around 6 to 8 months, **separation anxiety** and use of the parent as a secure base indicate that a true attachment bond has formed. As representation and language develop, toddlers try to alter the parent's coming and going through requests and persuasion. Out of early caregiving experiences, children construct an **internal working model** that serves as a guide for all future close relationships.

Describe the Strange Situation and the Attachment Q-Sort, along with factors that affect attachment security.

>> The **Strange Situation** is a laboratory technique for assessing the quality of attachment between 1 and 2 years. Using it, researchers have identified four attachment patterns: **secure attachment, avoidant attachment, resistant attachment,** and **disorganized/disoriented attachment.** The **Attachment Q-Sort,** a home observation method suitable for 1- to 4-year-olds, yields a score ranging from high to low in security.

>> Securely attached babies in middle-SES families experiencing favorable life conditions more often maintain their attachment pattern than do insecure babies. An exception is the disorganized/disoriented pattern, which is highly stable. Cultural conditions must be considered in interpreting the meaning of attachment patterns.

>> Attachment quality is influenced by **sensitive caregiving,** the fit between the baby's temperament and parenting practices, and family circumstances. Parents' internal working models are good predictors of infant attachment patterns, but parents' childhood experiences do not transfer directly to quality of attachment with their own children.

>> Infants develop strong affectionate ties to fathers, who tend to engage in more exciting, physical play with babies than do mothers. Early in the first year, infants begin to build rich emotional relationships with siblings that mix affection and caring with rivalry and resentment. Individual differences in the quality of sibling relationships are influenced by temperament and parenting practices.

>> Continuity of caregiving is the crucial factor that determines whether attachment security is linked to later development. Children can recover from an insecure attachment history if caregiving improves.

Self-Development During the First Two Years

Describe the development of self-awareness in infancy and toddlerhood, along with the emotional and social capacities it supports.

>> Babies' capacity for intermodal perception supports early self-awareness. Around age 2, **self-recognition** is well under way. Two-year-olds point to themselves in photos and refer to themselves by name or with a personal pronoun.

>> Self-awareness is associated with the beginnings of **empathy.** As language strengthens, between 18 and 30 months toddlers develop a **categorical self** based on age, sex, physical characteristics, and goodness and badness.

>> Self-awareness also provides the foundation for the emergence of **compliance** between 12 and 18 months, and an increasing capacity for **delay of gratification** between ages 1½ and 3 years. Children who are advanced in development of attention and language and who have warm, encouraging parents tend to be more self-controlled.

Important Terms and Concepts

attachment (p. 150)
Attachment Q-Sort (p. 152)
autonomy versus shame and doubt (p. 141)
avoidant attachment (p. 152)
basic emotions (p. 142)
basic trust versus mistrust (p. 141)
categorical self (p. 158)
compliance (p. 159)
delay of gratification (p. 159)
difficult child (p. 146)
disorganized/disoriented attachment (p. 152)

easy child (p. 146)
effortful control (p. 147)
emotional self-regulation (p. 145)
empathy (p. 158)
ethological theory of attachment (p. 151)
goodness-of-fit model (p. 149)
inhibited, or shy, child (p. 147)
internal working model (p. 152)
resistant attachment (p. 152)
secure attachment (p. 152)
secure base (p. 143)

self-conscious emotions (p. 145)
self-recognition (p. 158)
sensitive caregiving (p. 154)
separation anxiety (p. 151)
slow-to-warm-up child (p. 146)
social referencing (p. 144)
social smile (p. 142)
stranger anxiety (p. 143)
Strange Situation (p. 152)
temperament (p. 146)
uninhibited, or sociable, child (p. 147)

Milestones
Development in Infancy and Toddlerhood

PHYSICAL

- Height and weight increase rapidly. (92–94)
- Newborn reflexes decline. (82–83)
- Distinguishes basic tastes and odors; shows preference for sweet-tasting foods. (86–87)
- Responses can be classically and operantly conditioned. (103–104)
- Habituates to unchanging stimuli; recovers to novel stimuli. (104)
- Sleep is increasingly organized into a night–day schedule. (98–99)
- Holds head up, rolls over, and grasps objects. (106, 107)
- Perceives auditory and visual stimuli as organized patterns. (109, 111–112)
- Shows sensitivity to motion and binocular depth cues. (110–111)
- Recognizes and prefers human facial pattern; recognizes features of mother's face. (111–112)
- By end of this period, moves from relying on motion and spatial arrangement to using shape, color, and texture to visually identify objects. (113)
- Masters a wide range of intermodal (visual, auditory, and tactile) relationships. (113)

COGNITIVE

- Engages in immediate and deferred imitation of adults' facial expressions. (104–105, 120)
- Repeats chance behaviors that lead to pleasurable and interesting results. (118–119)

- Violation-of-expectation tasks suggest some awareness of many physical properties (including object permanence) and basic numerical knowledge. (120, 122–123)
- Recognition memory for visual events improves. (125)
- Attention becomes more efficient and flexible. (124)
- Forms perceptual categories based on objects' similar features. (125, 127)

LANGUAGE

- Coos and, by end of this period, babbles. (135)
- Begins to establish joint attention with caregiver, who labels objects and events. (135)

EMOTIONAL/SOCIAL

- Social smile and laughter emerge. (142)
- Matches feeling tone of caregiver in face-to-face communication; later, expects matched responses. (143–145)
- Emotional expressions become well-organized and meaningfully related to environmental events. (142)

- Regulates emotion by shifting attention and self-soothing. (145–146)
- Awareness of self as physically distinct from surroundings increases. (157–158)

PHYSICAL

- Approaches adultlike sleep–wake schedule. (98–99)
- Sits alone, crawls, and walks. (106)

- Reaching and grasping improve in flexibility and accuracy; shows refined pincer grasp. (108)
- Develops sensitivity to pictorial depth cues. (111)
- Intermodal perception continues to improve. (113)

COGNITIVE

- Engages in intentional, or goal-directed, behavior. (119)
- Finds object hidden in an initial location. (119)
- Engages in deferred imitation of adults' actions with objects. (121)
- Solves simple problems by analogy to a previous problem. (121–122)
- Categorizes objects conceptually, by similar function and behavior. (125, 127)

LANGUAGE

- Babbling expands to include sounds of spoken languages and patterns of the child's language community. (135)
- Joint attention with caregiver becomes more accurate. (135)

Note: Numbers in parentheses indicate the page or pages on which each milestone is discussed.

- Takes turns in games, such as pat-a-cake and peekaboo. (135)
- Comprehends some word meanings. (136)
- Uses preverbal gestures (showing, pointing) to influence others' behavior. (135)

- Around end of this period, says first words. (136)

EMOTIONAL/SOCIAL

- Smiling and laughter increase in frequency and expressiveness. (142)
- Anger and fear increase in frequency and intensity. (142–143)
- Stranger anxiety and separation anxiety appear. (143)
- Uses caregiver as a secure base for exploration. (143)
- Shows "clear-cut" attachment to familiar caregivers. (151)
- Increasingly detects the meaning of others' emotional expressions and engages in social referencing. (144–145)
- Regulates emotion by approaching and retreating from stimulation. (145)

13–18 months

PHYSICAL

- Height and weight gain are rapid, but not as great as in first year. (92)
- Walking is better coordinated. (107)
- Manipulates small objects with improved coordination. (108)

COGNITIVE

- Explores the properties of objects by acting on them in novel ways. (118)
- Searches in several locations for a hidden object. (119)
- Engages in deferred imitation of adults' actions with objects over longer delays and across a change in context—for example, from child care to home. (121)
- Sustained attention improves. (124)
- Recall memory for people, places, and objects improves. (125)
- Sorts objects into categories. (125, 127)

LANGUAGE

- Steadily adds to vocabulary, with comprehension ahead of production. (135, 136)

EMOTIONAL/SOCIAL

- Joins in play with familiar adults and siblings. (156)
- Realizes that others' emotional reactions may differ from one's own. (144–145)
- Shows signs of empathy. (158)
- Complies with simple directives. (159)

19–24 months

PHYSICAL

- Jumps, walks on tiptoe, runs, and climbs. (106)
- Manipulates small objects with good coordination. (108)

COGNITIVE

- Solves simple problems using representation. (119–120)
- Finds a hidden object that has been moved while out of sight. (120)
- Engages in make-believe play, using simple actions experienced in everyday life. (120)

- Engages in deferred imitation of actions an adult tries to produce, even if not fully realized. (121, 123)
- Sorts objects into categories more effectively. (125, 127)

LANGUAGE

- Produces about 200 words. (136)
- Combines two words. (136)

EMOTIONAL/SOCIAL

- Self-conscious emotions (shame, embarrassment, guilt, envy, and pride) emerge. (145)
- Acquires a vocabulary for talking about feelings. (146)
- Begins to use language to assist with emotional self-regulation. (145–146)
- Begins to tolerate caregiver's absences more easily; separation anxiety declines. (151)
- Recognizes image of self and, by end of this period, uses own name or personal pronoun to refer to self. (158)
- Categorizes self and others on the basis of age, sex, physical characteristics, and goodness and badness. (158–159)
- Shows gender-stereotyped toy preferences. (158)
- Self-control, as indicated by delay of gratification, emerges. (159)

CHAPTER 7

Physical and Cognitive Development in Early Childhood

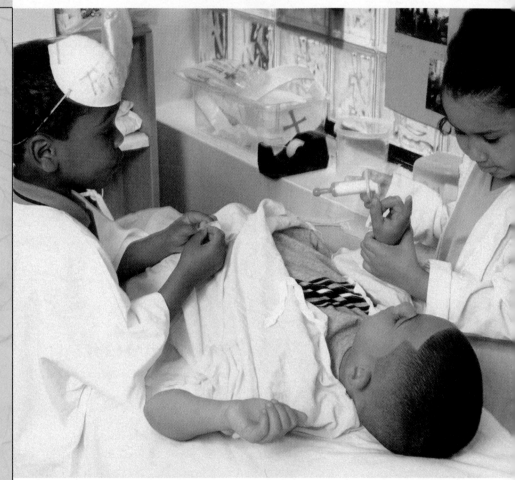

© LAURA DWIGHT PHOTOGRAPHY

Preschoolers draw on their rich array of everyday experiences when they engage in make-believe play. In turn, their make-believe contributes greatly to their rapidly advancing cognitive and language skills.

For more than a decade, my office window overlooked the preschool and kindergarten play yard of our university laboratory school. On mild fall and spring mornings, the doors of the classrooms swung open, and sand table, easels, and large blocks spilled out into a small courtyard. Alongside the building was a grassy area with jungle gyms, swings, a play-house, and a flower garden planted by the children; beyond it, a circular path lined with tricycles and wagons. Each day, the setting was alive with activity.

© DAVID YOUNG-WOLFF/PHOTOEDIT

The years from 2 to 6 are often called "the play years"—aptly so, since play blossoms during this time and supports every aspect of development. Our discussion opens with the physical achievements of early childhood—growth in body size and improvements in motor coordination. We look at biological and environmental factors that support these changes and at their intimate connection with other domains of development.

Then we explore early childhood cognition, beginning with Piaget's preoperational stage. Recent research, along with Vygotsky's sociocultural theory and information processing, extends our understanding of preschoolers' cognitive competencies. Next, we turn to factors that contribute to early childhood mental development—the home environment, the quality of preschool and child care, and educational media. We conclude with the most awesome achievement of early childhood—language development.

Physical Development

A Changing Body and Brain

In early childhood, body growth tapers off from the rapid rate of the first two years. On average, children add 2 to 3 inches in height and about 5 pounds in weight each year. Boys continue to be slightly larger than girls. As "baby fat" drops off further, children gradually become thinner, although girls retain somewhat more body fat than boys, who are slightly more muscular. As Figure 7.1 on page 166 shows, by age 5 the top-heavy, bowlegged, potbellied toddler has become a more stream-lined, flat-tummied, longer-legged child with body proportions similar to those of adults. Consequently, posture and balance improve—changes that support gains in motor coordination.

Individual differences in body size are even more apparent during early childhood than in infancy and toddlerhood. Speeding around the bike path in the play yard, 5-year-old Darryl—at 48 inches tall and 55 pounds—towered over his kindergarten classmates. (The average North American 5-year-old boy is 43 inches tall and weighs 42 pounds.) Priti, an Asian-Indian child, was unusually small because of genetic factors linked to her cultural ancestry. Lynette and Hal, two Caucasian children with impoverished home lives, were well below average for reasons we will discuss shortly.

Skeletal Growth

The skeletal changes of infancy continue throughout early childhood. Between ages 2 and 6, approximately 45 new *epiphyses*, or growth centers in which cartilage hardens into bone, emerge in various parts of the skeleton. X-rays of these growth centers enable doctors to estimate children's *skeletal age*, or progress toward physical maturity (see page 93 in Chapter 4).

By the end of the preschool years, children start to lose their primary, or "baby," teeth. Girls, who are ahead of boys in physical development, lose teeth earlier. Environmental influences also matter: Prolonged malnutrition delays the appearance of permanent teeth, whereas overweight and obesity accelerate it (Hilgers et al., 2006).

Diseased baby teeth can affect the health of permanent teeth, so preventing decay in primary teeth is essential—by brushing consistently, avoiding sugary foods, drinking fluoridated water, and getting topical fluoride treatments and sealants (plastic coatings that protect tooth surfaces). Another factor is exposure to tobacco smoke, which suppresses children's immune system, including the ability to fight bacteria responsible for tooth decay. Young children in homes with regular smokers are three times as likely as their agemates to have decayed teeth (Shenkin et al., 2004). Unfortunately, an estimated 30 percent of U.S. preschoolers have tooth decay, a figure that rises to 60 percent by age 18 (U.S. Department of Health and Human Services, 2007e).

Brain Development

Between ages 2 and 6, the brain increases from 70 percent of its adult weight to 90 percent. By age 4, many parts of the cerebral cortex have overproduced synapses, and fMRI evidence indicates that cerebral blood flow peaks, signifying a high energy need (Huttenlocher, 2002; Nelson, Thomas, & de Haan, 2006). As *formation of synapses, cell death, myelination,* and *synaptic pruning* occur (see Chapter 4), preschoolers improve in a wide variety of skills—physical coordination, perception, attention, memory, language, logical thinking, and imagination.

Chris at 4½ years

Chris at 3½ years

Chris at 3 years

Chris at 5 years

Mariel at 4 years

Mariel at 2½ years

Mariel at 4½ years

Mariel at 5 years

■ **FIGURE 7.1** ■ **Body growth during early childhood.** During the preschool years, children grow more slowly than in infancy and toddlerhood. Chris and Mariel's bodies became more streamlined, flat-tummied, and longer-legged. Boys continue to be slightly taller, heavier, and more muscular than girls. But generally, the two sexes are similar in body proportions and physical capacities.

EEG and fMRI measures of neural activity in various cortical regions reveal especially rapid growth from early to middle childhood in frontal-lobe areas devoted to inhibiting impulses and planning and organizing behavior (Bartgis, Lilly, & Thomas, 2003; Diamond, 2004). Furthermore, for most children, the left cerebral hemisphere is especially active between 3 and 6 years and then levels off. In contrast, activity in the right hemisphere increases steadily throughout early and middle childhood (Thatcher, Walker, & Giudice, 1987; Thompson et al., 2000).

In line with these developments, early childhood is a time of marked gains on tasks that depend on the frontal cortex—ones that require impulse control and thoughtful responses (Rothbart & Bates, 2006). Further, language skills (typically housed in the left hemisphere) increase at an astonishing pace. In contrast, spatial skills (usually located in the right hemisphere), such as giving directions, drawing pictures, and reading maps, develop gradually over childhood and adolescence. Differences in development of the two hemispheres suggest that they are continuing to *lateralize* (specialize in cognitive functions). Let's take a closer look at brain lateralization in early childhood by focusing on handedness.

■ **HANDEDNESS.** On one visit to the preschool, I observed 3-year-old Moira, who does most things—drawing, eating, and zipping her jacket—with her left hand. But she uses her right

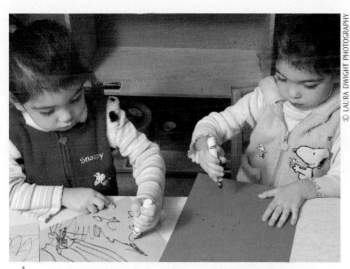

Twins are more likely than ordinary siblings to differ in hand preference, perhaps because twins usually lie in opposite orientations in the uterus.

hand for a few activities, such as throwing a ball. Research on handedness, along with other evidence covered in Chapter 4, supports the joint contribution of nature and nurture to brain lateralization.

By age 6 months, infants typically display a smoother, more efficient movement when reaching with their right than their left arm—a difference, believed to be biologically based, that may contribute to the right-hand preference evident in most children by the end of the first year (Hinojosa, Sheu, & Michael, 2003; Rönnqvist & Domellöf, 2006). Gradually, handedness extends to additional skills.

Handedness reflects the greater capacity of one side of the brain—the individual's **dominant cerebral hemisphere**—to carry out skilled motor action. Other important abilities are generally located on the dominant side as well. For right-handed people—in Western nations, 90 percent of the population—language is housed in the left hemisphere with hand control. For the left-handed 10 percent, language is occasionally located in the right hemisphere or, more often, shared between the hemispheres (Szaflarski et al., 2002). This indicates that the brains of left-handers tend to be less strongly lateralized than those of right-handers.

Left-handed parents show only a weak tendency to have left-handed children. One genetic theory proposes that most children inherit a gene that *biases* them for right-handedness and a left-dominant cerebral hemisphere, but this bias is not strong enough to overcome experiences that might sway children toward a left-hand preference (Annett, 2002). Even prenatal events may profoundly affect handedness. Both identical and fraternal twins are more likely than ordinary siblings to differ in hand preference, probably because twins usually lie in opposite orientations in the uterus (Derom et al., 1996). The orientation of most fetuses—facing toward the left—is believed to promote greater motor control on the body's right side (Previc, 1991).

Handedness also involves practice. Newborns' bias in head position causes them to spend more time looking at and using one hand, which contributes to greater skillfulness of that hand (Hinojosa, Sheu, & Michael, 2003). Furthermore, wide cultural differences exist: In Tanzania, Africa, where children are physically restrained and punished for favoring their left hand, less than 1 percent of adults are left-handed (Provins, 1997).

Most left-handers have no developmental problems. In fact, they are more likely than their right-handed agemates to develop outstanding verbal and mathematical talents (Flannery & Liederman, 1995). More even distribution of cognitive functions across both hemispheres may be responsible.

■ **OTHER ADVANCES IN BRAIN DEVELOPMENT.** In addition to the cerebral cortex, other parts of the brain make strides during early childhood (see Figure 7.2). All of these changes involve establishing links between parts of the brain, increasing the coordinated functioning of the central nervous system.

At the rear and base of the brain is the **cerebellum,** a structure that aids in balance and control of body movement. Fibers linking the cerebellum to the cerebral cortex grow and myelinate from birth through the preschool years, contributing to dramatic gains in motor coordination: By the end of the preschool years, children can play hopscotch, throw a ball with well-coordinated movements, and print letters of the alphabet. Connections between the cerebellum and cerebral cortex also support thinking: Children with damage to the cerebellum usually display both motor and cognitive deficits, including problems with memory, planning, and language (Noterdaeme et al., 2002; Riva & Giorgi, 2000).

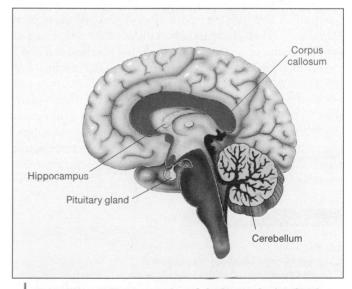

■ **FIGURE 7.2** ■ **Cross section of the human brain, showing the location of the cerebellum, the hippocampus, and the corpus callosum.** These structures undergo considerable development during early childhood. Also shown is the pituitary gland, which secretes hormones that control body growth (see page 168).

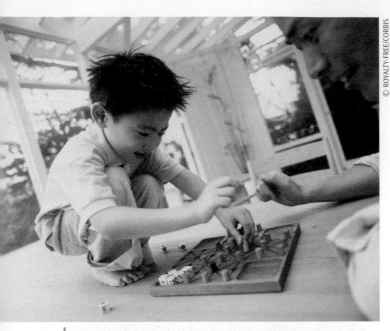

In early childhood, changes in the corpus callosum and other brain structures enhance communication between parts of the brain, enabling children to perform increasingly complex tasks—like this board game—that require integration of attention, memory, language, and problem solving.

An inner-brain structure called the **hippocampus,** which plays a vital role in memory and in images of space that help us find our way, undergoes rapid synapse formation and myelination in the second half of the first year, when recall memory and independent movement emerge. Over the preschool and school years, the hippocampus and surrounding areas of the cerebral cortex continue to develop swiftly, establishing connections with one another and with the frontal lobes (Nelson, Thomas, & de Haan, 2006). These changes support the dramatic gains in memory and spatial understanding of early and middle childhood.

The **corpus callosum** is a large bundle of fibers connecting the two cerebral hemispheres. Production of synapses and myelination of the corpus callosum peak between 3 and 6 years, then continue more slowly through adolescence (Thompson et al., 2000). The corpus callosum supports smooth coordination of movements on both sides of the body and integration of many aspects of thinking, including perception, attention, memory, language, and problem solving.

ASK YOURSELF

>> **REVIEW**
What aspects of brain development underlie the tremendous gains in language, thinking, and motor control of early childhood?

>> **REFLECT**
How early, and to what extent, did you experience tooth decay in childhood? What factors might have been responsible?

Influences on Physical Growth and Health

As we consider factors affecting growth and health in early childhood, you will encounter some familiar themes. Heredity remains important, but environmental factors—including good nutrition, relative freedom from disease, and physical safety—also are essential.

Heredity and Hormones

Children's physical size and rate of growth are related to those of their parents, reflecting the impact of heredity (Bogin, 2001). Genes influence growth by controlling the body's production of hormones. The **pituitary gland,** located at the base of the brain, plays a critical role by releasing two hormones that induce growth.

The first, **growth hormone (GH),** is necessary for development of all body tissues except the central nervous system and the genitals. Children who lack GH reach an average mature height of only 4 feet, 4 inches. When treated early with injections of GH, such children show catch-up growth and then grow at a normal rate, becoming much taller than they would have without treatment (Saenger, 2003).

A second pituitary hormone, **thyroid-stimulating hormone (TSH),** prompts the thyroid gland in the neck to release *thyroxine*, which is necessary for brain development and for GH to have its full impact on body size. Infants born with a deficiency of thyroxine must receive it at once, or they will be mentally retarded. Once the most rapid period of brain development is complete, children with too little thyroxine grow at a below-average rate, but the central nervous system is no longer affected. With prompt treatment, such children catch up in body growth and eventually reach normal size (Salerno et al., 2001).

Nutrition

With the transition to early childhood, many children become unpredictable, picky eaters. Preschoolers' appetites decline because growth has slowed. Their wariness of new foods is also adaptive. In sticking to familiar foods, they are less likely to swallow dangerous substances when adults are not around to protect them (Birch & Fisher, 1995). Parents need not worry about variations in amount eaten from meal to meal. Preschoolers compensate for a meal in which they eat little by eating more at a later meal (Hursti, 1999). Though they eat less, preschoolers require a high-quality diet, including the same foods adults need.

Children tend to imitate the food choices of people they admire, both adults and peers. Repeated, unpressured exposure to a new food also increases acceptance (Fuller et al., 2005). Serving broccoli or tofu increases children's liking for these healthy foods. In contrast, offering sweet fruit or soft drinks

© ROYALTY-FREE/CORBIS

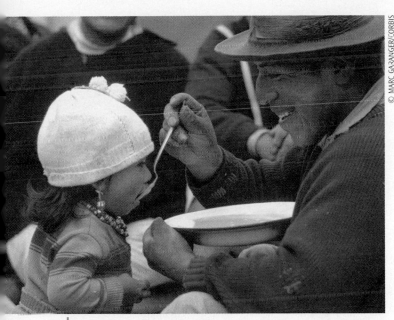

This Quechua child of the Peruvian highlands enthusiastically accepts a spoonful of soup made from bitter-tasting potatoes. She has already acquired a taste for the foods that are commonly served in her culture.

promotes "milk avoidance" (Black et al., 2002). Too much parental control limits children's opportunities to develop self-control. Offering bribes ("Finish your vegetables, and you can have an extra cookie") causes children to like the healthy food less and the treat more (Birch, Fisher, & Davison, 2003).

As indicated in earlier chapters, many children in North America and in developing countries lack access to sufficient high-quality food to support healthy development. Five-year-old Hal rode a bus from a poor neighborhood to our laboratory preschool. His mother's welfare check barely covered her rent, let alone food. Hal's diet was deficient in protein and in essential vitamins and minerals, and he was thin, pale, and tired. By the school years, low-SES North American children are, on average, ½ to 1 inch shorter than their economically advantaged counterparts (Cecil et al., 2005; Yip, Scanlon, & Trowbridge, 1993).

Infectious Disease

One day, I noticed that Hal had been absent from the play yard for several weeks, so I asked Leslie, his preschool teacher, what was wrong. "Hal's been hospitalized with a severe case of the measles," she explained. In well-nourished children, ordinary childhood illnesses have no effect on physical growth. But when children are poorly fed, disease interacts with malnutrition in a vicious spiral, with potentially severe consequences.

■ **INFECTIOUS DISEASE AND MALNUTRITION.** Hal's reaction to the measles is commonplace in developing nations, where many children live in poverty and do not receive routine immunizations. Poor diet depresses the body's immune system, making children far more susceptible to disease. Of the 10 million annual deaths of children under age 5 worldwide, 98 percent are in developing countries and 70 percent are due to infectious diseases (World Health Organization, 2008a).

Disease, in turn, is a major contributor to malnutrition, hindering both physical growth and cognitive development. Illness reduces appetite and limits the body's ability to absorb foods, especially in children with intestinal infections. In developing countries, widespread diarrhea, resulting from unsafe water and contaminated foods, leads to growth stunting and nearly two million childhood deaths each year (World Health Organization, 2008a). Studies carried out in Brazil and Peru reveal that the more persistent diarrhea is in early childhood, the shorter children are in height and the lower they score on mental tests during the school years (Checkley et al., 2003; Niehaus et al., 2002).

Most developmental impairments and deaths due to diarrhea can be prevented with nearly cost-free *oral rehydration therapy (ORT)*, in which sick children are given a solution of glucose, salt, and water that quickly replaces fluids the body loses. Since 1990, public health workers have taught nearly half the families in the developing world how to administer ORT. Also, supplements of zinc (essential for immune system functioning), which cost only 30 cents for a month's supply, substantially reduce the incidence of severe diarrhea (Aggarwal, Sentz, & Miller, 2007). Through these interventions, the lives of millions of children are saved each year.

■ **IMMUNIZATION.** In industrialized nations, childhood diseases have declined dramatically during the past half-century, largely as a result of widespread immunization of infants and young children. Hal got the measles because, unlike classmates from advantaged homes, he did not receive a full program of immunizations. About 23 percent of U.S. preschoolers lack essential immunizations. The rate rises to 26 percent for poverty-stricken children, who do not receive full protection until age 5 or 6, when it is required for school entry (U.S. Department of Health and Human Services, 2007c). In contrast, fewer than 10 percent of preschoolers lack immunizations in Denmark and Norway, and fewer than 7 percent in Great Britain, Canada, the Netherlands, and Sweden (United Nations, 2002; UNICEF, 2008).

Why does the United States lag behind in immunization? As noted in earlier chapters, many U.S. children do not have access to the health care they need. But inability to pay for vaccines is only one cause. Parents with stressful daily lives often fail to schedule vaccination appointments. And some parents have been influenced by media reports suggesting a link between the measles–mumps–rubella vaccine and a rise in the number of children diagnosed with autism, although large-scale studies show no such association (Richler et al., 2006; Stehr-Green et al., 2003). In areas where many parents have refused to immunize their children, disease outbreaks have occurred, with life-threatening consequences (Kennedy & Gust,

2008; Tuyen & Bisgard, 2003). Public education programs to increase parental knowledge about the importance and safety of timely immunizations are badly needed.

Childhood Injuries

Unintentional injuries are the leading cause of childhood mortality in industrialized nations. As Figure 7.3 reveals, the United States ranks poorly in these largely preventable events. Nearly 35 percent of U.S. childhood deaths and 50 percent of adolescent deaths result from injuries (Children's Defense Fund, 2008). And among injured children and youths who survive, thousands suffer pain, brain damage, and permanent physical disabilities.

Auto and traffic accidents, drownings, and burns are the most common injuries during early and middle childhood. Motor vehicle collisions are by far the most frequent source of injury across all ages, ranking as the leading cause of death among children over 1 year old.

■ **FACTORS RELATED TO CHILDHOOD INJURIES.** The common view of childhood injuries as "accidental" suggests they are due to chance and cannot be prevented. In fact, they occur within a complex *ecological system* of individual, family,

This Thai family—like many others—rides unprotected on the only form of transportation it has. In developing countries, heavy road traffic and weak safety measures contribute to an injury death rate before age 15 that is five times higher than in developed nations.

community, and societal influences—and we can do something about them.

Because of their higher activity level and greater impulsivity and risk taking, boys are 1.5 times more likely to be injured than girls (National Safe Kids Campaign, 2005). Children with certain temperamental and personality characteristics—inattentiveness, overactivity, irritability, defiance, and aggression—are also at greater risk (Ordonana, Caspi, & Moffitt, 2008; Schwebel & Gaines, 2007). They are likely to protest when placed in auto seat restraints or refuse to take a companion's hand when crossing the street—even after repeated instruction and discipline.

Poverty, single parenthood, and low parental education are also strongly associated with injury (Schwebel & Brezausek, 2007; World Health Organization, 2008c). Parents experiencing many daily stresses often have little energy to monitor the safety of their children. And their rundown homes and neighborhoods pose further risks (Dal Santo et al., 2004).

Childhood injury rates are high in the United States because of extensive poverty, shortages of high-quality child care (to supervise children in their parents' absence), and a high rate of births to teenagers, who are not ready for parenthood. But U.S. children from advantaged families are also at considerably greater risk for injury than children in Western Europe (World Health Organization, 2008c). This indicates that besides reducing poverty and teenage pregnancy and upgrading the status of child care, additional steps are needed to ensure children's safety.

■ **PREVENTING CHILDHOOD INJURIES.** Childhood injuries have many causes, so a variety of approaches are needed to reduce them. Laws prevent many injuries by requiring car safety seats, child-resistant caps on medicine bottles, flame-

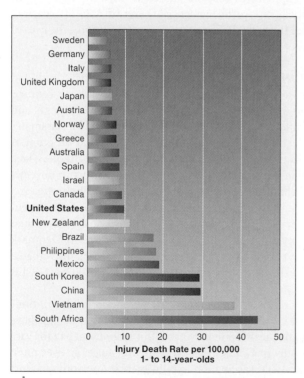

■ **FIGURE 7.3** ■ **International death rates due to unintentional injury among 1- to 14-year-olds.** Compared with other industrialized nations, the United States has a high injury death rate. Injury death rates are many times higher in developing nations, where poverty, rapid population growth, overcrowding in cities, and inadequate safety measures endanger children's lives. (Adapted from World Health Organization, 2008c.)

proof clothing, and fencing around backyard swimming pools (Brenner et al., 2003). Communities can help by modifying their physical environments. Playgrounds, a common site of injury, can be covered with protective surfaces (National Safe Kids Campaign, 2005). Free, easily installed window guards can be given to families in high-rise apartment buildings to prevent falls. And media campaigns can inform parents and children about safety issues.

But even though they know better, many parents and children behave in ways that compromise safety. About 40 percent of U.S. parents fail to place their preschoolers in car safety seats (Howard, 2002; National Safe Kids Campaign, 2005). Furthermore, many parents begin relying on children's knowledge of safety rules, rather than controlling access to hazards, as early as 2 or 3 years of age (Morrongiello, Ondejko, & Littlejohn, 2004). But even older preschoolers spontaneously recall only about half the safety rules their parents teach them. Even with well-learned rules, they need supervision to ensure they comply (Morrongiello, Midgett, & Shields, 2001). Attention must also be paid to family conditions that can prevent childhood injury: relieving crowding in the home, providing social supports to ease parental stress, and teaching parents to use effective discipline—a topic we take up in Chapter 8.

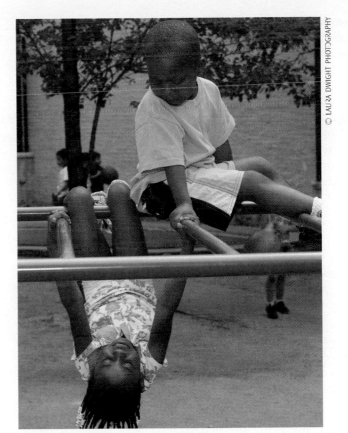

As preschoolers' bodies become more streamlined, their balance improves greatly, enabling children to combine upper- and lower-body skills into more refined actions.

© LAURA DWIGHT PHOTOGRAPHY

ASK YOURSELF

⟩⟩ REVIEW

Using research on malnutrition or on unintentional injuries, show how physical growth and health in early childhood result from a continuous, complex interplay between heredity and environment.

⟩⟩ APPLY

One day, Leslie prepared a new snack to serve at preschool: celery stuffed with ricotta cheese. The first time she served it, few children touched it. How can Leslie encourage her students to accept the snack? What tactics should she avoid?

⟩⟩ REFLECT

Ask a parent or other family member whether, as a preschooler, you were a picky eater, suffered from many infectious diseases, or sustained any serious injuries. In each instance, what factors might have been responsible?

Motor Development

TAKE A MOMENT... Observe several 2- to 6-year-olds at play in a neighborhood park, and you will see that an explosion of new motor skills occurs in early childhood. Preschoolers continue to integrate previously acquired skills into more complex, *dynamic systems.* Then they revise each new skill as their bodies grow larger and stronger, their central nervous systems develop, and their environments present new challenges.

Gross-Motor Development

As children's bodies become more streamlined and less top-heavy, their center of gravity shifts downward, toward the trunk. As a result, balance improves greatly, paving the way for new gross-motor skills. By age 2, preschoolers' gaits become smooth and rhythmic—secure enough that soon they leave the ground, at first by running and later by jumping, hopping, galloping, and skipping.

As children become steadier on their feet, their arms and torsos are freed to experiment with new skills—throwing and catching balls, steering tricycles, and swinging on horizontal bars and rings. Then upper- and lower-body skills combine into more refined actions. Five- and 6-year-olds simultaneously steer and pedal a tricycle and flexibly move their whole body when throwing, catching, hopping, and jumping. By the end of the preschool years, all skills are performed with greater speed and endurance.

Fine-Motor Development

Fine-motor skills, too, take a giant leap forward. As control of the hands and fingers improves, young children put puzzles together, build with small blocks, cut and paste, and improve in self-help skills—dressing and undressing, using a fork adeptly, and (at the end of early childhood) cutting food with a knife and tying shoes. Fine-motor progress is also apparent in drawings and first efforts to write.

■ **DRAWING.** A variety of factors combine with fine-motor control to influence changes in children's artful representations (Golomb, 2004). These include the realization that pictures can serve as symbols and improved planning and spatial understanding. Typically, drawing progresses through the following sequence:

1. *Scribbles.* At first, children's gestures rather than the resulting scribbles contain the intended representation. For example, one 18-month-old made her crayon hop and, as it produced a series of dots, explained, "Rabbit goes hophop" (Winner, 1986).

2. *First representational forms.* Around age 3, children's scribbles start to become pictures. Few 3-year-olds, however, spontaneously draw so others can tell what their picture represents. But when adults draw with children and point out resemblances between drawings and objects, preschoolers' pictures become more comprehensible and detailed (Braswell & Callanan, 2003).

   A major milestone in drawing occurs when children use lines to represent the boundaries of objects, enabling 3- and 4-year-olds to draw their first picture of a person. Fine-motor and cognitive limitations lead the preschooler to reduce the figure to the simplest form that still looks human: a circular shape with lines attached—the universal "tadpole" image shown on the left in Figure 7.4.

3. *More realistic drawings.* Greater realism in drawings develops gradually, as perception, language (ability to describe visual details), memory, and fine-motor capacities improve (Toomela, 2002). Five- and 6-year-olds create more complex drawings, like the one on the right in Figure 7.4,

containing more conventional human and animal figures, with the head and body differentiated. Older preschoolers' drawings still contain perceptual distortions because they have just begun to represent depth—a free depiction of reality makes their artwork look fanciful and inventive.

■ **EARLY PRINTING.** At first, preschoolers do not distinguish writing from drawing. Around age 4, writing shows some distinctive features of print, such as separate forms arranged in a line on the page. But children often include picturelike devices—for example, using a circular shape to write "sun" (Levin & Bus, 2003). Only gradually, between ages 4 and 6, do children realize that writing stands for language.

Preschoolers' first attempts to print often involve their name, generally using a single letter. "How do you make a *D?*" my older son, David, asked at age 3. When I printed a large uppercase *D* for him to copy, he was quite satisfied with his backward, imperfect creation. By age 5, David printed his name clearly enough for others to read but, like many children, continued to reverse some letters until well into second grade. Until children start to read, they do not find it useful to distinguish between mirror-image forms, such as *b* and *d* and *p* and *q* (Bornstein & Arterberry, 1999).

Individual Differences in Motor Skills

Wide individual differences exist in the ages at which children reach motor milestones. A tall, muscular child tends to move more quickly and to acquire certain skills earlier than a short, stocky youngster. And as in other domains, parents and teachers probably provide more encouragement to children with biologically based motor-skill advantages.

Sex differences in motor skills are evident in early childhood. Boys are ahead of girls in skills that emphasize force and power. By age 5, they can jump slightly farther, run slightly

■ **FIGURE 7.4** ■ **Examples of young children's drawings.** The universal tadpolelike shape that children use to draw their first picture of a person is shown on the left. The tadpole soon becomes an anchor for greater details that sprout from the basic shape. By the end of the preschool years, children produce more complex, differentiated pictures like the one on the right, drawn by a 6-year-old child. (*Left:* From H. Gardner, 1980, *Artful Scribbles: The Significance of Children's Drawings,* New York: Basic Books, p. 64. Reprinted by permission of Basic Books, a member of Perseus Books Group. *Right:* From E. Winner, "Where Pelicans Kiss Seals," *Psychology Today, 20*[8], August 1986, p. 35. Reprinted by permission from the collection of Ellen Winner.)

faster, and throw a ball about five feet farther. Girls have an edge in fine-motor skills and in certain gross-motor skills that require a combination of good balance and foot movement, such as hopping and skipping (Fischman, Moore, & Steele, 1992; Haywood & Getchell, 2005). Boys' greater muscle mass and, in the case of throwing, slightly longer forearms contribute to their skill advantages. And girls' greater overall physical maturity may be partly responsible for their better balance and precision of movement.

From an early age, boys and girls are usually encouraged into different physical activities. For example, fathers are more likely to play catch with their sons than with their daughters. Sex differences in motor skills increase with age, but they remain small throughout childhood. This suggests that social pressures for boys, more than girls, to be active and physically skilled exaggerate small, genetically based sex differences (Greendorfer, Lewko, & Rosengren, 1996).

Children master the motor skills of early childhood during everyday play. Aside from throwing (where direct instruction is helpful), preschoolers exposed to gymnastics, tumbling, and other formal lessons do not make faster progress. And when parents and teachers criticize a child's performance, push specific motor skills, or promote a competitive attitude, they risk undermining children's self-confidence and, in turn, their motor progress (Berk, Mann, & Ogan, 2006). Adults involved in young children's motor activities should focus on fun rather than on winning or perfecting the "correct" technique.

ASK YOURSELF

>> **REVIEW**
Describe typical changes in children's drawings during early childhood, along with factors that contribute to those changes.

>> **APPLY**
Mabel and Chad want to do everything they can to support their 3-year-old daughter's motor development. What advice would you give them?

Cognitive Development

One rainy morning, as I observed in our laboratory preschool, Leslie, the children's teacher, joined me at the back of the room for a moment. "Preschoolers' minds are such a blend of logic, fantasy, and faulty reasoning," Leslie reflected. "Every day, I'm startled by the maturity and originality of what they say and do. Yet at other times, their thinking seems limited and inflexible."

Leslie's comments sum up the puzzling contradictions of early childhood cognition. That day, for example, 3-year-old Sammy looked up, startled, after a loud crash of thunder outside. "A magic man turned on the thunder!" he pronounced. Even

when Leslie patiently explained that thunder is caused by lightning, not by a person turning it on or off, Sammy persisted: "Then a magic lady did it."

In other respects, Sammy's thinking was surprisingly advanced. At snack time, he accurately counted, "One, two, three, four!" and then got four cartons of milk, one for each child at his table. But when his snack group included more than four children, Sammy's counting broke down. And after Priti dumped out her raisins, scattering them in front of her on the table, Sammy asked, "How come you got lots, and I only got this little bit?" He didn't realize that he had just as many raisins; his were simply all bunched up in a tiny red box.

To understand Sammy's reasoning, we turn first to Piaget's and Vygotsky's theories and evidence highlighting the strengths and limitations of each. Then we consider additional research on young children's cognition, inspired by the information-processing perspective, and look at the dramatic expansion of language in early childhood.

Piaget's Theory: The Preoperational Stage

As children move from the sensorimotor to the **preoperational stage,** which spans the years 2 to 7, the most obvious change is an extraordinary increase in representational, or symbolic, activity. Recall that infants and toddlers have some ability to represent their world. During early childhood, this capacity blossoms.

Mental Representation

Piaget acknowledged that language is our most flexible means of mental representation. Despite the power of language, however, Piaget did not regard it as a major ingredient in childhood cognitive change. Instead, he believed that sensorimotor activity leads to internal images of experience, which children then label with words (Piaget, 1936/1952). In support of Piaget's view, recall from Chapter 5 that children's first words have a strong sensorimotor basis. In addition, infants and toddlers acquire an impressive range of categories long before they use words to label them (see page 127). But as we will see, other theorists regard Piaget's account of the link between language and thought as incomplete.

Make-Believe Play

Make-believe play is another example of the development of representation in early childhood. Piaget believed that through pretending, young children practice and strengthen newly acquired representational schemes. Drawing on his ideas, several investigators have traced changes in preschoolers' make-believe.

■ **DEVELOPMENT OF MAKE-BELIEVE.** One day, Sammy's 18-month-old brother, Dwayne, visited the classroom. Dwayne

Make-believe play increases in sophistication during the preschool years. Children pretend with less realistic toys, so a toy truck can stand for an electric hair clipper. And children increasingly coordinate make-believe roles.

wandered around, picked up a toy telephone receiver, said, "Hi, Mommy," and then dropped it. Next, he found a cup, pretended to drink, and then toddled off again. Meanwhile, Sammy joined Vance and Lynette in the block area for a space shuttle launch.

"That can be our control tower," Sammy suggested, pointing to a corner by a bookshelf. "Countdown!" he announced, speaking into his "walkie-talkie"—a small wooden block. "Five, six, two, four, one, blastoff!" Lynette made a doll push a pretend button, and the rocket was off!

Comparing Dwayne's pretend play with Sammy's, we see three important changes that reflect the preschool child's growing symbolic mastery:

- *Play detaches from the real-life conditions associated with it.* In early pretending, toddlers use only realistic objects—a toy telephone to talk into, a cup to drink from. Their first pretend acts imitate adults' actions and are not yet flexible. Children younger than age 2, for example, will pretend to drink from a cup but refuse to pretend a cup is a hat (Tomasello, Striano, & Rochat, 1999). They have trouble using an object (cup) that already has an obvious use as a symbol of another object (hat).

  After age 2, children pretend with less realistic toys—a block might stand for a telephone receiver (Striano, Tomasello, & Rochat, 2001). Gradually, they can flexibly imagine objects and events without any support from the real world, as Sammy's imaginary control tower illustrates.

- *Play becomes less self-centered.* At first, make-believe is directed toward the self—for example, Dwayne pretends to feed only himself. Soon, children begin to direct pretend actions toward other objects, as when a child feeds a doll.

Early in the third year, they become detached participants who make a doll feed itself or (in Lynette's case) push a button to launch a rocket (McCune, 1993).

- *Play includes more complex combinations of schemes.* Dwayne can pretend to drink from a cup, but he does not yet combine pouring and drinking. Later, children combine schemes with those of peers in **sociodramatic play,** the make-believe with others that is under way around age 2 and increases rapidly during the next few years (Kavanaugh, 2006). Already, Sammy and his classmates can create and coordinate several roles in an elaborate plot. By the end of early childhood, children have a sophisticated understanding of story lines (Göncü, 1993).

In sociodramatic play, children display awareness that make-believe is a representational activity—an understanding that improves steadily over early childhood (Lillard, 2003; Rakoczy, Tomasello, & Striano, 2004; Sobel, 2006). **TAKE A MOMENT...** Listen closely to a group of preschoolers as they assign roles and negotiate make-believe plans: "You *pretend to be* the astronaut, I'll *act like* I'm operating the control tower!" In communicating about pretend, children think about their own and others' fanciful representations—evidence that they have begun to reason about people's mental activities.

■ **BENEFITS OF MAKE-BELIEVE.** Today, Piaget's view of make-believe as mere practice of representational schemes is regarded as too limited. Play not only reflects but also contributes to children's cognitive and social skills. Compared with social nonpretend activities (such as drawing or putting puzzles together), during sociodramatic play preschoolers' interactions last longer, show more involvement, draw more children into the activity, and are more cooperative (Creasey, Jarvis, & Berk, 1998).

It is not surprising, then, that preschoolers who spend more time at sociodramatic play are seen as more socially competent by their teachers (Connolly & Doyle, 1984). And many studies reveal that make-believe strengthens a wide variety of mental abilities, including sustained attention, memory, logical reasoning, language and literacy skills, imagination, creativity, understanding of emotions, and the ability to reflect on one's own thinking, control one's own behavior, and take another's perspective (Berk, Mann, & Ogan, 2006; Elias & Berk, 2002; Hirsh-Pasek et al., 2009; Ruff & Capozzoli, 2003). We will return to the topic of early childhood play in this and the next chapter.

Symbol–Real-World Relations

To make believe and draw—and to understand other forms of representation, such as photographs, models, and maps—preschoolers must realize that each symbol corresponds to something specific in everyday life. When do children comprehend symbol–real-world relations?

In one study, 2½- and 3-year-olds watched an adult hide a small toy (Little Snoopy) in a scale model of a room and then

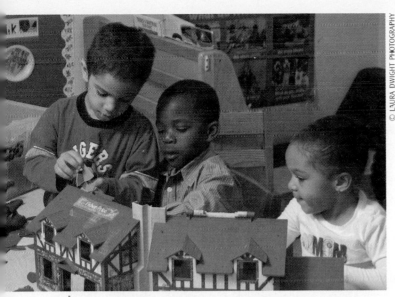

Children who experience a variety of symbols come to understand that one object, such as this play village, can stand for another—a full-sized real village that people live in.

were asked to retrieve it. Next, they had to find a larger toy (Big Snoopy) hidden in the room that the model represented. Not until age 3 could most children use the model as a guide to finding Big Snoopy in the real room (DeLoache, 1987). The 2½-year-olds did not realize that the model could be both *a toy room* and *a symbol of another room*. They had trouble with **dual representation**—viewing a symbolic object as both an object in its own right and a symbol (DeLoache, 2002).

Recall that in make-believe play, 1½- to 2-year-olds cannot use an object with an obvious use (cup) to stand for another object (hat). Likewise, 2-year-olds do not yet grasp that a drawing—an object in its own right—also represents real-world objects.

How do children grasp the dual representation of symbolic objects? When adults point out similarities between models and real-world spaces, 2½-year-olds perform better on the find-Snoopy task (Peralta de Mendoza & Salsa, 2003). Also, insight into one type of symbol–real-world relation helps preschoolers master others. For example, children regard photos and pictures in books as symbols early, around 1½ to 2 years, because a picture's primary purpose is to stand for something; it is not an interesting object in its own right (Preissler & Carey, 2004; Simcock & DeLoache, 2006). And 3-year-olds who can use a model of a room to locate Big Snoopy readily transfer their understanding to a simple map (Marzolf & DeLoache, 1994). In sum, experiences with diverse symbols—photos, picture books, make-believe, and maps—help preschoolers appreciate that one object can stand for another.

Limitations of Preoperational Thought

Aside from gains in representation, Piaget described preschoolers in terms of what they *cannot* understand. As the term *preoper-*

ational suggests, he compared them to older, more competent school-age children. According to Piaget, young children are not capable of *operations*—mental actions that obey logical rules. Rather, their thinking is rigid, limited to one aspect of a situation at a time, and strongly influenced by the way things appear at the moment.

■ **EGOCENTRISM.** For Piaget, the most fundamental deficiency of preoperational thinking is **egocentrism**—failure to distinguish the symbolic viewpoints of others from one's own. He believed that when children first mentally represent the world, they tend to focus on their own viewpoint and simply assume that others perceive, think, and feel the same way they do.

Piaget's most convincing demonstration of egocentrism involves his *three-mountains problem*, described in Figure 7.5. Egocentrism is responsible for preoperational children's **animistic thinking**—the belief that inanimate objects have lifelike qualities, such as thoughts, wishes, feelings, and intentions (Piaget, 1926/1930). Recall Sammy's firm insistence that someone must have turned on the thunder. According to Piaget, because young children egocentrically assign human purposes to physical events, magical thinking is common during the preschool years.

Piaget argued that preschoolers' egocentric bias prevents them from *accommodating*, or reflecting on and revising their faulty reasoning in response to their physical and social worlds. To understand this shortcoming, let's consider some additional tasks that Piaget gave to children.

■ **FIGURE 7.5** ■ **Piaget's three-mountains problem.** Each mountain is distinguished by its color and by its summit. One has a red cross, another a small house, and the third a snow-capped peak. Children at the preoperational stage respond egocentrically. They cannot select a picture that shows the mountains from the doll's perspective. Instead, they simply choose the photo that reflects their own vantage point.

■ **INABILITY TO CONSERVE.**   Piaget's famous conservation tasks reveal a variety of deficiencies of preoperational thinking. **Conservation** refers to the idea that certain physical characteristics of objects remain the same, even when their outward appearance changes. At snack time, Priti and Sammy had identical boxes of raisins, but when Priti spread her raisins out on the table, Sammy was convinced that she had more.

In another conservation task involving liquid, the child is shown two identical tall glasses of water and asked if they contain equal amounts. Once the child agrees, the water in one glass is poured into a short, wide container. Then the child is asked whether or not the amount of water has changed. Preoperational children think the quantity has changed. They explain, "There is less now because the water is way down here" (that is, its level is so low) or, "There is more now because it is all spread out." Figure 7.6 illustrates other conservation tasks that you can try with children.

The inability to conserve highlights several related aspects of preoperational children's thinking. First, their understanding is characterized by **centration.** They focus on one aspect of a situation, neglecting other important features. In conservation of liquid, the child *centers* on the height of the water, failing to realize that changes in width compensate for changes in height. Second, children are easily distracted by the *perceptual appearance* of objects. Third, children treat the initial and final states of the water as unrelated events, ignoring the *dynamic transformation* (pouring of water) between them.

The most important illogical feature of preoperational thought is its **irreversibility,** an inability to mentally go through a series of steps in a problem and then reverse direction, returning to the starting point. *Reversibility* is part of every logical operation. After Priti spills her raisins, Sammy cannot reverse by thinking, "I know that Priti doesn't have more raisins than I do. If we put them back in that little box, her raisins and my raisins would look just the same."

■ **LACK OF HIERARCHICAL CLASSIFICATION.**   Preoperational children have difficulty with **hierarchical classification**— the organization of objects into classes and subclasses on the basis of similarities and differences. Piaget's famous *class inclusion problem,* illustrated in Figure 7.7, demonstrates this limitation. Preoperational children center on the overriding feature, red. They do not think reversibly by moving from the whole class (flowers) to the parts (red and blue) and back again.

Follow-Up Research on Preoperational Thought

Over the past three decades, researchers have challenged Piaget's view of preschoolers as cognitively deficient. Because many Piagetian problems contain unfamiliar elements or too many pieces of information for young children to handle at once, preschoolers' responses do not reflect their true abilities. Piaget also missed many naturally occurring instances of effective reasoning by preschoolers.

■ **EGOCENTRIC, ANIMISTIC, AND MAGICAL THINKING.**   Even 2-year-olds realize that what they see sometimes differs from what another person sees. When asked to help an adult looking for a lost object, 24-month-olds—but not 18-month-olds—handed her a toy resting behind a bucket that was within the child's line of sight but not the adult's (Moll & Tomasello, 2006). And when researchers adapt the three-mountains problem to include familiar objects, 4-year-olds show clear awareness

■ **FIGURE 7.6** ■ **Some Piagetian conservation tasks.** Children at the preoperational stage cannot yet conserve. These tasks are mastered gradually over the concrete operational stage. Children in Western nations typically acquire conservation of number, mass, and liquid sometime between 6 and 7 years and of weight between 8 and 10 years.

Conservation Task	Original Presentation	Transformation
Number	Are there the same number of pennies in each row?	Now are there the same number of pennies in each row, or does one row have more?
Mass	Is there the same amount of clay in each ball?	Now does each piece have the same amount of clay, or does one have more?
Liquid	Is there the same amount of water in each glass?	Now does each glass have the same amount of water, or does one have more?
Weight	Does each of the two balls of clay weigh the same?	Now (without placing them back on the scale to confirm what is correct for the child) do the two pieces of clay weigh the same, or does one weigh more?

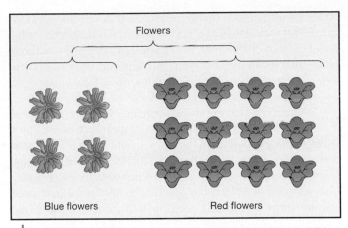

■ **FIGURE 7.7** ■ **A Piagetian class inclusion problem.** Children are shown 16 flowers, 4 of which are blue and 12 of which are red. Asked, "Are there more red flowers or flowers?" the preoperational child responds, "More red flowers," failing to realize that both red and blue flowers are included in the category "flowers."

of others' vantage points (Newcombe & Huttenlocher, 1992). Nonegocentric responses also appear in young children's everyday interactions. In Chapter 5, we saw that toddlers have already begun to infer others' intentions (see page 121).

In his later writings, Piaget (1945/1951) described preschoolers' egocentrism as a tendency rather than an inability. As we revisit the topic of perspective taking, we will see that it develops gradually throughout childhood and adolescence.

Piaget also overestimated preschoolers' animistic beliefs. Even young infants have begun to distinguish animate from inanimate, as indicated by their developing categorical distinctions between living and nonliving things (see page 127). By age 2½, children give psychological explanations ("he likes to"; "she wants to") for people and occasionally for animals, but rarely for objects (Hickling & Wellman, 2001). They do make errors when questioned about vehicles, such as trains and airplanes, which appear to be self-moving and have other lifelike features—for example, headlights that resemble eyes (Gelman & Opfer, 2002). But their responses result from incomplete knowledge, not from a belief that inanimate objects are alive.

The same is true for other fantastic beliefs of the preschool years. Most 3- and 4-year-olds say that magic accounts for unusual beings and events they cannot explain—fairies, goblins, ghosts and, for Sammy, thunder (Rosengren & Hickling, 2000). Furthermore, older 3-year-olds and 4-year-olds think that violations of physical laws (walking through a wall) and mental laws (turning on the TV just by thinking about it) require magic more than violations of social conventions (taking a bath with shoes on) (Browne & Woolley, 2004). These responses indicate that preschoolers' notions of magic are flexible and appropriate.

Between ages 4 and 8, as children gain familiarity with physical events and principles, their magical beliefs decline. They figure out who is really behind Santa Claus and the Tooth Fairy, and they realize that the antics of magicians are due to trickery (Subbotsky, 2004). Religion and culture also play a role. Jewish children are more likely than their Christian agemates to express disbelief in Santa Claus and the Tooth Fairy. Having learned at home that Santa is unreal, they seem to generalize this attitude to other magical figures (Woolley, 1997).

■ **ILLOGICAL THOUGHT.** Many studies show that when preschoolers are given tasks that are simplified and relevant to their everyday lives, they do not display the illogical characteristics that Piaget saw in the preoperational stage. For example, when a conservation-of-number task is scaled down to include only three items instead of six or seven, 3-year-olds perform well (Gelman, 1972). And when preschoolers are asked carefully worded questions about what happens to substances (such as sugar) after they are dissolved in water, they give accurate explanations. Most 3- to 5-year-olds know that the substance is conserved—that it continues to exist, can be tasted, and makes the liquid heavier, even though it is invisible in the water (Au, Sidle, & Rollins, 1993; Rosen & Rozin, 1993).

Preschoolers' ability to reason about transformations is evident on other problems. They can engage in impressive *reasoning by analogy* about physical changes. Presented with the picture-matching problem "Playdough is to cut-up playdough as apple is to . . . ?," even 3-year-olds choose the correct answer (a cut-up apple) from a set of alternatives, several of which (a bitten apple, a cut-up loaf of bread) share physical features with the right choice (Goswami, 1996).

Finally, even without detailed biological knowledge, preschoolers understand that the insides of animals are responsible for cause–effect sequences (such as willing oneself to move) that are impossible for nonliving things (Gelman, 2003; Keil & Lockhart, 1999). Preschoolers seem to use illogical reasoning only when grappling with unfamiliar topics, too much information, or contradictory facts that they cannot reconcile (Ruffman, 1999).

■ **CATEGORIZATION.** Although preschoolers have difficulty with Piagetian class inclusion tasks, they organize their everyday knowledge into nested categories at an early age. By the second half of the first year, children have formed a variety of global categories—for example, furniture, animals, vehicles, and plants (Mandler, 2004). The objects go together because of their common function or behavior, challenging Piaget's assumption that preschoolers' thinking is wholly governed by appearances. Indeed, 2- to 5-year-olds readily draw inferences about nonobservable characteristics shared by category members (Gopnik & Nazzi, 2003). For example, after being told that a bird has warm blood and that a stegosaurus (dinosaur) has cold blood, preschoolers infer that a pterodactyl (labeled a dinosaur) has cold blood, even though it closely resembles a bird.

During the second and third years, and perhaps earlier, children's global categories differentiate. They form many *basic-level categories*—ones at an intermediate level of generality,

© LAURA DWIGHT/PHOTOEDIT

Preschoolers devise many categories based on nonobservable characteristics that members share. This 4-year-old knows that despite wide variations in size and appearance, all dinosaurs share common inner features, such as cold blood.

such as "chairs," "tables," and "beds." By the third year, children easily move back and forth between basic-level categories and *general categories,* such as "furniture." And they break down basic-level categories into *subcategories,* such as "rocking chairs" and "desk chairs," "bluebirds" and "cardinals" (Mervis, Pani, & Pani, 2003).

Preschoolers' rapidly expanding vocabularies and general knowledge support their impressive skill at categorizing (Gelman & Koenig, 2003). Also, during picture-book reading, parents often label and explain categories to children ("Penguins live at the South Pole, swim, catch fish, and have thick layers of fat and feathers that help them stay warm") (Gelman et al., 1998).

In sum, preschoolers' category systems are not yet very complex. But they already have capacity to classify hierarchically and on the basis of nonobvious properties. And preschoolers use logical, causal reasoning to identify the interrelated features that form the basis of a category and to classify new members.

■ **APPEARANCE VERSUS REALITY.** What happens when preschoolers encounter objects that have two identities—a real one and an apparent one? In a series of studies, children were presented with objects that were disguised in various ways and asked what each "looks like" and what each "is really and truly." Preschoolers had difficulty. For example, when asked whether a candle that looks like a crayon "is really and truly" a crayon, they often responded, "Yes!" Not until age 6 or 7 did children do well on these tasks (Flavell, Green, & Flavell, 1987).

Younger children's poor performance, however, is not due to a general difficulty in distinguishing appearance from reality, as Piaget suggested. Rather, they have trouble with the *language* of these tasks (Deák, Ray, & Brenneman, 2003). When permitted to solve appearance–reality problems nonverbally, by choosing from an array of objects the one that "really" has a particular identity, most 3-year-olds perform well (Sapp, Lee, & Muir, 2000).

Note how the appearance–reality distinction involves an attainment discussed earlier: *dual representation*—the realization that an object can be one thing (a candle) while symbolizing another (a crayon). At first, however, children's understanding is fragile. Performing well on verbal appearance–reality tasks signifies a more secure understanding and is related to further progress in representational ability (Bialystok & Senman, 2004).

Evaluation of the Preoperational Stage

*TAKE A MOMENT...*Compare the cognitive attainments of early childhood, summarized in Table 7.1, with Piaget's description of the preoperational child on pages 175–176. The evidence as a whole indicates that Piaget was partly right and partly wrong about young children's cognitive capacities.

That preschoolers have some logical understanding suggests that they attain logical operations gradually, which poses yet another challenge to Piaget's stage concept of abrupt change toward logical reasoning around age 6 or 7. Does a preoperational stage really exist? Some no longer think so. Recall from Chapter 5 that according to the information-processing perspective, children work out their understanding of each type of task separately, and their thought processes are basically the same at all ages—just present to a greater or lesser extent.

Other experts think the stage concept is valid but must be modified. For example, some *neo-Piagetian theorists* combine Piaget's stage approach with the information-processing emphasis on task-specific change (Case, 1998; Halford & Andrews, 2006). They believe that Piaget's strict stage definition must be transformed into a less tightly knit concept, one in which a related set of competencies develops over an extended time period, depending on brain development and specific experiences. These investigators point to findings indicating that as long as the complexity of tasks and children's exposure to them are controlled, children approach those tasks in similar ways (Andrews & Halford, 2002; Case & Okamoto, 1996). For example, in drawing pictures, preschoolers depict objects separately, ignoring their spatial arrangement. In understanding stories, they grasp a single story line but have trouble with a main plot plus one or more subplots.

■ **TABLE 7.1** ■ *Some Cognitive Attainments of Early Childhood*

APPROXIMATE AGE	COGNITIVE ATTAINMENTS
2–4 years	Shows a dramatic increase in representational activity, as reflected in the development of language, make-believe play, drawing, understanding of dual representation, and categorization
	Takes the perspective of others in simplified, familiar situations and in everyday, face-to-face communication
	Distinguishes animate beings from inanimate objects; denies that magic can alter everyday experiences
	Grasps conservation, notices transformations, reverses thinking, and understands many cause-and-effect relationships in familiar contexts
	Categorizes objects on the basis of common function and behavior and devises ideas about underlying characteristics that category members share
	Sorts familiar objects into hierarchically organized categories
	Distinguishes appearance from reality
4–7 years	Becomes increasingly aware that make-believe (and other thought processes) are representational activities
	Replaces magical beliefs about fairies, goblins, and events that violate expectations with plausible explanations
	Solves verbal appearance-reality problems, signifying a more secure understanding

This flexible stage notion recognizes the unique qualities of early childhood thinking. At the same time, it provides a better account of why, as Leslie put it, "Preschoolers' minds are such a blend of logic, fantasy, and faulty reasoning."

Vygotsky's Sociocultural Theory

During early childhood, rapid growth of language broadens preschoolers' participation in social dialogues with more knowledgeable individuals, who encourage them to master culturally important tasks. According to Vygotsky's sociocultural theory, children start to communicate with themselves in much the same way they converse with others. This greatly enhances their thinking and ability to control their own behavior. Let's see how this happens.

Private Speech

TAKE A MOMENT... Watch preschoolers as they play and explore the environment, and you will see that they frequently talk out loud to themselves. For example, as Sammy worked a puzzle, he said, "Where's the red piece? Now, a blue one. No, it doesn't fit. Try it here."

Piaget (1923/1926) called these utterances *egocentric speech*, reflecting his belief that young children have difficulty taking the perspectives of others. Their talk, he said, is often "talk for self" in which they express thoughts in whatever form they happen to occur, regardless of whether a listener can understand. Piaget believed that cognitive development and certain social experiences eventually bring an end to egocentric speech. Specifically, through disagreements with peers, children see that others hold viewpoints different from their own.

Vygotsky (1934/1987) disagreed with Piaget's conclusions. Because language helps children think about their mental activities and behavior and select courses of action, Vygotsky saw it as the foundation for all higher cognitive processes, including controlled attention, deliberate memorization and recall, categorization, planning, problem solving, and self-reflection. In Vygotsky's view, children speak to themselves for self-guidance. As they get older and find tasks easier, their self-directed speech is internalized as silent, *inner speech*—the internal verbal dialogues we carry on while thinking and acting in everyday situations.

Over the past three decades, almost all studies have supported Vygotsky's perspective (Berk & Harris, 2003; Winsler, 2009). As a result, children's self-directed speech is now called **private speech** instead of egocentric speech. Research shows that children use more of it when tasks are appropriately challenging (neither too easy nor too hard), after they make errors, or when they are confused about how to proceed. With age, as Vygotsky predicted, private speech goes underground, changing into whispers and silent lip movements. Furthermore, children who freely use private speech during a challenging activity are more attentive and involved and show better task performance than their less talkative agemates (Al-Namlah, Fernyhough, & Meins, 2006; Berk & Spuhl, 1995; Fernyhough & Fradley, 2005; Winsler, Naglieri, & Manfra, 2006).

Social Origins of Early Childhood Cognition

Where does private speech come from? Recall from Chapter 5 that Vygotsky believed that children's learning takes place within the *zone of proximal development*—a range of tasks too difficult for the child to do alone but possible with the help of adults and more skilled peers. Consider the joint activity of Sammy and his mother, who helps him put together a difficult puzzle:

Sammy: I can't get this one in. [*Tries to insert a piece in the wrong place.*]

Mother: Which piece might go down here? [*Points to the bottom of the puzzle.*]

Sammy: His shoes. [*Finds a piece that resembles the clown's shoes, tries it, and it fits; then attempts another piece and looks at his mother.*]

Mother: Try turning it just a little. [*Gestures to show him.*]

Sammy: There! [*Puts in several more pieces while his mother watches.*]

Sammy's mother keeps the puzzle at a manageable level of difficulty. To do so, she engages in **scaffolding**—adjusting the support offered during a teaching session to fit the child's current level of performance. When the child has little notion of how to proceed, the adult uses direct instruction, breaking the task into manageable units and suggesting strategies. As the child's competence increases, effective scaffolders gradually and sensitively withdraw support, turning over responsibility to the child. Then children take the language of these dialogues, make it part of their private speech, and use this speech to organize their independent efforts.

Consistent with Vygotsky's ideas, in several studies, children whose parents were effective scaffolders used more private speech, were more successful when attempting difficult tasks on their own, and were advanced in overall cognitive development (Berk & Spuhl, 1995; Conner & Cross, 2003; Mulvaney et al., 2006). Adult cognitive support—teaching in small steps and offering strategies—predicts gains in children's thinking. And adult emotional support—offering encouragement and allowing the child to take over the task—predicts children's effort (Neitzel & Stright, 2003).

Other research shows that although children benefit from working on tasks with same-age peers, their planning and problem solving improve more when their partner is either

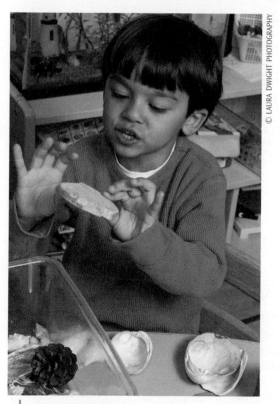

© LAURA DWIGHT PHOTOGRAPHY

This 4-year-old talks to himself as he explores a collection of shells, pine cones, and other natural objects. Research supports Vygotsky's theory that children use private speech to guide their own thinking and behavior.

an "expert" peer (especially capable at the task) or an adult. And peer disagreement (emphasized by Piaget) seems less important in fostering cognitive development than the extent to which children resolve differences of opinion and cooperate (Kobayashi, 1994; Tudge, 1992).

Vygotsky's View of Make-Believe Play

Vygotsky (1933/1978) saw make-believe play as the ideal social context for fostering cognitive development in early childhood. As children create imaginary situations, they learn to follow internal ideas and social rules rather than their immediate impulses. For example, a child pretending to go to sleep follows the rules of bedtime behavior. A child imagining himself as a father conforms to the rules of parental behavior. According to Vygotsky, make-believe play is a unique, broadly influential zone of proximal development in which children try out a wide variety of challenging activities and acquire many new competencies.

Turn back to page 174 to review findings that make-believe play enhances cognitive and social skills. Pretending is also rich in private speech—a finding that supports its role in helping children bring action under the control of thought (Krafft & Berk, 1998). And preschoolers who spend more time engaged in sociodramatic play are better at taking personal responsibility for following classroom rules and at regulating emotion (Berk, Mann, & Ogan, 2006; Lemche et al., 2003). These findings support the role of make-believe in children's increasing self-control.

Evaluation of Vygotsky's Theory

In granting social experience a fundamental role in cognitive development, Vygotsky's theory underscores the vital role of teaching and the wide cultural variation in children's cognitive skills. Nevertheless, it has not gone unchallenged. Verbal communication may not be the only means through which children's thinking develops—or even, in some cultures, the most important means. When Western parents scaffold, their verbal communication resembles the teaching that takes place in school, where their children will spend years preparing for adult life. In cultures that place less emphasis on schooling and literacy, parents often expect children to acquire new skills through keen observation and participation in community activities (see the Cultural Influences box on page 182).

To account for children's diverse ways of learning through involvement with others, Barbara Rogoff (1998, 2003) suggests the term **guided participation,** a broader concept than scaffolding. It refers to shared endeavors between more expert and less expert participants, without specifying the precise features of communication. Consequently, it allows for variations across situations and cultures.

According to Vygotsky, make-believe play is a zone of proximal development that promotes many new competencies. In this preschool classroom, 4- and 5-year-olds form a pretend music ensemble. Following their conductor's signals, the young musicians learn to collaborate and stay on beat.

Finally, Vygotsky's theory says little about how basic motor, perceptual, attention, memory, and problem-solving skills, discussed in Chapters 4 and 5, contribute to socially transmitted higher cognitive processes. For example, his theory does not address how these elementary capacities spark changes in children's social experiences, from which more advanced cognition springs (Miller, 2001; Moll, 1994). Piaget paid far more attention than Vygotsky to the development of basic cognitive processes. It is intriguing to speculate about the broader theory that might exist today if Piaget and Vygotsky—the two twentieth-century giants of cognitive development—had had a chance to meet and weave together their extraordinary accomplishments.

ASK YOURSELF

>> **REVIEW**
Describe characteristics of social interaction that support children's cognitive development. How does such interaction create a zone of proximal development?

>> **APPLY**
Tanisha sees her 5-year-old son talking aloud to himself as he plays. She wonders whether she should discourage this behavior. Using Vygotsky's theory and related research, how would you advise Tanisha?

>> **REFLECT**
When do you use private speech? Does it serve a self-guiding function for you, as it does for children? Explain.

■ CULTURAL INFLUENCES ■

Children in Village and Tribal Cultures Observe and Participate in Adult Work

In Western societies, schools equip children with the skills they need to become competent workers. In early childhood, middle-SES parents focus on preparing their children for school success by engaging in child-focused conversations and play that enhance language, literacy, and other academic knowledge. In village and tribal cultures, children receive little or no schooling, spend their days in contact with adult work, and assume mature responsibilities in early childhood (Rogoff et al., 2003). Consequently, parents have little need to rely on conversation and play to teach children.

A study comparing 2- and 3-year-olds' daily lives in four cultures—two U.S. middle-SES suburbs, the Efe hunters and gatherers of the Republic of Congo, and a Mayan agricultural town in Guatemala—documented these differences (Morelli, Rogoff, & Angelillo, 2003). In the U.S. communities, young children had little access to adult work and spent much time conversing and playing with adults. In contrast, the Efe and Mayan children spent their days close to—and frequently observing—adult work, which often took place in or near the Efe campsite or the Mayan family home.

An ethnography of a remote Mayan village in Yucatán, Mexico, shows that when young children are legitimate onlookers and participants in a daily life structured around adult work, their competencies differ from those of Western preschoolers (Gaskins, 1999; Gaskins, Haight, & Lancy, 2007). Yucatec Mayan adults are subsistence farmers. Men tend cornfields, aided by sons age 8 and older. Women prepare meals, wash clothes, and care for the livestock and garden, assisted by daughters and by sons too young to work in the fields. Children join in these activities from the second year on. When not participating, they are expected to be self-sufficient. Young children make many nonwork decisions for themselves—how much to sleep and eat, what to wear, and even when to start school. As a result, Yucatec Mayan preschoolers are highly competent at self-care. In contrast, their make-believe play is limited; when it occurs, they usually enact adult work. Otherwise, they watch others—for hours each day.

Yucatec Mayan parents rarely converse or play with preschoolers or scaffold their learning. Rather, when children imitate adult tasks, parents conclude that they are ready for more responsibility. Then they assign chores, selecting tasks the child can do with little help so that adult work is not disturbed. If a child cannot do a task, the adult takes over and the child observes, reengaging when able to contribute.

Expected to be autonomous and helpful, Yucatec Mayan children seldom ask others for something interesting to do. From an early age, they can sit quietly for long periods—through a long religious service or a ride to town. And when an adult directs them to do a chore, they respond eagerly to the type of command that Western children frequently resent. By age 5, Yucatec Mayan children spontaneously take responsibility for tasks beyond those assigned.

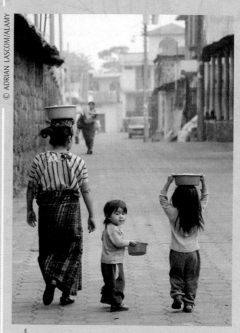

A Mayan 3-year-old imitates her mother in balancing a basin of water on her head, while her younger sibling prepares to attempt the skill. Children in Yucatec Mayan culture join in the work of their community from an early age, spending many hours observing adults.

![tree icon] Information Processing

Recall from Chapter 5 that information processing focuses on *mental strategies* that children use to transform stimuli flowing into their mental systems. During early childhood, advances in representation and in children's ability to guide their own behavior lead to more efficient ways of attending, manipulating information, and solving problems. Preschoolers also become more aware of their own mental life and begin to acquire academically relevant knowledge important for school success.

Attention

Although preschoolers are often easily distracted, sustained attention improves considerably in early childhood. A major reason is a steady gain in children's ability to inhibit impulses and keep their mind on a competing goal. Consider a task in which the child must say "night" to a picture of the sun and "day" to a picture of the moon with stars. Whereas 3- and 4-year-olds make many errors, by age 6 to 7, children find such tasks easy (Kirkham, Cruess, & Diamond, 2003; Zelazo et al., 2003). They can resist the "pull" of their attention toward a dominant stimulus—a skill that, as early as age 3 to 5, predicts reading and math achievement from kindergarten through high school (Blair & Razza, 2007; Duncan et al., 2007).

During early childhood, children also become better at *planning*—thinking out a sequence of acts ahead of time and allocating attention accordingly to reach a goal. As long as tasks are familiar and not too complex, preschoolers can generate and follow a plan. For example, 4-year-olds can search for a lost object in a play area systematically if possible locations are few

(McColgan & McCormack, 2008). But when asked to compare detailed pictures, preschoolers fail to search thoroughly. And on tasks with several steps, they rarely decide what to do first and what to do next in an orderly fashion (Friedman & Scholnick, 1997; Ruff & Rothbart, 1996).

Children learn much from cultural tools that support planning—directions for playing games, patterns for construction, and recipes for cooking—especially when they collaborate with more expert planners. When 4- to 7-year-olds were observed jointly constructing a toy with their mothers, the mothers provided basic information about the usefulness of plans and how to implement specific steps: "Do you want to look at the picture and see what goes where? What piece do you need first?" After working with their mothers, younger children more often referred to the plan when building on their own (Gauvain, 2004; Gauvain, de la Ossa, & Hurtado-Ortiz, 2001). When parents encourage planning in everyday activities, from loading the dishwasher to packing for a vacation, they help children plan more effectively.

Memory

Unlike infants and toddlers, preschoolers have the language skills to describe what they remember, and they can follow directions on memory tasks. As a result, memory becomes easier to study in early childhood.

■ **RECOGNITION AND RECALL. *TAKE A MOMENT...*** Show a young child a set of 10 pictures or toys. Then mix them up with some unfamiliar items, and ask the child to point to the ones in the original set. You will find that preschoolers' *recognition* memory—ability to tell whether a stimulus is the same as or similar to one they have seen before—is remarkably good. In fact, 4- and 5-year-olds perform nearly perfectly. Now keep the items out of view, and ask the child to name the ones she saw. This more demanding task requires *recall*—that the child generate a mental image of an absent stimulus. Young children's recall is much poorer than their recognition. At age 2, they can recall no more than one or two items, at age 4 only about three or four (Perlmutter, 1984).

Better recall in early childhood is strongly associated with language development, which greatly enhances long-lasting representations of past experiences (Simcock & Hayne, 2003). But even preschoolers with good language skills recall poorly because they are not skilled at using **memory strategies,** deliberate mental activities that improve our chances of remembering. Preschoolers do not yet *rehearse,* or repeat items over and over to remember. Nor do they *organize,* grouping together items that are alike (all the animals together, all the vehicles together) so they can easily retrieve the items by thinking of their similar characteristics—even when they are trained to do so (Gathercole, Adams, & Hitch, 1994).

Why do young children seldom use memory strategies? One reason is that strategies tax their limited working memories. *Digit span* tasks, in which children try to repeat an adult-provided string of numbers, assess the size of working memory, which improves slowly, from an average of two digits at age 2½ to five digits at age 7 (Kail, 2003). With such limits, preschoolers have difficulty holding on to pieces of information and applying a strategy at the same time.

■ **MEMORY FOR EVERYDAY EXPERIENCES.** Think about the difference between your recall of listlike information and your memory for everyday experiences. In remembering lists, you recall isolated bits, reproducing them exactly as you originally learned them. In remembering everyday experiences, you recall complex, meaningful events.

Memory for Familiar Events. Like adults, preschoolers remember familiar, repeated events—what you do when you go to preschool or have dinner—in terms of **scripts,** general descriptions of what occurs and when it occurs in a particular situation. Young children's scripts begin as a structure of main acts. For example, when asked to tell what happens at a restaurant, a 3-year-old might say, "You go in, get the food, eat, and then pay." Although first scripts contain only a few acts, they are almost always recalled in correct sequence (Bauer, 2002, 2006). With age, scripts become more elaborate, as in this 5-year-old's account of going to a restaurant: "You go in. You can sit in a booth or at a table. Then you tell the waitress what you want. You eat. If you want dessert, you can have some. Then you pay and go home." (Hudson, Fivush, & Kuebli, 1992).

Scripts help children (and adults) organize and interpret everyday experiences. Once formed, they can be used to predict what will happen in the future. Children rely on scripts in make-believe play and when listening to and telling stories. Scripts also support children's earliest efforts at planning by helping them represent sequences of actions that lead to desired goals (Hudson, Sosa, & Shapiro, 1997).

Memory for One-Time Events. In Chapter 5, we considered a second type of everyday memory—*autobiographical memory,* or representations of personally meaningful, one-time events. As preschoolers' cognitive and conversational skills improve, their descriptions of special events become better organized in time and more detailed (Fivush, 2001).

Adults use two styles to elicit children's autobiographical narratives. In the *elaborative style,* they follow the child's lead, ask varied questions, add information to the child's statements, and volunteer their own recollections and evaluations of events. For example, after a trip to the zoo, the parent might say, "What was the first thing we did?" "Why weren't the parrots in their cages?" "I thought the lion was scary. What did you think?" In contrast, adults who use the *repetitive style* provide little information and keep repeating the same questions, regardless of the child's interest: "Do you remember the zoo? What did we do at the zoo?" Preschoolers who experience the elaborative style recall more information about past events, and they also produce more organized and detailed personal stories when followed up one to two years later (Cleveland & Reese, 2005; Farrant & Reese, 2000).

As children talk with adults about the past, they not only improve their autobiographical memory but also create a

If this father of Shanghai, China, uses an elaborative style to elicit his daughter's past-event narratives, she is likely to construct a richer autobiographical memory, recalling more information and producing more organized and detailed personal stories.

shared history that strengthens close relationships and self-understanding. Parents and preschoolers with secure attachment bonds engage in more elaborate reminiscing (Bost et al., 2006). And children of elaborative-style parents describe themselves in clearer, more consistent ways (Bird & Reese, 2006). When, in past-event conversations, a child discovers that she finds swimming and going to the zoo fun, she can begin to connect these specific experiences into a general understanding of "what I enjoy," yielding a clearer self-image.

The Young Child's Theory of Mind

As representation of the world, memory, and problem solving improve, children reflect on their own thought processes. They begin to construct a *theory of mind,* or coherent set of ideas about mental activities. This understanding is also called **metacognition,** or "thinking about thought" (the prefix *meta-* means "beyond" or "higher"). As adults, we have a complex appreciation of our inner mental worlds, which we use to interpret our own and others' behavior and to improve our performance on various tasks. How early are children aware of their mental lives, and how complete and accurate is their knowledge?

■ **AWARENESS OF MENTAL LIFE.** At the end of the first year, babies view people as intentional beings who can share and influence one another's mental states, a milestone that

opens the door to new forms of communication—joint attention, social referencing, preverbal gestures, and spoken language. These interactive skills, in turn, enhance toddlers' mental understandings (Tomasello & Rakoczy, 2003).

As 2-year-olds' vocabularies expand, their first verbs include such words as *think, remember,* and *pretend* (Wellman, 2002). By age 3, children realize that thinking takes place inside their heads and that a person can think about something without seeing, touching, or talking about it (Flavell, Green, & Flavell, 1995). But 2- to 3-year-olds have only a beginning grasp of the distinction between mental life and behavior. They think that people always behave in ways consistent with their *desires* and do not understand that less obvious, more interpretive mental states, such as *beliefs,* also affect behavior.

From age 4 on, children understand that both *beliefs* and *desires* determine behavior. Dramatic evidence comes from games that test whether preschoolers realize that *false beliefs*—ones that do not represent reality accurately—can guide people's actions. **TAKE A MOMENT...** For example, show a child two small closed boxes—a familiar Band-Aid box and a plain, unmarked box. Then say, "Pick the box you think has the Band-Aids in it." Children usually pick the marked container. Next, open the boxes and show the child that, contrary to her own belief, the marked one is empty and the unmarked one contains the Band-Aids. Finally, introduce the child to a hand puppet and explain, "Pam has a cut, see? Where do you think she'll look for Band-Aids? Why would she look in there? Before you looked inside, did you think that the plain box contained Band-Aids? Why?" (Bartsch & Wellman, 1995). Only a handful of 3-year-olds can explain Pam's—and their own—false beliefs, but many 4-year-olds can.

Among children of diverse cultural and SES backgrounds, false-belief understanding strengthens after age 3½, becoming more secure between ages 4 and 6 (Amsterlaw & Wellman, 2006; Callaghan et al., 2005; Flynn, 2006). During that time, it becomes a powerful tool for understanding oneself and others and a good predictor of social skills (Harwood & Farrar, 2006; Watson et al., 1999).

■ **FACTORS CONTRIBUTING TO PRESCHOOLERS' THEORY OF MIND.** How do children develop a theory of mind at such a young age? Language, cognitive abilities, make-believe play, and social experiences all contribute.

Understanding the mind requires the ability to reflect on thoughts, which language makes possible. Many studies indicate that language ability strongly predicts preschoolers' grasp of false belief (Milligan, Astington, & Dack, 2007). Children who spontaneously use, or who are trained to use, complex sentences with mental-state words are especially likely to pass false-belief tasks (de Villiers & de Villiers, 2000; Hale & Tager-Flusberg, 2003). Among the Quechua of the Peruvian highlands, whose language lacks mental-state terms, children have difficulty with false-belief tasks for years after children in industrialized nations have mastered them (Vinden, 1996). Chinese languages, in contrast, have verb markers that can label the word *believe* as decidedly false. When adults use those markers within false-belief tasks, Chinese preschoolers perform better (Tardif, Wellman, & Cheung, 2004).

The ability to inhibit inappropriate responses, think flexibly, and plan fosters mastery of false belief (Carlson, Moses, & Claxton, 2004; Sabbagh et al., 2006). To do well on false-belief tasks, children must suppress an irrelevant response—the tendency to assume that others share their own knowledge and beliefs.

Social experience also promotes understanding of the mind. In longitudinal research, mothers of securely attached babies were more likely to comment appropriately on their infants' mental states: "Do you *remember* Grandma?" "You really *like* that swing!" These mothers continued to describe their children, when they reached preschool age, in terms of mental characteristics: "She's got a mind of her own!" This maternal "mind-mindedness" was positively associated with later performance on false belief and other theory-of-mind tasks (Meins et al., 1998, 2003; Ruffman et al., 2006).

Also, preschoolers with siblings who are children (but not infants)—especially older siblings or two or more siblings—tend to be more aware of false belief because they are exposed to more family talk about others' perspectives (Jenkins et al., 2003; McAlister & Peterson, 2006, 2007). Similarly, preschool friends who often engage in mental-state talk—as children do during make-believe play—are ahead in false-belief understanding (de Rosnay & Hughes, 2006).

Core knowledge theorists (see Chapter 5, page 122) believe that to profit from the social experiences just described, children must be biologically prepared to develop a theory of mind. They claim that children with *autism*, for whom mastery of false belief is either greatly delayed or absent, are deficient in the brain mechanism that enables humans to detect mental states. See the Biology and Environment box on page 186 to find out more about the biological basis of reasoning about the mind.

■ LIMITATIONS OF PRESCHOOLERS' UNDERSTANDING OF MENTAL LIFE.

Though surprisingly advanced, preschoolers' awareness of mental activities is far from complete. For example, 3- and 4-year-olds are unaware that people continue to think while they wait, look at pictures, listen to stories, or read books—when there are no obvious cues that they are thinking (Flavell, Green, & Flavell, 1995, 2000). And children younger than age 6 pay little attention to the *process* of thinking. When asked about subtle distinctions between mental states, such as *know* and *forget*, they express confusion (Lyon & Flavell, 1994). And they believe that all events must be directly observed to be known. They do not understand that *mental inferences* can be a source of knowledge (Miller, Hardin, & Montgomery, 2003).

These findings suggest that preschoolers view the mind as a passive container of information. Consequently, they greatly underestimate the amount of mental activity that people engage in and are poor at inferring what people know or are thinking about. In contrast, older children view the mind as an active, constructive agent—a change we will consider further in Chapter 9.

Early Childhood Literacy

One week, Leslie's students created a make-believe grocery store. They placed empty food boxes on shelves in the classroom, labeled items with prices, and made paper money for use at the cash register. A sign at the entrance announced the daily specials: "APLS BNS 5¢" ("apples bananas 5¢").

As such play reveals, preschoolers understand a great deal about written language long before they learn to read or write in conventional ways. This is not surprising: Children in industrialized nations live in a world filled with written symbols. Their active efforts to construct literacy knowledge through informal experiences are called **emergent literacy.**

Young preschoolers search for units of written language as they "read" memorized versions of stories and recognize familiar signs, such as "PIZZA." But they do not yet understand the symbolic function of the elements of print (Bialystok & Martin, 2003). Many preschoolers think that a single letter stands for a whole word or that each letter in a person's signature represents a separate name. Children revise these ideas as their cognitive capacities improve, as they encounter writing in many contexts, and as adults help them with written communication.

Eventually, children figure out that letters are parts of words and are linked to sounds in systematic ways, as seen in the invented spellings that are typical between ages 5 and 7. At first, children rely on sounds in the names of letters, as in "ADE

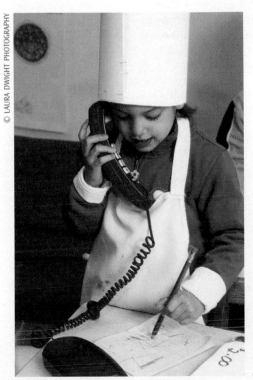

Preschoolers acquire literacy knowledge informally through participating in everyday activities involving written symbols. Here a young chef "jots down" a phone order for a take-out meal.

■ BIOLOGY AND ENVIRONMENT ■

"Mindblindness" and Autism

Michael stood at the water table in Leslie's classroom, repeatedly filling a plastic cup and dumping out its contents—dip–splash, dip–splash—until Leslie came over and redirected his actions. Without looking at Leslie's face, Michael moved to a new repetitive pursuit: pouring water from one cup into another and back again. As other children entered the play space and conversed, Michael hardly noticed.

Michael has *autism* (a term that means "absorbed in the self"), the most severe behavior disorder of childhood. Like other children with autism, by age 3 he displayed deficits in three core areas of functioning. First, he had only limited ability to engage in nonverbal behaviors required for successful social interaction, such as eye contact, facial expressions, gestures, and give-and-take. Second, his language was delayed and stereotyped. He used words to echo what others said and to get things he wanted, not to exchange ideas. Third, he engaged in much less make-believe play than other children (Frith, 2003; Walenski, Tager-Flusberg, & Ullman, 2006). And Michael showed another typical feature of autism: His interests were narrow and overly intense. For example, one day he sat for more than an hour spinning a toy Ferris wheel.

Researchers agree that autism stems from abnormal brain functioning, usually due to genetic or prenatal environmental causes. From the first year on, children with the disorder have larger-than-average brains, perhaps due to massive overgrowth of synapses and lack of synaptic pruning (Courchesne, Carper, & Akshoomoff, 2003). Furthermore, fMRI studies reveal that autism is associated with reduced activity in areas of the cerebral cortex known to mediate emotional and social responsiveness and thinking about mental activities, including mirror neurons, discussed

in Chapter 4 (see page 105) (Mundy, 2003; Théoret et al., 2005).

Growing evidence reveals that children with autism have a deficient theory of mind. Long after they reach the intellectual level of an average 4-year-old, they have great difficulty with false-belief tasks. Most find it hard to attribute mental states to themselves or others (Steele, Joseph, & Tager-Flusberg, 2003).

As early as the second year, children with autism show deficits in capacities believed to contribute to an understanding of mental life. Compared with other children, they less often establish joint attention, engage in social referencing, or imitate an adult's novel behaviors (Mundy & Stella, 2000; Vivanti et al., 2008). Furthermore, they are relatively insensitive to eye gaze as a cue to what a speaker is talking about. Instead, they often assume that another person's language refers to what they themselves are looking at—a possible reason for their frequent nonsensical expressions (Baron-Cohen, Baldwin, & Crowson, 1997).

Do these findings indicate that autism is due to impairment of an innate, core brain function, which leaves the child "mindblind" and therefore deficient in human sociability? Some researchers think so (Baron-Cohen & Belmonte, 2005; Scholl & Leslie, 2000). But others point out that individuals with mental retardation but not autism also do poorly on tasks assessing mental understanding (Yirmiya et al., 1998). This suggests that some kind of general intellectual impairment may be involved.

One conjecture is that children with autism are impaired in *executive processing* (refer to

This child, who has autism, is barely aware of his teacher and classmates. Researchers disagree on whether the "mindblindness" accompanying autism results from a specific deficit in social understanding or a general impairment in executive processing.

the *central executive* in the information-processing model on page 125 in Chapter 5). This leaves them deficient in skills involved in flexible, goal-oriented thinking, including shifting attention to relevant aspects of a situation, inhibiting irrelevant responses, applying strategies to hold information in working memory, and generating plans (Geurts et al., 2004; Joseph & Tager-Flusberg, 2004). An inability to think flexibly would interfere with understanding the social world, since social interaction requires quick integration of information from various sources and evaluation of alternative possibilities.

It is not clear which of these hypotheses is correct. Perhaps several biologically based deficits underlie the tragic social isolation of children like Michael.

LAFWTS KRMD NTU A LAVATR" ("eighty elephants crammed into a[n] elevator"). Over time, they grasp sound–letter correspondences (McGee & Richgels, 2008).

Literacy development builds on a broad foundation of spoken language and knowledge about the world. Over time, children's language and literacy progress facilitate one another.

Phonological awareness—the ability to reflect on and manipulate the sound structure of spoken language, as indicated by sensitivity to changes in sounds within words, to rhyming, and to incorrect pronunciation—is a strong predictor of emergent literacy knowledge (Dickinson et al., 2003; Paris & Paris, 2006). When combined with sound–letter knowledge, it enables children to isolate speech segments and link them with their written symbols. Vocabulary and grammatical skills are also influential.

The more informal literacy-related experiences young children have, the better their language and emergent literacy development and their later reading skills (Dickinson & McCabe, 2001; Speece et al., 2004). Pointing out letter–sound correspondences and playing language–sound games enhance children's awareness of the sound structure of language and how it is represented in print (Foy & Mann, 2003). *Interactive* reading, in which adults discuss storybook content with preschoolers, promotes many aspects of language and literacy development (Wasik & Bond, 2001).

Preschoolers from low-SES families have fewer home and preschool language and literacy learning opportunities—a major reason that they are behind in reading achievement throughout the school years (Foster et al., 2005; Foster & Miller, 2007). Providing child-care centers and parents with children's books, along with guidance in how to stimulate early literacy learning, greatly enhances low-income preschoolers' emergent literacy skills (High et al., 2000; Neuman, 1999).

Young Children's Mathematical Reasoning

Mathematical reasoning, like literacy, builds on informally acquired knowledge. Between 14 and 16 months, toddlers display a beginning grasp of **ordinality,** or order relationships between quantities—for example, that 3 is more than 2, and 2 is more than 1. Soon they attach verbal labels (*lots, little, big, small*) to amounts and sizes. Sometime in the third year, they begin to count. By the time children turn 3, most can count rows of about five objects, although they do not yet know exactly what the words mean. But 2½- to 3½-year-olds realize that when a number label changes (for example, from *five* to *six*), the number of items should also change (Sarnecka & Gelman, 2004).

By age 3½ to 4, most children have mastered the meaning of numbers up to ten, count correctly, and grasp the vital principle of **cardinality**—that the last number in a counting sequence indicates the quantity of items in a set (Geary, 2006a). Mastery of cardinality increases the efficiency of children's counting.

Around age 4, children use counting to solve arithmetic problems. At first, their strategies are tied to the order of numbers as presented; to add 2 + 4, they count on from 2 (Bryant & Nunes, 2002). But soon they experiment with other strategies and eventually arrive at the most efficient, accurate approach—in this example, beginning with the higher digit. Around this time, children realize that subtraction cancels out addition. Knowing, for example, that 4 + 3 = 7, they can infer without counting that 7 − 3 = 4 (Rasmussen, Ho, & Bisanz, 2003). Grasping basic arithmetic rules facilitates rapid computation, and with enough practice, children recall answers automatically. When adults provide many occasions for counting, comparing quantities, and talking about number concepts, children acquire these understandings sooner (Ginsburg, Lee, & Boyd, 2008).

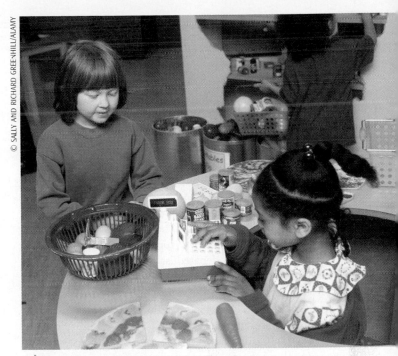

Preschoolers construct basic arithmetic understandings sooner when they have many opportunities to count, compare quantities, and talk about number concepts.

ASK YOURSELF

>> **REVIEW**
Describe a typical 4-year-old's understanding of mental activities, noting both strengths and limitations.

>> **APPLY**
Lena wonders why her son's preschool teacher provides extensive playtime in learning centers instead of formal lessons in literacy and math skills. Explain to Lena why adult-supported play is the best way for preschoolers to develop academically.

>> **REFLECT**
Describe informal experiences while you were growing up that may have contributed to your literacy and math development.

Individual Differences in Mental Development

Five-year-old Hal sat in a testing room while Sarah gave him an intelligence test. Some of Sarah's questions were *verbal*. For example, she showed him a picture of a shovel and said, "Tell me what this is"—an item measuring vocabulary. She tested his memory by asking him to repeat sentences and lists of numbers back to her. To assess Hal's spatial reasoning, Sarah used *nonverbal* tasks: Hal copied designs with special blocks, figured out the pattern in a series of shapes, and indicated what a piece of paper folded and cut would look like when unfolded (Roid, 2003; Wechsler, 2002).

Sarah knew that Hal came from an economically disadvantaged family. When low-SES and certain ethnic minority preschoolers are bombarded with questions by an unfamiliar adult, they sometimes react with anxiety. Also, such children may not define the testing situation in achievement terms, settling for lower performance than their abilities allow. Sarah spent time playing with Hal before she began testing and encouraged him while testing was in progress. Under these conditions, low-SES preschoolers improve in performance (Bracken, 2000).

The questions Sarah asked Hal tap knowledge and skills that not all children have equal opportunity to learn. In Chapter 9, we will take up the hotly debated issue of *cultural bias* in mental testing. For now, keep in mind that intelligence tests do not sample all human abilities, and performance is affected by cultural and situational factors (Sternberg, 2005). Nevertheless, test scores remain important: By age 6 to 7, they are good predictors of later IQ and academic achievement, which are related to vocational success. Let's see how the environments in which preschoolers spend their days—home, preschool, and child care—affect mental test performance.

Home Environment and Mental Development

A special version of the *Home Observation for Measurement of the Environment (HOME)*, covered in Chapter 5, assesses aspects of 3- to 6-year-olds' home lives that support mental development. Preschoolers who develop well intellectually have homes rich in educational toys and books. Their parents are warm and affectionate, stimulate language and academic knowledge, and arrange interesting outings. They also make reasonable demands for socially mature behavior—for example, that the child perform simple chores and behave courteously toward others. And these parents resolve conflicts with reason instead of physical force and punishment (Bradley & Caldwell, 1982; Espy, Molfese, & DiLalla, 2001; Roberts, Burchinal, & Durham, 1999).

As we saw in Chapter 2, these characteristics are less often seen in poverty-stricken families. When low-SES parents manage, despite daily pressures, to obtain high HOME scores, their preschoolers do substantially better on tests of intelligence and emergent literacy skills (Foster et al., 2005; Klebanov et al., 1998). And in a study of low-SES African-American 3- and 4-year-olds, HOME cognitive stimulation and emotional support subscales predicted reading achievement four years later (Zaslow et al., 2006).

Preschool, Kindergarten, and Child Care

Largely because of the rise in maternal employment, over the past several decades the number of young children enrolled in preschool or child care has steadily increased to more than 60 percent in the United States (U.S. Census Bureau, 2009b). The line between preschool and child care is fuzzy. Responding to the needs of employed parents, many U.S. preschools, as well as public school kindergartens, have increased their hours from half to full days (U.S. Department of Education, 2009). At the same time, good child care should provide the same high-quality educational experiences that an effective preschool does.

■ **TYPES OF PRESCHOOL AND KINDERGARTEN.** Preschool and kindergarten programs range along a continuum, from child-centered to teacher-directed. In **child-centered programs,** teachers provide a variety of activities from which children select, and much learning takes place through play. In contrast, in **academic programs,** teachers structure children's learning, teaching letters, numbers, colors, shapes, and other academic skills through formal lessons, often using repetition and drill.

Despite evidence that formal academic training in early childhood undermines motivation and emotional well-being, preschool and kindergarten teachers have felt increased pressure to take this approach. Preschoolers and kindergartners who spend much time passively sitting and completing worksheets display more stress behaviors (such as wiggling and rocking), have less confidence in their abilities, prefer less challenging tasks, and are less advanced in motor, academic, language, and social skills at the end of the school year (Marcon, 1999a; Stipek et al., 1995). Follow-ups reveal lasting effects through elementary school in poorer study habits and achievement (Burts et al., 1992; Hart et al., 1998, 2003). These outcomes are strongest for low-SES children.

A special type of child-centered approach is Montessori education, devised a century ago by Italian physician and child development researcher Maria Montessori, who originally applied her method to poverty-stricken children. Features of Montessori schooling include materials designed to promote exploration and discovery, child-chosen activities, and equal emphasis on academic and social development (Lillard, 2007). In an evaluation of public preschools serving mostly urban minority children in Milwaukee, researchers compared students randomly assigned to either Montessori or other classrooms (Lillard & Else-Quest, 2006). Five-year-olds who had completed two years of Montessori education outperformed controls in literacy and math skills, false-belief understanding, concern with fairness in solving conflicts with peers, and cooperative play with classmates.

■ **EARLY INTERVENTION FOR AT-RISK PRESCHOOLERS.** In the 1960s, as part of the "War on Poverty" in the United States, many intervention programs for low-SES preschoolers were initiated in an effort to address learning problems before formal schooling begins. The most extensive of these federal programs, **Project Head Start,** began in 1965. A typical Head Start center provides children with a year or two of preschool, along with nutritional and health services. Parent involvement is central to the Head Start philosophy. Parents serve on policy

Project Head Start provides preschoolers from poverty-stricken families with preschool education and nutritional and health services. High-quality, early educational intervention has benefits lasting into adulthood.

councils, contribute to program planning, work directly with children in classrooms, attend special programs on parenting and child development, and receive services directed at their own emotional, social, and vocational needs. Currently, more than 18,000 U.S. Head Start centers serve about 908,000 children (Head Start Bureau, 2008).

Several decades of research have established the long-term benefits of preschool intervention. The most extensive of these studies combined data from seven interventions implemented by universities or research foundations. Results showed that poverty-stricken children who attended programs scored higher in IQ and achievement than controls during the first two to three years of elementary school. After that, differences declined (Lazar & Darlington, 1982). But on real-life measures of school adjustment, children and adolescents who had received intervention remained ahead. They were less likely to be placed in special education or retained in grade, and a greater number graduated from high school.

A separate report on one program—the High/Scope Perry Preschool Project—revealed benefits lasting well into adulthood. Two years' exposure to cognitively enriching preschool was associated with increased employment and reduced pregnancy and delinquency rates in adolescence. At age 27, those who had attended preschool were more likely than no-preschool controls to have graduated from high school and college, have higher earnings, be married, and own their own home—and less likely to have been involved with the criminal justice system (see Figure 7.8) (Weikart, 1998). In the most recent follow-up, at age 40, the intervention group sustained its advantage on all

measures of life success, including education, income, family life, and law-abiding behavior (Schweinhart et al., 2005).

Do the effects of these well-designed and well-delivered programs generalize to Head Start and other community-based preschool interventions? Gains are similar, though not as strong because quality of services is more variable (Barnett, 2004; NICHD Early Child Care Research Network, 2001). But interventions of high quality are associated with diverse favorable outcomes, including greater year-end gains in academic skills and—in the long term—higher rates of high school graduation and college enrollment and lower rates of adolescent drug use and delinquency (Garces, Thomas, & Currie, 2002; Love et al., 2006; Mashburn, 2008).

A consistent finding is that gains in IQ and achievement test scores from attending Head Start and other interventions quickly dissolve. These children typically enter inferior public schools in poverty-stricken neighborhoods, an experience that undermines the benefits of preschool education (Brooks-Gunn, 2003; Ramey, Ramey, & Lanzi, 2006). Still, the gains in school adjustment that result from attending a one- or two-year Head Start program are impressive. Program effects on parents may contribute: The more involved parents are in Head Start, the better their child-rearing practices and the more stimulating their home learning environments—factors positively related to preschoolers' task persistence and year-end academic, language, and social skills (Marcon, 1999b; McLoyd, Aikens, & Burton, 2006; Parker et al., 1999).

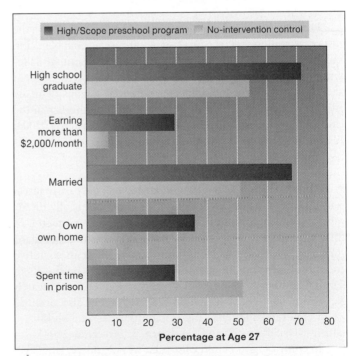

■ **FIGURE 7.8** ■ **Some outcomes of the High/Scope Perry Preschool Project on follow-up at age 27.** Children who received intervention were advantaged over no-intervention controls on all measures of life success when they reached adulthood. (Adapted from Schweinhart et al., 2005.)

Applying What We Know

Signs of Developmentally Appropriate Early Childhood Programs

Program Characteristics	Signs of Quality
Physical setting	Classroom space is divided into richly equipped activity areas, including make-believe play, blocks, science, math, games and puzzles, books, art, and music. Fenced outdoor play space is equipped with swings, climbing equipment, tricycles, and sandbox.
Group size	In preschools and child-care centers, group size is no greater than 18 to 20 children with two teachers.
Caregiver–child ratio	In child-care centers, teacher is responsible for no more than eight to ten children. In family child care, caregiver is responsible for no more than six children.
Daily activities	Children mainly work individually or in small groups, selecting their own activities and learning through experiences relevant to their own lives. Teachers facilitate children's involvement and adjust expectations to children's developing capacities.
Interactions between adults and children	Teachers move among groups and individuals, asking questions, offering suggestions, and adding more complex ideas. Teachers use positive guidance techniques, such as modeling and encouraging expected behavior and redirecting children to more acceptable activities.
Teacher qualifications	Teachers have college-level specialized preparation in early childhood development, early childhood education, or a related field.
Relationships with parents	Parents are encouraged to observe and participate. Teachers talk frequently with parents about children's behavior and development.
Licensing and accreditation	Child-care setting, whether a center or a home, is licensed by the state. In the United States, voluntary accreditation by the National Academy of Early Childhood Programs *(www.naeyc.org/accreditation)* or the National Association for Family Child Care *(www.nafcc.org)* is evidence of a high-quality program.

Source: Copple & Bredekamp, 2009.

Head Start is highly cost-effective when compared with the cost of providing special education, treating criminal behavior, and supporting unemployed adults. Economists estimate a lifetime return to society of more than $250,000 on an investment of $15,000 per preschool child—a potential savings of many billions of dollars if every poverty-stricken preschooler in the United States were enrolled (Heckman & Masterov, 2004; Temple & Reynolds, 2006). Because of funding shortages, however, many eligible children do not receive services.

■ **CHILD CARE.** We have seen that high-quality early intervention can enhance the development of economically disadvantaged children. As noted in Chapter 5, however, much U.S. child care lacks quality. Preschoolers exposed to substandard child care, especially for long hours, score lower in cognitive and social skills and higher in behavior problems (Belsky, 2006; Lamb & Ahnert, 2006; NICHD Early Child Care Research Network, 2003, 2006). Psychological well-being also declines when children experience the instability of several child-care settings (De Schipper, van IJzendoorn, & Tavecchio, 2004).

In contrast, good child care enhances cognitive, language, and social development, especially for low-SES children—effects that persist into the early school years (Lamb & Ahnert, 2006; NICHD Early Child Care Research Network, 2006; Peisner-Feinberg et al., 2001). In an investigation that followed very-low-income children over the preschool years, center-based care was more strongly associated with cognitive gains than were other child-care arrangements, probably because centers are more likely to provide a systematic educational program (Loeb et al., 2004). Applying What We Know above summarizes characteristics of high-quality early childhood programs, based on standards for developmentally appropriate practice devised by the U.S. National Association for the Education of Young Children.

Educational Media

Besides home and preschool, young children spend much time in another learning environment: electronic media, including both television and computers. In the United States and other industrialized nations, nearly all homes have at least one television set, and most have two or more. And about 85 percent of U.S. children live in homes with one or more computers (Roberts, Foehr, & Rideout, 2005; U.S. Census Bureau, 2009b).

■ **EDUCATIONAL TELEVISION.** Sammy's favorite TV program, *Sesame Street,* uses lively visual and sound effects to stress basic literacy and number concepts and puppet and human characters to teach general knowledge, emotional and social understanding, and social skills. Today, *Sesame Street* is broadcast in more than 120 countries, making it the most widely viewed children's program in the world (Sesame Workshop, 2008).

Time devoted to watching children's educational programs is associated with gains in early literacy and math skills and academic progress in elementary school (Ennemoser & Schneider, 2007; Linebarger et al., 2004; Wright et al., 2001). Consistent with these findings, one study reported a link between preschool viewing of *Sesame Street* and other similar educational programs and getting higher grades, reading more books, and placing more value on achievement in high school (Anderson et al., 2001). In recent years, *Sesame Street* has modified its rapid-paced format in favor of more leisurely episodes with a clear story line. Watching children's programs with slow-paced action and easy-to-follow narratives, such as *Barney and Friends,* leads to more elaborate make-believe play than viewing programs that present quick, disconnected bits of information (Singer & Singer, 2005).

Despite the spread of computers, television remains the dominant form of youth media, with children first becoming viewers in early infancy. About 40 percent of U.S. 3-month-olds regularly watch either TV or videos, a figure that rises to 90 percent by age 2 (Zimmerman, Christakis, & Meltzoff, 2007). The average U.S. 2- to 6-year-old watches TV programs and videos from 1½ to 2 hours a day. In middle childhood, viewing time increases to an average of 3½ hours a day, then declines slightly in adolescence (Rideout & Hamel, 2006; Scharrer & Comstock, 2003).

Low-SES children are more frequent viewers, perhaps because few alternative forms of entertainment are available in their neighborhoods or affordable for their parents. Also, parents with limited education are more likely to engage in practices that heighten TV viewing, including eating family meals in front of the set and failing to limit children's TV access (Hesketh et al., 2007). About one-third of U.S. preschoolers and two-thirds of school-age children and adolescents have a TV set in their bedroom; these children spend from 40 to 90 more minutes per day watching than agemates without one (Rideout & Hamel, 2006). And if parents watch a lot of TV, their children do, too.

Does extensive TV viewing take children away from worthwhile activities? The more preschool and school-age children watch prime-time shows and cartoons, the less time they spend reading and interacting with others and the poorer their academic skills (Ennemoser & Schneider, 2007; Wright et al., 2001). Whereas educational programs can be beneficial, watching entertainment TV—especially heavy viewing—detracts from children's school success and social experiences.

■ **LEARNING WITH COMPUTERS.** Because computers can have rich educational benefits, many early childhood classrooms include computer learning centers. Word-processing programs can support emergent literacy, enabling preschool and young school-age children to experiment with letters and words without having to struggle with handwriting. As a result, their written products tend to be longer and of higher quality (Clements & Sarama, 2003).

Simplified computer languages that children can use to make designs or build structures introduce them to programming skills. As long as adults support children's efforts, computer programming promotes improved problem solving and metacognition because children must plan and reflect on their thinking to get their programs to work. Furthermore, while programming, children are especially likely to help one another and to persist in the face of challenge (Nastasi & Clements, 1994; Resnick & Silverman, 2005).

As with television, children spend much time using computers for entertainment purposes, especially game playing. Both media are rife with gender stereotypes and violence. We will consider their impact on emotional and social development in the next chapter.

ASK YOURSELF

>> **REVIEW**
What findings indicate that child-centered rather than academic preschools and kindergartens are better suited to fostering academic development?

>> **APPLY**
Your senator has heard that IQ gains resulting from Head Start do not last, so he plans to vote against additional funding. Write a letter explaining why he should support Head Start.

>> **REFLECT**
How much and what kinds of TV viewing and computer use did you engage in as a child? How do you think your home media environment influenced your development?

Language Development

Language is intimately related to virtually all the cognitive changes discussed in this chapter. Between ages 2 and 6, children make momentous advances.

Vocabulary

At age 2, Sammy had a spoken vocabulary of 200 words. By age 6, he will have acquired around 10,000 words (Bloom, 1998). To accomplish this feat, Sammy will learn about five new words each day. How do children build their vocabularies so quickly? Research shows that they can connect new words with their underlying concepts after only a brief encounter, a process called **fast-mapping.** Preschoolers can even fast-map two or more new words encountered in the same situation (Wilkinson, Ross, & Diamond, 2003).

■ **TYPES OF WORDS.** Children in many Western and non-Western language communities fast-map labels for objects especially rapidly because these refer to concepts that are easy to perceive. Soon children add verbs (*go, run, broke*), which require understandings of relationships between objects and actions. Children learning Chinese, Japanese, and Korean—languages in which nouns are often omitted from adult sentences, while verbs are stressed—acquire verbs especially quickly (Kim, McGregor, & Thompson, 2000; Tardif, 2006). Gradually, preschoolers add modifiers (*red, round, sad*). Among those that are related in meaning, general distinctions (which are easier) appear before specific ones. Thus, children first acquire *big–small*, then *tall–short*, *high–low*, and *wide–narrow* (Stevenson & Pollitt, 1987).

To fill in for words they have not yet learned, children as young as age 3 coin new words using ones they already know—for example, "plant-man," for a gardener, "crayoner" for a child using crayons. Preschoolers also extend language meanings through metaphor—like the 3-year-old who described a stomachache as a "fire engine in my tummy" (Winner, 1988). Young preschoolers' metaphors involve concrete sensory comparisons: "Clouds are pillows," "Leaves are dancers." Once vocabulary and general knowledge expand, children also appreciate nonsensory comparisons: "Friends are like magnets," "Time flies by" (Keil, 1986; Özçaliskan, 2005).

■ **STRATEGIES FOR WORD LEARNING.** Preschoolers figure out the meanings of new words by contrasting them with words they already know. But exactly how they discover which concept each word picks out is not yet fully understood. One speculation is that early in vocabulary growth, children adopt a *mutual exclusivity bias;* they assume that words refer to entirely separate (nonoverlapping) categories (Markman, 1992). Consistent with this idea, when 2-year-olds hear the labels for two distinct novel objects (for example, *clip* and *horn*), they assign each word correctly, to the whole object and not just a part of it (Waxman & Senghas, 1992).

Indeed, children's first several hundred nouns refer mostly to objects well-organized by shape. And learning of nouns based on the perceptual property of shape heightens young children's attention to the distinctive shapes of other objects (Smith et al., 2002; Yoshida & Smith, 2003). This *shape bias* helps preschoolers master additional names of objects, and vocabulary accelerates.

But mutual exclusivity and object shape cannot account for preschoolers' remarkably flexible responses when objects have more than one name. In these instances, children often call on other components of language. According to one proposal, they figure out many word meanings by observing how words are used in the structure of sentences (Gleitman et al., 2005; Naigles & Swenson, 2007). Consider an adult who says, "This is a *citron* one," while showing the child a yellow car. Two- and 3-year-olds conclude that a new word used as an adjective for a familiar object (car) refers to a property of that object (Hall & Graham, 1999; Imai & Haryu, 2004).

Young children also take advantage of the rich social information that adults frequently provide when they introduce new words. For example, they often draw on their expanding ability to infer others' intentions, desires, and perspectives (Akhtar & Tomasello, 2000). In one study, an adult performed an action on an object and then used a new label while looking back and forth between the child and the object, as if inviting the child to play. Two-year-olds concluded that the label referred to the

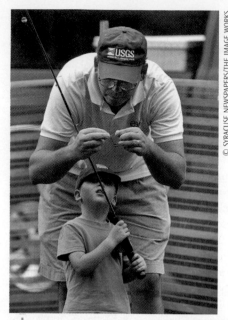

Young children rely on any useful information available to add to their vocabularies. As his father prepares a hook, this 3-year-old attends to a variety of perceptual, social, and linguistic cues to grasp the meanings of unfamiliar fishing words, such as bait, line, bobber, and sinker.

action, not the object (Tomasello & Akhtar, 1995). By age 3, children can even use a speaker's recently expressed desire (which of two novel objects the adult said she liked) to figure out a word's meaning ("I really want to play with the *riff*") (Saylor & Troseth, 2006).

According to a recent theory of early vocabulary development, children draw on a *coalition* of cues—perceptual, social, and linguistic—which shift in importance with age (Golinkoff & Hirsh-Pasek, 2006). Infants rely solely on perceptual features. Toddlers and young preschoolers, while still sensitive to perceptual features (such as object shape), increasingly attend to social cues—the speaker's direction of gaze, gestures, and expressions of desire and intention (Hollich, Hirsh-Pasek, & Golinkoff, 2000; Pruden et al., 2006). And as language develops further, linguistic cues—sentence structure and intonation (stress, pitch, and loudness)—play larger roles.

Preschoolers are most successful at figuring out new word meanings when several kinds of information are available (Saylor, Baldwin, & Sabbagh, 2005). Researchers have just begun to study the multiple cues that children use for different kinds of words and how their combined strategies change with development.

Grammar

Between ages 2 and 3, English-speaking children use simple sentences that follow a subject–verb–object word order. Children learning other languages adopt the word orders of the adult speech to which they are exposed.

■ **BASIC RULES.** Studies of children acquiring diverse languages reveal that their first use of grammatical rules is piecemeal—limited to just a few verbs. As children listen for familiar verbs in adults' speech, they expand their own utterances containing those verbs, relying on adult speech as their model (Gathercole, Sebastián, & Soto, 1999; Lieven, Pine, & Baldwin, 1997). Sammy, for example, added the preposition *with* to the verb *open* ("You open with scissors") because he often heard his parents say, "open with." But he failed to add *with* to the verb *hit* ("He hit me stick").

To test preschoolers' ability to generate novel sentences that conform to basic English grammar, researchers had them use a new verb in the subject–verb–object form after hearing it in a different construction, such as passive: "Ernie is getting *gorped* by the dog." The percentage of children who, when asked what the dog was doing, could respond, "He's *gorping* Ernie," rose steadily with age. But not until 3½ to 4 could the majority of children apply the subject–verb–object structure broadly, to newly acquired verbs (Tomasello, 2003, 2006).

As soon as children form three-word sentences, they make small additions and changes to words that enable us to express meanings flexibly and efficiently. For example, they add *-s* for plural *(cats),* use prepositions *(in* and *on),* and form various tenses of the verb *to be (is, are, were, has been, will).* All English-speaking children master these grammatical markers in a regular sequence, starting with those that involve the simplest meanings and structures (Brown, 1973; de Villiers & de Villiers, 1973).

Once children acquire these markers, they sometimes overextend the rules to words that are exceptions—a type of error called **overregularization.** "My toy car *breaked*" and "We each have two *feets*" are expressions that appear between ages 2 and 3 (Maratsos, 2000; Marcus, 1995).

■ **COMPLEX STRUCTURES.** Gradually, preschoolers master more complex grammatical structures, although they do make mistakes. In first creating questions, 2- to 3-year-olds use many formulas: "Where's *X?*" "Can I *X?*" (Dabrowska, 2000; Tomasello, 1992, 2003). Question asking remains variable for the next couple of years. An analysis of one child's questions revealed that he inverted the subject and verb when asking certain questions but not others ("What she will do?" "Why he can go?") The correct expressions were the ones he heard most often in his mother's speech (Rowland & Pine, 2000). And sometimes children produce errors in subject–verb agreement ("Where does the dogs play?") and in subject case ("Where can me sit?") (Rowland, 2007).

Similarly, children have trouble with some passive sentences. When told, "The car was pushed by the truck," young preschoolers often make a toy car push a truck. By age 5, they understand such expressions, but full mastery of the passive form is not complete until the end of middle childhood (Horgan, 1978; Lempert, 1990).

Nevertheless, 4- and 5-year-olds form embedded sentences ("I think *he will come*"), tag questions ("Dad's going to be home soon, *isn't he?*"), and indirect objects ("He showed *his friend* the

present"). As the preschool years draw to a close, children use most of the grammatical constructions of their language competently (Tager-Flusberg & Zukowski, 2009).

Conversation

Besides acquiring vocabulary and grammar, children must learn to engage in effective and appropriate communication. This practical, social side of language is called **pragmatics,** and preschoolers make considerable headway in mastering it.

As early as age 2, children are skilled conversationalists. In face-to-face interaction, they take turns and respond appropriately to their partners' remarks (Pan & Snow, 1999). With age, the number of turns over which children can sustain interaction and their ability to maintain a topic over time increase. By age 4, children adjust their speech to fit the age, sex, and social status of their listeners. For example, in acting out roles with hand puppets, they use more commands when playing socially dominant and male roles (teacher, doctor, father) but speak more politely and use more indirect requests when playing less dominant and female roles (student, patient, mother) (Anderson, 2000).

Preschoolers' conversational skills occasionally do break down—for example, when talking on the phone. Here is an excerpt from one 4-year-old's phone conversation with his grandfather:

Grandfather:	How old will you be?
John:	Dis many. *[Holding up four fingers.]*
Grandfather:	Huh?
John:	Dis many. *[Again holding up four fingers.]* (Warren & Tate, 1992, pp. 259–260)

Young children's conversations appear less mature in highly demanding situations in which they cannot see their

Preschool children are skilled conversationalists. In face-to-face interaction, they take turns and respond appropriately to their partners' remarks.

listeners' reactions or rely on typical conversational aids, such as gestures and objects to talk about. But when asked to tell a listener how to solve a simple puzzle, 3- to 6-year-olds give more specific directions over the phone than in person, indicating that they realize the need for more verbal description on the phone (Cameron & Lee, 1997). Between ages 4 and 8, both conversing and giving directions over the phone improve greatly. Telephone talk provides yet another example of how preschoolers' competencies depend on the demands of the situation.

Supporting Language Development in Early Childhood

How can adults foster preschoolers' language development? As in toddlerhood, interaction with more skilled speakers is vital. Conversational give-and-take with adults, either at home or in preschool, is consistently related to language progress (Hart & Risley, 1995; NICHD Early Child Care Research Network, 2000b).

Sensitive, caring adults use additional techniques that promote early language skills. When children use words incorrectly or communicate unclearly, they give helpful, explicit feedback, such as, "I can't tell which ball you want. Do you mean the large red one?" But they do not overcorrect, especially when children make grammatical mistakes. Criticism discourages children from freely using language in ways that lead to new skills.

Instead, adults often provide indirect feedback about grammar by using two strategies, often in combination: **recasts**—restructuring inaccurate speech into correct form, and **expansions**—elaborating on children's speech, increasing its complexity (Bohannon & Stanowicz, 1988; Chouinard & Clark, 2003). For example, if a child says, "I gotted new red shoes," the parent might respond, "Yes, you got a pair of new red shoes." But these techniques do not consistently affect children's usage (Strapp & Federico, 2000; Valian, 1999). Rather than eliminating errors, perhaps expansions and recasts model grammatical alternatives and encourage children to experiment with them.

Do the findings just described remind you once again of Vygotsky's theory? In language, as in other aspects of intellectual growth, parents and teachers gently prompt children to take the next step forward. Children strive to master language because they want to connect with other people. Adults, in turn, respond to children's desire to become competent speakers by listening attentively, elaborating on what children say, modeling correct usage, and stimulating children to talk further. In the next chapter, we will see that this combination of warmth and encouragement of mature behavior is at the heart of early childhood emotional and social development as well.

ASK YOURSELF

>> **REVIEW**
Explain how children's strategies for word learning support the interactionist perspective on language development, described on pages 134–135 in Chapter 5.

>> **APPLY**
Sammy's mother explained to him that the family would take a vacation in Miami. The next morning, Sammy announced, "I gotted my bags packed. When are we going to Your-ami?" What explains Sammy's error?

Summary

PHYSICAL DEVELOPMENT

A Changing Body and Brain

Describe body growth and brain development during early childhood.

>> Children grow more slowly in early childhood than they did in the first two years. As body fat declines, they become longer and leaner. New growth centers appear in the skeleton, and by the end of early childhood, children start to lose their primary teeth.

>> In early childhood, frontal-lobe areas of the cerebral cortex devoted to planning and organizing behavior develop rapidly. The left cerebral hemisphere shows more neural activity than the right, supporting young children's expanding language skills.

>> Hand preference strengthens during early and middle childhood, indicating that lateralization is increasing. Handedness reflects an individual's **dominant cerebral hemisphere.** One theory proposes that most children are genetically biased for right-handedness but that experience can sway them toward a left-hand preference.

>> In early childhood, connections are established between brain structures. Fibers linking the **cerebellum** to the cerebral cortex myelinate, enhancing balance and motor control. The **hippocampus,** which plays a vital role in memory and spatial orientation, and the **corpus callosum,** connecting the two cerebral hemispheres, also develop rapidly.

Influences on Physical Growth and Health

Describe the effects of heredity, nutrition, and infectious disease on physical growth in early childhood.

>> Heredity influences physical growth by controlling the release of hormones from the **pituitary gland.** Two hormones are especially influential: **growth hormone (GH)** and **thyroid-stimulating hormone (TSH).**

>> As preschoolers' growth rate slows, their appetites decline, and they may become picky eaters. Repeated exposure to new foods and a positive atmosphere at mealtimes can encourage healthy, varied eating.

>> Infectious diseases affect children who do not receive routine immunizations, both in the developing world and in industrialized nations. Illness, especially intestinal infections, can lead to malnutrition. Immunization rates are lower in the United States than in other industrialized nations because many economically disadvantaged children do not have access to health care.

What factors increase the risk of unintentional injuries, and how can childhood injuries be prevented?

>> Unintentional injuries are the leading cause of childhood mortality in industrialized countries. Injury victims are more likely to be boys; to be temperamentally inattentive, overactive, and defiant; and to be growing up in stressed, poverty-stricken families.

© AUTHORS IMAGES/ALAMY

>> Approaches to preventing childhood injuries include passing laws that promote child safety, creating safer home and community environments, improving public education; and reducing poverty and other sources of parental stress.

Motor Development

Cite major milestones of gross- and fine-motor development in early childhood.

>> During early childhood, the child's center of gravity shifts toward the trunk, and balance improves, paving the way for many gross-motor achievements. Preschoolers run, jump, hop, gallop, eventually skip, throw and catch, and generally become better coordinated.

>> Increasing control of the hands and fingers leads to dramatic improvements in fine-motor skills. Preschoolers gradually become self-sufficient at dressing and using a knife and fork.

>> By age 3, children's scribbles become pictures. With age, their drawings increase in complexity and realism. Preschoolers also try to print letters of the alphabet and, later, words.

>> Sex differences that favor boys in skills requiring force and power and girls in skills requiring good balance and fine movements are partly genetic, but environmental pressures exaggerate them. Children master the motor skills of early childhood through informal play experiences.

COGNITIVE DEVELOPMENT

Piaget's Theory: The Preoperational Stage

Describe advances in mental representation and limitations of thinking during the preoperational stage.

>> Rapid advances in mental representation mark the beginning of Piaget's **preoperational stage.** With age, make-believe becomes increasingly complex, evolving into **socio-dramatic play** with others. Preschoolers' make-believe supports many aspects of development. Gradually, children become capable of **dual representation**—viewing a symbolic object as both an object in its own right and a symbol.

>> Piaget also described preoperational children in terms of deficits. According to his theory, preoperational children are egocentric, often failing to imagine others' perspectives. **Egocentrism** contributes to **animistic thinking, centration,** a focus on perceptual appearances, and **irreversibility.** These difficulties cause preschoolers to fail **conservation** and **hierarchical classification** tasks.

What are the implications of follow-up research for the accuracy of the preoperational stage?

>> When young children are given simplified problems relevant to their everyday lives, they recognize differing perspectives, distinguish animate and inanimate objects, reason about physical transformations, understand cause-and-effect relationships, and organize knowledge into hierarchical categories, including categories based on nonobvious features.

>> Evidence that operational thinking develops gradually over the preschool years challenges Piaget's stage concept. Some theorists propose a more flexible view of stages.

Vygotsky's Sociocultural Theory

Explain Vygotsky's perspective on children's private speech and make-believe play, and note how cross-cultural research has expanded his ideas.

>> Vygotsky regarded language as the foundation for all higher cognitive processes. In his view, **private speech,** or language used for self-guidance, emerges out of social communication as adults and more skilled peers help children master challenging tasks. Private speech is gradually internalized as inner, verbal thought.

>> **Scaffolding** is a form of social interaction that promotes transfer of cognitive processes to children. Make-believe play serves as a vital zone of proximal development that enhances many new competencies.

>> **Guided participation,** a broader term than scaffolding, recognizes cultural and situational variations in adult support of children's efforts.

Information Processing

How do attention and memory change during early childhood?

>> Although preschoolers are easily distracted, attention gradually becomes more sustained. With adult support, planning also improves.

>> Preschoolers' recognition memory is very accurate, but their recall for listlike information is poor because they are not skilled at using **memory strategies.** Like adults, preschoolers remember recurring experiences in terms of **scripts,** which become more elaborate with age. When adults use an elaborative style of conversing with children about the past, their autobiographical memory becomes better organized and detailed.

Describe the young child's theory of mind.

>> Preschoolers begin to construct a theory of mind, indicating that they are capable of **metacognition.** Around age 4, they understand that people can hold false beliefs.

>> Language, cognitive abilities, make-believe play, and diverse social experiences with adults, siblings, and peers all contribute to development of a theory of mind. Preschoolers regard the mind as a passive container of information rather than as an active, constructive agent.

Summarize children's literacy and mathematical knowledge during early childhood.

>> Young children attempt to figure out how written symbols convey meaning—an active effort known as **emergent literacy.** Preschoolers gradually revise incorrect ideas about the meaning of written symbols as their cognitive and language capacities improve, as they encounter writing in many contexts, and as adults help them with written communication. **Phonological awareness** is a strong predictor of emergent literacy knowledge.

© LAURA DWIGHT PHOTOGRAPHY

>> In the second year, children have a beginning grasp of **ordinality.** Soon they discover additional mathematical principles, including **cardinality,** and experiment with counting strategies to solve arithmetic problems, eventually arriving at the most efficient, accurate technique. Many occasions for counting, comparing quantities, and talking about number promote mathematical knowledge in early childhood.

Individual Differences in Mental Development

Describe early childhood intelligence tests and the impact of home, educational programs, child care, and media on mental development in early childhood.

>> By age 5 to 6, intelligence test scores are good predictors of later IQ and academic achievement. Children growing up in warm, stimulating homes with parents who make reasonable demands for mature behavior score higher on mental tests.

>> Preschools and kindergartens range from **child-centered programs** to **academic programs.** A heavy stress on formal academic training undermines young children's motivation and negatively influences later school achievement.

>> **Project Head Start** is the largest U.S. federally funded preschool program for low-income children. High-quality preschool intervention results in immediate test score gains and long-term improvements in school adjustment.

© SASSYSTOCK/FOTOSEARCH

>> Poor-quality child care impairs children's cognitive and social development. In contrast, good child care enhances development, especially among low-SES children.

>> Children pick up many cognitive skills from educational television programs. Programs with slow-paced action and easy-to-follow story lines foster more elaborate make-believe play. But heavy viewing, especially prime-time shows and cartoons, is related to weaker academic skills.

>> Computer word-processing programs can support preschoolers' emergent literacy skills. Introducing young children to simplified computer languages fosters problem solving and metacognition.

Language Development

Trace the development of vocabulary, grammar, and conversational skills in early childhood.

>> Supported by **fast-mapping,** children's vocabularies grow dramatically during early childhood. Preschoolers draw on diverse cues—perceptual, social, and linguistic—to figure out the meanings of new words.

>> Between ages 2 and 3, children adopt the basic word order of their language. As they master grammatical rules, they may overextend them in a type of error called **overregularization.** By the end of early childhood, children have acquired complex grammatical forms.

>> To communicate effectively, children must master the practical, social side of language, known as **pragmatics.** Two-year-olds are already skilled conversationalists in face-to-face interaction. By age 4, children adapt their speech to their listeners in culturally accepted ways.

Cite factors that support language learning in early childhood.

>> Conversational give-and-take with more skilled speakers fosters language progress. Adults often provide explicit feedback on the clarity of children's language and indirect feedback about grammar through **recasts** and **expansions.**

Important Terms and Concepts

academic programs (p. 188)
animistic thinking (p. 175)
cardinality (p. 187)
centration (p. 176)
cerebellum (p. 167)
child-centered programs (p. 188)
conservation (p. 176)
corpus callosum (p. 168)
dominant cerebral hemisphere (p. 167)
dual representation (p. 175)
egocentrism (p. 175)

emergent literacy (p. 185)
expansions (p. 194)
fast-mapping (p. 191)
growth hormone (GH) (p. 168)
guided participation (p. 181)
hierarchical classification (p. 176)
hippocampus (p. 168)
irreversibility (p. 176)
memory strategies (p. 183)
metacognition (p. 184)
ordinality (p. 187)
overregularization (p. 193)

phonological awareness (p. 186)
pituitary gland (p. 168)
pragmatics (p. 193)
preoperational stage (p. 173)
private speech (p. 180)
Project Head Start (p. 188)
recasts (p. 194)
scaffolding (p. 180)
scripts (p. 183)
sociodramatic play (p. 174)
thyroid-stimulating hormone (TSH) (p. 168)

Emotional and Social Development in Early Childhood

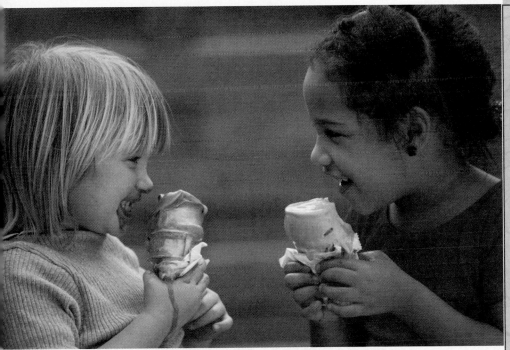

CHAPTER 8

© BENN MITCHELL/GETTY IMAGES/PHOTOGRAPHER'S CHOICE

During the preschool years, children make great strides in understanding the thoughts and feelings of others, and they build on these skills as they form first friendships—special relationships marked by attachment and common interests.

As the children in Leslie's classroom moved through the preschool years, their personalities took on clearer definition. By age 3, they voiced firm likes and dislikes as well as new ideas about themselves. "See, I'm great at this game," Sammy announced with confidence, as he aimed a beanbag toward the mouth of a large clown face—an attitude that kept him trying, even though he missed most of the throws.

The children's conversations also revealed early notions about morality. Often they combined adults' statements about right and wrong with forceful attempts to defend their own desires. "You're 'posed to share," stated Mark, grabbing the beanbag out of Sammy's hand.

"I was here first! Gimme it back," demanded Sammy, pushing Mark. The two boys struggled until Leslie intervened, provided another beanbag, and showed them how both could play.

As the interaction between Sammy and Mark reveals, preschoolers quickly become complex social beings. Between ages 2 and 6, first friendships form, in which children converse, act out complementary roles, and learn that their own desires for companionship and toys are best met when they consider others' needs and interests.

The children's developing understanding of their social world was especially evident in their growing attention to gender roles. While Lynette and Karen cared for a sick baby doll in the housekeeping area, Sammy, Vance, and Mark transformed the block corner into a busy intersection. "Green light, go!" shouted police officer Sammy as Vance and Mark pushed large wooden cars and trucks across the floor. Already, the children preferred same-sex peers and, in their play, mirrored their culture's gender stereotypes.

This chapter is devoted to the many facets of early childhood emotional and social development. We begin with Erikson's view of personality change in the preschool years. Then we consider children's concepts of themselves, their insights into their social and moral worlds, their gender typing, and their increasing ability to manage their emotional and social behaviors. Finally, we ask, What is effective child rearing? And we discuss the complex conditions that support good parenting or lead it to break down.

Erikson's Theory: Initiative versus Guilt

According to Erikson (1950), once children have a sense of autonomy, they become less contrary than they were as toddlers. Their energies are freed for tackling the psychological conflict of the preschool years: **initiative versus guilt.** As the word *initiative* suggests, young children have a new sense of purposefulness. They are eager to tackle new tasks, join in activities with peers, and discover what they can do with the help of adults. They also make strides in conscience development.

Erikson regarded play as a means through which young children learn about themselves and their social world. Play creates a small social organization of children who try out culturally meaningful roles and skills and who cooperate to achieve common goals. Around the world, children act out family scenes and highly visible occupations—police officer, doctor, and nurse in Western societies, hut builder and spear maker among the Baka of West Africa (Göncü, Patt, & Kouba, 2004).

Through patient, reasonable adult guidance and play experiences with peers, preschoolers also adopt both moral and gender-role standards of their society. For Erikson, the negative outcome of early childhood is an overly strict conscience, or superego (see Chapter 1, page 12), that causes children to feel too much guilt because they have been threatened, criticized,

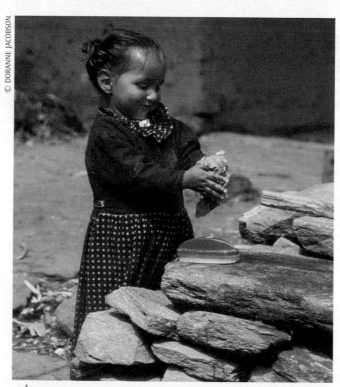

This 3-year-old in India pretends to do the laundry on the washing stone outside her family's home. Around the world, young children act out family scenes and highly visible occupations, developing a sense of initiative as they gain insight into what they can do.

and punished excessively by adults. When this happens, preschoolers' exuberant play and bold efforts to master new tasks break down.

As we will see, Erikson's image of initiative captures the diverse changes in young children's emotional and social lives. Early childhood is, indeed, a time when children develop a confident self image, more effective control over their emotions, new social skills, the foundations of morality and a sense of themselves as boy or girl.

Self-Understanding

In Chapter 7, we noted that young children acquire a vocabulary for talking about their mental lives and refine their understanding of mental states. As self-awareness strengthens, preschoolers focus more intently on qualities that make the self unique. They begin to develop a **self-concept,** the set of attributes, abilities, attitudes, and values that an individual believes defines who he or she is.

Foundations of Self-Concept

Ask a 3- to 5-year-old to tell you about himself, and you are likely to hear something like this: "I'm Tommy. I got this new red T-shirt. I'm 4 years old. I have a new Tinkertoy set, and I made this big, big tower." Preschoolers' self-concepts are very concrete. Usually, they mention observable characteristics, such as their name, physical appearance, possessions, and everyday behaviors (Harter, 2006; Watson, 1990).

By age 3½, preschoolers also describe themselves in terms of typical emotions and attitudes—"I'm happy when I play with my friends"; "I don't like being with grownups"—suggesting a beginning understanding of their unique psychological characteristics (Eder & Mangelsdorf, 1997). But preschoolers do not say, "I'm helpful" or "I'm shy." Direct references to personality traits must wait for greater cognitive maturity.

In fact, very young preschoolers' concepts of themselves are so bound up with specific possessions and actions that they spend much time asserting their rights to objects ("Mine!"), as Sammy did in the beanbag incident at the beginning of this chapter. The stronger children's self-definition, the more possessive they tend to be (Fasig, 2000; Levine, 1983). A firmer sense of self also enables children to cooperate in resolving disputes over objects, playing games, and solving simple problems (Caplan et al., 1991). Accordingly, rather than simply insisting on sharing, parents and teachers can accept young children's possessiveness as a sign of self-assertion ("Yes, that's your toy") and then encourage compromise ("but in a little while, would you give someone else a turn?").

Recall from Chapter 7 that adult–child conversations about personally experienced events contribute to the development of an autobiographical memory, in which children represent the self in relation to their social context (see page 183). Consequently, narratives serve as a rich source of early self-knowledge and as a major means of imbuing the self-concept with cultural values. In an observational study of middle-SES Irish-American families in Chicago and Chinese families in Taiwan, Chinese parents frequently told their preschoolers long stories about the child's misdeeds. In a warm, caring tone, they stressed the impact of the child's misbehavior on others ("You made Mama lose face"). Irish-American parents, in contrast, rarely dwelt on children's transgressions in storytelling and, when they did, interpreted these acts positively (Miller et al., 1997, 2002). Consistent with these narrative differences, the Chinese child's self-image emphasizes obligations to others, whereas the American child's is more autonomous.

Emergence of Self-Esteem

Another aspect of self-concept emerges in early childhood: **self-esteem,** the judgments we make about our own worth and the feelings associated with those judgments. ***TAKE A MOMENT...*** Make a list of your own self-judgments. Notice that, besides a global appraisal of your worth as a person, you have a variety of separate self-evaluations concerning how well you perform at different activities. These evaluations are among the most important aspects of self-development because they affect emotional experiences, future behavior, and long-term psychological adjustment.

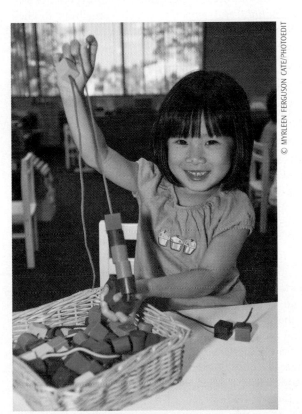

A preschooler proudly displays a string of beads she has assembled. Her high self-esteem contributes greatly to her initiative in mastering many new skills.

By age 4, preschoolers have several self-judgments—for example, about learning things in school, making friends, getting along with parents, and treating others kindly (Marsh, Ellis, & Craven, 2002). But because preschoolers cannot distinguish between their desired and their actual competence, they usually rate their own ability as extremely high and underestimate task difficulty, as when Sammy asserted, despite his many misses, that he was great at beanbag throwing (Harter, 2006).

High self-esteem contributes greatly to preschoolers' initiative. By age 3, children with a history of parental criticism of their worth and performance give up easily when faced with a challenge and express shame and despondency after failing (Kelley, Brownell, & Campbell, 2000). Adults can avoid promoting these self-defeating reactions by adjusting their expectations to children's capacities, scaffolding children's attempts at difficult tasks (see Chapter 7, page 180), and pointing out effort and improvement in children's behavior.

Emotional Development

Gains in representation, language, and self-concept support emotional development in early childhood. Between ages 2 and 6, children achieve a better understanding of their own and others' feelings, and emotional self-regulation improves. In addition, preschoolers more often experience *self-conscious emotions* and *empathy,* which contribute to their developing sense of morality.

Understanding Emotion

Early in the preschool years, children refer to causes, consequences, and behavioral signs of emotion, and over time their understanding becomes more accurate and complex (Stein & Levine, 1999). By age 4 to 5, children correctly judge the causes of many basic emotions ("He's sad because he misses his mother"). Preschoolers' explanations tend to emphasize external factors over internal states, a balance that changes with age (Levine, 1995). After age 4, children better understand that both desires and beliefs motivate behavior (see page 184 in Chapter 7). Then their grasp of how internal factors can trigger emotion expands.

Preschoolers can also predict what a playmate expressing a certain emotion might do next. Four-year-olds know that an angry child might hit someone and that a happy child is more likely to share (Russell, 1990). And they realize that thinking and feeling are interconnected—that a person reminded of a previous sad experience is likely to feel sad (Lagattuta, Wellman, & Flavell, 1997). Furthermore, they come up with effective ways to relieve others' negative feelings, such as hugging to reduce sadness (Fabes et al., 1988).

Preschoolers whose parents frequently acknowledge their emotional reactions and talk about diverse emotions are better able to judge others' emotions when tested at later ages (Denham & Kochanoff, 2002). Furthermore, 3- to 5-year-olds who are securely attached to their mothers better understand emotion. Attachment security is related to warmer, more elaborative parent–child narratives, including discussions of feelings that highlight the emotional significance of events (Laible & Song, 2006; Raikes & Thompson, 2006).

As preschoolers learn about emotion from interacting with adults, they engage in more emotion talk with siblings and friends, especially during make-believe play (Hughes & Dunn, 1998). Make-believe, in turn, contributes to emotional understanding, especially when children play with siblings (Youngblade & Dunn, 1995). The intense nature of the sibling relationship, combined with frequent acting out of feelings, makes pretending an excellent context for learning about emotions. Also, the more preschoolers refer to feelings when interacting with playmates, the better liked they are by their peers (Fabes et al., 2001). Children seem to recognize that acknowledging others' emotions and explaining their own enhance the quality of relationships.

Emotional Self-Regulation

Language also contributes to preschoolers' improved *emotional self-regulation.* By age 3 to 4, children verbalize a variety of strategies for adjusting their emotional arousal to a more comfortable level. For example, they know they can blunt emotions by restricting sensory input (covering their eyes or ears to block out a scary sight or sound), talking to themselves ("Mommy said she'll be back soon"), or changing their goals (deciding that they don't want to play anyway after being excluded from a game) (Thompson & Goodvin, 2007). *Effortful control*—in particular, inhibiting impulses and shifting attention—also continues to be vital in managing emotion. Three-year-olds who can distract themselves when frustrated tend to become cooperative school-age children with few problem behaviors (Gilliom et al., 2002).

Warm, patient parents who explain strategies for controlling feelings strengthen children's capacity to handle stress (Gottman, Katz, & Hooven, 1997). In contrast, when parents rarely express positive emotion, dismiss children's feelings as unimportant, and have difficulty controlling their own anger, children have continuing problems managing emotion (Eisenberg et al., 2001; Gilliom et al., 2002; Katz & Windecker-Nelson, 2004).

Temperament affects the development of emotional self-regulation. Children who experience negative emotion intensely find it harder to inhibit feelings and shift attention away from disturbing events. They are more likely to be anxious and fearful, respond with irritation to others' distress, react angrily or aggressively when frustrated, and get along poorly with teachers and peers (Chang et al., 2003; Denham et al., 2002; Rothbart & Bates, 2006).

Self-Conscious Emotions

One morning in Leslie's classroom, a group of children crowded around for a bread-baking activity. Leslie asked them to wait patiently while she got a baking pan. But Sammy reached over to feel the dough, and the bowl tumbled off the table. When Leslie returned, Sammy looked at her, then covered his eyes with his hands. He felt ashamed and guilty.

As their self-concepts develop, preschoolers become increasingly sensitive to praise and blame or to the possibility of such feedback. They more often experience *self-conscious emotions*—feelings that involve injury to or enhancement of their sense of self (see Chapter 6). By age 3, self-conscious emotions are clearly linked to self-evaluation (Stipek, 1995; Thompson, Meyer, & McGinley, 2006). But because preschoolers are still developing standards of excellence and conduct, they depend on adults' messages to know when to feel proud, ashamed, or guilty (Stipek, 1995; Thompson, Meyer, & McGinley, 2006).

Parents whose feedback labels the worth of the child and her performance ("That's a bad job! I thought you were a good girl!") have children who experience self-conscious emotions intensely—more shame after failure, more pride after success. In contrast, parents who focus on how to improve performance ("You did it this way; now try doing it that way") induce moderate, more adaptive levels of shame and pride and greater persistence on difficult tasks (Kelley, Brownell, & Campbell, 2000; Lewis, 1998).

Among Western children, intense shame is associated with feelings of personal inadequacy ("I'm stupid"; "I'm a terrible person") and with maladjustment—withdrawal and depression as well as intense anger and aggression toward those who shamed them (Mills, 2005). In contrast, guilt—when it occurs in appropriate circumstances and is not accompanied by shame—is related to good adjustment. Guilt helps children resist harmful impulses, and it motivates a misbehaving child to repair the damage and behave considerately (Mascolo & Fischer, 2007; Tangney, 2001).

The consequences of shame for children's adjustment, however, may vary across cultures. As Chinese parents' narratives about their child's misdeeds illustrate (see page 199), adults in Asian collectivist societies more often induce shame in children, viewing it as an adaptive reminder of the importance of others' judgments (Bedford, 2004).

Empathy

In early childhood, another emotional capacity, *empathy,* serves as an important motivator of **prosocial,** or **altruistic, behavior**—actions that benefit another person without any expected reward for the self (Eisenberg, Fabes, & Spinrad, 2006). Compared with toddlers, preschoolers rely more on words to communicate empathic feelings. And as the ability to take another's perspective improves, empathic responding increases.

Yet empathy—*feeling with* another person and responding emotionally in a similar way—does not always yield acts of kindness and helpfulness. For some children, empathizing with an upset adult or peer escalates into personal distress. In trying to reduce these feelings, the child focuses on his own anxiety rather than the person in need. As a result, empathy does not lead to **sympathy**—feelings of concern or sorrow for another's plight.

As children's language skills and ability to take the perspective of others improve, empathy also increases, motivating prosocial, or altruistic, behavior.

Temperament plays a role in whether empathy prompts sympathetic, prosocial behavior or self-focused personal distress. Children who are sociable, assertive, and good at regulating emotion are more likely to help, share, and comfort others in distress. But poor emotion regulators, who are often overwhelmed by their feelings, less often display sympathetic concern and prosocial behavior (Bengtsson, 2005; Eisenberg et al., 1998).

As with emotional self-regulation, parenting affects empathy and sympathy. When parents show sensitive concern for their preschoolers' feelings, children are likely to react similarly to others' distress—relationships that persist into adolescence and early adulthood (Koestner, Franz, & Weinberger, 1990; Michalik et al., 2007). Besides modeling sympathy, parents can teach children the importance of kindness and can intervene when they display inappropriate emotion—strategies that predict high levels of sympathetic responding (Eisenberg, 2003).

Peer Relations

As children become increasingly self-aware and better at communicating and understanding the thoughts and feelings of others, their skill at interacting with peers improves rapidly. Because peers interact on an equal footing, children must learn to keep a conversation going, cooperate, and set goals in play. With peers, children form friendships—special relationships marked by attachment and common interests.

Advances in Peer Sociability

Mildred Parten (1932), one of the first to study peer sociability among 2- to 5-year-olds, noticed a dramatic rise with age in joint, interactive play. She concluded that social development

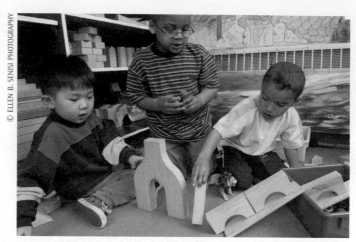

These 4-year-olds (left) engage in parallel play. Cooperative play (right) develops later than parallel play, but preschool children continue to move back and forth between the two types of sociability, sometimes using parallel play as a respite from the complex demands of cooperation.

proceeds in a three-step sequence. It begins with **nonsocial activity**—unoccupied, onlooker behavior and solitary play. Then it shifts to **parallel play,** in which a child plays near other children with similar materials but does not try to influence their behavior. At the highest level are two forms of true social interaction. In **associative play,** children engage in separate activities but exchange toys and comment on one another's behavior. Finally, in **cooperative play,** a more advanced type of interaction, children orient toward a common goal, such as acting out a make-believe theme.

■ **FOLLOW-UP RESEARCH ON PEER SOCIABILITY.** Longitudinal evidence indicates that these play forms emerge in the order suggested by Parten but that later-appearing ones do not replace earlier ones (Rubin, Bukowski, & Parker, 2006). Rather, all types coexist in early childhood.

TAKE A MOMENT... Watch preschoolers move from one type of play to another in a play group or preschool classroom, and you will see that they often transition from onlooker to parallel to cooperative play and back again (Robinson et al., 2003). Preschoolers seem to use parallel play as a respite from the demands of complex social interaction and a crossroad to

new activities. Also, both solitary and parallel play remain fairly stable from 3 to 6 years, accounting for as much of the child's play as cooperative interaction (Rubin, Fein, & Vandenberg, 1983).

We now understand that the *type,* not the amount, of solitary and parallel play changes in early childhood. In studies of preschoolers' play in Taiwan and the United States, researchers rated the *cognitive maturity* of nonsocial, parallel, and cooperative play, using the categories shown in Table 8.1. Within each play type, older children displayed more cognitively mature behavior than younger children (Pan, 1994; Rubin, Watson, & Jambor, 1978).

Often parents wonder if a preschooler who spends much time playing alone is developing normally. But only *certain types* of nonsocial activity—aimless wandering, hovering near peers, and functional play involving repetitive motor action—are cause for concern. Children who watch peers without playing are usually temperamentally inhibited—high in social fearfulness (Coplan et al., 2004; Rubin, Burgess, & Hastings, 2002). But most preschoolers with low rates of peer interaction simply like to play alone, and their solitary activities are positive and constructive. When they do play with peers, they show socially skilled behavior (Rubin & Coplan, 1998).

■ **TABLE 8.1** ■ *Developmental Sequence of Cognitive Play Categories*

PLAY CATEGORY	DESCRIPTION	EXAMPLES
Functional play	Simple, repetitive motor movements with or without objects, especially common during the first two years	Running around a room, rolling a car back and forth, kneading clay with no intent to make something
Constructive play	Creating or constructing something, especially common between 3 and 6 years	Making a house out of toy blocks, drawing a picture, putting together a puzzle
Make-believe play	Acting out everyday and imaginary roles, especially common between 2 and 6 years	Playing house, school, or police officer; acting out storybook or television characters

Source: Rubin, Fein, & Vandenberg, 1983.

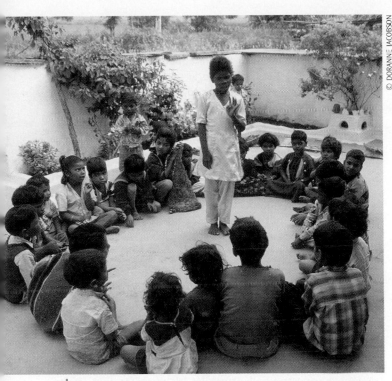

Village children in India, varying widely in age, play a "circle tapping" game to help one another learn that requires high levels of cooperation. The child in the center recites a poem, the alphabet, or numbers, then walks around the outside of the circle, saying, "Whomever I tap, whomever I tap, it will be their turn." The tapped child moves to the center to recite.

■ **CULTURAL VARIATIONS.** Peer sociability in collectivist societies, which stress group harmony, differs from that in individualistic cultures. For example, children in India generally play in large groups that require high levels of cooperation. Much of their behavior occurs in unison and involves close physical contact. In a game called Bhatto Bhatto, children act out a script about a trip to the market, touching one another's elbows and hands as they pretend to share a tasty vegetable (Roopnarine et al., 1994).

Cultural beliefs about the importance of play also affect early peer associations. Adults who view play as mere entertainment are less likely to provide props or to encourage pretend than those who value its cognitive and social benefits (Gaskins, 2000). Preschoolers of Korean-American parents, who emphasize task persistence as vital for learning, spend less time than Caucasian-American children in joint make-believe and more time unoccupied and in parallel play (Farver, Kim, & Lee, 1995).

First Friendships

As preschoolers interact, first friendships form that serve as important contexts for emotional and social development. Preschoolers understand that a friend is someone "who likes you" and with whom you spend a lot of time. But 4- to 7-year-olds regard friendship as based on pleasurable play and sharing of toys. As yet, it does not have a long-term, enduring quality based on mutual trust (Damon, 1988a; Hartup, 2006). Indeed, Sammy would declare, "Mark's my best friend," on days when the boys got along well. But when a dispute arose, he would reverse himself: "Mark, you're not my friend!"

Nevertheless, interactions between young friends are unique. Preschool friends are more emotionally expressive, talking, laughing, and looking at each other more often than nonfriends do (Hartup, 2006). Furthermore, the ease with which kindergartners make new friends predicts cooperative participation in classroom activities and self-directed completion of learning tasks—behaviors linked to gains in achievement (Ladd, Birch, & Buhs, 1999; Ladd, Buhs, & Seid, 2000). The capacity to form friendships enables children to integrate themselves into classroom environments in ways that foster both academic and social competence. In one study, 4-year-olds of average intelligence but with above-average social skills fared better in academic achievement when they reached first grade than did agemates of equal mental ability who were socially below average (Konold & Pianta, 2005).

Because social maturity in early childhood contributes to later academic performance, a growing number of experts propose that kindergarten readiness be assessed in terms of not just academic skills but also social skills (Ladd, Herald, & Kochel, 2006; Thompson & Raikes, 2007). Preschool interventions, too, should attend to these vital social prerequisites.

Parental Influences on Early Peer Relations

Children first acquire skills for interacting with peers within the family. Parents influence children's peer sociability both *directly,* through attempts to influence children's peer relations, and *indirectly,* through their child-rearing practices and play behaviors (Ladd & Pettit, 2002; Rubin et al., 2005).

■ **DIRECT PARENTAL INFLUENCES.** Preschoolers whose parents frequently arrange informal peer play activities tend to have larger peer networks and to be more socially skilled (Ladd, LeSieur, & Profilet, 1993). In providing play opportunities, parents show children how to initiate their own peer contacts. And parents' skillful suggestions for entering play groups and managing conflict are associated with preschoolers' social competence and peer acceptance (Parke et al., 2004b).

■ **INDIRECT PARENTAL INFLUENCES.** Many parenting behaviors not directly aimed at promoting peer sociability nevertheless influence it. For example, secure attachments to parents are linked to more responsive, harmonious peer interaction, larger peer networks, and warmer, more supportive friendships during the preschool and school years (Laible, 2007; Lucas-Thompson & Clarke-Stewart, 2007; Wood, Emmerson, & Cowan, 2004). The sensitive, expressive communication that contributes to attachment security may be responsible. In several studies, involved, emotionally positive parent–child

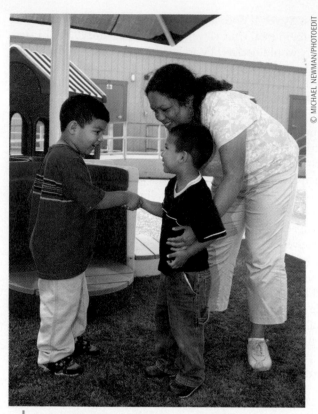

Parents influence preschoolers' peer interaction skills by offering advice, guidance, and examples of how to behave. These children receive a lesson in how to greet a friend by shaking hands.

conversations and play predicted preschoolers' prosocial behavior and positive peer relations (Clark & Ladd, 2000; Lindsey & Mize, 2000).

Some preschoolers already have great difficulty with peer relations. In Leslie's classroom, Robbie was one of them. Wherever he happened to be, comments like "Robbie ruined our block tower" and "Robbie hit me for no reason" could be heard. As we take up moral development in the next section, you will learn more about how parenting contributed to Robbie's peer problems.

ASK YOURSELF

》REVIEW
Among children who spend much time playing alone, what factors distinguish those who are likely to have adjustment difficulties from those who are well-adjusted and socially skilled?

》APPLY
Three-year-old Ben lives in the country, with no other preschoolers nearby. His parents wonder whether it is worth driving Ben into town once a week to participate in a peer play group. What advice would you give Ben's parents, and why?

》REFLECT
What did your parents do, directly and indirectly, that might have influenced your earliest peer relationships?

Foundations of Morality

Children's conversations and behavior provide many examples of their developing moral sense. By age 2, they use words to evaluate behavior as "good" or "bad" and react with distress to aggressive or otherwise harmful acts (Kochanska, Casey, & Fukumoto, 1995).

Adults everywhere take note of this budding capacity to distinguish right from wrong. Some cultures have special terms for it. The Utku Indians of Hudson Bay say the child develops *ihuma* (reason). The Fijians believe that *vakayalo* (sense) appears. In response, parents hold children more responsible for their behavior (Dunn, 2005). By the end of early childhood, children can state many moral rules: "Don't take someone's things without asking!" "Tell the truth!" And they argue over matters of justice: "It's not fair. He got more!"

All theories of moral development recognize that conscience begins to take shape in early childhood. And most agree that at first, the child's morality is *externally controlled* by adults. Gradually, it becomes regulated by *inner standards*. Truly moral individuals do not do the right thing just to conform to others' expectations. Rather, they have developed compassionate concerns and principles of good conduct, which they follow in many situations.

Each major theory emphasizes a different aspect of morality. Psychoanalytic theory stresses the *emotional side* of conscience development—in particular, identification and guilt as motivators of good conduct. Social learning theory focuses on how *moral behavior* is learned through reinforcement and modeling. Finally, the cognitive-developmental perspective emphasizes *thinking*—children's ability to reason about justice and fairness.

The Psychoanalytic Perspective

Recall that according to Freud, young children form a *superego*, or conscience, by *identifying* with the same-sex parent, whose moral standards they adopt. Children obey the superego to avoid *guilt*, a painful emotion that arises each time they are tempted to misbehave. Moral development, Freud believed, is largely complete by 5 to 6 years of age.

Today, most researchers disagree with Freud's view of conscience development. In his theory, fear of punishment and loss of parental love motivate conscience formation and moral behavior (Tellings, 1999). Yet children whose parents frequently use threats, commands, or physical force tend to violate standards often and feel little guilt, whereas parental warmth and responsiveness predict greater guilt following transgressions (Kochanska et al., 2005, 2008). And if a parent withdraws love after misbehavior—for example, refuses to speak to or states a dislike for the child—children often respond with high levels of self-blame, thinking "I'm no good." or "Nobody loves me." Eventually, to protect themselves from overwhelming guilt, these children may deny the emotion and, as a result, also develop a weak conscience (Kochanska, 1991).

This teacher uses inductive discipline to explain to a child the impact of his transgression on others. She indicates how the child should behave, encouraging empathy and sympathetic concern.

■ **INDUCTIVE DISCIPLINE.**   In contrast, conscience formation is promoted by a type of discipline called **induction,** in which an adult helps the child notice feelings by pointing out the effects of the child's misbehavior on others. For example, a parent might say, "She's crying because you won't give back her doll" (Hoffman, 2000). Preschoolers with warm parents who use induction are more likely to refrain from wrongdoing, confess and repair damage after misdeeds, and display prosocial behavior (Kerr et al., 2004; Zahn-Waxler, Radke-Yarrow, & King, 1979).

The success of induction may lie in its power to motivate children's active commitment to moral standards. By emphasizing the impact of the child's actions on others, it encourages empathy and sympathy (Krevans & Gibbs, 1996). And giving children reasons for changing their behavior encourages them to adopt moral standards because they make sense.

■ **THE CHILD'S CONTRIBUTION.**   Although good discipline is crucial, children's characteristics affect the success of parenting techniques. Twin studies suggest a modest genetic contribution to empathy (Knafo & Plomin, 2006; Zahn-Waxler et al., 2001). A highly empathic child is more responsive to induction.

Temperament is also influential. Mild, patient tactics—requests, suggestions, and explanations—are sufficient to prompt guilt reactions in anxious, fearful preschoolers (Kochanska et al., 2002). But with fearless, impulsive children, gentle discipline has little impact. Power assertion also works poorly. It undermines the child's capacity for effortful control, which strongly predicts good conduct, empathy, sympathy, and pro-

social behavior. Parents of impulsive children can foster conscience development by ensuring a secure attachment relationship and combining firm correction with induction (Kochanska & Aksan, 2006; Kochanska, Aksan, & Joy, 2007). When children are so low in anxiety that parental disapproval causes them little discomfort, a close parent–child bond motivates them to listen to parents as a means of preserving an affectionate, supportive relationship.

■ **THE ROLE OF GUILT.**   Although little support exists for Freudian ideas about conscience development, Freud was correct that guilt is an important motivator of moral action. Inducing *empathy-based guilt* (expressions of personal responsibility and regret, such as "I'm sorry I hurt him") by explaining that the child is harming someone and has disappointed the parent is a means of influencing children without using coercion (Baumeister, 1998). At the same time, parents must help children deal with guilt feelings constructively—by guiding them to make up for immoral behavior rather than minimizing or excusing it.

But contrary to Freud's belief, guilt is not the only force that compels us to act morally. Nor is moral development complete by the end of early childhood. Rather, it is a gradual process, extending into adulthood.

Social Learning Theory

According to social learning theory, moral behavior is acquired just like any other set of responses: through reinforcement and modeling.

■ **THE IMPORTANCE OF MODELING.**   Operant conditioning—reinforcement for good behavior, in the form of approval, affection, and other rewards—is not enough for children to acquire moral responses. To be reinforced, a behavior must first occur spontaneously. Yet many prosocial acts, such as sharing, helping, or comforting an unhappy playmate, occur so rarely at first that reinforcement cannot explain their rapid development in early childhood. Rather, social learning theorists believe that children learn to behave morally largely through *modeling*—observing and imitating people who demonstrate appropriate behavior (Bandura, 1977; Grusec, 1988). Once children acquire a moral response, such as sharing or telling the truth, reinforcement in the form of praise increases its frequency (Mills & Grusec, 1989).

Many studies show that having helpful or generous models increases young children's prosocial responses. Models are most influential in the early years. In one study, toddlers' eager, willing imitation of their mothers' behavior predicted moral conduct (not cheating in a game) and guilt following transgressions at age 3 (Forman, Aksan, & Kochanska, 2004). At the end of early childhood, children who have had consistent exposure to caring adults have internalized prosocial rules and follow them whether or not a model is present (Mussen & Eisenberg-Berg, 1977).

■ THE EFFECTS OF PUNISHMENT.

A sharp reprimand or physical force to restrain or move a child is justified when immediate obedience is necessary—for example, when a 3-year-old is about to run into the street. In fact, parents are most likely to use forceful methods under these conditions. But to foster long-term goals, such as acting kindly toward others, they tend to rely on warmth and reasoning (Kuczynski, 1984). And in response to very serious transgressions, such as lying and stealing, they often combine power assertion with reasoning (Grusec, 2006; Grusec & Goodnow, 1994).

Frequent punishment, however, promotes only momentary compliance. For example, Robbie's parents often hit, criticized, and shouted at him. But as soon as they were out of sight, Robbie usually engaged in the unacceptable behavior again. The more harsh threats, angry physical control, and physical punishment children experience, the more likely they are to develop serious, lasting mental health problems. These include weak internalization of moral rules; depression, aggression, antisocial behavior, and poor academic performance in childhood and adolescence; and depression, alcohol abuse, criminality, and partner and child abuse in adulthood (Afifi et al., 2006; Bender et al., 2007; Gershoff, 2002a; Lynch et al., 2006).

Harsh punishment has several undesirable side effects:

- It models aggression.

- It induces a chronic sense of being personally threatened, which prompts children to focus on their own distress rather than respond sympathetically to others.

- It causes children to avoid the punishing adult, who, as a result, has little opportunity to teach desirable behaviors.

- By stopping children's misbehavior temporarily, it offers immediate relief to adults, who may then punish more often—a course of action that can spiral into abuse.

- Adults whose parents used corporal punishment are more accepting of it (Deater-Deckard et al., 2003). In this way, use of physical punishment may transfer to the next generation.

Parents with conflict-ridden marriages and with mental health problems are more likely to be punitive and also to have hard-to-manage children (Erath et al., 2006; Knafo & Plomin, 2006). These parent–child similarities suggest that heredity contributes to the link between punitive discipline and children's adjustment difficulties. But heredity is not a complete explanation because parental harshness and corporal punishment predict emotional and behavior problems in children of diverse temperaments (Mulvaney & Mebert, 2007). Negative outcomes are simply more pronounced among temperamentally difficult children.

A survey of a nationally representative sample of U.S. households revealed that although corporal punishment increases from infancy to age 5 and then declines, it is high at all ages (see Figure 8.1) (Straus & Stewart, 1999). And more than one-fourth of physically punishing parents report having used a hard object, such as a brush or a belt (Gershoff, 2002b).

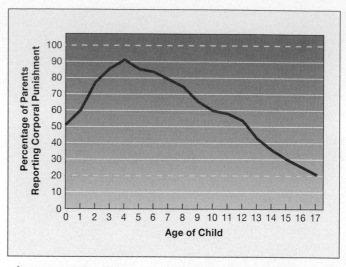

■ **FIGURE 8.1** ■ **Prevalence of corporal punishment by children's age.** Estimates are based on the percentage of parents in a nationally representative U.S. sample of nearly 1,000 reporting one or more instances of spanking, slapping, pinching, shaking, or hitting with a hard object in the past year. Physical punishment increases sharply during early childhood and then declines, but it is high at all ages. (From M. A. Straus & J. H. Stewart, 1999, "Corporal Punishment by American Parents: National Data on Prevalence, Chronicity, Severity, and Duration in Relation to Child and Family Characteristics," *Clinical Child and Family Psychology Review, 2,* p. 59. Adapted with kind permission from Springer Science and Business Media and Murray Straus.)

A prevailing American belief is that corporal punishment, if implemented by caring parents, is harmless, perhaps even beneficial. But as the Cultural Influences box on the following page reveals, this assumption is valid only under conditions of limited use in certain social contexts.

■ ALTERNATIVES TO HARSH PUNISHMENT.

Alternatives to criticism, slaps, and spankings can reduce the side effects of punishment. A technique called **time out** involves removing children from the immediate setting—for example, by sending them to their rooms—until they are ready to act appropriately. When a child is out of control, a few minutes in time out can be enough to change behavior while also giving angry parents a cooling-off period. Another approach is *withdrawal of privileges,* such as watching a favorite TV program. When parents decide to use these forms of punishment, they can increase their effectiveness in three ways:

- *Consistency.* Permitting children to act inappropriately on some occasions confuses them, and the unacceptable act persists (Acker & O'Leary, 1996).

- *A warm parent–child relationship.* Children of involved, caring parents find the interruption in parental affection that accompanies punishment especially unpleasant. They want to regain parental warmth and approval as quickly as possible.

■ CULTURAL INFLUENCES ■

Ethnic Differences in the Consequences of Physical Punishment

In an African-American community, six elders, who had volunteered to serve as mentors for parents facing child-rearing challenges, met to discuss parenting issues at a social service agency. Their attitudes toward discipline were strikingly different from those of the white social workers who had brought them together. Each elder argued that successful child rearing required use of appropriate physical tactics. At the same time, they voiced strong disapproval of screaming or cursing at children, calling such out-of-control parental behavior "abusive." Ruth, the oldest and most respected member of the group, characterized good parenting as a complex combination of warmth, teaching, talking nicely, and disciplining physically. She related how an older neighbor advised her to handle her own children when she was a young parent:

> She said to me says, don't scream . . . you talk to them real nice and sweet and when they do something ugly . . . she say you get a nice little switch and you won't have any trouble with them and from that day that's the way I raised 'em. (Mosby et al., 1999, pp. 511–512.)

Use of physical punishment is highest among low-SES ethnic minority parents, who are more likely than middle-SES white parents to advocate slaps and spankings (Pinderhughes et al., 2000; Straus & Stewart, 1999). And although corporal punishment is linked to a wide array of negative child outcomes, exceptions do exist.

In one longitudinal study, researchers followed several hundred families for 12 years, collecting information on disciplinary strategies and youth problem behaviors. Even after many child and family characteristics were controlled, the findings were striking: In Caucasian-American families, physical punishment was positively associated with adolescent aggression and antisocial behavior. In African-American families, by contrast, the more mothers had disciplined physically in childhood, the less their teenagers displayed angry, acting-out behavior and got in trouble at school and with the police (Lansford et al., 2004).

African-American and Caucasian-American parents seem to mete out physical punishment differently. In black families, such discipline is typically culturally approved, mild, delivered in a context of parental warmth, and aimed at helping children become responsible adults. White parents, in contrast, usually consider physical punishment to be wrong, so when they resort to it, they are often highly agitated and rejecting of the child (Dodge, McLoyd, & Lansford, 2006). As a result, most black children may view spanking as a practice carried out with their best interests in mind, whereas white children may regard it as an "act of personal aggression" (Gunnoe & Mariner, 1997, p. 768; McLoyd et al., 2007).

These findings are not an endorsement of physical punishment. Other forms of discipline, including the positive strategies listed on page 208, are far more effective. But it is noteworthy that the meaning and impact of physical discipline varies sharply with cultural context.

In African-American families, physical discipline is typically culturally approved, mild, and delivered in a context of parental warmth. As a result, African-American children may view spanking as a practice carried out with their best interests in mind, not as an act of aggression.

■ *Explanations.* Providing reasons for mild punishment helps children relate the misdeed to expectations for future behavior, resulting in far greater reduction in misbehavior than using punishment alone (Larzelere et al., 1996).

■ **POSITIVE DISCIPLINE.** The most effective forms of discipline encourage good conduct—by building a mutually respectful bond with the child, letting the child know ahead of time how to act, and praising mature behavior (Zahn-Waxler & Robinson, 1995). When sensitivity, cooperation, and shared positive emotion are evident between parents and preschoolers, children show firmer conscience development—expressing empathy after transgressions, playing fairly in games, and considering others' welfare (Kochanska et al., 2005, 2008).

Consult Applying What We Know on page 208 for ways to discipline positively. Parents who use these strategies focus on long-term social and life skills. This greatly reduces the need for punishment.

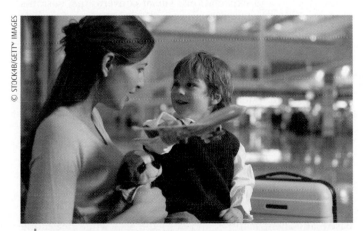

Parents who engage in positive discipline encourage good conduct and reduce opportunities for misbehavior. By bringing along toys and joining in his make-believe, this mother helps her young child behave appropriately during a long wait at the airport.

Applying What We Know

Using Positive Discipline

Strategy	Explanation
Use transgressions as opportunities to teach.	When a child engages in harmful or unsafe behavior, intervene firmly, and then use induction, which motivates children to make amends and behave prosocially.
Reduce opportunities for misbehavior.	On a long car trip, bring back-seat activities that relieve children's restlessness. At the supermarket, converse with children and let them help with shopping. As a result, children learn to occupy themselves constructively when options are limited.
Provide reasons for rules.	When children appreciate that rules are fair to all concerned, not arbitrary, they strive to follow the rules because these are reasonable and rational.
Arrange for children to participate in family routines and duties.	By joining with adults in preparing a meal, washing dishes, or raking leaves, children develop a sense of responsible participation in family and community life and acquire many practical skills.
When children are obstinate, try compromising and problem solving.	When a child refuses to obey, express understanding of the child's feelings, suggest a compromise, and help the child think of ways to avoid the problem in the future. Responding firmly but kindly and respectfully increases the likelihood of willing cooperation.
Encourage mature behavior.	Express confidence in children's capacity to learn and appreciation for effort and cooperation, as in "You gave that your best!" Adult encouragement fosters pride and satisfaction in succeeding, thereby inspiring children to improve further.

The Cognitive-Developmental Perspective

The psychoanalytic and behaviorist approaches to morality focus on how children acquire ready-made standards of good conduct from adults. In contrast, the cognitive-developmental perspective regards children as *active thinkers* about social rules. As early as the preschool years, children make moral judgments, deciding what is right or wrong on the basis of concepts they construct about justice and fairness (Gibbs, 2010; Turiel, 2006).

Furthermore, preschoolers distinguish **moral imperatives,** which protect people's rights and welfare, from two other types of rules and expectations: **social conventions,** customs determined solely by consensus, such as table manners; and **matters of personal choice,** which do not violate rights and are up to the individual, such as choice of friends and leisure activities (Killen, Margie, & Sinno, 2006; Nucci, 1996; Smetana, 2006). Interviews with 3- and 4-year-olds reveal that they judge moral violations (stealing an apple) as more wrong than violations of social conventions (eating ice cream with your fingers). And preschoolers' concern with personal choice, conveyed through such statements as "I'm gonna wear *this* shirt," serves as the springboard for moral concepts of individual rights (Nucci, 2005).

Within the moral domain, however, preschool and young school-age children tend to reason *rigidly*, making judgments based on salient features and consequences while neglecting other important information. For example, they are more likely than older children to claim that stealing and lying are always wrong, even when a person has a morally sound reason for en-gaging in these acts (Lourenco, 2003). They view inflicting physical damage (breaking a peer's toy) as a more serious transgression than treating others unfairly (not sharing) (Nucci, 2002). And their focus on outcomes means that they fail to realize that a promise is still a promise, even if it is unfulfilled (Maas, 2008; Maas & Abbeduto, 2001).

Cognition and language support preschoolers' moral understanding, but social experiences are vital. Disputes with siblings and peers over rights and possessions allow preschoolers to negotiate, compromise, and work out their first ideas about justice and fairness (Killen & Nucci, 1995). And children who are advanced in moral thinking tend to have parents who adapt their communications about fighting, honesty, and ownership to what their children can understand, tell stories with moral implications, encourage prosocial behavior, and gently stimulate the child to think further, without being hostile or critical (Janssens & Deković, 1997; Walker & Taylor, 1991a).

Preschoolers who verbally and physically assault others, often without provocation, are already delayed in moral reasoning (Helwig & Turiel, 2004). Without special help, such children show long-term disruptions in moral development.

The Other Side of Morality: Development of Aggression

Beginning in late infancy, all children display aggression at times. As interactions with siblings and peers increase, so do aggressive outbursts (Dodge, Coie, & Lynam, 2006; Tremblay, 2004). By the second year, two general types of aggression emerge. Initially, the most common is **proactive** (or *instrumental*)

aggression, in which children act to fulfill a need or desire—obtain an object, privilege, space, or social reward, such as adult or peer attention—and unemotionally attack a person to achieve their goal. The other type, **reactive** (or *hostile*) **aggression,** is an angry, defensive response to provocation or a blocked goal and is meant to hurt another person.

Proactive and reactive aggression come in three forms:

- **Physical aggression** harms others through physical injury—pushing, hitting, kicking, or punching others or destroying another's property.

- **Verbal aggression** harms others through threats of physical aggression, name-calling, or hostile teasing.

- **Relational aggression** damages another's peer relationships through social exclusion, malicious gossip, or friendship manipulation.

In early childhood, verbal aggression gradually replaces physical aggression (Alink et al., 2006; Tremblay et al., 1999). And proactive aggression declines as preschoolers' improved capacity to delay gratification enables them to avoid grabbing others' possessions. But reactive aggression in verbal and relation forms tends to rise over early and middle childhood (Côté et al., 2007; Tremblay, 2000). Older children are better able to recognize malicious intentions and, as a result, more often respond in hostile ways.

By age 17 months, boys are more physically aggressive than girls—a difference found throughout childhood in many cultures (Baillargeon et al., 2007; Card et al., 2008). The sex difference is due in part to biology—in particular, to male sex hormones (androgens) and temperamental traits (activity level, irritability, impulsivity) on which boys score higher. Gender-role conformity is also important. Once preschoolers are aware of gender stereotypes—that males and females are expected to behave differently—physical aggression drops off more sharply in girls than in boys (Fagot & Leinbach, 1989). Parents also respond far more negatively to physical fighting in girls (Arnold, McWilliams, & Harvey-Arnold, 1998).

Although girls have a reputation for being both more verbally and relationally aggressive than boys, the sex difference is small (Crick et al., 2004, 2006; Crick, Ostrov, & Werner, 2006). Beginning in the preschool years, girls concentrate most of their aggressive acts in the relational category. Boys inflict harm in more variable ways: Physically and verbally aggressive boys also tend to be relationally aggressive (Card et al., 2008). Therefore, boys display overall rates of aggression that are much higher than girls'.

At the same time, girls more often select indirect relational tactics, such as rumor spreading, refusing to speak to a peer, or saying behind someone's back, "Don't play with her," that—in disrupting intimate bonds especially important to girls—can be particularly mean. And whereas physical attacks are usually brief, acts of indirect relational aggression may extend for hours, weeks, or even months (Nelson, Robinson, & Hart, 2005; Underwood, 2003).

As early as 17 months of age, boys are more physically aggressive than girls—a difference found throughout childhood in many cultures.

Children who are emotionally negative, impulsive, and disobedient are prone to early, high rates of physical or relational aggression (or both) that often persist, resulting in serious conduct problems in middle childhood and adolescence (Coté et al., 2007; Vaillancourt et al., 2003). These negative outcomes, however, depend on child-rearing conditions.

■ **THE FAMILY AS TRAINING GROUND FOR AGGRESSIVE BEHAVIOR.** "I can't control him, he's impossible," Robbie's mother, Nadine, complained to Leslie one day. When Leslie asked if Robbie might be troubled by something happening at home, she discovered that his parents fought constantly and resorted to harsh, inconsistent discipline. The same child-rearing practices that undermine moral internalization—love withdrawal, power assertion, physical punishment, and inconsistency—are linked to aggression from early childhood through adolescence, in children of both sexes and in many cultures, with most of these practices predicting both physical and relational forms (Bradford et al., 2003; Côté et al., 2007; Nelson et al., 2006a).

In families like Robbie's, anger and punitiveness quickly create a conflict-ridden family atmosphere and an "out-of-control" child. The pattern begins with forceful discipline, which occurs more often with stressful life experiences, a parent with an unstable personality, or a difficult child (Dodge, Coie, & Lynam, 2006). Typically, the parent threatens, criticizes, and punishes, and the child whines, yells, and refuses until the parent "gives in." As these cycles become more frequent, they generate anxiety and irritability among other family members, including siblings, who soon join in the hostile interactions. Destructive sibling conflict, in turn, quickly spreads to peer relationships, contributing to poor impulse control and antisocial behavior (Garcia et al., 2000; Ostrov, Crick, & Stauffacher, 2006).

Boys are more likely than girls to be targets of harsh, inconsistent discipline because they are more active and impulsive and therefore harder to control. Children who are products of these family processes come to view the world from a violent perspective, seeing hostile intent where it does not exist (Lochman & Dodge, 1998; Orbio de Castro et al., 2002). As a result, they make many unprovoked attacks and soon conclude that aggression "works" to control others.

■ **VIOLENT MEDIA AND AGGRESSION.** In the United States, 57 percent of television programs between 6 A.M. and 11 P.M. contain violent scenes, often portraying repeated aggressive acts that go unpunished. TV victims of violence are rarely shown experiencing serious harm, and few programs condemn violence or depict other ways of solving problems. Violent content is 9 percent above average in children's programming, and cartoons are the most violent (Center for Communication and Social Policy, 1998).

Reviewers of thousands of studies have concluded that TV violence increases the likelihood of hostile thoughts and emotions and of verbally, physically, and relationally aggressive behavior (Comstock & Scharrer, 2006; Ostrov, Gentile, & Crick, 2006). And a growing number of studies show that playing violent video and computer games has similar effects (Anderson, 2004).

Violent programming not only creates short-term difficulties in parent and peer relations but also has lasting negative consequences. In longitudinal research, time spent watching TV in childhood and adolescence predicted aggressive behavior in adulthood, after other factors linked to TV viewing (such as prior child and parent aggression, IQ, parent education, family income, and neighborhood crime) were controlled (see Figure 8.2) (Graber et al., 2006; Huesmann, 1986; Huesmann et al., 2003; Johnson et al., 2002). Aggressive children and adolescents have

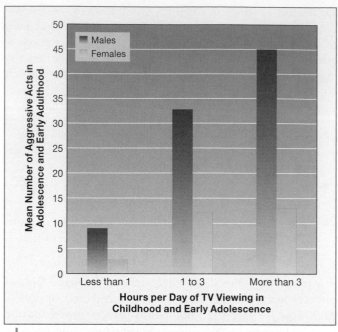

■ **FIGURE 8.2** ■ **Relationship of television viewing in childhood and early adolescence to aggressive acts in adolescence and early adulthood.** Interviews with more than 700 parents and youths revealed that the more TV watched in childhood and early adolescence, the greater the annual number of aggressive acts committed by the young person, as reported in follow-up interviews at ages 16 and 22. (Adapted from Johnson et al., 2002.)

a greater appetite for violent TV and computer games. And boys devote more time to violent media than girls, in part because of male-oriented themes of conquest and adventure and use of males as lead characters. But even in nonaggressive children, violent TV sparks hostile thoughts and behavior; its impact is simply less intense (Bushman & Huesmann, 2001).

Furthermore, media violence "hardens" children to aggression. Viewers quickly habituate, responding with reduced arousal to real-world instances, tolerating more aggression in others, and believing that violence is widespread in society (Anderson et al., 2003). As these responses indicate, exposure to violent media modifies children's attitudes so they increasingly match media images.

The ease with which television and computer fare can manipulate children's beliefs and behavior has led to strong public pressure for media regulation. In the United States, the First Amendment right to free speech has hampered efforts to regulate TV. Instead, all programs must be rated for violent and sexual content, and all new TV sets are required to contain the V-chip, which allows parents to block undesired material. In contrast, Canada's nationwide broadcasting code bans from children's shows realistic scenes of violence that minimize consequences and cartoons with violence as the central theme. Further, violent programming intended for adults cannot be shown on Canadian channels before 9 P.M. (Canadian children, however, can access violent TV fare on U.S. channels.)

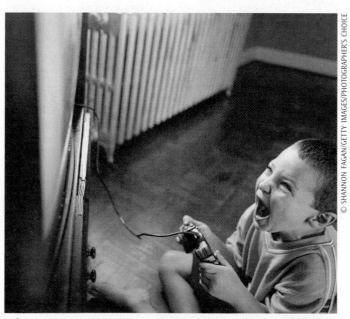

TV violence increases the likelihood of hostile thoughts and emotions and tolerance of real-world aggression. And playing violent video and computer games has similar effects.

At present, parents bear most responsibility for protecting their children from exposure to media violence and other inappropriate content. Although the Internet poses additional risks, parents can control children's access by using filters or programs that monitor website visits. Yet surveys of U.S. parents indicate that 20 to 30 percent of preschoolers and 40 percent of school-age children experience no limits on TV or computer use at home (Rideout & Hamel, 2006; Roberts, Foehr, & Rideout, 2005; Varnhagen, 2007).

■ HELPING CHILDREN AND PARENTS CONTROL AGGRESSION.

Treatment for aggressive children is best begun early, before their antisocial behavior becomes well-practiced and difficult to change. Breaking the cycle of hostilities between family members, promoting effective ways of relating to others, and monitoring and limiting TV and computer use are crucial.

Leslie suggested that Robbie's parents see a family therapist, who observed their inept practices and taught them alternatives. They learned not to give in to Robbie, to pair commands with reasons, and to replace verbal insults and harsh physical punishment with more effective strategies, such as time out and withdrawal of privileges. After several weeks of such training, children's aggression declines, and parents view their children more positively—benefits still evident one to four years later (Kazdin, 2003; Patterson & Fisher, 2002).

Leslie also began coaching Robbie in how to interact successfully with peers, encouraging him to talk about a playmate's emotions and to express his own. As Robbie practiced taking the perspective of others and feeling sympathetic concern, his angry lashing out at peers declined (Izard et al., 2004). Robbie participated in social problem-solving training as well. Over several months, he met with Leslie and a small group of classmates to act out common conflicts using puppets, discuss alternatives for resolving disputes, and practice successful strategies. Children who receive such training show gains in social competence still present several months later (Shure & Aberson, 2005).

Finally, Robbie's parents sought counseling for their marital problems. When parents receive help in coping with stressors in their own lives, interventions aimed at reducing children's aggression are even more effective (Kazdin & Whitley, 2003).

ASK YOURSELF

≫ REVIEW
What must parents do to foster conscience development in fearless, impulsive children? Does this remind you of the concept of goodness of fit (see page 149 in Chapter 6)? Explain.

≫ APPLY
Alice and Wayne want their two children to become morally mature, caring individuals. List some parenting practices they should use and some they should avoid.

≫ REFLECT
Which types of punishment for a misbehaving preschooler do you endorse, and which types do you reject? Why?

Gender Typing

Gender typing refers to any association of objects, activities, roles, or traits with one sex or the other in ways that conform to cultural stereotypes (Liben & Bigler, 2002). Already, the children in Leslie's classroom had acquired many gender-linked beliefs and preferences and tended to play with peers of their own sex.

Social learning theory, with its emphasis on modeling and reinforcement, and *cognitive-developmental theory*, with its focus on children as active thinkers about their social world, offer contemporary explanations of children's gender typing. We will see, however, that neither is adequate by itself. *Gender schema theory*, a third perspective that combines elements of both, has gained favor. In the following sections, we consider the early development of gender typing.

Gender-Stereotyped Beliefs and Behavior

Recall from Chapter 6 that around age 2, children use such words as *boy, girl, lady,* and *man* appropriately. As soon as gender categories are established, children sort out what they mean in terms of activities and behavior. Preschoolers associate toys, articles of clothing, tools, household items, games, occupations, colors (blue and pink), and behaviors (physical and relational aggression) with one sex or the other (Giles & Heyman, 2005; Poulin-Dubois et al., 2002; Ruble, Martin, & Berenbaum, 2006). And their actions reflect their beliefs, not only in play preferences but in personality traits as well. As we have seen, boys tend to be more active, impulsive, assertive, and physically aggressive. Girls tend to be more fearful, dependent, emotionally sensitive, compliant, advanced in effortful control, and skilled at understanding self-conscious emotions and at inflicting indirect relational aggression (Bosacki & Moore, 2004; Else-Quest et al., 2006; Underwood, 2003).

During early childhood, children's gender-stereotyped beliefs strengthen—so much so that many children apply them as blanket rules rather than as flexible guidelines. When children were asked whether gender stereotypes could be violated, half or more of 3- and 4-year-olds answered "no" to clothing, hairstyle, and play with certain toys (such as Barbie dolls and GI Joes) (Blakemore, 2003). Furthermore, most 3- to 6-year-olds are firm about not wanting to be friends with a child who violates a gender stereotype (a boy who wears nail polish, a girl who plays with trucks) or to attend a school where such violations are allowed (Ruble et al., 2007). These one-sided judgments are a joint product of gender stereotyping in the environment and young children's cognitive limitations (Trautner et al., 2005). Most preschoolers do not yet realize that characteristics *associated with* being male or female—activities, toys, occupations, hairstyle, and clothing—do not *determine* a person's sex.

Early in the preschool years, gender typing is well under way. Girls tend to play with girls and are drawn to toys and activities that emphasize nurturance, cooperation, and physical attractiveness.

Genetic Influences on Gender Typing

The sex differences just described appear in many cultures around the world (Munroe & Romney, 2006). Certain ones— male activity level and physical aggression, female emotional sensitivity, and preference for same-sex playmates—are widespread among mammalian species (de Waal, 1993, 2001). According to an evolutionary perspective, the adult life of our male ancestors was largely oriented toward competing for mates, that of our female ancestors toward rearing children. Therefore, males became genetically primed for dominance and females for intimacy, responsiveness, and cooperativeness (Geary, 1999; Maccoby, 2002).

Experiments with animals reveal that prenatally administered androgens increase active play and aggression and suppress caregiving in both male and female mammals (Sato et al., 2004). Eleanor Maccoby (1998) argues that hormones also affect human play styles, leading to rough, noisy movements among boys and calm, gentle actions among girls. Then, as children interact with peers, they choose partners whose interests and behaviors are compatible with their own. Preschool girls increasingly seek out other girls and like to play in pairs because they share a preference for quieter activities involving cooperative roles. Boys come to prefer larger-group play with other boys, who share a desire to run, climb, play-fight, and compete (Fabes, Martin, & Hanish, 2003). By age 6, children spend 11 times as much time with same-sex as with other-sex playmates (Martin & Fabes, 2001).

Even stronger support for the role of biology in human gender typing comes from research on girls exposed prenatally to high levels of androgens, due either to normal variation in hormone levels or to a genetic defect. In both instances, these girls

showed more "masculine" behavior—a preference for trucks and blocks, for active play, and for boys as playmates—even when parents encouraged gender-typical play (Cohen-Bendahan, van de Beek, & Berendbaum, 2005; Pasterski et al., 2005).

And additional evidence for the role of biology in gender typing comes from a case study of a boy who experienced serious sexual-identity and adjustment problems because his biological makeup and sex of rearing were at odds. Turn to the Lifespan Vista box on the following page to find out about David's development.

Environmental Influences on Gender Typing

In a study following almost 14,000 British children from ages 2½ to 8, gender-typed behavior rose steadily over early childhood, with the most gender-typed young preschoolers showing the sharpest increase (Golombok et al., 2008). A wealth of evidence reveals that environmental forces—at home, at school, and in the community—build on genetic influences to promote vigorous gender typing in early childhood.

■ **PARENTS.** Beginning at birth, parents have different expectations of sons than of daughters. Many describe achievement, competition, and control of emotion as important for sons and warmth, "ladylike" behavior, and closely supervised activities as important for daughters (Brody, 1999; Turner & Gervai, 1995).

Parenting practices reflect these beliefs. Parents typically give their sons toys that stress action and competition (cars, tools, footballs) and their daughters toys that emphasize nurturance, cooperation, and physical attractiveness (dolls, tea sets, jewelry) (Leaper, 1994; Leaper & Friedman, 2007). Parents also actively reinforce independence in boys and closeness and dependency in girls. For example, parents react more positively when a son plays with cars and trucks, demands attention, runs and climbs, or tries to take toys from others. When interacting with a daughter, they more often direct play activities, provide help, encourage participation in household tasks, refer to emotions, and express approval and agreement (Clearfield & Nelson, 2006; Fagot & Hagan, 1991; Kuebli, Butler, & Fivush, 1995; Leaper et al., 1995).

Furthermore, parents provide children with indirect cues about gender categories and stereotypes through the language they use. In one study, researchers observed mothers talking about picture books with their 2- to 6-year-olds (Gelman, Taylor, & Nguyen, 2004). Mothers often labeled gender, even when they did not have to do so ("That's a boy." "Is that a she?"). And they frequently expressed *generic utterances*, which referred to many, or nearly all, males or females as alike, ignoring exceptions: "Boys can be sailors." "Most girls don't like trucks." At age 2, mothers introduced these sweeping generalizations nearly three times as often as children. By age 6, children were producing these generics more often than mothers, suggesting that children picked up many of these expressions from

■ A LIFESPAN VISTA: Looking Forward, Looking Back ■

David: A Boy Who Was Reared as a Girl

As a married man and father in his mid-thirties, David Reimer talked freely about his everyday life: his problems at work and the challenges of child rearing. But when asked about his first 15 years, he distanced himself, speaking as if the child of his early life were another person. In essence, she was.

David—named Bruce at birth—underwent the first infant sex reassignment ever reported on a genetically and hormonally normal child. To find out about David's development, researchers interviewed him and studied his medical and psychotherapy records (Colapinto, 2001; Diamond & Sigmundson, 1999).

When Bruce was 8 months old, his penis was accidentally severed during circumcision. Soon afterward, his desperate parents heard about psychologist John Money's success in assigning a sex to children born with ambiguous genitals. They traveled from their home in Canada to Johns Hopkins University in Baltimore, where, under Money's oversight, 22-month-old Bruce had surgery to remove his testicles and sculpt his genitals to look like those of a girl. The operation complete, Bruce's parents named their daughter Brenda.

Brenda's upbringing was tragic. From the outset, she resisted her parents' efforts to steer her in a "feminine" direction. A dominant, rough-and-tumble child, Brenda picked fights with other children and usually won. Brian (Brenda's identical twin brother) recalled that Brenda looked like a girl—until she moved or spoke: "She walked like a guy. Sat with her legs apart. She talked about guy things. . . . She played with my toys: Tinkertoys, dump trucks" (Colapinto, 2001, p. 57).

At school, Brenda's boyish behavior led classmates to taunt and tease her. When she played with girls, she tried organizing large-group, active games, but they weren't interested. Friendless and uncomfortable as a girl, Brenda increasingly displayed behavior problems. During periodic medical follow-ups, she drew pictures of herself as a boy and refused additional surgery to create a vagina.

As adolescence approached, Brenda's parents moved her from school to school and from therapist to therapist in an effort to help her fit in socially and accept a female identity—pressures that increased Brenda's anxiety and conflict with her parents. At puberty, when Brenda's shoulders broadened and her

COURTESY OF DAVID REIMER

Because of a medical accident when he was a baby, David Reimer underwent the first sex reassignment on a genetically and hormonally normal child: He was reared as a girl. David's case shows the overwhelming impact of biology on gender identity. At age 36, as shown here, he was a married man and father. But two years later, the troubled life that sprang from David's childhood ended tragically, in suicide.

body added muscle, her parents insisted that she begin estrogen therapy to feminize her appearance. Soon she grew breasts and added fat around her waist and hips. Repelled by her feminizing shape, Brenda began overeating to hide it. Her classmates reacted to her confused appearance with stepped-up brutality.

At last, Brenda was transferred to a therapist who recognized her despair and encouraged her parents to tell her about her infancy. When Brenda was 14, her father explained the circumcision accident. David recalled reacting with relief. Deciding to return to his biological sex immediately, he named himself David, after the biblical lad who slew a giant and overcame adversity. David soon started injections of the androgen hormone testosterone to masculinize his body, and he underwent surgery to remove his breasts and to construct a penis. Although his adolescence continued to be troubled, in his twenties he fell in love with Jane, a single mother of three children, and married her.

David's case confirms the impact of genetic sex and prenatal hormones on a person's sense of self as male or female. His gender reassignment failed because his male biology overwhelmingly demanded a consistent sexual identity. At the same time, his childhood highlights the importance of experience. David expressed outrage at adult encouragement of dependency in girls—after all, he had experienced it firsthand.

Although David tried to surmount his tragic childhood, the troubled life that sprang from it persisted. When David was in his mid-thirties, his twin brother, Brian, committed suicide. Then, after David had lost his job and had been swindled out of his life savings in a shady investment deal, his wife left him, taking the children. Grief-stricken, David sank into a deep depression. On May 4, 2004, at age 38, he shot himself.

parental speech. And 4- to 6-year-olds frequently made stereotyped generic statements, which their mothers often affirmed (*Child:* "Only boys can drive trucks." *Mother:* "OK.").

Of the two sexes, boys are more gender-typed, and fathers, especially, insist that boys conform to gender roles (Wood, Desmarais, & Gugula, 2002). But parents who hold nonstereotyped values and consciously avoid promoting gender-role learning have children who are less gender-typed (Tenenbaum & Leaper, 2002). And in homes where fathers devote as much or more time to caregiving as mothers, children tend to be less

gender-typed in emotional style—sons more emotionally sensitive, daughters more self-confident (Brody, 1997).

■ **TEACHERS.** Like parents, preschool teachers give girls more encouragement to participate in adult-structured activities. Girls frequently cluster around the teacher, following directions, while boys are attracted to areas of the classroom where teachers are minimally involved (Campbell, Shirley, & Candy, 2004; Powlishta, Serbin, & Moller, 1993). As a result, boys and girls engage in different social behaviors. Compliance

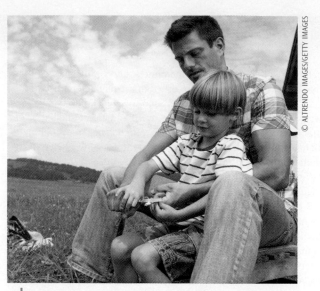

Gender-typed behavior rises steadily over early childhood, due to a mix of genetic and environmental forces. On the environmental side, fathers, especially, are more insistent that boys conform to gender roles. This father shows his son how to cut shavings of wood for kindling a campfire.

and bids for help occur more often in adult-structured contexts; assertiveness, leadership, and creative use of materials in unstructured pursuits.

Teachers also use more disapproval and controlling discipline with boys. When girls misbehave, teachers tend to negotiate, coming up with a joint plan to improve behavior (Erden & Wolfgang, 2004). Teachers seem to expect boys to misbehave more often—a belief based partly on boys' actual behavior and partly on gender stereotypes.

■ **PEERS.** Children's same-sex peer associations make the peer context a potent source of gender-role learning (Martin & Fabes, 2001). By age 3, same-sex peers positively reinforce one another for gender-typed play by praising, imitating, or joining in. In contrast, when preschoolers engage in "cross-gender" activities—for example, when boys play with dolls or girls with cars and trucks—peers criticize. Boys are especially intolerant of cross-gender play in other boys (Fagot, 1984).

Children also develop different styles of social influence in gender-segregated peer groups. To get their way in large-group play, boys often rely on commands, threats, and physical force. Girls' preference for playing in pairs leads to greater concern with a partner's needs, evident in polite requests, persuasion, and acceptance. Girls soon find that these tactics succeed with other girls but not with boys, who ignore their courteous overtures (Leaper, 1994; Leaper, Tenenbaum, & Shaffer, 1999). Boys' unresponsiveness gives girls another reason to stop interacting with them.

As boys and girls separate, *in-group favoritism*—more positive evaluations of members of one's own gender—becomes another factor that sustains the separate social worlds of boys

and girls. As a result, "two distinct subcultures" of knowledge, beliefs, interests, and behaviors form (Maccoby, 2002).

Gender Identity

As adults, each of us has a **gender identity**—an image of oneself as relatively masculine or feminine in characteristics. By middle childhood, researchers can measure gender identity by asking children to rate themselves on personality traits. A child or adult with a "masculine" identity scores high on traditionally masculine items (such as *ambitious, competitive,* and *self-sufficient*) and low on traditionally feminine items (such as *affectionate, cheerful,* and *soft-spoken*). Someone with a "feminine" identity does the reverse. And a substantial minority (especially females) have a gender identity called **androgyny,** scoring high on both masculine and feminine personality characteristics.

"Masculine" and androgynous children and adults have higher self-esteem than "feminine" individuals (Bronstein, 2006; Harter, 2006). Also, androgynous individuals are more adaptable—able to show masculine independence or feminine sensitivity, depending on the situation (Huyck, 1996; Taylor & Hall, 1982). The existence of an androgynous identity demonstrates that children can acquire a mixture of positive qualities traditionally associated with each gender—an orientation that may best help them realize their potential.

■ **EMERGENCE OF GENDER IDENTITY.** How do children develop a gender identity? According to *social learning theory,* behavior comes before self-perceptions. Preschoolers first acquire gender-typed responses through modeling and reinforcement and only later organize these behaviors into gender-linked ideas about themselves. In contrast, *cognitive-developmental theory* maintains that self-perceptions come before behavior. Over the preschool years, children acquire a cognitive appreciation of the permanence of their sex. They develop **gender constancy**—a full understanding of the biologically based permanence of their gender, including the realization that sex remains the same even if clothing, hairstyle, and play activities change. Then children use this knowledge to guide their behavior (Kohlberg, 1966).

Children younger than age 6 who watch an adult dress a doll in "other-gender" clothing typically insist that the doll's sex has also changed (Chauhan, Shastri, & Mohite, 2005; Fagot, 1985). Attainment of gender constancy is strongly related to ability to pass Piagetian conservation and verbal appearance–reality tasks (see page 178 in Chapter 7) (De Lisi & Gallagher, 1991; Trautner, Gervai, & Nemeth, 2003). Indeed, gender constancy tasks can be considered a type of appearance–reality problem, in that children must distinguish what a person looks like from who he or she really is.

Is cognitive-developmental theory correct that gender constancy is responsible for children's gender-typed behavior? Evidence for this assumption is weak. "Gender-appropriate" behavior appears so early in the preschool years that its initial appearance must result from modeling and reinforcement, as social learning theory suggests. Although outcomes are not entirely consistent, some evidence suggests that gender constancy actually contributes to more flexible gender-role attitudes during the school years (Ruble et al., 2007). But overall, the impact of gender constancy on gender typing is not great. As research in the following section reveals, gender-role adoption is more powerfully affected by children's beliefs about how close the connection must be between their own gender and their behavior.

■ **GENDER SCHEMA THEORY.** **Gender schema theory** is an information-processing approach to gender typing that combines social learning and cognitive-developmental features. It explains how environmental pressures and children's cognitions work together to shape gender-role development (Martin & Halverson, 1987; Martin, Ruble, & Szkrybalo, 2002). At an early age, children pick up gender-typed preferences and behaviors from others. At the same time, they organize their experiences into *gender schemas,* or masculine and feminine categories, that they use to interpret their world. As soon as preschoolers can label their own sex, they select gender schemas consistent with it ("Only boys can be doctors" or "Cooking is a girl's job") and apply those categories to themselves. Their self-perceptions then become gender-typed and serve as additional schemas that children use to process information and guide their own behavior.

We have seen that individual differences exist in the extent to which children endorse gender-typed views. Children who acquire rigid gender schemas use them to filter their experiences (Liben & Bigler, 2002). When such children see others behaving in "gender-inconsistent" ways, they often cannot remember the information or distort it to make it "gender-consistent." For example, when shown a picture of a male nurse, they may remember him as a doctor (Liben & Signorella, 1993; Martin & Ruble, 2004). And because gender-schematic preschoolers typically conclude, "What I like, children of my own sex will also like," they often use their own preferences to add to their gender biases! For example, a girl who dislikes oysters may conclude that only boys like oysters even though she has never actually been given information promoting such a stereotype (Liben & Bigler, 2002).

Reducing Gender Stereotyping in Young Children

How can we help young children avoid rigid gender schemas? No easy recipe exists. Biology clearly affects children's gender typing, channeling boys toward active, competitive play and girls toward quieter, more intimate interaction. But most aspects of gender typing are not built into human nature (Ruble, Martin, & Berenbaum, 2006).

Because young children's cognitive limitations lead them to assume that cultural practices determine gender, adults are wise to try to delay preschoolers' exposure to gender-stereotyped messages. Parents and teachers can begin by limiting traditional

gender roles in their own behavior and by providing children with nontraditional alternatives—for example, giving boys and girls both trucks and dolls, avoiding use of language that conveys gender stereotypes, and shielding children from media presentations that do the same.

Once children notice the vast array of gender stereotypes in their society, parents and teachers can point out exceptions. For example, they can arrange for children to see men and women pursuing nontraditional careers and can explain that interests and skills, not sex, should determine a person's occupation. Research shows that such reasoning is highly effective in reducing children's tendency to view the world in a gender-biased fashion. By middle childhood, children who hold flexible beliefs about what boys and girls can do are more likely to notice instances of gender discrimination (Bigler & Liben, 1992; Brown & Bigler, 2004). And, as we will see next, a rational approach to child rearing promotes healthy, adaptable functioning in many other areas as well.

ASK YOURSELF

>> **REVIEW**
Explain how the social environment and young children's cognitive limitations contribute to rigid gender stereotyping in early childhood.

>> **APPLY**
List findings indicating that language and communication—between parents and children, between teachers and children, and between peers—powerfully affect children's gender typing. What recommendations would you make to counteract these influences?

>> **REFLECT**
Would you describe your own gender identity as "masculine," "feminine," or androgynous? What biological and social factors might have influenced your gender identity?

Child Rearing and Emotional and Social Development

In this and previous chapters, we have seen how parents can foster children's competence—by building a parent–child relationship based on affection and cooperation, by serving as models and reinforcers of mature behavior, by using reasoning and inductive discipline, and by guiding and encouraging children's mastery of new skills. Now let's put these practices together into an overall view of effective parenting.

Styles of Child Rearing

Child-rearing styles are combinations of parenting behaviors that occur over a wide range of situations, creating an enduring child-rearing climate. In a landmark series of studies, Diana

■ **TABLE 8.2** ■ *Features of Child-Rearing Styles*

CHILD-REARING STYLE	ACCEPTANCE AND INVOLVEMENT	CONTROL	AUTONOMY GRANTING
Authoritative	Is warm, responsive, attentive, patient, and sensitive to the child's needs	Makes reasonable demands for maturity and consistently enforces and explains them	Permits the child to make decisions in accord with readiness Encourages the child to express thoughts, feelings, and desires When parent and child disagree, engages in joint decision making when possible
Authoritarian	Is cold and rejecting and frequently degrades the child	Makes many demands coercively, using force and punishment Often uses psychological control, withdrawing love and intruding on the child's individuality	Makes decisions for the child Rarely listens to the child's point of view
Permissive	Is warm but overindulgent or inattentive	Makes few or no demands	Permits the child to make many decisions before the child is ready
Uninvolved	Is emotionally detached and withdrawn	Makes few or no demands	Is indifferent to the child's decision making and point of view

Baumrind gathered information on child rearing by watching parents interact with their preschoolers (Baumrind, 1971). Her findings, and those of others who have extended her work, reveal three features that consistently differentiate an effective style from less effective ones: (1) acceptance and involvement, (2) control, and (3) autonomy granting (Gray & Steinberg, 1999; Hart, Newell, & Olsen, 2003). Table 8.2 shows how child-rearing styles differ in these features.

■ **AUTHORITATIVE CHILD REARING.** The **authoritative child-rearing style**—the most successful approach—involves high acceptance and involvement, adaptive control techniques, and appropriate autonomy granting. Authoritative parents are warm, attentive, and sensitive to their child's needs. They establish an enjoyable, emotionally fulfilling parent–child relationship that draws the child into close connection. At the same time, authoritative parents exercise firm, reasonable control. They insist on mature behavior and give reasons for their expectations. Finally, authoritative parents engage in gradual, appropriate autonomy granting, allowing the child to make decisions in areas where he is ready to do so (Kuczynski & Lollis, 2002; Russell, Mize, & Bissaker, 2004).

Throughout childhood and adolescence, authoritative parenting is linked to many aspects of competence—an upbeat mood, self-control, task persistence, cooperativeness, high self-esteem, social and moral maturity, and favorable school performance (Amato & Fowler, 2002; Gonzalez & Wolters, 2006; Mackey, Arnold, & Pratt, 2001; Milevsky et al., 2007; Steinberg, Darling, & Fletcher, 1995).

■ **AUTHORITARIAN CHILD REARING.** The **authoritarian child-rearing style** is low in acceptance and involvement, high in coercive control, and low in autonomy granting. Authoritarian

parents appear cold and rejecting. To exert control, they yell, command, criticize, and threaten, demanding unquestioning obedience. If the child resists, authoritarian parents resort to force and punishment.

Children of authoritarian parents are anxious, unhappy, and low in self-esteem and self-reliance and tend to react with hostility when frustrated. Boys, especially, show high rates of anger and defiance. Although girls also engage in acting-out behavior, they are more likely to be dependent and overwhelmed by challenging tasks (Hart, Newell, & Olsen, 2003; Thompson, Hollis, & Richards, 2003).

In addition to unwarranted direct control, authoritarian parents engage in a more subtle type called **psychological control**—behaviors that intrude on and manipulate children's verbal expression, individuality, and attachments to parents. In an attempt to decide virtually everything for the child, these parents frequently interrupt or put down the child's ideas, decisions, and choice of friends. When they are dissatisfied, they withdraw love, making their affection contingent on the child's compliance. They also hold excessively high expectations that do not fit the child's developing capacities. Children and adolescents subjected to psychological control exhibit adjustment problems involving both anxious, withdrawn and defiant, aggressive behaviors (Barber & Harmon, 2002; Silk et al., 2003).

■ **PERMISSIVE CHILD REARING.** The **permissive child-rearing style** is warm and accepting but uninvolved. Permissive parents are either overindulging or inattentive and, thus, engage in little control. They allow children to make many of their own decisions at an age when they are not yet capable of doing so. Their children can go to bed whenever they wish and can watch as much television as they want. They do not have to learn good manners or do any household chores. Although some permissive parents truly believe in this approach, many others simply lack confidence in their ability to influence their child's behavior.

Children of permissive parents are impulsive, disobedient, and rebellious. Compared with children whose parents exert more control, they are also overly demanding and dependent on adults, and they show less persistence on tasks, poorer school achievement, and more antisocial behavior (Barber & Olsen, 1997; Baumrind, 1971; Steinberg, Blatt-Eisengart, & Cauffman, 2006).

■ **UNINVOLVED CHILD REARING.** The **uninvolved child-rearing style** combines low acceptance and involvement with little control and general indifference to issues of autonomy. Often these parents are emotionally detached and depressed, so overwhelmed by life stress that they have little time and energy for children. At its extreme, uninvolved parenting is a form of child maltreatment called *neglect*. Especially when it begins early, it disrupts virtually all aspects of development (see Chapter 6, page 144). Even with less extreme parental disengagement, children and adolescents display many problems—poor emotional self-regulation, school achievement difficulties, and antisocial behavior (Aunola, Stattin, & Nurmi, 2000; Kurdek & Fine, 1994).

What Makes Authoritative Child Rearing Effective?

Longitudinal research indicates that authoritative child rearing promotes maturity and adjustment in children of diverse temperaments (Hart, Newell, & Olson, 2003; Olson et al., 2000; Rubin, Burgess, & Coplan, 2002). It seems to create a positive emotional context for parental influence in the following ways:

■ Warm, involved parents who are secure in the standards they hold for their children provide models of caring concern as well as confident, self-controlled behavior.

■ Children are far more likely to comply with and internalize control that appears fair and reasonable, not arbitrary.

■ Authoritative parents appropriately make demands and grant autonomy. By letting children know that they are competent individuals who can do things successfully for themselves, these parents foster favorable self-esteem and cognitive and social maturity.

■ Supportive aspects of the authoritative style help protect children from the negative effects of family stress and poverty (Beyers et al., 2003).

Over time, the relationship between parenting and children's attributes becomes increasingly bidirectional (Kuczynski, 2003). When parents intervene patiently but firmly, they promote favorable adjustment, setting the stage for a positive parent–child relationship.

Cultural Variations

Although authoritative child rearing is broadly advantageous, ethnic groups often have distinct parenting beliefs and practices that reflect cultural values. Let's take some examples.

Compared with Western parents, Chinese parents are more directive in teaching and scheduling their children's time, as a way of fostering self-control and high achievement. Chinese parents may appear less warm than Western parents because they withhold praise, which they believe results in self-satisfied, poorly motivated children (Chen et al., 2001). But Chinese parents report expressing affection and using induction and other reasoning-oriented discipline as much as North American parents do (Jose et al., 2000; Shwalb et al., 2004). When Chinese parents engage in harsh, excessive control, however, their children display the same negative outcomes seen in Western children: anxiety, depression, and aggression (Nelson et al., 2005, 2006a, 2006b; Wang, Pomerantz, & Chen, 2007).

In Hispanic families, Asian Pacific Island families, and Caribbean families of African and East Indian origins, firm insistence on respect for parental authority is paired with high parental warmth—a combination suited to promoting competence and family loyalty (Harrison et al., 1994; Roopnarine & Evans, 2007). Hispanic fathers typically spend much time with their children and are warm and sensitive (Cabrera & Garcia-Coll, 2004; Jambunathan, Burts, & Pierce, 2000). In Caribbean families that have immigrated to the United States, fathers' authoritativeness—but not mothers'—predicted preschoolers'

This father encourages his daughter to help with recycling. By letting children know they are competent individuals, authoritative parents foster high self-esteem and social maturity.

literacy and math skills, probably because Caribbean fathers take a larger role in guiding their children's academic progress (Roopnarine et al., 2006).

In low-SES African-American families, parents tend to expect immediate obedience, regarding strictness as fostering self-control and a watchful attitude in risky surroundings. Consistent with these beliefs, African-American parents who use more controlling strategies tend to have more cognitively and socially competent children (Brody & Flor, 1998). Recall, also, that a history of physical punishment is associated with a reduction in antisocial behavior among African-American youths but with an increase among Caucasian Americans. Most African-American parents who use "no-nonsense" discipline use physical punishment sparingly and combine it with warmth and reasoning.

These cultural variations remind us that child-rearing styles must be viewed in their larger context. As we have seen, many factors contribute to good parenting: personal characteristics of the child and parent, SES, access to extended family and community supports, cultural values and practices, and public policies. As we turn to the topic of child maltreatment, our discussion will underscore, once again, that effective child rearing is sustained not just by the desire of mothers and fathers to be good parents. Almost all want to be. Unfortunately, when vital supports for parenting break down, children—as well as parents—can suffer terribly.

Child Maltreatment

Child maltreatment is as old as human history, but only recently has the problem been widely acknowledged and research aimed at understanding it. Perhaps public concern has increased because child maltreatment is especially common in large industrialized nations. In the most recently reported year, 905,000

U.S. children (12 out of every 1,000) were identified as victims (U.S. Department of Health and Human Services, 2008d). Most cases go unreported, so the true figures are much higher.

Child maltreatment takes the following forms:

- *Physical abuse:* Assaults, such as kicking, biting, shaking, punching, or stabbing, that inflict physical injury
- *Sexual abuse:* Fondling, intercourse, exhibitionism, commercial exploitation through prostitution or production of pornography, and other forms of exploitation
- *Neglect:* Failure to meet a child's basic needs for food, clothing, medical attention, or supervision
- *Emotional abuse:* Acts that could cause serious mental or behavioral disorders, including social isolation, repeated unreasonable demands, ridicule, humiliation, intimidation, or terrorizing

Parents commit more than 80 percent of abusive incidents. Other relatives account for about 7 percent. The remainder are perpetrated by parents' unmarried partners, school officials, camp counselors, and other adults. Maternal and paternal rates of physical and emotional abuse are fairly similar, but mothers commit more neglect, fathers more sexual abuse. Infants and young preschoolers are at greatest risk for neglect, preschool and school-age children for physical, emotional, and sexual abuse (Trocomé & Wolfe, 2002; U.S. Department of Health and Human Services, 2008d). Because most sexual abuse victims are identified in middle childhood, we will pay special attention to this form of maltreatment in Chapter 10.

■ **ORIGINS OF CHILD MALTREATMENT.** For help in understanding child maltreatment, researchers turned to ecological systems theory (see Chapters 1 and 2). They discovered that many interacting variables—at the family, community, and

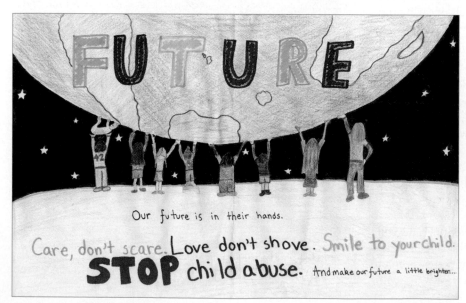

Each year, fourth to sixth graders across Los Angeles County enter a poster contest to celebrate Child Abuse Prevention Month. This 2008 winner appeals to parents to treat children with warmth and caring. (Lisa Valicente and Madeline Zauss, 6th Grade, Jefferson Elementary School, Redondo Beach, CA. Courtesy ICAN Associates, Los Angeles County Inter-Agency Council on Child Abuse & Neglect, *ican4kids.org*.)

cultural levels—contribute. The more risks present, the greater the likelihood of abuse or neglect.

The Family. Within the family, children whose characteristics make them more challenging to rear are at increased risk of abuse. These include premature or very sick babies and children who are temperamentally difficult, are inattentive and overactive, or have other developmental problems (Sidebotham et al., 2003). But whether such children actually are maltreated depends on parents' characteristics.

Although child maltreatment is more common among disturbed parents, no single "abusive personality type" exists. Maltreating parents tend to have a history of abuse as a child, to be inept at handling discipline confrontations, and to believe in harsh physical discipline (Wekerle & Wolfe, 2003). They also suffer from biased thinking about their child. For example, they often attribute their baby's crying or their child's misdeeds to a stubborn or bad disposition, evaluate child transgressions as worse than they are, and feel powerless in parenting— perspectives that lead them to move quickly toward physical force (Bugental & Happaney, 2004; Crouch et al., 2008).

Most parents have enough self-control not to respond with abuse to their child's misbehavior or developmental problems. Other factors combine with these conditions to prompt an extreme response. Abusive parents react to stressful situations with high emotional arousal. And low income, low education (less than a high school diploma), unemployment, young maternal age, alcohol and drug use, marital conflict, overcrowded living conditions, frequent moves, and extreme household disorganization are common in abusive homes (Wekerle & Wolfe, 2003; Wekerle et al., 2007). These conditions increase the chances that parents will be too overwhelmed to meet basic child-rearing responsibilities or will vent their frustrations by lashing out at their children.

The Community. The majority of abusive and neglectful parents are isolated from both formal and informal social supports. Because of their life histories, many have learned to mistrust and avoid others and are poorly skilled at establishing and maintaining positive relationships. Also, maltreating parents are more likely to live in unstable, rundown neighborhoods that provide few links between family and community, such as parks, child-care centers, preschool programs, recreation centers, and religious institutions (Coulton et al., 2007; Zielinski & Bradshaw, 2006). They lack "lifelines" to others during stressful times.

The Larger Culture. Cultural values, laws, and customs profoundly affect the chances that child maltreatment will occur when parents feel overburdened. Although the United States has laws to protect children from maltreatment, widespread support exists for use of physical force with children (refer back to page 206). Many countries—including Austria, Croatia, Cyprus, Denmark, Finland, Germany, Israel, Italy, Latvia, Norway, and Sweden— have outlawed physical punishment, a measure that dampens both physical discipline and

abuse (Bugental & Grusec, 2006). Furthermore, every industrialized nation except the United States and Canada now prohibits corporal punishment in schools (Center for Effective Discipline, 2005). The U.S. Supreme Court has twice upheld the right of school officials to use corporal punishment. Fortunately, some U.S. states and Canadian provinces have passed laws that ban it.

■ **CONSEQUENCES OF CHILD MALTREATMENT.** The family circumstances of maltreated children impair the development of emotional self-regulation, empathy and sympathy, self-concept, social skills, and academic motivation. Over time, these youngsters show serious learning and adjustment problems, including academic failure, severe depression, aggressive behavior, peer difficulties, substance abuse, and delinquency, including violent crime (Cicchetti & Toth, 2006; Shonk & Cicchetti, 2001; Wolfe et al., 2001).

Furthermore, the trauma of repeated abuse is associated with central nervous system damage, including abnormal EEG brain-wave activity, fMRI-detected reduced size and impaired functioning of the cerebral cortex and corpus callosum, and atypical production of the stress hormone cortisol—initially too high but, after months of abuse, often too low. Over time, the massive trauma of persistent abuse seems to blunt children's normal physiological response to stress (Cicchetti, 2007; Teicher et al., 2004; Watts-English et al., 2006). These effects increase the chances that cognitive and emotional problems will endure.

■ **PREVENTING CHILD MALTREATMENT.** Because child maltreatment is embedded in families, communities, and society as a whole, efforts to prevent it must be directed at each of these levels. Suggested approaches include teaching high-risk parents effective child-rearing strategies and developing broad social programs aimed at improving economic conditions for low-SES families.

Providing social supports to families eases parental stress, sharply reducing child maltreatment. A trusting relationship with another person is the most important factor in preventing mothers with childhood histories of abuse from repeating the cycle with their own children (Egeland, Jacobvitz, & Sroufe, 1988). Parents Anonymous, a U.S. organization with affiliate programs around the world, helps child-abusing parents learn constructive parenting practices, largely through social supports. Its local chapters offer self-help group meetings, daily phone calls, and regular home visits to relieve social isolation and teach parenting skills.

Early intervention aimed at strengthening both child and parent competencies can reduce child maltreatment substantially. Healthy Families America, a program that began in Hawaii and has spread to 440 sites across the United States and Canada, identifies at-risk families during pregnancy or at birth. Each receives three years of home visitation, in which a trained worker helps parents manage crises, encourages effective child rearing, and puts parents in touch with community services

(PCA America, 2009). In an evaluation of its effectiveness, Healthy Families home visitation alone reduced only neglect, not abuse (Duggan et al., 2004). But adding a *cognitive component* dramatically increased its impact. When home visitors helped parents change negative appraisals of their children—by countering inaccurate interpretations (for example, that the baby is behaving with malicious intent) and by working on solving child-rearing problems—physical punishment and abuse dropped sharply after one year of intervention (Bugental et al., 2002).

Child maltreatment is a sad note on which to end our discussion of a period of childhood that is so full of excitement, awakening, and discovery. But there is reason to be optimistic. Great strides have been made over the past several decades in understanding and preventing child maltreatment.

ASK YOURSELF

>> **REVIEW**

Summarize findings on ethnic variations in child-rearing styles. Is the concept of authoritative parenting useful for understanding effective parenting across cultures? Explain.

>> **APPLY**

Chandra heard a news report about ten severely neglected children living in squalor in an inner-city tenement. She wondered, "Why would parents mistreat their children?" How would you answer Chandra?

>> **REFLECT**

How would you classify your parents' child-rearing styles? What factors might have influenced their approach to parenting?

Summary

Erikson's Theory: Initiative versus Guilt

What personality changes take place during Erikson's stage of initiative versus guilt?

>> Erikson's image of **initiative versus guilt** captures the emotional and social changes of early childhood. A healthy sense of initiative depends on exploring the social world through play, forming a conscience, and experiencing supportive child rearing.

Self-Understanding

Describe preschoolers' self-concepts and self-esteem.

>> As preschoolers think more intently about themselves, they construct a **self-concept** that consists largely of observable characteristics and typical emotions and attitudes. Their increasing self-awareness underlies struggles over objects as well as first efforts to cooperate.

>> During early childhood, high **self-esteem** contributes to a mastery-oriented approach to the environment. But adult criticism can undermine a young child's self-esteem and enthusiasm for learning.

Emotional Development

Cite changes in understanding and expression of emotion during early childhood, along with factors that influence those changes.

>> Preschoolers have an impressive understanding of the causes, consequences, and behavioral signs of basic emotions, supported by conversations about feelings with parents and make-believe play, especially with siblings. By age 3 to 4, children are aware of various strategies for emotional self-regulation. Temperament and parental modeling influence preschoolers' capacity to handle negative emotion.

>> As their self-concepts develop, preschoolers experience self-conscious emotions more often. Parental messages affect the intensity of these emotions and the situations in which they occur. Empathy also becomes more common. Temperament and parenting affect the extent to which empathy leads to **sympathy** and **prosocial,** or **altruistic, behavior.**

Peer Relations

Describe peer sociability and friendship in early childhood, along with parental influences on early peer relations.

>> During early childhood, peer interaction increases, as children move from **nonsocial activity** to **parallel play,** then to **associative** and **cooperative play.** But even as associative and cooperative play increase, both solitary and parallel play remain common.

>> Preschoolers view friendship in concrete, activity-based terms. Parents affect peer sociability both directly, through attempts to influence their child's peer relations, and indirectly, through their child-rearing practices.

© MICHAEL NEWMAN/PHOTOEDIT

Foundations of Morality

What are the central features of psychoanalytic, social learning, and cognitive-developmental approaches to moral development?

>> Psychoanalytic and social learning approaches to morality focus on how children acquire ready-made standards held by adults. Contrary to the claims of Freud's theory, discipline based on fear of punishment and loss of parental love does not foster conscience development. Instead, **induction** is far more effective.

>> Social learning theory regards reinforcement and, especially, adult modeling as the basis for moral action. Alternatives such as **time out** and withdrawal of privileges can help parents avoid the undesirable side effects of harsh punishment. Punishment is more effective when parents are consistent, have a warm relationship with the child, and offer explanations.

>> The cognitive-developmental perspective views children as active thinkers about social rules. Although preschoolers tend to reason rigidly about moral matters, by age 4 they can consider people's intentions in making moral judgments. Preschoolers also distinguish **moral imperatives** from **social conventions** and **matters of personal choice.**

Describe the development of aggression in early childhood, including family and television as major influences.

>> Aggression first appears by the second year. During early childhood, **proactive aggression** declines, while **reactive aggression** increases. Proactive and reactive aggression come in at least three forms: **physical aggression, verbal aggression,** and **relational aggression.** Preschoolers gradually replace physical with verbal aggression. By the second year, boys are more physically aggressive than girls.

>> Ineffective discipline and a conflict-ridden family atmosphere promote and sustain aggression in children. Media violence, both on TV and in computer games, also triggers childhood aggression. Teaching parents effective child-rearing practices, providing children with social problem-solving training, reducing family hostility, and shielding children from violent media can reduce aggressive behavior.

Gender Typing

Discuss genetic and environmental influences on preschoolers' gender-stereotyped beliefs and behavior.

>> **Gender typing** is well under way in the preschool years. Prenatal male sex hormone (androgen) levels contribute to sex differences in play styles and, in turn, to preference for same-sex peers. But parents, teachers, and peers also encourage many gender-typed responses.

Describe and evaluate the accuracy of major theories that explain the emergence of gender identity.

>> Although most people have a traditional **gender identity,** some exhibit **androgyny,** combining both masculine and feminine characteristics. Masculine and androgynous identities are linked to higher self-esteem.

>> According to social learning theory, preschoolers first acquire gender-typed responses through modeling and reinforcement and then organize them into gender-linked ideas about themselves. Cognitive-developmental theory suggests that **gender constancy** must precede gender-typed behavior, though evidence for this assumption is weak.

>> **Gender schema theory** combines features of social learning and cognitive-developmental perspectives. As children acquire gender-stereotyped preferences and behaviors, they form masculine and feminine categories that they apply to themselves and use to interpret their world.

Child Rearing and Emotional and Social Development

Describe the impact of child-rearing styles on children's development, and note cultural variations in child rearing.

>> Three features distinguish **child-rearing styles:** (1) acceptance and involvement, (2) control, and 3) autonomy granting. In contrast to the **authoritarian, permissive,** and **uninvolved** styles, the **authoritative style** promotes cognitive, emotional, and social competence. **Psychological control** is associated with authoritarian parenting and contributes to adjustment problems.

>> Certain ethnic groups, including Chinese, Hispanic, Asian Pacific Island, Caribbean, and African-American, combine parental warmth with high levels of control. But when control becomes harsh and excessive, it impairs academic and social competence.

Discuss the multiple origins of child maltreatment, its consequences for development, and effective prevention.

>> Maltreating parents use ineffective discipline, hold a negatively biased view of their child, and feel powerless in parenting. Unmanageable parental stress and social isolation greatly increase the chances of abuse and neglect. Societal support for use of physical force promotes child abuse.

>> The trauma of repeated abuse is associated with central nervous system damage and serious learning and adjustment problems. Successful prevention requires efforts at the family, community, and societal levels.

Important Terms and Concepts

androgyny (p. 214)
associative play (p. 202)
authoritarian child-rearing style (p. 216)
authoritative child-rearing style (p. 216)
child-rearing styles (p. 215)
cooperative play (p. 202)
gender constancy (p. 214)
gender identity (p. 214)
gender schema theory (p. 215)
gender typing (p. 211)

induction (p. 205)
initiative versus guilt (p. 198)
matters of personal choice (p. 208)
moral imperatives (p. 208)
nonsocial activity (p. 202)
parallel play (p. 202)
permissive child-rearing style (p. 216)
physical aggression (p. 209)
proactive aggression (p. 208)
prosocial, or altruistic, behavior (p. 201)

psychological control (p. 216)
reactive aggression (p. 209)
relational aggression (p. 209)
self-concept (p. 199)
self-esteem (p. 199)
social conventions (p. 208)
sympathy (p. 201)
time out (p. 206)
uninvolved child-rearing style (p. 217)
verbal aggression (p. 209)

Milestones
Development in Early Childhood

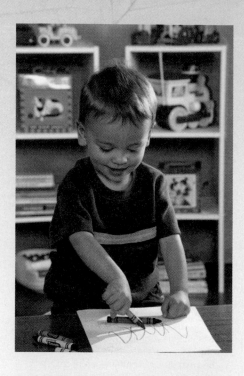

2 years

PHYSICAL

- Throughout early childhood, height and weight increase more slowly than in toddlerhood. (165)
- Balance improves; walks more rhythmically; hurried walk changes to run. (171)
- Jumps, hops, throws, and catches with rigid upper body. (171)
- Puts on and removes simple items of clothing. (171–172)
- Uses spoon effectively. (171–172)
- First drawings are gestural scribbles. (172)

COGNITIVE

- Make-believe becomes less dependent on realistic objects, less self-centered, and more complex (173); sociodramatic play increases. (174)
- Understands the symbolic function of photos and pictures in books. (174–175)
- Takes the perspective of others in simplified, familiar situations and in face-to-face communication. (176–177)

- Recognition memory is well-developed. (183)
- Shows awareness of the distinction between inner mental and outer physical events. (184)
- Begins to count. (187)

LANGUAGE

- Vocabulary increases rapidly. (191)
- Uses a coalition of cues—perceptual and, increasingly, social and linguistic—to figure out word meanings. (192)
- Speaks in simple sentences that follow basic word order of native language. (192)
- Adds grammatical markers. (193)
- Displays effective conversational skills. (193)

EMOTIONAL/SOCIAL

- Understands causes, consequences, and behavioral signs of basic emotions. (200)
- Begins to develop self-concept and self-esteem. (199–200)
- Shows early signs of developing moral sense—verbal evaluations of own and others' actions and distress at harmful behaviors. (204)
- May display proactive (instrumental) aggression. (208–209)
- Gender-stereotyped beliefs and behavior increase. (211)

3–4 years

PHYSICAL

- Running, jumping, hopping, throwing, and catching become better coordinated. (171)

- Galloping and one-foot skipping appear. (171)
- Pedals and steers tricycle. (171)
- Uses scissors. (171)
- Uses fork effectively. (172)
- Draws first picture of a person, using tadpole image. (172)

COGNITIVE

- Understands the symbolic function of drawings and of models of real-world spaces. (174–175)
- Grasps conservation, reasons about transformations, reverses thinking, and understands cause-and-effect relationships in familiar contexts. (177)
- Distinguishes appearance from reality. (178)
- Sorts familiar objects into hierarchically organized categories. (177–178)
- Uses private speech to guide behavior during challenging tasks. (179–180)
- Sustained attention and planning improve. (182–183)
- Uses scripts to recall familiar experiences. (183)
- Understands that both beliefs and desires determine behavior. (184)
- Knows meaning of numbers up to ten, counts correctly, grasps principle of cardinality. (187)

Note: Numbers in parentheses indicate the page or pages on which each milestone is discussed.

LANGUAGE

- Aware of some meaningful features of written language. (186–187)
- Coins new words based on known words; extends language meanings through metaphor. (192)
- Masters increasingly complex grammatical structures. (193)
- Occasionally overextends grammatical rules to exceptions. (193)
- Adjusts speech to fit the age, sex, and social status of listeners. (193)

EMOTIONAL/SOCIAL

- Describes self in terms of observable characteristics and typical emotions and attitudes. (199)
- Has several self-esteems, such as learning things in school, making friends, and getting along with parents. (200)
- Emotional self-regulation improves. (200)
- Experiences self-conscious emotions more often. (200–201)
- Relies more on language to express empathy. (201)
- Engages in associative and cooperative play with peers, in addition to parallel play. (201–202)

- Forms first friendships, based on pleasurable play and sharing of toys. (203)
- Distinguishes truthfulness from lying. (208)
- Distinguishes moral imperatives from social conventions and matters of personal choice. (208)
- Proactive aggression declines, while reactive aggression (verbal and relational) increases. (209)
- Preference for same-sex playmates strengthens. (212)

5–6 years

PHYSICAL

- Starts to lose primary teeth. (165)
- Increases running speed, gallops more smoothly, and engages in true skipping. (171)
- Displays mature throwing and catching patterns. (171)

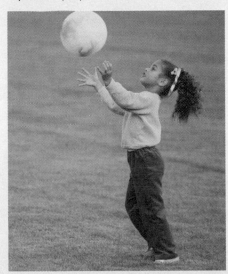

- Uses knife to cut soft foods. (172)
- Ties shoes. (172)
- Draws more complex pictures. (172)
- Copies some numbers and simple words. (172)

COGNITIVE

- Magical beliefs decline. (177, 179)
- Ability to distinguish appearance from reality improves. (178, 179)
- Attention and planning continue to improve. (182–183)
- Recognition, recall, scripted memory, and autobiographical memory improve. (183–184)

- Understanding of false belief strengthens. (184)

LANGUAGE

- Understands that letters and sounds are linked in systematic ways. (185–186)
- Uses invented spellings. (185–186)
- By age 6, vocabulary reaches about 10,000 words. (191)
- Uses most grammatical constructions competently. (193)

EMOTIONAL/SOCIAL

- Emotional understanding (ability to interpret, predict, and influence others' emotional reactions) improves. (200)
- Empathic responding increases. (201)
- Has acquired many morally relevant rules and behaviors. (204–205)
- Gender-stereotyped beliefs and behavior and preference for same-sex playmates continue to strengthen. (211–212)
- Understands gender constancy. (214)

CHAPTER 9

Physical and Cognitive Development in Middle Childhood

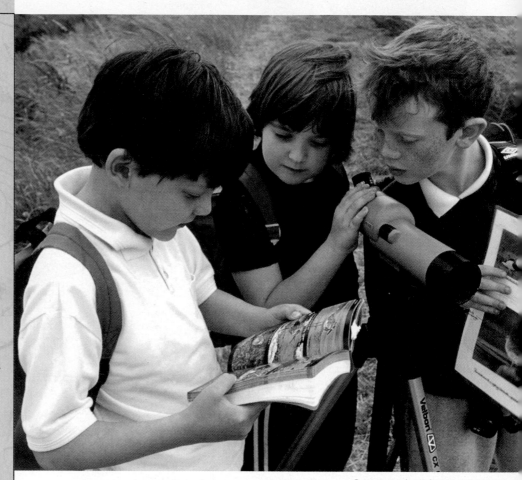

© IAN SHAW/NTPL/THE IMAGE WORKS

On a bird-watching field trip, fourth-grade classmates collaborate to identify an unfamiliar species. An improved capacity to remember, reason, and reflect on one's own thinking makes middle childhood a time of dramatic advances in academic learning and problem solving.

"I'm on my way, Mom!" hollered 10-year-old Joey as he slung his book bag over his shoulder, dashed out the door, jumped on his bike, and headed down the street for school. Joey's 8-year-old sister Lizzie followed, pedaling furiously until she caught up with Joey.

"They're branching out," Rena, the children's mother and one of my colleagues at the university, told me over lunch that day. Homework, household chores, soccer teams, music lessons, scouting, friends at school and in the neighborhood, and Joey's new paper route were all part of the children's routine. "It seems as if the basics are all there. Being a parent is still very challenging, but it's more a matter of refinements—helping them become independent, competent, and productive."

© DESIGNPICS INC./INDEX STOCK IMAGERY/PHOTOLIBRARY

Joey and Lizzie have entered middle childhood—the years from 6 to 11. Around the world, children of this age are assigned new responsibilities. For children in industrialized nations, middle childhood is often called the "school years" because its onset is marked by the start of formal schooling. In village and tribal cultures, the school may be a field or a jungle. But universally, children in this period are guided by mature members of society toward real-world tasks that increasingly resemble those they will perform as adults.

By age 6, the brain has reached 90 percent of its adult weight, and the body continues to grow slowly. In this way, nature gives school-age children the mental powers to master challenging tasks as well as added time to acquire the knowledge and skills essential for life in a complex social world. We begin by reviewing typical growth trends, gains in motor skills, and health concerns. Then we return to Piaget's theory and the information-processing approach for an overview of cognitive changes during the school years. Next, we examine the genetic and environmental roots of IQ scores and the further blossoming of language. Finally, we turn to the importance of schools in children's learning and development.

Physical Development

Body Growth

Physical growth during the school years continues at the slow, regular pace of early childhood. At age 6, the average North American child weighs about 45 pounds and is 3½ feet tall. Over the next few years, children add about 2 to 3 inches in height and 5 pounds in weight each year (see Figure 9.1). Between ages 6 and 8, girls are slightly shorter and lighter than boys. By age 9, this trend reverses as girls approach the dramatic adolescent growth spurt, which occurs two years earlier in girls than in boys.

Because the lower portion of the body is growing fastest, Joey and Lizzie appeared longer-legged than they had in early childhood. Girls continue to have slightly more body fat and boys more muscle. After age 8, girls begin accumulating fat at a faster rate, and they will add even more during adolescence (Siervogel et al., 2000).

During middle childhood, the bones of the body lengthen and broaden. But ligaments are not yet firmly attached to bones; this, combined with increasing muscle strength, gives children the unusual flexibility needed to perform cartwheels and handstands. As their bodies become stronger, many children experience a greater desire for physical exercise. Nighttime "growing pains"—stiffness and aches in the legs—are common as muscles adapt to an enlarging skeleton (Evans & Scutter, 2004).

Between ages 6 and 12, all 20 primary teeth are lost and replaced by permanent ones, with girls losing their teeth slightly earlier than boys. For a while, the permanent teeth seem much too large. Gradually, growth of facial bones, especially the jaw and chin, causes the child's face to lengthen and mouth to widen, accommodating the newly erupting teeth.

Health Issues

Children from economically advantaged homes, like Joey and Lizzie, are at their healthiest in middle childhood, full of energy and play. The cumulative effects of good nutrition, combined with rapid development of the body's immune system, offer greater protection against disease. At the same time, growth in lung size permits more air to be exchanged with each breath, so children are better able to exercise vigorously without tiring.

Poverty continues to be a powerful predictor of ill health during the school years. Because economically disadvantaged U.S. families often lack health insurance (see Chapter 2), many children do not have regular access to a doctor. A substantial number also lack such basic necessities as regular meals.

Nutrition

School-age children need a well-balanced, plentiful diet to provide energy for learning and increased physical activity. With their increasing focus on play, friendships, and new activities, many children spend little time at the table, and the percentage who eat dinner with their families drops sharply between ages 9 and 14. Yet eating an evening meal with parents leads to a diet higher in fruits and vegetables and lower in fried foods and soft drinks (Fiese & Schwartz, 2008; Neumark-Sztainer et al., 2003).

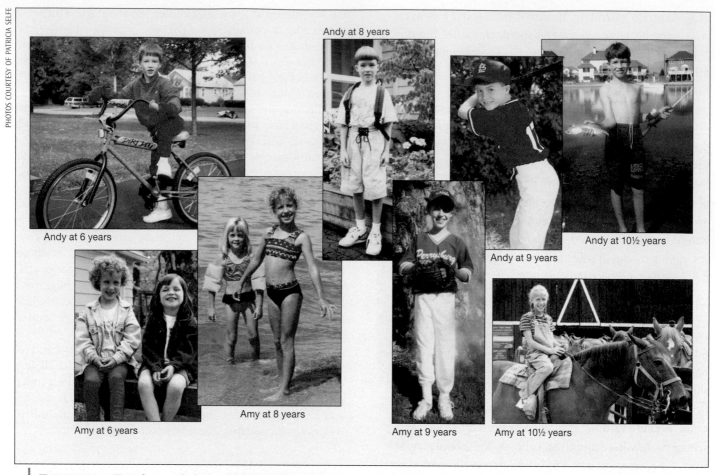

Andy at 8 years

Andy at 6 years

Andy at 9 years

Andy at 10½ years

Amy at 8 years

Amy at 6 years

Amy at 9 years

Amy at 10½ years

■ FIGURE 9.1 ■ Body growth during middle childhood. School-age children continue the slow, regular pattern of growth they showed in early childhood. But around age 9, girls begin to grow at a faster rate than boys. At age 10½, Amy was taller, heavier, and more mature looking than Andy.

As we saw in earlier chapters, many poverty-stricken children in developing countries and in North America suffer from serious and prolonged malnutrition. Unfortunately, malnutrition that persists from infancy or early childhood into the school years usually leads to permanent physical and mental damage (Grantham-McGregor, Walker, & Chang, 2000; Liu et al., 2003). Government-sponsored supplementary food programs from the early years through adolescence can prevent these effects. In studies carried out in Egypt, Kenya, and Mexico, quality of food (protein, vitamin, and mineral content) strongly predicted favorable cognitive development in middle childhood (Sigman, 1995; Watkins & Pollitt, 1998).

Obesity

Mona, a very heavy child in Lizzie's class, often watched from the sidelines during recess. When she did join in games, she was slow and clumsy. Most afternoons, she walked home from school alone while the other children gathered in groups, talking, laughing, and chasing. At home, Mona sought comfort in high-calorie snacks.

Mona suffers from **obesity,** a greater-than-20-percent increase over healthy weight, based on *body mass index (BMI)*—

a ratio of weight to height associated with body fat. (A BMI above the 85th percentile for a child's age and sex is considered overweight, a BMI above the 95th percentile obese.) During the past several decades, a rise in overweight and obesity has occurred in many Western nations. Today, 32 percent of U.S. children and adolescents are overweight, and 11 percent are obese (Ogden, Carroll, & Flegal, 2008; Shields, 2005).

Obesity rates are also increasing rapidly in developing countries, as urbanization shifts the population toward sedentary lifestyles and diets high in meats and refined foods (World Press Review, 2004; Wrotniak et al., 2004). In China, for example, 15 percent of children and adolescents are overweight, and 3 percent are obese—a fourfold increase over the past two decades, with boys affected more than girls (Wu, 2006). In addition to lifestyle changes, a prevailing belief in Chinese culture that excess body fat signifies prosperity and health—carried over from a half-century ago, when famine caused millions of deaths—has contributed to this upsurge. High valuing of sons may induce Chinese parents to offer boys especially generous portions of energy-dense foods.

■ CAUSES OF OBESITY.   Overweight children tend to have overweight parents, and identical twins are more likely to share the disorder than fraternal twins. But heredity accounts only for a *tendency* to gain weight (Salbe et al., 2002). The importance of environment is seen in the consistent relationship of low SES to obesity in industrialized nations, especially among ethnic minorities, including African-American, Hispanic, and Native-American children and adults (Anand et al., 2001; Ogden et al., 2006). Factors responsible include lack of knowledge about healthy diet; a tendency to buy high-fat, low-cost foods; and family stress, which can prompt overeating. Recall also that children who were malnourished in their early years are at increased risk for becoming overweight later (see page 101 in Chapter 4).

Parental feeding practices also play a role. Some parents anxiously overfeed, interpreting almost all their child's discomforts as a desire for food. Others are overly controlling, restricting when, what, and how much their child eats and constantly worrying about weight gain (Moens, Braet, & Soetens, 2007). Both types of parents fail to help children learn to regulate their own energy intake. Also, parents of overweight children often use high-fat, sugary foods to reinforce other behaviors—a practice that leads children to attach greater value to treats (Sherry et al., 2004). Because of these experiences, obese children develop maladaptive eating habits. They are more responsive than normal-weight individuals to external stimuli associated with food—taste, sight, smell, time of day, and food-related words— and less responsive to internal hunger cues (Jansen et al., 2003; Temple et al., 2007).

Sleep habits may also play a role. A study of 3- to 12-year-olds revealed that children who got less nightly sleep were more likely to be overweight five years later (Snell, Adam, & Duncan, 2007). Reduced sleep may increase time available for eating, leave children too fatigued for physical activity, or disrupt the brain's regulation of hunger and metabolism.

Overweight children also tend to be physically inactive, which is both cause and consequence of excessive weight gain. Research reveals that the rise in childhood obesity is due in part to the many hours U.S. children spend watching television. In a study that tracked children's TV viewing from ages 4 to 11, the more TV children watched, the more body fat they added (Proctor et al., 2003). Watching TV reduces time spent in physical exercise, and TV ads encourage children to eat fattening, unhealthy snacks. Children permitted to have a TV in their bedroom—a practice linked to especially high TV viewing— are at even further risk for overweight (Adachi-Mejia et al., 2007).

Finally, the broader food environment affects the incidence of obesity. Compared with a half-century ago, communities today are designed for automobile use, with fewer sidewalks and other walkways—a change that has contributed to reduced physical activity (Krishnamoorthy, Hart, & Jelalian, 2006). And over the past three decades, the number of families who frequently eat high-calorie meals outside the home has risen dramatically. Eating in restaurants or at relatives', neighbors', or friends' homes, as opposed to at home, substantially increases children's overall food consumption, including high-calorie drinks and snacks, and risk of weight gain (Ayala et al., 2008; French, Story, & Jeffrey, 2001).

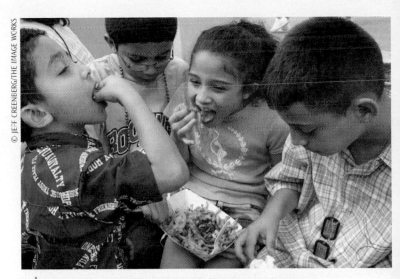

These children consume a snack of cheesy fries with joyous abandon. High-calorie, fatty foods are prominent in the family diets provided by overweight parents, leaving their children at high risk for excessive weight gain.

■ **CONSEQUENCES OF OBESITY.**   More than 80 percent of affected children become overweight adults, often with lifelong health problems. High blood pressure, high cholesterol levels, respiratory abnormalities, and insulin resistance begin to appear in the early school years—symptoms that are powerful predictors of heart disease, type 2 diabetes, gallbladder disease, sleep and digestive disorders, many forms of cancer, and early death (Krishnamoorthy, Hart, & Jelalian, 2006; World Cancer Research Fund, 2007). Furthermore, obesity has caused a dramatic rise in cases of diabetes in children, sometimes leading to early, severe complications, including stroke, kidney failure, and circulatory problems that heighten the risk of blindness and leg amputation (Hannon, Rao, & Arslanian, 2005).

Emotional and social problems are also severe. In Western societies, both children and adults stereotype obese youngsters as lazy, sloppy, ugly, stupid, self-doubting, and deceitful (Kilpatrick & Sanders, 1978; Penny & Haddock, 2007; Tiggemann & Anesbury, 2000). By middle childhood, they are socially isolated and display more achievement and behavior problems than normal-weight peers. Persistent obesity from childhood into adolescence predicts serious disorders, including defiance, aggression, and severe depression (Mustillo et al., 2003; Schwimmer, Burwinkle, & Varni, 2003; Young-Hyman et al., 2006). These psychological consequences combine with continuing discrimination to result in reduced life chances in adult close relationships and employment.

■ **TREATING OBESITY.**   Because childhood obesity is often a family disorder, the most effective interventions are family-based. In Mona's case, the school nurse suggested that Mona and her obese mother enter a weight-loss program together. In one study, both parent and child revised eating patterns, exercised daily, and reinforced each other with praise and special activities and times together. The more weight parents lost, the more their children lost (Wrotniak et al., 2004). Follow-ups after 5 and 10 years showed that children maintained their weight loss more effectively than adults, a finding that underscores the importance of early intervention (Epstein, Roemmich, & Raynor, 2001). But diet and lifestyle interventions work best when parents' and children's weight problems are not severe (Nemet et al., 2005).

Illnesses

Children experience a somewhat higher rate of illness during the first two years of elementary school than later because of exposure to sick children and an immune system that is still developing. About 15 to 20 percent of American children have chronic diseases and conditions (including physical disabilities). By far the most common—accounting for about one-third of childhood chronic illness and the most frequent cause of school absence and childhood hospitalization—is *asthma,* in which the bronchial tubes (passages that connect the throat and lungs) are highly sensitive (Bonilla et al., 2005). In response to a variety of stimuli, such as cold weather, infection, exercise, allergies, and emotional stress, they fill with mucus and contract, leading to coughing, wheezing, and serious breathing difficulties.

During the past three decades, the number of children with asthma has more than doubled. Although heredity contributes, environmental factors seem necessary to spark the illness. Boys, African-American children, and children who were born underweight, whose parents smoke, or who live in poverty are at greatest risk (Federico & Liu, 2003; Pearlman et al., 2006). For African-American and poverty-stricken youngsters, pollution in inner-city areas (which triggers allergic reactions), stressful home lives, and lack of access to good health care are implicated. Childhood obesity is also related to asthma, perhaps due to high levels of blood-circulating inflammatory substances associated with body fat (Saha, Riner, & Liu, 2005).

About 2 percent of American youngsters have more severe chronic illnesses, such as sickle cell anemia, diabetes, arthritis, cancer, and AIDS. Painful medical treatments, physical discomfort, and changes in appearance often disrupt the sick child's daily life, making it difficult to concentrate in school and separating the child from peers. As the illness worsens, family stress increases (LeBlanc, Goldsmith, & Patel, 2003). For these reasons, chronically ill children are at risk for academic, emotional, and social difficulties.

A strong link between good family functioning and child well-being exists for chronically ill children, just as it does for physically healthy children (Drotar et al., 2006). Interventions that foster positive family relationships help parent and child cope with the disease and improve children's adjustment. These include health education, counseling, social support, and disease-specific summer camps, which teach children self-help skills and give parents time off from the demands of caring for a chronically ill youngster.

Motor Development and Play

TAKE A MOMENT... Visit a park on a pleasant weekend afternoon, and watch several preschool and school-age children at play. You will see that gains in body size and muscle strength support improved motor coordination in middle childhood. And greater cognitive and social maturity enables older children to use their new motor skills in more complex ways.

Gross-Motor Development

During the school years, running, jumping, hopping, and ball skills become more refined. Third to sixth graders burst into sprints as they race across the playground, jump quickly over rotating ropes, kick and dribble soccer balls, and balance adeptly as they walk heel-to-toe across narrow ledges. These diverse skills reflect gains in four basic motor capacities:

- *Flexibility.* Compared with preschoolers, school-age children are physically more pliable and elastic, a difference evident as they swing bats, kick balls, jump over hurdles, and execute tumbling routines.

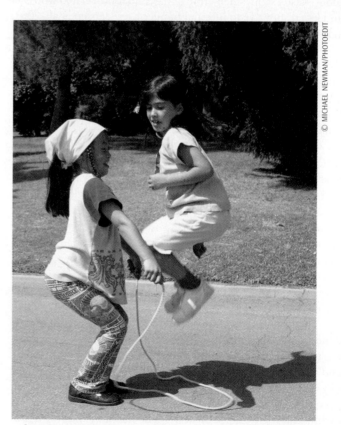

A fancy twist of the rope following each revolution complicates this game of jump rope. During the school years, improved physical flexibility, balance, agility, and force combine with more efficient information processing to promote gains in many gross-motor skills.

© MICHAEL NEWMAN/PHOTOEDIT

- *Balance.* Improved balance supports many athletic skills, including running, skipping, throwing, kicking, and the rapid changes of direction required in team sports.

- *Agility.* Quicker and more accurate movements are evident in the fancy footwork of dance and cheerleading and in the forward, backward, and sideways motions used to dodge opponents in tag and soccer.

- *Force.* Older youngsters can throw and kick a ball harder and propel themselves farther off the ground when running and jumping (Haywood & Getchell, 2005).

Along with body growth, more efficient information processing contributes greatly to improved motor performance. During middle childhood, the capacity to react only to relevant information increases. And steady gains in reaction time occur, with 11-year-olds responding twice as quickly as 5-year-olds (Band et al., 2000; Kail, 2003). Because 6 and 7-year-olds are seldom successful at batting a thrown ball, T-ball is more appropriate than baseball at this age. Likewise, handball, four-square, and kickball should precede instruction in tennis, basketball, and football.

Fine-Motor Development

Fine-motor development also improves over the school years. By age 6, most children can print the alphabet, their first and last names, and the numbers from 1 to 10 with reasonable clarity. Their writing is large, however, because they make strokes with the entire arm rather than just the wrist and fingers. Children usually master uppercase letters first because their horizontal and vertical motions are easier to control than the small curves of the lowercase alphabet. Legibility of writing gradually increases as children produce more accurate letters with uniform height and spacing. These improvements prepare children for mastering cursive writing by third grade.

By the end of the preschool years, children can accurately copy many two-dimensional shapes, and they integrate these into their drawings. Some depth cues have also begun to appear, such as making distant objects smaller than near ones (Braine et al., 1993). Around 9 to 10 years, the third dimension is clearly evident through overlapping objects, diagonal placement, and converging lines. Furthermore, as Figure 9.2 shows, school-age children not only depict objects in considerable detail but also relate them to one another as part of an organized whole (Case, 1998).

Sex Differences

Sex differences in motor skills extend into middle childhood and, in some instances, become more pronounced. Girls have an edge in fine-motor skills of handwriting and drawing and in gross-motor capacities that depend on balance and agility, such as hopping and skipping. But boys outperform girls on all other gross-motor skills and, in throwing and kicking, the gender gap is large (Cratty, 1986; Haywood & Getchell, 2005).

■ **FIGURE 9.2** ■ **Organization, detail, and depth in school-age children's drawings.** Integration of depth cues increases dramatically over the school years, as shown in this drawing by a 10-year-old artist from Singapore. Here, depth is indicated by overlapping objects, diagonal placement, and converging lines, as well as by making distant objects smaller than near ones.

School-age boys' genetic advantage in muscle mass is not large enough to account for their gross-motor superiority. Rather, social experiences play a larger role. Research confirms that parents hold higher expectations for boys' athletic performance, and children readily absorb these messages. From first through twelfth grades, girls are less positive than boys about the value of sports and their own sports ability—differences explained in part by parental beliefs (Fredricks & Eccles, 2002).

Educating parents about the minimal differences between school-age boys' and girls' physical capacities and sensitizing them to unfair biases against promotion of girls' athletic ability may help increase girls' self-confidence and participation in athletics. And greater emphasis on skill training for girls, along with increased attention to their athletic achievements, is also likely to help. As a positive sign, compared with a generation ago, many more girls now participate in individual and team sports such as gymnastics and soccer (National Council of Youth Sports, 2008).

Games with Rules

The physical activities of school-age children reflect an important advance in their play: Games with rules become common. Children around the world engage in an enormous variety of informally organized games, such as tag, jacks, hopscotch, and

With their coach's encouragement, these young softball players are likely to evaluate their own sports ability positively and to continue playing, thereby narrowing the gender gap in athletic participation.

variants of popular sports. They have also invented hundreds of other games, including red rover, statues, leapfrog, kick the can, and prisoner's base (Kirchner, 2000).

Gains in perspective taking—in particular, the ability to understand the roles of several players in a game—permit this transition to rule-oriented games. These play experiences, in turn, contribute greatly to emotional and social development. Child-invented games usually rely on simple physical skills and a sizable element of luck. As a result, they rarely become contests of individual ability. Instead, they permit children to try out different styles of cooperating, competing, winning, and losing with little personal risk. Also, in their efforts to organize a game, children discover why rules are necessary and which ones work well—experiences that foster more mature concepts of fairness and justice.

Partly because of parents' concerns about safety and because of the attractions of TV, video games, and the Internet, today's children devote less time to informal outdoor play. At the same time, organized sports, such as Little League baseball and soccer and hockey leagues, have expanded tremendously, filling many hours that children used to devote to spontaneous play. About half of U.S. children—66 percent of boys and 37 percent of girls—participate at some time between ages 5 and 18 (National Council of Youth Sports, 2008).

For most children, playing on a community athletic team is associated with increased self-esteem and social competence (Daniels & Leaper, 2006; Fletcher, Nickerson, & Wright, 2003). And children who view themselves as good at sports are more likely to continue playing on teams in adolescence, which predicts greater participation in sports and other physical fitness activities in early adulthood (Marsh et al., 2007; McHale et al., 2005).

In some cases, though, youth sports overemphasize competition and adult control. Coaches and parents who criticize

and react angrily to defeat can prompt intense anxiety in some children, setting the stage for emotional difficulties and early athletic dropout (Tofler, Knapp, & Drell, 1998; Wall & Côté, 2007). By permitting children to select an appropriate sport on the basis of their interests, encouraging them to contribute to rules and strategies, and emphasizing effort, skill gains, and teamwork rather than winning, adults can ensure that athletic leagues provide positive learning experiences.

Shadows of Our Evolutionary Past

TAKE A MOMENT... While watching children in your neighborhood park, notice how they sometimes wrestle, roll, hit, and run after one another, alternating roles while smiling and laughing. This friendly chasing and play-fighting is called **rough-and-tumble play.** It emerges in the preschool years and peaks in middle childhood, and children in many cultures engage in it with peers whom they like especially well (Pellegrini, 2004).

Children's rough-and-tumble play resembles the social behavior of many other young mammals. It is more common among boys, probably because prenatal exposure to androgens (male sex hormones) predisposes boys toward active play (see Chapter 8). In our evolutionary past, rough-and-tumble play may have been important for developing fighting skill. Children seem to use play-fighting as a safe context to assess the strength of peers so they can refrain from challenging agemates with whom they are not well-matched physically (Pellegrini & Smith, 1998; Roseth et al., 2007).

As children reach puberty, individual differences in strength become apparent, and rough-and-tumble play declines. When it does occur, its meaning changes: Adolescent boys' rough-and-tumble is linked to aggression (Pellegrini, 2003). Unlike children, teenage rough-and-tumble players "cheat," hurting their opponent. In explanation, boys often say that they are retaliating, apparently to reestablish dominance. Thus, a play behavior that limits aggression in childhood becomes a context for hostility in adolescence.

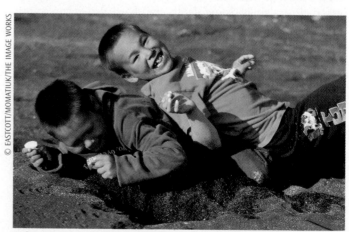

On an Alaskan beach, these 6- and 7-year-old brothers engage in rough-and-tumble play, which can be distinguished from aggression by its good-natured quality.

SOCIAL ISSUES

School Recess—A Time to Play, a Time to Learn

When 7-year-old Whitney's family moved to a new city, she left a school with three daily recess periods for one with just a single 15-minute break per day, which her second-grade teacher cancelled if any child misbehaved. Whitney, who had previously enjoyed school, complained daily of headaches and an upset stomach. Her mother, Jill, thought, "My child is stressing out because she can't move all day!" After Jill and other parents successfully appealed to the school board to add a second recess period, Whitney's symptoms vanished (Rauber, 2006).

In recent years, recess—with its rich opportunities for child-organized play and peer interaction—has diminished or disappeared in many U.S. elementary schools (Pellegrini, 2005; Pellegrini & Holmes, 2006). Under the assumption that extra time for academics will translate into achievement gains, 7 percent of U.S. schools no longer provide recess to students as young as second grade. And over half of schools that do have

recess now schedule it just once a day (U.S. Department of Education, 2009).

Yet rather than subtracting from classroom learning, recess periods boost it! Research dating back more than a century confirms that distributing cognitively demanding tasks over a longer time by introducing regular breaks enhances attention and performance at all ages. Such breaks are particularly important for children. In a series of studies, elementary school students were more attentive in the classroom after recess than before it—an effect that was greater for second than fourth graders (Pellegrini, Huberty, & Jones, 1995).

In other research, kindergartners' and first graders' engagement in peer conversation and games during recess predicted gains in academic achievement, even after other factors that might explain the relationship (such as previous achievement) were controlled (Pellegrini, 1992; Pellegrini et al., 2002). Recall from Chapter 8 that children's social maturity contributes substantially to academic competence. Recess is one of the few remaining contexts devoted to child-organized games that provide practice in vital social skills—cooperation, leadership, followership,

Recess offers rich opportunities for child-organized play and games that promote academic achievement and social competence.

and inhibition of aggression—under adult supervision rather than adult direction. As children transfer these skills to the classroom, they may participate in discussions, collaborate, follow rules, and enjoy academic pursuits more—factors that enhance motivation and achievement.

Physical Education

Physical activity supports many aspects of children's development—health, sense of self-worth, and the cognitive and social skills necessary for getting along with others. Yet to devote more time to academic instruction, U.S. elementary schools have cut back on recess, despite its contribution to all domains of development (see the Social Issues box above). Similarly, only 15 percent of U.S. elementary and middle schools provide students with physical education at least three days a week, a figure that drops to 3 percent in high school (Lee et al., 2007). Not surprisingly, only 42 percent of school-age boys and 11 percent of girls are active enough for good health—that is, engage in at least moderate-intensity exercise for one hour or more per day (Metcalf et al., 2008).

Many experts believe that schools should not only offer more frequent physical education classes but also change the content of these programs. Training in competitive sports, often a high priority, is unlikely to reach the least physically fit youngsters. Instead, programs should emphasize enjoyable, informal games and individual exercise—pursuits most likely to endure.

Physically fit children tend to become active adults who reap many benefits (Dennison et al., 1998; Tammelin et al., 2003). These include greater physical strength, resistance to many illnesses, enhanced psychological well-being, and a longer life.

ASK YOURSELF

>> **REVIEW**
Select either obesity or asthma, and explain how both genetic and environmental factors contribute to this common health problem of middle childhood.

>> **APPLY**
Nine-year-old Allison thinks she isn't good at sports, and she doesn't like physical education class. Suggest some strategies her teacher can use to improve her pleasure and involvement in physical activity.

>> **REFLECT**
Did you participate in organized sports as a child? If so, what kind of climate for learning did coaches and parents create? What impact do you think your experiences had on your development?

Cognitive Development

"Finally!" 6-year-old Lizzie exclaimed the day she entered first grade. "Now I get to go to real school, just like Joey!" Lizzie walked into her classroom confidently, pencils, crayons, and writing pad in hand, ready for a more disciplined approach to learning than she had experienced in early childhood.

Lizzie was entering a whole new world of challenging mental activities. In a single morning, she and her classmates wrote in journals, met in reading groups, worked on addition and subtraction, and sorted leaves gathered for a science project. As Lizzie and Joey moved through the elementary school grades, they tackled increasingly complex tasks and became more accomplished at reading, writing, math skills, and general knowledge of the world. To understand the cognitive attainments of middle childhood, we turn to research inspired by Piaget's theory and by the information-processing perspective. And we look at expanding definitions of intelligence that help us appreciate individual differences.

Piaget's Theory: The Concrete Operational Stage

When Lizzie visited my child development class as a 4-year-old, Piaget's conservation problems confused her (see Chapter 7, page 176). But when she returned at age 8, she found these tasks easy. When water was poured from a tall, narrow container into a short, wide one, she exclaimed, "Of course it's still the same amount! The water in the short glass is lower, but it's also wider. Pour it back," she instructed the college student who was interviewing her. "You'll see."

Concrete Operational Thought

Lizzie has entered Piaget's **concrete operational stage,** which extends from about 7 to 11 years and marks a major turning point in cognitive development. Thought is far more logical, flexible, and organized than it was earlier.

■ **CONSERVATION.** The ability to pass *conservation tasks* provides clear evidence of *operations*—mental actions that obey logical rules. Notice how Lizzie is capable of *decentration,* focusing on several aspects of a problem and relating them, rather than centering on just one. Lizzie also demonstrates **reversibility,** the capacity to think through a series of steps and then mentally reverse direction, returning to the starting point. Recall from Chapter 7 that reversibility is part of every logical operation. It is solidly achieved in middle childhood.

■ **CLASSIFICATION.** Between ages 7 and 10, children pass Piaget's *class inclusion problem* (see page 177). This indicates that they are more aware of classification hierarchies and can

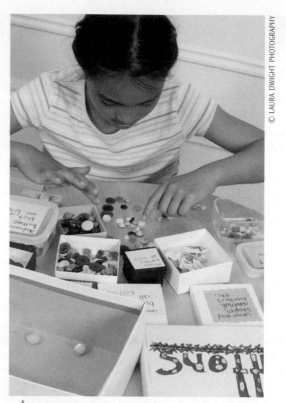

An improved ability to categorize underlies children's interest in collecting objects during middle childhood. Here, an 8-year-old sorts and organizes buttons in her extensive collection.

focus on relations between a general category and two specific categories at the same time—that is, on three relations at once (Hodges & French, 1988; Ni, 1998). Collections—stamps, coins, baseball cards, rocks, and bottle caps—become common in middle childhood. At age 10, Joey spent hours sorting and re-sorting his baseball cards, grouping them first by league and team, then by playing position and batting average. He could separate the players into a variety of classes and subclasses and easily rearrange them.

■ **SERIATION.** The ability to order items along a quantitative dimension, such as length or weight, is called **seriation.** To test for it, Piaget asked children to arrange sticks of different lengths from shortest to longest. Older preschoolers can put the sticks in a row, but they do so haphazardly, making many errors. In contrast, 6- to 7-year-olds create the series efficiently, moving in an orderly sequence from the smallest stick, to the next largest, and so on.

The concrete operational child can also seriate mentally, an ability called **transitive inference.** In a well-known transitive inference problem, Piaget showed children pairings of sticks of different colors. From observing that Stick A is longer than Stick B and Stick B is longer than Stick C, children must infer that A is longer than C. Like Piaget's class inclusion task, transitive inference requires children to integrate three relations at once—in this instance, A–B, B–C, and A–C. When researchers take steps to ensure that children remember the premises (A–B and B–C), 7-year-olds can grasp transitive inference (Andrews & Halford, 1998; Wright, 2006).

■ **SPATIAL REASONING.** Piaget found that school-age children's understanding of space is more accurate than that of preschoolers. Let's consider children's **cognitive maps**—their mental representations of familiar large-scale spaces, such as their neighborhood or school. Drawing a map of a large-scale space requires considerable perspective-taking skill. Because the entire space cannot be seen at once, children must infer its overall layout by relating its separate parts.

Preschoolers and young school-age children include *landmarks* on the maps they draw, but their arrangement is not always accurate. They do better when asked to place stickers showing the location of desks and people on a map of their classroom. But if the map is rotated to a position other than the orientation of the classroom, they have difficulty (Liben & Downs, 1993).

Around age 8 to 10, maps become better organized, showing landmarks along an *organized route of travel*. At the same time, children become able to give clear, well-organized instructions for getting from one place to another by using a "mental walk" strategy—imagining another person's movements along a route (Gauvain & Rogoff, 1989). At the end of middle childhood, children form an *overall view of a large-scale space*. And they readily draw and read maps, even when the orientation of the map and the space it represents do not match (Liben, 1999). Ten- to 12-year olds also grasp the notion of *scale*—the proportional relation between a space and its representation on a map (Liben, 2006).

Limitations of Concrete Operational Thought

Concrete operational thinking suffers from one important limitation: Children think in an organized, logical fashion only when dealing with concrete information they can perceive directly. Their mental operations work poorly with abstract ideas—ones not apparent in the real world. Consider children's solutions to transitive inference problems. When shown pairs of sticks of unequal length, Lizzie easily engaged in transitive inference. But she had difficulty with a hypothetical version of this task: "Susan is taller than Sally, and Sally is taller than Mary. Who is the tallest?" Not until age 11 or 12 can children solve this problem.

That logical thought is at first tied to immediate situations helps account for a special feature of concrete operational reasoning: School-age children master concrete operational tasks step by step, not all at once. For example, they usually grasp conservation of number first, followed by conservation of length, liquid, and mass, and then weight. This *continuum of acquisition* (or gradual mastery) of logical concepts is another indication of the limitations of concrete operational thinking (Fischer & Bidell, 1991). Rather than coming up with general

logical principles that they apply to all relevant situations, school-age children seem to work out the logic of each problem separately.

Follow-Up Research on Concrete Operational Thought

According to Piaget, brain development combined with experience in a rich and varied external world should lead children everywhere to reach the concrete operational stage. Yet recent evidence indicates that specific cultural and school practices have much to do with mastery of Piagetian tasks (Rogoff, 2003; Rogoff & Chavajay, 1995). And information-processing research helps explain the gradual mastery of logical concepts in middle childhood.

■ **THE IMPACT OF CULTURE AND SCHOOLING.** In tribal and village societies, conservation is often delayed. For example, among the Hausa of Nigeria, who live in small agricultural settlements and rarely send their children to school, even the most basic conservation tasks—number, length, and liquid—are not understood until age 11 or later (Fahrmeier, 1978). This suggests that taking part in relevant everyday activities helps children master conservation and other Piagetian problems.

The very experience of going to school seems to promote mastery of Piagetian tasks. When children of the same age are tested, those who have been in school longer do better on transitive inference problems (Artman & Cahan, 1993). Opportunities to seriate objects, to learn about order relations, and to remember the parts of complex problems are probably responsible. Yet certain informal nonschool experiences can

This Zinacanteco Indian girl of southern Mexico learns the centuries-old practice of backstrap weaving, which requires complex mental transformations. Although North American children perform better on Piaget's tasks, Zinacanteco children are far more adept at figuring out how to transform warp strung on a loom into woven cloth.

also foster operational thought. Around age 7 to 8, Zinacanteco Indian girls of southern Mexico, who learn to weave elaborately designed fabrics as an alternative to schooling, engage in mental transformations to figure out how a warp strung on a loom will turn out as woven cloth—reasoning expected at the concrete operational stage. American children of the same age, who do much better than Zinacanteco children on Piagetian tasks, have great difficulty with these weaving problems (Maynard & Greenfield, 2003).

On the basis of such findings, some investigators have concluded that the forms of logic required by Piagetian tasks do not emerge spontaneously but, rather, are heavily influenced by training, context, and cultural conditions. Does this view remind you of Vygotsky's sociocultural theory, discussed in earlier chapters?

■ **AN INFORMATION-PROCESSING VIEW OF CONCRETE OPERATIONAL THOUGHT.** The gradual mastery of logical concepts in middle childhood raises a familiar question about Piaget's theory: Is an abrupt stagewise transition to logical thought the best way to describe cognitive development in middle childhood?

Some *neo-Piagetian theorists* argue that the development of operational thinking can best be understood in terms of gains in information-processing speed rather than a sudden shift to a new stage. For example, Robbie Case (1996, 1998) proposed that, with practice, cognitive schemes demand less attention and become more automatic. This frees up space in *working memory* (see page 124) so children can focus on combining old schemes and generating new ones. For instance, the child who sees water poured from one container to another recognizes that the height of the liquid changes. As this understanding becomes routine, the child notices that the width of the water changes as well. Soon children coordinate these observations, and they conserve liquid. Then, as this logical idea becomes well-practiced, the child transfers it to more demanding situations.

Once the schemes of a Piagetian stage are sufficiently automatic, enough working memory is available to integrate them into an improved representation. As a result, children acquire *central conceptual structures*—networks of concepts and relations that permit them to think more effectively about a wide range of situations (Case, 1996, 1998). The central conceptual structures that emerge from integrating concrete operational schemes are broadly applicable principles that result in increasingly complex, systematic reasoning, which we will discuss in Chapter 11 in the context of formal operational thought.

Case and his colleagues—along with other information-processing researchers—have examined children's performance on a wide variety of tasks, including solving arithmetic problems, understanding stories, drawing pictures, and interpreting social situations. In each task, preschoolers typically focus on only one dimension. In understanding stories, for example, they grasp only a single story line. In drawing pictures, they

depict objects separately. By the early school years, children coordinate two dimensions—two story lines in a single plot and drawings that show both the features of objects and their relationships. Around 9 to 11 years, children integrate multiple dimensions (Case, 1998; Halford & Andrews, 2006). Children tell coherent stories with a main plot and several subplots. And their drawings follow a set of rules for representing perspective and, therefore, include several points of reference, such as near, midway, and far.

Case's theory helps explain why many understandings appear in specific situations at different times rather than being mastered all at once. First, different forms of the same logical insight, such as the various conservation tasks, vary in their processing demands, with those acquired later requiring more space in working memory. Second, children's experiences vary widely. A child who often listens to and tells stories but rarely draws pictures displays more advanced thinking in storytelling. Compared with Piaget's, Case's theory better accounts for unevenness in cognitive development.

Evaluation of the Concrete Operational Stage

Piaget was correct that school-age children approach many problems in organized, rational ways not possible in early childhood. But disagreement continues over whether this difference occurs because of *continuous* improvement in logical skills or *discontinuous* restructuring of children's thinking (as Piaget's stage idea assumes). Many researchers think that both types of change may be involved (Carey, 1999; Case, 1998; Demetriou et al., 2002; Fischer & Bidell, 2006; Halford & Andrews, 2006). During the school years, children apply logical schemes to many more tasks. In the process, their thought seems to undergo qualitative change—toward a comprehensive grasp of the underlying principles of logical thought.

ASK YOURSELF

》 **REVIEW**
Children's performance on conservation tasks illustrates a continuum of acquisition of logical concepts. Review the preceding sections, and list additional examples of gradual development of logical reasoning.

》 **APPLY**
Nine-year-old Adrienne spends many hours helping her father build furniture in his woodworking shop. How might this experience facilitate Adrienne's performance on Piagetian seriation problems?

》 **REFLECT**
Which aspects of Piaget's description of the concrete operational child do you accept? Which do you doubt? Explain, citing research evidence.

Information Processing

In contrast to Piaget's focus on overall cognitive change, the information-processing perspective examines separate aspects of thinking. Attention and memory, which underlie every act of cognition, are central concerns in middle childhood, just as they were during infancy and the preschool years. Advances in metacognition and opportunities for self-regulation aid development. Also, increased understanding of how school-age children process information is being applied to their academic learning—in particular, to reading and mathematics.

Researchers believe that brain development contributes to the following basic changes in information processing that facilitate diverse aspects of thinking:

■ *Increases in information-processing speed and capacity.* Time needed to process information on a wide variety of cognitive tasks declines rapidly between ages 6 and 12 (Kail & Park, 1992, 1994). This suggests a biologically based gain in speed of thinking, possibly due to myelination and synaptic pruning in the brain (Kail, 2003). Some researchers believe this greater efficiency contributes to more complex, effective thinking because a faster thinker can hold on to and operate on more information in working memory (Halford & Andrews, 2006; Luna et al., 2004). Indeed, *digit span,* which assesses the basic capacity of working memory (see page 183), improves from about five digits at age 7 to seven digits at age 12 (Kail, 2003).

■ *Gains in inhibition.* As indicated in earlier chapters, inhibition—the ability to control internal and external distracting stimuli—improves from infancy on. But additional strides occur in middle childhood as the frontal lobes of the cerebral cortex develop further (Luna et al., 2004; Nelson, Thomas, & de Haan, 2006). Individuals skilled at inhibition can prevent their minds from straying to irrelevant thoughts, an ability that supports many information-processing skills by preserving space in working memory for the task at hand (Dempster & Corkill, 1999; Klenberg, Korkman, & Lahti-Nuuttila, 2001).

Besides brain development, strategy use contributes to more effective information processing. As we will see, school-age children think far more strategically than preschoolers.

Attention

In middle childhood, attention becomes more selective, adaptable, and planful. First, children become better at deliberately attending to just those aspects of a situation that are relevant to their goals. When researchers introduce irrelevant stimuli into a task and see how well children attend to its central elements, performance improves sharply between ages 6 and 10 (Goldberg, Maurer, & Lewis, 2001; Gomez-Perez & Ostrosky-Solis, 2006; Tabibi & Pfeffer, 2007).

Second, older children flexibly adapt their attention to task requirements. When asked to sort cards with pictures that vary in both color and shape, children age 5 and older can switch their basis of sorting from color to shape; younger children typically persist in sorting in just one way (Brooks et al., 2003; Zelazo, Frye, & Rapus, 1996).

Finally, planning improves greatly in middle childhood (Gauvain, 2004; Scholnick, 1995). School-age children scan detailed pictures and written materials for similarities and differences more thoroughly than preschoolers. And on tasks with many parts, they make decisions about what to do first and what to do next in an orderly fashion.

The attentional strategies just considered are crucial for success in school. Unfortunately, some children have great difficulty paying attention. See the Biology and Environment box on page 236 for a discussion of the serious learning and behavior problems of children with attention-deficit hyperactivity disorder.

Memory Strategies

As attention improves, so do *memory strategies,* deliberate mental activities we use to store and retain information. When Lizzie had a list of things to learn—for example, the state capitals of the United States—she immediately used **rehearsal**—repeating the information to herself, a memory strategy first appears in the early school years. Soon after, a second strategy becomes common: **organization**—grouping related items together (for example, all state capitals in the same part of the country), an approach that improves recall dramatically (Schneider, 2002).

Perfecting memory strategies requires time and effort. Eight-year-old Lizzie rehearsed in a piecemeal fashion. After being given the word *cat* in a list of items, she said, "Cat, cat, cat." But 10-year-old Joey used a more effective approach: He combined previous words with each new item, saying, "Desk, man, yard, cat, cat" (Kunzinger, 1985). Joey also organized more skillfully, grouping items into fewer categories. And he used organization in a wide range of memory tasks, whereas Lizzie used it only when categorical relations among items were obvious (Bjorklund et al., 1994).

Furthermore, Joey often combined several strategies—for example, organizing items, then stating the category names, and finally rehearsing. The more strategies children apply simultaneously and consistently, the better they remember (DeMarie et al., 2004). Younger school-age children often try out various memory strategies, but they use them less systematically and with less success than older children. Still, the tendency to experiment allows younger children to discover which strategies work best and how to combine them effectively. Indeed, children experiment with strategies when faced with many cognitive challenges—an approach that enables them to gradually "home in" on the most effective techniques (Siegler, 1996, 2007).

▪ BIOLOGY AND ENVIRONMENT ▪

Children with Attention-Deficit Hyperactivity Disorder

While the other fifth graders worked quietly at their desks, Calvin squirmed, looked out the window, and fiddled with his shoelaces. "Hey Joey," he yelled across the room, "wanna play ball after school?" But the other children weren't eager to play with Calvin, who was physically awkward and failed to follow the rules of the game. He had trouble taking turns at bat. In the outfield, he looked elsewhere when the ball came his way. Calvin's desk was a chaotic mess. He often lost pencils, books, and other school materials and forgot to do his assignments.

Symptoms of ADHD

Calvin is one of 3 to 6 percent of school-age children with **attention-deficit hyperactivity disorder (ADHD),** which involves inattention, impulsivity, and excessive motor activity resulting in academic and social problems (American Psychiatric Association, 1994; Barkley, 2006). Boys are diagnosed about four times as often as girls. However, many girls with ADHD seem to be overlooked, either because their symptoms are less flagrant or because of a gender bias: A disruptive boy is more likely to be referred for treatment (Abikoff et al., 2002; Biederman et al., 2005).

Children with ADHD cannot stay focused on a task requiring mental effort for more than a few minutes. They often act impulsively, lashing out with hostility when frustrated. Many, though not all, are *hyperactive*, exhausting parents and teachers and irritating other children with their excessive motor activity. For a child to be diagnosed with ADHD, these symptoms must have appeared before age 7 as a persistent problem.

Because of their difficulty concentrating, children with ADHD score 7 to 15 points lower than other children on intelligence tests (Barkley, 2002a). Researchers agree that deficient executive processing (see page 124 in Chapter 5) underlies ADHD symptoms. According to one view, children with ADHD are impaired in capacity to inhibit action in favor of thought (Barkley, 2003a). Another hypothesis is that ADHD results from a cluster of executive processing problems that interfere with

ability to guide one's own actions (Brown, 2005, 2006). Research confirms that children with ADHD do poorly on tasks requiring sustained attention; find it hard to ignore irrelevant information; have difficulty with memory, planning, reasoning, and problem solving; and often fail to manage frustration and intense emotion (Barkley, 2003b, 2006).

Origins of ADHD

ADHD runs in families and is highly heritable: Identical twins share it more often than fraternal twins (Rasmussen et al., 2004). Children with ADHD show abnormal brain functioning, including reduced electrical and blood-flow activity and structural abnormalities in the frontal lobes of the cerebral cortex and in other areas involved in attention, inhibition of behavior, and other aspects of motor control (Mackie et al., 2007; Sowell et al., 2003). Also, the brains of children with ADHD grow more slowly and are about 3 percent smaller in overall volume than those of unaffected agemates (Durston et al., 2004; Shaw et al., 2007). Several genes affecting neural communication have been implicated in the disorder (Quist & Kennedy, 2001).

At the same time, ADHD is associated with environmental factors. Exposure to prenatal teratogens—such as illegal drugs, alcohol, and tobacco—are linked to inattention and hyperactivity (Milberger et al., 1997). Furthermore, children with ADHD are more likely to come from homes in which marriages are unhappy and family stress is high (Bernier & Siegel, 1994). But a stressful home life rarely causes ADHD. Rather, these children's behaviors can contribute to family problems, which intensify the child's preexisting difficulties.

Treating ADHD

Calvin's doctor eventually prescribed stimulant medication, the most common treatment for ADHD. As long as dosage is carefully regulated, these drugs reduce symptoms in 70 percent of children who take them (Greenhill, Halperin, & Abikoff, 1999). Stimulant medication seems to increase activity in the frontal lobes, thereby improving the child's capacity to sustain attention and to inhibit off-task behavior.

But drug treatment is not enough: The most effective intervention approach combines medication with modeling and reinforcement

of appropriate academic and social behavior (Smith, Barkley, & Shapiro, 2006). Family intervention is also important. Inattentive, overactive children strain the patience of parents, who are likely to react punitively and inconsistently—a child-rearing style that strengthens defiant, aggressive behavior. In fact, in 45 to 65 percent of cases, these two sets of behavior problems occur together (Barkley, 2002b).

ADHD is usually a lifelong disorder. Affected individuals are at risk for persistent antisocial behavior, depression, and other problems (Kessler et al., 2005, 2006). Adults with ADHD continue to need help in structuring their environments, regulating negative emotion, selecting appropriate careers, and understanding their condition as a biological deficit rather than a character flaw.

© DAVID YOUNG-WOLFF/PHOTOEDIT

This child frequently engages in disruptive behavior at school. Children with ADHD have great difficulty staying on task and often act impulsively, ignoring social rules.

By the end of middle childhood, children start to use **elaboration**—creating a relationship, or shared meaning, between two or more pieces of information that do not belong to the same category. For example, if two of the words you must learn are *fish* and *pipe*, you might generate the verbal statement or mental image, "The fish is smoking a pipe." This highly effective memory technique, which requires considerable effort and space in working memory, becomes increasingly common in adolescence and early adulthood (Schneider & Pressley, 1997). Because organization and elaboration combine items into *meaningful chunks,* they permit children to hold onto much more information and also to *retrieve* it easily by thinking of other items associated with it.

The Knowledge Base and Memory Performance

During middle childhood, the long-term knowledge base grows larger and becomes organized into increasingly elaborate, hierarchically structured networks. This rapid growth of knowledge helps children use strategies and remember (Schneider, 2002). Knowing more about a topic makes new information more meaningful and familiar so it is easier to store and retrieve.

To test this idea, researchers classified fourth graders as either experts or novices in knowledge of soccer and gave both groups lists of soccer and nonsoccer items to learn. Experts remembered far more items on the soccer list (but not on the nonsoccer list) than novices. And during recall, experts' listing of items was better organized, as indicated by clustering of items into categories (Schneider & Bjorklund, 1992). This better organization at retrieval suggests that highly knowledgeable children organize information in their area of expertise with little or no effort. Consequently, experts can devote more working-memory resources to using recalled information for reasoning and problem solving (Bjorklund & Douglas, 1997).

By the end of the school years, extensive knowledge and use of memory strategies support one another. Children who are expert in an area are usually highly motivated. As a result, they not only acquire knowledge more quickly but also *actively use what they know* to add more. In contrast, academically unsuccessful children fail to ask how previously stored information can clarify new material. This, in turn, interferes with the development of a broad knowledge base (Schneider & Bjorklund, 1998).

Culture and Memory Strategies

A repeated finding is that people in non-Western cultures who lack formal schooling do not use or benefit from instruction in memory strategies (Rogoff, 2003). Tasks that require children to recall isolated bits of information, which are common in classrooms, strongly motivate use of memory strategies. In fact, Western children get so much practice with this type of learning that they do not refine techniques relying on cues available in everyday life, such as spatial location and arrangement of objects. For example, Guatemalan Mayan 9-year-olds do slightly better than their American agemates when told to remember the placement of 40 familiar objects in a play scene. American children often rehearse object names when it would be more effective to keep track of spatial relations (Rogoff & Waddell, 1982). The development of memory strategies, then, is not just a product of a more competent information-processing system. It also depends on task demands and cultural circumstances.

The School-Age Child's Theory of Mind

During middle childhood, children's *theory of mind,* or set of ideas about mental activities, becomes more elaborate and refined. Recall from Chapter 7 that this awareness of thought is often called *metacognition.* School-age children's improved ability to reflect on their own mental life is another reason that their thinking advances.

Unlike preschoolers, who view the mind as a passive container of information, older children regard it as an active, constructive agent that selects and transforms information (Kuhn, 2000). Consequently, they have a much better understanding of cognitive processes and their impact on performance. School-age children, for example, know that doing well on a task depends on focusing attention—concentrating and exerting effort (Miller & Bigi, 1979). With age, they also become increasingly aware of effective memory strategies and why they work (Alexander et al., 2003). And children gradually grasp relationships between mental activities—for example, that remembering is crucial for understanding and that understanding strengthens memory (Schwanenflugel, Henderson, & Fabricius, 1998).

Furthermore, school-age children's understanding of sources of knowledge expands. They realize that people can extend their knowledge not just by directly observing events and talking to others but also by making *mental inferences* (Miller, Hardin, & Montgomery, 2003). This grasp of inference enables knowledge of *false belief* to expand. By age 7, children are aware that people form beliefs about other people's beliefs ("Joe thinks Andy thinks the kitten is lost ") and that these second-order beliefs can be wrong! Appreciation of *second-order false belief* enables children to pinpoint the reasons that another person arrived at a certain belief (Astington, Pelletier, & Homer, 2002; Naito & Seki, 2009). This assists them greatly in understanding others' perspectives.

School-age children's capacity for more complex thinking contributes greatly to their more reflective, process-oriented view of the mind. But experiences that foster awareness of mental activities are also involved. In a study of rural children of Cameroon, Africa, those who attended school performed much better on theory-of-mind tasks (Vinden, 2002). In school, teachers often call attention to the workings of the mind when they remind children to pay attention, remember mental steps, and evaluate their reasoning. And as children engage in reading, writing, and math, they often use *private speech,* at first speaking out loud and then silently to themselves. As they "hear themselves think," they probably detect many aspects of mental life.

Cognitive Self-Regulation

Although metacognition expands, school-age children often have difficulty putting what they know about thinking into action. They are not yet good at **cognitive self-regulation,** the process of continuously monitoring progress toward a goal, checking outcomes, and redirecting unsuccessful efforts. For example, Lizzie knows she should group items when memorizing and that she should reread a complicated paragraph to make sure she understands. But she does not always engage in these activities.

Why does cognitive self-regulation develop gradually? Monitoring learning outcomes is cognitively demanding, requiring constant evaluation of effort and progress. By adolescence, self-regulation is a strong predictor of academic success, and parents and teachers can foster it (Joyner & Kurtz-Costes, 1997). In one study, researchers observed parents helping their children with problem solving during the summer before third grade. Parents who patiently pointed out important features of the task and suggested strategies had children who, in the classroom, more often discussed ways to approach problems and monitored their own performance (Stright et al., 2002). Explaining the effectiveness of strategies is particularly helpful because it provides a rationale for future action.

Children who acquire effective self-regulatory skills develop a sense of *academic self-efficacy*—confidence in their own ability, which supports future self-regulation (Schunk & Pajares, 2005). Unfortunately, some children receive messages from parents and teachers that seriously undermine their academic self-esteem and self-regulatory skills. We will consider these *learned-helpless* children, along with ways to help them, in Chapter 10.

Applications of Information Processing to Academic Learning

Fundamental discoveries about the development of information processing have been applied to children's learning of reading and mathematics. Researchers are identifying the cognitive ingredients of skilled performance, tracing their development, and pinpointing differences in cognitive skills between good and poor learners. They hope, as a result, to design teaching methods that will improve children's learning.

■ **READING.** Reading makes use of many skills at once, taxing all aspects of our information-processing systems. Joey and Lizzie must perceive single letters and letter combinations, translate them into speech sounds, recognize the visual appearance of many common words, hold chunks of text in working memory while interpreting their meaning, and combine the meanings of various parts of a text passage into an understandable whole. If one or more of these skills are poorly developed, they will compete for space in our limited working memories, and reading performance will decline.

As children make the transition from emergent literacy to conventional reading, *phonological awareness* continues to

facilitate their progress (see page 185 in Chapter 7). Other information-processing activities also contribute. Gains in processing speed foster children's rapid conversion of visual symbols into sounds (McBride-Chang & Kail, 2002). And visual scanning and discrimination are also important and improve with reading experience (Rayner, Pollatsek, & Starr, 2003). Performing all these skills efficiently releases working memory for higher-level activities involved in comprehending the text's meaning.

Until recently, researchers were involved in an intense debate over how to teach beginning reading. Those who took a **whole-language approach** argued that reading should be taught in a way that parallels natural language learning. From the beginning, children should be exposed to text in its complete form—stories, poems, letters, posters, and lists—so that they can appreciate the communicative function of written language (Watson, 1989). Other experts advocated a **phonics approach,** believing that children should first be coached on *phonics*—the basic rules for translating written symbols into sounds. Only after mastering these skills should they get complex reading material (Rayner & Pollatsek, 1989).

Many studies show that, in fact, children learn best with a mixture of both approaches. In kindergarten, first, and second grades, teaching that includes phonics boosts reading scores, especially for children who lag behind in reading progress (Stahl & Miller, 2006; Xue & Meisels, 2004). And when teachers combine real reading and writing with teaching of phonics and engage in other excellent teaching practices—encouraging children to tackle reading challenges and integrating reading into all school subjects—first graders show far greater literacy progress (Pressley et al., 2002).

Why might combining phonics with whole language work best? Learning relationships between letters and sounds enables children to decipher words they have never seen before. Consequently, it promotes children's belief that they can succeed at challenging reading tasks (Tunmer & Chapman, 2002). Yet too much emphasis on basic skills may cause children to lose sight of the goal of reading: understanding. Children who read aloud fluently without registering meaning know little about effective reading strategies—for example, that they must read more carefully if they will be tested than if they are reading for pleasure, or that explaining a passage in their own words is a good way to assess comprehension. Providing instruction aimed at increasing knowledge and use of reading strategies enhances reading performance from third grade on (Paris & Paris, 2006; Van Keer, 2004).

■ **MATHEMATICS.** Mathematics teaching in elementary school builds on and greatly enriches children's informal knowledge of number concepts and counting. Written notation systems and formal computational procedures enhance children's ability to represent numbers and compute. Over the early elementary school years, children acquire basic math facts through a combination of frequent practice, experimentation with diverse computational procedures (through which they discover faster, more accurate techniques), reasoning about number concepts, and teaching that conveys effective strategies (Alibali, 1999; Siegler,

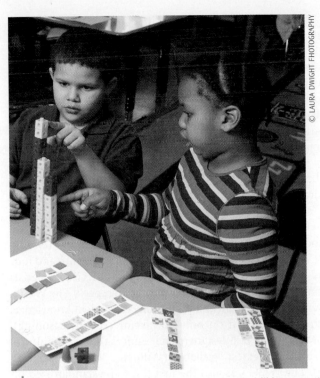

Arguments about how to teach mathematics pit drill in computing against "number sense," or understanding. A blend of both approaches is most beneficial, including opportunities to experiment with problem solving, grasp the reasons behind strategies, and evaluate solution techniques.

2007). For example, when first graders realize that regardless of the order in which two sets are combined, they yield the same result ($2 + 6 = 8$ and $6 + 2 = 8$), they more often start with the higher digit (6) and count on $(7, 8)$, a strategy that minimizes the work involved. Eventually children retrieve answers automatically and apply this knowledge to more complex problems.

Arguments about how to teach mathematics resemble those about reading, pitting drill in computing against "number sense," or understanding. Again, a blend of both approaches is most beneficial. In learning basic math, poorly performing students use cumbersome techniques or try to retrieve answers from memory too soon. They have not sufficiently experimented with strategies to see which are most effective and to reorganize their observations in logical, efficient ways—for example, noticing that multiplication problems involving 2 (2×8) are equivalent to addition doubles ($8 + 8$) (Canobi, 2004; Canobi, Reeve, & Pattison, 2003). This suggests that encouraging students to apply strategies and making sure they understand why certain strategies work well are essential for solid mastery of basic math. In one study, second graders taught in these ways not only mastered correct procedures but even invented their own successful strategies, some of which were superior to standard, school-taught methods (Fuson & Burghard, 2003).

In Asian countries, students receive a variety of supports for acquiring mathematical knowledge and often excel at math computation and reasoning. Use of the metric system helps Asian children grasp place value. The consistent structure of number words in Asian languages (*ten-two* for 12, *ten-three* for 13) also makes this idea clear (Miura & Okamoto, 2003). And because Asian number words are shorter and more quickly pronounced, more digits can be held in working memory at once, increasing the speed of thinking. Furthermore, Chinese parents provide their preschoolers with extensive practice in counting and adding—experiences that contribute to the superiority of Chinese over U.S. children's math knowledge even before school entry (Siegler & Mu, 2008; Zhou et al., 2006). Finally, as we will see later in this chapter, compared with lessons in the United States, those in Asian classrooms devote more time to exploring math concepts and less to drill and repetition.

ASK YOURSELF

≫ REVIEW
Cite evidence that school-age children view the mind as an active, constructive agent.

≫ APPLY
After viewing a slide show on endangered species, second and fifth graders were asked to remember as many animals as they could. Explain why fifth graders recalled much more than second graders.

≫ REFLECT
In your elementary school math education, how much emphasis was placed on computational drill and how much on understanding of concepts? How do you think that balance affected your interest and performance in math?

Individual Differences in Mental Development

Around age 6, IQ becomes more stable than it was at earlier ages, and it correlates moderately well with academic achievement, typically around .50 to .60. And children with higher IQs are more likely when they grow up to attain higher levels of education and enter more prestigious occupations (Brody, 1997; Deary et al., 2007). Because IQ predicts school performance and educational attainment, it often enters into educational decisions. Do intelligence tests accurately assess the school-age child's ability to profit from academic instruction? Let's look closely at this controversial issue.

Defining and Measuring Intelligence

Virtually all intelligence tests provide an overall score (the IQ), which represents *general intelligence*, or reasoning ability, along with an array of separate scores measuring specific mental abilities (see page 130 in Chapter 5). But intelligence is a collection of many capacities, not all of which are included on currently available tests (Carroll, 2005; Sternberg, 2005). See Figure 9.3 on page 240 for items typically included in intelligence tests for children.

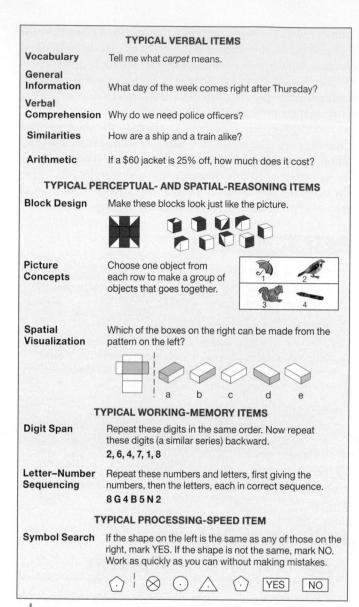

TYPICAL VERBAL ITEMS

Vocabulary   Tell me what *carpet* means.

General Information   What day of the week comes right after Thursday?

Verbal Comprehension   Why do we need police officers?

Similarities   How are a ship and a train alike?

Arithmetic   If a $60 jacket is 25% off, how much does it cost?

TYPICAL PERCEPTUAL- AND SPATIAL-REASONING ITEMS

Block Design   Make these blocks look just like the picture.

Picture Concepts   Choose one object from each row to make a group of objects that goes together.

Spatial Visualization   Which of the boxes on the right can be made from the pattern on the left?

TYPICAL WORKING-MEMORY ITEMS

Digit Span   Repeat these digits in the same order. Now repeat these digits (a similar series) backward.
2, 6, 4, 7, 1, 8

Letter–Number Sequencing   Repeat these numbers and letters, first giving the numbers, then the letters, each in correct sequence.
8 G 4 B 5 N 2

TYPICAL PROCESSING-SPEED ITEM

Symbol Search   If the shape on the left is the same as any of those on the right, mark YES. If the shape is not the same, mark NO. Work as quickly as you can without making mistakes.

■ **FIGURE 9.3** ■ **Test items like those on commonly used intelligence tests for children.** The verbal items emphasize culturally loaded, fact-oriented information. The perceptual- and spatial-reasoning, working-memory, and processing-speed items emphasize aspects of information processing and are assumed to assess more biologically based skills.

The intelligence tests given from time to time in classrooms are *group-administered tests.* They permit large numbers of students to be tested at once and are useful for identifying children who require more extensive evaluation with *individually administered tests,* which require extensive training and experience to give well. The examiner not only considers the child's answers but also observes the child's behavior, noting such reactions as attention to and interest in the tasks and wariness of the adult. These observations provide insight into whether the test results accurately reflect the child's abilities. Two individual tests—the Stanford-Binet and the Wechsler—are often used to identify highly intelligent children and to diagnose children with learning problems.

The modern descendant of Alfred Binet's first successful intelligence test is the *Stanford-Binet Intelligence Scales,* Fifth Edition, for individuals from age 2 to adulthood (Roid, 2003). It assesses general intelligence and five intellectual factors, each of which includes a verbal and a nonverbal mode of testing. (The nonverbal mode is useful when assessing individuals with limited English or communication disorders.) Knowledge and quantitative reasoning factors emphasize culturally loaded, fact-oriented information, such as vocabulary and arithmetic problems. In contrast, visual–spatial processing, working-memory, and basic information-processing factors are assumed to be less culturally biased because they require little specific information (see the spatial visualization item in Figure 9.3).

The *Wechsler Intelligence Scale for Children (WISC-IV)* is the fourth edition of a widely used test for 6- through 16-year-olds (Wechsler, 2003). It measures general intelligence and four broad factors: verbal reasoning, perceptual (or visual–spatial) reasoning, working memory, and processing speed. The WISC-IV was designed to downplay culturally dependent knowledge, which is emphasized on only one factor (verbal reasoning). According to the test designers, the result is the most "culture-fair" intelligence test available (Williams, Weis, & Rolfhus, 2003). The WISC was also the first test to be standardized on children representing the total population of the United States, including ethnic minorities.

Recent Efforts to Define Intelligence

As we have seen, mental tests now tap important aspects of information processing. In line with this trend, some researchers are combining the mental testing approach to defining intelligence with the information-processing approach. They believe that once we identify the processing skills that separate individuals who test well from those who test poorly, we will know more about how to intervene to improve performance. These investigators conduct *componential analyses* of children's test scores. This means that they look for relationships between aspects (or components) of information processing and children's intelligence test scores.

Measures of basic working-memory capacity (such as digit span) correlate well with mental test scores (de Ribaupierre & Lecerf, 2006). And processing speed, assessed in terms of reaction time on diverse cognitive tasks, is moderately related to IQ (Deary, 2001; Li et al., 2004). Individuals whose nervous systems permit them to take in more information and manipulate it quickly have an edge in intellectual skills.

But flexible attention, memory, and reasoning strategies are as important as efficient thinking in predicting IQ, and they explain some of the association between response speed and good test performance (Lohman, 2000; Miller & Vernon, 1992). Children who apply strategies effectively acquire more knowledge and can retrieve it rapidly. Similarly, recall that available space in working memory depends in part on effective inhibition (see page 235). Inhibition and sustained and selective attention are among a wide array of attentional skills that are good predictors of IQ (Schweizer, Moosbrugger, & Goldhammer, 2006).

The componential approach has one major shortcoming: It regards intelligence as entirely due to causes within the child. Yet throughout this book, we have seen how cultural and situational factors affect children's thinking. Robert Sternberg has expanded the componential approach into a comprehensive theory that regards intelligence as a product of inner and outer forces.

■ **STERNBERG'S TRIARCHIC THEORY OF SUCCESSFUL INTELLIGENCE.** As Figure 9.4 shows, Sternberg's (2001, 2002, 2005) **triarchic theory of successful intelligence** identifies three broad, interacting intelligences: (1) *analytical intelligence,* or information-processing skills; (2) *creative intelligence,* the capacity to solve novel problems; and (3) *practical intelligence,* application of intellectual skills in everyday situations. Intelligent behavior involves balancing all three intelligences to achieve success in life according to one's personal goals and the requirements of one's cultural community.

Analytical Intelligence. *Analytical intelligence* consists of the information-processing components that underlie all intelligent acts: applying strategies, acquiring task-relevant and metacognitive knowledge, and engaging in self-regulation. On mental tests, however, processing skills are used in only a few of their potential ways, resulting in a far too narrow view of intelligent behavior.

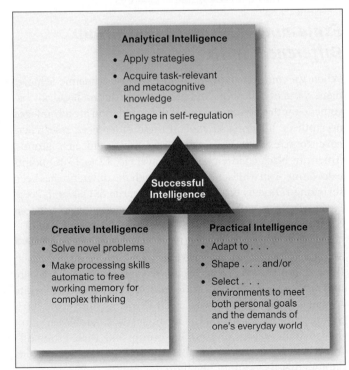

■ **FIGURE 9.4** ■ **Sternberg's triarchic theory of successful intelligence.** People who behave intelligently balance three interrelated intelligences—analytical, creative, and practical—to achieve success in life, defined by their personal goals and the requirements of their cultural communities.

Creative Intelligence. In any context, success depends not only on processing familiar information but also on generating useful solutions to new problems. People who are *creative* think more skillfully than others when faced with novelty. Given a new task, they apply their information-processing skills in exceptionally effective ways, rapidly making these skills automatic so that working memory is freed for more complex aspects of the situation.

Practical Intelligence. Finally, intelligence is a *practical,* goal-oriented activity aimed at *adapting to, shaping,* or *selecting environments.* Intelligent people skillfully *adapt* their thinking to fit with both their desires and the demands of their everyday worlds. When they cannot adapt to a situation, they try to *shape,* or change, it to meet their needs. If they cannot shape it, they *select* new contexts that better match their skills, values, or goals. Practical intelligence reminds us that children with certain life histories do well on intelligence tests and adapt easily to the testing conditions. Others, with different backgrounds, may misinterpret or reject the testing context. Yet such children often display sophisticated abilities in daily life—for example, engaging in complex artistic activities or interacting skillfully with people.

The triarchic theory highlights the limitations of current intelligence tests in assessing the complexity of intelligent behavior. For example, out-of-school, practical forms of intelligence are vital for life success and help explain why cultures vary widely in the behaviors they regard as intelligent (Sternberg et al., 2000). When researchers asked ethnically diverse parents to describe an intelligent first grader, Caucasian Americans mentioned cognitive traits. In contrast, ethnic minorities (Cambodian, Filipino, Vietnamese, and Mexican immigrants) identified noncognitive capacities—motivation, self-management, and social skills (Okagaki & Sternberg, 1993). According to Sternberg, mental tests can easily underestimate, and even overlook, the intellectual strengths of some children, especially ethnic minorities.

■ **GARDNER'S THEORY OF MULTIPLE INTELLIGENCES.** In yet another view of how information-processing skills underlie intelligent behavior, Howard Gardner's (1983, 1993, 2000) **theory of multiple intelligences** defines intelligence in terms of distinct sets of processing operations that permit individuals to engage in a wide range of culturally valued activities. Dismissing the idea of general intelligence, Gardner proposes at least eight independent intelligences (see Table 9.1 on page 242).

Gardner believes that each intelligence has a unique biological basis, a distinct course of development, and different expert performances. At the same time, he emphasizes that a lengthy process of education is required to transform any raw potential into a mature social role (Connell, Sheridan, & Gardner, 2003). Cultural values and learning opportunities affect the extent to which a child's intellectual strengths are realized and the ways they are expressed.

Gardner's list of abilities has yet to be firmly grounded in research. Neurological evidence for the independence of his

■ **TABLE 9.1** ■ *Gardner's Multiple Intelligences*

INTELLIGENCE	PROCESSING OPERATIONS	EXPERT PERFORMANCE POSSIBILITIES
Linguistic	Sensitivity to the sounds, rhythms, and meaning of words and the functions of language	Poet, journalist
Logico-mathematical	Sensitivity to, and capacity to detect, logical or numerical patterns; ability to handle long chains of logical reasoning	Mathematician
Musical	Ability to produce and appreciate pitch, rhythm (or melody), and aesthetic quality of the forms of musical expressiveness	Instrumentalist, composer
Spatial	Ability to perceive the visual–spatial world accurately, to perform transformations on those perceptions, and to re-create aspects of visual experience in the absence of relevant stimuli	Sculptor, navigator
Bodily-kinesthetic	Ability to use the body skillfully for expressive as well as goal-directed purposes; ability to handle objects skillfully	Dancer, athlete
Naturalist	Ability to recognize and classify all varieties of animals, minerals, and plants	Biologist
Interpersonal	Ability to detect and respond appropriately to the moods, temperaments, motivations, and intentions of others	Therapist, salesperson
Intrapersonal	Ability to discriminate complex inner feelings and to use them to guide one's own behavior; knowledge of one's own strengths, weaknesses, desires, and intelligences	Person with detailed, accurate self-knowledge

Sources: Gardner, 1993, 1998a, 2000.

abilities is weak. Some exceptionally gifted individuals have abilities that are broad rather than limited to a particular domain (Goldsmith, 2000). Nevertheless, Gardner calls attention to several abilities not measured by intelligence tests. For example, his interpersonal and intrapersonal intelligences include a set

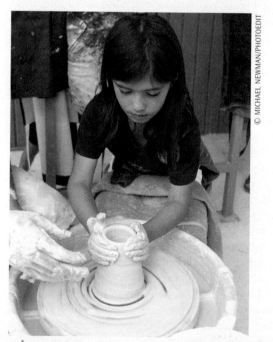

According to Gardner, children are capable of at least eight distinct intelligences. As this child learns pottery skills under the guidance of an expert potter, she enriches her spatial intelligence.

of capacities for dealing with people and understanding oneself that are vital for a satisfying, successful life.

Explaining Individual and Group Differences in IQ

When we compare individuals in terms of academic achievement, years of education, and occupational status, it quickly becomes clear that certain sectors of the population are advantaged over others. In trying to explain these differences, researchers have compared the IQ scores of ethnic and SES groups. American black children score, on average, 12 to 13 IQ points below American white children, although the difference has been shrinking (Dickens & Flynn, 2006; Edwards & Oakland, 2006; Hedges & Nowell, 1998). Hispanic children fall midway between black and white children (Ceci, Rosenblum, & Kumpf, 1998).

The IQ gap between middle-SES and low-SES children—about 9 points—accounts for some of the ethnic differences in IQ, but not all. When black children and white children are matched on parental education and income, the black–white IQ gap is reduced by a third to a half (Brooks-Gunn et al., 2003; Smith, Duncan, & Lee, 2003). Of course, considerable variation exists within each ethnic and SES group. Still, these group differences in IQ are large enough and their consequences serious enough that they cannot be ignored.

In the 1970s, the IQ nature–nurture controversy escalated after psychologist Arthur Jensen (1969) published a controversial monograph entitled, "How Much Can We Boost IQ and Scholastic Achievement?" Jensen argued—and still maintains—that heredity is largely responsible for individual, ethnic, and

SES variations in intelligence (Jensen, 1998, 2001; Rushton & Jensen, 2005, 2006). His work sparked an outpouring of research studies and responses, including ethical challenges reflecting deep concern that his conclusions would fuel social prejudices. Richard Herrnstein and Charles Murray rekindled the controversy with *The Bell Curve* (1994). Like Jensen, they argued that heredity contributes substantially to individual and SES differences (and possibly to ethnic differences) in IQ. Let's look closely at some important evidence.

■ **NATURE VERSUS NURTURE.** Recall from Chapter 2 that *heritability estimates* are obtained from *kinship studies,* which compare family members. The most powerful evidence on the heritability of IQ involves twin comparisons. The IQ scores of identical twins (who share all their genes) are more similar than those of fraternal twins (who are genetically no more alike than ordinary siblings). On the basis of this and other kinship evidence, researchers estimate that about half the differences in IQ among children can be traced to their genetic makeup.

But heritabilities risk overestimating genetic influences and underestimating environmental influences (see page 55). Although these measures offer convincing evidence that genes contribute to IQ, disagreement persists over how large the role of heredity really is (Grigorenko, 2000; Plomin, 2003). And heritability estimates do not reveal the complex processes through which genes and experiences influence intelligence as children develop.

Adoption studies offer a wider range of information. Findings consistently reveal that when young children are adopted into caring, stimulating homes, their IQs rise substantially compared with the IQs of nonadopted children who remain in economically deprived families (van IJzendoorn, Juffer, & Poelhuis, 2005). But adopted children benefit to varying degrees. In one investigation, children of two extreme groups of biological mothers—those with IQs below 95 and those with IQs above 120—were adopted at birth by parents who were well above average in income and education. During the school years, the children of the low-IQ biological mothers scored above average in IQ, indicating that test performance can be greatly improved by an advantaged home life. But they did not do as well as children of high-IQ biological mothers placed in similar adoptive families (Loehlin, Horn, & Willerman, 1997). Adoption research confirms that heredity and environment contribute jointly to IQ.

Adoption research also sheds light on the black–white IQ gap. In two studies, African-American children adopted into economically well-off white homes during the first year of life scored high on intelligence tests, attaining mean IQs of 110 and 117 by middle childhood—20 to 30 points higher than the typical scores of children growing up in low-income black communities (Moore, 1986; Scarr & Weinberg, 1983). In one investigation, the IQs of black adoptees declined in adolescence, perhaps because of the challenges faced by minority teenagers in forming an ethnic identity that blends birth and adoptive backgrounds (DeBerry, Scarr, & Weinberg, 1996). When this process is filled with emotional turmoil, it can dampen motivation on tests and in school. Still, the black adoptees remained above the IQ average for low-SES African Americans.

Adoption findings do not completely resolve questions about ethnic differences in IQ. Nevertheless, the IQ gains of black children "reared in the culture of the tests and schools" are consistent with a wealth of evidence that poverty severely depresses the intelligence of ethnic minority children.

■ **CULTURAL INFLUENCES.** A controversial question raised about ethnic differences in IQ has to do with whether they result from *test bias.* If a test samples knowledge and skills that not all groups of children have had equal opportunity to learn, or if the testing situation impairs the performance of some groups but not others, then the resulting score is a biased, or unfair, measure (Ceci & Williams, 1997; Sternberg, 2005).

Communication Styles. Ethnic minority families often foster unique language skills. In one study, a researcher spent many hours observing in low-SES black homes in a southeastern U.S. city (Heath, 1990). She found that African-American parents rarely asked their children the knowledge-training questions typical of middle-SES white parents and of tests and classrooms ("What color is it?" "What's this story about?"). Instead, the black parents asked only "real" questions, ones they themselves could not answer. Often these were analogy questions ("What's that like?") or story-starter questions ("Didja hear Miss Sally this morning?") that called for elaborate responses and had no "right" answer. Black children may be confused by the "objective" questions they encounter on tests and in classrooms.

Furthermore, many ethnic minority parents without extensive schooling prefer a *collaborative style of communication* when completing tasks with children. They work together in a coordinated, fluid way, each focused on the same aspect of the problem—a pattern observed in Native-American, Canadian Inuit, Hispanic, and Guatemalan Mayan cultures (Chavajay & Rogoff, 2002; Crago, Annahatak, & Ningiuruvik, 1993; Delgado-Gaitan, 1994). With increasing education, parents establish a *hierarchical style of communication,* like that of classrooms and tests. The parent directs each child to carry out an aspect of the task, and children work independently (Greenfield, Suzuki, & Rothstein-Fish, 2006). This sharp discontinuity between home and school practices may contribute to low-SES minority children's lower IQ and school performance.

Test Content. Many researchers argue that IQ scores are affected by specific information acquired as part of majority-culture upbringing. Unfortunately, attempts to change tests by eliminating verbal, fact-oriented items and relying only on spatial reasoning tasks (believed to be less culturally loaded) have not raised the scores of low-SES minority children much (Reynolds & Kaiser, 1990). Yet even these nonverbal test items depend on learning opportunities. For example, using small blocks to duplicate designs and playing video games increase success on spatial tasks (Dirks, 1982; Maynard, Subrahmanyam, & Greenfield, 2005). Low-income minority children, who often grow up in more "people-oriented" than "object-oriented" homes, may lack toys and games that promote certain intellectual skills.

Furthermore, the sheer amount of time a child spends in school predicts IQ. When children of the same age enrolled in different grades are compared, those who have been in school longer score higher on intelligence tests (Ceci, 1991, 1999). Taken together, these findings indicate that children's exposure to the factual knowledge and ways of thinking valued in classrooms has a sizable impact on their intelligence test performance.

Stereotypes. Imagine trying to succeed at an activity when the prevailing attitude is that members of your group are incompetent. **Stereotype threat**—the fear of being judged on the basis of a negative stereotype—can trigger anxiety that interferes with performance (Steele, 1997). Mounting evidence confirms that stereotype threat undermines test taking in children and adults. For example, researchers gave African-American, Hispanic-American, and Caucasian 6- to 10-year-olds verbal tasks. Some children were told that the tasks were "not a test." Others were told they were "a test of how good children are at school problems" (McKown & Weinstein, 2003). Among children who were aware of ethnic stereotypes (such as "black people aren't smart"), African Americans and Hispanics performed far worse in the "test" condition than in the "not a test" condition. Caucasian children, in contrast, performed similarly in both conditions (see Figure 9.5).

Over middle childhood, children become increasingly conscious of ethnic stereotypes, and those from stigmatized groups are especially mindful of them. By middle school, many low-SES minority students start to say that doing well in school is not important to them (Major et al., 1998; Osborne, 1994). Self-protective disengagement, sparked by stereotype threat, may be responsible. This weakening of motivation can have serious, long-term consequences. Research shows that self-discipline—effort and delay of gratification—predicts school performance at least as well as, and sometimes better than, IQ does (Duckworth & Seligman, 2005).

Reducing Cultural Bias in Testing. Although not all experts agree, many acknowledge that IQ scores can underestimate the intelligence of culturally different children. A special concern exists about incorrectly labeling minority children as slow learners and assigning them to remedial classes, which are far less stimulating than regular school experiences. To avoid this danger, test scores need to be combined with assessments of children's adaptive behavior—their ability to cope with the demands of their everyday environments. The child who does poorly on an intelligence test yet plays a complex game on the playground or figures out how to rewire a broken TV is unlikely to be mentally deficient.

In addition, culturally relevant testing procedures enhance minority children's test performance. In an approach called **dynamic assessment,** an innovation consistent with Vygotsky's zone of proximal development, an adult introduces purposeful teaching into the testing situation to find out what the child can attain with social support. Research shows that children's receptivity to teaching and their capacity to transfer what they have learned to novel problems contribute substantially to gains in test performance (Lidz, 2001; Sternberg & Grigorenko, 2002).

But rather than adapting testing to support ethnic minority children's learning needs, American education is placing greater emphasis on traditional test scores. To upgrade the academic achievement of poorly performing students, a *high-*

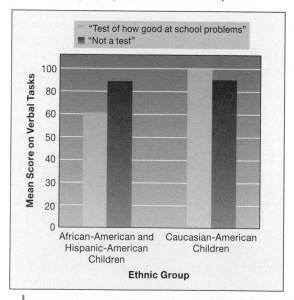

■ **FIGURE 9.5** ■ **Effect of stereotype threat on test performance.** Among African-American and Hispanic-American children who were aware of ethnic stereotypes, being told that verbal tasks were a "test of how good children are at school problems" led to far worse performance than being told the tasks were "not a test." These statements had little impact on the performance of Caucasian-American children. (Adapted from McKown & Weinstein, 2003.)

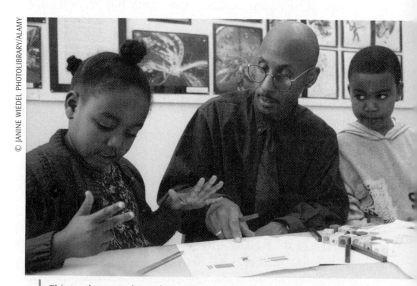

This teacher uses dynamic assessment, tailoring instruction to students' individual needs—an approach that reveals what a child can learn with social support.

⌐ SOCIAL ISSUES ⌐

High-Stakes Testing

To better hold schools accountable for educating students, during the past two decades many U.S. states mandated that students pass exams for high school graduation. As these high-stakes achievement tests spread, some states and school districts also made grade promotion and secondary-school academic course credits contingent on test scores (Gootman, 2005).

The U.S. No Child Left Behind Act, authorized by Congress in 2002, uses high-stakes testing to identify "passing" and "failing" schools. The law mandates that each state evaluate every public school's performance through annual achievement testing and publicize the results. Schools that consistently perform poorly (have a high percentage of failing students) must give parents options for upgrading their children's education, such as transfers to nearby, higher-performing schools or enrollment in remedial classes. Some states offer schoolwide rewards for high scores, including official praise and financial bonuses to school staff. Penalties imposed for low scores include withdrawal of accreditation, state takeover, and closure.

Proponents of high-stakes testing believe that it introduces greater rigor into classroom teaching, improves student motivation and achievement, and either turns around poor-performing schools or protects students from being trapped in them. But accumulating evidence indicates that high-stakes testing often undermines, rather than upgrades, the quality of education.

In a Canadian study, researchers examined the impact of requiring students to pass a high school exit exam on eighth-, tenth-, and twelfth-grade science teaching. They found that twelfth-grade teachers narrowed the scope of what they taught to strings of facts to be memorized for the test. As a result, eighth and tenth graders, in some respects, were doing more advanced work than twelfth graders—conducting more experiments, exploring topics in greater depth, and engaging in more critical thinking (Wideen et al., 1997).

An additional concern is that high-stakes testing promotes fear—a poor motivator for upgrading teaching and learning. Principals and teachers worry about losing funding and their jobs if students do poorly—punishments that have sparked unprecedented levels of adult cheating and other educationally detrimental behaviors. These range from giving students answers, changing students' scores, and offering students rewards (money, sweets, and expensive toys) for earning high scores to suspending or expelling students likely to perform poorly just before test administration (Nichols & Berliner, 2007).

Furthermore, many students who get passing school grades, even high grades, fail exams because a time-limited test can tap only a small sample of skills covered in the classroom (Hursh, 2007). Students most likely to score poorly are minority youths living in poverty. When they are punished with course failure and grade retention, their self-esteem and motivation drop sharply, and they are likely to drop out (Balfanz et al., 2007; Hursh, 2007).

Clearly, serious issues remain for lawmakers and educators to resolve about the use of high-stakes tests. These include their fairness to minority students and their questionable power to spark school reforms that make students better learners.

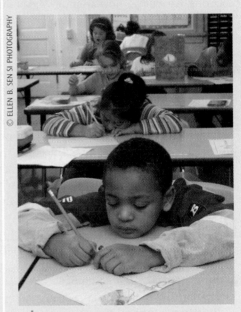

© ELLEN B. SEN SI PHOTOGRAPHY

In many U.S. classrooms, high-stakes testing has narrowed the focus of the curriculum to test preparation and promoted a one-size-fits-all education.

---

stakes testing movement has arisen, making progress through school contingent on test performance. As the Social Issues box above indicates, this stepped-up emphasis on passing standardized tests has narrowed the focus of instruction, and it may widen SES and ethnic differences in educational attainment.

In view of its many problems, should intelligence testing in schools be suspended? Most experts reject this solution. Without testing, important educational decisions would be based only on subjective impressions, perhaps increasing discriminatory placement of minority children. Intelligence tests are useful when interpreted carefully by psychologists and educators who are sensitive to cultural influences on test performance. And despite their limitations, IQ scores continue to be fairly accurate measures of school learning potential for the majority of Western children.

ASK YOURSELF

≫ REVIEW
Using Sternberg's triarchic theory and Gardner's theory of multiple intelligences, explain the limitations of current intelligence tests in assessing the diversity of human intelligence.

≫ APPLY
Josefina, a Hispanic fourth grader, does well on homework assignments. But when her teacher announces, "It's time for a test to see how much you've learned," Josefina usually does poorly. How might stereotype threat explain this inconsistency?

≫ REFLECT
Do you think that intelligence tests are culturally biased? What observations and evidence influenced your conclusions?

Language Development

Vocabulary, grammar, and pragmatics continue to develop in middle childhood, although less obviously than at earlier ages. In addition, school-age children's attitude toward language undergoes a fundamental shift. They develop language awareness.

Schooling contributes greatly to these language competencies. Reflecting on language is extremely common during reading instruction. And fluent reading is a major new source of language learning (Ravid & Tolchinsky, 2002). In the following sections, we will see how an improved ability to reflect on language grows out of literacy and supports language skills.

Vocabulary and Grammar

During the elementary school years, vocabulary increases fourfold, eventually exceeding 40,000 words, a rate of growth greater than in early childhood. In addition to the word-learning strategies discussed in Chapter 7, school-age children add to their vocabularies by analyzing the structure of complex words. From *happy* and *decide,* they quickly derive the meanings of *happiness* and *decision* (Larsen & Nippold, 2007). They also figure out many more word meanings from context (Nagy & Scott, 2000).

As at earlier ages, children benefit from conversations with more expert speakers, especially when their partners use complex words and explain them (Weizman & Snow, 2001). But because written language contains a far more diverse and complex vocabulary than spoken language, reading contributes enormously to vocabulary growth.

As their knowledge expands and becomes better organized, older school-age children think about and use words more precisely: In addition to the verb *fall,* for example, they also use *topple, tumble,* and *plummet* (Berman, 2007). Word definitions also illustrate this change. Five- and 6-year-olds offer concrete descriptions referring to functions or appearance: *knife:* "when you're cutting carrots"; *bicycle:* "it's got wheels, a chain, and handlebars." By the end of elementary school, synonyms and explanations of categorical relationships appear—for example, *knife:* "something you could cut with. A saw is like a knife. It could also be a weapon" (Wehren, De Lisi, & Arnold, 1981).

School-age children's more reflective and analytical approach to language permits them to appreciate the multiple meanings of words—to recognize, for example, that many words, such as *cool* or *neat,* have psychological as well as physical meanings: "What a cool shirt!" or "That movie was really neat!" This grasp of double meanings permits 8- to 10-year-olds to comprehend subtle metaphors, such as "sharp as a tack" and "spilling the beans" (Nippold, Taylor, & Baker, 1996; Wellman & Hickling, 1994). It also leads to a change in children's humor. Riddles and puns that alternate between different meanings of a key word are common: "Hey, did you take a bath?" "Why, is one missing?"

Mastery of complex grammatical constructions also improves. For example, English-speaking children use the passive voice more frequently, and they more often extend it from an abbreviated form ("It broke") into full statements ("The glass was broken by Mary") (Israel, Johnson, & Brooks, 2000; Tomasello, 2006). Although the passive form is challenging, language input makes a difference. When adults speak a language that emphasizes full passives, such as Inukitut (spoken by the Inuit people of Arctic Canada), children produce them earlier (Allen & Crago, 1996).

Another grammatical achievement of middle childhood is advanced understanding of infinitive phrases—the difference between "John is eager to please" and "John is easy to please" (Chomsky, 1969). Like gains in vocabulary, appreciation of these subtle grammatical distinctions is supported by an improved ability to analyze and reflect on language.

Pragmatics

Improvements in *pragmatics,* the communicative side of language, also occur. Conversational strategies become more refined. For example, school-age children are better at phrasing things to get their way. When an adult refuses to hand over a desired object, 9-year-olds, but not 5-year-olds, state their second requests more politely (Axia & Baroni, 1985).

Furthermore, as a result of improved memory and ability to take the perspective of listeners, children's narratives increase in organization, detail, and expressiveness. A typical 4- or 5-year-old's narrative states what happened: "We went to the lake. We fished and waited. Paul caught a huge catfish." Six- and 7-year-olds, in contrast, include orienting information (time, place, and participants) and many connectives that lend coherence to the story ("next," "then," "so," "finally"). Gradually, narratives lengthen into a *classic form* in which events not only build to a high point but resolve: "After Paul reeled in the catfish, Dad cleaned and cooked it. Then we ate it all up!" And

In families who regularly eat meals together, children are advanced in language and literacy development. Mealtimes offer many opportunities to relate complex, extended personal stories.

© JUPITERIMAGES/COMSTOCK IMAGES/ALAMY

evaluative comments rise dramatically, becoming common by age 8 to 9: "The catfish tasted great. Paul was so proud!" (Melzi & Ely, 2009; Ukrainetz et al., 2005).

Because children pick up the narrative styles of significant adults in their lives, their narrative forms vary widely across cultures. For example, instead of the *topic-focused style* of most Western school-age children, who describe an experience from beginning to end, African-American children often use a *topic-associating style* in which they blend several similar anecdotes. One 9-year-old related having a tooth pulled, then described seeing her sister's tooth pulled, next told how she had removed one of her baby teeth, and concluded, "I'm a pullin'-teeth expert . . . call me, and I'll be over" (McCabe, 1997, p. 164). As a result, African-American children's narratives are usually longer and more complex than those of white children (Champion, 2003b).

The ability to generate clear oral narratives enhances reading comprehension and prepares children for producing longer, more explicit written narratives. In families who regularly eat meals together, children are advanced in language and literacy development because mealtimes offer many opportunities to relate complex, extended personal stories (Snow & Beals, 2006).

Learning Two Languages at a Time

Throughout the world, many children grow up *bilingual*, learning two languages, and sometimes more than two, in childhood. An estimated 15 percent of U.S. children—6 million in all—speak a language other than English at home (U.S. Census Bureau, 2009b).

■ **BILINGUAL DEVELOPMENT.**   Children can become bilingual in two ways: (1) by acquiring both languages at the same time in early childhood or (2) by learning a second language after mastering the first. Children of bilingual parents who teach them both languages in infancy and early childhood separate the language systems from the start and attain early language milestones according to a typical timetable (Bosch & Sebastian-Galles, 2001; Conboy & Thal, 2006; Holowka, Brosseau-Lapré, & Petitto, 2002). When school-age children acquire a second language after they already speak a first language, they generally take five to seven years to attain speaking and writing skills on a par with those of native-speaking agemates (Paradis, 2007).

As with first-language development, a *sensitive period* for second-language development exists. Mastery must begin sometime in childhood for most second-language learners to attain full proficiency. But a precise age cutoff for a decline in second-language learning has not been established (Hakuta, Bialystok, & Wiley, 2003). Rather, a continuous age-related decrease from childhood to adulthood occurs.

A large body of research shows that bilingualism has positive consequences for development. Children who are fluent in two languages do better than others on tests of selective attention, analytical reasoning, concept formation, and cognitive flexibility (Bialystok, 2001; Bialystok & Martin, 2004). They are also advanced in certain aspects of language awareness, such as detection of errors in grammar and meaning. And children readily transfer their phonological awareness skills in one language to the other (Bialystok, McBride-Chang, & Luk, 2005; Snow & Kang, 2006). These capacities, as noted earlier, enhance reading achievement.

■ **BILINGUAL EDUCATION.**   The advantages of bilingualism provide strong justification for bilingual education programs in schools. In Canada, about 7 percent of elementary school students are enrolled in *language immersion programs*, in which English-speaking children are taught entirely in French for several years. This strategy has been successful in developing children who are proficient in both languages and who, by grade 6, achieve as well in reading, writing, and math as their counterparts in the regular English program (Harley & Jean, 1999; Holobow, Genesee, & Lambert, 1991; Turnbull, Hart, & Lapkin, 2003).

In the United States, fierce disagreement exists over the question of how best to educate ethnic minority children with limited English proficiency. Some believe that time spent communicating in the child's native tongue detracts from English-language achievement. Other educators, committed to developing minority children's native language while fostering mastery of English, note that providing instruction in the native tongue lets minority children know that their heritage is respected and prevents inadequate proficiency in both languages. Minority children who gradually lose the first language as a result of being taught the second end up limited in both languages for a time, a circumstance that leads to serious academic difficulties and increases the risk of later dropout (Ovando & Collier, 1998).

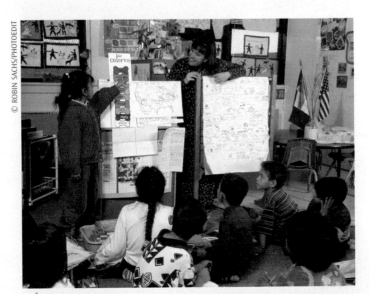

In this English–Spanish bilingual classroom, children are more involved in learning, participate more actively in class discussions, and acquire the second language more easily.

At present, public opinion and educational practice favor English-only instruction. Many U.S. states have passed laws declaring English to be their official language, creating conditions in which schools have no obligation to teach minority students in languages other than English. Yet in classrooms where both languages are integrated into the curriculum, minority children are more involved in learning and acquire the second language more easily. In contrast, when teachers speak only in a language children can barely understand, minority children display frustration, boredom, and withdrawal (Crawford, 1997).

Supporters of U.S. English-only education often point to the success of Canadian language immersion programs, in which classroom lessons are conducted in the second language. But Canadian parents enroll their children in immersion classrooms voluntarily, and both French and English are majority languages that are equally valued in Canada. For American non-English-speaking minority children, whose native languages are not valued by the larger society, a different strategy seems necessary: one that promotes children's native-language skills while they learn English.

ASK YOURSELF

》》 **REVIEW**
Cite examples of how language awareness fosters school-age children's language progress.

》》 **APPLY**
Ten-year-old Shana arrived home from soccer practice and remarked, "I'm wiped out!" Megan, her 5-year-old sister, looked puzzled. "What did'ya wipe out, Shana?" Megan asked. Explain Shana's and Megan's different understandings of this expression.

》》 **REFLECT**
Did you acquire a second language at home or study one in school? Considering research on bilingualism, what changes would you make in your own second-language learning, and why?

Learning in School

Evidence cited throughout this chapter indicates that schools are vital forces in children's cognitive development. How do schools exert such a powerful influence? Research looking at schools as complex social systems—educational philosophies, teacher–student relationships, and larger cultural context—provides important insights. As you read about these topics, refer to Applying What We Know on the following page, which summarizes characteristics of high-quality education in elementary school.

Educational Philosophies

Each teacher brings to the classroom an educational philosophy that plays a major role in children's learning. Two philosophical approaches have received most research attention.

They differ in what children are taught, the way they are believed to learn, and how their progress is evaluated.

■ **TRADITIONAL VERSUS CONSTRUCTIVIST CLASSROOMS.** In a **traditional classroom,** the teacher is the sole authority for knowledge, rules, and decision making. Students are relatively passive—listening, responding when called on, and completing teacher-assigned tasks. Their progress is evaluated by how well they keep pace with a uniform set of standards for their grade.

A **constructivist classroom,** in contrast, encourages students to *construct* their own knowledge. Although constructivist approaches vary, many are grounded in Piaget's theory, which views children as active agents who reflect on and coordinate their own thoughts rather than absorbing those of others. A glance inside a constructivist classroom reveals richly equipped learning centers, small groups and individuals solving self-chosen problems, and a teacher who guides and supports in response to children's needs. Students are evaluated by considering their progress in relation to their own prior development.

In the United States, the pendulum has swung back and forth between these two views. In the 1960s and early 1970s, constructivist classrooms gained in popularity. Then, as concern arose over the academic progress of children and youths, a "back-to-basics" movement arose. Classrooms returned to traditional instruction, a style still prevalent today.

Although older elementary school children in traditional classrooms have a slight edge in achievement test scores, constructivist settings are associated with many other benefits—gains in academic motivation, critical thinking, social and moral maturity, and positive attitudes toward school (DeVries, 2001; Rathunde & Csikszentmihalyi, 2005; Walberg, 1986). And as noted in Chapter 7, when teacher-directed instruction is emphasized in preschool and kindergarten, it actually undermines academic motivation and achievement, especially in low-SES children.

■ **NEW PHILOSOPHICAL DIRECTIONS.** New approaches to education, grounded in Vygotsky's sociocultural theory, capitalize on the rich social context of the classroom to spur children's learning. In these **social-constructivist classrooms,** children participate in a wide range of challenging activities with teachers and peers, with whom they jointly construct understandings. As children acquire knowledge and strategies from working together, they become competent, contributing members of their classroom community and advance in cognitive and social development (Bodrova & Leong, 2007; Palincsar, 2003). Vygotsky's emphasis on the social origins of higher cognitive processes has inspired the following educational themes:

■ *Teachers and children as partners in learning.* A classroom rich in both teacher–child and child–child collaboration transfers culturally valued ways of thinking to children.

■ *Experiences with many types of symbolic communication in meaningful activities.* As children master reading, writing,

Applying What We Know

Signs of High-Quality Education in Elementary School

Classroom Characteristics	Signs of Quality
Class size	Optimum class size is no larger than 18 children.
Physical setting	Space is divided into richly equipped activity centers—for reading, writing, playing math or language games, exploring science, using computers, and other academic pursuits. Spaces are used flexibly for individual and small-group activities and whole-class gatherings.
Curriculum	The curriculum helps children both achieve academic standards and make sense of their learning. Subjects are integrated so that children apply knowledge in one area to others. Learning activities are responsive to children's interests, ideas, and everyday lives, including their cultural backgrounds.
Interactions between teachers and children	Teachers foster each child's progress and use intellectually engaging strategies, including posing problems, asking thought-provoking questions, discussing ideas, adding complexity to tasks, and encouraging cooperative learning. They also demonstrate, explain, coach, and assist in other ways, depending on each child's learning needs.
Evaluations of progress	Teachers regularly evaluate children's progress through written observations and work samples, which they use to enhance and individualize teaching. They help children reflect on their work and decide how to improve it. They also seek information and perspectives from parents on how well children are learning and include parents' views in evaluations.
Relationship with parents	Teachers forge partnerships with parents. They hold periodic conferences and encourage parents to visit the classroom anytime, to observe and volunteer.

Source: Copple & Bredekamp, 2009.

and mathematics, they become aware of their culture's communication systems, reflect on their own thinking, and bring it under voluntary control.

- *Teaching adapted to each child's zone of proximal development.* Assistance that both responds to current understandings and encourages children to take the next step helps ensure that each child makes the best progress possible.

According to Vygotsky, besides teachers, more expert peers can spur children's learning, as long as they adjust the help they provide to fit the less mature child's zone of proximal development. Consistent with this idea, mounting evidence confirms that peer collaboration promotes development only under certain conditions. A crucial factor is **cooperative learning,** in which small groups of classmates work toward common goals—by resolving differences of opinion, sharing responsibilities, and providing one another with sufficient explanations to correct misunderstandings. And children profit more when their peer partner is an "expert"—especially capable at the task. When older or more expert students assist younger or less expert students, both benefit in achievement and self-esteem (Ginsburg-Block, Rohrbeck, & Fantuzzo, 2006; Renninger, 1998).

Because Western cultural-majority children regard competition and independent work as natural, they typically require extensive guidance to succeed at cooperative learning. In several studies, groups of students trained in collaborative processes displayed more cooperative behavior, gave clearer

explanations, and enjoyed learning more than did untrained groups (Gillies, 2000, 2003; Terwel et al., 2001). In other research, the quality of children's collaborative discussions predicted gains in diverse cognitive skills that persisted for

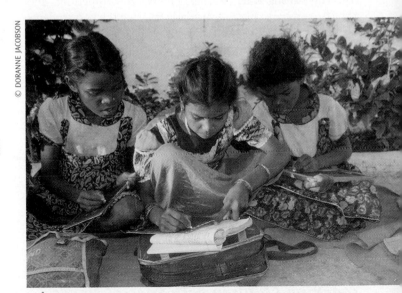

© DORANNE JACOBSON

These children attending a rural school in India cooperate easily while completing a reading assignment. Their Western cultural-majority agemates, in contrast, typically require extensive guidance to succeed at cooperative learning.

weeks beyond the cooperative learning experience (Fleming & Alexander, 2001).

Teacher–Student Interaction

Elementary school students describe good teachers as caring, helpful, and stimulating—behaviors associated with gains in motivation, achievement, and positive peer relations (Daniels, Kalkman, & McCombs, 2001; Hughes & Kwok, 2006, 2007; Hughes, Zhang, & Hill, 2006). But too many U.S. teachers emphasize repetitive drill over higher-level thinking, such as grappling with ideas and applying knowledge to new situations (Sacks, 2005). In a longitudinal investigation of middle-school students, those in more academically demanding classrooms showed better attendance and larger gains in math achievement over the following two years (Phillips, 1997).

Of course, teachers do not interact in the same way with all children. Well-behaved, high-achieving students typically get more encouragement and praise, whereas unruly students have more conflicts with teachers and receive more criticism (Henricsson & Rydell, 2004). Caring teacher–student relationships have an especially strong impact on the achievement and social behavior of low-SES minority students (Baker, 2006). But overall, higher-SES students—who tend to be higher-achieving and to have fewer discipline problems—have more supportive relationships with teachers (Pianta, Hamre, & Stuhlman, 2003).

Unfortunately, once teachers' attitudes toward students are established, they can become more extreme than is warranted by students' behavior. Of special concern are **educational self-fulfilling prophecies:** Children may adopt teachers' positive or negative views and start to live up to them. This effect is especially strong when teachers emphasize competition and publicly compare children, regularly favoring the best students (Kuklinski & Weinstein, 2001; Weinstein, 2002).

Teacher expectations have a greater impact on low achievers than high achievers (Madon, Jussim, & Eccles, 1997). When a teacher is critical, high achievers can fall back on their history of success. Low-achieving students' sensitivity to self-fulfilling prophecies can be beneficial when teachers believe in them. But biased teacher judgments are usually slanted in a negative direction. In one study, African-American children were especially responsive to negative teacher expectations in reading, and girls were especially responsive to negative teacher expectations in math (McKown & Weinstein, 2002). Recall our discussion of *stereotype threat.* A child in the position of confirming a negative stereotype may respond with anxiety and reduced motivation, increasing the likelihood of a negative self-fulfilling prophecy.

Teaching Children with Special Needs

We have seen that effective teachers flexibly adjust their teaching strategies to accommodate students with a wide range of characteristics. These adjustments are especially challenging at the very low and high ends of the ability distribution. How do schools serve children with special learning needs?

■ **CHILDREN WITH LEARNING DIFFICULTIES.** U.S. legislation mandates that schools place children who require special supports for learning in the "least restrictive" (as close to normal as possible) environments that meet their educational needs. In **inclusive classrooms,** students with learning difficulties are placed in regular classrooms for all or part of the school day, a practice designed to prepare them for participation in society and to combat prejudices against individuals with disabilities (Kugelmass & Ainscow, 2004). Largely as the result of parental pressures, an increasing number of students experience *full inclusion*—full-time placement in regular classrooms.

Some students in inclusive classrooms have *mild mental retardation:* Their IQs fall between 55 and 70, and they also show problems in adaptive behavior, or skills of everyday living (American Psychiatric Association, 1994). But the largest number—5 to 10 percent of school-age children—have **learning disabilities,** great difficulty with one or more aspects of learning, usually reading. As a result, their achievement is considerably behind what would be expected on the basis of their IQ. Sometimes deficits express themselves in other ways—for example, as severe inattention, which depresses both IQ and achievement (recall our discussion of ADHD on page 236). The problems of students with learning disabilities cannot be traced to any obvious physical or emotional difficulty or to environmental disadvantage. Instead, subtle deficits in brain functioning seem to be involved (Berninger, 2006). In many instances, the cause is unknown.

Although some included students benefit academically, many do not. Achievement gains depend on both the severity of

In this inclusive second-grade classroom, a teacher encourages a special-needs child to listen to his classmate read a story. The child is likely to do well if he receives support from a special education teacher and if his classroom teacher minimizes comparisons and promotes cooperative learning.

© ELLEN B. SENISI PHOTOGRAPHY

the disability and the support services available (Klingner et al., 1998). Furthermore, children with disabilities are often rejected by regular-classroom peers. Students with mental retardation are overwhelmed by the social skills of their classmates; they cannot interact adeptly in a conversation or game. And the processing deficits of some students with learning disabilities lead to problems in social awareness and responsiveness (Kelly & Norwich, 2004; Sridhar & Vaughn, 2001).

Does this mean that students with special needs cannot be served in regular classrooms? Not necessarily. Often these children do best when they receive instruction in a resource room for part of the day and in the regular classroom for the remainder (Weiner & Tardif, 2004). In the resource room, a special education teacher works with students on an individual and small-group basis. Then, depending on their progress, children join regular classmates for different subjects and amounts of time.

Special steps must to be taken to promote peer relations in inclusive classrooms. Cooperative learning and peer-tutoring experiences in which teachers guide children with learning difficulties and their classmates in working together lead to friendly interaction, improved peer acceptance, and achievement gains (Fuchs et al., 2002a, 2002b).

■ **GIFTED CHILDREN.** In Joey and Lizzie's school, some children are **gifted,** displaying exceptional intellectual strengths. One or two students in every grade have IQ scores above 130, the standard definition of giftedness based on intelligence test performance (Gardner, 1998b). High-IQ children, as we have seen, have keen memories and an exceptional capacity to solve challenging academic problems. Yet recognition that intelligence tests do not sample the entire range of human mental skills has led to an expanded conception of giftedness.

Creativity and Talent. **Creativity** is the ability to produce work that is original yet appropriate—something others have not thought of that is useful in some way (Lubart, 2003; Sternberg, 2003). Tests of creative capacity tap **divergent thinking**—the generation of multiple and unusual possibilities when faced with a task or problem. Divergent thinking contrasts with **convergent thinking,** which involves arriving at a single correct answer and is emphasized on intelligence tests (Guilford, 1985).

Because highly creative children (like high-IQ children) are often better at some tasks than others, a variety of tests of divergent thinking are available (Runco, 1992; Torrance, 1988). A verbal measure might ask children to name uses for common objects (such as a newspaper). A figural measure might ask them to create drawings based on a circular motif (see Figure 9.6). A "real-world problem" measure requires students to suggest solutions to everyday problems. Responses can be scored for the number of ideas generated and their originality.

Yet critics point out that these measures tap only one of the complex cognitive contributions to creative accomplishment in everyday life. Also involved are defining new and important

■ **FIGURE 9.6** ■ **Responses of an 8-year-old who scored high on a figural measure of divergent thinking.** This child was asked to make as many pictures as she could from the circles on the page. The titles she gave her drawings, from left to right, are as follows: "Dracula," "one-eyed monster," "pumpkin," "Hula-Hoop," "poster," "wheelchair," "Earth," "stop-light," "planet," "movie camera," "sad face," "picture," "beach ball," "the letter *O*," "car," "glasses." (Reprinted courtesy of Laura Berk.)

problems, evaluating divergent ideas, choosing the most promising, and calling on relevant knowledge to understand and solve problems (Sternberg, 2003; Guignard & Lubart, 2006).

Consider these ingredients, and you will see why people usually demonstrate creativity in only one or a few related areas. Even individuals designated as gifted by virtue of high IQ often show uneven ability across academic subjects. Partly for this reason, definitions of giftedness have been extended to include **talent**—outstanding performance in a specific field. Case studies reveal that excellence in writing, mathematics, science, music, visual arts, athletics, or leadership has roots in specialized interests and skills that first appear in childhood (Moran & Gardner, 2006; Winner, 2003). Highly talented children are biologically prepared to master their domain of interest, and they display a passion for doing so.

But talent must be nurtured. Studies of the backgrounds of talented children and highly accomplished adults often reveal parents who are warm and sensitive, provide a stimulating home life, are devoted to developing their child's abilities, and provide models of hard work. These parents are reasonably demanding but not driving or overambitious (Winner, 1996, 2000). They arrange for caring teachers while the child is young and for more rigorous master teachers as the talent develops.

Many gifted children and adolescents are socially isolated, partly because their highly driven, nonconforming, and independent styles leave them out of step with peers and partly because they enjoy solitude, which is necessary to develop their talents. Still, gifted children desire gratifying peer relationships, and some—more often girls than boys—try to become better liked by hiding their abilities. Compared with their ordinary agemates, gifted youths, especially girls, report more emotional and social difficulties, including low self-esteem and depression (Reis, 2004; Winner, 2000).

Finally, whereas many talented youths become experts in their fields, few become highly creative. Rapidly mastering an existing field requires different skills than innovating in that field (Moran & Gardner, 2006). The world, however, needs both experts and creators.

Educating the Gifted. Debate about the effectiveness of school programs for the gifted typically focuses on factors irrelevant to giftedness—whether to provide enrichment in regular classrooms, pull children out for special instruction (the most common practice), or advance brighter students to a higher grade. Overall, gifted children fare well academically and socially within each of these models (Moon & Feldhusen, 1994). Yet the extent to which programs foster creativity and talent depends on opportunities to acquire relevant skills.

Gardner's theory of multiple intelligences has inspired several model programs that provide enrichment to all students in diverse disciplines. Meaningful activities, each tapping a specific intelligence or set of intelligences, serve as contexts for assessing strengths and weaknesses and, on that basis, teaching new knowledge and original thinking (Gardner, 1993, 2000). For example, linguistic intelligence might be fostered through storytelling or playwriting; spatial intelligence through drawing, sculpting, or taking apart and reassembling objects; and kinesthetic intelligence through dance or pantomime.

Evidence is still needed on how effectively these programs nurture children's talent and creativity. But they have already succeeded in one way—by highlighting the strengths of some students who previously had been considered unexceptional or even at risk for school failure (Kornhaber, 2004). Consequently, they may be especially useful in identifying talented, low-SES ethnic minority children, who are underrepresented in school programs for the gifted (McBee, 2006).

How Well-Educated Are American Children?

Our discussion of schooling has largely focused on how teachers can support the education of children. Yet many factors—both within and outside schools—affect children's learning. Societal values, school resources, quality of teaching, and parental encouragement all play important roles. Nowhere are these multiple influences more apparent than when schooling is examined in cross-cultural perspective.

In international studies of reading, mathematics, and science achievement, young people in Hong Kong, Korea, Japan, and Taiwan are consistently top performers. Among Western nations, Canada, Finland, Netherlands, and Switzerland are also in the top tier. But U.S. students typically perform at the international average and sometimes below it (see Figure 9.7) (Programme for International Student Assessment, 2003, 2006).

Why do U.S. youths fall behind in academic accomplishment? In the Programme for International Student Assessment, which periodically assesses academic achievement of 15-year-olds in many countries, students were asked about their study habits. Compared with students in the top-achieving nations, many more U.S. students reported studying by memorizing rather than by relating information to previously acquired knowledge (Programme for International Student Assessment, 2005).

Researchers have conducted in-depth research on learning environments in Asian nations, such as Japan, Korea, and Taiwan, to clarify the factors that support high achievement. A

	Country	Average Math Achievement Score
High-Performing Nations	Taiwan	549
	Finland	548
	Hong Kong	547
	Korea, Republic of	547
	Netherlands	531
	Switzerland	530
	Canada	527
	Macao, China	525
	Japan	523
	New Zealand	522
	Belgium	520
	Australia	520
Intermediate-Performing Nations	Denmark	513
	Czech Republic	510
	Iceland	506
	Austria	505
	Germany	504
	Sweden	502
International Average = 498	Ireland	501
	France	496
	United Kingdom	495
	Poland	495
	Hungary	491
	Luxembourg	491
	Norway	490
	Spain	480
	United States	**474**
Low-Performing Nations	Portugal	466
	Italy	462
	Greece	459
	Turkey	424

■ **FIGURE 9.7** ■ **Average mathematics scores of 15-year-olds by country.** The Programme for International Student Assessment assessed achievement in many nations around the world. Taiwan, Hong Kong, Korea, and Japan were among the top performers in mathematics, whereas the United States performed below the international average. Similar outcomes occurred in reading and science. (Adapted from Programme for International Student Assessment, 2006.)

variety of social forces combine to foster a strong commitment to learning in Asian families and schools:

- *Emphasis on effort.* Whereas American parents and teachers tend to regard native ability as key to academic success, Japanese, Korean, and Taiwanese parents and teachers believe that all children can succeed academically with enough effort. Asian parents devote many more hours to helping their children with homework (Stevenson, Lee, & Mu, 2000). Furthermore, Asian youths, influenced by collectivist values, typically view striving to achieve as a moral obligation—a responsibility to family and community (Bempechat & Drago-Severson, 1999).

- *High-quality education for all.* All students in Japanese, Korean, and Taiwanese elementary schools receive the same nationally mandated, high-quality education, delivered by teachers who are better paid than in the United States (U.S. Department of Education, 2008). Academic lessons are particularly well-organized and presented in ways that capture children's attention and encourage high-level thinking (Grow-Maienza, Hahn, & Joo, 2001). And Japanese elementary school teachers are three times as likely as U.S. teachers to work outside class with students who need extra help (Woodward & Ono, 2004).

- *More time devoted to instruction.* In Japan, Hong Kong, and Taiwan, the school year is more than 50 days longer than in the United States (World Education Services, 2007).

The Asian examples underscore the need for families, schools, and the larger society to work together to upgrade education. Currently, the United States is investing more tax dollars in elementary and secondary education and strengthening teacher preparation. In addition, many schools are taking steps to increase parent involvement. Children whose parents create stimulating learning environments at home, monitor their child's academic progress, help with homework, and communicate often with teachers consistently show superior achievement (Hill & Taylor, 2004; Jeynes, 2005). The results of these efforts can be seen in recent national assessments of educational progress (U.S. Department of Education, 2003, 2005). After two decades of decline, U.S. students' overall academic achievement has risen, although not enough to enhance their standing internationally.

ASK YOURSELF

≫ REVIEW
List some teaching practices that foster children's achievement and some that undermine it. Provide a brief explanation of each practice.

≫ APPLY
Sandy wonders why her daughter Mira's teacher often has students work on assignments in small, cooperative groups. Explain the benefits of this approach to Sandy. What must Mira's teacher do to ensure that cooperative learning succeeds?

≫ REFLECT
What teaching philosophy characterized most of your elementary education—traditional, constructivist, or social constructivist? What impact do you think that approach had on your motivation and achievement?

Summary

PHYSICAL DEVELOPMENT

Body Growth

Describe major trends in body growth during middle childhood.

≫ Gains in body size during middle childhood continue at a slow, regular pace. Bones lengthen and broaden, and permanent teeth replace all 20 primary teeth. By age 9, girls overtake boys in physical size.

Health Issues

Describe the causes and consequences of serious nutritional problems in middle childhood, giving special attention to obesity.

≫ Many poverty-stricken children in developing countries and North America continue to suffer from serious and prolonged malnutrition, which can permanently impair physical and mental development.

≫ Overweight and **obesity** are growing problems in Western and developing nations, posing long-term health risks. Although heredity contributes to obesity, reduced sleep, parental feeding practices, maladaptive eating habits, and lack of exercise also play important roles. Obese children are rated as less likable by peers and adults and have serious adjustment problems. Family-based interventions to change parents' and children's eating patterns and lifestyles are the most effective treatment approaches.

©JEFF GREENBERG/THE IMAGE WORKS

What factors contribute to illness during the school years, and how can these health problems be reduced?

≫ Children experience more illnesses during the first two years of elementary school than later because of exposure to sick children and an immature immune system.

≫ The most common cause of school absence and childhood hospitalization is asthma. Although heredity contributes, environmental factors—pollution, stressful home lives, lack of access to good health care, and childhood obesity—have led to an increase in the disease, especially among African-American and poverty-stricken children.

>> Children with severe chronic illnesses are at risk for academic, emotional, and social difficulties, but positive family relationships improve adjustment.

Motor Development and Play

Cite major changes in motor development and play during middle childhood.

>> Gains in flexibility, balance, agility, and force, along with more efficient information processing, contribute to school-age children's improved motor performance.

>> Fine-motor development also improves. Children's writing becomes more legible, and their drawings increase in organization, detail, and representation of depth.

>> While girls outperform boys in fine-motor skills, boys outperform girls in all gross-motor skills except those requiring balance and agility. Higher expectations by parents for boys' athletic performance play a large role.

>> Games with rules become common during the school years, contributing to emotional and social development. Children, especially boys, also engage in **rough-and-tumble play,** through which they safely assess the strength of peers to avoid challenging stronger agemates.

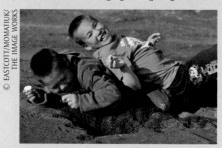

>> Most U.S. school-age children are not active enough for good health. With cutbacks in recess and physical education, they do not reap the health and social benefits of physical fitness.

COGNITIVE DEVELOPMENT

Piaget's Theory: The Concrete Operational Stage

What are the major characteristics of concrete operational thought?

>> Children in the **concrete operational stage** can reason logically about concrete, tangible information. Mastery of conservation demonstrates **reversibility** in thinking. School-age youngsters are also better at hierarchical classification and **seriation,** including **transitive inference.** Their spatial reasoning improves, as seen in their ability to give directions and to create **cognitive maps** representing familiar large-scale spaces.

>> School-age children master logical ideas gradually. Concrete operational thought is limited in that children do not come up with general logical principles.

Discuss follow-up research on concrete operational thought.

>> Specific cultural practices, especially those associated with schooling, affect children's mastery of Piagetian tasks.

>> Some researchers attribute the gradual development of operational thought to gains in information-processing speed. According to Case's neo-Piagetian theory, with practice, cognitive schemes demand less attention and become more automatic, freeing up space in working memory for combining old schemes and generating new ones. Eventually, children consolidate schemes into highly efficient, central conceptual structures, becoming increasingly able to coordinate and integrate multiple dimensions.

Information Processing

Cite basic changes in information processing, and describe the development of attention and memory in middle childhood.

>> Brain development contributes to increases in processing speed and capacity and to gains in inhibition, which facilitate many aspects of thinking.

>> During the school years, attention becomes more selective, adaptable, and planful. The serious symptoms of **attention-deficit hyperactivity disorder (ADHD)** lead to both academic and social problems.

>> Memory strategies also improve. **Rehearsal** appears first, followed by **organization** and then **elaboration.** With age, children combine memory strategies.

>> Development of the long-term knowledge base makes new information easier to store and retrieve. Memory strategies are promoted by learning activities in school.

Describe the school-age child's theory of mind and capacity to engage in self-regulation.

>> Metacognition expands over middle childhood. School-age children regard the mind as an active, constructive agent and, therefore, have a much better understanding of cognitive processes. **Cognitive self-regulation**—putting what one knows about thinking into action—develops gradually over middle childhood and adolescence. It improves with instructions to monitor cognitive activity.

Discuss current controversies in teaching reading and mathematics to elementary school children.

>> Skilled reading draws on all aspects of the information-processing system. Research showing that a mixture of **whole language** and **phonics** is most effective in teaching beginning reading has resolved a long-standing debate. Teaching that blends practice in basic skills with conceptual understanding also is best in mathematics.

Individual Differences in Mental Development

Describe major approaches to defining and measuring intelligence.

>> Most intelligence tests yield an overall score as well as scores for separate intellectual factors. During the school years, IQ becomes more stable, and it correlates moderately well with academic achievement.

>> The componential approach to defining intelligence seeks to identify information-processing skills that contribute to mental test performance. Memory span, speed of thinking, and effective strategy use are positively related to IQ.

>> Sternberg's **triarchic theory of successful intelligence** views intelligence as an interaction of inner and outer forces—analytical intelligence (information-processing skills), creative intelligence (capacity to solve novel problems), and practical intelligence (ability to succeed in one's everyday world).

>> Gardner's **theory of multiple intelligences** identifies at least eight mental abilities. The theory has been especially helpful in understanding and nurturing children's talents, although it has yet to be verified by research.

Describe evidence indicating that both heredity and environment contribute to intelligence.

>> Heritability estimates and adoption research indicate that intelligence is a product of both heredity and environment. Studies of black children adopted into well-to-do homes during the first year of life indicate that the black–white IQ gap is substantially influenced by environment.

>> IQ scores are affected by cultural forces, including exposure to certain communication styles and knowledge and ways of thinking sampled by the test. Among children aware of ethnic stereotypes, **stereotype threat** can trigger anxiety that interferes with test performance. **Dynamic assessment** helps many minority children perform more competently on mental tests.

Language Development

Describe changes in school-age children's vocabulary, grammar, and pragmatics, and cite the advantages of bilingualism for development.

>> During middle childhood, vocabulary continues to grow rapidly, and children have a more precise and flexible understanding of word meanings. They also use more complex grammatical constructions and conversational strategies, and their narratives increase in organization, detail, and expressiveness. Language awareness contributes to school-age children's language progress.

>> Mastery of a second language must begin in childhood for full proficiency to occur. Bilingualism has positive consequences for cognitive development and certain aspects of language awareness. In Canada, language immersion programs are highly successful in making children proficient in both English and French. In the United States, bilingual education that combines instruction in the native tongue and in English supports ethnic minority children's academic learning.

Learning in School

Describe the impact of educational philosophies and teacher–student interaction on children's motivation and academic achievement.

>> Older elementary school students in **traditional classrooms** have a slight edge in academic achievement over those in **constructivist classrooms,** who gain in academic motivation, critical thinking, social and moral maturity, and positive attitudes toward school.

>> Students in **social-constructivist classrooms** benefit from working collaboratively in meaningful activities and from teaching adapted to each child's zone of proximal development. **Cooperative learning** promotes achievement and self-esteem.

>> Caring, helpful, and stimulating teaching fosters children's motivation, academic achievement, and peer relations. **Educational self-fulfilling prophecies** have a greater impact on low than high achievers and are especially likely to occur in classrooms that emphasize competition and public evaluation.

Under what conditions is placement of children with learning difficulties in regular classrooms successful?

>> Students with mild mental retardation and **learning disabilities** are often placed in **inclusive classrooms.** The success of regular-classroom placement depends on meeting individual learning needs and positive peer relations.

Describe the characteristics of gifted children and current efforts to meet their educational needs.

>> **Giftedness** includes high IQ, **creativity,** and **talent.** Tests of creativity that tap **divergent** rather than **convergent thinking** focus on only one of the ingredients of creativity. Highly talented children have parents and teachers who nurture their exceptional abilities. Gifted children are best served by educational programs that build on their special strengths.

How well are American children achieving compared with children in other industrialized nations?

>> In international studies, young people in Asian nations are consistently top performers, whereas American students typically display an average or below-average performance. Asian parents and teachers emphasize effort over native ability, and Asian schools provide the same high-quality education to all students and devote more time to instruction.

Important Terms and Concepts

attention-deficit hyperactivity disorder (ADHD) (p. 236)

cognitive maps (p. 233)

cognitive self-regulation (p. 238)

concrete operational stage (p. 232)

constructivist classroom (p. 248)

convergent thinking (p. 251)

cooperative learning (p. 249)

creativity (p. 251)

divergent thinking (p. 251)

dynamic assessment (p. 244)

educational self-fulfilling prophecies (p. 250)

elaboration (p. 237)

gifted (p. 251)

inclusive classrooms (p. 250)

learning disabilities (p. 250)

obesity (p. 226)

organization (p. 235)

phonics approach (p. 238)

rehearsal (p. 235)

reversibility (p. 232)

rough-and-tumble play (p. 230)

seriation (p. 232)

social-constructivist classroom (p. 248)

stereotype threat (p. 244)

talent (p. 251)

theory of multiple intelligences (p. 241)

traditional classroom (p. 248)

transitive inference (p. 232)

triarchic theory of successful intelligence (p. 241)

whole-language approach (p. 238)

CHAPTER 10

Emotional and Social Development in Middle Childhood

© CHRISTIANE EISLER/PETER ARNOLD INC.

Social understanding expands greatly in middle childhood. Like others their age around the world, these Turkish children select friends based on personal qualities, and they become more responsive to one another's needs and desires.

ate one afternoon, Rena heard her son Joey burst through the front door, run upstairs, and phone his best friend. "Terry, gotta talk to you," Joey pleaded breathlessly. "Everything was going great until that word I got—*porcupine*," Joey went on, referring to the fifth-grade spelling bee at school that day. "Just my luck! *P-o-r-k*, that's how I spelled it! I can't believe it. Maybe I'm not so good at social studies," Joey confided, "but I *know* I'm better at spelling than that stuck-up Belinda Brown. I knocked myself out studying those spelling lists. Then *she* got all the easy words. If I *had* to lose, why couldn't it be to a nice person?"

Joey's conversation reflects his new emotional and social capacities. By entering the spelling bee, he shows *industriousness,* the energetic pursuit of meaningful achievement in his culture. Joey's social understanding has also expanded: He can size up strengths, weaknesses, and personality characteristics. Furthermore, friendship means something different than it did earlier—Joey counts on his best friend, Terry, for understanding and emotional support.

For an overview of personality change in middle childhood, we return to Erikson's theory. Then we look at children's views of themselves and of others, their moral understanding, and their peer relationships. Each increases in complexity as children reason more effectively and spend more time in school and with agemates.

Despite changing parent–child relationships, the family remains powerfully influential in middle childhood. Today, family lifestyles are more diverse than ever before. Through Joey's and his younger sister Lizzie's experiences with parental divorce, we will see that family functioning is far more important than family structure in ensuring children's well-being. Finally, we look at some common emotional problems of middle childhood.

Erikson's Theory: Industry versus Inferiority

According to Erikson (1950), children whose previous experiences have been positive enter middle childhood prepared to direct their energies toward realistic accomplishment.

Erikson believed that the combination of adult expectations and children's drive toward mastery sets the stage for the psychological conflict of middle childhood, **industry versus inferiority,** which is resolved positively when children develop a sense of competence at useful skills and tasks.

In industrialized nations, the beginning of formal schooling marks the transition to middle childhood. In school, children discover their own and others' unique capacities, learn the value of division of labor, and develop a sense of moral commitment and responsibility. The danger at this stage is *inferiority,* reflected in the pessimism of children who have little confidence in their ability to do things well. This sense of inadequacy can develop when family life has not prepared children for school life or when teachers and peers destroy children's feelings of competence and mastery with negative responses.

Erikson's sense of industry combines several developments of middle childhood: a positive but realistic self-concept, pride in accomplishment, moral responsibility, and cooperative participation with agemates. How do these aspects of self and social relationships change over the school years?

Self-Understanding

In middle childhood, children become able to describe themselves in terms of psychological traits, to compare their own characteristics with those of their peers, and to speculate about the causes of their strengths and weaknesses. These transformations in self-understanding have a major impact on children's self-esteem.

Self-Concept

During the school years, children refine their self-concept, organizing their observations of behaviors and internal states into general dispositions. A major change takes place between ages 8 and 11, as the following self-description by an 11-year-old illustrates:

> My name is A. I'm a human being. I'm a girl. I'm a truthful person. I'm not pretty. I do so-so in my studies. I'm a very good cellist. . . . I try to be helpful. I'm always ready to be friends with anybody. Mostly I'm good, but I lose my temper. (Montemayor & Eisen, 1977, pp. 317–318)

Instead of specific behaviors, this child emphasizes competencies: "I'm a very good cellist" (Damon & Hart, 1988). She also describes her personality, mentioning both positive and negative traits: "truthful" but short-tempered. Older school-age children are far less likely than younger children to describe themselves in extreme, all-or-none ways (Harter, 2003, 2006).

These qualified, trait-based self-descriptions result from cognitive advances—specifically, the capacity to combine typical experiences and behaviors into psychological dispositions.

Children also become better at *perspective taking*—inferring others' attitudes toward the child—and incorporating those attitudes into their self-definitions. These cognitive capacities, combined with more experiences in which children are evaluated against agemates, prompt **social comparisons**—judgments of one's own appearance, abilities, and behavior in relation to those of others. For example, Joey observed that he was better than his peers at spelling but not so good at social studies (Butler, 1998; Harter, 2006). As children internalize others' expectations and make social comparisons, they form an *ideal self* that they use to evaluate their *real self*. As we will see, a large discrepancy between the two can undermine self-esteem, leading to sadness, hopelessness, and depression.

In middle childhood, children look to more people beyond the family for information about themselves as they enter a wider range of settings in school and community. And self-descriptions now include frequent reference to social groups: "I'm a Boy Scout, a paperboy, and a Prairie City soccer player," said Joey. And as children move into adolescence, although parents and other adults remain influential, self-concept is increasingly vested in feedback from close friends (Oosterwegel & Oppenheimer, 1993).

But recall that the makeup of self-concept varies from culture to culture. In earlier chapters, we noted that Asian parents stress harmonious interdependence, whereas Western parents stress independence and self-assertion. When asked to recall personally significant past experiences (their last birthday, a time their parent scolded them), U.S. children gave longer accounts including more personal preferences, skills, and opinions. Chinese children, in contrast, more often referred to social interactions and to others. Similarly in their self-descriptions, U.S. children listed more personal attributes ("I'm smart,"

"I like hockey"), Chinese children more attributes involving group membership and relationships ("I'm in second grade," "My friends are crazy about me") (Wang, 2004, 2006).

Development of Self-Esteem

Recall that most preschoolers have extremely high self-esteem. But as children enter school and receive more feedback about how well they perform compared with their peers, self-esteem differentiates and also adjusts to a more realistic level.

Researchers have asked children to indicate the extent to which statements such as "I am good at homework" or "I'm usually the one chosen for games" are true of themselves. By age 6 to 7, children have formed at least four broad self-evaluations—academic competence, social competence, physical/athletic competence, and physical appearance. Within these are more refined categories that become increasingly distinct with age (Marsh, 1990; Marsh & Ayotte, 2003; Van den Bergh & De Rycke, 2003). Furthermore, the capacity to view the self in terms of stable dispositions permits school-age children to combine their separate self-evaluations into a general psychological image of themselves—an overall sense of self-esteem (Harter, 2003, 2006). As a result, self-esteem takes on the hierarchical structure shown in Figure 10.1.

Children attach greater importance to certain self-evaluations than to others. Although individual differences exist, during childhood and adolescence, perceived physical appearance correlates more strongly with overall self-worth than any other self-esteem factor (Klomsten, Skaalvik, & Espnes, 2004; Shapka & Keating, 2005). Emphasis on appearance, in the media and in society, has major implications for young people's general satisfaction with themselves.

Over the first few years of elementary school, level of self-esteem declines as children evaluate themselves in various areas (Marsh, Craven, & Debus, 1998; Wigfield et al., 1997). Typically, the drop is not great enough to be harmful. Most (but not all) children appraise their characteristics and competencies realistically while maintaining an attitude of self-respect. Then, from fourth grade on, self-esteem rises for the majority of young people, who feel especially good about their peer relationships and athletic capabilities (Cole et al., 2001; Twenge & Campbell, 2001).

Influences on Self-Esteem

From middle childhood on, individual differences in self-esteem become increasingly stable (Trzesniewski, Donnellan, & Robins, 2003). And positive relationships among self-esteem, valuing of various activities, and success at those activities emerge and strengthen (Denissen, Zarrett, & Eccles, 2007; Harter, 1999; Valentine, DuBois, & Cooper, 2004). What social influences might lead self-esteem to be high for some children and low for others?

■ **CULTURE.** An especially strong emphasis on social comparison in school may explain why Chinese and Japanese

As these young musicians participate in their school orchestra, they become more aware of their own competencies. The combination of cognitive gains and repeated evaluations against their peers prompts school-age children to make social comparisons. As a result, children refine their self-concepts, describing themselves as better at some endeavors than at others.

© TOM & DEE ANN MCCARTHY/CORBIS

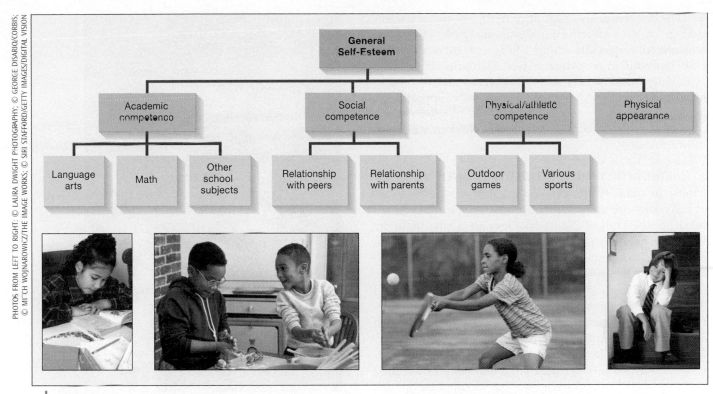

■ **FIGURE 10.1** ■ **Hierarchical structure of self-esteem in the mid-elementary school years.** From their experiences in different settings, children form at least four separate self-esteems: academic competence, social competence, physical/athletic competence, and physical appearance. These differentiate into additional self-evaluations and combine to form a general sense of self-esteem.

children, despite their higher academic achievement, score lower in self-esteem than North American children (Harter, 2006; Hawkins, 1994; Twenge & Crocker, 2002). And because their culture values social harmony, Asian children tend to be reserved about judging themselves positively but generous in their praise of others (Falbo et al., 1997).

Gender-stereotyped expectations also affect self-esteem. In one study, the more 5- to 8-year-old girls talked with friends about the way people look, watched TV shows focusing on physical appearance, and perceived their friends as valuing thinness, the lower their physical self-esteem and overall self-worth a year later (Dohnt & Tiggemann, 2006). In academic self-judgments, girls score higher in language arts self-esteem, whereas boys have higher math, science, and physical/athletic self-esteem—even when children of equal skill levels are compared (Fredricks & Eccles, 2002; Jacobs et al., 2002; Tennenbaum & Leaper, 2003). At the same time, girls exceed boys in self-esteem dimensions of close friendship and social acceptance. And despite a widely held assumption that boys' overall self-worth is much higher than girls', the difference is slight (Marsh & Ayotte, 2003; Young & Mroczek, 2003). Girls may think less well of themselves because they internalize this negative cultural message.

Compared with their Caucasian agemates, African-American children tend to have slightly higher self-esteem, possibly because of warm, extended families and a stronger sense of ethnic pride (Gray-Little & Hafdahl, 2000). Finally, children

and adolescents who attend schools or live in neighborhoods where their SES and ethnic groups are well-represented feel a stronger sense of belonging and have fewer self-esteem problems (Gray-Little & Carels, 1997).

■ **CHILD-REARING PRACTICES.** Children whose parents use an *authoritative* child-rearing style (see Chapter 8) feel especially good about themselves (Carlson, Uppal, & Prosser, 2000; Rudy & Grusec, 2006; Wilkinson, 2004). Warm, positive parenting lets children know that they are accepted as competent and worthwhile. And firm but appropriate expectations, backed up with explanations, help them evaluate their own behavior against reasonable standards.

Controlling parents—those who too often help or make decisions for their child—communicate a sense of inadequacy to children. Having parents who are repeatedly disapproving is also linked to low self-esteem (Kernis, 2002; Pomerantz & Eaton, 2000). Children subjected to such parenting need constant reassurance, and many rely heavily on peers to affirm their self-worth—a risk factor for adjustment difficulties, including aggression and antisocial behavior (Donnellan et al., 2005). In contrast, indulgent parenting is correlated with unrealistically high self-esteem, which also undermines development. These children tend to lash out at challenges to their overblown self-images and, thus, are also likely to be hostile and aggressive (Hughes, Cavell, & Grossman, 1997).

The best way to foster a positive, secure self-image is to encourage children to strive for worthwhile goals. Over time, achievement fosters self-esteem, which contributes to further effort and gains in performance (Gest, Domitrovich, & Welsh, 2005; Guay, Marsh, & Boivin, 2003). What can adults do to promote, and to avoid undermining, this mutually supportive relationship between motivation and self-esteem? Some answers come from research on adults' messages to children in achievement situations.

■ MAKING ACHIEVEMENT-RELATED ATTRIBUTIONS.

Attributions are our common, everyday explanations for the causes of behavior—our answers to the question, "Why did I or another person do that?" Notice how Joey, in talking about the spelling bee at the beginning of this chapter, attributes his disappointing performance to *luck* (Belinda got all the easy words) and his usual success to *ability* (he *knows* he's a better speller than Belinda). Joey also appreciates that *effort* matters: "I knocked myself out studying those spelling lists."

Cognitive development permits school-age children to separate all these variables in explaining performance (Dweck, 2002). Those who are high in academic self-esteem and motivation make **mastery-oriented attributions,** crediting their successes to ability—a characteristic they can improve through trying hard and can count on when facing new challenges. And they attribute failure to factors that can be changed or controlled, such as insufficient effort or a very difficult task (Heyman & Dweck, 1998). So whether these children succeed or fail, they take an industrious, persistent approach to learning.

In contrast, children who develop **learned helplessness** attribute their failures, not their successes, to ability. When they succeed, they conclude that external factors, such as luck, are responsible. Unlike their mastery-oriented counterparts, they believe that ability is fixed and cannot be improved by trying hard (Cain & Dweck, 1995). When a task is difficult, these children experience an anxious loss of control—in Erikson's terms, a pervasive sense of inferiority. They give up without really trying.

Children's attributions affect their goals. Mastery-oriented children seek information on how best to increase their ability through effort. Hence, their performance improves over time (Blackwell, Trzesniewski, & Dweck, 2007). In contrast, learned-helpless children focus on obtaining positive and avoiding negative evaluations of their fragile sense of ability. Over time, their ability no longer predicts how well they do (Pomerantz & Saxon, 2001). Because they fail to connect effort with success, learned-helpless children do not develop the metacognitive and self-regulatory skills necessary for high achievement (see Chapter 9). Lack of effective learning strategies, reduced persistence, low performance, and a sense of loss of control sustain one another in a vicious cycle (Chan & Moore, 2006).

■ INFLUENCES ON ACHIEVEMENT-RELATED ATTRIBUTIONS.

Adult communication plays a key role in the different attributions of mastery-oriented and learned-helpless children.

Mastery-oriented children credit their successes to ability, and they seek information on how best to increase their ability through effort. Hence, their performance improves over time.

Parents of children with a learned-helpless style usually believe that their child is incapable. When the child fails, the parent might say, "You can't do that, can you? It's OK if you quit" (Hokoda & Fincham, 1995). After the child succeeds, the parent might give feedback that evaluates the child's traits ("You're so smart"). Trait statements promote a fixed view of ability, leading children to question their competence in the face of setbacks and to retreat from challenge (Mueller & Dweck, 1998).

For some children, performance is especially likely to be undermined by adult feedback. Despite their higher achievement, girls more often than boys blame poor performance on ability. Girls tend to receive messages from teachers and parents that their ability is at fault when they do not do well, and negative stereotypes (for example, that girls are weak at math) reduce their interest and effort (Bleeker & Jacobs, 2004; Cole et al., 1999). And as Chapter 9 revealed, low-SES ethnic minority students often receive less favorable feedback from teachers—conditions that result in a drop in academic self-esteem and achievement (Harris and Graham, 2007).

Finally, cultural values affect the likelihood that children will develop learned helplessness. Because of the high value their culture places on effort and self-improvement, Asians attend more to failure than to success because failure indicates where corrective action is needed. Americans, in contrast, focus more on success because it enhances self-esteem. When researchers observed U.S. and Chinese mothers' responses to their fourth and fifth graders' puzzle solutions, the U.S. mothers offered more praise after success, whereas the Chinese mothers more often pointed out the child's inadequate performance. And regardless of success or failure, Chinese mothers made more task-relevant statements aimed at ensuring that children exerted sufficient effort to do well ("You concentrated on it": "You got only 6 out of 12"). When children continued with the task after mothers left the room, the Chinese children showed greater gains in performance (Ng, Pomerantz, & Lam, 2007).

■ **FOSTERING A MASTERY-ORIENTED APPROACH.** Attribution research suggests that well-intended messages from adults sometimes undermine children's competence. An intervention called *attribution retraining* encourages learned-helpless children to believe that they can overcome failure by exerting more effort. Children are given tasks difficult enough that they will experience some failure, followed by repeated feedback that helps them revise their attributions: "You can do it if you try harder." After they succeed, children receive additional feedback—"You're really good at this" or "You really tried hard on that one"—so that they attribute their success to both ability and effort, not chance. Another approach is to encourage low-effort students to focus less on grades and more on mastering a task for its own sake (Hilt, 2004; Horner & Gaither, 2004). Instruction in effective strategies and self-regulation is also vital, to compensate for development lost in this area and to ensure that renewed effort pays off (Wigfield et al., 2006).

ASK YOURSELF

>> **REVIEW**
How does level of self-esteem change in middle childhood, and what accounts for these changes?

>> **APPLY**
Should parents promote children's self-esteem by telling them they're "smart" or "wonderful"? Are children harmed if they do not feel good about everything they do? Why or why not?

>> **REFLECT**
Recall your own attributions for academic successes and failures when you were in elementary school. What are those attributions like now? What messages from others may have contributed to your attributions?

Emotional Development

Greater self-awareness and social sensitivity contribute to emotional development in middle childhood. Changes take place in experience of self-conscious emotions, emotional understanding, and emotional self-regulation.

Self-Conscious Emotions

In middle childhood, self-conscious emotions of pride and guilt become clearly governed by personal responsibility. Children experience pride in a new accomplishment and guilt over a transgression, even when no adult is present (Harter & Whitesell, 1989).

Pride motivates children to take on further challenges, whereas guilt prompts them to make amends and to strive for self-improvement. But harsh, insensitive reprimands from adults ("Everyone else can do it! Why can't you?") can lead to intense shame, which (as noted in Chapter 8) is particularly destructive. A shame-induced sharp drop in self-esteem can trigger withdrawal, depression, and intense anger at those who participated in the shame-evoking situation (Lindsay-Hartz, de Rivera, & Mascolo, 1995; Mills, 2005).

Emotional Understanding

School-age children's understanding of mental activity means that, unlike preschoolers, they are likely to explain emotion by referring to internal states, such as happy or sad thoughts (Flavell, Flavell, & Green, 2001). Also, around age 8, children become aware that they can experience more than one emotion at a time, each of which may be positive or negative and differ in intensity (Pons et al., 2003). For example, Joey reflected, "I was very happy that I got a birthday present from my grandma but a little sad that I didn't get just what I wanted."

Appreciating mixed emotions helps children realize that people's expressions may not reflect their true feelings (Misailidi, 2006). It also fosters awareness of self-conscious emotions. For example, between ages 6 and 7, children improve sharply in ability to distinguish pride from happiness and surprise (Tracy, Robins, & Lagattuta, 2005). And 8- and 9-year-olds understand that pride combines two sources of happiness—joy in accomplishment and joy that a significant person recognized that accomplishment (Harter, 1999).

As with self-understanding, gains in emotional understanding are supported by cognitive development and social experiences, especially adults' sensitivity to children's feelings and willingness to discuss emotions. Together, these factors lead to a rise in empathy as well. As children move closer to adolescence, advances in perspective taking permit an empathic response not just to people's immediate distress but also to their general life condition (Hoffman, 2000). As Joey and Lizzie imagined how people who are chronically ill or hungry feel and evoked those emotions in themselves, they gave part of their allowance to charity and joined in school and scouting fundraising projects.

Emotional Self-Regulation

Rapid gains in emotional self-regulation occur in middle childhood. As children engage in social comparison and care more

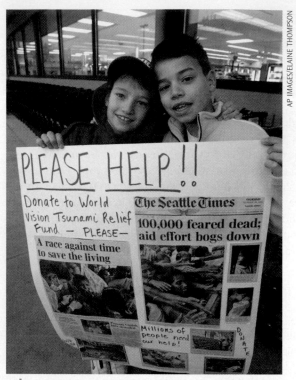

These 8-year-old twin brothers raised over $5,000 for victims of the devastating tsunami of 2005. Their gains in emotional understanding and perspective taking enable them to respond with empathy to people's immediate distress as well as to their general life condition.

about peer approval, they must learn to manage negative emotion that threatens their self-esteem.

By age 10, most children shift adaptively between two general strategies for managing emotion. In **problem-centered coping,** they appraise the situation as changeable, identify the difficulty, and decide what to do about it. If problem solving does not work, they engage in **emotion-centered coping,** which is internal, private, and aimed at controlling distress when little can be done about an outcome (Kliewer, Fearnow, & Miller, 1996; Lazarus & Lazarus, 1994). For example, when faced with an anxiety-provoking test or an angry friend, older school-age children view problem solving and seeking social support as the best strategies. But when outcomes are beyond their control—for example, after receiving a bad grade—they opt for distraction or try to redefine the situation: "Things could be worse. There'll be another test." School-age children's improved ability to reflect on thoughts and feelings means that, compared with preschoolers, they more often use these internal strategies to manage emotion (Brenner & Salovey, 1997).

When emotional self-regulation has developed well, school-age children acquire a sense of *emotional self-efficacy*—a feeling of being in control of their emotional experience (Saarni, 2000). This fosters a favorable self-image and an optimistic outlook, which further help children face emotional challenges. As at younger ages, school-age children whose parents respond sensitively and helpfully when the child is distressed are emo-

tionally well-regulated—generally upbeat in mood and also empathic and prosocial. In contrast, poorly regulated children often experience hostile, dismissive parental reactions to distress (Davidov & Grusec, 2006; Zeman, Shipman, & Suveg, 2002). These children are overwhelmed by negative emotion, a response that interferes with empathy and prosocial behavior.

Understanding Others: Perspective Taking

We have seen that middle childhood brings major advances in **perspective taking,** the capacity to imagine what other people may be thinking and feeling. These changes support self-concept and self-esteem, understanding of others, and a wide variety of social skills. Robert Selman's five-stage sequence describes changes in perspective-taking skill, based on children's and adolescents' responses to social dilemmas in which characters have differing information and opinions about an event.

As Table 10.1 indicates, at first children have only a limited idea of what other people might be thinking and feeling. Over time, they become more aware that people can interpret the same event quite differently. Soon, they can "step into another person's shoes" and reflect on how that person might regard their own thoughts, feelings, and behavior, as when they say something like, "I *thought you would think* I was just kidding when I said that." (Note the similarity between this level of perspective taking and second-order false belief, described on page 237 in Chapter 9.) Finally, older children and adolescents can evaluate two people's perspectives simultaneously, at first from the vantage point of a disinterested spectator and later by referring to societal values (Gurucharri & Selman, 1982). The following explanation reflects this ability: "I know why Joey hid the stray kitten in the basement, even though his mom was against keeping it. He believes in not hurting animals. If you put the kitten outside or give it to the pound, it might die."

Besides cognitive maturity, experiences in which adults and peers explain their viewpoints contribute greatly to children's perspective taking. Good perspective takers, in turn, are more likely to display empathy and sympathy and to handle difficult social situations effectively—among the reasons they are better-liked by peers (FitzGerald & White, 2003).

Moral Development

Recall from Chapter 8 that preschoolers pick up many morally relevant behaviors through modeling and reinforcement. By middle childhood, they have had time to internalize rules for good conduct: "It's good to help others in trouble" or "It's wrong to take something that doesn't belong to you." This change leads children to become considerably more independent and trustworthy.

■ **TABLE 10.1** ■ *Selman's Stages of Perspective Taking*

STAGE	APPROXIMATE AGE RANGE	DESCRIPTION
Level 0: Undifferentiated perspective taking	3–6	Children recognize that self and other can have different thoughts and feelings, but they frequently confuse the two.
Level 1: Social-informational perspective taking	4–9	Children understand that different perspectives may result because people have access to different information.
Level 2: Self-reflective perspective taking	7–12	Children can "step into another person's shoes" and view their own thoughts, feelings, and behavior from the other person's perspective. They also recognize that others can do the same.
Level 3: Third-party perspective taking	10–15	Children can step outside a two-person situation and imagine how the self and other are viewed from the point of view of a third, impartial party.
Level 4: Societal perspective taking	14–adult	Individuals understand that third-party perspective taking can be influenced by one or more systems of larger societal values.

Sources: Selman, 1976; Selman & Byrne, 1974.

In Chapter 8, we also saw that children do not just copy their morality from others but actively think about right and wrong. An expanding social world, the capacity to consider more information when reasoning, and perspective taking lead moral understanding to advance greatly in middle childhood.

Moral and Social-Conventional Understanding

During the school years, children construct a flexible appreciation of moral rules. By age 7 to 8, they no longer say truth telling is always good and lying is always bad but also consider prosocial and antisocial intentions. They evaluate certain types of truthfulness very negatively—for example, bluntly telling a classmate that you don't like her drawing (Bussey, 1999).

As children's ideas about justice take into account an increasing number of variables, they clarify and link moral imperatives and social conventions. School-age children, for example, distinguish social conventions with a clear *purpose* (not running in school hallways to prevent injuries) from ones with no obvious justification (crossing a "forbidden" line on the playground). They regard violations of purposeful social conventions as closer to moral transgressions (Buchanan-Barrow & Barrett, 1998). With age, they also realize that people's *intentions* and the *contexts* of their actions affect the moral implications of violating a social convention. In one study, 8- to 10-year-olds stated that because of a flag's symbolic value, burning it to express disapproval of a country or to start a cooking fire is worse than burning it accidentally. But they recognized that flag burning is a form of freedom of expression, and most agreed that it would be acceptable in a country that treated its citizens unfairly (Helwig & Prencipe, 1999).

Children in Western and non-Western cultures reason similarly about moral and social-conventional concerns (Neff & Helwig, 2002; Nucci, 2002, 2005). When a directive is fair and caring, such as telling children to stop fighting or to share

candy, school-age children view it as right, regardless of who states it—a principal, a teacher, or a child with no authority. In contrast, even in Korean culture, which places a high value on deference to authority, 7- to 11-year-olds evaluate negatively

School-age children recognize that certain social conventions have a clear purpose—such as separating recyclables from trash to prevent waste. And they regard violations of these kinds of conventions as closer to moral transgressions.

a teacher's or principal's order to engage in immoral acts, such as stealing or refusing to share (Kim, 1998; Kim & Turiel, 1996).

Understanding Individual Rights

When children in diverse cultures challenge adult authority, they typically do so within the personal domain. As their grasp of moral imperatives and social conventions strengthens, so does their conviction that certain choices, such as hairstyle, friends, and leisure activities, are up to the individual.

Notions of personal choice, in turn, enhance children's moral understanding. As early as age 6, children view freedom of speech and religion as individual rights, even if laws exist that deny those rights (Helwig, 2006). And they regard laws that discriminate against individuals—for example, denying certain people access to medical care or education—as wrong and worthy of violating (Helwig & Jasiobedzka, 2001). In justifying their responses, children appeal to personal privileges and, by the end of middle childhood, to the importance of individual rights for maintaining a fair society.

At the same time, older school-age children place limits on individual choice. Fourth graders faced with conflicting moral and personal concerns—such as whether or not to befriend a classmate of a different race or gender—typically decide in favor of kindness and fairness (Killen et al., 2002). Partly for this reason, prejudice usually declines in middle childhood (Ruble et al., 2004).

with these changes, aggression declines. But the drop is greatest for physical attacks (Côte et al., 2007). As we will see, verbal and relational aggression continue as children form peer groups.

Peer Groups

TAKE A MOMENT... Watch children in the schoolyard or neighborhood, and notice how often they gather in groups of three to a dozen or more. In what ways are members of the same group noticeably alike? By the end of middle childhood, children display a strong desire for group belonging. They form **peer groups,** collectives that generate unique values and standards for behavior and a social structure of leaders and followers. Peer groups organize on the basis of proximity (being in the same classroom) and similarity in sex, ethnicity, popularity, and aggression (Rubin, Bukowski, & Parker, 2006).

The practices of these informal groups lead to a "peer culture" that typically consists of a specialized vocabulary, dress code, and place to "hang out." These customs bind peers together, creating a sense of group identity. Within the group, children acquire many social skills—cooperation, leadership, followership, and loyalty to collective goals.

Most school-age children believe a group is wrong to exclude a peer (Killen, Crystal, & Watanabe, 2002). Nevertheless, children do exclude, often using relationally aggressive tactics. Peer groups—at the instigation of their leaders, who can be skillfully aggressive—frequently oust no longer "respected" children. Some, whose own previous behavior toward outsiders reduces their chances of being included elsewhere, turn to other

>> **REVIEW**
How does emotional self-regulation improve in middle childhood? What implications do these changes have for children's self-esteem?

>> **APPLY**
Seven-year-old Tracy heard her parents discussing an older cousin's fiancé. "Molly can marry whomever she wants," Tracy chimed in. "That's *her* choice." How is Tracy's reasoning contributing to her moral understanding?

Peer Relations

In middle childhood, the society of peers becomes an increasingly important context for development. Peer contact, as we have seen, contributes to perspective taking and understanding of self and others. These developments, in turn, enhance peer interaction. Compared with preschoolers, school-age children resolve conflicts more effectively, using persuasion and compromise (Mayeux & Cillessen, 2003). Sharing, helping, and other prosocial acts also increase. In line

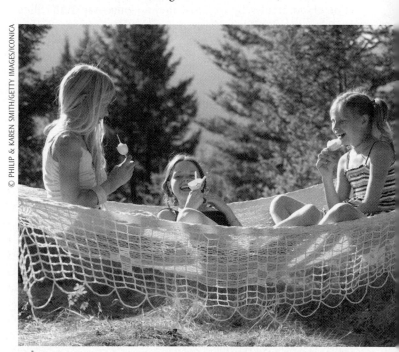

These girls have probably established a peer-group structure of leaders and followers as they gather for joint activities. Their relaxed body language and similar way of dressing suggest their strong sense of group belonging.

low-status peers with poor social skills (Werner & Crick, 2004). Socially anxious children, when ousted, often become increasingly peer-avoidant and thus more isolated (Gazelle & Rudolph, 2004). In either case, opportunities to acquire socially competent behavior diminish.

School-age children's desire for group membership can also be satisfied through formal group ties such as scouting, 4-H, and religious youth groups. Adult involvement holds in check the negative behaviors associated with children's informal peer groups (Vandell & Shumow, 1999).

Friendships

Whereas peer groups provide children with insight into larger social structures, friendships contribute to the development of trust and sensitivity. During the school years, friendship becomes more complex and psychologically based. Consider the following 8-year-old's ideas:

> *How come you like Shelly better than anyone else?* She's done the most for me. She never disagrees, she never eats in front of me, she never walks away when I'm crying, and she helps me with my homework. . . . *How do you get someone to like you?* . . . If you're nice to [your friends], they'll be nice to you. (Damon, 1988b, pp. 80–81)

As these responses show, friendship has become a mutually agreed-on relationship in which children like each other's personal qualities and respond to one another's needs and desires. And once a friendship forms, *trust* becomes its defining feature. Consequently, older children regard violations of trust, such as not helping when others need help, breaking promises, and gossiping behind the other's back, as serious breaches of friendship (Hartup & Abecassis, 2004; Selman, 1980).

Because of these features, school-age children's friendships are more selective. Whereas preschoolers say they have lots of friends, by age 8 or 9, children name only a handful of good friends, and their friendships last longer—sometimes for several years. Girls, who demand greater closeness than boys, are more exclusive in their friendships (Markovitz, Benenson, & Dolensky, 2001).

In addition, children tend to select friends similar to themselves in age, sex, race, ethnicity, and SES. Friends also resemble one another in personality (sociability, aggression), popularity, academic achievement, prosocial behavior, and judgments (including biased perceptions) of other people (Hartup, 2006; Mariano & Harton, 2005). But friendship opportunities offered by children's environments also affect their choices. In integrated classrooms with mixed-race collaborative learning groups, students form more cross-race friendships (Turner, Hewstone, & Voci, 2007).

Through friendship, children come to realize that close relationships can survive disagreements if friends are secure in their liking for one another (Rose & Asher, 1999). In this way, friendship provides an important context in which children learn to tolerate criticism and resolve disputes.

School-age children tend to select friends similar to themselves in age, sex, race, ethnicity, and SES. However, in integrated classrooms with mixed-race collaborative learning groups, students form more cross-race friendships.

Yet the impact of friendships on development depends on the nature of those friends. Children who bring kindness and compassion to their friendships strengthen each other's prosocial tendencies and form more lasting ties. When aggressive children make friends, the relationship is often riddled with hostile interaction and is at risk for breakup, especially when just one member of the pair is aggressive (Ellis & Zarbatany, 2007). Aggressive girls' friendships are full of jealousy, conflict, and betrayal (Werner & Crick, 2004). Aggressive boys' friendships involve frequent expressions of anger, coercive statements, physical attacks, and enticements to rule-breaking behavior (Bagwell & Coie, 2004; Crick & Nelson, 2002). These findings indicate that the social problems of aggressive children operate within their closest peer ties.

Peer Acceptance

Peer acceptance refers to likability—the extent to which a child is viewed by a group of agemates, such as classmates, as a worthy social partner. Unlike friendship, likability is not a mutual relationship but a one-sided perspective, involving the group's view of an individual. Nevertheless, certain social skills that contribute to friendship also enhance peer acceptance. Better-accepted children tend to have more friends and more positive relationships with them (Lansford et al., 2006).

To assess peer acceptance, researchers usually use self-reports that measure *social preferences*—for example, asking children to identify classmates whom they "like very much" or "like very little." Another approach assesses *social prominence*—children's judgments of whom most of their classmates admire. The classmates children identify as prominent (looked up to by many others) show only moderate correspondence with those they say they personally prefer (LaFontana & Cillessen, 1999).

Children's self-reports yield four general categories of peer acceptance:

- **Popular children,** who get many positive votes (are well-liked)
- **Rejected children,** who get many negative votes (are disliked)
- **Controversial children,** who get a large number of positive and negative votes (are both liked and disliked)
- **Neglected children,** who are seldom mentioned, either positively or negatively

About two-thirds of students in a typical elementary school classroom fit one of these categories (Coie, Dodge, & Coppotelli, 1982). The remaining one-third, who do not receive extreme scores, are *average* in peer acceptance.

Peer acceptance is a powerful predictor of psychological adjustment. Rejected children, especially, are anxious, unhappy, disruptive, and low in self-esteem. Both teachers and parents rate them as having a wide range of emotional and social problems. Peer rejection in middle childhood is also strongly associated with poor school performance, absenteeism, dropping out, substance use, depression, antisocial behavior, and delinquency in adolescence and with criminality in early adulthood (Laird et al., 2001; Rubin, Bukowski, & Parker, 2006).

However, earlier influences—children's characteristics combined with parenting practices—may largely explain the link between peer acceptance and adjustment. School-age children with peer-relationship problems are more likely to have experienced family stress due to low income, insensitive child rearing, and coercive discipline (Cowan & Cowan, 2004). Nevertheless, as we will see, rejected children evoke reactions from peers that contribute to their unfavorable development.

■ **DETERMINANTS OF PEER ACCEPTANCE.** Why is one child liked while another is rejected? A wealth of research reveals that social behavior plays a powerful role.

Popular Children. The majority of **popular-prosocial children** combine academic and social competence, performing well in school and communicating with peers in sensitive, friendly, and cooperative ways (Cillessen & Bellmore, 2004). But other popular children are admired for their socially adept yet belligerent behavior. This smaller subtype, **popular-antisocial children,** includes "tough" boys—athletically skilled but poor students who cause trouble and defy adult authority—and relationally aggressive boys and girls who enhance their own status by ignoring, excluding, and spreading rumors about other children (Cillessen & Mayeux, 2004; Rodkin et al., 2006; Rose, Swenson, & Waller, 2004). But with age, peers like these

high-status, aggressive youths less and less and may eventually reject them.

Rejected Children. Rejected children display a wide range of negative social behaviors. Most are **rejected-aggressive children,** who show high rates of conflict, physical and relational aggression, and hyperactive, inattentive, and impulsive behavior. They are even more belligerent than popular-aggressive children and are also deficient in perspective taking and emotion regulation (Crick, Casas, & Nelson, 2002; Dodge, Coie, & Lynam, 2006). In contrast, **rejected-withdrawn children** are passive and socially awkward. These timid children are overwhelmed by social anxiety and hold negative expectations for how peers will treat them (see the Biology and Environment box on the following page) (Hart et al., 2000; Ladd & Burgess, 1999; Troop-Gordon & Asher, 2005). As rejected children are excluded, their classroom participation declines, their feelings of loneliness rise, their academic achievement falters, and they want to avoid school (Buhs & Ladd, 2001). Most have few friends, and some have none—a circumstance that predicts severe adjustment difficulties (Ladd & Troop-Gordon, 2003).

Controversial and Neglected Children. Consistent with the mixed peer opinion they engender, controversial children display a blend of positive and negative social behaviors. They are hostile and disruptive, but they also engage in positive, prosocial acts (Newcomb, Bukowski, & Pattee, 1993). But like their popular-antisocial counterparts, they often bully others and engage in calculated relational aggression to sustain their dominance (DeRosier & Thomas, 2003; Putallaz et al., 2007).

Perhaps the most surprising finding is that neglected children, once thought to be in need of treatment, are usually well-adjusted. Although they engage in low rates of interaction, most are just as socially skilled as average children. They do not report feeling lonely or unhappy, and when they want to, they can break away from their usual pattern of playing by themselves (Harrist et al., 1997; Ladd & Burgess, 1999). Neglected children remind us that an outgoing, gregarious personality style is not the only path to emotional well-being.

■ **HELPING REJECTED CHILDREN.** A variety of interventions exist to improve the peer relations and psychological adjustment of rejected children. Most involve coaching, modeling, and reinforcing positive social skills, such as how to initiate interaction with a peer, cooperate in play, and respond to another child with friendly emotion and approval. Several of these programs have produced lasting gains in social competence and peer acceptance (Asher & Rose, 1997; DeRosier, 2007).

Still another approach focuses on training in perspective taking and in solving social problems. But many rejected-aggressive children are unaware of their poor social skills and do not take responsibility for their social failures (Mrug, Hoza, & Gerdes, 2001). Rejected-withdrawn children, in contrast, are likely to develop a *learned-helpless* approach to peer difficulties—concluding, after repeated rebuffs, that they will never be liked

▪ BIOLOGY AND ENVIRONMENT ▪

Bullies and Their Victims

Follow the activities of aggressive children over a school day, and you will see that they reserve their hostilities for certain peers. A particularly destructive form of interaction is **peer victimization,** in which certain children become targets of verbal and physical attacks or other forms of abuse. What sustains these repeated assault–retreat cycles?

About 10 to 20 percent of children are bullies, while 15 to 30 percent are repeatedly victimized. Most bullies are boys who use both physical and verbal attacks, but girls sometimes bombard a vulnerable classmate with verbal and relational hostility (Rigby, 2004). And in a study of several hundred middle school students, about one in four reported experiencing "cyberbullying" through text messages, e-mail, or other electronic tools (Li, 2006).

Some bullies are high-status youngsters who may be liked for their leadership or athletic abilities. But most are disliked, or become so, because of their cruelty (Vaillancourt, Hymel, & McDougall, 2003). Nevertheless, peers rarely intervene to help victims, and about 20 to 30 percent of onlookers actually encourage bullies, even joining in (Salmivalli & Voeten, 2004).

Chronic victims tend to be passive when active behavior is expected. On the playground, they hang around chatting or wander on their own. When bullied, they give in, cry, and assume defensive postures (Boulton, 1999). Biologically based traits—an inhibited temperament and a frail physical appearance—contribute to victimization. But victims also have histories of resistant attachment, overly controlling child rearing, and maternal overprotection—parenting that prompts anxiety, low self-esteem, and dependency, resulting in a fearful demeanor that marks these children as vulnerable (Snyder et al., 2003). Persistent bullying, in turn, further impairs victims' emotional self-regulation and social skills—outcomes that heighten victimization (Hoglund & Leadbeater, 2007; Rosen, Milich, & Harris, 2007). Victims' adjustment problems include depression, loneliness, poor school performance, disruptive behavior, and school avoidance (Paul & Cillessen, 2003).

Interventions that change victimized children's negative opinions of themselves and that teach them to respond in non-reinforcing ways to their attackers are helpful. Another way to assist victimized children is to help them form and maintain a gratifying friendship (Fox & Boulton, 2006). When children have a close friend to whom they can turn for help, bullying episodes usually end quickly.

Although modifying victimized children's behavior can help, this does not mean they are to blame. The best way to reduce bullying is to promote prosocial attitudes and behaviors. Effective approaches include developing school and community codes against bullying, teaching child bystanders to intervene, enlisting parents' assistance in changing bullies' behaviors, and (if necessary) moving socially prominent bullies to another class or school (Leadbeater & Hoglund, 2006; Smith, Ananiadou, & Cowie, 2003).

Some bullies are high-status youngsters, but most are disliked, or become so, because of their cruelty. Chronic victims tend to be physically weak, rejected by peers, and afraid to defend themselves—characteristics that make them easy targets.

(Wichmann, Coplan, & Daniels, 2004). Both types of children need help attributing their peer difficulties to internal, changeable causes.

Finally, because rejected children's social incompetence often originates in harsh, authoritarian parenting, interventions that focus on the child alone may not be sufficient (Rubin, Bukowski, & Parker, 2006). If parent–child interaction does not change, children may soon return to their old behavior patterns.

Gender Typing

Children's understanding of gender roles broadens in middle childhood, and their gender identities (views of themselves as relatively masculine or feminine) change as well. We will see that development differs for boys and girls.

Gender-Stereotyped Beliefs

Research in many countries reveals that stereotyping of personality traits increases steadily in middle childhood, becoming adultlike around age 11 (Best, 2001; Heyman & Legare, 2004). For example, children regard "tough," "aggressive," "rational," and "dominant" as masculine and "gentle," "sympathetic," and "dependent" as feminine (Serbin, Powlishta, & Gulko, 1993).

Children derive these distinctions from observing sex differences in behavior as well as from adult treatment. When helping a child with a task, for example, parents (especially fathers) behave in a more mastery-oriented fashion with sons, setting higher standards, explaining concepts, and pointing out important features of tasks—particularly during gender-typed pursuits, such as science activities (Tenenbaum & Leaper, 2003; Tenenbaum et al., 2005). Furthermore, parents less often encourage girls to make their own decisions. And both parents and teachers more often praise boys for knowledge and accomplishment, girls for obedience (Good & Brophy, 2003; Leaper, Anderson, & Sanders, 1998; Pomerantz & Ruble, 1998).

Also in line with adult stereotypes, school-age children quickly figure out which academic subjects and skill areas are "masculine" and which are "feminine." They often regard reading, spelling, art, and music as more for girls and mathematics, athletics, and mechanical skills as more for boys (Eccles, Jacobs, & Harold, 1990; Jacobs & Weisz, 1994). These attitudes influence children's preferences and sense of competence. For example, boys tend to feel more competent than girls at math and science, whereas girls feel more competent than boys at language arts—even when children of equal skill level are compared (Bhanot & Jovanovic, 2005; Freedman-Doan et al., 2000; Hong, Veach, & Lawrenz, 2003).

Although school-age children are aware of many stereotypes, they also develop a more open-minded view of what males and females *can do* (Trautner et al., 2005). The ability to classify flexibly underlies this change. School-age children realize that a person can belong to more than one social category—for example, be a "boy" yet "like to play house" (Bigler, 1995). By the end of middle childhood, children regard gender typing as socially rather than biologically influenced (Taylor, 1996). Nevertheless, they take a harsh view of certain violations—boys playing with dolls and wearing girls' clothing, girls acting noisily and roughly. They are especially intolerant when boys engage in "cross-gender" acts (Blakemore, 2003).

Gender Identity and Behavior

From third to sixth grade, boys strengthen their identification with "masculine" personality traits, whereas girls' identification with "feminine" traits declines. Girls often describe themselves as having some "other-gender" characteristics (Serbin, Powlishta, & Gulko, 1993). Whereas boys usually stick to "masculine" pursuits, girls now experiment with a wider range of options—from cooking and sewing to sports and science fairs—and more often consider traditionally male future work roles (Liben & Bigler, 2002).

These changes are due to a mixture of cognitive and social forces. School-age children of both sexes are aware that society attaches greater prestige to "masculine" characteristics. For example, they rate "masculine" occupations as having higher status than "feminine" occupations (Liben, Bigler, & Krogh, 2001). Messages from adults and peers are also influential. In Chapter 8, we saw that parents (especially fathers) are far less tolerant when sons, as opposed to daughters, cross gender lines. Similarly, a tomboyish girl can make her way into boys' activities without losing the approval of her female peers, but a boy who hangs out with girls is likely to be ridiculed and rejected.

As school-age children make social comparisons and characterize themselves in terms of stable dispositions, their gender identity expands to include the following self-evaluations, which greatly affect their adjustment:

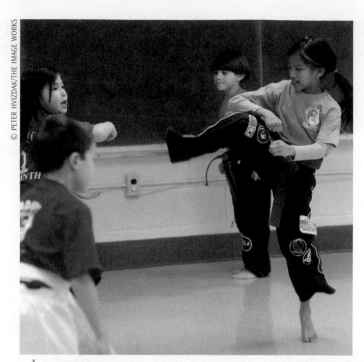

This 9-year-old girl enjoys karate lessons. Whereas school-age boys usually stick to "masculine" pursuits, girls experiment with a wider range of options.

- *Gender typicality*—the degree to which the child feels he or she "fits in" with others of the same gender (Egan & Perry, 2001).

- *Gender contentedness*—the degree to which the child feels satisfied with his or her gender assignment.

- *Felt pressure to conform to gender roles*—the degree to which the child feels parents and peers disapprove of his or her gender-related traits.

In a longitudinal study of third through seventh graders, *gender-typical* and *gender-contented* children gained in self-esteem over the following year. In contrast, children who were *gender-atypical* and *gender-discontented* declined in self-worth. Furthermore, gender-atypical children who reported *intense pressure to conform to gender roles* experienced serious difficulties—withdrawal, sadness, disappointment, and anxiety (Yunger, Carver, & Perry, 2004).

Currently, researchers and therapists are debating how best to help children who feel gender-atypical. Some advocate making them more gender-typical, through therapy that reinforces such children for engaging in traditional gender-role activities so they will feel more compatible with same-sex peers (Zucker, 2006). Others oppose this approach on grounds that it is likely to heighten felt pressure to conform (which predicts maladjustment) and—for children who fail to change—may result in parental rejection. These experts advocate intervening with parents and peers to help them become more accepting of children's gender-atypical interests and behaviors (Bigler, 2007; Conway, 2007; Crawford, 2003). ***TAKE A MOMENT...*** In view of what you have learned about the development of children's gender typing, which approach do you think would be more successful, and why?

ASK YOURSELF

>> **REVIEW**
How does friendship change in middle childhood?

>> **APPLY**
What changes in parent–child relationships are probably necessary to help rejected children?

>> **REFLECT**
As a school-age child, did you have classmates you would classify as popular-aggressive? What were they like, and why do you think peers admired them?

Family Influences

As children move into school, peer, and community contexts, the parent–child relationship changes. At the same time, children's well-being continues to depend on the quality of family interaction. In the following sections, we will see that contemporary changes in families—high rates of divorce, re-marriage, and maternal employment—can have positive as well as negative effects on children. In later chapters, we take up other family structures, including gay and lesbian families, never-married single-parent families, and the increasing numbers of grandparents rearing grandchildren.

Parent–Child Relationships

In middle childhood, the amount of time children spend with parents declines dramatically. The child's growing independence means that parents must deal with new issues. "I've struggled with how many chores to assign, how much allowance to give, whether their friends are good influences, and what to do about problems at school," Rena remarked. "And then there's the challenge of keeping track of them when they're out—or even when they're home and I'm not there to see what's going on."

Despite these new concerns, child rearing becomes easier for parents who established an authoritative style in the early years. Reasoning is more effective with school-age children be-cause of their greater capacity for logical thinking and their in-creased respect for parents' expert knowledge (Collins, Madsen, & Susman-Stillman, 2002).

As children demonstrate that they can manage daily activ-ities and responsibilities, effective parents engage in **coregulation,** a form of supervision in which parents exercise general over-sight while letting children take charge of moment-by-moment decision making. Coregulation grows out of a cooperative rela-tionship between parent and child based on give-and-take and mutual respect. Parents must guide and monitor from a distance

and effectively communicate expectations when they are with their children. And children must inform parents of their where-abouts, activities, and problems so parents can intervene when necessary (Maccoby, 1984).

As at younger ages, mothers spend more time than fathers with school-age children. Still, fathers are often highly involved. Each parent, however, tends to devote more time to children of his or her own sex (Lamb & Lewis, 2004). In parents' separate activities with children, mothers are more concerned with care-giving and ensuring that children meet responsibilities in homework, after-school lessons, and chores. Fathers, especially those with sons, focus on achievement-related and recreational pursuits (Collins & Russell, 1991). But when both parents are present, fathers engage in as much caregiving as mothers.

Siblings

Sibling rivalry tends to increase in middle childhood. As chil-dren participate in a wider range of activities, parents often compare siblings' traits and accomplishments. The child who

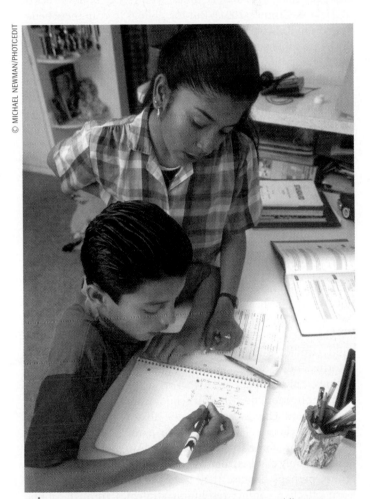

Although sibling rivalry tends to increase in middle childhood, siblings also provide one another with emotional support and help with difficult tasks.

gets less parental affection, more disapproval, or fewer material resources is likely to be resentful (Dunn, 2004; Tamrouti-Makkink et al., 2004).

For same-sex siblings who are close in age, parental comparisons are more frequent, resulting in more antagonism and poorer adjustment. This effect is particularly strong when parents are under stress as a result of financial worries, marital conflict, or single parenthood (Jenkins, Rasbash, & O'Connor, 2003). Parents whose energies are drained become less careful about being fair.

To reduce this rivalry, siblings often strive to be different from one another. For example, two brothers I know deliberately selected different athletic pursuits and musical instruments. Parents can limit the effects of rivalry by making an effort not to compare children, but some feedback about their competencies is inevitable. As siblings strive to win recognition for their own uniqueness, they shape important aspects of each other's development.

Although conflict rises, school-age siblings continue to rely on each other for companionship and assistance with academic and peer challenges and, at times, with family issues (Tucker, McHale, & Crouter, 2001). But for siblings to reap these benefits, parental encouragement of warm, considerate sibling ties is vital. Providing parents with training in mediation—how to get siblings to lay down ground rules, clarify their points of disagreement and common ground, and discuss possible solutions—increases siblings' awareness of each other's perspectives and reduces animosity (Smith & Ross, 2007). When siblings get along well, the older sibling's academic and social competence tends to "rub off on" the younger sibling, fostering more favorable achievement and peer relations (Brody & Murry, 2001; Lamarche et al., 2006). But older siblings with conflict-ridden peer relations tend to transmit their physically or relationally aggressive styles to their younger brothers and sisters (Ostrov, Crick, & Staffacher, 2006).

Only Children

Although sibling relationships bring many benefits, they are not essential for healthy development. Contrary to popular belief, only children are not spoiled, and in some respects, they are advantaged. U.S. children growing up in one-child and multi-child families do not differ in self-rated personality traits (Mottus, Indus, & Allik, 2008). And compared to children with siblings, only children are higher in self-esteem and achievement motivation, do better in school, and attain higher levels of education. One reason may be that only children have somewhat closer relationships with parents, who may exert more pressure for mastery and accomplishment (Falbo, 1992). However, only children tend to be less well-accepted in the peer group, perhaps because they have not had opportunities to learn effective conflict-resolution strategies through sibling interaction (Kitzmann, Cohen, & Lockwood, 2002).

Favorable development also characterizes only children in China, where a one-child family policy has been strictly enforced in urban areas for more than two decades to control

In China, a one-child family policy has been strictly enforced in urban areas for more than two decades to control population growth. However, Chinese only children do not differ from agemates with siblings in social skills and peer acceptance.

population growth (Yang, 2008). Compared with agemates who have siblings, Chinese only children are advanced in cognitive development and academic achievement. They also feel more emotionally secure, perhaps because government disapproval promotes tension in families with more than one child (Falbo & Poston, 1993; Jiao, Ji, & Jing, 1996). Chinese mothers usually ensure that their children have regular contact with first cousins (who are considered siblings). Perhaps as a result, Chinese only children do not differ from agemates with siblings in social skills and peer acceptance (Hart, Newell, & Olsen, 2003).

Divorce

Children's interactions with parents and siblings are affected by other aspects of family life. Joey and Lizzie's relationship, Rena told me, had been particularly negative only a few years before. Joey pushed, hit, and taunted Lizzie and called her names—fighting that coincided with Rena and her husband's growing marital unhappiness. When Joey was 8 and Lizzie 5, their father, Drake, moved out.

Between 1960 and 1985, divorce rates in Western nations rose dramatically before stabilizing in most countries. The United States has the highest divorce rate in the world (see Figure 10.2). Of the 45 percent of American marriages that end in divorce, half involve children. At any given time, one-fourth of U.S. children live in single-parent households. Although most reside with their mothers, the percentage in father-headed households has increased steadily, to about 12 percent (Federal Interagency Forum on Child and Family Statistics, 2008).

Children of divorce spend an average of five years in a single-parent home. About two-thirds of divorced parents marry again. Half their children eventually experience a third

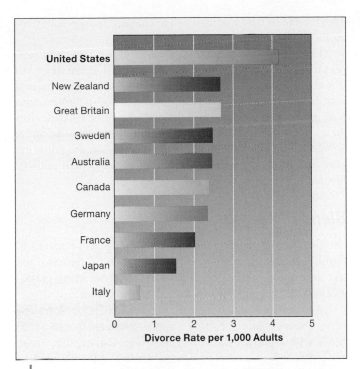

■ FIGURE 10.2 ■ Divorce rates in ten industrialized nations.
The U.S. divorce rate is the highest in the industrialized world, far exceeding divorce rates in other countries. (Adapted from U.S. Census Bureau, 2009a; United Nations, 2002.)

major change—the end of a parent's second marriage (Hetherington & Kelly, 2002).

These figures reveal that divorce is a transition that leads to a variety of new living arrangements, accompanied by changes in housing, income, and family roles and responsibilities. Since the 1960s, many studies have reported that marital breakup is stressful for children. But how well children fare depends on many factors: the custodial parent's psychological health, the child's characteristics, and social supports within the family and surrounding community (Hetherington, 2003).

■ IMMEDIATE CONSEQUENCES. "Things were worst during the period Drake and I decided to separate," Rena reflected. "We fought over division of our belongings and the custody of the children, and the kids suffered. Sobbing, Lizzie told me she was 'sorry she made Daddy go away.' Joey kicked and threw things at home and didn't do his work at school. In the midst of everything, I could hardly deal with their problems. We had to sell the house; I couldn't afford it alone. And I needed a better-paying job."

Family conflict often rises in newly divorced households as parents try to settle disputes over children and possessions. Once one parent moves out, additional events threaten supportive interactions between parents and children. Mother-headed households typically experience a sharp drop in income. In the United States, the majority of single mothers with young children live in poverty, getting less than the full amount of child support from the absent father or none at all (Children's Defense Fund, 2009).

The transition from marriage to divorce typically leads to high maternal stress, depression, and anxiety and to a disorganized family situation. Declines in well-being are greatest for mothers of young children (Williams & Dunne-Bryant, 2006). "Meals and bedtimes were at all hours, and I stopped taking Joey and Lizzie on weekend outings," said Rena. As children react with distress and anger to their less secure home lives, discipline may become harsh and inconsistent. Contact with noncustodial fathers often decreases over time (Hetherington & Kelly, 2002). Fathers who see their children only occasionally are inclined to be permissive and indulgent, making the mother's task of managing the child even more difficult.

The more parents argue and fail to provide children with warmth, involvement, and consistent guidance, the poorer children's adjustment. About 20 to 25 percent of children in divorced families display severe problems, compared with about 10 percent in nondivorced families (Gerard, Krishnakumar, & Buehler, 2006; Strohschein, 2005). At the same time, reactions vary with children's age, temperament, and sex.

Children's Age. Preschool and young school-age children often blame themselves for a marital breakup (as Lizzie did) and fear that both parents may abandon them (Pryor & Rodgers, 2001). Even many older children, with the cognitive maturity to understand that they are not responsible for their parents' divorce, react strongly, declining in school performance, becoming unruly, and escaping into undesirable peer activities (D'Onofrio et al., 2006; Lansford et al., 2006). But some older children—especially the oldest child in the family—display more mature behavior, willingly taking on extra household tasks as well as emotional support of a depressed, anxious mother. But if these demands are too great, these children may eventually become resentful and engage in angry, acting-out behavior (Hetherington, 1999).

Children's Temperament and Sex. Exposure to stressful life events and inadequate parenting magnifies the problems of temperamentally difficult children. In contrast, easy children are less often targets of parental anger and also cope more effectively with adversity.

These findings help explain sex differences in response to divorce. Girls sometimes respond as Lizzie did, with crying, self-criticism, and withdrawal. More often, children of both sexes show demanding, attention-getting, acting-out behavior. But in mother-custody families, boys are at greater risk for serious adjustment problems (Amato, 2001). Recall from Chapter 8 that boys are more active and noncompliant—behaviors that increase with exposure to parental conflict and inconsistent discipline.

■ LONG-TERM CONSEQUENCES. Rena eventually found better-paying work and gained control over the daily operation of the household. Her own feelings of anger and rejection also declined. And after several meetings with a counselor, Rena and Drake realized the harmful impact of their quarreling on Joey and Lizzie. Drake visited regularly and handled

Joey's unruliness with firmness and consistency. Soon Joey's school performance improved, his behavior problems subsided, and both children seemed calmer and happier.

Most children show improved adjustment by two years after divorce. Yet overall, children and adolescents of divorced parents continue to score slightly lower than children of continuously married parents in academic achievement, self-esteem, social competence, and emotional adjustment (Amato, 2001). And divorce is linked to problems with adolescent sexuality and development of intimate ties. Young people who experienced parental divorce—especially more than once—display higher rates of early sexual activity and adolescent parenthood (Wolfinger, 2000). Some experience other lasting difficulties—reduced educational attainment, troubled romantic relationships and marriages, and divorce in adulthood (Amato, 2006; Amato & Cheadle, 2005).

The overriding factor in positive adjustment following divorce is effective parenting—shielding the child from family conflict and using authoritative child rearing (Leon, 2003; Wolchik et al., 2000). Where the custodial parent is the mother, contact with fathers is important. The more paternal contact and the warmer the father–child relationship, the less children react with defiance and aggression (Dunn et al., 2004). For girls, a good father–child relationship protects against early sexual activity and unhappy romantic involvements. For boys, it seems to affect overall psychological well-being. In fact, several studies indicate that outcomes for sons are better when the father is the custodial parent (Clarke-Stewart & Hayward, 1996; McLanahan, 1999). Fathers' greater economic security and image of authority seem to help them engage in effective parenting with sons.

Although divorce is painful for children, remaining in an intact but high-conflict family is much worse than making the transition to a low-conflict, single-parent household (Greene et al., 2003; Strohschein, 2005). Divorcing parents who set aside their disagreements and support each other in their child-rearing roles greatly improve their children's chances of growing up competent, stable, and happy.

■ **DIVORCE MEDIATION, JOINT CUSTODY, AND CHILD SUPPORT.** Community-based services aimed at helping divorcing families include **divorce mediation,** a series of meetings between divorcing adults and a trained professional aimed at reducing family conflict. Research reveals that mediation increases out-of-court property and child-custody settlements, cooperation and involvement of both parents in child rearing, and parents' and children's feelings of well-being (Emery, Sbarra, & Grover, 2005).

Joint custody, which grants parents equal say in important decisions about the child's upbringing, is becoming increasingly common. In most instances, children reside with one parent and see the other on a fixed schedule, similar to the typical sole-custody situation. In other cases, parents share physical custody, and children move between homes—transitions that can be especially hard on some children. Joint-custody parents report little conflict—fortunately so, since the success of the arrangement depends on parental cooperation. And their chil-

dren tend to be better-adjusted than children in sole-maternal-custody homes (Bauserman, 2002).

Finally, many single-parent families depend on child support from the noncustodial parent to relieve financial strain. All U.S. states have procedures for withholding wages from parents who fail to make these payments. Noncustodial fathers who have generous visitation schedules and who often see their children are more likely to pay child support regularly (Amato & Sobolewski, 2004). Applying What We Know on the following page summarizes ways to help children adjust to their parents' divorce.

Blended Families

"If you get married to Wendell, and Daddy gets married to Carol," Lizzie wondered aloud to Rena, "then I'll have two sisters and one more brother. And let's see, how many grandmothers and grandfathers? A lot!" exclaimed Lizzie.

About 60 percent of divorced parents remarry within a few years. Others *cohabit,* or share a sexual relationship and a residence with a partner outside of marriage. Parent, stepparent, and children form a new family structure called the **blended,** or **reconstituted, family.** For some children, this expanded family network is positive, bringing more adult attention. But most have more problems than children in stable, first-marriage families. Switching to stepparents' new rules and expectations can be stressful, and children often view steprelatives as intruders. How well they adapt is, again, related to the quality of family functioning (Hetherington & Kelly, 2002). This depends on which parent forms a new relationship, the child's age and sex, and the complexity of blended-family relationships. As we will see, older children and girls seem to have the hardest time.

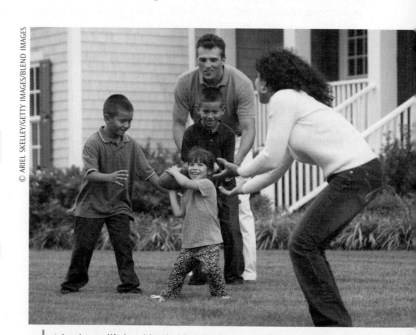

© ARIEL SKELLEY/GETTY IMAGES/BLEND IMAGES

Adapting to life in a blended family can be stressful for children. But the transition can be eased if stepparents move into their new roles gradually, first building warm relationships with children.

Applying What We Know

Helping Children Adjust to Their Parents' Divorce

Suggestion	Rationale
Shield children from conflict.	Witnessing intense parental conflict is very damaging to children. If one parent insists on expressing hostility, children fare better if the other parent does not respond in kind.
Provide children with as much continuity, familiarity, and predictability as possible.	Children adjust better during the period surrounding divorce when their lives have some stability—for example, the same school, bedroom, babysitter, playmates, and daily schedule.
Explain the divorce, and tell children what to expect.	Children are more likely to develop fears of abandonment if they are not prepared for their parents' separation. They should be told that their parents will not be living together anymore, which parent will be moving out, and when they will be able to see that parent. Parents should provide a reason for the divorce that the child can understand and assure children that they are not to blame.
Emphasize the permanence of the divorce.	Fantasies of parents getting back together can prevent children from accepting the reality of their current life. Children should be told that the divorce is final and that they cannot change this fact.
Respond sympathetically to children's feelings.	For children to adjust well, their painful emotions must be acknowledged, not denied or avoided.
Engage in authoritative parenting.	Provide children with affection and acceptance, reasonable demands for mature behavior, and consistent, rational discipline. Parents who engage in authoritative parenting greatly reduce their children's risk of maladjustment.
Promote a continuing relationship with both parents.	When parents disentangle their lingering hostility toward the former partner from the child's need for a continuing relationship with the other parent, children adjust well. Grandparents and other extended-family members can help by not taking sides.

Source: Teyber, 2001.

■ **MOTHER–STEPFATHER FAMILIES.** Because mothers generally retain custody of children, the most common form of blended family is a mother–stepfather arrangement. Boys tend to adjust quickly, welcoming a stepfather who is warm and who refrains from exerting his authority too quickly. Mothers' friction with sons also declines as a result of greater economic security, another adult to share household tasks, and an end to loneliness (Visher, Visher, & Pasley, 2003). Girls, however, often react with sulky, resistant behavior when a new stepfather disrupts the close ties they have established with their mothers (Bray, 1999).

But age affects these findings. Older school-age children and adolescents of both sexes display more irresponsible, acting-out behavior than their peers not in stepfamilies (Hetherington & Stanley-Hagan, 2000). Some parents are warmer and more involved with their biological children than with their stepchildren. Older children are more likely to notice and challenge unfair treatment. And adolescents often view the new stepparent as a threat to their freedom, especially if they experienced little parental monitoring in the single-parent family. Still, when teenagers have affectionate, cooperative relationships with their mothers, many eventually develop good relations with their stepfathers—a circumstance linked to better adjustment (Yuan & Hamilton, 2006).

■ **FATHER–STEPMOTHER FAMILIES.** Remarriage of noncustodial fathers often leads to reduced contact with their biological children, as these fathers tend to withdraw from their "previous" families (Dunn, 2002). When fathers have custody, children typically react negatively to remarriage. One reason is that children living with fathers often start out with more problems. Perhaps the biological mother could no longer handle the difficult child (usually a boy), so the father and his new partner are faced with a youngster who has behavior problems. In other instances, the father has custody because of a very close relationship with the child, and his remarriage disrupts this bond (Buchanan, Maccoby, & Dornbusch, 1996).

Girls, especially, have a hard time getting along with their stepmothers, either because the remarriage threatens the girl's bond with her father or because she becomes entangled in loyalty conflicts between the two mother figures. But the longer girls live in father–stepmother households, the more positive their interaction with stepmothers becomes (Hetherington & Jodl, 1994). Eventually, most girls benefit from the support of a second mother figure.

■ **SUPPORT FOR BLENDED FAMILIES.** Family life education and therapy can help parents and children adapt to the complexities of blended families. Effective approaches encourage stepparents to move into their new roles gradually by first building a warm relationship with the child (Visher, Visher, & Pasley, 2003). Counselors can help couples form a cooperative "parenting coalition" to limit loyalty conflicts and provide consistency in child rearing.

Unfortunately, the divorce rate for second marriages is even higher than for first marriages. Parents with antisocial tendencies and poor child-rearing skills are particularly likely to have several divorces and remarriages, and their children have greater adjustment difficulties (Dunn, 2002). These families usually require prolonged, intensive therapy.

Maternal Employment and Dual-Earner Families

Today, U.S. single and married mothers are in the labor market in nearly equal proportions, and more than three-fourths of those with school-age children are employed (U.S. Census Bureau, 2009b). In previous chapters, we saw that the impact of maternal employment on early development depends on the quality of child care and the continuing parent–child relationship. The same is true in middle childhood.

■ MATERNAL EMPLOYMENT AND CHILD DEVELOPMENT.
Children whose mothers enjoy their work and remain committed to parenting show favorable adjustment—higher self-esteem, more positive family and peer relations, less gender-stereotyped beliefs, and better grades in school. Girls, especially, profit from the image of female competence. Regardless of SES, daughters of employed mothers are more achievement- and career-oriented (Hoffman, 2000).

Parenting practices contribute to these benefits. Employed mothers who value their parenting role are more likely to use authoritative child rearing and coregulation. And maternal employment leads fathers—especially those who believe in the importance of the paternal role—to take on greater child-rearing responsibilities, with a small but increasing number staying home full-time (Gottfried, Gottfried, & Bathurst, 2002; Jacobs & Kelley, 2006). Paternal involvement is associated with higher intelligence and achievement, more mature social behavior, and a flexible view of gender roles in childhood and adolescence and with generally better mental health in adulthood (Coltrane, 1996; Pleck & Masciadrelli, 2004).

But when employment places heavy demands on a mother's schedule or is stressful for other reasons, children are at risk for ineffective parenting. Working many hours or experiencing a negative workplace atmosphere is associated with reduced parental sensitivity, fewer joint parent–child activities, and poorer cognitive development in children and adolescents (Brooks-Gunn, Han, & Waldfogel, 2002; Bumpus, Crouter, & McHale, 2006; Strazdins et al., 2006). Negative consequences are magnified when low-SES mothers spend long days at low-paying, physically exhausting jobs (Raver, 2003). In contrast, part-time employment and flexible work schedules, which help parents meet children's needs, are associated with good child adjustment (Hill et al., 2006).

■ CHILD CARE FOR SCHOOL-AGE CHILDREN.
High-quality child care is vital for children's well-being, even in middle childhood. An estimated 7 million 5- to 13-year-olds in the United States are **self-care children** who are without adult supervision for some period of time after school (Durlak &

Weissberg, 2007). Self-care increases with age and also with SES, perhaps because of the greater safety of higher-income neighborhoods. But when lower-SES parents lack alternatives, their children spend more hours on their own (Casper & Smith, 2002).

Younger school-age children who spend many hours alone have emotional and social difficulties (Vandell & Posner, 1999). As children become old enough to look after themselves, those who have a history of authoritative child rearing, are monitored by parental telephone calls, and have regular after-school chores appear responsible and well-adjusted. In contrast, children left to their own devices are more likely to bend to peer pressures and engage in antisocial behavior (Coley, Morris, & Hernandez, 2004; Vandell et al., 2006).

Before age 8 or 9, most children need supervision because they are not yet competent to handle emergencies (Galambos & Maggs, 1991). But throughout middle childhood, attending high-quality after-school programs with stimulating activities is linked to good school performance and emotional and social adjustment (Durlak & Weissberg, 2007; Granger, 2008). Low-SES children who participate in "after-care" programs offering academic assistance and enrichment activities (scouting, music and art lessons, clubs) show special benefits. They exceed their self-care counterparts in classroom work habits, academic achievement, and prosocial behavior and display fewer behavior problems (Lauer et al., 2006; Vandell et al., 2006).

Unfortunately, good after-care is in especially short supply in low-income neighborhoods (Afterschool Alliance, 2004). A special need exists for well-planned programs in these areas—ones that provide safe environments, warm relationships with adults, and enjoyable, goal-oriented activities.

In this after-school program, children learn about fossils from an AmeriCorps volunteer. Attending high-quality after-school programs is linked to good school performance and emotional and social adjustment.

>> **REVIEW**
Describe and explain changes in sibling relationships during middle childhood.

>> **APPLY**
Steve and Marissa are in the midst of an acrimonious divorce. Their 9-year-old son Dennis has become hostile and defiant. How can Steve and Marissa help Dennis adjust?

>> **REFLECT**
What after-school child-care arrangements did you experience in elementary school? How do you think they influenced your development?

Some Common Problems of Development

We have considered a variety of stressful experiences that place children at risk for future problems. Next, we address two more areas of concern: school-age children's fears and anxieties and the consequences of child sexual abuse. Finally, we sum up factors that help children cope effectively with stress.

Fears and Anxieties

Although fears of the dark, thunder and lightning, and supernatural beings persist into middle childhood, older children's anxieties are also directed toward new concerns. As children begin to understand the realities of the wider world, the possibility of personal harm (being robbed, stabbed, or shot) and media events (war and disasters) often trouble them. Other common worries include academic failure, parents' health, physical injuries, and peer rejection (Muris et al., 2000; Weems & Costa, 2005).

Children in Western nations mention exposure to negative information in the media as the most common source of their fears, followed by direct exposure to frightening events (Muris et al., 2001). Nevertheless, as we saw in Chapter 8, many parents have no rules about their children's TV viewing or computer use, including Internet access.

As long as fears are not too intense, most children handle them constructively, and they decline with age (Gullone, 2000). But about 5 percent of school-age children develop an intense, unmanageable fear called a **phobia.** Children with inhibited temperaments are at high risk (Ollendick, King, & Muris, 2002).

For example, in *school phobia,* children feel severe apprehension about attending school, often accompanied by physical complaints (dizziness, nausea, and stomachaches). About one third of children with school phobia are 5- to 7-year-olds for whom the real fear is maternal separation. Family therapy helps these children, whose difficulty can often be traced to parental overprotection (Elliott, 1999). Most cases of school phobia appear around age 11 to 13. These children usually find a particular aspect of school frightening—an overcritical teacher, a school bully, or too much parental pressure to achieve. A change in school environment or parenting practices may be needed. Firm insistence that the child return to school, along with training in how to cope with difficult situations, is also helpful (Silverman & Pina, 2008).

Severe childhood anxieties may arise from harsh living conditions. In inner-city ghettos and in war-torn areas of the world, many children live in the midst of constant danger and deprivation. As the Lifespan Vista box on page 276 reveals, these youngsters are at risk for long-term difficulties. Finally, as we saw in our discussion of child abuse in Chapter 8, too often violence and other destructive acts become part of adult–child relationships. During middle childhood, child sexual abuse increases.

Child Sexual Abuse

Until recently, adults often dismissed children's claims of sexual abuse as fantasy. In the 1970s, efforts by professionals and media attention led to recognition of child sexual abuse as a widespread problem. About 90,000 cases in the United States were confirmed in the most recently reported year (U.S. Department of Health and Human Services, 2008d).

■ **CHARACTERISTICS OF ABUSERS AND VICTIMS.** Sexual abuse is committed against children of both sexes, but more often against girls. Most cases are reported in middle childhood, but for some victims, abuse begins early in life and continues for many years (Hoch-Espada, Ryan, & Deblinger, 2006; Trickett & Putnam, 1998).

Typically, the abuser is male—a parent or someone the parent knows well—a father, stepfather, or live-in boyfriend, somewhat less often an uncle or older brother. But in about 25 percent of cases, mothers are the offenders, more often with sons (Boroughs, 2004). However, the Internet and mobile phones have become avenues through which other adults commit sexual abuse—for example, by exposing children and adolescents to pornography and online sexual advances as a way of "grooming" them for sexual acts offline (Wolak et al., 2008).

Many offenders blame the abuse on the willing participation of a seductive youngster. Yet children are not capable of making a deliberate, informed decision to enter into a sexual relationship! Even older children and adolescents are not free to say yes or no. Rather, the responsibility lies with abusers, who tend to have characteristics that predispose them toward sexual exploitation of children. They have great difficulty controlling their impulses and may suffer from psychological disorders, including alcohol and drug abuse. Often they pick out children who are unlikely to defend themselves or to be believed—those who are physically weak, emotionally deprived, socially isolated, or affected by disabilities (Bolen, 2001).

■ A LIFESPAN VISTA: Looking Forward, Looking Back ■

Impact of Ethnic and Political Violence on Children

Around the world, many children live with armed conflict, terrorism, and other acts of violence stemming from ethnic and political tensions. Some children may participate in fighting, either because they are forced or because they want to please adults. Others are kidnapped, assaulted, and tortured. Those who are bystanders often come under direct fire and may be killed or physically maimed. And many watch in horror as family members, friends, and neighbors flee, are wounded, or die. In the past decade, wars have left 6 million children physically disabled, 20 million homeless, and more than 1 million separated from their parents (Ursano & Shaw, 2007; Wexler, Branski, & Kerem, 2006).

When war and social crises are temporary, most children can be comforted and do not show long-term emotional difficulties. But chronic danger requires children to make substantial adjustments that can seriously disrupt their psychological functioning. Many children of war lose their sense of safety, become desensitized to violence, are haunted by terrifying memories, are impaired in moral reasoning, and build a pessimistic view of the future. Anxiety and depression increase, as do aggression and antisocial behavior—outcomes seen in every war zone studied, from Bosnia, Angola, Rwanda, and the Sudan to the West Bank, Afghanistan, and Iraq (Barenbaum, Ruchkin, & Schwab-Stone, 2004; Klingman, 2006).

Parental affection and reassurance are the best protection against lasting problems. When parents offer security and serve as role models of calm emotional strength, most children can withstand even extreme war-related violence (Smith et al., 2001). Children who are separated from parents must rely on help from their communities. Orphans in Eritrea who were placed in residential settings where they could form close emotional ties with an adult showed less emotional stress five years later than orphans placed in impersonal settings (Wolff & Fesseha, 1999). Education and recreation programs are powerful safeguards, too, providing children with consistency in their lives along with teacher and peer supports.

With the September 11, 2001, terrorist attacks on the World Trade Center, some U.S. children experienced extreme wartime violence firsthand. Children in Public School 31 in Brooklyn, New York, for example, watched through classroom windows as the planes struck the towers and were engulfed in flames and as the towers crumbled. Many worried about the safety of family members, and some lost them. In the aftermath, most expressed intense fears—for example, that terrorists were infiltrating their neighborhoods and that planes flying overhead might smash into nearby buildings.

Unlike many war-traumatized children in the developing world, Public School 31 students received immediate intervention—a "trauma curriculum" in which they expressed their emotions through writing, drawing, and discussion and participated in experiences aimed at restoring trust and tolerance (Lagnado, 2001). Older children learned about the feelings of their Muslim classmates, the dire condition of children in Afghanistan, and ways to help victims as a means of overcoming a sense of helplessness.

When wartime drains families and communities of resources, international organizations must step in and help children. Efforts to preserve children's physical, psychological, and educational well-being may be the best way to stop transmission of violence to the next generation.

AP IMAGES/ANJA NIEDRINGHAUS

A trauma counselor comforts a child standing amid the rubble of her neighborhood in the Gaza Strip. Many children of war lose their sense of safety, and without special support from caring adults, they are likely to have lasting emotional problems.

Reported cases of child sexual abuse are linked to poverty and marital instability. Children who live in homes with a constantly changing cast of characters—repeated marriages, separations, and new partners—are especially vulnerable. But children in economically advantaged, stable families are also victims, although their abuse is more likely to escape detection (Putnam, 2003).

■ **CONSEQUENCES.** The adjustment problems of child sexual abuse victims—including anxiety, depression, low self-esteem, mistrust of adults, and anger and hostility—are often severe and can persist for years after the abusive episodes. Younger children frequently react with sleep difficulties, loss of appetite, and generalized fearfulness. Adolescents may run away and show suicidal reactions, substance abuse, and delinquency (Feiring, Taska, & Lewis, 1999; Wolfe, 2006). And repeated sexual abuse, like physical abuse, is associated with central nervous system damage (Cicchetti, 2007).

Sexually abused children frequently display precocious sexual knowledge and behavior. In adolescence, abused young people often become promiscuous, and as adults, they show increased arrest rates for sex crimes (mostly against children) and prostitution (Salter et al., 2003; Whipple, 2006). Furthermore, women who were sexually abused are likely to choose partners who abuse them and their children, and they often engage in child abuse and neglect themselves (Pianta, Egeland, & Erickson, 1989). In all these ways, the harmful impact of sexual abuse is transmitted to the next generation.

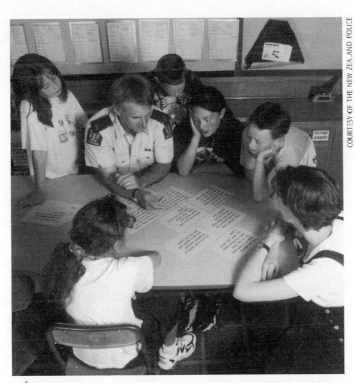

COURTESY OF THE NEW ZEALAND POLICE

Keeping Ourselves Safe is New Zealand's school-based child abuse prevention program. It involves teachers, police officers, and parents in protecting children by teaching them to recognize and respond to abusive adult behaviors.

■ **PREVENTION AND TREATMENT.** Because sexual abuse typically appears in the midst of other serious family problems, long-term therapy with both children and parents is usually needed (Olafson & Boat, 2000). The best way to reduce the suffering of victims is to prevent sexual abuse from continuing. Today, courts are prosecuting abusers more vigorously and taking children's testimony more seriously.

Educational programs that teach children to recognize inappropriate sexual advances and whom to turn to for help reduce the risk of abuse (Hebert & Tourigny, 2004). Yet because of controversies over educating children about sexual abuse, few schools offer these interventions. New Zealand is the only country with a national, school-based prevention program targeting sexual abuse. In Keeping Ourselves Safe, children and adolescents learn that abusers are rarely strangers. Parent involvement ensures that home and school collaborate in teaching children self-protection skills. Evaluations reveal that virtually all New Zealand parents and children support the program and that it has helped many children avoid or report abuse (Sanders, 2006).

Fostering Resilience in Middle Childhood

Throughout middle childhood—and other periods of development—children encounter challenging and sometimes threatening situations that require them to cope with psychological stress. In this and the previous chapter, we have considered such topics as chronic illness, learning disabilities, achievement expectations, divorce, wartime trauma, and sexual abuse. Each taxes children's coping resources, creating serious risks for development.

Nevertheless, only a modest relationship exists between stressful life experiences and psychological disturbance in childhood (Masten & Reed, 2002). Recall from Chapter 1 that four broad factors protect against maladjustment: (1) the child's personal characteristics, including an easy temperament and a mastery-oriented approach to new situations; (2) a warm parental relationship; (3) an adult outside the immediate family who offers a support system; and (4) community resources, such as good schools, social services, and youth organizations and recreation centers (Commission on Children at Risk, 2008; Wright & Masten, 2005).

Any one of these ingredients of resilience can account for why one child fares well and another poorly. Usually, however, personal and environmental factors are interconnected: Each resource favoring resilience strengthens others. For example, safe, stable neighborhoods with family-friendly community services reduce parents' daily hassles and stress, thereby promoting good parenting (Pinderhughes et al., 2001). In contrast, unfavorable home and neighborhood experiences increase the chances that children will act in ways that expose them to further hardship. And when negative conditions pile up, such as marital discord, poverty, crowded living conditions, neighborhood violence, and abuse, the rate of maladjustment multiplies (Wright & Masten, 2005).

Rather than a preexisting attribute, resilience is a capacity that develops, enabling children to use internal and external resources to cope with adversity (Roberts & Masten, 2004; Yates, Egeland, & Sroufe, 2003). As the next two chapters will reveal, young people whose childhood experiences helped them learn to overcome obstacles, strive for self-direction, and respond considerately and sympathetically to others meet the challenges of the next period—adolescence—quite well.

ASK YOURSELF

≫ REVIEW
Describe adjustment problems of victims of child sexual abuse. How can the harmful consequences of sexual abuse carry over to the next generation?

≫ APPLY
Claire told her 6-year-old daughter never to talk to or take candy from strangers. Why will Claire's warning not protect her daughter from sexual abuse?

≫ REFLECT
Describe a challenging time during your childhood. What aspects of the experience increased stress? What resources helped you cope with adversity?

Summary

Erikson's Theory: Industry versus Inferiority

What personality changes take place during Erikson's stage of industry versus inferiority?

>> According to Erikson, children who successfully resolve the psychological conflict of **industry versus inferiority** develop a sense of competence at skills and tasks, a positive but realistic self-concept, pride in accomplishment, moral responsibility, and the ability to work cooperatively with agemates.

Self-Understanding

Describe school-age children's self-concept and self-esteem and how they make achievement-related attributions.

>> During middle childhood, children's self-concepts include competencies, personality traits, and **social comparisons.**

>> Self-esteem differentiates further and becomes hierarchically organized and more realistic. Authoritative parenting is linked to favorable self-esteem.

>> Children who make **mastery-oriented attributions** credit success to ability and failure to controllable factors, such as insufficient effort. In contrast, children who receive negative feedback about their ability are likely to develop **learned helplessness,** attributing success to external factors, such as luck, and failure to low ability.

Emotional Development

Cite changes in self-conscious emotions and in understanding and management of emotion in middle childhood.

>> In middle childhood, self-conscious emotions of pride and guilt become clearly governed by personal responsibility. Experiencing intense shame can shatter self-esteem.

>> School-age children recognize that people can experience more than one emotion at a time. Because of advances in perspective taking, empathy increases.

>> By age 10, most children can shift adaptively between **problem-centered** and **emotion-centered coping** in regulating emotion. Emotionally well-regulated children are upbeat, empathic, and prosocial.

Understanding Others: Perspective Taking

How does perspective taking change in middle childhood?

>> As Selman's five-stage sequence indicates, **perspective taking** improves greatly, supported by cognitive maturity and experiences in which others explain their viewpoints. Good perspective takers have more positive social skills.

Moral Development

Describe changes in moral understanding during middle childhood.

>> By middle childhood, children have internalized rules for good conduct. They clarify and link moral imperatives and social conventions, considering the purpose of the rule, people's intentions, and the context of their actions. They also better understand individual rights.

Peer Relations

How do peer sociability and friendship change in middle childhood?

>> In middle childhood, prosocial acts increase while physical aggression declines. By the end of the school years, children organize themselves into **peer groups.**

>> Friendships develop into mutual relationships based on trust. Children tend to select friends similar to themselves in many ways.

Describe categories of peer acceptance and ways to help rejected children.

>> On measures of **peer acceptance, popular children** are well-liked by many agemates; **rejected children** are actively disliked; **controversial children** are both liked and disliked; and **neglected children** are seldom chosen, either positively or negatively.

>> Two subtypes of popular children exist: **popular-prosocial children,** who are academically and socially competent; and **popular-antisocial children,** who are aggressive but admired. Rejected children also divide into two subtypes: **rejected-aggressive children,** who are especially high in conflict and hostility, and **rejected-withdrawn children,** who are passive, socially awkward, and at risk for **peer victimization.**

>> Rejected children often experience lasting adjustment difficulties. Interventions involving coaching in social skills and training in perspective taking and solving social problems produce gains in social competence and peer acceptance.

Gender Typing

What changes in gender-stereotyped beliefs and gender identity occur during middle childhood?

>> School-age children extend their awareness of gender stereotypes to personality traits and academic subjects. But they also develop a more open-minded view of what males and females can do.

>> Boys strengthen their identification with the masculine role, whereas girls often experiment with "other-gender" activities. Gender identity includes self-evaluations based on typicality, contentedness, and felt pressure to conform to gender roles, each of which affects adjustment.

Family Influences

How do parent–child communication and sibling relationships change in middle childhood?

>> Despite declines in time spent with parents, effective **coregulation** allows parents to exercise general oversight over children, who increasingly make their own decisions.

>> Sibling rivalry tends to increase with greater participation in diverse activities and more frequent parental comparisons. Only children do not differ from children with siblings in self-rated personality traits and are higher in self-esteem, school performance, and educational attainment.

What factors influence children's adjustment to divorce and remarriage?

>> Although marital breakup is often quite stressful for children, individual differences exist based on parental psychological health, child characteristics (age, temperament, and sex), and social supports. Boys and children with difficult temperaments are at greater risk for adjustment problems. In both sexes, divorce is linked to early sexual activity, adolescent parenthood, and relationship difficulties.

>> The overriding factor in positive adjustment following divorce is effective parenting. Positive father–child relationships have protective value, as do extended-family supports.

>> **Divorce mediation** can be beneficial in the period surrounding divorce. The success of **joint custody** depends on a cooperative relationship between divorcing parents.

>> When divorced parents enter new relationships and form **blended,** or **reconstituted families,** girls, older children, and children in father–stepmother families display the greatest adjustment problems. Stepparents who move into their roles gradually and form a "parenting coalition" help children adjust.

How do maternal employment and life in dual-earner families affect school-age children?

>> When mothers enjoy their work and remain committed to parenting, their children benefit from higher self-esteem, more positive family and peer relations, less gender-stereotyped beliefs, and better school grades. In dual-earner families, the father's willingness to share in household responsibilities is linked to many positive child outcomes. Workplace supports help parents in their child-rearing roles.

>> Authoritative child rearing, parental monitoring, and regular after-school chores lead **self-care children** to be responsible and well-adjusted. Good "after-care" programs also aid school performance and emotional and social adjustment.

© BOB DAEMMRICH/PHOTOEDIT

Some Common Problems of Development

Cite common fears and anxieties in middle childhood.

>> School-age children's fears are directed toward new concerns, including personal harm, media events, academic failure, parents' health, and peer rejection. Children with inhibited temperaments are at higher risk of developing a **phobia.**

Discuss factors related to child sexual abuse and its consequences for children's development.

>> Child sexual abuse is generally committed by male family members, more often against girls than boys. Abusers have characteristics that predispose them toward sexual exploitation of children. Reported cases are strongly associated with poverty and marital instability. Abused children often have severe adjustment problems.

Cite factors that foster resilience in middle childhood.

>> Children's personal characteristics, a warm parental relationship, other supportive adults, and community resources predict resilience. But when negative factors pile up, the rate of maladjustment multiplies.

Important Terms and Concepts

blended, or reconstituted, families (p. 272)
controversial children (p. 266)
coregulation (p. 269)
divorce mediation (p. 272)
emotion-centered coping (p. 262)
industry versus inferiority (p. 257)
joint custody (p. 272)
learned helplessness (p. 260)

mastery-oriented attributions (p. 260)
neglected children (p. 266)
peer acceptance (p. 265)
peer group (p. 264)
peer victimization (p. 267)
perspective taking (p. 262)
phobia (p. 275)
popular children (p. 266)

popular-antisocial children (p. 266)
popular-prosocial children (p. 266)
problem-centered coping (p. 262)
rejected children (p. 266)
rejected-aggressive children (p. 266)
rejected-withdrawn children (p. 266)
self-care children (p. 274)
social comparisons (p. 258)

Milestones

Development in Middle Childhood

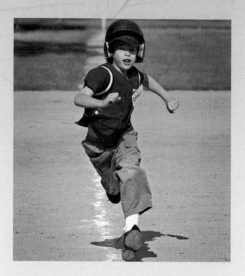

6–8 years

PHYSICAL

- Slow gains in height and weight continue until adolescent growth spurt. (225)
- Permanent teeth gradually replace primary teeth. (225)
- Legibility of writing increases, preparing children to master cursive writing. (229)
- Drawings become more organized and detailed and include some depth cues. (229)
- Games with rules and rough-and-tumble play become common. (229–230)

COGNITIVE

- Thought becomes more logical, as shown by the ability to pass Piagetian conservation, class inclusion, and seriation problems. (232)

- Spatial reasoning improves; gives clear, well-organized directions and draws coherent cognitive maps. (233)
- Attention becomes more selective, adaptable, and planful. (235)
- Uses memory strategies of rehearsal and then organization. (235)
- Views the mind as an active, constructive agent, capable of transforming information. (237)
- Awareness of memory strategies and the impact of psychological factors (such as focusing attention) on task performance improves. (237)
- Appreciates second-order false beliefs. (237)
- Uses informal knowledge of number concepts and counting to master more complex mathematical skills. (238–239)

LANGUAGE

- Vocabulary increases rapidly throughout middle childhood, eventually exceeding 40,000 words. (246)
- Word definitions are concrete, referring to functions and appearance. (246)
- Narratives increase in organization, detail, and expressiveness. (246)
- Transitions from emergent literacy to conventional reading. (238)
- Language awareness improves. (246)
- Conversational strategies become more refined. (246)

EMOTIONAL/SOCIAL

- Self-concept begins to include personality traits and social comparisons. (257–258)
- Self-esteem differentiates, becomes hierarchically organized, and declines to a more realistic level. (258)
- Self-conscious emotions of pride and guilt are governed by personal responsibility. (261)
- Understands that people may have different perspectives because they have access to different information. (262)
- Recognizes that individuals can experience more than one emotion at a time and that people's expressions may not reflect their true feelings. (261)
- Empathy increases. (261)
- Becomes more independent and trustworthy. (262)

- Constructs a flexible appreciation of moral rules, taking prosocial and antisocial intentions into account. (263)
- Physical aggression declines; verbal and relational aggression continue. (264)
- Resolves conflicts more effectively. (264)

9–11 years

PHYSICAL

- Adolescent growth spurt begins two years earlier in girls than in boys. (225)
- Executes gross motor skills of running, jumping, throwing, catching, kicking, batting, and dribbling more quickly and with better coordination. (228)

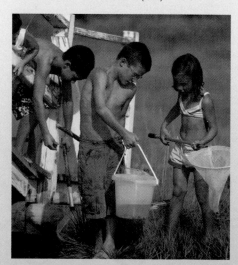

Note: Numbers in parentheses indicate the page or pages on which each milestone is discussed.

- Steady gains in reaction time contribute to improved motor performance. (229)
- Representation of depth in drawings expands. (229)

COGNITIVE

- Continues to master Piagetian tasks in a step-by-step fashion. (232)
- Spatial reasoning further improves; readily draws and reads maps, and grasps the notion of scale. (233)
- Selective attention and planning improve further. (235)
- Uses memory strategies of rehearsal and organization more effectively. (235)

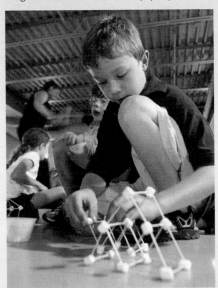

- Applies several memory strategies simultaneously; begins to use elaboration. (235, 237)
- Long-term knowledge base grows larger and becomes better organized. (237)
- Theory of mind becomes more elaborate and refined. (237)
- Cognitive self-regulation improves. (238)

LANGUAGE

- Thinks about and uses words more precisely; word definitions emphasize synonyms and categorical relations. (246)
- Grasps double meanings of words, as reflected in comprehension of metaphors and humor. (246)
- Continues to master complex grammatical constructions. (246)
- Continues to refine conversational strategies. (246)

- Narratives lengthen, become more coherent, and include more evaluative comments. (246–247)

EMOTIONAL/SOCIAL

- Self-esteem tends to rise (258)
- Distinguishes ability, effort, and external factors in attributions for success and failure. (260)
- Becomes more knowledgeable about socially approved ways to display negative emotion. (261–262)
- Empathic responding extends to general life conditions. (261)

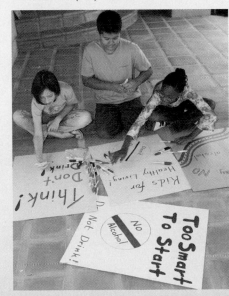

- Shifts adaptively between problem-centered and emotion-centered strategies in regulating emotion. (261–262)
- Can "step into another's shoes" and view the self from that person's perspective; later, can view the relationship between self and other from the perspective of a third, impartial party. (262)

- Clarifies and links moral rules and social conventions. (263–264)
- Convictions about matters of personal choice strengthen, and understanding of individual rights expands. (264)

- Friendships become more selective and are based on mutual trust. (265)
- Peer groups emerge. (264–265)
- Becomes aware of more gender stereotypes, including personality traits and achievement, but has a flexible appreciation of what males and females can do. (267–268)
- Gender identity expands to include self-evaluations of typicality, contentedness, and pressure to conform. (268)
- Sibling rivalry tends to increase. (269–270)

CHAPTER
11

Physical and Cognitive Development in Adolescence

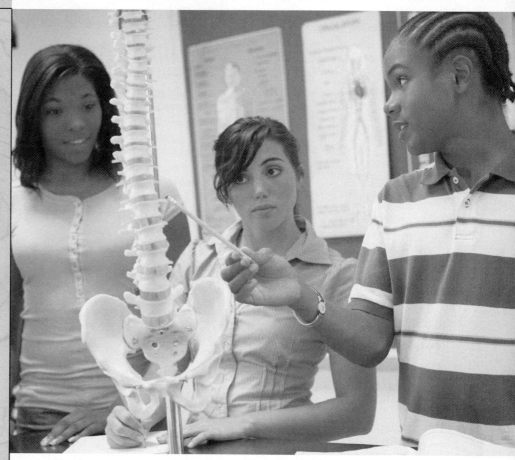

© JON FEINGERSH/JUPITER IMAGES

Adolescence brings momentous advances. A flood of biological events leads to an adult-sized body and sexual maturity. Cognitive changes allow teenagers to grasp complex scientific principles, grapple with political issues, and detect the deep meaning of a poem or story.

On Sabrina's eleventh birthday, her friend Joyce gave her a surprise party, but Sabrina seemed somber during the celebration. Although Sabrina and Joyce had been close friends since third grade, their relationship was faltering. Sabrina was much taller and 20 pounds heavier than most girls in her sixth-grade class. Her breasts were well-developed, her hips and thighs had broadened, and she had begun to menstruate. In contrast, Joyce still had the short, lean, flat-chested body of a school-age child.

Ducking into the bathroom while the other girls put candles on the cake, Sabrina frowned at her image in the mirror. "I'm so big and heavy," she whispered. At church youth group on Sundays, Sabrina broke away from Joyce and joined the eighth-grade girls. Around them, she didn't feel so large and awkward.

Once a month, parents gathered at Sabrina's and Joyce's school to discuss child-rearing concerns. Sabrina's parents, Franca and Antonio, attended whenever they could. "How you know they are becoming teenagers is this," volunteered Antonio. "The bedroom door is closed, and they want to be alone. Also, they contradict and disagree. I tell Sabrina, 'You have to go to Aunt Gina's for dinner with the family.' The next thing I know, she is arguing with me."

Sabrina has entered **adolescence,** the transition between childhood and adulthood. In industrialized societies, the skills young people must master are so complex and the choices confronting them so diverse that adolescence is greatly extended. But around the world, the basic tasks of this period are much the same. Sabrina must accept her full-grown body, acquire adult ways of thinking, attain greater independence from her family, develop more mature ways of relating to peers of both sexes, and begin to construct an identity—a secure sense of who she is in terms of sexual, vocational, moral, ethnic, religious, and other life values and goals.

The beginning of adolescence is marked by **puberty, a flood of biological events leading to an adult-sized body and sexual maturity.** As Sabrina's reactions suggest, entry into adolescence can be an especially trying time for some young people. In this chapter, we trace the events of puberty and take up a variety of health concerns—physical exercise,

nutrition, sexual activity, substance abuse, and other problems affecting teenagers who encounter difficulties on the path to maturity.

Adolescence also brings with it vastly expanded powers of reasoning. Teenagers can grasp complex scientific and mathematical principles, grapple with social and political issues, and delve into the meaning of a poem or story. The second part of this chapter traces these extraordinary changes from both Piaget's and the information-processing perspective. Next, we examine sex differences in mental abilities. Finally, we turn to the main setting in which adolescent thought takes shape: the school.

Physical Development

Conceptions of Adolescence

Why is Sabrina self-conscious, argumentative, and in retreat from family activities? Historically, theorists explained the impact of puberty on psychological development by resorting to extremes—either a biological or a social explanation.

In the early twentieth century, major theorists viewed adolescence from a "storm-and-stress" perspective. The most influential, G. Stanley Hall (1904), who based his ideas on Darwin's theory of evolution, described adolescence as a period so turbulent that it resembled the era in which humans evolved from savages into civilized beings. Similarly, Anna Freud (1969), who expanded the focus on adolescence of her father Sigmund Freud's theory, viewed the teenage years as a biologically based, universal "developmental disturbance."

Contemporary research shows that the storm-and-stress notion of adolescence is exaggerated. Certain problems, such as eating disorders, depression, suicide, and lawbreaking, do occur more often than earlier (Farrington, 2004; Graber, 2004). But the overall rate of psychological disturbance rises only slightly from childhood to adolescence (Roberts, Attkisson, & Rosenblatt, 1998). Although some teenagers do encounter serious difficulties, emotional turbulence is not routine.

The first researcher to point out the wide variability in adolescent adjustment was anthropologist Margaret Mead (1928). Returning from the Pacific islands of Samoa, she concluded that because of the culture's relaxed social relationships and openness toward sexuality, adolescence "is perhaps the pleasantest time the Samoan girl (or boy) will ever know" (p. 308). Mead offered an alternative view in which the social environment is entirely responsible for the range of teenage experiences, from erratic and agitated to calm and stress-free. Later researchers found that Samoan adolescence was not as untroubled as Mead had assumed (Freeman, 1983).

Today we know that biological, psychological, and social forces combine to influence adolescent development (Magnusson, 1999; Susman & Rogol, 2004). Biological changes are universal—found in all primates and all cultures. These internal stresses and the social expectations accompanying them—that the young person develop new interpersonal relationships and take on greater responsibility—are likely to prompt moments of self-doubt and disappointment in all teenagers. Adolescents' prior and current experiences affect their success in surmounting these challenges.

At the same time, the length of adolescence and its demands and pressures vary substantially among cultures. Most tribal and village societies have only a brief intervening phase between childhood and full assumption of adult roles (Weisfield, 1997). In industrialized nations, young people face prolonged dependence on parents and postponement of sexual gratification while they prepare for a productive work life. As a result, adolescence is greatly extended.

We will see that the more the social environment supports young people in achieving adult responsibilities, the better they fare. For all the biological tensions and uncertainties about the future that teenagers feel, most negotiate this period successfully.

Puberty: The Physical Transition to Adulthood

The changes of puberty are dramatic: Within a few years, the body of the school-age child is transformed into that of a full-grown adult. Genetically influenced hormonal processes regulate pubertal growth. Girls, who have been advanced in physical maturity since the prenatal period, reach puberty, on average, two years earlier than boys.

Hormonal Changes

The complex hormonal changes that underlie puberty occur gradually and are under way by age 8 or 9. Secretions of *growth hormone (GH)* and *thyroxine* (see Chapter 7, page 168) increase, leading to tremendous gains in body size and to attainment of skeletal maturity.

Sexual maturation is controlled by the sex hormones. Although we think of *estrogens* as female hormones and *androgens* as male hormones, both types are present in each sex but in different amounts. The boy's testes release large quantities of the androgen *testosterone,* which leads to muscle growth, body and facial hair, and other male sex characteristics. Androgens (especially testosterone for boys) also contribute to gains in body size. The testes secrete small amounts of estrogen as well. In both sexes, estrogens increase GH secretion, adding to the growth spurt and, in combination with androgens, stimulating gains in bone density, which continue into early adulthood (Cooper, Sayer, & Dennison, 2006; Styne, 2003).

Estrogens released by girls' ovaries cause the breasts, uterus, and vagina to mature, the body to take on feminine proportions, and fat to accumulate. Estrogens also contribute to regulation of the menstrual cycle. *Adrenal androgens,* released from the adrenal glands on top of each kidney, influence girls' height spurt and stimulate growth of underarm and pubic hair. They have little impact on boys, whose physical characteristics are influenced mainly by androgen and estrogen secretions from the testes.

As you can see, pubertal changes are of two broad types: (1) overall body growth and (2) maturation of sexual characteristics. Boys and girls differ in both aspects. In fact, puberty is the time of greatest sexual differentiation since prenatal life.

Body Growth

The first outward sign of puberty is the rapid gain in height and weight known as the **growth spurt.** On average, it is under way for North American girls shortly after age 10, for boys around age 12½. Because estrogens trigger and then restrain GH secretion more readily than androgens, the typical girl is taller and heavier during early adolescence (Archibald, Graber, & Brooks-Gunn, 2006; Bogin, 2001). At age 14, she is surpassed by the typical boy, whose adolescent growth spurt has now started, whereas hers is almost finished. Growth in body size is complete for most girls by age 16 and for boys by age 17½, when the epiphyses at the ends of the long bones close completely (see Chapter 7, page 165). Altogether, adolescents add 10 to 11 inches in height and 50 to 75 pounds—nearly 50 percent of adult body weight. Figure 11.1 illustrates pubertal changes in general body growth.

■ **BODY PROPORTIONS.** During puberty, the cephalocaudal growth trend of infancy and childhood reverses. The hands, legs, and feet accelerate first, followed by the torso, which accounts for most of the adolescent height gain (Sheehy et al., 1999). This pattern helps explain why early adolescents often appear awkward and out of proportion—long-legged, with giant feet and hands.

Sex differences in pubertal growth are obvious among these sixth graders. Although the children are the same age, the boy is much shorter and less mature looking than the girls.

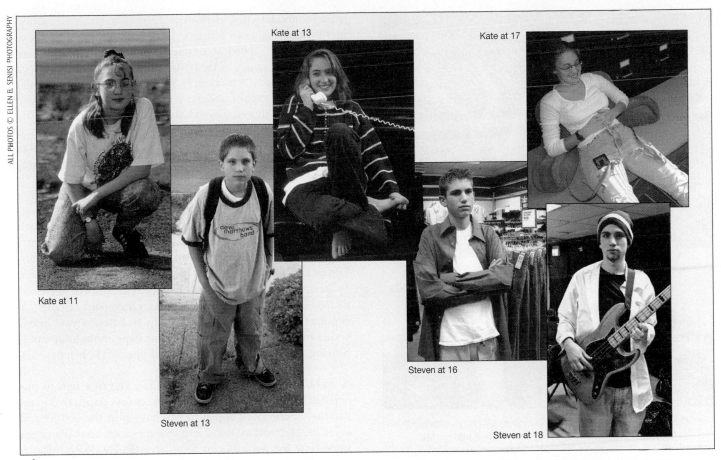

Kate at 13

Kate at 17

Kate at 11

Steven at 13

Steven at 16

Steven at 18

ALL PHOTOS © ELLEN B. SENISI PHOTOGRAPHY

■ **FIGURE 11.1** ■ **Body growth during adolescence.** Because the pubertal growth spurt takes place earlier for girls than for boys, Kate reached her adult body size earlier than Steven. During puberty, adolescents show large sex differences in body proportions.

Large sex differences in body proportions also appear, caused by the action of sex hormones on the skeleton. Boys' shoulders broaden relative to the hips, whereas girls' hips broaden relative to the shoulders and waist. Of course, boys also end up larger than girls, and their legs are longer in relation to the rest of the body—mainly because boys have two extra years of preadolescent growth, when the legs are growing the fastest.

■ **MUSCLE–FAT MAKEUP AND OTHER INTERNAL CHANGES.**
Sabrina worried about her weight because compared with her later-developing girlfriends, she had accumulated much more fat. Around age 8, girls start to add fat on their arms, legs, and trunk, a trend that accelerates between ages 11 and 16. In contrast, arm and leg fat decreases in adolescent boys. Although both sexes gain in muscle, this increase is much greater in boys, who develop larger skeletal muscles, hearts, and lung capacity (Rogol, Roemmich, & Clark, 2002). Also, the number of red blood cells—and therefore the ability to carry oxygen from the lungs to the muscles—increases in boys but not in girls. Altogether, boys gain far more muscle strength than girls, a difference that contributes to teenage boys' superior athletic performance (Ramos et al., 1998).

Motor Development and Physical Activity

Puberty brings steady improvement in gross motor performance, but changes differ for boys and girls. Girls' gains are slow and gradual, leveling off by age 14. In contrast, boys show a dramatic spurt in strength, speed, and endurance that continues through the teenage years. By midadolescence, few girls perform as well as the average boy in running speed, broad jump, and throwing distance (Haywood & Getchell, 2005; Malina & Bouchard, 1991).

Among boys, athletic competence is strongly related to peer admiration and self-esteem. Some adolescents are so obsessed with physical prowess that they turn to performance-enhancing drugs. About 8 percent of U.S. high school seniors, mostly boys, reported using creatine, an over-the-counter substance that enhances short-term muscle power but carries a risk of serious side effects, including muscle tissue disease, brain seizures, and heart irregularities (Castillo & Comtock, 2007). About 2 percent of seniors, again mostly boys, have taken anabolic steroids or a related substance, androstenedione—powerful prescription medications that boost muscle mass and strength

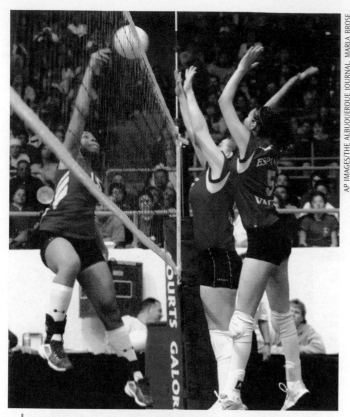

Although high school girls' participation in sports has increased, it still falls far short of boys'. Yet intraschool and intramural athletics yield many benefits—not just gains in motor skills but important lessons in teamwork, problem solving, assertiveness, and competition.

(Johnston et al., 2008). Teenagers usually obtain steroids illegally, ignoring side effects, which range from acne, excess body hair, and high blood pressure to mood swings, aggressive behavior, and damage to the liver, circulatory system, and reproductive organs (Casavant et al., 2007). Coaches and health professionals should inform teenagers of the dangers of these performance-enhancing substances.

Besides improving motor performance, sports and exercise influence cognitive and social development, providing lessons in teamwork, problem solving, assertiveness, and competition. And regular, sustained physical activity has lifelong health benefits. Yet physical activity among U.S. adolescents declines dramatically with age. By age 15, less than one-third meet the U.S. government recommendation of at least 60 minutes of moderate to strenuous physical activity per day (Nader et al., 2008). In high school, only 58 percent of boys and 49 percent of girls are enrolled in any physical education, with less than 30 percent of all students experiencing a daily physical education class (U.S. Department of Health and Human Services, 2008k).

Sexual Maturation

Accompanying rapid body growth are changes in physical features related to sexual functioning. Some, called **primary** **sexual characteristics,** involve the reproductive organs (ovaries, uterus, and vagina in females; penis, scrotum, and testes in males). Others, called **secondary sexual characteristics,** are visible on the outside of the body and serve as additional signs of sexual maturity (for example, breast development in females and the appearance of underarm and pubic hair in both sexes). As Table 11.1 shows, these characteristics develop in a fairly standard sequence, although the ages at which each begins and is completed vary greatly. Typically, pubertal development takes about four years, but some adolescents complete it in two years, whereas others take five to six years.

■ **SEXUAL MATURATION IN GIRLS.** Female puberty usually begins with the budding of the breasts and the growth spurt. **Menarche,** or first menstruation, typically occurs around age 12½ for North American girls, 13 for Western Europeans. But the age range is wide, from 10½ to 15½ years. Following menarche, breast and pubic hair growth are completed, and underarm hair appears (Archibald, Graber, & Brooks-Gunn, 2006). Notice in Table 11.1 that nature delays sexual maturity until the girl's body is large enough for childbearing; menarche takes place after the peak of the height spurt.

■ **SEXUAL MATURATION IN BOYS.** The first sign of puberty in boys is the enlargement of the testes (glands that manufacture sperm), accompanied by changes in the texture and color of the scrotum. Pubic hair emerges soon after, about the same time the penis begins to enlarge (Rogol, Roemmich, & Clark, 2002).

As Table 11.1 reveals, the growth spurt occurs much later in the sequence of pubertal events for boys than for girls. When it reaches its peak around age 14, enlargement of the testes and penis is nearly complete, and underarm hair appears. So do facial and body hair, which increase gradually for several years. Another landmark of male physical maturity is the deepening of the voice as the larynx enlarges and the vocal cords lengthen. (Girls' voices also deepen slightly.) Voice change usually takes place at the peak of the male growth spurt and is often not complete until puberty is over (Archibald, Graber, & Brooks-Gunn, 2006).

While the penis is growing, the prostate gland and seminal vesicles (which together produce semen, the fluid containing sperm) enlarge. Then, around age 13½, **spermarche,** or first ejaculation, occurs (Rogol, Roemmich, & Clark, 2002).

Individual Differences in Pubertal Growth

Heredity contributes substantially to the timing of pubertal changes: Identical twins are more similar than fraternal twins in attainment of most pubertal milestones (Eaves et al., 2004; Mustanski et al., 2004). Nutrition and exercise also make a difference. In females, a sharp rise in body weight and fat may trigger sexual maturation. Fat cells release a protein called *leptin,* which is believed to signal the brain that a girl's energy stores are sufficient for puberty—a likely reason that breast and pubic hair growth and menarche occur earlier for heavier and, especially,

■ **TABLE 11.1** ■ *Pubertal Development in North American Girls and Boys*

GIRLS	AVERAGE AGE ATTAINED	AGE RANGE	BOYS	AVERAGE AGE ATTAINED	AGE RANGE
Breasts begin to "bud"	10	(8–13)	Testes begin to enlarge	11.5	(9.5–13.5)
Height spurt begins	10	(8–13)	Pubic hair appears	12	(10–15)
Pubic hair appears	10.5	(8–14)	Penis begins to enlarge	12	(10.5–14.5)
Peak strength spurt	11.6	(9.5–14)	Height spurt begins	12.5	(10.5–16)
Peak height spurt	11.7	(10–13.5)	Spermarche (first ejaculation) occurs	13.5	(12–16)
Menarche (first menstruation) occurs	12.5	(10.5–14)	Peak height spurt	14	(12.5–15.5)
Peak weight spurt	12.7	(10–14)	Peak weight spurt	14	(12.5–15.5)
Adult stature reached	13	(10–16)	Facial hair begins to grow	14	(12.5–15.5)
Pubic hair growth completed	14.5	(14–15)	Voice begins to deepen	14	(12.5–15.5)
Breast growth completed	15	(10–17)	Penis and testes growth completed	14.5	(12.5–16)
			Peak strength spurt	15.3	(13–17)
			Adult stature reached	15.5	(13.5–17.5)
			Pubic hair growth completed	15.5	(14–17)

Sources: Chumlea et al., 2003; Herman-Giddens, 2006; Rogol, Roemmich, & Clark, 2002; Wu, Mendola, & Buck, 2002.

Photos: (left) © David Young-Wolff/PhotoEdit; (right) © Rob Melnychuk/Getty Images/Taxi

obese girls. In contrast, girls who begin rigorous athletic training at an early age or who eat very little (both of which reduce the percentage of body fat) usually experience later puberty (Anderson, Dallal, & Must, 2003; Lee et al., 2007; Slyper, 2006).

In poverty-stricken regions where malnutrition and infectious disease are common, menarche is greatly delayed, occurring as late as age 14 to 16 in many parts of Africa. Within developing countries, girls from higher-income families reach menarche 6 to 18 months earlier than those living in economically disadvantaged homes (Parent et al., 2003).

Early family experiences may also affect pubertal timing. One theory suggests that humans have evolved to be sensitive to the emotional quality of their childhood environments. When children's safety and security are at risk, it is adaptive for them to reproduce early. Research indicates that girls and (less consistently) boys with a history of family conflict, harsh parenting, or parental separation tend to reach puberty early. In contrast, those with warm, stable family ties reach puberty relatively late (Belsky et al., 2007; Bogaert, 2005; Ellis, 2004; Ellis & Essex, 2007; Mustanski et al., 2004; Tremblay & Frigon, 2005).

A **secular trend,** or generational change, in pubertal timing lends added support to the role of physical well-being in pubertal development. In industrialized nations, age of menarche declined steadily—by about three to four months per decade—from 1900 to 1970, a period in which nutrition, health care,

sanitation, and control of infectious disease improved greatly. Boys, too, have reached puberty earlier in recent decades (Karpati et al., 2002). In North America and a few European countries, soaring rates of overweight and obesity are responsible for a modest, continuing trend toward earlier menarche (Kaplowitz, 2006). A worrisome consequence is that girls who reach sexual maturity at age 10 or 11 will experience pressure for unfavorable peer involvements, including sexual activity.

Brain Development

The physical transformations of adolescence include major changes in the brain. Brain-imaging research reveals continued pruning of unused synapses in the cerebral cortex, especially in the frontal lobes—the "governor" of thought and action. In addition, growth and myelination of stimulated neural fibers accelerate, strengthening connections among various brain regions—especially linkages between the two cerebral hemispheres through the corpus callosum, and between the frontal lobes and other brain areas, which attain rapid communication (Blakemore & Choudhury, 2006; Keating, 2004; Lenroot & Giedd, 2006). This sculpting of the adolescent brain supports diverse cognitive skills, including improved processing speed, attention, memory, planning, capacity to integrate information, and self-regulation.

In addition, in humans and other mammals, neurons become more responsive to excitatory neurotransmitters during puberty. As a result, adolescents react more strongly to stressful events and experience pleasurable stimuli more intensely (Casey, Getz, & Galvan, 2008; Spear, 2004, 2008). These changes probably contribute to teenagers' drive for novel experiences, including drug taking, especially among those who engage in reward seeking to counteract chronic emotional pain. Alterations in neurotransmitter activity may also be involved in adolescents' increased susceptibility to certain disorders, such as depression and eating disturbances.

At puberty, revisions occur in the brain's regulation of sleep, perhaps because of increased neural sensitivity to evening light. As a result, adolescents go to bed much later than they did as children. Yet they need almost as much sleep as they did in middle childhood—about nine hours. When the school day begins early, their sleep needs are not satisfied (Carskadon, Acebo, & Jenni, 2004; Carskadon et al., 2002). Sleep-deprived adolescents perform especially poorly on cognitive tasks during morning hours. And they are more likely to achieve less well in school, suffer from depressed mood, and engage in high-risk behaviors (Dahl & Lewin, 2002; Hansen et al., 2005). Delaying school start times, while helpful, does not fully solve the problem.

To what extent are the hormonal changes of puberty responsible for adolescent brain growth and reorganization? Researchers do not yet have a ready answer. But the transformations that occur enhance our understanding of both the cognitive advances and the troubling behaviors of adolescence, along with teenagers' need for adult patience, oversight, and guidance.

During puberty, neurons become more responsive to excitatory neurotransmitters. As a result, adolescents react more strongly to stressful events, such as disagreements with parents. This mother must try to be patient with her son, despite his intense resistance.

© SW PRODUCTIONS/GETTY IMAGES/PHOTODISC

The Psychological Impact of Pubertal Events

TAKE A MOMENT... Think back to your late elementary and middle school days. As you reached puberty, how did your feelings about yourself and your relationships with others change? Research reveals that pubertal events affect adolescents' self-image, mood, and interaction with parents and peers. Some outcomes are a response to dramatic physical change, whenever it occurs. Others have to do with pubertal timing.

Reactions to Pubertal Changes

Two generations ago, menarche was often traumatic. Today, girls commonly react with "surprise," undoubtedly due to the sudden onset of the event. Otherwise, they typically report a mixture of positive and negative emotions (DeRose & Brooks-Gunn, 2006). Yet wide individual differences exist that depend on prior knowledge and support from family members.

For girls who have no advance information, menarche can be shocking and disturbing. In the 1950s, up to 50 percent received no prior warning, and of those who did, many were given "grin-and-bear-it" messages (Costos, Ackerman, & Paradis, 2002; Shainess, 1961). Today, few girls are uninformed, a shift that is probably due to parents' greater willingness to discuss sexual matters and to the spread of health education classes (Omar, McElderry, & Zakharia, 2003). Almost all girls get some information from their mothers. And some evidence suggests that compared with Caucasian-American families, African-American families may better prepare girls for menarche, treat it as an important milestone, and express less conflict over girls reaching sexual maturity—factors that lead African-American girls to react more favorably (Martin, 1996; Scott et al., 1989).

Like girls' reactions to menarche, boys' responses to spermarche reflect mixed feelings. Virtually all boys know about ejaculation ahead of time, but many say that no one spoke to them before or during puberty about physical changes (Omar, McElderry, & Zakharia, 2003). Usually they get their information from their own reading. Even boys who had advance information often say that their first ejaculation occurred earlier than they expected and that they were unprepared for it. As with girls, boys who feel better prepared tend to react more positively (Stein & Reiser, 1994). But whereas almost all girls eventually tell a friend that they are menstruating, far fewer boys tell anyone about spermarche (DeRose & Brooks-Gunn, 2006; Downs & Fuller, 1991). Overall, boys get less social support than girls for the physical changes of puberty.

Many tribal and village societies celebrate the onset of puberty with an *initiation ceremony,* a ritualized announcement to the community that marks an important change in privilege and responsibility. Consequently, young people know that reaching puberty is valued in their culture. In contrast, Western societies grant little formal recognition to movement from childhood to adolescence or from adolescence to adulthood.

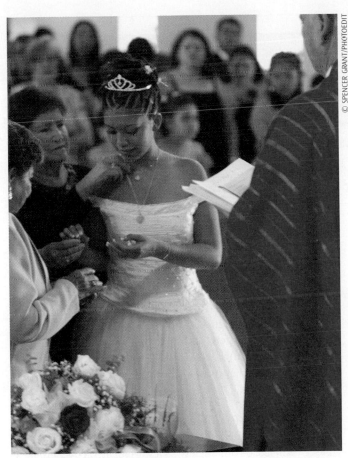

In Hispanic communities, the *quinceañera*, celebrated at age 15, is a rite of passage honoring a girl's journey from childhood to maturity. It usually begins with a mass in which the priest blesses gifts presented to the girl.

Ceremonies such as the Jewish bar or bat mitzvah and the *quinceañera* in Hispanic communities (celebrating a 15-year-old girl's sexual maturity and marriage availability) resemble initiation ceremonies, but only within the ethnic or religious subculture. They do not mark a significant change in social status in the larger society.

Instead, Western adolescents are granted partial adult status at many different ages—for example, an age for starting employment, for driving, for leaving high school, for voting, and for drinking. The absence of a widely accepted marker of physical and social maturity makes the process of becoming an adult more confusing.

Pubertal Change, Emotion, and Social Behavior

A common belief is that puberty has something to do with adolescent moodiness and the desire for greater physical and psychological separation from parents. Let's see what research says about these relationships.

■ **ADOLESCENT MOODINESS.** Biological, psychological, and social forces combine to make adolescence a time of deeper valleys and higher peaks in emotional experience. Higher pubertal hormone levels are linked to greater moodiness, but only modestly so (Buchanan, Eccles, & Becker, 1992; Graber, Brooks-Gunn, & Warren, 2006).

In several studies, the moods of children, adolescents, and adults were monitored by having them carry electronic pagers. Over a one-week period, they were beeped at random intervals and asked to write down what they were doing, whom they were with, and how they felt. As expected, adolescents reported less favorable moods than school-age children and adults (Larson et al., 2002; Larson & Lampman-Petraitis, 1989). But negative moods were linked to a greater number of negative life events, such as difficulties with parents, disciplinary actions at school, and breaking up with a boyfriend or girlfriend. Negative events increased steadily from childhood to adolescence, and teenagers also seemed to react to them with greater emotion than children (Larson & Ham, 1993).

Furthermore, compared with the moods of older adolescents and adults, those of younger adolescents (ages 12 to 16) were less stable and strongly related to situational changes. Low points of adolescents' days tended to occur in adult-structured settings—class, job, and religious services. High points were times spent with peers and coincided with Friday and Saturday evenings, especially in high school (see Figure 11.2 on page 290). Going out with friends and romantic partners increases so dramatically during adolescence that it becomes a "cultural script" for what is *supposed* to happen (Larson & Richards, 1998). Consequently, teenagers who spend weekend evenings at home often feel profoundly lonely.

■ **PARENT–CHILD RELATIONSHIPS.** Sabrina's father noticed that as his children entered adolescence, they kept their bedroom doors closed, resisted spending time with the family, and became more argumentative. Sabrina and her mother squabbled over Sabrina's messy room ("It's *my* room, Mom. You don't have to live in it!"). And Sabrina resisted the family's weekly visit to Aunt Gina's ("Why do I *always* have to go?"). Research in cultures as diverse as the United States and Turkey shows a rise in parent–child conflict at puberty (Gure, Ucanok, & Sayil, 2006; Laursen, Coy, & Collins, 1998; Steinberg & Morris, 2001). Frequency of arguing is surprisingly similar across North American subcultures, occurring as often in families of European descent as in immigrant Asian and Hispanic families whose traditions emphasize respect for parental authority (Fuligni, 1998).

Why should a youngster's more adultlike appearance trigger these disputes? The association may have adaptive value. Among nonhuman primates, the young typically leave the family group around the time of puberty. The same is true in many nonindustrialized cultures (Caine, 1986; Schlegel & Barry, 1991). Departure of young people discourages sexual relations between close blood relatives. But adolescents in industrialized nations, who are still economically dependent on parents, cannot leave

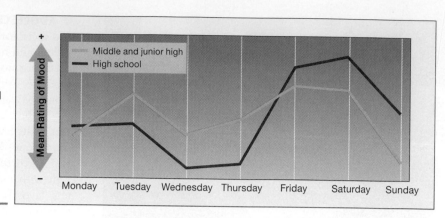

■ **FIGURE 11.2** ■ **Younger and older adolescents' emotional experiences across the week.** Adolescents' reports revealed that emotional high points are on Fridays and Saturdays. Mood drops on Sunday, before returning to school, and during the week, as students spend much time in adult-structured settings in school. (From R. Larson & M. Richards, 1998, "Waiting for the Weekend: Friday and Saturday Night as the Emotional Climax of the Week," in A. C. Crouter & R. Larson (Eds.), *Temporal Rhythms in Adolescence: Clocks, Calendars, and the Coordination of Daily Life.* San Francisco: Jossey-Bass, p. 41. Reprinted with permission from John Wiley & Sons, Inc.)

the family. Consequently, a modern substitute seems to have emerged: psychological distancing.

As children become physically mature, they demand to be treated in adultlike ways. And as we will see, adolescents' new powers of reasoning may also contribute to a rise in family tensions. Parent–adolescent disagreements focus largely on everyday matters such as driving, dating, and curfews (Adams & Laursen, 2001). But beneath these disputes lie serious concerns: parental efforts to protect teenagers from harm.

Parent–daughter conflict tends to be more intense than conflict with sons, perhaps because parents place more restrictions on girls (Allison & Schultz, 2004). But most disputes are mild. Parents and teenagers display both conflict and affection, and they usually agree on important values, such as honesty and the importance of education.

Pubertal Timing

"All our children were early maturers," said Franca during the parents' discussion group. "The boys were tall by age 13, but it was easier for them. They felt big and important. Sabrina was skinny as a little girl, but now she says she's too fat and needs to diet. She thinks about boys and doesn't concentrate on her schoolwork."

Findings of several studies match the experiences of Sabrina and her brothers. Both adults and peers viewed early-maturing boys as relaxed, independent, self-confident, and physically attractive. Popular with agemates, they tended to hold leadership positions in school and to be athletic stars. In contrast, both adults and peers viewed late-maturing boys as anxious, overly talkative, and attention-seeking (Brooks-Gunn, 1988; Clausen, 1975). However, early-maturing boys, though viewed as well-adjusted, report slightly more psychological stress and problem behaviors than their later-maturing agemates (Ge, Conger, & Elder, 2001; Huddleston & Ge, 2003).

In contrast, early-maturing girls were unpopular, withdrawn, lacking in self-confidence, anxious, and prone to depression, and they held few leadership positions (Ge, Conger, & Elder, 1996; Graber et al., 1997; Graber, Brooks-Gunn, & Warren, 2006; Jones & Mussen, 1958). They were more involved

in deviant behavior (getting drunk, participating in early sexual activity) and achieved less well in school (Caspi et al., 1993; Dick et al., 2000; Ge et al., 2006). Their late-maturing counterparts, however, were regarded as physically attractive, lively, sociable, and leaders at school.

Two factors largely account for these trends: (1) how closely the adolescent's body matches cultural ideals of physical attractiveness and (2) how well young people fit in physically with their peers.

■ **THE ROLE OF PHYSICAL ATTRACTIVENESS.** *TAKE A MOMENT...* Flip through your favorite popular magazine. You will see evidence of our society's view of an attractive female as thin and long-legged and a good-looking male as tall, broad-shouldered, and muscular. The female image is a girlish shape that favors the late developer. The male image fits the early-maturing boy.

Consistent with these preferences, early-maturing Caucasian girls tend to report a less positive **body image**—conception of and attitude toward their physical appearance—than their on-time and late-maturing agemates. Compared with African-American and Hispanic girls, Caucasian girls are more likely to have internalized the cultural ideal of female attractiveness: Most want to be thinner (Rosen, 2003; Stice, Presnell, & Bearman, 2001; Williams & Currie, 2000). Although boys are less consistent, early, rapid maturers are more likely to be satisfied with their physical characteristics (Alsaker, 1995; Sinkkonen, Anttila, & Siimes, 1998).

Body image is a strong predictor of young people's self-esteem (Harter, 2006). But the negative effects of pubertal timing on body image and—as we will see next—emotional adjustment are greatly amplified when accompanied by other stressors (Stice, 2003).

■ **THE IMPORTANCE OF FITTING IN WITH PEERS.** Physical status in relation to peers also explains differences in adjustment between early and late maturers. From this perspective, early-maturing girls and late-maturing boys have difficulty because they fall at the extremes of physical development and feel "out of place" when with their agemates. Not surprisingly, adolescents feel most comfortable with peers who match their own level of biological maturity (Stattin & Magnusson, 1990).

Because few agemates of the same pubertal status are available, early-maturing adolescents of both sexes seek out older companions, who often encourage them into activities they are not ready to handle emotionally, including sexual activity, drug and alcohol use, and minor delinquent acts (Ge et al., 2002). Perhaps as a result, early maturers of both sexes report feeling emotionally stressed and show declines in academic performance (Graber, 2003; Mendle, Turkheimer, & Emery, 2007).

At the same time, the young person's context greatly increases the likelihood that early pubertal timing will lead to negative outcomes. Early maturers in economically disadvantaged neighborhoods are especially vulnerable to establishing ties with deviant peers, which heightens their defiant, hostile behavior. And because families in such neighborhoods tend to be exposed to chronic, severe stressors and to have few social supports, these early maturers are also more likely to experience harsh, inconsistent parenting, which predicts both deviant peer associations and antisocial behavior (Conger et al., 2002; Ge et al., 2002).

■ **LONG-TERM CONSEQUENCES.** Follow-ups reveal that early-maturing girls, especially, are prone to lasting difficulties. In a study that followed young people from ages 14 to 24, early-maturing boys showed good adjustment. But early-maturing girls reported poorer-quality relationships with family and friends, smaller social networks, and lower life satisfaction into early adulthood than their on-time counterparts (Graber et al., 2004).

Recall that childhood family conflict and harsh parenting are linked to earlier pubertal timing, more so for girls than for boys (see page 287). Perhaps many early-maturing girls enter adolescence with emotional and social difficulties. As the stresses of puberty interfere with school performance and lead to unfavorable peer pressures, poor adjustment deepens (Graber, 2003). Clearly, interventions that target at-risk early-maturing youths are needed. These include educating parents and teachers and providing adolescents with counseling and social supports.

(see page 287)

ASK YOURSELF

》 REVIEW
Summarize the impact of pubertal timing on adolescent development.

》 APPLY
As a school-age child, Chloe enjoyed leisure activities with her parents. Now, at age 14, she spends hours in her room and resists going on weekend family excursions. Explain Chloe's behavior.

》 REFLECT
Recall your own reactions to the physical changes of puberty. Are they consistent with research findings? Explain.

Health Issues

The arrival of puberty brings new health issues related to the young person's efforts to meet physical and psychological needs. As adolescents attain greater autonomy, their personal decision making becomes important, in health as well as other areas. Yet none of the health concerns we are about to discuss can be traced to a single cause. Rather, biological, psychological, family, peer, and cultural factors jointly contribute.

Nutritional Needs

Puberty leads to a dramatic rise in food intake. During the growth spurt, boys require about 2,700 calories a day and much more protein than they did earlier, girls about 2,200 calories but somewhat less protein than boys because of their smaller size and muscle mass (Cortese & Smith, 2003).

Yet of all age groups, adolescents are the most likely to skip breakfast (a practice linked to obesity), consume empty calories, and eat on the run (Stockman et al., 2005; Striegel-Moore & Franko, 2006). Fast-food restaurants, where teenagers often gather, have begun to offer some healthy menu options. But adolescents need guidance in choosing these alternatives. Eating fast foods is strongly associated with excess fat and sugar consumption, indicating that teenagers often make unhealthy food choices (Bowman et al., 2004; Kubik et al., 2003).

As with school-age children, frequency of family meals is strongly associated with healthy eating in teenagers (Fiese & Schwartz, 2008). But families with adolescents eat fewer meals together.

© BOB DAEMMRICH/PHOTOEDIT

African-American early-maturing girls seem to escape the adjustment difficulties commonly associated with early pubertal timing. Their families and friends tend to be welcoming of menarche (see page 288), and they are more likely to report a positive body image than their Caucasian counterparts.

(see page 288)

Eating Disorders

Sabrina's desire to lose weight worried Franca. She explained to her daughter that her build was really quite average for an adolescent girl and reminded her that her Italian ancestors had considered a plump female body more beautiful than a thin one. Girls who reach puberty early, who are very dissatisfied with their body image, and who grow up in homes where concern with weight and thinness is high are at risk for serious eating problems. The two most serious are anorexia nervosa and bulimia nervosa.

■ ANOREXIA NERVOSA.

Anorexia nervosa is a tragic eating disturbance in which young people starve themselves because of a compulsive fear of getting fat. About 1 percent of North American and Western European teenage girls are affected. During the past half-century, cultural admiration of female thinness has fueled a sharp increase in cases. Anorexia nervosa is equally common in all SES groups, but Asian-American, Caucasian-American, and Hispanic girls are at greater risk than African-American girls, who tend to be more satisfied with their size and shape (Fairburn & Harrison, 2003; Granillo, Jones-Rodriguez, & Carvajal, 2005; Steinhausen, 2006). Boys account for about 10 percent of cases of anorexia; about half of these are homosexual or bisexual young people who are uncomfortable with a strong, muscular appearance (Robb & Dadson, 2002).

© LAUREN GREENFIELD/VII PHOTO

Aiva, age 16, an anorexia nervosa patient, is shown at left on the day she entered treatment. She weighed just 77 pounds—69 percent of her normal body weight. At right, Aiva appears 10 weeks later, on her last day of treatment. Only about 50 percent of young people with anorexia fully overcome the disorder.

Anorexics have an extremely distorted body image. Even after they have become severely underweight, they see themselves as too heavy. Most go on self-imposed diets so strict that they struggle to avoid eating in response to hunger. To enhance weight loss, they exercise strenuously.

In their attempt to reach "perfect" slimness, anorexics lose between 25 and 50 percent of their body weight. Because a normal menstrual cycle requires about 15 percent body fat, either menarche does not occur or menstrual periods stop. Malnutrition causes pale skin, brittle discolored nails, fine dark hairs all over the body, and extreme sensitivity to cold. If it continues, the heart muscle can shrink, the kidneys can fail, and irreversible brain damage and loss of bone mass can occur. About 6 percent of anorexics die of the disorder (Katzman, 2005).

Forces within the person, the family, and the larger culture give rise to anorexia nervosa. Identical twins share the disorder more often than fraternal twins, indicating a genetic influence. Abnormalities in neurotransmitters in the brain, linked to anxiety and impulse control, may make some individuals more susceptible (Kaye, 2008; Lock & Kirz, 2008). Many anorexics have extremely high standards for their own behavior and performance, are emotionally inhibited, and avoid intimate ties outside the family. Consequently, they are often excellent students who are responsible and well-behaved. But as we have also seen, the societal image of "thin is beautiful" contributes to the poor body image of many girls—especially early-maturing girls, who are at greatest risk for anorexia nervosa (Tyrka, Graber, & Brooks-Gunn, 2000).

In addition, parent–adolescent interactions reveal problems related to adolescent autonomy. Often the mothers of these girls have high expectations for physical appearance, achievement, and social acceptance and are overprotective and controlling. Fathers tend to be emotionally distant. These parental attributes may contribute to anorexic girls' persistent anxiety and fierce pursuit of perfection in achievement, respectable behavior, and thinness (Kaye, 2008). Nevertheless, it remains unclear whether maladaptive parent–child relationships precede the disorder, emerge in response to it, or both.

Because anorexic girls typically deny or minimize the seriousness of their disorder, treating it is difficult (Couturier & Lock, 2006). Hospitalization is often necessary to prevent life-threatening malnutrition. The most successful treatment is family therapy and medication to reduce anxiety and neurotransmitter imbalances (Fairburn, 2005; Treasure & Schmidt, 2005). Still, only about 50 percent of anorexics fully recover.

■ BULIMIA NERVOSA.

When Sabrina's 16-year-old brother, Louis, brought his girlfriend, Cassie, to the house, Sabrina admired her good figure. "What willpower!" Sabrina thought. "Cassie hardly touches food. But what's the matter with her teeth?"

Cassie's secret was not willpower. She actually had great difficulty controlling her appetite. Cassie suffered from **bulimia nervosa,** an eating disorder in which young people (again, mainly girls, but gay and bisexual boys are also vulnerable) engage in strict dieting and excessive exercise accompanied by binge eating, often followed by deliberate vomiting and purging with laxatives (Herzog, Eddy, & Beresin, 2006; Wichstrøm, 2006). When she was alone, Cassie often felt anxious and unhappy. She responded with eating rampages, consuming thousands of calories in an hour or two, followed by vomiting that eroded the enamel on her teeth. In some cases, life-threatening damage to the throat and stomach occurs.

Bulimia is more common than anorexia nervosa, affecting about 2 to 4 percent of teenage girls, only 5 percent of whom have previously been anorexic. Twin studies show that bulimia, like anorexia, is influenced by heredity (Klump, Kaye, & Strober, 2001). Overweight and early menarche increase the risk. Some bulimics, like anorexics, are perfectionists. But most are impulsive, sensation-seeking young people who lack self-control in many areas, engaging in petty shoplifting, alcohol abuse, and other risky behaviors (Kaye, 2008). And although bulimics share with anorexics pathological anxiety about gaining weight, they may have experienced their parents as disengaged and emotionally unavailable rather than controlling (Fairburn & Harrison, 2003).

Unlike anorexics, bulimics usually feel depressed and guilty about their abnormal eating habits. As a result, bulimia is usually easier to treat than anorexia, through support groups, nutrition education, training in changing eating habits, and anti-anxiety, antidepressant, and appetite-control medication (Hay & Bacaltchuk, 2004).

Sexuality

Louis and Cassie hadn't planned to have intercourse—it "just happened." But before and after, a lot of things passed through their minds. After they had dated for three months, Cassie began to wonder, "Will Louis think I'm normal if I don't have sex with him? If he wants to and I say no, will I lose him?" Both young people knew their parents wouldn't approve. But that Friday evening, Louis and Cassie's feelings for each other seemed overwhelming. "If I don't make a move," Louis thought, "will she think I'm a wimp?"

With the arrival of puberty, hormonal changes—in particular, the production of androgens in young people of both sexes—lead to an increase in sex drive (Halpern, Udry, & Suchindran, 1997). In response, adolescents become very concerned about managing sexuality in social relationships. New cognitive capacities involving perspective taking and self-reflection affect their efforts to do so. Yet like the eating behaviors we have just discussed, adolescent sexuality is heavily influenced by the young person's social context.

■ **THE IMPACT OF CULTURE.** *TAKE A MOMENT...* When did you first learn the "facts of life"—and how? Was sex discussed openly in your family, or was it treated with secrecy? Exposure to sex, education about it, and efforts to limit the sexual curiosity of children and adolescents vary widely around the world.

Adolescence is an especially important time for the development of sexuality, as these two young people demonstrate. But North American teenagers receive contradictory and confusing messages about the appropriateness of sex.

Despite the prevailing image of sexually free adolescents, sexual attitudes in North America are relatively restrictive. Typically, parents provide little or no information about sex, discourage sex play, and rarely talk about sex in children's presence. When young people become interested in sex, only about half report getting information from parents about intercourse, pregnancy prevention, and sexually transmitted disease. Many parents, fearing embarrassment or concerned that their teenager will not take them seriously, avoid meaningful discussions about sex. Yet warm, open give-and-take, as described in Applying What We Know on page 294, is associated with teenagers' adoption of parents' views and with reduced sexual risk taking (Jaccard, Dodge, & Dittus, 2003; Miller, Forehand, & Kotchick, 1999).

Adolescents who do not get information about sex from their parents are likely to learn from friends, books, magazines, movies, TV, and the Internet (Jaccard, Dodge, & Dittus, 2002; Sutton et al., 2002). On prime-time TV shows, which adolescents watch more than other TV offerings, 80 percent of programs contain sexual content. Most depict partners as spontaneous and passionate, taking no steps to avoid pregnancy or sexually transmitted disease, and experiencing no negative consequences (Roberts, Henriksen, & Foehr, 2004). In several studies, media

Applying What We Know

Communicating with Adolescents About Sexual Issues

Strategy	Explanation
Foster open communication.	Let the teenager know you are a willing and trustworthy resource by stating that you are available when questions arise and will answer fully and accurately.
Use correct terms for body parts.	Correct vocabulary gives the young person a basis for future discussion and also indicates that sex is not a secretive topic.
Use effective discussion techniques.	Listen, encourage the adolescent to participate, ask open-ended rather than yes/no questions, and give supportive responses. Avoid dominating and lecturing, which cause teenagers to withdraw.
Reflect before speaking.	When the adolescent asks questions or offers opinions about sex, remain nonjudgmental. If you differ with the teenager's views, convey your perspective in a nonthreatening manner, emphasizing that although you disagree, you are not attacking his or her character. Trying to dictate the young person's behavior generally results in alienation.
Keep conversations going.	Many parents regard their job as finished once they have had the "big talk" in early adolescence. But young people are more likely to be influenced by an accumulation of smaller discussions. If open communication is sustained, the teenager is more likely to return with thoughts and questions.

Source: Berkowitz, 2004.

exposure to sexual content predicted teenagers' current sexual activity, intentions to be sexually active in the future, and subsequent pregnancies, even after many other relevant factors were controlled (Chandra et al., 2008; Friedman, 2006; Pardum, L'Engle, & Brown, 2005).

The Internet is an especially hazardous "sex educator." In a survey of a large sample of U.S. 10- to 17-year-old Web users, 42 percent said they had viewed online pornographic websites (images of naked people or people having sex) while surfing the Internet in the past 12 months. Of these, 66 percent indicated they had encountered the images accidentally and did not want to view them. Youths who felt depressed, had been bullied by peers, or were involved in delinquent activities had more encounters with Internet pornography, which may have intensified their adjustment problems (Wolak, Mitchell, & Finkelhor, 2007).

Consider the contradictory messages young people receive. On one hand, adults express disapproval of sex at a young age and outside of marriage. On the other hand, the broader social environment extols the excitement and romanticism of sex. North American teenagers are left bewildered, poorly informed about sexual facts, and with little sound advice on how to conduct their sex lives responsibly.

■ CHARACTERISTICS OF SEXUALLY ACTIVE ADOLESCENTS.

Overall teenage sexual activity rates are similar in the United States and other Western countries: About half of adolescents have had intercourse. But quality of sexual experiences differs. U.S. youths become sexually active earlier than their Canadian and European counterparts (Boyce et al., 2006; U.S. Department of Health and Human Services, 2008k). As Figure 11.3

illustrates, a substantial percentage of U.S. young people are sexually active quite early, by ninth grade (age 14 to 15). Males tend to have their first intercourse earlier than females. And about 18 percent of adolescent boys in the United States—more than twice the percentage in Canada, France, and Great Britain—

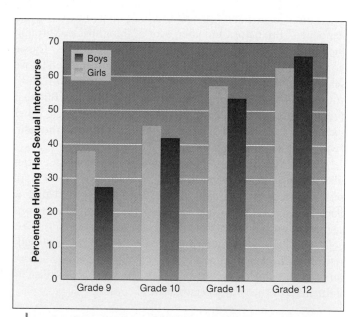

■ **FIGURE 11.3** ■ **U.S. adolescents who report ever having had sexual intercourse.** Many young adolescents are sexually active—more than in other Western nations. Boys tend to have their first intercourse earlier than girls. By the end of high school, rates of boys and girls having had sexual intercourse are similar. (From U.S. Department of Health and Human Services, 2008k.)

have had sexual relations with three or more partners in the past year (Alan Guttmacher Institute, 2004). Most teenagers, however, have had only one or two sexual partners by the end of high school.

Early and frequent teenage sexual activity is linked to personal, family, peer, and educational characteristics. These include childhood impulsivity, weak sense of personal control over life events, early pubertal timing, parental divorce, single-parent and stepfamily homes, large family size, little or no religious involvement, weak parental monitoring, disrupted parent–child communication, sexually active friends and older siblings, poor school performance, lower educational aspirations, and tendency to engage in norm-violating acts, including alcohol and drug use and delinquency (Crockett, Raffaelli, & Shen, 2006; Manlove et al., 2006; Siebenbruner, Zimmer-Gembeck, & Egeland, 2007; Silver & Bauman, 2006).

Notice that many of these factors are associated with growing up in a low-income family. Living in a neighborhood high in physical deterioration, crime, and violence also increases the likelihood that teenagers will be sexually active (Ge et al., 2002). In such neighborhoods, social ties are weak, adults exert little oversight and control over adolescents' activities, and negative peer influences are widespread. In fact, the high rate of sexual activity among African-American teenagers—67 percent compared with 48 percent of all U.S. young people—is largely accounted for by poverty in the black population (Darroch, Frost, & Singh, 2001; U.S. Department of Health and Human Services, 2008k).

■ **CONTRACEPTIVE USE.** Although adolescent contraceptive use has increased in recent years, about 20 percent of sexually active teenagers in the United States are at risk for unintended pregnancy because they do not use contraception consistently (Alan Guttmacher Institute, 2002, 2005). Why do so many fail to take precautions? Typically, teenagers respond, "I wasn't planning to have sex," or, "I didn't want to spoil the moment." As we will see when we take up adolescent cognitive development, although adolescents can consider multiple possibilities when faced with a problem, they often fail to apply this reasoning to everyday situations.

The social environment also contributes to teenagers' reluctance to use contraception. Those without the rewards of meaningful education and work are especially likely to engage in irresponsible sex, sometimes within relationships characterized by exploitation. About 11 percent of U.S. girls and 5 percent of boys say they were pressured to have intercourse when they were unwilling (U.S. Department of Health and Human Services, 2008k).

In contrast, teenagers who report good relationships with parents and who talk openly with them about sex and contraception are more likely to use birth control (Henrich et al., 2006; Kirby, 2002a). But few adolescents believe their parents would be understanding and supportive. School sex education classes, as well, often leave teenagers with incomplete or incorrect knowledge. Some do not know where to get birth control

counseling and devices; those who do often wor or family planning clinic might not keep their visits tial. About 20 percent of adolescents using health serv that if their parents were notified, they would still have sex without contraception (Jones et al., 2005).

■ **SEXUAL ORIENTATION.** So far, we have focused only on heterosexual behavior. About 2 to 3 percent of young people identify as lesbian, gay, or bisexual (Bailey, Dunne, & Martin, 2000; Savin-Williams & Diamond, 2004). An unknown number experience same-sex attraction but have not come out to friends or family (see the Social Issues box on page 296).

Heredity makes an important contribution to homosexuality: Identical twins of both sexes are much more likely than fraternal twins to share a homosexual orientation; so are biological (as opposed to adoptive) relatives (Kendler et al., 2000; Kirk et al., 2000). Furthermore, male homosexuality tends to be more common on the maternal than on the paternal side of families, suggesting that it might be X-linked (see Chapter 2) (Hamer et al., 1993).

How might heredity lead to homosexuality? According to some researchers, certain genes affect the level or impact of prenatal sex hormones, which modify brain structures in ways that induce homosexual feelings and behavior (Bailey et al., 1995; LeVay, 1993). Keep in mind, however, that environmental factors can also alter prenatal hormones. Girls exposed prenatally to very high levels of androgens or estrogens—either because of a genetic defect or from drugs given to the mother to prevent miscarriage—are more likely to become homosexual or bisexual (Meyer-Bahlburg et al., 1995). Furthermore, homosexual men tend to be later in birth order and to have a higher-than-average number of older brothers (Blanchard & Bogaert, 2004). Perhaps mothers with several male children sometimes produce antibodies to androgens, which reduces the prenatal impact of male sex hormones on the brains of later-born boys.

Stereotypes and misconceptions about homosexuality persist. For example, contrary to common belief, most homosexual adolescents are not "gender-deviant" in dress or behavior. And attraction to members of the same sex is not limited to gay, lesbian, and bisexual teenagers. About 50 to 60 percent of adolescents who report having engaged in homosexual acts identify as heterosexual (Savin-Williams & Diamond, 2004).

Sexually Transmitted Diseases

Sexually active adolescents, both homosexual and heterosexual, are at risk for sexually transmitted diseases (STDs). Adolescents have the highest rates of STDs of all age groups. Despite a recent decline in STDs in the United States, one out of six sexually active teenagers contracts one of these illnesses each year—a rate three or more times higher than that of Canada and Western Europe (Health Canada, 2006; U.S. Centers for Disease Control and Prevention, 2007). Left untreated, STDs can lead to sterility and life-threatening complications.

SOCIAL ISSUES

Cultures vary as much in their acceptance of homosexuality as in their approval of extramarital sex. In North America, homosexuals are stigmatized. This makes forming a sexual identity especially challenging for gay, lesbian, and bisexual youths.

Wide variations in sexual identity formation exist, depending on personal, family, and community factors. Yet interviews with gay and lesbian adolescents and adults reveal that many (though not all) move through a three-phase sequence in coming out to themselves and others.

Feeling Different

Typically, first sense of a biologically determined gay or lesbian sexual orientation appears between ages 6 and 12, in play interests more like those of the other gender (Rahman & Wilson, 2003). Boys may find that they are less interested in sports, more drawn to quieter activities, and more emotionally sensitive than other boys; girls may find that they are more athletic and active than other girls.

By age 10, many of these children start to engage in *sexual questioning*—wondering why the typical heterosexual orientation does not apply to them. Often, they experience their sense of being different as deeply distressing. Compared with children who are confident of their homosexuality, sexual-questioning children report greater anxiety about peer relationships and greater dissatisfaction with their biological gender over time (Carver, Egan, & Perry, 2004).

Confusion

With the arrival of puberty, feeling different clearly encompasses feeling sexually different. Awareness of a same-sex physical attraction occurs, on average, between ages 11 and 12 for boys and 14 and 15 for girls, perhaps because adolescent social pressures toward heterosexuality are particularly intense for girls (D'Augelli, 2006; Diamond, 1998).

Realizing that homosexuality has personal relevance sparks additional confusion. A few

adolescents resolve their discomfort by crystallizing a gay, lesbian, or bisexual identity quickly, with a flash of insight into their sense of being different. But most experience an inner struggle that is intensified by lack of role models and social support (D'Augelli, 2002; Safren & Pantalone, 2006).

Some throw themselves into activities they associate with heterosexuality. Boys may go out for athletic teams; girls may drop softball and basketball in favor of dance. And many homosexual youths (more females than males) try heterosexual dating (D'Augelli, 2006; Dubé, Savin-Williams, & Diamond, 2001). Those who are extremely troubled and guilt-ridden may escape into alcohol, drugs, and suicidal thinking. Suicide attempts are unusually high among gay, lesbian, and bisexual young people (McDaniel, Purcell, & D'Augelli, 2001; Morrow, 2006).

Self-Acceptance

By the end of adolescence, the majority of gay, lesbian, and bisexual teenagers accept their sexual identity. But they face another crossroad: whether to tell others. Powerful stigma against their sexual orientation leads some to decide that disclosure is impossible: While self-defining as gay, they otherwise "pass" as heterosexual (Savin-Williams, 2001). When homosexual youths do come out, they often experience intense hostility, including verbal abuse and physical attacks (D'Augelli, 2002).

Nevertheless, many eventually acknowledge their sexual orientation publicly, usually by telling trusted friends first. Once teenagers establish a same-sex sexual or romantic relationship, many come out to parents. Few parents respond with severe rejection; most are either positive or slightly negative and disbelieving (Savin-Williams & Ream, 2003). Parental understanding is the strongest predictor of favorable adjustment (Savin-Williams, 2003).

When people react positively, coming out strengthens the young person's view of homosexuality as a valid, meaningful, and

These teens prepare to celebrate ALLY week, designed to encourage students to be allies against anti-lesbian, gay, bisexual, and transgender language, bullying, and harassment in America's schools. When peers react with acceptance, coming out strengthens the young person's view of homosexuality as a valid and fulfilling identity.

fulfilling identity. Contact with other gays and lesbians is important for reaching this phase, and changes in society permit many adolescents in urban areas to attain it earlier than their counterparts did a decade or two ago. Gay and lesbian communities exist in large cities, but teenagers in small towns and rural areas may have difficulty meeting other homosexuals and finding a supportive environment. These adolescents have a special need for caring adults and peers who can help them find self- and social acceptance.

Gay, lesbian, and bisexual youths who succeed in coming out to themselves and others integrate their sexual orientation into a broader sense of identity, a process we will address in Chapter 12. As a result, their energy is freed for other aspects of psychological growth. In sum, coming out can foster many aspects of adolescent development, including self-esteem, psychological well-being, and relationships with family and friends.

By far the most serious STD is AIDS. In contrast to other Western nations, where the incidence of AIDS among people under age 30 is low, one-fifth of U.S. AIDS cases occur between ages 20 and 29. Because AIDS symptoms typically do not emerge until eight to ten years after infection with the HIV virus, nearly all these cases originated in adolescence. Drug-abusing adolescents who share needles and male adolescents who have sex with HIV-positive same-sex partners account for most cases, but heterosexual spread of the disease remains high (Kelley et al., 2003). It is at least twice as easy for a male to infect a female with any STD, including HIV, as for a female to infect a male. Currently, females account for about 37 percent of new U.S. HIV cases (Rangel et al., 2006).

As the result of school courses and media campaigns, about 60 percent of U.S. middle-school students and 90 percent of high school students are aware of basic facts about AIDS. But most have limited understanding of other STDs and are poorly informed about how to protect themselves (Coholl ct al., 2001; Ethier et al., 2003). Furthermore, high school students report engaging in oral sex much more often than intercourse and with more partners. But few report consistently using STD protection during oral sex, which is a significant mode of transmission of several STDs (Prinstein, Meade, & Cohen, 2003). Concerted efforts are needed to educate young people about the full range of STDs and risky sexual behaviors.

Adolescent Pregnancy and Parenthood

Cassie didn't get pregnant after having sex with Louis, but some of her classmates were less fortunate. About 800,000 teenage girls in the United States become pregnant annually, 25,000 of them younger than age 15. Despite a steady decline since 1991, the U.S. adolescent pregnancy rate is much higher than that of any other industrialized country (see Figure 11.4). Three factors heighten the incidence of adolescent pregnancy: (1) Effective sex education reaches too few teenagers; (2) convenient, low-cost contraceptive services for adolescents are scarce; and (3) many families live in poverty, which encourages young people to take risks.

Because 40 percent of U.S. adolescent pregnancies end in abortion, the number of American teenage births is actually lower than it was 50 years ago (U.S. Department of Health and Human Services, 2007a). But teenage parenthood is a much greater problem today because adolescents are far less likely to marry before childbirth. In 1960, only 15 percent of teenage births were to unmarried females, compared with 86 percent today (Child Trends, 2008). Increased social acceptance of single motherhood, along with the belief of many teenage girls that a baby might fill a void in their lives, means that very few girls give up their infants for adoption.

■ **CORRELATES AND CONSEQUENCES OF ADOLESCENT PARENTHOOD.** Teenage parents have both life conditions and personal attributes that interfere with their ability to parent effectively (Jaffee et al., 2001). They are far more likely to

be poverty-stricken than agemates who postpone childbearing. Their backgrounds often include low parental warmth and involvement, domestic violence and child abuse, repeated parental divorce and remarriage, adult models of early unmarried parenthood, and residence in neighborhoods where other adolescents also display these risks. Girls at risk for early pregnancy do poorly in school, engage in alcohol and drug use, have a childhood history of aggressive and antisocial behavior, associate with deviant peers, and experience high rates of depression (Elfenbein & Felice, 2003; Hillis et al., 2004; Luster & Haddow, 2005). A high percentage of out-of-wedlock births are to low-income ethnic minority teenagers. Many turn to early parenthood as a way to move into adulthood when educational and career avenues are unavailable.

After a baby is born, adolescents' lives often worsen in several respects:

- *Educational attainment.* Giving birth before age 18 reduces the likelihood of finishing high school. Only about 70 percent of U.S. adolescent mothers graduate, compared with 95 percent of girls who wait to become parents (National Women's Law Center, 2007).

- *Marital patterns.* Teenage motherhood reduces the chances of marriage and, for those who do marry, increases the likelihood of divorce compared with peers who delay childbearing (Moore & Brooks-Gunn, 2002). Consequently, teenage mothers spend more of their parenting years as single parents. About 35 percent become pregnant again within two years. Of these, about half go on to deliver a second child (Child Trends, 2008).

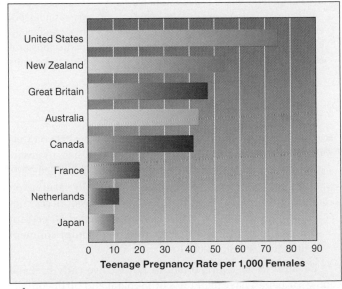

■ **FIGURE 11.4** ■ **Pregnancy rates among 15- to 19-year-olds in eight industrialized nations.** U.S. teenagers have the highest pregnancy rate. (Adapted from Alan Guttmacher Institute, 2001, 2006.)

FESPAN VISTA: Looking Forward, Looking Back ■

Parent, Like Child: Intergenerational Continuity in Adolescent Parenthood

Does adolescent parenthood increase the chances of teenage childbearing in the next generation? To find out, researchers have conducted several unique studies of mothers (first generation)—some who gave birth as teenagers and some who postponed parenting—and their children (second generation), who were followed longitudinally for several decades (Barber, 2001b; Campa & Eckenrode, 2006; Hardy et al., 1998; Manlove, 1997).

First-generation mothers' age at first childbirth strongly predicted the age at which second-generation young people—both daughters and sons—became parents. Yet becoming a second-generation teenage parent is not inevitable for individuals born to an adolescent mother. Rather, adolescent parenthood is linked to a set of related, unfavorable family conditions and personal characteristics, which negatively influence development over an extended time and, therefore, often transfer to the next generation:

■ *Home environmental quality and parenting skills.* The long-term poverty and unstable marital patterns linked to adolescent parenthood reduce the quality of the home environment—in terms of organization, play and learning materials, and parental warmth, encouragement, verbal stimula-tion, and acceptance of the child (as opposed to punitiveness and abuse). Compared with daughters in other fami-lies, the daughters of unmarried adoles-cent mothers live in families that obtain lower early childhood HOME scores (see page 188 in Chapter 7), even after mothers' prebirth SES is controlled (Campa & Eckenrode, 2006). Low HOME scores are associated with poorer language and IQ scores, which, in turn, contribute to the poor school performance and decision making associated with early sexual activ-ity, laxity in use of contraceptives, and adolescent childbearing.

■ *Intelligence and education.* Younger mothers' cognitive deficits and reduced educational attainment contribute to the likelihood their children will experience long-term, poor-quality home environ-ments and, thus, in adolescence will engage in the maladaptive behaviors just mentioned (Barber, 2001b; Hardy et al., 1998).

■ *Father absence.* In several studies, inter-generational continuity in adolescent parenthood—especially for daughters—was far greater when teenage mothers remained unmarried (Barber, 2001b; Campa & Eckenrode, 2006). Marriage may limit the negative impact of teenage child-bearing on development by strengthening parental financial resources and involve-ment and reducing family stress. It may be particularly protective for girls because unmarried fathers are less likely to remain in regular contact with daughters than with sons. Recall from Chapter 10 that a warm, involved noncustodial father is linked to reduced early sexual activity in girls (see page 272).

In sum, a life course of adversity—poverty, depleted and disorganized home environ-ments, poor parenting, father absence, intel-lectual deficits, poor academic performance, and limited educational opportunities—contributes to intergenerational continuity in adolescent pregnancy and parenthood.

© BILDERLOUNGE/SUPERSTOCK

Will the child of this teenage mother also become an adolescent parent? Negative family conditions and personal characteristics associated with early childbearing increase the likelihood that adolescent parenthood will recur in the next generation.

■ *Economic circumstances.* Many teenage mothers are on wel-fare. And limited education restricts many others to unsat-isfying, low-paid jobs. Adolescent fathers, too, are generally unemployed or work at unskilled jobs, usually earning too little to provide their children with basic necessities (Bunting & McAuley, 2004). And an estimated 50 percent have committed illegal offenses resulting in imprisonment (Elfenbein & Felice, 2003).

Because teenage girls often do not receive early prenatal care, their babies have high rates of prenatal and birth compli-cations—especially low birth weight (Dell, 2001). And com-pared with adult mothers, adolescent mothers know less about child development and interact less effectively with their babies (Moore & Florsheim, 2001; Pomerleau, Scuccimarri, & Malcuit,

2003). Their children tend to score low on intelligence tests, achieve poorly in school, and engage in disruptive social behav-ior. And as the Lifespan Vista box above indicates, adolescent parenthood frequently is repeated in the next generation (Brooks-Gunn, Schley, & Hardy, 2002). Even when children born to teenage mothers do not become early child bearers, their development is often compromised, in terms of likelihood of high school graduation, financial independence in adult-hood, and physical and mental health (Pogarsky, Thornberry, & Lizotte, 2006).

Still, outcomes vary widely. If a teenage parent finishes high school, secures gainful employment, avoids additional births, and finds a stable marriage partner, long-term disrup-tions in her own and her child's development will be less severe.

■ **PREVENTION STRATEGIES.** Preventing teenage pregnancy means addressing the many factors underlying early sexual activity and lack of contraceptive use. Sex education courses typically improve awareness of sexual facts—knowledge necessary for responsible sexual behavior. Knowledge, however, is not enough: Sex education must also help teenagers build a bridge between what they know and what they do. Effective prevention combines the following key elements:

- They teach techniques for handling sexual situations through role-playing and other activities.

- They deliver clear, accurate messages that are appropriate in view of participating adolescents' culture and sexual experiences.

- They last long enough to have an impact.

- They provide specific information about contraceptives and ready access to them.

Many studies show that these components can delay the initiation of sexual activity, increase contraceptive use, change attitudes (for example, strengthen future orientation), and reduce pregnancy rates (Kirby, 2002b; Manlove et al., 2006; Thomas & Dimitrov, 2007).

Proposals to increase access to contraceptives are the most controversial aspect of adolescent pregnancy prevention. Yet sex education programs focusing on abstinence have little or no impact on delaying teenage sexual activity or on preventing pregnancy (Bennett & Assefi, 2005; Underhill, Montgomery, & Operario, 2007). And in Canada and Western Europe, where community- and school-based clinics offer adolescents contraceptives and where universal health insurance helps pay for them, teenage sexual activity is no higher than in the United States—but pregnancy, childbirth, and abortion rates are much lower (Schalet, 2007).

Efforts to prevent adolescent pregnancy and parenthood must go beyond improving sex education and access to contraception to build academic and social competence (Allen, Seitz, & Apfel, 2007). In one intervention, at-risk high school students took a community service class in which they participated in at least 20 hours per week of volunteer work tailored to their interests and in discussions focused on coping with everyday challenges. At the end of the school year, pregnancy, school failure, and school suspension were substantially lower among intervention students than among high-risk students with regular classroom experiences (Allen et al., 1997).

Finally, teenagers who look forward to a promising future are far less likely to engage in early and irresponsible sex. By expanding educational, vocational, and employment opportunities, society can give young people good reasons to postpone childbearing.

■ **INTERVENING WITH ADOLESCENT PARENTS.** The most difficult and costly way to deal with adolescent parenthood is to wait until it happens. Young parents need health care, encouragement to stay in school, job training, instruction in parenting and life-management skills, and high-quality, affordable child care. Schools that provide these services reduce the incidence of low-birth-weight babies, increase educational success, and prevent additional childbearing (Barnet et al., 2004; Seitz & Apfel, 2005).

Adolescent mothers also benefit from relationships with family members who are sensitive to their developmental needs. In one study, teenage mothers who had a long-term "mentor" relationship—an aunt, neighbor, or teacher who provided emotional support and guidance—were far more likely than those without a mentor to stay in school and graduate (Klaw, Rhodes, & Fitzgerald, 2003).

Although nearly half of young fathers visit their children during the first few years, contact usually diminishes. As with teenage mothers, support from family members helps fathers stay involved (Bunting & McAuley, 2004). Teenage mothers who receive financial and child-care assistance and emotional support from their child's father are less distressed and more likely to sustain a relationship with him (Cutrona et al., 1998; Gee & Rhodes, 2003). And infants with lasting ties to their teenage fathers show better long-term adjustment (Florsheim & Smith, 2005; Furstenberg & Harris, 1993).

Substance Use and Abuse

At age 14, Louis waited until he was alone at home, took some cigarettes from his uncle's pack, and smoked. At an unchaperoned party, he and Cassie drank several cans of beer and lit up marijuana joints. Louis got little physical charge out of these experiences. A good student, who was well-liked by peers and got along well with his parents, he did not need drugs as an escape valve. But he knew of other teenagers who started with alcohol and cigarettes, moved on to harder substances, and eventually were hooked.

© JUPITERIMAGES/I2I/ALAMY

Encouragement from friends contributes to teenagers' alcohol and drug use and—among young people with family difficulties—increases the risk of drug abuse.

According to the most recent, nationally representative survey of U.S. high school students, by tenth grade, 40 percent of U.S. young people have tried cigarette smoking, 63 percent drinking, and 38 percent at least one illegal drug (usually marijuana). At the end of high school, 17 percent smoke cigarettes regularly, 28 percent have engaged in heavy drinking during the past two weeks, and 40 percent have experimented with illegal drugs. About 20 percent have tried at least one highly addictive and toxic substance, such as amphetamines, cocaine, phencyclidine (PCP), Ecstasy (MDMA), inhalants, heroin, sedatives (including barbiturates), or OxyContin (a narcotic painkiller) (Johnston et al., 2008).

These figures represent a substantial decline since the mid-1990s, probably resulting from greater parent, school, and media focus on the hazards of drug use. Still, drug use rises steadily over adolescence. Why do so many young people subject themselves to the health risks of these substances? In part, drug taking reflects the sensation seeking of these years. But teenagers also live in drug-dependent cultural contexts. They see adults relying on caffeine to stay alert, cigarettes to cope with daily hassles, and other remedies to relieve stress, depression, and physical discomfort. Furthermore, over 90 percent of teenagers say they are aware of cigarette and alcohol ads specifically targeting them (Alcohol Concern, 2007).

The majority of teenagers who dabble in alcohol, tobacco, and marijuana are not headed for a life of addiction. These minimal *experimenters* are usually psychologically healthy, sociable, curious young people (Shedler & Block, 1990). Poverty is linked to family and peer contexts that promote illegal drug use. At the same time, use of diverse drugs is lower among African Americans than among Hispanics and Caucasian Americans; Native-American youths rank highest in drug taking (Johnston et al., 2008; Wallace et al., 2003). Researchers have yet to explain these variations.

Adolescent experimentation with any drug should not be taken lightly. Because most drugs impair perception and thought processes, a single heavy dose can lead to permanent injury or death. And a worrisome minority of teenagers move from substance use to abuse—taking drugs regularly, requiring increasing amounts to achieve the same effect, moving on to harder substances, and using enough to interfere with their ability to meet daily responsibilities.

■ **CORRELATES AND CONSEQUENCES OF ADOLESCENT SUBSTANCE ABUSE.** Unlike experimenters, drug abusers are seriously troubled young people. Their impulsive, disruptive, hostile style is often evident in early childhood. Compared with other young people, their drug taking starts earlier and may have genetic roots (Chassin et al., 2004; Ellickson et al., 2005). But environmental factors also contribute. These include low SES, family mental health problems, parental and older sibling drug abuse, lack of parental warmth and involvement, physical and sexual abuse, and poor school performance. Especially among teenagers with family difficulties, encouragement from friends who use and provide drugs increases substance abuse (Goldstein, Davis-Kean, & Eccles, 2005; Prinstein, Boergers, & Spirito, 2001).

Teenagers who depend on alcohol and hard drugs to deal with daily stresses fail to learn responsible decision-making skills and alternative coping techniques. They show serious adjustment problems, including chronic anxiety, depression, and antisocial behavior, that are both cause and consequence of heavy drug taking (Kassel et al., 2005; Simons-Morton & Haynie, 2003). And they often enter into marriage, childbearing, and the work world prematurely and fail at them—painful outcomes that further promote addictive behavior.

■ **PREVENTION AND TREATMENT.** School and community programs that reduce drug experimentation typically teach adolescents skills for resisting peer pressure, emphasize health and safety risks of drug-taking, and get adolescents to commit to not using drugs (Cuijpers, 2002). But because some drug taking seems inevitable, interventions that prevent teenagers from harming themselves and others when they do experiment are essential. Many communities offer weekend on-call transportation services that any young person can contact for a safe ride home, with no questions asked.

Different strategies are required to prevent drug abuse. One approach is to work with parents early, reducing family adversity and improving parenting skills (Velleman, Templeton, & Copello, 2005). Programs that teach at-risk teenagers effective strategies for handling life stressors and that build competence through community service reduce alcohol and drug abuse, just as they reduce teenage pregnancy.

When an adolescent becomes a drug abuser, family and individual therapy are generally needed to treat maladaptive parent–child relationships, impulsivity, low self-esteem, anxiety, and depression. Academic and vocational training to improve life success also helps. But even comprehensive programs have alarmingly high relapse rates—from 35 to 85 percent (Brown & Ramo, 2005; Waldron, Turner, & Ozechowski, 2005). One recommendation is to start treatment gradually, through support-group sessions that focus on reducing drug taking (Myers et al., 2001). Modest improvements may increase young people's motivation to make longer-lasting changes through intensive treatment.

ASK YOURSELF

≫ **REVIEW**
Compare risk factors for anorexia nervosa and bulimia nervosa. How do treatments and outcomes differ for the two disorders?

≫ **APPLY**
After 17-year-old Veronica gave birth to Ben, her parents told her they didn't have room for the baby. Veronica dropped out of school and moved in with her boyfriend, who soon left. Why are Veronica and Ben likely to experience long-term hardships?

≫ **REFLECT**
Describe your experiences with peer pressure to experiment with alcohol and drugs. What factors influenced your response?

Cognitive Development

One mid-December evening, a knock at the front door announced the arrival of Franca and Antonio's oldest son, Jules, home for vacation after the fall semester of his sophomore year at college. The family gathered around the kitchen table. "How did it all go, Jules?" asked Antonio.

"Well, physics and philosophy were awesome," Jules responded with enthusiasm. "The last few weeks, our physics prof introduced us to Einstein's theory of relativity. Boggles my mind, it's so incredibly counterintuitive."

"Counter-what?" asked 11-year-old Sabrina.

"Counterintuitive. Unlike what you'd normally expect," explained Jules. "Imagine you're on a train, going unbelievably fast, like 160,000 miles a second. The faster you go, approaching the speed of light, the slower time passes and the denser and heavier things get relative to on the ground. The theory revolutionized the way we think about time, space, matter—the entire universe."

Sabrina wrinkled her forehead, baffled by Jules's otherworldly reasoning. "Time slows down when I'm bored, like right now, not on a train when I'm going somewhere exciting," Sabrina announced.

Sixteen-year-old Louis reacted differently. "Totally cool, Jules. So what'd you do in philosophy?"

"We studied the ethics of futuristic methods in human reproduction. For example, we argued the pros and cons of a world in which all embryos develop in artificial wombs."

"What do you mean?" asked Louis. "You order your kid at the lab?"

"That's right. I wrote my term paper on it. I had to evaluate it in terms of principles of justice and freedom...."

As this conversation illustrates, adolescence brings with it vastly expanded powers of reasoning. At age 11, Sabrina finds it difficult to move beyond her firsthand experiences to a world of possibilities. Over the next few years, her thinking will acquire the complex qualities that characterize the cognition of her older brothers. Jules considers multiple variables simultaneously and thinks about situations that are not easily detected in the real world or that do not exist at all. As a result, he can grasp advanced scientific and mathematical principles and grapple with social and political issues. Compared with school-age children's thinking, adolescent thought is more enlightened, imaginative, and rational.

Systematic research on adolescent cognitive development began with testing of Piaget's ideas (Keating, 2004). Recently, information-processing research has greatly enhanced our understanding.

Piaget's Theory: The Formal Operational Stage

According to Piaget, around age 11 young people enter the **formal operational stage,** in which they develop the capacity for abstract, systematic, scientific thinking. Whereas concrete operational children can "operate on reality," formal operational adolescents can "operate on operations." They no longer require concrete things and events as objects of thought. Instead, they can come up with new, more general logical rules through internal reflection (Inhelder & Piaget, 1955/1958). Let's look at two major features of the formal operational stage.

Hypothetico-Deductive Reasoning

Piaget believed that at adolescence, young people first become capable of **hypothetico-deductive reasoning.** When faced with a problem, they start with a *hypothesis*, or prediction about variables that might affect an outcome, from which they *deduce* logical, testable inferences. Then they systematically isolate and combine variables to see which of these inferences are confirmed in the real world. Notice how this form of problem solving begins with possibility and proceeds to reality. In contrast, concrete operational children start with reality—with the most obvious predictions about a situation. When these are not confirmed, they usually cannot think of alternatives and fail to solve the problem.

Adolescents' performance on Piaget's famous *pendulum problem* illustrates this approach. Suppose we present several school-age children and adolescents with strings of different lengths, objects of different weights to attach to the strings, and a bar from which to hang the strings (see Figure 11.5). Then we ask each of them to figure out what influences the speed with which a pendulum swings through its arc.

■ **FIGURE 11.5** ■ **Piaget's pendulum problem.** Adolescents who engage in hypothetico-deductive reasoning think of variables that might possibly affect the speed with which a pendulum swings through its arc. Then they isolate and test each variable, as well as testing the variables in combination. Eventually they deduce that the weight of the object, the height from which it is released, and how forcefully it is pushed have no effect on the speed with which the pendulum swings through its arc. Only string length makes a difference.

Formal operational adolescents hypothesize that four variables might be influential: (1) the length of the string, (2) the weight of the object hung on it, (3) how high the object is raised before it is released, and (4) how forcefully the object is pushed. By varying one factor at a time while holding the other three constant, they test each variable separately and, if necessary, also in combination. Eventually they discover that only string length makes a difference.

In contrast, concrete operational children cannot separate the effects of each variable. They may test for the effect of string length without holding weight constant—comparing, for example, a short, light pendulum with a long, heavy one. Also, they typically fail to notice variables that are not immediately suggested by the concrete materials of the task—for example, how high the object is raised or how forcefully it is released.

Propositional Thought

A second important characteristic of Piaget's formal operational stage is **propositional thought**—adolescents' ability to evaluate the logic of propositions (verbal statements) without referring to real-world circumstances. In contrast, children can evaluate the logic of statements only by considering them against concrete evidence in the real world.

In a study of propositional reasoning, a researcher showed children and adolescents a pile of poker chips and asked whether statements about the chips were true, false, or uncertain (Osherson & Markman, 1975). In one condition, the researcher hid a chip in her hand and presented the following propositions:

"*Either* the chip in my hand is green or it is not green."
"The chip in my hand is green *and* it is not green."

In Piaget's formal operational stage, adolescents engage in propositional thought. As these students discuss problems in a science class, they show that they can reason with symbols that do not necessarily represent objects in the real world.

In another condition, the experimenter made the same statements while holding either a red or a green chip in full view.

School-age children focused on the concrete properties of the poker chips. When the chip was hidden, they replied that they were uncertain about both statements. When it was visible, they judged both statements to be true if the chip was green and false if it was red. In contrast, adolescents analyzed the logic of the statements. They understood that the "either-or" statement is always true and the "and" statement is always false, regardless of the chip's color.

Although Piaget did not view language as playing a central role in children's cognitive development (see Chapter 7), he acknowledged its importance in adolescence. Formal operations require language-based and other symbolic systems that do not stand for real things, such as those in higher mathematics. Secondary school students use such systems in algebra and geometry. Formal operational thought also involves verbal reasoning about abstract concepts. Jules was thinking in this way when he pondered relationships among time, space, and matter in physics and wondered about justice and freedom in philosophy.

Follow-Up Research on Formal Operational Thought

Research on formal operational thought poses questions similar to those we discussed with respect to Piaget's earlier stages: Does formal operational thinking appear earlier than Piaget expected? Do all individuals reach formal operations during their teenage years?

■ **ARE CHILDREN CAPABLE OF HYPOTHETICO-DEDUCTIVE AND PROPOSITIONAL THINKING?** School-age children show the glimmerings of hypothetico-deductive reasoning, although they are less competent at it than adolescents. In simplified situations—ones involving no more than two possible causal variables—6-year-olds understand that hypotheses must be confirmed by appropriate evidence (Ruffman et al., 1993). But school-age children cannot sort out evidence that bears on three or more variables at once. And children have difficulty explaining why a pattern of observations supports a hypothesis, even when they recognize the connection between the two.

With respect to propositional thought, when a simple set of premises defies real-world knowledge ("All cats bark. Rex is a cat. Does Rex bark?"), 4- to 6-year-olds can reason logically in make-believe play. To justify their answer, they are likely to say, "We can pretend cats bark!" (Dias & Harris, 1988, 1990). But in an entirely verbal mode, children have great difficulty reasoning from premises that contradict reality or their own beliefs.

Consider this set of statements: "If dogs are bigger than elephants, and elephants are bigger than mice, then dogs are bigger than mice." Children younger than 10 judge this reasoning to be false because some of the relations specified do not occur in real life (Moshman & Franks, 1986; Pillow, 2002). They have more difficulty than adolescents inhibiting activation of well-learned knowledge ("Elephants are larger than dogs") that casts doubt on the truthfulness of the premises (Klaczynski, Schuneman, & Daniel, 2004; Simoneau & Markovits, 2003). Partly for this reason, they fail to grasp the *logical necessity* of propositional reasoning—that the accuracy of conclusions drawn from premises rests on the rules of logic, not on real-world confirmation.

As with hypothetico-deductive reasoning, in early adolescence, young people become better at analyzing the *logic* of propositions irrespective of their *content*. And as they get older, they handle problems requiring increasingly complex mental operations. In justifying their reasoning, they more often explain the logical rules on which it is based (Müller, Overton, & Reese, 2001; Venet & Markovits, 2001). But these capacities do not appear suddenly at puberty. Rather, gains occur gradually from childhood on—findings that call into question the emergence of a discrete new stage of cognitive development at adolescence (Keating, 2004; Kuhn & Franklin, 2006; Moshman, 2005).

■ **DO ALL INDIVIDUALS REACH THE FORMAL OPERATIONAL STAGE?** *TAKE A MOMENT...* Try giving one or two of the formal operational tasks just described to your friends. How well do they do? Even well-educated adults frequently have difficulty with such reasoning (Keating, 1979, 2004). One reason is that people are most likely to think abstractly and systematically on tasks in which they have had extensive guidance and practice in using such reasoning. This conclusion is supported by evidence that taking college courses leads to improvements in formal reasoning related to course content. Math and science prompt gains in propositional thought, social science in methodological and statistical reasoning (Lehman & Nisbett, 1990).

Individuals in tribal and village societies rarely master formal operational tasks (Cole, 1990). Piaget acknowledged that without the opportunity to solve hypothetical problems, people in some societies might not display formal operations. Still, these findings raise further questions about Piaget's stage sequence. Does formal operational thought largely result from children's and adolescents' independent efforts to make sense of their world, as Piaget claimed? Or is it a culturally transmitted way of thinking that is specific to literate societies and taught in school? In an Israeli study of middle school students, after controlling for participants' age, researchers found that years of schooling fully accounted for gains in propositional thought (Artman, Cahan, & Avni-Babad, 2006). School tasks, the investigators speculated, provide crucial experiences in setting aside the "if . . . then" logic of everyday conversations that is often used to convey intentions, promises, and threats ("If you don't do your chores, then you won't get your allowance") but that conflicts with the logic of academic reasoning. In school, then, adolescents encounter rich opportunities to realize their neurological potential to think more effectively.

An Information-Processing View of Adolescent Cognitive Development

Information-processing theorists refer to a variety of specific mechanisms, supported by brain development and experience, that underlie cognitive change in adolescence. Each was discussed in previous chapters (Case, 1998; Kuhn & Franklin, 2006; Luna et al., 2004). Now let's draw them together:

■ *Attention* becomes more selective (focused on relevant information) and better-adapted to the changing demands of tasks.

■ *Inhibition*—both of irrelevant stimuli and of well-learned responses in situations where they are inappropriate—improves, supporting gains in attention and reasoning.

■ *Strategies* become more effective, improving storage, representation, and retrieval of information.

■ *Knowledge* increases, easing strategy use.

■ *Metacognition* (awareness of thought) expands, leading to new insights into effective strategies for acquiring information and solving problems.

■ *Cognitive self-regulation* improves, yielding better moment-by-moment monitoring, evaluation, and redirection of thinking.

■ *Speed of thinking* and *processing capacity* increase. As a result, more information can be held at once in working memory and combined into increasingly complex, efficient representations, "opening possibilities for growth" in the capacities just listed and also improving as a result of gains in those capacities (Demetriou et al., 2002, p. 97).

As we look at influential findings from an information-processing perspective, we will see some of these mechanisms of change in action. And we will discover that researchers regard one of them—*metacognition*—as central to adolescent cognitive development.

Scientific Reasoning: Coordinating Theory with Evidence

During a free moment in physical education class, Sabrina wondered why more of her tennis serves and returns passed the net and dropped into her opponent's court when she used a particular brand of balls. "Is it something about their color or size?" she asked herself. "Hmm . . . or maybe it's their surface texture that might affect their bounce."

The heart of scientific reasoning is coordinating theories with evidence. Deanna Kuhn (2002) has conducted extensive research into the development of scientific reasoning, using problems that, like Piaget's tasks, involve several variables that might affect an outcome. In one series of studies, third, sixth, and ninth graders and adults were first given evidence—sometimes

■ **FIGURE 11.6** ■ **Which features of these sports balls—size, color, surface texture, or presence or absence of ridges—influence the quality of a player's serve?** This set of evidence suggests that color might be important, since light-colored balls are largely in the good-serve basket and dark-colored balls in the bad-serve basket. But the same is true for texture! The good-serve basket has mostly smooth balls; the bad-serve basket, rough balls. Since all light-colored balls are smooth and all dark-colored balls are rough, we cannot tell whether color or texture makes a difference. But we can conclude that size and presence or absence of ridges are not important, since these features are equally represented in the good-serve and bad-serve baskets. (Adapted from Kuhn, Amsel, & O'Loughlin, 1988.)

consistent and sometimes conflicting with theories—and then questioned about the accuracy of each theory.

For example, participants were given a problem much like the one Sabrina posed. They were asked to theorize about which of several features of sports balls—size (large or small), color (light or dark), texture (rough or smooth), or presence or absence of ridges on the surface—influences the quality of a player's serve. Next, they were told about the theory of Mr. (or Ms.) S, who believes that the ball's size is important, and the theory of Mr. (or Ms.) C, who thinks color makes a difference. Finally, the interviewer presented evidence by placing balls with certain characteristics in two baskets, labeled "good serve" and "bad serve" (see Figure 11.6).

The youngest participants often ignored conflicting evidence or distorted it in ways consistent with their preferred theory. Instead of viewing evidence as separate from and bearing on a theory, children often blend the two into a single representation of "the way things are." They are especially likely to overlook evidence that does not match their prior beliefs when a causal variable is implausible (like color affecting the performance of a sports ball) and when task demands (number of variables to be evaluated) are high (Zimmerman, 2005, 2007). The ability to distinguish theory from evidence and to use logical rules to examine their relationship improves steadily from childhood into adolescence, continuing into adulthood (Kuhn & Dean, 2004).

How Scientific Reasoning Develops

What factors support skill at coordinating theory with evidence? Greater working-memory capacity, permitting a theory and the effects of several variables to be compared at once, is vital. Adolescents also benefit from exposure to increasingly complex problems and to teaching that highlights critical fea-

tures of scientific reasoning—for example, why a scientist's expectations in a particular situation are inconsistent with everyday beliefs and experiences (Chinn & Malhotra, 2002). This explains why scientific reasoning is strongly influenced by years of schooling, whether individuals grapple with traditional scientific tasks (like the sports-ball problem) or engage in informal reasoning—for example, justifying a theory about what causes children to fail in school (Amsel & Brock. 1996).

Researchers believe that sophisticated *metacognitive understanding* is vital for scientific reasoning (Kuhn, 1999; Moshman, 1999). When adolescents regularly pit theory against evidence over many weeks, they experiment with various strategies, reflect on and revise them, and become aware of the nature of logic. Then they apply their appreciation of logic to an increasingly wide variety of situations. The ability to *think about* theories, *deliberately isolate* variables, and *actively seek* disconfirming evidence is rarely present before adolescence (Kuhn, 2000; Moshman, 1998).

But adolescents and adults vary widely in scientific reasoning skills. Many continue to show a self-serving bias, applying logic more effectively to ideas they doubt than to ideas they favor (Klaczynski & Narasimham, 1998). Reasoning scientifically requires the metacognitive capacity to evaluate one's objectivity—to be fair-minded rather than self-serving (Moshman, 1999). As we will see in Chapter 12, this flexible, open-minded approach is both a cognitive attainment and a personality trait—one that assists teenagers greatly in forming an identity and developing morally. Information-processing findings confirm that scientific reasoning is not the result of an abrupt, stagewise change. Instead, it develops out of many specific experiences that require children and adolescents to match theories against evidence and reflect on and evaluate their thinking.

Consequences of Adolescent Cognitive Changes

The development of increasingly complex, effective thinking leads to dramatic revisions in the way adolescents see themselves and others. But just as adolescents are occasionally awkward in using their transformed bodies, they initially falter in their abstract thinking. As we will see, teenagers' self-concern, idealism, criticism, and indecisiveness, though perplexing to adults, are usually beneficial in the long run.

Self-Consciousness and Self-Focusing

Adolescents' ability to reflect on their own thoughts, combined with physical and psychological changes, leads them to think more about themselves. Piaget's followers identified two distorted images of the relation between self and other that commonly appear.

The first is called the **imaginary audience,** adolescents' belief that they are the focus of everyone else's attention and concern (Elkind & Bowen, 1979). As a result, they become extremely self-conscious. When Sabrina woke up one Sunday

The personal fable leads adolescents to view themselves as special and unique. When combined with a sensation-seeking personality, it seems to reduce teenagers' sense of vulnerability and contribute to risky behaviors.

with a large pimple on her chin, her first thought was, "I can't possibly go to church! Everyone will notice how ugly I look." The imaginary audience helps explain why adolescents spend long hours inspecting every detail of their appearance and why they are so sensitive to public criticism. To teenagers, who believe that everyone is monitoring their performance, a critical remark from a parent or teacher can be mortifying.

A second cognitive distortion is the **personal fable.** Certain that others are observing and thinking about them, teenagers develop an inflated opinion of their own importance—a feeling that they are special and unique. Many adolescents view themselves as reaching great heights of omnipotence and also sinking to unusual depths of despair—experiences that others cannot possibly understand (Elkind, 1994). One teenager wrote in her diary, "My parents' lives are so ordinary, so stuck in a rut. Mine will be different. I'll realize my hopes and ambitions."

Imaginary-audience and personal-fable ideation are partly an outgrowth of advances in perspective taking, which cause teenagers to be more concerned with what others think (Vartanian & Powlishta, 1996). When asked why they worry about the opinions of others, adolescents responded that others' evaluations have important *real* consequences—for self-esteem, peer acceptance, and social support (Bell & Bromnick, 2003). With respect to the personal fable, in a study of sixth through tenth graders, sense of omnipotence predicted favorable self-esteem and overall positive adjustment. Viewing the self as highly capable and influential may help young people cope with challenges of adolescence. In contrast, sense of personal uniqueness was modestly associated with depression and suicidal thinking (Aalsma, Lapsley, & Flannery, 2006). Focusing on the distinctiveness of one's own experiences may interfere with forming close, rewarding relationships, which provide social support in stressful times.

Idealism and Criticism

Adolescents' capacity to think about possibilities opens up the world of the ideal. Teenagers can imagine alternative family, religious, political, and moral systems, and they want to explore them. They often construct grand visions of a world with no injustice, discrimination, or tasteless behavior. The disparity between teenagers' idealism and adults' greater realism creates tension between parent and child. Envisioning a perfect family against which their parents and siblings fall short, adolescents become fault-finding critics.

Overall, however, teenage idealism and criticism are advantageous. Once adolescents come to see other people as having both strengths and weaknesses, they have a much greater capacity to work constructively for social change and to form positive and lasting relationships (Elkind, 1994).

Decision Making

Although adolescents handle many cognitive tasks more effectively than they did when younger, they often do not think rationally during decision making: (1) identifying the pros and cons of each alternative; (2) assessing the likelihood of various outcomes; (3) evaluating their choice in terms of whether their goals were met; and, if not, (4) learning from the mistake and making a better future decision. In one study, researchers gave adolescents and adults hypothetical dilemmas—whether to have cosmetic surgery, which parent to live with after divorce—and asked them to explain how they would decide. Adults outperformed adolescents, more often considering alternatives, weighing benefits and risks, and suggesting advice-seeking (Halpern-Felsher & Cauffman, 2001).

Furthermore, in making decisions, adolescents, more often than adults (who also have difficulty), fall back on well-learned intuitive judgments (Jacobs & Klaczynski, 2002). Consider a hypothetical problem requiring a choice, on the basis of two arguments, between taking a traditional lecture class and taking a computer-based class. One argument contains large-sample information: course evaluations from 150 students, 85 percent of whom liked the computer class. The other argument contains small-sample personal reports: complaints of two honor-roll students who both hated the computer class and enjoyed the traditional class. Most adolescents, even those who knew that selecting the large-sample argument was "more intelligent," based their choice on the small-sample argument, which resembled the informal opinions they depend on in everyday life (Klaczynski, 2001).

Why is decision making so challenging for adolescents? As "first-timers" at many experiences, they do not have sufficient knowledge to predict potential outcomes. They also face many complex situations involving competing goals, such as how to maintain social status while avoiding getting drunk at a party. In unfamiliar circumstances and when making a good decision would mean inhibiting "feel-good" behavior (smoking, overeating, unsafe sex), adolescents are far more likely than adults to emphasize short-term over long-term goals (Boyer, 2006; Reyna & Farley, 2006). Furthermore, teenagers often feel overwhelmed

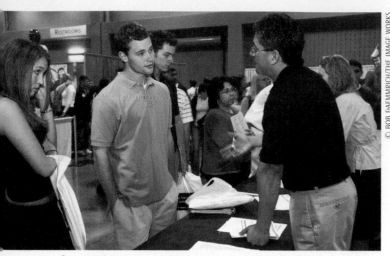

These high school students attending a college fair will face many choices over the next few years. In unfamiliar situations, teenagers are more likely than adults to fall back on intuitive judgments rather than to use sound decision-making strategies.

by their expanding range of options—abundant school courses, extracurricular activities, social events, and material goods. As a result, their efforts to choose frequently break down, and they resort to habit, act on impulse, or postpone decisions.

Over time, young people learn from their successes and failures, gather information from others about factors that affect decision making, and reflect on the decision-making process (Byrnes, 2003; Jacobs & Klaczynski, 2002). Consequently, their confidence and performance improve.

ASK YOURSELF

>> **REVIEW**
Describe research findings that challenge Piaget's notion of a new, discrete stage of cognitive development at adolescence.

>> **APPLY**
Clarissa, age 14, is convinced that no one appreciates how hurt she feels at not being invited to the homecoming dance. Meanwhile, 15-year-old Justine, alone in her room, pantomimes being sworn in as student body president with her awestruck parents looking on. Which aspect of the personal fable is each girl displaying? Which girl is more likely to be well-adjusted, which poorly adjusted? Explain.

>> **REFLECT**
Do you recall engaging in idealistic thinking or poor decision making as a teenager? Cite examples.

Learning in School

In complex societies, adolescence coincides with entry into secondary school. Most young people move into either a middle or a junior high school and then into a high school. With each change, academic achievement increasingly determines higher education options and job opportunities. In the following sections, we take up various aspects of secondary school life.

School Transitions

When Sabrina started junior high, she left a small, intimate, self-contained sixth-grade classroom for a much larger school. "I don't know most of the kids in my classes, and my teachers don't know me," Sabrina complained to her mother at the end of the first week. "Besides, there's too much homework. I get assignments in all my classes at once. I can't do all this!" she shouted, bursting into tears.

■ **IMPACT OF SCHOOL TRANSITIONS.** As Sabrina's reactions suggest, school transitions can create adjustment problems. With each school change—from elementary to middle or junior high and then to high school—adolescents' grades decline. The drop is partly due to tighter academic standards. At the same time, the transition to secondary school often means less personal attention, more whole-class instruction, and less chance to participate in classroom decision making (Seidman, Aber, & French, 2004).

It is not surprising, then, that students rate their middle or junior high school learning experiences less favorably than their elementary school experiences, stating that their teachers care less about them, grade less fairly, and stress competition more (Wigfield & Eccles, 1994). Consequently, many young people feel less academically competent and decline in motivation (Barber & Olsen, 2004; Gutman & Midgley, 2000; Otis, Grouzet, & Pelletier, 2005).

Inevitably, students must readjust their feelings of self-confidence and self-worth as they encounter revised academic expectations and a more complex social world. But adolescents who face added strains—family disruption, poverty, low parental involvement, or learned helplessness on academic tasks—are at greatest risk for self-esteem and academic difficulties (de Bruyn, 2005; Rudolph et al., 2001; Seidman et al., 2003).

Distressed young people whose school performance either remains low or drops sharply after school transition often show a persisting pattern of poor self-esteem, motivation, and achievement. In one study, researchers compared "multiple-problem" youths (those having both academic and mental health problems), youths having difficulties in just one area (either academic or mental health), and well-adjusted youths (those doing well in both areas) across the transition to high school. Although all groups declined in grade point average, well-adjusted students continued to get high marks and multiple-problem youths low marks, with the others falling in between. And as Figure 11.7 shows, the multiple-problem youths showed a far greater rise in truancy and out-of-school problem behaviors (Roeser, Eccles, & Freedman-Doan, 1999). For some, school transition initiates a downward spiral in academic performance and school involvement that leads to dropping out.

■ **HELPING ADOLESCENTS ADJUST TO SCHOOL TRANSITIONS.** As these findings reveal, school transitions often lead to environmental changes that fit poorly with adolescents' developmental needs (Eccles, 2004). They disrupt close relationships with teachers at a time when adolescents need adult support. They emphasize competition during a period of heightened self-focusing. They reduce decision making and choice as the desire for autonomy is increasing. And they interfere with peer networks as young people become more concerned with peer acceptance.

Support from parents, teachers, and peers can ease these strains. Parental involvement, monitoring, gradual autonomy granting, and emphasis on mastery rather than merely good grades are associated with better adjustment (Grolnick et al., 2000; Gutman, 2006). Adolescents with close friends are more likely to sustain these friendships across the transition, which increases social integration and academic motivation in the new school (Aikens, Bierman, & Parker, 2005). Forming smaller units within larger schools promotes closer relationships with both teachers and peers and greater extracurricular involvement (Seidman, Aber, & French, 2004).

Other, less extensive changes are also effective. In the first year after a school transition, homerooms can be provided in which teachers offer academic and personal counseling. Assigning students to classes with several familiar peers or a constant group of new peers strengthens emotional security and social support. In schools that took these steps, students were less likely to decline in academic performance or display other adjustment problems (Felner et al., 2002).

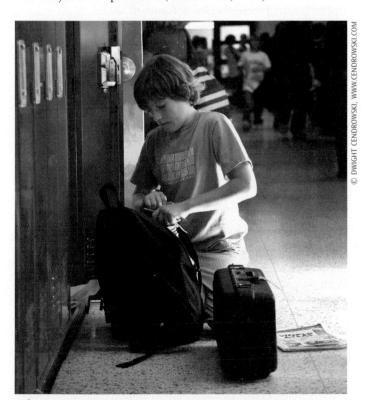

This seventh grader hurries at his locker so he won't be late for class at his new middle school. Moving from a small, self-contained elementary school classroom to a large, impersonal secondary school is stressful for adolescents.

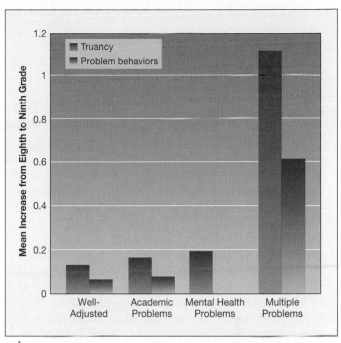

■ **FIGURE 11.7** ■ **Increase in truancy and out-of-school problem behaviors across the transition to high school in four groups of students.** Well-adjusted students, students with only academic problems, and students with only mental health problems showed little change. (Good students with mental health problems actually declined in problem behaviors, so no purple bar is shown for them.) In contrast, multiple-problem students—with both academic and mental health difficulties—increased sharply in truancy and problem behaviors after changing schools from eighth to ninth grade. (Adapted from Roeser, Eccles, & Freedman-Doan, 1999.)

Finally, teenagers' perceptions of the sensitivity and flexibility of their school learning environments are influential. When schools minimize competition and differential treatment based on ability, middle school students are less likely to feel angry and depressed, to be truant, or to show declines in academic values, self-esteem, and achievement (Roeser, Eccles, & Sameroff, 2000).

Academic Achievement

Adolescent achievement is the result of a long history of cumulative effects. Early on, positive educational environments, both family and school, lead to personal traits that support achievement—intelligence, confidence in one's own abilities, the desire to succeed, and high educational aspirations. Nevertheless, improving an unfavorable environment can foster resilience among poorly performing young people. Let's look at environmental factors that enhance achievement during the teenage years.

■ **CHILD-REARING PRACTICES.** As in childhood, authoritative parenting is linked to higher grades among adolescents varying widely in SES, just as it predicts mastery-oriented behavior in childhood. In contrast, authoritarian and permissive styles are associated with lower grades (Collins & Steinberg, 2006; Vazsonyi, Hibbert, & Snider, 2003). Uninvolved parenting (low in both warmth and maturity demands) predicts the poorest grades and worsening school performance over time (Glasgow et al., 1997; Kaisa, Stattin, & Nurmi, 2000).

Adolescents whose parents engage in joint decision making, gradually permitting more autonomy with age, achieve especially well (Spera, 2005; Wang, Pomerantz, & Chen, 2007). Warmth, open discussion, firmness, and monitoring of the adolescents' whereabouts and activities make young people feel cared about and valued, encourage reflective thinking and self-regulation, and increase awareness of the importance of doing well in school. These factors, in turn, are related to mastery-oriented attributions, effort, achievement, and high educational aspirations (Aunola, Stattin, & Nurmi, 2000; Gregory & Weinstein, 2004; Trusty, 1999).

■ **PARENT–SCHOOL PARTNERSHIPS.** High-achieving students typically have parents who keep tabs on their child's progress, communicate with teachers, and make sure that their child is enrolled in challenging, well-taught classes (Hill & Taylor, 2004). In a nationally representative sample of U.S. adolescents, parents' school involvement in eighth grade strongly predicted students' grade point average in tenth grade, beyond the influence of SES and previous academic achievement (Keith et al., 1998). Parents who are in frequent contact with the school send their teenager a message about the value of education, model constructive solutions to academic problems, and promote wise educational decisions.

The daily stresses of living in low-income, high-risk neighborhoods reduce parents' energy for school involvement (Bowen, Bowen, & Ware, 2002). Yet stronger home–school links could relieve some of this stress. Schools can build parent–school partnerships by strengthening personal relationships between teachers and parents, tapping parents' talents to improve the quality of school programs, and including parents in school governance so they remain invested in school goals.

■ **PEER INFLUENCES.** Peers play an important role in adolescent achievement, in a way that relates to both family and school. Teenagers whose parents value achievement generally choose friends who share those values (Rubin, Bukowski, & Parker, 2006). For example, when Sabrina began to make new friends in junior high, she often studied with her girlfriends. Each girl wanted to do well and reinforced this desire in the others.

Peer support for high achievement also depends on the overall climate of the peer culture, which, for ethnic minority youths, is powerfully affected by the surrounding social order. In one study, integration into the school peer network predicted higher grades among Caucasians and Hispanics but not among Asians and African Americans (Faircloth & Hamm, 2005). Asian cultural values stress respect for family and teacher expectations over close peer ties (Chao & Tseng, 2002; Chen, 2005). African-American minority adolescents may observe that their ethnic group is worse off than the white majority in educational attainment, jobs, income, and housing. And discriminatory treatment by teachers and peers, often resulting from stereotypes that they are "not intelligent," triggers anger, anxiety, self-doubt, declines in achievement, association with peers who are not interested in school, and increases in problem behaviors (Wong, Eccles, & Sameroff, 2003).

Yet not all economically disadvantaged minority students respond this way. Case studies of inner-city, poverty-stricken African-American adolescents who were high-achieving and optimistic about their future revealed that they were intensely aware of oppression but believed in striving to alter their social position (O'Connor, 1997). How did they develop this sense of agency? Parents, relatives, and teachers had convinced them through discussion and example that injustice should not be tolerated and that, together, African Americans could overcome it—a perspective that encouraged both strong ethnic identity and high academic motivation, even in the face of peer pressures against excelling academically.

■ **CLASSROOM LEARNING EXPERIENCES.** Adolescents need school environments that are responsive to their expanding powers of reasoning and their emotional and social needs. Without appropriate learning experiences, their cognitive potential is unlikely to be realized.

As noted earlier, in large, departmentalized secondary schools, many adolescents report that their classes lack warmth and supportiveness—a circumstance that dampens their motivation. Reduced teacher–student closeness is partly due to students' movement from class to class throughout the school day. But a benefit of separate classes is that adolescents can be taught by subject-matter experts, who are more likely to encourage high-level thinking and emphasize content relevant to students' experiences—factors that promote interest, effort, and

This parent is involved in his adolescent son's schooling. By keeping tabs on his progress, the father sends a message to his child about the importance of education and teaches skills for solving academic problems.

achievement (Eccles, 2004). Secondary school classrooms, however, do not consistently provide challenging, interesting teaching.

Because of the uneven quality of instruction, many seniors graduate from high school deficient in basic academic skills. Although the achievement gap separating African-American, Hispanic, and Native-American students from white students has declined since the 1970s, mastery of reading, writing, mathematics, and science by low-SES ethnic minority students remains disappointing (U.S. Department of Education, 2007b, 2007c, 2007d). Too often these young people attend underfunded schools with rundown buildings, outdated equipment, and textbook shortages. In some, crime and discipline problems receive more attention than teaching and learning.

By middle school, many low-SES minority students have been placed in low academic tracks, compounding their learning difficulties. Longitudinal research following thousands of U.S. students from eighth to twelfth grade reveals that assignment to a college preparatory track accelerates academic progress, whereas assignment to a vocational or general education track decelerates it (Hallinan & Kubitschek, 1999). Even in secondary schools with no formal tracking program, low-SES minority students tend to be assigned to lower course levels in most or all academic subjects, resulting in *de facto* (unofficial) *tracking* (Lucas & Behrends, 2002).

Breaking out of a low academic track is difficult. Track or course enrollment is generally based on past performance, which is limited by placement history. Interviews with African-American students in one high school revealed that many thought their previous performance did not reflect their ability (Ogbu, 2003). Yet teachers and counselors, overburdened with other responsibilities, had little time to reconsider individual cases.

High school students are separated into academic and vocational tracks in virtually all industrialized nations. In China, Japan, and most Western European countries, students' placement in high school is determined by their performance on a national exam. The outcome usually fixes the young person's future possibilities. In the United States, students who are not assigned to a college preparatory track or who do poorly in high school can still attend college. Ultimately, however, many young people do not benefit from the more open U.S. system. By adolescence, SES differences in quality of education and academic achievement are greater in the United States than in most other industrialized countries (Marks, Cresswell, & Ainley, 2006). And the United States has a higher percentage of young people who see themselves as educational failures and drop out of high school (see Figure 11.8).

Dropping Out

Across the aisle from Louis in math class sat Norman, who daydreamed, crumpled his notes into his pocket after class, and rarely did his homework. On test days, he twirled a rabbit's foot for good luck but left most questions blank. To Louis, who was quick at schoolwork, Norman seemed to live in another world.

Once or twice a week, Norman cut class; one spring day, he stopped coming altogether.

Norman is one of about 10 percent of U.S. 16- to 24-year-olds who dropped out of high school and remain without a diploma or a GED (U.S. Department of Education, 2009). The dropout rate is higher among boys than girls and is particularly high among low-SES ethnic minority youths, especially Native-American and Hispanic teenagers. The decision to leave school has dire consequences. Youths without upper secondary education have much lower literacy scores than high school graduates; they lack the skills employers value in today's knowledge-based economy. Consequently, dropouts have much lower employment rates than high school graduates. Even when employed, dropouts are far more likely to remain in menial, low-paying jobs.

■ **FACTORS RELATED TO DROPPING OUT.** Although many dropouts achieve poorly and show high rates of norm-violating acts, a substantial number are like Norman—young people with few behavior problems who experience academic difficulties and quietly disengage from school (Janosz et al., 2000; Newcomb et al., 2002). The pathway to dropping out starts early. Risk factors in first grade predict dropout nearly as well as risk factors in secondary school (Entwisle, Alexander, & Olson, 2005).

Norman had a long history of marginal-to-failing school grades and low academic self-esteem. Faced with a challenging task, he gave up, relying on luck—his rabbit's foot—to get by. As Norman got older, he attended class less regularly, paid little attention when he was there, and rarely did his homework. He

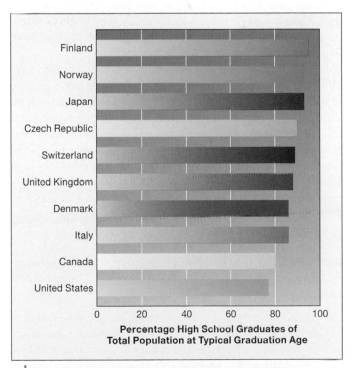

■ **FIGURE 11.8** ■ **High school graduation rates in ten industrialized nations.** The United States ranks below many other developed countries. (From OECD, 2008a.)

A baking and pastry student puts the finishing touches on a cake at a technical high school in Pennsylvania. High-quality vocational education, integrated with academic instruction, helps students at risk for dropping out see the relevance of school learning to their future goals.

didn't join school clubs or participate in sports. As a result, few teachers or students got to know him well. By the day he left, Norman felt alienated from all aspects of school life.

As with other dropouts, Norman's family background contributed to his problems. Compared with other students, even those with the same grade profile, dropouts are more likely to have parents who are uninvolved in their teenager's education and engage in little monitoring of their youngster's daily activities. Many are single parents, never finished high school themselves, and are unemployed (Englund, Egeland, & Collins, 2008; Pagani et al., 2008).

Academically marginal students who drop out often have school experiences that undermine their chances for success: grade retention, which marks them as academic failures; large, impersonal secondary schools; and classes with unsupportive teachers and few opportunities for active participation (Hardre & Reeve, 2003; Lee & Burkam, 2003). Recent reports indicate that over 60 percent of adolescents in some U.S. inner-city high schools do not graduate. Students in general education and vocational tracks, where teaching tends to be the least stimulating, are three times as likely to drop out as those in a college preparatory track (U.S. Department of Education, 2009).

■ **PREVENTION STRATEGIES.** Among the diverse strategies available for helping teenagers at risk of dropping out, several common themes are related to success:

■ *Remedial instruction and counseling that offer personalized attention.* To overcome the negative psychological effects of repeated school failure, academic assistance must be combined with social support (Christenson & Thurlow, 2004). In one successful approach, at-risk students are matched with retired adults, who serve as tutors, mentors, and role models in addressing academic and vocational needs (Prevatt, 2003).

■ *High-quality vocational training.* For many marginal students, the real-life nature of vocational education is more comfortable and effective than purely academic work. To work well, vocational education must carefully integrate academic and job-related instruction so students see the relevance of classroom experiences to their future goals (Harvey, 2001).

■ *Efforts to address the many factors in students' lives related to leaving school early.* Programs that strengthen parent involvement, offer flexible work–study arrangements, and provide on-site child care for teenage parents can make staying in school easier for at-risk adolescents.

■ *Participation in extracurricular activities.* Another way of helping marginal students is to draw them into the community life of the school. In small high schools (500 to 700 students or less), potential dropouts are far more likely to be needed to help staff and operate school activities. Creation of smaller "schools within schools" has the same effect (Feldman & Matjasko, 2007). Participation focusing on the arts, community service, and vocational development promotes improved academic performance, reduced antisocial behavior, more favorable self-esteem and initiative, and increased peer acceptance (Fredricks & Eccles, 2005, 2006; Mahoney, 2000).

As we conclude our discussion of academic achievement, let's place the school dropout problem in historical perspective. Over the past half-century, the percentage of U.S. young people completing high school by age 24 increased steadily, from less than 50 percent to 90 percent. College attendance also rose during this period: Today, nearly 40 percent of U.S. young people earn college degrees—among the highest rates in the world (U.S. Department of Education, 2007a).

Finally, although many dropouts get caught in a vicious cycle in which their lack of self-confidence and skills prevents them from seeking further education and training, about one-third return to finish their secondary education within a few years (U.S. Department of Education, 2008). And some extend their schooling further, realizing how essential education is for a rewarding job and a satisfying adult life.

ASK YOURSELF

≫ REVIEW
List ways that parents can promote their adolescent's academic achievement. Explain why each is effective.

≫ APPLY
Tanisha is finishing sixth grade. She can either continue in her current school through eighth grade or switch to a much larger seventh- to ninth-grade middle school. Which choice would you suggest, and why?

≫ REFLECT
Describe your own experiences in making the transition to middle or junior high school and then to high school. What did you find stressful? What helped you adjust?

Summary

PHYSICAL DEVELOPMENT

Conceptions of Adolescence

How have conceptions of adolescence changed over the past century?

» **Adolescence,** initiated by **puberty,** is the period of transition between childhood and adulthood. Early theories explained the impact of puberty on psychological development in terms of either biological or social forces. Contemporary research shows that adolescence is a product of biological, psychological, and social forces.

Puberty: The Physical Transition to Adulthood

Describe pubertal changes in body size, proportions, sleep patterns, motor performance, and sexual maturity.

» Hormonal changes beginning in middle childhood initiate puberty, on average, two years earlier for girls than for boys. The first outward sign is the **growth spurt.** As the body enlarges, girls' hips and boys' shoulders broaden. Girls add more fat, boys more muscle.

» Puberty brings improvement in gross motor performance—slow and gradual for girls, more dramatic for boys. Preoccupation with physical prowess leads some boys to use dangerous performance-enhancing drugs.

» Besides motor performance, sports and exercise foster cognitive and social development. Yet a substantial minority of teenagers are not enrolled in regular physical education.

» At puberty, changes in **primary** and **secondary sexual characteristics** accompany rapid body growth. **Menarche** occurs late in the girl's sequence of pubertal events, after the growth spurt peaks. In boys, the peak in growth occurs later, preceded by enlargement of the sex organs and **spermarche.**

What factors influence the timing of puberty?

» Heredity, nutrition, exercise, and overall physical health contribute to pubertal timing. A **secular trend** toward earlier menarche has occurred in industrialized nations as physical well-being increased.

What changes in the brain take place during adolescence?

» Pruning of unused synapses in the cerebral cortex continues in adolescence, and growth and myelination of stimulated neural fibers accelerate, supporting cognitive advances. Increased responsiveness of neurons to excitatory neurotransmitters may play a role in teenagers' drive for novel experiences.

» Changes also occur in brain regulation of sleep. Consequently, adolescents go to bed much later than they did as children, and sleep deprivation increases.

The Psychological Impact of Pubertal Events

Explain adolescents' reactions to the physical changes of puberty.

» Girls generally react to menarche with mixed emotions. Their feelings lean in a positive direction when they receive advance information and support from family members. Boys also react to spermarche with mixed feelings but receive less social support than girls.

» Besides higher hormone levels, negative life events and adult-structured situations are associated with adolescents' negative moods. In contrast, teenagers feel upbeat when with peers and in self-chosen leisure activities.

» Puberty is accompanied by psychological distancing between parent and child. The reaction may be a modern substitute for physical departure from the family, which typically occurs at sexual maturity in primate species and in nonindustrialized cultures.

Describe the impact of pubertal timing on adolescent adjustment, noting sex differences.

» Early-maturing boys and late-maturing girls, whose appearance closely matches cultural standards of physical attractiveness, have a more positive **body image** and usually adjust well. In contrast, early-maturing girls and late-maturing boys, who fit in least well with peers, experience emotional and social difficulties, which—for girls—persist into early adulthood.

Health Issues

Describe nutritional needs during adolescence, and cite factors that contribute to eating disorders.

» Nutritional requirements increase with rapid body growth. Poor eating habits lead many adolescents to have deficient diets. Frequency of family meals is associated with healthy eating.

» Early puberty, maladaptive family interactions, and societal emphasis on thinness heighten risk of eating disorders. **Anorexia nervosa** tends to appear in girls with perfectionist, inhibited personalities; overprotective, controlling mothers; and emotionally distant fathers. **Bulimia nervosa** is associated with disengaged parenting. Some bulimics are perfectionists; others lack self-control in many areas of their lives.

Discuss factors that influence adolescent sexual attitudes and behavior.

» North American attitudes toward adolescent sex remain relatively restrictive, and the social environment—parents, schools, and mass media—delivers contradictory messages.

» Early, frequent sexual activity is linked to factors associated with economic disadvantage. Many sexually active teenagers do not practice contraception consistently. Adolescent cognitive processes and a lack of social support for responsible sexual behavior, including access to birth control, underlie this failure to take precautions against pregnancy.

Describe factors involved in the development of homosexuality.

» About 2 to 3 percent of young people identify as lesbian, gay, or bisexual. Biological factors, including heredity and prenatal hormone levels, play an important role in homosexuality. Lesbian and gay teenagers face special challenges in developing a positive sexual identity.

Discuss factors related to sexually transmitted diseases and to teenage pregnancy and parenthood.

» Early sexual activity combined with inconsistent contraceptive use results in high rates of sexually transmitted diseases (STDs) among U.S. adolescents. Aside from AIDS, most teenagers have limited knowledge about STDs.

» Adolescent pregnancy and parenthood rates are higher in the United States than in most other industrialized nations. Adolescent parenthood is associated with school dropout, reduced chances of marriage, greater likelihood of divorce, and poverty, jeopardizing the well-being of both parent and child.

» Effective sex education, access to contraceptives, and programs that build academic and social competence help prevent early pregnancy. Adolescent mothers need school programs that provide job training, instruction in life-management skills, and child care. They also benefit from family support. When teenage fathers stay involved, children develop more favorably.

What personal and social factors are related to adolescent substance use and abuse?

» Teenage alcohol and drug use is pervasive in industrialized nations, reflecting the sensation seeking of adolescence as well as a drug-dependent cultural context. The minority who move from use to abuse have serious psychological, family, and school problems. Effective prevention programs work with parents early, to reduce family adversity, strengthen parenting skills, and build teenagers' competence.

COGNITIVE DEVELOPMENT

Piaget's Theory: The Formal Operational Stage

What are the major characteristics of formal operational thought?

» During Piaget's **formal operational stage,** adolescents engage in **hypothetico-deductive reasoning.** When faced with a problem, they start with a hypothesis about variables that might affect an outcome; deduce logical, testable inferences; and systematically isolate and combine variables to see which inferences are confirmed.

» **Propositional thought** also develops. Adolescents can evaluate the logic of verbal statements apart from real-world circumstances.

© CRAIG WITKOWSKI/ INDEX STOCK/PHOTOLIBRARY

Discuss recent research on formal operational thought and its implications for the accuracy of Piaget's formal operational stage.

» Adolescents and adults are most likely to think abstractly and systematically in situations in which they have had extensive guidance and practice in using such reasoning. Individuals in tribal and village societies rarely master formal operational tasks. Piaget's highest stage seems to depend on specific learning opportunities made available in school.

An Information-Processing View of Adolescent Cognitive Development

How do information-processing researchers account for cognitive changes in adolescence?

» Information-processing researchers believe that a variety of specific mechanisms underlie cognitive gains in adolescence: improved attention and inhibition, more effective strategies, greater knowledge, improved cognitive self-regulation, gains in speed of thinking and processing capacity, and, especially, advances in metacognition.

» Research on scientific reasoning indicates that the ability to coordinate theory with evidence improves over adolescence and into adulthood. Gradually, young people solve increasingly complex problems and reflect on their thinking, acquiring more mature metacognitive understanding.

Consequences of Adolescent Cognitive Changes

Describe typical reactions of adolescents that result from their advancing cognition.

» As adolescents reflect on their own thoughts, they think more about themselves, and two distorted images of the relation between self and other appear—the **imaginary audience** and the **personal fable.** Teenagers' capacity to think about possibilities prompts idealistic visions at odds with everyday reality, and they often become fault-finding critics. Compared with adults, adolescents have difficulty with decision making, more often falling back on well-learned, intuitive judgments.

Learning in School

Discuss the impact of school transitions on adolescent adjustment.

» School transitions in adolescence can be stressful. Teenagers who must cope with added stresses—especially those with both academic and mental health difficulties—are at greatest risk for adjustment problems.

Discuss family, peer, school, and employment influences on academic achievement during adolescence.

» Authoritative parenting and parents' school involvement promote high achievement. Teenagers whose parents encourage achievement are likely to choose friends from similar families.

» Warm, supportive learning environments with activities that emphasize high-level thinking enable adolescents to reach their academic potential. Poor-quality school environments and assignment to non-college-preparatory tracks often dampen low-SES students' academic progress.

What factors increase the risk of high school dropout?

» About 10 percent of U.S. young people leave high school and remain without a diploma, many of whom are low-SES minority youths. Contributing factors include a long history of poor school performance, lack of parental support for academic achievement, large impersonal classes, and unstimulating teaching.

Important Terms and Concepts

adolescence (p. 283)
anorexia nervosa (p. 292)
body image (p. 290)
bulimia nervosa (p. 292)
formal operational stage (p. 301)
growth spurt (p. 284)

hypothetico-deductive reasoning (p. 301)
imaginary audience (p. 304)
menarche (p. 286)
personal fable (p. 305)
primary sexual characteristics (p. 286)

propositional thought (p. 302)
puberty (p. 283)
secondary sexual characteristics (p. 286)
secular trend (p. 287)
spermarche (p. 286)

Emotional and Social Development in Adolescence

© ROLF BRUDERER/CORBIS

As adolescents spend less time with family, peer groups become more tightly knit into cliques. Mixed-sex cliques provide boys and girls with models of how to interact and a chance to do so without having to be intimate.

ouis sat on the grassy hillside overlooking the high school, waiting for his best friend, Darryl, to arrive from his fourth-period class. Watching as hundreds of students poured onto the school grounds, Louis reflected on what he had learned in government class that day. "Suppose I *had* been born in the People's Republic of China. I'd be sitting here, speaking a different language, being called by a different name, and thinking about the world in different ways. Wow," Louis pondered. "I am who I am through some quirk of fate."

Louis awoke from his thoughts with a start to see Darryl standing in front of him. "Hey, dreamer! I've been shouting and waving from the bottom of the hill for five minutes. How come you're so spaced out lately, Louis?"

"Oh, just wondering about stuff—what I want, what I believe in. You ever feel that way?"

"Yeah, a lot," Darryl admitted, looking at Louis seriously. "I wonder, who will I become?"

Louis and Darryl's introspective remarks are signs of a major reorganization of the self at adolescence: the development of identity. Both young people are attempting to formulate their personal values and the directions they will pursue in life.

We begin this chapter with Erikson's account of identity development and the research it has stimulated on teenagers' thoughts and feelings about themselves. The quest for identity extends to many aspects of development. We will see how a sense of cultural belonging, moral understanding, and masculine and feminine self-images are refined during adolescence. And as parent–child relationships are revised and young people become increasingly independent of the family, friendships and peer networks become crucial contexts for bridging the gap between childhood and adulthood. Our chapter concludes with a discussion of several serious adjustment problems: depression, suicide, and delinquency.

Erikson's Theory: Identity versus Role Confusion

Erikson (1950, 1968) was the first to recognize **identity** as the major personality achievement of adolescence and as a crucial step toward becoming a productive, content adult. Constructing an identity involves defining who you are, what you value, and the directions you choose to pursue in life.

One expert described it as an explicit theory of oneself as a rational agent—one who acts on the basis of reason, takes responsibility for those actions, and can explain them (Moshman, 2005). This search for what is true and real about the self drives many choices—vocation, interpersonal relationships, community involvement, ethnic-group membership, and expression of one's sexual orientation, as well as moral, political, and religious ideals.

Although the seeds of identity formation are planted early, not until late adolescence and early adulthood do young people become absorbed in this task. According to Erikson, in complex societies, teenagers experience an *identity crisis*—a temporary period of distress as they experiment with alternatives before settling on values and goals. They go through a process of inner soul-searching, sifting through characteristics that defined the self in childhood and combining them with emerging traits, capacities, and commitments. Then they mold these into a solid inner core that provides a mature identity—a sense of self-continuity as they move through various roles in daily life. Once formed, identity continues to be refined in adulthood as people reevaluate earlier commitments and choices.

Erikson called the psychological conflict of adolescence **identity versus role confusion.** If young people's earlier conflicts were resolved negatively or if society limits their choices to ones that do not match their abilities and desires, they may appear shallow, directionless, and unprepared for the challenges of adulthood.

Current theorists agree with Erikson that questioning of values, plans, and priorities is necessary for a mature identity, but they no longer describe this process as a "crisis" (Grotevant, 1998; Kroger, 2005). For most young people, identity development is not traumatic and disturbing but, rather, a process of *exploration* followed by *commitment*. As young people try out life possibilities, they gather important information about themselves and their environment and move toward making enduring decisions. In doing so, they forge an organized self-structure (Arnett, 2000, 2006; Moshman, 2005). In the following sections, we will see that adolescents go about the task of defining the self in ways that closely match Erikson's description.

Self-Understanding

During adolescence, the young person's vision of the self becomes more complex, well-organized, and consistent, setting the stage for a unified personal identity (Harter, 2003, 2006). Compared with younger children, adolescents have more or less positive feelings about an increasing variety of aspects of the self. Over time, they form a balanced, integrated representation of their strengths and limitations.

Changes in Self-Concept

In describing themselves, adolescents unify separate personality traits ("smart," "talented") into more abstract descriptors ("intelligent"). But at first, their generalizations are not interconnected and are often contradictory. For example, 12- to 14-year-olds might mention opposing traits—"intelligent" and "airhead," "shy" and "outgoing." These disparities result from adolescents' expanding social world, which creates pressure to display different selves in different relationships—with parents, classmates, close friends, and romantic partners. As they become increasingly aware of these inconsistencies, teenagers agonize over "which is the real me" (Harter, 2003, 2006).

Gradually, cognitive changes enable teenagers to combine their traits into an organized system. Their use of qualifiers ("I have a *fairly* quick temper," "I'm not *thoroughly* honest") reveals their awareness that psychological qualities can change from one situation to the next. Older adolescents also add integrating principles that make sense out of formerly troublesome contradictions. "I'm very adaptable," said one young person. "When I'm around my friends, who think that what I say is important, I'm talkative; but around my family I'm quiet because they're never interested enough to really listen to me" (Damon, 1990, p. 88).

Compared with school-age children, teenagers place more emphasis on social virtues, such as being friendly, considerate, kind, and cooperative (Damon & Hart, 1988). Among older adolescents, personal and moral values also appear as key themes, as young people revise their views of themselves to include enduring beliefs and plans.

Changes in Self-Esteem

Self-esteem, the evaluative side of self-concept, continues to differentiate. Teenagers add several new dimensions of self-evaluation—close friendship, romantic appeal, and job competence—to those of middle childhood (see Chapter 10, page 259) (Harter, 2003, 2006).

Level of self-esteem also changes. Though some adolescents experience temporary or persisting declines after school transitions (see Chapter 11, page 306), self-esteem rises for most young people (Cole et al., 2001; Twenge & Campbell, 2001). Teenagers often assert that they have become more mature, capable, personable, and attractive. In a study of adolescents in 13 industrialized nations, most were optimistic and expressed confidence in their ability to cope with life's challenges (Grob & Flammer, 1999).

At the same time, individual differences in self-esteem become increasingly stable in adolescence (Trzesniewski, Donnellan, & Robins, 2003). And positive relationships among self-esteem, valuing of various activities, and success at those activities strengthen. For example, academic self-esteem is a powerful predictor of teenagers' judgments of the importance and usefulness of school subjects, willingness to exert effort, achievement, and eventual career choice (Bleeker & Jacobs, 2004; Denissen, Zarrett, & Eccles, 2007; Whitesell et al., 2009).

In adolescence as in childhood, authoritative parenting predicts high self-esteem, as does encouragement from teachers (Carlson, Uppal, & Prosser, 2000; McKinney, Donnelly, & Renk, 2008; Wilkinson, 2004). In contrast, feedback that is negative, inconsistent, or not contingent on performance triggers, at

During adolescence, self-esteem rises for most young people, who feel especially good about their peer relationships and athletic capabilities.

best, uncertainty about the self's capacities and, at worst, a sense of being incompetent and unloved (Kernis, 2002). Teenagers who experience such parenting tend to rely only on peers, not on adults, to affirm their self-esteem—a risk factor for adjustment difficulties (DuBois et al., 1999, 2002).

Paths to Identity

Adolescents' well-organized self-descriptions and differentiated sense of self-esteem provide the cognitive foundation for forming an identity. Through interviews or questionnaires, researchers commonly evaluate progress in identity development on two key criteria derived from Erikson's theory: *exploration* and *commitment* (Marcia, 1980). Their various combinations yield four *identity statuses*, summarized in Table 12.1 on page 316: **identity achievement,** commitment to values, beliefs, and goals following a period of exploration; **identity moratorium,** exploration without having reached commitment; **identity foreclosure,** commitment in the absence of exploration; and **identity diffusion,** an apathetic state characterized by lack of both exploration and commitment.

Identity development follows many paths. Some young people remain in one status, whereas others experience many status transitions. And the pattern often varies across *identity domains,* such as sexual orientation, vocation, and religious and political values. Most young people change from "lower" statuses (foreclosure or diffusion) to higher ones (moratorium or achievement) between their mid-teens and mid-twenties, but some move in the reverse direction (Kroger, 2001, 2005; Meeus, 1996).

■ **TABLE 12.1** ■ *The Four Identity Statuses*

IDENTITY STATUS	DESCRIPTION	EXAMPLE
Identity achievement	Having already explored alternatives, identity-achieved individuals are committed to a clearly formulated set of self-chosen values and goals. They feel a sense of psychological well-being, of sameness through time, and of knowing where they are going.	When asked how willing she would be to give up going into her chosen occupation if something better came along, Lauren responded, "Well, I might, but I doubt it. I've thought long and hard about law as a career. I'm pretty certain it's for me."
Identity moratorium	*Moratorium* means "delay or holding pattern." These individuals have not yet made definite commitments. They are in the process of exploring—gathering information and trying out activities, with the desire to find values and goals to guide their lives.	When asked whether he had ever had doubts about his religious beliefs, Ramón said, "Yes, I guess I'm going through that right now. I just don't see how there can be a God and yet so much evil in the world."
Identity foreclosure	Identity-foreclosed individuals have committed themselves to values and goals without exploring alternatives. They accept a ready-made identity chosen for them by authority figures—usually parents but sometimes teachers, religious leaders, or romantic partners.	When asked if she had ever reconsidered her political beliefs, Hillary answered, "No, not really, our family is pretty much in agreement on these things."
Identity diffusion	Identity-diffused individuals lack clear direction. They are neither committed to values and goals nor actively trying to reach them. They may never have explored alternatives or may have found the task too threatening and overwhelming.	When asked about his attitude toward nontraditional gender roles, Joel responded, "Oh, I don't know. It doesn't make much difference to me. I can take it or leave it."

Because attending college provides opportunities to explore career options and lifestyles, college students make more identity progress than they did in high school (Montgomery & Côté, 2003). After college, they often sample a broad range of life experiences before choosing a life course. Those who go to work immediately after high school graduation settle on a self-definition earlier. But if they encounter obstacles to realizing their occupational goals because of lack of training or vocational choices, they are at risk for identity foreclosure or diffusion (Cohen et al., 2003; Eccles et al., 2003).

Identity Status and Psychological Well-Being

A wealth of research verifies that both identity achievement and moratorium are psychologically healthy routes to a mature self-definition. Long-term foreclosure and diffusion, in contrast, are maladaptive.

Adolescents in moratorium resemble identity-achieved individuals in using an active, *information-gathering cognitive style* when making personal decisions and solving problems: They seek out relevant information, evaluate it carefully, and critically reflect on and revise their views (Berzonsky, 2003; Berzonsky & Kuk, 2000). Young people who are identity-achieved or exploring have higher self-esteem, feel more in control of their own lives, are more likely to view school and work as feasible avenues for realizing their aspirations, and are more advanced in moral reasoning (Adams & Marshall, 1996; Kroger, 2007; Serafini & Adams, 2002).

Adolescents stuck in either foreclosure or diffusion are passive in the face of identity concerns and have adjustment

difficulties. Foreclosed individuals display a *dogmatic, inflexible cognitive style*, internalizing the values and beliefs of parents and others without deliberate evaluation and resisting information that threatens their position (Berzonsky & Kuk, 2000). Most fear rejection by people on whom they depend for affection and self-esteem.

Long-term diffused individuals are the least mature in identity development. They typically use a *diffuse-avoidant cognitive style* in which they avoid dealing with personal decisions and problems and, instead, allow current situational pressures to dictate their reactions (Berzonsky & Kuk, 2000; Krettenauer, 2005). Taking an "I don't care" attitude, they entrust themselves to luck or fate and tend to go along with the crowd. As a result, they experience time management and academic difficulties and, of all young people, are most likely to use and abuse drugs (Archer & Waterman, 1990; Schwartz et al., 2005). Often at the heart of their apathy is a sense of hopelessness about the future.

Factors Affecting Identity Development

Adolescent identity formation begins a lifelong dynamic process in which a change in either the individual or the context opens up the possibility of reformulating identity (Kunnen & Bosma, 2003). A wide variety of factors influence identity development.

Identity status, as we have just seen, is both cause and consequence of personality characteristics. Adolescents who assume that absolute truth is always attainable tend to be foreclosed, while those who doubt that they will ever feel certain about anything are more often identity-diffused. Young people who

■ CULTURAL INFLUENCES ■

Identity Development Among Ethnic Minority Adolescents

Most adolescents are aware of their cultural ancestry but relatively unconcerned about it. However, for teenagers who are members of minority groups, **ethnic identity**—a sense of ethnic-group membership and attitudes and feelings associated with that membership—is central to the quest for identity. As they develop cognitively and become more sensitive to feedback from the social environment, minority youths become painfully aware that they are targets of discrimination and inequality. This discovery complicates their efforts to develop a sense of cultural belonging and a set of personally meaningful goals.

In many immigrant families from collectivist cultures, adolescents' commitment to obeying their parents and fulfilling family obligations lessens the longer the family has been in the immigrant-receiving country—a circumstance that induces **acculturative stress,** psychological distress resulting from conflict between the minority and the host culture (Phinney, Ong, & Madden, 2000). When immigrant parents tightly restrict their teenagers through fear that assimilation into the larger society will undermine their

cultural traditions, their youngsters often rebel, rejecting aspects of their ethnic background.

At the same time, discrimination can interfere with the formation of a positive ethnic identity. In one study, Mexican-American youths who had experienced more discrimination were less likely to explore their ethnicity and to report feeling good about it (Romero & Roberts, 2003).

Young people with parents of different ethnicities face extra challenges. In a large survey of high school students, part-black biracial teenagers reported as much discrimination as their monoracial black counterparts, yet they felt less positively about their ethnicity. And compared with monoracial minorities, many biracials—including black–white, black–Asian, white–Asian, black–Hispanic, and white–Hispanic—regarded ethnicity as less central to their identities (Herman, 2004). Perhaps these adolescents encountered fewer opportunities in their homes and communities to forge a strong sense of belonging to either culture.

When family members encourage adolescents to disprove ethnic stereotypes of low achievement or antisocial behavior, young people typically surmount the threat that discrimination poses to a favorable ethnic identity. These teenagers manage unfair

treatment effectively, by seeking social support and engaging in direct problem solving (Phinney & Chavira, 1995; Scott, 2003). Also, adolescents whose families taught them the history, traditions, values, and language of their ethnic group and who frequently interact with same-ethnicity peers are more likely to forge a favorable ethnic identity (Hughes et al., 2006; McHale et al., 2006).

How can society help minority adolescents resolve identity conflicts constructively? Here are some relevant approaches:

- Promote effective parenting, in which children and adolescents benefit from family ethnic pride yet are encouraged to explore the meaning of ethnicity in their own lives.
- Ensure that schools respect minority youths' native languages, unique learning styles, and right to high-quality education.
- Foster contact with peers of the same ethnicity, along with respect between ethnic groups (García Coll & Magnuson, 1997).

A strong, secure ethnic identity is associated with higher self-esteem, optimism, and sense of mastery over the environment (St. Louis & Liem, 2005; Umana-Taylor & Updegraff, 2007; Worrell & Gardner-Kitt, 2006). For these reasons, adolescents with a positive connection to their ethnic group cope more effectively with stress, show higher achievement in school, and have fewer emotional and behavior problems than agemates who identify only weakly with their ethnicity (Greene, Way, & Pahl, 2006; Seaton, Scottham, & Sellers, 2006; Umana-Taylor & Alfaro, 2006).

Forming a **bicultural identity**—by exploring and adopting values from both the adolescent's subculture and the dominant culture—offers additional benefits. Biculturally identified adolescents tend to be achieved in other areas of identity as well and to have especially favorable relations with members of other ethnic groups (Phinney, 2007; Phinney et al., 2001). In sum, achievement of ethnic identity enhances many aspects of emotional and social development.

© DAVID GROSSMAN/THE IMAGE WORKS

These adolescents celebrate their cultural heritage by participating in a Filipino parade in New York City. When minority youths encounter respect for their ethnic heritage in schools and communities, they are more likely to retain ethnic values and customs as an important part of their identity.

Applying What We Know

Supporting Healthy Identity Development

Strategy	Explanation
Engage in warm, open communication.	Provides both emotional support and freedom to explore values and goals
Initiate discussions that promote high-level thinking at home and at school.	Encourages rational and deliberate selection among beliefs and values
Provide opportunities to participate in extracurricular activities and vocational training programs.	Permits young people to explore the real world of adult work
Provide opportunities to talk with adults and peers who have worked through identity questions.	Offers models of identity achievement and advice on how to resolve identity concerns
Provide opportunities to explore ethnic heritage and learn about other cultures in an atmosphere of respect.	Fosters identity achievement in all areas and ethnic tolerance, which supports the identity explorations of others

appreciate that they can use rational criteria to choose among alternatives are likely to be exploring or identity achieved (Berzonsky & Kuk, 2000; Boyes & Chandler, 1992).

Parenting practices are associated with identity statuses. Adolescents who feel attached to their parents but free to voice their own opinions tend to be in a state of moratorium or identity achievement (Berzonsky, 2004; Luyckx, Goossens, & Soenens, 2006). Foreclosed teenagers usually have close bonds with parents but lack opportunities for healthy separation. And diffused young people report the lowest levels of parental support and warm, open communication (Reis & Youniss, 2004; Zimmerman & Becker-Stoll, 2002).

Interaction with diverse peers through school and community activities encourages adolescents to explore values and role possibilities (Barber et al., 2005). In one study, 15-year-olds with warm, trusting peer ties were more involved in exploring relationship issues—for example, thinking about what they valued in close friends and in a life partner (Meeus, Oosterwegel, & Vollebergh, 2002). In another study, young people's attachment to friends predicted progress in choosing a career (Felsman & Blustein, 1999).

Schools and communities can help by offering rich and varied opportunities for exploration. Supportive experiences include classrooms that promote high-level thinking, extracurricular activities that enable teenagers to take on responsible roles, teachers and counselors who encourage low-SES students to go to college, and vocational training that immerses young people in the real world of adult work (Coatsworth et al., 2005; McIntosh, Metz, & Youniss, 2005).

Finally, societal forces also are responsible for the special challenges faced by gay, lesbian, and bisexual youths (see Chapter 11) and by ethnic minority adolescents in forming a secure identity (see the Cultural Influences box on page 318). Applying What We Know above summarizes ways that adults can support adolescents in their quest for identity.

© PIXLAND/JUPITERIMAGES

This adolescent feels attached to her father but also free to voice her own opinions—circumstances that foster healthy identity development.

ASK YOURSELF

>> **REVIEW**
List personal and contextual factors that promote identity development.

>> **APPLY**
Return to the conversation between Louis and Darryl in the opening of this chapter. Which identity status best characterizes each of the two boys, and why?

>> **REFLECT**
Does your identity status vary across the domains of sexuality, close relationships, vocation, religious beliefs, and political values? Describe factors that may have influenced your identity development in an important domain.

Moral Development

Eleven-year-old Sabrina sat at the kitchen table reading the Sunday newspaper. "You gotta see this," she said to 16-year-old Louis, who sat munching cereal. Sabrina held up a page of large photos showing a 70-year-old woman standing in her home. The floor and furniture were piled with stacks of newspapers, cardboard boxes, tin cans, glass containers, food, and clothing. The accompanying article described crumbling plaster on the walls, frozen pipes, and nonfunctioning sinks, toilet, and furnace. The headline read: "Loretta Perry: My Life Is None of Their Business."

"Look what they're trying to do to this poor lady," exclaimed Sabrina. "They wanna throw her out of her house and tear it down! Those city inspectors must not care about anyone. Here it says, 'Mrs. Perry has devoted much of her life to doing favors for people.' Why doesn't someone help *her?*"

"Sabrina, you're missing the point," Louis responded. "Mrs. Perry is violating law—30 building code standards! And she's not just a threat to herself—she's a danger to her neighbors, too. Suppose her house caught on fire. You can't live around other people and say your life is nobody's business."

"You don't just knock someone's home down," Sabrina replied angrily. "Why aren't her friends and neighbors over there fixing up that house? You're just like those building inspectors, Louis. You've got no feelings!"

As Louis and Sabrina's disagreement over Mrs. Perry's plight illustrates, cognitive development and expanding social experiences permit adolescents to better understand larger social structures—societal institutions and law-making systems—that govern moral responsibilities. As their grasp of social arrangements expands, adolescents construct new ideas about what should be done when the needs and desires of people conflict. As a result, they move toward increasingly just, fair, and balanced solutions to moral problems.

Kohlberg's Theory of Moral Development

Early work by Piaget on the moral judgment of the child inspired Lawrence Kohlberg's more comprehensive cognitive-developmental theory of moral understanding. Kohlberg used a clinical interviewing procedure in which he presented a sample of 10- to 16-year-old boys with hypothetical *moral dilemmas*—stories presenting a conflict between two moral values—and asked them what the main actor should do and why. Then he followed the participants longitudinally, reinterviewing them at 3- to 4-year intervals over the next 20 years. The best known of Kohlberg's dilemmas, the "Heinz dilemma," pits the value of obeying the law (not stealing) against the value of human life (saving a dying person):

In Europe a woman was near death from cancer. There was one drug the doctors thought might save her. A druggist in the same town had discovered it, but he was charging ten times what the drug cost him to make. The sick woman's husband, Heinz, went to everyone he knew to borrow the money, but he could only get together half of what it cost. The druggist refused to sell the drug for less or let Heinz pay later. So Heinz became desperate and broke into the man's store to steal the drug for his wife. Should Heinz have done that? Why or why not? (paraphrased from Colby et al., 1983, p. 77)

Kohlberg emphasized that it is *the way an individual reasons* about the dilemma, not *the content of the response* (whether or not to steal), that determines moral maturity. Individuals who believe Heinz should take the drug and those who think he should not can be found at each of Kohlberg's first four stages. Only at the two highest stages do moral reasoning and content come together in a coherent ethical system (Kohlberg, Levine, & Hewer, 1983). Given a choice between obeying the law and preserving individual rights, the most advanced moral thinkers support individual rights (in the Heinz dilemma, stealing the drug to save a life).

■ **KOHLBERG'S STAGES.**   Kohlberg organized moral development into three levels, each with two stages, yielding six stages in all. He believed that moral understanding is promoted by the same factors Piaget thought were important for cognitive development: (1) actively grappling with moral issues and noticing weaknesses in one's current reasoning and (2) gains in perspective taking, which permit individuals to resolve moral conflicts in more effective ways. **TAKE A MOMENT...** As we examine Kohlberg's developmental sequence in light of possible responses to the Heinz dilemma, look for changes in perspective taking that each stage assumes.

The Preconventional Level.   At the **preconventional level,** morality is externally controlled. Children accept the rules of authority figures and judge actions by their consequences. Behaviors that result in punishment are viewed as bad, those that lead to rewards as good.

■ *Stage 1: The punishment and obedience orientation.* Children at this stage find it difficult to consider two points of view in a moral dilemma. As a result, they overlook people's intentions. Instead, they focus on fear of authority and avoidance of punishment as reasons for behaving morally.

> *Prostealing:* "If you let your wife die, you will . . . be blamed for not spending the money to help her and there'll be an investigation of you and the druggist for your wife's death." (Kohlberg, 1969, p. 381)

> *Antistealing:* "You shouldn't steal the drug because you'll be caught and sent to jail if you do. If you do get away, [you'd be scared that] the police would catch up with you any minute." (Kohlberg, 1969, p. 381)

■ *Stage 2: The instrumental purpose orientation.* Children become aware that people can have different perspectives in a moral dilemma, but at first this understanding is con-

If the 12-year-old on the right expects a favor in return for carrying her injured friend's backpack, she is at Kohlberg's preconventional level. If she is guided by the Golden Rule, "Do unto others as you would have them do unto you," then she understands ideal reciprocity and has advanced to the conventional level.

crete. They view right action as flowing from self-interest and understand reciprocity as equal exchange of favors: "You do this for me and I'll do that for you."

Prostealing: "[I]f Heinz decides to risk jail to save his wife, it's his life he's risking; he can do what he wants with it. And the same goes for the druggist; it's up to him to decide what he wants to do." (Rest, 1979, p. 26)

Antistealing: "[Heinz] is running more risk than it's worth [to save a wife who is near death]." (Rest, 1979, p. 27)

The Conventional Level. At the **conventional level,** individuals continue to regard conformity to social rules as important, but not for reasons of self-interest. They believe that actively maintaining the current social system ensures positive relationships and societal order.

- *Stage 3: The "good boy–good girl" orientation, or the morality of interpersonal cooperation.* The desire to obey rules because they promote social harmony first appears in the context of close personal ties. Stage 3 individuals want to maintain the affection and approval of friends and relatives by being a "good person"—trustworthy, loyal, respectful,

helpful, and nice. The capacity to view a two-person relationship from the vantage point of an impartial, outside observer supports this new approach to morality. At this stage, individuals understand *ideal reciprocity:* They express the same concern for the welfare of another as they do for themselves—a standard of fairness summed up by the Golden Rule: "Do unto others as you would have them do unto you."

Prostealing: "No one will think you're bad if you steal the drug, but your family will think you're an inhuman husband if you don't. If you let your wife die, you'll never be able to look anyone in the face again." (Kohlberg, 1969, p. 381)

Antistealing: "It isn't just the druggist who will think you're a criminal, everyone else will too. . . . [Y]ou'll feel bad thinking how you've brought dishonor on your family and yourself." (Kohlberg, 1969, p. 381)

- *Stage 4: The social-order-maintaining orientation.* At this stage, the individual takes into account a larger perspective— that of societal laws. Moral choices no longer depend on close ties to others. Instead, rules must be enforced in the same evenhanded fashion for everyone, and each member of society has a personal duty to uphold them. The Stage 4 individual believes that laws should never be disobeyed because they are vital for ensuring societal order and cooperative relations between individuals.

Prostealing: "Heinz has a duty to protect his wife's life; it's a vow he took in marriage. But it's wrong to steal, so he would have to take the drug with the idea of paying the druggist for it and accepting the penalty for breaking the law later."

Antistealing: "Even if his wife is dying, it's still [Heinz's] duty as a citizen to obey the law. . . . If everyone starts breaking the law in a jam, there'd be no civilization, just crime and violence." (Rest, 1979, p. 30)

The Postconventional or Principled Level. Individuals at the **postconventional level** move beyond unquestioning support for their own society's rules and laws. They define morality in terms of abstract principles and values that apply to all situations and societies.

- *Stage 5: The social contract orientation.* At Stage 5, individuals regard laws and rules as flexible instruments for furthering human purposes. They can imagine alternatives to their own social order, and they emphasize fair procedures for interpreting and changing the law. When laws are consistent with individual rights and the interests of the majority, each person follows them because of a *social contract orientation*—free and willing participation in the system because it brings about more good for people than if it did not exist.

Prostealing: "Although there is a law against stealing, the law wasn't meant to violate a person's right to life. . . . If

Heinz is prosecuted for stealing, the law needs to be reinterpreted to take into account situations in which it goes against people's natural right to keep on living."

- **Stage 6: The universal ethical principle orientation.** At this highest stage, right action is defined by self-chosen ethical principles of conscience that are valid for all people, regardless of law and social agreement. Stage 6 individuals typically mention such principles as respect for the worth and dignity of each person.

  Prostealing: "It doesn't make sense to put respect for property above respect for life itself. [People] could live together without private property at all. Respect for human life and personality is absolute and accordingly [people] have a mutual duty to save one another from dying." (Rest, 1979, p. 37)

■ **RESEARCH ON KOHLBERG'S STAGE SEQUENCE.** Kohlberg's original research and other longitudinal studies provide the most convincing evidence for his stage sequence. With few exceptions, individuals move through the first four stages in the predicted order (Colby et al., 1983; Dawson, 2002; Walker & Taylor, 1991b). Moral development is slow and gradual: Reasoning at Stages 1 and 2 decreases in early adolescence, while Stage 3 increases through midadolescence and then declines. Stage 4 reasoning rises over the teenage years until, by early adulthood, it is the typical response.

Few people move beyond Stage 4. In fact, postconventional morality is so rare that no clear evidence exists that Kohlberg's Stage 6 actually follows Stage 5. This poses a key challenge to Kohlberg's theory: If people must reach Stages 5 and 6 to be considered truly morally mature, few individuals anywhere would measure up! According to one reexamination of Kohlberg's stages, moral maturity can be found in a revised understanding of Stages 3 and 4 (Gibbs, 1991, 2010). These stages are not "conventional"—based on social conformity—as Kohlberg assumed. Rather, they require profound moral constructions—an understanding of ideal reciprocity as the basis for relationships (Stage 3) and for widely accepted moral standards, set forth in rules and laws (Stage 4). In this view, "postconventional" morality is a highly reflective endeavor limited to a handful of people who have attained advanced education, usually in philosophy.

TAKE A MOMENT... Think of an actual moral dilemma you faced recently. How did you solve it? Did your reasoning fall at the same stage as your thinking about Heinz? Real-life conflicts often elicit moral reasoning below a person's actual capacity because they involve practical considerations and mix cognition with intense emotion (Carpendale, 2000; Walker, 2004). The influence of situational factors on moral judgments indicates that like Piaget's cognitive stages, Kohlberg's moral stages are loosely organized and overlapping. People draw on a range of moral responses that vary with context. With age, this range shifts upward as less mature moral reasoning is gradually replaced by more advanced moral thought.

Are There Sex Differences in Moral Reasoning?

In the discussion at the beginning of this section, notice how Sabrina's moral argument focuses on caring and commitment to others. Carol Gilligan (1982) is the best known of those who have argued that Kohlberg's theory—originally formulated on the basis of interviews with males—does not adequately represent the morality of girls and women. Gilligan believes that feminine morality emphasizes an "ethic of care" that Kohlberg's system devalues. Sabrina's reasoning falls at Stage 3 because it is based on mutual trust and affection, whereas Louis's is at Stage 4 because he emphasizes following the law. According to Gilligan, a concern for others is a *different* but no less valid basis for moral judgment than a focus on impersonal rights.

Most studies, however, do not support the claim that Kohlberg's approach underestimates the moral maturity of females (Turiel, 2006; Walker, 2006). On hypothetical dilemmas as well as everyday moral problems, adolescent and adult females display reasoning at the same stage as their male agemates and often at a higher stage. Themes of justice and caring appear in the responses of both sexes, and when girls do raise interpersonal concerns, they are not downgraded in Kohlberg's system (Jadack et al., 1995; Kahn, 1992; Walker, 1995).

Still, Gilligan makes a powerful claim that research on moral development has been limited by too much attention to rights and justice (a "masculine" ideal) and too little to care and responsiveness (a "feminine" ideal). Some evidence shows that although the morality of males and females taps both orientations, females do tend to emphasize care, whereas males either stress justice or focus equally on justice and care (Jaffee & Hyde, 2000; Wark & Krebs, 1996; Weisz & Black, 2002). This difference in emphasis, which appears more often in real-life dilemmas than in hypothetical ones, may reflect women's greater involvement in daily activities involving care and concern for others.

Coordinating Moral, Social-Conventional, and Personal Concerns

Adolescents' moral advances are also evident in their reasoning about situations that raise competing moral, social-conventional, and personal issues. In diverse Western and non-Western cultures, teenagers express great concern with matters of personal choice—a reflection of their quest for identity and strengthening independence (Neff & Helwig, 2002; Nucci, 2002). More firmly than at younger ages, they assert that dress, hairstyle, diary records, and friendships are solely the province of the individual and not subject to control by authority figures (such as parents) (Nucci, 2001, 2005). As adolescents enlarge the range of issues they regard as personal, they think more intently about conflicts between personal choice and community obligation—for example, whether, and under what conditions, it is permissible for laws to restrict speech, religion, marriage, childbearing, group membership, and other individual rights (Helwig, 1995; Wainryb, 1997).

Teenagers display more subtle thinking than school-age children on such issues. When asked if it is OK to exclude a child from a peer group on the basis of race or gender, fourth graders usually say exclusion is always unfair. But by tenth grade, young people, though increasingly mindful of fairness, indicate that under certain conditions—within friendship more often than peer groups, and on the basis of gender more often than race—exclusion is OK (Killen et al., 2002). In explaining, they mention the right to personal choice as well as concerns about effective group functioning.

As adolescents integrate personal rights with ideal reciprocity, they demand that protections they want for themselves extend to others. For example, with age, adolescents are more likely to defend the government's right to limit the personal right to engage in risky health behaviors such as smoking and drinking, in the interest of the larger public good (Flanagan, Stout, & Gallay, 2008). Similarly, they become mindful of the overlap between moral imperatives and social conventions. Eventually they see that violating strongly held conventions—showing up at a wedding in a T-shirt, talking out of turn at a student council meeting—can harm others, either by inducing distress or by undermining fair treatment. As their grasp of fairness deepens, teenagers realize that many social conventions are vital for maintaining a just and peaceful society (Nucci, 2001). Notice

These teenagers are making signs for an anti-war demonstration. Adolescent moral development involves thinking more intently about conflicts between personal choice and community obligation— for example, whether, and under what conditions, it is permissible to challenge a decision by one's country to go to war.

how this understanding is central to Kohlberg's Stage 4, which is typically attained as adolescence draws to a close.

Influences on Moral Reasoning

Many factors influence moral understanding, including child-rearing practices, schooling, peer interaction, and culture. As Kohlberg believed, these experiences work by presenting young people with cognitive challenges, which stimulate them to think about moral problems in more complex ways.

■ **PARENTING PRACTICES.** Adolescents who gain most in moral understanding have parents who engage in moral discussions, encourage prosocial behavior, and create a supportive atmosphere by listening sensitively, asking clarifying questions, and presenting higher-level reasoning (Pratt, Skoe, & Arnold, 2004; Wyatt & Carlo, 2002). In one study, 11-year-olds were asked what they thought an adult would say to justify a moral rule, such as not lying or breaking a promise. Those with warm, demanding, communicative parents were far more likely than their agemates to point to the importance of ideal reciprocity: "You wouldn't like it if I did it to you" (Leman, 2005). In contrast, when parents lecture, use threats, or make sarcastic remarks, adolescents show little or no change in moral reasoning over time (Walker & Taylor, 1991a).

■ **SCHOOLING.** Years of schooling is a powerful predictor of movement to Kohlberg's Stage 4 or higher (Dawson et al., 2003; Gibbs et al., 2007). Higher education introduces young people to social issues that extend beyond personal relationships to entire political or cultural groups. Consistent with this idea, college students who report more perspective-taking opportunities (for example, classes that emphasize open discussion of opinions, friendships with others of different cultural backgrounds) and who indicate that they have become more aware of social diversity tend to be advanced in moral reasoning (Comunian & Gielen, 2006; Mason & Gibbs, 1993a, 1993b).

■ **PEER INTERACTION.** Interaction among peers who present differing viewpoints promotes moral understanding. When young people negotiate and compromise with agemates, they realize that social life can be based on cooperation between equals rather than authority relations (Killen & Nucci, 1995). Peer discussions of moral problems have provided the basis for interventions aimed at improving high school and college students' moral understanding. But for these to be effective, young people must be highly engaged—confronting and critiquing one another's viewpoints, as Sabrina and Louis did when they argued over Mrs. Perry's plight (Berkowitz & Gibbs, 1983; Comunian & Gielen, 2006). And because moral development occurs gradually, many peer interaction sessions over weeks or months are needed to produce moral change.

■ **CULTURE.** Individuals in industrialized nations move through Kohlberg's stages more quickly and advance to a higher level than individuals in village societies, who rarely move

Growing up in a small village in the Pamir Mountains of China, these adolescents view moral cooperation as based on direct relations between people. Consequently, their moral reasoning is unlikely to advance beyond Kohlberg's Stage 3.

beyond Stage 3. One explanation is that in village societies, moral cooperation is based on direct relations between people and does not allow for the development of advanced moral understanding (Stages 4 to 6), which depends on appreciating the role of larger social structures, such as laws and government institutions (Gibbs et al., 2007).

A second possible reason for cultural variation is that responses to moral dilemmas in collectivist cultures (including village societies) are often more other-directed than in Western Europe and North America (Miller, 2006). In both village and industrialized cultures that highly value interdependency, statements portraying the individual as vitally connected to the social group are common. In one study, Japanese male and female adolescents, who almost always integrated caring and justice-based reasoning, placed greater weight on caring, which they regarded as a communal responsibility (Shimizu, 2001). Similarly, in research conducted in India, even highly educated people (expected to have attained Kohlberg's Stages 4 and 5) viewed solutions to moral dilemmas as the responsibility of the entire society, not of a single person (Miller & Bersoff, 1995).

These findings raise the question of whether Kohlberg's highest level represents a culturally specific way of thinking—one limited to Western societies that emphasize individualism and an appeal to an inner, private conscience. At the same time, a review of over 100 studies confirmed an age-related trend consistent with Kohlberg's Stages 1 to 4 across diverse societies (Gibbs et al., 2007). A common justice morality is clearly evident in the dilemma responses of people from vastly different cultures.

Moral Reasoning and Behavior

A central assumption of the cognitive-developmental perspective is that moral understanding should affect moral action.

According to Kohlberg, mature moral thinkers realize that behaving in line with their beliefs is vital for creating and maintaining a just social world (Gibbs, 2010). Consistent with this idea, higher-stage adolescents more often act prosocially by helping, sharing, and defending victims of injustice (Carlo et al., 1996; Comunian & Gielen, 2000, 2006). Also, they less often engage in cheating, aggression, and other antisocial behaviors (Gregg, Gibbs, & Fuller, 1994; Raaijmakers, Engels, & Van Hoof, 2005; Stams et al., 2006).

Yet the connection between mature moral reasoning and action is only modest. As we have seen, moral behavior is influenced by many factors besides cognition, including the emotions of empathy, sympathy, and guilt; individual differences in temperament; and a long history of experiences that affect moral decision making. **Moral self-relevance**—the degree to which morality is central to self-concept—also affects moral behavior (Walker, 2004). In a study of low-SES African-American and Hispanic teenagers, those who emphasized moral traits and goals in their self-descriptions displayed exceptional levels of community service (Hart & Fegley, 1995). But they did not differ from their agemates in moral reasoning.

Research has yet to identify the origins of a sense of moral self-relevance. Close relationships with parents, teachers, and friends may play a vital role by modeling prosocial behavior and fostering morally relevant emotions of empathy and guilt, which combine with moral cognition to powerfully motivate moral action (Arsenio, 2006; Hoffman, 2000). Another possibility is that *just educational environments*—in which teachers guide students in democratic decision making and rule setting, resolving disputes civilly, and taking responsibility for others' welfare—are influential (Atkins, Hart, & Donnelly, 2004).

Religious Involvement and Moral Development

Religion is especially important in U.S. family life. In recent national polls, nearly two-thirds of Americans reported being religious, compared with one-half of those in Canada, one-third of those in Great Britain and Italy, and even fewer elsewhere in Europe (Gallup News Service, 2006; Jones, 2003). As adolescents search for a personally meaningful identity, formal religious involvement tends to decline (Donahue & Benson, 1995; Kerestes & Youniss, 2003). Nevertheless, teenagers who remain part of a religious community are advantaged in moral values and behavior. Compared with nonaffiliated youths, they are more involved in community service activities aimed at helping the less fortunate (Kerestes, Youniss, & Metz, 2004). And religious involvement promotes responsible academic and social behavior and discourages misconduct (Dowling et al., 2004).

A variety of factors probably contribute to these favorable outcomes. In a study of inner-city high school students, religiously involved young people were more likely to report trusting relationships with parents, other adults, and friends who hold similar worldviews. The more activities they shared with this network, the higher they scored in empathy and prosocial behavior (King & Furrow, 2004). Furthermore, religious education

These teenagers gather with other religious groups to voice their support for world peace. Involvement in a religious community promotes teens' moral values and behavior, encouraging responsible academic work and community service.

and youth activities directly teach concern for others and provide opportunities for moral discussions and civic engagement. And adolescents who feel connected to a higher being may develop certain inner strengths, including moral self-relevance and prosocial values, that help them translate their thinking into action (Hardy & Carlo, 2005; Sherrod & Spiewak, 2008). An exception to these findings is seen in religious cults, where rigid indoctrination into the group's beliefs, suppression of individuality, and estrangement from society all work against moral maturity (Richmond, 2004).

Further Challenges to Kohlberg's Theory

Although much evidence is consistent with the cognitive-developmental approach to morality, Kohlberg's theory has faced challenges. The most radical opposition comes from researchers who—referring to wide variability in moral reasoning across situations—claim that Kohlberg's stage sequence inadequately accounts for morality in everyday life (Krebs and Denton, 2005). These investigators favor a *pragmatic approach to morality*. They assert that everyday moral judgments—rather than being efforts to arrive at just solutions—are practical tools that people use to achieve their goals. To benefit personally, people often must advocate cooperation with others. And, the pragmatists assert, people frequently act first and then invoke moral judgments to rationalize their actions, regardless of whether their behavior is self-centered or prosocial (Haidt, 2001).

Is the pragmatic approach correct that people strive to resolve moral conflicts fairly only when they themselves have nothing to lose? Supporters of the cognitive-developmental perspective point out that people frequently rise above self-interest to defend others' rights. For example, moral leaders in business—rather than resorting to Stage 2 reasoning—

endorse trust, integrity, good faith, and just laws and codes of conduct (Damon, 2004; Gibbs, 2006). Also, when presented with moral justifications varying in maturity, adolescents and adults are well aware of the greater adequacy of higher-stage thinking, which some people act on despite highly corrupt environments. Furthermore, individuals who engage in sudden altruistic action may have previously considered relevant moral issues so thoroughly that their moral judgment activates automatically, triggering an immediate response (Gibbs et al., 2009; Pizzaro & Bloom, 2003). In these instances, people who appear to be engaging in after-the-fact moral justification are actually behaving with great forethought.

In sum, the cognitive-developmental approach to morality has done much to clarify our profound moral potential. And despite opposition, Kohlberg's central assumption—that with age, humans everywhere construct a deeper understanding of fairness and justice that guides moral action—remains powerfully influential.

Gender Typing

As Sabrina entered adolescence, she began to place more emphasis on excelling in literature, art, and music—traditionally feminine subjects. When with peers, she worried about walking, talking, eating, dressing, laughing, and competing in ways consistent with gender roles.

Early adolescence is a period of **gender intensification**—increased gender stereotyping of attitudes and behavior and movement toward a more traditional gender identity (Basow & Rubin, 1999; Galambos, Almeida, & Petersen, 1990). Both sexes experience gender intensification, but it is stronger for girls, who feel less free to experiment with "other-gender" activities and behavior than they did in middle childhood (Huston & Alvarez, 1990).

What accounts for gender intensification? Biological, social, and cognitive factors are involved. As puberty magnifies sex differences in appearance, teenagers spend more time thinking about themselves in gender-linked ways. Pubertal changes also prompt gender-typed pressures from others. Parents—especially those with traditional gender-role beliefs—may encourage "gender-appropriate" activities and behavior more than they did earlier (Shanahan et al., 2007). And when adolescents start to date, they often become more gender-typed as a way of increasing their attractiveness (Maccoby, 1998). Finally, cognitive changes—in particular, greater concern with what others think—make young teenagers more responsive to gender-role expectations.

Gender intensification declines by middle to late adolescence, but not all young people move beyond it to the same degree. Teenagers who are encouraged to explore non-gender-typed options and to question the value of gender stereotypes for themselves and society are more likely to build an androgynous gender identity (see Chapter 8, page 214). Overall, androgynous adolescents, especially girls, tend to be psychologically

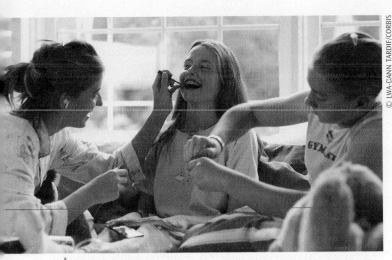

In early adolescence, young people, especially girls, move toward more traditional gender identities. By the late teens, gender intensification declines, especially among adolescents encouraged to explore non-gender-typed options.

healthier—more self-confident, more willing to speak their own mind, better-liked by peers, and identity-achieved (Bronstein, 2006; Dusek, 1987; Harter, 2006).

ASK YOURSELF

≫ REVIEW
How does an understanding of ideal reciprocity contribute to moral development? Why are Kohlberg's Stages 3 and 4 morally mature constructions?

≫ APPLY
Tam grew up in a small village culture, Lydia in a large industrial city. At age 15, Tam reasons at Kohlberg's Stage 3, Lydia at Stage 4. What factors might account for the difference?

≫ REFLECT
Do you favor a cognitive-developmental or a pragmatic approach to morality, or both? What research evidence and personal experiences influenced your viewpoint?

The Family

Franca and Antonio remember their son Louis's freshman year of high school as a difficult time. Because of a demanding project at work, Franca was away from home many evenings and weekends. In her absence, Antonio took over, but when business declined and he had to cut costs at his hardware store, he, too, had less time for the family. That year, Louis and two friends used their computer know-how to crack the code of a long-distance telephone service. From the family basement, they made calls around the country. Louis's grades fell, and he often left the house without saying where he was going. When the telephone company traced the illegal calls to their phone number, Franca and Antonio knew they had cause for concern.

Development at adolescence involves striving for **autonomy**—a sense of oneself as a separate, self-governing individual. Teenagers strive to rely more on themselves and less on parents for decision making (Collins & Laursen, 2004; Steinberg & Silk, 2002). Nevertheless, parent–child relationships remain vital for helping adolescents become autonomous, responsible individuals.

Parent–Child Relationships

A variety of changes within the adolescent support autonomy. In Chapter 11, we saw that puberty triggers psychological distancing from parents. In addition, as young people look more mature, parents give them more independence and responsibility. Gradually, adolescents solve problems and make decisions more effectively. And an improved ability to reason about social relationships leads teenagers to *deidealize* their parents, viewing them as "just people." Consequently, they no longer bend as easily to parental authority as they did when younger. Yet as Franca and Antonio's episode with Louis reveals, teenagers still need guidance and, at times, protection from dangerous situations.

In diverse ethnic groups and cultures, warm, supportive parent–adolescent ties that permit young people to explore ideas and social roles foster autonomy, predicting high self-reliance, work orientation, academic competence, favorable self-esteem, and ease of separation in the transition to college (Bean, Barber, & Crane, 2007; Eisenberg et al., 2005b; Wang, Pomerantz, & Chen, 2007). Conversely, parents who are coercive or psychologically controlling interfere with the development of autonomy. These tactics are consistently linked to low self-esteem, depression, drug and alcohol use, and antisocial behavior—outcomes that often persist into early adulthood (Barber, Stolz, & Olsen, 2005; Bronte-Tinkew, Moore, & Carrano, 2006; Wissink, Deković, & Meijer, 2006).

In Chapter 2, we described the family as a *system* that must adapt to changes in its members. The rapid physical and psychological changes of adolescence trigger conflicting expectations in parent–child relationships—a major reason that many parents find rearing teenagers to be stressful. Parents and teenagers—especially young teenagers—differ sharply on the appropriate age for granting certain privileges, such as control over clothing, school courses, and going out with friends (Smetana, 2002). Consistent parental monitoring of the young person's daily activities, through a cooperative relationship in which the adolescent willingly discloses information, is linked to a variety of positive outcomes—prevention of delinquency, reduction in sexual activity, improved school performance, and positive psychological well-being (Crouter & Head, 2002; Jacobson & Crockett, 2000).

Throughout adolescence, the quality of the parent–child relationship is the single most consistent predictor of mental health. In well-functioning families, teenagers remain attached to parents and seek their advice, but they do so in a context of greater freedom (Collins & Steinberg, 2006). The mild conflict that arises facilitates adolescent identity and autonomy by

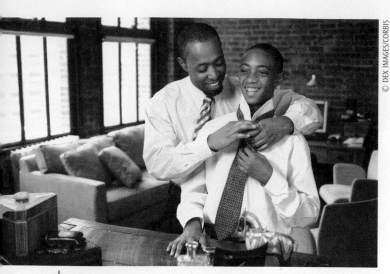

This teenager and his father share an affectionate moment. Adolescents may resist parental authority, especially in matters of personal choice such as dress. But most maintain close family ties, particularly when parents give them the freedom to explore ideas and social roles.

helping family members express and tolerate disagreement and informing parents of teenagers' changing needs and expectations.

By middle to late adolescence, most parents and children achieve this mature, mutual relationship, and harmonious interaction is on the rise. Teenagers living in risky neighborhoods tend to have more trusting relationships with parents and adjust more favorably when parents maintain tighter control (McElhaney & Allen, 2001). In harsh surroundings, young people seem to interpret more measured granting of autonomy as a sign of parental caring.

Family Circumstances

As Franca and Antonio's experience with Louis reminds us, adult life stress can interfere with warm, involved parenting and, in turn, with children's adjustment at any period of development. But parents who are financially secure, not overloaded with job pressures, and content with their marriages usually find it easier to grant teenagers appropriate autonomy and experience less conflict with them (Cowan & Cowan, 2002; Crouter & Bumpus, 2001). When Franca and Antonio's work stress eased and they recognized Louis's need for more involvement and guidance, his problems subsided.

Less than 10 percent of families with adolescents have seriously troubled relationships. Of these, most have difficulties that began in childhood (Collins & Laursen, 2004). Teenagers who develop well despite family stresses continue to benefit from factors that fostered resilience in earlier years: an appealing, easy-going disposition; a parent who combines warmth with high expectations; and (especially if parental supports are lacking) bonds with prosocial adults outside the family who care deeply about the adolescent's well-being (Masten, 2001; Masten & Shaffer, 2006).

Siblings

Like parent–child relationships, sibling interactions adapt to development at adolescence. As younger siblings become more self-sufficient, they accept less direction from their older brothers and sisters, and sibling influence declines. Also, as teenagers become more involved in friendships and romantic relationships, they invest less time and energy in siblings, who are part of the family from which they are trying to establish autonomy. As a result, sibling relationships often become less intense, in both positive and negative feelings (Hetherington, Henderson, & Reiss, 1999; Kim et al., 2006).

Nevertheless, attachment between siblings remains strong for most young people. Brothers and sisters who established a positive bond in early childhood continue to express affection and caring—an outcome linked to more favorable emotional and social adjustment (Branje et al., 2004; Kim et al., 2007). Also, mild sibling differences in perceived parental affection no longer trigger jealousy but, instead, predict greater sibling warmth (Feinberg et al., 2003). Perhaps adolescents interpret a unique parental relationship, as long as it is generally accepting, as a gratifying sign of their own individuality.

Peer Relations

As adolescents spend less time with family members, peers become increasingly important. In industrialized nations, young people spend most of each weekday with agemates in school. Teenagers also spend much out-of-class time together, more in some cultures than others. For example, U.S. young people have about 50 hours of free time per week, Europeans about 45 hours, and East Asians about 33 hours (Larson, 2001). A shorter school year and less demanding academic standards, which lead American youths to devote much less time to schoolwork, account for this difference.

In the following sections, we will see that adolescent peer relations can be both positive and negative. At their best, peers serve as critical bridges between the family and adult social roles.

Friendships

Number of "best friends" declines from about four to six in early adolescence to one or two in adulthood (Hartup & Stevens, 1999). At the same time, the nature of the relationship changes.

■ **CHARACTERISTICS OF ADOLESCENT FRIENDSHIPS.** When asked about the meaning of friendship, teenagers stress three characteristics. The most important is *intimacy,* or psychological closeness, which is supported by *mutual understanding* of each other's values, beliefs, and feelings. In addition, more than younger children, teenagers want their friends to be *loyal*—to stick up for them and not to leave them for somebody else (Buhrmester, 1996; Hartup & Abecassis, 2004).

As frankness and faithfulness increase, *self-disclosure* (sharing of private thoughts and feelings) between friends rises steadily over the adolescent years (see Figure 12.1). As a result, teenage friends get to know each other better as personalities. In addition to the many characteristics that school-age friends share (see page 265 in Chapter 10), adolescent friends tend to be alike in identity status, educational aspirations, political beliefs, and willingness to try drugs and engage in lawbreaking acts (Akers, Jones, & Coyl, 1998; Berndt & Murphy, 2002). Occasionally, however, teenagers choose friends with differing attitudes and values, which permits them to explore new perspectives within the security of a compatible relationship.

During adolescence, cooperation and mutual affirmation between friends increase—changes that reflect greater skill at preserving the relationship and sensitivity to a friend's needs and desires (Phillipsen, 1999). Adolescents also are less possessive of their friends than they were in childhood (Parker et al., 2005). Desiring a certain degree of autonomy for themselves, they recognize that friends need this, too.

■ SEX DIFFERENCES IN FRIENDSHIPS. *TAKE A MOMENT...* Ask several adolescents to describe their close friendships. You are likely to find a consistent sex difference: Emotional closeness is more common between girls than between boys (Markovits, Benenson, & Dolensky, 2001). Girls frequently get together to "just talk," and their interactions contain more self-disclosure and supportive statements. In contrast, boys more often gather for an activity—usually sports and competitive games. Boys' discussions usually focus on accomplishments and involve more competition and conflict (Brendgen et al., 2001; Rubin, Bukowski, & Parker, 2006).

Friendship closeness, though usually beneficial, can have costs. When focusing on deeper thoughts and feelings, adolescent

© MYRLEEN FERGUSON CATE/PHOTOEDIT

Compared to boys, girls place a higher value on emotional closeness, engaging in more self-disclosure and mutually supportive statements with friends.

friends tend to *coruminate*, or repeatedly mull over problems and negative emotions—an activity that sparks anxiety and depression (Rose, Carlson, & Waller, 2007). And when conflicts arise between intimate friends, more potential exists for one party to harm the other through relational aggression—for example, by divulging sensitive personal information to outsiders. For this reason, girls' closest same-sex friendships tend to be of shorter duration than boys' (Benenson & Christakos, 2003).

■ FRIENDSHIPS ON THE INTERNET. Teenagers frequently use the Internet to communicate with friends. Instant messaging—their preferred means of online interaction—seems to

■ FIGURE 12.1 ■ Age changes in reported self-disclosure to parents and peers, based on findings of several studies.
Self-disclosure to friends increases steadily during adolescence, reflecting intimacy as a major basis of friendship. Self-disclosure to romantic partners also rises. However, not until the college years does it surpass intimacy with friends. Self-disclosure to parents declines in early adolescence, a time of mild parent–child conflict. As family relationships readjust to the young person's increasing autonomy, self-disclosure to parents rises. (From D. Buhrmester, 1996, "Need Fulfillment, Interpersonal Competence, and the Developmental Contexts of Early Adolescent Friendship," in W. M. Bukowski, A. F. Newcomb, & W. W. Hartup, Eds., *The Company They Keep: Friendship in Childhood and Adolescence,* New York: Cambridge University Press, p. 168. Reprinted with the permission of Cambridge University Press.)

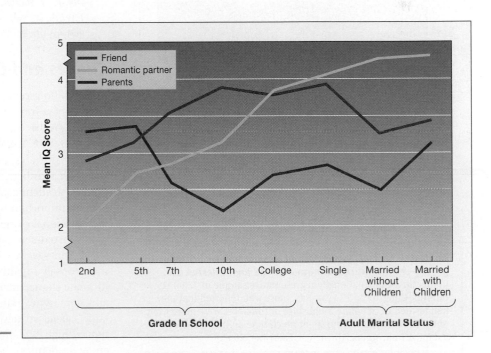

support friendship closeness. As amount of instant messaging between preexisting friends increases, so do young people's perceptions of intimacy in the relationship and feelings of well-being (Hu et al., 2004; Valkenburg & Peter, 2007a, 2007b).

Although mostly communicating with friends they know, teenagers are also drawn to meeting new people over the Internet. Chat rooms, blogs, message boards, and social networking sites open up vast alternatives beyond their families, schools, and communities. Through these online ties, young people explore central adolescent issues—sexuality, challenges in parent and peer relationships, and attitudes and values—in contexts that may feel less threatening than similar everyday conversations (Subrahmanyam, Smahel, & Greenfield, 2006). Online interactions with strangers also offer some teenagers vital social support. Young people suffering from eating disorders, depression, and other problems can access message boards where participants provide mutual assistance (Whitlock, Powers, & Eckenrode, 2006).

But online communication also poses dangers. In unmonitored chat rooms, teenagers are likely to encounter degrading racial and ethnic slurs and sexually obscene and harassing remarks (Tynes, Reynolds, & Greenfield, 2004). Furthermore, in a survey of a nationally representative sample of U.S. 10- to 17-year-olds, 14 percent reported online close friendships or romances (Wolak, Mitchell, & Finkelhor, 2003). Although some well-adjusted adolescents formed these bonds, many were youths who reported high levels of conflict with parents, peer victimization, depression, and delinquency, and who spent extensive time on the Internet (see Figure 12.2). They also more often

had been asked by online friends for face-to-face meetings and had attended those meetings—without telling their parents.

The Internet's value for enabling convenient and satisfying communication among teenage friends must be weighed against its potential for facilitating harmful social experiences. Parents are wise to point out the risks of Internet communication, including harassment and exploitation, and to insist that teenagers follow Internet safety rules (see *www.safeteens.com*).

■ **FRIENDSHIPS AND ADJUSTMENT.** As long as adolescent friendships are not characterized by jealousy, relational aggression, or attraction to antisocial behavior, they are related to many aspects of psychological health and competence into early adulthood (Bagwell et al., 2001; Bukowski, 2001), for several reasons:

- *Close friendships provide opportunities to explore the self and develop a deep understanding of another.* Through open, honest communication, friends become sensitive to each other's strengths and weaknesses, needs and desires—a process that supports the development of self-concept, perspective taking, and identity.

- *Close friendships provide a foundation for future intimate relationships.* Conversations with teenage friends about sexuality and romance, along with the intimacy of friendship itself, may help adolescents establish and work out problems in romantic partnerships (Connolly & Goldberg, 1999).

- *Close friendships help young people deal with the stresses of adolescence.* Supportive friendships promote empathy, sympathy, and prosocial behavior. As a result, friendships contribute to involvement in constructive youth activities, avoidance of antisocial acts, and psychological well-being (Lansford et al., 2003; Wentzel, Barry, & Caldwell, 2004).

- *Close friendships can improve attitudes toward and involvement in school.* When teenagers enjoy interacting with friends at school, they may begin to view all aspects of school life more positively (Berndt & Murphy, 2002).

Cliques and Crowds

In early adolescence, *peer groups* (see Chapter 10) become increasingly common and tightly knit. They are organized into **cliques,** groups of about five to seven members who are friends and, therefore, usually resemble one another in family background, attitudes, and values. At first, cliques are limited to same-sex members. Among girls but not boys, being in a clique predicts academic and social competence. Clique membership is more important to girls, who use it as a context for expressing emotional closeness (Henrich et al., 2000). By midadolescence, mixed-sex cliques are common.

Often several cliques with similar values form a larger, more loosely organized group called a **crowd.** Unlike the more intimate clique, membership in a crowd is based on reputation and stereotype, granting the adolescent an identity within the larger social structure of the school. Prominent crowds in a typical high school might include "brains" (nonathletes who enjoy academics), "jocks" (who are very involved in sports),

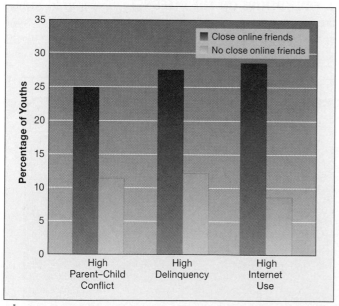

■ **FIGURE 12.2** ■ **Association of close online friendships with parent–child conflict, delinquency, and high Internet use.** In this survey of a nationally representative sample of 1,500 U.S. Internet-using 10- to 17-year-olds, those who reported that they had formed close online friendships or romances were more likely to be troubled youths who spent much time on the Internet. (Adapted from Wolak, Mitchell, & Finkelhor, 2003.)

Members of this Ultimate Frisbee team form a crowd. Unlike the more intimate clique, the larger, more loosely organized crowd grants the adolescent an identity within the larger social structure of the school.

"populars" (class leaders who are highly social and involved in activities), "partyers" (who value socializing but care little about schoolwork), "nonconformists" (who like unconventional clothing and music), and "burnouts" (who cut school and get into trouble) (Kinney, 1999; Stone & Brown, 1999).

What influences the sorting of teenagers into cliques and crowds? Crowd affiliations are linked to strengths in adolescents' self-concepts, which reflect their abilities and interests (Prinstein & La Greca, 2002). Family factors are important, too. In a study of 8,000 ninth to twelfth graders, adolescents who described their parents as authoritative were members of "brain," "jock," and "popular" groups that accepted both adult and peer reward systems. In contrast, boys with permissive parents aligned themselves with the "partyers" and "burnouts," suggesting lack of identification with adult reward systems (Durbin et al., 1993). These findings indicate that many peer-group values are extensions of ones acquired at home.

As interest in dating increases, boys' and girls' cliques come together. Mixed-sex cliques provide models of how to interact with the other sex and a chance to do so without having to be intimate (Connolly et al., 2004). By late adolescence, when boys and girls feel comfortable enough about approaching each other directly, mixed-sex cliques disappear (Connolly & Goldberg, 1999).

Crowds also decline in importance. As adolescents settle on personal values and goals, they no longer feel a need to broadcast, through dress, language, and activities, who they are. From tenth to twelfth grade, about half of young people switch crowds, mostly in favorable directions (Strouse, 1999). "Brains" and "normal" crowds grow and deviant crowds lose members as teenagers focus more on their future.

Dating

The hormonal changes of puberty increase sexual interest, but cultural expectations determine when and how dating begins. Asian youths start dating later and have fewer dating partners than young people in Western societies, which tolerate and even encourage romantic involvements from middle school on. At age 12 to 14, these relationships last only briefly, but by age 16 they continue, on average, for nearly two years (Carver, Joyner, & Udry, 2003). Young adolescents tend to mention recreation and achieving peer status as reasons for dating. By late adolescence, as young people are ready for greater psychological intimacy, they look for someone who offers companionship, affection, and social support (Brown, 2004; Collins & van Dulmen, 2006b).

The achievement of intimacy between dating partners typically lags behind that between friends. Recall from Chapter 6 that according to ethological theory, early attachment bonds lead to an *internal working model* that guides later close relationships. Consistent with this idea, secure attachment to parents in infancy and childhood—together with recollections of that security in adolescence—predicts quality of teenagers' friendships and romantic ties (Collins & van Dulmen, 2006a; Weimer, Kerns, & Oldenburg, 2004).

Perhaps because early adolescent dating relationships are shallow and stereotyped, early dating is related to drug use, delinquency, and poor academic achievement (Eaton et al., 2007; Zimmer-Gembeck, Siebenbruner, & Collins, 2001). These factors, along with a history of uninvolved parenting and aggression in family and peer relationships, increase the likelihood of dating violence (Arriaga & Foshee, 2004; Cyr, McDuff, & Wright, 2006). Young teenagers are better off sticking with group activities, such as parties and dances, before becoming involved with a steady boyfriend or girlfriend.

Gay and lesbian youths face special challenges in initiating and maintaining visible romances. Their first dating relationships seem to be short-lived and to involve little emotional commitment, but for reasons different from those of heterosexuals: They fear peer harassment and rejection (Diamond &

As long as dating does not begin too soon, it extends the benefits of adolescent friendships. Besides being fun, dating promotes sensitivity, empathy, and identity development as teenagers relate to someone whose needs differ from their own.

Lucas, 2004). In addition, many have difficulty finding a same-sex partner because their homosexual peers have not yet come out. Often their first contacts with other sexual minority youths occur in support groups, where they are free to date publicly (Diamond, 2003).

As long as it does not begin too soon, dating promotes sensitivity, empathy, self-esteem, social support, and identity development (Collins, 2003; Furman & Shaffer, 2003). Still, about half of first romances do not survive high school graduation, and those that do usually become less satisfying (Shaver, Furman, & Buhrmester, 1985). Because young people are still forming their identities, high school couples often find that they have little in common later.

ASK YOURSELF

>> **REVIEW**
Describe the distinct positive functions of friendships, cliques, and crowds in adolescence. What factors lead some friendships and peer-group ties to be harmful?

>> **APPLY**
Thirteen-year-old Mattie's parents are warm, firm in their expectations, and consistent in monitoring her activities. At school, Mattie met some girls who want her to tell her parents she's going to a friend's house and then, instead, join them at the beach for a party, where there will be drinking. Is Mattie likely to comply? Explain.

>> **REFLECT**
How did family experiences influence your crowd membership in high school? How did your crowd membership influence your behavior?

Problems of Development

Most young people move through adolescence with little disturbance. But as we have seen, some encounter major disruptions in development, such as early parenthood, substance abuse, and school failure. In each instance, biological and psychological changes, families, schools, peers, communities, and culture combine to yield particular outcomes. Serious difficulties rarely occur in isolation but are usually interrelated—as is apparent in three additional problems of the teenage years: depression, suicide, and delinquency.

Depression

Depression—feeling sad, frustrated, and hopeless about life, accompanied by loss of pleasure in most activities and disturbances in sleep, appetite, concentration, and energy—is the most common psychological problem of adolescence. About 15 to 20 percent of teenagers have had one or more major depressive episodes, a rate comparable to that of adults. From 2 to 8 percent are chronically depressed—gloomy and self-critical

for many months and sometimes years (Rushton, Forcier, & Schectman, 2002).

Serious depression affects only 1 to 2 percent of children, many of whom remain depressed in adolescence. In addition, depression increases sharply from ages 12 to 16 in industrialized nations, with many more girls than boys displaying adolescent onset. Teenage girls are twice as likely as boys to report persistent depressed mood—a difference sustained throughout the lifespan (Dekker et al., 2007; Hankin & Abela, 2005; Nolen-Hoeksema, 2002).

■ **FACTORS RELATED TO DEPRESSION.** Kinship studies of twins and other close relatives reveal that heredity plays an important role in depression (Glowinski et al., 2003). Genes can induce depression by affecting the balance of neurotransmitters in the brain, the development of brain regions involved in inhibiting negative emotion, or the body's hormonal response to stress.

But experience can also promote these biological changes. In earlier chapters we saw that depressed or otherwise stressed parents often engage in maladaptive parenting. As a result, their child's emotional self-regulation, attachment, and self-esteem may be impaired, with serious consequences for many cognitive and social skills (Abela et al., 2005; Yap, Allen, & Ladouceur, 2008). Depressed youths usually display a learned-helpless attributional style (see Chapter 10) (Graber, 2004). In a vulnerable young person, numerous events can spark depression—for example, failing at something important, parental divorce, or the end of a close friendship or romantic partnership.

■ **SEX DIFFERENCES.** Why are girls more prone to depression than boys? Biological changes associated with puberty cannot be responsible because the gender difference is limited to industrialized nations. In developing countries, rates of depression are similar for males and females and occasionally higher in males (Culbertson, 1997). Even when females do exceed

© DAVID GROSSMAN/THE IMAGE WORKS

In industrialized nations, stressful life events and gender-typed coping styles—passivity, dependency, and rumination—make adolescent girls more susceptible to depression than boys.

males in depression, the size of the difference varies. For example, it is smaller in China than in North America, perhaps because of decades of efforts by the Chinese government to eliminate gender inequalities (Greenberger et al., 2000).

Instead, gender-typed coping styles seem to be responsible. Early-maturing girls are especially prone to depression (see Chapter 11). And the gender intensification of early adolescence often strengthens girls' passivity, dependency, and tendency to ruminate on their anxieties and problems—maladaptive approaches to tasks expected of teenagers in complex cultures. Consistent with this explanation, adolescents who identify strongly with "feminine" traits ruminate more and are more depressed, regardless of their sex (Broderick & Korteland, 2004; Papadakis et al., 2006). Girls who repeatedly feel overwhelmed develop an overly reactive physiological stress response and cope more poorly with future challenges (Nolen-Hoeksema, 2006). In this way, stressful experiences and stress reactivity feed on one another, sustaining depression. Profound depression can lead to suicidal thoughts, which all too often are translated into action.

Suicide

The suicide rate increases over the lifespan, from childhood to old age, but it jumps sharply at adolescence. Currently, suicide is the third-leading cause of death among American youths (after motor vehicle collisions and homicides) (U.S. Census Bureau, 2009b). At the same time, rates of adolescent suicide vary widely among industrialized nations—low in Greece, Italy, the Netherlands, and Spain; intermediate in Australia, Canada, Japan, and the United States; and high in Finland, New Zealand, and Singapore (Bridge, Goldstein, & Brent, 2006). These differences remain unexplained.

■ **FACTORS RELATED TO ADOLESCENT SUICIDE.** Despite girls' higher rates of depression, the number of boys who kill themselves exceeds the number of girls by a ratio of 3 or 4 to 1. Girls make more unsuccessful suicide attempts and use methods from which they are more likely to be revived, such as a sleeping pill overdose. In contrast, boys tend to choose techniques that lead to instant death, such as firearms. Gender-role expectations may contribute; less tolerance exists for feelings of helplessness and failed efforts in males (Canetto & Sakinofsky, 1998).

Perhaps because of greater extended-family support, African Americans and Hispanics have lower suicide rates than Caucasian Americans. Recently, however, suicide has risen among African-American adolescent males; the current rate approaches that of Caucasian-American males. And Native-American youths commit suicide at rates two to six times national averages (U.S. Census Bureau, 2009b). High rates of profound family poverty, school failure, alcohol and drug use, and depression probably underlie these trends. Gay, lesbian, and bisexual youths are also at high risk, attempting suicide three times as often as other adolescents. Those who have tried to kill themselves report more family conflict over their gender-atypical

behavior, inner turmoil about their sexuality, and peer victimization (D'Augelli et al., 2005).

Suicide tends to occur in two types of young people. The first group includes adolescents who are highly intelligent but solitary, withdrawn, and unable to meet their own standards or those of important people in their lives. Members of a second, larger group show antisocial tendencies (Evans, Hawton, & Rodham, 2004). Besides being hostile and destructive, they turn their anger and disappointment inward.

Suicidal adolescents often have a family history of emotional and antisocial disorders. In addition, they are likely to have experienced multiple stressful life events, including economic disadvantage, parental divorce, frequent parent–child conflict, and abuse and neglect (Beautrais, 2003; Pfeffer, 2006). Triggering events include parental blaming of the teenager for family problems, the breakup of an important peer relationship, or the humiliation of having been caught engaging in antisocial acts.

Why does suicide increase in adolescence? One factor seems to be teenagers' improved ability to plan ahead. Although some act impulsively, many young people take purposeful steps toward killing themselves. Other cognitive changes also contribute. Belief in the personal fable leads many depressed young people to conclude that no one could possibly understand their intense pain.

■ **PREVENTION AND TREATMENT.** To prevent suicides, parents and teachers must be trained to pick up on the signals that a troubled teenager sends (see Table 12.2). Schools and

■ **TABLE 12.2** ■ *Warning Signs of Suicide*

Efforts to put personal affairs in order—smoothing over troubled relationships, giving away treasured possessions
Verbal cues—saying goodbye to family members and friends, making direct or indirect references to suicide ("I won't have to worry about these problems much longer"; "I wish I were dead")
Feelings of sadness, despondency, "not caring" anymore
Extreme fatigue, lack of energy, boredom
No desire to socialize; withdrawal from friends
Easily frustrated
Emotional outbursts—spells of crying or laughing, bursts of energy
Inability to concentrate, distractible
Decline in grades, absence from school, discipline problems
Neglect of personal appearance
Sleep change—loss of sleep or excessive sleepiness
Appetite change—eating more or less than usual
Physical complaints—stomachaches, backaches, headaches

recreational and religious organizations can provide counseling and support (Spirito et al., 2003). Once a teenager takes steps toward suicide, staying with the young person, listening, and expressing compassion until professional help arrives are essential.

Treatments for depressed and suicidal adolescents range from antidepressant medication to individual, family, and group therapy. On a broader scale, gun-control legislation that limits adolescents' access to the most frequent and deadly suicide method in the United States would greatly reduce both the number of suicides and the high teenage homicide rate (Commission on Adolescent Suicide Prevention, 2005).

Teenage suicides often occur in clusters, with one death increasing the likelihood of others among depressed peers who knew the young person (Bearman & Moody, 2004; Gould, Jamieson, & Romer, 2003). In view of this trend, a watchful eye must be kept on vulnerable adolescents after a suicide happens.

Delinquency

Juvenile delinquents are children or adolescents who engage in illegal acts. Although youth crime has declined in the United States since the mid-1990s, 12- to 17-year-olds account for about 15 percent of police arrests, although they constitute only 8 percent of the population (U.S. Department of Justice, 2008). When asked directly and confidentially about lawbreaking, almost all teenagers admit to having committed some sort of offense—usually a minor crime, such as petty stealing or disorderly conduct (Flannery et al., 2003).

Both police arrests and self-reports show that delinquency rises over the early teenage years, remains high in middle adolescence, and then declines (Farrington, 2004; U.S. Department of Justice, 2008). Among young teenagers, antisocial behavior increases as a result of desire for peer approval. Over time, peers become less influential, moral reasoning improves, and young people enter social contexts (such as higher education, work, and marriage) that are less conducive to lawbreaking.

For most adolescents, a brush with the law does not forecast long-term antisocial behavior. But repeated arrests are cause for concern. Teenagers are responsible for 18 percent of violent offenses in the United States (U.S. Department of Justice, 2008). A small percentage become recurrent offenders, and some enter a life of crime.

■ **FACTORS RELATED TO DELINQUENCY.** In adolescence, the gender gap in physical aggression widens (Chesney-Lind, 2001). Although girls account for about one in five adolescent arrests for violence, their offenses are largely limited to simple assault (such as pushing or spitting). Violent crime is mostly the domain of boys (Dahlberg & Simon, 2006). SES and ethnicity are strong predictors of arrests but only mildly related to teenagers' self-reports of antisocial acts. The difference is due to the tendency to arrest, charge, and punish low-SES ethnic minority youths more often than their higher-SES white and Asian counterparts (Farrington, 2004; U.S. Department of Justice, 2008).

Delinquency rises during the early teen years and remains high during middle adolescence. Although most of the time it involves petty stealing and disorderly conduct, a small percentage of young people engage in repeated, serious offenses and are at risk for a life of crime.

Difficult temperament, low intelligence, poor school performance, peer rejection in childhood, and association with antisocial peers are linked to delinquency (Laird et al., 2005). How do these factors fit together? One of the most consistent findings about delinquent youths is that their families are low in warmth, high in conflict, and characterized by harsh, inconsistent discipline and low monitoring (Barnes et al., 2006; Capaldi et al., 2002). Our discussion on page 209 in Chapter 8 explained how ineffective parenting can promote and sustain children's aggression. Boys are more likely than girls to be targets of angry, inconsistent discipline because they are more active and impulsive and therefore harder to control. When children who are extreme in these characteristics are exposed to emotionally negative, inept parenting, aggression rises during childhood, leads to violent offenses in adolescence, and persists into adulthood (see the Lifespan Vista box on the following page).

Teenagers commit more crimes in poverty-stricken neighborhoods with limited recreational and employment opportunities and high adult criminality (Kroneman, Loeber, & Hipwell, 2004). In such neighborhoods, adolescents have easy access to deviant peers, drugs, and firearms and are likely to be recruited into antisocial gangs, whose members commit the vast majority of violent delinquent acts. Furthermore, schools in these locales typically fail to meet students' developmental needs (Flannery et al., 2003). Large classes, weak instruction, and lax enforcement of rules increase teenagers' inclination toward aggression and violence.

■ **PREVENTION AND TREATMENT.** Because delinquency has roots in childhood and results from events in several contexts, prevention must start early and take place at multiple levels (Frey et al., 2009). Positive family relationships, authoritative parenting, high-quality teaching in schools, and communities

■ A LIFESPAN VISTA: Looking Forward, Looking Back ■

Two Routes to Adolescent Delinquency

Persistent adolescent delinquency follows two paths, one involving a small number of youths with an onset of conduct problems in childhood, the second a larger number with an onset in adolescence. The early-onset type is far more likely to lead to a life-course pattern of aggression and criminality (Moffitt, 2006). The late-onset type usually does not persist beyond the transition to early adulthood.

Why does antisocial activity more often continue and escalate into violence in the first group? Longitudinal studies yield similar answers to this question. Most research has focused on boys, but several investigations report that girls who were physically aggressive in childhood are also at risk for later problems—occasionally violent delinquency but more often other norm-violating behaviors and psychological disorders (Broidy et al., 2003; Chamberlain, 2003).

Early-Onset Type

Early-onset youngsters seem to inherit traits that predispose them to aggressiveness (Pettit, 2004). For example, violence-prone boys are emotionally negative, restless, willful, and physically aggressive as early as age 2. They also show subtle deficits in cognitive functioning that seem to contribute to disruptions in the development of language, memory, and cognitive and emotional self-regulation (Moffitt, 2006; Shaw et al., 2003). Some have attention-deficit hyperactivity disorder (ADHD), which compounds their learning and self-control problems (see Chapter 9, page 236).

Yet these biological risks are not sufficient to sustain antisocial behavior: Most early-onset boys decline in aggression over time. Among those who follow the life-course path, inept parenting transforms their undercontrolled style into defiance and persistent aggression (Brame, Nagin, & Tremblay, 2001; Broidy et al., 2003). As they fail academically and are rejected by peers, they befriend other deviant youths, who facilitate one another's violent behavior (see Figure 12.3) (Lacourse et al., 2003). Limited cognitive and social skills result in high rates of school dropout and unemployment, contributing further to antisocial involvements (Patterson & Yoerger, 2002).

Preschoolers high in relational aggression also tend to be hyperactive and frequently in conflict with peers and adults (Willoughby, Kupersmidt, & Bryant, 2001). As these behaviors trigger peer rejection, relationally aggressive girls befriend other girls high in relational hostility, and their relational aggression rises (Werner & Crick, 2004). Adolescents high in relational aggression are often angry, vengeful, and defiant of adult rules. Among teenagers who combine physical and relational hostility, these oppositional reactions intensify, increasing the likelihood of serious antisocial activity (Harachi et al., 2006; Prinstein, Boergers, & Vernberg, 2001).

Late-Onset Type

Other youths first display antisocial behavior around the time of puberty, gradually increasing their involvement. Their conduct problems arise from the peer context, not from biological deficits and a history of unfavorable development. For some, quality of parenting may decline for a time, perhaps due to family stresses or the challenges of disciplining an unruly teenager (Moffitt, 2006). When age brings gratifying adult privileges, these youths draw on prosocial skills mastered before adolescence and abandon their antisocial ways.

A few late-onset youths do continue to engage in antisocial acts. The seriousness of their adolescent offenses seems to trap them in situations that close off opportunities for responsible behavior. Being employed or in school and forming positive, close relationships predict an end to criminal offending by age 20 to 25 (Clingempeel & Henggeler, 2003; Stouthamer-Loeber et al., 2004). In contrast, the longer antisocial young people spend in prison, the more likely they are to sustain a life of crime.

These findings suggest a need for a fresh look at policies aimed at stopping youth crime. Keeping youth offenders locked up for many years disrupts their vocational lives and access to social support during a crucial period of development, condemning them to a bleak future.

■ **FIGURE 12.3** ■ **Path to chronic delinquency for adolescents with childhood-onset antisocial behavior.** Difficult temperament and cognitive deficits characterize many of these youths in early childhood; some have attention-deficit hyperactivity disorder. Inept parenting transforms biologically based self-control difficulties into hostility and defiance.

with healthy economic and social conditions go a long way toward reducing adolescent antisocial acts.

Lacking resources for effective prevention, many U.S. schools have implemented *zero tolerance policies,* which punish all disruptive and threatening behavior, usually with suspension or expulsion. Yet often they are implemented inconsistently: Low-SES minority students are two to three times as likely to be punished, especially for minor misbehaviors (Goode & Goode, 2007; Skiba & Rausch, 2006). No evidence exists that zero tolerance reduces youth misconduct (Stinchcomb, Bazemore, & Riestenberg, 2006). To the contrary, some studies find that these policies heighten high school dropout and antisocial behavior.

Treating serious offenders requires an intensive, often lengthy approach, also directed at the multiple determinants of delinquency. In a program called *multisystemic therapy,* counselors combined family intervention with integrating violent youths into positive school, work, and leisure activities and disengaging them from deviant peers. Compared with conventional services or individual therapy, the intervention led to greater improvement in parent–child relations and school performance and a dramatic and sustained drop in number of arrests (Borduin, 2007; Henggeler, Sheidow, & Lee, 2007). Efforts to create nonaggressive environments—at the family, community, and cultural levels—are needed to help delinquent youths and to foster healthy development of all young people.

ASK YOURSELF

>> **REVIEW**
Why are adolescent girls at greater risk for depression and adolescent boys at greater risk for suicide?

>> **APPLY**
Zeke had been well-behaved in elementary school, but at age 13 he started spending time with the "wrong crowd." At age 16, he was arrested for property damage. Is Zeke likely to become a long-term offender? Why or why not?

Summary

Erikson's Theory: Identity versus Role Confusion

According to Erikson, what is the major personality achievement of adolescence?

>> Erikson's theory regards **identity** as the major personality achievement of adolescence. Young people who successfully resolve the psychological conflict of **identity versus role confusion** construct a solid self-definition consisting of self-chosen values and goals.

Self-Understanding

Describe changes in self-concept and self-esteem during adolescence.

>> Cognitive changes lead adolescents' self-descriptions to become more organized and consistent. Personal and moral values appear as key themes.

>> Self-esteem further differentiates and, for most adolescents, rises. Authoritative parenting and encouragement from teachers support positive self-esteem.

Describe the four identity statuses, along with factors that promote identity development.

>> Identity development is often measured by exploration of alternatives and commitment to self-chosen values and goals. **Identity achievement** (commitment, preceded by exploration) and **identity moratorium** (exploration without having reached commitment) are psychologically healthy identity statuses.

>> Long-term **identity foreclosure** (commitment without exploration) and **identity diffusion** (lack of both exploration and commitment) are related to adjustment difficulties.

>> An information-gathering cognitive style, healthy parental attachment, interaction with diverse peers, close friendships, and schools and communities that provide rich and varied opportunities promote healthy identity development. Similarly, supportive parents, peers, and schools can foster a strong, secure **ethnic identity** among minority adolescents. A **bicultural identity** offers additional emotional and social benefits.

© DAVID GROSSMAN/THE IMAGE WORKS

Moral Development

Describe Kohlberg's theory of moral development, and evaluate its accuracy.

>> According to Kohlberg, moral reasoning develops gradually through three levels, each of which contains two stages: At the **preconventional level,** morality is externally controlled by rewards, punishments, and authority figures; at the **conventional level,** conformity to laws and rules preserves positive human relationships and societal order; and at the **postconventional level,** morality is defined by abstract, universal principles of justice.

>> A reexamination of Kohlberg's stages suggests that moral maturity can be found at Stages 3 and 4; few people move beyond to the postconventional level. The influence of situational factors on moral judgment indicates that Kohlberg's moral stages are loosely organized and overlapping.

>> Contrary to Gilligan's claim, Kohlberg's theory does not underestimate the moral reasoning of females but instead taps both justice and caring moralities.

>> Compared with children, teenagers display more subtle reasoning about conflicts between personal choice and community obligation. They are also increasingly aware of the moral implications of following social conventions.

Describe influences on moral reasoning and its relationship to moral behavior.

>> Experiences contributing to moral maturity include warm, rational parenting, years of schooling, and peer discussions of moral issues. In village societies, where moral cooperation is based on direct relations between people, moral reasoning rarely moves beyond Kohlberg's Stage 3. In collectivist cultures, dilemma responses are more other-directed than in Western societies.

>> Maturity of moral reasoning is only modestly related to moral behavior. Moral action is also influenced by the individual's empathy and guilt, temperament, history of morally relevant experiences, and **moral self-relevance.**

© JEFF GREENBERG/ALAMY

>> Despite declines in formal religious involvement in adolescence, most religiously affiliated teenagers are advantaged in moral values and behavior.

Gender Typing

Why is early adolescence a period of gender intensification?

>> Biological, social, and cognitive factors jointly contribute to **gender intensification.** As pubertal changes occur and concern with what others think strengthens, teenagers focus on gender-linked attributes. Also, parents and dating partners encourage gender-appropriate behavior.

The Family

Discuss changes in parent–child and sibling relationships during adolescence.

>> In their quest for **autonomy,** adolescents strive to rely more on themselves and less on parents for decision making. As teenagers deidealize their parents, they often question parental authority. Warm, supportive parenting and consistent monitoring as part of a cooperative parent–adolescent relationship predict favorable outcomes.

>> Sibling relationships become less intense as adolescents separate from the family and turn toward peers. Still, attachment to siblings remains strong for most young people.

Peer Relations

Describe adolescent friendships, peer groups, and dating relationships and their consequences for development.

>> Adolescent friendships are based on greater intimacy, mutual understanding, and loyalty and contain more self-disclosure. Girls' friendships place greater emphasis on emotional closeness, boys' on shared activities and accomplishments.

>> As long as they are not characterized by jealousy, relational aggression, or attraction to antisocial behavior, adolescent friendships promote self-concept, perspective taking, identity, and the capacity for intimate relationships. They also help young people deal with stress and can improve attitudes toward school.

>> Adolescent peer groups are organized into more intimate **cliques,** particularly important to girls, and **crowds,** which grant teenagers an identity within the larger social structure of the school. Parenting styles influence the assortment of teenagers into cliques and crowds. With interest in dating, mixed-sex cliques grow in importance and then decline. Crowds also diminish, as teenagers settle on personal values and goals.

>> Intimacy in dating relationships lags behind that of same-sex friendships. Positive relationships with parents and friends contribute to secure romantic ties, which enhance emotional and social development in older teenagers.

© NICO KAI/ICONICA/GETTY IMAGES

Problems of Development

What factors are related to adolescent depression and suicide?

>> Depression is the most common psychological problem of the teenage years, with girls at greater risk in industrialized nations. Various combinations of biological and environmental factors are implicated—heredity, maladaptive parenting, a learned-helpless attributional style, and negative life events.

>> The suicide rate increases dramatically at adolescence. Boys account for most deaths by suicide, while girls make more unsuccessful suicide attempts. Teenagers at risk for suicide may be intelligent, solitary, and withdrawn, but more often, they are antisocial. Family turmoil is common in the backgrounds of suicidal adolescents.

Discuss factors related to delinquency.

>> Although almost all teenagers engage in some delinquent activity, only a few are serious repeat offenders. Most are boys with a childhood history of conduct problems.

>> A consistent factor related to delinquency is a family environment low in warmth, high in conflict, and characterized by inconsistent discipline and low monitoring. Poverty-stricken neighborhoods with high crime rates and ineffective schools also promote lawbreaking.

Important Terms and Concepts

Milestones
Development in Adolescence

Early Adolescence: 11–14

PHYSICAL

- If a girl, reaches peak of growth spurt. (284)
- If a girl, adds more body fat than muscle. (285)
- If a girl, starts to menstruate. (286)
- If a boy, begins growth spurt. (284)
- If a boy, starts to ejaculate seminal fluid. (286)
- Is likely to be aware of sexual orientation. (295)
- If a girl, motor performance increases gradually, leveling off by age 14. (285)
- Shows heightened stress response and novelty-seeking. (288)

COGNITIVE

- Shows gains in hypothetico-deductive reasoning and propositional thought. (301–302)
- Improves in scientific reasoning—coordinating theory with evidence—on complex, multivariable tasks. (303–304)
- Becomes more self-conscious and self-focused. (304–305)

- Becomes more idealistic and critical. (305)
- Metacognition and self-regulation continue to improve. (303)

EMOTIONAL/SOCIAL

- Self-concept includes abstract descriptors unifying separate personality traits, but these are are often contradictory and not interconnected. (314–315)
- Shows gender intensification—increased gender stereotyping of attitudes and behavior. (324)
- In striving for autonomy, spends less time with parents and siblings, more time with peers. (326)
- Friendships decline in number and are based on intimacy, mutual understanding, and loyalty. (326)
- Peer groups become organized around same-sex cliques. (328)
- Cliques with similar values form crowds. (328–329)
- Conformity in response to peer pressure increases. (332)

Middle Adolescence: 14–16

PHYSICAL

- If a girl, completes growth spurt. (284)
- If a boy, reaches peak of growth spurt. (284)
- If a boy, voice deepens. (286)
- If a boy, adds muscle while body fat declines. (285)
- If a boy, motor performance improves dramatically. (285)
- May have had sexual intercourse. (294–295)

COGNITIVE

- Continues to improve in hypothetico-deductive reasoning and propositional thought. (301–302)

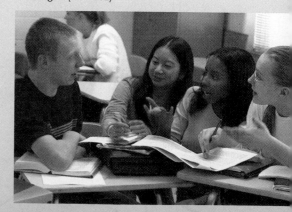

Note: Numbers in parentheses indicate the page or pages on which each milestone is discussed.

- Continues to improve in scientific reasoning, following a similar sequential order on different types of tasks. (304)
- Becomes less self-conscious and self-focused. (304–305)
- Improves in everyday decision making. (305–306)

EMOTIONAL/SOCIAL

- Combines features of the self into an organized self-concept. (315)
- Self-esteem differentiates further and tends to rise. (315)

- In most cases, begins to move from "lower" to "higher" identity statuses. (316)
- Is likely to engage in societal perspective taking. (262, 320)
- Increasingly emphasizes ideal reciprocity and societal laws as the basis for resolving moral dilemmas. (320)
- Engages in more subtle reasoning about conflicts between moral, social-conventional, and personal-choice issues. (321–322)
- Gender intensification declines. (324)
- Mixed-sex cliques become common. (328)
- Has probably started dating. (329)

PHYSICAL

- If a boy, completes growth spurt. (284)
- If a boy, gains in motor performance continue. (285)

COGNITIVE

- Continues to improve in metacognition, scientific reasoning, and decision making. (303–304, 305)

EMOTIONAL/SOCIAL

- Self-concept emphasizes personal and moral standards. (315)
- Continues to construct an identity, typically moving to higher identity statuses. (315–317)
- Continues to advance in maturity of moral reasoning. (319–321)
- Conformity to peer pressure may decline. (332)
- Cliques and crowds decline in importance. (329)
- Seeks psychological intimacy in romantic ties, which last longer. (329–330)

CHAPTER
13

Physical and Cognitive Development in Early Adulthood

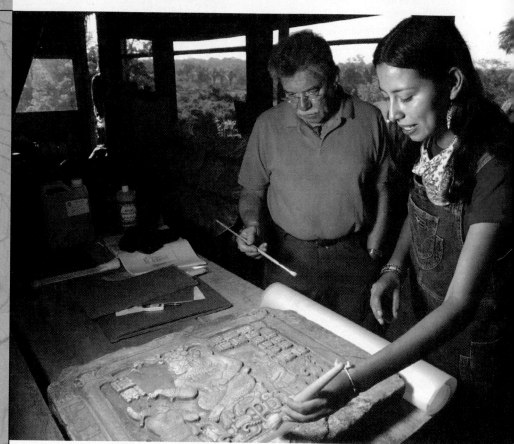

© DANIEL LECLAIR/REUTERS/CORBIS

Early adulthood brings momentous changes— among them, selecting a vocation, starting full-time work, and attaining economic independence. Once young adults embark on a career path, as this young Guatemalan archaeologist has, strong ties with mentors are vital for success.

The back seat and trunk piled high with belongings, 23-year-old Sharese hugged her mother and brother goodbye, jumped in the car, and headed toward the interstate with a sense of newfound freedom mixed with apprehension. Three months earlier, the family had watched proudly as Sharese received her bachelor's degree in chemistry from a small university 40 miles from her home. Her college years had been a time of gradual release from economic and psychological dependency on her family. She returned home periodically on weekends and lived there

during the summer months. But this day marked a turning point. She was moving to her own apartment in a city 800 miles away, with plans to work on a master's degree. With a teaching assistantship and a student loan, Sharese felt more "on her own" than at any previous time.

During her college years, Sharese made lifestyle changes and settled on a vocational direction. Overweight throughout high school, she lost 20 pounds in her sophomore year, revised her diet, and began an exercise regimen by joining the university's Ultimate Frisbee team, eventually becoming its captain. A summer spent as a counselor at a camp for chronically ill children helped convince Sharese to apply her background in science to a career in public health.

Still, two weeks before she was to leave, Sharese confided in her mother that she was having doubts about her decision. "Sharese," her mother advised, "we never know if our life choices are going to suit us just right, and most times they aren't perfect. It's what we make of them—how we view and mold them—that turns them into successes." So Sharese embarked on her journey and found herself face-to-face with a multitude of exciting challenges and opportunities.

In this chapter, we take up the physical and cognitive sides of early adulthood, which extends from about age 18 to 40. As noted in Chapter 1, the adult years are difficult to divide into discrete periods because the timing of important milestones varies greatly among individuals. But for most people, early adulthood involves a common set of tasks: leaving home, completing education, beginning full-time work, attaining economic independence, establishing a long-term sexually and emotionally intimate relationship, and starting a family. These are energetic decades filled with momentous decisions that—more than any other time of life—offer the potential for living to the fullest.

Physical Development

We have seen that throughout childhood and adolescence, the body grows larger and stronger, coordination improves, and sensory systems gather information more effectively. Once body structures reach maximum capacity and efficiency, **biological aging,** or **senescence,** begins—genetically influenced declines in the functioning of organs and systems that are universal in all members of our species. Like physical growth, however, biological aging varies widely across parts of the body, and individual differences are great—variation that the *lifespan perspective* helps us understand. A host of contextual factors—including each person's unique genetic makeup, lifestyle, living environment, and historical period—influence biological aging, each of which can accelerate or slow age-related declines (Arking, 2006). As a result, the physical changes of the adult years are, indeed, *multidimensional* and *multidirectional* (see page 6 in Chapter 1).

In the following sections, we examine the process of biological aging. Then we turn to physical and motor changes already under way in early adulthood. As you will see, biological aging can be modified substantially through behavioral and environmental interventions. Over the past century, improved

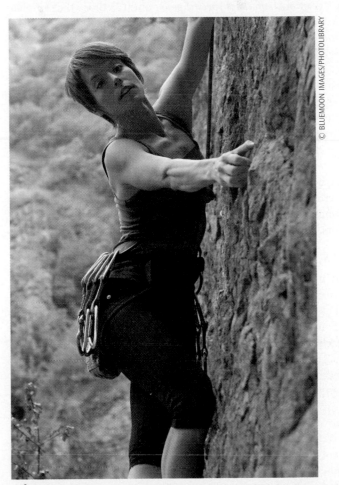

This rock climber, in her early twenties, is at her peak in strength, endurance, sensory acuteness, and immune system responsiveness.

nutrition, medical treatment, sanitation, and safety have added 25 to 30 years to *average life expectancy* in industrialized nations (see Chapter 1, page 5).

Biological Aging Is Under Way in Early Adulthood

In her early twenties, Sharese is at her peak in strength, endurance, sensory acuteness, and immune system responsiveness. Yet over the next two decades, she will age and, as she moves into middle and late adulthood, will show more noticeable declines.

Biological aging is the combined result of many causes, some operating at the level of DNA, others at the level of cells, and still others at the level of tissues, organs, and the whole organism. Hundreds of theories exist, indicating that our understanding is still in an early stage (Arking, 2006).

Aging at the Level of DNA and Body Cells

Current explanations of biological aging at the level of DNA and body cells are of two types: (1) those that emphasize the *programmed effects of specific genes* and (2) those that emphasize the *cumulative effects of random events* that damage genetic and cellular material. Evidence for both views exists, and a combination may eventually prove to be correct.

Genetically programmed aging receives some support from kinship studies indicating that longevity is a family trait. People whose parents had long lives tend to live longer themselves. And greater similarity exists in the lifespans of identical than fraternal twins. But the heritability of longevity is modest, ranging from .15 to .25 for age at death and from .27 to .57 for various measures of current biological age, such as strength of hand grip, respiratory capacity, blood pressure, and bone density (Cevenini et al., 2008; Kerber et al., 2001; Mitchell et al., 2001). Rather than inheriting longevity directly, people probably inherit one or more risk factors, which influence their chances of dying earlier or later.

One "genetic programming" theory proposes the existence of "aging genes" that control certain biological changes, such as menopause, gray hair, and deterioration of body cells. The strongest evidence for this view comes from research showing that human cells allowed to divide in the laboratory have a lifespan of 50 divisions, plus or minus 10 (Hayflick, 1998). With each duplication, a special type of DNA called **telomeres**—located at the ends of chromosomes, serving as a "cap" to protect the ends from destruction—shortens. Eventually, so little remains that the cells no longer duplicate at all. Telomere shortening acts as a brake against somatic mutations (such as those involved in cancer), which become more likely as cells duplicate (Wright & Shay, 2005). But an increase in the number of senescent cells (ones with short telomeres) also contributes to age-related disease, loss of function, and earlier mortality (Epel et al., 2009; Shin et al., 2006). As the Biology and Environment box on the following page reveals, researchers have begun to

identify health behaviors and psychological states that accelerate telomere shortening—powerful biological evidence that certain life circumstances compromise longevity.

According to an alternative, "random events" theory, DNA in body cells is gradually damaged through spontaneous or externally caused mutations. As these accumulate, cell repair and replacement become less efficient, and abnormal cancerous cells are often produced. Animal studies confirm an increase in DNA breaks and deletions and damage to other cellular material with age. Similar evidence is accruing for humans (Schumacher, Garinis, & Hoeijmakers, 2007).

One probable cause of age-related DNA and cellular abnormalities is the release of **free radicals**—naturally occurring, highly reactive chemicals that form in the presence of oxygen. (Radiation and certain pollutants and drugs can trigger similar effects.) When oxygen molecules break down within the cell, the reaction strips away an electron, creating a free radical. As it seeks a replacement from its surroundings, it destroys nearby cellular material, including DNA, proteins, and fats essential for cell functioning. Free radicals are thought to be involved in more than 60 disorders of aging, including cardiovascular disease, neurological disorders, cancer, cataracts, and arthritis (Barja, 2004; Cutler & Mattson, 2006). Although our bodies produce substances that neutralize free radicals, some harm occurs, and it accumulates over time.

Animal species with longer life expectancies display slower rates of free-radical damage to DNA (Sanz, Pamplona, & Barja, 2006). Some researchers believe that genes for longevity work by defending against free radicals. In this way, a programmed genetic response may limit random DNA and cellular deterioration.

Kinship studies indicate that longevity is a family trait. In addition to favorable heredity, these grandsons will likely benefit from the model of a fit, active grandfather who buffers stress by enjoying life.

© RONNIE KAUFMAN/LARRY HIRSHOWITZ/GETTY IMAGES/BLEND IMAGES

▪ BIOLOGY AND ENVIRONMENT ▪

Telomere Length: A New Marker of the Impact of Life Circumstances on Biological Aging

In the not-too-distant future, your annual physical exam may include an assessment of the length of your *telomeres*—DNA at the ends of chromosomes, which safeguard the stability of your cells. Telomeres shorten with each cell duplication; when they drop below a critical length, the cell can no longer divide and becomes senescent. Although telomeres shorten with age, the rate at which they do so varies greatly. An enzyme called *telomerase* prevents shortening and can even reverse the trend, causing telomeres to lengthen and, thus, protecting the aging cell.

Over the past decade, research examining the influence of life circumstances on telomere length has exploded. A well-established finding is that chronic illnesses, such as cardiovascular disease and cancer, hasten telomere shortening in white blood cells, which play a vital role in the immune response (see page 344). Telomere shortening, in turn, predicts more rapid disease progression and earlier death (Fuster & Andres, 2006).

Accelerated telomere shortening has been linked to a variety of unhealthy behaviors, including cigarette smoking and the physical inactivity and overeating that lead to obesity and to insulin resistance, which often precedes type 2 diabetes (Epel et al., 2006; Gardner et al., 2005). Unfavorable health conditions may alter telomere length as early as

the prenatal period, with possible long-term negative consequences for biological aging. In research on rats, poor maternal nutrition during pregnancy resulted in low birth weight and development of shorter telomeres in kidney and heart tissue (Jennings et al., 1999; Tarry-Adkins et al., 2008). In a human investigation, preschoolers who had been low-birth-weight as infants had shorter telomeres in their white blood cells than did their normal-birth-weight agemates (Raqib et al., 2007).

Persistent psychological stress—parenting a child with a chronic illness, caring for an elder with dementia, or severe depression—is linked to reduced telomerase activity and telomere shortness in white blood cells (Damjanovic et al., 2007; Epel et al., 2004; McEwen, 2007; Simon et al., 2006). Can stress actually modify telomeres? In a laboratory experiment, researchers exposed human white blood cells to the stress hormone cortisol. The cells responded by decreasing production of telomerase (Choi, Fauce, & Effros, 2008).

Fortunately, when adults make positive lifestyle changes, telomeres seem to respond accordingly. In one study, declines in psychological stress were associated with telomere lengthening in white blood cells (Epel et al., 2009). In an investigation of men with low-risk prostate cancer, three months of intensive improvement in diet and exercise led to

Accelerated telomere shortening has been linked to a variety of unhealthy behaviors. Fortunately, positive lifestyle changes, including healthy diet and exercise, seem to trigger a positive response in telomeres.

decreased blood cholesterol and psychological stress, along with increased white blood cell telomerase activity (Ornish et al., 2008).

Currently, researchers are working on identifying sensitive periods of telomere change—times when telomeres are most susceptible to modification. Early intervention—for example, enhanced prenatal care and interventions to reduce obesity in childhood—may be particularly powerful. But telomeres are changeable well into late adulthood (Epel et al., 2009). As our understanding of predictors and consequences of telomere length expands, it may become an important index of health and aging throughout life.

Foods rich in vitamins C and E and beta-carotene also forestall free-radical damage—a reason that improved diet contributes to gains in life expectancy (Milbury & Richer, 2008).

Aging at the Level of Tissues and Organs

What consequences might the DNA and cellular deterioration just described have for the structure and functioning of organs and tissues? There are many possibilities. Among those with clear support is the **cross-linkage theory of aging.** Over time, protein fibers that make up the body's connective tissue form bonds, or links, with one another. When these normally separate fibers cross-link, tissue becomes less elastic, leading to many negative outcomes, including loss of flexibility in the skin and other

organs, clouding of the lens of the eye, clogging of arteries, and damage to the kidneys. Like other aspects of aging, cross-linking can be reduced by external factors, including regular exercise and a vitamin-rich, low-fat diet (Schneider, 1992; Wickens, 2001).

Gradual failure of the endocrine system, which produces and regulates hormones, is yet another route to aging. An obvious example is decreased estrogen production in women, which culminates in menopause. Because hormones affect many body functions, disruptions in the endocrine system can have widespread effects on health and survival. For example, a gradual drop in growth hormone (GH) is associated with loss of muscle and bone mass, addition of body fat, thinning of the skin, and decline in cardiovascular functioning. In adults with abnormally low levels of GH, hormone therapy can slow these symptoms, but it has serious side effects, including increased risk of muscle pain and cancer (Harman & Blackman, 2004). So far, diet and physical activity are safer ways to limit these aspects of biological aging.

Finally, declines in immune system functioning contribute to many conditions of aging, including increased susceptibility to infectious disease and cancer and changes in blood vessel walls associated with cardiovascular disease. Decreased vigor of the immune response seems to be genetically programmed, but other aging processes we have considered (such as weakening of the endocrine system) can intensify it (Hawkley & Cacioppo, 2004; Malaguarnera et al., 2001).

Physical Changes

The physical changes of aging are summarized in Table 13.1. During the twenties and thirties, they are so gradual that most are hardly noticeable. We will examine several in detail here and take up others in later chapters.

Cardiovascular and Respiratory Systems

During her first month in graduate school, Sharese pored over research articles on cardiovascular functioning. In her African-American extended family, her father, an uncle, and three aunts had died of heart attacks in their forties and fifties. These tragedies prompted Sharese to reconsider her own health-related behaviors. She also decided to enter the field of public health in hopes of finding ways to relieve health problems among black Americans. *Hypertension,* or high blood pressure, occurs 12 percent more often in the U.S. black than in the U.S. white population; the rate of death from heart disease among African Americans is 30 percent higher (American Heart Association, 2009).

Sharese was surprised to learn that fewer age-related changes occur in the heart than we might expect, given that heart disease is a leading cause of death throughout adulthood, responsible for as many as 10 percent of U.S. male and 5 percent of U.S. female deaths between ages 20 and 34—figures that more than double in the following decade (Lloyd-Jones et al., 2009). In healthy individuals, the heart's ability to meet the body's oxygen requirements under typical conditions (as measured by heart rate in relation to volume of blood pumped) does not change during adulthood. Only during stressful exercise does heart performance decline with age—a change due to a decrease in maximum heart rate and greater rigidity of the heart muscle (Arking, 2006).

One of the most serious diseases of the cardiovascular system is *atherosclerosis,* in which heavy deposits of plaque containing cholesterol and fats collect on the walls of the main arteries. If present, it usually begins early in life, progresses during middle adulthood, and culminates in serious illness. Atherosclerosis is multiply determined, making it hard to separate the contributions of biological aging from individual genetic and environ-

mental influences. The complexity of causes is illustrated by animal research indicating that before puberty, a high-fat diet produces only fatty streaks on the artery walls (Olson, 2000). In sexually mature adults, however, it leads to serious plaque deposits, suggesting that sex hormones may heighten the insults of a high-fat diet.

Heart disease has decreased considerably since the mid-twentieth century, with a larger drop in the last 20 years due to a decline in cigarette smoking, to improved diet and exercise among at-risk individuals, and to better medical detection and treatment of high blood pressure and cholesterol (American Heart Association, 2008). Later, when we consider health and fitness, we will see why heart attacks were so common in Sharese's family—and why they occur at especially high rates in the African-American population.

Like the heart, lung capacity decreases during physical exertion. Maximum vital capacity (amount of air that can be forced in and out of the lungs) declines by 10 percent per decade after age 25 (Mahanran et al., 1999). Connective tissue in the lungs, chest muscles, and ribs stiffens with age, making it more difficult for the lungs to expand to full volume (Smith & Cotter, 2008). Fortunately, under normal conditions, we use less than half our vital capacity. Nevertheless, aging of the lungs contributes to older adults' difficulty in meeting the body's oxygen needs while exercising.

Motor Performance

Declines in heart and lung functioning under conditions of exertion, combined with gradual muscle loss, lead to changes in motor performance. In most people, the impact of biological aging on motor skills is difficult to separate from decreases in motivation and practice. Therefore, researchers study outstanding athletes, who try to attain their very best performance in real life (Tanaka & Seals, 2003).

In several investigations, the mean ages for best performance of Olympic and professional athletes in a variety of sports were charted over time. Absolute performance in most events improved over the past century, suggesting improved training methods. But ages of best performance remained relatively constant. Athletic tasks that require speed of limb movement, explosive strength, and gross-motor coordination—sprinting, jumping, and tennis—typically peak in the early twenties. Those that depend on endurance, arm–hand steadiness, and aiming—long-distance running, baseball, and golf—usually peak in the late twenties and early thirties. Because these skills require either stamina or precise motor control, they take longer to perfect (Schulz & Curnow, 1988).

These findings tell us that the upper biological limit of motor capacity is reached in the first part of early adulthood. How quickly do athletic skills weaken in later years? Longitudinal research on master runners reveals that as long as practice continues, speed drops only slightly from the mid-thirties into the sixties, when performance falls off at an accelerating pace (see Figure 13.1 on page 344) (Tanaka & Higuchi, 1998; Trappe,

■ **TABLE 13.1** ■ *Physical Changes of Aging*

ORGAN OR SYSTEM	TIMING OF CHANGE	DESCRIPTION
Sensory		
Vision	From age 30	As the lens stiffens and thickens, ability to focus on close objects declines. Yellowing of the lens, weakening of muscles controlling the pupil, and clouding of the vitreous (gelatin-like substance that fills the eye) reduce light reaching the retina, impairing color discrimination and night vision. Visual acuity, or fineness of discrimination, decreases, with a sharp drop between ages 70 and 80.
Hearing	From age 30	Sensitivity to sound declines, especially at high frequencies but gradually extending to all frequencies. Change is more than twice as rapid for men as for women.
Taste	From age 60	Sensitivity to the four basic tastes—sweet, salty, sour, and bitter—is reduced. This may be due to factors other than aging, since number and distribution of taste buds do not change.
Smell	From age 60	Loss of smell receptors reduces ability to detect and identify odors.
Touch	Gradual	Loss of touch receptors reduces sensitivity on the hands, particularly the fingertips.
Cardiovascular	Gradual	As the heart muscle becomes more rigid, maximum heart rate decreases, reducing the heart's ability to meet the body's oxygen requirements when stressed by exercise. As artery walls stiffen and accumulate plaque, blood flow to body cells is reduced.
Respiratory	Gradual	Under physical exertion, respiratory capacity decreases and breathing rate increases. Stiffening of connective tissue in the lungs and chest muscles makes it more difficult for the lungs to expand to full volume.
Immune	Gradual	Shrinking of the thymus limits maturation of T cells and disease-fighting capacity of B cells, impairing the immune response.
Muscular	Gradual	As nerves stimulating them die, fast-twitch muscle fibers (responsible for speed and explosive strength) decline in number and size to a greater extent than slow-twitch fibers (which support endurance). Tendons and ligaments (which transmit muscle action) stiffen, reducing speed and flexibility of movement.
Skeletal	Begins in the late thirties, accelerates in the fifties, slows in the seventies	Cartilage in the joints thins and cracks, leading bone ends beneath it to erode. New cells continue to be deposited on the outer layer of the bones, and mineral content of bone declines. The resulting broader but more porous bones weaken the skeleton and make it more vulnerable to fracture. Change is more rapid in women than in men.
Reproductive	In women, accelerates after age 35; in men, begins after age 40	Fertility problems (including difficulty conceiving and carrying a pregnancy to term) and risk of having a baby with a chromosomal disorder increase.
Nervous	From age 50	Brain weight declines as neurons lose water content and die, mostly in the cerebral cortex, and as ventricles (spaces) within the brain enlarge. Development of new synapses and limited generation of new neurons can, in part, compensate for these declines.
Skin	Gradual	Epidermis (outer layer) is held less tightly to the dermis (middle layer); fibers in the dermis and hypodermis (inner layer) thin; fat cells in the hypodermis decline. As a result, the skin becomes looser, less elastic, and wrinkled. Change is more rapid in women than in men.
Hair	From age 35	Grays and thins.
Height	From age 50	Loss of bone strength leads to collapse of disks in the spinal column, leading to a height loss of as much as 2 inches by the seventies and eighties.
Weight	Increases to age 50; declines from age 60	Weight change reflects a rise in fat and a decline in muscle and bone mineral. Since muscle and bone are heavier than fat, the resulting pattern is weight gain followed by loss. Body fat accumulates on the torso and decreases on the extremities.

Sources: Arking, 2006; Whalley, 2001; Whitbourne, 1996.

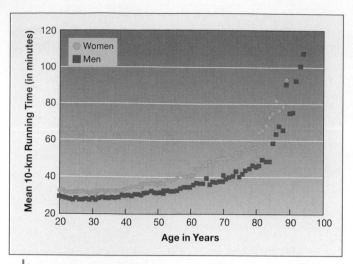

■ FIGURE 13.1 ■ Ten-kilometer running times with advancing age, based on longitudinal performances of hundreds of master athletes. Runners maintain their speed into the mid-thirties, followed by modest increases in running times into the sixties, with a progressively steeper increase thereafter. (From H. Tanaka & D. R. Seals, 2003, "Dynamic Exercise Performance in Masters Athletes: Insight into the Effects of Primary Human Aging on Physiological Functional Capacity," *Journal of Applied Physiology, 5*, p. 2153. Adapted with permission of The American Physiological Society.)

2007). In the case of long-distance swimming—a non-weight-bearing exercise with a low incidence of injury—the decline in speed is even more gradual: The accelerating performance drop-off is delayed until the seventies (Tanaka & Seals, 1997).

In sum, before late adulthood, biological aging accounts for only a small part of age-related decline until advanced old age. Lower levels of performance by healthy people into their sixties and seventies largely reflect reduced capacities resulting from a less physically demanding lifestyle.

In 2009, 37-year-old Lance Armstrong attempted the near-impossible by going for an eighth victory in the Tour de France, the world's toughest cycling race. He scored an impressive third place; first and second place went to cyclists more than ten years younger. Sustained training leads to adaptations in body structures that minimize motor decline into the sixties.

Immune System

The immune response is the combined work of specialized cells that neutralize or destroy antigens (foreign substances) in the body. Two types of white blood cells play vital roles. *T cells*, which originate in the bone marrow and mature in the thymus (a small gland located in the upper part of the chest), attack antigens directly. *B cells*, manufactured in the bone marrow, secrete antibodies into the bloodstream that multiply, capture antigens, and permit the blood system to destroy them. Since receptors on their surfaces recognize only a single antigen, T and B cells come in great variety. They join with additional cells to produce immunity.

The capacity of the immune system to offer protection against disease increases through adolescence and declines after age 20. The trend is partly due to changes in the thymus, which is largest during the teenage years, then shrinks until it is barely detectable by age 50. As a result, production of thymic hormones is reduced, and the thymus is less able to promote full maturity and differentiation of T cells. Because B cells release far more antibodies when T cells are present, the immune response is compromised further (Weng, 2008).

Withering of the thymus is not the only reason that the body gradually becomes less effective in warding off illness. The immune system interacts with the nervous and endocrine systems. For example, psychological stress can weaken the immune response (Coe & Laudenslager, 2007; Larbi et al., 2008). During final exams, for example, Sharese was less resistant to colds. And in the month after her father died, she had great difficulty recovering from the flu. Divorce, caring for an ill aging parent, sleep deprivation, and chronic depression can also reduce immunity (Hamer, Wolvers, & Albers, 2004; Robles & Kiecolt-Glaser, 2003). And physical stress—from pollution, allergens, poor nutrition, and rundown housing—undermines immune functioning throughout adulthood. When physical and psychological stress combine, the risk of illness is magnified (Friedman & Lawrence, 2002).

Reproductive Capacity

Many people believe that pregnancy during the twenties is ideal, not only because of lower risk of miscarriage and chromosomal disorders (see Chapter 2) but also because younger parents have more energy to keep up with active children. However, first births to women in their thirties have increased greatly over the past three decades. Many people are delaying childbearing until their education is complete and their careers are well-established.

Nevertheless, reproductive capacity does decline with age. Fertility problems among women increase from age 15 to 50. Between ages 15 and 29, 8 percent of U.S. women surveyed report difficulties, a figure that rises to 14 percent among 30- to 34-year-olds and 18 percent among 35- to 44-year-olds, when the success of reproductive technologies drops sharply (see page 42 in Chapter 2) (U.S. Department of Health and Human Services, 2009a). In many mammals, including humans, a certain level of reserve ova in the ovaries is necessary for conception. Some women have normal menstrual cycles but do not conceive because their reserve of ova is too low—the major cause of the female age-related decline in fertility (Djahanbakhch, Ezzati, & Zosmer, 2007). In males, semen volume, sperm motility, and percentage of normal sperm decrease gradually after age 35, contributing to reduced fertility rates in older men (Lambert, Masson, & Fisch, 2006).

ASK YOURSELF

≫ REVIEW
How do life conditions that accelerate telomere shortening illustrate the joint influence of heredity and environment on biological aging?

≫ APPLY
Penny is a long-distance runner for her college track team. She wonders what her running performance will be like 30 years from now. What factors will affect Penny's future athletic skill?

≫ REFLECT
Before reading this chapter, had you thought of early adulthood as a period of aging? Why is it important for young adults to be conscious of factors that contribute to biological aging?

Health and Fitness

Figure 13.2 displays leading causes of death in early adulthood in the United States. Death rates for all causes exceed those of other industrialized nations—a difference believed to be due to a combination of factors, including higher rates of poverty and extreme obesity, more lenient gun-control policies, and lack of universal, government-sponsored health insurance (OECD, 2008b; Torrey & Haub, 2004). But, as we have noted, wide individual and group differences in physical changes are linked to environmental risks and health-related behaviors.

SES variations in health over the lifespan reflect these influences. Income, education, and occupational status show strong and continuous relationships with almost every disease and health indicator (Adler & Newman, 2002; Alwin & Wray, 2005; Geiger, 2007). Longitudinal evidence confirms that economically advantaged and well-educated individuals sustain better health over most of their adult lives, whereas the health of lower-income individuals with limited education steadily declines (Lantz et al., 1998, 2001). SES differences in health-related circumstances and habits—stressful life events, crowding, pollution, diet, exercise, overweight and obesity, substance abuse, jobs with numerous health risks, availability of supportive social relationships, and (in the United States) access to affordable health care—are largely responsible (Brand et al., 2007; Evans & Kantrowitz, 2002; Wray, Alwin, & McCammon, 2005).

SES disparities in health and mortality are larger in the United States than in other industrialized nations (Mackenbach, 2002). Besides the lack of universal health insurance, poverty-stricken U.S. families have lower incomes than those classified as poor in other countries. In addition, SES groups are more likely to be segregated by neighborhood in the United States, resulting in greater inequalities in environmental factors that affect health, such as housing, pollution, education, and community services.

These findings reveal, once again, that the living conditions that nations and communities provide combine with those that people create for themselves to affect physical aging. Because the incidence of health problems is much lower during the twenties and thirties than later on, early adulthood is an excellent time to prevent later problems. In the following sections, we take up a variety of major health concerns—nutrition, exercise, substance abuse, sexuality, and psychological stress.

Nutrition

Bombarded with advertising claims and an extraordinary variety of food choices, adults find it increasingly difficult to make wise dietary decisions. An abundance of food, combined with a heavily scheduled life, means that most Americans eat because they feel like it or because it is time to do so rather than to maintain the body's functions (Donatelle, 2009). Overweight

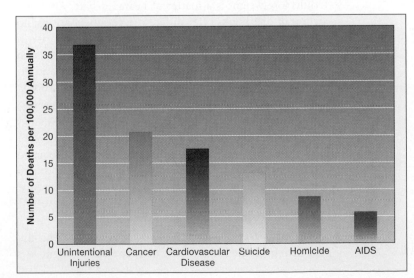

■ **FIGURE 13.2** ■ **Leading causes of death between 25 and 44 years of age in the United States.** Nearly half of unintentional injuries are motor vehicle accidents. As later chapters will reveal, unintentional injuries remain a leading cause of death at older ages, rising sharply in late adulthood. Rates of cancer and cardiovascular disease rise steadily over middle and late adulthood. (Adapted from U.S. Census Bureau, 2009b.)

and obesity and a high-fat diet are widespread nutritional problems with long-term consequences for health in adulthood.

■ OVERWEIGHT AND OBESITY.

In Chapter 9, we noted that obesity (a greater than 20 percent increase over average body weight, based on age, sex, and physical build) has increased dramatically in many Western nations. Among adults, a body mass index (BMI) of 25 to 29 constitutes overweight, a BMI of 30 or greater (amounting to 30 or more excess pounds) constitutes obesity. Today, 34 percent of U.S. adults are obese. The rate rises to 35 percent among Native Americans, 36 percent among Hispanics, and 45 percent among African Americans. In the United States and Western Europe, 5 to 7 percent more women than men suffer from obesity (Tjepkema, 2005; U.S. Department of Health and Human Services, 2009a, 2009c).

Overweight—a less extreme but nevertheless unhealthy condition—affects an additional 33 percent of Americans. Combine the rates of overweight and obesity and the total, 67 percent, makes Americans the heaviest people in the world. **TAKE A MOMENT...** Notice in these figures that the U.S. obesity rate now exceeds its rate of overweight, a blatant indicator of the growing severity of the problem.

Recall from Chapter 9 that overweight children are very likely to become overweight adults. But a substantial number of people show large weight gains in adulthood, most often between ages 25 and 40. And young adults who were already overweight or obese typically get heavier, leading obesity rates to rise steadily between ages 20 and 60 (Tjepkema, 2005; U.S. Department of Health and Human Services, 2009a).

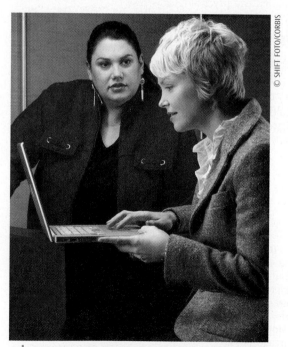

Overweight adults suffer enormous social discrimination. Which of these two young career women is more likely to find a mate, successfully vie for a new job, and be treated kindly by others?

Causes and Consequences. With the decline in need for physical labor in the home and workplace, our lives have become more sedentary. Meanwhile, the average number of calories and amount of sugar and fat consumed by Americans rose over most of the twentieth and early twenty-first century, with a sharp increase after 1970.

Adding some weight between ages 25 and 50 is a normal part of aging because **basal metabolic rate (BMR), the amount of energy the body uses at complete rest,** gradually declines as the number of active muscle cells (which create the greatest energy demand) drops off. But excess weight is strongly associated with serious health problems (see page 227 in Chapter 9)—including type 2 diabetes, heart disease, and many forms of cancer—and with early death. Furthermore, overweight adults suffer enormous social discrimination. Compared with their normal-weight agemates, they are less likely to find mates, be rented apartments, receive financial aid for college, or be offered jobs. And they report frequent mistreatment by family members, peers, co-workers, and health professionals (Andreyeva, Puhl, & Brownell, 2008; Puhl & Brownell, 2006).

Treatment. Because obesity climbs in early and middle adulthood, treatment for adults should begin as soon as possible. Even moderate weight loss reduces health problems substantially (Orzano & Scott, 2004). But most individuals who start a weight-loss program return to their original weight, and often to a higher weight, within two years (Vogels, Diepvens, & Westerterp-Plantenga, 2005). The high rate of failure is partly due to limited knowledge of just how obesity disrupts the complex neural, hormonal, and metabolic factors that maintain a normal body-weight set point. Until more information is available, researchers are examining the features of treatments and participants associated with greater success. The following elements promote lasting behavior change:

■ *A well-balanced diet lower in calories and fat, plus exercise.* To lose weight, Sharese sharply reduced calories, sugar, and fat in her diet and exercised regularly. The precise balance of dietary protein, carbohydrates, and fats that best helps adults lose weight is a matter of heated debate. Although scores of diet books offer different recommendations, no clear-cut evidence exists for the long-term superiority of one approach over others (Tsai & Wadden, 2005). Research does confirm that restricting calorie and fat intake and increasing physical activity are essential (Franz et al., 2007).

■ *Training participants to keep an accurate record of what they eat.* About 30 to 35 percent of obese people sincerely believe they eat less than they do, and from 25 to 45 percent report problems with binge eating—a behavior associated with weight-loss treatment failure (Blaine & Rodman, 2007; Wadden & Foster, 2000). When Sharese became aware of how often she ate when she was not actually hungry, she was better able to limit her food intake.

■ *Social support.* Group or individual counseling and encouragement from friends and relatives help sustain weight-loss efforts by fostering self-esteem (Dansinger et al., 2007). Once Sharese decided to act, with the support of her family and a weight-loss counselor, she began to feel better about herself even before the first pounds were shed.

■ *Teaching problem-solving skills.* Acquiring cognitive and behavioral strategies for coping with tempting situations and periods of slowed progress is associated with long-term change. Weight-loss maintainers are more likely than individuals who relapse to be conscious of their behavior, to use social support, and to confront problems directly (Cooper & Fairburn, 2002).

■ *Extended intervention.* Longer treatments (from 25 to 40 weeks) that include the components listed here grant people time to develop new habits.

■ **DIETARY FAT.** During college, Sharese altered the diet of her childhood and adolescent years, sharply limiting red meat, eggs, butter, and fried foods. U.S. national dietary recommendations include reducing dietary fat to 30 percent of total caloric intake, with no more than 10 percent made up of saturated fat, which generally comes from meat and dairy products and is solid at room temperature (U.S. Department of Health and Human Services, 2009a). Many researchers believe that fat consumption plays a role in breast cancer and (when it includes large amounts of red meat) is linked to colon cancer (Blackburn & Wang, 2007; Kono, 2004). But the main reasons for limiting dietary fat are the strong connection of total fat with obesity and of saturated fat with cardiovascular disease (Bruner et al., 2007). Nevertheless, despite a slight drop in fat consumption, most American adults eat too much.

Moderate fat consumption is essential for normal body functioning. But when we consume too much, some is converted

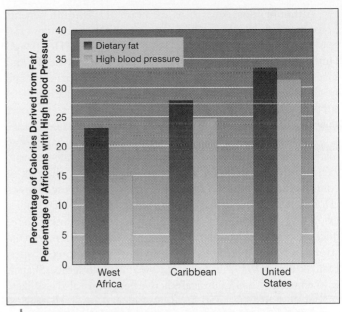

■ **FIGURE 13.3** ■ **Dietary fat and prevalence of high blood pressure among Africans in West Africa, the Caribbean, and the United States.** The three regions represent the historic path of the slave trade and, therefore, have genetically similar populations. As dietary fat increases, high blood pressure and heart disease rise. Both are particularly high among African Americans. (Adapted from Luke et al., 2001.)

to cholesterol, which accumulates as plaque on the arterial walls in atherosclerosis. Earlier in this chapter, we noted that atherosclerosis is determined by multiple biological and environmental factors. But excess fat consumption (along with other societal conditions) is a major contributor to the high rate of heart disease in the U.S. black population. When researchers compare Africans in West Africa, the Caribbean, and the United States (the historic path of the slave trade), dietary fat increases, and so do high blood pressure and heart disease (see Figure 13.3) (Luke et al., 2001). Indeed, West Africans have one of the lowest rates of heart disease in the world.

The best rule of thumb is to eat less fat of all kinds and to substitute unsaturated for saturated fat when possible. Furthermore, regular exercise can reduce the harmful influence of dietary fat because it creates chemical byproducts that help eliminate cholesterol from the body.

Exercise

Three times a week, over the noon hour, Sharese delighted in running, making her way to a wooded trail that cut through a picturesque area of the city. Regular exercise kept her fit and slim, and she noticed that she caught fewer respiratory illnesses than in the days when she had been sedentary and overweight. As Sharese explained to a friend, "Exercise gives me a positive outlook and calms me down. Afterward, I feel a burst of energy that gets me through the day."

A balanced, low-fat diet promotes physical and psychological well-being and contributes to a normal body weight.

Although most Americans are aware of the health benefits of exercise, about 40 percent are inactive, with no regular brief sessions of even light activity (U.S. Department of Health and Human Services, 2009a). More women than men are inactive. And inactivity is greater among low-SES adults, who live in less safe neighborhoods, have more health problems, experience less social support for exercising regularly, and feel less personal control over their health (Grzywacz & Marks, 2001; Wilson et al., 2004).

Besides reducing body fat and building muscle, exercise fosters resistance to disease. Frequent bouts of moderate-intensity exercise enhance the immune response, lowering the risk of colds or flu and promoting faster recovery from these illnesses (Donatelle, 2009). Furthermore, in several longitudinal studies extending over 10 to 20 years, physical activity was linked to reduced incidence of cancer at all body sites except the skin, with the strongest findings for cancer of the rectum and colon (Albanes, Blair, & Taylor, 1989; Tardon et al., 2005; Wannamethee, Shaper, & Macfarlane, 1993). Physically active people are also less likely to develop diabetes and cardiovascular disease (Bassuk & Manson, 2005). If they do, these illnesses typically occur later and are less severe than among their inactive agemates.

How does exercise help prevent these serious illnesses? First, it reduces the incidence of obesity. In addition, people who exercise probably adopt other healthful behaviors, thereby lowering the risk of diseases associated with high-fat diets, alcohol consumption, and smoking. Exercise also promotes

cardiovascular functioning by strengthening the heart muscle, decreasing blood pressure, and producing a form of "good cholesterol" (high-density lipoproteins, or HDLs) that helps remove "bad cholesterol" (low-density lipoproteins, or LDLs) from the artery walls (Donatelle, 2009).

Yet another way that exercise may guard against illness is through its mental health benefits. Physical activity reduces anxiety and depression and improves mood, alertness, and energy. Furthermore, as EEG and fMRI evidence indicates, exercise enhances neural activity in the cerebral cortex and improves overall cognitive functioning (Hillman, Erickson, & Kramer, 2008; Johnson & Krueger, 2007; Penedo & Dahn, 2005). The stress-reducing properties of exercise undoubtedly strengthen immunity to disease. And as physical activity enhances cognitive functioning and psychological well-being, it promotes on-the-job productivity, self-esteem, ability to cope with stress, and life satisfaction.

How much exercise is recommended for a healthier, happier, and longer life? Moderately intense physical activity—for example, 30 minutes of brisk walking—on most days leads to health benefits for previously inactive people. Adults who exercise at greater intensity—enough to build up a sweat—derive even greater protection against cardiovascular disease, diabetes, colon cancer, and obesity (Hu & Manson, 2001; Yu et al., 2003). Currently, the U.S. government recommends 30 minutes of moderate-intensity physical activity on five or more days per week or 20 or more minutes of vigorous-intensity exercise (for example, jogging, biking uphill, fast swimming) on three or more days per week (U.S. Department of Health and Human Services, 2009d).

Substance Abuse

Eager to try a wide range of experiences before settling down to the responsibilities of adulthood, U.S. 19- to 22-year-olds are more likely than younger or older individuals to smoke cigarettes, chew tobacco, use marijuana, and take stimulants to enhance cognitive or physical performance (U.S. Department of Health and Human Services, 2009b). Binge drinking and experimentation with prescription drugs (such as OxyContin, a highly addictive painkiller) and "party drugs" (such as LSD and MDMA, or Ecstasy) also increase, at times with tragic consequences. Risks include brain damage, lasting impairments in mental functioning, and unintentional injury and death (Burgess, O'Donohoe, & Gill, 2000; Montoya et al., 2002).

Furthermore, when alcohol and drug taking become chronic, they intensify the psychological problems that underlie addiction. As many as 20 percent of U.S. 21- to 25-year-olds are substance abusers (U.S. Department of Health and Human Services, 2009b). The same personal and situational conditions that lead to abuse in adolescence are predictive in the adult years (see page 300 in Chapter 11). Cigarette smoking and alcohol consumption are the most common substance disorders.

© LORI ADAMSKI PEEK/GETTY IMAGES/STONE

Regular, moderate-to-vigorous exercise predicts a healthier, longer life. Participants in this kickboxing class reap both physical and mental health benefits.

■ **CIGARETTE SMOKING.** Dissemination of information on the harmful effects of cigarette smoking has helped reduce its prevalence among U.S. adults from 40 percent in 1965 to 24 percent in 2007 (U.S. Department of Health and Human Services, 2009b). Still, smoking has declined very slowly, and most of the drop is among college graduates, with very little change for those who did not finish high school. Furthermore, although more men than women smoke, the gender gap is much smaller today than in the past, reflecting a sharp increase in smoking among young women who did not finish high school. Smoking among college students has also risen—for students of both sexes and of diverse ethnicities. More than 90 percent of men and 85 percent of women who smoke started before age 21 (U.S. Department of Health and Human Services, 2009b). And the earlier people start smoking, the greater their daily cigarette consumption and likelihood of continuing, an important reason that preventive efforts with adolescents and young adults are vital.

The ingredients of cigarette smoke—nicotine, tar, carbon monoxide, and other chemicals—leave their damaging mark throughout the body, in deterioration of the retina of the eye; skin abnormalities, including premature aging, poor wound healing, and hair loss; decline in bone mass; decrease in reserve ova and earlier menopause in women; and reduced sperm count and higher rate of sexual impotence in men (American Society for Reproductive Medicine, 2004; Freiman et al., 2004; Thornton et al., 2005). Other deadly outcomes include increased risk of heart attack, stroke, acute leukemia, melanoma, and cancer of the mouth, throat, larynx, esophagus, lungs, stomach, pancreas, kidneys, and bladder.

Cigarette smoking is the most preventable cause of death in industrialized nations (U.S. Department of Health and Human Services, 2008a). Benefits of quitting include return of most disease risks to nonsmoker levels within three to eight years. Although millions of people have stopped smoking without help, those who enter treatment programs or use cessation aids (for example, nicotine gum, nasal spray, or patches, designed to reduce dependency gradually) often fail: After one year, 70 to 90 percent start smoking again (Ludvig, Miner, & Eisenberg, 2005). Unfortunately, too few treatments last long enough or teach skills for avoiding relapse.

■ **ALCOHOL.** National surveys reveal that about 11 percent of men and 3 percent of women in the United States are heavy drinkers (U.S. Department of Health and Human Services, 2009b). About one-third of this group are *alcoholics*—people who cannot limit their alcohol use. In men, alcoholism usually begins in the teens and early twenties and worsens over the following decade. In women, its onset is typically later, in the twenties and thirties, and its course is more variable (John et al., 2003).

Twin studies support a genetic contribution to alcoholism (Tsuang et al., 2001). But whether a person comes to deal with life's problems through drinking is greatly affected by personal characteristics and circumstances: Half of hospitalized alcoholics have no family history of problem drinking (Hawkins, Catalano, & Miller, 1992). Alcoholism crosses SES and ethnic lines but is higher in some groups than others. In cultures where alcohol is a traditional part of religious or ceremonial ac-

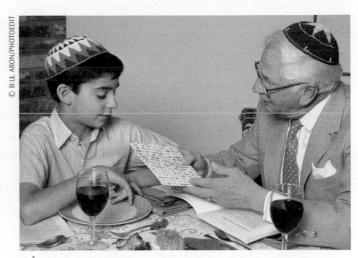

In cultures where alcohol is a traditional part of religious or ceremonial activities, people are less likely to abuse it. This Jewish grandfather teaches his grandson the customs of the Passover Seder, which include blessing and drinking wine.

tivities, people are less likely to abuse it. Where access to alcohol is carefully controlled and viewed as a sign of adulthood, dependency is more likely—factors that may, in part, explain why college students drink more heavily than young people not enrolled in college (Slutske et al., 2004). Poverty and hopelessness also promote excessive drinking (U.S. Department of Health and Human Services, 2009b).

Alcohol acts as a depressant, impairing the brain's ability to control thought and action. In a heavy drinker, it relieves anxiety at first but then induces it as the effects wear off, so the alcoholic drinks again. The best-known complication of chronic alcohol use is liver disease, but it is also linked to cardiovascular disease, inflammation of the pancreas, irritation of the intestinal tract, bone marrow problems, disorders of the blood and joints, and some forms of cancer. Over time, alcohol causes brain damage, leading to confusion, apathy, inability to learn, and impaired memory (Brun & Andersson, 2001). The costs to society are enormous. About 40 percent of fatal motor vehicle crashes in the United States involve drivers who have been drinking (Pickrell, 2006). About half of police activities in large cities involve alcohol-related offenses (McKim, 2002). Alcohol frequently plays a part in sexual coercion, including date rape, and in domestic violence.

The most successful treatments combine personal and family counseling, group support, and aversion therapy (use of medication that produces a physically unpleasant reaction to alcohol). Nevertheless, breaking an addiction that has dominated a person's life is difficult; about 50 percent of alcoholics relapse within a few months (Volpicelli, 2001).

Sexuality

At the end of high school, about 65 percent of U.S. young people have had sexual intercourse; by age 25, nearly all have done so, and the gender and SES differences that were apparent in adolescence (see pages 294–295 in Chapter 11) have diminished (U.S. Department of Health and Human Services, 2008k). Compared with earlier generations, contemporary adults display a wider range of sexual choices and lifestyles, including cohabitation, marriage, extramarital experiences, and orientation toward a heterosexual or homosexual partner. In this chapter, we explore the attitudes, behaviors, and health concerns that arise as sexual activity becomes a regular event in young people's lives. In Chapter 14, we focus on the emotional side of close relationships.

■ HETEROSEXUAL ATTITUDES AND BEHAVIOR.

One Friday evening, Sharese accompanied her roommate Heather to a young singles bar. Shortly after they arrived, two young men joined them. Faithful to her boyfriend, Ernie, whom she had met in college and who worked in another city, Sharese remained aloof for the next hour. In contrast, Heather was talkative and gave one of the men, Rich, her phone number. The next weekend, Heather went out with Rich. On the second date, they had intercourse, but the romance lasted only a few weeks. Aware of Heather's more adventurous sex life, Sharese wondered whether her own was normal. Only after several months of dating exclusively had she and Ernie slept together.

What are the sexual attitudes and behaviors of contemporary adults? Answers were difficult to find until the National Health and Social Life Survey, the first in-depth study of U.S. adults' sex lives based on a nationally representative sample, was carried out in the early 1990s. Nearly four out of five randomly chosen 18- to 59-year-olds agreed to participate—3,400 in all. Findings were remarkably similar to those of surveys conducted at about the same time in France, Great Britain, and Finland, and to a more recent U.S. survey (Langer, 2004; Laumann et al., 1994; Michael et al., 1994).

Although their sexual practices are diverse, adults in Western nations are far less sexually active than we have come to believe on the basis of widespread display of sexuality in the media. Monogamous, emotionally committed couples like Sharese and Ernie are more typical (and more satisfied) than couples like Heather and Rich.

Sexual partners, whether dating, cohabiting, or married, usually do not select each other arbitrarily. They tend to be similar in age (within five years), education, ethnicity, and (to a lesser extent) religion. In addition, people who establish lasting relationships usually meet in conventional ways—either through family members or friends, or at work, school, or social events where people similar to themselves congregate. Sustaining an intimate relationship is easier when adults share interests and values and people they know approve of the match.

Over the past decade, Internet dating services have become an increasingly popular way to initiate relationships. According to one estimate, over 40 percent of single U.S. adults visit these matchmaking websites (Mazzarella, 2007). Although success rates are lower than with conventional strategies, adults who

Sexual partners tend to be similar in age, education, ethnicity, and religion. And those who establish lasting relationships usually meet through family members or friends, or at work, school, or social events where people similar to themselves congregate.

form an online relationship and then meet face-to-face often go on to see each other again, with 18 percent of such ties lasting for more than a year (Gavin, Scott, & Duffield, 2005).

Consistent with popular belief, Americans today have more sexual partners over their lifetimes than they did a generation ago. For example, one-third of adults over age 50 have had five or more partners, whereas half of 30- to 50-year-olds have accumulated that many in much less time. And although women are more opposed to casual sex then men, after excluding a small number of men (less than 3 percent) with a great many sexual partners, contemporary men and women differ little in average number of lifetime sexual partners (Langer, 2004). Why is this so? From an evolutionary perspective, contemporary effective contraception has permitted sexual activity with little risk of pregnancy, enabling women to have as many partners as men without risking the welfare of their offspring.

But when adults of any age are asked how many partners they have had in the past year, the usual reply (for about 70 percent) is one. What explains the trend toward more relationships in the context of sexual commitment? In the past, dating several partners was followed by marriage. Today, dating more often gives way to cohabitation, which leads either to marriage or to breakup. In addition, people are marrying later, and the divorce rate remains high. Together, these factors create more opportunities for new partners. Still, surveys of college students reveal that almost all want to settle down with a mutually exclusive sexual partner eventually (Pedersen et al., 2002). In line with this goal, most people spend the majority of their lives with one partner.

How often do Americans have sex? Not nearly as frequently as the media suggest. One-third of 18- to 59-year-olds have intercourse as often as twice a week, another third have it a few times a month, and the remaining third have it a few times a year or not at all. Three factors affect frequency of sexual activity: age, whether people are cohabiting or married, and how long the couple has been together. Single people have more partners, but this does not translate into more sex! Sexual activity increases through the twenties as people either cohabit or marry. Then, around age 30, it declines as the demands of daily life—working, commuting, taking care of home and children—intensify.

Most adults say they are happy with their sex lives. For those in committed relationships, more than 80 percent report feeling "extremely physically and emotionally satisfied," a figure that rises to 88 percent for married couples. In contrast, as number of sex partners increases, satisfaction declines sharply. These findings challenge two stereotypes—that marriage is sexually dull and that people with many partners have the "hottest" sex.

Only a minority of adults—women more often than men—report persistent sexual problems. For women, the two most frequent difficulties are lack of interest in sex (33 percent) and inability to achieve orgasm (24 percent); for men, climaxing too early (29 percent) and anxiety about performance (16 percent). Sexual difficulties are linked to low SES and psychological stress and are more common among people who are not married, have had more than five partners, and have experienced sexual abuse during childhood or (for women) sexual coercion in adulthood (Laumann, Paik, & Rosen, 1999). As these findings suggest, a history of unfavorable personal relationships and sexual experiences increases the risk of sexual dysfunction.

But overall, a completely untroubled physical experience is not essential for sexual happiness. Surveys of adults repeatedly show that satisfying sex involves more than technique; it is attained in the context of love, affection, and fidelity (Bancroft, 2002; Santtila et al., 2008).

■ **HOMOSEXUAL ATTITUDES AND BEHAVIOR.** The majority of Americans support civil liberties and equal employment opportunities for gay men, lesbians, and bisexuals (Brooks, 2000). And attitudes toward sexual relations between two adults of the same sex have gradually become more accepting: In one survey, 55 to 65 percent of U.S. 18- to 65-year-olds agreed "it is OK" (Langer, 2004). Homosexuals' political activism and greater openness about their sexual orientation have contributed to slow gains in acceptance. Exposure and interpersonal contact reduce negative attitudes. But perhaps because they are especially concerned with gender-role conformity, heterosexual men judge homosexuals (and especially gay men) more harshly than do heterosexual women (Kite & Whitley, 2003; Lim, 2002).

In the National Health and Social Life Survey, 2.8 percent of men and 1.4 percent of women identified themselves as homosexual or bisexual—figures similar to those of other national surveys conducted in the United States, France, and Great Britain (Black, Gates, & Sanders, 2000; Mercer et al., 2007; Mosher, Chandra, & Jones, 2005; Spira, 1992). But an estimated 30 percent of same-sex couples do not report themselves as such in survey research. This unwillingness to answer questions, engendered by a climate of persecution, has limited researchers' access to information about the sex lives of gay men and lesbians. The little evidence available indicates that homosexual sex follows many of the same rules as heterosexual sex: People tend to seek out partners similar in education and background to themselves; partners in committed relationships have sex more often and are more satisfied; and the overall frequency of sex is modest (Laumann et al., 1994; Michael et al., 1994).

Homosexuals tend to live in large cities, where many others share their sexual orientation, or in college towns, where attitudes are more accepting. Living in small communities where prejudice is intense and no social network exists through which to find compatible homosexual partners is isolating, lonely, and predictive of mental health problems (Meyer, 2003).

■ **SEXUAL COERCION.** After a long day of classes, Sharese flipped on the TV and caught a talk show discussion on sex without consent. Karen, a 25-year-old woman, described her husband Mike pushing, slapping, verbally insulting, and forcing her to have sex. "It was a control thing," Karen explained tearfully. "He complained that I wouldn't always do what he wanted. I didn't leave because I was sure he'd come after me and get more violent."

One day, as Karen was speaking long distance to her mother on the phone, Mike grabbed the receiver and shouted, "She's not the woman I married! I'll kill her if she doesn't shape up!" Alarmed, Karen's parents arrived by plane the next day to rescue her, then helped her start divorce proceedings and get treatment.

An estimated 15 to 20 percent of U.S. women have endured *rape,* legally defined as intercourse by force, by threat of harm, or when the victim is incapable of giving consent (because of mental illness, mental retardation, or alcohol consumption). From 22 to 57 percent of women have experienced other forms of sexual aggression. The majority of victims (eight out of ten) are under age 30 (Schewe, 2007; Testa et al., 2003; U.S. Department of Health and Human Services, 2009a). Women are vulnerable to partners, acquaintances, and strangers, but in most instances their abusers are men they know well. Sexual coercion crosses SES and ethnic lines; people of all walks of life are offenders and victims.

Personal characteristics of the man with whom a woman is involved are far better predictors of her chances of becoming a victim than her own characteristics. Men who engage in sexual assault tend to believe in traditional gender roles, approve of violence against women, and accept rape myths (for example, "Women really want to be raped"). Perpetrators also tend to interpret women's social behavior inaccurately, viewing friendliness as seductiveness, assertiveness as hostility, and resistance as desire. Frequently reasoning that "she brought it on herself," they express little remorse (Abbey & McAuslan, 2004; Scully & Marolla, 1998). Furthermore, sexual abuse in childhood, promiscuity in adolescence, and alcohol abuse in adulthood are associated with sexual coercion. Approximately half of all sexual assaults take place while people are intoxicated (Abbey et al., 2004; Kalof, 2000).

Cultural forces also contribute. When men are taught from an early age to be dominant, competitive, and aggressive and women to be submissive, cooperative, and passive, the themes of rape are reinforced. Under these conditions, men may view a date not as a chance to get to know a partner but as a potential sexual conquest. Societal acceptance of violence also sets the stage for rape, which typically occurs in relationships in which other forms of aggression are commonplace.

About 15 to 30 percent of U.S. young adult samples report female-initiated coercive sexual behavior against men, with 3 to 10 percent of male respondents indicating threats of physical force or actual force. Victimized men often say that women who committed these acts encouraged them to get drunk and threatened to end the relationship unless they complied (Anderson & Savage, 2005). Unfortunately, authorities rarely recognize female-initiated forced sex as illegal, and few men report these crimes.

Consequences.   Psychological reactions to rape resemble those of survivors of extreme trauma. Immediate responses—shock, confusion, withdrawal, and psychological numbing—eventually give way to chronic fatigue, tension, disturbed sleep, depression, substance abuse, social anxiety, and suicidal thoughts (Schewe, 2007; Stein et al., 2004). Victims of ongoing sexual coercion may fall into a pattern of extreme passivity and fear.

One-third to one-half of female rape victims are physically injured. From 4 to 30 percent contract sexually transmitted diseases, and pregnancy results in 5 to 20 percent of cases. Furthermore, women victimized by rape (and other crimes) report more symptoms of illness across almost all body systems. And they are more likely to engage in negative health behaviors, including smoking and alcohol use (McFarlane et al., 2005; Schewe, 2007).

A counselor and client talk at a rape crisis center. A variety of community services, including safe houses, crisis hotlines, and support groups, help women take refuge from abusive partners.

Prevention and Treatment.   A variety of community services, including safe houses, crisis hotlines, support groups, and legal assistance, exist to help women take refuge from abusive partners, but most are underfunded and cannot reach out to everyone in need. Practically no services are available for victimized men, who are often too embarrassed to come forward (Anderson & Savage, 2005).

The trauma induced by rape is severe enough that therapy is important—both individual treatment to reduce anxiety and depression and group sessions where contact with other survivors helps counter isolation and self-blame (Neville & Heppner, 2002). Other critical features that foster recovery include

- *Routine screening for victimization* during health-care visits to ensure referral to community services and protection from future harm
- *Validation of the experience,* by acknowledging that many others have been physically and sexually assaulted by intimate partners; that such assaults lead to a wide range of persisting symptoms, are illegal and inappropriate, and should not be tolerated; and that the trauma can be overcome
- *Safety planning,* even when the abuser is no longer present, to prevent recontact and reassault.

Finally, many steps can be taken at the level of the individual, the community, and society to prevent sexual coercion. Some are listed in Applying What We Know on the following page.

■ **MENSTRUAL CYCLE.**   The menstrual cycle is central to women's lives and presents unique health concerns. Although almost all women experience some discomfort during menstruation, others have more severe difficulties. **Premenstrual syndrome (PMS)** refers to an array of physical and psychological symptoms that usually appear six to ten days prior to menstruation. The most common are abdominal cramps, fluid retention, diarrhea, tender breasts, backache, headache, fatigue, tension, irritability, and depression; the precise combination varies from person to person. Nearly 40 percent of women have some form of PMS, usually beginning sometime after age 20. For most, symptoms are mild, but for 10 to 20 percent, PMS is severe enough to interfere with academic, occupational, and social functioning. PMS affects women of all SES levels and is a worldwide phenomenon—just as common in Italy and the Islamic nation of Bahrain as it is in the United States (Brody, 1992; Halbreich, 2004).

The causes of PMS are not well-established, but evidence for a genetic predisposition is accumulating. Identical twins are twice as likely as fraternal twins to share the syndrome (Treloar, Heath, & Martin, 2002). PMS is related to hormonal changes that follow ovulation and precede menstruation. But hormone therapy is not consistently effective, suggesting that sensitivity of brain centers to these hormones, rather than the hormones themselves, is probably responsible (Indusekhar, Usman, & O'Brien, 2007). Common treatments include analgesics for pain, antidepressant medication, vitamin/mineral supplements,

© GERI ENGBERG/THE IMAGE WORKS

Applying What We Know

Preventing Sexual Coercion

Suggestion	Description
Reduce gender stereotyping and gender inequalities.	The roots of men's sexual coercion of women lie in the historically subordinate status of women. Unequal educational and employment opportunities keep many women economically dependent on men and therefore poorly equipped to avoid partner violence. At the same time, there is a need for increased public awareness that women sometimes commit sexually aggressive acts.
Mandate treatment for men and women who physically or sexually assault their partners.	Ingredients of effective intervention include combating rape myths and inducing personal responsibility for violent behavior; teaching social awareness, social skills, and anger management; and developing a support system to prevent future attacks.
Expand interventions for children and adolescents who have witnessed violence between their parents.	Although most child witnesses to parental violence do not become involved in abusive relationships as adults, they are at increased risk.
Teach both men and women to take precautions that lower the risk of sexual assault.	Risk of sexual assault can be reduced by communicating sexual limits clearly to a date and, among women, developing neighborhood ties to other women; increasing the safety of the immediate environment (for example, installing deadbolt locks, checking the back seat of the car before entering); avoiding deserted areas; not walking alone after dark; and leaving parties where alcohol use is high.
Broaden definitions of rape to be gender-neutral.	In some U.S. states, where the definition of rape is limited to vaginal or anal penetration, a woman legally cannot rape a man. A broader definition is needed to encompass women as both receivers and perpetrators of sexual aggression.

Sources: Anderson & Savage, 2005; Schewe, 2007.

exercise, and other strategies for reducing stress. Although each of these approaches is helpful in certain cases, no method has been devised for curing PMS.

Psychological Stress

A final health concern, threaded throughout previous sections, has such a broad impact that it merits a comment of its own. Psychological stress, measured in terms of adverse social conditions, negative life events, or daily hassles, is related to a wide variety of unfavorable health outcomes—both unhealthy behaviors and clear physical consequences.

Chronic stress resulting from economic hardship is consistently linked to hypertension, a relationship that contributes to the high incidence of heart disease in low-income groups, especially African Americans. As it mobilizes the body for action, stress elevates blood pressure. Compared with higher-SES individuals, low-SES adults show a stronger cardiovascular response to stress, perhaps because they more often perceive stressors as unsolvable (Almeida et al., 2005; Carroll et al., 2007). Earlier we mentioned that psychological stress interferes with immune system functioning, a link that may underlie its relationship to several forms of cancer. And by reducing digestive activity as blood flows to the brain, heart, and extremities, stress can cause gastrointestinal difficulties, including constipation, diarrhea, colitis, and ulcers (Donatelle, 2009).

The many challenging tasks of early adulthood make it a particularly stressful time of life. Young adults more often report depressive feelings than middle-aged people, many of whom have attained vocational success and financial security and are enjoying more free time as parenting responsibilities decline (Schieman, Van Gundy, & Taylor, 2001; Wade & Cairney, 1997). Also, as we will see in Chapters 15 and 16, middle-aged adults are better than young adults at coping with stress (Aldwin & Levenson, 2002).

In previous chapters, we repeatedly noted the stress-buffering effect of social support, which continues throughout life. Helping stressed young adults establish and maintain satisfying social ties is as important a health intervention as any we have mentioned.

ASK YOURSELF

≫ REVIEW
Why are people in committed relationships likely to be more sexually active and satisfied than those who are dating several partners?

≫ APPLY
Tom had been going to a health club three days a week after work, but job pressures convinced him that he no longer had time for regular exercise. Explain to Tom why he should keep up his exercise regimen, and suggest ways to fit it into his busy life.

≫ REFLECT
List three strategies that you can implement now to enhance your health in future decades, noting research that supports the importance of each change in your behavior.

Cognitive Development

The cognitive changes of early adulthood are supported by further development of the cerebral cortex, especially the frontal lobes. Pruning of synapses along with growth and myelination of stimulated neural fibers continue, though at a slower pace than in adolescence (Nelson, Thomas, & De Haan, 2006). As we will see, cognitive advances (and underlying brain growth) are promoted by major life events, including attaining higher education, establishing a career, and grappling with the demands of marriage and child rearing. fMRI evidence reveals that as young adults become increasingly proficient in a field of endeavor, cortical regions specialized for those activities undergo further *experience-dependent brain growth* (see page 98 in Chapter 4). In addition to functioning more efficiently, structural changes may occur as skill refinement results in increased cortical tissue devoted to the task and, at times, reorganization of brain areas governing the activity (Hill & Schneider, 2006).

How does cognition change in early adulthood? Lifespan theorists have examined this question from three familiar vantage points. First, they have proposed transformations in the structure of thought—new, qualitatively distinct ways of thinking that extend the cognitive-developmental changes of childhood and adolescence. Second, adulthood is a time of attaining advanced knowledge in a particular area, an accomplishment that has important implications for information processing and creativity. Finally, researchers have been interested in the extent to which the diverse mental abilities assessed by intelligence tests remain stable or change during the adult years—a topic we will address in Chapter 15.

Changes in the Structure of Thought

Sharese described her first year in graduate school as a "cognitive turning point." As part of her internship in a public health clinic, she observed firsthand the many factors that affect human health-related behaviors. For a time, the realization that everyday dilemmas did not have clear-cut solutions made her intensely uncomfortable. "Working in this messy reality is so different from the problem solving I did in my undergraduate classes," she told her mother over the phone one day.

Piaget (1967) acknowledged the possibility that important advances in thinking follow the attainment of formal operations. He observed that adolescents prefer an idealistic, internally consistent perspective on the world to one that is vague, contradictory, and adapted to particular circumstances (see Chapter 11, page 305). Sharese's reflections fit the observations of researchers who have studied **postformal thought**—cognitive development beyond Piaget's formal operations. To clarify how thinking is restructured in adulthood, let's look at some influential theories, along with supportive research. Together, they show how personal effort and social experiences spark increasingly rational, flexible, and practical ways of thinking that accept uncertainties and vary across situations.

Perry's Theory: Epistemic Cognition

The work of William Perry (1981, 1970/1998) provided the starting point for an expanding research literature on the development of *epistemic cognition*. *Epistemic* means "of or about knowledge," and **epistemic cognition** refers to our reflections on how we arrived at facts, beliefs, and ideas. When mature, rational thinkers reach conclusions that differ from those of others, they consider the justifiability of their conclusions. When they cannot justify their approach, they revise it, seeking a more balanced, adequate route to acquiring knowledge.

■ **DEVELOPMENT OF EPISTEMIC COGNITION.** Perry interviewed Harvard University undergraduates at the end of each of their four years of college, asking "what stood out" during the previous year. Responses indicated that students' reflections on knowing changed as they experienced the complexities of university life and moved closer to adult roles—findings confirmed in many subsequent studies (King & Kitchener, 1994, 2002; Magolda, 2002; Moore, 2002).

Younger students regarded knowledge as made up of separate units (beliefs and propositions), whose truth could be determined by comparing them to objective standards—standards that exist apart from the thinking person and his or her situation. As a result, they engaged in **dualistic thinking,** dividing information, values, and authority into right and wrong, good and bad, we and they. As one college freshman stated, "When I went to my first lecture, what the man said was just like God's word. I believe everything he said because he is a professor . . . and this is a respected position" (Perry, 1981, p. 81). And when asked, "If two people disagree on the interpretation of a poem, how would you decide which one is right?" a sophomore replied, "You'd have to ask the poet. It's his poem" (Clinchy, 2002, p. 67).

Older students, in contrast, had moved toward **relativistic thinking**—viewing all knowledge as embedded in a framework of thought. Aware of a diversity of opinions on many topics, they gave up the possibility of absolute truth in favor of multiple truths, each relative to its context. As a result, their thinking became more flexible and tolerant. As one college senior put it, "Just seeing how [famous philosophers] fell short of an all-encompassing answer, [you realize] that ideas are really individualized. And you begin to have respect for how great their thought could be, without its being absolute" (Perry, 1970/1998, p. 90). The relativistic thinker is acutely aware that each person, in arriving at a position, creates his or her own "truth"—that is, chooses one of many possible positions, each of which is defensible (Moore, 2002; Sinnott, 2003).

Eventually, the most mature individuals progress to **commitment within relativistic thinking.** Instead of choosing between opposing views, they try to formulate a more satisfying perspective that synthesizes contradictions. When consid-

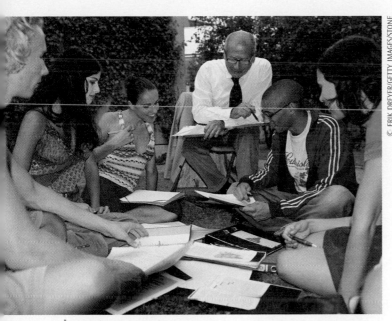

© ERIK DREYER/GETTY IMAGES/STONE

When college students challenge one another's reasoning while tackling realistic, ambiguous problems, they are likely to gain in epistemic cognition.

ering which of two theories studied in a college course is better or which of several movies most deserves an Oscar, the individual moves beyond the stance that everything is a matter of opinion and generates rational criteria against which options can be evaluated (Moshman, 2003, 2005). Few college students reach this extension of relativism. Adults who attain it generally display a more sophisticated approach to learning, in which they actively seek out differing perspectives to advance their knowledge and understanding.

■ **IMPORTANCE OF PEER INTERACTION AND REFLECTION.** Advances in epistemic cognition depend on further gains in metacognition, which are likely to occur in situations that challenge young peoples' perspectives and induce them to consider the rationality of their thought processes (Moshman, 2005). In a study of the college learning experiences of seniors who scored low and high in Perry's scheme, high-scoring students frequently reported activities that encouraged them to struggle with realistic but ambiguous problems in a supportive environment, in which faculty offered encouragement and guidance. For example, an engineering major, describing an airplane-design project that required advanced epistemic cognition, noted his discovery that "you can design 30 different airplanes and each one's going to have its benefits and there's going to be problems with each one" (Marra & Palmer, 2004, p. 116). The low-scoring students rarely mentioned such experiences.

When students tackle challenging, ill-structured problems, interaction among individuals who are roughly equal in knowledge and authority is beneficial because it prevents acceptance of another's reasoning simply because of greater power or

expertise. When college students were asked to devise the most effective solution to a difficult logical problem, only 3 out of 32 students (9 percent) in a "work alone" condition succeeded. But in an "interactive" condition, 15 out of 20 small groups (75 percent) arrived at the correct solution following extensive discussion (Moshman & Geil, 1998). Most groups engaged in a process of "collective rationality" in which members challenged one another to justify their reasoning and collaborated in working out the most defensible strategy.

Of course, reflection on one's own thinking can also occur individually. But peer interaction fosters the necessary type of individual reflection: arguing with oneself over competing ideas and strategies and coordinating opposing perspectives into a new, more effective structure. **TAKE A MOMENT...** Return to page 249 in Chapter 9 to review how peer collaboration fosters cognitive development in childhood. It remains a highly effective basis for education in early adulthood.

Labouvie-Vief's Theory: Pragmatic Thought and Cognitive-Affective Complexity

Gisella Labouvie-Vief's (1980, 1985) portrait of adult cognition echoes features of Perry's theory. Adolescents, she points out, operate within a world of possibility. Adulthood involves movement from hypothetical to **pragmatic thought,** a structural advance in which logic becomes a tool for solving real-world problems.

According to Labouvie-Vief, the need to specialize motivates this change. As adults select one path out of many alternatives, they become more aware of the constraints of everyday life. And in the course of balancing various roles, they accept contradictions as part of existence and develop ways of thinking that thrive on imperfection and compromise. Sharese's friend Christy, a student and mother of two young children, illustrates:

> I've always been a feminist, and I wanted to remain true to my beliefs in family and career. But this is Gary's first year of teaching high school, and he's saddled with four preparations and coaching the school's basketball team. At least for now, I've had to settle for "give-and-take feminism"— going to school part-time and shouldering most of the responsibility for the kids while he gets used to his new job. Otherwise, we'd never make it financially.

Labouvie-Vief (2003, 2006) also points out that young adults' enhanced reflective capacities alter the dynamics of their emotional lives: They become more adept at integrating cognition with emotion and, in doing so, again make sense of discrepancies. Examining the self-descriptions of several hundred 10- to 80-year-olds diverse in SES, Labouvie-Vief found that from adolescence through middle adulthood, people gained in **cognitive affective complexity**—awareness of positive and negative feelings and coordination of them into a complex,

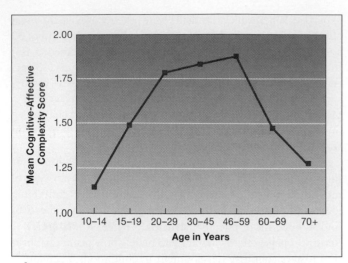

■ **FIGURE 13.4** ■ **Changes in cognitive-affective complexity from adolescence to late adulthood.** Performance, based on participants' descriptions of their roles, traits, and emotions, increased steadily from adolescence through early adulthood, peaked in middle age, and fell off in late adulthood when (as we will see in later chapters) basic information-processing skills decline. (From G. Labouvie-Vief, 2004, "Dynamic Integration: Affect, Cognition, and the Self in Adulthood." *Current Directions in Psychological Science, 12,* p. 203. Reprinted by permission of Blackwell Publishing Ltd.)

organized structure (see Figure 13.4) (Labouvie-Vief, 2008; Labouvie-Vief et al., 1995; Labouvie-Vief, DeVoe, & Bulka, 1989). For example, one 34-year-old combined roles, traits, and diverse emotions into this coherent self-description: "With the recent birth of our first child, I find myself more fulfilled than ever, yet struggling in some ways. My elation is tempered by my gnawing concern over meeting all my responsibilities in a satisfying way while remaining an individualized person with needs and desires."

Cognitive-affective complexity promotes greater awareness of one's own and others' perspectives and motivations. As Labouvie-Vief (2003) notes, it is valuable in solving many pragmatic problems. Individuals high in cognitive-affective complexity view events and people in a tolerant, open-minded fashion. And because cognitive-affective complexity involves accepting and making sense of both positive and negative feelings, it helps people regulate intense emotion and, therefore, think rationally about real-world dilemmas (Labouvie-Vief & Gonzalez, 2004). As we will see next, adults' increasingly specialized and context-bound thought, although it closes off certain options, opens new doors to higher levels of competence.

Expertise and Creativity

In Chapter 9, we noted that children's expanding knowledge improves their ability to remember new information related to what they already know. For young adults, **expertise**—acquisition of extensive knowledge in a field or endeavor—is supported by the specialization that begins with selecting a college major or an occupation, since it takes many years for a person to master any complex domain. Once attained, expertise has a profound impact on information processing.

Compared with novices, experts remember and reason more quickly and effectively. The expert knows more domain-specific concepts and represents them at a deeper and more abstract level and as having more features that can be linked to other concepts. As a result, unlike novices, whose understanding is superficial, experts approach problems with underlying principles in mind. For example, a highly trained physicist notices when several problems deal with conservation of energy and can therefore be solved similarly. In contrast, a beginning physics student focuses only on surface features—whether the problem contains a disk, a pulley, or a coiled spring (Chi, 2006; Chi, Glaser, & Farr, 1988). Experts can use what they know to arrive at many solutions automatically—through quick and easy remembering. And when a problem is challenging, they tend to plan ahead, systematically analyzing and categorizing elements and selecting the best from many possibilities, while the novice proceeds more by trial and error.

Expertise is necessary for creativity (Weissberg, 2006). Mature creativity requires a unique cognitive capacity—the ability to formulate new, culturally meaningful problems and to ask significant questions that have not been posed before. Case studies support the 10-year rule in development of master-level creativity—a decade between initial exposure to a field and sufficient expertise to produce a creative work (Simonton, 2000; Winner, 2003). Furthermore, a century of research reveals

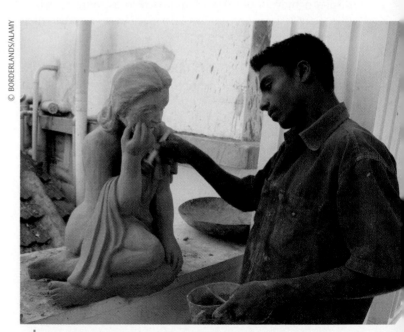

A sculptor works on a statue to honor those who died in the Asian tsunami of 2004. The creative products of adulthood differ from those of childhood in that they are not just original but also directed at a social or aesthetic need.

that creative accomplishment rises in early adulthood, peaks in the late thirties or early forties, and gradually declines, though rarely so substantially as to turn a creative person into a noncreative person (Dixon, 2003). And exceptions to this pattern exist. Those who get an early start in creativity tend to peak and drop off sooner, whereas "late bloomers" reach their full stride at older ages. This suggests that creativity is more a function of "career age" than of chronological age.

The course of creativity also varies across disciplines (Simonton, 1991, 2006). For example, artists and musicians typically show an early rise in creativity, perhaps because they do not need extensive formal education before they begin to produce. Academic scholars and scientists, who must earn higher academic degrees and spend years doing research to make worthwhile contributions, usually display their achievements later and over a longer time.

Though creativity is rooted in expertise, it also requires other qualities—an innovative thinking style, tolerance of ambiguity, a special drive to succeed, and a willingness to experiment and try again after failure (Lubart, 2003; Sternberg & Lubart, 1996). And creativity demands time and energy. For women especially, it may be postponed or disrupted by child rearing, divorce, or an unsupportive partner (Vaillant & Vaillant, 1990). In sum, creativity is multiply determined. When personal and situational factors jointly promote it, creativity can continue for many decades, well into old age.

ASK YOURSELF

>> **REVIEW**
How does expertise affect information processing? Why is expertise necessary for, but not the same as, creativity?

>> **APPLY**
For her human development course, Marcia wrote a paper in which she discussed differing implications of Piaget's and Vygotsky's theories for education. Then she presented evidence that combining both perspectives yields a more effective approach than either position by itself. Explain how Marcia's reasoning illustrates advanced epistemic cognition.

>> **REFLECT**
Describe a classroom experience or assignment in one of your college courses that promoted relativistic thinking.

The College Experience

Looking back at the trajectory of their lives, many people view the college years as formative—more influential than any other period of adulthood. This is not surprising. College serves as a "developmental testing ground," a time for devoting full attention to exploring alternative values, roles, and behaviors. To facilitate this exploration, college exposes students to a form of "culture shock"—encounters with new ideas and beliefs, new freedoms and opportunities, and new academic and

social demands. About two-thirds of U.S. high school graduates enroll in an institution of higher education (U.S. Department of Education, 2009). Besides offering a route to a high-status career and its personal and monetary rewards, colleges and universities have a transforming impact on young people.

Psychological Impact of Attending College

Thousands of studies reveal broad psychological changes from the freshman to the senior year of college (Montgomery & Côté, 2003; Pascarella & Terenzini, 1991). As research inspired by Perry's theory indicates, students become better at reasoning about problems that have no clear solution, identifying the strengths and weaknesses of opposing sides of complex issues, and reflecting on the quality of their thinking. Their attitudes and values also broaden. They show increased interest in literature, the performing arts, and philosophical and historical issues and greater tolerance for ethnic and cultural diversity. Also, as noted in Chapter 12, college leaves its mark on moral reasoning by fostering concern with individual rights and human welfare. Finally, exposure to multiple worldviews encourages young people to look more closely at themselves. During the college years, students develop greater self-understanding, enhanced self-esteem, and a firmer sense of identity.

Residence hall living is one of the most consistent predictors of cognitive change because it maximizes involvement in the educational and social systems of the institution (Terenzini, Pascarella, & Blimling, 1999). These findings underscore the importance of programs that integrate commuting students into out-of-class campus life. Quality of academic experiences

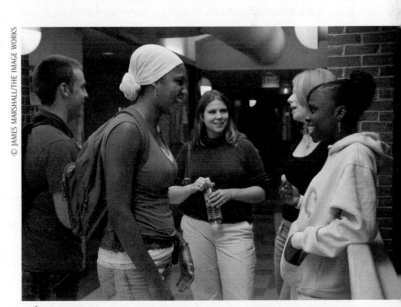

© JAMES MARSHALL/THE IMAGE WORKS

Interacting with other college students in academic and extracurricular settings yields rich benefits. Residence hall living in particular predicts cognitive change because it maximizes involvement in the educational and social systems of the institution.

also affects college outcomes. Psychological benefits increase with students' effort and willingness to participate in class and with challenging teaching that integrates learning in separate courses, offers extensive contact with faculty, and connects course work with real workplace activities (Franklin, 1995).

Dropping Out

Completing a college education has enduring effects on people's postcollege opportunities and worldview. Yet 45 percent of U.S. students at two-year institutions and 30 percent of students at four-year institutions drop out, most within the first year and many within the first six weeks (ACT, 2008). Dropout rates are higher in colleges with less selective admission requirements; in some, the first-year dropout rate approaches 50 percent. And ethnic minority students from low-SES families are at increased risk for dropping out (Montgomery & Côté, 2003).

Both personal and institutional factors contribute to college leaving. First-year students who have trouble adapting—because of lack of motivation, poor study skills, financial pressures, or emotional dependence on parents—quickly develop negative attitudes toward the college environment. Often these exit-prone students do not meet with their advisors or professors. At the same time, colleges that do little to help high-risk students, through developmental courses and other support services, have a higher percentage of dropouts (Moxley, Najor-Durack, & Dumbrigue, 2001).

Reaching out to students, especially during the early weeks and throughout the first year, is crucial. Programs that forge bonds between teachers and students and that provide academic support, part-time work opportunities, and meaningful extracurricular roles increase retention. Membership in campus-based social and religious organizations is especially helpful in strengthening minority students' sense of belonging (Fashola & Slavin, 1998). Young people who feel that they have entered a college community that is concerned about them as individuals are far more likely to graduate.

Vocational Choice

Young adults, college-bound or not, face a major life decision: the choice of a suitable work role. What influences young people's decisions about careers? What is the transition from school to work like, and what factors make it easy or difficult?

Selecting a Vocation

In societies with an abundance of career possibilities, occupational choice is a gradual process that begins early. Major theorists view the young person as moving through several periods of vocational development (Gottfredson, 2005; Super, 1990, 1994):

1. The **fantasy period:** In early and middle childhood, children gain insight into career options by fantasizing about

them. Their preferences, guided largely by familiarity, glamour, and excitement, bear little relation to the decisions they will eventually make.

2. The **tentative period:** Between ages 11 and 16, adolescents think about careers in more complex ways, at first in terms of their *interests,* and soon—as they become more aware of personal and educational requirements for different vocations—in terms of their *abilities* and *values.* "I like science and the process of discovery," Sharese thought as she neared high school graduation. "But I'm also good with people, and I'd like to do something to help others. So maybe teaching or medicine would suit my needs."

3. The **realistic period:** By the late teens and early twenties, with the economic and practical realities of adulthood just around the corner, young people start to narrow their options. A first step is often further *exploration*—gathering more information about possibilities that blend with their personal characteristics. In the final phase, *crystallization,* they focus on a general vocational category and experiment for a time before settling on a single occupation. As a college sophomore, Sharese pursued her interest in science, but she had not yet selected a major. Once she decided on chemistry, she considered whether to pursue teaching, medicine, or public health.

Factors Influencing Vocational Choice

Most, but not all, young people follow this pattern of vocational development. A few know from an early age just what they want to be and follow a direct path to a career goal. Some decide and later change their minds, and still others remain undecided for an extended period. College students are granted added time to explore various options. In contrast, the life conditions of many low-SES youths restrict their range of choices.

Making an occupational choice is not simply a rational process in which young people weigh abilities, interests, and values against career options. Like other developmental milestones, it is the result of a dynamic interaction between person and environment (Gottfredson & Duffy, 2008).

■ **PERSONALITY.** People are attracted to occupations that complement their personalities. John Holland (1985, 1997) identified six personality types that affect vocational choice:

- The *investigative person,* who enjoys working with ideas, is likely to select a scientific occupation (for example, anthropologist, physicist, or engineer).

- The *social person,* who likes interacting with people, gravitates toward human services (counseling, social work, or teaching).

- The *realistic person,* who prefers real-world problems and working with objects, tends to choose a mechanical occupation (construction, plumbing, or surveying).

- The *artistic person,* who is emotional and high in need for individual expression, looks toward an artistic field (writing, music, or the visual arts).

- The *conventional person,* who likes well-structured tasks and values material possessions and social status, has traits well-suited to certain business fields (accounting, banking, or quality control).

- The *enterprising person,* who is adventurous, persuasive, and a strong leader, is drawn to sales and supervisory positions or to politics.

TAKE A MOMENT... Does one of these personality types describe you? Or do you have aspects of more than one type? Research confirms a relationship between personality and vocational choice in diverse cultures, but it is only moderate. Many people are blends of several personality types and can do well at more than one kind of occupation (Holland, 1997; Spokane & Cruza-Guet, 2005). Furthermore, career decisions are made in the context of family influences, educational opportunities, and current life circumstances. For example, Sharese's friend Christy scored high on Holland's investigative dimension. But when she married and had children early, she postponed her dream of becoming a college professor and chose a human services career that required fewer years of education.

■ **FAMILY INFLUENCES.** Individuals who grew up in higher-SES homes are more likely to select high-status, white-collar occupations, such as doctor, lawyer, scientist, or engineer. In contrast, those with lower-SES backgrounds tend to choose less prestigious, blue-collar careers—for example, plumber, construction worker, food service employee, or secretary. Parent–child vocational similarity is partly a function of similarity in personality, intellectual abilities, and—especially— educational attainment (Ellis & Bonin, 2003; Schoon & Parsons,

2002). Years of schooling completed powerfully predicts occupational status.

Other factors also promote family resemblance in occupational choice. Higher-SES parents are more likely to give their children important information about the world of work and to have connections with people who can help the young person obtain a high-status position (Kalil, Levine, & Ziol-Guest, 2005). Parenting practices also shape work-related values. Recall from Chapter 2 that higher-SES parents tend to promote curiosity and self-direction, which are required in many high-status careers. Lower-SES parents, in contrast, are more likely to emphasize conformity and obedience. Eventually, young people may choose careers that dovetail with these differences.

Still, parents can foster higher aspirations. Parental pressure to do well in school and encouragement toward high-status occupations predict vocational attainment beyond SES (Bryant, Zvonkovic, & Reynolds, 2006).

■ **TEACHERS.** Young adults preparing for or in careers requiring extensive education often report that teachers influenced their choice (Bright et al., 2005; Reddin, 1997). College-bound high school students tend to have closer relationships with teachers than do other students—relationships that are especially likely to foster high career aspirations in young women (Wigfield et al., 2002). These findings provide yet another reason to promote positive teacher–student relations, especially for high school students from low-SES families. The power of teachers in offering encouragement and acting as role models can serve as an important source of resilience for these young people.

■ **GENDER STEREOTYPES.** Over the past three decades, young women have expressed increasing interest in occupations largely held by men (Gottfredson, 2005). Changes in gender-role attitudes, along with a dramatic rise in numbers of employed mothers who serve as career-oriented models for their daughters, are common explanations for women's attraction to nontraditional careers.

But women's progress in entering and excelling at male-dominated professions has been slow. As Table 13.2 on page 360 shows, although the percentage of women engineers, lawyers, doctors, and business executives increased between 1983 and 2007 in the United States, it still falls far short of equal representation. Women remain concentrated in less well-paid, traditionally feminine professions, such as writing, social work, education, and nursing (U.S. Census Bureau, 2009b). In virtually all fields, their achievements lag behind those of men, who write more books, make more discoveries, hold more positions of leadership, and produce more works of art.

Ability cannot account for these dramatic sex differences. In elementary and secondary school, girls are advantaged in reading and writing achievement, and the gender gap favoring boys in math is small (Halpern et al., 2007; Halpern, Wai, & Saw, 2005). Rather, gender-stereotyped messages play a key role. Although girls earn higher grades than boys, they reach secondary school less confident of their abilities, more likely to

This young man has followed his father's career path to become an emergency medical technician. Parent–child vocational similarity is partly a function of similarity in personality, intellectual abilities, and—especially—educational attainment.

© PBNJ PRODUCTIONS/GETTY IMAGES/BLEND IMAGES

■ **TABLE 13.2** ■ *Percentage of Women in Various Professions in the United States, 1983 and 2007*

PROFESSION	1983	2007
Engineer	5.8	9.7
Lawyer	15.8	32.6
Doctor	15.8	30.0
Business executive	32.4	37.5[a]
Author, artist, entertainer	42.7	47.1
Social worker	64.3	82.0
Elementary or middle school teacher	93.5	80.9
Secondary school teacher	62.2	56.9
College or university professor	36.3	46.2
Librarian	84.4	83.2
Registered nurse	95.8	91.7
Psychologist	57.1	64.4

Source: U.S. Census Bureau, 2009b.

[a]This percentage includes executives and managers at all levels. Women make up only 25 percent of chief executive officers at large corporations, although that figure represents a sixfold increase over the past 25 years.

underestimate their achievement, and less likely to express interest in math and science careers (Wigfield et al., 2002). In college, the career aspirations of many women decline further as they question their capacity and opportunities to succeed in male-dominated fields and worry about combining a highly demanding career with family responsibilities (Chhin, Bleeker, & Jacobs, 2008; Wigfield et al., 2006). Research indicates that many mathematically talented college women settle on non-science majors. And those who remain in the sciences more often choose medicine or another health profession and less often choose engineering or a math or physical science career than their male counterparts (Benbow et al., 2000; Halpern et al., 2007).

These findings reveal a pressing need for programs that sensitize high school and college personnel to the special problems women face in developing and maintaining high vocational aspirations and selecting nontraditional careers. Those who continue to achieve usually have four experiences in common:

- A college environment that values women's accomplishments and attempts to enhance women's experiences in its curriculum

- Frequent interaction with faculty and professionals in their chosen fields

- Models of accomplished women who have successfully dealt with family–career role conflict (Swanson & Fouad, 1999; Zeldin & Pajares, 2000)

Compared to women, men have changed little in their interest in nontraditional occupations. See the Social Issues box on the following page for research on the motivations and experiences of men who do choose female-dominated careers.

Vocational Preparation of Non-College-Bound Young Adults

Sharese's younger brother Leon graduated from high school in a vocational track. Like approximately one-third of American young people with a high school diploma, he had no current plans to go to college. He hoped to work in data processing after graduation, but six months later he was still a part-time sales clerk at a candy store. Although Leon had filled out many job applications, he got no interviews or offers. He soon despaired of discovering any relationship between his schooling and a career.

Leon's inability to find a job other than the one he held as a student is typical for U.S. non-college-bound high school graduates. Although they are more likely to find employment than youths who drop out, they have fewer work opportunities than high school graduates of several decades ago. About 20 percent of recent high school graduates who do not continue their education are unemployed (U.S. Department of Education, 2009). When they do find work, most hold low-paid, unskilled jobs. In addition, they have few alternatives for vocational counseling and job placement as they transition from school to work (Shanahan, Mortimer, & Krüger, 2002).

American employers regard recent high school graduates as poorly prepared for skilled business and industrial occupations and manual trades. And there is some truth to this impression. Unlike European nations, the United States has no widespread training system for non-college-bound youths. As a result, most graduate without work-related skills and experience a "floundering period" that lasts for several years.

In Germany, young people who do not go to a Gymnasium (college-preparatory high school) have access to one of the most successful work–study apprenticeship systems in the world for entering business and industry. About two-thirds of German youths participate. After completing full-time schooling at age 15 or 16, they spend the remaining two years of compulsory education in the Berufsschule, combining part-time vocational courses with an apprenticeship that is jointly planned by educators and employers (Deissinger, 2007). Apprentices who complete the program and pass a qualifying examination are certified as skilled workers and earn union-set wages. Businesses provide financial support because they know that the program guarantees a competent, dedicated work force (Heinz, 1999; Kerckhoff, 2002). Many apprentices are hired into well-paid jobs by the firms that train them.

The success of the German system—and of similar systems in Austria, Denmark, Switzerland, and several East European countries—suggests that a national apprenticeship program would improve the transition from high school to work for U.S. young people. The many benefits of bringing together the worlds of schooling and work include helping non-college-bound young people establish productive lives right after grad-

SOCIAL ISSUES

Masculinity at Work: Men Who Choose Nontraditional Careers

Ross majored in engineering through his sophomore year of college, when he startled his family and friends by switching to nursing. "I've never looked back," Ross said. "I love the work." He noted some benefits of being a male in a female work world, including the high regard of women colleagues and rapid advancement. "But as soon as they learn what I do," Ross remarked with disappointment, "guys on the outside question my abilities and masculinity."

What factors influence the small but increasing number of men who, like Ross, enter careers dominated by women? Compared to their traditional-career counterparts, these men are less gender-typed, less focused on the social status of their work, and more interested in working with people (Dodson & Borders, 2006; Jome, Surething, & Taylor, 2005). When several hundred men were assessed in their first year of college and again four years later, those who chose traditionally feminine occupations had more liberal social attitudes, including attitudes about gender roles, than those who chose traditionally masculine occupations. They also less often rated occupational prestige as important in their choice and were less likely to aspire to graduate education (Lease, 2003).

In one study, 40 men who were primary school teachers, nurses, airline stewards, or librarians, when asked how they arrived at their choice, described diverse pathways (Simpson, 2005). Some actively sought the career, others happened on it while exploring possibilities, and still others first spent time in another occupation (usually male-dominated), found it unsatisfying, and then settled into their current career.

The men also confirmed Ross's observations: Because of their male minority status, co-workers often assumed they were more knowledgeable than they actually were. They also had opportunities to move quickly into supervisory positions, although many did not seek advancement (Simpson, 2004). As one teacher commented, "I just want to be a good classroom teacher. What's wrong with that?" Furthermore, while in training and on the job, virtually all the men reported feeling socially accepted—relaxed and comfortable working with women.

But when asked to reflect on how others reacted to their choice, many men expressed anxiety about being stigmatized by other men. To reduce these feelings, they frequently described their job in ways that minimized its

© PAUL CONKLIN/PHOTOEDIT

This nurse exemplifies the increasing number of men entering careers dominated by women. Compared with his traditional-career counterparts, he is likely to be less gender-typed, less focused on the social status of his work, and more interested in working with people.

feminine image. Several librarians emphasized technical requirements by referring to their title as "information scientist" or "researcher." The teachers often highlighted the sports aspect of their work. And nurses sometimes distanced themselves from a feminine work identity by specializing in "adrenaline-charged" areas such as accident or emergency.

Despite these tensions, the men uniformly derived enjoyment and self-esteem from their nontraditional career choice. As with Ross, their high level of private comfort seemed to prevail over uneasiness about the feminine public image of their work.

---

uation, motivating at-risk youths to stay in school, and contributing to the nation's economic growth. Nevertheless, implementing an apprenticeship system poses major challenges: overcoming the reluctance of employers to assume part of the responsibility for vocational training, ensuring cooperation between schools and businesses, and preventing low-SES youths from being concentrated in the lowest-skilled apprenticeship placements (Hamilton & Hamilton, 2000). Currently, small-scale school-to-work projects in the United States are attempting to solve these problems and build bridges between learning and working.

Although vocational development is a lifelong process, adolescence and early adulthood are crucial periods for defining occupational goals and launching a career. The support of families, schools, businesses, communities, and society as a whole can contribute greatly to a positive outcome. In Chapter 14, we will take up the challenges of establishing a career and integrating it with other life tasks.

ASK YOURSELF

≫ REVIEW
What student and college-environment characteristics contribute to favorable psychological changes during the college years?

≫ APPLY
Diane, a high school senior, knows that she wants to "work with people" but doesn't yet have a specific career in mind. Diane's father is a chemistry professor, her mother a social worker. What steps can Diane's parents take to broaden her awareness of the world of work and help her focus on an occupational goal?

≫ REFLECT
Describe your progress in choosing a vocation. What personal and environmental factors have been influential?

Summary

PHYSICAL DEVELOPMENT

Biological Aging Is Under Way in Early Adulthood

Describe current theories of biological aging, including those at the level of DNA and body cells and those at the level of tissues and organs.

>> Once body structures reach maximum capacity and efficiency, **biological aging,** or **senescence,** begins.

>> The programmed effects of specific genes may control certain age-related biological changes in DNA and body cells. For example, **telomere** shortening results in senescent cells, which contribute to disease and loss of function.

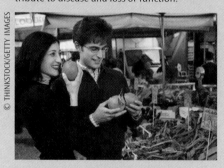

>> DNA may also be damaged as random mutations accumulate, leading to less efficient cell repair and replacement and to abnormal cancerous cells. Release of **free radicals** is a likely cause of age-related DNA and cellular damage.

>> Genetic and cellular deterioration affects tissues and organs. The **cross-linkage theory of aging** suggests that over time, protein fibers form links and become less elastic, producing negative changes in many organs. Declines in the endocrine and immune systems also contribute to aging.

Physical Changes

Describe the physical changes of aging, paying special attention to the cardiovascular and respiratory systems, motor performance, the immune system, and reproductive capacity.

>> Gradual physical changes take place in early adulthood and later accelerate. Declines in heart and lung performance are evident during exercise. Heart disease is a leading cause of death in adults. Atherosclerosis is a serious, multiply determined cardiovascular disease involving fatty deposits on artery walls.

>> Athletic skills requiring speed, strength, and gross body coordination peak in the early twenties; those requiring endurance, arm–hand steadiness, and aiming peak in the late twenties and early thirties. Less active lifestyles rather than biological aging account for most of the age-related decline in athletic skill and motor performance.

>> The immune response strengthens through adolescence and declines after age 20. This trend is partly due to shrinking of the thymus gland. Psychological stress may also contribute.

>> Women's reproductive capacity declines with age due to reduced quality and quantity of ova. Men show a gradual decrease in semen volume and sperm quality after age 35.

Health and Fitness

Describe the impact of SES, nutrition, and exercise on health, and discuss obesity in adulthood.

>> Economically advantaged, well-educated individuals tend to sustain good health over most of their adult lives, whereas the health of lower-income individuals with limited education declines. SES differences in health-related living conditions and habits are largely responsible.

>> Overweight and obesity have increased dramatically in Western nations, especially in the United States. Some weight gain between ages 25 and 50 results from a decrease in **basal metabolic rate (BMR),** but many young adults show large increases because of sedentary lifestyles and diets high in sugar and fat.

>> Regular exercise reduces body fat, builds muscle, helps prevent disease, and enhances psychological well-being. Moderately intense exercise on most days leads to health benefits, which increase with greater intensity of exercise.

What are the most commonly abused substances, and what health risks may result?

>> Cigarette smoking and alcohol consumption are the two most common substance abuses. Most adults who smoke began before age 21 and are at increased risk for a wide variety of serious health problems.

>> About one-third of heavy drinkers suffer from alcoholism, to which both heredity and environment contribute. Alcohol is implicated in numerous diseases and physical disorders and in such social problems as highway fatalities, crime, and sexual coercion.

Describe sexual attitudes and behavior of young adults, and discuss sexual coercion and premenstrual syndrome.

>> Most adults are less sexually active than popular media images suggest, but compared with earlier generations, they display a wider range of sexual choices and lifestyles and have had more sexual partners. Nevertheless, most people spend the majority of their lives with one partner.

>> Adults in committed relationships report high satisfaction with their sex lives. Only a minority of adults report persistent sexual problems—difficulties linked to low SES and stress.

>> Negative attitudes toward homosexual men and women have begun to change, largely as a result of greater exposure and interpersonal contact. Homosexual relationships, like heterosexual relationships, are characterized by similarity between partners in education and background, greater satisfaction in committed relationships, and modest frequency of sexual activity.

>> Most rape victims have been harmed by men they know well. Men who commit sexual assault typically hold traditional gender roles, approve of violence against women, accept rape myths, and have difficulty interpreting women's social behavior accurately. Cultural acceptance of strong gender typing and of violence contributes to sexual coercion, which leads to psychological trauma. Female-initiated coercive sexual behavior also occurs, although it is less often reported and recognized by the legal system.

>> Nearly 40 percent of women experience **premenstrual syndrome (PMS),** usually in mild form. Evidence for a genetic predisposition is accumulating.

How does psychological stress affect health?

>> Chronic psychological stress induces physical responses that contribute to heart disease, cancer, and gastrointestinal problems. Because early adulthood is a highly stressful time of life, interventions that help stressed young people form supportive social ties are especially important.

COGNITIVE DEVELOPMENT

Changes in the Structure of Thought

Describe characteristics of adult thought, and explain how thinking changes in adulthood.

>> Cognitive development beyond Piaget's formal operations is known as **postformal thought.** According to Perry's theory of **epistemic cognition,** college students move from **dualistic thinking,** dividing information into right and wrong, to **relativistic thinking,** awareness of multiple truths. Eventually, the most mature individuals progress to **commitment within relativistic thinking,** a perspective that synthesizes contradictions.

>> Advances in epistemic cognition depend on gains in metacognition. Peer collaboration on challenging, ill-structured problems is especially beneficial.

>> According to Labouvie-Vief's theory, the need to specialize motivates adults to progress from the world of possibilities to **pragmatic thought,** which uses logic as a tool to solve real-world problems. As a result of enhanced reflective capacities, adults also gain in **cognitive-affective complexity**—coordination of positive and negative feelings into a complex, organized structure.

Expertise and Creativity

What roles do expertise and creativity play in adult thought?

>> Specialization in college and in an occupation leads to **expertise,** which enhances problem solving and is necessary for creativity. Although creativity tends to rise in early adulthood and to peak in the late thirties or early forties, its development varies across disciplines and individuals. In addition to expertise, diverse personal and situational factors jointly promote creativity.

© BORDERLANDS/ALAMY

The College Experience

Describe the impact of a college education on young people's lives, and discuss the problem of dropping out.

>> Through involvement in academic programs and campus life, college students gain in knowledge and reasoning ability, broaden their attitudes and values, and show enhanced self-understanding and self-esteem.

>> Dropout rates are higher in less selective colleges and for ethnic minority students from low-SES families. Personal and institutional factors contribute to college leaving, which is especially likely during the first year.

Vocational Choice

Trace the development of vocational choice, and cite factors that influence it.

>> Vocational choice moves through a **fantasy period,** in which children explore career options by fantasizing about them; a **tentative period,** in which teenagers weigh different careers against their interests, abilities, and values; and a **realistic period,** in which young people settle on a vocational category and then a specific occupation.

>> Vocational choice is influenced by personality; parents' provision of educational opportunities, vocational information, and encouragement; and close relationships with teachers. Women's progress in male-dominated professions has been slow, and their achievements lag behind those of men in virtually all fields. Gender-stereotyped messages play a key role. Although some men choose careers in female-dominated fields, this is still uncommon.

© PAUL CONKLIN/PHOTOEDIT

What problems do U.S. non-college-bound young people face in preparing for a vocation?

>> Most U.S. non-college-bound high school graduates are limited to low-paid, unskilled jobs, and too many are unemployed. Youth apprenticeships, like those widely available in European countries, would address the need for vocational training and improve the transition from school to work for these young people.

Important Terms and Concepts

basal metabolic rate (BMR) (p. 346)
biological aging, or senescence (p. 339)
cognitive-affective complexity (p. 355)
commitment within relativistic thinking (p. 354)
cross-linkage theory of aging (p. 341)

dualistic thinking (p. 354)
epistemic cognition (p. 354)
expertise (p. 356)
fantasy period (p. 358)
free radicals (p. 340)
postformal thought (p. 354)

pragmatic thought (p. 355)
premenstrual syndrome (PMS) (p. 352)
realistic period (p. 358)
relativistic thinking (p. 354)
telomeres (p. 340)
tentative period (p. 358)

CHAPTER 14

Emotional and Social Development in Early Adulthood

COURTESY OF AMÉLIE GRYSOLE, HAITI 2009, AGRYSOLE@YAHOO.FR, CLOWNS WITHOUT BORDERS

For many young people in industrialized nations, the transition to early adulthood is a time of prolonged exploration of attitudes, values, and life possibilities. This young adult has interrupted his education to volunteer for Clowns Without Borders, an organization that brings joy to children living in refugee camps and conflict zones. Here he entertains a Haitian audience, most of whom endure harsh and often dangerous living conditions.

After completing her master's degree at age 26, Sharese returned to her hometown, where she and Ernie would soon be married. During their year-long engagement, Sharese had vacillated about whether to follow through. At times, she looked with envy at Heather, still unattached and free to choose from an array of options before her. After graduating from college, Heather accepted a Peace Corps assignment in a remote region of Ghana and then traveled for eight months before returning to the United States to contemplate next steps.

© JUPITERIMAGES/COMSTOCK IMAGES/ALAMY

Sharese also pondered the life circumstances of Christy and her husband, Gary—married their junior year in college and parents of two children born within the next few years. Financial pressures and the demands of parenthood had put Christy's education and career plans on hold. Sharese wondered whether it was really possible to combine family and career.

As her wedding approached, Sharese's ambivalence intensified, and she admitted to Ernie that she didn't feel ready to marry. But Ernie reassured her of his love. His career had been under way for two years, he had received a company promotion, and at age 28, he looked forward to marriage and starting a family. Uncertain and conflicted, Sharese felt swept toward the altar as relatives, friends, and gifts arrived. On the appointed day, she walked down the aisle.

In this chapter, we take up the emotional and social sides of early adulthood. Notice that Sharese, Ernie, and Heather moved toward adult roles slowly, at times wavering along the way. Not until their mid- to late twenties did they make lasting career and romantic choices and attain full economic independence—markers of adulthood that young people of previous generations reached considerably earlier. Each of these young people received financial and other forms of support from parents and other family members, which enabled them to postpone taking on adult roles. We consider whether prolonged exploration of life options has become so widespread that we must posit a new developmental period—*emerging adulthood*—to describe and understand it.

Recall from Chapter 12 that identity development continues to be a central focus from the late teens into the mid-twenties (see page 316). As they achieve a secure identity and independence from parents, young adults seek close, affectionate ties. Yet the decade of the twenties is accompanied by a sharp rise in the extent to which people feel they are personally in control of events in their lives. Indeed, 20- to 29-year-olds report a greater sense of control than they ever will again (Grob, Krings, & Bangerter, 2001). Perhaps for this reason, like Sharese, they often fear losing their freedom. Once this struggle is resolved, early adulthood leads to new family units and parenthood, accomplished in the context of diverse lifestyles. At the same time, young adults must master the skills and tasks of their chosen career.

Our discussion will reveal that identity, love, and work are intertwined. In negotiating these arenas, young adults do more choosing, planning, and changing course than any other age group. When their decisions are in tune with themselves and their social worlds, they acquire many new competencies, and life is full and rewarding.

A Gradual Transition: Emerging Adulthood

TAKE A MOMENT... Think about your own development. Do you consider yourself to have reached adulthood? When a large sample of American 18- to 25-year-olds was asked this question, the majority gave an ambiguous answer: "yes and no" (see Figure 14.1). Only after reaching their late twenties and

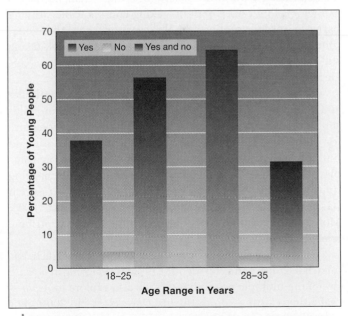

■ FIGURE 14.1 ■ American young people's responses to the question, "Do you feel that you have reached adulthood?" Between ages 18 and 25, the majority answered "yes and no," reflecting their view that they had left adolescence but were not yet fully adult. Even in their late twenties and early thirties, about one-third of young people judged that they had not completed the transition to adulthood. (Adapted from Arnett, 2001.)

early thirties did most feel that they were truly adult—findings evident in a wide range of industrialized nations (Arnett, 1997, 2001, 2003, 2007a; Buhl & Lanz, 2007; Macek, Bejĉek, & Vaníĉková, 2007). The life pursuits and subjective judgments of many contemporary young people indicate that the transition to adult roles has become so delayed and prolonged that it has spawned a new transitional period, extending from the late teens to the mid-twenties, called **emerging adulthood.**

Unprecedented Exploration and Advances in Identity

The late teens and early twenties are a time of great challenge and uncertainty. Emerging adults have left adolescence but are some distance from taking on adult responsibilities, and their parents agree: In a survey of parents of a large sample of ethnically and religiously diverse U.S. undergraduate and graduate students, most viewed their children as not yet fully adult (Nelson et al., 2007). Rather, young people who have the economic resources to do so explore alternatives in education, work, personal beliefs and values, and love more intensively than they did as teenagers (Arnett, 2006, 2007b).

Emerging adulthood greatly prolongs identity development. Released from the oversight of parents but not yet immersed in adult roles, 18- to 25-year-olds can engage in activities of the widest possible scope. Because so little is normative, or socially expected, routes to adult responsibilities are highly diverse in timing and order across individuals (Côté, 2006). For example, many more college students than in past generations pursue their education in a drawn-out, nonlinear way—changing majors as they explore career options, taking courses while working part-time, or interrupting school to work or travel. About one-third of U.S. college graduates enter graduate school, taking still more years to settle into their desired career track (U.S. Department of Education, 2009).

As a result of these experiences, young people's attitudes and values broaden. They express increased interest in philosophical, historical, and political issues and greater tolerance for ethnic and cultural diversity. Furthermore, exposure to multiple viewpoints encourages development of a more complex self-concept that includes awareness of their own changing traits and values over time, along with enhanced self-esteem (Galambos, Barker, & Krahn, 2006; Labouvie-Vief, 2006; Montgomery & Côté, 2003). Together, these changes contribute to advances in identity.

During the college years, young people refine their approach to constructing an identity. Besides exploring in *breadth* (weighing multiple possibilities), they also explore in *depth*—evaluating existing commitments (Luyckx et al., 2006). For example, if you have not yet selected your major, you may be taking classes in a broad array of disciplines. Once you choose a major, you are likely to embark on an in-depth evaluation of your choice—reflecting on your interest, motivation, and performance and on your career prospects as you take additional

classes in that field. As a result, either your commitment to your major strengthens, or you return to broad exploration of options. In a longitudinal study extending over the first two years of college, most students cycled between making commitments and evaluating commitments in various identity domains. Fluctuations in students' certainty about their commitments sparked movement between these two states (Luyckx, Goossens, & Soenens, 2006).

TAKE A MOMENT... Consider your own identity progress. Does it fit this *dual-cycle model,* in which identity formation is a lengthy process of feedback loops? Notice how the model helps explain the movement between identity statuses displayed by many young people, described in Chapter 12. College students who move toward exploration in depth and certainty of commitment are better-adjusted, academically and socially. Those who spend much time exploring in breadth without making commitments tend to be poorly adjusted—depressed and higher in drug use (Luyckx et al., 2006).

Many aspects of the life course that were once socially structured—marriage, parenthood, religious beliefs, and career paths—are increasingly left to individual decision. During the college years, for example, attendance at religious services drops to its lowest level—about 30 percent in the United

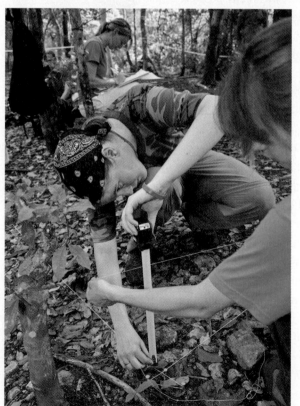

Identity development during the college years involves exploring in depth—evaluating current commitments. As these archaeology majors excavate a Mayan site in Belize, they mull over their interest, motivation, and career prospects as future archaeologists.

States—as young people continue to evaluate beliefs acquired in their families against alternatives. Many emerging adults work on constructing their own individualistic faith, often weaving together beliefs and practices from a variety of sources, including Eastern and Western religious traditions, science, and popular culture (Shipman et al., 2002).

Identity progress in emerging adulthood requires a sense of purpose, self efficacy (belief in one's ability to succeed), determination to overcome obstacles, and responsibility for outcomes. Among young people of diverse ethnicities and SES levels, this set of qualities—called *personal agency*—is positively related to an information-gathering cognitive style and to identity exploration and commitment, and negatively related to identity diffusion (Schwartz, Côté, & Arnett, 2005).

Cultural Change, Cultural Variation, and Emerging Adulthood

Rapid cultural change explains the recent appearance of this rich, complex bridge between adolescence and assumption of adult responsibilities. First, entry-level positions in many fields require more education than in the past, prompting young adults to seek higher education in record numbers and thus delaying financial independence and career commitment. Second, wealthy nations with longer-lived populations have no pressing need for young people's labor, freeing 18- to 25-year-olds for extended exploration.

Indeed, emerging adulthood is limited to cultures that postpone entry into adult roles until the twenties. In developing nations such as China and India, only a privileged few—usually those from wealthier families who are admitted to universities—experience emerging adulthood, often for a shorter time span than their Western counterparts (Badger, Nelson, & Barry, 2006; Nelson & Chen, 2007). Furthermore, the overwhelming majority of young people in traditional non-Western countries—those who have few economic resources or who remain in rural regions where they grew up—have no "emerging adulthood." With limited education, they typically enter marriage, parenthood, and lifelong work early (UNICEF, 2009).

In industrialized countries, where many benefit from these transitional years, young people nevertheless vary in their beliefs about what it means to become an adult. Reflecting on the self-searching of these years, respondents from diverse cultures, ethnicities, and religious backgrounds emphasize psychological qualities, especially self-sufficiency—accepting responsibility for one's actions, deciding on personal beliefs and values, establishing an equal relationship with parents, and becoming financially independent (Facio & Micocci, 2003; Mayseless & Sharf, 2003; Nelson et al., 2007). Youths from collectivist minority groups also include self-control, becoming more considerate of others, and attaining certain roles, such as marital partner and parent (Arnett, 2003; Cheah & Nelson, 2004).

Nevertheless, for low-SES young people in Western nations who are burdened by early parenthood, do not finish high school, are otherwise academically unprepared for college, or do not have access to vocational training, emerging adulthood is limited or nonexistent (see Chapters 11 and 13) (Cohen et al., 2003; Eccles et al., 2003). As the Cultural Influences box on page 368 indicates, because of its strong association with SES and higher education, some researchers reject the notion of emerging adulthood as a distinct period of development. Others disagree, predicting that emerging adulthood will become increasingly common as *globalization*—the exchange of ideas, information, trade, and immigration among nations—accelerates (Arnett, 2007a; Nelson & Chen, 2007). As globalization proceeds, gains in financial security and higher education and the formation of a common "global identity" among young people may make emerging adulthood a typical experience around the world.

Risk and Resilience in Emerging Adulthood

In grappling with momentous choices, emerging adults play a more active role in their own development than at any earlier time (Arnett, 2006; Eccles et al., 2003). As they experiment, they often encounter disappointments in love and work that require them to adjust, and sometimes radically change, their life path.

Emerging adults' vigorous explorations also extend earlier risks, including unprotected sexual activity, substance use, and hazardous driving behavior. For example, drug taking peaks during these years (see Chapter 13). And as we will see later, feelings of loneliness are higher than at any other time of life.

Longitudinal research shows that the personal attributes and social supports listed in Applying What We Know on page 369 foster successful passage through these years, as indicated by completing a college education, forging a warm, stable intimate relationship, finding and keeping a well-paying job, and volunteering in one's community (Benson et al., 2006; Eccles & Gootman, 2002). Notice how factors in the table overlap with ones discussed in previous chapters that promote *resilience*, the capacity to overcome challenge and adversity.

Relationships with parents have an especially wide-ranging influence. A secure, affectionate parent–emerging adult bond that extends the balance of connection and separation established in adolescence promotes many aspects of adaptive functioning: favorable self-esteem, identity progress, successful transition to college life, higher academic achievement, more rewarding friendships and romantic ties, and reduced anxiety, depression, loneliness, and drug abuse (Aquilino, 2006).

In addition, emerging adults who feel securely attached to parents and who view them as having used an authoritative child-rearing style are more likely to have integrated their parents' religious or spiritual beliefs into their own personal world view (Okagaki, Hammond, & Seamon, 1999). Then, as young people seek their place in an increasingly complex, ever-changing world, a religious or spiritual ideology helps anchor them. It serves as a reminder of social injustices, motivating—as it did

▪ CULTURAL INFLUENCES ▪

Is Emerging Adulthood Really a Distinct Period of Development?

Although broad consensus exists that cultural change has prolonged the transition to adult roles for many young people, disagreement exists over whether these years of "emergence" merit the creation of a new developmental period (Hendry & Kloep, 2007). Critics of the concept of emerging adulthood offer the following arguments.

First, burgeoning higher education enrollment, delayed career entry, and later marriage and parenthood are cultural trends that began as early as the 1970s in industrialized nations, only gradually becoming more conspicuous. At no time has adulthood in complex societies been attained at a distinct moment. Rather, young people have in the past and continue today to reach adult status earlier in some domains, later in others. And they may reverse direction. For example, after finishing college or being laid off from a job, they might move back to the parental home to get their bearings (Cohen et al., 2003). In accord with the lifespan perspective, development is multidimensional and multidirectional for 18- to 25-year-olds, as it is for adults of all ages. Transitions occur during all periods of the lifespan, with societal conditions heavily influencing their length and complexity.

Second, emerging adulthood fails to describe the experiences of most of the world's youths (Bynner, 2005). In many developing countries, young people—particularly women—are limited in education and marry and have children early (see page 48 in Chapter 2). According to one estimate, nearly 1.5 billion individuals—86 percent of young people—follow this traditional route to adulthood, with no prospect of alternatives (Lloyd, 2005). And as we have seen, many low-SES young people in industrialized nations lack the academic preparation and financial resources to experience an emerging adulthood.

Third, research on emerging adulthood largely emphasizes its personal and societal benefits. But the extended exploration that defines this period, though opening opportunities, might be risky for those without the personal agency to make effective choices and acquire adult skills (Levine, 2005). These young people may remain uncommitted for too long—an outcome that would impede the focused learning required for a successful work life. A favorable emerging adulthood, then, depends on whether it is used effectively to acquire the competencies needed for modern living.

Proponents of emerging adulthood as a distinct developmental period respond that, though not universal, it applies to most young people in industrialized societies and is spreading rapidly in developing nations that play major roles in our global economy (Arnett, 2007a). Furthermore, the concept reminds us that the lives of many people in their early twenties differ vastly from those in their thirties and of the need to clarify the contextual factors that contribute to their experiences.

This married man and father living in a rural region of India has few economic resources. Like the majority of young people in developing countries, he has no emerging adulthood.

But—as skeptics note—age-graded influences have declined in favor of nonnormative influences throughout contemporary adulthood (see page 9 in Chapter 1 to review) (Hendry & Kloep, 2007). In their view, rather than being unique, emerging adults are part of a general trend toward blurring of age-related expectations, yielding multiple transitions and increased diversity in development across the adult years.

---

in adolescence—community service. It also offers an image of ideal character traits toward which they can strive (Kerestes & Youniss, 2003).

As one reviewer of research concluded, "What seems advantageous for emerging adults' achievement of independence is feeling connected, secure, understood, and loved in their families, and having the willingness to call on parental resources" (Aquilino, 2006, p. 201). In contrast, exposure to multiple negative life events—family conflict, abusive intimate relationships, repeated romantic breakups, academic or employment difficulties,

and financial strain—undermines development, even in emerging adults whose childhood and adolescence prepared them well for this transition (Cui & Vaillant, 1996).

In sum, supportive family, school, and community environments are crucial, just as they were at earlier ages. The overwhelming majority of young people with access to these resources are highly optimistic—convinced that, despite challenges, they will eventually attain happiness in work and close relationships (Arnett, 2000, 2006). Now let's turn to theories of psychosocial development in early adulthood.

Applying What We Know

Resources That Foster Resilience in Emerging Adulthood

Type of Resource	Description
Cognitive attributes	Effective planning and decision making
	Information gathering cognitive style
	Good school performance
	Knowledge of vocational options and skills
Emotional and social attributes	Positive self-esteem
	Good emotional self-regulation and flexible coping strategies
	Good conflict-resolution skills
	Confidence in one's ability to reach one's goals
	Sense of personal responsibility for outcomes
	Persistence and good use of time
	Healthy identity development—movement toward exploration in depth and commitment certainty
	Strong moral character
	Sense of meaning and purpose in life, engendered by religion, spirituality, or other sources
	Desire to contribute meaningfully to one's community
Social supports	Positive relationships with parents, peers, teachers, and mentors
	Sense of connection to social institutions, such as school, church, workplace, and community center

Sources: Benson et al., 2006; Eccles and Gootman, 2002.

ASK YOURSELF

≫ **REVIEW**
What cultural changes have led to the emergence of the period known as emerging adulthood?

≫ **APPLY**
List supports that your college environment offers emerging adults in its health and counseling services, academic advising, residential living, and extracurricular activities. How does each help young people master the challenges of this period?

≫ **REFLECT**
Should emerging adulthood be considered a distinct developmental period? Why or why not?

Erikson's Theory: Intimacy versus Isolation

Erikson's vision has influenced all contemporary theories of adult personality development. His psychological conflict of early adulthood is **intimacy versus isolation,** reflected in the young person's thoughts and feelings about making a permanent commitment to an intimate partner.

As Sharese discovered, establishing a mutually gratifying close relationship is challenging. Intimacy requires that young people redefine their identity to include both partners' values and interests. Those in their teens and early twenties frequently say they don't feel ready for a lasting tie (Collins & van Dulmen, 2006b). During their first year of marriage, Sharese separated from Ernie twice as she tried to reconcile her desire for self-determination with her desire for intimacy. Maturity involves balancing these forces. Without intimacy, young adults face the negative outcome of Erikson's early adulthood stage: loneliness and self-absorption. Ernie's patience and stability helped Sharese realize that committed love requires generosity and compromise but not total surrender of the self.

Research confirms that—as Erikson emphasized—a secure identity fosters attainment of intimacy. Commitment to personally meaningful values and goals prepares young adults for interpersonal commitments, which increase as early adulthood progresses (Kroger, 2007). Among large samples of college students, identity achievement was positively correlated with fidelity (loyalty in relationships) and love, for both men and women. In contrast, identity moratorium—a state of searching prior to commitment—was negatively associated with fidelity and love (Markstrom et al., 1997; Markstrom & Kalmanir, 2001). Other studies show that advanced identity development strongly predicts involvement in a deep, committed love partnership or readiness to establish such a partnership (Montgomery, 2005). Still, the coordination of identity and intimacy is more complex for women, who are more likely than men to consider the impact of their personal goals on important relationships (Archer, 2002).

Erikson believed that successful resolution of intimacy versus isolation prepares the individual for the middle adulthood stage, which focuses on *generativity*—caring for the next generation and helping to improve society. But childbearing and child rearing usually occur in the twenties and thirties, and contributions to society through work are also under way.

In sum, identity, intimacy, and generativity are concerns of early adulthood, with shifts in emphasis that differ among individuals. Recognizing that Erikson's theory provides only a broad sketch of adult personality development, other theorists have expanded and modified his stage approach, adding detail and flexibility.

Other Theories of Adult Psychosocial Development

In the 1970s, growing interest in adult development led to several widely read books on the topic. Daniel Levinson's *The Seasons of a Man's Life* (1978) and George Vaillant's *Adaptation to Life* (1977) and *Aging Well* (2002) present psychosocial theories in the tradition of Erikson. Each is summarized in Table 14.1.

Levinson's Seasons of Life

Seeking an underlying order to the life course, Levinson (1978) conducted in-depth biographical interviews with 40 35- to 45-year-old men from four occupational subgroups: hourly workers in industry, business executives, university biologists, and novelists. Later he interviewed 45 women, also 35 to 45 years of age, from three subgroups: homemakers, business executives, and university professors. His results and those of others suggest a common path of change within which men and women approach developmental tasks in somewhat different ways (Levinson, 1996; Roberts & Newton, 1987).

Like Erikson, Levinson (1978, 1996) saw development as a sequence of qualitatively distinct eras (stages or seasons). Each begins with a *transition*, followed by a stable phase during which individuals build a life structure aimed at harmonizing inner personal and outer societal demands. Eventually people question the current structure, and a new transition ensues.

The **life structure,** a key concept in Levinson's theory, is the underlying design of a person's life, consisting of relationships with significant others—individuals, groups, and institutions. Of its many components, usually only a few, relating to marriage/family and occupation, are central. But wide individual differences exist in the weight of central and peripheral components.

Men's and women's accounts of their lives offer support for Levinson's description. They also reveal that early adulthood is the era of "greatest energy and abundance, contradiction and stress" (Levinson, 1986, p. 5). These years involve serious decisions about work, marriage, children, and lifestyle before many people have enough experience to choose wisely.

Levinson reported that during the early adult transition, most young people construct a *dream*—an image of themselves in the adult world that guides their decision making. For men, the dream usually emphasizes an independent achiever in an occupational role. In contrast, most career-oriented women display "split dreams" involving both marriage and career. Also, women's dreams tend to define the self in terms of relationships with husband, children, and colleagues. Men's dreams are usually more individualistic: They view significant others, especially wives, as vital supporters of their goals and less often see themselves as supporting others' goals.

■ **TABLE 14.1** ■ *Theories of Adult Psychosocial Development*

PERIOD OF DEVELOPMENT	ERIKSON	LEVINSON	VAILLANT
Early adulthood (18–40 years)	Intimacy versus isolation	Early adult transition: 17–22 years	Intimacy
		Entry life structure for early adulthood: 22–28 years	
		Age-30 transition: 28–33 years	Career consolidation
		Culminating life structure for early adulthood: 33–40 years	
Middle adulthood (40–65 years)	Generativity versus stagnation	Midlife transition: 40–45 years	Generativity
		Entry life structure for middle adulthood: 45–50 years	
		Age-50 transition: 50–55 years	Keeper of meaning
		Culminating life structure for middle adulthood: 55–60 years	
Late adulthood (65 years–death)	Ego integrity versus despair	Late adult transition: 60–65 years	Ego integrity
		Late adulthood: 65 years–death	

Although both of these young scientists are deeply committed to their careers, their images of their future lives may differ. Men more often see themselves as independent achievers in their occupational role, whereas women tend to have "split dreams" involving both marriage and career.

Young adults also form a relationship with a *mentor* who facilitates realization of their dream—often a senior colleague at work but occasionally a more experienced friend, neighbor, or relative. As we will see when we take up vocational development, finding a supportive mentor is easier for men than for women.

During the age-30 transition, young people who had been preoccupied with career and are still single usually focus on finding a life partner, while women who had emphasized marriage and motherhood often develop more individualistic goals. For example, Christy, who had dreamed of becoming a professor, finally earned her doctoral degree in her mid-thirties and secured a college teaching position. For young people without a satisfying intimate tie or vocational direction or who question the personal meaning of their life structure, this can be a time of considerable inner conflict and instability.

To create the culminating life structure of early adulthood, men usually "settle down" by focusing on certain relationships and aspirations, setting others aside. Their goal is to establish a stable niche in society that is consistent with their values, whether those be wealth, prestige, artistic or scientific achievement, or forms of family or community participation. In his thirties, Sharese's husband, Ernie, expanded his knowledge of real estate accounting, became a partner in his firm, coached his son's soccer team, and was elected treasurer of his church. He paid less attention to golf, travel, and playing the guitar than he had in his twenties.

Many women, however, remain unsettled in their thirties, often because they have added an occupational or relationship commitment (Levinson, 1996). When her two children were born, Sharese felt torn between her research position in the state health department and her family. She took three months off after the arrival of each baby. When she returned to work, she did not pursue attractive administrative openings that required travel and time away from home. And shortly after Christy began teaching, she and Gary divorced. Becoming a single parent while starting her professional life introduced new strains. Not until middle age do many women attain the stability typical of men in their thirties—reaching career maturity and taking on more authority in the community.

Vaillant's Adaptation to Life

Vaillant (1977) examined the development of nearly 250 men born in the 1920s, selected for study while they were students at a highly competitive liberal arts college, and followed as many as possible over the lifespan. In college, the participants underwent extensive interviews. During each succeeding decade, they answered lengthy questionnaires. Then Vaillant (2002) interviewed the men at ages 47, 60, and 70 about work, family, and physical and mental health.

Other than denying a strict age-related schedule of change, Vaillant's theory is compatible with Levinson's. Both agree that quality of relationships with important people shape the life course. In studying how the men altered themselves and their social world to adapt to life, Vaillant confirmed Erikson's stages but filled gaps between them. After a period in their twenties devoted to intimacy concerns, the men focused on career consolidation in their thirties. During their forties, they pulled back from individual achievement and became more generative—giving to and guiding others. In their fifties and sixties, they became "keepers of meaning," or guardians of their culture, expressing concern about the values of the younger generation and the state of their society. Many felt a deep need to preserve and pass on cultural traditions by teaching others what they had learned from life experience (Vaillant & Koury, 1994). Finally, in their seventies, the men became more spiritual and reflective.

Although Vaillant initially studied only men, eventually he examined the development of a sample of bright, well-educated women who were participants in another lifelong study. His findings, and those of others, suggest that women undergo a series of changes similar to those just described (Block, 1971; Oden & Terman, 1968; Vaillant, 2002).

Limitations of Levinson's and Vaillant's Theories

The patterns Levinson and Vaillant identified are based largely on interviews with people born in the first few decades of the twentieth century. As our discussion of emerging adulthood illustrates, young adults' development is more variable today than in past generations. Furthermore, Levinson's sample included only a few non-college-educated, low-income adults, and low-SES women remain almost entirely uninvestigated. Examining longitudinal archives on low-SES men who had grown up in the 1940s, Vaillant (1993) reported evidence for his stage sequence. Still, he acknowledged that the sample was limited.

Finally, Levinson's participants, interviewed in middle age, might not have remembered all aspects of their early adulthoods accurately. Studies of new generations—both men and women, of diverse backgrounds—are needed to discern the extent to which the developmental paths just described apply to most or all young people.

The Social Clock

As we have seen, changes in society from one generation to the next can affect the life course. Bernice Neugarten (1968a, 1979) identified an important cultural and generational influence on adult development: the **social clock**—age-graded expectations for major life events, such as beginning a first job, getting married, birth of the first child, buying a home, and retiring. All societies have such timetables. Being on time or off time can affect self-esteem because adults (like children and adolescents) make social comparisons, measuring their progress against that of agemates.

Conformity to or departure from the social clock can be a major source of adult personality change. In a study of college women born in the 1930s who were followed up at ages 27 and 43, researchers determined how closely participants followed a "feminine" social clock (marriage and parenthood in the early or mid-twenties) or a "masculine" one (entry into a high-status career and advancement by the late twenties). Those who started families on time became more responsible, self-controlled, tolerant, and caring but declined in self-esteem and felt more vulnerable as their lives progressed. Those who followed a "masculine" occupational timetable became more dominant, sociable, independent, and intellectually effective, a trend also found in a cohort born a decade later (Vandewater & Stewart, 1997). And women who had neither married nor begun a

career by age 30 suffered from self-doubt, feelings of incompetence, and loneliness (Helson, 1992; Helson, Mitchell, & Moane, 1984).

Following a social clock of some kind seems to foster confidence during early adulthood because it guarantees that young people will engage in the work of society, develop skills, and gain in understanding of the self and others (Helson, 1997; Hendry & Kloep, 2007). As Neugarten (1979) suggested, the stability of society depends on having people committed to social-clock patterns. With this in mind, let's take a closer look at how young men and women traverse the major tasks of young adulthood.

Close Relationships

To establish an intimate tie to another person, people must find a partner and build a lasting emotional bond. Although young adults are especially concerned with romantic love, the need for intimacy can also be satisfied through other relationships involving mutual commitment—with friends, siblings, and co-workers.

Romantic Love

Finding a life partner is a major milestone of early adult development, with profound consequences for self-concept and psychological well-being (Meeus et al., 2007). It is also a complex process that unfolds over time and is affected by a variety of events.

■ **SELECTING A MATE.** Recall from Chapter 13 that intimate partners generally meet in places where they find people of their own age, ethnicity, SES, and religion or (somewhat less often) connect through Internet dating services. People usually select partners who resemble themselves in other ways—attitudes, personality, educational plans, intelligence, physical attractiveness, and even height (Keith & Schafer, 1991; Simpson & Harris, 1994). Overall, little support exists for the idea that "opposites attract." In fact, many studies confirm that the more

Being on time or off time for major life events, such as parenthood, can affect self-esteem because adults make social comparisons, measuring their progress against that of agemates.

similar partners are, the more satisfied they tend to be with their relationship and the more likely they are to stay together (Blackwell & Lichter, 2004; Lucas et al., 2004).

Nevertheless, men and women differ in the importance they place on certain characteristics. In diverse industrialized and developing countries, women assign greater weight to intelligence, ambition, financial status, and moral character, whereas men place more emphasis on physical attractiveness and domestic skills. In addition, women prefer a same-age or slightly older partner, men a younger partner (Buunk, 2002; Cramer, Schaefer, & Reid, 2003; Stewart, Stinnett, & Rosenfeld, 2000).

Evolutionary theory helps us understand these findings. Recall from Chapter 13 that because their capacity to reproduce is limited, women seek a mate with traits, such as earning power and emotional commitment, that help ensure children's survival and well-being. In contrast, men look for a mate with traits that signal youth, health, sexual pleasure, and ability to give birth to and care for offspring. As further evidence for this difference, men often want a relationship to move quickly toward physical intimacy, while women typically prefer to take the time to achieve psychological intimacy first (Buss, 2008).

From an alternative, social learning perspective, gender roles profoundly influence criteria for mate selection. Beginning in childhood, men learn to be assertive and independent—behaviors needed for success in the work world. Women acquire nurturant behaviors, which facilitate caregiving. Then each sex learns to value traits that fit with this traditional division of labor (Eagly & Wood, 1999; Wood & Eagly, 2000). In support of this theory, in cultures and in younger generations experiencing greater gender equity, men and women are more alike in their mate preferences. For example, compared with men in China and Japan, American men place more emphasis on their mate's financial prospects, less on her domestic skills. And both sexes care somewhat less about their mate's age relative to their own. Instead, they place a high value on relationship satisfaction (Buss et al., 2001; Toro-Morn & Sprecher, 2003).

As the Lifespan Vista box on page 374 reveals, young people's choice of an intimate partner and the quality of their relationship also are affected by memories of their early parent–child bond. Finally, for romance to lead to a lasting partnership, it must happen at the right time. If one or both do not feel ready to marry, the relationship is likely to dissolve.

■ THE COMPONENTS OF LOVE.

How do we know that we are in love? Robert Sternberg's (1988, 2000, 2006) **triangular theory of love** identifies three components—intimacy, passion, and commitment—that shift in emphasis as romantic relationships develop. *Intimacy,* the emotional component, involves warm, tender communication, expressions of concern about the other's well-being, and a desire for the partner to reciprocate. *Passion,* the desire for sexual activity and romance, is the physical- and psychological-arousal component. *Commitment* is the cognitive component, leading partners to decide that they are in love and to maintain that love.

At the beginning of a relationship, **passionate love**—intense sexual attraction—is strong. Gradually, passion declines in favor of intimacy and commitment, which form the basis for **companionate love**—warm, trusting affection and caregiving (Acker & Davis, 1992; Fehr, 1994). Each aspect of love, however, helps sustain the relationship. Early passionate love is a strong predictor of whether partners keep dating. But without the quiet intimacy, predictability, and shared attitudes and values of companionate love, most romances eventually break up (Hendrick & Hendrick, 2002).

Couples whose relationships endure generally report that they love each other more than they did earlier (Sprecher, 1999). In the transformation of romantic involvements from passionate to companionate, *commitment* may be the aspect of love that determines whether a relationship survives. Communicating that commitment—through warmth, attentiveness, empathy, caring, acceptance, and respect—strongly predicts relationship maintenance (Rusbult et al., 2006). For example, Sharese's doubts about getting married subsided largely because of Ernie's expressions of commitment.

Intimate partners who consistently express their commitment report higher-quality and longer-lasting relationships (Fitzpatrick & Sollie, 1999). An important feature of their communication is constructive conflict resolution—directly expressing wishes and needs, listening patiently, asking for clarification, compromising, accepting responsibility, forgiving their partner, and avoiding the escalation of negative interaction sparked by criticism, contempt, defensiveness, and stonewalling (Johnson et al., 2005; Schneewind & Gerhard, 2002). How men handle conflict is particularly important because they tend to be less skilled than women at negotiating it, often avoiding discussion (Gayle, Preiss, & Allen, 2002).

■ CULTURE AND THE EXPERIENCE OF LOVE.

Passion and intimacy, which form the basis for romantic love, became the dominant basis for marriage in twentieth-century Western nations as the value of individualism strengthened. From this vantage point, mature love is based on autonomy, appreciation of the partner's unique qualities, and intense emotion. Trying to satisfy dependency needs through an intimate bond is regarded as immature (Hatfield, Rapson, & Martel, 2007).

This Western view contrasts sharply with the collectivist perspectives of Eastern cultures, such as China and Japan, where dependency throughout life is viewed positively because the self is defined through role relationships—son or daughter, brother or sister, husband or wife. Furthermore, in choosing a mate, Chinese and Japanese young people are expected to consider obligations to others, especially parents. College students of Asian heritage are less likely than those of American or European descent to endorse a view of love based solely on physical attraction and deep emotion (Hatfield, Rapson, & Martel, 2007). Instead, they stress companionship and practical matters—similarity of background, career promise, and likelihood of being a good parent.

Still, even in countries where arranged marriages are still fairly common (including China, India, and Japan), parents and prospective brides and grooms consult one another before moving forward (Goodwin & Pillay, 2006). If parents try to force

■ A LIFESPAN VISTA: Looking Forward, Looking Back ■

Childhood Attachment Patterns and Adult Romantic Relationships

Recall from Chapter 6 (page 152) that according to Bowlby's ethological theory of attachment, the early attachment bond leads to the construction of an *internal working model,* or set of expectations about attachment figures, that serves as a guide for close relationships throughout life. We also saw that adults' evaluations of their early attachment experiences are related to their parenting behaviors—specifically, to the quality of attachments they build with their children (see pages 154–156). Additional evidence indicates that recollections of childhood attachment patterns strongly predict romantic relationships in adulthood.

In studies carried out in Australia, Israel, and the United States, researchers asked people to recall and evaluate their early parental bonds (attachment history), their attitudes toward intimate relationships (internal working model), and their actual experiences with romantic partners. In a few studies, investigators also observed couples' behaviors. Consistent with Bowlby's theory, adults' memories and interpretations of childhood attachment patterns were good indicators of internal working models and relationship experiences. (To review patterns of attachment, see page 152.)

Secure Attachment

Adults who described their attachment history as secure (warm, loving, and supportive parents) had internal working models that reflected this security. They viewed themselves as likable and easy to get to know, were comfortable with intimacy, and rarely worried about abandonment or someone getting too close to them. In line with these attitudes, they characterized their most important love relationship in terms of trust, happiness, and friendship (Cassidy, 2001). Furthermore, their behaviors toward their partner were empathic and supportive and their conflict resolution strategies constructive. They were also at ease in turning to their partner for comfort and assistance (Collins et al., 2006; Creasey, 2002; Creasey & Ladd, 2004; Roisman et al., 2002).

Avoidant Attachment

Adults who reported an avoidant attachment history (demanding, disrespectful, and critical parents) displayed internal working models that stressed independence, mistrust of love partners, and anxiety about people getting too close. They were convinced that others disliked them and that romantic love is hard to find and rarely lasts. Jealousy, emotional distance, lack of support in response to their partner's distress, and little enjoyment of physical contact pervaded their most important love relationship (Collins et al., 2006). Along with resistant individuals, avoidant adults endorse many unrealistic beliefs about relationships—for example, that partners cannot change, that males' and females' needs differ, and that "mind reading" is expected (Stackert & Bursik, 2003).

Resistant Attachment

Adults recalling a resistant attachment history (parents who responded unpredictably and unfairly) presented internal working models in which they sought to merge completely with another person and fall in love quickly (Cassidy, 2001). At the same time, they worried that their intense feelings would overwhelm others, who really did not love them and would not want to stay with them. Their most important love relationship was riddled with jealousy, emotional highs and lows, and desperation about whether the partner would return their affection (Feeney, 1999). Resistant adults, though offering a distressed partner

support, do so in ways that fit poorly with their partner's needs (Collins et al., 2006).

Are adults' descriptions of their childhood attachment experiences accurate? In several longitudinal studies, quality of parent–child interactions, observed or assessed through family interviews 5 to 23 years earlier, were good predictors of internal working models and romantic-relationship quality in early adulthood (Allen & Hauser, 1996; Donnellan, Larsen-Rife, & Conger, 2005; Ogawa et al., 1997; Roisman et al., 2001). However, quality of attachment to parents is not the only factor that influences later internal working models and intimate ties. Characteristics of the partner and current life conditions also are important. In one study, adults with an inner sense of security fostered security in their partners as well as in their adolescent and young adult children (Cook, 2000).

In sum, negative parent–child experiences can be carried forward into adult relationships, predisposing people to believe that they are undeserving of love or that their intimate partners cannot be trusted. At the same time, internal working models are continuously "updated." When adults with unhappy love lives have a chance to form more satisfying intimate ties, they may revise their internal working models.

How might the internal working model constructed by this baby, held tenderly by his father, have influenced the relationship he forged as a young adult with his wife? Research indicates that early attachment pattern is one among several factors that predicts the quality of later intimate ties.

In this Hindu wedding ceremony, a relative symbolizes the marriage knot by tying the groom's scarf to the bride's dress. Although arranged marriages are still common in India, parents and prospective brides and grooms usually consult one another before moving forward.

their children into an unappealing marriage, sympathetic extended family members may come to children's defense. Today, young people in many countries consider love to be a prerequisite for marriage, though Westerners assign greater importance to it—especially, its passionate component.

Friendships

Like romantic partners and childhood friends, adult friends are usually similar in age, sex, and SES—factors that contribute to common interests, experiences, and needs and therefore to the pleasure derived from the relationship. As in earlier years, friends in adulthood enhance self-esteem through affirmation and acceptance and provide support in times of stress (Bagwell et al., 2005; Collins & Madsen, 2006). Friends also make life more interesting by expanding social opportunities and access to knowledge and points of view.

Trust, intimacy, and loyalty continue to be important in adult friendships, as they were in middle childhood and adolescence. Sharing thoughts and feelings is sometimes greater in friendship than in marriage, although commitment is less strong as friends come and go over the life course. Even so, some adult friendships continue for many years, at times throughout life. Female friends see one another more often, which contributes to greater friendship continuity for women (Sherman, de Vries, & Lansford, 2000).

■ **SAME-SEX FRIENDSHIPS.** Extending a pattern evident in childhood and adolescence, women have more intimate same-sex friendships than men. Barriers to intimacy between male friends include competitiveness, which may make men unwilling

to disclose weaknesses, and concern that if they tell about themselves, their friends will not reciprocate (Reid & Fine, 1992). Because a balance of power and give-and-take is basic to a good friendship, women generally evaluate their same-sex friendships more positively than men do (Veniegas & Peplau, 1997).

Of course, individual differences in friendship quality exist. The longer-lasting men's friendships are, the closer they become and the more they involve disclosure of personal information (Sherman, de Vries, & Lansford, 2000). And gay and lesbian romantic relationships often develop out of close same-sex friendships, with lesbians, especially, forging compatible friendships based on gratifying communication before becoming involved romantically (Diamond, 2006).

As they develop romantic ties and marry, young adults—especially men—direct more of their disclosures toward their partners (Carbery & Buhrmester, 1998; Kito, 2005). Still, friendships continue to be vital contexts for personal sharing throughout adulthood. Turn back to Figure 12.2 on page 328 to view developmental trends in self-disclosure to romantic partners and friends.

■ **OTHER-SEX FRIENDSHIPS.** During the college years, other-sex friendships are as common as romantic relationships. After marriage, they decline with age for men but increase for women, who tend to form them in the workplace. Highly educated, employed women have the largest number of other-sex friends. Through these relationships, young adults often gain in companionship and self-esteem and learn a great deal about masculine and feminine styles of intimacy (Bleske & Buss, 2000). Because men confide especially easily in their female friends, such friendships offer them a unique opportunity to broaden their expressive capacity. And women sometimes say male friends offer objective points of view on problems and situations—perspectives not available from female friends (Monsour, 2002).

Many people try to keep other-sex friendships platonic to safeguard their integrity (Messman, Canary, & Hause, 2000). Still, about half of college students engage in sexual activity with an other-sex friend whom they have no intention of dating (Kaplan & Keys, 1997). If both sexual attraction and intimacy persist, the relationship often changes into a romantic bond (Afifi & Faulkner, 2000). When a solid other-sex friendship does evolve into a romance, it may be more stable and enduring than a romantic relationship formed without a foundation in friendship (Hendrick & Hendrick, 1993).

■ **SIBLINGS AS FRIENDS.** As young people marry and invest less time in developing a romantic partnership, siblings—especially sisters whose earlier bond was positive—become more frequent companions. A childhood history of intense parental favoritism and sibling rivalry can disrupt sibling bonds in adulthood (Panish & Stricker, 2002). But when family experiences have been positive, relationships between adult same-sex siblings can be especially close. A shared background promotes similarity in values and perspectives and the possibility of deep mutual understanding. Warm sibling relationships in adulthood

© HUMMER/GETTY IMAGES/DIGITAL VISION

As young people marry and invest less time in developing romantic partnerships, siblings—especially sisters whose earlier bond was positive—become more frequent companions than in adolescence. Often, friend and sibling roles merge.

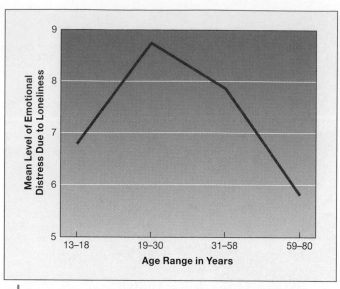

■ **FIGURE 14.2** ■ **Changes in emotional distress due to loneliness from adolescence to late adulthood.** More than 700 Canadian 13- to 80-year-olds responded to a questionnaire assessing the extent to which they experienced emotional distress due to loneliness. Loneliness rose sharply from the early teens to the late teens and early twenties and then declined. (Adapted from Rokach, 2001.)

are important sources of psychological well-being (Sherman, Lansford, & Volling, 2006).

Loneliness

Young adults are at risk for **loneliness**—unhappiness resulting from a gap between the social relationships we currently have and those we desire—when they either do not have an intimate partner or lack gratifying friendships. Though both situations give rise to similar emotions, they are not interchangeable. For example, even though she had several enjoyable friendships, Heather sometimes felt lonely because she was not dating someone she cared about. And although Sharese and Ernie were happily married, they felt lonely after moving to a new town where they did not know anyone.

Loneliness peaks in the late teens and early twenties, then declines steadily into the seventies (see Figure 14.2) (Rokach, 2001). The rise in loneliness during early adulthood is understandable. As young people move through school and employment settings, they must constantly develop new relationships. Also, young adults may expect more from their intimate ties than older adults, who have learned to live with imperfections. With age, people become better at accepting loneliness and using it for positive ends—to sharpen awareness of their personal fears and needs (Rokach, 2003).

Loneliness is intense after loss of an intimate tie: Separated, divorced, or widowed adults are lonelier than their married, co-habiting, or single counterparts. Men not involved in a romantic relationship feel lonelier than women, perhaps because they have fewer alternatives for satisfying intimacy needs (Stroebe et al., 1996). And immigrants from collectivist cultures report

higher levels of loneliness than people born in the United States and Canada (DiTommaso, Brannen, & Burgess, 2005). Leaving a large, close-knit family system for an individualistic society seems to prompt intense feelings of isolation.

Personal characteristics also contribute to loneliness. Young adults who are socially anxious or who have insecure working models of attachment to parents are more often intensely lonely (Jackson et al., 2002). But as long as loneliness is not overwhelming, it can motivate young people to reach out to others. It can also encourage them to find ways to be comfortably alone and to use this time to understand themselves better (Rokach & Neto, 2006). Healthy personality development involves striking this balance between gratifying relationships with others and contentment within ourselves.

ASK YOURSELF

≫ REVIEW
Describe gender differences in traits usually desired in a long-term partner. What findings indicate that both biological and social forces contribute to those differences?

≫ APPLY
After dating for two years, Mindy and Graham reported greater love and relationship satisfaction than during their first few months of dating. What features of communication probably deepened their bond, and why is it likely to endure?

≫ REFLECT
Do you have a nonromantic, close other-sex friendship? If so, how has it enhanced your emotional and social development?

The Family Life Cycle

For most young people, the life course takes shape within the **family life cycle**—a sequence of phases characterizing the development of most families around the world. In early adulthood, people typically live on their own, marry, and bear and rear children. In middle age, as their children leave home, their parenting responsibilities diminish. Late adulthood brings retirement, growing old, and (more often for women) death of one's spouse (Carter & McGoldrick, 2005).

But today, wide variations exist in the sequence and timing of family life-cycle phases—high rates of out-of-wedlock births, delayed marriage and childbearing, divorce, and remarriage, among others. And some people, voluntarily or involuntarily, do not experience all phases. Still, the family life-cycle model offers an organized way of thinking about how the family system changes over time and the impact of each phase on the family unit and its members.

Leaving Home

Departure from the parental home is a major step toward assuming adult responsibilities. The average age of leaving has decreased in recent years as more young people live independently before marriage. In 1940, over 80 percent of Americans in their twenties resided with their parents; today, only about 50 percent of 18- to 25-year-olds do. Residential independence rises steadily with age—a trend evident in most industrialized nations (Cohen et al., 2003).

Departures for education tend to occur at earlier ages, those for full-time work and marriage later. Because the majority of U.S. young adults enroll in higher education, many leave home around age 18. Other young people leave early to escape family friction (Stattin & Magnusson, 1996). Those from divorced, single-parent homes tend to be early leavers, perhaps because of family stress (Cooney & Mortimer, 1999). Compared with the previous generation, fewer North American and Western European young people leave home to marry; more do so just to be "independent"—to express their adult status. But difficult job markets and high housing costs mean that many must take undesirable work or remain financially dependent on parents (Lindsay, Almey, & Normand, 2002).

Nearly half of young adults return home for a brief time after initial leaving. As people encounter unexpected twists and turns on the road to independence, the parental home offers a safety net and base of operations for launching adult life. Failures in work or marriage can prompt a move back. Usually, though, role transitions, such as the end of college or military service, bring people back. Contrary to popular belief, returning home usually is not a sign of weakness but a common event (Ward & Spitze, 2007).

The extent to which young people live on their own before marriage varies with SES and ethnicity. Those who are economically well-off are more likely to establish their own residence. Among African-American, Hispanic, and Native-American groups, poverty and a cultural tradition of extended family living lead to lower rates of leaving home, even among young people in college or working (De Marco & Berzin, 2008; Fussell & Furstenberg, 2005). Unmarried Asian young adults also tend to live with their parents. But the longer Asian families have lived in the United States and thus been exposed to individualistic values, the more likely young people are to move out after finishing high school (Goldscheider & Goldscheider, 1999).

When young adults are prepared for independence and feel securely attached to their parents, departure from the home is linked to more satisfying parent–child interaction and successful transition to adult roles, even among ethnic minorities that strongly emphasize family loyalty and obligations (Smetana, Metzger, & Campione-Barr, 2004). In contrast, leaving home very early because of lack of parental financial and social support is associated with long-term disadvantage—less successful marriage and work life (White, 1994).

Joining of Families in Marriage

The average age of first marriage in the United States has risen from about 20 for women and 23 for men in 1950 to 25½ for women and 27½ for men today. The number of first and second marriages has declined over the last few decades as more people stay single, cohabit, or do not remarry after divorce. Still, nearly 90 percent of Americans marry at least once. At present, 58 percent of U.S. adults live together as married couples (U.S. Census Bureau, 2009b).

Same-sex marriages are recognized nationwide in Belgium, Canada, the Netherlands, Norway, South Africa, Spain, and Sweden. In the United States, Connecticut, Iowa, Massachusetts, and Vermont have legalized same-sex marriage. California, Hawaii, Maine, New Hampshire, New Jersey, Washington, and the District of Columbia grant people in same-sex unions the same legal status as married couples. Because legalization is so recent, research on same-sex couples in the context of marriage is scant. But evidence on cohabiting same-sex couples suggests that the same factors that contribute to happiness in other-sex marriages do so in same-sex unions (Diamond, 2006).

Marriage involves the joining of two individuals. It also requires that two systems—the spouses' families—adapt and overlap to create a new subsystem. Consequently, marriage presents complex challenges.

■ **MARITAL ROLES.** Their honeymoon over, Sharese and Ernie turned to a multitude of issues that they had previously decided individually or that their families of origin had prescribed—from everyday matters (when and how to eat, sleep, talk, work, relax, have sex, and spend money) to family traditions and rituals (which to retain, which to work out for themselves). And as they related to their social world as a couple, they modified relationships with parents, siblings, extended family, friends, and co-workers.

© ROLF BRUDERER/CORBIS

In an egalitarian marriage, husband and wife share power and authority. Both are equally concerned with the balance between work, children, and their relationship.

Contemporary alterations in the context of marriage, including changing gender roles and living farther away from family members, mean that couples must work harder to define their relationships. Although partners are usually similar in religious and ethnic background, "mixed" marriages have become more common. For example, nearly half of American Jews who marry today select a non-Jewish spouse (Fishman, 2004). And other-race unions now account for nearly 4 percent of the married population in the United States (U.S. Census Bureau, 2009b). Couples whose backgrounds differ greatly face extra challenges in making the transition to married life.

Because many couples live together before marriage, it has become less of a turning point in the family life cycle. Still, defining marital roles can be difficult. Age of marriage is the most consistent predictor of marital stability. Young people who marry in their teens and early twenties are far more likely to divorce than those who marry later (Heaton, 2002). Both early marriage followed by childbirth and the reversal of family life-cycle events (childbirth before marriage) are more common among low-SES adults (U.S. Census Bureau, 2009b). This acceleration of family formation complicates adjustment to life as a couple.

Despite progress in the area of women's rights, **traditional marriages,** involving a clear division of husband's and wife's roles, still exist in Western nations. The man is the head of household; his primary responsibility is the economic well-being of his family. The woman devotes herself to caring for her husband and children and to creating a nurturant, comfortable home. In recent decades, however, these marriages have changed, with many women who focused on motherhood while their children were young returning to the work force later.

In **egalitarian marriages,** partners relate as equals, sharing power and authority. Both try to balance the time and energy they devote to their occupations, their children, and their relationship. Most well-educated, career-oriented women expect this form of marriage. And college-student couples who eventually intend to marry often plan in advance how they will coordinate work and family roles, especially if the woman intends to enter a male-dominated career (Botkin, Weeks, & Morris, 2000; Peake & Harris, 2002).

In Western nations, men in dual-earner marriages participate much more in child care than in the past. U.S. fathers in such marriages put in 85 percent as much time as mothers do. But housework—cleaning, shopping, cooking, laundry, picking up clutter—reveals a different story. Recent surveys indicate that women in the United States and Canada spend nearly twice as much time as men on housework, women in Australia nearly three times as much (see Figure 14.3). In Sweden, which places a high value on gender equality, men do more than in other nations. In contrast, men typically do little housework or child care in Japan, where corporate jobs typically demand long work hours (Institute for Social Research, 2002; Shwalb et al., 2004). In sum, true equality in marriage is still rare, and couples who strive for it usually attain a form of marriage in between traditional and egalitarian.

■ **MARITAL SATISFACTION.** Despite its rocky beginnings, Sharese and Ernie's marriage grew to be especially happy. In contrast, Christy and Gary became increasingly discontented. Differences between these two couples mirror the findings of a large body of research on personal and contextual factors, summarized in Table 14.2.

Christy and Gary had a brief courtship, married and had children early, and struggled financially. Gary's negative, critical personality led him to get along poorly with Christy's parents and to feel threatened when he and Christy disagreed. Christy tried to offer Gary encouragement and support, but her own needs for nurturance and individuality were not being met. Gary felt threatened by Christy's career aspirations. As she came closer to attaining them, the couple grew further apart. In contrast, Sharese and Ernie married later, after their educations were complete. They postponed having children until their careers were under way and they had built a sense of togetherness that allowed each to thrive as an individual. Patience, caring, common values, enjoyment of each other's company, sharing of personal experiences through conversation, cooperating in household responsibilities, and good conflict-resolution skills contributed to their compatibility.

Quality of the marital relationship predicts mental health similarly for both genders (Kurdek, 2005; Williams, 2003). But men tend to feel slightly happier with their marriages than women do (Dillaway & Broman, 2001; Kurdek, 2005). Women feel particularly dissatisfied when the demands of husband, children, housework, and career are overwhelming (Forry, Leslie, & Letiecq, 2007; Saginak & Saginak, 2005). Research in both Western and non-Western industrialized nations reveals

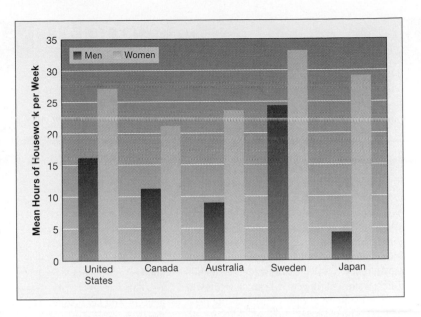

■ **FIGURE 14.3** ■ **Average hours per week of housework reported by men and women in five nations.** In each nation, women devote considerably more time than men to housework. Men's participation is greater in Sweden, which places a high value on gender equality. In Japan, where traditional gender roles prevail, men devote the least time to housework. (Data for the United States, Sweden, and Japan from Institute for Social Research, 2002; for Canada from Statistics Canada, 2006; for Australia from Baxter, Hewett, & Haynes, 2008.)

that equal power in the relationship and sharing of family responsibilities usually enhances both men's and women's satisfaction, largely by strengthening marital harmony (Amato & Booth, 1995; Xu & Lai, 2004).

At their worst, marital relationships can become contexts for intense opposition, dominance–submission, and emotional and physical violence. As the Social Issues box on page 380 explains, although women are more often targets of severe partner abuse, both men and women play both roles: perpetrator and victim.

In view of its long-term implications, it is surprising that most couples spend little time before their wedding day reflecting on the decision to marry. High school and college courses in family life education can promote better mate selection. And

counseling aimed at helping couples discuss their desires openly and use positive, respectful conflict-resolution strategies is highly effective in easing adjustment to marriage and enhancing relationship quality (Gordon, Temple, & Adams, 2005).

Parenthood

For many adults, the decision to have children used to be "a biological given or an unavoidable cultural demand" (Michaels, 1988, p. 23). Today, in Western industrialized nations, parenthood is a matter of true individual choice. Effective birth control techniques enable adults to avoid having children in most instances. And changing cultural values allow people to remain childless with little fear of social criticism.

■ **TABLE 14.2** ■ *Factors Related to Marital Satisfaction*

FACTOR	HAPPY MARRIAGE	UNHAPPY MARRIAGE
Family backgrounds	Partners similar in SES, education, religion, and age	Partners very different in SES, education, religion, and age
Age at marriage	After age 23	Before age 23
Length of courtship	At least six months	Less than six months
Timing of first pregnancy	After first year of marriage	Before or within first year of marriage
Relationship to extended family	Warm and positive	Negative; wish to maintain distance
Marital patterns in extended family	Stable	Unstable; frequent separations and divorces
Financial and employment status	Secure	Insecure
Family responsibilities	Shared; perception of fairness	Largely the woman's responsibility; perception of unfairness
Personality characteristics	Emotionally positive; good conflict-resolution skills	Emotionally negative and impulsive; poor conflict-resolution skills

Note: The more factors present, the greater the likelihood of marital happiness or unhappiness.

Sources: Bradbury, Fincham, & Beach, 2000; Johnson et al., 2005; Waldinger et al., 2004.

SOCIAL ISSUES

Partner Abuse

Violence in families is a widespread health and human rights issue, occurring in all cultures and SES groups. Often one form of domestic violence is linked to others. Recall the story of Karen in Chapter 13. Her husband, Mike, not only assaulted her sexually and physically but also abused her psychologically—isolating, humiliating, and demeaning her (Dutton, 2007; Dutton & Nicholls, 2005). Violent adults also break their partner's favorite possessions, punch holes in walls, or throw objects. If children are present, they may become victims.

Partner abuse in which husbands are perpetrators and wives are physically injured is the type most likely to be reported to authorities. But many acts of family violence are not reported. When researchers ask American couples about fights that led to acts of hostility, men and women report similar rates of assault (Archer, 2002; Dutton, 2007). Women victims are more often physically injured, but sex differences in severity of abuse are not great (Archer, 2002; Ehrensaft, Moffitt, & Caspi, 2004). Partner abuse occurs at about the same rate in same-sex relationships as in heterosexual relationships (Schwartz & Waldo, 2004). "Getting my partner's attention," "gaining control," and "expressing anger" are reasons that partners typically give for abusing each other (Dutton, 2007).

Factors Related to Partner Abuse

In abusive relationships, dominance–submission sometimes proceeds from husband to wife, sometimes from wife to husband. In about one-third to one-half of cases, both partners are violent (Dutton, Nicholls, & Spidel, 2005). Marvin's and Pat's relationship helps us understand how partner abuse escalates. Shortly after their wedding, Pat began complaining about the demands of Marvin's work and insisted that he come home early to spend time with her. When he resisted, she hurled epithets, threw objects, and slapped him. One evening, Marvin became so angry at Pat's hostilities that he smashed a dish against the wall, threw his wedding ring at her, and left the house. The next morning, Pat apologized and promised not to attack again. But her outbursts became more frequent and desperate.

These violence–remorse cycles, in which aggression escalates, characterize many abusive relationships. Personality and developmental history, family circumstances, and cultural factors combine to make partner

abuse more likely (Dixon & Browne, 2003).

Many abusers are overly dependent on their spouses as well as jealous, possessive, and controlling. For example, the thought of Karen ever leaving induced such high anxiety in Mike that he monitored all her activities. Depression, anxiety, and low self-esteem also characterize abusers. And because they have great difficulty managing anger, trivial events—such as an unwashed shirt or a late meal—can trigger abusive episodes. When asked to explain their offenses, they attribute greater blame to their partner than to themselves (Henning, Jones, & Holdford, 2005).

A high proportion of abusers grew up in homes where parents engaged in hostile interactions, used coercive discipline, and were abusive toward their children (Bevan & Higgins, 2002; Ehrensaft, Cohen, & Johnson, 2006). Perhaps this explains why conduct problems in childhood and violent delinquency in adolescence also predict partner abuse (Dutton, 2007). Stressful life events, such as job loss or financial difficulties, increase its likelihood (Emery & Laumann-Billings, 1998). Because of widespread poverty, African Americans and Native Americans report high rates of partner violence (Hoff, 2001). Alcohol abuse is another related factor.

At a societal level, cultural norms that endorse male dominance and female submissiveness promote partner abuse (World Health Organization, 2000, 2005). As Figure 14.4 shows, in countries with widespread poverty that also sanction gender inequality, partner violence against women is especially high, affecting nearly half or more of the female population.

Victims are chronically anxious and depressed and experience frequent panic attacks (Stuart et al., 2006). Yet a variety of situational factors discourage them from leaving these destructive relationships. A victimized wife may depend on her husband's earning power or fear even worse harm to

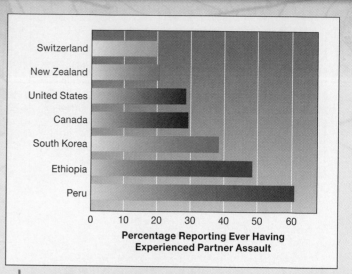

■ **FIGURE 14.4** ■ **Assaults by intimate partners against women in seven nations.** In each country, samples of women were asked to indicate whether they had ever experienced partner physical abuse. The incidence, always underreported, is high in all nations. It is especially high in countries that endorse traditional gender roles and suffer from widespread poverty. (From World Health Organization, 2000, 2005.)

herself or her children. Extreme assaults, including homicide, tend to occur after partner separation. And victims of both sexes, but especially men, are deterred by the embarrassment of going to the police.

Intervention and Treatment

Community services available to battered women include crisis telephone lines that provide anonymous counseling and social support and shelters that offer protection and treatment (see page 352). Because many women return to their abusive partners several times before making their final move, community agencies usually offer therapy to male batterers. Most rely on several months to a year of group sessions that confront rigid gender stereotyping; teach communication, problem solving, and anger control; and use social support to motivate behavior change (Whitaker, Baker, & Arias, 2007).

Although existing treatments are better than none, most are not effective at dealing with relationship difficulties or alcohol abuse. At present, few interventions acknowledge that men also are victims. Yet ignoring their needs perpetuates domestic violence. When victims do not want to separate from a violent partner, a whole-family treatment approach that focuses on changing partner interaction and reducing high life stress is crucial.

In 1950, 78 percent of American married couples were parents. Today, 70 percent bear children, and they tend to be older when they have their first child. Consistent with this pattern of delayed childbearing and with the decision of most women to divide their energies between family and work, family size in industrialized nations has declined. In 1950, the average number of children per couple was 3.1. Currently, it is 1.8 in the United States and Canada; 1.7 in Australia, Great Britain, and Sweden; 1.4 in Japan and Germany; and 1.3 in Italy (U.S. Census Bureau, 2009a, 2009b). Nevertheless, the vast majority of married people continue to embrace parenthood as one of life's most meaningful experiences.

■ **THE DECISION TO HAVE CHILDREN.** The choice of parenthood is affected by a complex array of factors, including financial circumstances, personal and religious values, and health conditions. Women with traditional gender identities usually decide to have children. Whether a woman is employed has less impact on childbearing than her occupation. Women with high-status, demanding careers less often choose parenthood and, when they do, more often delay it than women with less consuming jobs (Barber, 2001a; Tangri & Jenkins, 1997).

When Americans are asked about their desire to have children, they mention a variety of advantages and disadvantages. Some ethnic and regional differences exist, but in all groups, the most important reasons for having children include the warm, affectionate relationship and the stimulation and fun that children provide. Also frequently mentioned are growth and learning experiences that children bring to the lives of adults, the desire to have someone carry on after one's own death, and feelings of accomplishment and creativity that come from helping children grow (Cowan & Cowan, 2000; O'Laughlin & Anderson, 2001).

Most young adults also realize that having children means years of extra burdens and responsibilities. Among disadvantages of parenthood, they cite "loss of freedom" most often, followed by "financial strain." According to a conservative estimate, new parents in the United States today will spend about $200,000 to rear a child from birth to age 18, and many will incur substantial additional expense for higher education and financial dependency during emerging adulthood (U.S. Department of Agriculture, 2007).

■ **TRANSITION TO PARENTHOOD.** The early weeks after a baby enters the family are full of profound changes: constant caregiving, added financial responsibilities, and less time for the couple's relationship. These demands usually cause the gender roles of husband and wife to become more traditional—even for couples like Sharese and Ernie who are strongly committed to gender equality (Cowan & Cowan, 2000; Salmela-Aro et al., 2001).

For most new parents, however, the arrival of a baby does not cause significant marital strain. Marriages that are gratifying and supportive tend to remain so (Feeney et al., 2001; Miller, 2000). But troubled marriages usually become more unhappy and distressed (Houts et al., 2008; Kluwer & Johnson, 2007). In a study of newlyweds who were interviewed annually for six years, the husband's affection, expression of "we-ness" (values and goals similar to his wife's), and awareness of his wife's daily life predicted mothers' stable or increasing marital satisfaction after childbirth (Shapiro, Gottman, & Carrere, 2000). When expectant couples anticipate lack of partner support in parenting, their prediction generally becomes reality, yielding an especially difficult post-birth adjustment (McHale & Rotman, 2007).

Violated expectations about division of labor in the home powerfully affect new parents' well-being. In dual-earner marriages, the larger the difference in men's and women's caregiving responsibilities, the greater the decline in marital satisfaction after childbirth, especially for women—with negative consequences for parent–infant interaction. In contrast, sharing caregiving predicts greater parental happiness and sensitivity to the baby (McHale et al., 2004; Moller, Hwang, & Wickberg, 2008).

Postponing childbearing until the late twenties or thirties, as more couples do today, eases the transition to parenthood. Waiting permits couples to pursue occupational goals, gain life experience, and strengthen their relationship. Under these circumstances, men are more enthusiastic about becoming fathers and therefore more willing to participate. And women whose careers are well under way and whose marriages are happy are more likely to encourage their husbands to share housework and child care, which fosters fathers' involvement (Lee & Dougherty, 2007; Schoppe-Sullivan et al., 2008).

A second birth typically requires that fathers take an even more active role in parenting—by caring for the firstborn while the mother is recuperating and by sharing in the high demands of tending to both a baby and a young child. Consequently,

Compared to a first birth, a second birth typically requires that fathers become more actively involved in parenting, sharing in the high demands of tending to both a baby and a young child.

well-functioning families with a newborn second child typically pull back from the traditional division of responsibilities that occurred after the first birth. In a study that tracked parents from the end of pregnancy through the first year after their second child's birth, fathers' willingness to place greater emphasis on the parenting role was strongly linked to mothers' adjustment after the arrival of a second baby (Stewart, 1990).

Generous, paid employment leave—widely available in other industrialized nations but not in the United States—is crucial for parents of newborns (see Chapter 3, pages 81–82). But financial pressures mean that many new mothers who are eligible for unpaid work leave take far less than they are guaranteed by U.S. federal law, while new fathers take little or none (Han & Waldfogel, 2003). When favorable workplace policies exist and parents take advantage of them, couples are more likely to support each other and experience family life as gratifying (Feldman, Sussman, & Zigler, 2004). As a result, the stress caused by the birth of a baby stays at manageable levels.

■ **FAMILIES WITH YOUNG CHILDREN.**   In today's complex world, men and women are less certain about how to rear children than in previous generations. Clarifying child-rearing values and implementing them in warm, involved, and appropriately demanding ways are crucial for the welfare of the next generation and society. Yet cultures do not always place a high priority on parenting, as indicated by the lack of many societal supports for children and families (see Chapter 2, page 51). Furthermore, changing family forms mean that the lives of today's parents differ substantially from those of past generations.

In previous chapters, we discussed a wide variety of influences on child-rearing styles, including personal characteristics of children and parents, SES, and ethnicity. The couple's relationship is also vital. Parents who work together as a *coparenting team*, cooperating and showing solidarity and respect for each other in parenting roles, are more likely to gain in warm marital interaction, feel competent as parents, use effective child-rearing practices, and have children who are developing well (McHale et al., 2002a; Schoppe-Sullivan et al., 2004).

For employed parents, a major struggle is finding good child care and, when their child is ill or otherwise in need of emergency care, taking time off from work or making other urgent arrangements. The younger the child, the greater parents' sense of risk and difficulty—especially low-income parents, who must work longer hours to pay bills; who often, in the United States, have no workplace benefits (health insurance or paid sick leave); and who typically cannot afford the cost of child care (Halpern, 2005b). When competent, convenient child care is not available, the woman usually faces added pressures. She must either curtail or give up her work, with profound financial consequences in low-income families, or endure unhappy children, missed workdays, and constant searches for new arrangements.

Despite its challenges, rearing young children is a powerful source of adult development. Parents report that it expands their emotional capacities and enriches their lives. For example,

Ernie remarked that through sharing in child rearing, he felt "rounded out" as a person. Other involved parents say that parenthood helped them tune in to others' feelings and needs, required that they become more tolerant, self-confident, and responsible, and broadened their extended family, friendship, and community ties (Knoester & Eggebeen, 2006; Nomaguchi & Milkie, 2003).

■ **FAMILIES WITH ADOLESCENTS.**   Adolescence brings sharp changes in parental roles. In Chapters 11 and 12, we noted that parents must establish a revised relationship with their adolescent children—blending guidance with freedom and gradually loosening control. As adolescents gain in autonomy and explore values and goals in their search for identity, parents often complain that their teenager is too focused on peers and no longer cares about being with the family. Heightened parent–child bickering over everyday issues takes a toll, especially on mothers, who do most of the negotiating with teenagers.

Overall, children seem to navigate the challenges of adolescence more easily than parents, many of whom report a dip in marital and life satisfaction. More people seek family therapy during this period of the family life cycle than during any other (Steinberg & Silk, 2002).

■ **PARENT EDUCATION.**   In the past, family life changed little from one generation to the next, and adults learned what they needed to know about parenting through modeling and direct experience. Today's world confronts adults with a host of factors that impinge on their ability to succeed as parents.

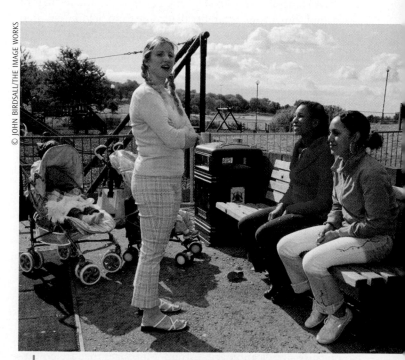

Contemporary parents eagerly seek information on child rearing, and women often reach out to a network of friends for knowledge and assistance.

Contemporary parents eagerly seek information on child rearing. New mothers often regard popular parenting books and magazines as particularly valuable. They also reach out to a network of other women for knowledge and assistance. Fathers, by contrast, rarely have social networks through which they can learn about child care and child rearing. Consequently, they frequently turn to mothers to figure out how to relate to their child, especially if they have a close, confiding marriage (Lamb & Lewis, 2004; McHale, Kuersten-Hogan, & Rao, 2004). Recall from Chapter 6 that marital harmony fosters both parents' positive engagement with babies, but it is especially important for fathers.

Parent education courses exist to help parents clarify child-rearing values, improve family communication, understand how children develop, and apply more effective parenting strategies. A variety of programs yield positive outcomes, including enhanced knowledge of effective parenting practices, improved parent–child interaction, and heightened awareness by parents of their role as educators of their children (Bert, Ferris, & Borkowski, 2008; Smith, Perou, & Lesesne, 2002). Another benefit is social support—opportunities to discuss concerns with experts and other dedicated parents.

ASK YOURSELF

>> **REVIEW**
What strategies can couples use to ease the transition to parenthood?

>> **APPLY**
After her wedding, Sharese was convinced she had made a mistake. Cite factors that sustained her marriage and led it to become especially happy.

>> **REFLECT**
Do you live with your parents or on your own? What factors contributed to your current living arrangements? If you live independently, has your relationship with your parents changed in ways that match the findings of research?

The Diversity of Adult Lifestyles

The current array of adult lifestyles dates back to the 1960s, when young people began to question the conventional wisdom of previous generations and to ask, "What kinds of commitments should I make to live a full and rewarding life?" As the public became more accepting of diverse lifestyles, choices such as staying single, cohabiting, remaining childless, and divorcing seemed more available.

Today, nontraditional family options have penetrated the American mainstream. As we will see, some adults make a deliberate decision to adopt a lifestyle, whereas others drift into it.

The lifestyle may be imposed by society, as is the case for cohabiting same-sex couples in the United States, who cannot marry legally in most states. Or people may choose a certain lifestyle because they feel pushed away from another, such as a marriage gone sour. In sum, the adoption of a lifestyle can be within or beyond the person's control.

Singlehood

On finishing her education, Heather joined the Peace Corps and spent four years in Ghana. Though open to a long-term relationship, she had only fleeting romances. After she returned to the United States, she accepted a management position with an insurance company. At age 35, over lunch with Sharese, she reflected on her life: "I was open to marriage, but after my career took off, it would have interfered. Now I'm so used to independence that I question whether I could adjust to living with another person. I like being able to pick up and go where I want, when I want. But there's a tradeoff: I sleep alone, eat most of my meals alone, and spend a lot of my leisure time alone."

Singlehood—not living with an intimate partner—has increased in recent years, especially among young adults. For example, rates of never-married American 30- to 34-year-olds have risen sixfold since 1970, to about one-third of males and one-fourth of females. More people marry later or not at all, and divorce has added to the number of singles. In view of these trends, it is likely that most Americans will spend a substantial part of their adult lives single, and a growing minority—about 8 to 10 percent—will stay that way (U.S. Census Bureau, 2009b).

© BILL BACHMANN/THE IMAGE WORKS

Compared with single men, single women more easily come to terms with their lifestyle, in part because of the greater social support available to women through intimate same-sex friendships.

Because they marry later, more young adult men than women are single. But women are far more likely than men to remain single for many years or their entire life. With age, fewer men are available with characteristics that most women seek in a mate—the same age or older, equally or better educated, and professionally successful. In contrast, men can choose partners from a large pool of younger unmarried women. Because of the tendency for women to "marry up" and men to "marry down," men in blue-collar occupations and women in prestigious careers are overrepresented among singles after age 30.

Ethnic differences also exist. For example, the percentage of never-married African Americans is nearly twice as great as that of Caucasian Americans in early adulthood. As we will see later, high unemployment among black men interferes with marriage. Many African Americans eventually marry in their late thirties and forties, a period in which black and white marriage rates come closer together (U.S. Census Bureau, 2009b).

The most commonly mentioned advantages of singlehood are freedom and mobility. But singles also recognize drawbacks—loneliness, the dating grind, limited sexual and social life, reduced sense of security, and feelings of exclusion from the world of married couples. Single men have more physical and mental health problems than single women, who more easily come to terms with their lifestyle, in part because of the greater social support available to women through intimate same-sex friendships (Pinquart, 2003). But overall, people who have always been single are content with their lives. Though not quite as happy as married people, they report feeling considerably happier than people recently widowed or divorced (DePaulo & Morris, 2005; Lucas et al., 2003).

Nevertheless, many single people go through a stressful period in their late twenties, when most of their friends have married. Widespread veneration of marriage, along with negative stereotyping of singles as socially immature and self-centered, probably contributes (DePaulo & Morris, 2006). For single women, the mid-thirties is another trying time, as the biological deadline for childbearing approaches. A few decide to become parents through artificial insemination or a love affair. And an increasing number are adopting, often from overseas countries.

Cohabitation

Cohabitation refers to the lifestyle of unmarried couples who have a sexually intimate relationship and who share a residence. Until the 1960s, cohabitation in Western nations was largely limited to low-SES adults. Since then, it has increased in all groups, with an especially dramatic rise among well-educated, economically advantaged young people. Today's young adults are much more likely than those of a generation ago to form their first conjugal union through cohabitation. Among Americans in their twenties, cohabitation is now the preferred mode of entry into a committed intimate partnership, chosen by more than 50 percent of couples (U.S. Census Bureau,

Cohabitation has increased dramatically in the United States since the 1960s. However, the practice is not as thoroughly integrated into American society as it is in Western Europe, where couples like these Dutch partners report that they are nearly as committed as married people.

2009b). Cohabitation rates are even higher among adults with failed marriages (Cohan & Kleinbaum, 2002).

Although Americans are more open to cohabitation than in the past, their attitudes are not yet as positive as those of Western Europeans. Furthermore, American couples who cohabit before they are engaged to be married are more prone to divorce than couples who wait to live together until after they have made a commitment to each other. But this association is less strong or absent in Western European nations, where cohabitation is thoroughly integrated into society and cohabiters are nearly as devoted to each other as married people (Kline et al., 2004; Rhoades, Stanley, & Markman, 2006). U.S. young people who cohabit prior to engagement tend to have less conventional values. They have had more sexual partners and are more politically liberal, less religious, and more androgynous. In addition, a larger number have parents who divorced (Axinn & Barber, 1997; Kurdek, 2006).

These personal characteristics may contribute to the negative outcomes associated with cohabitation. But the cohabitation experience itself also plays a role. American cohabiters are less likely than married people to pool finances or jointly own a house. In addition, they have poorer-quality relationships (Cohan & Kleinbaum, 2002; Kline et al., 2004). Perhaps the open-ended nature of the cohabiting relationship reduces motivation to develop effective conflict-resolution skills. When cohabiters carry negative communication into marriage, it undermines marital satisfaction.

Certain couples, however, are exceptions to the trends just described. People who cohabit after separation or divorce often test a new relationship carefully to prevent another failure, especially when children are involved. As a result, they cohabit longer and are less likely to move toward marriage (Smock & Gupta, 2002). Similarly, cohabitation is often an alternative to marriage among low-SES couples. Many regard their earning power as too uncertain for marriage and continue living together, sometimes giving birth to children and marrying when their financial status improves (Jayakody & Cabrera, 2002).

Finally, cohabiting gay and lesbian couples report strong commitment, equal to that of married people. When their relationships become difficult, they end more often than marriages only because of fewer barriers to separating, including children in common, financial dependence on a partner, or concerns about the costs of divorce (Kurdek, 1998, 2006). In a study in which same-sex couples in Vermont were followed over three years, cohabiters were more likely than couples in civil unions to have ended their relationships (Balsam et al., 2008). Civil unions were as stable as heterosexual marriages.

Childlessness

At work, Sharese got to know Beatrice and Daniel. Married for seven years and in their mid-thirties, they did not have children and were not planning any. To Sharese, their relationship seemed especially caring and affectionate. "At first, we were open to becoming parents," Beatrice explained, "but eventually we decided to focus on our marriage."

Some people are *involuntarily childless* because they did not find a partner with whom to share parenthood or their efforts at fertility treatments did not succeed. Beatrice and Daniel are in another category—men and women who are *voluntarily childless*.

Childlessness in the United States has increased steadily, from 9 percent of women between ages 20 and 44 in 1975 to about 20 percent in the mid-2000s, with similar trends occurring in other Western nations (Rowland, 2007; Sewall & Burns, 2006). Current figures vary somewhat, perhaps because voluntary childlessness is not always a permanent condition. A few people decide early that they do not want to be parents and stick to their plans. But most, like Beatrice and Daniel, make their decision after they are married and have developed a lifestyle they do not want to give up. Later, some change their minds.

Besides marital satisfaction and freedom from child-care responsibilities, common reasons for not having children include the woman's career and economic security. Consistent with these motives, the voluntarily childless are usually college-educated, have prestigious occupations, and are highly committed to their work (Amba & Martinez, 2006; Kemkes-Grottenhaler, 2003).

Negative stereotypes of nonparenthood—as a sign of self-indulgence and irresponsibility—have weakened in Western nations (Dykstra & Hagestad, 2007). In line with this trend, voluntarily childless adults are just as content with their lives as parents who have good relationships with their children. But adults who cannot overcome infertility are likely to be dissatisfied—some profoundly disappointed, others more

ambivalent, depending on compensations in other areas of their lives (Letherby, 2002; Nichols & Pace-Nichols, 2000). Childlessness interferes with adjustment only when it is beyond a person's control.

Divorce and Remarriage

Divorce rates have stabilized since the mid-1980s, partly because of rising age of marriage, which is linked to greater financial stability and marital satisfaction. In addition, the increase in cohabitation has curtailed divorce: Many relationships break up before marriage (Bumpass, 2004; Heaton, 2002). Still, 45 percent of U.S. marriages dissolve. Because most divorces occur within seven years of marriage, many involve young children. Divorces are also common during the transition to midlife, when people have adolescent children—a period (as noted earlier) of reduced marital satisfaction.

■ **FACTORS RELATED TO DIVORCE.** Why do so many marriages fail? As Christy and Gary's divorce illustrates, the most obvious reason is a disrupted husband–wife relationship. Christy and Gary did not argue more than Sharese and Ernie. But their problem-solving style was ineffective. When Christy raised concerns, Gary reacted with resentment, defensiveness, and retreat—a demand–withdraw pattern found in many partners who split up (Haltzman, Holstein, & Moss, 2007). Another typical style involves little conflict, but partners increasingly lead separate lives because they have different expectations of family life and few shared interests, activities, or friends (Gottman & Levenson, 2000).

What problems underlie these maladaptive communication patterns? In a nine-year longitudinal study, researchers asked a U.S. national sample of 2,000 married people about marital problems and followed up three, six, and nine years later to find out who had separated or divorced (Amato & Rogers, 1997). Wives reported more problems than husbands, with the gender difference largely involving the wife's emotions, such as anger and hurt feelings. Husbands seemed to have difficulty sensing their wife's distress, which contributed to her view of the marriage as unhappy. Regardless of which spouse reported the problem or was judged responsible for it, the strongest predictors of divorce during the following decade were infidelity, spending money foolishly, drinking or using drugs, expressing jealousy, engaging in irritating habits, and moodiness.

Background factors that increase the chances of divorce are younger age at marriage, not attending religious services, being previously divorced, and having parents who had divorced. Low religious involvement subtracts an influential context for instilling positive marital attitudes and behaviors. And research following families over two decades reveals that parental divorce elevates risk of divorce in at least two succeeding generations, in part because it promotes child adjustment problems and reduces commitment to the norm of lifelong marriage (Amato & Cheadle, 2005; Wolfinger, 2005).

© NOEL HENDRICKSON/PHOTODISC RED/GETTY IMAGES

An ineffective problem-solving style can lead to divorce. Many partners who split up follow a pattern in which one partner raises concerns, and the other reacts with resentment, anger, and retreat.

Poorly educated, economically disadvantaged couples who suffer multiple life stresses are especially likely to split up (Clarke-Stewart & Brentano, 2006). But Christy's case represents another trend—rising marital breakup among well-educated, career-oriented, economically independent women. When a woman's workplace status and income exceed her husband's, the risk of divorce increases—an association explained by differing gender-role beliefs between the spouses. A husband's lack of support for his wife's career can greatly heighten her unhappiness and, therefore, the chances that she will end the marriage (Popenoe, 2006). Overall, women are twice as likely as men to initiate divorce proceedings.

■ **CONSEQUENCES OF DIVORCE.** Divorce involves the loss of a way of life and therefore a part of the self sustained by that way of life. As a result, it provides opportunities for both positive and negative change.

Immediately after separation, both men and women experience disrupted social networks, a decline in social support, and increased anxiety, depression, and impulsive behavior (Amato, 2000). For most, these reactions subside within two years. Nonworking women who organized their identities around their husbands have an especially hard time. And some noncustodial fathers feel disoriented and rootless as a result of decreased contact with their children. Others distract themselves with a frenzy of social activity (Coleman, Ganong, & Leon, 2006).

Finding a new partner contributes most to the life satisfaction of divorced adults (Forste & Heaton, 2004; Wang & Amato, 2000). But it is more crucial for men, who adjust less well than women to living on their own. Despite loneliness and a drop in income (see Chapter 10), women tend to bounce back more easily from divorce. Christy, for example, developed new friendships and a sense of self-reliance that might not have emerged had she remained married to Gary. However, a few

women—especially those who are anxious and fearful, who remain strongly attached to their ex-spouses, or who lack education and job skills—experience a drop in self-esteem and persistent depression and sometimes enter into unsuccessful relationships repeatedly (Amato, 2000; Coleman, Ganong, & Leon, 2006). Job training, continued education, career advancement, and social support from family and friends play vital roles in the economic and psychological well-being of many divorced women.

■ **REMARRIAGE.** On average, people remarry within four years of divorce, men somewhat faster than women. Remarriages are especially vulnerable to breakup for several reasons. First, practical matters—financial security, help in rearing children, relief from loneliness, and social acceptance—figure more heavily into a second marriage. These concerns do not provide a sound footing for a lasting partnership. Second, some people transfer the negative patterns of interaction and problem solving learned in their first marriage to the second. Third, people with a failed marriage behind them are more likely to view divorce as an acceptable solution when marital difficulties resurface. Finally, remarried couples experience more stress from stepfamily situations (Coleman, Ganong, & Leon, 2006). As we will see, stepparent–stepchild ties are powerful predictors of marital happiness.

Blended families generally take three to five years to develop the connectedness and comfort of intact biological families (Ihinger-Tallman & Pasley, 1997). Family life education, couples counseling, and group therapy can help divorced and remarried adults adapt to the complexities of their new circumstances (Whiteside, 2006).

Variant Styles of Parenthood

Diverse family forms result in varied styles of parenthood. Each type of family—blended, never-married, gay or lesbian, among others—presents unique challenges to parenting competence and adult psychological well-being.

■ **STEPPARENTS.** Whether stepchildren live in the household or visit only occasionally, stepparents are in a difficult position. Stepparents enter the family as outsiders and, too often, move into their new parental role too quickly. Lacking a warm attachment bond to build on, their discipline is usually ineffective. Stepparents frequently criticize the biological parent for being too lenient, while the biological parent may view the stepparent as too harsh (Ganong & Coleman, 2004). Compared with first-marriage parents, remarried parents typically report higher levels of tension and disagreement, most centering on child-rearing issues. When both adults have children from prior marriages, rather than only one, more opportunities for conflict exist and relationship quality is poorer (Coleman, Ganong, & Fine, 2000).

Stepmothers are especially likely to experience conflict. Those who have not previously been married and had children may have an idealized image of family life, which is quickly shattered. Expected to be in charge of family relationships, stepmothers quickly find that stepparent–stepchild ties do not develop instantly. After divorce, biological mothers are frequently jealous, uncooperative, and possessive of their children. Even when their husbands do not have custody, stepmothers feel stressed (Church, 2004; MacDonald & DeMaris, 1996). As stepchildren go in and out of the home, stepmothers find life easier without resistant children and then feel guilty about their "unmaternal" feelings.

Stepfathers with children of their own tend to establish positive bonds with stepchildren relatively quickly, perhaps because they are experienced in building warm parent–child ties and feel less pressure than stepmothers to plunge into parenting. And stepchildren generally respond favorably to stepfathers' efforts to connect with them through enjoyable activities (Ganong et al., 1999). But stepfathers without biological children (like their stepmother counterparts) can have unrealistic expectations. Or their wives may push them into the father role, sparking negativity from children.

A caring marital relationship, cooperation from the biological parent, and children's willingness to accept their parent's new spouse are crucial for stepparent adjustment. Over time, many couples strengthen their relationship and build a coparenting partnership that improves interactions with stepchildren (Church, 2004). But because stepparent–stepchild bonds are hard to establish, the divorce rate is higher for remarried couples with stepchildren than for those without them.

■ **NEVER-MARRIED SINGLE PARENTS.** About 10 percent of U.S. children live with a single parent who has never married and does not have a partner. Of these parents, about 85 percent are mothers, 15 percent fathers (U.S. Census Bureau, 2009b). In the United States, African-American young women make up the largest group of never-married parents. Over 60 percent of births to black mothers in their twenties are to women without a partner, compared with 13 percent of births to white women (U.S. Census Bureau, 2009b). African-American women postpone marriage more and childbirth less than women in other U.S. ethnic groups. Job loss, persisting unemployment, and consequent inability of many black men to support a family have contributed to the postponement of marriage.

Never-married black mothers tap the extended family, especially their own mothers and sometimes male relatives, for help in rearing their children (Gasden, 1999; Jayakody & Kalil, 2002). For about one-third, marriage—not necessarily to the child's biological father—occurs within nine years after birth of the first child (Wu, Bumpass, & Musick, 2001). These couples function much like other first-marriage parents. Their children are often unaware that the father is a stepfather, and parents do not report the child-rearing difficulties typical of blended families (Ganong & Coleman, 1994).

Still, for low-SES women, never-married parenthood generally increases financial hardship. And children of low-SES never-married mothers who lack father involvement achieve less well in school and display more antisocial behavior than children in low-SES first-marriage families—problems that make life more difficult for mothers (Coley, 1998). But marriage to the child's biological father benefits children only when the father is a reliable source of economic and emotional support. When a mother pairs up with an antisocial father, her child is at greater risk for conduct problems than if she had reared the child alone (Jaffee et al., 2003). Strengthening social support, education, and employment opportunities for low-SES parents would greatly enhance the well-being of unmarried mothers and their children.

■ **GAY AND LESBIAN PARENTS.** Several million American gay men and lesbians are parents, most through previous heterosexual marriages, some through adoption, and a growing number through reproductive technologies (Ambert, 2005; Patterson, 2002). In the past, because of laws assuming that homosexuals could not be adequate parents, those who divorced a heterosexual partner lost custody of their children. Today, some U.S. states hold that sexual orientation by itself is irrelevant to custody. A few U.S. states, however, ban gay and lesbian couples from adopting children.

Most research on homosexual parents and children is limited to volunteer samples. Findings indicate that gay and lesbian parents are as committed to and effective at child rearing as heterosexual parents and sometimes more so (Bos, van Balen, & van den Boom, 2007; Tasker, 2005). Also, whether born to or adopted by their parents or conceived through donor insemination, children in gay and lesbian families did not differ from children of heterosexuals in mental health, peer relations, or gender identity (Allen & Burrell, 1996; Flaks et al., 1995; Golombok & Tasker, 1996).

Two additional studies, which surmounted the potential bias associated with a volunteer sample by including all

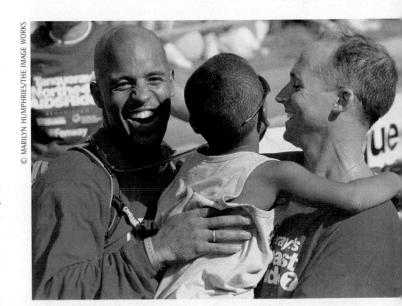

© MARILYN HUMPHRIES/THE IMAGE WORKS

Gay and lesbian parents are as committed to and effective at child rearing as heterosexual parents. Overall, families headed by same-sex partners can be distinguished from other families only by issues related to living in a nonsupportive society.

lesbian-mother families who had conceived children at a fertility clinic, also reported that children were developing favorably (Brewaeys et al., 1997; Chan, Raboy, & Patterson, 1998). Likewise, among participants drawn from a representative sample of British mothers and their 7-year-olds, children reared in lesbian-mother families did not differ from children reared in heterosexual families in adjustment and gender-role preferences (Golombok et al., 2003). Furthermore, children of gay and lesbian parents do not differ from other children in sexual orientation; the large majority are heterosexual (Tasker, 2005).

When extended-family members have difficulty accepting them, homosexual mothers and fathers often build "families of choice" through friends, who assume the roles of relatives. Usually, however, parents of gays and lesbians cannot endure a permanent rift (Fisher, Easterly, & Lazear, 2008). With time, interactions between homosexual parents and their families of origin become more positive and supportive.

A major concern of gay and lesbian parents is that their children will be stigmatized by their parents' sexual orientation. Most studies indicate that incidents of teasing or bullying are rare because parents and children carefully manage the information they reveal to others (Tasker, 2005). But in an Australian study, even though most third to tenth graders were guarded about discussing their parents' relationship with peers, nearly half reported harassment (Ray & Gregory, 2001). Overall, families headed by homosexuals can be distinguished from other families only by issues related to living in a nonsupportive society.

ASK YOURSELF

>> **REVIEW**
Return to Chapter 10, pages 270–272, and review the impact of divorce and remarriage on children and adolescents. How do those findings resemble outcomes for adults? What might account for the similarities?

>> **APPLY**
After dating for a year, Wanda and Scott decided to live together. Their parents worried that cohabitation would reduce the couple's chances for a successful marriage. Is this fear justified? Why or why not?

>> **REFLECT**
Do your own experiences or those of your friends match research findings on cohabitation, singlehood, never-married parents, or gay and lesbian parents? Select one instance and discuss.

Career Development

Besides family life, vocational life is a vital domain of social development in early adulthood. Young people must learn how to perform work tasks well, get along with co-workers, respond to authority, and protect their own interests. When work experiences go well, adults develop new competencies, feel a sense of personal accomplishment, make new friends, and become financially independent and secure. And as we have seen, especially for women but also for men who support their partner's career development, aspirations and accomplishments in the workplace and the family are interwoven.

Establishing a Career

Our discussion of Levinson's and Vaillant's theories highlighted diverse paths and timetables for career development. Consider the wide variations among Sharese, Ernie, Christy, and Gary. As is typical for men, Ernie's and Gary's career lives were long and *continuous,* from completion of formal education to retirement. Sharese and Christy, like many women, had *discontinuous* career paths—ones that were interrupted or deferred by child rearing and other family needs (Huang & Sverke, 2007; Moen & Roehling, 2005). Furthermore, not all people embark on the vocation of their dreams. In an Australian study that followed 1,200 young people after they finished their schooling, at any given time during the next seven years, only 20 percent were working in a field consistent with their greatest interest (Athanasou, 2002).

Even for those who enter their chosen field, initial experiences can be discouraging. At the health department, Sharese discovered that committee meetings and paperwork consumed much of her day. Because each project had a deadline, the pressure of productivity weighed heavily on her. Adjusting to unanticipated disappointments in salary, supervisors, and co-workers is difficult. As new workers become aware of the gap between their expectations and reality, resignations are common. On average, people in their twenties move to a new job every two years (Petersen & Gonzales, 1999).

After a period of evaluation and adjustment, young adults generally settle into their work. In careers with opportunities for promotion, high aspirations must often be revised downward because the structure of most work settings resembles a pyramid, with few high-level executive and supervisory jobs. Besides opportunity, personal characteristics affect career progress. As we will see, a sense of self-efficacy is influential. Young people who are very anxious about on-the-job failure tend to set their career aspirations either too high or too low. When they encounter obstacles, they quickly conclude that career tasks are too hard and give up (Lent & Brown, 2002). As a result, they achieve far less than their abilities would permit.

Recall from Levinson's theory that career success often depends on the quality of a mentoring relationship. Access to an effective mentor is jointly affected by the availability of willing people and the individual's capacity to select an appropriate individual (Ramaswami & Dreher, 2007). The best mentors are seldom top executives, who tend to be preoccupied and therefore less helpful and sympathetic. Usually, young adults fare better with lower-level mentors—more experienced co-workers or members of their professional associations (Allen & Finkelstein, 2003).

Women and Ethnic Minorities

Although women and ethnic minorities have penetrated nearly all professions, their talents often are not developed to the fullest. Women, especially those who are members of economically disadvantaged minorities, remain concentrated in occupations that offer little opportunity for advancement, and they are underrepresented in executive and managerial roles (see Chapter 13, pages 359–360). And although the overall difference between men's and women's earnings is smaller today than 30 years ago, it remains considerable. U.S. government surveys following 9,000 U.S. college-educated workers for a decade revealed that a year after receiving their bachelor's degrees, women working full time earned just 80 percent as much as men. The difference was largely (but not entirely) due to gender differences in college majors: Women more often chose education and service fields, men higher-paying scientific and technical fields. Ten years after graduation, the gender pay gap had widened: Women's pay was only 69 percent of men's (Dey & Hill, 2007). Gender disparities in career development accounted for about 90 percent of the gap, with the remaining 10 percent attributed to on-the-job discrimination.

Especially for women in traditionally feminine occupations, career planning is often short-term and subject to change. Many enter and exit the labor market several times as they give birth to and rear children. Between ages 18 and 34, the typical woman has been out of the labor force 26 percent of the time, in contrast to 11 percent for the typical man (Furchtgott-Roth,

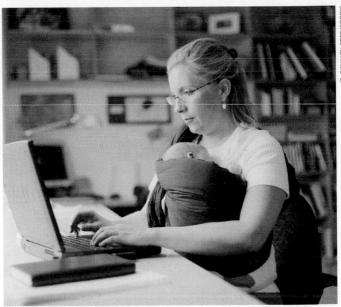

Women in prestigious, male-dominated careers often delay or avoid childbearing. But thanks to her employer's generous parental leave policies, this university professor is able to work from home while caring for her infant.

2009; U.S. Department of Labor, 2004). Time away from a career greatly hinders advancement—a major reason that women in prestigious, male-dominated careers tend to delay or avoid childbearing (Blair-Loy & DeHart, 2003).

In addition, low self-efficacy with respect to male-dominated fields limits women's career progress. Women who pursue nontraditional careers usually have "masculine" traits—high achievement orientation, self-reliance, and belief that their efforts will result in success. But even those with high self-efficacy are less certain than their male counterparts that they can overcome barriers to career success (Lindley, 2005). In a study of women scientists on university faculties, those reporting a sexist work climate (sexual harassment or discrimination in salary, promotion, or resources) were less satisfied with their jobs and less productive (Settles et al., 2006). Gender-stereotyped images of women as followers rather than leaders slow advancement into top-level management positions. And because men dominate high-status fields, fewer women are available to serve as mentors (Stewart & Lavaque-Manty, 2008).

Despite laws guaranteeing equal opportunity, racial bias in the labor market remains strong. In one study, researchers responded to more than 1,300 help-wanted newspaper ads with fictitious résumés, some containing higher qualifications and some lower qualifications. Half the résumés were assigned a white-sounding name (Emily Walsh, Brendan Baker) and half a black-sounding name (Lakisha Washington, Jamal Jones). At all job levels, from clerical work to top management, résumés with "white" names evoked 50 percent more callbacks than résumés with "black" names. And although whites received substantially more callbacks in response to high-quality than to

Ethnic minority women, such as this scientist, must surmount combined gender and racial discrimination to realize their career potential. Those who succeed often display an unusually high sense of self-efficacy.

low-quality résumés, having a high-quality résumé made little difference for blacks As the researchers noted, "Discrimination appears to bite twice, making it harder for African Americans to find a job and to improve their employability" (Bertrand & Mullainathan, 2004, p. 3). Consistent with this conclusion, African Americans spend more time searching for work, experience less stable employment, and acquire less work experience than Caucasian Americans with equivalent job qualifications (Pager & Shepherd, 2008).

Ethnic minority women must surmount combined gender and racial discrimination to realize their career potential. Those who succeed often display an unusually high sense of self-efficacy, attacking problems head-on despite repeated obstacles to achievement (Byars & Hackett, 1998). In an interview study of African-American women who had become leaders in diverse fields, all reported intense persistence, fueled by supportive relationships with other women, including teachers, colleagues, and friends who countered their sense of professional isolation (Richie et al., 1997). Many described their mothers as inspiring role models who had set high standards for them. Others felt empowered by a deep sense of connection to their African-American communities.

Combining Work and Family

Whether women work because they want to or have to (or both), the dominant family form today is the dual-earner marriage. Most dual-earner couples are also parents, since the majority of women with children are in the work force (see page 274 in Chapter 10). But many more women than men experience moderate to high levels of stress in trying to meet both work and family responsibilities (Cinamon & Rich, 2002).

© SMITH COLLECTION/GETTY IMAGES/ICONICA

Dual-earner couples can better balance work and family if they share both the pleasures and the burdens of child rearing.

TAKE A MOMENT... Think about a dual-earner family you know well. What are the main sources of strain? When Sharese returned to her job after her children were born, she felt a sense of *role overload,* or conflict between work and family responsibilities. In addition to a demanding career, she also (like most employed women) shouldered most of the household and child-care tasks. And both Sharese and Ernie felt torn between the desire to excel at their jobs and the desire to spend more time with each other, their children, and their friends and relatives. Role overload is linked to increased psychological stress, poorer marital relations, less effective parenting, and child behavior problems (Perry-Jenkins, Repetti, & Crouter, 2000; Saginak & Saginak, 2005).

Workplace supports can greatly reduce role overload, yielding substantial payoffs for employers. Among a large, nationally representative sample of U.S. working adults, the greater the number of time-flexible policies available in their work settings (for example, time off to care for a sick child, choice in start and stop times, and opportunities to work from home), the better their work performance (Halpern, 2005a). Employees with several time-flexible options missed fewer days of work, less often arrived at work late or left early, felt more committed to their employer, and worked harder. They also reported fewer stress-related health symptoms.

Effectively balancing work and family brings many benefits—a better standard of living, improved work productivity, enhanced psychological well-being, greater self-fulfillment, and happier marriages. Ernie took great pride in Sharese's career accomplishments, which contributed to his view of her as an interesting, capable helpmate. Multiple roles also granted both young people expanded contexts for experiencing success and greater similarity in everyday experiences, which fostered gratifying communication (Barnett & Hyde, 2001). Applying What We Know on the following page lists strategies that help dual-earner couples combine work and family roles in ways that promote mastery and pleasure in both spheres of life.

ASK YOURSELF

≫ REVIEW
Why do professionally accomplished women, especially those who are members of economically disadvantaged minorities, typically display high self-efficacy?

≫ APPLY
Heather climbed the career ladder of her company quickly, reaching a top-level executive position by her early thirties. In contrast, Sharese and Christy did not attain managerial roles in early adulthood. What factors might account for this disparity in career progress?

≫ REFLECT
Contact a major employer in your area and ask about its policies for helping employees combine work and family roles. What improvements would you suggest? Why are family-friendly policies "win-win" situations for both workers and employers?

Applying What We Know

Strategies That Help Dual-Earner Couples Combine Work and Family Roles

Strategy	Description
Devise a plan for sharing household tasks.	As soon as possible in the relationship, discuss relative commitment to work and family and division of household responsibilities. Decide who does a particular chore on the basis of who has the needed skill and time, not on the basis of gender. Schedule regular times to rediscuss your plan.
Begin sharing child care right after the baby's arrival.	For fathers, strive to spend equal time with the baby early. For mothers, refrain from imposing your standards on your partner. Instead, share the role of "child-rearing expert" by discussing parenting values and concerns often. Attend a parent education course together.
Talk over conflicts about decision making and responsibilities.	Face conflict through communication. Clarify your feelings and needs and express them to your partner. Listen and try to understand your partner's point of view. Then be willing to negotiate and compromise.
Establish a balance between work and family.	Critically evaluate the time you devote to work in view of your values and priorities. If it is too much, cut back.
Press for workplace and public policies that assist dual-earner family roles.	Encourage your employer to provide benefits that help combine work and family, such as flexible work hours, parental leave with pay, and on-site high-quality, affordable child care. Communicate with lawmakers and other citizens about improving public policies for children and families.

Summary

A Gradual Transition: Emerging Adulthood

What is emerging adulthood, and how has cultural change contributed to it?

>> In **emerging adulthood,** young adults from about age 18 to 25 are released from parental oversight but have not yet taken on adult roles. During these years of extended exploration, young people prolong identity development as they explore alternatives in breadth and depth.

© JIM WEST/THE IMAGE WORKS

>> Increased education required for entry-level positions in many fields, gains in economic prosperity, reduced need for young people's labor, and globalization have prompted the appearance and spread of emerging adulthood.

>> In trying out possibilities, emerging adults must adjust to disappointments in love and work, and their explorations also extend risky behaviors of adolescence. A wide array of personal attributes and social supports foster resilience.

Erikson's Theory: Intimacy versus Isolation

According to Erikson, what personality changes take place during early adulthood?

>> In Erikson's theory, young adults must resolve the conflict of **intimacy versus isolation,** balancing independence and intimacy as they form a close relationship with a partner. Research confirms that a secure identity fosters attainment of intimacy.

>> Young people also focus on aspects of generativity, including parenting and contributions to society through work.

Other Theories of Adult Psychosocial Development

Describe and evaluate Levinson's and Vaillant's theories of adult personality development.

>> Levinson described a series of eras, each consisting of a transition and a stable phase, in which people revise their **life structure.** Young adults usually construct a dream, typically involving career for men and both marriage and career for women, and form a relationship with a mentor to help them realize their dream. In their thirties, men tend to settle down, whereas many women remain unsettled into middle adulthood.

>> Vaillant refined Erikson's stages, portraying the twenties as devoted to intimacy, the thirties to career consolidation, the forties to generativity, and the fifties and sixties to cultural values.

>> The patterns Levinson and Vaillant identified are based on limited samples of people born in the first few decades of the twentieth century. Young adults' development is more variable today than in past generations.

What is the social clock, and how does it affect personality in adulthood?

>> Conformity to or departure from the **social clock**—age-graded expectations for major life events—can be a major source of personality change. Following a social clock grants confidence to young adults; deviating from it can bring psychological distress.

Close Relationships

Describe factors affecting mate selection and the role of romantic love in the young adult's quest for intimacy.

>> Romantic partners tend to resemble one another in age, ethnicity, SES, religion, and various personal and physical attributes. According to evolutionary theory, women seek a mate with traits that help ensure children's survival, while men look for characteristics signaling sexual pleasure and ability to bear offspring. An alternative, social learning perspective emphasizes that gender roles profoundly influence criteria for mate selection. Research suggests that both biological and social forces are involved.

>> According to the **triangular theory of love,** the balance among intimacy, passion, and commitment changes as romantic relationships move from the intense sexual attraction of **passionate love** toward more settled **companionate love.** Commitment is key to a satisfying, enduring relationship.

Describe adult friendships and sibling relationships and the role of loneliness in adult development.

>> Adult friendships have characteristics and benefits similar to earlier friendships and are based on trust, intimacy, and loyalty. Women's same-sex friendships tend to be more intimate than men's. After college, other-sex friendships decline with age for men but increase for highly educated, employed women. Adult sibling relationships often resemble friendships, especially among sisters with positive early experiences.

>> Young adults are vulnerable to **loneliness,** which declines with age as they form satisfying intimate ties. As long as it is not too intense, loneliness can encourage young people to reach out to others and better understand themselves.

The Family Life Cycle

Trace phases of the family life cycle that are prominent in early adulthood, and cite factors that influence these phases today.

>> Wide variations exist in the sequence and timing of phases of the **family life cycle.** Leaving home is a major step in assuming adult responsibilities. Departures for education occur earlier than those for full-time work and marriage. SES and ethnicity influence the likelihood that a young person will live independently before marriage. Many unmarried young adults return home for a period of time.

>> Nearly 90 percent of Americans marry, at later ages than in the past. Today, couples must work harder to define their marital roles. Both **traditional marriages** and **egalitarian marriages** are affected by women's participation in the workforce. Even in dual-earner marriages, North American women spend nearly twice as much time as men on housework.

>> Quality of the marital relationship predicts mental health similarly for both men and women. Women, however, feel particularly dissatisfied when the combined demands of work and family roles are overwhelming. Although most couples become parents, they do so at a later age and have fewer children than in the past.

>> The arrival of a child requires couples to adjust to increased responsibilities and often prompts a shift to more traditional roles, though this may reverse after the birth of a second child. Shared caregiving predicts greater parental happiness and positive parent–infant interaction.

>> Families with young children face challenges of clarifying and implementing child-rearing values. Couples who work together as a co-parenting team are more likely to gain in warm marital interaction, feel competent as parents, use effective child-rearing practices, and have children who are developing well.

>> In families with adolescents, parents must blend guidance with freedom and gradually loosen control. Marital satisfaction often declines in this phase. Parent education programs can help parents clarify their child-rearing values and use more effective strategies.

The Diversity of Adult Lifestyles

Discuss the diversity of adult lifestyles, focusing on singlehood, cohabitation, and childlessness.

>> Singlehood has risen in recent years because of a trend toward later marriage and a high divorce rate. Despite certain drawbacks, singles appreciate their freedom and mobility. Women tend to adjust more favorably than men.

>> **Cohabitation** has risen dramatically, especially among well-educated, economically advantaged young adults. Compared with their Western European counterparts, American cohabiters tend to be less conventional in values and behavior and less committed to their partner, and their subsequent marriages are more likely to fail. However, gay and lesbian couples who cohabit because they cannot marry report commitment equal to that of married couples.

>> Voluntarily childless adults tend to be well-educated and career-oriented and are as satisfied with their lives as parents who have good relationships with their children. But when childlessness is beyond a person's control, it interferes with adjustment.

Discuss today's high rates of divorce and remarriage, and cite factors that contribute to them.

>> Nearly half of U.S. marriages dissolve, often while children are at home. About two-thirds of divorced people remarry. Maladaptive communication patterns, younger ages at marriage, a family history of divorce, poverty, and the changing status of women all contribute to divorce.

≫ Finding a new partner is important to many divorced adults, especially men. Remarriages break up for several reasons, including the prominence of practical concerns rather than love in the decision to remarry, the persistence of negative styles of communication, the acceptance of divorce as a solution to marital difficulties, and problems adjusting to a stepfamily.

Discuss the challenges associated with variant styles of parenthood, including stepparents, never-married parents, and gay and lesbian parents.

≫ Establishing stepparent–stepchild ties is difficult, especially for stepmothers and for stepfathers without children of their own. A caring husband–wife relationship, cooperation from the biological parent, and children's acceptance are crucial for stepparent adjustment.

≫ Never-married single parenthood is especially high among low-income African-American women in their twenties. Unemployment among black men contributes to this trend. Although these mothers often receive help from extended family members, they find it difficult to overcome poverty.

≫ Gay and lesbian parents are as committed to and effective at child rearing as heterosexual parents, and their children are as well-adjusted as those reared by heterosexual parents.

© MARILYN HUMPHRIES/THE IMAGE WORKS

Career Development

Discuss patterns of career development, and cite difficulties faced by women, ethnic minorities, and couples seeking to combine work and family.

≫ Men's career paths are usually continuous, whereas women's are often discontinuous because of child rearing and other family needs. After adjusting to the realities of the work world, young adults settle into an occupation. Their progress is affected by opportunities for promotion, personal characteristics such as self-efficacy, and access to an effective mentor.

≫ Women and ethnic minorities have penetrated nearly all professions but have made limited progress in career advancement. Women are hampered by time away from the labor market, low self-efficacy and lack of mentoring in traditionally male-dominated fields, and gender stereotypes of women as followers rather than leaders. Racial bias in the labor market remains strong, and ethnic minority women who succeed display an unusually high sense of self-efficacy.

≫ Couples, particularly women, in dual-earner marriages often experience role overload. Effectively balancing work and family brings a better standard of living, enhanced psychological well-being, and happier marriages. Time-flexible workplace policies reduce stress while augmenting work performance.

Important Terms and Concepts

cohabitation (p. 384)
companionate love (p. 373)
egalitarian marriage (p. 378)
emerging adulthood (p. 366)

family life cycle (p. 377)
intimacy versus isolation (p. 369)
life structure (p. 370)
loneliness (p. 376)

passionate love (p. 373)
social clock (p. 372)
traditional marriage (p. 378)
triangular theory of love (p. 373)

Milestones
Development in Early Adulthood

- As basal metabolic rate declines, gradual weight gain begins in the middle of this decade and continues through middle adulthood. (346)
- Sexual activity increases. (349–351)

COGNITIVE

- If college educated, dualistic thinking declines in favor of relativistic thinking. (354)

- Moves from hypothetical to pragmatic thought. (355)
- Narrows vocational options and settles on a specific career. (358)
- Shows gains in cognitive–affective complexity, which continue through middle adulthood. (355–356)

- Develops expertise in a field of endeavor, which enhances problem solving. (356)

- May increase in creativity. (356–357)

EMOTIONAL/SOCIAL

- In the first half of this decade, if life circumstances permit, may engage in the extended exploration that characterizes emerging adulthood. (365–367)
- Feels increasingly in control of life events. (365)
- Is likely to achieve a personally meaningful identity. (366–367)
- Leaves the parental home permanently. (377)

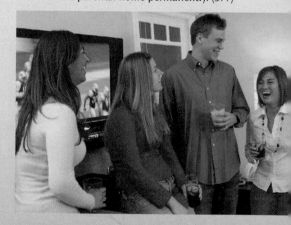

- Strives to make a permanent commitment to an intimate partner. (369–370, 372–373)
- Usually constructs a dream—an image of the self in the adult world that guides decision making. (370)

18–30 years

PHYSICAL

- Athletic skills that require speed of limb movement, explosive strength, and gross motor coordination peak early in this decade, then decline. (342)
- Athletic skills that depend on endurance, arm–hand steadiness, and aiming peak at the end of this decade, then decline. (342)
- Declines in touch sensitivity, cardiovascular and respiratory capacity, immune system functioning, and skin elasticity begin and continue throughout adulthood. (343)

Note: Numbers in parentheses indicate the page or pages on which each milestone is discussed.

- Typically forms a relationship with a mentor. (371)
- If in a high-status career, acquires professional skills, values, and credentials. (356, 370–371)
- Begins to develop mutually gratifying adult friendships and work ties. (375–376)
- May cohabit, marry, and bear children. (377–382)

- Sibling relationships become more companionate. (375–376)
- Loneliness peaks early in this decade, then declines steadily throughout adulthood. (376)

30–40 years

PHYSICAL

- Declines in vision, hearing, and the skeletal system begin and continue throughout adulthood. (343)
- In women, reproductive capacity continues to decline, and fertility problems increase sharply after the middle of this decade. (344–345)

- In men, semen volume, sperm motility, and percentage of normal sperm decrease gradually in the second half of this decade. (345)
- Hair begins to gray and thin in the middle of this decade. (343)
- Sexual activity declines, probably as a result of the demands of daily life. (351)

COGNITIVE

- May develop commitment within relativistic thinking. (354–355)
- Creative accomplishment often peaks in the second half of this decade, although this varies across disciplines. (356–357)

EMOTIONAL/SOCIAL

- Reevaluates life structure and tries to change components that are inadequate. (371)
- Establishes a stable niche in society through family, occupation, and community activities. (For women, career maturity and authority in the community may be delayed.) (371)

CHAPTER 15

Physical and Cognitive Development in Middle Adulthood

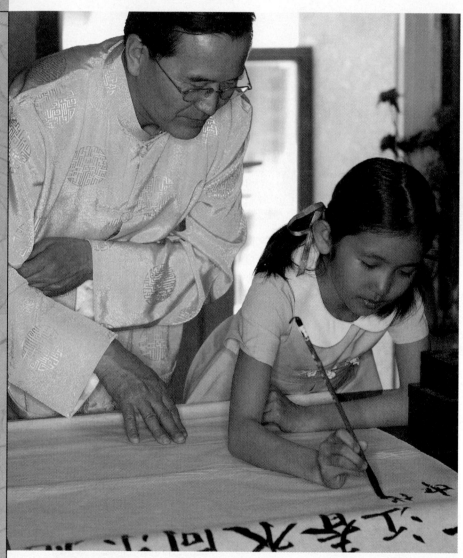

© FLORESCO PRODUCTIONS/CORBIS

In middle adulthood, expertise—accumulated knowledge that supports high-level performance in vocational or leisure pursuits—reaches its height. As this master calligrapher shares his expertise with a young student, he transfers knowledge, skill, and passion for the art to a new generation.

On a snowy December evening, Devin and Trisha sat down to read the holiday cards piled high on the kitchen counter. Devin's 55th birthday had just passed; Trisha would turn 48 in a few weeks. During the past year, they had celebrated their 24th wedding anniversary. These milestones, along with the annual updates they received from friends, brought the changes of midlife into bold relief.

Instead of new births, children starting school, or a first promotion at work, holiday cards and letters sounded new themes. Jewel's recap of the past year reflected a growing awareness of a finite lifespan, one in which time had become more precious. She wrote:

© WESTEND61/CORBIS

> My mood has been lighter ever since my birthday. There was some burden I laid down by turning 49. My mother passed away when she was 48, so it all feels like a gift now. Blessed be!

George and Anya reported on their son's graduation from law school and their daughter Michelle's first year of university:

> Anya is filling the gap created by the children's departure by returning to college for a nursing degree. After enrolling this fall, she was surprised to find herself in the same psychology class as Michelle. At first, Anya worried about handling the academic work, but after a semester of success, she's feeling more confident.

Tim's message reflected continuing robust health, acceptance of physical changes, and a new burden—caring for aging parents:

> I used to be a good basketball player in college, but recently I noticed that my 20-year-old nephew, Brent, can dribble and shoot circles around me. It must be my age! But I ran our city marathon in September and came in seventh in the over-50 division. Brent ran, too, but he opted out a few miles short of the finish line to get some pizza while I pressed on. That must be my age, too!

> The saddest news is that my dad had a bad stroke. His mind is clear, but his body is partially paralyzed. It's really upsetting because he was getting to enjoy the computer I gave him, and it was so upbeat to talk with him about it in the months before the stroke.

Middle adulthood, which begins around age 40 and ends at about 65, is marked by narrowing life options and a shrinking future as children leave home and career paths become more determined. In other ways, middle age is hard to define because wide variations in attitudes and behaviors exist. Some individuals seem physically and mentally young at age 65—active and optimistic, with a sense of serenity and stability. Others feel old at age 40—as if their lives had peaked and were on a downhill course.

In this chapter, we trace physical and cognitive development from the fifth into the seventh decade of life. In both domains, we will encounter not just progressive declines but also sustained performance and compensating gains. As in earlier chapters, we will see that change occurs in manifold ways. Besides heredity and biological aging, our personal approach to passing years combines with family, community, and cultural contexts to affect the way we age.

Physical Development

Physical development in midlife is a continuation of the gradual changes under way in early adulthood. Hair grays and thins, new lines appear on the face, and a fuller, less youthful body shape is evident. During midlife, most individuals begin to experience life-threatening health episodes—if not in themselves, then in their partners and friends. And a change in time orientation, from "years since birth" to "years left to live," adds to consciousness of aging (Neugarten, 1968b).

These factors lead to a revised physical self-image, with somewhat less emphasis on hoped-for gains and more on feared declines (Bybee & Wells, 2003). Prominent concerns among 40- to 65-year-olds include getting a fatal disease, being too ill to maintain independence, and losing mental capacities. Unfortunately, many middle-aged adults fail to embrace realistic alternatives. People can do much to promote physical vigor and good health in midlife.

Physical Changes

As she dressed for work one morning, Trisha remarked jokingly to Devin, "I think I'll leave the dust on the mirror so I can't see the wrinkles and gray hairs." Catching sight of her image, she continued in a more serious tone. "And look at this fat—it just doesn't want to go! I need to figure out how to fit some regular exercise into my life." In response, Devin glanced down soberly at his own enlarged midriff.

At breakfast, Devin took his glasses on and off and squinted while reading the paper. "I've gotta get these bifocals adjusted again." As they conversed between the kitchen and the adjoining den, Devin sometimes asked Trisha to repeat herself. And he kept turning up the radio and TV volume. "Does it need to be that loud?" Trisha frequently asked.

In the following sections, we look closely at major physical changes of midlife. As we do so, you may find it helpful to refer back to Table 13.1 on page 343, which provides a summary.

Vision

By the forties, difficulty reading small print is common, due to thickening of the lens combined with weakening of the muscle that enables the eye to *accommodate* (adjust its focus) to nearby objects. As new fibers appear on the surface of the lens, they compress older fibers toward the center, creating a thicker, denser, less pliable structure that eventually cannot be transformed at all. By age 50, the accommodative ability of the lens is one-sixth of what it was at age 20. Around age 60, the lens loses its capacity to adjust to objects at varying distances entirely, a condition called **presbyopia** (literally, "old eyes"). As the lens enlarges, the eye rapidly becomes more farsighted between ages 40 and 60 (Charman, 2008). Corrective lenses—or, for nearsighted people, bifocals—ease reading problems.

A second set of changes limits ability to see in dim light, which declines at twice the rate of daylight vision (Jackson & Owsley, 2000). Throughout adulthood, the size of the pupil shrinks and the lens yellows. In addition, starting at age 40, the *vitreous* (transparent gelatin-like substance that fills the eye) develops opaque areas, reducing the amount of light reaching the retina. Changes in the lens and vitreous also cause light to scatter within the eye, increasing sensitivity to glare. While driving at night, Devin sometimes had trouble making out signs and moving objects. And his vision was more disrupted by bright light sources, such as headlights of oncoming cars (Owsley et al., 1998).

Yellowing of the lens and increasing density of the vitreous also limit color discrimination, especially at the green–blue–violet end of the spectrum (Kraft & Werner, 1999). Occasionally, Devin had to ask whether his sport coat, tie, and socks matched.

Besides structural changes in the eye, neural changes in the visual system occur. Gradual loss of rods and cones (light- and color-receptor cells) in the retina and of neurons in the optic nerve (the pathway between the retina and the cerebral cortex) contributes to visual declines (Bonnel, Mohand-Said, & Sahel, 2003).

Middle-aged adults are at increased risk of **glaucoma,** a disease in which poor fluid drainage leads to a buildup of pressure within the eye, damaging the optic nerve. Glaucoma affects nearly 2 percent of people over age 40, more often women than men. It typically progresses without noticeable symptoms and is a leading cause of blindness. Glaucoma runs in families: Siblings of people with glaucoma have a tenfold increased risk, and the disease occurs three to four times as often in African Americans and Hispanics as in Caucasians (Friedman, 2006; Kwon et al., 2009). Starting in midlife, eye exams should include a glaucoma test. Drugs that promote re-

lease of fluid and surgery to open blocked drainage channels prevent vision loss.

Hearing

An estimated 14 percent of Americans between ages 45 and 64 suffer from hearing loss, often resulting from adult-onset hearing impairments. Although some conditions run in families and may be hereditary, most are age-related, a condition called **presbycusis** ("old hearing") (Gratton & Vásquez, 2003).

As we age, inner-ear structures that transform mechanical sound waves into neural impulses deteriorate through natural cell death or reduced blood supply caused by atherosclerosis. Processing of neural messages in the auditory cortex also declines. The first sign, at around age 50, is a noticeable hearing loss at high frequencies, which gradually extends to all frequencies. Late in life, human speech becomes more difficult to make out (Liu & Yan, 2007). Still, throughout middle adulthood, most people hear reasonably well across a wide frequency range. And African tribal peoples display little age-related hearing loss (Jarvis & van Heerden, 1967; Rosen, Bergman, & Plester, 1962). These findings suggest factors other than biological aging are involved.

Men's hearing declines earlier and more rapidly than women's, a difference associated with cigarette smoking, intense noise and chemical pollutants in some male-dominated occupations, and (at older ages) high blood pressure and cerebrovascular disease, or strokes that damage brain tissue (Heltzner et al., 2005; Van Eyken, Van Camp, & Van Laer, 2007). Most middle-aged and elderly people with hearing difficulties benefit from sound amplification with hearing aids.

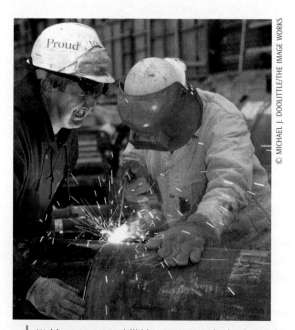

Welders prepare a drill bit to penetrate bedrock. Men's hearing declines more rapidly than women's, a difference associated with several factors, including intense noise in some male-dominated occupations.

Skin

Our skin consists of three layers: (1) the *epidermis,* or outer protective layer, where new skin cells are constantly produced; (2) the *dermis,* or middle supportive layer, consisting of connective tissue that stretches and bounces back, giving the skin flexibility; and (3) the *hypodermis,* an inner fatty layer that adds to the soft lines and shape of the skin. As we age, the epidermis becomes less firmly attached to the dermis, fibers in the dermis thin, cells in both the epidermis and dermis decline in water content, and fat in the hypodermis diminishes, leading the skin to wrinkle, loosen, and feel dry.

In the thirties, lines develop on the forehead as a result of smiling, furrowing the brow, and other facial expressions. In the forties, these become more pronounced, and "crow's-feet" appear around the eyes. Gradually, the skin loses elasticity and begins to sag, especially on the face, arms, and legs. After age 50, "age spots," collections of pigment under the skin, increase. Blood vessels in the skin become more visible as the fatty layer thins.

Because sun exposure hastens wrinkling and spotting, individuals who have spent much time outdoors without proper skin protection look older than their contemporaries (Landau, 2007). And partly because the dermis of women is not as thick as that of men, women's skin ages more quickly (Makrantonaki & Xouboulis, 2007).

Muscle–Fat Makeup

As Trisha and Devin make clear, weight gain—"middle-age spread"—is a concern for both men and women. A common pattern of change is an increase in body fat and a loss of lean body mass (muscle and bone). The rise in fat largely affects the torso and occurs as fatty deposits within the body cavity; as noted earlier, fat beneath the skin on the limbs declines. On average, the size of the abdomen increases 6 to 16 percent in men, 25 to 35 percent in women from early through middle adulthood (Whitbourne, 1996). Sex differences in fat distribution also appear. Men accumulate more on the back and upper abdomen, women around the waist and upper arms (Sowers et al., 2007). Muscle mass declines very gradually in the forties and fifties, largely due to atrophy of fast-twitch fibers, responsible for speed and explosive strength.

Yet, as indicated in Chapter 13, large weight gain and loss of muscle power are not inevitable. With age, people must gradually reduce caloric intake to adjust for the age-related decline in basal metabolic rate (see page 346). In a longitudinal study of nearly 30,000 U.S. 50- to 79-year-old women diverse in SES and ethnicity, a low-fat diet involving increased consumption of vegetables, fruits, and grains was associated with greater initial weight loss and success at maintaining that loss over a seven-year period (Howard et al., 2006). In nonhuman animals, dietary restraint dramatically increases longevity while sustaining health and vitality. Currently, researchers are identifying the biological mechanisms involved and studying their relevance to humans (see the Biology and Environment box on page 400).

Furthermore, weight-bearing exercise that includes resistance training (a strength-training routine that places a moderately stressful load on the muscles) offsets both excess weight and muscle loss (Macaluso & De Vito, 2004; Rivlin, 2007). Consider Devin's 57-year-old friend Tim, who for years has ridden his bike to and from work and jogged on weekends, averaging an hour of vigorous activity per day. Like many endurance athletes, he maintained the same weight and muscular physique throughout early and middle adulthood.

Skeleton

As new cells accumulate on their outer layers, the bones broaden, but their mineral content declines, so they become more porous. This leads to a gradual loss in bone density that begins in the late thirties and accelerates in the fifties, especially among women. Women's reserve of bone minerals is lower than men's to begin with. And following menopause, the favorable impact of estrogen on bone mineral absorption is lost. Reduction in bone density during adulthood is substantial—about 8 to 12 percent in men and 20 to 30 percent in women (Seeman, 2002, 2008).

Loss of bone strength causes the disks in the spinal column to collapse. Consequently, height may drop by as much as 1 inch by age 60, a change that will hasten thereafter. In addition, the weakened bones cannot support as much load: They fracture more easily and heal more slowly. A healthy lifestyle—including weight-bearing exercise, adequate calcium and vitamin D intake, and avoidance of smoking and heavy alcohol consumption—can slow bone loss in postmenopausal women by as much as 30 to 50 percent (Borer, 2005; Cooper et al., 2009).

When bone loss is very great, it leads to a debilitating disorder called *osteoporosis.* We will take up this condition shortly when we consider illness and disability.

Reproductive System

The midlife transition in which fertility declines is called the **climacteric.** In women, it brings an end to reproductive capacity; in men, by contrast, fertility diminishes but is retained.

■ **REPRODUCTIVE CHANGES IN WOMEN.** The changes involved in women's climacteric occur gradually over a 10-year period, during which the production of estrogen decreases. As a result, the number of days in a woman's monthly cycle shortens from about 28 in her twenties and thirties to perhaps 23 by her late forties, and her cycles become more irregular. In some, ova are not released; when they are, more are defective (see Chapter 2, page 41). The climacteric concludes with **menopause,** the end of menstruation and reproductive capacity. This occurs, on average, in the early fifties among North American, European, and East Asian women, although the age range extends from the late thirties to the late fifties. Women who smoke or who have not borne children tend to reach menopause earlier (Avis, Crawford, & Johannes, 2002; Rossi, 2005).

■ BIOLOGY AND ENVIRONMENT ■

Anti-Aging Effects of Dietary Calorie Restriction

For nearly 70 years, scientists have known that dietary calorie restriction in nonhuman animals slows aging while maintaining good health and body functions. Rats and mice fed 30 to 40 percent fewer calories than they would freely eat beginning in early life show various physiological health benefits, lower incidence of chronic diseases, and a 60 percent increase in length of life (Fontana, 2009). Mild to moderate calorie restriction begun after rodents reach physical maturity also slows aging and extends longevity, though to a lesser extent. Other studies reveal similar dietary-restriction effects in mice, dogs, fleas, spiders, worms, fish, and yeast.

Primate Research

Would primates, especially humans, also benefit from a restricted diet? Researchers are tracking health indicators in rhesus monkeys and squirrel monkeys ranging from 1 to 20 years of age, after placing some on regimens of 30 percent reduced calories, supplemented with vitamins and minerals to ensure a healthy diet. Two decades of longitudinal findings reveals that, compared with freely eating controls, dietary-restricted monkeys are smaller but not overly thin. They accumulate body fat differently—less on the torso, a type of fat distribution that reduces middle-aged humans' risk of heart disease.

Calorie-restricted monkeys also have a lower body temperature and basal metabolic rate—changes that suggest they shift physiological processes away from growth to life-maintaining functions. Consequently, like calorie-restricted rodents, they seem better able to withstand severe physical stress, such as surgery and infectious disease, perhaps because their bodies more easily repair damaged cells (Weindruch et al., 2001).

Among physiological processes mediating the benefits of calorie restriction, three seem most powerful. First, calorie restriction inhibits production of free radicals, thereby limiting cellular deterioration, which contributes to many diseases of aging (see page 340 in Chapter 13) (Carter et al., 2007; Yu, 2006). Second, calorie restriction reduces blood glucose and insulin levels, which protects against diabetes and cardiovascular disease. Lower blood pressure and cholesterol and a high

ratio of "good" to "bad" cholesterol in calorie-restricted primates strengthen these effects (Fontana, 2008). Third, calorie restriction combined with limited consumption of dietary protein reduces levels of IGF-1, an insulin-like hormone produced primarily in the liver, by 30 to 40 percent—a physiological effect consistently linked to increased longevity (Fontana et al., 2009).

The earlier monkeys are placed on calorie restriction, the more favorable its physiological consequences. So far, fully fed monkeys have been three times more likely to die of aging-related diseases than their calorie-restricted counterparts (Colman et al., 2009).

Human Parallels

The laboratory experimental strategies used to study calorie restriction in animals cannot be applied to humans. But natural experiments indicate that people who limit their food intake may benefit similarly.

Compared with mainland Japanese citizens, residents of the island of Okinawa consume an average of 20 percent fewer calories, while maintaining a healthy diet. This restricted diet is associated with a 60 to 70 percent reduction in incidence of deaths due to cancer and cardiovascular disease and a two- to forty-fold increase in seniors living to age 100 over other regions of Japan (Kagawa, 1978). Although other differences between Okinawans and mainland Japanese may play a role, Okinawans who move away from the island and, presumably, give up their calorie-limited lifestyle show increased mortality rates (Mizushima & Yapori, 1992).

In the early 1990s, eight American men and women ranging in age from 25 to 67 entered the Biosphere, an enclosed three-acre natural habitat, where they lived and raised their own food for two years. Eating 1,800 calories a day and engaging in three to four hours of daily heavy labor, the Biospherians experienced physiological changes similar to those observed in calorie-restricted rodents and monkeys, including reduced blood glucose, insulin, cholesterol, and blood pressure; a stronger immune-system response; and decreased fat mass (Heilbronn & Ravussin, 2003). Measures taken on normal and overweight people placed on high-quality, energy-restricted diets show the same effects (Fontana, 2009; Redman et al., 2008).

Why might calorie restriction be an anti-aging strategy? Researchers speculate that the

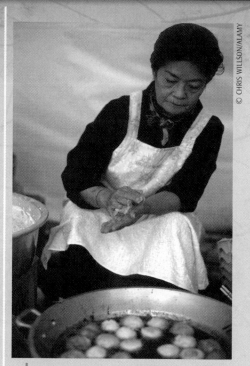

Residents of Okinawa—like this elderly street vendor preparing dumplings for the day's customers—consume 20 percent fewer calories, on average, than mainland Japanese citizens. Their diet is associated with longer life.

body's response to food scarcity evolved to increase the chances of surviving adversity.

Nevertheless, calorie restriction may add only two to three years to the extended longevity already conferred by human improvements in living conditions and medical treatment (de Grey, 2005). Also, to be effective, calorie restriction in humans may need to involve substantial reductions in protein intake to induce the decline in IGF-1 consistently linked to longevity in animal research. Yet ethical considerations, including insufficient energy to meet requirements of daily life and risks of malnutrition, argue against trying to get people to modify the quantity and makeup of their food intake substantially. Finally, very few people would be willing to maintain a drastically reduced diet for most of their lifespan. As a result, scientists have begun to explore *calorie-restriction mimetics*—agents such as natural food substances, herbs, and vigorous exercise regimens—that might yield the same benefits as calorie restriction, without dieting (Barzilai & Bartke, 2009; Ingram et al., 2006). These investigations are still in their early stages.

Following menopause, estrogen declines further, causing the reproductive organs to shrink, the genitals to be less easily stimulated, and the vagina to lubricate more slowly during arousal. As a result, complaints about sexual functioning increase, with about 35 to 40 percent of women reporting difficulties, especially among those with health problems or whose partners have sexual performance difficulties (Lindau et al., 2007; Walsh & Berman, 2004). The drop in estrogen also contributes to decreased elasticity of the skin and loss of bone mass. Also lost is estrogen's ability to help protect against accumulation of plaque on the walls of the arteries, by boosting "good cholesterol" (high-density lipoprotein).

The period leading up to and following menopause is often accompanied by emotional and physical symptoms, including mood fluctuations and *hot flashes*—sensations of warmth accompanied by a rise in body temperature and redness in the face, neck, and chest, followed by sweating. Hot flashes—which may occur during the day and also, as *night sweats*, during sleep—affect more than 50 percent of women in Western industrialized nations (Nelson, 2008). Typically, they are not severe: Only about 1 in 12 experiences them every day.

Although menopausal women tend to report increased irritability and less satisfying sleep, research using EEG and other physiological measures finds no links between menopause and changes in quantity or quality of sleep (Lamberg, 2007; Young et al., 2002). Also, many studies reveal no association between menopause and depression in the general population (Avis, 2003; Soares, 2007; Vesco et al., 2007). Rather, women who have a previous history of depression, are physically inactive, or are experiencing highly stressful life events are more likely to report depressive episodes during the climacteric. In view of these findings, sleep difficulties or depression should not be dismissed as temporary byproducts of menopause: These problems merit serious evaluation and treatment.

As Figure 15.1 illustrates, compared with North American, European, African, and Middle Eastern women, Asian women report fewer menopausal complaints, including hot flashes. Asian diets, which are low in fat and high in soy-based foods (a rich source of plant estrogen) may be involved (Obermeyer, 2000).

■ **HORMONE THERAPY.** To reduce the physical discomforts of menopause, doctors may prescribe **hormone therapy, or low daily doses of estrogen.** Hormone therapy comes in two types: (1) estrogen alone, or *estrogen replacement therapy (ERT)*, for women who have had hysterectomies (surgical removal of the uterus); and (2) estrogen plus progesterone, or *hormone replacement therapy (HRT)*, for other women. Combining estrogen with progesterone lessens the risk of cancer of the endometrium (lining of the uterus), which has long been known as a serious side effect of hormone therapy.

Hormone therapy is highly successful at counteracting hot flashes and vaginal dryness. It also offers some protection against bone deterioration and colon cancer (Nelson et al., 2002). Nevertheless, a large-scale experiment, in which more than 16,000 50- to 79-year-olds randomly assigned to take HRT or a sugar pill were followed for five years, revealed two negative consequences. First, HRT caused a mild increase in heart attacks, stroke, and blood clots. Second, HRT taken for more than four years slightly elevated the incidence of breast cancer (Women's Health Initiative, 2002, 2004). In other studies, ERT, as well, increased the risk of breast cancer and blood clots (Bhavnani & Strickler, 2005; Prentice et al., 2008). Furthermore, an additional experiment involving 4,500 65- to 79-year-olds indicated that HRT slightly elevated the risk of mild cognitive declines and nearly doubled the risk of Alzheimer's disease and other dementias (Rapp et al., 2003; Shumaker et al., 2003).

But timing of intervention may make a difference. Hormone therapy begun before menopausal age may actually reduce the risk of cardiovascular disease. And hormone therapy begun around the time of menopause, rather than a decade or two later, may reduce the risk of Alzheimer's (Henderson, 2009; Rossouw et al., 2007).

Fortunately, the number of alternative treatments for menopausal symptoms is increasing. At present, however, hormone therapy continues to provide the most reliable relief. Therefore, some experts argue that prescribing it to low-risk women on a short-term basis (no longer than five years) is justified because it improves quality of life (Col et al., 2004).

■ **WOMEN'S PSYCHOLOGICAL REACTIONS TO MENOPAUSE.** How do women react to menopause—a clear-cut signal that their childbearing years are over? The answer lies in how they interpret the event in relation to their past and future lives.

For Jewel, who had wanted marriage and family but never attained these goals, menopause was traumatic. Her sense of physical competence was still bound up with the ability to have children. Physical symptoms can also make menopause a difficult

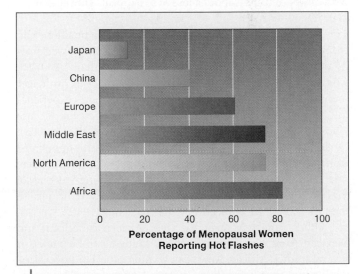

■ **FIGURE 15.1** ■ **Percentage of menopausal women in different regions of the world reporting hot flashes.** Findings are derived from interviews with large samples in each region. Women in Asian nations, especially Japanese women, are less likely to suffer from hot flashes, perhaps because they eat soy-based foods, a rich source of plant estrogen. (Adapted from Obermeyer, 2000; Shea, 2006.)

African-American women generally speak of menopause as normal, inevitable, even welcome. They also experience less irritability and moodiness during this transition than Caucasian-American women.

time (Elavsky & McAuley, 2007). And in a society that values a youthful appearance, some women respond to the climacteric with disappointment about a loss of sex appeal (Howell & Beth, 2002).

Many women, however, find menopause to be little or no trouble, regard it as a new beginning, and report improved quality of life (Mishra & Kuh, 2006). When more than 2,000 U.S. women were asked what their feelings were about no longer menstruating, nearly 50 percent of those currently experiencing changes in their menstrual cycles, and 60 percent of those whose periods had ceased, said they felt relieved (Rossi, 2005). Most do not want more children and are thankful to be freed from worry about birth control. And highly educated, career-oriented Caucasian-American women with fulfilling lives outside the home usually have more positive attitudes toward menopause than those with less education (Theisen et al., 1995).

Other research suggests that African-American and Mexican-American women hold especially favorable views. In several studies, African-American women experienced less irritability and moodiness than Caucasian Americans. They rarely spoke of menopause in terms of physical aging but, instead, regarded it as normal, inevitable, even welcome (Holmes-Rovner et al., 1996; Melby, Lock, & Kaufert, 2005; Sampselle et al., 2002). Some African Americans expressed exasperation at society's readiness to label as "crazy" women's authentic reactions to work-

or family-based stressors that often coincide with menopause. Among Mexican-American women who have not yet adopted the language (and perhaps certain beliefs) of the larger society, attitudes toward menopause are especially positive (Bell, 1995). And in an investigation of a large sample of ethnically diverse 40- to 55-year-old U.S. women, other factors—SES, physical health, lifestyle factors (smoking, diet, exercise, weight gain), and especially psychological stress—overshadowed menopausal status and symptoms (hot flashes, night sweats, and vaginal dryness) in impact on self-rated quality of life (Avis et al., 2004).

The wide variation in physical symptoms and attitudes indicates that menopause is not just a hormonal event. It is also affected by cultural beliefs and practices.

■ **REPRODUCTIVE CHANGES IN MEN.** Although men also experience a climacteric, no male counterpart to menopause exists. Both quantity and motility of sperm decrease from the twenties on, and quantity of semen diminishes after age 40, negatively affecting fertility in middle age (Sloter et al., 2006). Still, sperm production continues throughout life, and men in their nineties have fathered children. Testosterone production also declines with age, but the change is minimal in healthy men who continue to engage in sexual activity, which stimulates cells that release testosterone (Hermann et al., 2000).

Nevertheless, because of reduced blood flow to and changes in connective tissue in the penis, more stimulation is required for an erection, and it may be harder to maintain. Difficulty attaining an erection becomes more common in midlife, affecting about 30 percent of men by age 60 (Lindau et al., 2007). Viagra and other drugs that increase blood flow to the penis offer temporary relief from erectile dysfunction. Publicity surrounding these drugs has prompted open discussion of erectile dysfunction and encouraged more men to seek treatment (Berner et al., 2008). But those taking the medications are often not adequately screened for the host of factors besides declining testosterone that contribute to impotence, including disorders of the nervous, circulatory, and endocrine systems; anxiety and depression; pelvic injury; and loss of interest in one's sexual partner (Montorsi, 2005).

ASK YOURSELF

≫ **REVIEW**
What factors influence women's psychological reactions to menopause?

≫ **APPLY**
At age 42, Stan began to wear bifocals, and over the next 10 years, he required an adjustment to his corrective lenses almost every year. What physical changes account for his recurring need for new eyewear?

≫ **REFLECT**
In view of the benefits and risks of hormone therapy, what factors would you consider, or advise others to consider, before taking such medication?

Health and Fitness

In midlife, nearly 85 percent of Americans rate their health as either "excellent" or "good"—still a large majority, but lower than the 95 percent figure in early adulthood (U.S. Department of Health and Human Services, 2009a). Whereas younger people usually attribute health complaints to temporary infections, middle-aged adults more often point to chronic diseases. As we will see, among those who rate their health unfavorably, men are more likely to suffer from fatal illnesses, women from nonfatal, limiting health problems.

In addition to typical negative indicators—major diseases and disabling conditions—our discussion takes up sexuality as a positive indicator of health. Before we begin, it is important to note that our understanding of health in middle and late adulthood is limited by insufficient research on women and ethnic minorities. Fortunately, this situation is changing. For example, the Women's Health Initiative (WHI)—a commitment by the U.S. federal government, extending from 1993 to 2005, to study factors influencing the health of nearly 162,000 postmenopausal women of all ethnic groups and SES levels—has led to important findings, including the risks of hormone therapy, discussed earlier. A five-year extension, involving annual health updates from 115,000 WHI participants, continues to yield vital information.

Sexuality

Frequency of sexual activity among married couples tends to decline in middle adulthood, but for most, the drop is slight. Longitudinal research reveals that stability of sexual activity is far more typical than dramatic change. Couples who have sex often in early adulthood continue to do so in midlife (Dennerstein & Lehert, 2004; Walsh & Berman, 2004). And the best predictor of sexual frequency is marital happiness, an association that is probably bidirectional (Edwards & Booth, 1994). Sex is more likely to occur in the context of a good marriage, and couples who have sex often probably view their relationship more positively.

Nevertheless, *intensity* of sexual response declines in midlife due to physical changes of the climacteric. Both men and women take longer to feel aroused and to reach orgasm (Bartlik & Goldstein, 2001; Walsh & Berman, 2004). If partners perceive each other as less attractive, this may contribute to a drop in sexual desire. Yet in the context of a positive outlook, sexual activity can become more satisfying. Devin and Trisha, for example, viewed each other's aging bodies with acceptance and affection—as a sign of their enduring and deepening relationship. And with greater freedom from the demands of work and family, their sex life became more spontaneous. The majority of married people over age 50 say that their sex life is an important component of their relationship, and most find ways to overcome difficulties with sexual functioning. One happily married 52-year-old woman commented, "We know what we are doing, we've had plenty of practice (laughs), and I would

never have believed that it gets better as you get older, but it does" (Gott & Hinchliff, 2003, p. 1625; Kingsberg, 2002).

Illness and Disability

As Figure 15.2 shows, cancer and cardiovascular disease are the leading causes of death in middle age. Unintentional injuries, though still a major health threat, occur at a lower rate than in early adulthood, largely because motor vehicle collisions decline. But falls resulting in bone fractures and death nearly double from early to middle adulthood (U.S. Census Bureau, 2009b).

Men are more vulnerable than women to most health problems. Among middle-aged men, cancer deaths exceed cardiovascular disease deaths by a small margin; among women, cancer is by far the leading cause of death (refer again to Figure 15.2). And largely because of more severe poverty and lack of universal health insurance, the United States continues to exceed most other industrialized nations in death rates from major causes (OECD, 2008b). Finally, as we take a closer look at illness and disability in the following sections, we will encounter yet another familiar theme: the close connection between psychological and physical well-being. Personality traits that magnify stress—especially hostility and anger—are serious threats to health in midlife.

■ **CANCER.** From early to middle adulthood, the death rate due to cancer multiplies tenfold, accounting for about one-third of all midlife deaths in the United States. Although the incidence of many types of cancer is currently leveling off or declining, cancer mortality was on the rise for many decades, largely because of a dramatic increase in lung cancer due to cigarette smoking. In the past 15 years, the incidence of lung cancer has dropped in men; 50 percent fewer smoke today than

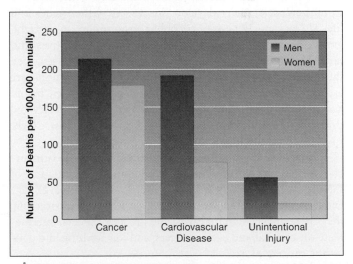

■ **FIGURE 15.2** ■ **Leading causes of death among people age 45 to 64 in the United States.** Men are more vulnerable than women to each leading cause of death. Cancer is the leading killer of both sexes, by a far smaller margin over cardiovascular disease for men than for women. (Adapted from U.S. Census Bureau, 2009b.)

in the 1950s. In contrast, lung cancer has increased in women, many of whom took up smoking in the decades after World War II (U.S. Department of Health and Human Services, 2009a).

Cancer occurs when a cell's genetic program is disrupted, leading to uncontrolled growth and spread of abnormal cells that crowd out normal tissues and organs. Cancer-causing mutations can be either *germline* (due to an inherited predisposition) or *somatic* (occurring in a single cell, which then multiplies) (see page 40 in Chapter 2 to review). Recall from Chapter 13 that according to one theory, error in DNA duplication increases with age, either occurring spontaneously or resulting from the release of free radicals or breakdown of the immune system. Environmental toxins may initiate or intensify this process.

For cancers that affect both sexes, men are generally more vulnerable than women. The difference may be due to genetic makeup, exposure to cancer-causing agents as a result of lifestyle or occupation, and a tendency to delay going to the doctor. Although the relationship of SES to cancer varies with site (for example, lung and stomach cancers are linked to lower SES, breast and prostate cancers to higher SES), cancer death rates increase sharply as SES decreases and are especially high among low-income ethnic minorities (Jemal et al., 2008). Poorer medical care and reduced ability to fight the disease, due to inadequate diet and high life stress, underlie this trend.

Overall, a complex interaction of heredity, biological aging, and environment contributes to cancer. For example, many patients with familial breast cancer who respond poorly to treatment have defective forms of particular tumor-suppressor genes (either BRCA1 or BRCA2). Genetic screening for these mutations is available, permitting prevention efforts to begin early. Even though women with one of these faulty genes are at much greater risk for breast cancer than other women, only 35 to 50 percent actually develop the disease. Other genes and lifestyle factors—including alcohol consumption, overweight, greater number of pregnancies, use of oral contraceptives, and hormone therapy to treat menopausal symptoms—heighten their risk. Women with BRCA1 or BRCA2 mutations are especially likely to develop early-onset breast cancer, before age 30 (Ripperger et al., 2009). But their risk remains elevated throughout middle and late adulthood, when breast cancer rises among women in general.

People often fear cancer because they believe it is incurable. Yet 40 percent of affected individuals are cured—free of the disease for five years or longer. Survival rates, however, vary widely with type of cancer (Jemal et al., 2008). For example, they are relatively high for breast and prostate cancers, intermediate for cervical and colon cancers, and low for lung and pancreatic cancers.

Breast cancer is the leading malignancy for women, prostate cancer for men. Lung cancer—largely preventable through avoiding tobacco—ranks second for both sexes, followed closely by colon and rectal cancer. Scheduling annual medical checkups and learning risk factors—a change in bowel or bladder habits, a sore that does not heal, unusual bleeding or discharge, thickening or lump in a breast or elsewhere in your body, indigestion or swallowing difficulty, change in a wart or mole, nagging cough or hoarseness—can reduce cancer illness and death rates considerably.

Surviving cancer is a triumph, but it also brings emotional challenges. During cancer treatment, relationships focus on the illness. Afterward, they must refocus on health and full participation in daily life. Friends, family, and co-workers may need reminders that cancer is not contagious and that with patience and support from supervisors and co-workers, cancer survivors regain their on-the-job productivity (Mains et al., 2005).

■ **CARDIOVASCULAR DISEASE.** Each year, about 25 percent of middle-aged American deaths are caused by cardiovascular disease (U.S. Department of Health and Human Services, 2009a). We associate cardiovascular disease with heart attacks, but Devin, like many middle-aged and older adults, learned of the condition during an annual checkup. His doctor detected high blood pressure, high blood cholesterol, and *atherosclerosis*—a buildup of plaque in his coronary arteries, which encircle the heart and provide its muscles with oxygen and nutrients. These indicators of cardiovascular disease are known as "silent killers" because they often have no symptoms.

When symptoms *are* evident, they take different forms. The most extreme is a *heart attack*—blockage of normal blood supply to an area of the heart, usually brought on by a blood clot in one or more plaque-filled coronary arteries. Intense pain results as muscle in the affected region dies. A heart attack is a medical emergency; over 50 percent of victims die before reaching the hospital, another 15 percent during treatment, and an additional 15 percent over the next few years (American Heart Association, 2009). Among other, less extreme symptoms of cardiovascular disease are *arrhythmia*, or irregular heartbeat. When it persists, it can prevent the heart from pumping enough blood and result in faintness. It can also allow clots to form within the heart's chambers, which may break loose and travel to the brain. In some individuals, indigestion-like pain or crushing chest pain, called *angina pectoris*, reveals an oxygen-deprived heart.

Today, cardiovascular disease can be treated in many ways—including coronary bypass surgery, medication, and pacemakers to regulate heart rhythm. To relieve arterial blockage, Devin had *angioplasty*, a procedure in which a surgeon threaded a needle-thin catheter into his arteries and inflated a balloon at its tip, which flattened fatty deposits to allow blood to flow more freely. But unless Devin took other measures to reduce his risk, his doctor warned, the arteries would clog again within a year. Some risk factors, such as heredity, advanced age, and being male, cannot be changed. But adults can prevent heart disease or slow its progress by engaging in such measures as quitting smoking, maintaining a healthy body weight, exercising regularly, and reducing hostility and other forms of psychological stress.

Because men account for over 70 percent of cases of cardiovascular disease in middle adulthood, doctors often view a heart condition as a "male problem" and frequently overlook women's symptoms, which tend to be milder, more often taking the form of angina than a heart attack (Mosca et al., 2005). In one study, researchers had male and female actors present identical symptoms of angina to a sample of over 700 doctors. The doctors were far less likely to suspect heart problems in women—especially African-American women, who are at greater risk for heart disease than Caucasian-American women (Schulman et al., 1999). In follow-ups of victims of full-blown heart attacks, once again women—and especially African-American women—were less likely to be offered costly, invasive treatments, such as angioplasty and bypass surgery (Dey et al., 2009; Jneid et al., 2008; Steiner & Miller, 2008). As a result, treatment outcomes—including rehospitalization and death—tend to be worse for women.

■ **OSTEOPOROSIS.** When age-related bone loss is severe, a condition called **osteoporosis** develops. The disorder, affecting about 10 million U.S. adults, 80 percent of whom are women, greatly magnifies the risk of bone fractures. An estimated 55 percent of people over age 50 are at risk for osteoporosis because they have bone density levels low enough to be of concern, and 12 percent have been diagnosed with it (National Osteoporosis Foundation, 2008). After age 70, osteoporosis affects the majority of people of both sexes (Donatelle, 2009). Although we associate it with a slumped-over posture, a shuffling gait, and a "dowager's hump" in the upper back, this extreme is rare. Because the bones gradually become more porous over many years, osteoporosis may not be evident until fractures—typically in the spine, hips, and wrist—occur or are discovered through X-rays.

A major factor related to osteoporosis is the decline in estrogen associated with menopause. In middle and late adulthood, women lose about 50 percent of their bone mass, about half of it in the first 10 years following menopause—a decline that, by the late sixties, is two to five times greater than in men (Bonnick, 2008). In men, the age-related decrease in testosterone—though much more gradual than estrogen loss in women—contributes to bone loss because the body converts some to estrogen.

Heredity, too, plays an important role. A family history of osteoporosis increases risk, with identical twins more likely than fraternal twins to share the disorder (Williams & Spector, 2006). People with thin, small-framed bodies are more likely to be affected because they attain a lower peak bone mass in adolescence. In contrast, higher bone density makes African Americans less susceptible than Asian Americans, Caucasians, Hispanics, and Native Americans (Pothiwala, Evans, & Chapman-Novakofski, 2006). An unhealthy lifestyle also contributes: A calcium-deficient diet, excess intake of sodium and caffeine, and physical inactivity reduce bone mass, as do cigarette smoking and alcohol consumption, which interfere with the replacement of bone cells (National Osteoporosis Foundation, 2008).

When major bone fractures (such as the hip) occur, 10 to 20 percent of patients die within a year (Reginster & Burlet, 2006). Because osteoporosis has become known as a "women's disease," men are far less likely to be screened and treated, even after a hip fracture (Bonnick, 2008; Kiebzak et al., 2002).

Physical inactivity increases the chances of osteoporosis. More than half of people over age 50, mostly women, are at risk. Weightbearing exercise and strength training are recommended for both prevention and treatment.

And compared with women, men with hip fractures tend to be older. Probably for these reasons, the one-year mortality rate after hip fracture is nearly twice as great for men as for women—a gap that widens with age (Campion & Maricic, 2003; Gennari & Bilezikian, 2007).

To treat osteoporosis, doctors recommend a diet enriched with calcium and vitamin D (which promotes calcium absorption), weight-bearing exercise (walking rather than swimming), strength training (weight lifting), and bone-strengthening medications (National Osteoporosis Foundation, 2009). A better way to reduce lifelong risk is through early prevention: maximizing peak bone density by increasing calcium and vitamin D intake and engaging in regular exercise in childhood, adolescence, and early adulthood.

Hostility and Anger

Whenever Trisha's sister Dottie called, she seemed like a powder keg ready to explode. Dottie was critical of her boss at work and dissatisfied with the way Trisha, a lawyer, had handled the family's affairs after their father died. Inevitably, Dottie's anger surfaced, exploding in hurtful remarks: "Any lawyer knows that, Trisha. How could you be so stupid! I should have called a *real* lawyer."

After listening as long as she could bear, Trisha would warn, "Dottie, if you continue, I'm going to hang up!"

At age 53, Dottie had high blood pressure, difficulty sleeping, and back pain. In the past five years, she had been hospitalized five times—twice for treatment of digestive problems, twice for an irregular heartbeat, and once for a benign tumor on her thyroid gland. Trisha often wondered whether Dottie's personal style was partly responsible for her health problems.

That hostility and anger might have negative effects on health is a centuries-old idea. Several decades ago, researchers first tested this notion by identifying 35- to 59-year-old men who displayed the **Type A behavior pattern**—extreme competitiveness, ambition, impatience, hostility, angry outbursts, and a sense of time pressure. They found that within the next eight years, Type As were more than twice as likely as Type Bs (people with a more relaxed disposition) to develop heart disease (Rosenman et al., 1975).

Later studies, however, often failed to confirm these results. Type A is actually a mix of behaviors, only one or two of which affect health. Current evidence pinpoints hostility as a "toxic" ingredient of Type A, since isolating it from global Type A consistently predicts heart disease and other health problems in both men and women (Aldwin et al., 2001; Eaker et al., 2004; Matthews et al., 2004; Smith et al., 2004). *Expressed hostility* in particular—frequent angry outbursts; rude, disagreeable behavior; critical and condescending nonverbal cues during social interaction, including glares; and expressions of contempt and disgust—leads to greater cardiovascular arousal, health complaints, and illness (Chesney et al., 1997; Julkunen & Ahlström, 2006). As people get angry, heart rate, blood pressure, and stress hormones escalate until the body's response is extreme.

Can Dottie preserve her health by bottling up her hostility instead of expressing it? Repeatedly suppressing overt anger or ruminating about past anger-provoking events is also associated with high blood pressure and heart disease (Hogan & Linden, 2004; Julkunen, 1996). A better alternative, as we will see, is to develop effective ways of handling stress and conflict.

Adapting to the Challenges of Midlife

Middle adulthood is often a productive time of life, when people attain their greatest accomplishments and satisfactions. Nevertheless, it takes considerable stamina to cope with the full array of changes this period can bring. Devin responded to his expanding waistline and cardiovascular symptoms by leaving his desk twice a week to attend a low-impact aerobics class and by reducing job-related stress through daily 10-minute meditation sessions. Aware of her sister Dottie's difficulties, Trisha resolved to handle her own hostile feelings more adaptively. And her generally optimistic outlook enabled her to cope successfully with the physical changes of midlife, the pressures of her legal career, and Devin's chronic illness.

Stress Management

TAKE A MOMENT... Turn back to Chapter 13, page 353, and review the negative consequences of psychological stress on the cardiovascular, immune, and gastrointestinal systems. Stress management is important at any age, but in middle adulthood

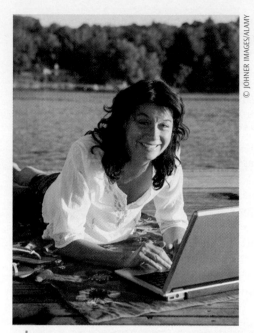

Stress management is important at any age, but in middle adulthood, it can limit the age-related rise in illness. This midlifer reduces stress by periodically leaving her high-pressure office environment to work in a tranquil, picturesque setting.

it can limit the age-related rise in illness and, when disease strikes, reduce its severity.

Applying What We Know on the following page summarizes effective ways to reduce stress. Even when stressors cannot be eliminated, people can change how they handle some and view others. At work, Trisha focused on problems she could control—not on her boss's irritability but on ways to delegate routine tasks to her staff so she could focus on problems that required her knowledge and skills. When Dottie phoned, Trisha reminded herself of Dottie's difficult temperament and hard life instead of interpreting Dottie's anger as a sign of her own incompetence. And greater life experience helped Trisha accept change as inevitable, so that she was better-equipped to deal with the jolt of sudden events, such as Devin's hospitalization for treatment of arterial blockage.

Notice how Trisha called on two general strategies for coping with stress, discussed in Chapter 10: (1) *problem-centered coping*, in which she appraised the situation as changeable, identified the difficulty, and decided what to do about it; and (2) *emotion-centered coping*, which is internal, private, and aimed at controlling distress when little can be done about a situation. Longitudinal research shows that adults who effectively reduce stress move flexibly between problem-centered and emotion-centered techniques, depending on the situation (Zakowski et al., 2001). Their approach is deliberate, thoughtful, and respectful of both themselves and others. In contrast, ineffective coping is largely emotion-centered and either impulsive or escapist (Brennan, Schutte, & Moos, 2006; Lazarus, 1999).

Applying What We Know

Managing Stress

Strategy	Description
Reevaluate the situation.	Learn to differentiate normal reactions from those based on irrational beliefs.
Focus on events you can control.	Don't worry about things you cannot change or that may never happen; focus on strategies for handling events under your control.
View life as fluid.	Expect change and accept it as inevitable; then many unanticipated changes will have less emotional impact.
Consider alternatives.	Don't rush into action; think before you act.
Set reasonable goals for yourself.	Aim high, but be realistic about your capacities, motivation, and the situation.
Exercise regularly.	A physically fit person can better handle stress, both physically and emotionally.
Master relaxation techniques.	Relaxation helps refocus energies and reduce the physical discomfort of stress. Classes and self-help books teach these techniques.
Use constructive approaches to anger reduction.	Delay responding ("Let me check into that and get back to you"); use mentally distracting behaviors (counting to 10 backwards) and self-instruction (a covert "Stop!") to control anger arousal, then engage in calm, self-controlled problem solving ("I should call him rather than confront him personally").
Seek social support.	Friends, family members, co-workers, and organized support groups can offer information, assistance, and suggestions for coping with stressful situations.

Constructive approaches to anger reduction are a vital health intervention (refer again to Applying What We Know). Teaching people to be assertive rather than hostile and to negotiate rather than explode interrupts the intense physiological response that intervenes between psychological stress and illness.

As noted in Chapter 13, people tend to cope with stress more effectively as they move from early to middle adulthood. They may become more realistic about their ability to change situations and more skilled at anticipating stressful events and at preparing to manage them (Aldwin & Levenson, 2002). Furthermore, when middle-aged adults surmount a highly stressful experience, they often report lasting personal benefits—for some, a greater sense of mastery as they look back with amazement at what they were able to accomplish under extremely trying conditions.

Exercise

Regular exercise, as noted in Chapter 13, has a range of physical and psychological benefits—among them, equipping adults to handle stress more effectively and reducing the risk of many diseases. Heading for his first aerobics class, Devin wondered, Can starting to exercise at age 50 counteract years of physical inactivity? His question is important: Nearly 70 percent of U.S. middle-aged adults are sedentary, and half of those who begin an exercise program discontinue it within the first six months. (U.S. Department of Health and Human Services, 2009a).

A person beginning to exercise in midlife must overcome initial barriers and ongoing obstacles—lack of time and energy, inconvenience, work conflicts, and health factors (such as overweight). *Self-efficacy* is just as vital in adopting, maintaining, and exerting oneself in an exercise regimen as it is in career progress (see Chapter 14). An important outcome of starting an exercise program is that sedentary adults gain in self-efficacy, which further promotes physical activity (McAuley & Elavsky, 2008; Wilbur et al., 2005). Enhanced physical fitness, in turn,

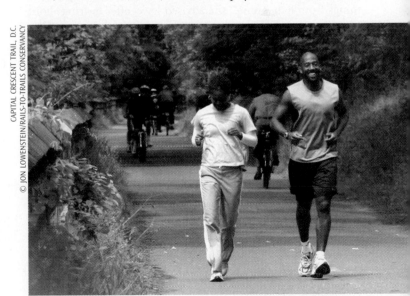

Attractive, safe parks and trails, like this hiking and biking trail built on a former rail line in Washington, D.C., can help encourage sedentary adults to develop beneficial exercise regimens.

prompts middle-aged adults to feel better about their physical selves. Over time, their physical self-esteem—sense of body conditioning and attractiveness—rises (Elavsky & McAuley, 2007; McAuley, Mihalko, & Bane, 1997).

The exercise format that works best depends on the beginning exerciser's characteristics. Normal-weight adults are more likely to stick with group classes than are overweight adults, who may feel embarrassed and struggle to keep up with the pace. Overweight people do better with an individualized, home-based routine planned by a consultant (King, 2001). However, adults with highly stressful lives are more likely to persist in group classes, which offer a regular schedule and the face-to-face support of others, than in a home-based program (King et al., 1997).

Accessible, attractive, and safe exercise environments— parks, walking and biking trails, and community recreation centers—and frequent opportunities to observe others using them also promote physical activity (King et al., 2000). Besides health problems and daily stressors, low-SES adults often mention inconvenient access to facilities, expense, unsafe neighborhoods, and unclean streets as barriers to exercise—important reasons that activity level declines sharply with SES (Taylor et al., 2007; Wilbur et al., 2003).

An Optimistic Outlook

What type of individual is likely to cope adaptively with stress brought on by inevitable life changes? Researchers have identified a set of three personal qualities—control, commitment, and challenge—that, together, they call **hardiness** (Maddi, 1999, 2005, 2007).

Trisha fit the pattern of a hardy individual. First, she regarded most experiences as *controllable.* "You can't stop all bad things from happening," she advised Jewel after hearing about her menopausal symptoms, "but you can try to do something about them." Second, Trisha displayed a *committed,* involved approach to daily activities, finding interest and meaning in almost all of them. Finally, she viewed change as a *challenge*—a chance for personal growth.

Hardiness influences the extent to which people appraise stressful situations as manageable, interesting, and enjoyable. These optimistic appraisals, in turn, predict health-promoting behaviors, tendency to seek social support, and fewer physical symptoms (Maddi, 2006; Smith, Young, & Lee, 2004). Furthermore, high-hardy individuals are likely to use active, problem-centered coping strategies in situations they can control. In contrast, low-hardy people more often use emotion-centered and avoidant coping strategies—for example, saying, "I wish I could change how I feel," denying that the stressful event occurred, or eating and drinking to forget about it (Maddi, 2007; Maddi & Hightower, 1999; Soderstrom et al., 2000).

In this and previous chapters, we have seen that many factors act as stress-resistant resources—among them heredity, diet, exercise, social support, and coping strategies. Research on hardiness adds yet another ingredient: a generally optimistic outlook and zest for life.

Gender and Aging: A Double Standard

Negative stereotypes of aging, which lead many middle-aged adults to fear physical changes, are more likely to be applied to women than to men, yielding a double standard. Though many women in midlife say they have "hit their stride"—feel assertive, confident, versatile, and capable of resolving life's problems— people often rate them as less attractive and as having more negative personality characteristics than middle-aged men (Denmark & Klara, 2007; Kite et al., 2005). And men tend to judge an aging female more harshly than women do (Kogan & Mills, 1992).

These effects appear more often when people rate photos as opposed to verbal descriptions. The ideal of a sexually attractive woman—smooth skin, good muscle tone, lustrous hair— may be at the heart of the double standard of aging. Some evidence suggests that the end of a woman's ability to bear children contributes to negative judgments of physical appearance, especially by men (Marcus-Newhall, Thompson, & Thomas, 2001). Yet societal forces exaggerate this view. For example, middle-aged people in media ads are usually male executives, fathers, and grandfathers—handsome images of competence and security. And many more cosmetic products designed to hide signs of aging are offered for women than for men.

Fortunately, recent surveys suggest that the double standard is declining—that more people are viewing middle age as a potentially upbeat, satisfying time for both genders (Menon, 2001; Narayan, 2008). Models of older women with lives full of intimacy, accomplishment, hope, and imagination are promoting acceptance of physical aging and a new vision of growing older— one that emphasizes gracefulness, fulfillment, and inner strength.

ASK YOURSELF

>> **REVIEW**
Cite evidence that biological aging, individual heredity, and environmental factors contribute to osteoporosis.

>> **APPLY**
During a routine physical exam, Dr. Furrow gave 55-year-old Bill a battery of tests for cardiovascular disease but did not assess his bone density. In contrast, when 60-year-old Cara complained of chest pains, Dr. Furrow opted to "wait and see" before initiating further testing. What might account for Dr. Furrow's different approaches to Cara and Bill?

>> **REFLECT**
Which midlife health problem is of greatest personal concern to you? What steps can you take now to help prevent it?

Cognitive Development

In middle adulthood, the cognitive demands of everyday life extend to new and sometimes more challenging situations. Consider a typical day in the lives of Devin and Trisha. Recently appointed dean of faculty at a small college, Devin was at his desk by 7:00 A.M. In between strategic-planning meetings, he reviewed files of applicants for new positions and worked on the coming year's budget. Meanwhile, Trisha prepared for a civil trial, participated in jury selection, and then joined other top lawyers at her firm for a conference about management issues. That evening, Trisha and Devin advised their 20-year-old son, Mark, who had dropped by to discuss his uncertainty over whether to change his college major. By 7:30 P.M., Trisha was off to an evening meeting of the local school board. And Devin left for a biweekly gathering of an amateur quartet in which he played the cello.

Middle adulthood is a time of expanding responsibilities—on the job, in the community, and at home. To juggle diverse roles effectively, Devin and Trisha called on a wide array of intellectual abilities, including accumulated knowledge, verbal fluency, memory, rapid analysis of information, reasoning, problem solving, and expertise in their areas of specialization. What changes in thinking take place in middle adulthood? How does vocational life—a major arena in which cognition is expressed—influence intellectual skills? And what can be done to support the rising tide of adults who are returning to college in hopes of enhancing their knowledge and quality of life?

Changes in Mental Abilities

At age 50, when he occasionally couldn't recall a name or had to pause in the middle of a lecture or speech to think about what to say next, Devin wondered, Are these signs of an aging mind? Twenty years earlier, he had taken little notice of the same events. His questioning stems from widely held stereotypes of older adults as forgetful and confused. Most cognitive aging research has focused on deficits while neglecting cognitive stability and gains.

As we examine midlife cognitive changes, we will revisit the theme of diversity in development. Although declines occur in some aspects of functioning, most people display cognitive competence, especially in familiar contexts, and some attain outstanding accomplishment. Overall, the evidence supports an optimistic view of adult cognitive potential.

The research we are about to consider illustrates core assumptions of the lifespan perspective: development as *multidimensional*, or the combined result of biological, psychological, and social forces; development as *multidirectional*, or the joint expression of growth and decline, with the precise mix varying across abilities and individuals; and development as *plastic*, or open to change, depending on how a person's biological and environmental history combines with current life conditions. You may find it helpful to return to pages 5–7 in Chapter 1 to review these ideas.

Cohort Effects

Research using intelligence tests sheds light on the widely held belief that intelligence inevitably declines in middle and late adulthood as the brain deteriorates. Many early cross-sectional studies showed this pattern—a peak in performance at age 35

followed by a steep drop into old age. But widespread testing of college students and soldiers in the 1920s provided a convenient opportunity to conduct longitudinal research, retesting participants in middle adulthood. These findings revealed an age-related increase! To explain this contradiction, K. Warner Schaie (1998, 2005) used a sequential design, combining longitudinal and cross-sectional approaches (see pages 30–31 in Chapter 1) in the Seattle Longitudinal Study.

In 1956, people ranging in age from 22 to 70 were tested cross-sectionally. Then, at regular intervals, longitudinal follow-ups were conducted and new samples added, yielding a total of 5,000 participants, five cross-sectional comparisons, and longitudinal data spanning more than 60 years. Findings on five mental abilities showed the typical cross-sectional drop after the mid-thirties. But longitudinal trends for those abilities revealed modest gains in midlife, sustained into the fifties and the early sixties, after which performance decreased gradually.

Cohort effects are largely responsible for this difference. In cross-sectional research, each new generation experienced better health and education than the one before it. Also, the tests given may tap abilities less often used by older individuals, whose lives no longer require that they learn information for its own sake but, instead, skillfully solve real-world problems.

Crystallized and Fluid Intelligence

A close look at diverse mental abilities shows that only certain ones follow the longitudinal pattern just described. To appreciate this variation, let's consider two broad mental abilities, each of which includes an array of specific intellectual factors.

In 2009, 58-year-old Chesley "Sully" Sullenberger successfully landed a distressed commercial airliner in the Hudson River just off-shore of New York City, saving all its passengers and crew. As we will see, midlife is a time when some of the most complex mental abilities are at their peak.

The first of these broad abilities, **crystallized intelligence,** refers to skills that depend on accumulated knowledge and experience, good judgment, and mastery of social conventions—abilities acquired because they are valued by the individual's culture. Devin made use of crystallized intelligence when he expressed himself articulately at an alumni luncheon and suggested effective ways to save money in budget planning. On intelligence tests, vocabulary, general information, verbal comprehension, and logical reasoning items measure crystallized intelligence.

In contrast, **fluid intelligence** depends more heavily on basic information-processing skills—ability to detect relationships among visual stimuli, speed of analyzing information, and capacity of working memory. Though fluid intelligence often combines with crystallized intelligence to support effective reasoning and problem solving, it is believed to be influenced less by culture than by conditions in the brain and by learning unique to the individual (Horn & Noll, 1997). Intelligence test items reflecting fluid abilities include spatial visualization, digit span, letter-number sequencing, and symbol search. (Refer to page 240 in Chapter 9 for examples.)

Many cross-sectional studies show that crystallized intelligence increases steadily through middle adulthood, whereas fluid intelligence begins to decline in the twenties. These trends have been found repeatedly in investigations in which younger and older participants had similar education and general health status, largely correcting for cohort effects (Horn, Donaldson, & Engstrom, 1981; Kaufman & Horn, 1996; Park et al., 2002). In one such investigation, including nearly 2,500 mentally and physically healthy 16- to 85-year-olds, verbal (crystallized) IQ peaked between ages 45 and 54 and did not decline until the eighties! Nonverbal (fluid) IQ, in contrast, dropped steadily over the entire age range (Kaufman, 2001).

The midlife rise in crystallized abilities makes sense because adults are constantly adding to their knowledge and skills at work, at home, and in leisure activities. In addition, many crystallized skills are practiced almost daily. But does longitudinal evidence confirm the progressive fall-off in fluid intelligence?

■ SCHAIE'S SEATTLE LONGITUDINAL STUDY.

Figure 15.3 shows Schaie's longitudinal findings in detail. The five factors that gained in early and middle adulthood—verbal ability, inductive reasoning, verbal memory, spatial orientation, and numeric ability—include both crystallized and fluid skills. Their paths of change confirm that midlife is a time of peak performance on some of the most complex mental abilities (Willis & Schaie, 1999). According to these findings, middle-aged adults are intellectually "in their prime," not—as stereotypes would have it—"over the hill."

Figure 15.3 also shows a sixth ability, *perceptual speed*—a fluid skill in which participants must, for example, identify within a time limit which of five shapes is identical to a model or whether pairs of multidigit numbers are the same or different. Perceptual speed decreased from the twenties to the late eighties—a pattern that fits with a wealth of research indicating

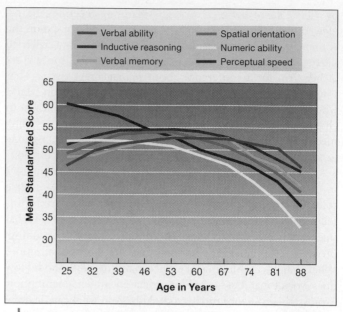

■ FIGURE 15.3 ■ Longitudinal trends in six mental abilities, from the Seattle Longitudinal Study. In five abilities, modest gains occurred into the fifties and early sixties, followed by gradual declines. The sixth ability—perceptual speed—decreased steadily from the twenties to the late eighties. And late in life, fluid factors (spatial orientation, numeric ability, and perceptual speed) showed greater decrements than crystallized factors (verbal ability, inductive reasoning, and verbal memory). (From K. W. Schaie, 1994, "The Course of Adult Intellectual Development," *American Psychologist, 49,* p. 308. Copyright © 1994 by the American Psychological Association. Reprinted with permission of American Psychological Association.)

that cognitive processing slows as people get older (Schaie, 1994, 1996, 1998). Also notice in Figure 15.3 how, late in life, fluid factors (spatial orientation, numeric ability, and perceptual speed) show greater decrements than crystallized factors (verbal ability, inductive reasoning, and verbal memory).

■ EXPLAINING CHANGES IN MENTAL ABILITIES.

Some theorists believe that a general slowing of central nervous system functioning underlies nearly all age-related declines in cognitive performance (Salthouse, 1996, 2006). Many studies offer at least partial support for this idea. Researchers have also identified other important changes in information processing, some of which may be triggered by declines in speed.

Before we turn to this evidence, let's clarify why research reveals gains followed by stability in crystallized abilities, despite a much earlier decline in fluid intelligence, or basic information-processing skills. First, the decrease in basic processing, while substantial after age 45, may not be great enough to affect many well-practiced performances until quite late in life. Second, as we will see, adults can often compensate for cognitive limitations by drawing on their cognitive strengths. Finally, as people discover that they are no longer as good as they once were at certain tasks, they accommodate, shifting to activities that depend less on cognitive efficiency and more on accumulated knowledge. Thus, the basketball player becomes a coach, the once quick-witted salesperson a manager.

Information Processing

As processing speed slows, certain aspects of attention and memory decline. Yet midlife is also a time of great expansion in cognitive competence as adults apply their vast knowledge and life experience to problem solving in the everyday world.

Speed of Processing

Devin watched with fascination as his 20-year-old son, Mark, played a computer game, responding to multiple on-screen cues in rapid-fire fashion. When Devin tried it, although he practiced over several days, his performance remained well behind Mark's. Similarly, on a family holiday in Australia, Mark adjusted quickly to driving on the left side of the road, but after a week, Trisha and Devin still felt confused at intersections, where rapid responses were needed.

These real-life experiences fit with laboratory findings. On both simple reaction-time tasks (pushing a button in response to a light) and complex ones (pushing a left-hand button to a blue light, a right-hand button to a yellow light), response time increases steadily from the early twenties into the nineties. The more complex the situation, the more disadvantaged older adults are. Though small—less than 1 second in most studies—the decline in speed is nevertheless of practical significance (Deary & Der, 2005; Der & Deary, 2006).

Researchers agree that changes in the brain are responsible for age-related cognitive slowing but disagree on the precise explanation (Hartley, 2006; Salthouse & Caja, 2000). According to the **neural network view,** as neurons in the brain die, breaks in neural networks occur. The brain adapts by forming bypasses—new synaptic connections that go around the breaks but are less efficient (Cerella, 1990). Another hypothesis, the **information-loss view,** suggests that older adults experience greater loss of information as it moves through the cognitive system. As a result, the whole system must slow down to inspect and interpret the information. Imagine making a photocopy, then using it to make another copy. Each subsequent copy is less clear. Similarly, with each step of thinking, information degrades. The older the adult, the more exaggerated this effect. Complex tasks, which have more processing steps, are more affected by information loss (Myerson et al., 1990).

At present, researchers are not sure whether just one or two neural changes, or multiple changes that vary across individuals, underlie declines in processing speed (Hartley, 2006). What is clear is that processing speed predicts adults' performance on many tests of complex abilities. The slower their reaction time, the lower people's scores on memory, reasoning, and problem-solving tasks, with relationships greater for fluid- than crystallized-ability items (Finkel et al., 2007; Salthouse, 2005, 2006). Indeed, as adults get older, correlations between processing speed and other cognitive performances strengthen. This suggests that processing speed contributes broadly to declines in cognitive functioning (Li et al., 2004).

Yet processing speed correlates only moderately with older adults' performances, including fluid-ability tasks. And it is not the only major predictor of age-related cognitive changes. Other factors—declines in vision and hearing and in attentional resources, inhibition, working-memory capacity, and use of memory strategies—also predict diverse age-related cognitive performances (Hartley, 2006; Luo & Craik, 2008). Nevertheless, processing speed, as we will see in the following sections, does contribute to the decrements in attention and memory just mentioned (Levitt, Fugelsang, & Crossley, 2006; Salthouse, Fristoe, & Rhee, 1996). But disagreement persists over whether age-related cognitive changes have just one common cause, best represented by processing speed, or multiple independent causes.

Furthermore, processing speed is a weak predictor of the skill with which older adults perform complex, familiar tasks in everyday life, which they continue to do with considerable proficiency. Devin, for example, played a Mozart quartet on his cello with great speed and dexterity, keeping up with three other players 10 years his junior. How did he manage? Compared with the others, he more often looked ahead in the score (Krampe & Charness, 2007). Using this compensatory approach, he could prepare a response in advance, thereby minimizing the importance of speed. Knowledge and experience can also compensate for impairments in processing speed. Devin's many years of playing the cello undoubtedly supported his ability to play swiftly and fluidly.

Because older adults find ways to compensate for cognitive slowing on familiar tasks, their reaction time is considerably better on verbal items (indicating as quickly as possible whether a string of letters forms a word) than on nonverbal items (responding to a light or other signal) (Hultsch, MacDonald, & Dixon, 2002; Wingfield & Stine-Morrow, 2000). Finally, as we will see in Chapter 17, older adults' processing speed can be improved through training, though age differences remain.

Attention

Studies of attention focus on how much information adults can take into their mental systems at once; the extent to which they can attend selectively, ignoring irrelevant information; and the ease with which they can adapt their attention, switching from one task to another as the situation demands. Trisha sometimes tried to prepare dinner or continue working on a legal brief while talking on the phone. But with age, she found it harder to engage in the two activities simultaneously. Consistent with Trisha's experience, laboratory research reveals that sustaining two complex tasks at once becomes more challenging with age.

An age-related decrement also occurs in the ability to switch back and forth between mental operations, such as judging one of a pair of numbers as "odd or even" on some trials, "more or less" on others (Kramer & Kray, 2006; Radvansky, Zacks, & Hasher, 2005). These declines in attention might be due to the slowdown in information processing described earlier, which limits the amount of information a person can attend to at once (Kramer & Madden, 2008).

As adults get older, *inhibition*—resistance to interference from irrelevant information—is also harder (Gazzaley et al., 2005; Hasher, Zacks, & May, 1999). On *continuous performance tasks,* in which participants are shown a series of stimuli on a computer screen and asked to press the space bar only after a particular sequence occurs (for example, the letter *K* immediately followed by the letter *A*), performance declines steadily from the thirties into old age, with older adults making more errors of commission (pressing the space bar in response to incorrect letter sequences). And when extraneous noise is introduced, errors of omission (not pressing the space bar after a *K–A* sequence) also rise with age (Mani, Bedwell, & Miller, 2005). In everyday life, inhibitory difficulties cause older adults to appear distractible—inappropriately diverted from the task at hand by a thought or a feature of the environment.

Again, adults can compensate for these changes. People highly experienced in attending to critical information and performing several tasks at once, such as air traffic controllers and pilots, know exactly what to look for. As a result, they show smaller age-related attentional declines (Tsang & Shaner, 1998). Similarly, older adults focus on relevant information and handle two tasks proficiently when they have extensively practiced those activities over their lifetimes (Kramer & Madden, 2008). Furthermore, practice can improve the ability to divide attention between two tasks, selectively focus on relevant information, and switch back and forth between mental operations.

Conductors and teachers must focus on relevant information within a complex field of stimulation and divide their attention among competing tasks—well-practiced skills that may help slow age-related declines in attention.

When older adults receive training in these skills, their performance improves as much as that of younger adults, although training does not close the gap between age groups (Bherer et al., 2006; Erickson et al., 2007; Kramer, Hahn, & Gopher, 1998).

Memory

From the twenties into the sixties, the amount of information people can retain in working memory diminishes. Whether given lists of words or digits or meaningful prose passages to learn, middle-aged and older adults recall less than young adults, although memory for prose suffers less than memory for list items (Hultsch et al., 1998; Old & Naveh-Benjamin, 2008a).

This change is largely due to a decline in use of memory strategies on these tasks. Older individuals rehearse less than younger individuals—a difference believed to be due to a slower rate of thinking (Salthouse, 1996). Older people cannot repeat new information to themselves as quickly as younger people. Reduced working-memory capacity is another likely influence, leading to difficulties in retaining to-be-remembered items and processing them at the same time (Park & Payer, 2006).

Memory strategies of organization and elaboration, which require people to link incoming information with already stored information, are also applied less often and less effectively with age (Dunlosky & Hertzog, 2001; Troyer et al., 2006). An additional reason older adults are less likely to use these techniques is that they find it harder to retrieve information from long-term memory that would help them recall. For example, given a list of words containing *parrot* and *blue jay,* they don't immediately access the category "bird," even though they know it well (Hultsch et al., 1998). Greater difficulty keeping one's attention on relevant information seems to be involved. As irrelevant stimuli take up space in working memory, less is available for the memory task at hand (O'Connor & Kaplan, 2003; Radvansky, Zacks, & Hasher, 2005).

But keep in mind that the memory tasks given by researchers require strategies that many adults seldom use and may not be motivated to use, since most are not in school (see Chapter 9, page 236). When a word list has a strong category-based structure, older adults organize as well as younger adults do (Naveh-Benjamin, 2000; Naveh-Benjamin et al., 2005). And when given training in strategic memorizing, middle-aged and older people use strategies willingly, and they show improved performance over long periods, though age differences remain (Derwinger, Neely, & Bäckman, 2005).

Furthermore, tasks can be designed to help older people compensate for age-related declines in working memory—for example, by slowing the pace at which information is presented. In one study, adults ranging in age from 19 to 68 were shown a video and immediately tested on its content (a pressured, classroomlike condition). Then they were given a packet of information on the same topic as the video to study at their leisure and told to return three days later to be tested (a self-paced condition) (Beier & Ackerman, 2005). Performance declined with age only in the pressured condition, not in the

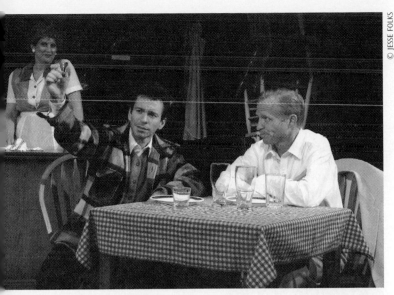

Age-related changes in memory vary widely across tasks and individuals. Bringing decades of experience to the task, these actors in a community theater production retain the ability to memorize hundreds of lines and perform demanding roles.

self-paced condition. And although topic-relevant knowledge predicted better recall in both conditions, it did so more strongly in the self-paced condition, which granted participants ample time to retrieve and apply what they already knew.

Finally, middle-aged people who have trouble recalling something often draw on decades of accumulated *metacognitive knowledge* about how to maximize performance—reviewing major points before an important presentation, organizing notes and files so information can be found quickly, and parking the car in the same area of the parking lot each day. Research suggests that aging has little impact on metacognition (Berg, 2000; Schwartz & Frazier, 2005).

In sum, age-related changes in memory vary widely across tasks and individuals as people use their cognitive capacities to meet the requirements of their everyday worlds. ***TAKE A MOMENT...*** Does this remind you of Sternberg's *theory of successful intelligence,* described in Chapter 9—in particular, his notion of *practical intelligence* (see page 241)? To understand memory development (and other aspects of cognition) in adulthood, we must view it in context. As we turn to problem solving, expertise, and creativity, we will encounter this theme again.

Practical Problem Solving and Expertise

One evening, as Devin and Trisha sat in the balcony of the Chicago Opera House awaiting curtain time, the announcement came that 67-year-old Ardis Krainik, the opera company's general director and "life force," had died. After a shocked hush, members of the audience began turning to one another, asking about the woman who had made the opera company into one of the world's greatest.

Starting as a chorus singer and clerk typist, Ardis rose rapidly through the ranks, becoming assistant to the director and

developing a reputation for tireless work and unmatched organizational skill. When the opera company fell deeply in debt, Ardis—now the newly appointed general director—erased the deficit within a year and restored the company's sagging reputation. She charmed donors into making large contributions, attracted world-class singers, and filled the house to near capacity (Rhein, 1997).

Ardis's story is a dramatic one, but all middle-aged adults encounter opportunities to display continued cognitive growth in the realm of **practical problem solving,** which requires people to size up real-world situations and analyze how best to achieve goals that have a high degree of uncertainty. Gains in *expertise*—an extensive, highly organized, and integrated knowledge base that can be used to support a high level of performance—help us understand why practical problem solving takes this leap forward.

The development of expertise is under way in early adulthood and reaches its height in midlife, leading to highly efficient and effective approaches to solving problems. This rapid, implicit application of knowledge is the result of years of learning, experience, and effortful practice (Krampe & Charness, 2007; Wagner, 2000). It cannot be assessed by laboratory tasks or mental tests that do not call on this knowledge.

Expertise is not just the province of the highly educated and of those who rise to the top of administrative ladders. In a study of food service workers, researchers identified the diverse ingredients of expert performance in terms of physical skills (strength and dexterity); technical knowledge (of menu items, ordering, and food presentation); organizational skills (setting priorities, anticipating customer needs); and social skills (confident presentation and a pleasant, polished manner). Next, 20- to 60-year-olds with fewer than two to more than ten years of experience were evaluated on these qualities. Although physical strength and dexterity declined with age, job knowledge and organizational and social skills increased (Perlmutter, Kaplan, & Nyquist, 1990). Compared to younger adults with similar years of experience, middle-aged employees performed more competently, serving customers in especially adept, attentive ways.

Age-related advantages are also evident in solutions to everyday problems—for example, how to resolve a disagreement between two friends, or whether to make a costly repair to one's home (Denney, 1990; Denney & Pearce, 1989). From middle age on, adults place greater emphasis on thinking through a practical problem—trying to understand it better, interpreting it from different perspectives, and solving it through logical analysis (Kim & Hasher, 2005). Perhaps for this reason, they are more rational decision makers—less likely than young adults to select attractive-looking options that, on further reflection, are not the best.

Creativity

As noted in Chapter 13, creative accomplishment tends to peak in the late thirties or early forties and then decline, but with considerable variation across individuals and disciplines. Some people produce highly creative works in later decades: In her early sixties, Martha Graham choreographed *Clytemnestra,*

© BRIANA ORR

In middle adulthood, creativity becomes more thoughtful, integrative, and altruistic. Author Masha Hamilton's travels to northeastern Kenya to research her novel, *The Camel Bookmobile,* led her to help organize the Camel Book Drive. It has funded the purchase of camels, books, and equipment for nomadic schools in the area.

into unique ways of thinking (Abra, 1989; Sasser-Coen, 1993). Creative works by older adults more often sum up or integrate ideas. Mature academics typically devote less energy to new discoveries in favor of writing memoirs, histories of their field, and other reflective works. And in older creators' novels, scholarly writings, paintings, and musical compositions, living with old age and facing death are common themes (Beckerman, 1990; Sternberg & Lubart, 2001).

Finally, creativity in middle adulthood frequently reflects a transition from a largely egocentric concern with self-expression to more altruistic goals (Tahir & Gruber, 2003). As the middle-aged person overcomes the youthful illusion that life is eternal, the desire to give to humanity and enrich the lives of others increases.

Taken together, these changes may contribute to an overall decline in creative output in later decades. In reality, however, creativity takes new forms.

ASK YOURSELF

>> **REVIEW**
How do slowing of cognitive processing, reduced working-memory capacity, and difficulties with inhibition affect memory in midlife? What can older adults do to compensate for these declines?

>> **APPLY**
Asked about hiring older sales personnel, a department store manager replied, "They're my best employees!" Why does this manager find older employees desirable, despite the age-related decline in speed of processing?

Vocational Life and Cognitive Development

Vocational settings are vital contexts for maintaining previously acquired skills and learning new ones. Yet work environments vary in the degree to which they are cognitively stimulating and promote autonomy. And inaccurate, negative stereotypes of age-related problem-solving and decision-making skills can result in older employees being assigned less challenging work.

In a study of over 600 U.S. men representing a wide range of occupations, researchers asked about the task complexity and self-direction of their jobs. During the interview, they also assessed cognitive flexibility, based on logical reasoning, awareness of both sides of an issue, and independence of judgment. A decade later, the job and cognitive variables were remeasured, permitting a look at their effects on each other. As expected, cognitively flexible men sought work that offered challenge and autonomy. But the relationship was reciprocal—complex work also led to gains in cognitive flexibility (Kohn & Schooler, 1978).

These same findings emerged in large-scale studies carried out in Japan and Poland—cultures quite different from the United States (Kohn, 2006; Kohn et al., 1990; Kohn & Slomczynski, 1990). In each nation, having a stimulating, nonroutine

recognized as one of the great full-length modern-dance dramas. Charles Darwin finished *On the Origin of Species* at age 50 and continued to write groundbreaking books and papers in his sixties and seventies. After abandoning a career in embroidery because of arthritis, Anna Mary Robertson Moses (known as Grandma Moses) began painting scenes of country life, producing about 1,600 works between ages 75 and 101 (Antonini et al., 2008; Tahir & Gruber, 2003). And as with problem solving, the *quality* of creativity may change with advancing age—in at least three ways.

First, youthful creativity in literature and the arts is often spontaneous and intensely emotional, while creative works produced after age 40 often appear more deliberately thoughtful (Lubart & Sternberg, 1998). Perhaps for this reason, poets produce their most frequently cited works at younger ages than do authors of fiction and nonfiction (Cohen-Shalev, 1986). Poetry depends more on language play and "hot" expression of feelings, whereas story- and book-length works require extensive planning and molding.

Second, with age, many creators shift from generating unusual products to combining extensive knowledge and experience job helped explain the relationship between SES and flexible, abstract thinking. And people who do intellectually demanding work seek out stimulating leisure pursuits, which also foster cognitive flexibility (Kohn et al., 2000).

Is the impact of a challenging job on cognitive growth greatest for young adults, who are in the early phase of career development? In fact, research shows that people in their fifties and early sixties gain as much as those in their twenties and thirties (Avolio & Sosik, 1999; Miller, Slomczynski, & Kohn, 1985). Once again, we are reminded of the plasticity of development. Cognitive flexibility is responsive to vocational experience well into middle adulthood and perhaps beyond.

Adult Learners: Becoming a Student in Midlife

Adults are returning to undergraduate and graduate study in record numbers. During the past quarter-century, students over age 25 in U.S. colleges and universities increased from 27 to 45 percent of total enrollment, with an especially sharp rise in those over age 35 (U.S. Department of Education, 2009). Life transitions often trigger a return to formal education, as with Devin and Trisha's friend Anya, who entered a nursing program after her last child left home. Divorce, widowhood, a job layoff, a family move, and a youngest child reaching school age are examples of other changes that commonly precede reentry (Moen & Roehling, 2005). Among a sample of African-American women, additional motivations included serving as a role model for children and enriching their ethnic community as a whole (Coker, 2003).

Characteristics of Returning Students

About 60 percent of adult learners are women (U.S. Department of Education, 2009). First-year reentry women report feeling more self-conscious, inadequate, and hesitant to talk in class than either returning men or traditional-age students (under age 25) (Wilke & Thompson, 1993). Their anxiety is due in part to not having practiced academic learning for many years but is also prompted by negative aging and gender stereotypes—erroneous beliefs that traditional-age students are smarter or that men are more logical and therefore more academically capable. And for minority students, ethnic stereotypes about ability to learn and prejudicial treatment are also factors (Coker, 2003).

Role demands outside of school—from spouses, children, other family members, friends, and employers—pull many returning women in conflicting directions. Those reporting high psychological stress typically have career rather than enrichment goals, young children, limited financial resources, and nonsupportive husbands (Padula & Miller, 1999). When couples fail to rework divisions of household and child-care responsibilities to accommodate the woman's return to school, marital satisfaction declines (Sweet & Moen, 2007). As a classmate told Anya one day, "I tried keeping the book open and

In this Wayne State University labor studies class for union members, students benefit from an approachable teacher who uses small-group discussion. Active engagement with the subject matter and personal relationships with faculty and other students help middle-aged learners succeed.

reading, cooking, and talking to the kids. It didn't work. They felt I was ignoring them." Because of multiple demands on their time, mature-age women tend to take fewer credits, experience more interruptions in their academic programs, and progress at a slower pace than mature-age men. Role overload is the most common reason for not completing their degrees (Jacobs & King, 2002). But many express high motivation to work through those difficulties, referring to the excitement of learning, to the fulfillment academic success brings, and to their hope that a college education will improve both their work and family lives (Kinser & Deitchman, 2007).

Supporting Returning Students

As these findings suggest, social supports for returning students can make the difference between continuing in school and dropping out. Adult students need family members and friends who encourage their efforts and enable them to find time for uninterrupted study. Anya's classmate explained, "My doubts subsided when one day, my husband volunteered, 'You take your books and do what you need to do. I can cook dinner and do the laundry.'" Institutional services for returning students are also essential. Personal relationships with faculty, peer networks enabling adults to get to know one another, conveniently scheduled evening and Saturday classes, online courses, and financial aid for part-time students increase the chances of academic success.

Although nontraditional students rarely require assistance in settling on career goals, they report a strong desire for help in choosing the most appropriate courses and in exploring jobs related to their talents (Luzzo, 1999). Academic advising and professional internship opportunities responsive to their needs are vital. Low-income students often need special assistance, such as academic tutoring, sessions in confidence building and assertiveness, and—in the case of ethnic minorities—help adjusting to styles of learning that are at odds with their cultural background.

When support systems are in place, most returning students gain in self-efficacy and do well academically (Chao & Good, 2004). After finishing her degree, Anya secured a position as a parish nurse with creative opportunities to counsel members of a large congregation about health concerns. Education granted her new life options, financial rewards, and higher self-esteem as she reevaluated her own competencies. Sometimes (though not in Anya's case) these revised values and increased self-reliance can spark other changes, such as a divorce or a new intimate partnership (Esterberg, Moen, & Dempster-McClain, 1994). In middle adulthood as in earlier years, education transforms development, often powerfully reshaping the life course.

ASK YOURSELF

>> **REVIEW**
In view of the impact of vocational and educational experiences on midlife cognitive development, evaluate the saying "You can't teach an old dog new tricks."

>> **APPLY**
Marcella completed one year of college in her twenties. Now, at age 42, she has returned to earn a degree. Plan a set of experiences for Marcella's first semester that will increase her chances of success.

>> **REFLECT**
Interview a nontraditional student in one of your classes about the personal challenges and rewards of working toward a degree at a later age. What services does your institution offer to support returning students?

Summary

PHYSICAL DEVELOPMENT

Physical Changes

Describe the physical changes of middle adulthood, paying special attention to vision, hearing, the skin, muscle–fat makeup, and the skeleton.

>> The gradual physical changes begun in early adulthood continue in midlife, contributing to a revised physical self-image, with less emphasis on hoped-for gains and more on feared declines.

>> Vision is affected by **presbyopia,** or loss of the accommodative ability of the lens, reduced ability to see in dim light, increased sensitivity to glare, and diminished color discrimination. After age 40, risk of **glaucoma,** a buildup of pressure in the eye that damages the optic nerve, increases.

>> Hearing loss, or **presbycusis,** first affects detection of high frequencies and then spreads to other tones.

>> The skin wrinkles, loosens, dries, and starts to develop age spots. Muscle mass declines, and fat deposits increase. A low-fat diet and regular exercise that includes resistance training can offset excess weight and muscle loss.

>> Bone density declines in both sexes, but to a greater extent in women, especially after menopause. Height loss and bone fractures can result.

Describe reproductive changes in middle adulthood, and discuss women's psychological reactions to menopause.

>> The **climacteric** in women, which occurs gradually over a 10-year period as estrogen production drops, concludes with **menopause,** sometimes accompanied by emotional and physical symptoms.

>> Though **hormone therapy** is successful in reducing the discomforts of menopause, it remains controversial because of increased risks of cardiovascular disease, certain cancers, and cognitive declines.

>> Menopause is affected by cultural beliefs and practices as well as hormonal changes. Physical symptoms and psychological reactions vary widely.

© DAVID BURCH/UPPERCUT IMAGES/PHOTOLIBRARY

>> Though sperm production continues throughout life, quantity of semen diminishes after age 40. Erections become harder to attain and maintain, but drugs are available to combat impotence.

Health and Fitness

Discuss sexuality in middle adulthood and its association with psychological well-being.

>> Frequency of sexual activity among married couples declines only slightly in middle adulthood and is associated with marital happiness. Intensity of sexual response declines more, due to physical changes of the climacteric. Most married people over age 50 find ways to overcome difficulties with sexual functioning.

Discuss cancer, cardiovascular disease, and osteoporosis, noting risk factors and interventions.

>> The death rate from cancer increases tenfold from early to middle adulthood. A complex interaction of heredity, biological aging, and environment contributes to cancer. Annual screenings and various preventive steps can reduce the incidence of cancer and cancer deaths.

>> Although cardiovascular disease has declined in recent decades, it remains a major cause of death in middle adulthood, especially among men. Symptoms include high blood pressure, high blood cholesterol, atherosclerosis, heart attack, arrhythmia, and angina pectoris. Quitting smoking, reducing blood cholesterol through diet and drug therapy, exercising, and reducing stress can decrease risk and aid in treatment.

>> **Osteoporosis** affects 12 percent of people over age 50, most of whom are postmenopausal women. Adequate calcium and vitamin D, weight-bearing and strength-training exercise, and bone-strengthening medications can help prevent and treat osteoporosis.

Discuss the association of hostility and anger with heart disease and other health problems.

>> Expressed hostility is a component of the **Type A behavior pattern** that predicts heart disease and other health problems. Because anger suppression is also related to health problems, a better alternative is to develop effective ways of handling stress and conflict.

Adapting to the Challenges of Midlife

Discuss the benefits of stress management, exercise, and an optimistic outlook in dealing effectively with challenges of midlife.

>> Effective stress management includes both problem-centered and emotion-centered coping, depending on the situation; constructive approaches to anger reduction; and social support. In middle adulthood, people tend to cope with stress more effectively.

>> Regular exercise confers many physical and psychological advantages, making it worthwhile for sedentary middle-aged people to begin exercising. Developing a sense of self-efficacy, choosing an appropriate exercise format, and making exercise environments accessible, attractive, and safe promote physical activity.

>> **Hardiness** is made up of three personal qualities: control, commitment, and challenge. By inducing a generally optimistic outlook on life, hardiness helps people cope with stress adaptively.

Explain the double standard of aging.

>> Although negative stereotypes of aging discourage older adults of both sexes, middle-aged women are more likely to be viewed unfavorably, especially by men. New surveys suggest that the double standard of aging is declining as both genders view middle age more positively.

COGNITIVE DEVELOPMENT

Changes in Mental Abilities

Describe cohort effects on intelligence revealed by Schaie's Seattle Longitudinal Study.

>> Early cross-sectional research showed a peak in intelligence test performance around age 35 followed by a steep decline, whereas longitudinal evidence revealed modest gains in midlife. Using a sequential design, Schaie found that the cross-sectional, steep drop-off largely resulted from cohort effects, as each new generation experienced better health and education.

Describe changes in crystallized and fluid intelligence in middle adulthood, and discuss individual and group differences in intellectual development.

>> In cross-sectional studies that correct for cohort effects, **crystallized intelligence** (which depends on accumulated knowledge and experience) gains steadily through middle adulthood. In contrast, **fluid intelligence** (which depends more on basic information-processing skills) declines starting in the twenties.

AP IMAGES/AMY SANCETTA

>> In the Seattle Longitudinal Study, perceptual speed follows a pattern of steady, continuous decline. But other fluid skills, in addition to crystallized abilities, increase through middle adulthood, confirming that midlife is a time of peak performance on a variety of complex abilities.

Information Processing

How does information processing change in midlife?

>> Speed of cognitive processing slows with age, a change explained by either the **neural network view** or the **information-loss view.** As reaction time slows, people perform less well on complex memory, reasoning, and problem-solving tasks, and especially on fluid-ability items. But other factors also predict diverse, age-related cognitive changes.

>> Middle-aged people show declines in ability to divide their attention, focus on relevant stimuli, and switch from one task to another as the situation demands. Cognitive inhibition becomes more difficult, at times prompting distractibility.

>> Adults in midlife retain less information in working memory, largely due to a decline in use of memory strategies. But training, improved design of tasks, and metacognitive knowledge enable older adults to compensate for age-related decrements.

Discuss the development of practical problem solving, expertise, and creativity in middle adulthood.

>> As expertise increases, middle-aged adults in all walks of life often become good at **practical problem solving.** Creativity becomes more deliberately thoughtful, and it shifts from generating unusual products to integrating ideas and from concern with self-expression to more altruistic goals.

Vocational Life and Cognitive Development

Describe the relationship between vocational life and cognitive development.

>> At all ages and in different cultures, the relationship between vocational life and cognitive development is reciprocal. Stimulating, complex work and flexible, abstract thinking support each other.

Adult Learners: Becoming a Student in Midlife

Discuss the challenges that adults face in returning to college and the benefits of earning a degree in midlife.

>> Adults are returning to college and graduate school in record numbers. The majority are women, who are often motivated by life transitions. Returning students must cope with a lack of recent practice at academic work; stereotypes of aging, gender, and ethnicity; and demands of multiple roles.

© JIM WEST/ALAMY

>> Social support from family and friends and institutional services suited to their needs can help returning students succeed. Further education results in enhanced competencies, new relationships, and reshaped life paths.

Important Terms and Concepts

climacteric (p. 399)
crystallized intelligence (p. 410)
fluid intelligence (p. 410)
glaucoma (p. 398)
hardiness (p. 408)

hormone therapy (p. 401)
information-loss view (p. 411)
menopause (p. 399)
neural network view (p. 411)
osteoporosis (p. 405)

practical problem solving (p. 413)
presbycusis (p. 398)
presbyopia (p. 398)
Type A behavior pattern (p. 406)

CHAPTER
16

Emotional and Social Development in Middle Adulthood

© JIM WEST/PHOTOEDIT

Midlife is a time of increased generativity—giving to and guiding younger generations. As these volunteers build a playground for children in a low-income neighborhood, their exuberance conveys the deep sense of satisfaction they derive from generative activities.

One weekend when Devin, Trisha, and their 24-year-old son, Mark, were vacationing together, the two middle-aged parents knocked on Mark's hotel room door. "Your dad and I are going off to see a crafts exhibit," Trisha explained. "Feel free to stay behind," she offered, recalling Mark's antipathy toward attending such events as an adolescent.

"That exhibit sounds great!" Mark replied. "I'll meet you in the lobby. We've got so little time together as it is."

"Sometimes I forget he's an adult!" exclaimed Trisha as she and Devin re-

© THOMAS NORTHCUT/GETTY IMAGES/RISER

turned to their room to grab their coats. "It's been great to have Mark with us these few days—like spending time with a good friend."

In their forties and fifties, Trisha and Devin built on earlier strengths and intensified their commitment to leaving a legacy for those who would come after them. As Mark graduated from college, took his first job, fell in love, and married, they felt a sense of pride at having escorted a member of the next generation into responsible adult roles. Family activities, which had declined during Mark's adolescent and college years, now increased as Trisha and Devin related to their son and daughter-in-law not just as kin but as enjoyable adult companions. Challenging work and more time for community involvement, leisure pursuits, and each other contributed to a richly diverse and gratifying time of life.

The midlife years were not as smooth for two of Trisha and Devin's friends. Fearing that she might grow old alone, Jewel frantically pursued her quest for an intimate partner. She attended singles events, registered with dating services, and traveled in hopes of meeting a like-minded companion. "I can't stand the thought of turning 50," she lamented in a letter to Trisha. But Jewel also had compensating satisfactions—friendships that had grown more meaningful, warm relationships with a nephew and niece, and a successful consulting business.

Tim, Devin's best friend from graduate school, had been divorced for over 15 years. Recently, he had met Elena and had come to love her deeply. But in addition to her own divorce, Elena was dealing with a troubled daughter, a new

career, and other life changes. Whereas Tim had reached the peak of his career and was ready to enjoy life, Elena wanted to recapture much of what she had missed in earlier decades—not just a gratifying intimate relationship, but opportunities to realize her talents. "I don't know where I fit into Elena's plans," Tim wondered aloud on the phone with Trisha.

Increasing awareness of limited time ahead prompts middle-aged adults to reevaluate the meaning of their lives, refine and strengthen their identities, and reach out to future generations. Most make modest adjustments in their outlook, goals, and daily lives. But a few experience profound inner turbulence and initiate major changes, often in an effort to make up for lost time. Together with advancing years, family and work transitions contribute greatly to emotional and social development.

More midlifers are addressing these tasks than ever before, now that the baby boomers have reached their forties, fifties, and early sixties. Indeed, 45- to 54-year-olds are currently the largest age sector of the U.S. population (U.S. Census Bureau, 2009b). As our discussion will reveal, the baby boomers have brought increased self-confidence, social consciousness, and vitality—along with great developmental diversity—to this period of the lifespan.

A monumental survey called *Midlife Development in the United States (MIDUS),* conducted in the mid-1990s, has contributed enormously to our understanding of midlife emotional and social development. Its nationally representative sample included nearly 3,500 U.S. 25- to 75-year-olds, enabling those in the middle years to be compared with younger and older individuals. Through telephone interviews and self-administered questionnaires, participants responded to over 1,100 items addressing wide-ranging psychological, health, and background factors, yielding unprecedented breadth of information in a single study (Brim, Ryff, & Kessler, 2005). The research endeavor also included "satellite" studies, in which subsamples of respondents were questioned in greater depth on key topics. And it is now being extended longitudinally.

MIDUS has greatly expanded our knowledge of the *multidimensional* and *multidirectional* nature of midlife change, and it promises to be a rich source of information for many years to come. Hence, our discussion repeatedly draws on MIDUS, at times delving into its findings, at other times citing them alongside those of other investigations. Let's turn now to Erikson's theory and related research, to which MIDUS has contributed.

Erikson's Theory: Generativity versus Stagnation

Erikson's psychological conflict of midlife is called **generativity versus stagnation.** Generativity involves reaching out to others in ways that give to and guide the next generation. It is under way in early adulthood, typically through childbearing and child rearing and establishing a niche in the occupational world. But it expands greatly in midlife, when commitment extends beyond oneself and one's life partner to a larger group— family, community, or society (McAdams & Logan, 2004). The generative adult combines the need for self-expression with the need for communion, integrating personal goals with the welfare of the larger social world.

Erikson (1950) selected the term *generativity* to encompass everything generated that can outlive the self and ensure society's continuity and improvement: children, ideas, products, and works of art. Although parenting is a major means of realizing generativity, it is not the only means: Adults can be generative in other family relationships (as Jewel was with her nephew and niece), as mentors in the workplace, in volunteer endeavors, and through many forms of productivity and creativity.

Notice, from what we have said so far, that generativity brings together personal desires and cultural demands. On the personal side, middle-aged adults feel a need to be needed—to attain symbolic immortality by making a contribution that will survive their death (Kotre, 1999; McAdams, Hart, & Maruna,

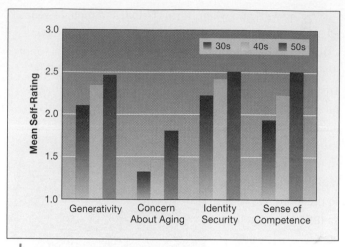

■ **FIGURE 16.1** ■ **Age-related changes in self-rated generativity, concern about aging, identity security, and sense of competence.** In a longitudinal study of over 300 college-educated women, self-rated generativity increased from the thirties to the fifties, as did concern about aging. The rise in generativity was accompanied by other indicators of psychological health—greater security with one's identity and sense of competence. (Adapted from Stewart, Ostrove, & Helson, 2001.)

1998). This desire may stem from a deep-seated evolutionary urge to protect and advance the next generation. On the cultural side, society imposes a social clock for generativity in midlife, requiring adults to take responsibility for the next generation through their roles as parents, teachers, mentors, leaders, and coordinators (McAdams & Logan, 2004). And according to Erikson, a culture's "belief in the species"—the conviction that life is good and worthwhile, even in the face of human destructiveness and deprivation—is a major motivator of generative action, which has improving humanity as its goal.

The negative outcome of this stage is stagnation: Once people attain certain life goals, such as marriage, children, and career success, they may become self-centered and self-indulgent. Adults may express a sense of stagnation through lack of interest in young people (including their own children), through a focus on what they can get from others rather than what they can give, and through taking little interest in being productive at work, developing their talents, or bettering the world in other ways.

Much research indicates that generativity increases in midlife (Keyes & Ryff, 1998; Rossi, 2001, 2004). For example, in longitudinal and cross-sectional studies of college-educated women, and in an investigation of middle-aged adults diverse in SES, self-rated generativity rose from the thirties into the forties and fifties (see Figure 16.1). At the same time, participants expressed greater concern about aging, increased security with their identities, and a stronger sense of competence (Miner-Rubino, Winter, & Stewart, 2004; Stewart, Ostrove, & Helson, 2001; Zucker, Ostrove, & Stewart, 2002).

Just as Erikson's theory suggests, highly generative people appear especially well-adjusted—low in anxiety and depression; high in autonomy, self-acceptance, and life satisfaction; and

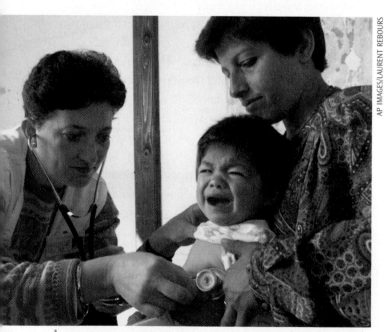

Albanian doctor Besa Basha works in Kosovo for Doctors Without Borders, a Nobel Prize–winning organization that treats patients, distributes food and medicine, and builds medical facilities in troubled regions throughout the world. Her generative work integrates personal goals with concern for societal welfare.

AP IMAGES/LAURENT REBOURS

more likely to have successful marriages and close friends (Ackerman, Zuroff, & Moskowitz, 2000; An & Cooney, 2006; Grossbaum & Bates, 2002; Westermeyer, 2004). They are also more open to differing viewpoints, possess leadership qualities, desire more from work than financial rewards, and care greatly about the welfare of their children, their partner, their aging parents, and the wider society (Peterson, 2002; Peterson, Smirles, & Wentworth, 1997). Furthermore, generativity is associated with more effective child rearing—higher valuing of trust, open communication, transmission of values to children, and an authoritative style (Hart et al., 2001; Peterson & Duncan, 2007; Pratt et al., 2008).

Although these findings characterize adults of all backgrounds, individual differences in contexts for generativity exist. Having children seems to foster men's generative development more than women's. In several studies, including the MIDUS survey, fathers scored higher in generativity than childless men (Marks, Bumpass, & Jun, 2004; McAdams & de St. Aubin, 1992; Snarey et al., 1987). Perhaps parenting awakens in men a tender, caring attitude toward the next generation that women have opportunities to develop in other ways. And for low-SES men with troubled pasts, fatherhood can provide a context for highly generative, positive life change (Roy & Lucas, 2006). As one former gang member, who earned an associate's degree and struggled to keep his teenage sons off the streets, explained, "I came through the depths of hell to try to be a father. I let my sons know, 'You're never without a daddy. . . .' I tell them that if me and your mother separate, I make sure that wherever I go, I build something for you to come to" (p. 153).

Finally, compared with Caucasians, African Americans more often engage in certain types of generativity. They are more involved in religious groups and activities, offer more social support to members of their community, and are more likely to view themselves as role models and sources of wisdom for their children (Hart et al., 2001). A life history of strong support from church and extended family may strengthen these generative values and actions. In samples of Caucasian Americans, religiosity and spirituality are also linked to greater generative activity (Dillon & Wink, 2004; Wink & Dillon, 2003). Highly generative middle-aged adults often indicate that as children and adolescents, they internalized moral values rooted in a religious tradition, which provided lifelong encouragement for generative action (McAdams, 2006). Especially in individualistic societies, belonging to a religious community or believing in a higher being may help preserve generative commitments.

Other Theories of Psychosocial Development in Midlife

Erikson's theory provides only a broad sketch of adult personality development. For a closer look at psychosocial change in midlife, let's revisit Levinson's and Vaillant's theories, which were introduced in Chapter 14.

Levinson's Seasons of Life

Return to page 370 to review Levinson's eras (stages or seasons). Like early adulthood, middle adulthood begins with a transitional period (age 40 to 45), during which people evaluate their success in meeting early adulthood goals. Realizing that from now on, more time will lie behind than ahead, they regard the remaining years as increasingly precious. Consequently, some make drastic revisions in their life structure: divorcing, remarrying, changing careers, or displaying enhanced creativity. Others make smaller changes while staying in the same marriage, surroundings, occupation, and workplace.

Whether these years bring a gust of wind or a storm, most people turn inward for a time, focusing on personally meaningful living (Neugarten, 1968b). According to Levinson, for middle-aged adults to reassess their relation to themselves and the external world and rebuild their life structure, they must confront four developmental tasks. Each requires the individual to reconcile two opposing tendencies within the self, attaining greater internal harmony.

- *Young–old:* The middle-age person must seek new ways of being both young and old. This means giving up certain youthful qualities, retaining and transforming others, and finding positive meaning in being older. Perhaps because of the double standard of aging (see page 408 in Chapter 15), most middle-aged women express concern about appearing less attractive (Rossi, 2005). But middle-aged men—particularly non-college-educated men, who often hold blue-collar jobs requiring physical strength and stamina—are also highly sensitive to physical aging. In one study, they were more concerned about physical changes than both college- and non-college-educated women, who exceeded college-educated men (Miner-Rubino, Winter, & Stewart, 2004). Compared with previous midlife cohorts, the baby boomers are especially interested in controlling physical changes—a desire that has helped energize a huge industry of anti-aging cosmetic products and medical procedures (Lachman, 2004; Jones, Whitbourne, & Skultety, 2006).

- *Destruction–creation:* With greater awareness of mortality, the middle-aged person focuses on ways he or she has acted destructively and how others have done the same. Past hurtful acts toward family members, friends, and co-workers are countered by a strong desire to participate in activities that advance human welfare, thereby leaving a legacy for future generations. The image of a legacy can be satisfied in many ways—through charitable gifts, creative products, volunteer service, or mentoring young people.

- *Masculinity–femininity:* The middle-aged person must create a better balance between masculine and feminine parts of the self. For men, this means greater acceptance of "feminine" traits of nurturance and caring, which enhance close relationships and compassionate exercise of authority in the workplace. For women, it generally means being more open to "masculine" characteristics of autonomy and assertiveness (Gilligan, 1982; Harris, Ellicott, & Holmes, 1986). Recall from Chapter 8 that people who combine masculine and feminine traits have an androgynous gender identity, which is associated with favorable adjustment.

- *Engagement–separateness:* The middle-aged person must forge a better balance between engagement with the external world and separateness. For many men, and for women who have had successful careers, this may mean reducing concern with ambition and achievement and attending more fully to the self. But women who have been devoted to child rearing or an unfulfilling job often feel compelled to move in the other direction (Levinson, 1996). At age 48, Elena left her position as a reporter for a small-town newspaper, pursued an advanced degree in creative writing, accepted a college teaching position, and began writing a novel. Tim, in contrast, recognized his overwhelming desire for a gratifying romantic partnership. By scaling back his career, he realized he could grant Elena the time and space she needed to build a rewarding work life.

People who flexibly modify their identities in response to age-related changes yet maintain a sense of self-continuity are more aware of their own thoughts and feelings and are higher in self-esteem (Jones, Whitbourne, & Skultety, 2006; Sneed & Whitbourne, 2001, 2003). But when poverty, unemployment, and lack of a respected place in society dominate the life course, energies are directed toward survival rather than realistically approaching age-related changes. Even adults whose jobs are secure and who live in pleasant neighborhoods may find that employment conditions restrict possibilities for growth by placing too much emphasis on productivity and profit and too little on the meaning of work. In her early forties, Trisha left a large law firm, where she felt constant pressure to bring in high-fee clients and received little acknowledgment of her efforts, for a small practice.

Opportunities for advancement ease the transition to middle adulthood. Yet these are far less available to women than to men. Individuals of both sexes in blue-collar jobs also have few possibilities for promotion. Many find compensating rewards in mentoring younger workers and in moving to the senior generation of their families (Christensen & Larsen, 2008; Levinson, 1978).

Vaillant's Adaptation to Life

Whereas Levinson interviewed 35- to 45-year-olds, Vaillant (1977, 2002)—in his longitudinal research on well-educated men and women—followed participants past the half-century mark. Recall from Chapter 14 how adults in their late forties and fifties take on peak responsibility for the functioning of society, eventually becoming "keepers of meaning," or guardians of their culture (see page 371). Vaillant reported that the most-successful and best-adjusted entered a calmer, quieter time of life. "Passing the torch"—concern that the positive aspects of their culture survive—became a major preoccupation.

In societies around the world, older people are guardians of traditions, laws, and cultural values. This stabilizing force holds in check too-rapid change sparked by the questioning and challenging of adolescents and young adults. As people approach the end of middle age, they focus on longer-term, less personal goals, such as the state of human relations in their society. And they become more philosophical, accepting the fact that not all problems can be solved in their lifetime.

Is There a Midlife Crisis?

Levinson (1978, 1996) reported that most men and women in his samples experienced substantial inner turmoil during the transition to middle adulthood. Yet Vaillant (1977, 2002) saw few examples of crisis but, rather, slow and steady change. These contrasting findings raise the question of how much personal upheaval actually accompanies entry to midlife. Are self-doubt and stress especially great during the forties, and do they prompt major restructuring of the personality, as the term **midlife crisis** implies?

Consider the reactions of Trisha, Devin, Jewel, Tim, and Elena to middle adulthood. Trisha and Devin moved easily into this period, whereas Jewel, Tim, and Elena sought alternative life paths. Clearly, wide individual differences exist in response to midlife. **TAKE A MOMENT...** Now ask several individuals in their twenties and thirties whether they expect to encounter a

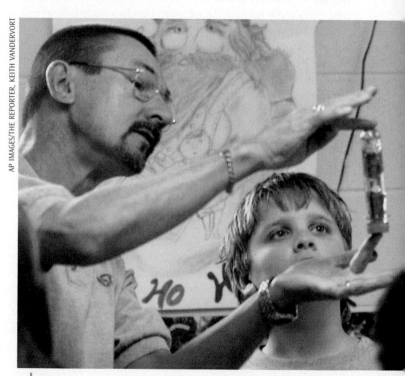

As is typical for midlifers, elementary school teacher Jaime Malwitz modified his career in ways that resemble a turning point, not a crisis. He designed a scientist-in-residence program, which is currently being implemented in many school districts. Here he serves as a resident physicist, discussing a density experiment with a fifth grader.

midlife crisis between ages 40 and 50. You are likely to find that Americans often anticipate it, perhaps because of culturally induced apprehension of aging (Menon, 2001; Wethington, Kessler, & Pixley, 2005). Yet little evidence supports this view of middle age as a turbulent time.

When MIDUS participants were asked to describe "turning points" (major changes in the way they felt about an important aspect of their lives) that had occurred during the past five years, most of the ones reported concerned work. Women's work-related turning points peaked in early adulthood, when many adjusted their work lives to accommodate marriage and childrearing (see Chapter 14). The peak for men, in contrast, came at midlife, a time of increased career responsibility and advancement. Other common turning points in early and middle adulthood were positive: They involved fulfilling a dream and learning something good about oneself (Wethington, Kessler, & Pixley, 2005). Overall, turning points rarely resembled midlife crises. Even negative work-related turning points generally led to personal growth—for example, a layoff that sparked a positive career change or a shift in energy from career to personal life.

Asked directly if they had ever experienced something they would consider a midlife crisis, only one-fourth of the MIDUS respondents said yes. And they defined such events much more loosely than researchers do. Some reported a crisis well before age 40, others well after age 50. And most attributed it not to age but rather to challenging life events (Wethington, 2000).

Another way of exploring midlife questioning is to ask adults about life regrets—attractive opportunities they did not pursue or lifestyle changes they did not make. In two investigations of women in their early forties, those who acknowledged regret without making life changes, compared to those who modified their lives, reported less favorable psychological well-being and poorer physical health over time (Landman et al., 1995; Stewart & Vandewater, 1999).

By late midlife, with less time ahead to make life changes, people's interpretation of regrets plays a major role in their well-being. Mature, contented adults acknowledge a past characterized by some losses but are able to disengage from them, investing in personally rewarding goals (King & Hicks, 2007). Among a sample of several hundred 60- to 65-year-olds diverse in SES, about half expressed at least one regret. Compared to those who had not resolved their disappointments, those who had come to terms with them (accepted and identified some eventual benefits) or had "put the best face on things" (identified benefits but still had some lingering regret) reported better physical health and greater life satisfaction (Torges, Stewart, & Miner-Rubino, 2005).

In sum, life evaluation is common during middle age. Most people make changes that are best described as turning points rather than drastic alterations of their lives. Those who cannot modify their life paths often look for the "silver lining" in life's difficulties (Wethington, Kessler, & Pixley, 2005). The few midlifers who are in crisis typically have had early adulthoods in which gender roles, family pressures, or low income severely limited their ability to fulfill personal needs and goals.

ASK YOURSELF

≫ **REVIEW**
What personal and cultural forces motivate generativity? Why does it increase and contribute vitally to favorable adjustment in midlife?

≫ **APPLY**
After years of experiencing little personal growth at work, 42-year-old Mel looked for a new job and received an attractive offer in another city. Although he felt torn between leaving close friends and pursuing a long-awaited career opportunity, after several weeks of soul searching, he took the new job. Was Mel's dilemma a midlife crisis? Why or why not?

≫ **REFLECT**
Think of a middle-aged adult whom you admire. Describe the various ways that individual expresses generativity.

Stability and Change in Self-Concept and Personality

Midlife changes in self-concept and personality reflect growing awareness of a finite lifespan, longer life experience, and generative concerns. Yet certain aspects of personality remain stable, revealing the persistence of individual differences established during earlier periods.

Possible Selves

On a business trip, Jewel found a spare afternoon to visit Trisha. Sitting in a coffee shop, the two women reminisced about the past and thought aloud about the future. "It's been tough living on my own and building the business," Jewel said. "What I hope for is to become better at my work, to be more community-oriented, and to stay healthy and available to my friends. Of course, I would rather not grow old alone, but if I don't find that special person, I suppose I can take comfort in the fact that I'll never have to face divorce or widowhood."

Jewel is discussing **possible selves**, future-oriented representations of what one hopes to become and what one is afraid of becoming. Possible selves are the temporal dimension of self-concept—what the individual is striving for and attempting to avoid. To lifespan researchers, these hopes and fears are just as vital in explaining behavior as people's views of their current characteristics. Indeed, possible selves may be an especially strong motivator of action in midlife, as more meaning becomes attached to time (Frazier & Hooker, 2006). As we age, we may rely less on social comparisons in judging our self-worth and more on temporal comparisons—how well we are doing in relation to what we had planned.

Throughout adulthood, the personality traits people assign to their current selves show considerable stability. A 30-year-old who says he is cooperative, competent, outgoing, or successful is likely to report a similar picture at a later age. But reports of possible selves change greatly. Adults in their early twenties mention many possible selves, and their visions are lofty and idealistic—being "perfectly happy," "rich and famous," "healthy throughout life," and not being "a person who does nothing important." With age, possible selves become fewer in number and more modest and concrete. They are largely concerned with performance of roles and responsibilities already begun—"being competent at work," "being a good husband and father," "putting my children through the colleges of their choice," "staying healthy," and not being "a burden to my family" or "without enough money to meet my daily needs" (Bybee & Wells, 2003; Cross & Markus, 1991; Ryff, 1991).

What explains these shifts in possible selves? Because the future no longer holds limitless opportunities, adults preserve mental health by adjusting their hopes and fears. To stay motivated, they must maintain a sense of unachieved possibility, yet they must still manage to feel good about themselves and their lives despite disappointments (Lachman & Bertrand, 2002). For example, although Jewel feared loneliness in old age, she reminded herself that marriage can lead to equally negative outcomes, such as divorce and widowhood—possibilities that made not having attained an important interpersonal goal easier to bear.

Self-Acceptance, Autonomy, and Environmental Mastery

An evolving mix of competencies and experiences leads to changes in certain aspects of personality during middle adulthood. In Chapter 15, we noted that midlife brings gains in expertise and practical problem solving. Middle-aged adults also offer more complex, integrated descriptions of themselves than do younger and older individuals (Labouvie-Vief, 2003). Furthermore, midlife is typically a period in which the number of social roles peaks—spouse, parent, worker, and engaged community member. And status at work and in the community typically rises, as adults take advantage of opportunities for leadership and other complex responsibilities (Helson, Soto, & Cate, 2006).

These changes in cognition and breadth of roles undoubtedly contribute to other gains in personal functioning. In research on well-educated adults ranging in age from the late teens into the seventies, three qualities increased from early to middle adulthood and then leveled off:

- *Self-acceptance:* More than young adults, middle-aged people acknowledged and accepted both their good and bad qualities and felt positively about themselves and life.

- *Autonomy:* Middle-aged adults saw themselves as less concerned about others' expectations and evaluations and more concerned with following self-chosen standards.

- *Environmental mastery:* Middle-aged people saw themselves as capable of managing a complex array of tasks easily and effectively (Ryff, 1991, 1995).

As these findings indicate, midlife is generally a time of increased comfort with the self, independence, assertiveness, commitment to personal values, and life satisfaction (Helson, Jones, & Kwan, 2002; Helson & Wink, 1992; Keyes, Shmotkin, & Ryff, 2002; Mitchell & Helson, 1990). Perhaps because of these personal attributes, people sometimes refer to middle age as "the prime of life."

At the same time, factors contributing to psychological well-being differ substantially among cohorts, as self-reports gathered from 25- to 65-year-old MIDUS survey respondents reveal (Carr, 2004). Among women who were born during the baby-boom years or later, and who thus benefited from the women's movement, balancing career with family predicted greater self-acceptance and environmental mastery. But also consider that women born before or during World War II who sacrificed career to focus on child rearing—expected of young mothers in the 1950s and 1960s—were similarly advantaged in self-acceptance. Likewise, men who were in step with prevailing social expectations scored higher in well-being. Baby-boom and younger men who modified their work schedules to make room for family responsibilities—who fit their cohort's image of the "good father"—were more self-accepting. But older men who made this accommodation scored much lower in self-acceptance than those who focused on work and thus conformed to the "good provider" ideal of their times. (See the Biology and Environment box on the following page for additional influences on midlife psychological well-being.)

Coping with Daily Stressors

In a MIDUS satellite study in which more than 1,000 participants were interviewed on eight consecutive evenings, researchers found an early- to mid-adulthood plateau in frequency of daily stressors, followed by a decline as work and family responsibilities ease and leisure time increases (see Figure 16.2 on page 426) (Almeida & Horn, 2004). Compared with older people, young and midlife adults also perceived their stressors as more disruptive and unpleasant, perhaps because they often experienced several at once, and many involved financial risks and children.

But recall from Chapter 15 that midlife brings an increase in effective coping strategies. Middle-aged individuals are more likely to identify the positive side of difficult situations, postpone action to permit evaluation of alternatives, anticipate and plan ways to handle future discomforts, and use humor to express ideas and feelings without offending others (Diehl, Coyle, & Labouvie-Vief, 1996). Notice how these efforts flexibly draw on both problem-centered and emotion-centered strategies.

Why might effective coping increase in middle adulthood? Other personality changes seem to support it. In one study, complex, integrated self-descriptions—which increase in midlife, indicating an improved ability to blend strengths and weaknesses into an organized picture—predicted good coping strategies (Labouvie-Vief & Diehl, 2000). Midlife gains in emotional stability and confidence in handling life's problems may also contribute (Roberts et al., 2007; Roberts & Mroczek, 2008).

▪ BIOLOGY AND ENVIRONMENT ▪

What Factors Promote Psychological Well-Being in Midlife?

For Trisha and Devin, midlife brought contentment and high life satisfaction. But the road to happiness was rockier for Jewel, Tim, and Elena. What factors contribute to individual differences in psychological well-being at midlife? Consistent with the lifespan perspective, biological, psychological, and social forces are involved, and their effects are interwoven.

Good Health and Exercise

Good health affects energy and zest for life at any age. But during middle and late adulthood, taking steps to improve health and prevent disability becomes a better predictor of psychological well-being. Middle-aged adults who maintain an exercise regimen are likely to perceive themselves as particularly active for their age and, therefore, to feel a special sense of accomplishment (Netz et al., 2005). As an extra psychological benefit, exercise may reduce feelings of vulnerability to chronic illness and disability—a strong contributor to poor psychological well-being at midlife (Barsky, Cleary, & Klerman, 1992).

Sense of Control and Personal Life Investment

Middle-aged adults who report a high sense of control over events in various aspects of their lives—health, family, and work—also report more favorable psychological well-being, as MIDUS and other survey findings reveal. A sense of control fosters self-efficacy—a belief in one's ability to surmount challenges—and, consequently, helps sustain a positive outlook in the face of health, family, and work difficulties (Lachman & Firth, 2004; Smith et al., 2000).

Personal life investment—firm commitment to goals and involvement in pursuit of those goals—also adds to mental health and life satisfaction (Staudinger, Fleeson, & Baltes, 1999). According to Mihaly Csikszentmihalyi, a vital wellspring of happiness is *flow*—the psychological state of being so engrossed in a demanding, meaningful activity that one loses all sense of time and self-awareness. People describe flow as the height of enjoyment, even as an ecstatic state. The more people experience flow, the more they judge their lives to be gratifying (Nakamura & Csikszentmihalyi, 2002). Flow depends on perseverance and skill at complex

endeavors that offer potential for growth. These qualities are well-developed in middle adulthood.

Positive Social Relationships

Developing gratifying social ties is closely linked to midlife psychological well-being. In a survey of college alumni, those who preferred occupational prestige and high income to close friends were twice as likely as other respondents to describe themselves as "fairly" or "very" unhappy (Perkins, 1991, as cited by Myers, 2000).

Enjoyable social ties can strengthen the impact of an exercise regimen on well-being. Among an ethnically diverse sample of women using a private gym or an African Caribbean community center, exercising with likeminded companions contributed to their happiness and life satisfaction (Wray, 2007). The social side of going to the gym appeared especially important to minority women, who were less concerned with physical-appearance benefits than their Caucasian agemates.

A Good Marriage

Although friendships and positive relationships with co-workers are important, a good marriage boosts psychological well-being even more. The role of marriage in mental health increases with age, becoming a powerful predictor by late midlife (Marks, Bumpass, & Jun, 2004; Westermeyer, 1998).

Longitudinal studies tracking people as they move in and out of intimate relationships suggest that marriage actually brings about well-being. For example, when interviews with over 13,000 U.S. adults were repeated five years later, people who remained married reported greater happiness than those who remained single. Those who separated or divorced became less happy, reporting considerable depression. Men and women who married for the first time experienced a sharp increase in happiness, those who entered their second marriage a modest increase (Marks & Lambert, 1998).

Although not everyone is better off married, the link between marriage and well-being is similar in many nations, suggesting that marriage changes people's behavior in ways that make them better off (Diener et al., 2000; Lansford et al., 2005). Married partners monitor each other's health and offer care in times of illness. They also earn and save more money than single people, and higher income is modestly linked to psychological well-being (Myers, 2000; Waite, 1999). Furthermore, sexual satisfaction predicts mental health, and married

After crossing a marathon finish line, these middle-aged runners express a joyful sense of accomplishment. Maintaining an exercise regimen contributes greatly to midlife psychological well-being.

couples have more satisfying sex lives than unmarried couples and singles (see Chapter 14).

Mastery of Multiple Roles

Finally, success in handling multiple roles is linked to psychological well-being. In a study of nearly 300 middle-aged women, researchers asked about feelings of competence and control in four roles: wife, mother, caregiver of an impaired parent, and employee. Participants experienced the highest levels of mastery in their work roles. But competence and control in all four roles predicted life satisfaction and reduced depression (Christensen, Stephens, & Townsend, 1998). And women who occupied several roles—in work and family arenas—seemed to benefit from added opportunities to enhance their sense of mastery.

In the MIDUS survey, as role involvement increased, both men and women reported greater environmental mastery, more rewarding social relationships, heightened sense of purpose in life, and more positive emotion. Once again, adults who occupied multiple roles and who also reported high control (suggesting effective role management) scored especially high in well-being—an outcome that was stronger for less-educated adults (Ahrens & Ryff, 2006). Control over roles may be vital for individuals with lower educational attainment, whose role combinations may be particularly stressful and who have fewer economic resources.

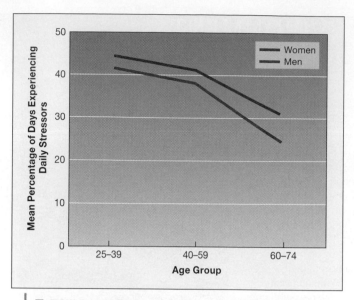

■ **FIGURE 16.2** ■ **Age-related change in daily stressors among men and women.** In a MIDUS satellite study, researchers interviewed more than 1,000 adults on eight consecutive evenings. Findings revealed an early- to mid-adulthood plateau, followed by a decline as work and family responsibilities ease and leisure time increases. (From D. M. Almeida & M. C. Horn, 2004, "Is Daily Life More Stressful During Middle Adulthood?" in O. G. Brim, C. D. Ryff, & R. C. Kessler (Eds.), *How Healthy Are We? A National Study of Well-Being at Midlife,* Chicago: The University of Chicago Press, p. 438. Adapted by permission of The University of Chicago Press.)

These attributes predict work and relationship effectiveness—outcomes that reflect the sophisticated, flexible coping of middle age.

Gender Identity

In her forties and early fifties, Trisha appeared more assertive at work, taking on leadership roles and speaking out freely. She was also more dominant in family relationships, expressing her opinions more readily than she had 10 or 15 years earlier. In contrast, Devin's sense of empathy became more apparent, and he was less assertive and more accommodating to Trisha's wishes.

Many studies report an increase in "masculine" traits in women and "feminine" traits in men across middle age (Huyck, 1990; James et al., 1995). Women become more confident, self-sufficient, and forceful, men more emotionally sensitive, caring, considerate, and dependent. These trends appear in not just Western industrialized nations but also village societies such as the Maya of Guatemala, the Navajo of the United States, and the Druze of the Middle East (Fry, 1985; Gutmann, 1977; Turner, 1982). Consistent with Levinson's theory, gender identity in midlife becomes more androgynous—a mixture of "masculine" and "feminine" characteristics.

Although the existence of these changes is well-accepted, explanations for them are controversial. A well-known evolutionary view, **parental imperative theory,** holds that identification with traditional gender roles is maintained during the active parenting years to help ensure the survival of children.

Men become more goal-oriented, while women emphasize nurturance. After children reach adulthood, parents are free to express the "other-gender" side of their personalities (Gutmann & Huyck, 1994).

But these biological accounts have been criticized. As discussed in earlier chapters, parents need both warmth and assertiveness (in the form of firmness and consistency) to rear children effectively. And although children's departure from the home is related to men's openness to the "feminine" side of their personalities, the link to a rise in "masculine" traits among women is less apparent (Huyck, 1996, 1998). In longitudinal research, college-educated women in the labor force became more independent by their early forties, regardless of whether they had children; those who were homemakers did not (Helson & Picano, 1990; Wink & Helson, 1993). Furthermore, cohort effects may contribute to this trend: In one study, middle-aged women of the baby-boom generation—who experienced new career opportunities as a result of the women's movement—more often described themselves as having masculine and androgynous traits than did older women (Strough et al., 2007).

Additional demands of midlife may prompt a more androgynous orientation. For example, among men, a need to enrich a marital relationship after children have departed, along with reduced chances for career advancement, may be involved in the awakening of emotionally sensitive traits. Compared with men, a greater number of women remain divorced, are widowed, and encounter discrimination in the workplace. Self-reliance and assertiveness are vital for coping with these circumstances.

In adulthood, androgyny is associated with advanced moral reasoning and psychosocial maturity (Prager & Bailey, 1985; Waterman & Whitbourne, 1982). People who do not integrate the masculine and feminine sides of their personalities tend to have mental health problems, perhaps because they are unable to adapt flexibly to the challenges of aging (Huyck, 1996).

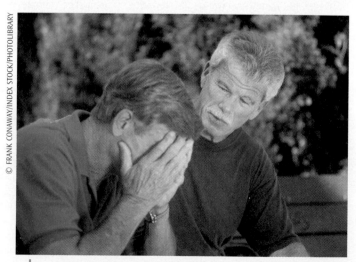

In middle age, gender identity becomes more androgynous for both sexes. Men tend to show an increase in "feminine" traits, becoming more emotionally sensitive, caring, considerate, and dependent.

■ **TABLE 16.1** ■ *The "Big Five" Personality Traits*

TRAIT	DESCRIPTION
Neuroticism	Individuals who are high on this trait are worrying, temperamental, self-pitying, self-conscious, emotional, and vulnerable. Individuals who are low are calm, even-tempered, self-content, comfortable, unemotional, and hardy.
Extroversion	Individuals who are high on this trait are affectionate, talkative, active, fun-loving, and passionate. Individuals who are low are reserved, quiet, passive, sober, and emotionally unreactive.
Openness to experience	Individuals who are high on this trait are imaginative, creative, original, curious, and liberal. Individuals who are low are down-to-earth, uncreative, conventional, uncurious, and conservative.
Agreeableness	Individuals who are high on this trait are soft-hearted, trusting, generous, acquiescent, lenient, and good-natured. Individuals who are low are ruthless, suspicious, stingy, antagonistic, critical, and irritable.
Conscientiousness	Individuals who are high on this trait are conscientious, hard-working, well-organized, punctual, ambitious, and persevering. Individuals who are low are negligent, lazy, disorganized, late, aimless, and nonpersistent.

Source: McCrae & Costa, 2006.

Individual Differences in Personality Traits

Although Trisha and Jewel both became more self-assured and assertive in midlife, in other respects they differed. Trisha had always been more organized and hard-working, Jewel more gregarious and fun-loving. Once, the two women traveled together. At the end of each day, Trisha was disappointed if she had not kept to a schedule and visited every tourist attraction. Jewel liked to "play it by ear"—wandering through streets and stopping to talk with shopkeepers and residents.

In previous sections, we considered personality changes common to many middle-aged adults, but individual differences also exist. The hundreds of personality traits on which people differ have been organized into five basic factors, called the **"big five" personality traits:** neuroticism, extroversion, openness to experience, agreeableness, and conscientiousness. Table 16.1 provides a description of each. Notice that Trisha is high in conscientiousness, whereas Jewel is high in extroversion.

Longitudinal and cross-sectional studies of men and women in many countries varying widely in cultural traditions reveal that agreeableness and conscientiousness increase from the teenage years through middle age, whereas neuroticism declines, and extroversion and openness to experience do not change or decrease slightly—changes that reflect "settling down" and greater maturity (McCrae & Costa, 2006; Roberts et al., 2003; Roberts, Walton, & Viechtbauer, 2006; Srivastava et al., 2003). The consistency of these cross-cultural findings has led some researchers to conclude that adult personality change is genetically influenced. They note that individual differences in the "big five" traits are large and highly stable: A person who scores high or low at one age is likely to do the same at another, over intervals ranging from 3 to 30 years (McCrae & Costa, 2006). In a reanalysis of more than 150 longitudinal studies including more than 50,000 participants, personality-trait stability increased from early to middle adulthood, reaching a peak in the decade of the fifties (Roberts & DelVecchio, 2000).

How can there be high stability in personality traits, yet significant changes in aspects of personality discussed earlier? We can think of adults as changing in overall organization and integration of personality but doing so on a foundation of basic, enduring dispositions that support a coherent sense of self as people adapt to changing life circumstances. When more than 2,000 individuals in their forties were asked to reflect on their personalities during the previous six years, 52 percent said they had "stayed the same," 39 percent said they had "changed a little," and 9 percent said they had "changed a lot" (Herbst et al., 2000).

Again, these findings contradict a view of middle adulthood as a period of great turmoil and change. But they also underscore that personality remains an "open system," responsive to the pressures of life experiences. Indeed, certain midlife personality changes may strengthen trait consistency! Improved self-understanding, self-acceptance, and skill at handling challenging situations may result in less need to modify basic personality dispositions over time.

ASK YOURSELF

≫ **REVIEW**
Summarize personality changes at midlife. How can these changes be reconciled with increasing stability of the "big five" personality traits?

≫ **APPLY**
Jeff, age 46, suggested to his wife, Julia, that they set aside time once a year to discuss their relationship—both positive aspects and ways to improve. Julia was surprised because Jeff had never before expressed interest in working on their marriage. What developments at midlife probably fostered this new concern?

≫ **REFLECT**
List your hoped-for and feared possible selves. Then ask family members in the early and middle adulthood periods to do the same. Are their reports consistent with age-related research findings? Explain.

Relationships at Midlife

The emotional and social changes of midlife take place within a complex web of family relationships and friendships. Although a few middle-aged people live alone, the vast majority—90 percent in the United States—live in families, most with a spouse (U.S. Census Bureau, 2009b). Partly because they have ties to older and younger generations in their families and partly because their friendships are well-established, people tend to have a larger number of close relationships during midlife than at any other period (Antonucci, Akiyama, & Takahashi, 2004).

The middle adulthood phase of the family life cycle is often referred to as "launching children and moving on." In the past, it was called the "empty nest," but this phrase implies a negative transition, especially for women. When adults devote themselves entirely to their children, the end of active parenting can trigger feelings of emptiness and regret. But for many people, middle adulthood is a liberating time, offering a sense of completion and an opportunity to strengthen existing ties and build new ones.

Because increased life expectancy has caused this period to lengthen, it is marked by the greatest number of exits and entries of family members. As adult children leave home and marry, middle-aged people must adapt to new roles of parent-in-law and grandparent. At the same time, they must establish a different type of relationship with their aging parents, who may become ill or infirm and die. Let's see how ties within and beyond the family change during this time of life.

Marriage and Divorce

Although not all couples are financially comfortable, middle-aged households are well-off compared with other age groups. Americans between 45 and 54 have the highest average annual income. And the baby boomers—more of whom have earned college and postgraduate degrees and live in dual-earner families—are financially better off than previous midlife generations (Eggebeen & Sturgeon, 2006; U.S. Census Bureau, 2009b). Partly because of increased education and financial security, the contemporary social view of marriage in midlife is one of expansion and new horizons.

These forces strengthen the need to review and adjust the marital relationship. For Devin and Trisha, this shift was gradual. By middle age, their marriage had permitted satisfaction of family and individual needs, endured many changes, and culminated in deeper feelings of love. Elena's marriage, in contrast, became more conflict-ridden as her teenage daughter's problems introduced added strains and as departure of children made marital difficulties more obvious. Tim's failed marriage revealed yet another pattern. With passing years, the number of problems declined, but so did the love expressed. As less happened in the relationship, good or bad, the couple had little to keep them together (Rokach, Cohen, & Dreman, 2004).

As the Biology and Environment box on page 425 revealed, marital satisfaction is a strong predictor of midlife psychological well-being. As in early adulthood, divorce is one way of resolving an unsatisfactory marriage. Although most divorces occur within five to ten years of marriage, about 10 percent take place after 20 years or more (U.S. Department of Health and Human Services, 2002). Divorce at any age takes a heavy psychological toll, but midlifers seem to adapt more easily than younger people (Marks & Lambert, 1998). Midlife gains in practical problem solving and effective coping strategies may reduce the stressful impact of divorce.

Nevertheless, for many women, marital breakup—especially when it is repeated—severely reduces standard of living (see page 271 in Chapter 10). For this reason, in midlife and earlier, it is a strong contributor to the **feminization of poverty**—a trend in which women who support themselves or their families have become the majority of the adult population living in poverty, regardless of age and ethnic group. Because of weak public policies safeguarding families (see Chapter 2), the gender gap in poverty is higher in the United States than in other Western industrialized nations (U.S. Census Bureau, 2009b).

Longitudinal evidence reveals that middle-aged women who weather divorce successfully tend to become more tolerant, comfortable with uncertainty, nonconforming, and self-reliant in personality—factors believed to be fostered by divorce-forced independence. And both men and women reevaluate what they consider important in a healthy relationship, placing greater weight on equal friendship and less on passionate love than they had the first time. As in earlier periods, divorce represents both a time of trauma and a time of growth (Baum, Rahav, & Sharon, 2005; Schneller & Arditti, 2004). Little is known about long-term adjustment following divorce among middle-aged men, perhaps because most enter new relationships and remarry within a short time.

© JEFF GREENBERG/PHOTOEDIT

For many middle-aged couples, having forged a relationship that permits satisfaction of both family and individual needs results in deep feelings of love.

Changing Parent–Child Relationships

Parents' positive relationships with their grown children are the result of a gradual process of "letting go," culminating in children's independent living. As mentioned earlier, most middle-aged parents adjust well to the launching phase of the family life cycle. Investment in nonparental relationships and roles, children's characteristics, parents' marital and economic circumstances, and cultural forces affect the extent to which this transition is expansive and rewarding or sad and distressing.

After moving their son Mark into his college dormitory at the start of his freshman year, Devin and Trisha felt a twinge of nostalgia. Driving home, they recalled his birth, first day of school, and high school graduation and commented on their suddenly tranquil household. Beyond this, they returned to rewarding careers and community participation and delighted in having more time for each other. Parents who have developed gratifying alternative activities typically welcome their children's adult status (Dennerstein, Dudley, & Guthrie, 2002).

Whether or not they reside with parents, adolescent and young-adult children who are "off-time" in development—not showing expected signs of independence and accomplishment—can prompt parental strain (Aquilino, 1996; Pillemer & Suitor, 2002). Consider Elena, whose daughter was frequently truant from high school and in danger of not graduating. The need for greater parental oversight and guidance caused anxiety and unhappiness for Elena, who was ready to focus on her own personal and vocational development.

However, wide variations exist in the social clock for children's departure. Recall from Chapter 13 that many young people from low-SES homes and with cultural traditions of extended-family living do not leave home early. In the Southern European countries of Greece, Italy, and Spain, parents often actively delay their children's leaving. In Italy, for example, parents believe that moving out without a "justified" reason signifies that something is wrong in the family. Hence, many more Italian young adults reside with their parents until marriage than in other Western nations. At the same time, Italian parent–adult-child relationships are usually positive, making shared living attractive (Rusconi, 2004).

With the end of parent–child coresidence, parental authority declines sharply. But continued communication is important to middle-aged adults. Departure of children is a relatively minor event when parent–child contact and affection are sustained. When it results in little or no communication, parents' life satisfaction declines (White, 1994). In a large longitudinal study of New Zealand families, parents who had been warm and supportive in middle childhood and adolescence were more likely to experience contact and closeness with their child in early adulthood (Belsky et al., 2001).

When children marry, parents face additional challenges in enlarging the family network to include in-laws. Difficulties occur when parents do not approve of their child's partner or when the young couple adopts a way of life inconsistent with the parents' values. But as MIDUS findings confirm, when warm, supportive relationships endure, intimacy between parents and children increases over the adult years, with great benefits for parents' life satisfaction (Ryff, Singer, & Seltzer, 2002). Once young adults strike out on their own, members of the middle generation, especially mothers, usually take on the role of **kinkeeper,** gathering the family for celebrations and making sure everyone stays in touch.

Grandparenthood

Two years after Mark married, Devin and Trisha were thrilled to learn that a granddaughter was on the way. Although the stereotypical image of grandparents as elderly persists, today the average age of becoming a grandparent is 50 years for American women, 52 for American men (Legacy Project, 2009). A longer life expectancy means that many adults will spend one-third or more of their lifespan in the grandparent role.

■ **MEANINGS OF GRANDPARENTHOOD.** Middle-aged adults typically rate grandparenthood as highly important, following closely behind the roles of parent and spouse but ahead of worker, son or daughter, and sibling (Reitzes & Mutran, 2002). Why did Trisha and Devin, like many others their age, greet the announcement of a grandchild with such enthusiasm? Most people experience grandparenthood as a significant milestone, mentioning one or more of the following gratifications:

- *Valued elder*—being perceived as a wise, helpful person
- *Immortality through descendants*—leaving behind not just one but two generations after death
- *Reinvolvement with personal past*—being able to pass family history and values to a new generation
- *Indulgence*—having fun with children without major child-rearing responsibilities (AARP, 2002; Miller & Cavanaugh, 1990)

■ **GRANDPARENT–GRANDCHILD RELATIONSHIPS.** Grandparents' styles of relating to grandchildren vary as widely as the meanings they derive from their new role. The grandparent's and grandchild's age and sex make a difference. When their granddaughter was young, Trisha and Devin enjoyed an affectionate, playful relationship with her. As she got older, she looked to them for information and advice in addition to warmth and caring. By the time their granddaughter reached adolescence, Trisha and Devin had become role models, family historians, and conveyers of social, vocational, and religious values.

Living nearby is the strongest predictor of frequent, face-to-face interaction with young grandchildren. Most grandparents in Western nations live close enough to at least one grandchild to enable regular visits, but because time and resources are limited, number of "grandchild sets" (households with grandchildren) reduces contact (Uhlenberg & Hammill, 1998). A strong desire to affect the development of grandchildren can motivate grandparents' involvement. As grandchildren get older, distance becomes less influential and relationship quality

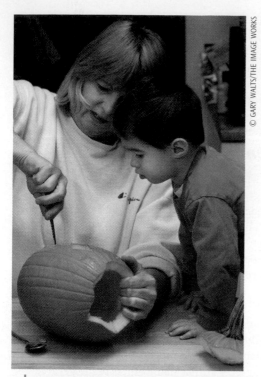

Many grandparents derive great joy from an affectionate, playful relationship with young grandchildren. As this grandchild gets older, he may look to his grandmother for advice, as a role model, and for family history in addition to warmth and caring.

more so: The extent to which adolescent or young-adult grandchildren believe their grandparent values contact is a good predictor of a close bond (Brussoni & Boon, 1998).

As Figure 16.3 shows, maternal grandmothers report more frequent visits with grandchildren than do paternal grandmothers, who are slightly advantaged over both maternal and paternal grandfathers (Uhlenberg & Hammill, 1998). Typically, relationships are closer between grandparents and grandchildren of the same sex and, especially, between maternal grandmothers and granddaughters (Brown & Rodin, 2004). Grandmothers also report higher satisfaction with the grandparent role than grandfathers, perhaps because grandmothers are more likely to participate in recreational, religious, and family activities with grandchildren (Silverstein & Marenco, 2001; Somary & Stricker, 1998). The grandparent role may be a vital means through which women satisfy their kinkeeping function.

SES and ethnicity also influence grandparent–grandchild ties. In low-income families, grandparents are more likely to perform essential activities. For example, many single parents live with their families of origin and depend on grandparents' financial and caregiving assistance to reduce the impact of poverty. Compared with grandchildren in intact families, grandchildren in single-parent and stepparent families report engaging in more diverse, higher-quality activities with their grandparents (Kennedy & Kennedy, 1993).

In some cultures, grandparents are absorbed into an extended-family household and become actively involved in

child rearing. When a Chinese, Korean, or Mexican-American maternal grandmother is a homemaker, she is the preferred caregiver while parents of young children are at work (Kamo, 1998; Williams & Torrez, 1998). Similarly, involvement in child care is high among Native-American grandparents. In the absence of a biological grandparent, an unrelated elder may be integrated into the family to serve as a mentor and disciplinarian for children (Werner, 1991).

Increasingly, grandparents have stepped in as primary caregivers in the face of serious family problems. As the Social Issues box on the following page reveals, a rising number of North American children live apart from their parents in grandparent-headed households. Despite their willingness to help and their competence at child rearing, grandparents who take full responsibility for young children experience considerable emotional and financial strain. They need much more assistance from community and government agencies than is currently available.

Because parents usually serve as gatekeepers of grandparents' contact with grandchildren, relationships between grandparents and their daughter-in-law or son-in-law strongly affect the closeness of grandparent–grandchild ties. A positive bond with a daughter-in-law seems particularly important in the relationship between grandparents and their son's children (Fingerman, 2004). And after a marital breakup, grandparents related to the custodial parent (typically the mother) have more frequent contact with grandchildren (Johnson, 1998).

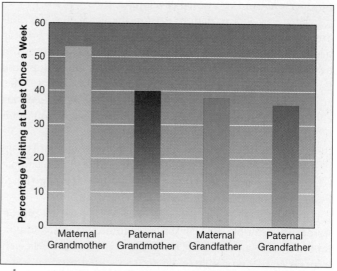

■ **FIGURE 16.3** ■ **Influence of grandparent sex and lineage on frequent visiting of grandchildren.** When a nationally representative sample of 4,600 U.S. grandparents were asked how often they visited a particular set of grandchildren, maternal grandmothers were especially likely to report visiting frequently (at least once a week). Paternal grandmothers slightly exceeded both maternal and paternal grandfathers. (From P. Uhlenberg & B. G. Hammill, 1998, "Frequency of Grandparent Contact with Grandchild Sets: Six Factors That Make a Difference," *Gerontologist*, 38, p. 281. Copyright © 1998 by The Gerontological Society of America. Reprinted by permission of Oxford University Press and Peter Uhlenberg.)

SOCIAL ISSUES

Grandparents Rearing Grandchildren: The Skipped-Generation Family

Nearly 2.4 million U.S. children—4 to 5 percent of the child population—live with grandparents but apart from parents, in **skipped-generation families** (U.S. Census Bureau, 2009b). The number of grandparents rearing grandchildren has increased over the past two decades. The arrangement occurs in all ethnic groups, though more often in African-American, Hispanic, and Native-American families than in Caucasian families (Fuller-Thomson & Minkler, 2005, 2007; Minkler & Fuller-Thomson, 2005). Although grandparent caregivers are more likely to be women than men, many grandfathers participate. Often these families take in two or more children.

In about half of skipped-generation families, grandparents step in because of parental substance-abuse problems. In most other instances, parental emotional or physical illness is involved (Pruchno & McKenney, 2000; Weber & Waldrop, 2000). Child abuse and neglect is often a factor. Occasionally child welfare authorities, out of a preference for placing the child with relatives rather than in a foster home, approach the grandparent, who assumes temporary or permanent legal custody. More often, grandparents offer their assistance, sometimes with and sometimes without legal responsibility. Most say they took action to protect the child only when the parents' situation became intolerable.

Because the skipped-generation family structure is not freely chosen, many custodial grandparents face highly stressful life circumstances. Unfavorable child-rearing experiences have left their mark on the children, who show high rates of learning difficulties, depression, and antisocial behavior. Absent parents' adjustment difficulties strain family relationships. These youngsters also introduce financial burdens into households that often are already low-income (Mills, Gomez-Smith, & De Leon, 2005; Williamson, Softas-Nall, & Miller, 2003). All these factors heighten grandparents' emotional distress.

Child-rearing tasks leave grandparents with less time for spouses, friends, and leisure when they had expected to have more time. Many report feeling emotionally drained, depressed, and worried about what will happen to the children if their own health fails (Hayslip & Kaminski, 2005; Kolomer & McCallion, 2005). Some families are extremely burdened. Native-American caregiving grandparents are especially likely to be unemployed, to have a disability, to be caring for several grandchildren, and to be living in extreme poverty (Fuller-Thomson & Minkler, 2005).

Despite great hardship, these grandparents seem to realize their widespread image as "silent saviors," often forging close emotional bonds with their grandchildren and using effective child-rearing practices (Fuller-Thomson & Minkler, 2000; Gibson, 2005). A survey of a large, representative sample of U.S. families revealed that compared with children in divorced, single-parent families or in blended families, children reared by grandparents were better behaved in school, less

A custodial grandmother helps her 8-year-old granddaughter with homework. Grandparents in skipped-generation families face shattered dreams of freedom and considerable emotional and financial strain. But most find compensating rewards in rearing grandchildren.

susceptible to physical illness, and doing just as well academically (Solomon & Marx, 1995).

Skipped-generation families have a tremendous need for social and financial support and intervention services for troubled children. But although their daily existence is often stressful, custodial grandparents—even those rearing children with serious problems—report as much satisfaction with the grandparent role as typical grandparents (Hayslip et al., 2002). Many mention joy from sharing children's lives and feelings of pride at children's progress, which help compensate for difficult circumstances. And some grandparents view the rearing of grandchildren as a "second chance"—an opportunity to make up for earlier, unfavorable parenting experiences and "do it right" (Dolbin-MacNab, 2006; Waldrop & Weber, 2001).

When family relationships are positive, grandparenthood provides an important means of fulfilling personal and societal needs in midlife and beyond. And it is a vital context for sharing between generations. Grandparents provide the young with firsthand experience in how older people think and function. In return, grandchildren become deeply attached to grandparents and keep them abreast of social change.

Middle-Aged Children and Their Aging Parents

The percentage of middle-aged Americans with living parents has risen dramatically—from 10 percent in 1900 to 50 percent at the beginning of the twenty-first century (U.S. Census Bureau, 2009b). A longer life expectancy means that adult children and their parents are increasingly likely to grow old together.

FREQUENCY AND QUALITY OF CONTACT.

Approximately two-thirds of older adults in the United States live close to at least one of their children, and frequency of contact is high through both visits and telephone calls (U.S. Census Bureau, 2009b). Proximity increases with age: Elders who move usually do so in the direction of kin, and younger people tend to move in the direction of their aging parents.

Middle age is a time when adults reassess relationships with their parents, just as they rethink other close ties. Many adult children become more appreciative of their parents' strengths and generosity and mention positive changes in the quality of the relationship, even after parents show physical declines (Fingerman et al., 2007). Trisha, for example, felt closer to her parents and made an effort to learn more about their early lives. And she recalled her mother's sound advice just before her marriage to Devin nearly three decades earlier: "Build a life together, but also forge your own life. You'll be happier." At several turning points, that advice influenced Trisha's decisions.

As Trisha's rapport with her mother conveys, mother–daughter relationships tend to be closer than other parent–child ties (Fingerman, 2001b). As the tensions of the adolescent years ease, many young-adult daughters and mothers build rewarding, intimate bonds. When daughters move into middle age, their descriptions of the mother–daughter bond become more complex, reflecting both positive and negative aspects—a change that may stem from daughters' more mature perspective and from growing relationship tensions (Fingerman, 2000). Although middle-aged daughters love their aging mothers, they face many competing demands on their time and energy (Fingerman, 2001a).

In collectivist cultures, older adults most often live with their married children. For example, traditionally, Chinese, Japanese, and Korean elderly moved in with a son and his wife and children; today, many live with a daughter and her family, too. This tradition of coresidence, however, is declining in some parts of Asia and in the United States, as more Asian and Asian-American elders choose to live on their own (Takagi, Silverstein, & Crimmins, 2007; Zhan & Montgomery, 2003; Zhang, 2004). Whether or not coresidence and daily contact are typical, relationship quality usually reflects patterns established earlier: Positive parent–child ties generally remain so, as do conflict-ridden interactions.

Help exchanged between adult children and their aging parents is responsive to past and current family circumstances. The more positive the history of the parent–child tie, the more help given and received (Whitbeck, Hoyt, & Huck, 1994). Also, parents give more help to unmarried children and to children with disabilities. Children give more to widowed parents and parents in poor health—usually emotional support and practical help, less often financial assistance. At the same time, a shift in helping occurs over the adult years. Parent-to-child assistance declines, while child-to-parent aid increases (Kunemund, Motel-Klingebiel, & Kohli, 2005; Rossi & Rossi, 1990; Zarit & Eggebeen, 2002).

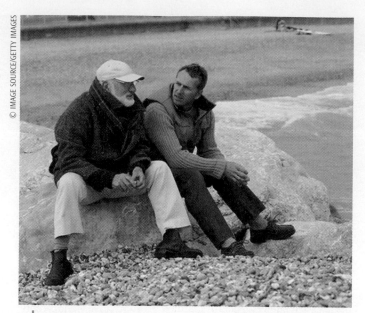

In midlife, many adults become more appreciative of their parents' strengths and generosity. They also mention positive changes in relationship quality—feeling closer and desiring to learn more about their parents' early lives.

Even when parent–child relationships have been emotionally distant, adult children offer more support as their parents age, out of a sense of altruism and family duty (Silverstein et al., 2002). And although the baby-boom generation is often described as self-absorbed, in surveys of large samples of U.S. adults repeated over time, baby-boom midlifers actually expressed a stronger commitment to caring for their aging parents than did the preceding middle-aged generation (Gans & Silverstein, 2006).

CARING FOR AGING PARENTS.

About 16 percent of the U.S. adult population provides unpaid care to an aging adult, and 25 to 35 percent of those in the work force report doing so (AARP, 2004; Family Caregiver Alliance, 2009). The burden of caring for aging parents can be great. In Chapter 2, we noted that as birthrates have declined, the family structure has become more "top-heavy," with more generations alive but fewer younger members. Consequently, more than one older family member is likely to need assistance, with fewer younger adults available to provide it.

The term **sandwich generation** is widely used to refer to the idea that middle-aged adults must care for multiple generations above and below them at the same time (Riley & Bowen, 2005). Although only a minority of contemporary middle-aged adults who care for elderly parents have children younger than age 18 at home, many are providing assistance to young-adult children and to grandchildren—obligations that, when combined with work and community responsibilities, can lead middle-aged caregivers to feel "sandwiched," or squeezed, between the pressures of older and younger generations. As the baby boomers move into late adulthood and as their adult children continue to delay childbearing, the number of sandwiched midlifers will increase.

Middle-aged adults living far from aging parents who are in poor health often substitute financial help for direct care, if they have the means. But when parents live nearby and have no spouse to meet their needs, adult children usually engage in direct care. Regardless of family income level, African-American, Asian-American, and Hispanic adults give aging parents more direct care and financial support than Caucasian-American adults do (AARP, 2004; Shuey & Hardy, 2003). And minority families typically build a large and strong support network in their ethnic communities that helps ensure financial or caregiving assistance.

In all ethnic groups, responsibility for providing care to aging parents falls more on daughters than on sons. Families turn to the person who seems most available—living nearby and with fewer commitments regarded as interfering with the ability to assist. These unstated rules, in addition to parents' preference for same-sex caregivers (aging mothers live longer), lead more women to fill the role. Daughters also feel more obligated than sons to care for aging parents (Gans & Silverstein, 2006).

About 50 percent of American women caregivers are employed; another 10 to 30 percent quit their jobs to provide care. And the time they devote to caring for a disabled aging parent is substantial, averaging 10 to 20 hours per week (AARP, 2004; Takamura & Williams, 2002). Nevertheless, men—although doing less than women—do contribute. In one investigation, employed men spent an average of $7\frac{1}{2}$ hours per week caring for parents or parents-in-law (Neal & Hammer, 2007). Tim, for example, looked in on his father, a recent stroke victim, every evening, reading to him, running errands, making household

© PAMELA MOORE/ISTOCKPHOTO

Caring for a chronically ill or disabled aging parent is highly stressful. But social support reduces physical and emotional strain, enabling adult children to find satisfactions and rewards in tending to parents' needs.

repairs, and taking care of finances. His sister, however, provided more hands-on care—cooking, feeding, and bathing. The care sons and daughters provide tends to be divided along gender-role lines (Harris, 1998; Pinquart & Sörensen, 2006).

As adults move from early to later middle age, the sex difference in parental caregiving declines. Perhaps as men reduce their vocational commitments and feel less need to conform to a "masculine" gender role, they grow more able and willing to provide basic care (Marks, 1996). At the same time, parental caregiving may contribute to men's greater openness to the "feminine" side of their personalities. A man who cared for his mother, severely impaired by Alzheimer's disease, commented on how the experience altered his outlook:

> Having to do personal care, becoming a male nurse, was a great adjustment. It was so difficult to do these tasks; things a man, a son, is not supposed to do. But, I had to alter, since charity must come before maintaining a selfish, conventional view. I have definitely modified my views on conventional expectations. (Hirsch, 1996, p. 112)

Although most adult children help willingly, caring for a chronically ill or disabled parent is highly stressful—and radically different from caring for a young child. The need for parental care typically arises suddenly, after a heart attack, fall, stroke, or diagnosis of cancer, leaving little time for preparation. Whereas children become increasingly independent, the parent usually gets worse, and the caregiving task and its cost escalate. As Tim explained to Devin and Trisha, "One of the hardest aspects is the emotional strain of seeing my father's physical and mental decline up close." Tim also felt a sense of grief over the loss of a cherished relationship, as his father no longer seemed to be his former self. Because duration of caregiving is uncertain, caregivers often feel they no longer have control over their lives (Gatz, Bengtson, & Blum, 1990).

Adults who share a household with ill parents—about 10 percent of American caregivers—experience the most stress. When a parent and child who have lived separately for years must move in together, conflicts generally arise over routines and lifestyles. But the greatest source of stress is problem behavior, especially for caregivers of parents who have deteriorated mentally (Alzheimer's Association, 2009). Tim's sister reported that their father would wake during the night, ask repetitive questions, follow her around the house, and become agitated and combative.

Parental caregiving often has emotional and physical health consequences. It leads to role overload, high job absenteeism, exhaustion, inability to concentrate, feelings of hostility, anxiety about aging, and rates of depression as high as 30 to 50 percent (Killian, Turner, & Cain, 2005; Neal & Hammer, 2007). In cultures and subcultures where adult children feel an especially strong sense of obligation to care for aging parents, the toll tends to be greater. In research on Korean, Korean-American, and Caucasian-American caregivers of parents with mental disabilities, the Koreans and Korean Americans reported higher levels of family obligation and care burden—and also higher levels of anxiety and depression—than the Caucasian Americans (Lee & Farran, 2004; Youn et al., 1999). And among

Applying What We Know

Relieving the Stress of Caring for an Aging Parent

Strategy	Description
Use effective coping strategies.	Use problem-centered coping to manage the parent's behavior and caregiving tasks. Delegate responsibilities to other family members, seek assistance from friends and neighbors, and recognize the parent's limits while calling on capacities the parent does have. Use emotion-centered coping to reinterpret the situation in a positive way, such as emphasizing the opportunity it offers for personal growth. Avoid denial of anger, depression, and anxiety in response to the caregiver work burden, which heightens stress.
Seek social support.	Confide in family members and friends about the stress of caregiving, seeking their encouragement and help. So far as possible, avoid quitting work to care for an ill parent, because doing so leads to social isolation and loss of financial resources.
Make use of community resources.	Contact community organizations to seek information and assistance, in the form of caregiver support groups, in-home respite help, home-delivered meals, transportation, and adult day care.
Press for workplace and public policies that relieve the emotional and financial burdens of caring for an aging parent.	Encourage your employer to provide elder care benefits, such as flexible work hours and employment leave for caregiving. Communicate with lawmakers and other citizens about the need for additional government funding to help pay for elder care. Emphasize the need for improved health insurance plans that reduce the financial strain of elder care on middle- and low-income families.

African-American caregivers, women who strongly endorsed cultural reasons for providing care ("It's what my people have always done") fared less well in mental health two years later than women who moderately endorsed cultural reasons (Dilworth-Anderson, Goodwin, & Williams, 2004).

Social support is highly effective in reducing caregiver stress. In Denmark, Sweden, and Japan, a government-sponsored home helper system eases the burden of parental care by making specially trained nonfamily caregivers available, based on the elder's needs (Blomberg, Edebalk, & Petersson, 2000; Lechner & Neal, 1999). In the United States, in-home care by a nonfamily caregiver is too costly for most families; only 10 to 20 percent arrange it (Family Caregiver Alliance, 2009). And unless they must, few people want to place their parents in formal care, such as nursing homes, which also are expensive. Applying What We Know above summarizes ways to relieve the stress of caring for an aging parent—at the individual, family, community, and societal levels. We will address additional elder care options, along with interventions for caregivers, in Chapter 17.

Siblings

A survey of a large sample of ethnically diverse Americans revealed that sibling contact and support decline from early to middle adulthood, rebounding only after age 70 for siblings living near one another (White, 2001). Decreased midlife contact is probably due to the demands of middle-aged adults' diverse roles. However, most adult siblings report getting together or talking on the phone at least monthly (Antonucci, Akiyama, & Merline, 2002).

Despite reduced contact, many siblings feel closer in midlife, often in response to major life events (Stewart et al., 2001). Launching and marriage of children seem to prompt siblings to think more about one another. When a parent becomes seriously ill, brothers and sisters who previously had little to do with one another may find themselves in touch about parental care. And when parents die, adult children realize they have become the oldest generation and must look to one another to sustain family ties (Gold, 1996).

Not all sibling bonds improve, of course. Recall Trisha's negative encounters with her sister, Dottie (see Chapter 15, page 405). Dottie's difficult temperament had made her hard to get along with since childhood, and her temper flared when their father died and problems arose over family finances. When siblings do not help with parental caregiving, the child shouldering the burden can unleash powerful negative feelings (Merrill, 1997). As one expert expressed it, "As siblings grow older, good relationships [often] become better and rotten relationships get worse" (Moyer, 1992, p. 57).

In industrialized nations, sibling relationships are voluntary. In village societies, they are generally involuntary and basic to family functioning. For example, among Asian Pacific Islanders, family social life is organized around strong brother–sister attachments. A brother–sister pair is often treated as a unit in exchange marriages with another family. After marriage, brothers are expected to protect sisters, and sisters serve as spiritual mentors to brothers (Cicirelli, 1995). In village societies, cultural norms reduce sibling conflict, thereby ensuring family cooperation.

Friendships

As family responsibilities declined in middle age, Devin had more time to spend with friends. On Friday afternoons, he met several male friends at a coffee house, and they chatted for a couple of hours. But most of Devin's friendships were couple-based—relationships he shared with Trisha. Compared with Devin, Trisha more often got together with friends on her own.

Middle-aged friendships reflect the same trends discussed in Chapter 14. At all ages, friendships between men are less intimate than those between women. Men tend to talk about sports, politics, and business, whereas women focus on feelings and life problems. Women report a greater number of close friends and say they both receive and provide their friends with more emotional support (Antonucci, 1994).

Nevertheless, for both sexes, number of friends declines with age, probably because people become less willing to invest in nonfamily ties unless they are very rewarding (Carbery & Buhrmester, 1998). As selectivity of friendship increases, older adults try harder to get along with friends (Antonucci & Akiyama, 1995). Having chosen a friend, middle-aged people attach great value to the relationship and take extra steps to protect it.

By midlife, family relationships and friendships support different aspects of psychological well-being. Family ties protect against serious threats and losses, offering security within a long-term timeframe. In contrast, friendships serve as current sources of pleasure and satisfaction (Antonucci, Akiyama, & Merline, 2002). As middle-aged couples renew their sense of companionship, they may combine the best of family and friendship. Indeed, research indicates that viewing a spouse as a best friend contributes greatly to marital happiness (Bengtson, Rosenthal, & Burton, 1990).

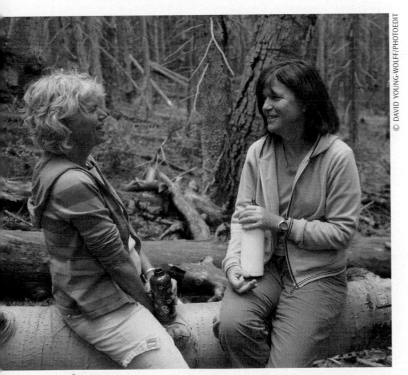

Friendships become more selective in midlife. Compared with younger people, middle-aged adults are less willing to invest in friendships unless they are very rewarding.

ASK YOURSELF

≫ REVIEW
How do age, sex, proximity, and culture affect grandparent–grandchild ties?

≫ APPLY
Raylene and her brother Walter live in the same city as their aging mother, Elsie. When Elsie could no longer live independently, Raylene took primary responsibility for her care. What factors probably contributed to Raylene's involvement in caregiving and Walter's lesser role?

≫ REFLECT
Ask a middle-aged couple you know well to describe the number and quality of their friendships today compared to their friendships in early adulthood. Does their report match research findings? Explain.

Vocational Life

Work continues to be a salient aspect of identity and self-esteem in middle adulthood. More so than in earlier or later years, people attempt to increase the personal meaning and self-direction of their vocational lives. The large tide of baby boomers currently moving through midlife and (as we will see in Chapter 18) the desire of most to work longer than the previous generation means that the number of older workers will rise dramatically over the next few decades (HSBC & Oxford Institute of Ageing, 2007). Yet a favorable transition from adult worker to older worker is hindered by negative stereotypes of aging—incorrect beliefs about limited learning capacity, slower decision making, and resistance to change and supervision (Maurer, 2007). Furthermore, gender discrimination continues to restrict the career attainments of many women. Let's take a close look at middle-aged work life.

Job Satisfaction

Job satisfaction increases in midlife in diverse nations and at all occupational levels, from executives to hourly workers (Hochwarter et al., 2001). The trend is weaker for women than for men, probably because women's reduced chances for advancement result in a sense of unfairness. It is also weaker for blue-collar than for white-collar workers, perhaps because blue-collar workers have less control over their own work schedules and activities (Avolio & Sosik, 1999). When different aspects of jobs are considered, intrinsic satisfaction—happiness with the work itself—shows a strong age-related gain. Extrinsic satisfaction—contentment with supervision, pay, and promotions—changes very little (Barnes-Farrell & Matthews, 2007).

What explains the rise in job satisfaction? An improved capacity to cope effectively with difficult situations and a broader time perspective probably contribute. "When I first started teaching, I complained a lot," remarked Devin. "Now I can tell a big problem from a trivial one." Moving out of unrewarding work roles, as Trisha did when she transitioned from a large to a small law firm, can also boost morale. And older people tend to have greater access to key job characteristics that predict well-being—involvement in decision making, reasonable workloads, and good physical working conditions. Furthermore, having fewer alternative positions into which they can move, older workers generally reduce their career aspirations (Barnes-Farrell & Matthews, 2007). As the perceived gap between actual and possible achievements narrows, job involvement—importance of one's work to self-esteem—increases (Warr, 1994, 2001).

Although emotional engagement with work is usually seen as psychologically healthy, it can also result in **burnout**—a condition in which long-term job stress leads to mental exhaustion, a sense of loss of personal control, and feelings of reduced accomplishment. Burnout occurs more often in the helping professions, including health care, human services, and teaching, which place high emotional demands on employees. And it is especially likely to occur in unsupportive work environments, where work assignments exceed time available to complete them and encouragement and feedback from supervisors are scarce (Schmidt, Neubach, & Heuer, 2007; Zapf et al., 2001). Burnout is a greater problem in the United States than in Western Europe, perhaps because of Americans' greater achievement orientation (Maslach, Schaufeli, & Leiter, 2001).

Career Development

After several years as a parish nurse, Anya felt a need for additional training to do her job better. Trisha appreciated her firm's generous support of workshop and course attendance, which helped her keep abreast of new legal developments. As these experiences reveal, career development is vital throughout work life.

■ **JOB TRAINING.** When Anya asked her supervisor, Roy, for time off to upgrade her skills, he replied, "You're in your fifties. What're you going to do with so much new information

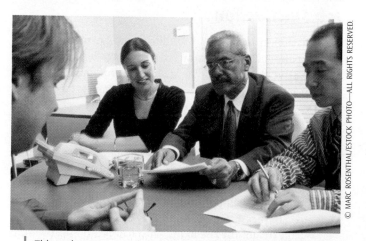

This project team, consisting of two young and two middle-aged adults, works on a challenging assignment. Age-balanced work groups foster communication and, in turn, on-the-job learning and enhanced performance.

at this point in your life?" Roy's insensitive, narrow-minded response, though usually unspoken, is all too common among managers—even some who are older themselves! Training and on-the-job career counseling are less available to older workers. And when career development activities are offered, older employees may be less likely to volunteer for them (Barnes-Farrell & Matthews, 2007; Hedge, Borman, & Lammlein, 2006). What influences willingness to engage in job training and updating?

Personal characteristics are important, starting with the degree to which an individual wants to change. With age, growth needs give way somewhat to security needs. Perhaps for this reason, older employees depend more on co-worker and supervisor encouragement for vocational development. Yet as we have seen, they are less likely to have supportive supervisors. Furthermore, negative stereotypes of aging reduce older workers' self-efficacy, or confidence that they can renew and expand their skills (Maurer, 2001; Maurer, Wrenn, & Weiss, 2003).

Workplace characteristics matter, too. An employee given work that requires new learning must pursue that learning to complete the assignment. Unfortunately, older workers sometimes receive more routine tasks than younger workers. Interaction among co-workers can also have a profound impact. Within project teams, people similar in age communicate more often. Age-balanced work groups (with more than one person in each age range) foster on-the-job learning and engagement because communication is a source of support as well as a means of acquiring job-relevant information (Avery, McKay, & Wilson, 2007; Zenger & Lawrence, 1989).

■ **GENDER AND ETHNICITY: THE GLASS CEILING.** In her thirties, Jewel became a company president by starting her own business. She had concluded that, as a woman, her chances of rising to a top executive position in a large corporation were low, so she didn't even try. In a longitudinal study of 1,500 U.S. adults, the probability of attaining a managerial position climbed substantially over 30 years of career experience for white men. By contrast, it rose modestly for white women and black men, and hardly at all for black women—findings that held after work skills and work productivity factors were controlled (Maume, 2004). When the most prestigious high-level management positions are considered, white men are even more advantaged: They account for 75 percent of chief executive officers at large corporations and 98 percent at Fortune 500 companies (U.S. Census Bureau, 2009b).

Women and ethnic minorities face a **glass ceiling,** or invisible barrier to advancement up the corporate ladder. Why is this so? Management is an art and skill that must be taught. Yet women and members of ethnic minorities have less access to mentors, role models, and informal networks that serve as training routes. And because of stereotyped doubts about women's career commitment and managerial ability, large companies spend less money on formal training programs for their female employees (Lyness & Thompson, 1997).

Furthermore, women who demonstrate qualities linked to leadership and advancement—assertiveness, confidence, forcefulness, and ambition—encounter prejudice because they

Indra K. Nooyi, CEO of PepsiCo, is among a handful of women who have shattered the glass ceiling at Fortune 500 companies, attaining the top leadership position. The recipient of numerous honors and awards, she has amassed an outstanding record in advancing PepsiCo's international business operations and in humanitarian service.

deviate from traditional gender roles (Carli & Eagly, 2000; Eagly & Karau, 2002). To overcome this bias, women in line for top positions must demonstrate greater competence than their male counterparts. In an investigation of several hundred senior managers at a multinational financial services corporation, promoted female managers had earned higher performance ratings than promoted male managers (Lyness & Heilman, 2006). In contrast, no gender difference existed in performance of managers not selected for promotion.

Like Jewel, many women have dealt with the glass ceiling by going around it. Largely because of lack of advancement opportunities, nearly twice as many female as male middle managers quit their jobs in large corporations, with most going into business for themselves (Mergenhagen, 1996). Today, more than half of all startup businesses in the United States are owned and successfully operated by women (Ahuja, 2005; U.S. Census Bureau, 2009b). But when women and ethnic minorities leave the corporate world, companies not only lose valuable talent but also fail to address the leadership needs of an increasingly diverse work force.

Planning for Retirement

One evening, Devin and Trisha met George and Anya for dinner. Halfway through the meal, Devin inquired, "George, tell us what you and Anya are going to do about retirement. Are you planning to work part-time or stop entirely? Do you think you'll stay here or move out of town?"

Three or four generations ago, the two couples would not have had this conversation. In 1900, about 70 percent of American men age 65 and over were in the labor force. By 1970, however, the figure had dropped to 27 percent, and in the early twenty-first century it declined to 16 percent (U.S. Census

Bureau, 2009b). Because of government-sponsored retirement benefits (begun in the United States in 1935), retirement is no longer a privilege reserved for the wealthy. The federal government pays Social Security to the majority of the aged, and others are covered by employer-based private pension plans (Chappell et al., 2003).

As the trend just noted suggests, the average age of retirement declined during the past several decades. Currently, it is age 62 in the United States and hovers between 60 and 63 in other Western nations (U.S. Census Bureau, 2009b). As indicated earlier, the healthy, active, long-lived baby-boom generation is expected to work longer. Still, up to one-fourth of their lives may lie ahead after they leave their career jobs.

Retirement is a lengthy, complex process that begins as soon as the middle-aged person first thinks about it (Kim & Moen, 2002b). Because retirement leads to a loss of two important work-related rewards—income and status—and to change in many other aspects of life, planning is important, resulting in better retirement adjustment and satisfaction. Yet nearly half of middle-aged people engage in no concrete retirement planning (Hershey et al., 2007; Jacobs-Lawson, Hershey, & Neukam, 2004; Quick & Moen, 1998).

Since income typically drops by 50 percent, more people engage in financial planning than in other forms of preparation. But even those who attend financial education programs often fail to look closely at their financial well-being and to make wise decisions (Hershey et al., 1998). Many could benefit from expert financial counsel.

Retirement leads to ways of spending time that are largely guided by one's interests rather than one's obligations. Planning for an active life has an even greater impact on happiness after retirement than financial planning. Participation in activities promotes many factors essential for psychological well-being, including a structured time schedule, social contact, and self-esteem (Schlossberg, 2004). Carefully considering whether or not to relocate at retirement is related to an active life, since it affects access to health care, friends, family, recreation, entertainment, and part-time work.

Devin retired at age 62, George at age 66. Though several years younger, Trisha and Anya—like many married women—coordinated their retirements with those of their husbands (Ruhm, 1996). In contrast, Jewel—in good health but without an intimate partner to share her life—kept her consulting business going until age 75. Tim took early retirement and moved to be near Elena, where he devoted himself to public service—tutoring second graders in a public school and coaching after-school and weekend youth sports.

Unfortunately, less well-educated people with lower lifetime earnings are least likely to attend retirement preparation programs—yet they stand to benefit the most. Although baby boomers as a whole are financially better off than their age-mates of the previous generation, the lowest-income quartile are actually worse off than their predecessors (Lusardi & Mitchell, 2007). And women often depend on their husband's preparations—a finding that may change as women increasingly become equal, rather than secondary, family earners (Han

& Moen, 1999). Employers must take extra steps to encourage lower-paid workers and women to participate in planning activities (Jacobs-Lawson, Hershey, & Neukam, 2004). In addition, enhancing retirement adjustment among the economically disadvantaged depends on access to better health care, vocational training, and jobs at early ages. Clearly, a lifetime of opportunities and experiences affects the transition to retirement. In Chapter 18, we will consider the decision to retire and retirement adjustment in greater detail.

ASK YOURSELF

>> **REVIEW**
What factors lead job satisfaction to increase with age?

>> **APPLY**
An executive wonders how his large corporation can foster advancement of women and ethnic minorities to upper management positions. What strategies would you recommend?

Summary

Erikson's Theory: Generativity versus Stagnation

According to Erikson, how does personality change in middle age?

>> Generativity begins in early adulthood but expands greatly as middle-aged adults face Erikson's psychological conflict of **generativity versus stagnation.** Generative people find fulfillment as they make contributions to society through parenthood, other family relationships, the workplace, and volunteer activities.

>> Personal desires and cultural demands jointly shape adults' generative activities. Highly generative people appear especially well-adjusted. The negative outcome, stagnation, occurs when people become self-centered and self-indulgent in midlife.

Other Theories of Psychosocial Development in Midlife

Describe Levinson's and Vaillant's views of psychosocial development in middle adulthood, and discuss similarities and differences between men and women.

>> According to Levinson, middle-aged adults reassess their relation to themselves and the external world. They confront four developmental tasks, each requiring them to reconcile two opposing tendencies within the self: young–old, destruction–creation, masculinity–femininity, and engagement–separateness.

>> Perhaps because of the double standard of aging, women express concern about appearing less attractive. But non-college-educated men, even more than women, show a rise in sensitivity to physical aging.

>> Middle-aged men may adopt "feminine" traits of nurturance and caring, while women may take on "masculine" traits of autonomy and assertiveness. Men and successful career-oriented women often reduce their focus on ambition and achievement. Women who have devoted themselves to child rearing or an unfulfilling job typically increase their involvement in work and community.

>> Vaillant found that adults in their late forties and fifties take on responsibility as guardians of their culture, seeking to "pass the torch" to later generations.

AP IMAGES/THE REPORTER, KEITH VANDERVORT

Does the term midlife crisis fit most people's experience of middle adulthood?

>> Most people respond to midlife with changes that are better described as "turning points" than as a crisis. Only a minority experience a **midlife crisis** characterized by intense self-doubt and stress that lead to drastic life alterations.

Stability and Change in Self-Concept and Personality

Describe changes in self-concept and personality in middle adulthood.

>> Middle-aged individuals maintain self-esteem and stay motivated by revising their **possible selves,** which become fewer in number as well as more modest and concrete as people adjust their hopes and fears to their life circumstances.

>> Midlife typically leads to greater self-acceptance, autonomy, and environmental mastery—changes that lead to greater psychological well-being and life satisfaction. As a result, middle age is sometimes called the "prime of life."

>> Coping with daily stressors becomes more effective with midlife gains in emotional stability and confidence in handling life's problems.

Describe changes in gender identity in midlife.

>> Both men and women become more androgynous in middle adulthood. Biological explanations, such as **parental imperative theory,** are controversial. A complex combination of social roles and life conditions is more likely responsible.

Discuss stability and change in the "big five" personality traits in adulthood.

>> Among the **"big five" personality traits,** neuroticism, extroversion, and openness to experience show stability or modest declines during adulthood, while agreeableness and conscientiousness increase. But individual differences in the "big five" traits are large and highly stable: Although adults change in overall organization and integration of personality, they do so on a foundation of basic, enduring dispositions.

Relationships at Midlife

Describe the middle adulthood phase of the family life cycle, including relationships with a marriage partner, adult children, grandchildren, and aging parents.

>> "Launching children and moving on" is the newest and longest phase of the family life cycle. Middle-aged adults must adapt to many entries and exits of family members as their children leave, marry, and produce grand-children and as their own parents age and die.

>> Midlife changes prompt many adults to review and adjust their marriages. When divorce occurs, middle-aged adults seem to adapt more easily than younger people. For women, marital breakup usually brings significant economic disadvantage, contributing to the **feminization of poverty.**

>> Most middle-aged parents adjust well to launch-ing adult children, especially if they have gratify-ing alternative activities and if parent–child contact and affection are sustained. As children marry and bring in-laws into the family network, middle-aged parents, especially mothers, often become **kinkeepers.**

>> Grandparenthood is an important means of ful-filling personal and societal needs. Proximity, number of grandchild sets, sex of grandparent and grandchild, and in-law relationships affect grandparent–grandchild contact and closeness. In low-income families and in some ethnic groups, grandparents provide essential financial and child-care assistance. When serious family problems exist, grandparents may become pri-mary caregivers in **skipped-generation families.**

>> Middle-aged adults reassess their relationships with aging parents, often becoming more appre-ciative. Mother–daughter relationships tend to be closer than other parent–child ties. Yet quality of the early parent–child relationship—positive or conflict-ridden—usually persists, affecting help exchanged.

>> Middle-aged adults, often caught between car-ing for ill or frail parents, assisting young-adult children and grandchildren, and meeting work and community responsibilities, are called the **sandwich generation.** The burden of caring for aging parents falls most heavily on adult daugh-ters, though in later middle age, the sex differ-ence declines.

>> Parental caregiving has emotional and health consequences. The toll is greatest in cultures and subcultures where adult children feel an especially strong obligation to provide care. Social support is highly effective in relieving caregiver stress.

Describe midlife sibling relationships and friendships.

>> Sibling contact and support decline from early to middle adulthood. However, most middle-aged siblings tend to feel closer, often in response to major life events. Sister–sister ties are typically closest in industrialized nations. In nonindustrialized societies, where sibling rela-tionships are basic to family functioning, other attachments (such as brother–sister) may be stronger.

>> In midlife, friendships become fewer, more selective, and more deeply valued. Men con-tinue to be less expressive with their friends than women, who have more close friendships. Viewing a spouse as a best friend can contribute greatly to marital happiness.

Vocational Life

Discuss job satisfaction and career development in middle adulthood, with special attention to sex differences and experiences of ethnic minorities.

>> Vocational readjustments are common as middle-aged people seek to increase the personal meaning and self-direction of their work lives. Job satisfaction increases at all occupational levels, more so for men than for women. Still, **burnout** is a serious occu-pational hazard, especially for those in help-ing professions and in unsupportive work environments.

>> Older workers engage in less career develop-ment because of negative stereotypes of aging, which impair self-efficacy; lack of encourage-ment from supervisors; and less challenging work assignments.

>> Women and ethnic minorities face a **glass ceiling** because of limited access to manage-ment training and prejudice against women who demonstrate qualities linked to leadership and advancement. Many women further their careers by leaving the corporate world, often to start their own businesses.

Discuss the importance of planning for retirement, noting various issues that middle-aged adults should address.

>> Many workers in the United States and Western nations retire from full-time work in midlife. Besides financial planning, planning for an active life is vital, with an especially strong impact on happiness after retirement. Low-paid workers and women need extra encour-agement to participate in retirement planning activities.

Important Terms and Concepts

"big five" personality traits (p. 427)
burnout (p. 436)
feminization of poverty (p. 428)
generativity versus stagnation (p. 420)

glass ceiling (p. 436)
kinkeeper (p. 429)
midlife crisis (p. 422)
parental imperative theory (p. 426)

possible selves (p. 423)
sandwich generation (p. 432)
skipped-generation family (p. 431)

Milestones

Development in Middle Adulthood

40–50 years

PHYSICAL

- Accommodative ability of the lens of the eye, ability to see in dim light, and color discrimination decline; sensitivity to glare increases. (398)
- Hearing loss at high frequencies occurs. (398)
- Hair grays and thins. (397)
- Lines on the face become more pronounced; skin loses elasticity and begins to sag. (399)
- Weight gain continues, accompanied by a rise in fatty deposits in the torso, while fat beneath the skin declines. (399)
- Loss of lean body mass (muscle and bone) occurs. (399)
- In women, production of estrogen drops, leading to shortening and irregularity of the menstrual cycle. (399, 401)

- In men, quantity of semen and sperm declines. (402)
- Intensity of sexual response declines, but frequency of sexual activity drops only slightly. (403)
- Rates of cancer and cardiovascular disease increase. (403–405)

COGNITIVE

- Consciousness of aging increases. (397, 421)
- Crystallized intelligence increases; fluid intelligence declines. (409–410)

- Cognitive-processing speed declines, but adults can compensate through experience and practice. (411)
- On complex tasks, ability to divide and control attention declines, but adults can compensate through experience and practice. (411–412)
- Amount of information retained in working memory declines, largely because of reduced use of memory strategies. (412–413)

- Retrieving information from long-term memory becomes more difficult. (413–413)

- General factual knowledge and knowledge related to one's occupation remain unchanged or may increase. (410, 413)
- Practical problem solving and expertise increase. (413)
- Creativity may emphasize integrating ideas and shift from self-expression to more altruistic goals. (414)

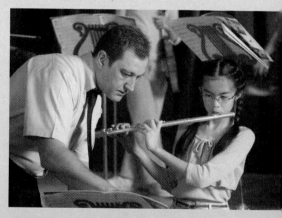

- If occupation offers challenge and autonomy, may show gains in cognitive flexibility. (414–415)

EMOTIONAL/SOCIAL

- Generativity increases. (420–421)
- Focus shifts toward personally meaningful living. (420–421)

Note: Numbers in parentheses indicate the page or pages on which each milestone is discussed.

- Possible selves become fewer in number and more modest and concrete. (423–424)
- Self-acceptance, autonomy, and environmental mastery increase. (424)
- Strategies for coping with stressors become more effective. (424, 426)
- Gender identity becomes more androgynous; "masculine" traits increase in women, "feminine" traits in men. (421–422, 426)
- Agreeableness and conscientiousness increase, while neuroticism declines. (427)
- May launch children. (428)
- May become a kinkeeper, especially if a mother. (429)

- May become a parent-in-law and a grandparent. (429–430)
- May care for a parent with a disability or chronic illness. (432–433)
- Siblings may feel closer. (434)
- Number of friends generally declines. (435)
- Job satisfaction typically increases. (435–436)

50–65 years

PHYSICAL

- Lens of the eye loses its capacity to adjust to objects at varying distances entirely. (398)
- Hearing loss extends to all frequencies but remains greatest for high frequencies. (398)
- Skin continues to wrinkle and sag, "age spots" increase, and blood vessels in the skin become more visible. (399)
- In women, menopause occurs; as estrogen declines further, genitals are less easily stimulated, and the vagina lubricates more slowly during arousal. (399, 401)

- In men, inability to attain an erection when desired becomes more common. (402)
- Loss of bone mass continues; rates of osteoporosis rise. (399, 405)
- Collapse of disks in the spinal column causes height to drop by as much as 1 inch. (399)

- Rates of cancer and cardiovascular disease continue to increase. (403–405)

COGNITIVE

- Cognitive changes previously listed continue.

EMOTIONAL/SOCIAL

- Emotional and social changes previously listed continue.

- Parent-to-child help-giving declines, and child-to-parent aid increases. (431–434)
- May retire. (437–438)

Physical and Cognitive Development in Late Adulthood

© ANDREW MILLIGAN/PA PHOTOS/LANDOV

Cultures around the world connect age with wisdom. Elders' extensive life experience enhances their ability to solve human problems and fill leadership positions, both of which are endeavors of South African anti-Apartheid activist Archbishop Desmond Tutu. Here, he gives high fives to students after an honorary degree ceremony at Edinburgh University.

At age 67, Walt gave up his photography business and looked forward to more spare time with 64-year-old Ruth, who retired from her position as a social worker at the same time. For Walt and Ruth, this culminating period of life was filled with volunteer work, golfing three times a week, and joint vacations with Walt's older brother Dick and his wife, Goldie. Walt also took up activities he had always loved but had little time to pursue—writing poems and short stories, attending theater performances, enrolling in a class on world politics, and cultivating a garden that became the envy of the neighborhood. Ruth read voraciously, served on the board of directors of an adoption agency, and had more time to visit her sister Ida in a nearby city.

Over the next 20 years, Walt and Ruth amazed nearly everyone who met them with their energy and vitality. Then, in their early eighties, the couple's lives changed profoundly. Walt had surgery to treat a cancerous prostate gland and within three months was hospitalized again after a heart attack. He lingered for six weeks and then died. Ruth's grieving was interrupted by the need to care for Ida. Alert and spry at age 78, Ida deteriorated mentally in her seventy-ninth year, despite otherwise excellent physical health. Meanwhile, Ruth's arthritis worsened, and her vision and hearing weakened.

As Ruth turned 85, certain activities had become difficult—but not impossible. "It just takes a little adjustment!" Ruth exclaimed in her usual upbeat manner. Reading was harder, so she checked out "talking books" from her local library. At dinner in a noisy restaurant with her daughter and family, Ruth felt overwhelmed and participated little in the fast-moving conversation. But in one-to-one interactions in a calm environment, she showed the same intelligence and wit that she had displayed all her life.

Late adulthood stretches from age 65 to the end of the lifespan. Unfortunately, popular images fail to capture the quality of these final decades. Instead, many myths prevail—that the elderly have entered a period of deterioration and dependency and that they are no longer able to learn. Young people who have little contact with older adults are often surprised that elders like Walt and Ruth even exist—active and involved in the world around them.

As we trace physical and cognitive development in late adulthood, we will see that the balance of gains and declines shifts as death approaches. But in industrialized nations, the typical 65-year-old can anticipate nearly two healthy, rewarding decades before this shift affects everyday life. And as Ruth illustrates, even after older adults become frail, many find ways to surmount physical and cognitive challenges.

Late adulthood is best viewed as an extension of earlier periods, not a break with them. As long as social and cultural contexts give elders support, respect, and purpose in life, these years are a time of continued potential.

Physical Development

TAKE A MOMENT... Do you know an older person who "seems young" or "seems old" for his or her age? In using these descriptors, we acknowledge that chronological age is an imperfect indicator of **functional age,** or actual competence and performance. Because people age biologically at different rates, some 80-year-olds appear younger than many 65-year-olds (Neugarten & Neugarten, 1987). Also, recall from Chapter 13 that within each person, change differs across parts of the body. For example, Ruth became infirm physically but remained active mentally, whereas Ida, though physically fit for her age, found it hard to engage in familiar tasks.

So much variation exists between and within individuals that researchers have not yet identified any single biological measure that predicts the overall rate at which an elderly person will age. But we do have estimates of how much longer older adults can expect to live, and our knowledge of factors affecting longevity in late adulthood has increased rapidly.

Two friends enjoy a stroll and conversation in Tokyo, Japan. How old are they? How old do they look and feel? Because people age biologically at different rates, the elder on the right appears younger than the elder on the left, though they are both in their early eighties.

Life Expectancy

"I wonder how many years I have left," Ruth asked herself each time a major life event, such as retirement or widowhood, occurred. Dramatic gains in **average life expectancy**— the number of years that an individual born in a particular year can expect to live, starting at any given age—provide powerful support for the multiplicity of factors considered in previous chapters that slow biological aging, including improved nutrition, medical treatment, sanitation, and safety. Recall from Chapter 1 that a U.S. baby born in 1900 had an average life expectancy of just under 50 years. In 2008, this figure reached 78.1 (75 for men and nearly 81 for women). Twentieth-century gains in life expectancy were extraordinary—equal to those of the previous 5,000 years! Steady declines in infant mortality (see Chapter 3) are a major factor. But death rates among adults have decreased as well, due mostly to advances in medical treatment (U.S. Department of Health and Human Services, 2009a).

Variations in Life Expectancy

Consistent group differences in life expectancy underscore the joint contribution of heredity and environment to biological aging. In almost all cultures, women can look forward to 4 to 7 more years of life than men. The protective value of the female's extra X chromosome (see Chapter 2) is believed to be responsible.

© JON BURBANK/THE IMAGE WORKS

These spry veterans tie a rope around a cherry tree to honor Japanese citizens who died in World War II. Japan's low-fat diet, which contributes to its low rates of obesity and heart disease, along with its favorable health-care policies, makes it the world's leader in average healthy life expectancy.

Yet since the early 1970s, the gender gap in life expectancy has narrowed in industrialized nations (Conti et al., 2003; Leung, Zhang, & Zhang, 2004). Because men are at higher risk for disease and early death, they reap somewhat larger generational gains from positive lifestyle changes and new medical discoveries.

Life expectancy varies substantially with SES, ethnicity, and nationality. As education and income increase, so does length of life (De Vogli et al., 2005). In the United States, a white child born in 2007 is likely to live 5 to 7 years longer than an African-American child and 4 to 5 years longer than a Native-American child (U.S. Department of Health and Human Services, 2009a). Accounting for these differences are higher rates of infant mortality, unintentional injuries, life-threatening disease, poverty-linked stress, and violent death in low-SES minority groups.

Length of life—and, even more important, *quality of life* in old age—can be predicted by a country's health care, housing, and social services, along with lifestyle factors. When researchers estimate **average healthy life expectancy,** the number of years a person born in a particular year can expect to live in full health, without disease or injury, Japan ranks first, the United States a disappointing twenty-ninth (see Figure 17.1). Japan's low rates of obesity and heart disease, linked to its low-fat diet, along with its favorable health-care policies, are largely responsible for its leading status. In developing nations with widespread poverty, malnutrition, disease, and armed conflict, average life expectancy hovers around 50 years, and healthy life expectancy is reduced by three to four decades compared with the industrialized world—for example, 75 years in Japan, 73 years in Sweden, 70 years in the United States, but only 44 in Haiti, 38 in Rwanda, 36 in Afghanistan, and 29 in Sierra Leone (World Health Organization, 2009).

Life Expectancy in Late Adulthood

Although poverty-stricken groups lag behind the economically advantaged, the number of people age 65 and older has risen dramatically in the industrialized world. Because the baby-boom generation makes 45- to 54-year-olds the currently fastest-growing segment of the population, older adults are projected to rise from nearly 13 percent of the U.S. population today to 18 percent by 2025. The second fastest-growing segment is the 85-and-older group, who currently make up nearly 2 percent of Americans. By the year 2050, the proportion of U.S. seniors age 85 and older will more than double, reaching 4.3 percent (U.S. Census Bureau, 2009b).

Americans reaching age 65 in the early twenty-first century can look forward, on average, to 19 more years of life. Although women outnumber men by a greater margin as elders advance in age, differences in average life expectancy between the sexes decline. An American newborn girl can expect to live about 5½ years longer than a newborn boy. At age 65, the difference narrows to just under 3 years; at age 85, to just over 1 year. Over age 100, the gender gap in life expectancy disappears (U.S. Census Bureau, 2009b). Similarly, differences in rates of chronic illness

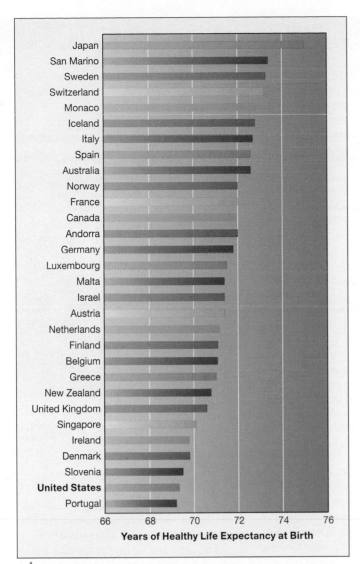

■ FIGURE 17.1 ■ Average healthy life expectancy at birth in 30 nations. The United States ranks a disappointing twenty-ninth in the world. In each nation, women's healthy life expectancy is 2 to 3 years longer, men's 2 to 3 years shorter, than the average depicted. (From World Health Organization, 2009.)

and in life expectancy between higher-SES whites and low-SES ethnic minorities decline with age. Around age 85, a *life expectancy crossover* occurs—surviving members of low-SES ethnic minority groups live longer than members of the white majority (House, Lantz, & Herd, 2005; Liang et al., 2002). Researchers speculate that among males and members of low-SES groups, only the biologically sturdiest survive into very old age.

Most Americans age 65 and older are capable of living active, independent, productive lives, but with age, growing numbers need assistance. After age 75, about 9 percent have difficulty carrying out **activities of daily living (ADLs)**—basic self-care tasks required to live on one's own, such as bathing, dressing, getting in and out of bed or a chair, or eating. And about 17 percent cannot carry out **instrumental activities of daily living (IADLs)**—tasks necessary to conduct the business

of daily life and also requiring some cognitive competence, such as telephoning, shopping, food preparation, housekeeping, and paying bills. The proportion of elders with these limitations rises sharply with age (U.S. Department of Health and Human Services, 2009a).

Throughout this book, we have seen that genetic and environmental factors jointly affect aging. With respect to heredity, identical twins typically die within 3 years of each other, whereas fraternal twins of the same sex differ by more than 6 years. Also, longevity runs in families. When both parents survive to age 70 or older, the chances that their children will live to 90 or 100 are double that of the general population (Cevenini et al., 2008; Hayflick, 1994; Mitchell et al., 2001). At the same time, evidence from twin studies suggests that once people pass 75 to 80 years, the contribution of heredity to length of life decreases in favor of environmental factors—a healthy diet; normal body weight; regular exercise; little or no tobacco, alcohol, and drug use; an optimistic outlook; low psychological stress; and social support (Yates et al., 2008; Zaretsky, 2003). As the Lifespan Vista box on page 446 reveals, the study of centenarians—people who cross the 100-year mark—offers special insights into how biological, psychological, and social influences work together to promote a long, satisfying life.

Maximum Lifespan

Finally, perhaps you are wondering: What is the **maximum lifespan,** or the genetic limit to length of life for a person free of external risk factors? According to current estimates, it varies between 70 and 110 for most people, with 85 about average (Harman, 2002). As the Lifespan Vista box indicates, the oldest verified age to which an individual has lived is 122 years.

Do these figures reflect the upper bound of human longevity, or can our lifespans be extended further? At present, scientists disagree on the answer (Arking, Novoseltsev, & Novoseltseva, 2004). But the controversy raises another issue: *Should* the lifespan be increased as far as possible? **_TAKE A MOMENT..._** How would you answer this question? Many people respond that quality, not just quantity, of life is the important goal—that is, doing everything possible to extend healthy life expectancy. Most experts agree that only after reducing the high rates of preventable illness and disability among low-SES individuals and wiping out age-related diseases should we invest in lengthening the maximum lifespan.

Physical Changes

Physical declines become more apparent in late adulthood, as more organs and systems of the body are affected. Nevertheless, most body structures can last into our eighties and beyond, if we take good care of them. For an overview of the physical changes we are about to discuss, return to Table 13.1 on page 343.

■ A LIFESPAN VISTA: Looking Forward, Looking Back ■

What Can We Learn About Aging from Centenarians?

Jeanne Louise Calment, listed in *Guinness World Records* as the longest-lived person whose age could be documented, was born in Arles, France, in 1875 and died there in 1997, 122 years later. Heredity may have contributed to her longevity: Her father lived to age 94, her mother to 86. As a young woman, she was healthy and energetic; she bicycled, swam, roller-skated, played tennis, and ran up the steps of the cathedral to attend daily Mass.

Jeanne's friends attributed her longevity to her easy-going disposition and resistance to stress. "If you can't do anything about it," she once said, "don't worry about it." Jeanne took up fencing at age 85 and rode a bicycle until age 100. Shortly thereafter, she moved into assisted living (see page 462), where she blossomed, becoming a celebrity because of both her age and her charming personality. Alert and quick-witted until her final year, she recommended laughter as the best recipe for long life. Asked once about the effects of aging, she quipped, "I've only one wrinkle, and I am sitting on it."

The past 40 years have seen a tenfold increase in centenarians in the industrialized world—a trend expected to accelerate (U.S. Census Bureau, 2009b). Women centenarians outnumber men by five to one. About 60 to 70 percent have physical and mental impairments that interfere with independent functioning. But the rest lead active, autonomous lives (Hagberg et al., 2001; Perls & Terry, 2003). These robust centenarians are of special interest because they represent the ultimate potential of the human species. Results of several longitudinal studies reveal that they are diverse in years of education (none to postgraduate), economic well-being (very poor to very rich), and ethnicity. At the same time, their physical condition and life stories reveal common threads.

Health

Centenarians usually have grandparents, parents, and siblings who reached very old age,

suggesting a genetically based survival advantage (Coles, 2004; Perls et al., 2002). Some centenarians share with their siblings a segment of identical DNA on the fourth chromosome, suggesting that a certain gene, or several genes, may increase the likelihood of exceptionally long life (Perls & Terry, 2003).

Most robust centenarians escape age-related chronic illnesses. Genetic testing reveals a low incidence of genes associated with immune-deficiency disorders, cancer, and Alzheimer's disease. Consistent with these findings, robust centenarians usually have efficiently functioning immune systems, and after-death examinations reveal few brain abnormalities (Silver & Perls, 2000). Others live successfully despite underlying chronic illness—typically atherosclerosis and other cardiovascular problems (Berzlanovich et al., 2005).

As a group, robust centenarians are of average or slender build and practice moderation in eating. Many have most or all of their own teeth—another sign of unusual physical health. The large majority have never smoked, and most report lifelong physical activity extending past age 100 (Kropf & Pugh, 1995).

Personality

In personality, these very senior citizens appear highly optimistic (Jopp & Rott, 2006). In a study in which robust centenarians retook personality tests after 18 months, they reported more fatigue and depression, perhaps in response to increased frailty at the very end of their lives. But they also scored higher in toughmindedness, independence, emotional security, and openness to experience—traits that may be vital for surviving beyond 100 (Martin, Long, & Poon, 2002).When asked about contributors to their longevity, these extremely long-lived elders often mention close family bonds and a long and happy marriage. An unusually large percentage of centenarian men—about one-fourth—are still married (Velkoff, 2000).

Activities

Robust centenarians have a history of community involvement—working for personally

Jeanne Louise Calment, shown here at age 121, took up fencing at age 85, rode a bicycle until age 100, and maintained a quick wit until her final year. The longest-lived person on record, she died at age 122.

rewarding just causes. Their current activities often include stimulating work, leisure pursuits, and learning, which may help sustain their good cognition and life satisfaction (Samuelsson et al., 1997). Writing letters, poems, plays, and memoirs; making speeches; teaching music lessons and Sunday school; nursing the sick; chopping wood; selling merchandise, bonds, and insurance; painting; practicing medicine; and preaching sermons are among robust centenarians' varied involvements.

As their numbers increase, robust centenarians are likely to be viewed less as curiosities and more as examples of typical development at its best. These independent, mentally alert, happy 100-year-olds illustrate how a healthy lifestyle, personal resourcefulness, and close ties to family and community can build on biological strengths, thereby pushing the limits of an active, fulfilling life.

Nervous System

On a routine office visit, 80-year-old Ruth told her doctor, "I think I might be losing my mind. Yesterday, I forgot the name of the family who just moved in next door. And the day before,

I had trouble finding the right words to explain to a delivery service how to get to my house."

"Ruth, everyone forgets those sorts of things from time to time," Dr. Wiley reassured her. "When we were young and had a memory lapse, we reprimanded ourselves for being scatterbrained and thought no more about it. Now, when we do the same thing, we attribute it to having 'a senior moment,' and we worry."

Aging of the central nervous system affects a wide range of complex activities. Although brain weight declines throughout adulthood, brain-imaging research and after-death autopsies reveal that the loss becomes greater starting in the sixties and may amount to as much as 5 to 10 percent by age 80, due to death of neurons and enlargement of ventricles (spaces) within the brain (Vinters, 2001).

Neuron loss occurs throughout the cerebral cortex but at different rates among different regions. In longitudinal studies, the frontal lobes (responsible for integration of information, judgment, and reflective thought) and the corpus callosum (which connects the two cortical hemispheres) tended to show the greatest shrinkage (Resnick et al., 2003; Smith et al., 2007). The cerebellum (which controls balance and coordination) also loses neurons—in all, about 25 percent. Glial cells, which myelinate neural fibers, decrease as well (Raz, 2005). And EEG measures reveal gradual slowing and reduced intensity of brain waves—signs of diminished efficiency of the central nervous system (Kramer, Fabiani, & Colcombe, 2006).

But the brain can overcome some of these declines. In several studies, growth of neural fibers in the brains of older adults unaffected by illness took place at the same rate as in middle-aged people. Aging neurons established new synapses after other neurons had degenerated (Flood & Coleman, 1988). Furthermore, the aging cerebral cortex can, to some degree, generate new neurons (Gould, 2007; Gould et al., 1999). And fMRI evidence reveals that compared with younger adults, elders who do well on cognitive tasks show more widely distributed activity across areas of the cerebral cortex (Reuter-Lorenz & Cappell, 2008). This suggests that one way older adults compensate for neuron loss is to call on additional brain regions to support cognitive processing.

The autonomic nervous system, involved in many life-support functions, also performs less well, putting the elderly at risk during heat waves and cold spells. For example, Ruth's reduced tolerance for hot weather was due to decreased sweating. And her body found it harder to raise its core temperature during cold exposure. However, among physically fit elders who are free of disease, these declines are mild (Whitbourne, 2001). The autonomic nervous system also releases higher levels of stress hormones into the bloodstream than it did earlier, perhaps to arouse body tissues that have become less responsive to these hormones over the years (Whitbourne, 2002). As we will see, this change may contribute to decreased immunity and to sleep problems.

Sensory Systems

Changes in sensory functioning become increasingly noticeable in late life. Older adults see and hear less well, and their taste, smell, and touch sensitivity may also decline. As Figure 17.2 shows, hearing impairments are more common than visual impairments. Extending trends for middle adulthood,

more women than men report being visually impaired, more men than women hearing impaired.

■ **VISION.**   In Chapter 15, we noted that structural changes in the eye make it harder to focus on nearby objects, see in dim light, and perceive color. In late adulthood, vision diminishes further. The cornea (clear covering of the eye) becomes more translucent and scatters light, which blurs images and increases sensitivity to glare. The lens continues to yellow, leading to further impairment in color discrimination.

The number of individuals with **cataracts**—cloudy areas in the lens, resulting in foggy vision and (without surgery) eventual blindness—increases tenfold from middle to late adulthood, affecting 25 percent of people in their seventies and 50 percent of those in their eighties (U.S. Census Bureau, 2009b). Besides biological aging, heredity, sun exposure, cigarette smoking, and certain diseases (such as diabetes) increase the risk of cataracts (Hammond et al., 2000; Klein et al., 2003). Fortunately, removal of the lens and replacement with an artificial lens implant or corrective eyewear are highly successful in restoring vision.

Impaired eyesight in late adulthood largely results from a reduction in light reaching the retina and from cell loss in the retina and optic nerve (refer again to Chapter 15). Dark adaptation—moving from a brightly lit to a dim environment, such as a movie theater—becomes harder. A decline in binocular vision (the brain's ability to combine images received from both eyes) makes depth perception less reliable (Brabyn et al., 2001).

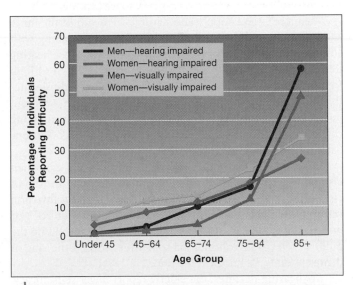

■ **FIGURE 17.2** ■ **Rates of visual and hearing impairments among U.S. men and women by age.** Among a large, nationally representative sample, those reporting that they had trouble seeing, even when wearing glasses or contact lenses, were judged visually impaired; those reporting "a lot of trouble" hearing were judged hearing impaired. Women report more visual impairments; men report more hearing impairments, a gap that widens considerably in late adulthood. In late life, hearing impairments become more common than visual impairments. (Adapted from U.S. Department of Health and Human Services, 2008i.)

And visual acuity (fineness of discrimination) worsens, dropping sharply after age 70 (Fozard & Gordon-Salant, 2001).

When light-sensitive cells in the *macula,* or central region of the retina, break down, older adults may develop **macular degeneration,** in which central vision blurs and gradually is lost. Macular degeneration is the leading cause of blindness among older adults. About 10 percent of 65- to 74-year-olds, and 30 percent of 75- to 85-year-olds, have symptoms. If diagnosed early, macular degeneration can sometimes be treated with laser therapy. As with cataracts, heredity (including several identified genes) increases risk, especially when combined with cigarette smoking or obesity (Chu et al., 2008; Rhone & Basu, 2008; Wysong, Lee, & Sloan, 2009). Atherosclerosis also contributes by constricting blood flow to the retina. Protective factors—believed to exert their effects by shielding cells in the macula from free-radical damage—include regular, brisk physical activity and a diet rich in green, leafy vegetables, which are excellent sources of vitamins A, C, E, and carotenoids (yellow and red plant pigments) (Feret et al., 2007). But vitamin pills, once thought to help reduce the incidence of both cataracts and macular degeneration, show no consistent benefits in carefully designed, experimental studies (Evans, 2008).

■ **HEARING.** "Mom, I'd like you to meet Joe's cousin Leona," said Ruth's daughter Sybil at a Thanksgiving gathering. But in the clamor of boisterous children, television sounds, and nearby conversations, 85-year-old Ruth didn't catch Leona's name or her relationship to Sybil's husband, Joe.

"Tell me your name again?" Ruth asked, adding, "Let's go into the other room, where it's quieter, so we can speak a bit."

Reduced blood supply and natural cell death in the inner ear and auditory cortex, discussed in Chapter 15, along with stiffening of membranes (such as the eardrum), cause hearing to decline in late adulthood. Decrements are greatest at high frequencies, although detection of soft sounds diminishes throughout the frequency range (see page 398). In addition, responsiveness to startling noises lessens, and discriminating complex tone patterns becomes harder (Fitzgibbons & Gordon-Salant, 1998; Hietanen et al., 2004).

Although hearing loss has less impact on self-care than vision loss, it affects safety and enjoyment of life. In the din of city traffic, 80-year-old Ruth didn't always correctly interpret warnings, whether spoken ("Watch it, don't step out yet") or nonspoken (the beep of a horn). And when she turned up the radio or television volume, she sometimes missed the ring of the telephone or a knock at the door.

As hearing declines, the elderly report lower self-efficacy, more loneliness and depressive symptoms, and a smaller social network than their normally hearing peers (Kramer et al., 2002). Of all hearing difficulties, the age-related decline in speech perception has the greatest impact on life satisfaction. After age 70, ability to detect the content and emotionally expressive features of conversation declines, especially in noisy settings (Schneider et al., 2000). Although Ruth used problem-centered coping to increase her chances of hearing conversa-

This adult son's patient guidance helps his elderly father feel included at a boisterous family reunion. Declines in hearing make it difficult for elders to socialize in noisy settings.

tion, she wasn't always successful. And sometimes people were inconsiderate. On a dinner outing, Joe raised his voice impatiently when Ruth asked him to repeat himself. At the family's Thanksgiving reunion, fewer relatives took time to talk with Ruth, and she felt pangs of loneliness.

As with vision, most older adults do not suffer from hearing loss great enough to disrupt their daily lives. For those who do, compensating with a hearing aid and minimizing background noise are helpful. When family members and others speak in quiet environments, older people are far more likely to convey an image of alertness and competence.

■ **TASTE AND SMELL.** Walt's brother Dick was a heavy smoker. In his sixties, he poured salt and pepper over his food, took his coffee with extra sugar, and asked for "extra hot" in Mexican and Indian restaurants.

Dick's reduced sensitivity to the four basic tastes—sweet, salty, sour, and bitter—is evident in many adults after age 60. Older adults also have greater difficulty recognizing familiar foods by taste alone (Fukunaga, Uematsu, & Sugimoto, 2005; Mojet, Christ-Hazelhof, & Heidema, 2001). But no change in the number or distribution of taste buds occurs late in life, so this drop in taste sensitivity may be due to factors other than aging. Cigarette smoking, dentures, medications, and environmental pollutants can affect taste perception. When taste is harder to detect, food is less enjoyable, increasing the likelihood of deficiencies in the elderly person's diet. Flavor additives can help make food more attractive (Drewnowski & Shultz, 2001).

Besides enhancing food enjoyment, smell has a self-protective function. An aging person who has difficulty detecting rancid food, gas fumes, or smoke may be in a life-threatening situation. A decrease in the number of smell receptors after age 60 contributes to declines in odor sensitivity. Researchers believe that odor perception not only wanes but becomes distorted, a change that may promote complaints that "food no longer smells and tastes right" (Seiberling & Conley, 2004).

But other factors may make this decline appear greater than it actually is. For example, older adults experiencing greater difficulty with verbal recall, including retrieval of odor labels, have greater difficulty with odor recognition tasks (Larsson & Bäckman, 1998; Larsson, Öberg, & Bäckman, 2005).

■ **TOUCH.**   Touch sensitivity is especially crucial for certain adults, such as the severely visually impaired who must read in Braille and people who must make fine judgments about texture in their occupations or leisure pursuits—for example, in art and handicraft activities. After age 70, nearly all elders experience a decline in touch perception on the hands, especially the fingertips, believed to be due to loss of touch receptors in certain regions of the skin and slowing of blood circulation to the extremities (Stevens & Cruz, 1996).

Cardiovascular and Respiratory Systems

In late adulthood, signs of change in the cardiovascular and respiratory systems become more apparent. In their sixties, Ruth and Walt noticed that they felt more physically stressed after running to catch a bus or to cross a street before the light changed.

As the years pass, the heart muscle becomes more rigid, and some of its cells die while others enlarge, leading the walls of the left ventricle (the largest heart chamber, from which blood is pumped to the body) to thicken. In addition, artery walls stiffen and accumulate some plaque (cholesterol and fats) due to normal aging (much more in those with atherosclerosis).

© KRISTI J. BLACK/CORBIS

After an uphill stretch, this biker needs a rest to catch his breath and feel re-energized. Aging of the cardiovascular and respiratory systems means that sufficient oxygen may not be delivered to body tissues during physical exertion.

Finally, the heart muscle becomes less responsive to signals from pacemaker cells within the heart, which initiate each contraction (Smith & Cotter, 2008). As a combined result of these changes, the heart pumps with less force, maximum heart rate decreases, and blood flow throughout the circulatory system slows. This means that sufficient oxygen may not be delivered to body tissues during high physical activity.

Changes in the respiratory system compound the effects of reduced oxygenation. Because lung tissue gradually loses its elasticity, vital capacity (amount of air that can be forced in and out of the lungs) is reduced by half between ages 25 and 80. As a result, the lungs fill and empty less efficiently, causing the blood to absorb less oxygen and give off less carbon dioxide. This explains why older people increase their breathing rate more and feel more out of breath while exercising—deficiencies that are more extreme in lifelong smokers and in people who have failed to reduce dietary fat or have had many years of exposure to environmental pollutants.

Immune System

As the immune system ages, T cells, which attack antigens (foreign substances) directly, become less effective (see Chapter 13, page 344). In addition, the immune system is more likely to malfunction by turning against normal body tissues in an **autoimmune response.** A less competent immune system can increase the elderly person's risk for a variety of illnesses, including infectious diseases (such as the flu), cardiovascular disease, certain forms of cancer, and various autoimmune disorders, such as rheumatoid arthritis and diabetes (Hasler & Zouali, 2005).

Older adults vary greatly in immunity. A few have sturdy immune systems that continue to respond nearly as well as in early adulthood. But most experience some loss of function, ranging from partial to profound (Pawelec et al., 1999). A healthy diet and exercise help protect the immune response in old age, whereas obesity aggravates the age-related decline (Chandra, 2002b; Drela, Kozdron, & Szczypiorski, 2004; Senchina & Kohut, 2007).

Sleep

When Walt went to bed at night, he usually lay awake for a half-hour to an hour before falling asleep, remaining in a drowsy state longer than when he was younger. During the night, he spent less time in the deepest phase of NREM sleep (see Chapter 3, page 83) and awoke several times.

Older adults require about as much total sleep as younger adults: around seven hours per night. Yet as people age, they have more difficulty falling asleep, staying asleep, and sleeping deeply. Insomnia affects nearly half of older adults at least a few nights per month. The timing of sleep tends to change as well, toward earlier bedtime and earlier morning awakening (Wolkove et al., 2007). Changes in brain structures controlling sleep and higher levels of stress hormones in the bloodstream, which have an alerting effect on the central nervous system, are believed to be responsible.

Fortunately, there are ways to foster restful sleep, such as establishing a consistent bedtime and waking time, exercising regularly, and using the bedroom only for sleep (not for eating, reading, or watching TV) (McCurry et al., 2007). Explaining that even very healthy older adults have trouble sleeping lets people know that age-related changes in the sleep–wake pattern are normal. The elderly receive more prescription sedatives for sleep complaints than do 40- to 65-year-olds. Used briefly, these drugs can help relieve temporary insomnia. But long-term medication can make matters worse by inducing rebound insomnia after the drug is discontinued (Feinsilver, 2003).

Physical Appearance and Mobility

In earlier chapters, we saw that changes leading to an aged appearance are under way as early as the twenties and thirties. Because these occur gradually, older adults may not notice their elderly appearance until it has become obvious.

Creasing and sagging of the skin, described in Chapter 15, extends into old age. In addition, oil glands that lubricate the skin become less active, leading to dryness and roughness. "Age spots" increase; in some individuals, the arms, backs of the hands, and face may be dotted with these pigmented marks. Moles and other small skin growths may also appear. Blood vessels can be seen beneath the more transparent skin, which has largely lost its layer of fatty support (Whitbourne, 2002).

The face is especially likely to show these effects because it is frequently exposed to the sun, which accelerates aging. Other factors that contribute to facial wrinkling and age spots include long-term alcohol use, cigarette smoking, and stress. In a study of identical twins, those who had been divorced appeared almost two years older than their married or widowed siblings (Guyuron et al., 2009). Additional facial changes occur: The nose and ears broaden as new cells are deposited on the outer layer of the skeleton. And especially in elders with a history of poor dental care, teeth may be yellowed, cracked, and chipped, and gums may have receded. As hair follicles under the skin's surface die, hair on the head thins in both sexes, and the scalp may be visible. In men with hereditary pattern baldness, follicles do not die but, instead, begin to produce fine, downy hair (Whitbourne, 2002).

Body build changes as well. Height continues to decline, especially in women, as loss of bone mineral content leads to further collapse of the spinal column. Weight generally drops after age 60 because of additional loss of lean body mass (bone density and muscle), which is heavier than the fat deposits accumulating on the torso.

Several factors affect mobility. The first is muscle strength, which generally declines at a faster rate in late adulthood than in middle age (Whitbourne, 2001, 2002). Second, bone strength deteriorates because of reduced bone mass. Third, strength and flexibility of the joints and the ligaments and tendons (which connect muscle to bone) diminish. In her eighties, Ruth's reduced ability to support her body, flex her limbs, and rotate her hips made walking at a steady, moderate pace, climbing stairs, and rising from a chair difficult. A carefully planned exercise program can minimize declines in strength, joint flexibility, and range of movement.

Adapting to Physical Changes of Late Adulthood

Great diversity exists in older adults' adaptation to the physical changes of aging. People who are more anxious about growing older monitor their physical state more closely and are more concerned about their appearance (Montepare, 2006). Dick and Goldie took advantage of an enormous industry designed to stave off outward signs of old age, including cosmetics, wigs,

Changes in appearance that accompany aging are evident in these portraits of Jimmy Carter—former U.S. president—at ages 52, 63, and 85. The skin creases and sags, "age spots" increase, the nose and ears broaden as new cells are deposited on the outer layer of the skeleton, and hair follicles die, causing hair on the head to thin.

and plastic surgery, plus various "anti-aging" dietary supplements, herbal products, and hormonal medications offered by "longevity" clinics—none with any demonstrated benefits and some of them harmful (Olshansky, Hayflick, & Perls, 2004). In contrast, Ruth and Walt were relatively unconcerned about their thinning white hair and wrinkled skin. Their identities were less bound up with their appearance than with their ability to remain active. Like Ruth and Walt, most elders say they feel younger than they look and than they actually are—self-evaluations that promote satisfaction with growing older (Kleinspehn-Ammerlahn, Grühn, & Smith, 2008; Rubin & Berntsen, 2006).

The most obvious outward signs of aging—graying hair, facial wrinkles, and baldness—bear no relationship to sensory, cognitive, and motor functioning or to longevity (Schnohr et al., 1998). In contrast, neurological, sensory, cardiovascular, respiratory, immune-system, and skeletal and muscular health strongly predict cognitive performance and both quality and length of later life (Anstey, Luszcz, & Sanchez, 2001; Bergman, Blomberg, & Almkvist, 2007; Reyes-Ortiz et al., 2005). Furthermore, people can do more to prevent declines in the functioning of internal body systems than they can do to prevent gray hair and baldness!

■ **EFFECTIVE COPING STRATEGIES.** Think back to our discussion of problem-centered and emotion-centered coping in Chapter 15. It applies here as well. As Walt and Ruth prevented and compensated for age-related changes through diet, exercise, environmental adjustments, and an active, stimulating lifestyle, they felt a sense of personal control over their fates. This prompted additional positive coping and improved physical functioning. In contrast, older adults who consider age-related declines inevitable and uncontrollable tend to be passive when faced with them and to report more physical and psychological adjustment difficulties (Kraaij, Pruymboom, & Garnefski, 2002; Morrison, 2008).

■ **ASSISTIVE TECHNOLOGY.** A rapidly expanding **assistive technology,** or array of devices that permit people with disabilities to improve their functioning, is available to help older people cope with physical declines. Computers are the greatest source of these innovative products. People with sensory impairments can use special software to enlarge text or have it read aloud. Phones that can be dialed and answered by voice commands help elders who have difficulty pushing buttons or getting across a room to answer the phone. And for elders who take multiple medications, a tiny computer chip called a "smart cap" can be placed on medicine bottles. It beeps on a programmed schedule as a reminder to take the drug and tracks how many and at what time pills have been taken.

Architects are also designing homes that can adapt to changing physical needs—equipping them with movable walls that expand and contract, plumbing that enables a full bathroom to be added on the main floor, and "smart-home" technologies that promote safety and mobility, such as sensors in floors that activate room lights when an older person gets up at night and alarm

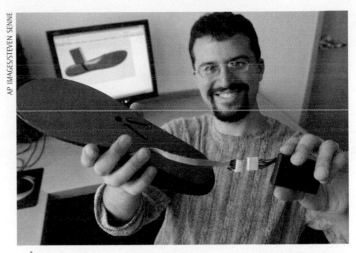

Erez Lieberman, Massachusetts Institute of Technology graduate student, displays the "iShoe" insole he invented. The device, designed to prevent catastrophic falls in the elderly, contains sensors that detect a wearer's balance. Data collected can be reported to the elder's doctor. The iShoe also can be outfitted with an alarm that alerts family members when a fall occurs.

systems that detect falls. Elders with disabilities who use assistive devices require fewer hours of personal caregiving (Hoenig, Taylor, & Sloan, 2003). Yet U.S. government-sponsored health-care coverage is largely limited to essential medical equipment. Sweden's health-care system, in contrast, covers many assistive devices that promote function and safety, and its building code requires that new homes include a full bathroom on the main floor (Hooyman & Kiyak, 2008). In this way, Sweden helps older adults remain as independent as possible.

A motorized chair allows this 90-year-old to remain in her own home despite its long staircase.

■ **OVERCOMING STEREOTYPES OF AGING.** Stereotypes of late adulthood, which view "deterioration as inevitable," are widespread in Western nations. Overcoming this pessimistic picture is vital for helping people adapt favorably to late-life physical changes.

Like gender stereotypes, aging stereotypes often operate automatically, without awareness; people "see" elders in stereotypical ways, even when they appear otherwise. As seniors encounter these negative messages, they experience *stereotype threat,* which results in diminished performance on tasks related to the stereotype (see page 244 in Chapter 9). In several studies, researchers exposed older adults to words associated with either negative aging stereotypes ("decrepit," "confused") or positive aging stereotypes ("sage," "enlightened"). Those in the negative-stereotype condition displayed a more intense physiological response to stress along with worse handwriting, memory performance, self-efficacy, and will to live (Hess & Hinson, 2006; Hess, Hinson, & Statham, 2004; Levy & Banaji, 2002; Levy et al., 2000).

As these findings indicate, negative stereotypes have a stressful, disorganizing impact on elders' functioning. Positive stereotypes, in contrast, reduce stress and foster competence (Levy, 2003). In a longitudinal investigation, people with positive self-perceptions of aging—who, for example, agreed with such statements as "As I get older, things are better than I thought they'd be"—lived, on average, 7½ years longer than those with negative self-perceptions. This survival advantage remained after gender, SES, loneliness, and physical health status were controlled (Levy et al., 2002). Adults with less education are especially susceptible to the detrimental effects of aging stereotypes, perhaps because they tend to accept those messages uncritically (Andreoletti & Lachman, 2004).

In cultures where the elderly are treated with deference and respect, an aging appearance can be a source of pride. In one study, Chinese adults diverse in age were less likely than

Canadian adults to stereotype elders, either positively or negatively (Ryan et al., 2004). In the native language of the Inuit people of Canada, the closest word to "elder" is *isumataq,* or "one who knows things"—a high status that begins when a couple becomes head of the extended family unit. When Inuit older adults were asked for their thoughts on aging well, they mentioned attitudes—a positive approach to life, interest in transmitting cultural knowledge to young people, and community involvement—nearly twice as often as physical health (Collings, 2001).

Despite inevitable declines, physical aging can be viewed with either optimism or pessimism. As Walt commented, "You can think of your glass as half full or half empty." Cultural valuing of elders greatly increases the likelihood that they will adopt the "half full" alternative.

ASK YOURSELF

>> **REVIEW**
Cite examples of how older adults can compensate for age-related physical declines.

>> **APPLY**
"The best way to adjust to this is to learn to like it," thought 65-year-old Herman, inspecting his thinning hair in the mirror. "I remember reading that bald older men are regarded as leaders." What type of coping is Herman using, and why is it effective?

>> **REFLECT**
While watching TV during the coming week, keep a log of portrayals of older adults. How many images were positive? How many conveyed negative stereotypes of aging?

Health, Fitness, and Disability

At Walt and Ruth's fiftieth wedding anniversary, 77-year-old Walt thanked a roomful of well-wishers for joining in the celebration. Then, with emotion, he announced, "I'm so grateful Ruth and I are in good health and still able to give to our family, friends, and community."

As Walt's remarks affirm, health is central to psychological well-being in late life. When researchers ask the elderly about possible selves (see Chapter 16, page 423), number of hoped-for physical selves declines with age and number of feared physical selves increases. Nevertheless, because older adults compare themselves to same-age peers, the majority rate their health favorably (U.S. Department of Health and Human Services, 2009a). As for protecting their health, elders' sense of self-efficacy is as high as that of young adults and higher than that of middle-aged people (Frazier, 2002; Hooker, 1992). The stronger elders' sense of control in coping with physical challenges, and the more optimistic they are about health outcomes, the better they are at overcoming threats to health, which promotes

This Inuit elder of northern Canada enjoys a visit with her daughter. In Inuit culture, aging is associated with expert knowledge and high status. Hence, changes in physical appearance can be a source of pride.

© EASTCOTT-MOMATIUK/THE IMAGE WORKS

further optimism and continued health-enhancing behaviors (Kubzansky et al., 2002; Morrison, 2008).

As mentioned earlier, SES and ethnic variations in health diminish in late adulthood. Nevertheless, before age 85, SES continues to predict physical functioning (House, Lantz, & Herd, 2005; Yao & Robert, 2008). African-American and Hispanic elderly (one-fifth of whom live in poverty) remain at greater risk for various health problems, including cardiovascular disease, diabetes, and certain cancers. Native-American older adults are even worse off. The majority are poor, and chronic health conditions—including diabetes, kidney disease, liver disease, tuberculosis, and hearing and vision impairments—are so widespread that the U.S. federal government grants Native Americans special health benefits. These begin as early as age 45, reflecting a much harder and shorter lifespan. Unfortunately, low-SES elders are less likely than their higher-SES counterparts to seek medical treatment, partly because they feel less in control of their health and less optimistic that treatment will work (Hopper, 1993).

The sex differences noted in Chapter 15 extend into late adulthood: Men are more prone to fatal diseases, women to non-life-threatening disabling conditions. By very old age (80 to 85 and beyond), women are more impaired than men because only the sturdiest men have survived (Murtagh & Hubert, 2004; Morrison, 2008). In addition, with fewer physical limitations, older men are better able to remain independent and to engage in exercise, hobbies, and involvement in the social world, all of which promote better health.

Widespread health-related optimism among the elderly suggests that substantial inroads into preventing disability can be made even in the last few decades of life. Ideally, as life expectancy extends, we want the average period of diminished vigor before death to decrease—a public health goal called the **compression of morbidity.** Several large-scale studies indicate that over the past two decades, compression of morbidity has occurred in industrialized nations despite rising rates of obesity and sedentary lifestyles, suggesting that medical advances and improved socioeconomic conditions are largely responsible (Fries, 2003; Hessler et al., 2003).

Yet the impact of good health habits on postponement of disability is large, indicating that compression of morbidity can be greatly extended. In a longitudinal investigation following university alumni from their late sixties on, disability was delayed by nearly eight years in those who were lean, who exercised, and who did not smoke compared with those who were obese, sedentary, or addicted to tobacco. Elders with these risks surged to extremely high levels of disability in the two years before death (Hubert et al., 2002; Vita et al., 1998).

More comprehensive strategies are needed in the developing world, where 70 percent of older people will reside by 2025. In these nations, poverty is rampant, chronic diseases occur earlier, even routine health interventions are unavailable or too costly for all but a few, and most public health programs do not focus on the elderly (Kalache, Aboderin, & Hoskins, 2002). As a result, disability rates among old people are especially high, and as yet, no progress has been made in compression of morbidity.

Nutrition and Exercise

The physical changes of late life lead to an increased need for certain nutrients—calcium and vitamin D to protect the bones; zinc and vitamins B_6, C, and E to protect the immune system; and vitamins A, C, and E to prevent free radicals (see Chapter 13, page 340). Yet declines in physical activity, in the senses of taste and smell, and in ease of chewing (because of deteriorating teeth) can reduce the quantity and quality of food eaten (Morley, 2001). Furthermore, the aging digestive system has greater difficulty absorbing certain nutrients, such as protein, calcium, and vitamin D. And older adults who live alone may have problems shopping or cooking and may feel less like eating by themselves. Together, these physical and environmental conditions increase the risk of dietary deficiencies.

In several studies, a daily vitamin–mineral tablet resulted in an enhanced immune response and a 50 percent drop in days of infectious illness (Chandra, 2002a; Wintergest, Maggini, & Hornig, 2007). But vitamin–mineral supplements do not protect against cardiovascular disease or cancer (Huang et al., 2006; Neuhouser et al., 2009). Furthermore, supplemental nutrients and herbs identified as "cognitive enhancers"—including B and E vitamins, folic acid, and ginkgo biloba—do not improve cognitive functioning (Aisen et al., 2008; DeKosky et al., 2008; Morris et al., 2006). At the same time, regularly eating fish high in polyunsaturated fatty acids (which promote vascular health) offers some protection against mental disabilities (Issa et al., 2006; Morris et al., 2005).

In addition to a healthy diet, exercise continues to be a powerful health intervention. Sedentary healthy older adults up to age 80 who begin endurance training (walking, cycling, aerobic

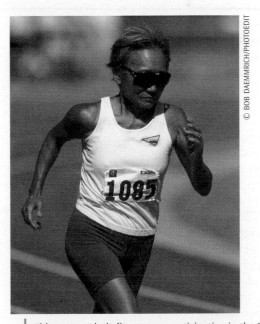

© BOB DAEMMRICH/PHOTOEDIT

This spectacularly fit woman, participating in the Senior Olympics, has likely been exercising for most of her life. However, even exercise programs begun in late adulthood can promote muscle size and strength and preservation of brain structures and behavioral capacities.

dance) show gains in vital capacity that compare favorably with those of much younger individuals. And weight-bearing exercise begun in late adulthood—even as late as age 90—promotes muscle size and strength. This translates into improved walking speed, balance, posture, and ability to carry out everyday activities (deJong & Franklin, 2004; Goldberg, Dengel, & Hagberg, 1996; Pyka et al., 1994).

Furthermore, exercise increases blood circulation to the brain, which helps preserve brain structures and behavioral capacities (Colcombe et al., 2003). In a series of studies, researchers used fMRI to assess changes in brain activity resulting from a six-month program of regular, moderate to vigorous exercise for healthy but sedentary seniors. Compared to a physically inactive group, the new exercisers displayed increased activity in areas of the cerebral cortex governing control of attention, as well as improved sustained and selective attention during mental testing, yielding better performance (Colcombe et al., 2004). They also showed gains in volume of the cerebral cortex—clear biological evidence for the role of physical activity in preserving central nervous system health (Colcombe et al., 2006).

Although good nutrition and physical activity are most beneficial when they are lifelong, it is never too late to change. Elders who come to value the intrinsic benefits of exercise—feeling stronger, healthier, and more energetic—are likely to engage in it regularly (Caserta & Gillett, 1998). Yet 75 percent of elderly men and 80 percent of elderly women are not active enough (Stewart et al., 2001).

Sexuality

When Walt turned 60, he asked his 90-year-old Uncle Louie at what age sexual desire and activity cease. Walt's question stemmed from a widely held myth that sex drive disappears among the elderly (Hillman, 2000). Louie corrected this impression. "My sexual interest has never gone away," he explained. "I can't do it as often, and it's a quieter experience than it was in my youth. But Rachella and I have led a happy intimate life, and it's still that way."

As in previous cross-sectional studies, a recent survey of a large, nationally representative sample of U.S. 57- to 85-year-olds reported a decline in frequency of sexual activity in older people—especially among women, who are less likely than men to be in a marital or other intimate relationship. At the same time, the majority of respondents attributed at least some importance to sex, and those who had been sexually active in the previous year mostly rated sex as "very" or "extremely" important. Consistent with these attitudes, most healthy couples reported continued, regular sexual enjoyment. More than half of the oldest respondents with an intimate partner indicated that they engaged in some type of sexual activity (usually intercourse) at least two to three times per month (see Figure 17.3) (Lindau et al., 2007). Note that these trends are probably influenced by cohort effects: A new generation of elders, accustomed to viewing sexuality positively, will probably be more sexually active.

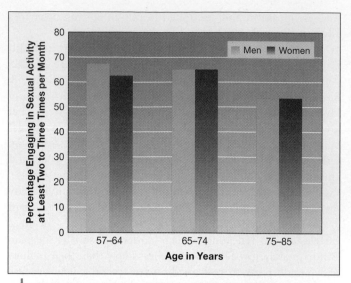

■ FIGURE 17.3 ■ Age-related changes in sexual activity among adults with an intimate partner. In a nationally representative sample of more than 3,000 U.S. 57- to 85-year-olds, most men and women with an intimate partner reported engaging in sexual activity (usually intercourse) at least two to three times per month. Sexual activity declined during late adulthood. Still, more than half of partnered 75- to 85-year-olds reported regular sexual activity. (Adapted from Lindau et al., 2007.)

The same generalization we discussed for midlife applies to late life: Good sex in the past predicts good sex in the future. Furthermore, using intercourse as the only measure of sexual activity promotes a narrow view of pleasurable sex. Even at the most advanced ages, there is more to sexuality than the sex act itself—feeling sensual, enjoying close companionship, and being loved and wanted. Both older men and older women report that the male partner is usually the one who ceases to interact sexually (Burgess, 2004; DeLamater & Moorman, 2007; Lindau et al., 2007). In a culture that emphasizes an erection as necessary for being sexual, a man may withdraw from all erotic activity when he finds that erections are harder to achieve and more time must elapse between them.

Disabilities that disrupt blood flow to the penis—most often, disorders of the autonomic nervous system, cardiovascular disease, and diabetes—are largely responsible for dampening sexuality in older men. But as noted in Chapter 15, availability of drug treatments, such as Viagra, has increased men's willingness to discuss erectile dysfunction with their doctors. In both sexes, cigarette smoking, excessive alcohol intake, poor health, and a variety of prescription medications also lead to diminished sexual performance (Gott & Hinchliff, 2003; Lindau, 2007). And because the sex ratio increasingly favors females, aging heterosexual women have fewer and fewer opportunities for sexual encounters.

In most tribal and village cultures, sexual activity among elders is expected and is common for both men and women until very late life (Winn & Newton, 1982). But in Western nations, sex in old age often meets with disapproval. Educational

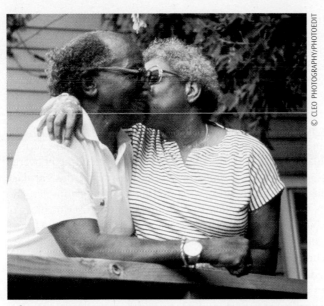

Most healthy older couples report continued, regular sexual enjoyment. In addition to intercourse, feeling sensual, enjoying close companionship, and being loved and wanted all are part of sexuality at the most advanced ages.

programs informing older adults about normal, age-related changes in sexual functioning and fostering a view of sex as extending throughout adulthood promote positive sexual attitudes (Hillman & Stricker, 1994). In nursing homes, education for caregivers is vital for ensuring residents' rights to privacy and other living conditions that permit sexual expression (Hajjar & Kamel, 2004).

Physical Disabilities

TAKE A MOMENT... Compare the death rates shown in Figure 17.4 with those in Figure 15.2 on page 403. You will see that illness and disability climb as the end of the lifespan approaches. Cardiovascular disease and cancer remain the leading causes of

death, increasing dramatically from mid- to late life. As before, death rates from cardiovascular disease and cancer are higher for men than for women, although the sex difference declines with advancing age (U.S. Census Bureau, 2009b).

The third most common killer among the aged is *stroke*—the only leading cause that is more prevalent among women. It occurs when a blood clot blocks a blood vessel or a blood vessel hemorrhages in the brain, causing damage to brain tissue. Stroke is a major cause of late-life disability and, after age 75, death. Respiratory diseases also rise sharply with age. And as the longest-lived people escape chronic diseases or weaken because of them, the immune system eventually encounters an infection it cannot fight. Consequently, many of the very old succumb to one of the more than 50 lung inflammations classified as *pneumonia*. Doctors recommend that people age 65 and older be vaccinated against the most common type.

Other diseases are less frequent killers, but they limit older adults' ability to live fully and independently. We have already noted the increase after age 65 in macular degeneration, which severely impairs vision and leads to blindness (see page 448). Osteoporosis, discussed in Chapter 15 (see page 405), continues to rise in late adulthood; recall that it affects the majority of men and women after age 70. Yet another bone disorder—*arthritis*—adds to the physical limitations of many elders. And *type 2 diabetes* and *unintentional injuries* also multiply in late adulthood. In the following sections, we take up these last three conditions.

Finally, an important point must be kept in mind as we discuss physical and mental disabilities of late adulthood: The fact that these conditions are *related to age* does not mean that they are *entirely caused by aging*. To clarify this distinction, experts distinguish between **primary aging** (another term for *biological aging*), or genetically influenced declines that affect all members of our species and take place even in the context of overall good health, and **secondary aging**, declines due to hereditary defects and negative environmental influences, such as poor diet, lack of exercise, disease, substance abuse, environmental pollution, and psychological stress.

■ **FIGURE 17.4** ■ **Leading causes of death among people age 65 and older in the United States.** In late adulthood, cardiovascular disease is the leading cause of death, followed by cancer. Stroke (unique in being more prevalent among women), respiratory diseases, and unintentional injuries also claim the lives of many elders. (Adapted from U.S. Census Bureau, 2009b.)

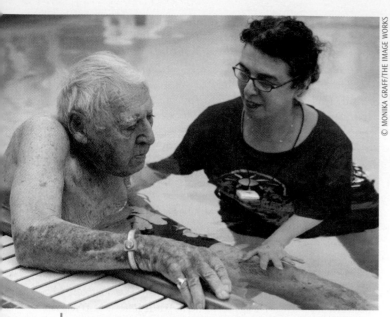

This frail elder, working with a physical therapist, suffers from wasted muscle mass and strength, weight loss, severe mobility problems, and perhaps cognitive impairment. Although biological aging contributes to his frailty, secondary aging—through genetic disorders, unhealthy lifestyle, and chronic disease—plays a larger role.

Throughout this book, we have seen that it is difficult to distinguish primary from secondary aging. Undoubtedly you have, at one time or another, encountered a *frail elder*—a person of extreme infirmity who displays wasted muscle mass and strength, weight loss, severe mobility problems, and perhaps cognitive impairment. **Frailty** involves weakened functioning of diverse organs and body systems, which profoundly interferes with everyday competence and leaves the older adult highly vulnerable in the face of an infection, extremely hot or cold weather, or an injury (Walston et al., 2006). Although primary aging contributes to frailty, researchers agree that secondary aging plays a larger role, through genetic disorders, unhealthy lifestyle, and chronic disease (Bergman et al., 2007; Hogan, MacKnight, & Bergman, 2003). The serious conditions we are about to discuss are major sources of frailty in the elderly.

■ **ARTHRITIS.** Beginning in her fifties, Ruth felt a slight morning stiffness in her neck, back, hips, and knees. In her sixties, she developed bony lumps on the end joints of her fingers. As the years passed, she experienced periodic joint swelling and some loss of flexibility—changes that affected her ability to move quickly and easily.

Arthritis, a condition of inflamed, painful, stiff, and sometimes swollen joints and muscles, becomes more common in late adulthood. It occurs in several forms. Ruth has **osteoarthritis**, the most common type, which involves deteriorating cartilage on the ends of bones of frequently used joints. Otherwise known as "wear-and-tear arthritis" or "degenerative joint disease," it is one of the few age-related disabilities in which years of use make a difference. Although a genetic proneness seems to exist, the disease usually does not appear until the forties or fifties. In frequently used joints, cartilage on the ends of the bones, which reduces friction during movement, gradually deteriorates. Or obesity places abnormal pressure on the joints and damages cartilage. Almost all older adults show some osteoarthritis on X-rays, although wide individual differences in severity exist (Fajardo & Di Cesare, 2005).

Unlike osteoarthritis, which is limited to certain joints, **rheumatoid arthritis** involves the whole body. An autoimmune response leads to inflammation of connective tissue, particularly the membranes that line the joints, resulting in overall stiffness, inflammation, and aching. Tissue in the cartilage tends to grow, damaging surrounding ligaments, muscles, and bones. The result is deformed joints and often serious loss of mobility. Sometimes other organs, such as the heart and lungs, are affected. Worldwide, about 2 percent of older adults have rheumatoid arthritis (Rasch et al., 2003).

Overall, disability due to arthritis affects 45 percent of U.S. men over age 65 and rises modestly with age. Among women, the incidence is higher and increases sharply with age: About 50 percent of 65- to 84-year-olds and 70 percent of those over age 85 are affected (U.S. Census Bureau, 2009b). Although rheumatoid arthritis can strike at any age, it rises after age 60. Twin studies support a strong hereditary contribution. Presence of certain genes heightens disease risk, possibly by triggering a late-life defect in the immune system (Turesson & Matteson, 2006). However, identical twins differ widely in disease severity, indicating that environment makes a difference. So far, cigarette smoking is the only confirmed lifestyle influence (Klareskog et al., 2006). Early treatment with powerful anti-inflammatory medications helps slow the course of the disease.

Managing arthritis requires a balance of rest when the disease flares, pain relief, and physical activity involving gentle stretching of all muscles to maintain mobility. Twice a week, 84-year-old Ruth attended a water-based exercise class. Within two months, her symptoms lessened, and she no longer needed a walker (Kettunen & Kujala, 2004). With proper analgesic medication, joint protection, and lifestyle changes, many people with either form of the illness lead long, productive lives. If hip or knee joints are badly damaged or deformed, they can be surgically rebuilt or replaced with plastic or metal devices.

■ **DIABETES.** After a meal, the body breaks down the food, releasing glucose (the primary energy source for cell activity) into the bloodstream. Insulin, produced by the pancreas, keeps the blood concentration of glucose within set limits by stimulating muscle and fat cells to absorb it. When this balance system fails, either because not enough insulin is produced or because body cells become insensitive to it, *type 2 diabetes* (otherwise known as *diabetes mellitus*) results. Over time, abnormally high blood glucose damages the blood vessels, increasing the risk of stroke, heart attack, circulatory problems in the legs, and injury to the eyes, kidneys, and nerves.

Excessive blood glucose also reduces blood flow to the hippocampus, a brain structure that plays an important role in memory (see page 168 in Chapter 7) (Wu et al., 2008). In several longitudinal studies, diabetes was associated with more rapid cognitive declines in the elderly and an elevated risk of Alzheimer's disease—an association we will soon revisit when we take up Alzheimer's (Arvanitakis et al., 2004; Logroscino, Kang, & Grodstein, 2004; Yaffe et al., 2004).

From middle to late adulthood, the incidence of type 2 diabetes doubles; it affects 10 percent of the elderly in the United States (U.S. Census Bureau, 2009b). Diabetes runs in families, suggesting that heredity is involved. But inactivity and abdominal fat deposits greatly increase the risk. Higher rates of type 2 diabetes are found among African-American, Mexican-American, and Native-American minorities for both genetic and environmental reasons, including high-fat diets and obesity associated with poverty.

Treating type 2 diabetes requires lifestyle changes, including a carefully controlled diet, regular exercise, and weight loss (Meneilly, 2006). By promoting glucose absorption and reducing abdominal fat, physical activity lessens disease symptoms.

■ **UNINTENTIONAL INJURIES.** At age 65 and older, the death rate from unintentional injuries is at an all-time high—more than twice as great as in adolescence and early adulthood. Motor vehicle collisions and falls are largely responsible.

Motor Vehicle Accidents. Older adults have higher rates of traffic violations, accidents, and fatalities per mile driven than any other age group, with the exception of drivers under age 25. The high rate of injury persists, even though many elders, especially women, limit their driving after noticing that their ability to drive safely is slipping (Silvi, 2004; U.S. Census Bureau, 2009b).

The greater elders' visual processing difficulties, the higher their rate of moving violations and crashes (Wood, 2002). Compared with young drivers, the elderly are less likely to drive quickly and recklessly but more likely to fail to heed signs, yield the right of way, and turn appropriately. They often try to compensate for their difficulties by being more cautious. Slowed reaction time, declines in capacity to attend selectively and engage in two activities at once, and resulting indecisiveness pose hazards, too (Makishita & Matsunaga, 2008). Elders are at high risk for collisions at busy intersections and in other complex traffic situations.

Nevertheless, older adults usually try to drive as long as possible. Giving up driving results in loss of freedom, control over one's life, and self-esteem (Wood, 2002). Specially trained driver rehabilitation consultants—affiliated with hospitals, drivers' licensing agencies, or U.S. Area Agencies on Aging (see page 52 in Chapter 2)—can help assess an elder's capacity to continue driving, provide driver retraining, or counsel elders to retire from driving and to arrange other transportation options.

The elderly also make up more than 30 percent of all pedestrian deaths (U.S. Census Bureau, 2009b). Confusing intersections, especially crossing signals that do not allow older people enough time to get to the other side of the street, are often involved.

Falls. One day, Ruth fell down the basement steps and lay there with a broken ankle until Walt arrived home an hour later. Ruth's tumble represents the leading type of accident among the elderly. About 30 percent of adults over age 65 and 50 percent over age 80 have experienced a fall within the last year. Declines in vision, hearing, mobility, muscle strength, and cognitive functioning; depressed mood; use of medications that affect mental processing; and development of certain chronic illnesses (such as arthritis) increase the risk of falling (Rubenstein, Stevens, & Scott, 2008).

Because of weakened bones and difficulty breaking a fall, serious injury results about 10 percent of the time. Among the most common is hip fracture. It increases twentyfold from age 65 to 85 and is associated with a 20 percent increase in mortality. Of those who survive, half never regain the ability to walk without assistance (U.S. Department of Health and Human Services, 2008i).

Falling can also impair health indirectly, by promoting fear of falling. Almost half of older adults who have fallen admit that they purposefully avoid activities because they are afraid of falling again (Health and Disability Research Institute, 2006). In this way, a fall can limit mobility and social contact, undermining both physical and psychological well-being. Although an active lifestyle may expose the elderly to more situations that can cause a fall, the health benefits of activity far outweigh the risk of serious injury due to falling.

Mental Disabilities

Normal age-related cell death in the brain, described earlier, does not lead to loss of ability to engage in everyday activities. But when cell death and structural and chemical abnormalities are profound, serious deterioration of mental and motor functions occurs.

Dementia refers to a set of disorders occurring almost entirely in old age in which many aspects of thought and behavior are so impaired that everyday activities are disrupted. Dementia strikes 13 percent of adults over age 65, both sexes about equally. Approximately 1 percent of people in their sixties are affected; the rate increases with age, rising sharply after age 80 until it reaches about 50 percent after age 85—trends that apply to the United States and other Western nations (Berr, Wancata, & Ritchie, 2005; Matthews & Brayne, 2005; Plassman et al., 2007). Although dementia rates are similar across most ethnic groups, African Americans have an elevated incidence—a difference explained by associated risk factors, not by race, as we will see shortly (Alzheimer's Association, 2009).

About a dozen types of dementia have been identified. Some are reversible with proper treatment, but most are irreversible and incurable. A few forms, such as Parkinson's disease,[1] involve deterioration in subcortical brain regions (primitive structures below the cortex) that often extends to the cerebral cortex and, in many instances, results in brain abnormalities

---

[1]In Parkinson's disease, neurons in the part of the brain that controls muscle movements deteriorate. Symptoms include tremors, shuffling gait, loss of facial expression, rigidity of limbs, difficulty maintaining balance, and stooped posture.

resembling Alzheimer's disease (Gallardo, Schlüter, & Südhoff, 2008). But in the large majority of dementia cases, subcortical brain regions are intact, and progressive damage occurs only to the cerebral cortex. *Cortical dementia* comes in two varieties: Alzheimer's disease and cerebrovascular dementia.

■ ALZHEIMER'S DISEASE.

When Ruth took 79-year-old Ida to the ballet, an occasion the two sisters anticipated eagerly each year, she noticed a change in Ida's behavior. Ida, who had forgotten the engagement, reacted angrily when Ruth arrived unannounced at her door. Driving to the theater, which was in a familiar part of town, Ida got lost—all the while insisting that she knew the way perfectly well. As the lights dimmed and the music began, Ida talked loudly and dug noisily in her purse.

"Shhhhhh," responded a dozen voices from surrounding seats.

"It's just the music!" Ida snapped at full volume. "You can talk all you want until the dancing starts." Ruth was astonished and embarrassed at the behavior of her once socially sensitive sister.

Six months later, Ida was diagnosed with **Alzheimer's disease,** the most common form of dementia, in which structural and chemical brain deterioration is associated with gradual loss of many aspects of thought and behavior. Alzheimer's accounts for 60 percent of all dementia cases and, at older ages, for an even higher percentage. Approximately 8 to 10 percent of people over age 65—about 5.1 million Americans—have the disorder. Of those over age 85, close to 45 percent are affected. In 2030, when all baby boomers will have reached late adulthood, the number of Americans with Alzheimer's is expected to rise to 7.7 million—an increase of more than 50 percent. About 5 percent of all deaths among the elderly involve Alzheimer's, making it a significant cause of late-life mortality (Alzheimer's Association, 2009).

Symptoms and Course of the Disease. The earliest symptoms are often severe memory problems—forgetting names, dates, appointments, familiar routes of travel, or the need to turn off the kitchen stove. At first, recent memory is most impaired, but as serious disorientation sets in, recall of distant events and such basic facts as time, date, and place evaporates. Faulty judgment puts the person in danger. For example, Ida insisted on driving after she was no longer competent to do so. Personality changes occur—loss of spontaneity and sparkle, anxiety in response to uncertainties created by mental problems, aggressive outbursts, reduced initiative, and social withdrawal. Depression often appears in the early phase of Alzheimer's and in other forms of dementia and worsens (Yaari & Corey-Bloom, 2007; Zubenko et al., 2003).

As the disease progresses, skilled and purposeful movements disintegrate. When Ruth took Ida into her home, she had to help her dress, bathe, eat, brush her teeth, and (eventually) walk and use the bathroom. Ida's sleep was disrupted by delusions and imaginary fears. She often awoke in the night and banged on the wall, insisting that it was dinnertime, or cried out that someone was choking her. Over time, Ida lost the ability to comprehend and produce speech. And when her brain ceased to process information, she could no longer recognize objects and familiar people. In the final months, Ida became increasingly vulnerable to infections, lapsed into a coma, and died.

The course of Alzheimer's varies greatly, from a year to as long as 15 years. The average life expectancy for a 70-year-old man with the disease is about $4\frac{1}{2}$ years, for a 70-year-old woman about 8 years (Larson et al., 2004).

Brain Deterioration. A diagnosis of Alzheimer's disease is made through exclusion, after ruling out other causes of dementia by a physical examination and psychological testing—an approach that is more than 90 percent accurate. To confirm Alzheimer's, doctors inspect the brain after death for a set of abnormalities that either cause or result from the disease (Yaari & Corey-Bloom, 2007). In nearly 90 percent of cases, however,

Computer images compare a brain scan of an Alzheimer's patient (left) with one of a healthy older adult (right). The Alzheimer's brain is shrunken, due to massive degeneration and death of neurons. Activity and blood flow (marked by yellow and green coding in the right scan) are also greatly reduced in the Alzheimer's brain.

Alzheimer's Cells

Healthy Cells

An image of tissue in the Alzheimer's brain (left) reveals amyloid plaques between neurons, dead and dying neurons containing neurofibrillary tangles, and far fewer neurons and synapses than in the healthy brain (right).

brain-imaging techniques (MRI and PET), which yield three-dimensional pictures of brain volume and activity, predict whether elders who do not yet show symptoms will receive an after-death confirmation of Alzheimer's (Mosconi et al., 2007; Vitali et al., 2008).

Two major structural changes in the cerebral cortex, especially in memory and reasoning areas, are associated with Alzheimer's. Inside neurons, **neurofibrillary tangles** appear bundles of twisted threads that are the product of collapsed neural structures and that contain abnormal forms of a protein called *tau.* Outside neurons, **amyloid plaques,** dense deposits of a deteriorated protein called *amyloid,* surrounded by clumps of dead nerve and glial cells, develop. Although some neurofibrillary tangles and amyloid plaques are present in the brains of normal middle-aged and older people and increase with age, they are far more abundant in Alzheimer's victims.

Recent findings suggest that a major culprit in the disease is abnormal breakdown of amyloid within neurons and that plaques reflect the brain's effort to eject harmful amyloid from neurons (Cleary et al., 2005; National Institute on Aging, 2008). In both Alzheimer's disease and Parkinson's disease, disruptions occur in a key neuronal structure responsible for chopping up and disposing of abnormal proteins (Ding et al., 2004). These damaged proteins (including amyloid) build to toxic levels, causing cell damage and death.

A major thrust of current research is understanding exactly how amyloid damages neurons, so treatments can be developed to slow or block this process. Several studies suggest that amyloid causes synapses—tiny gaps between neurons essential for neuronal communication—to malfunction (Lacor et al., 2007). Amyloid also induces heightened, abnormal electrical activity throughout the brain, contributing to neural network malfunctioning (Palop et al., 2007). And new evidence suggests that abnormal tau in neurofibrillary tangles facilitates amyloid-induced damage (Roberson et al., 2007)

As synapses deteriorate, levels of neurotransmitters—vital for sustaining neuronal communication—decline, neurons die in massive numbers, and brain volume shrinks. Destruction of neurons that release the neurotransmitter acetylcholine, involved in transporting messages between distant brain regions, further disrupts neuronal networks. As a result, many complex functions, including perception, memory, reasoning, and judgment, are impaired. A drop in serotonin, a neurotransmitter that regulates arousal and mood, may contribute to sleep disturbances, aggressive outbursts, and depression (Lanctot et al., 2002; Mintzer, 2001).

Risk Factors. Alzheimer's disease comes in two types: *familial,* which runs in families, and *sporadic,* which has no obvious family history. Familial Alzheimer's generally has an early onset (before age 65) and progresses more rapidly than the later-appearing sporadic type. Researchers have identified genes on chromosomes 1, 14, and 21, involved in generation of harmful amyloid, that are linked to familial Alzheimer's. In each case, the abnormal gene is dominant; if it is present in only one of the pair of genes inherited from parents, the person will

develop early-onset Alzheimer's (Ertekin-Tanner, 2007; National Institute on Aging, 2008). Recall that chromosome 21 is involved in Down syndrome. Individuals with this chromosomal disorder who live past age 40 almost always have the brain abnormalities and symptoms of Alzheimer's.

Heredity plays a different role in sporadic Alzheimer's, through somatic mutation. About half of people with this form of the disease have an abnormal gene on chromosome 19, which results in excess levels of *ApoE4,* a blood protein that carries cholesterol throughout the body. Researchers believe that a high blood concentration of ApoE4 affects the expression of a gene involved in regulating insulin. Deficient insulin and resulting glucose buildup in the bloodstream (conditions that, when extreme, lead to diabetes) are linked to brain damage, especially in areas regulating memory, and to abnormally high buildup of amyloid in brain tissue (National Institute on Aging, 2008; Neuman et al., 2008). In line with these findings, elders with diabetes have a 65 percent increased risk of developing Alzheimer's (Arvanitakis et al., 2004).

At present, the abnormal ApoE4 gene is the most commonly known risk factor for sporadic Alzheimer's. Nevertheless, many sporadic Alzheimer's victims show no currently known genetic marker, and some individuals with the ApoE4 gene do not develop the disease. Evidence is increasing for the role of a variety of other factors, including excess dietary fat, physical inactivity, overweight and obesity, chronic psychological stress, cardiovascular disease, and stroke (Kivipelto et al., 2008; Pasinetti & Eberstein, 2008; Whitmer et al., 2007; Wilson et al., 2006). Head injury, by accelerating deterioration of amyloid, may also increase Alzheimer's risk, especially among people with the ApoE4 gene (Jellinger, 2004).

The high incidence of Alzheimer's and other forms of dementia among African-American elderly illustrates the complexity of potential causes. Compared with African Americans, Yoruba village dwellers of Nigeria show a much lower Alzheimer's incidence and no association between the ApoE4 gene and the disease (Gureje et al., 2006). Some investigators speculate that intermarriage with Caucasians heightened genetic risk among African Americans and that environmental factors translated that risk into reality (Hendrie, 2001). Whereas the Yoruba of Nigeria eat a low-fat diet, the African-American diet is high in fat. Eating fatty foods may increase the chances that the ApoE4 gene will lead to Alzheimer's. The more fat consumed and the higher the blood level of "bad" cholesterol (low-density lipoproteins), the greater the incidence of Alzheimer's (Hall et al., 2006).

Protective Factors. Researchers are testing both drug and nondrug approaches to preventing or slowing the progress of Alzheimer's. A variety of factors once thought to be protective—hormone therapy for women (see Chapter 15, page 401), vitamins B and E and folate supplements, and anti-inflammatory drugs—have yielded contrary findings (National Institute on Aging, 2005). But a "Mediterranean diet" emphasizing fish, unsaturated fat (olive oil), and moderate consumption of red wine is linked to a 13 percent reduced incidence of Alzheimer's disease and also to a reduction in cerebrovascular dementia (which we will turn to next) (Scarmeas et al., 2007; Sofi et al., 2008). These foods contain fatty acids and other substances that help maintain the cardiovascular system, and they also promote the health of neural structures.

Education and an active lifestyle are beneficial as well. The rate of Alzheimer's is reduced by more than half in elders with higher education, though this protective effect is not as great for those with the ApoE4 gene (Qiu et al., 2001; Seeman et al., 2005). Some researchers speculate that education leads to more synaptic connections, which act as a *cognitive reserve,* giving the aging brain greater tolerance for injury before it crosses the threshold into mental disability. In support of this view, compared to their less educated counterparts, highly educated elders show a faster rate of decline following an Alzheimer's diagnosis, suggesting that they show symptoms only after very advanced brain deterioration (Andel et al., 2006; Hall et al., 2007). Late-life engagement in social and leisure activities also reduces the risk of Alzheimer's and of dementia in general, perhaps by stimulating synaptic growth (Bennett et al., 2006; Verghese et al., 2003). Finally, persistence, intensity, and variety of physical activity are associated with decreased risk for Alzheimer's and cerebrovascular dementia, but again, benefits are reduced for elders with the ApoE4 gene (Larson et al., 2006; Podewils et al., 2005).

Helping Alzheimer's Victims and Their Caregivers. As Ida's Alzheimer's worsened, the doctor prescribed a mild sedative and an antidepressant to help control her behavior. Drugs that increase levels of the neurotransmitters acetylcholine and serotonin show promise in limiting challenging dementia symptoms—especially agitation and disruptive behaviors, which are particularly stressful for caregivers (National Institute on Aging, 2008).

But with no cure available, family interventions ensure the best adjustment possible for the Alzheimer's victim, spouse, and other relatives. Dementia caregivers devote substantially more time to caregiving and experience more stress than do people caring for elders with physical disabilities (Alzheimer's Association, 2009). They need assistance and encouragement from extended-family members, friends, and community agencies. The Social Issues box on the following page describes a variety of helpful interventions for family caregivers. In addition to these strategies, avoiding dramatic changes in living conditions, such as moving to a new location, rearranging furniture, or modifying daily routines, helps elders with Alzheimer's disease feel as secure as possible in a cognitive world that is disintegrating.

■ **CEREBROVASCULAR DEMENTIA.** In **cerebrovascular dementia,** a series of strokes leaves areas of dead brain cells, producing step-by-step degeneration of mental ability, with each step occurring abruptly after a stroke. About 20 percent of all cases of dementia in Western nations are cerebrovascular, and about 10 percent are due to a combination of Alzheimer's and repeated strokes (Knopman, 2006). Heredity indirectly affects cerebrovascular dementia, through high blood pressure,

In this Japanese rehabilitation center, staff provide care for elderly stroke patients. High intake of alcohol and salt, coupled with low intake of animal protein, increases the risk of stroke among the Japanese.

cardiovascular disease, and diabetes, each of which increases the risk of stroke. And environmental influences—including cigarette smoking, heavy alcohol use, high salt intake, very low dietary protein, obesity, inactivity, and psychological stress—also heighten stroke risk (Román, 2003).

Because of their susceptibility to cardiovascular disease, more men than women have cerebrovascular dementia by their late sixties. Women are not at great risk until after age 75 (Sachdev, Brodaty, & Looi, 1999). The disease also varies among countries. For example, deaths due to stroke are high in Japan. Although a low-fat diet reduces Japanese adults' risk of cardiovascular disease, high intake of alcohol and salt and a diet very low in animal protein increase the risk of stroke. As Japanese consumption of alcohol and salt declined and intake of meat rose in recent decades, rates of cerebrovascular dementia and stroke-caused deaths improved (Goldman & Takahashi, 1996; Jellinger, 2008).

Although Japan presents a unique, contradictory picture (there, cardiovascular disease is low, and stroke is high), in most cases cerebrovascular dementia is caused by atherosclerosis. Prevention is the only effective way to stop the disease. The incidence of cerebrovascular dementia has dropped in the last two decades, largely as a result of the decline in heart disease and more effective stroke prevention methods (Manton, Gu, & Ukraintseva, 2005; U.S. Department of Health and Human Services, 2009a).

■ **MISDIAGNOSED AND REVERSIBLE DEMENTIA.** Careful diagnosis of dementia is crucial because other disorders can be mistaken for it. And some forms of dementia can be treated and a few reversed.

Depression is the disorder most often misdiagnosed as dementia. The depressed (but not demented) older adult is likely to exaggerate his or her mental difficulties, whereas the demented person minimizes them and is not fully aware of cognitive declines. About 1 to 2 percent of people over age 65 are

SOCIAL ISSUES

Interventions for Caregivers of Elders with Dementia

Margaret, wife and caregiver of a 71-year-old Alzheimer's patient, sent a desperate plea to an advice columnist at her local newspaper: "My husband can't feed or bathe himself, or speak to anyone or ask for assistance. I must constantly anticipate his needs and try to meet them. Please help me. I'm at the end of my rope."

The effects of Alzheimer's disease are devastating not just to elderly victims but also to family members who provide care with little or no outside assistance. Caregiving under these conditions has been called the "36-hour day." Although the majority of home caregivers are middle-aged, an estimated 15 to 25 percent are elders caring for a spouse or an aging parent. One-third of them are in poor health themselves, yet the number of hours dedicated to caregiving increases with the age of the caregiver (Chappell et al., 2003; Family Caregiver Alliance, 2005). Family members who exceed their caregiving capacities suffer greatly in physical and mental health and are at risk for early mortality (Schultz & Beach, 1999; Sörensen & Pinquart, 2005).

Most communities offer interventions designed to support family caregivers, but these need to be expanded and made more cost-effective. Those that work best address multiple needs: knowledge, coping strategies, caregiving skills, and respite.

Knowledge

Virtually all interventions try to enhance knowledge about the disease, caregiving challenges, and available community assistance. Knowledge is usually delivered through classes, but websites with wide-ranging information on caregiving, and online message boards and chat rooms through which caregivers can share information, also exist. Gains in knowledge, however, must be combined with other approaches to improve caregivers' well-being.

Coping Strategies

Many interventions teach caregivers everyday problem-solving strategies for managing the dependent elder's behavior, along with techniques for dealing with their own negative thoughts and feelings, such as resentment about having to provide constant care. Modes of delivery include support groups, individual therapy, and "coping with frustration" classes. All yield improvements in caregivers' adjustment and in patients' disturbing behaviors, both immediately and in follow-ups more than a year later (Selwood et al., 2007). Individual approaches are most effective because assistance can be tailored to the specific situation.

Caregiving Skills

Caregivers benefit from lessons in how to communicate with elders who can no longer express thoughts and emotions clearly and handle everyday tasks—for example, speaking slowly, with short, simple words; using gestures to reinforce meaning; waiting patiently for a response; refraining from interrupting, correcting, and criticizing; and introducing pleasant activities, such as music and slow-paced children's TV programs, that relieve agitation (Alzheimer's Association, 2005). Interventions that teach communication skills through active practice reduce elders' troublesome behavior and, as a result, lessen caregivers' distress and boost their sense of self-efficacy (Done & Thomas, 2001; Irvine, Ary, & Bourgeois, 2003).

Respite

Although caregivers usually say that *respite*— time away from providing care—is the assistance they most desire, they may be reluctant to use available services, such as adult day care or temporary placement in a care facility, because of cost, worries about the elder's adjustment, and guilt. Yet respite at least twice a week for several hours improves physical and mental health by permitting caregivers to maintain friendships, engage in enjoyable activities, and sustain a balanced life (Jeon, Brodaty, & Chesterson, 2005; Lund, Wright, & Caserta, 2005).

Multifaceted Interventions

Multifaceted interventions that are tailored to caregivers' individual needs make a substan-

This daughter cares for her father, who has Alzheimer's disease. Although the task has compensating rewards, it is physically demanding and emotionally draining. A great need exists for interventions that support caregivers.

tial difference in caregivers' lives. The Resources for Enhancing Alzheimer's Caregiver Health (REACH) initiative is an evaluation of nine "active" intervention programs, each including some or all of the ingredients just described, versus five "passive" interventions providing only information and referral to community agencies. Among more than 1,200 participating caregivers, those receiving six months of active intervention declined more in self-reported burden. And one program providing family therapy in the home— through a telephone system facilitating frequent communication among therapist, caregiver, family members, and other support systems—substantially reduced caregiver depressive symptoms (Gitlin et al., 2003; Schultz et al., 2003). Caregivers with greater care responsibility—women versus men, lower-SES versus higher-SES, spouses versus non-spouses—benefited most. In an additional evaluation with more than 600 participants, REACH active intervention programs enhanced quality of life among caregivers of diverse ethnicities—African-American, Caucasian, and Hispanic (Belle et al., 2006).

---

severely depressed, and another 2 percent are moderately depressed—rates lower than those for young and middle-aged adults (Nordhus, 2008). As we will see in Chapter 18, however, depression rises with age. It is often related to physical illness and pain and can lead to cognitive deterioration. However, U.S. older adults often do not receive the mental health services they need—partly because Medicare offers reduced coverage for treating mental health problems and partly because doctors rarely refer elders to mental health specialists (Knight et al., 2006). These circumstances increase the chances that depression will deepen and be confused with dementia.

The older we get, the more likely we are to be taking drugs that may have side effects resembling dementia. For example, some medications for coughs, diarrhea, and nausea inhibit the neurotransmitter acetylcholine, leading to Alzheimer's-like symptoms. In addition, some diseases can cause temporary memory loss and mental symptoms (Fong, Tulevaev, & Inouye, 2009). Treatment of the underlying illness relieves the problem. Finally, environmental changes and social isolation can trigger mental declines (Maynard, 2003). When supportive ties are restored, cognitive functioning usually bounces back.

Health Care

Health-care professionals and lawmakers in industrialized nations worry about the economic consequences of rapid increase in the elderly population. Rising government-supported health-care costs and demand for certain health-care services, particularly long-term care, are of greatest concern.

■ COST OF HEALTH CARE FOR THE ELDERLY.

Adults age 65 and older make up just under 13 percent of the North American population but account for over 40 percent of U.S. government health-care expenditures in the United States (U.S. Department of Health and Human Services, 2008g). According to current estimates, the cost of government-sponsored health insurance, or Medicare, for the elderly will double by 2025 and nearly triple by 2050, outpacing growth of the overall economy as the baby boom generation enters late adulthood and average life expectancy extends further (Social Security and Medicare Board of Trustees, 2009).

Because U.S. Medicare funds only about half of older adults' medical needs, American elders devote nearly 13 percent of their annual expenditures to health care—several times the proportion spent by older adults in other industrialized nations (OECD, 2008b; U.S. Department of Labor, 2008). And Medicare provides far less support for long-term care than elders with severe disabilities need.

■ LONG-TERM CARE.

When Ida moved into Ruth's home, Ruth promised never to place Ida in an institution. But as Ida's condition worsened and Ruth faced health problems of her own, she couldn't keep her word. Reluctantly, Ruth placed her in a nursing home.

Advancing age is strongly associated with use of long-term care services, especially nursing homes. Nearly half of U.S. nursing home residents are age 85 and older (U.S. Department of Health and Human Services, 2004). Among disorders of aging, dementia—especially Alzheimer's disease—most often leads to nursing home placement, followed by arthritis, hip fracture, and stroke (Agüero-Torres et al., 2001).

Overall, only 5 percent of Americans age 65 and older are institutionalized, about half the rate in other industrialized nations, such as the Netherlands and Sweden, which provide more

generous public financing of institutional care (OECD, 2008b). Unless nursing home placement follows hospitalization for an acute illness, older adults must pay for it until their resources are exhausted. At that point, Medicaid (health insurance for the poor) takes over. Consequently, the largest users of nursing homes in the United States are people with either very low or high incomes. Middle-income elderly and their families are more likely to try to protect their savings from being drained by high nursing home costs.

Nursing home use also varies across ethnic groups. For example, Caucasian Americans are nearly twice as likely as African Americans to be institutionalized. African-American older adults are more likely to have large, close-knit extended families. As a result, over 70 percent do not live alone, and over one-third reside with their adult children. Similarly, Asian, Hispanic, and Native-American elders use nursing homes less often than Caucasian Americans because of families' strong sense of caregiving responsibility (Yaffe et al., 2002). Overall, families provide at least 60 to 80 percent of all long-term care in Australia, Canada, New Zealand, the United States, and Western Europe.

To reduce institutionalized care of the elderly and its associated high cost, experts advocate alternatives, such as publicly funded in-home help for family caregivers (see Chapter 16, page 434). Another option rapidly becoming more widely available is **assisted living**—a homelike housing arrangement for seniors who require more care than can be provided at home but less than is usually provided in nursing homes. Assisted living is a cost-effective alternative to nursing homes that prevents unnecessary institutionalization (Stone & Reinhard, 2007). It also can enhance residents' autonomy, social life,

© MITCH WOJNAROWICZ/AMSTERDAM RECORDER/THE IMAGE WORKS

Nursing home residents exercise together in physical therapy. Unless nursing home placement follows hospitalization for an acute illness, U.S. Medicare does not cover it. Hence, American elders with severe disabilities must pay nursing home costs until their resources are exhausted.

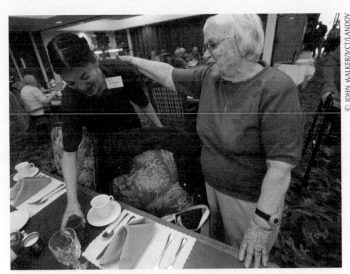

A resident greets a server in the dining room of an assisted living facility. This homelike environment enhances older adults' autonomy, social life, community involvement, and life satisfaction.

community involvement, and life satisfaction—benefits that we will take up in Chapter 18.

In Denmark, the combination of a government-sponsored home-helper system and expansion of assisted-living housing resulted in a 30 percent reduction in the need for nursing home beds over a 15-year period. At the same time, the Danish government saved money: Public expenditures for long-term care declined by 8 percent (Hastrup, 2007; Stuart & Weinrich, 2001).

When nursing home placement is necessary, steps can be taken to improve its quality. For example, the Netherlands has established separate facilities designed to meet the different needs of patients with mental and physical disabilities. Institutionalized elderly—like older people everywhere—desire a sense of personal control, gratifying social relationships, and meaningful and enjoyable daily activities (Alkema, Wilber, & Enguidanos, 2007). As Chapter 18 will reveal, designing nursing homes to meet these needs promotes both physical and psychological well-being.

ASK YOURSELF

>> **REVIEW**
Cite evidence that both genetic and environmental factors contribute to Alzheimer's disease and cerebrovascular dementia.

>> **APPLY**
Marissa complained to a counselor that at age 68, her husband, Wendell, no longer initiated sex or cuddled her. Why might Wendell have ceased to interact sexually? What interventions—both medical and educational—could be helpful to Marissa and Wendell?

>> **REFLECT**
What care and living arrangements have been made for elders needing assistance in your family? How did culture, personal values, financial means, health, and other factors influence those decisions?

Cognitive Development

Ruth's complaints to her doctor about difficulties with memory and verbal expression reflect common concerns about cognitive functioning in late adulthood. Decline in speed of processing, under way throughout the adult years, is believed to affect many aspects of cognition in old age. In Chapter 15, we noted that reduced efficiency of thinking compromises attention, amount of information that can be held in working memory, use of memory strategies, and retrieval from long-term memory. These decrements continue in the final decades of life.

TAKE A MOMENT... Return to Figure 15.3 on page 410, and note that the more a mental ability depends on fluid intelligence (biologically based information-processing skills), the earlier it starts to decline. In contrast, mental abilities that rely on crystallized intelligence (culturally based knowledge) are sustained longer. But maintenance of crystallized intelligence depends on continued opportunities to enhance cognitive skills. When these are available, crystallized abilities—general information and expertise in specific endeavors—can offset losses in fluid intelligence.

Look again at Figure 15.3. In advanced old age, decrements in fluid intelligence limit what people can accomplish even with cultural supports, including a rich background of experience, knowledge of how to remember and solve problems, and a stimulating daily life (Berg & Sternberg, 2003; Kaufman, 2001). Consequently, crystallized intelligence shows a modest decline.

Overall, loss outweighs improvement and maintenance as people approach the end of life, but plasticity is still possible (Baltes & Smith, 2003). Research reveals greater individual variation in cognitive functioning in late adulthood than at any other time of life (Hultsch, MacDonald, & Dixon, 2002; Riediger et al., 2006). Besides fuller expression of genetic and lifestyle influences, increased freedom to pursue self-chosen courses of action—some that enhance and others that undermine cognitive skills—may be responsible.

How can older adults make the most of their cognitive resources? According to one view, elders who sustain high levels of functioning engage in **selective optimization with compensation:** Narrowing their goals, they *select* personally valued activities to *optimize* (or maximize) returns from their diminishing energy. They also find new ways to *compensate* for losses (Baltes, 1997; Freund & Baltes, 2000). When 80-year-old concert pianist Arthur Rubinstein was asked how he managed to sustain such extraordinary piano playing at his advanced age, he described being *selective;* he played fewer pieces. This enabled him to *optimize* his energy; he could practice each piece more. He also developed new, *compensatory* techniques for decline in playing speed. For example, before a fast passage, he played extra slowly, so the fast section appeared to his audience to move more quickly.

In late adulthood, personal goals—while still including gains—increasingly focus on maintaining abilities and preventing losses (Freund & Ebner, 2005). In one study, researchers

Elders can sustain high levels of functioning through selective optimization with compensation. This retired theater teacher has done so by creating a studio at home where he focuses on composing music.

asked people to rate their most important physical and cognitive goals for emphasis on growth ("With this goal, I want to improve something or achieve something new") and maintenance/prevention of losses ("With this goal, I want to maintain something or prevent a loss"). As Figure 17.5 shows, compared

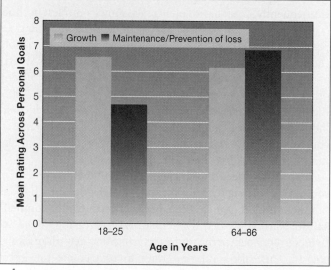

■ **FIGURE 17.5** ■ **Personal goal orientation toward growth and maintenance/prevention of loss in young and older adults.** Participants were asked to list two physical and two cognitive goals and then to rate each for emphasis on growth and on maintenance or prevention of loss, using an 8-point scale. Elders—while continuing to pursue growth—placed much greater emphasis on maintenance and loss prevention than did young adults. (From N. C. Ebner, A. M. Freund, & P. B. Baltes, 2006, "Developmental Changes in Personal Goal Orientation from Young to Late Adulthood: From Striving for Gains to Maintenance and Prevention of Losses," *Psychology and Aging, 21,* p. 671. Adapted by permission of American Psychological Association.)

with young adults, older adults accentuated maintenance and loss prevention (Ebner, Freund, & Baltes, 2006). Additional evidence revealed that the high-energy demands of growth goals induced this shift toward balancing losses—an orientation that predicted elders' psychological well-being.

As we review major changes in memory, language processing, and problem solving, we will consider ways that older adults optimize and compensate in the face of declines. We will also see that certain abilities that depend on extensive life experience, not processing efficiency, are sustained or increase in old age.

Memory

As older adults take in information more slowly and find it harder to apply strategies, inhibit irrelevant information, and retrieve relevant knowledge from long-term memory, the chances of memory failure increase (Luo & Craik, 2008; Old & Naveh-Benjamin, 2008b). A reduced capacity to hold material in working memory while operating on it means that memory problems are especially evident on complex tasks.

Deliberate versus Automatic Memory

"Ruth, you know that movie we saw—the one with the little 5-year-old boy who did such a wonderful acting job. What was it called?" asked Walt.

"I can't think of it, Walt. Which theater was it at? Who'd we go with? Tell me more about the little boy—maybe it'll come to me."

Although we all occasionally have memory failures like this, difficulties with recall rise in old age. When Ruth and Walt watched the movie, their slower cognitive processing meant that they retained fewer details. And because their working memories could hold less at once, they attended poorly to *context*—where they saw the movie and who went with them (Wegesin et al., 2000; Zacks & Hasher, 2006). When we try to remember, context serves as an important retrieval cue.

These memory difficulties mean that elders sometimes cannot distinguish an experienced event from one they imagined (Rybash & Hrubi-Bopp, 2000). They also have difficulty remembering the source of information—which member of their bridge club made a certain statement, in what magazine they read about a particular news event, and to whom and on which occasion they previously told a certain joke or story (Simons et al., 2004). Temporal memory—recall of the order in which events occurred or how recently they happened—suffers as well (Dumas & Hartman, 2003; Hartman & Warren, 2005).

A few days later, when Ruth saw an ad for the movie on TV, she recognized its title immediately. Recognition—a fairly automatic type of memory that demands little mental effort—suffers less than recall in late adulthood because a multitude of environmental supports for remembering are present (Hoyer & Verhagen, 2006).

Consider another automatic form of memory: **implicit memory,** or memory without conscious awareness. In a typical implicit memory task, you would be shown a list of words, then asked to fill in a word fragment (such as $t - - k$). You would probably complete the sequence with a word you had just seen (*task*) rather than another word (*took* or *teak*). Without trying to do so, you would engage in recall.

Age differences in implicit memory are much smaller than in explicit, or deliberate, memory. Memory that depends on familiarity rather than on conscious use of strategies is largely spared in old age (Fleischman et al., 2004; Hudson, 2008). The memory problems elders report—for names of people, places where they put important objects, directions for getting from one place to another, and (as we will see) appointments and medication schedules—all place substantial demands on their more limited working memories.

Associative Memory

The memory deficits just described are part of a general, age-related decline in binding information into complex memories. Researchers call this an **associative memory deficit,** or difficulty creating and retrieving links between pieces of information—for example, two items or an item and its context, such as Ruth's attempt to remember the name of the movie with the child actor or where she had seen the movie.

To find out whether older adults have greater difficulty with associative memory than younger adults, researchers showed them pairs of unrelated words or pictures of objects (such as *table–overcoat* or *sandwich–radio*) and asked that they study the pairs for an upcoming memory test. During the test, one group of participants was given a page of *single items,* some that had appeared in the study phase and some that had not, and asked to circle the ones they had studied. The other group was given a page of *item pairs,* some intact from the study phase (*table–overcoat*) and some that had been rearranged (*overcoat–radio*), and asked to circle pairs they had studied. Older adults did almost as well as younger adults on the single-item memory test. But they performed far worse on the item-pair test—findings that support an associative memory deficit (Naveh-Benjamin, 2000; Naveh-Benjamin et al., 2003).

Providing older adults with repeated presentations of information to be learned and more memory cues improves their associative memory (Naveh-Benjamin et al., 2003; Simons et al., 2004). For example, to associate names with faces, elders profit from mention of relevant facts about those individuals. When older adults are directed to use the memory strategy of *elaboration* (relating word pairs by generating a sentence linking them) during both study and retrieval, the young–old difference in memory nearly disappears (Naveh-Benjamin, Brav, & Levy, 2007). Clearly, elders' associative deficits are greatly affected by lack of spontaneous use of strategies that help bind information into integrated wholes.

Remote Memory

Although older people often say that their **remote memory,** or very long-term recall, is clearer than their memory for recent events, research does not support this conclusion.

For example, to assess autobiographical memory, researchers typically give a series of words (such as *book, machine, sorry, surprised*) and ask adults to report a personal memory cued by each. Or they present participants with a time line on a piece of paper, representing birth to present age, and ask them to place important life events on the line and note the age at which each occurred. People between ages 50 and 90 recall both remote and recent events more frequently than intermediate events, with recent events mentioned most often in the word-cue studies (see Figure 17.6). Among remote events recalled using either word-cue or time-line procedures, most happened between ages 10 and 30 (Rubin, 2002; Rubin & Schulkind, 1997; Schroots, van Dijkum, & Assink, 2004).

Why do older adults recall youthful events? Adolescence and early adulthood are times of rapid life change and identity development, when many personally significant experiences occur. Even public events linked to this period—World Series champions, Academy Award winners, and current events—are especially salient to elders (Rubin, Rahhal, & Poon, 1998).

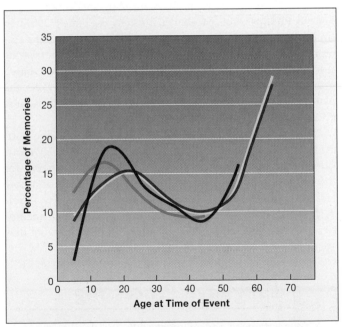

■ FIGURE 17.6 ■ Distribution of older adults' autobiographical memories by reported age at time of the event. In the four studies of 50- to 90-year-olds represented here, later events were remembered better than early events. Among early events, most of those recalled occurred between ages 10 and 30. (Adapted from D. C. Rubin, T. A. Rahhal, & L. W. Poon, 1998, "Things Learned in Early Adulthood Are Remembered Best," *Memory and Cognition, 26,* p. 4. Copyright © 1998 by the Psychonomic Society, Inc. Adapted by permission.)

Nevertheless, older adults recall recent personal experiences more readily than remote ones, probably because of interference produced by years of additional experience (Kausler, 1994). As we accumulate more memories, some inevitably resemble others. As a result, certain early memories become less clear than they once were.

Prospective Memory

So far, we have considered various aspects of *retrospective memory* (remembrance of things past). **Prospective memory** refers to remembering to engage in planned actions in the future. Because Ruth and Walt knew they were more likely to forget an appointment, they would ask about it repeatedly. "Sybil, what time is our dinner engagement?" Walt asked several times during the two days before the event. The amount of mental effort required determines whether older adults have trouble with prospective memory. Remembering the dinner date was challenging for Walt because he typically ate dinner with his daughter on Thursday evenings at 6 P.M., but this time, dinner was set for Tuesday at 7:15 P.M.

In the laboratory, older adults do better on *event-based* than on *time-based* prospective memory tasks. In an event-based task, an event (such as a certain word appearing on a computer screen) serves as a cue for remembering to do something (pressing a key) while the participant engages in an ongoing activity (reading paragraphs) (Einstein et al., 2000; Kliegel, Jäger, & Phillips, 2008; McDaniel, Einstein, & Rendell, 2007). In time-based tasks, the adult must engage in an action after a certain time interval has elapsed, without any obvious external cue (for example, pressing a key every 10 minutes). Time-based prospective memory requires considerable initiative to keep the planned action in mind, and declines in late adulthood are large (West & Craik, 1999).

But difficulties with prospective memory seen in the laboratory do not appear in real life, where adults are highly motivated to remember and good at setting up reminders for themselves, such as a buzzer ringing in the kitchen or a note tacked up prominently (Henry et al., 2004). In this way, the elderly compensate for their reduced-capacity working memories and the challenge of dividing attention between what they are doing now and what they must do in the future.

Language Processing

Language and memory skills are closely related. In language comprehension (understanding the meaning of spoken or written prose), we recollect what we have heard or read without conscious awareness. Like implicit memory, language comprehension changes very little in late life, as long as conversational partners do not speak too quickly and elders are given enough time to process written text accurately (Stine-Morrow et al., 2008; Thornton & Light, 2006). Successful older readers make a variety of adjustments to ensure comprehension, such as attending more closely to features of text prose, pausing more

Older adults compensate for their language-production problems: They speak more slowly, simplify their grammatical structures, and represent information in terms of gist rather than details. These strategies enable them to extract the essence of a message and enrich it with personal interpretations.

often to integrate information, and making good use of story organization to help them recall both main ideas and details.

Two aspects of language production do show age-related losses. The first is retrieving words from long-term memory (Connor et al., 2004). When conversing with others, Ruth and Walt sometimes had trouble finding the right words to convey their thoughts—even well-known words they had used many times in the past. Consequently, their speech contained more pronouns and other unclear references than it did at younger ages. They also spoke more slowly and paused more often, partly because they needed time to search their memories for certain words. And compared to younger people, they more often reported a *tip-of-the-tongue state*—certainty that they knew a word accompanied by an inability to produce it (Burke & Shafto, 2004).

Second, planning what to say and how to say it is harder in late adulthood. As a result, Walt and Ruth displayed slightly more hesitations, false starts, word repetitions, and sentence fragments as they aged (Bortfeld et al., 2001). Their statements were also less well-organized than before (Kemper, Kynette, & Norman, 1992).

As with memory, older adults develop compensatory techniques for their language production problems. For example, they speak more slowly and simplify their grammatical structures so they can devote more effort to retrieving words and organizing their thoughts. Sacrificing efficiency for greater clarity, they use more sentences to convey their message (Griffin & Spieler, 2006; Kemper, Thompson, & Marquis, 2001). As elders monitor their word-retrieval failures and try hard to overcome them, they show a greater frequency of tip-of-the-tongue states—but they resolve tip-of-the-tongues at a higher rate than do younger people (Schwartz & Frazier, 2005).

Problem Solving

Problem solving is yet another cognitive skill that illustrates how aging brings not only deterioration but also adaptive changes. Problem solving in the laboratory declines in late adulthood (Finucane et al., 2005). Older adults' memory limitations make it hard to keep all relevant facts in mind when dealing with a complex hypothetical problem.

Yet the everyday problems the elderly encounter differ from hypothetical problems devised by researchers—and also from the problems they experienced at earlier ages. After retirement, older adults do not have to deal with workplace problems. Their children are typically grown and living on their own, and their marriages have endured long enough to have fewer difficulties (Berg et al., 1998). With age, major concerns involve dealing with extended-family relationships (for example, expectations of adult children that they babysit grandchildren) and managing IADLs, such as preparing nutritious meals, handling finances, and attending to health concerns.

As long as they perceive problems as under their control and as important, elders are active and effective in solving problems of everyday life (Artistico, Cervone, & Pezzuti, 2003; Berg, 2008). The health arena, especially salient for elders, illustrates the adaptiveness of everyday problem solving. Older adults make faster decisions about whether they are ill, seek medical care sooner, and select treatments more quickly. In contrast, young and middle-aged adults are more likely to adopt a "wait and see" approach in favor of gathering more facts, even when the health problem is serious (Leventhal et al., 1993; Meyer, Russo, & Talbot, 1995). This swift response of the elderly is interesting in view of their slower cognitive processing. Research reveals that they have accumulated more health-related knowledge, which enables them to move ahead with greater certainty (Meyer, Talbot, & Ranalli, 2007). Acting decisively when faced with health risks is sensible in old age.

Finally, older adults report that they often consult others—generally spouses and adult children but also friends, neighbors, and members of their religious congregation—for advice about everyday problems (Strough et al., 2003). And compared with younger married couples, older married couples more often collaborate in problem solving, using highly effective strategies (Meegan & Berg, 2002). In jointly solving problems, elders seem to compensate for moments of cognitive difficulty.

Wisdom

A wealth of life experience underlies another capacity, believed to reach its height in old age: **wisdom.** When researchers ask people to describe wisdom, most mention breadth and depth of practical knowledge, ability to reflect on and apply that knowledge in ways that make life more bearable and worthwhile; emotional maturity, including the ability to listen, evaluate, and give advice; and altruistic creativity that contributes to humanity and enriches others' lives. One group of researchers summed up the multiple cognitive and personality traits that make up wisdom as "expertise in the conduct and meaning of life" (Baltes & Staudinger, 2000, p. 124; Baltes & Smith, 2008; Staudinger, Dörner, & Mickler, 2005).

During her college years, Ruth and Walt's granddaughter Marci telephoned with a pressing personal dilemma. Ruth's advice reflected the features of wisdom just mentioned. After her boyfriend Ken moved to another city to attend medical school, Marci, unsure whether her love for Ken would endure, had begun dating another student. "I can't stand being pulled in two directions," she exclaimed. "I'm thinking of calling Ken and telling him about Steve. Do you think I should?"

"This is not a good time, Marci," Ruth advised. "You'll break Ken's heart before you've had a chance to size up your feelings for Steve. And you said Ken's taking some important exams in two weeks. If you tell him now and he's distraught, it could affect the rest of his life."

Wisdom—whether applied to personal problems or to community, national, and international concerns requires the "pinnacle of insight into the human condition" (Baltes & Staudinger, 2000; Birren, 2009). Not surprisingly, cultures around the world assume that age and wisdom go together. In village and tribal societies, the most important social positions, such as chieftain and shaman (religious leader), are reserved for the old. Similarly, in industrialized nations, older adults are chief executive officers of large corporations, high-level religious leaders, members of legislatures, and supreme court justices. According to an evolutionary view, the genetic program of our species grants health, fitness, and strength to the young. Culture tames this youthful advantage in physical power with the insights of the old, ensuring balance and interdependence between generations (Assmann, 1994; Csikszentmihalyi & Rathunde, 1990).

© NAJLAH FEANNY/CORBIS SABA

Beaming as she hosts the annual conference for the Children's Defense Fund, Maya Angelou—revered author, teacher, and activist—exemplifies wisdom. She embodies the altruistic form of creativity that involves contributing to humanity and enriching others' lives. Her work on behalf of women and African Americans has continuously challenged sexism and racism.

In the most extensive research to date on development of wisdom, adults ranging in age from 20 to 89 responded to uncertain real-life situations—for example, what to consider and do if a good friend is about to commit suicide or if, after reflecting on your life, you discover that you have not achieved your goals (Staudinger, Dörner, & Mickler, 2005). Responses were rated for five ingredients of wisdom:

- Knowledge about fundamental concerns of life, including human nature, social relations, and emotions

- Effective strategies for applying that knowledge to making life decisions, handling conflict, and giving advice

- A view of people that considers the multiple demands of their life contexts

- A concern with ultimate human values, such as the common good, as well as respect for individual differences in values

- Awareness and management of the uncertainties of life—that many problems have no perfect solution

Results revealed that age is no guarantee of wisdom. A small number of adults of diverse ages ranked among the wise. But type of life experience made a difference. People in human-service careers who had extensive training and practice in grappling with human problems tended to attain high wisdom scores. Other high-scorers held leadership positions (Staudinger, Smith, & Baltes, 1992; Staudinger, 1996). And when age and relevant life experiences were considered together, more older than younger people scored in the top 20 percent.

In addition to age and life experience, having faced and overcome adversity appears to contribute to late-life wisdom (Brugman, 2006; Linley, 2003). In a longitudinal study of people who were young adults during the Great Depression of the 1930s, those who experienced economic hardship and surmounted it scored especially high in wisdom nearly 40 years later, as indicated by thoughtful interview responses about life events, insights into their own motives and behavior, and warmth and compassion (Ardelt, 1998).

Compared to their agemates, older adults with the cognitive, reflective, and emotional qualities that make up wisdom are better educated and physically healthier, forge more positive relations with others, and score higher on the personality dimension of openness to experience (Kramer, 2003). Wisdom is also a strong predictor of psychological well-being (Peterson & Seligman, 2004). Wise elders seem to flourish, even when faced with physical and cognitive challenges. This suggests that finding ways to promote wisdom would be a powerful means of both contributing to human welfare and fostering a gratifying old age.

Factors Related to Cognitive Change

A mentally active life—above-average education; frequent, supportive contact with family members and friends; stimulating leisure pursuits; community participation; and a flexible personality—predicts maintenance of mental abilities into advanced old age (Hughes et al., 2008; Schaie, 2005). Today's elders in industrialized nations are better educated than any previous generation. Since 1950, the rate of high school completion among U.S. adults age 65 and older has quadrupled, reaching 76 percent. Those with at least a bachelor's degree have increased more than fivefold, to 19 percent (National Institute on Aging, 2008). As the baby boomers enter late adulthood, these trends are expected to continue, forecasting improved preservation of cognitive functions.

As noted earlier, health status powerfully predicts elders' intellectual performance. A wide variety of chronic conditions, including vision and hearing impairments, cardiovascular disease, diabetes, osteoporosis, and arthritis, are strongly associated with cognitive declines (Anstey & Christensen, 2000; Baltes, Lindenberger, & Staudinger, 2006). But we must be cautious in interpreting this link between physical and cognitive deterioration, which may be exaggerated by the fact that brighter adults are more likely to engage in health-protective behaviors.

Retirement also affects cognitive change, both positively and negatively. When people leave routine jobs for stimulating leisure activities, outcomes are favorable. In contrast, retiring from a highly complex job without developing challenging substitutes accelerates intellectual declines (Schaie, 1996). In fact, complex, challenging work in late adulthood has an even stronger, facilitating impact on intellectual functioning than in middle adulthood (see page 415 in Chapter 15) (Schooler, Mulatu, & Oates, 1999).

As elders grow older, their scores on cognitive tasks show larger fluctuations from one occasion to the next. This rising instability of performance—especially in speed of response—accelerates in the seventies and is associated with cognitive declines. Researchers speculate that it signals end-of-life degeneration in wide-ranging areas of the brain (Hultsch, MacDonald, & Dixon, 2002; McDonald, Hultsch, & Dixon, 2003).

Terminal decline refers to marked acceleration in deterioration of cognitive functioning prior to death. Some longitudinal studies indicate that it is limited to a few aspects of intelligence, others that it occurs generally, across many abilities. Findings also differ greatly in its estimated length. Some report that it lasts only 1 to 3 years, others that it extends for as long as 14 years. The average is 4 to 5 years (Hassing et al., 2002; Lövdén et al., 2005; Rabbitt, Lunn, & Wong, 2008; Wilson et al., 2003). In one investigation, a sharp drop in life satisfaction predicted mortality. The downturn appeared, on average, four years in advance of death, was especially steep in people age 85 and older, and showed only a weak relationship to mental deterioration or chronic illnesses (Gerstorf et al., 2008).

Perhaps different kinds of terminal decline exist—one type arising from disease processes, another as part of a general biological breakdown due to normal aging. What we know for sure is that an extended, steep falloff in cognitive performance or in emotional investment in life is a sign of loss of vitality and impending death.

Cognitive Interventions

For most of late adulthood, cognitive declines are gradual. Although aging of the brain contributes to them, recall from our earlier discussion that the brain can compensate by growing new neural fibers. Furthermore, some cognitive decrements may be due to disuse of particular skills rather than biological aging. If plasticity of development is possible in old age, then interventions that train the elderly in cognitive strategies should at least partially reverse the age-related declines we have discussed.

The Adult Development and Enrichment Project (ADEPT) is the most extensive cognitive intervention program conducted to date. By using participants in the Seattle Longitudinal Study (see Chapter 15, page 409), researchers were able to do what no other investigation has done: assess the effects of cognitive training on long-term development (Schaie, 2005).

Intervention began with adults over age 64, some of whom had maintained their scores on two mental abilities (inductive reasoning and spatial orientation) over the previous 14 years and others who had shown declines. After just five one-hour training sessions in one of two types of mental test items, two-thirds of participants improved their performance on the trained skill. Gains for decliners were dramatic. Forty percent returned to the level at which they had been functioning 14 years earlier! A follow-up after 7 years revealed that although scores dropped somewhat, elders remained advantaged in their trained skill over agemates trained in the other ability. Finally, "booster" training at this time led to further gains, although these were smaller than the earlier gains.

In another large-scale intervention study called ACTIVE (Advanced Cognitive Training for Independent and Vital Elderly), more than 2,800 65- to 84-year-olds were randomly assigned to a ten-session training program focusing on one of three abilities—speed of processing, memory, or reasoning—or to a no-intervention control group. Again, trained elders showed an immediate advantage in the trained skill over controls that was still evident—though smaller in magnitude—at one- and two-year follow-ups (Ball et al., 2002). Five years after intervention, cognitive training was associated with reduced declines in general health and ability to engage in social and leisure pursuits—outcomes that were strongest for the speed-of-processing group (Wolinsky et al., 2006). The investigators speculated that speed-of-processing training induces a broad pattern of brain activation, affecting many regions.

Clearly, many cognitive skills can be enhanced in old age. A vital goal is to transfer intervention from the laboratory to the community, weaving it into the daily experiences of elderly people.

Lifelong Learning

The competencies that older adults need to live in our complex, changing world are the same as those of younger people—communicating effectively through spoken and written systems; locating information, sorting through it, and selecting what is needed; using math strategies, such as estimation; planning and organizing activities, including making good use of time and resources; mastering new technologies; and understanding past and current events and the relevance of each to their own lives. The elderly also need to develop new, problem-centered coping strategies—ways to sustain health and operate their households efficiently and safely—and updated vocational skills, for those who continue to work.

Participation of the elderly in continuing education has increased substantially over the past few decades. Elderhostel programs and their Canadian counterpart, Routes to Learning, attract over a quarter million North American older adults annually. Local educational institutions serve as hosts, combining stimulating one- to three-week courses with recreational pursuits. Some programs make use of community resources through classes on local ecology or folk life. Others involve travel abroad. Still others focus on innovative topics and experiences—writing one's own life story, discussing contemporary films with screenwriters, whitewater rafting, Chinese painting and calligraphy, and acquiring French language skills.

Other similar educational programs have sprung up in North America and elsewhere. The Bernard Osher Foundation collaborates with more than 120 U.S. universities to establish Osher Lifelong Learning Institutes on campuses. Each offers older adults a wide array of stimulating learning experiences, from auditing regular courses, to forming learning communities that address common interests, to helping to solve community problems. Participants in these programs tend to be active, well-educated, and financially well-off (Abraham, 1998). Much less is available for elders with little education and limited income. Community senior centers with inexpensive offerings related to everyday living attract more low-SES people than programs such as Elderhostel. Regardless of course content and which seniors attend, using the techniques summarized in

© JEFF GREENBERG/PHOTOEDIT

Elderhostel programs, like this class on U.S. folk cultures, respond to older adults' intense desire to learn. Besides acquiring new knowledge and skills, participants often make new friends and abandon stereotypes of aging as they see that they can still engage in complex learning.

Applying What We Know

Increasing the Effectiveness of Instruction for Older Adults

Technique	Description
Provide a positive learning environment.	Some elders have internalized negative stereotypes of their abilities and come to the learning environment with low self-esteem. A supportive group atmosphere, in which the instructor acts as a colleague, helps convince older adults that they can learn.
Allow ample time to learn new information.	Rate of learning varies widely among older adults, and some master new material at a fairly slow rate. Presenting information over several sessions or allowing for self-paced instruction aids mastery.
Present information in a well-organized fashion.	Older adults do not organize information as effectively as younger adults. Material that is outlined, presented, and then summarized enhances memory and understanding. Digressions make a presentation harder to comprehend.
Relate information to elders' experiences.	Relating new material to what elders have already learned, by drawing on their experiences and giving many vivid examples, enhances recall.

Source: Illeris, 2004.

Applying What We Know above increases the effectiveness of instruction.

Elderly participants in continuing education report a rich array of benefits—learning interesting facts, understanding new ideas in many disciplines, making new friends, and developing a broader perspective on the world (Kim & Merriam, 2004; Preece & Findsen, 2007). Furthermore, seniors come to see themselves differently. Many abandon their own ingrained stereotypes of aging when they realize that adults in late life—including themselves—can still engage in complex learning.

The educational needs of seniors are likely to be given greater attention in coming decades, as their numbers grow and they assert their right to lifelong learning. Once this happens, false stereotypes—"the elderly are too old to learn" or "education is for the young"—are likely to weaken and, perhaps, disappear.

ASK YOURSELF

>> **REVIEW**
Describe cognitive functions that are maintained or improve in late adulthood. What aspects of aging contribute to them?

>> **APPLY**
Estelle complained that she had recently forgotten two of her regular biweekly hair appointments and sometimes had trouble finding the right words to convey her thoughts. What cognitive changes account for Estelle's difficulties? What can she do to compensate?

>> **REFLECT**
Interview an older adult in your family, asking about ways the individual engages in selective optimization with compensation to make the most of declining cognitive resources. Describe several examples.

Summary

PHYSICAL DEVELOPMENT

Life Expectancy

Distinguish between chronological age and functional age, and discuss changes in life expectancy over the past century.

>> Because people age biologically at different rates, chronological age is an imperfect indicator of **functional age,** or actual competence and performance. Dramatic twentieth-century gains in **average life expectancy**—resulting from declines in both infant mortality and death rates among adults—confirm that biolog-ical aging can be modified by environmental factors, including improved nutrition, medical treatment, sanitation, and safety.

>> Length of life and, even more important, **average healthy life expectancy** can be predicted by a country's health care, housing, and social services, along with lifestyle factors.

>> With advancing age, the gender gap in average life expectancy declines as do differences between higher-SES whites and low-SES ethnic minorities. Around age 85, a life-expectancy crossover occurs, with longer life expectancy for low-SES minority groups.

>> About 9 percent of Americans over age 75 have difficulty carrying out **activities of daily living (ADLs),** or basic self-care tasks, and about 17 percent cannot perform **instrumental activities of daily living (IADLs),** which are tasks requiring some cognitive competence. The proportion of elders with these limitations increases sharply with age.

>> Longevity runs in families, but environmental factors become increasingly important with age. Scientists disagree on whether **maximum life-span** can be extended beyond about 85 to 90 years.

Physical Changes

Describe changes in the nervous system and the senses in late adulthood.

>> Loss of neurons occurs throughout the cerebral cortex, with greater shrinkage in the frontal lobes and the corpus callosum. The cerebellum also loses neurons. But the brain compensates by forming new synapses and, to some extent, generating new neurons. The autonomic nervous system functions less well and releases more stress hormones.

>> Older adults—more women than men—tend to suffer from impaired vision and may experience **cataracts** and **macular degeneration.**

>> In late life, hearing impairments are more common than visual impairments, especially in men. Impaired speech perception has the greatest impact on life satisfaction.

>> Taste and odor sensitivity decline, making food less appealing. Touch sensitivity also deteriorates, particularly on the fingertips.

Describe cardiovascular, respiratory, immune system, and sleep changes in late adulthood.

>> Reduced capacity of the cardiovascular and respiratory systems becomes more apparent. As at younger ages, not smoking, reducing dietary fat, avoiding environmental pollutants, and exercising can slow aging of these systems.

© KRISTI J. BLACK/CORBIS

>> The immune system functions less effectively, permitting diseases to progress and making **autoimmune responses** and stress-induced infection more likely.

>> Older adults find it harder to fall asleep, stay asleep, and sleep deeply. Timing of sleep shifts toward earlier bedtime and morning awakening.

Describe changes in physical appearance and mobility in late adulthood, along with effective adaptations to these changes.

>> Outward signs of aging, such as white hair, wrinkled and sagging skin, age spots, and decreased height and weight, become more noticeable. Mobility diminishes as muscle and bone strength and joint flexibility decline.

>> Problem-centered coping strategies yield improved physical functioning in the elderly. A rapidly expanding **assistive technology** is available to help older people cope with physical declines.

>> Negative stereotypes of aging have a stressful, disorganizing impact on elders' functioning, whereas positive ones reduce stress and foster competence.

Health, Fitness, and Disability

Discuss health and fitness in late life, paying special attention to nutrition, exercise, and sexuality.

>> Most elders rate their health favorably and, with respect to protecting it, have a high sense of self-efficacy. Low-SES ethnic minority elders remain at greater risk for certain health problems.

>> In late life, men continue to be more prone to fatal diseases and women to disabling conditions. By very old age, women are more impaired than surviving men. In industrialized nations, **compression of morbidity** has occurred, largely as a result of medical advances and improved socioeconomic conditions.

>> Because risk of dietary deficiencies increases, a daily vitamin–mineral supplement is beneficial, preventing infectious illness. Exercise, even when begun in late adulthood, continues to be a powerful health intervention.

>> Though sexual activity declines, especially among women, most elder couples report continued, regular sexual enjoyment.

Discuss physical disabilities common in late adulthood.

>> Illness and disability increase toward the end of life. Cardiovascular disease, cancer, stroke, and respiratory diseases claim many lives. **Primary aging** (species-wide genetically influenced declines) contributes to **frailty** in the elderly. But **secondary aging** (declines due to hereditary defects and negative environmental influences) plays a larger role.

>> **Osteoarthritis** and **rheumatoid arthritis** are widespread among older adults, especially women. Type 2 diabetes also increases.

>> The death rate from unintentional injuries reaches an all-time high in those age 65 and older, largely due to motor vehicle collisions, pedestrian accidents, and falls. Declines in visual processing and selective attention and slowed reaction time contribute.

Discuss mental disabilities common in late adulthood.

>> **Alzheimer's disease** is the most common form of **dementia.** Often starting with severe memory problems, it brings personality changes, depression, disintegration of purposeful movements, loss of ability to comprehend and produce speech, and death. Underlying these changes are abundant **neurofibrillary tangles** and **amyloid plaques** and lowered neurotransmitter levels in the brain.

>> Familial Alzheimer's generally has an early onset, progresses rapidly, and is linked to dominant genes on chromosomes 1, 14, and 21. About half of sporadic Alzheimer's victims have an abnormal ApoE4 gene on chromosome 19, resulting in insulin deficiency linked to brain damage.

>> Diverse environmental factors, including a high-fat diet, physical inactivity, chronic psychological stress, and cardiovascular disease, increase the risk of Alzheimer's. A "Mediterranean diet," education, and an active lifestyle are associated with lower incidence.

>> Heredity contributes to **cerebrovascular dementia** indirectly, through high blood pressure, cardiovascular disease, and diabetes. Many environmental influences also heighten stroke risk. Because of their greater susceptibility to cardiovascular disease, men are affected more than women.

>> Treatable problems, such as depression, side effects of medication, and reactions to social isolation, can be mistaken for dementia.

Discuss health-care issues that affect senior citizens.

>> Only a small percentage of American seniors are institutionalized, a rate about half that of other industrialized nations that offer more generous public financing of nursing home care. Though ethnic differences exist, family members provide most long-term care in Western nations. Publicly funded in-home help and **assisted living** can reduce the high costs of institutional placement and increase elders' life satisfaction.

© JOHN WALKER/MCT/LANDOV

COGNITIVE DEVELOPMENT

Describe overall changes in cognitive functioning in late adulthood.

>> Individual differences in cognitive functioning are greater in late adulthood than at any other time of life. With opportunities to enhance cognitive skills, crystallized intelligence can offset losses in fluid intelligence. Older adults can make the most of their cognitive resources through **selective optimization with compensation.**

Memory

How does memory change in late life?

>> Memory failures become more apparent, especially on tasks that are complex and require deliberate processing. Recall of context, source, and temporal order of events declines. Automatic forms of memory, such as recognition and **implicit memory,** suffer less. In general, an **associative memory deficit,** or difficulty creating and retrieving links between pieces of information, seems to characterize older adults' memory problems.

>> Contrary to what older people often report, **remote memory** is not clearer than recent memory. Autobiographical memory is best for recent experiences, followed by personally meaningful events that happened between ages 10 and 30, a period of rapid life change and identity development. In the laboratory, older adults do better on event-based than on time-based **prospective memory** tasks. In everyday life, they compensate for declines in prospective memory by using external memory aids.

Language Processing

Describe changes in language processing in late adulthood.

>> Age-related losses occur in two aspects of language production: retrieving words from long-term memory and planning what to say and how to say it. Elders compensate by simplifying their grammatical structures.

Problem Solving

How does problem solving change in late life?

>> Although hypothetical problem solving declines, in everyday problem solving, older adults are active and effective as long as they perceive problems as important and under their control. In matters of health, elders make quicker decisions than younger people. And they more often consult others about everyday problems.

Wisdom

What capacities make up wisdom, and how is it affected by age and life experience?

>> **Wisdom** involves extensive practical knowledge, ability to reflect on and apply that knowledge in ways that make life more bearable and worthwhile, emotional maturity, and altruistic creativity. When age and life experience in grappling with human problems are combined, more older than younger people rank among the wise.

Factors Related to Cognitive Change

List factors related to cognitive change in late adulthood.

>> Mentally active people are likely to maintain their cognitive abilities into advanced old age. A wide array of chronic conditions are associated with cognitive decline. Stimulating leisure activities and complex, challenging work facilitate intellectual functioning.

>> As elders grow older, their scores on cognitive tasks become increasingly unstable. As death approaches, **terminal decline**—a marked acceleration in deterioration of cognitive functioning—often occurs.

Cognitive Interventions

Can cognitive interventions help older adults sustain their mental abilities?

>> Large-scale interventions like ADEPT and ACTIVE demonstrate that training can enhance cognitive skills in older adults, with large benefits for those who had experienced cognitive declines.

Lifelong Learning

Discuss types of continuing education and benefits of such programs in late life.

>> Increasing numbers of older people continue their education through university courses, community offerings, and programs such as Elderhostel and Osher Lifelong Learning Institutes. Participants acquire new knowledge, new friends, a broader perspective on the world, and an image of themselves as more competent. Unfortunately, fewer continuing-education opportunities are available to low-SES seniors.

Important Terms and Concepts

activities of daily living (ADLs) (p. 445)
Alzheimer's disease (p. 458)
amyloid plaques (p. 459)
assisted living (p. 462)
assistive technology (p. 451)
associative memory deficit (p. 465)
autoimmune response (p. 449)
average healthy life expectancy (p. 444)
average life expectancy (p. 444)

cataracts (p. 447)
cerebrovascular dementia (p. 460)
compression of morbidity (p. 453)
dementia (p. 457)
frailty (p. 456)
functional age (p. 443)
implicit memory (p. 465)
instrumental activities of daily living (IADLs) (p. 445)
macular degeneration (p. 448)
maximum lifespan (p. 445)

neurofibrillary tangles (p. 459)
osteoarthritis (p. 456)
primary aging (p. 455)
prospective memory (p. 466)
remote memory (p. 465)
rheumatoid arthritis (p. 456)
secondary aging (p. 455)
selective optimization with compensation (p. 463)
terminal decline (p. 468)
wisdom (p. 467)

Emotional and Social Development in Late Adulthood

CHAPTER 18

© SEAN SPRAGUE/THE IMAGE WORKS

As family responsibilities and vocational pressures lessen, friendships—like the close tie between these Honduran elders—take on increasing importance. Having friends is an especially strong predictor of mental health in late adulthood.

With Ruth at his side, Walt spoke to the guests at their sixtieth-anniversary party. "Even when things were hard," he reflected, "the time of life I liked best always seemed to be the one I was currently experiencing. When I was a kid, I adored playing baseball. In my twenties, I loved learning the photography business. And of course," Walt continued, glancing affectionately at Ruth, "our wedding was the most memorable day of all."

He went on: "And then Sybil was born. Looking back at my parents and grandparents and forward at Sybil, Marci, and Marci's son Jamel, I feel a sense of unity with past and future generations."

Walt and Ruth greeted old age with calm acceptance, grateful for the gift of long life and loved ones. Yet not all older adults find such peace of mind. Walt's brother Dick was contentious, complaining about petty issues and major disappointments alike: "Goldie, why'd you serve cheesecake? No one eats cheesecake on birthdays!" "Know why we've got financial worries? Uncle Louie wouldn't lend me the money to keep the bakery going, so I *had* to retire."

A mix of gains and losses characterizes these twilight years, extending the multidirectionality of development. On one hand, old age is a time of pleasure and tranquility, when children are grown, life's work is nearly done, and responsibilities are lightened. On the other hand, it brings concerns about declining physical functions, unwelcome loneliness, and the growing specter of imminent death.

In this chapter, we consider how older adults reconcile these opposing forces. Although some are weary and discontented, most attach deeper significance to life and reap great benefits from family and friendship bonds, leisure activities, and community involvement. We will see how personal attributes and life history combine with home, neighborhood, community, and societal conditions to mold emotional and social development in late life.

Erikson's Theory: Ego Integrity versus Despair

The final psychological conflict of Erikson's (1950) theory, **ego integrity versus despair,** involves coming to terms with one's life. Adults who arrive at a sense of integrity feel whole, complete, and satisfied with their achievements. They have adapted to inevitable triumphs and disappointments and

realize that the paths they followed, abandoned, and never selected were necessary for fashioning a meaningful life course.

The capacity to view one's life in the larger context of all humanity—as the chance combination of one person and one segment in history—contributes to the serenity and contentment that accompany integrity. "These last few decades have been the happiest," Walt murmured, clasping Ruth's hand—only weeks before the heart attack that would end his life. At peace with himself, his wife, and his children, Walt had accepted his life course as something that had to be the way it was. In a study that followed a sample of women diverse in SES throughout adulthood, midlife generativity predicted ego integrity in late adulthood. Ego integrity, in turn, was associated with more favorable psychological well-being—a more upbeat mood, greater self-acceptance, higher marital satisfaction, closer relationships with adult children, greater community involvement, and increased ease in accepting help from others when it is needed (James & Zarrett, 2007).

Scanning the newspaper, Walt pondered, "I keep reading these percentages: One out of five people will get heart disease, one out of three will get cancer. But the truth is, one out of one will die. We are all mortal and must accept this fate." The year before, Walt had given his granddaughter, Marci, his collection of prized photos, which had absorbed him for over half a century. With the realization that the integrity of one's own life is part of an extended chain of human existence, death loses its sting (Vaillant, 1994, 2002).

Erik Erikson and his wife Joan exemplified the ideal of Erikson's final stage. They aged gracefully, felt satisfied with their achievements, and could often be seen walking hand in hand, deeply in love.

The negative outcome of this stage, despair, occurs when elders feel they have made many wrong decisions, yet time is too short to find an alternate route to integrity. Without another chance, the despairing person finds it hard to accept that death is near and is overwhelmed with bitterness, defeat, and hopelessness. According to Erikson, these attitudes are often expressed as anger and contempt for others, which disguise contempt for oneself. Dick's argumentative, fault-finding behavior, tendency to blame others for his personal failures, and regretful view of his own life reflect this deep sense of despair.

Other Theories of Psychosocial Development in Late Adulthood

As with Erikson's stages of early and middle adulthood, other theorists have clarified and refined his vision of late adulthood, specifying the tasks and thought processes that contribute to a sense of ego integrity. All agree that optimal development involves greater integration and deepening of the personality.

Peck's Tasks of Ego Integrity and Joan Erikson's Gerotranscendence

According to Robert Peck (1968), attaining ego integrity involves three distinct tasks:

- *Ego differentiation:* For those who invested heavily in their careers, finding other ways to affirm self-worth—through family, friendship, and community life.
- *Body transcendence:* Surmounting physical limitations by emphasizing the compensating rewards of cognitive, emotional, and social powers.
- *Ego transcendence:* As contemporaries die, facing the reality of death constructively through efforts to make life more secure, meaningful, and gratifying for younger generations.

In Peck's theory, ego integrity requires older adults to move beyond their life's work, their bodies, and their separate identities. Research suggests that as elders grow older, both *body transcendence* (focusing on psychological strengths) and *ego transcendence* (orienting toward a larger, more distant future) increase. In a study of elderly women, those in their eighties and nineties stated with greater certainty than those in their sixties that they "accept the changes brought about by aging," "have moved beyond fear of death," "have a clearer sense of the meaning of life," and "have found new, positive spiritual gifts to explore" (Brown & Lowis, 2003).

Erikson's widow Joan Erikson proposed that these attainments actually represent development beyond ego integrity (which requires satisfaction with one's past life) to an additional psychosocial stage that she calls **gerotranscendence**—a cosmic and transcendent perspective directed forward and outward, beyond the self. Drawing on her own experience of aging, her observations of her husband's final years, and the work of others on the positive potential of the years shortly before death, Joan Erikson speculated that success in attaining gerotranscendence is apparent in heightened inner calm and contentment and additional time spent in quiet reflection (Erikson, 1998; Tornstam, 1997, 2000).

Although interviews with people in their ninth and tenth decades reveal that many (but not all) experience this peaceful, contemplative state, more research is needed to confirm the existence of a distinct, transcendent late-life stage. Besides focusing more intently on life's meaning, many of the very old continue to report investments in the real world—visiting friends, keeping up with current events, striving to be a good neighbor, and engaging in rewarding leisure and volunteer pursuits (Adams, 2004).

Labouvie-Vief's Emotional Expertise

Recall from Chapter 13 that cognitive-affective complexity (awareness and coordination of positive and negative feelings into an organized self-description) increases from adolescence through middle adulthood and then declines as basic information-processing skills diminish in late adulthood.

But elders, as Gisella Labouvie-Vief points out, display a compensating emotional strength: They improve in **affect optimization,** the ability to maximize positive emotion and dampen negative emotion, which contributes to their remarkable resilience (Labouvie-Vief, 2003, 2005; Labouvie-Vief et al., 2007; Labouvie-Vief & Medler, 2002). Despite physical declines, increased health problems, a restricted future, and death of

© JULIA CUMES/THE IMAGE WORKS

Although she suffers from serious medical problems, this older adult asserted, "Being an invalid does not invalidate your life." She adopted this rescue dog, who gives her great pleasure. The ability of elders to maximize positive emotion and dampen negative emotion contributes to their remarkable resilience.

loved ones, most older adults sustain a sense of optimism (Diehl, Coyle, & Labouvie-Vief, 1996; Mroczek & Kolarz, 1998). And about 30 to 40 percent of elders not only are high in affect optimization but also retain considerable capacity for cognitive-affective complexity—a combination related to especially effective emotional self-regulation.

Furthermore, many middle-aged and elderly individuals describe their emotional reactions to personal experiences more vividly than do younger people—evidence that they are more in touch with their feelings. Older adults' emotional perceptiveness helps them separate interpretations from objective aspects of situations. Consequently, their coping strategies often include making sure they fully understand their own feelings before deciding on a course of action. And they readily use emotion-centered coping strategies (controlling distress internally) in negatively charged situations (Blanchard-Fields, 2007). In sum, a significant late-life psychosocial attainment is becoming expert at reflecting on one's own feelings and regulating negative affect (Labouvie-Vief & Diehl, 1999; Lawton, 2001).

Reminiscence

We often think of the elderly as engaged in **reminiscence**—telling stories about people and events from their past and reporting associated thoughts and feelings. Indeed, the widespread image of a reminiscing elder, living in the past to escape the realities of a shortened future, ranks among negative stereotypes of aging. But current theory and research indicate that reflecting on the past can be positive and adaptive.

In his comments on major events in his life at the beginning of this chapter, Walt was engaging in a special form of reminiscence called *life review*—calling up past experiences with the goal of achieving greater self-understanding. According to Robert Butler (1968), most older adults engage in life review as part of attaining ego integrity. Research indicates that older adults who participate in counselor-led life review report increased self-esteem, greater sense of purpose in life, and reduced depression (Watt & Cappeliez, 2000; Westerhof, Bohlmeijer, & Valenkamp, 2004).

But many elders who are high in self-acceptance and life satisfaction spend little time evaluating their pasts (Wink, 2007; Wink & Schiff, 2002). Indeed, in several studies in which older adults were asked what they considered to be the best time of life, 10 to 30 percent identified one of the decades of late adulthood. Early and middle adulthood received especially high marks, whereas childhood and adolescence ranked as less satisfying (Field, 1997; Mehlson, Platz, & Fromholt, 2003). These findings challenge the widespread belief that older adults inevitably focus on the past and wish to be young again. To the contrary, today's elders in industrialized nations are largely present- and future-oriented: They seek avenues for personal growth and fulfillment (see the Lifespan Vista box the following page).

Clearly, life review is not essential for adapting well to late adulthood. Indeed, reminiscence that is *self-focused*, engaged in to reduce boredom and revive bitter events, is linked to

adjustment problems. Despairing elders tend to ruminate, sustaining their negative emotion by dwelling on painful past experiences (Cully, LaVoie, & Gfeller, 2001). In contrast, extraverted elders tend to engage in *other-focused* reminiscence directed at social goals, such as solidifying family and friendship ties and reliving relationships with lost loved ones. And at times, older adults—especially those who score high in openness to experience—engage in *knowledge-based* reminiscence, drawing on their past for effective problem-solving strategies and for teaching younger people. These socially engaged, mentally stimulating forms of reminiscence help make life rich and rewarding (Cappeliez & O'Rourke, 2002).

Stability and Change in Self-Concept and Personality

Longitudinal research reveals continuing stability of the "big five" personality traits from mid- to late life (see Chapter 16, page 427). Yet the ingredients of ego integrity—wholeness, contentment, and image of the self as part of a larger world order—are reflected in several significant late-life changes in both self-concept and personality.

Secure and Multifaceted Self-Concept

Elders have accumulated a lifetime of self-knowledge, leading to more secure and complex conceptions of themselves than at earlier ages (Labouvie-Vief & Diehl, 1999). Ruth, for example, knew with certainty that she was good at growing a flower garden, budgeting money, and figuring out who could be trusted and who couldn't. Furthermore, when young and older adults were asked for several life-defining memories, 65- to 85-year-olds were more likely to mention events with a consistent theme such as the importance of relationships or personal independence—and to explain how the events were interrelated (McLean, 2008). Their autobiographical selves emphasized coherence and consistency, despite physical, cognitive, and occupational changes.

Ruth's firm and multifaceted self-concept allowed for self-acceptance—a key feature of integrity. In a study of German 70- to 103-year-olds asked to respond to the question "Who am I?," participants throughout the entire age range mentioned more positive than negative self-evaluations. And positive, multifaceted self-definitions predicted psychological well-being (Freund & Smith, 1999).

As the future shortens, most elders, into their eighties and nineties, continue to mention—and actively pursue—hoped-for selves in the areas of physical health, cognitive functioning, personal characteristics, relationships, and social responsibility (Frazier, 2002; Markus & Herzog, 1992). At the same time, possible selves reorganize well into old age. When the German elders just mentioned were followed longitudinally for four years, the majority deleted some possible selves and replaced them with new ones (Smith & Freund, 2002). Elders often characterize

■ A LIFESPAN VISTA: Looking Forward, Looking Back ■

The New Old Age

After retiring, pediatrician Jack McConnell, tried a relaxing lifestyle near a lake and golf course, but it worked poorly for the energetic 64-year-old. As his desire for a more fulfilling retirement grew, he noticed that outside his comfortable, gated community were many people serving community needs as gardeners, laborers, fast-food workers, and the like, yet who lived in or near poverty. The contrast galvanized Jack to found Volunteers in Medicine, a free clinic for working-poor adults and their families who lack health insurance (Croker, 2007). Five years later, at age 69, Jack was overseeing a highly cost-effective operation involving 200 retired doctors, nurses, and lay volunteers, who treat 6,000 patients a year.

Increasingly, older adults are using their newfound freedom from work and parenting responsibilities to pursue personally enriching interests and goals. In doing so, they are giving back to their communities in significant ways and serving as role models for younger generations.

Added years of longevity and health plus financial stability have granted this active, opportunistic time of life to so many contemporary seniors that some experts believe a new phase of late adulthood has evolved called the **Third Age**—a term originating over a decade ago in France that spread through Western Europe and recently has stretched to North America. According to this view, the First Age is childhood, the Second Age is the adult period of earning a living and rearing children, and the Third Age—extending from ages 65 to 79, and sometimes longer—is a time of personal fulfillment (James & Wink, 2007). The Fourth Age brings physical decline and need for care.

The baby boomers—healthier and financially better off than any preceding aging generation—are approaching late life with the conviction that their old age will not begin until 80 (Gergen & Gergen, 2003; Winter et al., 2007). This self-perception has helped define the Third Age as a time of self-realization and high life satisfaction. As we will see later in this chapter, retirement is no longer a one-way, age-graded event. In one survey of 300 older Americans, very few self-identified as retired (Trafford, 2004). Instead, they were building hybrid lives—leaving career jobs to work at different jobs that utilized their skills, and devoting themselves to community service (Moen & Altobelli, 2007).

Although policy makers often express concern about the huge, impending baby-boomer burden on Social Security and Medicare, this large pool of vigorous, publicly minded future seniors has the potential to make enormous economic and social contributions. Today's Third Agers donate billions to the global economy in volunteer work and continue to participate in the work force in large numbers.

But as midlife roles shrink and terminate, too few alternatives are available for the many aging adults eager to make a difference (Freedman, 1999; Wink & James, 2007). Societies need to provide abundant volunteer, national service, and other public interest opportunities, thereby harnessing their rich elder resources. The U.S. Serve America Act, signed into law in 2009, offers expanded

Retired pediatrician Jack McConnell founded Volunteers in Medicine, a free clinic for uninsured working-poor adults and their families. Added years of longevity and health plus financial stability have made late adulthood a time of personal enrichment and new goal-setting for many older adults.

service incentives and options to American adults of all ages and, thus, is a major step in that direction.

---

hoped-for selves in terms of "improving," "achieving," or "attaining," and those with hoped-for goals usually take concrete steps to attain them. Engaging in hope-related activities, in turn, is associated with gains in life satisfaction and with longer life (Hoppmann et al., 2007). Clearly, late adulthood is not a time of withdrawal from future planning!

Resilience: Agreeableness and Acceptance of Change

A flexible, optimistic approach to life, which fosters resilience in the face of adversity, is common in old age. Both open-ended interviews and personality tests reveal that elders gain in *agreeableness*, becoming increasingly generous, acquiescent, and good-natured well into late life (Allemand, Zimprich, & Martin, 2008; Field & Millsap, 1991; Weiss et al., 2005). Agreeableness seems to characterize people who have come to terms with life despite its imperfections.

At the same time, elders show modest age-related dips in *extraversion* and *openness to experience* (Allemand, Zimprich, & Martin, 2008; Roberts, Walton, & Viechtbauer, 2006). Perhaps this reflects a narrowing of social contacts as people become more selective about relationships and as family members and friends die. Still, older adults who were extraverted and open to experience throughout their lives tend to remain so—personality traits associated with greater life satisfaction (Mroczek & Spiro, 2005).

A related development is greater *acceptance of change*—an attribute the elderly frequently mention as important to psychological well-being (Ryff, 1989). When asked about dissatisfactions in their lives, many older adults respond that they are not unhappy about anything! Acceptance of change is also evident in most elders' effective coping with the loss of loved ones, including death of a spouse. The capacity to accept life's twists and turns, many of which are beyond one's control, is vital for adaptive functioning in late adulthood.

Most older adults are resilient, bouncing back in the face of adversity—especially if they did so earlier in their lives. And elders' heightened capacity for positive emotion contributes greatly to their resilience. Older adults' general cheerfulness strengthens their physiological resistance to stress, enabling them to conserve physical and mental resources needed for effective coping (Ong & Allaire, 2005). The minority of elders who are high in neuroticism—emotionally negative, short-tempered, and dissatisfied—tend to cope poorly with stressful events, experience mounting negative affect, and are at risk for health problems and earlier death (Mroczek & Spiro, 2007; Ong, Edwards, & Bergeman, 2006).

Spirituality and Religiosity

How do older adults manage to accept declines and losses yet still feel whole and complete and anticipate death with calm composure? One possibility, consistent with Peck's and Erikson's emphasis on a transcendent perspective among the elderly, is the development of a more mature sense of spirituality. Spirituality is not the same as religion: An inspirational sense of life's meaning can be found in art, nature, and social relationships. But for many people, religion provides beliefs, symbols, and rituals that guide this quest for meaning.

Older adults attach great value to religious beliefs and behaviors. According to a recent national survey, 72 percent of Americans age 65 and older say that religion is very important in their lives—the highest of any age group (Gallup News Service, 2006). Over half of U.S. elders attend religious services or other events weekly, nearly two-thirds watch religious TV programs, and about one-fourth pray at least three times a day (Princeton Religion Research Center, 1999).

Although health and transportation difficulties reduce organized religious participation in advanced old age, U.S. elders generally become more religious or spiritual as they age (Argue, Johnson, & White, 1999; Wink & Dillon, 2002). But this trend is far from universal. In a British 20-year longitudinal study, the majority of elders showed stability in religiosity over time, with nearly half indicating that religion was very important to them. One-fourth, however, said they had become less religious, with some citing disappointment at the support they had received from their religious institution during stressful times (such as bereavement) as the reason (Coleman, Ivani-Chalian, & Robinson, 2004). Despite these differences, spirituality and faith may advance to a higher level in late adulthood—away from prescribed beliefs toward a more reflective approach that emphasizes links to others, that is at ease with mystery and uncertainty, and that accepts one's own belief system as one of many possible worldviews (Fowler, 1981; McFadden, 1996).

Involvement in both organized and informal religious activities is especially high among low-SES ethnic minority elders, including African-American, Hispanic, and Native-American groups. African-American elders look to religion as a powerful resource for social support beyond the family and for the inner strength to withstand daily stresses and physical impairments (Armstrong & Crowther, 2002; Husaini, Blasi, & Miller, 1999). Compared with their Caucasian agemates, more African-American older adults report collaborating with God to overcome life problems (Krause, 2005; Lee & Sharpe, 2007).

Throughout adulthood, women are more likely than men to report that religion is very important to them, to participate in religious activities, and to engage in a personal quest for connectedness with a higher power (Gallup News Service, 2006; Levin, Taylor, & Chatters, 1994; Wink & Dillon, 2002). Women's higher rates of poverty, widowhood, and participation in caregiving expose them to higher levels of stress and anxiety. As with ethnic minorities, they turn to religion for social support and for a larger vision of community that places life's challenges in perspective.

Religious involvement is associated with diverse benefits, including better physical and psychological well-being, more time devoted to exercising and leisure activities, greater sense of closeness to family and friends, and greater generativity (care for others) (Boswell, Kahana, & Dilworth-Anderson, 2006; Lee, 2007; Wink, 2006, 2007). In longitudinal research, both organized and informal religious participation predicted longer

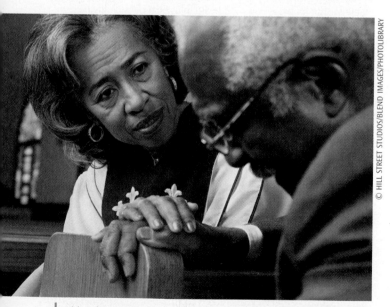

This minister takes time to offer a senior parishioner emotional support. African-American elders often look to religion as a powerful resource for the inner strength to withstand the challenges of late life.

© HILL STREET STUDIOS/BLEND IMAGES/PHOTOLIBRARY

survival, after family background, health, social, and psychological factors known to affect mortality were controlled (Helm et al., 2000; Strawbridge et al., 2001).

Contextual Influences on Psychological Well-Being

Personal and situational factors often combine to affect psychological well-being in late adulthood. Identifying these contextual influences is vital for designing interventions that foster positive adjustment.

Control versus Dependency

As Ruth's eyesight, hearing, and mobility declined in her eighties, Sybil visited daily to help with self-care and household tasks. During the hours mother and daughter were together, Sybil interacted most often with Ruth when she asked for help with activities of daily living. When Ruth handled tasks on her own, Sybil usually withdrew.

Observations of people interacting with older adults in both private homes and institutions reveal two highly predictable, complementary behavior patterns. In the first, called the **dependency–support script,** dependent behaviors are attended to immediately. In the second, the **independence–ignore script,** independent behaviors are mostly ignored. Notice how these sequences reinforce dependent behavior at the expense of independent behavior, regardless of the older person's competencies. Even a self-reliant elder like Ruth did not always resist Sybil's unnecessary help because it brought about social contact (Baltes, 1995, 1996).

Among elders who experience no difficulty with daily activities, opportunities to interact with others are related to high satisfaction with everyday life. In contrast, among elders who have trouble performing daily activities, social contact is linked to a less positive everyday existence (Lang & Baltes, 1997). This suggests that social interaction while assisting elders with physical care, household chores, and errands is often not meaningful and rewarding but, rather, demeaning and unpleasant. Consider these typical reactions of care recipients to a spouse's help with daily activities: "felt indebted," "felt like a weak, incapable person" (Newsom, 1999).

Longitudinal research shows that negative reactions to caregiving can result in persisting depression (Newsom & Schulz, 1998). But whether assistance from others undermines well-being depends on many factors, including the quality of help, the caregiver–elder relationship, and the social and cultural context in which helping occurs. In Western societies, which highly value independence, many elders fear relinquishing control and becoming dependent on others. This is especially so for older adults with a high need for self-determination (Curtiss, Hayslip, & Dolan, 2007; Frazier, 2002). And, respond-

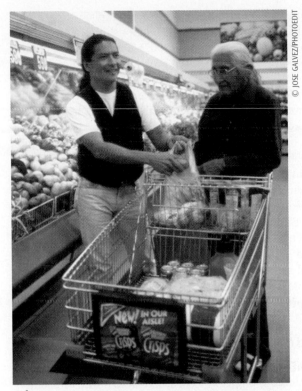

Will this Apache elder become too dependent by letting his son help with grocery shopping? Not necessarily. When older adults assume personal control over areas of dependency, they can conserve their strength and invest it in highly valued activities.

ing to stereotypes of the elderly as incapable, family members and other caregivers often act in ways that promote excessive dependency.

Does this mean we should encourage elders to be as independent as possible? According to Mary Baltes (1996), this alternative is as counterproductive as promoting passivity and incompetence. Aging brings diminished energy at a time when people confront many challenging developmental tasks. Dependency can be adaptive if it permits older people to remain in control by choosing those areas in which they desire help. In this way, they can conserve their strength by investing it in highly valued activities, using a set of strategies we considered in Chapter 17: *selective optimization with compensation.*

Physical Health

Physical declines and chronic disease can lead to a sense of loss of personal control—a major factor in adult mental health. Furthermore, physical illness resulting in disability is among the strongest risk factors for late-life depression (Morrison, 2008; Schieman & Plickert, 2007). Although fewer older than young and middle-aged adults are depressed (see Chapter 17), profound feelings of hopelessness rise with age as physical disability and consequent social isolation increase. But more than actual physical limitations, *perceived negative physical health* predicts depressive symptoms (Jang et al., 2007). This helps explain the stronger physical impairment–depression relationship among higher-SES elders (Schieman & Plickert, 2007). Because of their lifetime of better physical health, they probably experience physical limitations as more unexpected and challenging.

Depression in old age is often lethal. People age 65 and older have the highest suicide rate of all age groups (see the Social Issues box on the following page). What factors enable elders like Ruth to surmount the physical impairment–depression relationship, remaining content? Personal characteristics discussed in this and earlier chapters—optimism, effective coping, and a sense of self-efficacy—are vitally important (Morrison, 2008). But for frail elders to display these attributes, families and caregivers must grant them autonomy by avoiding the dependency–support script. When older adults remain in charge of personally important areas of their lives, they retain essential aspects of their identity in the face of change, view their past and future more favorably, and are emotionally more upbeat (Kunzmann, Little, & Smith, 2002).

Negative Life Changes

Ruth lost Walt to a heart attack, cared for his sister Ida as her Alzheimer's symptoms worsened, and faced health problems of her own—all within a span of a few years. Elders are at risk for a variety of negative life changes—death of loved ones, illness and physical disabilities, declining income, and greater dependency. Negative life changes are difficult for everyone but may actually evoke less stress and depression in older than in younger adults (Gatz, Kasl-Godley, & Karel, 1996). Many elders have learned to cope with hard times, to appraise negative changes as common and expected in late life, and to accept loss as part of human existence.

Still, when negative changes pile up, they test the coping skills of older adults (Kraaij, Arensman, & Spinhoven, 2002). In very old age, such changes are greater for women than for men. Women over age 75 are far less likely to be married, more often have lower incomes, and suffer from more illnesses—especially ones that restrict mobility. Furthermore, elderly women (as at younger ages) more often say that others depend on them for caregiving and emotional support. Thus, their social relations, even in very old age, are more often a source of stress (Antonucci, Ajrouch, & Birditt, 2008). And because of failing health, older women may not be able to meet others' needs for care, with negative consequences for their self-esteem. Not surprisingly, women of very advanced age tend to report a lower sense of psychological well-being than men (Pinquart & Sörensen, 2001).

Social Support

In late adulthood, social support continues to reduce stress, thereby promoting physical health and psychological well-being and increasing the odds of living longer (Fry & Debats, 2006; Liang et al., 1999; Temkin-Greener et al., 2004). Usually, elders receive informal assistance with tasks of daily living from family members—first from their spouse or, if none exists, from children and then from siblings or other relatives and friends.

Nevertheless, many older adults place such high value on independence that they do not want a great deal of help from people close to them unless they can reciprocate. When assistance is excessive or cannot be returned, it often results in psychological distress (Liang, Krause, & Bennett, 2001). Perhaps for this reason, adult children express a deeper sense of obligation toward their aging parents than their parents expect from them (see Chapter 16, page 432). Formal support—a paid home helper or agency-provided services—as a complement to informal assistance not only helps relieve caregiving burden but also spares elders from feeling overly dependent in their close relationships (Krause, 1990).

Ethnic minority elders are more willing to accept assistance when home helpers are connected to a familiar neighborhood organization, especially the church. Although African-American seniors say they rely more on their families than on the church for assistance, those with support and meaningful roles in both contexts score highest in mental health (Coke, 1992; Taylor, Lincoln, & Chatters, 2005; Walls & Zarit, 1991). Support from religious congregants has psychological benefits for elders of all backgrounds, perhaps because recipients feel that it is motivated by genuine care and concern, not just obligation (Krause, 2001). Also, the warm atmosphere of religious organizations fosters a sense of social acceptance and belonging.

Overall, for social support to foster well-being, elders need to assume personal control of it. This means consciously giving up primary control in some areas to remain in control of other, highly valued pursuits. For example, although she could handle dressing, financial matters, shopping, and food preparation for herself, Ruth allowed her daughter Sybil to assist with these activities, leaving Ruth with more stamina for pleasurable reading and outings with friends. Help that is not wanted or needed or that exaggerates weaknesses can undermine mental health, and—if existing skills fall into disuse—can also accelerate physical disability. In contrast, help that frees up energy for endeavors that are personally satisfying and that lead to growth enhances elders' quality of life. These findings clarify why *perceived social support* (elders' sense of being able to count on family or friends in times of need) is associated with a positive outlook in older adults with disabilities, whereas sheer *amount* of help family and friends provide has little impact (Taylor & Lynch, 2004).

Finally, besides tangible assistance, elders benefit from social support that offers affection, affirmation of their self-worth, and sense of belonging. Extraverted elders are more likely to take advantage of opportunities to engage with others, thereby reducing loneliness and depression and fostering self-esteem and life satisfaction (Mroczek & Spiro, 2005). But as we will see in the next section, supportive social ties in old age have little to do with quantity of contact. Instead, high-quality relationships, involving expressions of kindness, encouragement, respect, and emotional closeness, have the greatest impact on mental health in late life.

SOCIAL ISSUES

Elder Suicide

When 65-year-old Abe's wife died, he withdrew from life. Living far from his two daughters, he spent his nonworking days alone, watching television and reading mystery novels. As grandchildren were born, Abe visited his daughters' homes from time to time, carrying his unresponsive, despondent behavior with him.

After arthritis made walking difficult, Abe retired. With more empty days, his depression deepened. Gradually, he developed painful digestive difficulties, but he refused to see a doctor. Answering her invitation to a grandson's tenth birthday party, Abe wrote, "Maybe—if I'm still around next month. By the way, when I go, I want my body cremated." Two weeks later, Abe died from an intestinal blockage. His body was found in the living room chair where he habitually spent his days. Although it may seem surprising, Abe's self-destructive acts are a form of suicide.

Factors Related to Elder Suicide

Recall from Chapter 12 that suicide increases over the lifespan. It continues to climb during the elder years, reaching its highest rate among people age 75 and older (World Health Organization, 2002).

The higher suicide rate among males persists through late adulthood. Five times as many U.S. elderly men as women take their own lives (U.S. Census Bureau, 2009b). Compared with the white majority, most ethnic minority elders have low suicide rates.

What explains these trends? Despite the lifelong pattern of higher rates of depression and more suicide attempts among females, elderly women's closer ties to family and friends, greater willingness to seek social support, and religiosity prevent many from taking their own lives. High levels of social support through extended families and church affiliations may also prevent suicide among ethnic minorities. And within certain minority groups, deep respect for older adults fosters self-esteem and social integration (Kettl, 1998). This reduces elder suicide, making it nonexistent after age 80.

As in earlier years, the methods favored by elderly males (firearms, hanging) offer less chance of revival than those by elder females

(poisoning or drug overdose). Nevertheless, failed suicides are much rarer in old age than in adolescence (Conwell, Duberstein, & Caine, 2002). When elders decide to die, they seem especially determined to succeed.

Underreporting of suicides probably occurs at all ages, but it is more common in old age. Medical examiners are less likely to pursue suicide as a cause of death when a person is old. And many elders, like Abe, engage in indirect self-destructive acts rarely classified as suicide—deciding not to go to a doctor when ill or refusing to eat or take prescribed medications. Among institutionalized elders, these efforts to hasten death are widespread (Reiss & Tishler, 2008). Consequently, elder suicide is an even larger problem than official statistics indicate.

Two types of events prompt suicide in late life. Losses—retirement from a highly valued occupation, widowhood, or social isolation—place elders who have difficulty coping with change at risk for persistent depression. Risks of another type arise when chronic and terminal illnesses severely reduce physical functioning or cause intense pain (Woods, 2008). As comfort and quality of life diminish, feelings of hopelessness and helplessness deepen.

Prevention and Treatment

Warning signs of suicide in late adulthood, like those at earlier ages, include efforts to put personal affairs in order, statements about dying, despondency, and sleep and appetite changes. But family members, friends, and caregivers must also watch for indirect self-destructive acts that are unique to old age, such as refusing food or medical treatment. Too often, people in close touch with the elderly incorrectly assume that these symptoms are a "natural" consequence of aging.

Communities are beginning to recognize the importance of additional preventive steps, such as telephone hot lines with trained volunteers who provide emotional support and agencies that arrange for regular home visitors or "buddy system" phone calls. In institutions, providing residents with privacy, autonomy, and space helps prevent self-destructive behavior (Conwell & Duberstein, 2001).

When suicidal elders are depressed, the most effective treatment combines antidepressant medication with therapy, including help in coping with role transitions, such as retire-

Suicide reaches its highest rate among people age 75 and older. Warning signs include efforts to put personal affairs in order, statements about dying, despondency, and sleep and appetite changes.

ment, widowhood, and dependency brought about by illness. Distorted ways of thinking ("I'm old, and nothing can be done about my problems") must be countered and revised. Meeting with the family to find ways to reduce loneliness and desperation is also helpful.

Elder suicide raises a controversial ethical issue: Do people with incurable illnesses have the right to take their own lives? We will take up this topic in Chapter 19.

A Changing Social World

Walt and Ruth's outgoing personalities led many family members and friends to seek them out, and they often reciprocated. In contrast, Dick's stubborn nature meant that he and Goldie, for many years, had had a far more restricted network of social ties.

As noted earlier, extraverts (like Walt and Ruth) continue to interact with a wider range of people than do introverts and people (like Dick) with poor social skills. Nevertheless, both cross-sectional and longitudinal research reveals that size of social networks and, therefore, amount of social interaction decline for virtually everyone (Antonucci, Akiyama, & Takahashi, 2004; Lang, Staudinger, & Carstensen, 1998). This finding presents a curious paradox: If social interaction and social support are essential for mental health, how is it possible for elders to interact less yet be generally satisfied with life and less depressed than younger adults?

Social Theories of Aging

Social theories of aging offer explanations for changes in elders' social activity. Two older perspectives—disengagement theory and activity theory—interpret declines in social interaction in opposite ways. More recent approaches—continuity theory and socioemotional selectivity theory—account for a wider range of findings.

■ **DISENGAGEMENT THEORY.** According to **disengagement theory,** mutual withdrawal between elders and society takes place in anticipation of death (Cumming & Henry, 1961). Older people decrease their activity levels and interact less frequently, becoming more preoccupied with their inner lives. At the same time, society frees elders from employment and family responsibilities. The result is viewed as beneficial for both sides. Elders are granted a life of tranquility. And once they disengage, their deaths are less disruptive to society.

Clearly, however, not everyone disengages! As we saw in Chapter 17 when we discussed wisdom, older adults in many cultures move into new positions of prestige and power because of their long life experience. Even after retirement, many people sustain aspects of their work; others develop new, rewarding roles in their communities. Disengagement by the elderly, then, may represent not their personal preference but, rather, a failure of the social world to provide opportunities for engagement.

As we will see shortly, older adults' retreat from interaction is more complex than disengagement theory implies. Instead of disengaging from all social ties, they let go of unsatisfying contacts and maintain satisfying ones.

■ **ACTIVITY THEORY.** Attempting to overcome the flaws of disengagement theory, **activity theory** states that social barriers to engagement, not the desires of elders, cause declining rates of interaction. When older people lose certain roles (for example, through retirement or widowhood), they try to find others in an effort to stay about as active and busy as they were in middle age. In this view, elders' life satisfaction depends on conditions that permit them to remain engaged in roles and relationships (Maddox, 1963).

Although people do seek alternative sources of meaning and gratification in response to social losses, activity theory fails to acknowledge any psychological change in old age. Many studies show that merely offering elders opportunities for social contact does not lead to greater social activity. In nursing homes, for example, where social partners are abundant, social interaction is very low, even among the healthiest residents—a circumstance we will examine when we discuss housing arrangements for the elderly. Especially troubling for activity theory is the repeated finding that when health status is controlled, elders who have larger social networks and engage in more activities are not necessarily happier (Lee & Markides, 1990; Ritchey, Ritchey, & Dietz, 2001). Recall that quality, not quantity, of relationships predicts psychological well-being in old age.

■ **CONTINUITY THEORY.** According to **continuity theory,** rather than maintaining a certain activity level, most aging adults strive to maintain a personal system—an identity and a set of personality dispositions, interests, roles, and skills—that promotes life satisfaction by ensuring consistency between their past and anticipated future. This striving for continuity does not mean that elders' lives are static. To the contrary, aging produces inevitable change, but most older adults try to minimize stress and disruptiveness by integrating those changes into a coherent, consistent life path. As much as possible, they choose to use familiar skills and engage in familiar activities with familiar people—preferences that provide a secure sense of routine and direction in life.

Research on the daily lives of older adults confirms a high degree of continuity in everyday pursuits and relationships. Even after a change (such as retirement), people usually make choices that extend the previous direction of their lives, engag-

These sisters—ages 93 and 89—greet each other with enthusiasm. The one on the right traveled from Poland to New York City to make possible this reunion. To preserve emotional equilibrium and reduce stress, elders increasingly emphasize familiar, emotionally rewarding relationships.

processes. In middle adulthood, marital relationships deepen, siblings feel closer, and number of friendships declines. In old age, contacts with family and long-term friends are sustained until the eighties, when they diminish gradually in favor of a few very close relationships. In contrast, as Figure 18.1 shows, contacts with acquaintances and willingness to form new social ties fall off steeply from middle through late adulthood (Carstensen, Fung, & Charles, 2003; Fung, Carstensen, & Lang, 2001).

What explains these changes? Socioemotional selectivity theory states that physical and psychological aspects of aging lead to changes in the functions of social interaction. **TAKE A MOMENT...** Consider the reasons you interact with members of your social network. At times, you approach them to get information. At other times, you seek affirmation of your worth as a person. You also choose social partners to regulate emotion, approaching those who evoke positive feelings and avoiding those who make you feel sad, angry, or uncomfortable. For older adults, who have gathered a lifetime of information, the information-gathering function becomes less significant. And elders realize it is risky to approach people they do not know for self-affirmation: Stereotypes of aging increase the odds of receiving a condescending, hostile, or indifferent response.

Instead, as physical fragility makes it more important to avoid stress, older adults emphasize the emotion-regulating function of interaction. In one study, younger and older adults were asked to categorize their social partners. Younger people more often sorted them on the basis of information seeking and

ing in new activities but often within familiar domains. For example, a retired manager of a children's bookstore collaborated with friends to build a children's library and donate it to an overseas orphanage. A musician who, because of arthritis, could no longer play the violin arranged regular get-togethers with musically inclined friends to listen to and talk about music. Robert Atchley (1989), originator of continuity theory, noted, "Everyday life for most older people is like long-running improvisational theater in which . . . changes are mostly in the form of new episodes [rather] than entirely new plays" (p. 185).

Elders' reliance on continuity has many benefits. Participation in familiar activities with familiar people provides repeated practice that helps preserve physical and cognitive functioning, fosters self-esteem and mastery, and affirms identity (Finchum & Weber, 2000). Investing in long-standing, close relationships provides comfort, pleasure, and a network of social support. Finally, striving for continuity is essential for attaining Erikson's sense of ego integrity, which depends on preserving a sense of personal history (Atchley, 1999).

■ **SOCIOEMOTIONAL SELECTIVITY THEORY.** A final perspective addresses how people's social networks sustain continuity while also narrowing as they age. According to **socioemotional selectivity theory,** social interaction extends lifelong selection

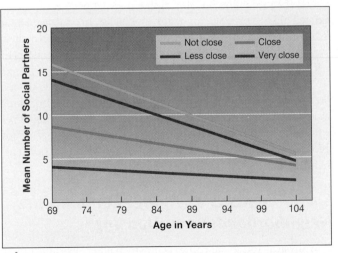

■ **FIGURE 18.1** ■ **Age-related change in number of social partners varying in closeness.** In interviews with over 500 elders ranging in age from 69 to 104, the number of "not close" and "less close" partners fell off steeply with age, whereas the number of "close" and "very close" partners declined minimally. (From F. R. Lang, U. M. Staudinger, & L. L. Carstensen, 1998, "Perspectives on Socioemotional Selectivity in Late Life: How Personality and Social Context Do (and Do Not) Make a Difference," *Journal of Gerontology, 53B,* p. 24. Copyright © 1998 The Gerontological Society of America. Adapted by permission of Oxford University Press and F. R. Lang.)

future contact, while older people emphasized anticipated feelings (Frederickson & Carstensen, 1990). They appeared highly motivated to approach pleasant relationships and avoid unpleasant ones. Interacting mostly with relatives and friends increases the chances that elders' emotional equilibrium will be preserved.

Consistent with these findings, older adults are less likely than younger people to respond to tensions with destructive tactics (yelling, arguing) and more likely to use constructive strategies, such as expressing affection or calmly letting the situation blow over (Birditt & Fingerman, 2005; Carstensen, Gottman, & Levenson, 1995). Elders also reinterpret conflict in less stressful ways—often by identifying something positive in the situation (Labouvie-Vief, 2003). Consequently, despite their smaller social networks, they are happier than younger people with their number of friends and report fewer problematic relationships (Akiyama et al., 2003; Fingerman & Birditt, 2003).

Research confirms that people's perception of time is strongly linked to their social goals. When remaining time is limited, adults of all ages place more emphasis on the emotional quality of their social experiences (Fung & Carstensen, 2004). This emphasis on *relationship quality* in late life helps explain an exception to the restriction of social relationships just described. In collectivist cultures, where people value an interdependent self and, thus, attach great importance to remaining embedded in their social group, elders may be motivated to sustain high-quality ties with all partners! In a Hong Kong study, older adults scoring high in interdependence both expanded their number of emotionally close social partners and sustained the same number of peripheral social partners into advanced old age (Yeung, Fung, & Lang, 2008). In contrast, Hong Kong elders scoring low in interdependence resembled their Western counterparts: They gradually limited their social ties to a few close relationships.

In sum, socioemotional selectivity theory views elders' preference for high-quality, emotionally fulfilling relationships to result from changing life conditions. But the meaning of relationship quality and, therefore, the number and variety of people to whom elders turn for pleasurable interaction and self-affirmation vary with culture.

Social Contexts of Aging: Communities, Neighborhoods, and Housing

The physical and social contexts in which elders live affect their social experiences and, consequently, their development and adjustment. Communities, neighborhoods, and housing arrangements vary in the extent to which they enable aging residents to satisfy their social needs.

■ **COMMUNITIES AND NEIGHBORHOODS.** About half of U.S. ethnic minority older adults live in cities, compared with only one-third of Caucasians. The majority of senior citizens reside in suburbs, where they moved earlier in their lives and usually remain after retirement. Suburban elders have higher incomes and report better health than inner-city elders do. But inner-city elders are better off in terms of transportation and

Like many older adults, these Spanish men reap great satisfaction from residing in a neighborhood with like-minded senior residents. Presence of family is less crucial when neighbors and nearby friends provide social support.

proximity to social services, and they are not as disadvantaged in terms of health, income, and availability of services as the one-fifth of American seniors who live in small towns and rural areas (U.S. Department of Health and Human Services, 2007a). In addition, small-town and rural elderly are less likely to live near their children, who often leave these communities in early adulthood.

Yet small-town and rural elderly compensate for distance from children and social services by establishing closer relationships with nearby extended family and by interacting more with neighbors and friends (Schilling & Wahl, 2002; Shaw, 2005). Smaller communities have features that foster gratifying relationships—stability of residents, shared values and lifestyles, willingness to exchange social support, and frequent social visits as country people "drop in" on one another. And many suburban and rural communities have responded to elder residents' needs by developing transportation programs (such as special buses and vans) to take elders to health and social services, senior centers, and shopping centers.

Both urban and rural older adults report greater life satisfaction when many senior citizens reside in their neighborhood and are available as like-minded companions. Presence of family is less crucial when neighbors and nearby friends provide social support (Gabriel & Bowling, 2004). This does not mean that neighbors replace family relationships. But elders are content as long as their children and other relatives who live far away arrange occasional visits (Hooyman & Kiyak, 2008).

■ **HOUSING ARRANGEMENTS.** Elders' housing preferences reflect a strong desire for **aging in place**—remaining in a familiar setting where they have control over their everyday life. Overwhelmingly, older adults in Western nations want to stay in the neighborhoods where they spent their adult lives; in fact, 90 percent remain in or near their old home. In the United States, fewer than 5 percent relocate to other communities (U.S. Department of Health and Human Services, 2007b). These moves are usually motivated by a desire to live closer to children or, among the more economically advantaged and healthy, a desire for a more temperate climate and a place to pursue leisure interests.

Most elder relocations occur within the same town or city and are prompted by declining health, widowhood, or disability (Sergeant, Ekerdt, & Chapin, 2008). As we look at housing arrangements for older adults, we will see that the more a setting deviates from home life, the harder it is for elders to adjust.

Ordinary Homes. For the majority of elders, who are not physically impaired, staying in their own homes affords the greatest possible personal control. More elders in Western countries live on their own today than ever before—a trend due to improved health and economic well-being (U.S. Department of Health and Human Services, 2009a). But when health and mobility problems appear, independent living poses risks. Most homes are not modified to suit the physical capacities of elder residents. And living alone in ill health is linked to social isolation and loneliness (Victor et al., 2000).

When Ruth reached her mid-eighties, Sybil begged her to move into her home. Like many adult children of Southern, Central, and Eastern European descent, Sybil felt an especially strong obligation to care for her frail mother. Older adults of these cultural backgrounds, as well as African Americans, Asians, Hispanics, and Native Americans, more often live in extended families (Gabrel, 2000; Hays & George, 2002).

Yet increasing numbers of ethnic minority elders want to live on their own, although poverty often prevents them from doing so. For example, two decades ago, most Asian-American older adults were living with their children, whereas today half live independently—a trend also evident in certain Asian nations, such as Japan (Takagi, Silverstein, & Crimmins, 2007; Wilmoth, 2001). With sufficient income to keep her home, Ruth refused to move in with Sybil. Continuity theory helps us understand why many elders react this way. As the site of memorable life events, the home strengthens continuity with the past, sustaining elders' sense of identity in the face of physical declines and social losses. And it permits older adults to adapt to their surroundings in familiar, comfortable ways (Atchley, 1999). Elders also value their independence, privacy, and network of nearby friends and neighbors.

During the past half century, the number of unmarried, divorced, and widowed elders living alone has risen dramatically. Approximately 30 percent of U.S. elders live by themselves, a figure that rises to nearly 50 percent for those age 85 and older (U.S. Census Bureau, 2009b). Over 40 percent of American elders who live alone are poverty-stricken—rates many times greater than among elderly couples. More than 70 percent are widowed women. Because of lower earnings in earlier years, some entered old age this way. Others became poor for the first time, often because they outlived a spouse who suffered a lengthy, costly illness. With age, their financial status worsens as their assets shrink and their own health-care costs rise (Biegel & Liebbrant, 2006; U.S. Census Bureau, 2009b). Poverty among lone elderly women is deeper in the United States than in other Western nations because of less generous government-sponsored income and health benefits.

This Chinese-American elder lives in her son and daughter-in-law's home, helping to rear their children—a traditional arrangement common in China. But increasingly, Asian-American older adults are choosing to live independently.

Residential Communities. About 15 percent of U.S. senior citizens live in residential communities, which come in great variety (Schafer, 1999; U.S. Department of Health and Human Services, 2007b). Housing developments for the aged, either single-dwelling or apartment complexes, differ from ordinary homes only in that they have been modified to suit elders' capacities (featuring, for example, single-level living space and grab bars in bathrooms).

For elders who need more help with everyday tasks, *assisted-living* arrangements are available (see Chapter 17, page 462). **Congregate housing**—an increasingly popular long-term care option—provides a variety of support services, including meals in a common dining room, along with watchful oversight of residents with physical and mental disabilities. **Life-care communities** offer a range of housing alternatives, from independent or congregate housing to full nursing home care. For a large initial payment and additional monthly fees, life care guarantees that elders' changing needs will be met within the same facility as they age.

Dick and Goldie decided in their late sixties to move to nearby congregate housing. For Dick, the move was a positive turn of events that permitted him to set aside past failures and relate to peers on the basis of their current life together. Dick found gratifying leisure pursuits—leading an exercise class, organizing a charity drive with Goldie, and using his skills as a baker to make cakes for birthday and anniversary celebrations.

Studies of diverse residential options for older adults reveal that they can have positive effects on physical and mental health. A specially designed physical space and care on an as-needed basis help elders overcome mobility limitations, thereby enabling greater social participation and a more active lifestyle (Fonda, Clipp, & Maddox, 2002; Jenkins, Pienta, & Horgas, 2002). And in societies where old age leads to reduced status, age-segregated living can be gratifying, opening up useful roles and leadership opportunities. Also, the more older adults perceive the environment as socially supportive, the more they collaborate with one another in coping with stressors of aging and in providing assistance to other residents (Lawrence & Schigelone, 2002).

Nevertheless, no U.S. federal regulations govern assisted-living facilities, which vary widely in quality. Low-income ethnic minority elders are less likely to use assisted living and, when they do, usually enter lower-quality settings. And in some states, assisted-living facilities are prohibited from providing any nursing care and monitoring, requiring elders to move when their health declines (Hawes & Phillips, 2007; Hernandez & Newcomer, 2007). Yet physical designs and support services that enable aging in place are vital for elders' well-being. These include homelike surroundings, division of large environments into smaller units to facilitate meaningful activities and social relationships, and the latest assistive technologies (Cutler, 2007).

Shared values and goals among residents with similar backgrounds also enhance life satisfaction. Older adults who feel socially integrated into the setting are more likely to consider it their home. But those who lack like-minded companions are at high risk for loneliness and depression (Adams, Sanders, & Auth, 2004; Young, 1998).

Nursing Homes. The 5 percent of Americans age 65 and older who live in nursing homes experience the most extreme restriction of autonomy and social integration. Although potential companions are abundant, interaction is low. To regulate emotion in social interaction (so important to elders), personal control over social experiences is vital. Yet nursing home residents have little opportunity to choose their social partners, and timing of contact is generally determined by staff, not by elders. Social withdrawal is an adaptive response to these often overcrowded, hospital-like settings. Not surprisingly, nursing home residents with physical but not mental impairments are far more depressed, anxious, and lonely than their community-dwelling counterparts (Guildner et al., 2001).

Designing more homelike nursing homes could help increase residents' sense of security and control. U.S. nursing homes, usually operated for profit, are often packed with residents and institutional in their operation. In contrast, European facilities are liberally supported by public funds and resemble high-quality assisted living.

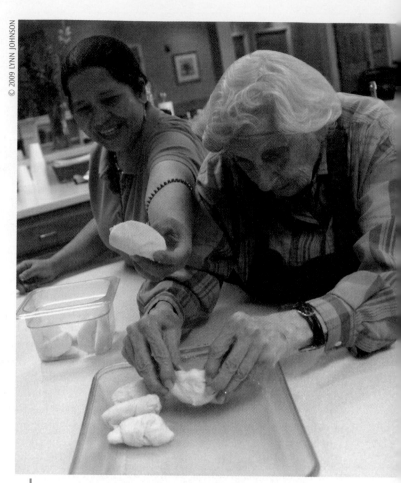

© 2009 LYNN JOHNSON

THE GREEN HOUSE® model blurs distinctions among nursing home, assisted living, and "independent" living. In this homelike setting, residents determine their own daily schedules and are invited to help with household tasks. Green House living environments, including this one in San Angelo, Texas, now exist in more than 20 U.S. states.

In a radically changed U.S. nursing-home concept called THE GREEN HOUSE® model, a large, outdated nursing home in Mississippi was replaced by ten small houses, each with ten or fewer residents who live in private bedroom-bathroom suites surrounding a family-style communal space (Rabig et al., 2006). Besides providing personal care, a stable staff of nursing assistants fosters elders' control and independence. Residents determine their own daily schedules and are invited to join in both recreational and household activities. A professional support team—including licensed nurses, therapists, social workers, physicians, and pharmacists—visits regularly to serve residents' health needs.

In a comparison of Green House residents with traditional nursing home residents, Green House elders reported substantially better quality of life, and they also showed less decline over time in ability to carry out activities of daily living (ADLs) (Kane et al., 2007). By making the home a central, organizing principle, The Green House approach includes all the aging-in-place features that ensure late-life well-being.

Relationships in Late Adulthood

The **social convoy** is an influential model of changes in our social networks as we move through life. **TAKE A MOMENT...** Picture yourself in the midst of a cluster of ships traveling together, granting one another safety and support. Ships in the inner circle represent people closest to you, such as a spouse, best friend, parent, or child. Those less close but still important travel on the outside. With age, ships exchange places in the convoy, and some drift off while others join the procession (Antonucci, Akiyama, & Takahashi, 2004). As long as the convoy continues to exist, you adapt positively.

In the following sections, we examine the ways elders with diverse lifestyles sustain social networks of family members and friends. Although the size of the convoy decreases as agemates die, elders are rarely left without people in their inner circle who contribute to their well-being—a testament to their resilience in maintaining effective social networks (Fiori, Smith, & Antonucci, 2007). But tragically, for some older adults the social convoy breaks down. We will also explore the circumstances in which elders experience abuse and neglect at the hands of those close to them.

Marriage

Even with the high U.S. divorce rate, one in every four or five first marriages is expected to last at least 50 years. Walt's comment to Ruth that "the last few decades have been the happiest" characterizes the attitudes and behaviors of many elderly couples who have spent their adult lives together. Marital satisfaction rises from middle to late adulthood, when it is at its peak (Ko et al., 2007; Levenson, Carstensen, & Gottman, 1993). Several changes in life circumstance and couples' communication underlie this trend.

First, late-life marriages involve fewer stressful responsibilities that can negatively affect relationships, such as rearing children and balancing demands of career and family (Kemp & Kemp, 2002). Second, perceptions of fairness in the relationship increase as men participate more in household tasks after retirement (Kulik, 2001). Third, with extra time together, the majority of couples engage in more joint leisure activities, which—especially for women—enhances a sense of marital closeness (Trudel et al., 2008).

Fourth, greater emotional understanding and emphasis on regulating emotion in relationships lead to more positive interactions between spouses. Compared to younger couples, elderly couples rate their relationship as higher in quality, disagree less often, and resolve their differences in more constructive ways. Even in unhappy marriages, elders are less likely to let their disagreements escalate into expressions of anger and resentment (Carstensen, Isaacowitz, & Charles, 1999; Hatch & Bulcroft, 2004). As in other relationships, the elderly protect themselves from stress by molding marital ties to make them as pleasant as possible.

Finally, compared to their single agemates, married elders generally have larger social networks of both family members and friends, which provide social engagement and support (Birditt & Antonucci, 2007; Fiori, Smith, & Antonucci, 2007). When marital dissatisfaction exists, however, even having close friendships cannot reduce its profoundly negative impact on adjustment. A poor marriage often takes a greater toll on women than on men (Birditt & Antonucci, 2007; Whisman et al., 2006). Recall from Chapter 14 that women more often try to work on a troubling relationship. In old age, expending energy in this way is especially taxing, both physically and mentally. Men, in contrast, often protect themselves by avoiding discussion.

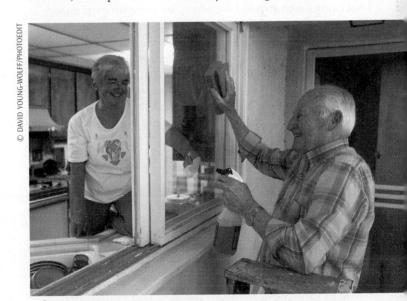

© DAVID YOUNG-WOLFF/PHOTOEDIT

After retirement, men's increased participation in household tasks results in a greater sense of equity in marriage, contributing to the rise in marital satisfaction from middle to late adulthood.

Gay and Lesbian Partnerships

Most elderly gays and lesbians in long-term partnerships report happy, highly fulfilling relationships, pointing to their partner as their most important source of social support (Grossman, D'Augelli, & Hershberger, 2000; Wojciechowski, 1998). A lifetime of effective coping with an oppressive social environment may have strengthened homosexuals' skill at dealing with latelife physical and social changes, thereby contributing to a satisfying partnership (Gabbay & Wahler, 2002). And changing social conditions, including the greater ease with which younger generations embrace their sexual minority identities and "come out," may have encouraged more older adults to do the same, with benefits for their well-being. Also, greater gender-role flexibility enables gay and lesbian couples to adapt easily to sharing household tasks following retirement (Cohler & Hostetler, 2007).

Nevertheless, because of continuing prejudice, aging gays and lesbians face unique challenges (Woolf, 2001). Health-care systems are often unresponsive to their unique needs. And where gay and lesbian unions are not legally recognized (in most U.S. states), if one partner becomes frail or ill, the other may not be welcome in hospitals or nursing homes or be allowed to participate in health-care decisions—an issue we will return to in Chapter 19. These circumstances can make late-life declines and losses especially painful.

Divorce, Remarriage, and Cohabitation

When Walt's uncle Louie was 61, he divorced his wife Sandra after 17 years of marriage. Although she knew the marriage was far from perfect, Sandra had lived with Louie long enough that the divorce came as a shock. A year later, Louie married Rachella, a divorcée who shared his enthusiasm for sports and dance.

Couples who divorce in late adulthood constitute less than 1 percent of all divorces in any given year. But the divorce rate among people age 65 and older is increasing as new generations of elders become more accepting of marital breakup and as the divorce risk rises for second and subsequent marriages. When asked about the reasons for divorce, elderly men typically mention lack of shared interests and activities, whereas women frequently cite emotional distance and their partner's refusal to communicate (Weingarten, 1988). "We never talked," Sandra said. "I felt isolated."

Compared with younger adults, longtime married elders faced with divorce find it harder to separate their identity from that of their former spouse, and they suffer more from a sense of personal failure. Relationships with family and friends shift at a time when close bonds are crucial for psychological well-being. Women, overall, suffer more than men because they are more likely to spend their remaining years living alone. The financial consequences are severe—greater than for widowhood because many accumulated assets are lost in property settlements (McDonald & Robb, 2004; Miller, Hemesath, & Nelson, 1997).

In younger individuals, divorce often leads to greater awareness of negative patterns of behavior and determination to change. In contrast, self-criticism in divorced elders heightens guilt and depression because their self-worth depends more on past than on future accomplishments. "I was always miserable with Sandra," Louie claimed, even though the couple's earlier days had been reasonably happy. Although blaming the partner may distort the marital history, it is a common coping strategy that enables older adults to preserve integrity and self-esteem (Weingarten, 1989).

Remarriage rates are low in late adulthood and decline with age, although they are considerably higher among divorced than widowed elders. Older men's opportunities for remarriage are far greater than women's. Nevertheless, the gender gap in elder remarriage is much smaller after divorce than after widowhood. Perhaps because their previous relationship was disappointing, divorcées find it easier than widows to enter a new relationship (Huyck, 1995). Also, divorced older women may be more motivated to remarry because of their more extreme economic circumstances.

Compared with younger people who remarry, elders who do so enter more stable relationships, as their divorce rate is much lower. In Louie and Rachella's case, the second marriage lasted for 32 years! Perhaps late-life remarriages are more successful because they involve more maturity, patience, and a better balance of romantic with practical concerns (Kemp & Kemp, 2002).

Rather than remarrying, today more elders choose cohabitation, a trend expected to continue as the baby boomers—the first generation to cohabit at high rates in early adulthood—reach late life. Like elder remarriages, cohabitation in late adulthood results in more stable relationships and higher relationship quality than it did at younger ages. But compared with younger people, fewer cohabiting elders have plans to marry. Reasons frequently given are concerns about acceptance of the new partner by adult children and negative financial consequences with respect to taxes, social security or pension benefits, and adult children's inheritance (King & Scott, 2005; Kemp & Kemp, 2002). In addition, like younger cohabiters, U.S. cohabiting elders tend to have less conventional values—for example, are less religious—than their married agemates (Brown, Lee, & Bulanda, 2006).

Widowhood

Walt died shortly after Ruth turned 80. Like over 70 percent of widowed elders, Ruth described the loss of her spouse as the most stressful event of her life. Being widowed means that the survivor has "lost the role and identity of being a spouse (being married and doing things as a couple), which is potentially one of the most pervasive, intense, intimate, and personal roles that they have ever had" (Lund & Caserta, 2004a, p. 29).

Widows make up about one-third of the elderly population in industrialized nations. Because women live longer than men and are less likely to remarry, more than 40 percent of U.S. women age 65 and older are widowed, compared with only 13 percent of men. Ethnic minorities with high rates of poverty and chronic disease are more likely to be widowed (U.S. Census Bureau, 2009b).

The greatest problem for recently widowed elders is profound loneliness (Lund, 1993). But adaptation varies widely, depending on age, social support, and personality. Elders have fewer lasting problems than younger widowed individuals, probably because death in later life is viewed as less unfair. And most widowed elders—especially those with outgoing personalities and high self-esteem—are resilient in the face of loneliness (Moore & Stratton, 2002; van Baarsen, 2002). To sustain continuity with their past, they try to preserve social relationships that were important before the spouse's death and report that relatives and friends respond in kind, contacting them at least as often as before (Utz et al., 2002). Also, the stronger elders' sense of self-efficacy in handling tasks of daily living, the more favorably they adjust (Fry, 2001).

Nevertheless, widowed individuals must reorganize their lives, reconstructing an identity that is separate from the deceased spouse. Overall, men show more physical and mental health problems and greater risk of mortality than women, for several reasons (Bennett, Smith, & Hughes, 2005; Pinquart, 2003). First, because most men relied on their wives for social connectedness, household tasks, promotion of healthy behaviors, and coping with stressors, they are less prepared than women for the challenges of widowhood. Second, because of gender-role expectations, men feel less free to express their emotions or to ask for help with meals, household tasks, and social relationships (Bennett, 2007; Lund & Caserta, 2004b). Finally, men tend to be less involved in religious activities—a vital source of social support and inner strength (Lee et al., 2001).

In two studies of older widowers, those in their seventies reported the most depression and showed the slowest rate of improvement over the following two years. The death of their wives occurred around the time they were adjusting to retirement, resulting in two major changes at once (Lund & Caserta, 2001, 2004a). African-American widowers, however, show no elevated risk of mortality over African-American married elders, and they report less depression than Caucasian widowers (Balaswamy & Richardson, 2001; Elwert & Christakis, 2006). Perhaps greater support from extended family and church is responsible.

Sex differences in the experience of widowhood contribute to men's higher remarriage rate. Women's kinkeeper role (see Chapter 16, page 429) and ability to form close friendships may lead them to feel less need to remarry. In addition, because many elderly women share the widowed state, they probably offer one another helpful advice and sympathy. In contrast, men often lack skills for maintaining family relationships, forming emotionally satisfying ties outside marriage, and handling the chores of their deceased wives.

Still, widowed elders with high self-esteem and a sense of purpose in life fare well within a few years, resembling their married counterparts in psychological well-being (Lund & Caserta, 2001). Older widows and widowers who participated in several months of weekly classes providing information and support in acquiring daily living skills felt better prepared to manage the challenges of widowed life (Caserta, Lund, & Obray, 2004). Applying What We Know on page 490 suggests ways to foster adaptation to widowhood in old age.

Most men rely on their wives for social connectedness, household tasks, and promotion of healthy behaviors, so they are less prepared than women for the challenges of widowhood. This man, however, appears to be managing well—in part because he is skilled at preparing nutritious meals.

Never-Married, Childless Older Adults

Shortly after Ruth and Walt's marriage in their twenties, Ruth's father died. Her sister Ida continued to live with and care for their mother, who was in ill health until she died 16 years later. When, at age 25, Ida received a marriage proposal, she responded, "I can't marry while my mother is still living. I'm expected to look after her." Ida's decision was not unusual for a daughter of her day. She never married or had children.

About 5 percent of older Americans have remained unmarried and childless throughout their lives. Almost all are conscious of being different from the norm, but most have developed alternative meaningful relationships. Ida, for example, formed a strong bond with a neighbor's son. In his childhood, she provided emotional support and financial assistance, which helped him overcome a stressful home life. He included Ida in family events and visited her regularly until she died. Other nonmarried elders also speak of the centrality of younger people—often nieces and nephews—in their social networks and of influencing them in enduring ways (Rubinstein et al., 1991). In addition, same-sex friendships are key in never-married elderly women's lives (McDill, Hall, & Turell, 2006). These tend to be unusually close and often involve joint travel, periods of coresidence, and associations with one another's extended families.

Nonmarried, childless men are more likely than women to feel lonely and depressed. And without pressure from a spouse to maintain a healthy lifestyle, they engage in more unhealthy

Applying What We Know

Fostering Adaptation to Widowhood in Late Adulthood

Suggestion	Description
Family and Friends	
Social support and interaction	Social support and interaction must extend beyond the grieving period to ongoing assistance and caring relationships. Family members and friends can help most by making support available while encouraging the widowed elder to use effective coping strategies.
Community	
Senior centers	Senior centers offer communal meals and other social activities, enabling widowed and other elders to connect with people in similar circumstances and to gain access to other community resources, such as listings of part-time employment and available housing.
Support groups	Support groups can be found in senior centers, religious institutions, and other agencies. Besides new relationships, they offer an accepting atmosphere for coming to terms with loss, effective role models, and assistance with developing skills for daily living.
Religious activities	Involvement in a church, synagogue, or mosque can help relieve loneliness and offer social support, new relationships, and meaningful roles.
Volunteer activities	One of the best ways for widowed elders to find meaningful roles is through volunteer activities. Some are sponsored by formal service organizations, such as the Retired and Senior Volunteer Program. Other volunteer programs exist in hospitals, senior centers, schools, and charitable organizations.

behaviors (Kendig et al., 2007). Never-married elderly women report a level of well-being equivalent to that of married elders and greater than that of divorcées and recently widowed elders. Only when they agree with the stereotype that "life is empty without a partner," or when they cannot maintain social contacts because of declining health, do they report feeling lonely (Baumbusch, 2004; Dykstra, 2006). These single women often state that they avoided many problems associated with being a wife and mother, and they view their enhanced friendships as an advantage of not marrying. At the same time, they realize that friendships are not the same as blood ties when it comes to caregiving in old age.

Siblings

Nearly 80 percent of Americans over age 65 have at least one living sibling. Most elder siblings live within 100 miles of each other, communicate regularly, and visit at least several times a year. Both men and women perceive bonds with sisters to be closer than bonds with brothers. Perhaps because of women's greater emotional expressiveness and nurturance, the closer the tie to a sister, the higher elders' psychological well-being (Cicirelli, 1989; Van Volkom, 2006).

Elderly siblings in industrialized nations are more likely to socialize than to provide one another with direct assistance because most turn first to their spouse and children. Nevertheless, siblings seem to be an important "insurance policy" in late adulthood. Figure 18.2 shows the extent to which, in a large na-

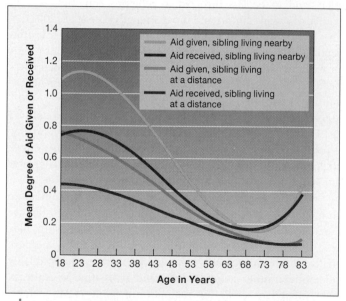

■ **FIGURE 18.2** ■ **Age-related changes in aid given to or received from a sibling.** In a large, nationally representative American survey, adults reported a rise in sibling aid in early adulthood, a decline during middle adulthood, and then a rise after age 70 for siblings living near one another (within 25 miles). In late life, siblings seem to be an important "insurance policy" when help is not available from a spouse or child. (Adapted from L. White, 2001, "Sibling Relationships over the Life Course: A Panel Analysis," *Journal of Marriage and the Family, 63,* p. 564. Adapted by permission of Blackwell Publishing, Ltd., publisher, and Lynn K. White.)

tionally representative U.S. survey, individuals ranging in age from 16 to 85 reported giving or receiving aid from a sibling. As we saw in earlier chapters, sibling support rises in early adulthood and then declines in middle adulthood. After age 70, it increases for siblings living within 25 miles of each other (White, 2001). Most elders say they would turn to a sibling for help in a crisis, less often in other situations (Connidis, 1994).

Widowed and never-married elders have more contacts with siblings, perhaps because they have fewer competing family relationships. They are also more likely to receive sibling support during illness (Connidis & Campbell, 1995). For example, when Ida's Alzheimer's symptoms worsened, Ruth came to her aid. Although Ida had many friends, Ruth was her only living relative.

Friendships

As family responsibilities and vocational pressures lessen, friendships take on increasing importance. Having friends is an especially strong predictor of mental health among the elderly (Nussbaum, 1994; Rawlins, 2004). Older adults report more favorable experiences with friends than with family members, in part because of the pleasurable leisure activities they share with friends (Larson, Mannell, & Zuzanek, 1986). Unique qualities of friendship interaction—openness, spontaneity, mutual caring, and common interests—are also influential.

■ **FUNCTIONS OF ELDER FRIENDSHIPS.** The diverse functions of friendship in late adulthood clarify its profound significance:

- *Intimacy and companionship.* As Ida and her best friend, Rosie, took walks, went shopping, or visited each other, they engaged in pleasurable conversation and disclosed their deepest sources of happiness and worry (Crohan & Antonucci, 1989). Mutual interests, feelings of belongingness, and opportunities to express feelings and confide in another sustain these bonds over time (Field, 1999).

- *Acceptance.* Late-life friends shield one another from negative judgments about their capabilities and worth as a person, which frequently stem from stereotypes of aging (Adams, 1985–1986). "Where's your cane, Rosie?" Ida asked when the two women were about to leave for a restaurant. "Come on, don't be self-conscious. Just remember: In the Greek village where my mother grew up, there was no separation between generations, so the young ones got used to wrinkled skin and weak knees and recognized older women as the wise ones. Why, they were midwives, matchmakers, experts in herbal medicine; they knew about everything!" (Deveson, 1994).

- *A link to the larger community.* For elders who cannot go out as often, interactions with friends can keep them abreast of events in the wider world. "Rosie," Ida reported, "did you know the Thompson girl was named high school valedictorian?" Friends can also open up new experiences that older adults

might not take part in alone. Often a first trip to a senior citizens' center takes place with a friend (Nussbaum, 1994).

- *Protection from the psychological consequences of loss.* Older adults in declining health who remain in contact with friends through phone calls and visits show improved psychological well-being. Similarly, when close relatives die, friends offer compensating social supports (Fiori, Smith, & Antonucci, 2007).

■ **CHARACTERISTICS OF ELDER FRIENDSHIPS.** Although older adults prefer familiar, established relationships over new ones, friendship formation continues throughout life. But with age, elders report that the friends they feel closest to are fewer in number and live in the same community. As in earlier years, elders tend to choose friends whose age, sex, race, ethnicity, and values are like their own. Compared with younger people, fewer report other-sex friendships. But some have them—usually longstanding ones dating back several decades (Monsour, 2002). As agemates die, the very old report more intergenerational friends—both same- and other-sex (Johnson & Troll, 1994). In her eighties, Ruth spent time with Margaret, a 55-year-old widow she met while serving on the board of directors of an adoption agency. Two or three times a month, Margaret came to Ruth's home for tea and lively conversation.

© RICHARD LIST/CORBIS

These men often meet to chat on a village street on the Greek island of Corfu. Even after physical mobility declines, many elders find ways to sustain ties with friends, who offer companionship, links to the larger community, and social support in the face of loss.

Sex differences in friendship, discussed in previous chapters, extend into late adulthood. Women are more likely to have intimate friends; men depend on their wives and, to a lesser extent, their sisters for warm, open communication. Also, older women have more **secondary friends**—people who are not intimates but with whom they spend time occasionally, such as a group that meets for lunch, bridge, or museum tours. Through these associates, elders meet new people, remain socially involved, and gain in psychological well-being (Adams, Bleiszner, & De Vries, 2000).

Relationships with Adult Children

About 80 percent of older adults in Western nations are parents of living children, most of whom are middle-aged. In Chapter 16, we noted that exchanges of help vary with the closeness of the parent–child bond and the needs of the parent and adult child. Recall, also, that over time, parent-to-child help declines, whereas child-to-parent assistance increases. Elders and their adult children are often in touch, even when they live far from each other. But as with other ties, quality rather than quantity of interaction affects older adults' life satisfaction. In diverse ethnic groups and cultures, warm bonds with adult children reduce the negative impact of physical impairments and other losses (such as death of a spouse) on psychological well-being. Alternatively, conflict or unhappiness with adult children contributes to poor physical and mental health (Ajrouch, 2007; Milkie, Bierman, & Schieman, 2008; Silverstein & Bengtson, 1991).

Although aging parents and adult children in Western nations provide each other with various forms of help, level of assistance is typically modest. Older adults in their sixties and seventies—especially those who own their own home and who are married or widowed as opposed to divorced—are more likely to be providers than recipients of help, suggesting SES variations in the balance of support (Grundy, 2005). This balance shifts as elders age, but well into late adulthood, elders in Western nations give more than they receive, especially in financial support but also in practical assistance—a circumstance that contradicts stereotypes of older adults as "burdens" on younger generations (HSBC & Oxford Institute of Ageing, 2007).

Interviews with parents age 75 and older in five Western nations revealed that in all countries, aid received from adult children most often took the form of emotional support. Fewer than one-third said their children assisted with household chores and errands. Elders who provided more help of various kinds than they received scored highest in life satisfaction, those receiving more help than they gave scored lowest, while those in a balanced exchange fell in between (Lowenstein, Katz, & Gur-Yaish, 2007). To avoid dependency, older parents usually do not seek children's practical assistance in the absence of a pressing need, and they express annoyance when children are overprotective or help unnecessarily (Spitze & Gallant, 2004). Moderate support, with many opportunities to reciprocate, is beneficial, fostering self-esteem and sense of family connection.

As social networks shrink in size, relationships with adult children become more important sources of family involvement. Elders 85 years and older with children have substantially more contacts with relatives than do those without children (Hooyman & Kiyak, 2008). Why is this so? Consider Ruth, whose daughter Sybil linked her to grandchildren, great-grandchildren, and relatives by marriage. When childless elders reach their eighties, siblings, other same-age relatives, and close friends may have become frail or died and hence may no longer be available as companions.

Elder Maltreatment

Although the majority of older adults enjoy positive relationships with family members, friends, and professional caregivers, some suffer maltreatment at the hands of these individuals. Reports from many industrialized nations reveal widely varying rates of maltreatment, from 3 to 28 percent in general population studies. Overall, more than 6 percent of elders say they were targets during the past month, amounting to about 2 million victims in the United States (Cooper, Selwood, & Livingston, 2008). Elder maltreatment crosses ethnic lines, although it is lower in Asian, Hispanic, and Native-American groups with strong traditions of respect for and obligation to the aged and highly disapproving attitudes toward harming them (Rittman, Kuzmeskus, & Flum, 2000; Sherman, Rosenblatt, & Antonucci, 2008). Yet all figures underestimate the actual incidence because most abusive acts take place in private and victims are often unable or unwilling to complain.

Elder maltreatment usually takes the following forms:

- *Physical abuse.* Intentional infliction of pain, discomfort, or injury, through hitting, cutting, burning, physical force, restraint, and other acts

- *Physical neglect.* Intentional or unintentional failure to fulfill caregiving obligations, resulting in lack of food, medication, or health services or in the elderly person being left alone or isolated

- *Emotional abuse.* Verbal assaults (such as name calling), humiliation (being treated as a child), and intimidation (threats of isolation or placement in a nursing home)

- *Sexual abuse.* Unwanted sexual contact of any kind

- *Financial abuse.* Illegal or improper exploitation of the elder's property or financial resources, through theft or use without the elder's consent

Financial abuse, emotional abuse, and neglect are the most frequently reported types (Anetzberger, 2005; World Health Organization, 2002). The perpetrator is usually a person the older adult trusts and depends on for care and assistance. Most abusers are family members—spouses (usually men), followed by children of both sexes and then by other relatives. Some are friends, neighbors, and in-home caregivers (U.S. Administration on Aging, 2009). Abuse in nursing homes is a major concern. In one survey, one-third of nurses indicated that they had ob-

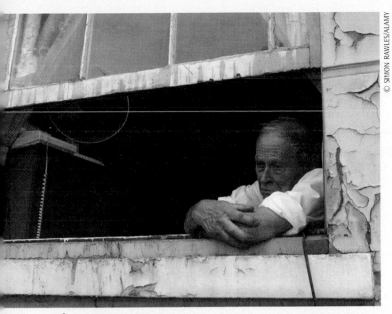

This older adult, who suffers from depression and physical disabilities, lives in a dilapidated rooming house. When conditions are ripe for elder maltreatment, those with physical or cognitive impairments are least able to protect themselves.

served it, while 10 percent admitted to at least one act of physical abuse and 40 percent to at least one act of emotional abuse (Wilber & McNeilly, 2001).

Over the past several decades, another form of neglect—referred to in the media as "granny dumping"—has increased: abandonment of elders with severe disabilities by family caregivers, usually at hospital emergency rooms (Fulmer, 2008). According to one U.S. hospital survey, between 100,000 and 200,000 older adults—most suffering from dementia—are left in hospital waiting rooms each year (Tanne, 1992). Overwhelmed, their caregivers seem to have concluded that they have no other option but to take this drastic step. (See pages 433–434 in Chapter 16 and page 461 in Chapter 17 for related research.)

■ **RISK FACTORS.** Characteristics of the victim, the abuser, their relationship, and its social context are related to the incidence and severity of elder maltreatment. The more of the following risk factors that are present, the greater the likelihood that abuse and neglect will occur.

Dependency of the Victim. When other conditions are ripe for maltreatment, elders who are frail or severely disabled are at greater risk because they are least able to protect themselves (Reay & Browne, 2008). Those with physical or cognitive impairments may also have personality traits that make them vulnerable—a tendency to lash out when angry or frustrated, a passive or avoidant approach to handling problems, and a low sense of self-efficacy (Comijs et al., 1999).

Dependency of the Perpetrator. Many abusers are dependent, emotionally or financially, on their victims. Frequently the perpetrator–victim relationship is one of mutual dependency

(Henderson, Buchanan, & Fisher, 2002). The abuser needs the older person for money or housing, and the older person needs the abuser for assistance with everyday tasks or to relieve loneliness.

Psychological Disturbance and Stress of the Perpetrator. Abusers are more likely than other caregivers to have psychological problems and to be dependent on alcohol or other drugs (Pillemer et al., 2007). Often they are socially isolated, have difficulties at work, or are unemployed. These factors increase the likelihood that they will lash out when caregiving is highly demanding or the behavior of an elder with dementia is irritating or hard to manage.

History of Family Violence. Elder abuse is often part of a long history of family violence. Adults who were abused as children are at increased risk of harming elders (Reay & Browne, 2008). In many instances, elder abuse is an extension of years of partner abuse (Walsh et al., 2007).

Institutional Conditions. Elder maltreatment is more likely to occur in nursing homes that are rundown and overcrowded and that have staff shortages, minimal staff supervision, high staff turnover, and few visitors (Payne & Fletcher, 2005). Highly stressful work conditions combined with minimal oversight of caregiving quality set the stage for abuse and neglect.

■ **PREVENTING ELDER MALTREATMENT.** Preventing elder maltreatment by family members is especially challenging. Victims may fear retribution; wish to protect abusers who are spouses, sons, or daughters; or feel embarrassed that they cannot control the situation. And they may be intimidated into silence or not know where to turn for help (Summers & Hoffman, 2006). Once abuse is discovered, intervention involves immediate protection and provision of unmet needs for the elder and of mental health services and social support for the spouse or caregiver.

Prevention programs offer caregivers counseling, education, and respite services, such as elder day care and in-home help. Trained volunteer "buddies" who make visits to the home can combat social isolation among elders and assist them with problem solving to avoid further harm. Support groups help seniors identify abusive acts, practice appropriate responses, and form new relationships. And agencies that provide informal financial services to older adults who are unable to manage on their own, such as writing and cashing checks and holding valuables in a safe, reduce financial abuse (Rabiner, O'Keeffe, & Brown, 2004).

When elder abuse is extreme, legal action offers elders the best protection, yet many victims are reluctant to initiate court procedures or, because of mental impairments, cannot do so. In these instances, social service professionals must help caregivers rethink their role, even if it means that the aging person might be institutionalized. In nursing homes, improving staff selection, training, and working conditions can greatly reduce abuse and neglect.

Combating elder maltreatment also requires efforts at the level of the larger society, including public education to encourage reporting of suspected cases and improved understanding of the needs of older people. Finally, countering negative stereotypes of aging reduces maltreatment because recognizing elders' dignity, individuality, and autonomy is incompatible with acts of harm.

ASK YOURSELF

>> **REVIEW**

Why is adjustment to late-life divorce usually more difficult for women and adjustment to widowhood more difficult for men?

>> **APPLY**

At age 51, Mae lost her job and moved in with her 78-year-old widowed mother, Beryl. Although Beryl welcomed Mae's companionship, Mae grew depressed and drank heavily. When Beryl complained about Mae's failure to look for work, Mae pushed and slapped her. Explain why this mother–daughter relationship led to elder abuse.

>> **REFLECT**

Select one elderly member of your extended family whom you know well, and describe that person's social convoy, or cluster of close relationships. In what ways has the convoy changed over the past five to ten years? How well has the person adapted to those changes? Explain.

Retirement

In Chapter 16, we noted that the period of retirement has lengthened because of increased life expectancy and a steady decline in average age of retirement—trends occurring in all Western industrialized nations. Because mandatory retirement no longer exists for most workers in Western countries, older adults have more choices about when to retire and how they spend their time.

Indeed, the trend toward earlier retirement may soon reverse, and not just because of a decline in older adults' retirement savings due to the recent global economic recession. According to a survey of 21,000 adults in 21 countries, most baby boomers say they want to work longer (HSBC & Oxford Institute of Ageing, 2007). Currently, 45 percent of U.S. adults in their sixties, and nearly 20 percent of those in their seventies, are still working in some capacity.

As these figures suggest, the contemporary retirement process is highly variable: It may include a planning period, the decision itself, diverse acts of retiring, and continuous adjustment and readjustment of activities for the rest of the life course. The majority of U.S. older adults with career jobs retire gradually by cutting down their hours and responsibilities. Many take *bridge jobs*—new part-time jobs or full-time jobs of shorter duration—that serve as transitions between full-time career and retirement (Moen & Altobelli, 2007). Others leave

their jobs but later return to paid work to introduce interest and challenge into the retirement years, to supplement limited financial resources, or both.

In the following sections, we examine factors that affect the decision to retire, happiness during the retirement years, and leisure and volunteer pursuits. We will see that the process of retirement and retired life reflect an increasingly diverse retired population.

The Decision to Retire

When Walt and Ruth retired, both had worked long enough to be eligible for comfortable income-replacement benefits—Walt's through the government-sponsored Social Security program, Ruth's through a private pension plan. In addition, they had planned for retirement (see Chapter 16, pages 437–438) and decided on a date for leaving the work force. They wanted to retire early enough to pursue leisure activities while they were both in good health and could enjoy them together. In contrast, Walt's brother Dick was forced to retire as the operating costs of his bakery rose and his clientele dropped off. He looked for temporary employment in sales while his wife, Goldie, kept her part-time job as a bookkeeper to help cover living expenses.

Affordability of retirement is usually the first consideration in the decision to retire. Yet despite economic concerns, many preretirees decide to let go of a steady work life in favor of alternative, personally meaningful work, leisure, or volunteer activities. "I was working since I was 10 years old," said one retired auto worker. "I wanted a rest." Exceptions to this favorable outlook are people like Dick—forced into retirement or earning very low wages—who often take bridge jobs reluctantly to make ends meet (Cahill, Giandrea, & Quinn, 2006; Warr et al., 2004).

Figure 18.3 summarizes personal and workplace factors in addition to income that influence the decision to retire. People in good health, for whom vocational life is central to self-esteem, and whose work environments are pleasant and interesting, are likely to keep on working. For these reasons, individuals in high-earning professional occupations usually retire later than those in blue-collar or clerical positions. And when they do retire, they more often shift to stimulating bridge jobs (Cahill, Giandrea, & Quinn, 2006; Siegrist et al., 2007). Self-employed elders also stay with their jobs longer, probably because they can flexibly adapt their working hours to changing needs (Helson & Cate, 2006). In contrast, people in declining health; who are engaged in routine, boring work; and who have compelling leisure interests often opt for retirement.

In most Western nations, generous social security benefits make retirement feasible for the economically disadvantaged and sustain the standard of living of most workers after they retire. The United States is an exception: Many U.S. retirees, especially those who held low-income jobs without benefits, experience falling living standards (Hungerford, 2003). Den-

Retire
- Adequate retirement benefits
- Compelling leisure interests
- Low work commitment
- Declining health
- Spouse retiring
- Routine, boring job

Continue Working
- Limited or no retirement benefits
- Few leisure interests
- High work commitment
- Good health
- Spouse working
- Flexible work schedule
- Pleasant, stimulating work environment

A recent retiree enjoys an adult-education class in bookbinding.

This doctor, in her 60s, plans to keep practicing medicine indefinitely.

■ **FIGURE 18.3** ■ **Personal and workplace factors that influence the decision to retire.**

mark, France, Germany, Finland, and Sweden have gradual retirement programs in which older employees reduce their work hours, receive a partial pension to make up income loss, and continue to accrue pension benefits. Besides strengthening financial security, this approach introduces a transitional phase that fosters retirement planning and well-being (Reday-Mulvey, 2000). And some countries' retirement policies are sensitive to women's more interrupted work lives. In Canada, France, and Germany, for example, time devoted to child rearing is given some credit when figuring retirement benefits (Service Canada, 2009).

In sum, individual preferences shape retirement decisions. At the same time, older adults' opportunities and limitations greatly affect their choices.

Adjustment to Retirement

Because retirement involves giving up roles that are a vital part of identity and self-esteem, it usually is assumed to be a stressful process that contributes to declines in physical and mental health. Consider Dick, who reacted to the closing of his bakery with anxiety and depression. But recall that Dick had a cranky, disagreeable personality. In this respect, his psychological well-being after retirement was similar to what it had been before! We must be careful not to assume a cause-and-effect relationship each time retirement is paired with an unfavorable reaction. For example, a wealth of evidence confirms that physical health problems lead elders to retire, rather than the reverse (Shultz & Wang, 2007).

The widely held belief that retirement inevitably leads to adjustment problems is contradicted by countless research findings. Contemporary elders view retirement as a time of opportunity and personal growth and describe themselves as active and socially involved—major determinants of retirement satisfaction (HSBC & Oxford Institute of Ageing, 2007; Kloep & Hendry, 2007). Still, about 10 to 30 percent mention some adjustment difficulties.

Workplace factors—especially financial worries and having to give up one's job— predict stress following retirement. And older adults who find it hard to give up the predictable schedule and social contacts of the work setting experience discomfort with their less structured way of life. But a sense of personal control over life events, including deciding to retire for internally motivated reasons (to do other things), is strongly linked to retirement satisfaction (Quine et al., 2007; Kim & Moen, 2002c). Well-educated people in high-status careers typically adjust favorably, perhaps because the satisfactions derived from challenging, meaningful work readily transfer to nonwork pursuits (Kim & Moen, 2002a).

As with other major life events, social support reduces stress associated with retirement. Although social-network size typically shrinks as relationships with co-workers decline, quality of relationships remains fairly stable. And many elders add to their social networks through leisure and volunteer pursuits (Kloep & Hendry, 2007). In Dick's case, entering congregate housing eased a difficult postretirement period, leading to new friends and rewarding leisure activities, some of which he shared with Goldie.

Finally, earlier in this chapter we noted that marital happiness tends to rise after retirement. When a couple's relationship is positive, it can buffer the uncertainty of retirement. And retirement can enhance marital satisfaction by granting husband and wife more time for companionship (Kim & Moen, 2002a; van Solinge & Henkens, 2008). Consequently, a good marriage not only promotes adjustment to retirement but also benefits from the greater freedom of the retirement years. In line with continuity theory, people try to sustain earlier lifestyle patterns, self-esteem, and values following retirement and, in favorable economic and social contexts, usually succeed in doing so (Atchley, 2003).

Leisure and Volunteer Activities

After a "honeymoon period" of trying out new options, many new retirees find that interests and skills do not develop suddenly. Instead, meaningful leisure and community service pursuits are usually formed earlier and sustained or expanded during retirement (HSBC & Oxford Institute of Ageing, 2007; Mannell, 1999). For example, Walt's fondness for writing, theater, and gardening dated back to his youth. And Ruth's strong focus on her vocation of social work led her to become an avid community volunteer.

Involvement in leisure activities and, especially, volunteer service is related to better physical and mental health and reduced mortality (Avlund et al., 2004; Cutler & Hendricks, 2001; Moen, 2003). But simply participating does not explain this relationship. Instead, elders select these pursuits because they permit self-expression, new achievements, the rewards of helping others, or pleasurable social interaction. And those high in sense of self-efficacy are more engaged (Diehl & Berg, 2007). These factors account for gains in well-being.

Older adults contribute enormously to society through volunteer work, a trend that is strengthening. About one-third of 60- and 70-year-olds in industrialized nations report volunteering. Of those who do, over half give 200 or more hours per year (HSBC & Oxford Institute of Ageing, 2007; Kloep & Hendry, 2007). Younger, better-educated, and financially secure elders with social interests are more likely to volunteer, women more often than men. Although most extend an earlier pattern of civic engagement, nonvolunteers are especially receptive to volunteer activities in the first few years after retiring—a prime time to recruit them into these personally rewarding and socially useful pursuits (Mutchler, Burr, & Caro, 2003).

In a survey of a large, nationally representative U.S. sample, time spent volunteering did not decline until the eighties (Hendricks & Cutler, 2004). Even then, it remained higher than at any other time of life! In accord with socioemotional selectivity theory, older adults eventually narrowed their volunteering to fewer roles, concentrating on one or two that meant the most to them. They seemed to recognize that excessive volunteering reduces its emotional rewards and, thus, its benefits to well-being (Windsor, Anstey, & Rodgers, 2008).

Finally, older adults report greater awareness of and interest in public affairs and vote at a higher rate than any other age group. After retiring, elders have more time to keep abreast of current events through reading and watching TV. Elders' political concerns are far broader than those that serve their own age group, and their voting behavior is not driven by self-interest (Binstock & Quadagno, 2001). Rather, their political involvement may stem from a deep desire for a safer, more secure world for future generations.

Optimal Aging

Walt, Ruth, Dick, Goldie, and Ida, and the research findings they illustrate, reveal great diversity in development during the final decades of life. Walt and Ruth fit contemporary experts' view of **optimal aging,** in which gains are maximized and losses minimized. Both were actively engaged with their families and communities, coped well with negative life changes, enjoyed a happy intimate partnership and other close relationships, and led daily lives filled with gratifying activities. Ida, too, experienced optimal aging until the onset of Alzheimer's symptoms. As a single adult, she built a rich social network that sustained her

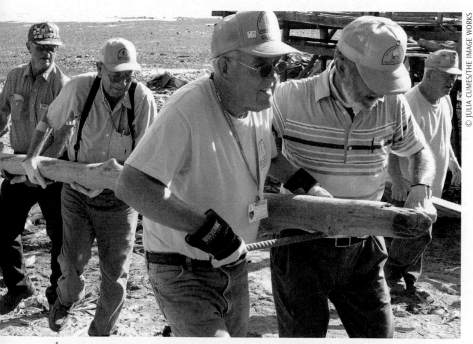
Volunteering grants elders a gratifying sense of making valuable contributions to society. These older adults, who range in age from 65 to 80, traveled to Thailand to help rebuild homes along the seacoast after the devastating tsunami of 2005.

into old age, despite the hardship of having spent many years caring for her ailing mother.

People age optimally when their growth, vitality, and striving limit and, at times, overcome physical, cognitive, and social declines. Researchers want to know more about factors that contribute to optimal aging so they can help more seniors experience it. Yet theorists disagree on the precise ingredients of a satisfying old age. Some focus on easily measurable outcomes, such as excellent cardiovascular functioning, absence of disability, superior cognitive performance, and creative achievements. But this view has been heavily criticized (Aldwin, Spiro, & Park, 2006). Not everyone can become an outstanding athlete, an innovative scientist, or a talented artist. And many older adults do not want to keep on accomplishing and producing—the main markers of success in Western nations.

Recent views of a contented, fulfilling late adulthood have turned away from specific achievements toward processes people use to reach personally valued goals (Freund & Baltes, 1998; Kahana et al., 2005; Lund, 1998). In research on three samples of adults followed over the lifespan, George Vaillant found that factors people could control to some degree (such as health habits, coping strategies, marital stability, and years of education) far outweighed uncontrollable factors (parental SES, family warmth in childhood, early physical health, and longevity of family members) in predicting a happy, active old age (Vaillant & Mukamal, 2001). Consider the following description of one participant, who in childhood had experienced low SES, parental discord, a depressed mother, and seven siblings crowded into a tenement apartment. Despite these early perils, he became happily married and, through the GI bill, earned an accounting degree. At 70, he was aging well:

Anthony Pirelli may have been *ill* considering his heart attack and open-heart surgery, but he did not feel *sick*. He was physically active as ever, and he continued to play tennis. Asked what he missed about his work, he exulted, "I'm so busy doing other things that I don't have time to miss work. . . . Life is not boring for me." He did not smoke or abuse alcohol; he loved his wife; he used mature [coping strategies]; he obtained 14 years of education; he watched his waistline; and he exercised regularly. (Adapted from Vaillant, 2002, pp. 12, 305)

Vaillant concluded, "The past often predicts but never determines our old age" (p. 12). Optimal aging is an expression of remarkable resilience during this final phase of the lifespan.

In this and the previous chapter, we have considered the many ways that older adults realize their goals. ***TAKE A MOMENT...*** Look back and review the most important ones:

■ Optimism and sense of self-efficacy in improving health and physical functioning (pages 452–453)

■ Selective optimization with compensation to make the most of limited physical energies and cognitive resources (pages 463 and 479)

■ Strengthening of self-concept, which promotes self-acceptance and pursuit of hoped-for possible selves (pages 476–478)

■ Enhanced emotional understanding and emotional self-regulation, which support meaningful, rewarding social ties (pages 475–476)

■ Acceptance of change, which fosters life satisfaction (page 478)

■ A mature sense of spirituality and faith, permitting anticipation of death with calmness and composure (page 478)

■ Personal control over domains of dependency and independence (pages 479–480, 492)

■ High-quality relationships, which offer social support and pleasurable companionship (pages 483–484)

Optimal aging is facilitated by societal contexts that permit elders to manage life changes effectively. Older adults need well-funded social security plans, good health care, safe housing, and diverse social services. Yet because of inadequate funding and difficulties reaching rural communities, many older adults' needs remain unmet. Furthermore, the U.S. Medicare system of sharing health-care costs with senior citizens strains their financial resources. And housing that adjusts to changes in elders' capacities, permitting them to age in place without disruptive and disorienting moves, is available only to the economically well-off.

Besides improving policies that meet older adults' basic needs, new future-oriented approaches must prepare for increased aging of the population. More emphasis on lifelong learning for workers of all ages would help people maintain and even increase skills as they grow older. Also, reforms that prepare for expected growth in the number of frail elders are vital, including affordable help for family caregivers, adapted housing, and sensitive nursing home care.

All these changes involve recognizing, supporting, and enhancing the contributions that seniors make to society. A nation that takes care of its senior citizens maximizes the chances that each of us, when our time comes to be old, will age optimally.

ASK YOURSELF

REVIEW
What psychological and workplace factors predict favorable adjustment to retirement?

APPLY
Nate, happily married to Gladys, adjusted well to retirement, and his marriage became even happier. How can a good marriage ease the transition to retirement? How can retirement enhance marital satisfaction?

REFLECT
Think of someone you know who is aging optimally. What personal qualities led you to select that person?

Summary

Erikson's Theory: Ego Integrity versus Despair

According to Erikson, how does personality change in late adulthood?

» The final psychological conflict of Erikson's theory, **ego integrity versus despair,** involves coming to terms with one's life. Adults who arrive at a sense of integrity feel whole and satisfied with their achievements. Despair occurs when elders feel time is too short to find an alternate route to integrity.

Other Theories of Psychosocial Development in Late Adulthood

Describe Peck's, Joan Erikson's, and Labouvie-Vief's views of psychosocial development in late adulthood, and discuss reminiscence in older adults' lives.

» According to Peck, attaining ego integrity involves three distinct tasks: ego differentiation, body transcendence, and ego transcendence. Joan Erikson believes these attainments represent an additional psychosocial stage, **gerotranscendence,** evident in inner calm and quiet reflection.

» Labouvie-Vief points out that older adults improve in **affect optimization**—the ability to maximize positive emotion and dampen negative emotion. Full understanding of their own feelings contributes to expertise in processing emotional information and regulating negative affect.

» **Reminiscence** can be positive and adaptive for older people. But many well-adjusted elders spend little time in life review to achieve greater self-understanding. Rather, as the term **Third Age** conveys, they are largely present- and future-oriented, seeking opportunities for personal fulfillment.

Stability and Change in Self-Concept and Personality

Cite stable and changing aspects of self-concept and personality, and discuss spirituality and religiosity in late adulthood.

» The "big five" personality traits show continuing stability from mid- to late life. With the accumulation of a lifetime of self-knowledge, elders have more secure and complex self-concepts. Those who continue to strive toward hoped-for possible selves improve in life satisfaction. In late adulthood, resilience is fostered by gains in agreeableness and acceptance of change.

» While U.S. elders generally become more religious or spiritual as they age, this trend is not universal: Some elders decline in religiosity.

» Religious involvement is especially high among low-SES ethnic minority elders and women and is linked to improved physical and psychological well-being and longer survival.

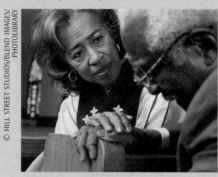

© HILL STREET STUDIOS/BLEND IMAGES/ PHOTOLIBRARY

Contextual Influences on Psychological Well-Being

Discuss the influence of control versus dependency, physical health, negative life changes, and social support on older adults' psychological well-being.

» In patterns of behavior called the **dependency–support script** and the **independence–ignore script,** older adults' dependency behaviors are attended to immediately while their independent behaviors are ignored. But dependency can be adaptive if elders remain in control by selecting areas in which they desire help. This enables them to conserve their strength for highly valued activities.

» Physical illness can lead to a sense of loss of personal control and, when disability results, is among the strongest risk factors for late-life depression. Older adults have the highest suicide rate of all age groups.

» Although elders are at risk for a variety of negative life changes, these events may evoke less stress and depression in older than in younger adults. But when negative changes pile up, they test elders' coping resources.

» Social support eases stress, thereby fostering older adults' physical health and psychological well-being. But if assistance is excessive or cannot be returned, it often sparks feelings of dependency and distress. Consequently, perceived social support, rather than sheer amount of help, is associated with a positive outlook.

A Changing Social World

Describe social theories of aging, including disengagement theory, activity theory, continuity theory, and socioemotional selectivity theory.

» **Disengagement theory** holds that social interaction declines because of mutual withdrawal between elders and society in anticipation of death. However, not everyone disengages, and elders' retreat from interaction is more complex than this theory implies.

» According to **activity theory,** social barriers to engagement, not the desires of elders, cause declining rates of interaction. Yet opportunities for social contact do not guarantee greater social activity.

» **Continuity theory** proposes that most aging adults strive to maintain consistency between their past and anticipated future. By using familiar skills and engaging in familiar activities with familiar people, elders minimize stress and disruptiveness by integrating late-life changes into a coherent, consistent life path.

» **Socioemotional selectivity theory** states that social networks become more selective as we age. Older adults emphasize the emotion-regulating function of interaction, preferring high-quality, emotionally fulfilling relationships.

How do communities, neighborhoods, and housing arrangements affect elders' social lives and adjustment?

» Suburban elders are better off in terms of income and health, whereas inner-city elders have easier access to social services. Small-town and rural elders are least well-off in these ways. Older adults living in neighborhoods with many like-minded seniors and in smaller communities report greater life satisfaction. For urban elders living alone, fear of crime restricts activities and undermines morale.

» Most elders prefer **aging in place,** remaining in a familiar setting where they have control over everyday life. For healthy elders, staying in one's own home offers the greatest personal control. But for those with health and mobility problems, independent living poses risks. Many older adults who live alone, especially widowed women, are poverty-stricken and suffer from unmet needs.

» Residential communities for seniors come in great variety. Among assisted-living arrangements, **congregate housing** offers a variety of support services, including meals in a common dining room, and is well-suited to promoting social participation. **Life-care communities** offer a range of options, from independent or congregate housing to full nursing home care.

» The small number of U.S. elders who live in nursing homes experience extreme restriction of autonomy. Typically, social interaction among residents is low. Designing homelike nursing homes with aging-in-place features fosters late-life well-being.

© 2009 LYNN JOHNSON

Relationships in Late Adulthood

Describe changes in social relationships in late adulthood, including marriage, gay and lesbian partnerships, divorce, remarriage, and widowhood, and discuss never-married, childless older adults.

» As we move through life, a **social convoy,** or cluster of family members and friends, provides safety and support. Though relationships change with age, elders do their best to sustain close, high-quality ties, which predicts positive adaptation.

» Marital satisfaction peaks in late adulthood as stressful responsibilities decline and gains in perceptions of relationship fairness, shared leisure activities, and positive communication increase. Most gay and lesbian elders also report happy, highly fulfilling relationships.

» When divorce occurs, stress is higher for older than for younger adults. Because of greater financial hardship and less likelihood of remarrying, women suffer more than men.

» Although elders' remarriage rates are low, those who do remarry enter into more stable relationships. Increasingly, older adults are choosing cohabitation over remarriage, for financial and personal reasons.

» Wide variation exists in adaptation to widowhood. Efforts to maintain social ties, an outgoing personality, high self-esteem, and a sense of self-efficacy in handling tasks of daily living foster adjustment. Women fare better than men.

» Most older adults who remain unmarried and childless throughout their lives develop alternative meaningful relationships. Never-married childless women are better-adjusted than men, but—despite smaller social networks—both find social support.

How do sibling relationships, friendships, and relationships with adult children change in late life?

» In late adulthood, most siblings live nearby, communicate regularly, and visit several times a year. Socialization is more common than direct assistance, though siblings provide an important "insurance policy." Sibling support increases for siblings living very near.

» Friendships grow in importance in late adulthood and serve a variety of functions: intimacy and companionship, acceptance, a link to the larger community, and protection from the psychological consequences of loss. Women are more likely than men to have both intimate friends and **secondary friends**—people with whom they spend time occasionally.

» Elders are often in touch with their adult children, who more often provide emotional support than direct assistance. Older adults often give more help than they receive, especially financial and practical assistance—an arrangement that is psychologically beneficial to elders.

Discuss elder maltreatment, including risk factors and strategies for prevention.

» Some elders suffer maltreatment at the hands of family members, friends, or professional caregivers. Risk factors include a dependent perpetrator–victim relationship, perpetrator psychological disturbance and stress, a history of family violence, and inadequate nursing homes.

» Elder-abuse prevention programs offer caregivers counseling, education, and respite services. Elders benefit from trained volunteers and support groups that help them avoid future harm. Societal efforts, including public education to encourage reporting of suspected cases and improved understanding of the needs of older people, are also vital.

Retirement

Discuss the decision to retire, adjustment to retirement, and involvement in leisure and volunteer activities.

» The decision to retire depends on affordability, health status, nature of the work environment, opportunities to pursue meaningful activities, and societal factors such as retirement benefits.

» Most older adults adapt well to retirement, especially those who view it as a time of personal growth and remain active and socially involved. Factors affecting adjustment include health status, financial stability, satisfactions previously derived from work, a sense of personal control over life events (including the retirement decision), social support, and marital happiness.

» Meaningful leisure and community service pursuits are typically formed earlier and sustained or expanded during retirement. Involvement is related to better physical and mental health and to reduced mortality.

© JULIA CUMES/THE IMAGE WORKS

Optimal Aging

Discuss the meaning of optimal aging.

» Elders who experience **optimal aging** have developed many ways to minimize losses and maximize gains. Societal contexts that permit older adults to manage life changes effectively foster optimal aging. These include well-funded social security plans, good health care, housing that adjusts to changes in elders' capacities, social services, and opportunities for lifelong learning.

Important Terms and Concepts

activity theory (p. 482)
affect optimization (p. 475)
aging in place (p. 484)
congregate housing (p. 485)
continuity theory (p. 482)
dependency–support script (p. 479)

disengagement theory (p. 482)
ego integrity versus despair (p. 474)
gerotranscendence (p. 475)
independence–ignore script (p. 479)
life-care communities (p. 485)
optimal aging (p. 496)

reminiscence (p. 476)
secondary friends (p. 492)
social convoy (p. 487)
socioemotional selectivity theory (p. 483)
Third Age (p. 477)

Milestones
Development in Late Adulthood

65–80 years

PHYSICAL

- Performance of autonomic nervous system declines, impairing tolerance for extremes of heat and cold. (447)
- Declines in vision continue, with increased sensitivity to glare and impaired color discrimination, dark adaptation, depth perception, and visual acuity. (447–448)
- Declines in hearing continue throughout the frequency range. (448)
- Sensitivity to taste and odor may decline. (448)
- Touch sensitivity declines on the hands, especially the fingertips. (449)
- Declines in cardiovascular and respiratory functioning lead to greater physical stress during exercise. (449)

- Aging of the immune system increases risk for a variety of illnesses, including infectious diseases, cardiovascular disease, certain forms of cancer, and various autoimmune disorders. (449)
- Sleep difficulties increase. (449–450)
- Graying and thinning of the hair continue; the skin wrinkles further and becomes more transparent as it loses its fatty layer of support; "age spots" increase. (450, 451)
- Height and weight decline because of loss of lean body mass. (450)

- Continued loss of bone mass leads to rising rates of osteoporosis. (450, 455)
- Intensity of sexual response and sexual activity decline, although most healthy married couples report regular sexual enjoyment. (454–455)

COGNITIVE

- Processing speed continues to decline, but crystallized intelligence is largely sustained. (463)
- Ability to control and divide attention continues to decline. (463)

- Amount of information that can be held in working memory, use of memory strategies, and retrieval from long-term memory diminish further; problems are greatest on tasks requiring deliberate processing and associative memory. (463–465)
- Modest forgetting of remote memories occurs. (465–466)

- Use of external aids for prospective memory increases. (466)
- Retrieving words from long-term memory and planning what to say and how to say it become more difficult. (466)
- Information is more likely to be represented in terms of gist rather than details. (466)
- Hypothetical problem solving declines, but everyday problem solving remains adaptive. (467)

Note: Numbers in parentheses indicate the page or pages on which each milestone is discussed.

- May hold an important position of leadership in society, such as chief executive officer, religious leader, or supreme court justice. (467)
- May develop wisdom. (467–468)
- Can improve a wide range of cognitive skills through training. (469)

EMOTIONAL/SOCIAL

- Comes to terms with life, developing ego integrity. (474)
- Cognitive-affective complexity declines as basic information-processing skill diminish. (475)

- Affect optimization, the ability to maximize positive emotion and dampen negative emotion, increases. (475–476)
- May engage in reminiscence and life review, but continues to seek avenues for personal growth and fulfillment. (476)
- Self-concept strengthens, becoming more secure and complex. (476–477)
- Agreeableness and acceptance of change increase, while extroversion and openness to experience decline modestly. (477–478)
- Spirituality and faith may advance to a higher level, away from prescribed beliefs toward a more reflective approach. (478)

- Perceived negative physical health may lead to depression. (479–480)
- Size of social network and amount of social interaction decline. (482–484)

- Selection of social partners is based on anticipated feelings, including pursuit of pleasant relationships and avoidance of unpleasant ones. (483–484)
- Marital satisfaction increases, peaking in late adulthood. (487)

- May be widowed. (488)
- Sibling closeness and mutual support may increase. (490–491)
- Number of friends generally declines. (491)
- May become a great-grandparent. (492)
- May retire. (494–495)
- Likely to increase involvement in leisure and volunteer activities (496)
- More likely to be knowledgeable about politics and to vote. (496)

80 years and older

PHYSICAL

- Physical changes previously listed continue.

- Mobility diminishes as muscle and bone strength and joint flexibility decline. (450)

COGNITIVE

- Cognitive changes previously listed continue.

- Fluid abilities decline further; crystallized abilities drop as well, though only modestly. (463)

EMOTIONAL/SOCIAL

- Emotional and social changes previously listed continue.
- May develop gerotranscendence, a cosmic perspective directed beyond the self. (475)
- Relationships with adult children become more important. (492)

- Frequency and variety of leisure and volunteer activities decline. (496)

CHAPTER
19

Death, Dying, and Bereavement

© CHRISTOPHE BOISVIEUX/CORB

All cultures have rituals for celebrating the end of life and helping the bereaved cope with profound loss. Here, community members perform a lion dance in front of a coffin during a traditional Han funeral in China. In Buddhist lore, the lion is a guardian, ensuring peace and good luck to those who cross its path.

As every life is unique, so each death is unique. The final forces of the human spirit separate themselves from the body in manifold ways.

My mother Sofie's death was the culmination of a five-year battle against cancer. In her last months, the disease invaded organs throughout her body, attacking the lungs in its final fury. She withered slowly, with the mixed blessing of time to prepare against certain knowledge that death was just around the corner. My father, Philip, lived another 18 years. At age 80, he was outwardly healthy, active, and about to depart on a long-awaited vacation when a heart attack snuffed out his life suddenly, without time for last words or deathbed reconciliations.

As I set to work on this chapter, my 65-year-old neighbor Nicholas gambled for a higher quality of life. To be eligible for a kidney transplant, he elected bypass surgery to strengthen his heart. Doctors warned that his body might not withstand the operation. But Nicholas knew that without taking a chance, he would live only a few years, in debilitated condition. Shortly after the surgery, infection set in, so weakening him that only extreme measures—a respirator to sustain breathing and powerful drugs to elevate his fading blood pressure—could keep him alive.

© MYRLEEN FERGUSON CATE/PHOTOEDIT

"Come on, Dad, you can do it," encouraged Nicholas's daughter Sasha, standing by his bedside and stroking his hand. But Nicholas could not. After two months in intensive care, he experienced brain seizures and slipped into a coma. Three doctors met with his wife, Giselle, to tell her there was no hope. She asked them to disconnect the respirator, and within half an hour Nicholas drifted away.

Death is essential for the survival of our species. We die so that our own children and the children of others may live. As hard as it is to accept the reality that we too will die, our greatest solace lies in the knowledge that death is part of ongoing life.

In this chapter, we address the culmination of lifespan development. Over the past century, technology has provided us with so many means to keep death at bay that many people regard it as a forbidden topic. But pressing social and economic dilemmas that are an outgrowth of the dramatic increase in life expectancy are forcing us to attend to life's end—its quality, its timing, and ways to help people adjust to their own and others' final leave taking.

Our discussion addresses the physical changes of dying, attitudes toward death, the thoughts and feelings of people as they stand face to face with death, where people die, hopelessly ill patients' right to die, and coping with the death of a loved one. The experiences of Sofie, Philip, Nicholas, their families, and others illustrate how each person's life history joins with social and cultural contexts to shape death and dying, lending great diversity to this universal experience.

How We Die

In industrialized countries, opportunities to witness the physical aspects of death are less available today than in previous generations. Most people in the developed world die in hospitals, where doctors and nurses, not loved ones, typically attend their last moments. Nevertheless, many want to know how we die, either to anticipate their own end or to grasp what is happening to a dying loved one.

Physical Changes

When asked how they would like to die, most people say they want "death with dignity"—either a quick, agony-free end during sleep or a clear-minded final few moments in which they can say farewell and review their lives. In reality, death is the culmination of a straightforward biological process. For about 20 percent of people, it is gentle—especially when narcotic drugs ease pain (Nuland, 1993). But most of the time it is not.

Of the one-quarter of people in industrialized nations who die suddenly, within a few hours of experiencing symptoms, 80 to 90 percent are victims of heart attacks (Winslow, Mehta, & Fuster, 2005). Though I longed for reassurance that my father's death had been painless, my wish was probably not fulfilled. Undoubtedly he felt the sharp, crushing sensation of a heart deprived of oxygen. As his heart twitched uncontrollably (called *fibrillation*) or stopped entirely, blood circulation slowed and ceased, and he was thrust into unconsciousness. A brain starved of oxygen for more than two to four minutes is irreversibly damaged. Other oxygen-deprived organs stop functioning as well.

Death is long and drawn out for three-fourths of people—many more than in times past, as a result of life-saving medical technology. Of those with heart disease, most have congestive heart failure, the cause of Nicholas's death (Gruenewald & White, 2006). His scarred heart could no longer contract with the force needed to deliver enough oxygen to his tissues. As it tried harder, its muscle weakened further. Without sufficient blood pressure, fluid backed up in Nicholas's lungs. This hampered his breathing and created ideal conditions for inhaled bacteria to multiply, enter the bloodstream, and run rampant in his system, leading many organs to fail.

Cancer also chooses diverse paths to inflict its damage. When it metastasizes, bits of tumor travel through the bloodstream and implant and grow in vital organs, disrupting their functioning. Medication made my mother's final days as comfortable as possible. But the preceding weeks involved physical suffering, including impaired breathing and digestion.

In the days or hours before death, activity declines; the person moves and communicates less and shows little interest in food, water, and surroundings. At the same time, body temperature, blood pressure, and circulation to the limbs fall, so the hands and feet feel cool and skin color changes to a duller, grayish hue (Hospice Foundation of America, 2005). When the transition from life to death is imminent, the person moves through three phases:

1. The **agonal phase.** The Greek word *agon* means "struggle." Here agonal refers to gasps and muscle spasms during the first moments in which the regular heartbeat disintegrates (Manole & Hickey, 2006).
2. **Clinical death.** A short interval follows in which heartbeat, circulation, breathing, and brain functioning stop, but resuscitation is still possible.
3. **Mortality.** The individual passes into permanent death.

Defining Death

TAKE A MOMENT... Consider what we have said so far, and note the dilemma of identifying just when death occurs. Death is not an event that happens at a single point in time but, rather, a process in which organs stop functioning in a sequence that varies from person to person. Because the dividing line between life and death is fuzzy, societies need a definition of death to help doctors decide when life-saving measures should be terminated, to signal survivors that they must begin to grieve their loss and reorganize their lives, and to establish when donated organs can be removed.

Several decades ago, loss of heartbeat and respiration signified death. But these criteria are no longer adequate because resuscitation techniques frequently permit vital signs to be restored. Today, **brain death,** irreversible cessation of all activity

A monk prays with mourners during a Shinto funeral in Japan. Shinto beliefs, which stress ancestor worship and time for the spirit to leave the corpse, may be partly responsible for the Japanese discomfort with the brain death standard and organ donation.

© MICHAEL S. YAMASHITA/CORBIS

in the brain and the brain stem (which controls reflexes), is used in most industrialized nations.

But not all countries accept this standard. In Japan, for example, doctors rely on traditional criteria—absence of heartbeat and respiration. This approach stands in the way of a national organ transplant program because few organs can be salvaged from bodies without artificially maintaining vital signs. Buddhist, Confucian, and Shinto beliefs about death, which stress ancestor worship and time for the spirit to leave the corpse, may be partly responsible for the Japanese discomfort with brain death and organ donation. Marring the body to harvest organs violates respect for the deceased. Today, Japanese law allows people who want to be organ donors to choose the standard of brain death, as long as their families do not object (Bagheri, 2007). Otherwise, they are considered to be alive until the heart stops beating.

Often the brain death standard does not solve the problem of when to halt treatment. Consider Nicholas, who, though not brain dead, had entered a **persistent vegetative state,** in which the cerebral cortex no longer registered electrical activity but the brain stem remained active. Doctors were certain they could not restore consciousness or body movement. Because thousands of people in the United States and other nations are in a persistent vegetative state, with health-care costs totaling many millions of dollars annually, some experts believe that absence of activity in the cerebral cortex should be sufficient to declare a person dead. But others point to a few cases in which patients who had been vegetative for months regained cortical responsiveness and consciousness, though usually with very limited functioning (Kotchoubey et al., 2005; Laureys & Boly, 2007). In still other instances of illness, a fully conscious but suffering person refuses life-saving measures—an issue we will consider later when we take up the right to die.

Death with Dignity

We have seen that nature rarely delivers the idealized, easy end most people want, nor can medical science guarantee it. Therefore, the greatest dignity in death is in the integrity of the life that precedes it—an integrity we can foster by the way we communicate with and care for the dying person.

First, we can provide the majority of dying people, who succumb gradually, with the utmost in humane and compassionate care. This includes treating them with esteem and respect—for example, by taking interest in those aspects of their lives that they most value and by addressing their greatest concerns (Chochinov, 2006).

Second, we can be candid about death's certainty. Unless people are aware that they are dying and understand (as far as possible) the likely circumstances of their death, they cannot plan for end-of-life care and decision making and share the sentiments that bring closure to relationships they hold most dear. Because Sofie knew how and when her death would probably take place, she chose a time when she, Philip, and her children could express what their lives had meant to one another. Among

In Post Falls, Idaho, dying patient Dick Warner's wife Nancy wears a nurse's hat she crafted from paper to symbolize her dual roles as medical and emotional caregiver. The evening of this photo, Nancy heard Dick's breaths shortening. She kissed him and whispered, "It's time to let go." He smiled and died the way he wanted, with the gentle support of his wife at his bedside.

those precious bedside exchanges was Sofie's memorable last wish that Philip remarry after her death so he would not live out his final years alone. Openness about impending death granted Sofie a final generative act, helped her let go of the person closest to her, and offered comfort as she faced death.

Finally, doctors and nurses can help dying people learn enough about their condition to make reasoned choices about whether to fight on or say no to further treatment. An understanding of how the normal body works simplifies comprehension of how disease affects it—education that can begin as early as the childhood years.

In sum, we can ensure the most dignified exit possible by offering the dying person care, affection, and companionship; the truth about diagnosis; and the maximum personal control over this final phase of life (American Hospice Foundation, 2009). These are essential ingredients of a "good death," and we will revisit them throughout this chapter.

Attitudes Toward Death

A century ago, when most deaths occurred at home, people of all ages, including children, helped with care of the dying family member and were present at the moment of death. They saw their loved one buried on family property or in the local cemetery, where the grave could be visited regularly. Because infant and childhood mortality rates were high, all people were likely to know someone their own age, or even younger, who had died. And it was common for children to experience the death of a parent.

Compared with earlier generations, today more young people reach adulthood without having experienced the death of someone they know well. When a death does occur, professionals

in hospitals and funeral homes take care of most tasks that involve confronting it directly (Morgan & Laungani, 2005).

This distance from death undoubtedly contributes to a sense of uneasiness about it. Despite frequent images of death in television shows, movies, and news reports of accidents, murders, wars, and natural disasters, we live in a death-denying culture. Adults are often reluctant to talk about death. And substitute expressions, such as "passing away," "going out," or "departing," permit us to avoid acknowledging it candidly. Not surprisingly, **death anxiety**—fear and apprehension of death—is widespread. But even people who are very accepting of the reality of death may be anxious about it (Firestone, 1994).

What predicts whether thoughts of our own demise trigger intense distress, relative calm, or something in between? To answer this question, researchers measure both general death anxiety and a variety of specific factors, including fear of no longer existing, loss of control, a painful death, the body decaying, being separated from loved ones, and the unknown (Neimeyer, 1994). Findings reveal large individual and cultural variations in aspects of death that arouse fear. For example, in a study of devout Islamic Saudi Arabians, certain factors that appear repeatedly in the responses of Westerners, such as fear of the body decaying and of the unknown, were entirely absent (Long, 1985).

Among Westerners, spirituality—a sense of life's meaning—seems to be more important than religious commitment in

Death anxiety declines in old age, and this 81-year-old from the Netherlands seems to have very little! She had this coffin made to serve as a bookshelf because, she said, "It's a waste to use a coffin just for burial." The pillow on the top will support her head after she dies.

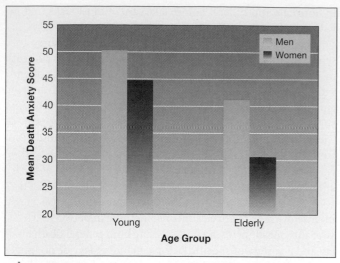

■ FIGURE 19.1 ■ Relationship of age and gender to death anxiety. In this study comparing young and elderly adults, death anxiety declined with age. At both ages, women expressed greater fear of death than men. Many other studies show similar findings. (Adapted from Tomer, Eliason, & Smith, 2000.)

limiting death anxiety (Rasmussen & Johnson, 1994). People with a well-developed personal philosophy of death are also less fearful. In one study, moderately religious middle-aged and older adults feared death more than those who were high or low in religiosity. And adults whose religious beliefs and behavior were contradictory—who believed in an afterlife but rarely prayed or attended services—were high in death anxiety. Together, these findings suggest that both firmness of beliefs and consistency between beliefs and practices, rather than religiousness itself, reduce fear of death (Wink & Scott, 2005). Death anxiety is especially low among adults with deep faith in some form of higher force or being—faith that may or may not be influenced by religion (Cicirelli, 1999, 2002).

TAKE A MOMENT... From what you have learned about adult psychosocial development, how do you think death anxiety might change with age? If you predicted it would decline, reaching its lowest level in late adulthood, you are correct (see Figure 19.1) (Russac et al., 2007; Tomer, Eliason, & Smith, 2000). This age-related drop has been found in many cultures and ethnic groups. Recall from Chapter 18 that older adults are especially effective at regulating negative emotion. As a result, most cope with anxieties, including fear of death, effectively. Furthermore, the attainment of ego integrity reduces death anxiety. Elders have had more time to develop symbolic immortality—the belief that one will continue to live on through one's children or through one's work or personal influence (see Chapter 16, page 420).

As long as it is not overly intense, death anxiety can motivate people to live up to internalized cultural values—for example, to be kind to others and to work hard to reach one's goals. These efforts increase adults' sense of self-esteem, self-efficacy, and purpose—powerful antidotes against the terrifying thought that, in the overall scheme of things, they "are no more

important or enduring than any individual potato, pineapple, or porcupine" (Fry, 2003; Pyszczynski et al., 2004, p. 436). In a study of Israeli adults, symbolic immortality predicted reduced fear of death, especially among those with secure attachments (Florian & Mikulincer, 1998). Gratifying, close interpersonal ties seem to help people feel worthwhile and forge a sense of symbolic immortality. And people who view death as an opportunity to pass a legacy to future generations are less likely to fear it (Cicirelli, 2001; Mikulincer, Florian, & Hirschberger, 2003).

Regardless of age, in both Eastern and Western cultures, women appear more anxious about death than men do (refer again to Figure 19.1) (Madnawat & Kachhawa, 2007; Tomer, Eliason, & Smith, 2000). Perhaps women are more likely to admit and men more likely to avoid troubled feelings about mortality—an explanation consistent with females' greater emotional expressiveness throughout the lifespan.

Experiencing some anxiety about death is normal and adaptive. But like other fears, very intense death anxiety can undermine effective adjustment. Although physical health in adulthood is not related to death anxiety, mental health clearly is. In cultures as different as China and the United States, people who are depressed or generally anxious are likely to have more severe death concerns (Neimeyer & Van Brunt, 1995; Wu, Tang, & Kwok, 2002). In contrast, people who are good at inhibition (keeping their minds from straying to irrelevant thoughts) and at emotional self-regulation report less death anxiety (Gailliot, Schmeichel, & Baumeister, 2006). They are better able to manage their concerns about death.

Death anxiety is largely limited to adolescence and adulthood. Children rarely display it unless they live in high-crime neighborhoods or war-torn areas where they are in constant danger (see the Lifespan Vista box on the impact of ethnic and political violence on children on page 276 in Chapter 10). Terminally ill children are also at risk for high death anxiety. Compared with other same-age patients, children with cancer express more destructive thoughts and negative feelings about death (Malone, 1982). For those whose parents make the mistake of not telling them they are going to die, loneliness and death anxiety can be extreme (O'Halloran & Altmaier, 1996).

ASK YOURSELF

≫ REVIEW
Explain why death anxiety typically declines in late adulthood.

≫ APPLY
Considering factors that influence death anxiety, suggest several experiences that religious institutions or senior centers could offer that might reduce fear in highly death-anxious people.

≫ REFLECT
Ask members of earlier generations in your family about their childhood experiences with death. Compare these to your own experiences. What differences did you find, and how would you explain them?

Thinking and Emotions of Dying People

In the year before her death, Sofie did everything possible to surmount her illness. In between treatments to control the cancer, she continued to teach high school, traveled to visit her children, cultivated a garden, and took weekend excursions with Philip. Hope pervaded Sofie's approach to her deadly condition, and she spoke often about the disease—so much so that her friends wondered how she could confront it so directly.

As Sofie deteriorated physically, she was frustrated, and at times angry and depressed, about her inability to keep on fighting. Once she asked when my husband and I, who were newly married, would have children. "If only I could live long enough to hold them in my arms!" she cried. In the last week, she appeared tired but free of struggle. Occasionally, she spoke of her love for us and commented on the beauty of the hills outside her window. But mostly, she looked and listened, rather than actively participating in conversation. One afternoon, she fell permanently unconscious.

Do Stages of Dying Exist?

As dying people move closer to death, are their reactions predictable? Do they go through a series of changes that are the same for everyone, or are their thoughts and feelings unique?

■ **KÜBLER-ROSS'S THEORY.** Although her theory has been heavily criticized, Elisabeth Kübler-Ross (1969) is credited with awakening society's sensitivity to the psychological needs of dying patients. From interviews with over 200 terminally ill people, she devised a theory of five typical responses—initially proposed as stages—to the prospect of death and the ordeal of dying:

■ *Denial.* On learning of the terminal illness, the person denies its seriousness. While the patient still feels reasonably well, denial is self-protective, allowing the individual to deal with the illness at his or her own pace. Kübler-Ross recommends that family members and health professionals not prolong denial by distorting the truth about the person's condition. In doing so, they prevent the dying person from adjusting to impending death and hinder necessary arrangements—for social support, for bringing closure to relationships, and for making decisions about medical interventions.

■ *Anger.* Recognition that time is short promotes anger at having to die without having had a chance to do all one wants to do. Family members and health professionals may be targets of the patient's rage, resentment, and envy. Even so, they must tolerate rather than lash out at the patient's behavior, recognizing that the underlying cause is the unfairness of death.

■ *Bargaining.* Realizing the inevitability of death, the terminally ill person attempts to bargain for extra time—a deal he or she may try to strike with family members, friends,

doctors, nurses, or God. The best response to these efforts to sustain hope is to listen sympathetically, as one doctor did to the pleas of a young AIDS-stricken father, whose wish was to live long enough to dance with his daughter—then 8 years old—at her wedding (Selwyn, 1996). Sometimes, bargains are altruistic acts. Tony, a 15-year-old leukemia patient, expressed to his mother:

> I don't want to die yet. Gerry [youngest brother] is only 3 and not old enough to understand. If I could live just one more year, I could explain it to him myself and he will understand. Three is just too young. (Komp, 1996, pp. 69–70)

Although many dying patients' bargains are unrealistic and impossible to fulfill, Tony lived for exactly one year—a gift to those who survived him.

■ *Depression.* When denial, anger, and bargaining fail to postpone the illness, the person becomes depressed about the loss of his or her life. Unfortunately, many experiences associated with dying, including physical and mental deterioration, pain, lack of control, and being hooked to machines, intensify despondency (Maier & Newman, 1995). Health care that responds humanely to the patient's wishes can limit despair.

■ *Acceptance.* Most people who reach acceptance, a state of peace and quiet about upcoming death, do so only in the last weeks or days. The weakened patient yields to death, disengaging from all but a few family members, friends, and caregivers. Some dying people, in an attempt to pull away from all they have loved, withdraw. "I'm getting my mental and emotional house in order," one patient explained (Samarel, 1995, p. 101).

■ **EVALUATION OF KÜBLER-ROSS'S THEORY.** Kübler-Ross cautioned that her five stages should not be viewed as a fixed sequence and that not all people display each response. But her use of the term *stages* has made it easy for her theory to be interpreted simplistically, as the series of steps a "normal" dying person follows. Some health professionals, unaware of diversity in dying experiences, have insensitively tried to push patients through Kübler-Ross's sequence. And caregivers, through callousness or ignorance, can too easily dismiss a dying patient's legitimate complaints about treatment as "just what you would expect in Stage 2" (Corr, 1993; Kastenbaum, 2009).

Rather than stages, the five reactions Kübler-Ross observed are best viewed as coping strategies that anyone may call on in the face of threat. Furthermore, dying people react in many additional ways—for example, through efforts to conquer the disease, as Sofie displayed; through an overwhelming need to control what happens to their bodies during the dying process; through acts of generosity and caring, as seen in Tony's concern for his brother; and through shifting their focus to living in a fulfilling way—"seizing the day" because so little time is left (Silverman, 2004; Wright, 2003).

As these examples suggest, the most serious drawback to Kübler-Ross's theory is that it looks at dying patients' thoughts and feelings outside the contexts that give them meaning. As we will see next, people's adaptations to impending death can be understood only in relation to the multidimensional influences that have contributed to their life course and also shape this final phase.

Contextual Influences on Adaptations to Dying

From the moment of her diagnosis, Sofie spent little time in denial. Instead, she met the deadly disease head on, just as she had dealt with other challenges of life. Her impassioned plea to hold her grandchildren was less a bargain with fate than an expression of profound defeat that on the threshold of late adulthood, she would not live to enjoy its rewards. At the end, her quiet, withdrawn demeanor was probably resignation, not acceptance. All her life, she had been a person with a fighting spirit.

According to recent theorists, a single strategy, such as acceptance, is not best for every dying patient. Rather, an **appropriate death** is one that makes sense in terms of the individual's pattern of living and values and, at the same time, preserves or restores significant relationships and is as free of suffering as possible (Samarel, 1995; Worden, 2000). When asked about a "good death," most patients mention the following goals:

- Maintaining a sense of identity, or inner continuity with one's past
- Clarifying the meaning of one's life and death

On September 18, 2007, Carnegie Mellon University computer science professor Randy Pausch, diagnosed with pancreatic cancer, gave his final lecture to a packed house. His message, which focused on achieving one's childhood dreams and enabling the dreams of others, can be viewed at *www.cmu.edu/homepage/multimedia/randy-pausch-lecture.shtml*. He died nine months later, at age 47, having approached his death in a way that suited his pattern of living and deepest values.

- Maintaining and enhancing relationships
- Achieving a sense of control over the time that remains
- Confronting and preparing for death (Goldsteen et al., 2006; Kleespies, 2004; Proulx & Jacelon, 2004)

Research reveals that biological, psychological, and social and cultural forces affect people's coping with dying and, therefore, the extent to which they attain these goals.

■ **NATURE OF THE DISEASE.**   The course of the illness and its symptoms affect the dying person's reactions. For example, the extended nature of Sofie's illness and her doctor's initial optimism about achieving a remission undoubtedly contributed to her attempts to try to conquer the disease. During the final month, when cancer had spread to Sofie's lungs and she could not catch her breath, she was agitated and fearful until oxygen and medication relieved her uncertainty about being able to breathe. In contrast, Nicholas's weakened heart and failing kidneys so depleted his strength that he responded only with passivity.

Because of the toll of the disease, about one-third of cancer patients experience severe depression—reactions distinct from the sadness, grief, and worry that typically accompany the dying process. Profound depression amplifies pain; impairs the immune response; interferes with the patient's capacity for pleasure, meaning, and connection; and is associated with poorer survival (Williams & Dale, 2006). It requires immediate treatment—through therapy, antidepressant medication, and patient and family education.

■ **PERSONALITY AND COPING STYLE.**   Understanding the way individuals view stressful life events and have coped with them in the past helps us appreciate the way they manage the dying process. In a study in which terminally ill patients discussed their images of dying, responses varied greatly:

- Beth regarded *dying as imprisonment:* "I felt like the clock started ticking . . . like the future has suddenly been taken. . . . In a way, I feel like I'm already dead."
- To Faith, dying was *a mandate to live ever more fully:* "I have a saying . . . 'You're not ready to live until you're ready to die' . . . It never meant much to me until I . . . looked death in the eye, and now I'm living. . . . This life is a lot better than the one before."
- Dawn viewed dying as *part of life's journey:* "I learned all about my disease . . . I would read, read, read . . . I wanted to know as much as I can about it, and I don't think hiding . . . behind the door . . . could help me at all. And, I realized for the first time in my life—*really, really, really realized* that I could handle anything."
- Patty approached dying as *an experience to be transformed* so as to make it more bearable: "I am an avid, rabid fan of *Star Trek*, a trekkie like there never has been . . . I watch it to the point that I've memorized it . . . [In my mind, I play the various characters so] I'm not [always] thinking about cancer or dying . . . I think that's how I get through it." (Wright, 2003, pp. 442–444, 447)

Each patient's view of dying helps explain her responses to worsening illness. Poorly adjusted individuals—those with conflict-ridden relationships and many disappointments in life—are usually more distressed (Kastenbaum, 2009).

■ FAMILY MEMBERS' AND HEALTH PROFESSIONALS' BEHAVIOR.

Earlier we noted that a candid approach, in which everyone close to and caring for the dying person acknowledges the terminal illness, is best. Yet this also introduces the burden of participating in the work of dying with the patient—bringing relationships to closure, reflecting on life, and dealing with fears and regrets.

People who find it hard to engage in these tasks may pretend that the disease is not as bad as it is. In patients inclined toward denial, a "game" can be set in motion in which participants are aware that the patient is dying but act as though it were not so. Though this game softens psychological pain for the moment, it makes dying much more difficult. Besides impeding communication, it frequently leads to futile medical interventions, in which the patient has little understanding of what is happening and is subjected to great physical and emotional suffering. One attending physician provided this account of a cancer patient's death:

> The problem was that she had a young husband and parents who were pretty much in complete denial. We were trying to be aggressive up to the end. To the point that we actually hung a new form of chemotherapy about four hours before she died, even though everybody knew except her immediate family that she was going to die within the next four to eight hours. (Jackson et al., 2005, p. 653)

When doctors want to inform patients of their prognosis, they may encounter resistance, especially within certain ethnic groups. Withholding information is common in Southern and Eastern Europe, Central and South America, much of Asia, and the Middle East. Japanese terminally ill cancer patients are seldom told the truth about their condition, partly because dying disrupts important interdependent relationships (Yamamoto, 2004). Many Mexican Americans and Korean Americans believe that informing patients is wrong and will hasten death (Blackhall et al., 1995, 2001). In these instances, providing information is complex. When a family insists that a patient not be told, the doctor can first offer information to the patient and then, if the patient refuses, ask who should receive information and make health-care decisions. The patient's preference can be honored and reassessed at regular intervals (Zane & Yeh, 2002).

Social support from family members also affects adaptation to dying. Dying patients who feel they have much unfinished business to attend to are more anxious about impending death. But family contact reduces their sense of urgency to prolong life, perhaps because it permits patients to work through at least some incomplete tasks (Mutran et al., 1997).

Effective communication with the dying person is honest, fostering a trusting relationship, yet also oriented toward maintaining hope. Many dying patients move through a hope trajectory—at first, hope for a cure; later, hope for prolonging life; and

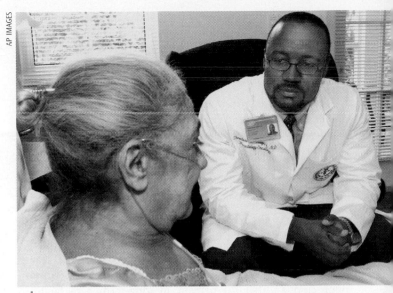

When doctors communicate openly and sensitively with terminally ill patients, they help them prepare for death by bringing relationships to closure, reflecting on life, and dealing with fears and regrets.

finally, hope for a peaceful death with as few burdens as possible (Fanslow, 1981). Once patients near death stop expressing hope, those close to them must accept this. Family members who find letting go very difficult may benefit from expert guidance.

■ SPIRITUALITY, RELIGION, AND CULTURE.

Earlier we noted that a sense of spirituality reduces fear of death. Informal reports from health professionals suggest that this is as true for dying patients as for people in general (Samarel, 1991). Vastly different cultural beliefs, guided by religious ideas, also shape people's dying experiences:

- Buddhism, widely practiced in China, India, and Southeast Asia, fosters acceptance of death. By reading sutras (teachings of Buddha) to the dying person to calm the mind and emphasizing that dying leads to rebirth in a heaven of peace and relaxation, Buddhists believe that it is possible to reach Nirvana, a state beyond the world of suffering (Kubotera, 2004; Yeung, 1996).

- In many Native-American groups, death is met with stoic self-control, an approach taught at an early age through stories that emphasize a circular, rather than linear, relationship between life and death and the importance of making way for others (Cox, 2002).

- For African Americans, a dying loved one signals a crisis that unites family members in caregiving. The terminally ill person remains an active and vital force within the family until he or she can no longer carry out this role—an attitude of respect that undoubtedly eases the dying process (Sullivan, 1995).

- Among the Maori of New Zealand, relatives and friends gather around the dying person to give spiritual strength and comfort. Elders, clergy, and other experts in tribal customs conduct a *karakia* ceremony, in which they recite prayers asking for peace, mercy, and guidance from the creator. After the ceremony, the patient is encouraged to discuss important matters with those closest to her—giving away of personal belongings, directions for interment, and completion of other unfinished tasks (Ngata, 2004).

In sum, dying prompts a multitude of thoughts, emotions, and coping strategies. Which ones are emphasized depends on a wide array of contextual influences. A vital assumption of the lifespan perspective—that development is multidimensional and multidirectional—is just as relevant to this final phase as to each earlier period.

A Place to Die

Whereas in the past most deaths occurred at home, in the United States today about 50 percent take place in hospitals and another 20 percent in long-term care facilities, mostly nursing homes (U.S. Department of Health and Human Services, 2008e). In the large, impersonal hospital environment, meeting the human needs of dying patients and their families is secondary, not because professionals lack concern, but because the work to be done focuses on saving lives. A dying patient represents a failure.

In the 1960s, a death awareness movement arose as a reaction to hospitals' death-avoiding practices—attachment of complicated machinery to patients with no chance of survival and avoidance of communication with dying patients. This movement led to medical care better suited to the needs of dying people and also to hospice programs, which have spread to many countries in the industrialized world. Let's visit each of these settings for dying.

Home

Had Sofie and Nicholas been asked where they wanted to die, undoubtedly each would have responded, "At home"—the preference of 80 to 90 percent of Americans (NHPCO, 2005; O'Connor, 2003). The reason is clear: The home offers an atmosphere of intimacy and loving care in which the terminally ill person is unlikely to feel abandoned.

However, only about one-fourth of Americans experience home death (U.S. Department of Health and Human Services, 2008e). And it is important not to romanticize dying at home. Because of dramatic improvements in medicine, dying people tend to be sicker or much older than in the past. Consequently, their bodies may be extremely frail, making ordinary activities—eating, sleeping, taking a pill, toileting, and bathing—major ordeals (Singer et al., 2005).

For many people, the chance to be with the dying person until the very end is a rewarding tradeoff for the high demands of caregiving. But the advantages and disadvantages of home death should be carefully weighed before undertaking it. Adequate support for the caregiver is essential (Germino, 2003). A home health aide is often necessary—a service (as we will see shortly) that hospice programs have made more accessible. Still, when family relationships are conflict-ridden, a dying

patient introduces additional strains, negating the benefits of home death. Finally, even with professional help, most homes are poorly equipped to handle the medical and comfort-care needs of the dying. To make home death possible, hospital-based equipment and technical support often must be transported to the home.

For all these reasons, older adults—although they view home as their ideal place to die—express concerns about quality of care, about burdening family and friends, and about the need for children to engage in unduly intimate caregiving tasks (Gott et al., 2004). And 10 months after a home death, family members continue to report more psychological stress than do family members whose loved one died elsewhere (Addington-Hall, 2000).

Hospital

Hospital dying takes many forms. Each is affected by the physical state of the dying person, the hospital unit in which it takes place, and the goal and quality of care.

Sudden deaths, due to injury or critical illness, typically occur in emergency rooms. Doctors and nurses usually have little time to speak with family members. When staff break the news of death in a sympathetic manner and provide explanations, family members are grateful. Otherwise, feelings of anger, frustration, and confusion can add to their grief. Crisis intervention services are needed to help survivors cope with sudden death (Walsh & McGoldrick, 2004).

Nicholas died on an intensive care ward focused on preventing death in patients whose condition can worsen quickly. Privacy and communication with the family were secondary to monitoring his condition. To prevent disruption of nurses' activities, Giselle and Sasha could be at Nicholas's side only at scheduled times. Dying in intensive care—an experience unique to technologically sophisticated societies—is especially

Dying in intensive care is a depersonalizing experience unique to technologically sophisticated societies. In such settings, medical responses supersede privacy and communication.

depersonalizing for patients like Nicholas, who linger between life and death while hooked to machines, often for months.

Cancer patients, who account for most cases of prolonged dying, typically die in general or specialized cancer care hospital units. When hospitalized for a long time, they reach out for help with physical and emotional needs, usually with mixed success. In these settings, the tasks associated with dying must be performed efficiently so that all patients can be served and health professionals are not drained emotionally by repeated attachments and separations.

Only one-fourth of U.S. hospitals have comprehensive treatment programs aimed at easing physical, emotional, and spiritual suffering at the end of life (Medina & Puntillo, 2006). And less than 1 percent of doctors and nurses are specially trained in managing pain in chronically ill and dying people. In 2006, such education became a formal medical subspecialty in the United States, an event that eventually may improve hospital care of the dying (Hallenbeck, 2006). But at present, many people die in painful, frightening, and depersonalizing hospital conditions, without their wishes being met.

Nursing Home

Though deaths in U.S. nursing homes—mostly elderly patients—are common, care emphasizes rehabilitation rather than high-quality terminal care. The few studies that have addressed what it is like to die in nursing homes concur that patients suffer from high levels of untreated pain (Bernabei et al., 1998; Ferrell, 1995).

In one investigation, researchers conducted after-death interviews with nursing staff and family members of all residents who died during a one-year period in two large North Carolina nursing homes (Reynolds et al., 2002). More than 50 percent had been in moderate to severe pain, 40 percent "very sad or depressed," 30 percent "very anxious or agitated," and 20 percent "very lonely" during their final three months. For the majority, "emotional and spiritual needs" had not been met. More than one-fourth of nursing staff and one-third of family members reported a need for improved communication about treatment decisions. As evidence of limited contact, more than one-third of family members could not identify the doctor in charge of their relative's care, and over half could not identify a nurse or nursing assistant.

The hospice approach—which we consider next—aims to reduce profound caregiving failures in hospitals and nursing homes. When combined with hospice, nursing home care of the dying improves greatly in pain management and in family satisfaction (Baer & Hanson, 2000; Miller et al., 2002).

The Hospice Approach

In medieval times, a *hospice* was a place where travelers could find rest and shelter. In the nineteenth and twentieth centuries, the word referred to homes for dying patients. Today, **hospice** is not a place but a comprehensive program of support services for terminally ill people and their families. It aims to provide a caring community sensitive to the dying person's needs so patients and family members can prepare for death in ways that

are satisfying to them. Quality of life is central to the hospice approach, which includes these main features:

- The patient and family as a unit of care

- Emphasis on meeting the patient's physical, emotional, social, and spiritual needs, including controlling pain, retaining dignity and self-worth, and feeling cared for and loved

- Care provided by an interdisciplinary team: the patient's doctor, a nurse or nurse's aide, a chaplain, a counselor or social worker, and a pharmacist

- The patient kept at home or in an inpatient setting with a homelike atmosphere where coordination of care is possible

- Focus on protecting the quality of remaining life with **palliative,** or **comfort, care** that relieves pain and other symptoms (nausea, breathing difficulties, insomnia, and depression) rather than prolonging life

- In addition to regularly scheduled home care visits, on-call services available 24 hours a day, 7 days a week

- Follow-up bereavement services offered to families in the year after a death

Hospice programs everywhere include a continuum of care, from home to inpatient options, including hospitals and nursing homes. Central to the hospice approach is that the dying person and his or her family be offered choices that guarantee an appropriate death. Some programs offer hospice day care, which permits caregivers to continue working or be relieved of the stresses of long-term care (Kernohan et al., 2006). Contact with others facing terminal illness is a supportive byproduct of many hospice arrangements. And to find out

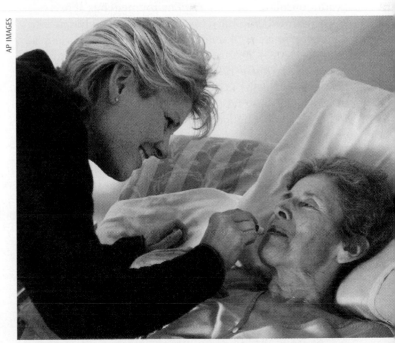

Hospice protects quality of life rather than extending it. This daughter applies lip balm for her mother—an act that increases her mother's comfort and enhances a sense of closeness and connection.

▪ BIOLOGY AND ENVIRONMENT ▪

Music as Palliative Care for Dying Patients

When Peter visits 82-year-old Stuart to play the harp, Stuart reports being transported to an idyllic place with water, children, and trees—far from the lung tumors that will soon take his life "When Peter plays for me . . . I am no longer frightened," Stuart says.

Peter is a specialist in *music thanatology,* an emerging specialty in music therapy that focuses on providing palliative care to the dying through music. He uses his harp, and sometimes his voice, to induce calm and give solace to the dying, their families, and their caregivers. Peter applies music systematically—matching it to each patient's breathing patterns and other responses, delivering different sounds to uplift or comfort, depending on his assessment of the patient's moment-by-moment needs.

Chaplains and counselors informally report that after music vigils, patients' conversations indicate that they more easily come to terms with their own death (Fyfe, 2006). And in a study of 65 dying patients in which pre- and postintervention physiological measures were compared, music vigils averaging an hour in length resulted in decreased agitation and wakefulness and slower, deeper, less effortful breathing (Freeman et al., 2006).

Why is music effective in easing the distress of those who are dying? In patients close to death, hearing typically functions longer than other senses. Thus, responsiveness to music may persist until the individual's final moments. Besides reducing anxiety, music can, in some instances, enhance the effects of medication administered to control pain (Starr, 1999). For these reasons, music vigils may be an especially effective end-of-life therapy.

© SIMON ODWYER/THE AGE PHOTO SALES

Music thanatology focuses on providing palliative care for the dying through music. This practitioner uses his harp, and sometimes his voice, to induce calm and provide solace.

about a comforting musical intervention for patients near death, consult the Biology and Environment box above.

Currently, the United States has over 4,700 hospices serving approximately 1.4 million terminally ill patients annually) (NHPCO, 2008). Because hospice care is a cost-effective alternative to expensive life-saving treatments, U.S. government health-care benefits (Medicare and Medicaid) cover it, as do most private insurance plans. In addition, community and foundation contributions allow many hospices to provide free services to uninsured patients who cannot pay (Hospice Foundation of America, 2009). Consequently, hospice is affordable for most dying patients and their families. Hospices also serve dying children—a tragedy so devastating that social support and bereavement intervention are vital.

Besides reducing patient physical suffering, hospice contributes to improved family functioning. The majority of patients and families report more effective coping, increased social support, and increased feelings of family closeness (Godkin, Krant, & Doster, 1984). In one study, family members experiencing hospice scored higher than nonhospice family members in psychological well-being one to two years after their loved one's death (Ragow-O'Brien, Hayslip, & Guarnaccia, 2000).

As a long-range goal, hospice organizations are striving for broader acceptance. Culturally sensitive approaches are needed to reach more ethnic minority patients, who are much less likely than white patients to participate in hospice (Crawley et al., 2000; Ngo-Metzger, Phillips, & McCarthy, 2007). In developing countries, where millions die of cancer, AIDS, and other devastating illnesses each year, community-based teams working under a nurse's supervision sometimes deliver palliative care. But they face many obstacles, including lack of funding, pain-relieving drugs, and professional and public education about hospice. As a result, they are small "islands of excellence," accessible to only a few families (Wright et al., 2008).

ASK YOURSELF

≫ REVIEW
Why is the stage notion an inaccurate account of dying patients' mental and emotional reactions?

≫ APPLY
When 5-year-old Timmy's kidney failure was diagnosed as terminal, his parents could not accept the tragic news. Their hospital visits became shorter, and they evaded his anxious questions. Eventually, Timmy blamed himself. He died with little physical pain, but alone, and his parents suffered prolonged guilt. How could hospice care have helped Timmy and his family?

≫ REFLECT
If you were terminally ill, where would you want to die? Explain.

The Right to Die

In 1990, 26-year-old Terri Schiavo's heart stopped briefly, temporarily cutting off oxygen to her brain. While Terri lay in a persistent vegetative state, her husband and guardian, Michael, claimed that she had earlier told him she would not want to be kept alive artificially, but Terri's parents disagreed. In 1998, the Florida Circuit Court granted Michael's petition to have Terri's feeding tube removed. In 2001, after her parents had exhausted their appeals, the tube was taken out. But on the basis of contradictory medical testimony, Terri's parents convinced a circuit court judge to order the feeding tube reinserted, and the legal wrangling continued. In 2002, Michael won a second judgment to remove the tube.

By that time, publicity over the case and its central question—who should make end-of-life decisions when the patient's wishes are unclear—had made Terri a political issue. In 2003, the Florida legislature passed a law allowing the governor to stay the circuit court's order to keep Terri alive, but on appeal, the law was declared unconstitutional. In 2005, the U.S. Congress entered the fray, passing a bill that transferred Terri's fate to the U.S. District Court. When the judge refused to intervene, the feeding tube was removed for a third time. In 2005—15 years after losing consciousness—Terri Schiavo died. The autopsy confirmed the original persistent vegetative state diagnosis: Her brain was half normal size.

The Schiavo case—and others like it—have brought right-to-die issues to the forefront of public attention. Today, all U.S. states have laws that honor patients' wishes concerning withdrawal of treatment in cases of terminal illness and, sometimes, in cases of a persistent vegetative state. But no uniform right-to-die policy exists, and heated controversy persists over how to handle the diverse circumstances in which patients and family members make requests.

Euthanasia is the practice of ending the life of a person suffering from an incurable condition. Its various forms are summarized in Table 19.1. As we will see, public acceptance of euthanasia is high, except when it involves ending the life of an anguished, terminally ill patient without his or her expressed permission.

Passive Euthanasia

In **passive euthanasia,** life-sustaining treatment is withheld or withdrawn, permitting a patient to die naturally. **TAKE A MOMENT...** Do you think Terri Schiavo should have been allowed to die sooner? Was it right for Nicholas's doctors to turn off his respirator at Giselle's request? When an Alzheimer's victim has lost all awareness and bodily functions, should life support be withheld?

In recent polls, more than three-fourths of Americans supported the right of patients or family members to end treatment when there is no hope of recovery (Pew Research Center, 2006). In 1986, the American Medical Association endorsed withdrawing all forms of treatment from the terminally ill when death is imminent and from those in a permanent vegetative state. Consequently, passive euthanasia is widely practiced as part of ordinary medical procedure, in which doctors exercise professional judgment.

Still, a minority of citizens do not endorse passive euthanasia. Religious denomination has surprisingly little effect on people's opinions. For example, most Catholics hold favorable views, despite slow official church acceptance because of fears that passive euthanasia might be a first step toward government-approved mercy killing. However, ethnicity makes a difference: Nearly twice as many African Americans as Caucasian Americans desire all medical means possible, regardless of the patient's condition, and African Americans more often receive life-sustaining intervention, such as feeding tubes (Bayer et al., 2006; Johnson et al., 2008). Their reluctance to forgo treatment reflects strong cultural and religious beliefs in overcoming adversity and in the power of God to promote healing (Johnson, Elbert-Avila, & Tulsky, 2005).

Because of controversial court cases like Terri Schiavo's, some doctors and health-care institutions are unwilling to end treatment without legal protection. In the absence of national consensus on passive euthanasia, people can best ensure that their wishes will be followed by preparing an **advance medical directive**—a written statement of desired medical treatment should they become incurably ill. U.S. states recognize two types of advance directives: a *living will* and a *durable power of*

■ **TABLE 19.1** ■ *Forms of Euthanasia*

FORM	DESCRIPTION
Passive euthanasia	At the patient's request, the doctor withholds or withdraws treatment, thereby permitting the patient to die naturally. For example, the doctor does not perform surgery or administer medication that could prolong life, or the doctor turns off the respirator of a patient who cannot breathe independently.
Voluntary active euthanasia	The doctor ends a suffering patient's life at the patient's request. For example, the doctor administers a lethal dose of drugs.
Assisted suicide	The doctor helps a suffering patient take his or her own life. For example, the doctor enables the patient to swallow or inject a lethal dose of drugs.
Involuntary active euthanasia	The doctor ends a suffering patient's life without the patient's permission. For example, without obtaining the patient's consent, the doctor administers a lethal dose of drugs.

attorney for health care. Sometimes these are combined into one document.

In a **living will,** people specify the treatments they do or do not want in case of a terminal illness, coma, or other near-death situation. For example, a person might state that without reasonable expectation of recovery, he or she should not be kept alive through medical intervention of any kind. In addition, a living will sometimes specifies that pain-relieving medication be given, even though it might shorten life. In Sofie's case, her doctor administered a powerful narcotic to relieve labored breathing and quiet her fear of suffocation. The narcotic suppressed respiration, causing death to occur hours or days earlier than if the medication had not been prescribed, but without distress. Such palliative care is accepted as appropriate and ethical medical practice.

Although living wills help ensure personal control, they do not guarantee it. Recognition of living wills is usually limited to patients who are terminally ill or are otherwise expected to die shortly. Only a few U.S. states cover people in a persistent vegetative state or elders who linger with many chronic problems, including Alzheimer's disease, because these conditions are not classified as terminal. Even when terminally ill patients have living wills, doctors often do not follow them for a variety of reasons, including fear of lawsuits, their own moral beliefs, failure to inquire about patients' directives, and inaccessibility of those directives—for example, located in the family safe or family members unaware of them (Gorman et al., 2005; van Asselt, 2006).

Because living wills cannot anticipate all future medical conditions and can easily be ignored, a second form of advance directive has become common. The **durable power of attorney for health care** authorizes appointment of another person (usually, though not always, a family member) to make health-care decisions on one's behalf. It is more flexible than the living will because it permits a trusted spokesperson to confer with the doctor as medical circumstances arise. Because authority to speak for the patient is not limited to terminal illnesses, more latitude exists for dealing with unexpected situations. And in gay and lesbian and other close relationships not sanctioned by law, the durable power of attorney can ensure the partner's role in decision making and in advocating for the patient's health-care needs.

Whether or not a person supports passive euthanasia, it is important to have a living will, durable power of attorney, or both, because most deaths occur in hospitals. Yet fewer than 30 percent of Americans have executed such documents, perhaps because of widespread uneasiness about bringing up the topic of death, especially with relatives (Pew Research Center, 2006). To encourage people to make decisions about potential treatment while they are able, U.S. federal law now requires that all medical facilities receiving federal funds provide information at admission about state laws and institutional policies on patients' rights and advance directives.

As happened with Terri Schiavo, health-care professionals—unclear about a patient's intent and fearing liability—will probably decide to continue treatment regardless of cost and a person's prior oral statements. Perhaps for this reason, some U.S. states permit appointment of a health-care proxy, or substitute decision maker, if a patient failed to provide an advance medical directive while competent. Proxies are an important means of covering children and adolescents, who cannot legally execute advance medical directives.

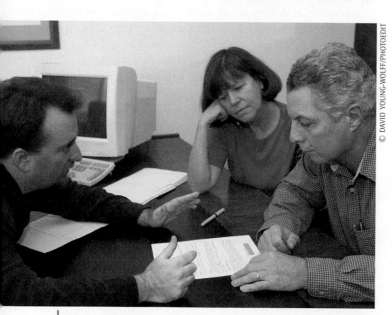

This couple discusses a durable power of attorney with a hospital chaplain. This advance directive authorizes a trusted spokesperson to make health-care decisions and helps ensure that one's desires will be granted.

© DAVID YOUNG-WOLFF/PHOTOEDIT

Voluntary Active Euthanasia

In recent years, the right-to-die debate has shifted from withdrawal of treatment for the hopelessly ill to more active alternatives. In **voluntary active euthanasia,** doctors or others act directly, at a patient's request, to end suffering before a natural end to life. The practice, a form of mercy killing, is a criminal offense in most countries, including almost all U.S. states. But support for voluntary active euthanasia is growing. As Figure 19.2 shows, about 70 to 90 percent of people in Western nations approve of it (World Federation of Right to Die Societies, 2006). When doctors engage in voluntary active euthanasia, judges in these countries are usually lenient, granting suspended sentences or probation—a trend reflecting rising public interest in self-determination in death as in life.

Nevertheless, attempts to legalize voluntary active euthanasia have prompted heated controversy. Supporters believe it represents the most compassionate option for terminally ill people in severe pain. Opponents stress the moral difference between "letting die" and "killing" and point out that at times, even very sick patients recover. They also argue that involving doctors in taking the lives of suffering patients may impair

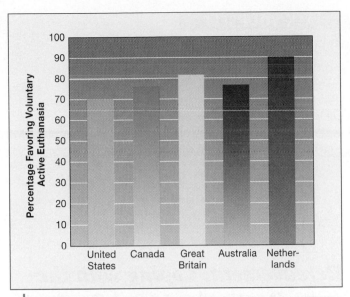

■ FIGURE 19.2 ■ Public opinion favoring voluntary active euthanasia in five nations. A struggle exists between public opinion, which has increasingly favored voluntary active euthanasia over the past 30 years, and legal statutes, which prohibit it. The majority of people in Western nations believe that a hopelessly ill, suffering patient who asks for a lethal injection should be granted that request. Public support for voluntary active euthanasia is highest in the Netherlands—the only nation in the world where the practice is legal under certain conditions. (From Pew Research Center, 2006, *Right to Die Societies.* Reprinted by permission.)

fering and honor self-determination by assisting a patient in dying, they should be subject to the most stringent monitoring possible.

Assisted Suicide

After checking Diane's blood count, Dr. Timothy Quill gently broke the news: leukemia. If she were to have any hope of survival, a strenuous course of treatment with only a 25 percent success rate would have to begin immediately. Convinced that she would suffer unspeakably from side effects and lack of control over her body, she chose not to undergo chemotherapy and a bone marrow transplant.

Diane insisted she wanted no part of a lingering death. She calmly stated that when the time came, she desired to take her own life in the least painful way possible—a choice she had discussed with her husband and son, who respected it. Realizing that Diane could get the most out of the time she had left only if her fears of prolonged pain were allayed, Dr. Quill granted her request for sleeping pills, making sure she knew the amounts needed for both sleep and suicide.

Diane's next few months were busy and fulfilling. Her son took leave from college to be with her, and her husband worked at home as much as possible. Gradually, bone pain, fatigue, and fever set in. Saying good-bye to her family and friends, Diane asked to be alone for an hour, took a lethal dose of medication, and died at home (Quill, 1991).

Assisting a suicide is illegal in Canada and in many, but not all, U.S. states. In Western Europe, doctor-assisted suicide is legal in Belgium, Germany, the Netherlands, and Switzerland and is tacitly accepted in many other countries (Hill, 2003; Scherer & Simon, 1999). In the United States, Oregon's 1997 Death with Dignity Act explicitly allows physicians to prescribe drugs so terminally ill patients can end their lives. To get a prescription, patients must have two doctors agree that they have less than six months to live and must request the drugs at least twice, with an interval of at least 15 days. In January 2006, the U.S. Supreme Court rejected a challenge to the Oregon law, but the Court has also upheld the right of other states to ban assisted suicide. In 2008, the state of Washington passed legislation—similar to Oregon's—permitting assisted suicide.

Only 46 percent of Americans approve of assisted suicide (Pew Research Center, 2006). And a survey of nearly 1,000 terminally ill U.S. patients ranging in age from 22 to 109 revealed that although they largely endorsed the practice, just one-tenth seriously considered asking for it; in a follow-up, many of them had changed their minds (Emanuel, Fairclough, & Emanuel, 2000).

In Oregon, assisted suicide accounts for only one-tenth of 1 percent of deaths (Niemeyer, 2006). But thousands of Oregonians say they find comfort in knowing the option is available (Hedberg, Hopkins, & Kohn, 2003).

Public interest in assisted suicide was sparked in the 1990s by Dr. Jack Kevorkian, a vigorous proponent of euthanasia who devised "suicide machines" that permitted more than 100 terminally ill patients, after brief counseling, to self-administer

people's trust in health professionals. Finally, a fear exists that legalizing this practice—even when strictly monitored to make sure it does not arise out of depression, loneliness, coercion, or a desire to diminish the burden of illness on others—could lead to a broadening of euthanasia (Loewy, 2004). Initially limited to the terminally ill, it might be applied involuntarily to the frail, demented, or disabled—outcomes that most people find unacceptable and immoral.

These concerns are warranted, as events in the Netherlands—where voluntary active euthanasia has been practiced for several decades and became legal in 2001—make clear. Dutch doctors are allowed to engage in it when there is no prospect of relief from physical or mental suffering, when no doubt exists about the patient's voluntary and well-informed desire to die, when all other options for care have been exhausted or refused, and when another doctor has been consulted. But despite these safeguards, some doctors admit to having actively caused a death when a patient did not ask for it, defending their action by referring to the impossibility of treating pain, a low quality of life, or drawn-out dying in a patient near death. And a small minority say they granted the euthanasia requests of physically healthy patients—usually elders who felt "weary of life" (Rurup et al., 2005).

Still, terminally ill individuals in severe pain continue to plead for legalization of voluntary active euthanasia. Probably all would agree that when doctors feel compelled to relieve suflethal drugs and carbon monoxide. Less publicity surrounded Dr. Quill's decision to assist Diane—a patient he knew well after serving for years as her personal doctor. After he told her story in a prestigious medical journal, reactions were mixed, as they are toward assisted suicide in general. Some view doctors who help suffering people who want to die as compassionate and respectful of patients' personal choices. Others oppose assisted suicide on religious and moral grounds or believe that the role of doctors should be limited to saving, not taking, lives.

Like euthanasia, assisted suicide poses grave dilemmas. Juries have seldom returned guilty verdicts in cases involving doctor-assisted suicide. Yet in April 1999, Kevorkian—after giving a terminally ill man a lethal injection, videotaping the death, and permitting the event to be broadcast on the CBS television program *60 Minutes*—was sentenced to 10 to 25 years in prison for second-degree murder and delivery of a controlled substance. The murder indictment prevented Kevorkian from introducing evidence indicating that the man wanted to kill himself—evidence that would have been permissible had the charge been assisted suicide or voluntary active euthanasia.

Public opinion consistently favors voluntary active euthanasia over assisted suicide. Yet in assisted suicide, the final act is solely the patient's, reducing the possibility of coercion. For this reason, some experts believe that legalizing assisted suicide is preferable to legalizing voluntary active euthanasia. However, in an atmosphere of high family caregiving burdens and intense pressure to contain health-care costs, legalizing either practice poses risks. The American Medical Association opposes both voluntary active euthanasia and assisted suicide. In a recent survey of 1,140 U.S. doctors, only 18 percent objected to sedating a dying patient to unconsciousness if pain can be controlled in no other way, whereas nearly 70 percent opposed assisted suicide (Curlin et al., 2008). Helping incurable, suffering patients who yearn for death poses profound moral and legal problems.

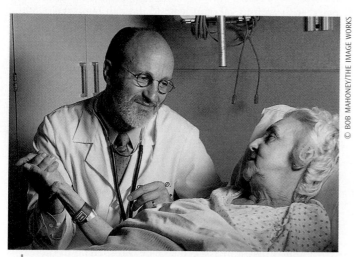

In a prestigious medical journal, Dr. Timothy Quill explained how and why he assisted a terminally ill patient in taking her own life. Doctor-assisted suicide is legal in the states of Oregon and Washington and in several Western European countries.

© BOB MAHONEY/THE IMAGE WORKS

Bereavement: Coping with the Death of a Loved One

Loss is an inevitable part of existence throughout the lifespan. Even when change is for the better, we must let go of some aspects of experience so we can embrace others. In this way, our development prepares us for profound loss.

Bereavement is the experience of losing a loved one by death. The root of this word means "to be robbed," suggesting unjust and injurious theft of something valuable. Consistent with this image, we respond to loss with **grief**—intense physical and psychological distress. When we say someone is grief-stricken, we imply that his or her total way of being is affected.

Because grief can be overwhelming, cultures have devised ways of helping their members move beyond it to deal with the life changes demanded by death of a loved one. **Mourning** is the culturally specified expression of the bereaved person's thoughts and feelings. Customs—such as gathering with family and friends, dressing in black, attending the funeral, and observing a prescribed mourning period with special rituals—vary greatly among societies and ethnic groups. But all have in common the goal of helping people work through their grief and learn to live in a world that does not include the deceased.

Clearly, grief and mourning are closely linked—in everyday language, we often use the two words interchangeably. Let's look closely at how people respond to the death of a loved one.

Grief Process

Theorists formerly believed that bereaved individuals—both children and adults—moved through three phases of grieving, each characterized by a different set of responses (Bowlby, 1980; Rando, 1995). In reality, however, people vary greatly in behavior and timing and often move back and forth between these reactions. A more accurate account compares grief to a roller-coaster ride, with many ups and downs and, over time, gradual resolution (Lund, 1996). Rather than phases, the grieving process is best conceived as a set of *tasks*—actions the person must take to recover and return to a fulfilling life: (1) accepting the reality of the loss; (2) working through the pain of grief; (3) adjusting to a world without the loved one; and (4) developing an inner bond with the deceased and moving on with life (Worden, 2009). According to this view, people can take active steps to overcome grief—a powerful remedy for the overwhelming feelings of vulnerability that the bereaved often experience.

■ **AVOIDANCE.** On hearing the news, the survivor experiences shock followed by disbelief, which may last from hours to weeks. A numbed feeling serves as "emotional anesthesia" while the person begins the first task of grieving: becoming painfully aware of the loss.

■ **CONFRONTATION.** As the mourner confronts the reality of the death, grief is most intense. The person often experiences a cascade of emotional reactions, including anxiety, sadness, protest, anger, helplessness, frustration, abandonment, and yearning for the loved one. Common responses include obsessively reviewing the circumstances of death, asking how it might have been prevented, and searching for meaning in it (Neimeyer, 2001b). In addition, the grief-stricken person may be absentminded, unable to concentrate, and preoccupied with thoughts of the deceased, and may experience loss of sleep and appetite. Self-destructive behaviors, such as taking drugs or driving too fast, may occur. Most of these responses are symptoms of depression—an invariable component of grieving.

Although confrontation is difficult, it enables the mourner to grapple with the second task: working through the pain of grief. Each surge of anguish brings the mourner closer to acceptance that the loved one is gone. As a result, the mourner makes progress on the third task: adjusting to a world in which the deceased is missing.

■ **RESTORATION.** Bereaved individuals must also deal with stressors that are secondary outcomes of the death—overcoming loneliness by reaching out to others; mastering skills (such as finances or cooking) that the deceased had performed; reorganizing daily life without the loved one; and revising one's identity from "spouse" to "widow" or from "parent" to "parent of a deceased child."

According to a recent perspective, called the **dual-process model of coping with loss,** effective coping requires people to oscillate between dealing with the emotional consequences of loss and attending to life changes, which—when handled successfully—have restorative, or healing, effects (Hansson & Stroebe, 2007; Stroebe & Schut, 1999). Much research indicates that confronting grief without relief has severe negative consequences for physical and mental health (Corr & Corr, 2007). Consistent with the dual-process model, in a study that assessed widowed older adults at 6, 18, and 48 months after the death of their spouses, both loss-oriented and restoration-oriented activities occurred throughout bereavement. As predicted, restoration-oriented events—such as visiting friends, attending religious services, and volunteering—reduced the stress of grieving (Richardson, 2007). Using the dual-process approach, one 14-session intervention for older adults grieving

the loss of a spouse addresses both emotional and life-change issues, alternating between them (Lund et al., 2004).

As grief subsides, emotional energies increasingly shift toward the fourth task—forging a symbolic bond with the deceased and moving on with life by meeting everyday responsibilities, investing in new activities and goals, strengthening old ties, and building new relationships. On certain days, such as family celebrations or the anniversary of death, grief reactions may resurface and require attention, but they do not interfere with a healthy, positive approach to life.

How long does grieving last? There is no single answer. Sometimes confrontation continues for a few months, at other times for several years. An occasional upsurge of grief may persist for a lifetime and is a common response to losing a much-loved spouse, partner, child, or friend (Sanders, 1999).

Personal and Situational Variations

Like dying, grieving is affected by many factors, including personality, coping style, and religious and cultural background. Sex differences are also evident. Compared with women, men typically express distress and depression less directly and seek social support less readily—factors that may contribute to the much higher mortality rate among bereaved men than women (Lund & Caserta, 2004b; McGoldrick, 2004).

Furthermore, the quality of the mourner's relationship with the deceased is important. An end to a loving, fulfilling bond may lead to anguished grieving, but it is unlikely to leave the residue of anger, guilt, and regret that often follows dissolution of a conflict-ridden, ambivalent tie. And end-of-life care makes a difference: Widowed older adults whose spouses experienced a painful death reported more anxiety, intrusive thoughts, and yearning for the loved one six months later (Carr, 2003).

Circumstances surrounding the death—whether it is sudden and unanticipated or follows a prolonged illness—also shape mourners' responses. The nature of the lost relationship and the timing of the death within the life course make a difference as well.

■ **SUDDEN, UNANTICIPATED DEATHS VERSUS PROLONGED, EXPECTED DEATHS.** In instances of sudden, unexpected deaths—usually the result of murder, suicide, war, accident, or natural disaster—avoidance may be especially pronounced and confrontation highly traumatic because shock and disbelief are extreme. In contrast, during prolonged dying, the bereaved person has had time to engage in **anticipatory grieving**—acknowledging that the loss is inevitable and preparing emotionally for it. Survivors may feel less overwhelmed immediately following the death. But they may display more persistent anxiety due to long-term stressors, such as highly demanding caregiving and having watched a loved one suffer from a debilitating illness (Carr et al., 2001).

Adjusting to a sudden death is easier when the survivor understands the reasons for it. This barrier to confronting loss is tragically apparent in cases of sudden infant death syndrome (SIDS), in which doctors cannot tell parents exactly why their apparently healthy baby died (see Chapter 3, page 85). That death seems "senseless" also complicates grieving after suicides, terrorist attacks, school and drive-by shootings, and natural disasters. In Western societies, people tend to believe that momentous events should be comprehensible and nonrandom (Lukas & Seiden, 2007). A death that is sudden and unexpected can threaten basic assumptions about a just, benevolent, and controllable world.

Suicide, particularly that of a young person, is especially hard to bear. Compared with survivors of other sudden deaths, people grieving a suicidal loss are more likely to conclude that they contributed to or could have prevented it—self-blame that can trigger profound guilt and shame. These reactions are likely to be especially intense and persisting when a mourner's culture or religion condemns suicide as immoral (Dunne & Dunne-Maxim, 2004; Sveen & Walby, 2008). Typically, recovery from grief after a suicide is prolonged.

■ **PARENTS GRIEVING THE LOSS OF A CHILD.** The death of a child, whether unexpected or foreseen, is the most difficult loss an adult can face (Dent & Stewart, 2004). Children are extensions of parents' feelings about themselves—the focus of hopes and dreams, including parents' sense of immortality. Also, because children depend on, admire, and appreciate their parents in a deeply gratifying way, they are an unmatched source of love. Finally, the death of a child is unnatural: Children are not supposed to die before their parents. Parents

Grieving parents find their children in a hospital morgue in Buenos Aires, Argentina, after a fire raced through a packed nightclub. The death of a child, whether unexpected or foreseen, is the most difficult loss an adult can face.

who have lost a child often report considerable distress many years later, along with frequent thoughts of the deceased.

If parents can reestablish a sense of life's meaning through valuing the lost child's impact on their lives and investing in other children and activities, then the result can be firmer family commitments and personal growth. The process, which often takes years, is associated with improved physical and mental health and gains in marital satisfaction (Murphy, 2008). Five years after her son's death, one parent reflected on her progress:

> I was afraid to let go [of my pain, which was] a way of loving him. . . . Finally I had to admit that his life meant more than pain, it also meant joy and happiness and fun—and living. . . . When we release pain we make room for happiness in our lives. My memories of S. became lighter and more spontaneous. Instead of hurtful, my memories brought comfort, even a chuckle. . . . I realized S. was still teaching me things. (Klass, 2004, p. 87)

■ **CHILDREN AND ADOLESCENTS GRIEVING THE LOSS OF A PARENT OR SIBLING.** The loss of an attachment figure has long-term consequences for children. When a parent dies, children's basic sense of security and being cared for is threatened. And the death of a sibling not only deprives children of a close emotional tie but also informs them, often for the first time, of their own vulnerability.

Children grieving a family loss describe frequent crying, trouble concentrating in school, sleep difficulties, headaches, and other physical symptoms several months to years after a death. And clinical studies reveal that persistent depression, anxiety, angry outbursts, social withdrawal, and worries about dying themselves are common (Dowdney, 2000; Luecken, 2008). At the same time, many children say they have actively maintained mental contact with their dead parent or sibling, dreaming about and speaking to them regularly. In a follow-up seven to nine years after sibling loss, thinking about the deceased brother or sister at least once a day was common (Martinson, Davies, & McClowry, 1987; Silverman & Nickman, 1996). These images, reported by bereaved adults as well, seem to facilitate coping with loss.

Cognitive development contributes to the ability to grieve. For example, children with an immature understanding of death may believe the dead parent left voluntarily, perhaps in anger, and that the other parent may also disappear. For these reasons, young children need careful, repeated explanations assuring them that the parent did not want to die and was not angry at them (Christ, Siegel, & Christ, 2002). Keeping the truth from children isolates them and often leads to profound regrets. One 8-year-old who learned only a half-hour in advance that his sick brother was dying reflected, "If only I'd known, I could have said goodbye."

Regardless of children's level of understanding, honesty, affection, and reassurance help them tolerate painful feelings of loss. Grief-stricken school-age children are usually more willing than adolescents to confide in parents. To appear normal, teenagers tend to keep their grieving from both adults and peers. Consequently, they are more likely than children to become depressed or to escape from grief through acting-out behavior (Granot, 2005). Overall, effective parenting—warmth combined with rational discipline—fosters adaptive coping and positive long-term adjustment in both children and adolescents (Luecken, 2008).

■ **ADULTS GRIEVING THE LOSS OF AN INTIMATE PARTNER.** Recall from Chapter 18 that after the death of a spouse, adaptation to widowhood varies greatly, with age, social support, and personality making a difference. After a period of intense grieving, most widowed elders in Western nations fare well, while younger individuals display more negative outcomes (see page 489 to review). Older widows and widowers have many more contemporaries in similar circumstances. And most have already attained important life goals or adjusted to the fact that some goals will not be attained.

In contrast, loss of a spouse or partner in early or middle adulthood is a nonnormative event that profoundly disrupts life plans. Interviews with a large, U.S. nationally representative sample of adults who had been widowed from less than 1 to 64 years previously (typically in middle adulthood) revealed that thoughts about and conversations with the lost spouse occurred often in the first few years and then declined gradually (Carnelley et al., 2006). But they did not reach their lowest level for several decades, when the typical respondent still thought about the deceased partner once every week or two and conversed with him or her about once a month. In addition to dealing with feelings of loss, young and middle-aged widows and widowers often must assume a greater role in comforting others, especially children (Lopata, 1996). They also face the stresses of single parenthood and rapid shrinking of the social network established during their life as a couple.

The death of an intimate partner in a gay or lesbian relationship presents unique challenges. When relatives limit or bar the partner from participating in funeral services, the survivor experiences *disenfranchised grief*—a sense of loss without the opportunity to mourn publicly and benefit from others' support—which can profoundly disrupt the grieving process (Lund & Caserta, 2004a). Fortunately, gay and lesbian communities provide helpful alternative support in the form of memorial services and other rituals.

■ **BEREAVEMENT OVERLOAD.** When a person experiences several deaths at once or in close succession, bereavement overload can occur. Multiple losses deplete the coping resources of even well-adjusted people, leaving them emotionally overwhelmed and unable to resolve their grief (Lattanzi-Licht & Doka, 2003).

Because old age often brings the death of spouse, siblings, and friends in close succession, elders are also at risk for bereavement overload. But recall from Chapter 18 that compared

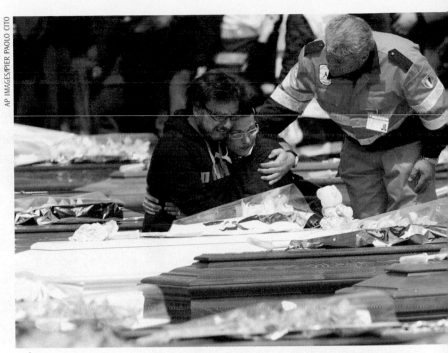

In the aftermath of the massive 2009 earthquake in L'Aquila, Italy, with a death toll of nearly 300, a couple mourns during the funeral service for quake victims. A public tragedy like this can spark bereavement overload, leaving mourners at risk for prolonged, overwhelming grief.

with young people, older adults are often better equipped to handle these losses. They know that decline and death are expected in late adulthood, and they have had a lifetime of experience through which to develop effective coping strategies.

Public tragedies—random murders in schools, terrorist attacks, natural disasters, or widely publicized kidnappings—can spark bereavement overload (Corr, 2003). Many survivors who lost loved ones, co-workers, or friends in the September 11, 2001, terrorist attacks (including an estimated 3,000 children who lost a parent) experienced repeated images of horror and destruction, which impeded coming to terms with loss (Nader, 2002; Webb, 2002). The greater the bereaved individual's exposure to the catastrophic death scene, the more severe these reactions.

Funerals and other bereavement rituals, illustrated in the Cultural Influences box on page 520, assist mourners of all ages in resolving grief with the help of family and friends. Bereaved individuals who remain preoccupied with loss and who have difficulty resuming interest in everyday activities benefit from special interventions designed to help them adjust.

Bereavement Interventions

Sympathy and understanding are sufficient to enable most people to undertake the tasks necessary to recover from grief (see Applying What We Know on page 521). Yet effective support is often difficult to provide, and relatives and friends can benefit from training in how to respond. Sometimes they give advice aimed at hastening recovery, an approach that most bereaved people dislike (Lehman, Ellard, & Wortman, 1986). Listening patiently and "just being there" are among the best ways to help.

■ CULTURAL INFLUENCES ■

Cultural Variations in Mourning Behavior

The ceremonies that commemorated Sofie's and Nicholas's deaths—the first Jewish, the second Quaker—were strikingly different. Yet they served common goals: announcing that a death has occurred, ensuring social support, commemorating the deceased, and conveying a philosophy of life after death.

At the funeral home, Sofie's body was washed and shrouded, a Jewish ritual signifying return to a state of purity. Then it was placed in a plain wooden (not metal) coffin, so as not to impede the natural process of decomposition. To underscore the finality of death, Jewish tradition does not permit viewing of the body; it remains in a closed coffin. Traditionally, the coffin is not left alone until burial; in honor of the deceased, the community maintains a day-and-night vigil.

To return the body quickly to the life-giving earth from which it sprang, Sofie's funeral was scheduled as soon as relatives could gather—just three days after death. Sofie's husband and children symbolized their anguish by cutting a black ribbon and pinning it to their clothing. The rabbi recited psalms of comfort, followed by a eulogy. The service continued at the graveside. Once the coffin had been lowered into the ground, relatives and friends took turns shoveling earth onto it, each participating in the irrevocable act of burial. The service concluded with the *Kaddish* prayer, which affirms life while accepting death.

At home, the family lit a memorial candle, which burned throughout *shiva,* the seven-day mourning period (Hazell, 2001). A meal of consolation prepared by others followed, creating a warm feeling of community. Jewish custom prescribes that after 30 days, life should gradually return to normal. When a parent dies, the mourning period is extended to 12 months.

In the Quaker tradition of simplicity, Nicholas was cremated promptly. During the next week, relatives and close friends gathered with Giselle and Sasha at their home.

The Balinese of Indonesia believe they must remain calm in the face of death so the gods can hear their prayers. While acknowledging their grief, these Balinese mourners work hard to maintain their composure as they participate in a cremation procession.

Together, they planned a memorial service to celebrate Nicholas's life.

When people arrived on the appointed day, a clerk of the Friends (Quaker) Meeting welcomed them and explained to newcomers the Quaker custom of worshipping silently, with those who feel moved to speak doing so at any time. Many mourners offered personal statements about Nicholas or read poems and selections from Scripture. After concluding comments from Giselle and Sasha, everyone joined hands to close the service. A reception for the family followed.

Variations in mourning behavior are vast, both within and across societies. At African-American funerals, for example, grief is expressed freely: Eulogies and music are usually designed to trigger release of deep emotion (McGoldrick et al., 2004). In contrast, the Balinese of Indonesia believe they must remain calm in the face of death so that the gods can hear their prayers. While acknowledging their underlying grief, Balinese mourners work hard to maintain their composure (Rosenblatt, 1993, 2008).

In recent years, a new ritual has arisen: "virtual cemeteries" on the Internet, which allow postings whenever bereaved individuals feel ready to convey their thoughts and feelings, creation of tributes at little or no cost, and continuous, easy access to the memorial. Most creators of Web tributes choose to tell personal stories, highlighting a laugh, a favorite joke, or a touching moment (Roberts & Vidal, 1999–2000). Some survivors use Web memorials to grieve openly, others to converse with the lost loved one. Cemetery guestbooks offer a place for visitors to connect with other mourners. Web cemeteries also provide a means for people excluded from traditional death rituals to engage in public mourning (Roberts, 2006; Stroebe, van der Houwen, & Schut, 2008). The following "gravesite" message captures the unique qualities of this highly flexible medium for mourning:

> I wish I could maintain contact with you, to keep alive the vivid memories of your impact on my life. . . . Because I cannot visit your grave today, I use this means to tell you how much you are loved.

Bereavement interventions typically encourage people to draw on their existing social network, while providing additional social support through group or individual counseling. Controversy exists over whether grief counseling benefits most bereaved people or whether it helps only those experiencing profound difficulties (Allumbaugh & Hoyt, 1999; CFAH, 2003; Jordan & Neimeyer, 2003). A recent analysis of research expressed optimism about broadly favorable effects (Larson & Hoyt, 2007).

Applying What We Know

Suggestions for Resolving Grief After a Loved One Dies

Suggestion	Description
Give yourself permission to feel the loss.	Permit yourself to confront all thoughts and emotions associated with the death. Make a conscious decision to overcome your grief, recognizing that this will take time.
Accept social support.	In the early part of grieving, let others reach out to you by making meals, running errands, and keeping you company. Be assertive; ask for what you need so people who would like to help will know what to do.
Be realistic about the course of grieving.	Expect to have some negative and intense reactions, such as feeling anguished, sad, and angry, that last from weeks to months and may occasionally resurface years after the death. There is no one way to grieve, so find the best way for you.
Remember the deceased.	Review your relationship to and experiences with the deceased, permitting yourself to see that you can no longer be with him or her as before. Form a new relationship based on memories, keeping it alive through photographs, commemorative donations, prayers, and other symbols and actions.
When ready, invest in new activities and relationships, and master new tasks of daily living.	Determine which roles you must give up and which ones you must assume as a consequence of the death, and take deliberate steps to incorporate these into your life. Set small goals at first, such as a night at the movies, a dinner date with a friend, a cooking or household repair class, or a week's vacation.

Self-help groups that bring together mourners who have experienced the same type of loss seem highly effective in reducing stress. In one such program for recently widowed elders, a participant expressed the many lasting benefits:

> We shared our anger at being left behind, . . . our fright of that aloneness. We shared our favorite pictures, so each of us could know the others' families and the fun we used to have. We shared our feelings of guilt if we had fun . . . and found out that it was okay to keep on living! . . . This group will always be there for me and I will always be there for them. I love you all! (Lund, 2005)

Effective interventions for children and adolescents following violent deaths protect them from unnecessary reexposure, help parents and teachers with their own distress so they can effectively offer comfort, and are culturally sensitive. After shootings on the grounds of one school, administrators arranged for a ceremony that removed "angry dead souls." Only then did the large number of Vietnamese Buddhist students return to their classrooms (Nader, Dubrow, & Stamm, 1999).

Sudden, violent, and unexplainable deaths; the loss of a child; a death that the mourner feels he or she could have prevented; or an ambivalent or dependent relationship with the deceased makes it harder for bereaved people to overcome their loss. In these instances, grief therapy, or individual counseling with a specially trained professional, can be helpful. One successful approach is to assist bereaved adults in finding some value in the grieving experience—for example, gaining insight into the meaning of relationships, discovering their own capacity to cope with adversity, or crystallizing a sense of purpose in their lives (Neimeyer, 2001a).

Nevertheless, most bereaved individuals do not participate in bereavement interventions, even when readily available to them. One study reported that only 30 percent of family members who had been caregivers for hospice patients made use of hospice bereavement services—consisting of phone support, onsite support groups, and referrals for counseling (Cherlin et al., 2007). Many who refused these services were severely distressed yet did not realize that intervention could be helpful.

Death Education

Preparatory steps can help people of all ages cope with death more effectively. The death awareness movement that sparked increased sensitivity to the needs of dying patients has also led to the rise of college and university courses in death, dying, and bereavement. Instruction has been integrated into the training of doctors, nurses, psychologists, and social workers, although most professional offerings are limited to only a few lectures (Wass, 2004). Death education is also found in adult education programs in many communities and even in a few elementary and secondary schools.

Death education at all levels has the following goals:

- Increasing students' understanding of the physical and psychological changes that accompany dying
- Helping students learn how to cope with the death of a loved one
- Preparing students to be informed consumers of medical and funeral services

■ Promoting understanding of social and ethical issues involving death

Educational format varies widely. Although using a lecture approach focused on conveying information leads to gains in knowledge, it often leaves students more uncomfortable about death than when they entered. In contrast, experiential programs that help people confront their own mortality—through discussions with the terminally ill, visits to mortuaries and cemeteries, and personal awareness exercises—are less likely to heighten death anxiety and may sometimes reduce it (Durlak & Riesenberg, 1991; Maglio & Robinson, 1994).

Whether acquired in the classroom or in our daily lives, our thoughts and feelings about death are forged through interactions with others. Dying people have at times confided in those close to them that awareness of the limits of their lifespan permitted them to focus on what is truly important in their lives. As one terminally ill patient summed up, "[It's] kind of like life, just speeded up"—an accelerated process in which, over a period of weeks to months, one grapples with issues that normally would have taken years or decades to resolve (Selwyn, 1996, p. 36). Applying this lesson to ourselves, we learn that by being in touch with death and dying, we can live ever more fully.

ASK YOURSELF

》 REVIEW
What circumstances are likely to induce bereavement overload? Cite examples.

》 APPLY
List features of self-help groups that contribute to their effectiveness in helping people cope with loss.

》 REFLECT
Visit a Web cemetery, such as Virtual Memorials, *virtualmemorials .com.* Select examples of Web tributes, guestbook entries, and testimonials that illustrate the unique ways in which virtual cemeteries help people cope with death.

Summary

How We Die

Describe the physical changes of dying, along with their implications for defining death and the meaning of death with dignity.

》 Death is long and drawn-out for three-fourths of people—many more than in times past, as a result of life-saving medical technology. Among those who die suddenly, 80 to 90 percent are victims of heart attacks.

》 In general, dying takes place in three phases: the **agonal phase,** in which regular heartbeat disintegrates; **clinical death,** a short interval in which resuscitation is still possible; and **mortality,** or permanent death.

》 In most industrialized nations, **brain death** is accepted as the definition of death. But for the thousands of incurable patients who remain in a **persistent vegetative state,** the brain death standard does not always solve the dilemma of when to halt treatment.

》 We can best ensure death with dignity by supporting dying patients through their physical and psychological distress, being candid about death's certainty, and helping them learn enough about their condition to make reasoned choices about treatment.

Attitudes Toward Death

Discuss factors that influence attitudes toward death, including death anxiety.

》 Compared with earlier generations, more young people reach adulthood having had little contact with death, contributing to a sense of unease about it.

© MICHEL PORRO/GETTY IMAGES

》 Wide individual and cultural variations exist in **death anxiety.** People with a sense of spirituality, a well-developed personal philosophy of death, and deep faith in a higher force or being experience less fear of death. With greater ability to regulate negative emotion and a sense of symbolic immortality, older adults are less anxious about death than younger adults. Across cultures, women exhibit more death anxiety than men.

Thinking and Emotions of Dying People

Describe and evaluate Kübler-Ross's theory, citing factors that influence dying patients' responses.

》 According to Kübler-Ross, dying people typically express five responses, initially proposed as "stages": denial, anger, bargaining, depression, and acceptance. These reactions do not occur in fixed sequence, and dying people often display other coping strategies.

》 An **appropriate death** is one that makes sense in terms of the individual's pattern of living and values, preserves or restores significant relationships, and is as free of suffering as possible. Many contextual variables—nature of the disease; personality and coping style; family members' and health professionals' truthfulness and sensitivity; and spirituality, religion, and cultural background—affect the way people respond to their own dying and, therefore, the extent to which they attain an appropriate death.

A Place to Die

Evaluate the extent to which homes, hospitals, nursing homes, and the hospice approach meet the needs of dying people and their families.

》 Although most people say they want to die at home, only about one-fourth of Americans do. Even with professional help and hospital-supplied equipment, caring for a dying patient is highly demanding.

>> Sudden deaths typically occur in hospital emergency rooms, where sympathetic explanations from staff can reduce family members' anger, frustration, and confusion. Intensive care is especially depersonalizing for patients, who linger between life and death while hooked to machines. Most U.S. hospitals still do not have comprehensive treatment programs aimed at easing suffering at the end of life.

>> Though deaths in U.S. nursing homes are common, high-quality terminal care is lacking. Too many patients die in pain without having their needs met.

>> Whether a person dies at home or in an institution, the **hospice** approach strives to meet the dying person's physical, emotional, social, and spiritual needs by providing **palliative, or comfort, care** focused on protecting the quality of remaining life rather than on prolonging life. Besides reducing patient physical suffering, hospice care contributes to improved family functioning and better psychological well-being among family survivors.

© SIMON ODWYER/THE AGE PHOTO SALES

The Right to Die

Discuss controversies surrounding euthanasia and assisted suicide.

>> **Euthanasia**—ending the life of a person suffering from an incurable condition—takes various forms.

>> **Passive euthanasia,** withholding or withdrawing life-sustaining treatment from a hopelessly ill patient, is widely accepted and practiced. People can best ensure that their wishes will be followed by preparing a written **advance medical directive.** A **living will** contains instructions for treatment, whereas the **durable power of attorney for health care** names another person to make health-care decisions on one's behalf.

>> Public support for **voluntary active euthanasia,** in which doctors or others comply with a suffering patient's request to die before a natural end to life, is high. Nevertheless, the practice remains a criminal offense in most countries and has sparked heated controversy.

>> Less public support exists for assisted suicide. But because the final act is solely the patient's, some experts believe that legalizing assisted suicide is preferable to legalizing voluntary active euthanasia.

Bereavement: Coping with the Death of a Loved One

Describe the phases of grieving, factors that underlie individual variations, and bereavement interventions.

>> **Bereavement** refers to the experience of losing a loved one by death, **grief** to the intense physical and psychological distress that accompanies loss. **Mourning** customs are culturally prescribed expressions of thoughts and feelings designed to help people work through their grief.

>> Although theorists previously regarded grieving as taking place in orderly phases—avoidance, confrontation, and finally restoration—a more accurate image is a roller-coaster ride, with the mourner completing a set of tasks to overcome grief. According to the **dual-process model of coping with loss,** effective coping involves oscillating between dealing with the emotional consequences of loss and attending to life changes, which offer temporary distraction and relief from painful grieving.

>> Like dying, grieving is affected by many personal and situational factors. Bereaved men express grief less directly than bereaved women. After a sudden, unanticipated death, avoidance may be especially pronounced and confrontation highly traumatic. In contrast, a prolonged, expected death grants the bereaved person time to engage in **anticipatory grieving.**

>> When a parent loses a child or a child loses a parent or sibling, grieving is generally intense and prolonged. Because loss of a spouse or partner in early or middle adulthood is a nonnormative event with a major impact on life plans, younger widowed individuals usually fare less well than widowed elders. Disenfranchised grief can profoundly disrupt the process of grieving.

AP IMAGES/DANIEL LUNA

>> People who experience several deaths at once or in close succession may suffer from bereavement overload.

>> Sympathy and understanding are sufficient for most people to recover from grief. Self-help groups can provide extra social support. Professional bereavement interventions can be helpful for those experiencing severe distress.

Death Education

Explain how death education can help people cope with death more effectively.

>> Instruction in death, dying, and bereavement is more likely to reach students cognitively and emotionally when, in addition to conveying information, it includes an experiential component.

Important Terms and Concepts

advance medical directive (p. 513)
agonal phase (p. 504)
anticipatory grieving (p. 517)
appropriate death (p. 508)
bereavement (p. 516)
brain death (p. 504)
clinical death (p. 504)

death anxiety (p. 505)
dual-process model of coping with loss (p. 517)
durable power of attorney for health care (p. 514)
euthanasia (p. 513)
grief (p. 516)
hospice (p. 511)
living will (p. 514)

mortality (p. 504)
mourning (p. 516)
palliative, or comfort, care (p. 511)
passive euthanasia (p. 513)
persistent vegetative state (p. 504)
voluntary active euthanasia (p. 514)

Glossary

A

academic programs Preschool and kindergarten programs in which teachers structure children's learning, teaching academic skills through formal lessons that often involve repetition and drill. Distinguished from *child-centered programs*. (p. 188)

accommodation In Piaget's theory, that part of adaptation in which new schemes are created and old ones adjusted to produce a better fit with the environment. Distinguished from *assimilation*. (p. 117)

acculturative stress Psychological distress resulting from conflict between an individual's minority culture and the host culture. (p. 318)

activities of daily living (ADLs) Basic self-care tasks required to live on one's own, such as bathing, dressing, getting in and out of bed or a chair, and eating. (p. 445)

activity theory A social theory of aging that states that declining rates of interaction in late adulthood reflect social barriers to engagement, not the desires of elders. Older people will try to preserve life satisfaction by finding roles that allow them to remain about as active and busy as they were in middle age. Distinguished from *disengagement theory, continuity theory,* and *socioemotional selectivity theory*. (p. 482)

adaptation In Piaget's theory, the process of building schemes through direct interaction with the environment. Consists of two complementary activities: *assimilation* and *accommodation*. (p. 117)

adolescence The transition between childhood and adulthood that begins with puberty. It involves accepting one's full-grown body, acquiring adult ways of thinking, attaining greater independence from one's family, developing more mature ways of relating to peers of both sexes, and beginning to construct an identity. (p. 283)

advance medical directive A written statement of desired medical treatment should a person become incurably ill. (p. 513)

affect optimization The ability to maximize positive emotion and dampen negative emotion. An emotional strength of late adulthood. (p. 475)

age-graded influences Influences on lifespan development that are strongly related to age and therefore fairly predictable in when they occur and how long they last. (p. 7)

age of viability The age at which the fetus can first survive if born early. Occurs sometime between 22 and 26 weeks. (p. 65)

aging in place In late adulthood, remaining in a familiar setting where one has control over one's everyday life. (p. 484)

agonal phase The phase of dying in which gasps and muscle spasms occur during the first moments in which the regular heart beat disintegrates. Distinguished from *clinical death* and *mortality*. (p. 504)

alcohol-related neurodevelopmental disorder (ARND) The least severe form of fetal alcohol spectrum disorder, involving brain injury but with typical physical growth and absence of facial abnormalities. Distinguished from *fetal alcohol syndrome (FAS)* and *partial fetal alcohol syndrome (p-FAS)*. (p. 69)

allele Each of two or more forms of a gene located at the same place on corresponding pairs of chromosomes. (p. 38)

Alzheimer's disease The most common form of dementia, in which structural and chemical brain deterioration is associated with gradual loss of many aspects of thought and behavior, including memory, skilled and purposeful movements, and comprehension and production of speech. (p. 458)

amnion The inner membrane that encloses the developing organism in amniotic fluid, which helps keep temperature constant and provides a cushion against jolts caused by the mother's movements. (p. 62)

amyloid plaques A structural change in the cerebral cortex associated with Alzheimer's disease, in which dense deposits of a deteriorated protein called *amyloid* develop, surrounded by clumps of dead nerve and glial cells. (p. 459)

androgyny The gender identity held by individuals who score high on both traditionally masculine and traditionally feminine personality characteristics. (p. 214)

animistic thinking The belief that inanimate objects have lifelike qualities, such as thoughts, wishes, feelings, and intentions. (p. 175)

anorexia nervosa An eating disorder in which young people, mainly females, starve themselves because of a compulsive fear of getting fat and an extremely distorted body image. (p. 292)

anoxia Inadequate oxygen supply during labor and delivery. (p. 77)

anticipatory grieving Before a prolonged, expected death, acknowledging and preparing emotionally for the inevitable loss. (p. 517)

Apgar Scale A rating system used to assess a newborn baby's physical condition immediately after birth on the basis of five characteristics: heart rate, respiratory effort, reflex irritability, muscle tone, and color. (p. 75)

appropriate death A death that makes sense in terms of the individual's pattern of living and values, preserves or restores significant relationships, and is as free of suffering as possible. (p. 508)

assimilation In Piaget's theory, that part of adaptation in which the external world is interpreted in terms of current schemes. Distinguished from *accommodation*. (p. 117)

assisted living A homelike housing arrangement for elders who require more care than can be provided at home but less than is usually provided in nursing homes. (p. 462)

assistive technology An array of devices that permits people with disabilities, including older adults, to improve their functioning. (p. 451)

associative memory deficit Age-related difficulty creating and retrieving links between pieces of information—for example, two items or an item and its context. (p. 465)

associative play A form of social interaction in which children engage in separate activities but interact by exchanging toys and commenting on one another's behavior. Distinguished from *nonsocial activity, parallel play,* and *cooperative play*. (p. 202)

attachment The strong, affectionate tie that humans have with special people in their lives, which leads them to feel pleasure when interacting with those people and to be comforted by their nearness in times of stress. (p. 150)

Attachment Q-Sort A method for assessing the quality of attachment in children between 1 and 4 years of age through home observations of a variety of attachment-related behaviors. (p. 152)

attention-deficit hyperactivity disorder (ADHD) A childhood disorder involving inattentiveness, impulsivity, and excessive motor activity. Often leads to academic and social problems. (p. 236)

authoritarian child-rearing style A child-rearing style that is low in acceptance and involvement, high in coercive and psychological control, and low in autonomy granting. Distinguished from *authoritative, permissive,* and *uninvolved child-rearing styles*. (p. 216)

authoritative child-rearing style A child-rearing style that is high in acceptance and involvement, emphasizes adaptive control techniques, and includes gradual, appropriate autonomy granting. Distinguished from *authoritarian, permissive,* and *uninvolved child-rearing styles*. (p. 216)

autobiographical memory Long-lasting representations of personally meaningful one-time events from both the recent and the distant past. (p. 126)

autoimmune response A malfunction of the immune system in which it turns against normal body tissues. (p. 449)

autonomy At adolescence, a sense of oneself as a separate, self-governing individual. Involves relying more on oneself and less on parents for support and guidance and engaging in careful, well-reasoned decision making. (p. 325)

autonomy versus shame and doubt In Erikson's theory, the psychological conflict of toddlerhood, which is resolved favorably when parents provide young children with suitable guidance and reasonable choices. (p. 141)

autosomes The 22 matching chromosome pairs in each human cell. (p. 37)

average healthy life expectancy The number of years a person born in a particular year can expect to live in full health, without disease or injury. (p. 444)

average life expectancy The number of years an individual born in a particular year can expect to live, starting at any given age. Distinguished from *maximum lifespan* and *average healthy life expectancy*. (p. 444)

avoidant attachment The attachment pattern characterizing infants who seem unresponsive to the parent when she is present, are usually not distressed by parental separation, and avoid or are slow to greet the parent when she returns. Distinguished from *secure, resistant,* and *disorganized/disoriented attachment*. (p. 152)

B

babbling Repetition of consonant–vowel combinations in long strings, beginning around 6 months of age. (p. 135)

basal metabolic rate (BMR) The amount of energy the body uses at complete rest. (p. 346)

basic emotions Emotions such as happiness, interest, surprise, fear, anger, sadness, and disgust that are universal in humans and other primates and have a long evolutionary history of promoting survival. (p. 142)

basic trust versus mistrust In Erikson's theory, the psychological conflict of infancy, which is resolved positively when the balance of care is sympathetic and loving. (p. 141)

behaviorism An approach that regards directly observable events—stimuli and responses—as the appropriate focus of study and views the development of behavior as taking place through classical and operant conditioning. (p. 13)

behavior modification Procedures that combine conditioning and modeling to eliminate undesirable behaviors and increase desirable responses. (p. 15)

bereavement The experience of losing a loved one by death. (p. 516)

bicultural identity The identity constructed by individuals who explore and adopt values from both their family's subculture and the dominant culture. (p. 318)

"big five" personality traits Five basic factors into which hundreds of personality traits have been organized: neuroticism, extroversion, openness to experience, agreeableness, and conscientiousness. (p. 427)

biological aging, or senescence Genetically influenced, age-related declines in the functioning of organs and systems that are universal in all members of our species. Sometimes called *primary aging*. (p. 339)

blended, or reconstituted, family A family structure resulting from cohabitation or remarriage that includes parent, child, and steprelatives. (p. 272)

body image Conception of and attitude toward one's physical appearance. (p. 290)

brain death Irreversible cessation of all activity in the brain and the brain stem. The definition of death accepted in most industrialized nations. (p. 504)

brain plasticity The capacity of various parts of the cerebral cortex to take over functions of damaged regions. Declines as hemispheres of the cerebral cortex lateralize. (p. 96)

breech position A position of the baby in the uterus that would cause the buttocks or feet to be delivered first. (p. 77)

bulimia nervosa An eating disorder in which individuals, mainly females, engage in strict dieting and excessive exercise accompanied by binge eating, often followed by deliberate vomiting and purging with laxatives. (p. 292)

burnout A condition in which long-term job stress leads to mental exhaustion, a sense of loss of personal control, and feelings of reduced accomplishment. (p. 436)

C

cardinality The mathematical principle specifying that the last number in a counting sequence indicates the quantity of items in the set. (p. 187)

carrier A heterozygous individual who can pass a recessive trait to his or her offspring. (p. 39)

cataracts Cloudy areas in the lens of the eye that increase from middle to old age, resulting in foggy vision and (without surgery) eventual blindness. (p. 447)

categorical self Classification of the self according to prominent ways in which people differ, such as age, sex, physical characteristics, and goodness and badness. Develops between 18 and 30 months. (p. 158)

central executive In information processing, the conscious part of working memory that directs the flow of information through the mental system by deciding what to attend to, coordinating incoming information with information already in the system, and selecting, applying, and monitoring strategies. (p. 124)

centration In Piaget's theory, the tendency of preoperational children to focus on one aspect of a situation while neglecting other important features. (p. 176)

cephalocaudal trend An organized pattern of physical growth and motor control that proceeds from head to tail. Distinguished from *proximodistal trend*. (p. 93)

cerebellum A structure at the rear and base of the brain that aids in balance and control of body movements. (p. 167)

cerebral cortex The largest, most complex structure of the human brain, containing the greatest number of neurons and synapses, which accounts for the highly developed intelligence of the human species. (p. 95)

cerebrovascular dementia A form of dementia that develops when a series of strokes leaves areas of dead brain cells, producing step-by-step degeneration of mental ability, with each step occurring abruptly after a stroke. (p. 460)

cesarean delivery A surgical delivery in which the doctor makes an incision in the mother's abdomen and lifts the baby out of the uterus. (p. 78)

child-centered programs Preschool and kindergarten programs in which teachers provide a variety of activities from which children select, and much learning takes place through play. Distinguished from *academic programs*. (p. 188)

child-directed speech (CDS) A form of language used by adults to speak to infants and toddlers, consisting of short sentences with high-pitched, exaggerated expression, clear pronunciation, distinct pauses between speech segments, and repetition of new words in a variety of contexts. (p. 137)

child-rearing styles Combinations of parenting behaviors that occur over a wide range of situations, creating an enduring child-rearing climate. (p. 215)

chorion The outer membrane that forms a protective covering around the prenatal organism. It sends out tiny hairlike villi, from which the placenta begins to develop. (p. 63)

chromosomes Rodlike structures in the cell nucleus that store and transmit genetic information. (p. 36)

chronosystem In ecological systems theory, temporal changes in environments, either externally imposed or arising from within the person, that produce new conditions affecting development. Distinguished from *microsystem*, *mesosystem*, *exosystem*, and *macrosystem*. (p. 21)

circular reaction In Piaget's theory, a means of building schemes in which infants try to repeat a chance event caused by their own motor activity. (p. 118)

classical conditioning A form of learning that involves associating a neutral stimulus with a stimulus that leads to a reflexive response. Once the nervous system makes the connection between the two stimuli, the neutral stimulus alone will produce the behavior. (p. 103)

climacteric The midlife transition in which fertility declines, bringing an end to reproductive capacity in women and diminished fertility in men. (p. 399)

clinical death The phase of dying in which heartbeat, circulation, breathing, and brain functioning stop, but resuscitation is still possible. Distinguished from *agonal phase* and *mortality*. (p. 504)

clinical interview An interview method in which the researcher uses a flexible, conversational style to probe for the participant's point of view. Distinguished from *structured interview*. (p. 24)

clinical, or case study, method A research method in which the aim is to obtain as complete a picture as possible of one individual's psychological functioning by bringing together interview data, observations, and sometimes test scores. (p. 24)

clique A group of about five to seven members who are good friends and, therefore, usually resemble one another in family background, attitudes, values, and interests. (p. 328)

cognitive-affective complexity A form of thinking that increases from adolescence through middle adulthood, involving awareness of positive and negative feelings and coordination of them into a complex, organized structure that integrates cognition with emotion. (p. 355)

cognitive-developmental theory An approach introduced by Piaget that views children as actively constructing knowledge as they manipulate and explore their world and that regards cognitive development as taking place in stages. (p. 15)

cognitive maps Mental representations of familiar large-scale spaces, such as neighborhood or school. (p. 233)

cognitive self-regulation The process of continuously monitoring progress toward a goal, checking outcomes, and redirecting unsuccessful efforts. (p. 238)

cohabitation The lifestyle of unmarried couples who have a sexually intimate relationship and who share a residence. (p. 384)

cohort effects Cultural–historical influences on the accuracy of longitudinal and cross-sectional research findings. Results based on one cohort—individuals developing in the same time period, who are influenced by particular historical and cultural conditions—may not apply to other cohorts. (p. 29)

collectivist societies Societies in which people define themselves as part of a group and stress group goals over individual goals. Distinguished from *individualistic societies*. (p. 51)

commitment within relativistic thinking In Perry's theory, the cognitive approach of the most mature adults, who, instead of choosing between opposing views, try to formulate a more satisfying perspective that synthesizes contradictions. (p. 354)

companionate love Love based on warm, trusting affection and caregiving. Distinguished from *passionate love*. (p. 373)

compliance Voluntary obedience to requests and commands. (p. 159)

compression of morbidity The public health goal of reducing the average period of diminished vigor before death as life expectancy extends. Medical advances, improved socioeconomic conditions, and good health habits all promote this goal. (p. 453)

concrete operational stage Piaget's third stage of cognitive development, extending from about 7 to 11 years of age, during which thought becomes logical, flexible, and organized in its application to concrete information, but the capacity for abstract thinking is not yet present. (p. 232)

conditioned response (CR) In classical conditioning, a new response produced by a conditioned stimulus (CS) that is similar to the unconditioned, or reflexive, response (UCR). (p. 103)

conditioned stimulus (CS) In classical conditioning, a neutral stimulus that through pairing with an unconditioned stimulus (UCS) leads to a new, conditioned response. (CR). (p. 103)

congregate housing Housing for the elderly that provides a variety of support services, including meals in a common dining room, along with watchful oversight of elders with physical and mental disabilities. (p. 485)

conservation The understanding that certain physical characteristics of objects remain the same, even when their outward appearance changes. (p. 176)

constructivist classroom A classroom grounded in Piaget's view of children as active agents who construct their own knowledge. Features include richly equipped learning centers, small groups and individuals solving self-chosen problems, a teacher who guides and supports in response to children's needs, and evaluation based on individual students' progress in relation to their own prior development. Distinguished from *traditional* and *social-constructivist classrooms*. (p. 248)

contexts Unique combinations of personal and environmental circumstances that can result in different paths of development. (p. 4)

continuity theory A social theory of aging that states that most aging adults, in their choice of everyday activities and social relationships, strive to maintain a personal system—an identity and a set of personality dispositions, interests, roles, and skills—that promotes life satisfaction by ensuring consistency between their past and anticipated future. Distinguished from *disengagement theory, activity theory,* and *socioemotional selectivity theory*. (p. 482)

continuous development The view that development is a process of gradually adding more of the same types of skills that were there to begin with. Distinguished from *discontinuous development*. (p. 4)

controversial children Children who receive many votes, both positive and negative, on self-report measures of peer acceptance, indicating that they are both liked and disliked. Distinguished from *popular, neglected,* and *rejected children*. (p. 266)

conventional level Kohlberg's second level of moral development, in which moral understanding is based on conforming to social rules to ensure positive human relationships and maintain societal order. (p. 320)

convergent thinking The type of cognition emphasized on intelligence tests, which involves arriving at a single correct answer to a problem. Distinguished from *divergent thinking*. (p. 251)

cooing Pleasant vowel-like noises made by infants beginning around 2 months of age. (p. 135)

cooperative learning Collaboration on a task by a small group of classmates who work toward common goals by resolving differences of opinion, sharing responsibilities, and providing one another with sufficient explanation to correct misunderstandings. (p. 249)

cooperative play A form of social interaction in which children orient toward a common goal, such as acting out a make-believe theme. Distinguished from *nonsocial activity, parallel play,* and *associative play*. (p. 202)

coregulation A form of supervision in which parents exercise general oversight while permitting children to take charge of moment-by-moment decision making. (p. 269)

core knowledge perspective A perspective that states that infants are born with a set of innate knowledge systems, or core domains of thought, each of which permits a ready grasp of new, related information and therefore supports early, rapid development of certain aspects of cognition. (p. 122)

corpus callosum The large bundle of fibers connecting the two hemispheres of the cerebral cortex. (p. 168)

correlational design A research design in which the investigator gathers information on individuals without altering their experiences and then examines relationships between participants' characteristics and their behavior or development. Does not permit inferences about cause and effect. (p. 27)

correlation coefficient A number, ranging from +1.00 to −1.00, that describes the strength and direction of the relationship between two variables. (p. 27)

creativity The ability to produce work that is original yet appropriate—something others have not thought of that is useful in some way. (p. 251)

cross-linkage theory of aging A theory of biological aging asserting that the formation of bonds, or links, between normally separate protein fibers causes the body's connective tissue to become less elastic over time, leading to many negative physical outcomes. (p. 341)

cross-sectional design A research design in which groups of participants of different ages are studied at the same point in time. Distinguished from *longitudinal design*. (p. 30)

crowd A large, loosely organized social group consisting of several cliques with similar values. Membership is based on reputation and stereotype. (p. 328)

crystallized intelligence Intellectual skills that depend on accumulated knowledge and experience, good judgment, and mastery of social conventions—abilities acquired because they are valued by the individual's culture. Distinguished from *fluid intelligence*. (p. 410)

D

death anxiety Fear and apprehension of death. (p. 505)

deferred imitation The ability to remember and copy the behavior of models who are not present. (p. 120)

delay of gratification The ability to wait for an appropriate time and place to engage in a tempting act. (p. 159)

dementia A set of disorders occurring almost entirely in old age in which many aspects of thought and behavior are so impaired that everyday activities are disrupted. (p. 457)

deoxyribonucleic acid (DNA) Long, double-stranded molecules that make up chromosomes. (p. 36)

dependency–support script A typical pattern of interaction in which caregivers attend to elders' dependent behaviors immediately, thereby reinforcing those behaviors. Distinguished from *independence–ignore script*. (p. 479)

dependent variable The variable the researcher expects to be influenced by the independent variable in an experiment. Distinguished from *independent variable*. (p. 28)

developmental cognitive neuroscience An area of investigation that brings together researchers from psychology, biology, neuroscience, and medicine to study the relationship between changes in the brain and the developing person's cognitive processing and behavior patterns. (p. 18)

developmentally appropriate practice A set of standards devised by the National Association for the Education of Young Children, specifying program characteristics that meet the developmental and individual needs of young children of varying ages, based on current research and the consensus of experts. (p. 132)

developmental science An interdisciplinary field devoted to the study of all changes humans experience throughout the lifespan. (p. 3)

differentiation theory The view that perceptual development involves the detection of increasingly fine-grained, invariant features in the environment. (p. 113)

difficult child A child whose temperament is characterized by irregular daily routines, slow acceptance of new experiences, and a tendency to react negatively and intensely. Distinguished from *easy child* and *slow-to-warm-up child*. (p. 146)

discontinuous development The view that development is a process in which new ways of understanding and responding to the world emerge at specific times. Distinguished from *continuous development*. (p. 4)

disengagement theory A social theory of aging that states that declines in social interaction in late adulthood are due to mutual withdrawal between elders and society in anticipation of death. Distinguished from *activity theory, continuity theory,* and *socioemotional selectivity theory*. (p. 482)

disorganized/disoriented attachment The attachment pattern reflecting the greatest insecurity, characterizing infants who show confused, contradictory responses when reunited with the parent after a separation. Distinguished from *secure, avoidant,* and *resistant attachment*. (p. 152)

divergent thinking The type of cognition associated with creativity, which involves generating multiple and unusual possibilities when faced with a task or problem. Associated with creativity. Distinguished from *convergent thinking*. (p. 251)

divorce mediation A series of meetings between divorcing adults and a trained professional that are aimed at reducing family conflict, including legal battles over property division and child custody. (p. 272)

dominant cerebral hemisphere The hemisphere of the cerebral cortex responsible for skilled motor action and other important abilities. In right-handed individuals, the left hemisphere is dominant; in left-handed individuals, motor and language skills are often shared between the hemispheres. (p. 167)

dominant–recessive inheritance A pattern of inheritance in which, under heterozygous conditions, the influence of only one allele is apparent. (p. 38)

dualistic thinking In Perry's theory, the cognitive approach typical of younger college students, who divide information, values, and authority into right and wrong, good and bad, we and they. Distinguished from *relativistic thinking*. (p. 354)

dual-process model of coping with loss A perspective that assumes that people cope most effectively with loss when they oscillate between dealing with the emotional consequences of loss and attending to life changes, which—when handled successfully—have restorative, or healing, effects. (p. 517)

dual representation The ability to view a symbolic object as both an object in its own right and a symbol. (p. 175)

durable power of attorney for health care A written statement authorizing appointment of another person (usually, though not always, a family member) to make health-care decisions on one's behalf. (p. 514)

dynamic assessment An approach to testing consistent with Vygotsky's zone of proximal development, in which purposeful teaching is introduced into the testing situation to find out what the child can attain with social support. (p. 244)

dynamic systems theory of motor development A theory that views new motor skills as reorganizations of previously mastered skills, which lead to more effective ways of exploring and controlling the environment. Each new skill is a joint product of central nervous system development, the body's movement possibilities, environmental supports for the skill, and the child's goal. (p. 106)

E

easy child A child whose temperament is characterized by establishment of regular routines in infancy, general cheerfulness, and easy adaptation to new experiences. Distinguished from *difficult child* and *slow-to-warm-up child*. (p. 146)

ecological systems theory Bronfenbrenner's approach, which views the person as developing within a complex system of relationships affected by multiple levels of the surrounding environment, from immediate settings of family and school to broad cultural values and programs. (p. 20)

educational self-fulfilling prophecies Teachers' positive or negative views of individual children, who tend to adopt and start to live up to those views. (p. 250)

effortful control The self-regulatory dimension of temperament, involving voluntary suppression of a dominant response in order to plan and execute a more adaptive response. (p. 147)

egalitarian marriage A form of marriage in which partners relate as equals, sharing power and authority. Both try to balance the time and energy they devote to their occupations, their children, and their relationship. Distinguished from *traditional marriage*. (p. 378)

egocentrism Failure to distinguish the symbolic viewpoints of others from one's own. (p. 175)

ego integrity versus despair In Erikson's theory, the psychological conflict of late adulthood, which is resolved positively when elders come to terms with their lives and feel whole, complete, and satisfied with their achievements, recognizing that the paths they followed, abandoned, or never selected were necessary for fashioning a meaningful life course. (p. 474)

elaboration A memory strategy that involves creating a relationship, or shared meaning, between two or more items of information that do not belong to the same category in order to improve recall. (p. 237)

embryo The prenatal organism from 2 to 8 weeks after conception—the period when the groundwork for all body structures and internal organs is laid down. (p. 64)

emergent literacy Children's active efforts to construct literacy knowledge through informal experiences. (p. 185)

emerging adulthood A new transitional period of development, extending from the late teens to the mid-twenties, during which young people have typically left adolescence but have not yet assumed adult responsibilities. Rather, they continue to explore alternatives in education, work, personal beliefs and values, and love. (p. 366)

emotional self-regulation Strategies for adjusting our emotional state to a comfortable level of intensity so we can accomplish our goals. (p. 145)

emotion-centered coping A strategy for managing emotion that is internal, private, and aimed at controlling distress when little can be done to change an outcome. Distinguished from *problem-centered coping*. (p. 262)

empathy The ability to understand another's emotional state and to *feel with* that person, or respond emotionally in a similar way. (p. 158)

epigenesis Development resulting from ongoing, bidirectional exchanges between heredity and all levels of the environment. (p. 57)

epistemic cognition Reflections on how one arrived at facts, beliefs, and ideas. (p. 354)

ethnic identity A sense of ethnic group membership and attitudes and feelings associated with that membership, as an enduring aspect of the self. (p. 318)

ethnography A method in which the researcher attempts to understand the unique values and social processes of a culture or a distinct social group through participant observation—living with its members and taking field notes for an extended time. (p. 25)

ethological theory of attachment Bowlby's theory, the most widely accepted view of attachment, which regards the infant's emotional tie to the caregiver as an evolved response that promotes survival. (p. 151)

ethology An approach concerned with the adaptive, or survival, value of behavior and its evolutionary history. (p. 18)

euthanasia The practice of ending the life of a person suffering from an incurable condition. (p. 513)

evolutionary developmental psychology An approach that seeks to understand the adaptive value of species-wide cognitive, emotional, and social competencies as those competencies change with age. (p. 19)

exosystem In ecological systems theory, social settings that do not contain the developing person but nevertheless affect experiences in immediate settings. Distinguished from *microsystem, mesosystem, macrosystem,* and *chronosystem*. (p. 21)

expansions Adult responses that elaborate on children's speech, increasing its complexity. (p. 194)

experience-dependent brain growth Growth and refinement of established brain structures as a result of specific learning experiences that vary widely across individuals and cultures. Distinguished from *experience-expectant brain growth*. (p. 98)

experience-expectant brain growth The young brain's rapidly developing organization, which depends on ordinary experiences—opportunities to see and touch objects, to hear language and other sounds, and to move about and explore the environment. Distinguished from *experience-dependent brain growth*. (p. 98)

experimental design A research design in which the investigator randomly assigns participants to two or more treatment conditions and studies the effect that manipulating an independent variable has on a dependent variable. Permits inferences about cause and effect. (p. 28)

expertise Acquisition of extensive knowledge in a field or endeavor. (p. 356)

expressive style of language learning A style of early language learning in which toddlers use language mainly to talk about their own and others' feelings and needs, with an initial vocabulary emphasizing social formulas and pronouns. Distinguished from *referential style of language learning*. (p. 137)

extended-family household A household in which one or more adult relatives live with the parent–child nuclear family. (p. 50)

F

family life cycle A sequence of phases characterizing the development of most families around the world. In early adulthood, people typically live on their own, marry, and bear and rear children. In middle age, parenting responsibilities diminish. Late adulthood brings retirement, growing old, and (more often for women) death of one's spouse. (p. 377)

fantasy period Period of vocational development in which children gain insight into career options by fantasizing about them. Distinguished from *tentative period* and *realistic period*. (p. 358)

fast-mapping Children's ability to connect new words with their underlying concepts after only a brief encounter. (p. 191)

feminization of poverty A trend in which women who support themselves or their families have become the majority of the adult population living in poverty, regardless of age and ethnic group. (p. 428)

fetal alcohol spectrum disorder (FASD) A range of physical, mental, and behavioral outcomes caused by prenatal alcohol exposure, including *fetal* *alcohol syndrome (FAS), partial fetal alcohol syndrome (p-FAS),* and *alcohol-related neurodevelopmental disorder (ARND).* (p. 69)

fetal alcohol syndrome (FAS) The most severe form of fetal alcohol spectrum disorder, distinguished by slow physical growth, facial abnormalities, and brain injury. Usually seen in children whose mothers consumed large amounts of alcohol during most or all of pregnancy. Distinguished from *partial fetal alcohol syndrome (p-FAS)* and *alcohol-related neurodevelopmental disorder (ARND).* (p. 69)

fetal monitors Electronic instruments that track the baby's heart rate during labor. (p. 77)

fetus The prenatal organism from the ninth week to the end of pregnancy—the period during which body structures are completed and dramatic growth in size occurs. (p. 64)

fluid intelligence Intellectual skills that largely depend on basic information-processing skills—ability to detect relationships among visual stimuli, speed of analyzing information, and capacity of working memory. Influenced less by culture than by conditions in the brain and by learning unique to the individual. Distinguished from *crystallized intelligence.* (p. 410)

formal operational stage Piaget's highest stage, beginning around 11 years of age, in which adolescents develop the capacity for abstract, systematic, scientific thinking. (p. 301)

frailty Weakened functioning of diverse organs and body systems, which profoundly interferes with everyday competence and leaves the older adult highly vulnerable in the face of an infection, extremely hot or cold weather, or an injury. (p. 456)

fraternal, or dizygotic, twins Twins resulting from the release and fertilization of two ova. They are genetically no more alike than ordinary siblings. Distinguished from *identical,* or *monozygotic, twins.* (p. 38)

free radicals Naturally occurring, highly reactive chemicals that form in the presence of oxygen and destroy nearby cellular material, including DNA, proteins, and fats essential for cell functioning. Believed to be involved in many disorders of aging. (p. 340)

functional age Actual competence and performance of an older adult, as distinguished from chronological age. (p. 443)

G

gametes Sex cells, or sperm and ova, which contain half as many chromosomes as regular body cells. (p. 37)

gender constancy A full understanding of the biologically based permanence of one's gender, including the realization that sex remains the same even if clothing, hairstyle, and play activities change. (p. 214)

gender identity An image of oneself as relatively masculine or feminine in characteristics. (p. 214)

gender intensification Increased gender stereotyping of attitudes and behavior and movement toward a more traditional gender identity, typical of early adolescence. (p. 324)

gender schema theory An information-processing approach to gender typing that explains how environmental pressures and children's cognitions work together to shape gender-role development. (p. 215)

gender typing Any association of objects, roles, or traits with one sex or the other in ways that conform to cultural stereotypes. (p. 211)

gene A segment of a DNA molecule that contains instructions for production of various proteins that contribute to growth and functioning of the body. (p. 37)

generativity versus stagnation In Erikson's theory, the psychological conflict of midlife, which is resolved positively if the adult can integrate personal goals with the welfare of the larger social world. The resulting strength is the capacity to give to and guide the next generation. (p. 420)

genetic counseling A communication process designed to help couples assess their chances of giving birth to a baby with a hereditary disorder and choose the best course of action in view of risks and family goals. (p. 42)

genetic–environmental correlation The idea that heredity influences the environments to which individuals are exposed. (p. 55)

genomic imprinting A pattern of inheritance in which alleles are imprinted, or chemically marked, in such a way that one pair member is activated, regardless of its makeup. (p. 39)

genotype An individual's genetic makeup. Distinguished from *phenotype.* (p. 36)

gerotranscendence According to Joan Erikson, a psychosocial stage characterizing the very old and representing development beyond ego integrity. Involves a cosmic, transcendent perspective directed forward and outward, beyond the self. Apparent in heightened inner calm and contentment and in additional time spent in quiet reflection. (p. 475)

gifted Displaying exceptional intellectual strengths. Includes high IQ, high creativity, and specialized talent. (p. 251)

glass ceiling Invisible barrier to advancement up the corporate ladder, faced by women and ethnic minorities. (p. 436)

glaucoma A disease in which poor fluid drainage leads to a buildup of pressure within the eye, damaging the optic nerve. A leading cause of blindness among older adults. (p. 398)

glial cells Cells that are responsible for myelination of neural fibers, improving the efficiency of message transfer. (p. 94)

goodness-of-fit model A model that describes how favorable adjustment depends on an effective match between a child's temperament and the child-rearing environment. (p. 149)

grief Intense physical and psychological distress following the death of a loved one. (p. 516)

growth hormone (GH) A pituitary hormone that affects the development of all body tissues except the central nervous system and the genitals. (p. 168)

growth spurt Rapid gain in height and weight that is the first outward sign of puberty. (p. 284)

guided participation Shared endeavors between more expert and less expert participants, without specifying the precise features of communication in order to allow for variations across situations and cultures. A broader concept than *scaffolding.* (p. 181)

H

habituation A gradual reduction in the strength of a response due to repetitive stimulation. (p. 104)

hardiness A set of three personal qualities—control, commitment, and challenge—that help people cope adaptively with stress brought on by inevitable life change. (p. 408)

heritability estimate A statistic that measures the extent to which individual differences in complex traits, such as intelligence or personality, in a specific population are due to genetic factors. (p. 54)

heterozygous Having two different alleles at the same place on a pair of chromosomes. Distinguished from *homozygous.* (p. 38)

hierarchical classification The organization of objects into classes and subclasses on the basis of similarities and differences between the groups. (p. 176)

hippocampus An inner-brain structure that plays a vital role in memory and in images of space we use to help us find our way. (p. 168)

history-graded influences Influences on lifespan development that are unique to a particular historical era and explain why people born around the same time (called a *cohort*) tend to be alike in ways that set them apart from people born at other times. (p. 9)

Home Observation for Measurement of the Environment (HOME) A checklist for gathering information about the quality of children's home lives through observation and parental interview. (p. 131)

homozygous Having two identical alleles at the same place on a pair of chromosomes. Distinguished from *heterozygous.* (p. 38)

hormone therapy Low daily doses of estrogen, either alone or in combination with progesterone, aimed at reducing the physical discomforts of menopause. (p. 401)

hospice A comprehensive program of support services for terminally ill people and their families, which regards the patient and family as a unit of care and emphasizes meeting the patient's physical, emotional, social, and spiritual needs while also providing follow-up bereavement services to the family. (p. 511)

hypothetico-deductive reasoning A formal operational problem-solving strategy in which adolescents begin with a *hypothesis,* or prediction, about variables that might affect an outcome. From the hypothesis, they *deduce* logical, testable inferences. Then they systematically isolate and combine variables to see which of those inferences are confirmed in the real world. (p. 301)

I

identical, or monozygotic, twins Twins that result when a zygote, during early cell duplication, separates into two clusters of cells that have the same genetic makeup. Distinguished from *fraternal,* or *dizygotic, twins.* (p. 38)

identity A well-organized conception of the self, consisting of values, beliefs, and goals, to which the individual is solidly committed. (p. 314)

identity achievement The identity status of individuals who, after a period of exploration, have committed themselves to a clearly formulated set of self-chosen values and goals. Distinguished from *identity moratorium, identity foreclosure,* and *identity diffusion.* (p. 315)

identity diffusion The identity status of individuals who do not engage in exploration and are not committed to values and goals. Distinguished from *identity achievement, identity moratorium,* and *identity foreclosure.* (p. 315)

identity foreclosure The identity status of individuals who do not engage in exploration but, instead are committed to ready-made values and goals chosen for them by authority figures. Distinguished from *identity achievement, identity moratorium,* and *identity diffusion.* (p. 315)

identity moratorium The identity status of individuals who are exploring but not yet committed to self-chosen values and goals. Distinguished from *identity achievement, identity foreclosure,* and *identity diffusion.* (p. 315)

identity versus role confusion In Erikson's theory, the psychological conflict of adolescence, which is resolved positively when adolescents achieve an identity after a period of exploration and inner soul-searching. (p. 314)

imaginary audience Adolescents' belief that they are the focus of everyone else's attention and concern. (p. 304)

imitation Learning by copying the behavior of another person. Also called *modeling* or *observational learning.* (p. 104)

implantation Attachment of the blastocyst to the uterine lining, which occurs 7 to 9 days after fertilization. (p. 62)

implicit memory Memory without conscious awareness. (p. 465)

inclusive classrooms Classrooms in which students with learning difficulties learn alongside typical students in a regular educational setting for part or all of the school day. (p. 250)

incomplete dominance A pattern of inheritance in which both alleles are expressed in the phenotype, resulting in a combined trait, or one that is intermediate between the two. (p. 39)

independence–ignore script A typical pattern of interaction in which elders' independent behaviors are mostly ignored and, as a result, occur less often. Distinguished from *dependency–support script.* (p. 479)

independent variable In an experiment, the variable the investigator expects to cause changes in another variable and that the researcher manipulates by randomly assigning participants to treatment conditions. Distinguished from *dependent variable.* (p. 28)

individualistic societies Societies in which people think of themselves as separate entities and are largely concerned with their own personal needs. Distinguished from *collectivist societies.* (p. 51)

induction A type of discipline in which an adult helps the child notice feelings by pointing out the effects of the child's misbehavior on others. (p. 205)

industry versus inferiority In Erikson's theory, the psychological conflict of middle childhood, which is resolved positively when experiences lead children to develop a sense of competence at useful skills and tasks. (p. 257)

infantile amnesia The inability of most older children and adults to remember events that happened before age 3. (p. 126)

infant mortality The number of deaths in the first year of life per 1,000 live births. (p. 81)

information-loss view A view that attributes age-related slowing of cognitive processing to greater loss of information as it moves through the system. As a result, the whole system must slow down to inspect and interpret the information. Distinguished from *neural network view.* (p. 411)

information processing An approach that views the human mind as a symbol-manipulating system through which information flows and that regards cognitive development as a continuous process. (p. 17)

inhibited, or shy, child A child whose temperament is such that he or she reacts negatively to and withdraws from novel stimuli. Distinguished from *uninhibited, or sociable, child.* (p. 147)

initiative versus guilt In Erikson's theory, the psychological conflict of early childhood, which is resolved positively through play experiences that foster a healthy sense of initiative and through development of a superego, or conscience, that is not overly strict and guilt-ridden. (p. 198)

instrumental activities of daily living (IADLs) Tasks that are necessary to conduct the business of daily life and that also require some cognitive competence, such as telephoning, shopping, food preparation, housekeeping, and paying bills. (p. 445)

intelligence quotient (IQ) A score that permits an individual's performance on an intelligence test to be compared to the performances of other individuals of the same age. (p. 130)

intentional, or goal-directed, behavior A sequence of actions in which schemes are deliberately coordinated to solve a problem. (p. 119)

intermodal perception Perception that combines information from more than one modality, or sensory system, resulting in an integrated whole. (p. 113)

internal working model A set of expectations about the availability of attachment figures and the likelihood that they will provide support in times of stress. It becomes a vital part of personality, serving as a guide for all future close relationships. (p. 152)

intimacy versus isolation In Erikson's theory, the psychological conflict of early adulthood, reflected in the young person's thoughts and feelings about making a permanent commitment to an intimate partner. (p. 369)

irreversibility The inability to mentally go through a series of steps in a problem and then reverse direction, returning to the starting point. Distinguished from *reversibility.* (p. 176)

J

joint attention A state in which the child and the caregiver attend to the same object or event and the caregiver comments verbally about what the child sees. Supports language development. (p. 135)

joint custody A child custody arrangement following divorce in which parents are granted equal say in important decisions about the child's upbringing. (p. 272)

K

kinkeeper Role assumed by members of the middle generation, especially mothers, who take responsibility for gathering the family for celebrations and making sure everyone stays in touch. (p. 429)

kinship studies Studies comparing the characteristics of family members to determine the importance of heredity in complex human characteristics. (p. 54)

kwashiorkor A disease caused by a diet low in protein that usually appears after weaning, between 1 and 3 years of age. Symptoms include an enlarged belly, swollen feet, hair loss, skin rash, and irritable, listless behavior. (p. 101)

L

language acquisition device (LAD) In Chomsky's theory, an innate system containing a universal grammar, or set of rules common to all languages, that enables children, no matter which language they hear, to understand and speak in a rule-oriented fashion as soon as they pick up enough words. (p. 134)

lanugo White, downy hair that covers the entire body of the fetus, helping the vernix stick to the skin. (p. 65)

lateralization Specialization of functions in the two hemispheres of the cerebral cortex. (p. 96)

learned helplessness Attribution of success to external factors, such as luck, and failure to low ability, which cannot be improved through effort. Distinguished from *mastery-oriented attributions.* (p. 260)

learning disabilities Great difficulty with one or more aspects of learning, usually reading, resulting in achievement considerably behind what would be expected on the basis of a child's IQ. (p. 250)

life-care communities Housing for the elderly that offers a range of alternatives, from independent or congregate housing to full nursing home care, guaranteeing that elders' needs will be met within the same facility as they age. (p. 485)

lifespan perspective A dynamic systems approach to development that assumes development is lifelong, multidimensional and multidirectional, highly plastic, and affected by multiple interacting forces. (p. 5)

life structure In Levinson's theory, the underlying design of a person's life, consisting of relationships with significant others—individuals, groups, and institutions. Includes both central components, such as marriage/family and occupation, and peripheral ones. (p. 370)

living will A written statement specifying the treatments a person does or does not want in case of a terminal illness, coma, or other near-death situation. (p. 514)

loneliness Unhappiness resulting from a gap between actual and desired social relationships. (p. 376)

longitudinal design A research design in which participants are studied repeatedly, and changes are noted as they get older. Distinguished from *cross-sectional design.* (p. 28)

long-term memory In information processing, the largest storage area in memory, containing our permanent knowledge base. (p. 124)

M

macrosystem In ecological systems theory, cultural values, laws, customs, and resources that influence experiences and interactions at inner levels of the environment. Distinguished from *microsystem, mesosystem, exosystem,* and *chronosystem.* (p. 21)

macular degeneration Blurring and eventual loss of central vision due to a breakdown of light-sensitive cells in the macula, or central region of the retina. (p. 448)

make-believe play A type of play in which children act out everyday and imaginary activities. (p. 120)

marasmus A disease caused by a diet low in all essential nutrients that usually appears in the first year of life and leads to a wasted condition of the body. (p. 101)

mastery-oriented attributions Attributions that credit success to ability, which can be improved through effort, and failure to insufficient effort. Distinguished from *learned helplessness.* (p. 260)

matters of personal choice Concerns that do not involve rights or the welfare of others and, therefore, are up to the individual, such as choice of friends, hairstyle, and leisure activities. Distinguished from *moral imperatives* and *social conventions.* (p. 208)

maximum lifespan The genetic limit to length of life for a person free of external risk factors. Distinguished from *average life expectancy* and *average healthy life expectancy.* (p. 445)

meiosis The process of cell division through which gametes are formed and in which the number of chromosomes in each cell is halved. (p. 37)

memory strategies Deliberate mental activities that improve the likelihood of remembering. (p. 183)

menarche First menstruation. (p. 286)

menopause The end of menstruation and, therefore, of a woman's reproductive capacity. (p. 399)

mental representation An internal depiction of information that the mind can manipulate, including images and concepts. (p. 119)

mental strategies In information processing, procedures that operate on and transform information, increasing the chances that we will retain information, use it efficiently, and think flexibly, adapting the information to changing circumstances. (p. 124)

mesosystem In ecological systems theory, connections between a person's microsystems, or immediate settings. Distinguished from *microsystem, exosystem, macrosystem,* and *chronosystem.* (p. 20)

metacognition Thinking about thought; a coherent set of ideas about mental activities. (p. 184)

microsystem In ecological systems theory, the innermost level of the environment, consisting of activities and interaction patterns in the person's immediate surroundings. Distinguished from *mesosystem, exosystem, macrosystem,* and *chronosystem.* (p. 20)

midlife crisis Inner turmoil and self-doubt that prompt major restructuring of the personality during the transition to middle adulthood. Characterizes the experience of only a minority of adults. (p. 422)

mirror neurons Specialized cells in motor areas of the cerebral cortex in primates that underlie the ability to imitate by firing identically when a primate hears or sees an action and when it carries out the action on its own. (p. 105)

mitosis The process of cell duplication, in which each new cell receives an exact copy of the original chromosomes. (p. 37)

moral imperatives Rules and expectations that protect people's rights and welfare. Distinguished from *social conventions* and *matters of personal choice.* (p. 208)

moral self-relevance The degree to which morality is central to an individual's self-concept. (p. 323)

mortality The phase of dying in which the individual passes into permanent death. Distinguished from *agonal phase* and *clinical death.* (p. 504)

mourning The culturally specified expression of the bereaved person's thoughts and feelings through funerals and other rituals. (p. 516)

mutation A sudden change in a segment of DNA. (p. 40)

myelination The coating of neural fibers with an insulating fatty sheath, called *myelin,* that improves the efficiency of message transfer. (p. 94)

N

naturalistic observation A research method in which the researcher goes into the natural environment to observe the behavior of interest. Distinguished from *structured observation.* (p. 23)

natural, or prepared, childbirth A group of techniques aimed at reducing pain and medical intervention and making childbirth as rewarding an experience as possible. Typically includes classes that provide information about the birth process, relaxation and breathing techniques designed to counteract the pain of uterine contractions, and a labor coach who offers encouragement and affection. (p. 76)

nature–nurture controversy Disagreement among theorists about whether genetic or environmental factors are more important influences on development. (p. 5)

neglected children Children who are seldom chosen, either positively or negatively, on self-report measures of peer acceptance. Distinguished from *popular, rejected,* and *controversial children.* (p. 266)

neural network view A view that attributes age-related slowing of cognitive processing to breaks in neural networks as neurons die. The brain adapts by forming bypasses—new synaptic connections that go around the breaks but are less efficient. Distinguished from *information-loss view.* (p. 411)

neural tube The primitive spinal cord that develops from the ectoderm, the top of which swells to form the brain. (p. 64)

neurofibrillary tangles A structural change in the cerebral cortex associated with Alzheimer's disease in which bundles of twisted threads appear that are the product of collapsed neural structures. (p. 459)

neurons Nerve cells that store and transmit information. (p. 94)

neurotransmitters Chemicals released by neurons that cross the synapse to send messages to other neurons. (p. 94)

niche-picking A type of genetic–environmental correlation in which individuals actively choose environments that complement their heredity. (p. 56)

nonnormative influences Influences on lifespan development that are irregular, in that they happen to just one or a few individuals and do not follow a predictable timetable. (p. 9)

nonorganic failure to thrive A growth disorder, usually present by 18 months of age, that is caused by lack of affection and stimulation. Affected infants show signs of marasmus although no organic cause exists for the failure to grow. (p. 102)

non-rapid-eye-movement (NREM) sleep A "regular" sleep state in which the body is almost motionless and heart rate, breathing, and brain wave activity are slow and regular. Distinguished from *rapid-eye-movement (REM) sleep.* (p. 83)

nonsocial activity Unoccupied, onlooker behavior and solitary play. Distinguished from *parallel, associative,* and *cooperative play.* (p. 202)

normal distribution The bell-shaped distribution that results when individual differences are measured in large samples. Most scores cluster around the mean, or average, with progressively fewer falling toward the extremes. (p. 130)

normative approach An approach in which measures of behavior are taken on large numbers of individuals and age-related averages are computed to represent typical development. (p. 11)

O

obesity A greater-than-20-percent increase over healthy body weight, based on the body mass index, a ratio of weight to height associated with body fat. (p. 226)

object permanence The understanding that objects continue to exist when they are out of sight. (p. 119)

operant conditioning A form of learning in which a spontaneous behavior is followed by a stimulus that changes the probability that the behavior will occur again. (p. 104)

optimal aging Aging in which gains are maximized and losses minimized. (p. 496)

ordinality The mathematical principle specifying order relationships between quantities, such as three is more than two and two is more than one. (p. 187)

organization In Piaget's theory, the internal rearrangement and linking together of schemes so that they form a strongly interconnected cognitive system. In information processing, a memory strategy that involves grouping related items together to improve recall. (p. 118, p. 235)

osteoarthritis A form of arthritis characterized by deteriorating cartilage on the ends of bones of frequently used joints, which leads to swelling, stiffness, and loss of flexibility. Otherwise known as "wear-and-tear" arthritis or "degenerative joint disease." Distinguished from *rheumatoid arthritis.* (p. 456)

osteoporosis Severe age-related bone loss, which greatly magnifies the risk of bone fractures. (p. 405)

overextension An early vocabulary error in which a word is applied too broadly, to a wider collection of objects and events than is appropriate. Distinguished from *underextension*. (p. 136)

overregularization Extension of regular grammatical rules to words that are exceptions. (p. 193)

P

palliative, or comfort, care Care for terminally ill, suffering patients that relieves pain and other symptoms (such as nausea, breathing difficulties, insomnia, and depression), with the goal of protecting the patient's quality of remaining life rather than prolonging life. (p. 511)

parallel play A form of limited social participation in which a child plays near other children with similar materials but does not interact with them. Distinguished from *nonsocial, associative,* and *cooperative play*. (p. 202)

parental imperative theory A theory that claims that identification with traditional gender roles is maintained during the active parenting years to help ensure the survival of children but that when children reach adulthood, parents are free to express the "other-gender" side of their personalities. (p. 426)

partial fetal alcohol syndrome (p-FAS) A form of fetal alcohol spectrum disorder characterized by facial abnormalities and brain injury, but less severe than fetal alcohol syndrome. Usually seen in children whose mothers drank alcohol in smaller quantities during pregnancy. (p. 69)

passionate love Love based on intense sexual attraction. Distinguished from *companionate love*. (p. 373)

passive euthanasia The practice of withholding or withdrawing life-sustaining treatment, permitting a patient to die naturally. Distinguished from *voluntary active euthanasia*. (p. 513)

peer acceptance Likability, or the extent to which a child is viewed by a group of agemates, such as classmates, as a worthy social partner. (p. 265)

peer group A collective of peers who generate unique values and standards for behavior and a social structure of leaders and followers. (p. 264)

peer victimization A destructive form of peer interaction in which certain children become frequent targets of verbal and physical attacks or other forms of abuse. (p. 267)

permissive child-rearing style A child-rearing style that is high in acceptance but overindulging or inattentive, low in control, and lenient rather than appropriate in autonomy granting. Distinguished from *authoritative, authoritarian,* and *uninvolved child-rearing styles*. (p. 216)

persistent vegetative state A state resulting from absence of brain-wave activity in the cerebral cortex in which the person is unconscious and displays no voluntary movements. (p. 504)

personal fable Adolescents' belief that they are special and unique. Leads them to conclude that others cannot possibly understand their thoughts and feelings and may promote a sense of invulnerability to danger. (p. 305)

perspective taking The capacity to imagine what other people may be thinking and feeling. (p. 262)

phenotype An individual's directly observable physical and behavioral characteristics, which are determined by both genetic and environmental factors. Distinguished from *genotype*. (p. 36)

phobia An intense, unmanageable fear that leads to persistent avoidance of the feared situation. (p. 275)

phonics approach An approach to beginning reading instruction that emphasizes coaching children on phonics—the basic rules for translating written symbols into sounds—before exposing them to complex reading material. Distinguished from the *whole-language approach*. (p. 238)

phonological awareness The ability to reflect on and manipulate the sound structure of spoken language, as indicated by sensitivity to changes in sounds within words, to rhyming, and to incorrect pronunciation. A strong predictor of emergent literacy. (p. 186)

physical aggression A form of aggression that harms others through physical injury to themselves or their property. Distinguished from *verbal aggression* and *relational aggression*. (p. 209)

pituitary gland A gland located at the base of the brain that releases hormones that induce physical growth. (p. 168)

placenta The organ that permits exchange of nutrients and waste products between the bloodstreams of the mother and the embryo, while also preventing the mother's and embryo's blood from mixing directly. (p. 63)

polygenic inheritance A pattern of inheritance in which many genes influence a characteristic. (p. 40)

popular-antisocial children A subgroup of popular children who are admired for their socially adept yet belligerent behavior. Includes "tough" boys who

are athletically skilled, aggressive, and poor students, as well as relationally aggressive boys and girls. Distinguished from *popular-prosocial children*. (p. 266)

popular children Children who receive many positive votes on self-report measures of peer acceptance, indicating they are well-liked. Distinguished from *rejected, controversial,* and *neglected children*. (p. 266)

popular-prosocial children A subgroup of popular children who combine academic and social competence. Distinguished from *popular-antisocial children*. (p. 266)

possible selves Future-oriented representations of what one hopes to become and what one is afraid of becoming. The temporal dimension of self-concept. (p. 423)

postconventional level Kohlberg's highest level of moral development, in which individuals define morality in terms of abstract principles and values that apply to all situations and societies. (p. 320)

postformal thought Cognitive development beyond Piaget's formal operational stage. (p. 354)

practical problem solving Problem solving that requires people to size up real-world situations and analyze how best to achieve goals that have a high degree of uncertainty. (p. 413)

pragmatics The practical, social side of language, concerned with how to engage in appropriate and effective communication. (p. 193)

pragmatic thought In Labouvie-Vief's theory, a structural advance in thinking in adulthood, characterized by the use of logic as a tool for solving real-world problems and by the acceptance of contradictions as part of existence. (p. 355)

preconventional level Kohlberg's first level of moral development, in which children accept the rules of authority figures and judge actions by their consequences, viewing behaviors that result in punishment as bad and those that lead to rewards as good. (p. 319)

premenstrual syndrome (PMS) An array of physical and psychological symptoms that usually appear 6 to 10 days prior to menstruation. The most common are abdominal cramps, fluid retention, diarrhea, tender breasts, backache, headache, fatigue, tension, irritability, and depression. (p. 352)

prenatal diagnostic methods Medical procedures that permit detection of developmental problems before birth. (p. 43)

preoperational stage Piaget's second stage of cognitive development, spanning 2 to 7 years of age, characterized by an extraordinary increase in representational, or symbolic, activity, although thought is not yet logical. (p. 173)

presbycusis Age-related hearing impairment, beginning around age 50 with noticeable hearing loss at high frequencies, which gradually extends to all frequencies. (p. 398)

presbyopia A condition of aging in which, around age 60, the lens of the eye loses its capacity to adjust to objects at varying distances. (p. 398)

preterm infants Infants born several weeks or more before their due date. (p. 78)

primary aging Genetically influenced age-related declines in the functioning of organs and systems that affect all members of our species and occur even in the context of overall good health. Also called *biological aging*. Distinguished from *secondary aging*. (p. 455)

primary sexual characteristics Physical features that involve the reproductive organs (ovaries, uterus, and vagina in females; penis, scrotum, and testes in males). Distinguished from *secondary sexual characteristics*. (p. 286)

private speech Self-directed speech that children use to plan and guide their own behavior. (p. 180)

proactive aggression A type of aggression in which children act to fulfill a need or desire—obtain an object, privilege, space, or social reward, such as adult attention—and unemotionally attack a person to achieve their goal. Also called *instrumental aggression*. Distinguished from *reactive aggression*. (p. 208)

problem-centered coping A strategy for managing emotion in which the individual appraises the situation as changeable, identifies the difficulty, and decides what to do about it. Distinguished from *emotion-centered coping*. (p. 262)

Project Head Start A U.S. federal early intervention program that provides children from low-income families with a year or two of preschool education, along with nutritional and health services, and that encourages parent involvement in program planning and children's learning and development. (p. 188)

propositional thought A type of formal operational reasoning involving the ability to evaluate the logic of propositions (verbal statements) without referring to real-world circumstances. (p. 302)

prosocial, or altruistic, behavior Actions that benefit another person without any expected reward for the self. (p. 201)

prospective memory Recall that involves remembering to engage in planned actions in the future. (p. 466)

proximodistal trend An organized pattern of physical growth and motor control that proceeds from the center of the body outward. Distinguished from *cephalocaudal trend*. (p. 93)

psychoanalytic perspective An approach to personality development introduced by Freud that assumes people move through a series of stages in which they confront conflicts between biological drives and social expectations. The way these conflicts are resolved determines the person's ability to learn, to get along with others, and to cope with anxiety. (p. 12)

psychological control Parental behaviors that intrude on and manipulate children's verbal expressions, individuality, and attachments to parents. (p. 216)

psychosexual theory Freud's theory, which emphasizes that how parents manage children's sexual and aggressive drives in the first few years is crucial for healthy personality development. (p. 12)

psychosocial theory Erikson's theory, which emphasizes that at each Freudian stage, individuals not only develop a unique personality but also acquire attitudes and skills that help them become active, contributing members of their society. Recognizes the lifespan nature of development and the impact of culture. (p. 12)

puberty Biological changes at adolescence that lead to an adult-sized body and sexual maturity. (p. 283)

public policies Laws and government programs designed to improve current conditions. (p. 51)

punishment In operant conditioning, removal of a desirable stimulus or presentation of an unpleasant stimulus, either of which decreases the occurrence of a response. (p. 104)

R

random assignment An evenhanded procedure for assigning participants to treatment conditions in an experiment, such as drawing numbers out of a hat or flipping a coin. Increases the chances that participants' characteristics will be equally distributed across treatment groups. (p. 28)

range of reaction Each person's unique, genetically determined response to a range of environmental conditions. (p. 55)

rapid-eye-movement (REM) sleep An "irregular" sleep state in which brain wave activity is similar to that of the waking state; eyes dart beneath the lids; heart rate, blood pressure, and breathing are uneven; and slight body movements occur. Distinguished from *non-rapid-eye-movement (NREM) sleep*. (p. 83)

reactive aggression An angry, defensive response to provocation or a blocked goal that is meant to hurt another person. Also called *hostile aggression*. Distinguished from *proactive aggression*. (p. 209)

realistic period Period of vocational development in which older adolescents and young adults narrow their vocational options, engaging in further exploration before focusing on a general vocational category and, slightly later, settling on a single occupation. Distinguished from *fantasy period* and *tentative period*. (p. 358)

recall A type of memory that involves remembering a stimulus that is not present. Distinguished from *recognition*. (p. 125)

recasts Adult responses that restructure children's grammatically inaccurate speech into correct form. (p. 194)

recognition A type of memory that involves noticing whether a stimulus is identical or similar to one previously experienced. Distinguished from *recall*. (p. 125)

recovery Following habituation, an increase in responsiveness to a new stimulus. (p. 104)

referential style of language learning A style of early language learning in which toddlers use language mainly to name things, producing many words that refer to objects. Distinguished from *expressive style of language learning*. (p. 137)

reflex An inborn, automatic response to a particular form of stimulation. (p. 82)

rehearsal A memory strategy that involves repeating information to oneself to improve recall. (p. 235)

reinforcer In operant conditioning, a stimulus that increases the occurrence of a response. (p. 104)

rejected-aggressive children A subgroup of rejected children who show high rates of conflict, physical and relational aggression, and hyperactive, inattentive, and impulsive behavior. Distinguished from *rejected-withdrawn children*. (p. 266)

rejected children Children who receive many negative votes on self-report measures of peer acceptance, indicating they are actively disliked. Distinguished from *popular, controversial,* and *neglected children*. (p. 266)

rejected-withdrawn children A subgroup of rejected children who are passive and socially awkward. Distinguished from *rejected-aggressive children*. (p. 266)

relational aggression A form of aggression that damages another's peer relationships through social exclusion, malicious gossip, or friendship manipulation. Distinguished from *physical aggression* and *verbal aggression*. (p. 209)

relativistic thinking In Perry's theory, the cognitive approach typical of older college students, who view all knowledge as embedded in a framework of thought and, therefore, give up the possibility of absolute truth in favor of multiple truths, each relative to its context. Distinguished from *dualistic thinking*. (p. 354)

reminiscence The process of telling stories about people and events from the past and reporting associated thoughts and feelings. (p. 476)

remote memory Recall of events that happened long ago. (p. 465)

resilience The ability to adapt effectively in the face of threats to development. (p. 8)

resistant attachment The attachment pattern characterizing infants who remain close to the parent and fail to explore before separation, are usually distressed when the parent leaves, and combine clinginess with angry, resistive behavior when the parent returns. Distinguished from *secure, avoidant,* and *disorganized/disoriented attachment*. (p. 152)

reversibility The ability to think through a series of steps in a problem and then mentally reverse direction, returning to the starting point. Distinguished from *irreversibility*. (p. 232)

rheumatoid arthritis A form of arthritis in which an autoimmune response leads to inflammation of connective tissue, particularly the membranes that line the joints, resulting in overall stiffness, inflammation, aching, deformed joints, and serious loss of mobility. Distinguished from *osteoarthritis*. (p. 456)

Rh factor incompatibility A condition that arises when the Rh protein is present in the fetus's blood but not in the mother's, causing the mother to build up antibodies. If these enter the fetus's system, they destroy red blood cells, reducing the oxygen supply to organs and tissues. Mental retardation, miscarriage, heart damage, or infant death can occur. (p. 72)

rough-and-tumble play A form of peer interaction involving friendly chasing and play-fighting that emerges in the preschool years and peaks in middle childhood. In our evolutionary past, it may have been important for the development of fighting skills. (p. 230)

S

sandwich generation A term used to describe middle-aged adults who must care for multiple generations above and below them at the same time. (p. 432)

scaffolding Adjusting the support offered during a teaching session to fit the learner's current level of performance. Direct instruction is offered when a task is new; less help is provided as competence increases, thereby keeping the task within the zone of proximal development. (p. 180)

scheme In Piaget's theory, a specific psychological structure, or organized way of making sense of experience, that changes with age. (p. 117)

scripts General descriptions of what occurs and when it occurs in a particular situation, used to organize and interpret everyday experiences. (p. 183)

secondary aging Declines due to hereditary defects and environmental influences, such as poor diet, lack of exercise, disease, substance abuse, environmental pollution, and psychological stress. Distinguished from *primary aging*. (p. 455)

secondary friends People who are not intimates but with whom an individual spends time occasionally, such as a group that meets for lunch, bridge, or museum tours. (p. 492)

secondary sexual characteristics Physical features visible on the outside of the body that serve as signs of sexual maturity but do not involve the reproductive organs (for example, breast development in females, appearance of underarm and pubic hair in both sexes). Distinguished from *primary sexual characteristics*. (p. 286)

secular trend A change from one generation to the next in an aspect of development, such as body size or pubertal timing. (p. 287)

secure attachment The attachment pattern characterizing infants who use the parent as a secure base from which to explore, may be distressed by parental separation, but actively seek contact and are easily comforted by the parent when she returns. Distinguished from *avoidant, resistant,* and *disorganized/disoriented attachment.* (p. 152)

secure base The familiar caregiver as a point from which the baby explores, venturing into the environment and then returning for emotional support. (p. 143)

selective optimization with compensation A set of strategies used by elders who sustain high levels of functioning. They narrow their goals, *selecting* personally valued activities as a way of *optimizing* returns from their diminishing energy while also finding new ways of *compensating* for losses. (p. 463)

self-care children Children who are without adult supervision for some period of time after school. (p. 274)

self-concept The set of attributes, abilities, attitudes, and values that an individual believes defines who he or she is. (p. 199)

self-conscious emotions Emotions involving injury to or enhancement of the sense of self, such as guilt, shame, embarrassment, envy, and pride. (p. 145)

self-esteem An aspect of self-concept that involves judgments about one's own worth and the feelings associated with those judgments. (p. 199)

self-recognition Identification of the self as a physically unique being. (p. 158)

sensitive caregiving Caregiving that involves responding promptly, consistently, and appropriately to infants and holding them tenderly and carefully. (p. 154)

sensitive period A time that is optimal for certain capacities to emerge and in which the individual is especially responsive to environmental influences. (p. 19)

sensorimotor stage Piaget's first stage, spanning the first two years of life, during which infants and toddlers "think" with their eyes, ears, hands, and other sensorimotor equipment. (p. 117)

sensory register The part of the information-processing system in which sights and sounds are represented directly and stored briefly. (p. 124)

separation anxiety An infant's distressed reaction to the departure of the familiar caregiver. (p. 151)

seriation The ability to order items along a quantitative dimension, such as length or weight. (p. 232)

sequential designs Developmental designs in which investigators conduct several similar cross-sectional or longitudinal studies (called *sequences*) at varying times. Some sequential designs combine longitudinal and cross-sectional strategies. (p. 30)

sex chromosomes The twenty-third pair of chromosomes, which determines the sex of the individual. In females, it is called *XX*; in males, *XY.* (p. 37)

skipped-generation family A family structure in which children live with grandparents but apart from parents. (p. 431)

slow-to-warm-up child A child whose temperament is characterized by inactivity; mild, low-key reactions to environmental stimuli; negative mood; and slow adjustment to new experiences. Distinguished from *easy child* and *difficult child.* (p. 146)

small-for-date infants Infants whose birth weight is below their expected weight considering the length of the pregnancy. Some are full term; others are preterm infants who are especially underweight. (p. 78)

social clock Age-graded expectations for major life events, such as beginning a first job, getting married, birth of the first child, buying a home, and retiring. (p. 372)

social comparisons Judgments of one's own appearance, abilities, and behavior in relation to those of others. (p. 258)

social-constructivist classroom A classroom grounded in Vygotsky's sociocultural theory, in which children participate in a wide range of challenging activities with teachers and peers, with whom they jointly construct understandings. Distinguished from *traditional* and *constructivist classrooms.* (p. 248)

social conventions Customs determined solely by consensus, such as table manners and politeness rituals. Distinguished from *moral imperatives* and *matters of personal choice.* (p. 208)

social convoy A model of age-related changes in social networks, which views the individual as moving through life within a cluster of relationships. Close ties are in the inner circle, less close ties on the outside. With age, people change places in the convoy, new ties are added, and some are lost entirely. (p. 487)

social learning theory An approach that emphasizes the role of modeling, otherwise known as imitation or observational learning, in the development of behavior. (p. 14)

social referencing Actively seeking emotional information from a trusted person in an uncertain situation. (p. 144)

social smile The infant's broad grin evoked by the parent's communication. First appears between 6 and 10 weeks of age. (p. 142)

sociocultural theory Vygotsky's theory, in which children acquire the ways of thinking and behaving that make up a community's culture through cooperative dialogues with more knowledgeable members of society. (p. 19)

sociodramatic play The make-believe play with others that is under way around age 2 and increases rapidly during the next few years. (p. 174)

socioeconomic status (SES) A measure of an individual's or a family's social position and economic well-being that combines three related, but not completely overlapping, variables: years of education, prestige of and skill required by one's job, and income. (p. 47)

socioemotional selectivity theory A social theory of aging that states that social interaction in late adulthood extends lifelong selection processes. According to this view, physical and psychological aspects of aging lead to an increased emphasis on the emotion-regulating function of social interaction. Consequently, older adults prefer familiar social partners with whom they have developed pleasurable relationships. Distinguished from *disengagement theory, activity theory,* and *continuity theory.* (p. 483)

spermarche First ejaculation of seminal fluid. (p. 286)

stage A qualitative change in thinking, feeling, and behaving that characterizes a specific period of development. (p. 4)

standardization The practice of giving a newly constructed test to a large, representative sample of individuals and using the results as the standard for interpreting individual scores. (p. 130)

states of arousal Different degrees of sleep and wakefulness. (p. 83)

statistical learning capacity Infants' ability to analyze the speech stream for regularly occurring sound sequences, through which they acquire a stock of speech structures for which they will later learn meanings. (p. 109)

stereotype threat The fear of being judged on the basis of a negative stereotype, which can trigger anxiety that interferes with performance. (p. 244)

stranger anxiety The infant's expression of fear in response to unfamiliar adults, which appears in many babies in the second half of the first year. (p. 143)

Strange Situation A laboratory procedure involving short separations from and reunions with the parent, designed to assess the quality of infant–caregiver attachment between 1 and 2 years of age. (p. 152)

structured interview An interview method in which each participant is asked the same questions in the same way. Distinguished from *clinical interview.* (p. 24)

structured observation A method in which the investigator sets up a laboratory situation that evokes the behavior of interest so that every participant has an equal opportunity to display the response. Distinguished from *naturalistic observation.* (p. 24)

subculture A group of people with beliefs and customs that differ from those of the larger culture. (p. 50)

sudden infant death syndrome (SIDS) The unexpected death, usually during the night, of an infant under 1 year of age that remains unexplained after thorough investigation. (p. 85)

sympathy Feelings of concern or sorrow for another's plight. (p. 201)

synapses The gaps between neurons, across which chemical messages are sent. (p. 94)

synaptic pruning Loss of synapses by seldom-stimulated neurons, thereby returning them to an uncommitted state so they can support future development. (p. 94)

T

talent Outstanding performance in a specific field. (p. 251)

telegraphic speech Toddlers' two-word utterances that, like a telegram, focus on high-content words while omitting smaller, less important words. (p. 136)

telomeres A special type of DNA located at the ends of chromosomes—serving as a "cap" to protect the ends from destruction—that shortens with each cell duplication. Eventually so little remains that the cells no longer duplicate at all. (p. 340)

temperament Early-appearing, stable individual differences in reactivity (quickness and intensity of emotional arousal, attention, and motor activity) and self-regulation (strategies that modify that reactivity). (p. 146)

tentative period Period of vocational development in which adolescents think about careers in more complex ways, at first in terms of their interests and soon—as they become more aware of personal and educational requirements for different vocations—in terms of their abilities and values. Distinguished from *fantasy period* and *realistic period*. (p. 358)

teratogen Any environmental agent that causes damage during the prenatal period. (p. 66)

terminal decline Marked acceleration in deterioration of cognitive functioning prior to death. (p. 468)

theory An orderly, integrated set of statements that describes, explains, and predicts behavior. (p. 3)

theory of multiple intelligences Gardner's theory, which identifies eight independent intelligences on the basis of distinct sets of processing operations that permit individuals to engage in a wide range of culturally valued activities. (p. 241)

Third Age A new phase of late adulthood extending from ages 65 to 79 or longer, resulting from added years of longevity plus good health and financial stability, in which older adults pursue personally enriching interests and goals. (p. 477)

thyroid-stimulating hormone (TSH) A pituitary hormone that stimulates the thyroid gland to release thyroxine, which is necessary for brain development and for growth hormone to have its full impact on body size. (p. 168)

time out A form of mild punishment that involves removing children from the immediate setting until they are ready to act appropriately. (p. 206)

traditional classroom A classroom in which the teacher is the sole authority for knowledge, rules, and decision making. Students are relatively passive—listening, responding when called on, and completing teacher-assigned tasks. Their progress is evaluated by how well they keep up with a uniform set of standards for their grade. Distinguished from *constructivist* and *social-constructivist classrooms*. (p. 248)

traditional marriage A form of marriage involving clear division of husband's and wife's roles. The man is the head of household and economic provider. The woman devotes herself to caring for her husband and children and creating a nurturant, comfortable home. Distinguished from *egalitarian marriage*. (p. 378)

transitive inference The ability to seriate, or order items along a quantitative dimension, mentally. (p. 232)

triarchic theory of successful intelligence Sternberg's theory, in which intelligent behavior involves balancing three broad, interacting intelligences—analytical intelligence, creative intelligence, and practical intelligence—to achieve success in life, according to one's personal goals and the requirements of one's cultural community. (p. 241)

triangular theory of love Sternberg's view of love as including three components—intimacy, passion, and commitment—that shift in emphasis as romantic relationships develop. (p. 373)

trimesters Three equal time periods into which prenatal development is sometimes divided, each of which lasts three months. (p. 65)

Type A behavior pattern A behavior pattern characterized by extreme competitiveness, ambition, impatience, hostility, angry outbursts, and a sense of time pressure. (p. 406)

U

umbilical cord The long cord connecting the prenatal organism to the placenta that delivers nutrients and removes waste products. (p. 63)

unconditioned response (UCR) In classical conditioning, a reflexive response that is produced by an unconditioned stimulus (UCS). Distinguished from *conditioned response*. (p. 103)

unconditioned stimulus (UCS) In classical conditioning, a stimulus that leads to a reflexive response. Distinguished from *conditioned stimulus*. (p. 103)

underextension An early vocabulary error in which a word is applied too narrowly, to a smaller number of objects and events than is appropriate. Distinguished from *overextension*. (p. 136)

uninhibited, or sociable, child A child whose temperament is such that he or she displays positive emotion to and approaches novel stimuli. Distinguished from *inhibited, or shy, child*. (p. 147)

uninvolved child-rearing style A child-rearing style that combines low acceptance and involvement with little control and general indifference to issues of autonomy. Distinguished from *authoritative, authoritarian*, and *permissive child-rearing styles*. (p. 217)

V

verbal aggression A type of aggression that harms others through threats of physical aggression, name-calling, or hostile teasing. Distinguished from *physical aggression* and *relational aggression*. (p. 209)

vernix A white, cheeselike substance that covers the fetus, preventing the skin from chapping due to constant exposure to amniotic fluid. (p. 65)

violation-of-expectation method A method in which researchers show babies an expected event (one that follows physical laws) and an unexpected event (a variation of the first event that violates physical laws). Heightened attention to the unexpected event suggests that the infant is "surprised" by a deviation from physical reality and, therefore, is aware of that aspect of the physical world. (p. 120)

visual acuity Fineness of visual discrimination. (p. 87)

voluntary active euthanasia The practice of acting directly, at a patient's request, to end suffering before a natural end to life. Distinguished from *passive euthanasia*. (p. 514)

W

whole-language approach An approach to beginning reading instruction that parallels natural language learning by exposing children to text in its complete form, using reading materials that are whole and meaningful to promote appreciation of the communicative function of written language. Distinguished from *phonics approach*. (p. 238)

wisdom A capacity made up of multiple cognitive and personality traits, combining breadth and depth of practical knowledge; the ability to reflect on and apply that knowledge in ways that make life more bearable and worthwhile; emotional maturity, including the ability to listen, evaluate, and give advice; and altruistic creativity, which involves contributing to humanity and enriching others' lives. (p. 467)

working, or short-term, memory The part of the information-processing system in which we "work" on a limited amount of information, actively applying mental strategies so the information will be retained and used effectively. (p. 124)

X

X-linked inheritance A pattern of inheritance in which a recessive gene is carried on the X chromosome, so that males are more likely to be affected. (p. 39)

Z

zone of proximal development In Vygotsky's theory, a range of tasks too difficult for a child to do alone but possible with the help of more-skilled partners. (p. 128)

zygote The newly fertilized cell formed by the union of sperm and ovum at conception. (p. 37)

References

A

Aalsma, M., Lapsley, D. K., & Flannery, D. J. (2006). Personal fables, narcissism, and adolescent adjustment. *Psychology in the Schools, 43,* 481–491.

AARP (American Association of Retired Persons). (2002). *The Grandparent Study 2002 report.* Washington, DC: Author.

AARP (American Association of Retired Persons). (2004) *Caregiving in the U.S.* Washington, DC: Author.

Abbey, A., & McAuslan, P. (2004). A longitudinal examination of male college students' perpetration of sexual assault. *Journal of Consulting and Clinical Psychology, 72,* 747–756.

Abbey, A., Zawacki, T., Buck, P. O., Clinton, A. M., & McAuslan, P. (2004). Sexual assault and alcohol consumption: What do we know about their relationship and what types of research are still needed? *Aggression and Violent Behavior, 9,* 271–303.

Abbott, S. (1992). Holding on and pushing away: Comparative perspectives on an eastern Kentucky child-rearing practice. *Ethos, 20,* 33–65.

Abel, E. (2004). Paternal contribution to fetal alcohol syndrome. *Addiction Biology, 9,* 127–133.

Abela, J. R. Z., Hankin, B. L., Haigh, E. A. P., Adams, P., Vinokuroff, T., & Trayhern, L. (2005). Interpersonal vulnerability to depression in high-risk children: The role of insecure attachment and reassurance seeking. *Journal of Clinical Child and Adolescent Psychology, 34,* 182–192.

Aber, J. L., Jones, S. M., & Raver, C. C. (2007). Poverty and child development: New perspectives on a defining issue. In J. L. Aber, S. J. Bishop-Josef, S. M. Jones, K. T. McLearn, & D. Phillips (Eds.), *Child development and social policy: Knowledge for action* (pp. 149–166). Washington, DC: American Psychological Association.

Abikoff, H. B., Jensen, P. S., Arnold, L. L., & Hoza, B. (2002). Observed classroom behavior of children with ADHD: Relationship to gender and comorbidity. *Journal of Abnormal Child Psychology, 30,* 349–359.

Abra, J. (1989). Changes in creativity with age: Data, explanations, and further predictions. *International Journal of Aging and Human Development, 28,* 105–126.

Abraham, S. (1998). Satisfaction of participants in university-administered elderhostel programs. *Educational Gerontology, 24,* 529–536.

Achenbach, T. M., Phares, V., Howell, C. T., Rauh, V. A., & Nurcombe, B. (1990). Seven-year outcome of the Vermont program for low-birthweight infants. *Child Development, 61,* 1672–1681.

Acker, M. M., & Davis, M. H. (1992). Intimacy, passion, and commitment in adult romantic relationships: A test of the triangular love theory. *Journal of Social and Personal Relationships, 9,* 21–50.

Acker, M. M., & O'Leary, S. G. (1996). Inconsistency of mothers' feedback and toddlers' misbehavior and negative affect. *Journal of Abnormal Child Psychology, 24,* 703–714.

Ackerman, S., Zuroff, D. C., & Moskowitz, D. S. (2000). Generativity in midlife and young adults: Links to agency, communion, and subjective well-being. *International Journal of Aging and Human Development, 50,* 17–41.

ACT. (2008). *2008 retention/completion summary tables.* Retrieved from www.act.org/research/policymakers/pdf/retain_trends.pdf

Adachi-Mejia, A. M., Longacre, M. R., Gibson, J. J., Beach, M. L., Titus-Ernstoff, L. T., & Dalton, M. A. (2007). Children with a TV in their bedroom at higher risk for being overweight. *International Journal of Obesity, 31,* 644–651.

Adams, G. R., & Marshall, S. (1996). A developmental social psychology of identity: Understanding the person in context. *Journal of Adolescence, 19,* 429–442.

Adams, K. B. (2004). Changing investment in activities and interests in elders' lives: Theory and measurement. *International Journal of Aging and Human Development, 58,* 87–108.

Adams, K. B., Sanders, S., & Auth, E. A. (2004). Loneliness and depression in independent living retirement communities: Risk and resilience factors. *Aging and Mental Health, 8,* 475–485.

Adams, R. G. (1985–1986). Emotional closeness and physical distance between friends: Implications for elderly women living in age-segregated and age-integrated settings. *International Journal of Aging and Human Development, 22,* 55–76.

Adams, R. G., Bleiszner, R., & De Vries, B. (2000). Definitions of friendship in the third age: Age, gender, and study location effects. *Journal of Aging Studies, 14,* 117–133.

Adams, R. G., & Laursen, B. (2001). The organization and dynamics of adolescent conflict with parents and friends. *Journal of Marriage and the Family, 63,* 97–110.

Adams, R. J., & Courage, M. L. (1998). Human newborn color vision: Measurement with chromatic stimuli varying in excitation purity. *Journal of Experimental Child Psychology, 68,* 22–34.

Addington-Hall, J. (2000). Do home deaths increase distress in bereavement? *Palliative Medicine, 14,* 161–162.

Adler, N. E., & Newman, K. (2002). Socioeconomic disparities in health: Pathways and policies. *Health Affairs, 21,* 60–76.

Adolph, K. E. (2000). Specificity of learning: Why infants fall over a veritable cliff. *Psychological Science, 11,* 290–295.

Adolph, K. E. (2002). Learning to keep balance. In R. V. Kail (Ed.), *Advances in child development and behavior* (Vol. 30, pp. 1–40). Boston: Academic Press.

Adolph, K. E., & Berger, S. E. (2006). Motor development. In D. Kuhn & R. Siegler (Eds.), *Handbook of child psychology: Vol. 2. Cognition, perception, and language* (6th ed., pp. 161–213). Hoboken, NJ: Wiley.

Adolph, K. E., & Eppler, M. A. (1998). Development of visually guided locomotion. *Ecological Psychology, 10,* 303–321.

Adolph, K. E., & Eppler, M. A. (1999). Obstacles to understanding: An ecological approach to infant problem solving. In E. Winograd, R. Fivush, & W. Hirst (Eds.), *Ecological approaches to cognition* (pp. 31–58). Mahwah, NJ: Erlbaum.

Adolph, K. E., Vereijken, B., & Shrout, P. E. (2003). What changes in infant walking and why. *Child Development, 74,* 475–497.

Afifi, T. O., Brownridge, D. A., Cox, B. J., & Sareen J. (2006). Physical punishment, childhood abuse and psychiatric disorders. *Child Abuse and Neglect, 30,* 1093–1103.

Afifi, W. A., & Faulkner, S. L. (2000). On being "just friends": The frequency and impact of sexual activity in cross-sex friendships. *Journal of Social and Personal Relationships, 17,* 205–222.

Afterschool Alliance. (2004). *America after 3 PM: A household survey on afterschool in America.* Retrieved from www.afterschoolalliance.org/researchFactSheets.cfm

Aggarwal, R., Sentz, J., & Miller, M. A. (2007). Role of zinc administration in prevention of childhood diarrhea and respiratory illnesses: A meta-analysis. *Pediatrics, 119,* 1120–1130.

Agüero-Torres, H., von Strauss, E., Viitanen, M., Winblad, B., & Fratiglioni, L. (2001). Institutionalization in the elderly: The role of chronic diseases and dementia. Cross-sectional and longitudinal data from a population-based study. *Journal of Clinical Epidemiology, 54,* 795–801.

Aguiar, A., & Baillargeon, R. (1999). 2.5-month-old infants' reasoning about when objects should and should not be occluded. *Cognitive Psychology, 39,* 116–157.

Aguiar, A., & Baillargeon, R. (2002). Developments in young infants' reasoning about occluded objects. *Cognitive Psychology, 45,* 267–336.

Ahrens, C. J. C., & Ryff, C. D. (2006). Multiple roles and well-being: Sociodemographic and psychological moderators. *Sex Roles, 55,* 801–815.

Ahuja, I. (2005). *Women's entrepreneurship in the United States.* Kansas City, MO: Kauffman Center for Entrepreneurial Leadership, Clearinghouse on Entrepreneurship Education. Retrieved from www.celcee.edu

Aikens, J. W., Bierman, K. L., & Parker, J. G. (2005). Navigating the transition to junior high school: The influence of pre-transition friendship and self-system characteristics. *Social Development, 14,* 42–60.

Ainsworth, M. D. S., Blehar, M. C., Waters, E., & Wall, S. (1978). *Patterns of attachment.* Hillsdale, NJ: Erlbaum.

Aisen, P. S., Schneider, L. S., Sano, M., Diaz-Arrastia, R., van Dyck, C. H., & Weiner, M. F. (2008). High-dose B vitamin supplementation and cognitive decline in Alzheimer disease: A randomized controlled trial. *Journal of the American Medical Association, 15,* 1774–1783.

Ajrouch, K. (2007). Health disparities and Arab-American elders: Does intergenerational support buffer the inequality-health link? *Journal of Social Issues, 63,* 745–758.

Akers, J. F., Jones, R. M., & Coyl, D. D. (1998). Adolescent friendship pairs: Similarities in identity status development, behaviors, attitudes, and intentions. *Journal of Adolescent Research, 13,* 178–201.

Akhtar, N., & Tomasello, M. (2000). The social nature of words and word learning. In R. Golinkoff & K. Hirsh-Pasek (Eds.), *Becoming a word learner: A debate on lexical acquisition.* Oxford, UK: Oxford University Press.

Akimoto, S. A., & Sanbonmatsu, D. M. (1999). Differences in self-effacing behavior between European and Japanese Americans: Effect on competence evaluations. *Journal of Cross-Cultural Psychology, 30,* 159–177.

Akiyama, H., Antonucci, T., Takahashi, K., & Langfahl, E. S. (2003). Negative interactions in close relationships across the lifespan. *Journal of Gerontology, 58B,* P70–P79.

Aksan, N., & Kochanska, G. (2004). Heterogeneity of joy in infancy. *Infancy, 6,* 79–94.

Akshoomoff, N. A., Feroleto, C. C., Doyle, R. E., & Stiles, J. (2002). The impact of early unilateral brain injury on perceptual organization and visual memory. *Neuropsychologia, 40,* 539–561.

Alan Guttmacher Institute. (2001). *Can more progress be made? Teenage sexual and reproductive behavior in developed countries.* New York: Author. Retrieved from www.guttmacher.org

Alan Guttmacher Institute. (2002). Teen pregnancy: Trends and lessons learned. Retrieved from http://www.agi-usa.org/pubs/ib_1-02.html

Alan Guttmacher Institute. (2004). Teen sexuality: Stats & facts. Retrieved from www.fotf.ca/familyfacts/issues/teensexuality/stats.html

Alan Guttmacher Institute. (2005). *Facts in brief: Contraceptive use.* Retrieved from www.guttmacher.org/pubs/fb_contr_use.html

Alan Guttmacher Institute. (2006). *U.S. teenage pregnancy statistics: National and state trends and trends by race and ethnicity.* New York: Author. Retrieved from www.guttmacher.org/pubs/2006/09/12/USTPstats.pdf

Albanes, D., Blair, A., & Taylor, P. R. (1989). Physical activity and risk of cancer in the NHANES I population. *American Journal of Public Health, 79,* 744–750.

Albers, C. A., & Grieve, A. J. (2007). Test review: Bayley, N. (2006). Bayley Scales of Infant and Toddler Development–Third Edition. San Antonio, TX: Harcourt Assessment. *Journal of Psychoeducational Assessment, 25,* 180–190.

Alcohol Concern. (2007). *Advertising alcohol.* Retrieved from www.alcoholconcern.org.uk

Aldwin, C. M., & Levenson, M. (2002). Stress, coping, and health at midlife: A developmental perspective. In M. E. Lachman (Ed.), *Handbook of midlife development* (pp. 188–214). New York: Wiley.

Aldwin, C. M., Spiro, A., III, Levenson, M. R., & Cupertino, A. P. (2001). Longitudinal findings from The Normative Aging Study: III. Personality, individual health trajectories, and mortality. *Psychology and Aging, 16,* 450–465.

Aldwin, C. M., Spiro, A., III, & Park, C. L. (2006). Health, behavior, and optimal aging: A life span developmental perspective. In J. E. Birren & K. W. Schaie (Eds.), *Handbook of the psychology of aging* (6th ed., pp. 85–104). Burlington, MA: Elsevier Academic Press.

Alessandri, S. M., Sullivan, M. W., & Lewis, M. (1990). Violation of expectancy and frustration in early infancy. *Developmental Psychology, 26,* 738–744.

Alexander, J. M., Fabricius, W. V., Fleming, V. M., Zwahr, M., & Brown, S. A. (2003). The development of metacognitive causal explanations. *Learning and Individual Differences, 13,* 227–238.

Alibali, M. W. (1999). How children change their minds: Strategy change can be gradual or abrupt. *Developmental Psychology, 35,* 127–145.

Alink, L. R. A., Mesman, J., van Zeijl, J., Stolk, M. N., Juffer, F., & Koot, H. M. (2006). The early childhood aggression curve: Development of physical aggression in 10- to 50-month-old children. *Child Development, 77,* 954–966.

Alkema, G. E., Wilber, K. H., & Enguidanos, S. M. (2007). Community- and facility-based care. In J. A. Blackburn & C. N. Dulmus (Eds.), *Handbook of gerontology: Evidence-based approaches to theory, practice, and policy* (pp. 455–497). Hoboken, NJ: Wiley.

Allemand, M., Zimprich, D., & Martin, M. (2008). Long-term correlated change in personality traits in old age. *Psychology and Aging, 23,* 545–557.

Allen, J. P., & Hauser, S. T. (1996). Autonomy and relatedness in adolescent–family interactions as predictors of young adults' states of mind regarding attachment. *Development and Psychopathology, 8,* 793–809.

Allen, J. P., Philliber, S., Herrling, S., & Kuperminc, G. P. (1997). Preventing teen pregnancy and academic failure: Experimental evaluation of a developmentally based approach. *Child Development, 64,* 729–742.

Allen, J. P., Seitz, V., & Apfel, N. H. (2007). The sexually mature teen as a whole person. In J. L. Aber, S. J. Bishop-Josef, S. M. Jones, K. T. McLearn, & D. A. Phillips (Eds.), *New directions in prevention and intervention for teen pregnancy and parenthood* (pp. 185–199). Washington, DC: American Psychological Association.

Allen, M., & Burrell, N. (1996). Comparing the impact of homosexual and heterosexual parents on children: Meta-analysis of existing research. *Journal of Homosexuality, 32,* 19–35.

Allen, S. E. M., & Crago, M. B. (1996). Early passive acquisition in Inuktitut. *Journal of Child Language, 23,* 129–156.

Allen, T. D., & Finkelstein, L. M. (2003). Beyond mentoring: Alternative sources and functions of developmental support. *Career Development Quarterly, 51,* 346–355.

Allison, B. N., & Schultz, J. B. (2004). Parent–adolescent conflict in early adolescence. *Adolescence, 39,* 101–119.

Allumbaugh, D. L., & Hoyt, W. T. (1999). Effectiveness of grief therapy: A meta-analysis. *Journal of Counseling Psychology, 46,* 370–380.

Almeida, D. M., & Horn, M. C. (2004). Is daily life more stressful during middle adulthood? In O. G. Brim, C. D. Ryff, & R. C. Kessler (Eds.), *How healthy are we? A national study of well-being at midlife* (pp. 425–451). Chicago: University of Chicago Press.

Almeida, D. M., Neupert, S. D., Banks, S. R., & Serido, J. (2005). Do daily stress processes account for socioeconomic health disparities? *Journal of Gerontology, 60B,* 34–39.

Al-Namlah, A. S., Fernyhough, C., & Meins, E. (2006). Sociocultural influences on the development of verbal mediation: Private speech and phonological recoding in Saudi Arabian and British samples. *Developmental Psychology, 42,* 117–131.

Alsaker, F. D. (1995). Timing of puberty and reactions to pubertal changes. In M. Rutter (Ed.), *Psychosocial disturbances in young people* (pp. 37–82). New York: Cambridge University Press.

Alter, J. (2008, September 29). It's not just about the boys. Get girls into school. *Newsweek,* pp. 50–51.

Althaus, J., & Wax, J. (2005). Analgesia and anesthesia in labor. *Obstetrics and Gynecology Clinics of North America, 32,* 231–244.

Alwin, D. F., & Wray, L. A. (2005). A life-span developmental perspective on social status and health. *Journal of Gerontology, 60B*(Special Issue II), 7–14.

Alzheimer's Association. (2005). *Communication: Best ways to interact with the person with dementia.* Chicago: Author.

Alzheimer's Association. (2009). 2009 *Alzheimer's disease facts and figures.* Retrieved from http://www.alz.org/national/documents/report_alzfactsfigures2009.pdf

Amato, P. R. (2000). The consequences of divorce for adults and children. *Journal of Marriage and Family, 62,* 1269–1287.

Amato, P. R. (2001). Children of divorce in the 1990s: An update of the Amato and Keith (1991) meta-analysis. *Journal of Family Psychology, 15,* 355–370.

Amato, P. R. (2006). Marital discord, divorce, and children's well-being: Results from a 20-year longitudinal study of two generations. In A. Clarke-Stewart & J. Dunn (Eds.), *Families count: Effects on child and adolescent development* (pp. 179–202). New York: Cambridge University Press.

Amato, P. R., & Booth, A. (1995). Change in gender role attitudes and perceived marital quality. *American Sociological Review, 60,* 58–66.

Amato, P. R., & Cheadle, J. (2005). The long reach of divorce: Divorce and child well-being across three generations. *Journal of Marriage and Family, 67,* 191–206.

Amato, P. R., & Fowler, F. (2002). Parenting practices, child adjustment, and family diversity. *Journal of Marriage and Family, 64,* 703–716.

Amato, P. R., & Rogers, S. J. (1997). A longitudinal study of marital problems and subsequent divorce. *Journal of Marriage and the Family, 59,* 612–624.

Amato, P. R., & Sobolewski, J. M. (2004). The effects of divorce on fathers and children: Nonresidential fathers and stepfathers. In M. E. Lamb (Ed.), *The role of the father in child development* (4th ed., pp. 341–367). Hoboken, NJ: Wiley.

Amba, J. C., & Martinez, G. M. (2006). Childlessness among older women in the United States: Trends and profiles. *Journal of Marriage and Family, 68,* 1045–1056.

Ambert, A.-M. (2005). *Same-sex couples and same-sex parent families: Relationships, parenting, and issues of marriage.* Ontario: Vanier Institute of the Family. Retrieved from www.vifamily.ca/library/publications/samesexd.html

American Academy of Pediatrics. (2005). Breastfeeding and the use of human milk. *Pediatrics, 115,* 496–506.

American Academy of Pediatrics. (2006). Folic acid for the prevention of neural tube defects. *Pediatrics, 104,* 325–327.

American Heart Association. (2008). *Heart and stroke death rates steadily decline; risks still too high.* Retrieved from www.americanheart.org/presenter.jhtml?identifier=3053235

American Heart Association. (2009). *Heart disease and stroke statistics: 2009 update-at-a-glance.* Dallas: Author.

American Hospice Foundation. (2009). *Talking about hospice: Tips for physicians.* Washington, DC: Author.

American Psychiatric Association. (1994). *Diagnostic and statistical manual of mental disorders* (4th ed.). Washington, DC: Author.

American Psychological Association. (2002). Ethical principles of psychologists and code of conduct. *American Psychologist, 57,* 1060–1073.

American Society for Reproductive Medicine. (2004). Smoking and infertility. *Fertility and Sterility, 81,* 1181–1186.

Amsel, E., & Brock, S. (1996). The development of evidence evaluation skills. *Cognitive Development, 11,* 523–550.

Amsterlaw, J., & Wellman, H. M. (2006). Theories of mind in transition: A micro-genetic study of the development of false belief understanding. *Journal of Cognition and Development, 7,* 139–172.

An, J. S., & Cooney, T. M. (2006). Psychological well-being in mid to late life: The role of generativity development and parent–child relationships across the lifespan. *International Journal of Behavioral Development, 30,* 410–421.

Anand, S. S., Yusuf, S., Jacobs, R., Davis, A. D., Yi, Q., & Gerstein, H. (2001). Risk factors, atherosclerosis, and cardiovascular disease among Aboriginal people in Canada: The study of health assessment and risk evaluation in Aboriginal peoples (SHARE-AP). *Lancet, 358,* 1147–1153.

Andel, R., Vigen, C., Mack, W. J., Clark, L. J., & Gatz, M. (2006). The effect of education and occupational complexity on rate of cognitive decline in Alzheimer's patients. *Journal of the International Neuropsychological Society, 12,* 147–152.

Anderson, C. A. (2004). An update on the effects of violent video games. *Journal of Adolescence, 27,* 113–122.

Anderson, C. A., Berkowitz, L., Donnerstein, E., Huesmann, R., Johnson, J. D., Linz, D., Malamuth, N. M., & Wartella, E. (2003). The influence of media violence on youth. *Psychological Science in the Public Interest, 4*(3), 81–106.

Anderson, D. M., Huston, A. C., Schmitt, K. L., Linebarger, D. L., & Wright, J. C. (2001). Early childhood television viewing and adolescent behavior. *Monographs of the Society for Research in Child Development, 66*(1, Serial No. 264).

Anderson, E. (2000). Exploring register knowledge: The value of "controlled improvisation." In L. Menn & N. B. Ratner (Eds.), *Methods for studying language production* (pp. 225–248). Mahwah, NJ: Erlbaum.

Anderson, J. L., Morgan, J. L., & White, K. S. (2003). A statistical basis for speech sound discrimination. *Language and Speech, 46,* 155–182.

Anderson, M. E., Johnson, D. C., & Batal, H. A. (2005). Sudden infant death syndrome and prenatal maternal smoking: Rising attributed risk in the Back to Sleep era. *BMC Medicine, 3,* 4.

Anderson, P. B., & Savage, J. S. (2005). Social, legal, and institutional context of heterosexual aggression by college women. *Trauma, Violence, and Abuse, 6,* 130–140.

Anderson, P. J., Wood, S. J., Francis, D. E., Coleman, L., Anderson, V., & Boneh, A. (2007). Are neuropsychological impairments in children with early-treated phenylketonuria (PKU) related to white matter abnormalities or elevated phenylalanine levels? *Developmental Neuropsychology, 32,* 645–668.

Anderson, S. E., Dallal, G. E., & Must, A. (2003). Relative weight and race influence average age at menarche: Results from two nationally representative surveys of U.S. girls studied 25 years apart. *Pediatrics, 111,* 844–850.

Andreoletti, C., & Lachman, M. E. (2004). Susceptibility and resilience to memory aging stereotypes: Education matters more than age. *Experimental Aging Research, 30,* 129–148.

Andrews, G., & Halford, G. S. (1998). Children's ability to make transitive inferences: The importance of premise integration and structural complexity. *Cognitive Development, 13,* 479–513.

Andrews, G., & Halford, G. S. (2002). A cognitive complexity metric applied to cognitive development. *Cognitive Psychology, 45,* 475–506.

Andreyeva, T., Puhl, R. M., & Brownell, K. D. (2008). Changes in perceived weight discrimination among Americans, 1995–1996 through 2004–2006. *Obesity, 16,* 1129–1134.

Anetzberger, G. J. (2005). The reality of elder abuse. *Clinical Gerontologist, 28,* 2–25.

Anisfeld, M., Turkewitz, G., Rose, S. A., Rosenberg, F. R., Shelber, F. J., Couturier-Fagan, D. A., Ger, J. S., & Sommer, I. (2001). No compelling evidence that newborns imitate oral gestures. *Infancy, 2,* 111–122.

Annett, M. (2002). *Handedness and brain asymmetry: The right shift theory.* Hove, UK: Psychology Press.

Anslow, P. (1998). Birth asphyxia. *European Journal of Radiology, 26,* 148–153.

Anson, D. S., & Fletcher, J. M. (2007). Gene therapy for disorders affecting children, progress and potential. *Journal of Paediatrics and Child Health, 43,* 323–330.

Anstey, K. J., & Christensen, H. (2000). Education, activity, health, blood pressure, and apolipoprotein E as predictors of cognitive change in old age: A review. *Gerontology, 46,* 163–177.

Anstey, K. J., Luszcz, M. A., & Sanchez, L. (2001). Two-year decline in vision but not hearing is associated with memory decline in very old adults in a population-based sample. *Gerontology, 47,* 289–293.

Antonini, F. M., Magnolfi, S. U., Petruzzi, E., Pinzani, P., Malentacchi, F., Petruzzi, I., & Masotti, G. (2008). Physical performance and creative activities of centenarians. *Archives of Gerontology and Geriatrics, 46,* 253–261.

Antonucci, T. C. (1994). A life-span view of women's social relations. In B. F. Turner & L. E. Troll (Eds.), *Women growing older* (pp. 239–269). Thousand Oaks, CA: Sage.

Antonucci, T. C., Ajrouch, K. J., & Birditt, K. (2008). Social relations in the Third Age: Assessing strengths and challenges using the convoy model. In J. B. James & P. Wink (Eds.), *Annual review of gerontology and geriatrics* (Vol. 26, pp. 193–209). New York: Springer.

Antonucci, T. C., & Akiyama, H. (1995). Convoys of social relations: Family and friendships within a life span context. In R. Blieszner & V. H. Bedford (Eds.), *Handbook of aging and the family* (pp. 355–371). Westport, CT: Greenwood Press.

Antonucci, T. C., Akiyama, H., & Merline, A. (2002). Dynamics of social relationships in midlife. In M. E. Lachman (Ed.), *Handbook of midlife development* (pp. 571–598). New York: Wiley.

Antonucci, T. C., Akiyama, H., & Takahashi, K. (2004). Attachment and close relationships across the lifespan. *Attachment and Human Development, 6,* 353–370.

Apgar, V. (1953). A proposal for a new method of evaluation in the newborn infant. *Current Research in Anesthesia and Analgesia, 32,* 260–267.

Aquilino, W. S. (1996). The returning adult child and parental experience at midlife. In C. D. Ryff & M. M. Seltzer (Eds.), *The parental experience in midlife* (pp. 423–458). Chicago: University of Chicago Press.

Aquilino, W. S. (2006). Family relationships and support systems in emerging adulthood. In J. J. Arnett & J. L. Tanner (Eds.), *Emerging adults in America: Coming of age in the 21st century* (pp. 193–218). Washington, DC: American Psychological Association.

Archer, J. (2002). Sex differences in aggression between heterosexual partners: A meta-analytic review. *Psychological Bulletin, 126,* 651–681.

Archer, S. L. (2002). Commentary on "Feminist Perspectives on Erikson's Theory: Their Relevance for Contemporary Identity Development Research." *Identity, 2,* 267–270.

Archer, S. L., & Waterman, A. S. (1990). Varieties of identity diffusions and foreclosures: An exploration of subcategories of the identity statuses. *Journal of Adolescent Research, 5,* 96–111.

Archibald, A. B., Graber, J. A., & Brooks-Gunn, J. (2006). Pubertal processes and physiological growth in adolescence. In G. R. Adams & M. D. Berzonsky (Eds.), *Blackwell handbook of adolescence* (pp. 24–48). Malden, MA: Blackwell.

Ardelt, M. (1998). Social crisis and individual growth: The long-term effects of the Great Depression. *Journal of Aging Studies, 12,* 291–314.

Argue, A., Johnson, D. R., & White, L. K. (1999). Age and religiosity: Evidence from a three-wave panel analysis. *Journal for the Scientific Study of Religion, 38,* 423–435.

Arking, R. (2006). *Biology of aging: Observations and principles* (3rd ed.). New York: Oxford University Press.

Arking, R., Novoseltsev, V., & Novoseltseva, J. (2004). The human life span is not that limited: The effect of multiple longevity phenotypes. *Journal of Gerontology, 59A,* 697–704.

Armstrong, T. D., & Crowther, M. R. (2002). Spirituality among older African Americans. *Journal of Adult Development, 9,* 3–12.

Arnett, J. J. (1997). Young people's conceptions of the transition to adulthood. *Youth and Society, 29,* 1–23.

Arnett, J. J. (2000). Emerging adulthood: A theory of development from the late teens through the twenties. *American Psychologist, 55,* 469–480.

Arnett, J. J. (2001). Conceptions of the transition to adulthood: Perspectives from adolescence to midlife. *Journal of Adult Development, 8,* 133–143.

Arnett, J. J. (2003). Conceptions of the transition to adulthood among emerging adults in American ethnic groups. In J. J. Arnett & N. L. Galambos (Eds.), *New directions for child and adolescent development* (No. 100, pp. 63–75). San Francisco: Jossey-Bass.

Arnett, J. J. (2006). Emerging adulthood: Understanding the new way of coming of age. In J. J. Arnett & J. L. Tanner (Eds.), *Emerging adults in America: Coming of age in the 21st century* (pp. 3–19). Washington, DC: American Psychological Association.

Arnett, J. J. (2007a). Emerging adulthood, a 21st century theory: A rejoinder to Hendry and Kloep. *Child Development Perspectives, 1,* 80–82.

Arnett, J. J. (2007b). Emerging adulthood: What is it and what is it good for? *Child Development Perspectives, 1,* 68–73.

Arnold, D. H., McWilliams, L., & Harvey-Arnold, E. (1998). Teacher discipline and child misbehavior in daycare: Untangling causality with correlational data. *Developmental Psychology, 34,* 276–287.

Arnon, S., Shapsa, A., Forman, L., Regev, R., Bauer, S., & Litmanovitz, I. (2006). Live music is beneficial to preterm infants in the neonatal intensive care unit. *Birth, 33,* 131–136.

Arriaga, X. B., & Foshee, V. A. (2004). Adolescent dating violence: Do adolescents follow in their friends' or their parents' footsteps? *Journal of Interpersonal Violence, 19,* 162–184.

Arsenio, W. F. (2006). Happy victimizers and moral responsibility: Sociocultural and developmental considerations. In M. Schleifer & C. Martiny (Eds.), *Talking to children about responsibility and control of emotions* (pp. 49–69). Calgary, Canada: Detselig Enterprises.

Artistico, D., Cervone, D., & Pezzuti, L. (2003). Perceived self-efficacy and everyday problem solving among young and older adults. *Psychology and Aging, 18,* 68–79.

Artman, L., & Cahan, S. (1993). Schooling and the development of transitive inference. *Developmental Psychology, 29,* 753–759.

Artman, L., Cahan, S., & Avni-Babad, D. (2006). Age, schooling, and conditional reasoning. *Cognitive Development, 21,* 131–145.

Arvanitakis, Z., Wilson, R. S., Bienias, J. L., Evans, D. A., & Bennett, D. A. (2004). Diabetes mellitus and risk of Alzheimer disease and decline in cognitive function. *Archives of Neurology, 61,* 661–666.

Asakawa, K. (2001). Family socialization practices and their effects on the internationalization of educational values for Asian and white American adolescents. *Applied Developmental Science, 5,* 184–194.

Asher, S. R., & Rose, A. J. (1997). Promoting children's social-emotional adjustment with peers. In P. Salovey & D. J. Sluyter (Eds.), *Emotional development and emotional intelligence* (pp. 193–195). New York: Basic Books.

Aslin, R. N., Jusczyk, P. W., & Pisoni, D. B. (1998). Speech and auditory processing during infancy: Constraints on and precursors to language. In D. Kuhn & R. S. Siegler (Eds.), *Handbook of child psychology: Vol. 2. Cognition, perception, and language* (5th ed., pp. 147–198). New York: Wiley.

Assmann, A. (1994). Wholesome knowledge: Concepts of wisdom in a historical and cross-cultural perspective. In D. L. Featherman, R. M. Lerner, & M. Perlmutter (Eds.), *Lifespan development and behavior* (pp. 187–224). Hillsdale, NJ: Erlbaum.

Astington, J. W., Pelletier, J., & Homer, B. (2002). Theory of mind and epistemological development: The relation between children's second-order false belief understanding and their ability to reason about evidence. *New Ideas in Psychology, 20,* 131–144.

Atchley, R. C. (1989). A continuity theory of normal aging. *Gerontologist, 29,* 183–190.

Atchley, R. C. (1999). *Continuity and adaptation in aging: Creating positive experiences.* Baltimore, MD: Johns Hopkins University Press.

Atchley, R. C. (2003). Why people cope well with retirement. In J. L. Ronch & J. A. Goldfield (Eds.), *Mental wellness in aging: Strengths-based approaches* (pp. 123–138). Baltimore, MD: Health Professions Press.

Athanasou, J. A. (2002). Vocational pathways in the early part of a career: An Australian study. *Career Development Quarterly, 52,* 78–88.

Atkins, R., Hart, D., & Donnelly, T. M. (2004). Moral identity development and school attachment. In D. Lapsley & D. Narvaez (Eds.), *Moral development, self, and identity* (pp. 65–82). Mahwah, NJ: Erlbaum.

Atkinson, R. C., & Shiffrin, R. M. (1968). Human memory: A proposed system and its control processes. In K. W. Spence & J. T. Spence (Eds.), *Advances in the psychology of learning and motivation* (Vol. 2, pp. 90–195). New York: Academic Press.

Au, T. K., Sidle, A. L., & Rollins, K. B. (1993). Developing an intuitive understanding of conservation and contamination: Invisible particles as a plausible mechanism. *Developmental Psychology, 29,* 286–299.

Aunola, K., Stattin, H., & Nurmi, J.-E. (2000). Parenting styles and adolescents' achievement strategies. *Journal of Adolescence, 23,* 205–222.

Avery, D. R., McKay, P. F., & Wilson, D. C. (2007). Engaging the aging workforce: The relationships between perceived age similarity, satisfaction with coworkers, and employee engagement. *Journal of Applied Psychology, 92,* 1542–1556.

Avis, N. E. (2003). Depression during the menopausal transition. *Psychology of Women Quarterly, 27,* 91–100.

Avis, N. E., Assmann, S. F., Kravitz, H. M., Ganz, P. A., & Ory, M. (2004). Quality of life in diverse groups of midlife women: Assessing the influence of menopause, health status and psychosocial and demographic factors. *Quality of Life Research, 13,* 933–946.

Avis, N. E., Crawford, S., & Johannes, C. B. (2002). Menopause. In G. M. Wingood & R. J. DeClemente (Eds.), *Handbook of women's sexual and reproductive health* (pp. 367–391). New York: Kluwer.

Avlund, K., Lund, R., Holstein, B. E., & Due, P. (2004). The impact of structural and functional characteristics of social relations as determinants of functional decline. *Journal of Gerontology, 59B,* 44–56.

Avolio, B. J., & Sosik, J. J. (1999). A lifespan framework for assessing the impact of work on white-collar workers. In S. L. Willis & J. D. Reid (Eds.), *Life in the middle* (pp. 249–274). San Diego, CA: Academic Press.

Axelin, A., Salanterä, S., & Lehtonen, L. (2006). 'Facilitated tucking by parents' in pain management of preterm infants—a randomized crossover trial. *Early Human Development, 82,* 241–247.

Axia, G., & Baroni, R. (1985). Linguistic politeness at different age levels. *Child Development, 56,* 918–927.

Axia, G., Bonichini, S., & Benini, F. (1999). Attention and reaction to distress in infancy: A longitudinal study. *Developmental Psychology, 35,* 500–504.

Axinn, W. G., & Barber, J. S. (1997). Living arrangements and family formation attitudes in early adulthood. *Journal of Marriage and the Family, 59,* 595–611.

Ayala, G. X., Rogers, M., Arredondo, E. M., Campbell, N. R., Baquero, B., Duerksen, S. C., & Elder, J. P. (2008). Away-from-home food intake and risk for obesity: Examining the influence of context. *Obesity, 16,* 1002–1008.

B

Bacallao, M. L., & Smokowski, P. R. (2007). The costs of getting ahead: Mexican family system changes after immigration. *Family Relations, 56,* 52–66.

Baddeley, A. (1993). Working memory and conscious awareness. In A. F. Collins, S. E. Gathercole, M. A. Conway, & P. E. Morris (Eds.), *Theories of memory* (pp. 11–28). Hove, UK: Erlbaum.

Baddeley, A. (2000). Short-term and working memory. In E. Tulving & R. I. M. Craik (Eds.), *The Oxford handbook of memory* (pp. 77–92). New York: Oxford University Press.

Badger, S., Nelson, L. J., & Barry, C. M. (2006). Perceptions of the transition to adulthood among Chinese and American emerging adults. *International Journal of Behavioral Development, 30,* 84–93.

Baer, W. M., & Hanson, L. C. (2000). Families' perception of the added value of hospice in the nursing home. *Journal of the American Geriatric Society, 48,* 879–882.

Bagheri, A. (2007). Individual choice in the definition of death. *Journal of Medical Ethics, 33,* 146–149.

Bagwell, C. L., Bender, S. E., Andreassi, C. L., Kinoshita, T. L., Montarello, S. A., & Muller, J. G. (2005). Friendship quality and perceived relationship changes predict psychosocial adjustment in early adulthood. *Journal of Social and Personal Relationships, 22,* 235–254.

Bagwell, C. L., & Coie, J. D. (2004). The best friendships of aggressive boys: Relationship quality, conflict management, and rule-breaking behavior. *Journal of Experimental Child Psychology, 88,* 5–24.

Bagwell, C. L., Schmidt, M. E., Newcomb, A. F., & Bukowski, W. M. (2001). Friendship and peer rejection as predictors of adult adjustment. In D. W. Nangle & C. A. Erdley (Eds.), *The role of friendship in psychological adjustment* (pp. 25–49). San Francisco: Jossey-Bass.

Bahrick, L. E., Gogate, L. J., & Ruiz, I. (2002). Attention and memory for faces and actions in infancy: The salience of actions over faces in dynamic events. *Child Development, 73,* 1629–1643.

Bahrick, L. E., Hernandez-Reif, M., & Flom, R. (2005). The development of infant learning about specific face–voice relations. *Developmental Psychology, 41,* 541–552.

Bahrick, L. E., Lickliter, R., & Flom, R. (2004). Intersensory redundancy guides the development of selective attention, perception, and cognition in infancy. *Current Directions in Psychological Science, 13,* 99–102.

Bahrick, L. E., Netto, D., & Hernandez-Reif, M. (1998). Intermodal perception of adult and child faces and voices by infants. *Child Development, 69,* 1263–1275.

Bahrick, L. E., & Pickens, J. N. (1995). Infant memory for object motion across a period of three months: Implications for a four-phase attention function. *Journal of Experimental Child Psychology, 59,* 343–371.

Bailey, J. M., Bobrow, D., Wolfe, M., & Mikach, S. (1995). Sexual orientation of adult sons of gay fathers. *Developmental Psychology, 31,* 124–129.

Bailey, J. M., Dunne, M. P., & Martin, N. G. (2000). Genetic and environmental influences on sexual orientation and its correlates in an Australian twin sample. *Journal of Personality and Social Psychology, 78,* 524–536.

Baillargeon, R. (2004). Infants' reasoning about hidden objects: Evidence for event-general and event-specific expectations. *Developmental Science, 7,* 391–424.

Baillargeon, R., & DeVos, J. (1991). Object permanence in young infants: Further evidence. *Child Development, 62,* 1227–1246.

Baillargeon, R., Zoccolillo, M., Keenan, K., Côté, S., Pérusse, D., Wu, H.-X., & Boivin, M. (2007). Gender differences in physical aggression: A prospective population-based survey of children before and after 2 years of age. *Developmental Psychology, 43,* 13–26.

Baker, J. A. (2006). Contributions of teacher–child relationships to positive school adjustment during elementary school. *Journal of School Psychology, 44,* 211–229.

Bakermans-Kranenburg, M. J., van IJzendoorn, M. H., & Juffer, F. (2003). Less is more: Meta-analyses of sensitivity and attachment interventions in early childhood. *Psychological Bulletin, 129,* 195–215.

Balaswamy, S., & Richardson, V. E. (2001). The cumulative effects of life event, personal, and social resources on subjective well-being of elderly widowers. *International Journal of Aging and Human Development, 53,* 311–327.

Balfanz, R., Legters, N., West, T. C., & Weber, L. M. (2007). Are NCLB's measures, incentives, and improvement strategies the right ones for the nation's low-performing high schools? *American Educational Research Journal, 44,* 559–593.

Ball, K., Berch, D. B., Helmers, K. F., Jobe, J. B., Leveck, M. D., & Marsiske, M. (2002). Effects of cognitive training interventions with older adults: A randomized controlled trial. *Journal of the American Medical Association, 288,* 2271–2281.

Balsam, K. F., Beauchaine, T. P., Rothblum, E. D., & Solomon, S. E. (2008). Three-year follow-up of same-sex couples who had civil unions in Vermont, same-sex couples not in civil unions, and heterosexual married couples. *Developmental Psychology, 44,* 102–116.

Baltes, M. M. (1995, February). Dependency in old age: Gains and losses. *Psychological Science, 4(1),* 14–19.

Baltes, M. M. (1996). *The many faces of dependency in old age.* New York: Cambridge University Press.

Baltes, P. B. (1997). On the incomplete architecture of human ontogeny: Selection, optimization, and compensation as foundation of developmental theory. *American Psychologist, 52,* 366–380.

Baltes, P. B., Lindenberger, U., & Staudinger, U. M. (2006). Life span theory in developmental psychology. In R. M. Lerner (Ed.), *Handbook of child psychology: Vol. 1. Theoretical models of human development* (6th ed., pp. 569–664). Hoboken, NJ: Wiley.

Baltes, P. B., & Smith, J. (2003). New frontiers in the future of aging: From successful aging of the young old to the dilemmas of the fourth age. *Gerontology, 49,* 123–135.

Baltes, P. B., & Smith, J. (2008). The fascination of wisdom. *Perspectives on Psychological Science, 3,* 56–64.

Baltes, P. B., & Staudinger, U. M. (2000). Wisdom: A metaheuristic (pragmatic) to orchestrate mind and virtue toward excellence. *American Psychologist, 55,* 122–136.

Bancroft, J. (2002). The medicalization of female sexual dysfunction: The need for caution. *Archives of Sexual Behavior, 31,* 451–455.

Band, G. P. H., van der Molen, M. W., Overtoom, C. C. E., & Verbaten, M. N. (2000). The ability to activate and inhibit speeded responses: Separate developmental trends. *Journal of Experimental Child Psychology, 75,* 263–290.

Bandura, A. (1977). *Social learning theory.* Englewood Cliffs, NJ: Prentice-Hall.

Bandura, A. (1999). Social cognitive theory of personality. In L. A. Pervin (Ed.), *Handbook of personality: Theory and research* (2nd ed., pp. 154–196). New York: Guilford.

Bandura, A. (2001). Social cognitive theory: An agentic perspective. *Annual Review of Psychology, 52,* 1–26.

Banish, M. T., & Heller, W. (1998). Evolving perspectives on lateralization of function. *Current Directions in Psychological Science, 7,* 1–2.

Banks, M. S. (1980). The development of visual accommodation during early infancy. *Child Development, 51,* 646–666.

Barber, B. K., & Harmon, E. L. (2002). Violating the self: Parental psychological control of children and adolescents. In B. K. Barber (Ed.), *Intrusive parenting: How psychological control affects children and adolescents* (pp. 15–52). Washington, DC: American Psychological Association.

Barber, B. K., & Olsen, J. A. (1997). Socialization in context: Connection, regulation, and autonomy in the family, school, and neighborhood, and with peers. *Journal of Adolescent Research, 12,* 287–315.

Barber, B. K., & Olsen, J. A. (2004). Assessing the transitions to middle and high school. *Journal of Adolescent Research, 19,* 3–30.

Barber, B. K., Stolz, H. E., & Olsen, J. A. (2005). Parental support, psychological control, and behavioral control: Assessing relevance across time, culture, and method. *Monographs of the Society for Research in Child Development, 70*(4, Serial No. 282).

Barber, B. L., Stone, M. R., Hunt, J. E., & Eccles, J. S. (2005). Benefits of activity participation: The roles of identity affirmation and peer group norm sharing. In J. L. Mahoney, R. W. Larson, & J. S. Eccles (Eds.), *Organized activities as contexts of development: Extracurricular activities, after-school and community programs* (pp. 185–210). Mahwah, NJ: Erlbaum.

Barber, J. S. (2001a). Ideational influences on the transition to parenthood: Attitudes toward childbearing and competing alternatives. *Social Psychology Quarterly, 64,* 101–127.

Barber, J. S. (2001b). The intergenerational transmission of age at first birth among married and unmarried men and women. *Social Sciences Research, 30,* 219–247.

Bard, K. A., Todd, B. K., Bernier, C., Love, J., & Leavens, D. A. (2006). Self-awareness in human and chimpanzee infants: What is measured and what is meant by the mark and mirror test? *Infancy, 9,* 191–219.

Barenbaum, J., Ruchkin, V., & Schwab-Stone, M. (2004). The psychosocial aspects of children exposed to war: Practice and policy initiatives. *Journal of Child Psychology and Psychiatry, 45,* 41–62.

Bar-Haim, Y., Ziv, T., Lamy, D., & Hodes, R. M. (2006). Nature and nurture in own-race face processing. *Psychological Science, 17,* 159–163.

Barja, G. (2004). Free radicals and aging. *Trends in Neuroscience, 27,* 595–600.

Barker, D. (2002). Fetal programming of coronary heart disease. *Trends in Endocrinology and Metabolism, 13,* 364.

Barkley, R. A. (2002a). Psychosocial treatments of attention-deficit/hyperactivity disorder in children. *Journal of Clinical Psychology, 63*(Suppl. 12), 36–43.

Barkley, R. A. (2002b). Major life activity and health outcomes associated with attention-deficit/hyperactivity disorder. *Journal of Clinical Psychiatry, 63*(Suppl. 12), 10–15.

Barkley, R. A. (2003a). Attention-deficit/hyperactivity disorder. In E. J. Mash & R. A. Barkley (Eds.), *Child psychopathology* (2nd ed., pp. 75–143). New York: Guilford Press.

Barkley, R. A. (2003b). Issues in the diagnosis of attention-deficit hyperactivity disorder in children. *Brain and Development, 25,* 77–83.

Barkley, R. A. (2006). Attention-deficit/hyperactivity disorder. In R. A. Barkley, D. A. Wolfe, & E. J. Mash (Eds.), *Behavioral and emotional disorders in adolescents: Nature, assessment, and treatment* (pp. 91–152). New York: Guilford.

Barnes, G. M., Hoffman, J. H., Welte, J. W., Farrell, M. P., & Dintcheff, B. A. (2006). Effects of parental monitoring and peer deviance on substance use and delinquency. *Journal of Marriage and Family, 68,* 1084–1104.

Barnes, J., Katz, I., Korbin, J. E., & O'Brien, M. (2007). *Children and families in communities: Theory, research, policy and practice.* Hoboken, NJ: Wiley.

Barnes-Farrell, J., & Matthews, R. A. (2007). Age and work attitudes. In K. S. Shultz & G. A. Adams (Eds.), *Aging and work in the 21st century* (pp. 139–162). Mahwah, NJ: Erlbaum.

Barnet, B., Arroyo, C., Devoe, M., & Duggan, A. K. (2004). Reduced school dropout rates among adolescent mothers receiving school-based prenatal care. *Archives of Pediatric and Adolescent Medicine, 158,* 262–268.

Barnett, D., & Vondra, J. I. (1999). Atypical patterns of early attachment: Theory, research, and current directions. In J. I Vondra & D. Barnett (Eds.), *Atypical attachment in infancy and early childhood among children at developmental risk. Monographs of the Society for Research in Child Development, 64*(3, Serial No. 258), 1–24.

Barnett, R. C., & Hyde, J. S. (2001). Women, men, work, family: An expansionist theory. *American Psychologist, 56,* 781–796.

Barnett, W. S. (2004). Does Head Start have lasting cognitive effects? The myth of fade-out. In E. Zigler & S. J. Styfco (Eds.), *The Head Start debates* (pp. 221–250). Baltimore: Brookes.

Baron-Cohen, S., Baldwin, D. A., & Crowson, M. (1997). Do children with autism use the speaker's direction of gaze strategy to crack the code of language? *Child Development, 68,* 48–57.

Baron-Cohen, S., & Belmonte, M. K. (2005). Autism: A window onto the development of the social and the analytic brain. *Annual Review of Neuroscience, 28,* 109–126.

Barr, H. M., Streissguth, A. P., Darby, B. L., & Sampson, P. D. (1990). Prenatal exposure to alcohol, caffeine, tobacco, and aspirin: Effects on fine and gross motor performance in 4-year-old children. *Developmental Psychology, 26,* 339–348.

Barr, R. G. (2001). "Colic" is something infants do, rather than a condition they "have": A developmental approach to crying phenomena patterns, pacification and (patho)genesis. In R. G. Barr, I. St. James-Roberts, & M. R. Keefe (Eds.), *New evidence on unexplained infant crying* (pp. 87–104). St. Louis: Johnson & Johnson Pediatric Institute.

Barr, R. G., & Hayne, H. (1999). Developmental changes in imitation from television during infancy. *Child Development, 70,* 1067–1081.

Barr, R. G, & Hayne, H. (2003). It's not what you know, it's who you know: Older siblings facilitate imitation during infancy. *International Journal of Early Years Education, 11,* 7–21.

Barr, R. G, Marrott, H., & Rovee-Collier, C. (2003). The role of sensory preconditioning in memory retrieval by preverbal infants. *Learning and Behavior, 31,* 111–123.

Barr, R. G., Paterson, J. A., MacMartin, L. M., & Lehtonen, L. (2005). Prolonged and unsoothable crying bouts in infants with and without colic. *Journal of Developmental and Behavioral Pediatrics, 26,* 14–23.

Barrett, K. C. (2005). The origins of social emotions and self-regulation in toddlerhood: New evidence. *Cognition and Emotion, 19,* 953–979.

Barsky, A. J., Cleary, P. D., & Klerman, G. L. (1992). Determinants of perceived health status of medical outpatients. *Social Science and Medicine, 34,* 1147–1154.

Bartgis, J., Lilly, A. R., & Thomas, D. G. (2003). Event-related potential and behavioral measures of attention in 5-, 7-, and 9-year-olds. *Journal of General Psychology, 130,* 311–335.

Bartlik, B., & Goldstein, M. Z. (2001). Men's sexual health after midlife. *Practical Geriatrics, 52,* 291–306.

Bartocci, M., Berggvist, L. L., Lagercrantz, H., & Anand, K. J. (2006). Pain activates cortical areas in the preterm newborn brain. *Pain, 122,* 109–117.

Bartrip, J., Morton, J., & de Schonen, S. (2001). Responses to mother's face in 3-week- to 5-month-old infants. *British Journal of Developmental Psychology, 19,* 219–232.

Bartsch, K., & Wellman, H. (1995). *Children talk about the mind.* New York: Oxford University Press.

Barzilai, N., & Bartke, A. (2009). Biological approaches to mechanistically understand the healthy life span extension achieved by calorie restriction and modulation of hormones. *Journal of Gerontology, 64A,* S187–S191.

Basow, S. A., & Rubin, L. R. (1999). Gender influences on adolescent development. In N. G. Johnson & M. C. Roberts (Eds.), *Beyond appearance: A new look at adolescent girls* (pp. 25–52). Washington, DC: American Psychological Association.

Bassuk, S. S., & Manson, J. E. (2005). Epidemiological evidence for the role of physical activity in reducing risk of type 2 diabetes and cardiovascular disease. *Journal of Applied Physiology, 99,* 1193–1204.

Bates, E. (2004). Explaining and interpreting deficits in language development across clinical groups: Where do we go from here? *Brain and Language, 88,* 248–253.

Bates, E., Marchman, V., Thal, D., Fenson, L., Dale, P., Reznick, J. S., Reilly, J., & Hartung, J. (1994). Developmental and stylistic variation in the composition of early vocabulary. *Journal of Child Language, 21,* 85–123.

Bates, J. E., Wachs, T. D., & Emde, R. N. (1994). Toward practical uses for biological concepts. In J. E. Bates & T. D. Wachs (Eds.), *Temperament: Individual differences at the interface of biology and behavior* (pp. 275–306). Washington, DC: American Psychological Association.

Bauer, C. R., Langer, J. C., Shakaran, S., Bada, H. S., & Lester, B. (2005). Acute neonatal effects of cocaine exposure during pregnancy. *Archives of Pediatrics and Adolescent Medicine, 159,* 824–834.

Bauer, P. J. (2002). Early memory development. In U. Goswami (Ed.), *Blackwell handbook of child cognitive development* (pp. 127–150). Malden, MA: Blackwell.

Bauer, P. J. (2006). Event memory. In D. Kuhn & R. Siegler (Eds.), *Handbook of child psychology: Vol. 2. Cognition, perception, and language* (6th ed., pp. 373–425). Hoboken, NJ: Wiley.

Bauer, P. J. (2007). Recall in infancy: A neurodevelopmental account. *Current Directions in Psychological Science, 16,* 142–146.

Bauer, P. J., Wiebe, S. A., Carver, L. J., Lukowski, A. F., Haight, J. C., Waters, J. M., & Nelson, C. A. (2006). Electrophysiological indexes of encoding and behavioral indexes of recall: Examining relations and developmental change late in the first year of life. *Developmental Neuropsychology, 29,* 293–320.

Baum, N., Rahav, G., & Sharon, D. (2005). Changes in the self-concepts of divorced women. *Journal of Divorce and Remarriage, 43,* 47–67.

Baumbusch, J. L. (2004). Unclaimed treasures: Older women's reflections on lifelong singlehood. *Journal of Women and Aging, 16,* 105–121.

Baumeister, R. F. (1998). Inducing guilt. In J. Bybee (Ed.), *Guilt and children* (pp. 185–213). San Diego: Academic Press.

Baumrind, D. (1971). Current patterns of parental authority. *Developmental Psychology Monograph, 4*(No. 1, Pt. 2).

Bauserman, R. (2002). Child adjustment in joint-custody versus sole-custody arrangements: A meta-analytic review. *Journal of Family Psychology, 16,* 91–102.

Baxter, J., Hewitt, B., & Haynes, M. (2008). Life course transitions and housework: Marriage, parenthood, and time on housework. *Journal of Marriage and Family, 70,* 259–272.

Baydar, N., Greek, A., & Brooks-Gunn, J. (1997). A longitudinal study of the effects of the birth of a sibling during the first 6 years of life. *Journal of Marriage and the Family, 59,* 939–956.

Bayer, A., & Tadd, W. (2000). Unjustified exclusion of elderly people from studies submitted to research ethics committee for approval: Descriptive study. *British Medical Journal, 321,* 992–993.

Bayer, W., Mallinger, J. B., Krishnan, A., & Shields, C. G. (2006). Attitudes toward life-sustaining interventions among ambulatory black and white patients. *Ethnicity and Disease, 16,* 914–919.

Bayless, S. (2007). Executive functions in school-age children born very prematurely. *Early Human Development, 83,* 247–254.

Bayley, N. (1969). *Bayley Scales of Infant Development.* New York: Psychological Corporation.

Bayley, N. (1993). *Bayley Scales of Infant Development* (2nd ed.). San Antonio, TX: Psychological Corporation.

Bayley, N. (2005). *Bayley Scales of Infant and Toddler Development, Third Edition* (Bayley-III). San Antonio, TX: Harcourt Assessment.

Bean, R. A., Barber, B. K., & Crane, D. R. (2007). Parental support, behavioral control, and psychological control among African American youth: The relationships to academic grades, delinquency, and depression. *Journal of Family Issues, 27,* 1335–1355.

Bearman, P. S., & Moody, J. (2004). Suicide and friendships among American adolescents. *American Journal of Public Health, 94,* 89–95.

Beautrais, A. L. (2003). Life course factors associated with suicidal behaviors in young people. *American Behavioral Scientist, 46,* 1137–1156.

Becker, G., Beyene, Y., Newsome, E., & Mayen, N. (2003). Creating continuity through mutual assistance: Intergenerational reciprocity in four ethnic groups. *Journal of Gerontology, 38B,* S151–S159.

Beckerman, M. B. (1990). Leos Janácek and "the late style" in music. *Gerontologist, 30,* 632–635.

Beckett, C., Maughan, B., Rutter, M., Castle, J., Colvert, E., & Groothues, C. (2006). Do the effects of early severe deprivation on cognition persist into early adolescence? Findings from the English and Romanian adoptees study. *Child Development, 77,* 696–711.

Bedford, O. A. (2004). The individual experience of guilt and shame in Chinese culture. *Culture and Psychology, 10,* 29–52.

Behnke, M., Eyler, F. D., Garvan, C. W., & Wobie, K. (2001). The search for congenital malformations in newborns with fetal cocaine exposure. *Pediatrics, 107,* e74.

Behnke, M., Eyler, F. D., Warner, T. D., Garvan, C. W., Hou, W., & Wobie, K. (2006). Outcome from a prospective, longitudinal study of prenatal cocaine use: Preschool development at 3 years of age. *Journal of Pediatric Psychology, 31,* 41–49.

Beier, M. E., & Ackerman, P. L. (2005). Age, ability, and the role of prior knowledge on the acquisition of new domain knowledge: Promising results in a real-world learning environment. *Psychology and Aging, 20,* 341–355.

Bell, J. H., & Bromnick, R. D. (2003). The social reality of the imaginary audience: A grounded theory approach. *Adolescence, 38,* 205–219.

Bell, M. A. (1998). Frontal lobe function during infancy: Implications for the development of cognition and attention. In J. E. Richards (Ed.), *Cognitive neuroscience of attention: A developmental perspective* (pp. 327–362). Mahwah, NJ: Erlbaum.

Bell, M. L. (1995). Attitudes toward menopause among Mexican American women. *Health Care for Women International, 16,* 425–435.

Bellamy, C. (2004). *The state of the world's children: 2004.* New York: UNICEF.

Bellamy, C. (2005). *The state of the world's children: 2005.* New York: UNICEF.

Belle, S. H., Burgio, L., Burns, R., Coon, D., Czaja, S. J., Gallagher-Thompson, D., & Gitlin, L. N. (2006). Enhancing quality of life of dementia caregivers from different ethnic or racial groups: A randomized, controlled trial. *Annals of Internal Medicine, 145,* 727–738.

Bellinger, D. C. (2005). Teratogen update: Lead and pregnancy. *Birth Defects Research: Part A, Clinical and Molecular Teratology, 73,* 409–420.

Belsky, J. (2001). Developmental risks (still) associated with child care. *Journal of Child Psychology and Psychiatry, 42,* 845–859.

Belsky, J. (2005). Attachment theory and research in ecological perspective: Insights from the Pennsylvania Infant and Family Development Project and the NICHD Study of Early Child Care. In K. E. Grossmann, K. Grossmann, & E. Waters (Eds.), *Attachment from infancy to adulthood: The major longitudinal studies* (pp. 71–97). New York: Guilford.

Belsky, J. (2006). Early child care and early child development: Major findings of the NICHD Study of Early Child Care. *European Journal of Developmental Psychology, 3,* 95–110.

Belsky, J., Campbell, S. B., Cohn, J. F., & Moore, G. (1996). Instability of infant–parent attachment security. *Developmental Psychology, 32,* 921–924.

Belsky, J., & Fearon, R. M. P. (2002). Early attachment security, subsequent maternal sensitivity, and later child development: Does continuity in development depend on caregiving? *Attachment and Human Development, 4,* 361–387.

Belsky, J., Jaffee, S., Hsieh, K., & Silva, P. A. (2001). Child-rearing antecedents of intergenerational relations in young adulthood: A prospective study. *Developmental Psychology, 37,* 801–813.

Belsky, J., Steinberg, L. D., Houts, R. M., Friedman, S. L., DeHart, G., Cauffman, E., Roisman, G. I., & Halpern-Felsher, B. (2007). Family rearing antecedents of pubertal timing. *Child Development, 78,* 1302–1321.

Bempechat, J., & Drago-Severson, E. (1999). Cross-national differences in academic achievement: Beyond etic conceptions of children's understandings. *Review of Educational Research, 69,* 287–314.

Benbow, C. P., Lubinski, D., Shea, D. L., & Eftekhara-Sanjani, H. (2000). Sex differences in mathematical reasoning ability at age 13: Their status 20 years later. *Psychological Science, 11,* 474–480.

Bender, H. L., Allen, J. P., McElhaney, K. B., Antonishak, J., Moore, C. M., Kelly, H. L., & Davis, S. M. (2007). Use of harsh physical discipline and developmental outcomes in adolescence. *Development and Psychopathology, 19,* 227–242.

Benenson, J. F., & Christakos, A. (2003). The greater fragility of females' versus males' closest same-sex friendships. *Child Development, 74,* 1123–1129.

Bengtson, V. L., Rosenthal, C. L., & Burton, L. (1990). Families and aging: Diversity and heterogeneity. In R. H. Binstock & L. K. George (Eds.), *Handbook of aging and the social sciences* (3rd ed., pp. 263–287). San Diego: Academic Press.

Bengtsson, H. (2005). Children's cognitive appraisal of others' distressful and positive experiences. *International Journal of Behavioral Development, 29,* 457–466.

Bennett, D. A., Schneider, J. A., Tang, Y., Arnold, S. E., & Wilson, R. S. (2006). The effect of social networks on the relation between Alzheimer's disease pathology and level of cognitive function in old people: A longitudinal cohort study. *Lancet Neurology, 5,* 406–412.

Bennett, K. M. (2007). "No sissy stuff": Toward a theory of masculinity and emotional expression in older widowed men. *Journal of Aging Studies, 21,* 347–356.

Bennett, K. M., Smith, P. T., & Hughes, G. M. (2005). Coping, depressive feelings and gender differences in late life widowhood. *Aging and Mental Health, 9,* 348–353.

Bennett, S. E., & Assefi, N. P. (2005). School-based teenage pregnancy prevention programs: A systematic review of randomized controlled trials. *Journal of Adolescent Health, 36,* 72–81.

Benson, P. L., Scales, P. C., Hamilton, S. F., & Sesma, A., Jr. (2006). Positive youth development: Theory, research, and applications. In R. M. Lerner (Ed.), *Handbook of child psychology: Vol. 1. Theoretical models of human development* (6th ed., pp. 894–941). Hoboken, NJ: Wiley.

Berg, C. A. (2000). Intellectual development in adulthood. In R. J. Sternberg (Ed.), *Handbook of intelligence* (pp. 117–137). New York: Cambridge University Press.

Berg, C. A. (2008). Everyday problem solving in context. In S. M. Hofer & D. F. Alwin (Eds.), *Handbook of cognitive aging: Interdisciplinary perspectives* (pp. 207–223). Thousand Oaks, CA: Sage.

Berg, C. A., & Sternberg, R. J. (2003). Multiple perspectives on the development of adult intelligence. In J. Demick & C. Andreoletti (Eds.), *Handbook of adult development* (pp. 103–119). New York: Springer.

Berg, C. A., Strough, J., Calderone, K. S., Sansone, C., & Weir, C. (1998). The role of problem definitions in understanding age and context effects on strategies for solving everyday problems. *Psychology and Aging, 13,* 29–44.

Bergman, H., Ferrucci, L., Guralnik, J., Hogan, D. B., Hummel, S., Karunananthan, S., & Wolfson. C. (2007). Frailty: An emerging research and clinical paradigm—issues and controversies. *Journal of Gerontology, 62A,* 731–737.

Bergman, I., Blomberg, M., & Almkvist, O. (2007). The importance of impaired physical health and age in normal cognitive aging. *Scandinavian Journal of Psychology, 48,* 115–125.

Berk, L. E., & Harris, S. (2003). Vygotsky, Lev. In L. Nadel (Ed.), *Encyclopedia of cognitive science.* London: Macmillan.

Berk, L. E., Mann, T., & Ogan, A. (2006). Make-believe play: Wellspring for development of self-regulation. In D. Singer, K. Hirsh-Pasek, & R. Golinkoff (Eds.), *Play = learning.* New York: Oxford University Press.

Berk, L. E., & Spuhl, S. (1995). Maternal interaction, private speech, and task performance in preschool children. *Early Childhood Research Quarterly, 10,* 145–169.

Berkowitz, C. M. (2004). *Talking to your kids about sex.* Somerville, NJ: Somerset Medical Center. Retrieved from www.somersetmedicalcenter.com/1817.cfm

Berkowitz, M. W., & Gibbs, J. C. (1983). Measuring the developmental features of moral discussion. *Merrill-Palmer Quarterly, 29,* 399–410.

Berman, R. A. (2007). Developing linguistic knowledge and language use across adolescence. In K. Hirsh-Pasek & R. M. Golinkoff (Eds.), *Action meets word: How children learn verbs* (pp. 347–367). New York: Oxford University Press.

Bernabei, R., Gambassi, G., Lapane, K., Landi, F., Gatsonis, C., & Dunlop, R. (1998). Management of pain in elderly cancer patients. *Journal of the American Medical Association, 279,* 1877–1882.

Berndt, T. J., & Murphy, L. M. (2002). Influences of friends and friendships: Myths, truths, and research recommendations. In R. V. Kail (Ed.), *Advances in child development and behavior* (Vol. 30, pp. 275–310). San Diego, CA: Academic Press.

Berner, M. M., Leiber, C., Kriston, L., Stodden, V., & Gunzler, C. (2008). Effects of written information material on help-seeking behavior in patients with erectile dysfunction: A longitudinal study. *Journal of Sexual Behavior, 5,* 436–447.

Bernier, J. C., & Siegel, D. H. (1994). Attention-deficit hyperactivity disorder: A family ecological systems perspective. *Families in Society, 75,* 142–150.

Berninger, V. W. (2006). A developmental approach to learning disabilities. In K. A. Renninger & I. E. Sigel (Eds.), *Handbook of child psychology: Vol. 4. Child psychology in practice* (6th ed., pp. 420–452). Hoboken, NJ: Wiley.

Berr, C., Wancata, J., & Ritchie, K. (2005). Prevalence of dementia in the elderly in Europe. *European Neuropsychopharmacology, 15,* 463–471.

Bert, S. C., Farris, J. R., & Borkowski, J. G. (2008). Parent training: Implementation strategies for adventures in parenting. *Journal of Primary Prevention, 29,* 243–261.

Bertenthal, B. I. (1993). Infants' perception of biomechanical motions: Intrinsic image and knowledge-based constraints. In C. Granrud (Ed.), *Visual perception and cognition in infancy* (pp. 175–214). Hillsdale, NJ: Erlbaum.

Bertenthal, B. I., & Longo, M. R. (2007). Is there evidence of a mirror neuron system from birth? *Developmental Science, 10,* 513–523.

Bertenthal, B. I., Longo, M. R., & Kenny, S. (2007). Phenomenal permanence and the development of predictive tracking in infancy. *Child Development, 78,* 350–363.

Bertrand, M., & Mullainathan, S. (2004). *Are Emily and Brendan more employable than Lakisha and Jamal? A field experiment on labor market discrimination.* Unpublished manuscript, University of Chicago.

Berzlanovich, A. M., Keil, W. W., Sim, T., Fasching, P., & Fazeny-Dorner, B. (2005). Do centenarians die healthy? An autopsy study. *Journal of Gerontology, 60A,* 862–865.

Berzonsky, M. D. (2003). Identity style and wellbeing: Does commitment matter? *Identity: An International Journal of Theory and Research, 3,* 131–142.

Berzonsky, M. D. (2004). Identity style, parental authority, and identity commitment. *Journal of Youth and Adolescence, 33,* 213–220.

Berzonsky, M. D., & Kuk, L. S. (2000). Identity status, identity processing style, and the transition to university. *Journal of Adolescent Research, 15,* 81–98.

Best, D. L. (2001). Gender concepts: Convergence in cross-cultural research and methodologies. *Cross-cultural Research: The Journal of Comparative Social Science, 35,* 23–43.

Betrán, A. P., Merialdi, M., Lauer, J. A., Bing-Shun, W., Thomas, J., Van Look, P., & Wagner, M. (2007). Rates of ceasarean section: Analysis of global, regional and national estimates. *Paediatric and Perinatal Epidemiology, 21,* 98–113.

Bevan, E., & Higgins, D. J. (2002). Is domestic violence learned? The contribution of child maltreatment to men's violence and adjustment. *Journal of Family Violence, 17,* 223–245.

Beyers, J. M., Bates, J. E., Pettit, G. S., & Dodge, K. A. (2003). Neighborhood structure, parenting processes, and the development of youths' externalizing behaviors: A multilevel analysis. *American Journal of Community Psychology, 31,* 35–53.

Bhanot, R., & Jovanovic, J. (2005). Parents' academic gender stereotypes influence whether they intrude on their children's work. *Sex Roles, 52,* 597–607.

Bhat, A., Heathcock, J., & Galloway, J. C. (2005). Toy-oriented changes in hand and joint kinematics during the emergence of purposeful reaching. *Infant Behavior and Development, 28,* 445–465.

Bhatt, R. S., Rovee-Collier, C., & Weiner, S. (1994). Developmental changes in the interface between perception and memory retrieval. *Developmental Psychology, 30,* 151–162.

Bhatt, R. S., Wilk, A., Hill, D., & Rovee-Collier, C. (2004). Correlated attributes and categorization in the first half-year of life. *Developmental Psychobiology, 44,* 103–115.

Bhavnani, B. R., & Strickler, R. C. (2005). Menopausal hormone therapy. *Journal of Obstetrics and Gynaecology Canada, 27,* 137–162.

Bherer, L., Kramer, A. F., Peterson, M. S., Colcombe, S., Erickson, K., & Becic, E. (2006). Training effects on dual-task performance: Are there age-related differences in plasticity of attentional control? *Psychology and Aging, 20,* 695–709.

Bialystok, E. (2001). *Bilingualism in development: Language, literacy, and cognition.* New York: Cambridge University Press.

Bialystok, E., & Martin, M. M. (2003). Notation to symbol: Development in children's understanding of print. *Journal of Experimental Child Psychology, 86,* 223–243.

Bialystok, E., & Martin, M. M. (2004). Attention and inhibition in bilingual children: Evidence from the dimensional change card sort task. *Developmental Science, 7,* 325–339.

Bialystok, E., McBride-Chang, C., & Luk, G. (2005). Bilingualism, language proficiency, and learning to read in two writing systems. *Journal of Educational Psychology, 97,* 580–590.

Bialystok, E., & Senman, L. (2004). Executive processes in appearance–reality tasks: The role of inhibition of attention and symbolic representation. *Child Development, 75,* 562–579.

Bianchi, D. W. (2005). Prenatal genetic diagnosis. In H. W. Taeusch, R. A. Ballard, & C. A. Gleason (Eds.), *Avery's diseases of the newborn* (8th ed., pp. 57–70). Philadelphia: Saunders.

Bianco, A., Stone, J., Lynch, L., Lapinski, R., Berkowitz, G., & Berkowitz, R. L. (1996). Pregnancy outcome at age 40 and older. *Obstetrics and Gynecology, 87,* 917–922.

Biederman, J., Kwon, A., Aleardi, M., Chouinard, V. A., Marino, T., & Cole, H. (2005). Absence of gender effects on attention-deficit hyperactivity disorder: Findings in nonreferred subjects. *American Journal of Psychiatry, 162,* 1083–1089.

Biegel, D., & Liebbrant, S. (2006). Elders living in poverty. In B. Berkman & S. D'Ambruoso (Eds.), *Handbook of social work in health and aging* (pp. 161–180). New York: Oxford University Press.

Bielawska-Batorowicz, E., & Kossakowska-Petrycka, K. (2006). Depressive mood in men after the birth of their offspring in relation to a partner's depression, social support, fathers' personality and prenatal expectations. *Journal of Reproductive and Infant Psychology, 24,* 21–29.

Bigler, R. S. (1995). The role of classification skill in moderating environmental influences on children's gender stereotyping: A study of the functional use of gender in the classroom. *Child Development, 66,* 1072–1087.

Bigler, R. S. (2007, June). Personal communication.

Bigler, R. S., & Liben, L. S. (1992). Cognitive mechanisms in children's gender stereotyping: Theoretical and educational implications of a cognitive-based intervention. *Child Development, 63,* 1351–1363.

Bimmel, N., Juffer, F., van IJzendoorn, M. H., & Bakermans-Kranenburg, M. J. (2003). Problem behavior of internationally adopted adolescents: A review and meta-analysis. *Harvard Review of Psychiatry, 11,* 64–77.

Binstock, R. H., & Quadagno, J. (2001). Aging and politics. In R. H. Binstock & L. K. George (Eds.), *Handbook of aging and the social sciences* (5th ed., pp. 333–351). San Diego, CA: Academic Press.

Bioethics Consultative Committee. (2003). *Comparison of ethics legislation in Europe.* Retrieved from www.synapse.net.mt/bioethics/euroleg1.htm

Birch, L. L., & Fisher, J. A. (1995). Appetite and eating behavior in children. *Pediatric Clinics of North America, 42,* 931–953.

Birch, L. L., Fisher, J. O., & Davison, K. K. (2003). Learning to overeat: Maternal use of restrictive feeding practices promotes girls' eating in the absence of hunger. *American Journal of Clinical Nutrition, 78,* 215–220.

Bird, A., & Reese, E. (2006). Emotional reminiscing and the development of an autobiographical self. *Developmental Psychology, 42,* 613–626.

Birditt, K. S., & Antonucci, T. C. (2007). Relationship quality profiles and well-being among married adults. *Journal of Family Psychology, 21,* 595–604.

Birditt, K. S., & Fingerman, K. L. (2005). Do we get better at picking our battles? Age group differences in descriptions of behavioral reactions to interpersonal tensions. *Journal of Gerontology, 60B,* P121–P128.

Biringen, Z., Emde, R. N., Campos, J. J., & Appelbaum, M. I. (1995). Affective reorganization in the infant, the mother, and the dyad: The role of upright locomotion and its timing. *Child Development, 66,* 499–514.

Birney, D. P., Citron-Pousty, J. H., Lutz, D. J., & Sternberg, R. J. (2005). The development of cognitive and intellectual abilities. In M. H. Bornstein & M. E. Lamb (Eds.), *Developmental science: An advanced textbook* (5th ed., pp. 327–358). Mahwah, NJ: Erlbaum.

Birren, J. E. (2009). Gifts and talents of elderly people: The persimmon's promise. In F. D. Horowitz, R. F. Subotnik, & D. J. Matthews (Eds.), *The development of giftedness and talent across the life span* (pp. 171–185). Washington, DC: American Psychological Association.

Bjorklund, D. F. (2004). *Children's thinking* (4th ed.). Belmont, CA: Wadsworth.

Bjorklund, D. F., & Blasi, C. (2005). Evolutionary developmental psychology. In D. Buss (Ed.), *Handbook of evolutionary psychology* (pp. 828–850). Hoboken, NJ: Wiley.

Bjorklund, D. F., & Douglas, R. N. (1997). The development of memory strategies. In N. Cowan (Ed.), *The development of memory in childhood* (pp. 83–111). Hove, UK: Psychology Press.

Bjorklund, D. F., Schneider, W., Cassel, W. S., & Ashley, E. (1994). Training and extension of a memory strategy: Evidence for utilization deficiencies in high- and low-IQ children. *Child Development, 65,* 951–965.

Black, D., Gates, G., & Sanders, S. (2000). Demographics of the gay and lesbian population in the United States: Evidence from available systematic data sources. *Demography, 37,* 139–154.

Black, M. M. (2005). Failure to thrive. In M. C. Roberts (Ed.), *Handbook of pediatric psychology and psychiatry* (3rd ed., pp. 499–511). New York: Guilford.

Black, R. E., Williams, S. M., Jones, I. E., & Goulding, A. (2002). Children who avoid drinking cow milk have low dietary calcium intakes and poor bone health. *American Journal of Clinical Nutrition, 76,* 675–680.

Blackburn, G. L., & Wang, K. A. (2007). Dietary fat reduction and breast cancer outcome: Results from the Women's Intervention Nutrition Study (WINS). *American Journal of Clinical Nutrition, 86,* s878–s881.

Blackhall, L. J., Frank, G., Murphy, S., & Michel, V. (2001). Bioethics in a different tongue: The case of truth-telling. *Journal of Urban Health, 78,* 59–71.

Blackhall, L. J., Murphy, S. T., Frank, G., Michel, V., & Azen, S. (1995). Ethnicity and attitudes toward patient autonomy. *Journal of the American Medical Association, 274,* 820–825.

Blackwell, D. L., & Lichter, D. T. (2004). Homogamy among dating, cohabiting, and married couples. *Sociological Quarterly, 45,* 719–737.

Blackwell, L. S., Trzesniewski, K. H., & Dweck, C. S. (2007). Implicit theories of intelligence predict achievement across an adolescent transition: A longitudinal study and an intervention. *Child Development, 78,* 246–263.

Blaine, B., & Rodman, J. (2007). Responses to weight loss treatment among obese individuals with and without BED: A matched-study meta-analysis. *Eating and Weight Disorders, 12,* 54–60.

Blair, C., & Razza, R. P. (2007). Relating effortful control, executive function, and false belief understanding to emerging math and literacy ability in kindergarten. *Developmental Psychology, 78,* 647–663.

Blair-Loy, M., & DeHart, G. (2003). Family and career trajectories among African-American female attorneys. *Journal of Family Issues, 24,* 908–933.

Blakemore, J. E. O. (2003). Children's beliefs about violating gender norms: Boys shouldn't look like girls, and girls shouldn't act like boys. *Sex Roles, 48,* 411–419.

Blakemore, S.-J., & Choudhury, S. (2006). Development of the adolescent brain: Implications for executive function and social cognition. *Journal of Child Psychology and Psychiatry, 47,* 296–312.

Blanchard, R., & Bogaert, A. F. (2004). Proportion of homosexual men who owe their sexual orientation to fraternal birth order: An estimate based on two national probability samples. *American Journal of Human Biology, 16,* 151–157.

Blanchard-Fields, F. (2007). Everyday problem solving and emotion: An adult developmental perspective. *Current Directions in Psychological Science, 16,* 26–31.

Blasi, C. H., & Bjorklund, D. F. (2003). Evolutionary developmental psychology: A new tool for better understanding human ontogeny. *Human Development, 46,* 259–281.

Blass, E. M., Ganchrow, J. R., & Steiner, J. E. (1984). Classical conditioning in newborn humans 2–48 hours of age. *Infant Behavior and Development, 7,* 223–235.

Bleeker, M. M., & Jacobs, J. E. (2004). Achievement in math and science: Do mothers' beliefs matter 12 years later? *Journal of Educational Psychology, 96,* 97–109.

Bleske, A. L., & Buss, D. M. (2000). Can men and women be just friends? *Personal Relationships, 7,* 131–151.

Block, J. (1971). *Lives through time.* Berkeley, CA: Bancroft.

Blomberg, S., Edebalk, P. G., & Petersson, J. (2000). The withdrawal of the welfare state: Elderly care in Sweden in the 1990s. *European Journal of Social Work, 3,* 151–163.

Bloom, L. (1998). Language acquisition in its developmental context. In D. Kuhn & R. S. Siegler (Eds.), *Handbook of child psychology: Vol. 2. Cognition, perception, and language* (5th ed., pp. 309–370). New York: Wiley.

Blumenfeld, P. C., Marx, R. W., & Harris, C. J. (2006). Learning environments. In K. A. Renninger & I. E. Sigel (Eds.), *Handbook of child psychology: Vol. 4. Child psychology in practice* (6th ed., pp. 297–342). Hoboken, NJ: Wiley.

Boardman, J. D. (2004). Stress and physical health: The role of neighborhoods as mediating and moderating mechanisms. *Social Science and Medicine, 58,* 2473–2483.

Bodrova, E., & Leong, D. J. (2007). *Tools of the mind: The Vygotskian approach to early childhood education* (2nd ed.). Upper Saddle River, NJ: Merrill/Prentice Hall.

Bogaert, A. F. (2005). Age at puberty and father absence in a national probability sample. *Journal of Adolescence, 28,* 541–546.

Bogartz, R. S., Shinskey, J. L., & Schilling, T. H. (2000). Object permanence in five-and-a-half-month-old infants. *Infancy, 1*, 403–428.

Bogin, B. (2001). *The growth of humanity.* New York: Wiley-Liss.

Bohannon, J. N., & Bonvillian, J. D. (2009). Theoretical approaches to language acquisition. In J. B. Gleason & B. Ratner (Ed.), *The development of language* (7th ed., pp. 227–284). Boston: Allyn and Bacon.

Bohannon, J. N., III, & Stanowicz, L. (1988). The issue of negative evidence: Adult responses to children's language errors. *Developmental Psychology, 24*, 684–689.

Bolen, R. M. (2001). *Child sexual abuse.* New York: Kluwer Academic.

Bolisetty, S., Bajuk, B., Me, A.-L., Vincent, T., Sutton, L., & Lui, K. (2006). Preterm outcome table (POT): A simple tool to aid counselling parents of very preterm infants. *Australian and New Zealand Journal of Obstetrics and Gynaecology, 46*, 189–192.

Bonilla, S., Kehl, S., Kwong, K. Y., Morphew, T., Kachru, R., & Jones, C. A. (2005). School absenteeism in children with asthma in a Los Angeles inner-city school. *Journal of Pediatrics, 147*, 802–806.

Bonnel, S., Mohand-Said, S., & Sahel, J.-A. (2003). The aging of the retina. *Experimental Gerontology, 38*, 825–831.

Bonnick, S. L. (2008). Osteoporosis in men and women. *Management of Osteoporosis, 8*, 28–36.

Bono, M. A., & Stifter, C. A. (2003). Maternal attention-directing strategies and infant focused attention during problem solving. *Infancy, 4*, 235–250.

Borduin, C. M. (2007). Multisystemic treatment of violent youth and their families. In T. A. Cavell & K. T. Malcolm (Eds.), *Anger, aggression and interventions for interpersonal violence* (pp. 239–265). Mahwah, NJ: Erlbaum.

Borer, K. T. (2005). Physical activity in the prevention and amelioration of osteoporosis in women: Interaction of mechanical, hormonal and dietary factors. *Sports Medicine, 35*, 779–830.

Bornstein, M. H. (1989). Sensitive periods in development: Structural characteristics and causal interpretations. *Psychological Bulletin, 105*, 179–197.

Bornstein, M. H. (2006). Parenting science and practice. In K. Renninger & I. E. Sigel (Eds.), *Handbook of child psychology: Vol. 4. Child psychology in practice* (6th ed., pp. 893–949). Hoboken, NJ: Wiley.

Bornstein, M. H., & Arterberry, M. E. (1999). Perceptual development. In M. H. Bornstein & M. E. Lamb (Eds.), *Developmental psychology: An advanced textbook* (pp. 231–274). Mahwah, NJ: Erlbaum.

Bornstein, M. H., & Arterberry, M. E. (2003). Recognition, discrimination, and categorization of smiling by 5-month-old infants. *Developmental Science, 6*, 585–599.

Bornstein, M. H., Vibbert, M., Tal, J., & O'Donnell, K. (1992). Toddler language and play in the second year: Stability, covariation, and influences of parenting. *First Language, 12*, 323–338.

Boroughs, D. S. (2004). Female sexual abusers of children. *Children and Youth Services Review, 26*, 481–487.

Borst, C. G. (1995). *Catching babies: The professionalization of childbirth, 1870–1920.* Cambridge, MA: Harvard University Press.

Bortfeld, H., Leon, S., Bloom, J., Schober, M., & Brennan, S. (2001). Disfluency rates in conversation: Effects of age, relationship, topic, role, and gender. *Language and Speech, 44*, 123–147.

Bos, H. M. W., van Balen, F., & van den Boom, D. C. (2007). Child adjustment and parenting in planned lesbian-parent families. *American Journal of Orthopsychiatry, 77*, 38–48.

Bosacki, S. L., & Moore, C. (2004). Preschoolers' understanding of simple and complex emotions: Links with gender and language. *Sex Roles, 50*, 659–675.

Bosch, L., & Sebastian-Galles, N. (2001). Evidence of early language discrimination abilities in infants from bilingual environments. *Infancy, 2*, 29–49.

Bost, K. K., Shin, N., McBride, B. A., Brown, G. L., Vaughn, B. E., & Coppola, G. (2006). Maternal secure base scripts, children's attachment security, and mother–child narrative styles. *Attachment and Human Development, 8*, 241–260.

Boswell, G. H., Kahana, E., & Dilworth-Anderson, P. (2006). Spirituality and healthy lifestyle behaviors: Stress counter-balancing effects on the well-being of older adults. *Journal of Religion and Health, 45*, 587–602.

Botkin, D. R., Weeks, M. O., & Morris, J. E. (2000). Changing marriage role expectations: 1961–1996. *Sex Roles, 42*, 933–942.

Botton, J., Heude, B., Maccario, J., Ducimetiére, P., & Charles, M. A. (2008). Postnatal weight and height growth velocities at different ages between birth and 5y and body composition in adolescent boys and girls. *American Journal of Clinical Nutrition, 87*, 1760–1768.

Bouchard, T. J. (2004). Genetic influence on human psychological traits: A survey. *Current Directions in Psychological Science, 13*, 148–151.

Bouchard, T. J., & Loehlin, J. C. (2001). Genes, evolution, and personality. *Behavior Genetics, 31*, 243–274.

Boulton, M. J. (1999). Concurrent and longitudinal relations between children's playground behavior and social preference, victimization, and bullying. *Child Development, 70*, 944–954.

Bowen, N. K., Bowen, G. L., & Ware, W. B. (2002). Neighborhood social disorganization, families, and the educational behavior of adolescents. *Journal of Adolescent Research, 17*, 468–490.

Bowlby, J. (1969). *Attachment and loss: Vol. 1. Attachment.* New York: Basic Books.

Bowlby, J. (1980). *Attachment and loss: Vol. 3. Loss: Sadness and depression.* New York: Basic Books.

Bowman, S. A., Gortmaker, S. L., Ebbeling, C. B., Pereira, M. A., & Ludwig, D. S. (2004). Effects of fast-food consumption on energy intake and diet quality among children in a national household survey. *Pediatrics, 113*, 112–113.

Boyce, W., Doherty-Poirier, M., MacKinnon, D., Fortin, C., Saab, H., King, M., & Gallupe, O. (2006). Sexual health of Canadian youth: Findings from the Canadian Youth, Sexual Health and HIV/AIDS Study. *Canadian Journal of Human Sexuality, 15*, 59–68.

Boyer, K., & Diamond, A. (1992). Development of memory for temporal order in infants and young children. In A. Diamond (Ed.), *Development and neural bases of higher cognitive function* (pp. 267–317). New York: New York Academy of Sciences.

Boyer, T. W. (2006). The development of risk-taking: A multi-perspective review. *Developmental Review, 26*, 291–345.

Boyes, M. C., & Chandler, M. (1992). Cognitive development, epistemic doubt, and identity formation in adolescence. *Journal of Youth and Adolescence, 21*, 277–304.

Boysson-Bardies, B. de, & Vihman, M. M. (1991). Adaptation to language: Evidence from babbling and first words in four languages. *Language, 67*, 297–319.

Brabyn, J., Schneck, M., Haegerstrom-Portnoy, G., & Lott, L. (2001). The Smith-Kettlewell Institute (SKI) longitudinal study of vision function and its impact among the elderly: An overview. *Optometry and Vision Science, 78*, 264–269.

Bracci, R., Perrone, S., & Buonocore, G. (2006). The timing of neonatal brain damage. *Biology of the Neonate, 90*, 145–155.

Bracken, B. A. (2000). Maximizing construct relevant assessment: The optimal preschool testing situation. In B. A. Bracken (Ed.), *The psychoeducational assessment of preschool children* (3rd ed., pp. 33–44). Upper Saddle River, NJ: Prentice-Hall.

Bradbury, T. N., Fincham, F. D., & Beach, S. R. H. (2000). Research on the nature and determinants of marital satisfaction: A decade in review. *Journal of Marriage and Family, 62*, 964–980.

Bradford, K., Barber, B. K., Olsen, J. A., Maughan, S. L., Erickson, L. D., Ward, D., & Stolz, H. E. (2003). A multi-national study of interparental conflict, parenting, and adolescent functioning: South Africa, Bangladesh, China, India, Bosnia, Germany, Palestine, Colombia, and the United States. *Marriage and Family Review, 35*, 107–137.

Bradley, R. H., & Caldwell, B. M. (1982). The consistency of the home environment and its relation to child development. *International Journal of Behavioral Development, 5*, 445–465.

Bradley, R. H., & Corwyn, R. F. (2003). Age and ethnic variations in family process mediators of SES. In M. H. Bornstein & R. H. Bradley (Eds.), *Socioeconomic status, parenting, and child development* (pp. 161–188). Mahwah, NJ: Erlbaum.

Bradley, R. H., Corwyn, R. F., McAdoo, H. P., & Garcia-Coll, C. (2001). The home environments of children in the United States. Part I: Variations by age, ethnicity, and poverty status. *Child Development, 72*, 1844–1867.

Bradley, R. H., Whiteside, L., Mundfrom, D. J., Casey, P. H., Kelleher, K. J., & Pope, S. K. (1994). Early indications of resilience and their relation to experiences in the home environments of low birthweight, premature children living in poverty. *Child Development, 65*, 346–360.

Bradshaw, R. A., & Burlingame, A. L. (2005). From proteins to proteomics. *IUBMB Life, 57*, 267–272.

Braine, L. G., Schauble, L., Kugelmass, S., & Winter, A. (1993). Representation of depth by children: Spatial strategies and lateral biases. *Developmental Psychology, 29*, 466–479.

Brame, B., Nagin, D. S., & Tremblay, R. E. (2001). Developmental trajectories of physical aggression from school entry to late adolescence. *Journal of Child Psychology and Psychiatry, 42*, 503–512.

Branca, F., & Ferrari, M. (2002). Impact of micronutrient deficiencies on growth: The stunting syndrome. *Annals of Nutrition and Metabolism, 46*(Suppl. 1), 8–17.

Brand, J. E., Warren, J. R., Carayon, P., & Hoonakker, P. (2007). Do job characteristics mediate the relationship between SES and health? Evidence from sibling models. *Social Science Research, 36*, 222–253.

Branje, S. J. T., van Lieshout, C. F. M., van Aken, M. A. G., & Haselager, G. J. T. (2004). Perceived support in sibling relationships and adolescent adjustment. *Journal of Child Psychology and Psychiatry, 45*, 1385–1396.

Braswell, G. S., & Callanan, M. A. (2003). Learning to draw recognizable graphic representations during mother–child interactions. *Merrill-Palmer Quarterly, 49*, 471–494.

Bray, J. H. (1999). From marriage to remarriage and beyond: Findings from the Developmental Issues in Stepfamilies Research Project. In E. M. Hetherington (Ed.), *Coping with divorce, single parenting, and remarriage: A risk and resiliency perspective* (pp. 295–319). Mahwah, NJ: Erlbaum.

Bremner, A. J., & Mareschal, D. (2004). Reasoning . . . what reasoning? *Developmental Science, 7*, 419–421.

Brendgen, M., Markiewicz, D., Doyle, A. B., & Bukowski, W. M. (2001). The relations between friendship quality, ranked-friendship preference, and adolescents' behavior with their friends. *Merrill-Palmer Quarterly, 47*, 395–415.

Brennan, P. L., Schutte, K. K., & Moos, R. H. (2006). Long-term patterns and predictors of successful stressor resolution in later life. *International Journal of Stress Management, 13*, 253–272.

Brenner, E., & Salovey, P. (1997). Emotional regulation during childhood: Developmental, interpersonal, and individual considerations. In P. Salovey & D. Sluyter (Eds.), *Emotional literacy and emotional development* (pp. 168–192). New York: Basic Books.

Brenner, R. A., & Committee on Injury, Violence, and Poison Prevention. (2003). Prevention of drowning in infants, children, and adolescents. *Pediatrics, 112,* 440-445.

Brenner, R. A., Simons-Morton, B. G., Bhaskar, B., Revenis, M., Das, A., & Clemens, J. D. (2003). Infant–parent bed sharing in an inner-city population. *Archives of Pediatrics and Adolescent Medicine, 157,* 33–39.

Bretherton, I., Fritz, J., Zahn-Waxler, C., & Ridgeway, D. (1986). Learning to talk about emotions: A functionalist perspective. *Child Development, 57,* 529–548.

Bretherton, I., & Munholland, K. A. (1999). Internal working models in attachment relationships: A construct revisited. In J. Cassidy & P. R. Shaver (Eds.), *Handbook of attachment* (pp. 89–111). New York: Guilford.

Brewaeys, A., Ponjaert, I., Van Hall, E. V., & Golombok, S. (1997). Donor insemination: Child development and family functioning in lesbian mother families. *Human Reproduction, 12,* 1349–1359.

Bridge, J. A., Goldstein, T. R., & Brent, D. A. (2006). Adolescent suicide and suicidal behavior. *Journal of Child Psychology and Psychiatry, 47,* 372–394.

Briefel, R. R., Reidy, K., Karwe, V., & Devaney, B. (2004). Feeding Infants and Toddlers Study: Improvements needed in meeting infant feeding recommendations. *Journal of the American Dietetic Association, 104*(Suppl. 1), s31–s37.

Bright, J. E. H., Pryor, R. G. L., Wilkenfeld, S., & Earl, J. (2005). The role of social context and serendipitous events in career decision making. *International Journal for Educational and Vocational Guidance, 5,* 19–36.

Brim, O. G., Ryff, C. D., & Kessler, R. C. (2005). The MIDUS National Survey: An overview. In O. G. Brim, C. D. Ryff, & R. C. Kessler (Eds.), *How healthy are we? A national study of well-being at midlife* (pp. 1–34). Chicago: University of Chicago Press.

Broderick, P. C., & Korteland, C. (2004). A prospective study of rumination and depression in early adolescence. *Clinical Child Psychology and Psychiatry, 9,* 383–394.

Brody, G. H., & Flor, D. L. (1998). Maternal resources, parenting practices, and child competence in rural, single-parent African American families. *Child Development, 69,* 803–816.

Brody, G. H., Ge, X., Kim, S. Y., Murry, V. M., Simons, R. L., & Gibbons, F. X. (2003). Neighborhood disadvantage moderates associations of parenting and older sibling problem attitudes and behavior with conduct disorders in African American children. *Journal of Consulting and Clinical Psychology, 71,* 211–222.

Brody, G. H., & Murry, V. M. (2001). Sibling socialization of competence in rural, single-parent African American families. *Journal of Marriage and Family, 63,* 996–1008.

Brody, G. H., Stoneman, Z., & McCoy, J. K. (1994). Forecasting sibling relationships in early adolescence from child temperaments and family processes in middle childhood. *Child Development, 65,* 771–784.

Brody, J. E. (1992, November 11). PMS is a worldwide phenomenon. *The New York Times,* p. C14.

Brody, L. R. (1997). Gender and emotion: Beyond stereotypes. *Journal of Social Issues, 53,* 369–393.

Brody, L. R. (1999). *Gender, emotion, and the family.* Cambridge, MA: Harvard University Press.

Brodzinsky, D. M., & Pinderhughes, E. (2002). Parenting and child development in adoptive families. In M. H. Bornstein (Ed.), *Handbook of parenting: Vol. 1* (2nd ed., pp. 279–311). Mahwah, NJ: Erlbaum.

Broidy, L. M., Nagin, D. S., Tremblay, R. E., Bates, J. E., Brame, B., Dodge, K. A., Fergusson, D., Horwood, J. L., Loeber, R., Laird, R., Lynam, D. R., Moffitt, T. E., Pettit, G. S., & Vitaro, F. (2003). Developmental trajectories of childhood disruptive behaviors and adolescent delinquency: A six-site, cross-national study. *Developmental Psychology, 39,* 222–245.

Bronfenbrenner, U., & Morris, P. A. (2006). The bio-ecological model of human development. In R. M. Lerner (Ed.), *Handbook of child psychology: Vol. 1. Theoretical models of human development* (6th ed., pp. 297–342). Hoboken, NJ: Wiley.

Bronson, G. W. (1994). Infants' transitions toward adult-like scanning. *Child Development, 65,* 1243–1261.

Bronstein, P. (2006). The family environment: Where gender role socialization begins. In J. Worell & C. D. Goodheart (Eds.), *Handbook of girls' and women's psychological health: Gender and well-being across the lifespan* (pp. 262–271). New York: Oxford University Press.

Bronte-Tinkew, J., Moore, K. A., & Carrano, J. (2006). The father–child relationship, parenting styles, and adolescent risk behaviors in intact families. *Journal of Family Issues, 27,* 850–881.

Brooks, C. (2000). Civil rights, liberalism, and the suppression of a Republican political realignment in the United States, 1972 to 1996. *American Sociological Review, 65,* 483–505.

Brooks, P. J., Hanauere, J. B., Padowska, B., & Rosman, H. (2003). The role of selective attention in preschoolers' rule use in a novel dimensional card sort. *Cognitive Development, 18,* 195–215.

Brooks, R., & Meltzoff, A. N. (2005). The development of gaze following and its relation to language. *Developmental Science, 8,* 535–543.

Brooks-Gunn, J. (1988). Antecedents and consequences of variations in girls' maturational timing. *Journal of Adolescent Health Care, 9,* 365–373.

Brooks-Gunn, J. (2003). Do you believe in magic? What we can expect from early childhood intervention programs. *Social Policy Report of the Society for Research in Child Development, 17,* 3–14.

Brooks-Gunn, J. (2004). Intervention and policy as change agents for young children. In P. L. Chase-Lansdale, K. Kiernan, & R. J. Friedman (Eds.), *Human development across lives and generations: The potential for change* (pp. 293–340). New York: Cambridge University Press.

Brooks-Gunn, J., Han, W.-J., & Waldfogel, J. (2002). Maternal employment and child cognitive outcomes in the first three years of life: The NICHD study of early child care. *Child Development, 73,* 1052–1072.

Brooks-Gunn, J., Klebanov, P. K., Smith, J., Duncan, G. J., & Lee, K. (2003). The black–white test score gap in young children. Contributions of test and family characteristics. *Applied Developmental Science, 7,* 239–252.

Brooks-Gunn, J., Schley, S., & Hardy, J. (2002). Marriage and the baby carriage: Historical change and intergenerational continuity in early parenthood. In L. J. Crockett & R. K. Sibereisen (Eds.), *Negotiating adolescence in times of social change* (pp. 36–57). New York: Cambridge University Press.

Brown, A. M., & Miracle, J. A. (2003). Early binocular vision in human infants: Limitations on the generality of the Superposition Hypothesis. *Vision Research, 43,* 1563–1574.

Brown, A. S. (2006). Prenatal infection as a risk factor for schizophrenia. *Schizophrenia Bulletin, 32,* 200–202.

Brown, B. B. (2004). Adolescents' relationships with peers. In R. Lerner & L. Steinberg (Eds.), *Handbook of adolescent psychology* (2nd ed., pp. 363–394). Hoboken, NJ: Wiley.

Brown, C., & Lewis, M. J. (2003). Psychosocial development in the elderly: An investigation into Erikson's ninth stage. *Journal of Aging Studies, 17,* 415–426.

Brown, C. S., & Bigler, R. S. (2004). Children's perceptions of gender discrimination. *Developmental Psychology, 40,* 714–726.

Brown, L. H., & Rodin, P. A. (2004). Grandparent–grandchild relationships and the life course perspective. In J. Demick & C. Andreoletti (Eds.), *Handbook of adult development* (pp. 459–474). New York: Springer.

Brown, R. W. (1973). *A first language: The early stages.* Cambridge, MA: Harvard University Press.

Brown, S. A., & Ramo, D. E. (2005). Clinical course of youth following treatment for alcohol and drug problems. In H. A. Liddle & C. L. Rowe (Eds.), *Adolescent substance abuse: Research and clinical advances* (pp. 79–103). Cambridge, UK: Cambridge University Press.

Brown, S. L., Lee, G. R., & Bulanda, J. R. (2006). Cohabitation among older adults: A national portrait. *Journal of Gerontology, 61B,* S71–S79.

Brown, T. E. (2005). *Attention deficit disorder: The unfocused mind in children and adults.* New Haven, CT: Yale University Press.

Browne, C. A., & Woolley, J. D. (2004). Preschoolers' magical explanations for violations of physical, social, and mental laws. *Journal of Cognition and Development, 5,* 239–260.

Bruer, J. T. (1999), *The myth of the first three years.* New York: Free Press.

Brugman, G. M. (2006). Wisdom and aging. In J. E. Birren & K. W. Schaie (Eds.), *Handbook of the psychology of aging* (6th ed., pp. 445–476). Burlington, MA: Elsevier Academic Press.

Brun, A., & Andersson, J. (2001). Frontal dysfunction and frontal cortical synapse loss in alcoholism: The main cause of alcohol dementia? *Dementia and Geriatric Cognitive Disorders, 12,* 289–294.

Bruner, E. J., Rees, K., Burke, M., & Thorogood, M. (2007). Dietary advice for reducing cardiovascular risk. *Cochrane Database of Systematic Reviews, Issue 4,* Art. No.: CD0021278.

Brussoni, M. J., and Boon, S. D. (1998). Grandparental impact in young adults' relationships with their closest grandparents: The role of relationship strength and emotional closeness. *International Journal of Aging and Human Development, 45,* 267–286.

Bruzzese, J.-M., & Fisher, C. B. (2003). Assessing and enhancing the research consent capacity of children and youth. *Applied Developmental Science, 7,* 13–26.

Bryant, B. K., Zvonkovic, A. M., & Reynolds, P. (2006). Parenting in relation to child and adolescent vocational development. *Journal of Vocational Behavior, 69,* 149–175.

Bryant, P., & Nunes, T. (2002). Children's understanding of mathematics. In U. Goswami (Ed.), *Blackwell handbook of childhood cognitive development* (pp. 412–439). Malden, MA: Blackwell.

Buchanan, C. M., Eccles, J. S., & Becker, J. B. (1992). Are adolescents the victims of raging hormones? Evidence for activational effects of hormones on moods and behavior at adolescence. *Psychological Bulletin, 111,* 62–107.

Buchanan, C. M., Maccoby, E. E., & Dornbusch, S. M. (1996). *Adolescents after divorce.* Cambridge, MA: Harvard University Press.

Buchanan-Barrow, E., & Barrett, M. (1998). Children's rule discrimination within the context of the school. *British Journal of Developmental Psychology, 16,* 539–551.

Buescher, E. S. (2001). Anti-inflammatory characteristics of human milk: How, where, why. *Advances in Experimental Medicine and Biology, 501,* 207–222.

Bugental, D. B., Ellerson, P. C., Lin, E. K., Rainey, B., & Kokotovic, A. (2002). A cognitive approach to child abuse prevention. *Journal of Family Psychology, 16,* 243–258.

Bugental, D. B., & Grusec, J. E. (2006). Socialization processes. In N. Eisenberg (Ed.), *Handbook of child psychology: Vol. 3. Social, emotional, and personality development* (6th ed., pp. 366–428). Hoboken, NJ: Wiley.

Bugental, D. B., & Happaney, K. (2004). Predicting infant maltreatment in low-income families: The interactive effects of maternal attributions and child status at birth. *Developmental Psychology, 40,* 234–243.

Buhl, H. M., & Lanz, M. (2007). Emerging adulthood in Europe: Common traits and variability across five European countries. *Journal of Adolescent Research, 22,* 439–443.

Buhrmester, D. (1996). Need fulfillment, interpersonal competence, and the developmental contexts of early adolescent friendship. In W. M. Bukowski, A. F. Newcomb, & W. W. Hartup (Eds.), *The company they keep: Friendship during childhood and adolescence* (pp. 158–185). New York: Cambridge University Press.

Buhrmester, D., & Furman, W. (1990). Perceptions of sibling relationships during middle childhood and adolescence. *Child Development, 61,* 1387–1398.

Buhs, E. S., & Ladd, G. W. (2001). Peer rejection as antecedent of young children's school adjustment: An examination of mediating processes. *Developmental Psychology, 37,* 550–560.

Bukowski, W. M. (2001). Friendship and the worlds of childhood. In D. W. Nangle & C. A. Erdley (Eds.), *The role of friendship in psychological adjustment* (pp. 93–105). San Francisco: Jossey-Bass.

Bumpass, L. L. (2004). Social change and the American family. *Annals of the New York Academy of Sciences, 1038,* 213–219.

Bumpus, M. F., Crouter, A. C., & McHale, S. M. (2006). Linkages between negative work-to-family spillover and mothers' and fathers' knowledge of their young adolescents' daily lives. *Journal of Early Adolescence, 26,* 36–59.

Bunting, L., & McAuley, C. (2004). Teenage pregnancy and parenthood: The role of fathers. *Child and Family Social Work, 9,* 295–303.

Burden, M. J., Jacobson, S. W., & Jacobson, J. L. (2005). Relation of prenatal alcohol exposure to cognitive processing speed and efficiency in childhood. *Alcoholism: Clinical and Experimental Research, 29,* 1473–1483.

Burgess, C., O'Donohoe, A., & Gill, M. (2000). Agony and ecstasy: A review of MDMA effects and toxicity. *European Psychiatry, 15,* 287–294.

Burgess, E. O. (2004). Sexuality in midlife and later life couples. In J. Harvey, A. Wenzel, & S. Sprecher (Eds.), *Handbook of sexuality in close relationships* (pp. 437–454). Mahwah, NJ: Erlbaum.

Burke, D. M., & Shafto, M. A. (2004). Aging and language production. *Current Directions in Psychological Science, 13,* 21–24.

Burts, D. C., Hart, C. H., Charlesworth, R., Fleege, P. O., Mosely, J., & Thomasson, R. H. (1992). Observed activities and stress behaviors of children in developmentally appropriate and inappropriate kindergarten classrooms. *Early Childhood Research Quarterly, 7,* 297–318.

Bushman, B. J., & Huesmann, L. R. (2001). Effects of televised violence on aggression. In D. G. Singer & J. L. Singer (Eds.), *Handbook of children and the media* (pp. 223–254). Thousand Oaks, CA: Sage.

Bushnell, E. W., & Boudreau, J. P. (1993). Motor development and the mind: The potential role of motor abilities as a determinant of aspects of perceptual development. *Child Development, 64,* 1005–1021.

Buss, D. M. (2008). *Evolutionary psychology: The new science of the mind* (3rd ed.). Boston: Allyn and Bacon.

Buss, D. M., Shackelford, T. K., Kirkpatrick, L. A., & Larsen, R. J. (2001). A half century of mate preferences: The cultural evolution of values. *Journal of Marriage and Family, 63,* 491–503.

Bussey, K. (1999). Children's categorization and evaluation of different types of lies and truths. *Child Development, 70,* 1338–1347.

Buswell, S. D., & Spatz, D. L. (2007). Parent–infant co-sleeping and its relationship to breastfeeding. *Journal of Pediatric Health Care, 21,* 22–28.

Butler, M., & Meaney, J. (Eds.). (2005). *Genetics of developmental disabilities.* Boca Raton, FL: Taylor & Francis.

Butler, R. (1998). Age trends in the use of social and temporal comparison for self-evaluation: Examination of a novel developmental hypothesis. *Child Development, 69,* 1054–1073.

Butler, R. N. (1968). The life review: An interpretation of reminiscence in the aged. In B. Neugarten (Ed.), *Middle age and aging* (pp. 486–496). Chicago: University of Chicago Press.

Buunk, B. P. (2002). Age and gender differences in mate selection criteria for various involvement levels. *Personal Relationships, 9,* 271–278.

Byard, R. W., & Krous, H. F. (2003). Sudden infant death syndrome: Overview and update. *Perspectives on Pediatric Pathology, 6,* 112–127.

Byars, A. M., & Hackett, G. (1998). Applications of social cognitive theory to the career development of women of color. *Applied and Preventive Psychology, 7,* 255–267.

Bybee, J. A., & Wells, Y. V. (2003). The development of possible selves during adulthood. In J. Demick & C. Andreoletti (Eds.), *Handbook of adult development* (pp. 257–270). New York: Springer.

Bynner, J. (2005). Rethinking the youth phase of the life course: The case for emerging adulthood? *Journal of Youth Studies, 8,* 367–384.

Byrnes, J. P. (2003). Cognitive development during adolescence. In G. R. Adams & M. D. Berzonsky (Eds.), *Blackwell handbook of adolescence* (pp. 227–246). Malden, MA: Blackwell.

C

Cabrera, N. J., & Garcia-Coll, C. (2004). Latino fathers: Uncharted territory in need of much exploration. In M. E. Lamb (Ed.), *The role of the father in child development* (4th ed., pp. 98–120). Hoboken, NJ: Wiley.

Cahill, K. E., Giandrea, M. D., & Quinn, J. F. (2006). Retirement patterns from career employment. *Gerontologist, 46,* 514–523.

Cain, K. M., & Dweck, C. S. (1995). The relation between motivational patterns and achievement cognitions through the elementary school years. *Merrill-Palmer Quarterly, 41,* 25–52.

Caine, N. (1986). Behavior during puberty and adolescence. In G. Mitchell & J. Erwin (Eds.), *Comparative primate biology: Vol. 2A. Behavior, conservation, and ecology* (pp. 327–361). New York: Liss.

Cairns, R. B., & Cairns, B. D. (2006). The making of developmental psychology. In R. M. Lerner (Ed.), *Handbook of child psychology: Vol. 1. Theoretical models of human development* (6th ed., pp. 89–165). Hoboken, NJ: Wiley.

Caldera, Y. M., & Lindsey, E. W. (2006). Coparenting, mother–infant interaction, and infant–parent attachment relationships in two-parent families. *Journal of Family Psychology, 20,* 275–283.

Caldwell, B. M., & Bradley, R. H. (1994). Environmental issues in developmental follow-up research. In S. L. Friedman & H. C. Haywood (Eds.), *Developmental follow-up* (pp. 235–256). San Diego: Academic Press.

Calkins, S. D. (2002). Does aversive behavior during toddlerhood matter? The effects of difficult temperament on maternal perceptions and behavior. *Infant Mental Health Journal, 23,* 381–402.

Callaghan, T., Rochat, P., Lillard, A., Claux, M. L., Odden, H., Itakura, S., Tapanya, S., & Singh, S. (2005). Synchrony in the onset of mental-state reasoning: Evidence from five cultures. *Psychological Science, 16,* 378–384.

Cameron, C. A., & Lee, K. (1997). The development of children's telephone communication. *Journal of Applied Developmental Psychology, 18,* 55–70.

Cameron-Faulkner, T., Lieven, E., & Tomasello, M. (2003). A construction based analysis of child-directed speech. *Cognitive Science, 27,* 843–873.

Campa, M. J., & Eckenrode, J. J. (2006). Pathways to intergenerational adolescent childbearing in a high-risk sample. *Journal of Marriage and Family, 68,* 558–572.

Campbell, A., Shirley, L., & Candy, J. (2004). A longitudinal study of gender-related cognition and behaviour. *Developmental Science, 7,* 1–9.

Campbell, F. A., Pungello, E. P., Miller-Johnson, S., Burchinal, M., & Ramey, C. T. (2001). The development of cognitive and academic abilities: Growth curves from an early childhood educational experiment. *Developmental Psychology, 37,* 231–242.

Campbell, F. A., Ramey, C. T., Pungello, E.P., Sparling, J., & Miller-Johnson, S. (2002). Early childhood education: Young adult outcomes from the Abecedarian Project. *Applied Developmental Science, 6,* 42–57.

Campbell, S. B., Brownell, C. A., Hungerford, A., Spieker, S. J., Mohan, R., & Blessing, J. S. (2004). The course of maternal depressive symptoms and maternal sensitivity as predictors of attachment security at 36 months. *Development and Psychopathology, 16,* 231–252.

Campion, J. M., & Maricic, M. J. (2003). Osteoporosis in men. *American Family Physician, 67,* 1521–1526.

Campos, J. J., Anderson, D. I., Barbu-Roth, M. A., Hubbard, E. M., Hertenstein, J. J., & Witherington, D. (2000). Travel broadens the mind. *Infancy, 1,* 149–219.

Campos, J. J., Witherington, D., Anderson, D. I., Frankel, C. I., Uchiyama, I., & Barbu-Roth, M. (2008). Rediscovering development in infancy. *Child Development, 79,* 1625–1632.

Camras, L. A., Oster, H., Campos, J. J., & Bakeman, R. (2003). Emotional facial expressions in European-American, Japanese, and Chinese infants. *Annals of the New York Academy of Sciences, 1000,* 1–17.

Camras, L. A., Oster, H., Campos, J. J., Miyake, K., & Bradshaw, D. (1992). Japanese and American infants' responses to arm restraint. *Developmental Psychology, 28,* 578–583.

Canada Campaign 2000. (2007). *Oh Canada! Too many children in poverty for too long . . . 2006 report card on child poverty in Canada from Campaign 2000.* Retrieved from http://campaign2000.ca/rc/rc06/index.html

Canetto, S. S., & Sakinofsky, I. (1998). The gender paradox in suicide. *Suicide and Life-Threatening Behavior, 28,* 1–23.

Canobi, K. H. (2004). Individual differences in children's addition and subtraction knowledge. *Cognitive Development, 19,* 81–93.

Canobi, K. H., Reeve, R. A., & Pattison, P. E. (2003). The role of conceptual understanding in children's addition problem solving. *Developmental Psychology, 39,* 521–534.

Capaldi, D., DeGarmo, D., Patterson, G. R., & Forgatch, M. (2002). Contextual risk across the early life span and association with antisocial behavior. In J. B. Reid, G. R. Patterson, & J. Snyder (Eds.), *Antisocial behavior in children and adolescents* (pp. 123–145). Washington, DC: American Psychological Association.

Capirci, O., Contaldo, A., Caselli, M. C., & Volterra, V. (2005). From action to language through gesture. *Gesture, 5,* 155–177.

Caplan, M., Vespo, J., Pedersen, J., & Hay, D. F. (1991). Conflict and its resolution in small groups of one- and two-year-olds. *Child Development, 62,* 1513–1524.

Cappeliez, P., & O'Rourke, N. (2002). Personality traits and existential concerns as predictors of the functions of reminiscence in older adults. *Journal of Gerontology, 57B,* P116–P123.

Carbery, J., & Buhrmester, D. (1998). Friendship and need fulfillment during three phases of young adulthood. *Journal of Social and Personal Relationships, 15,* 393–409.

Card, N. A., Stucky, B. D., Sawalani, G. M., & Little, T. D. (2008). Direct and indirect aggression during childhood and adolescence: A meta-analytic review of gender differences, intercorrelations, and relations to maladjustment. *Child Development, 79,* 1185–1229.

CARE Study Group. (2008). Maternal caffeine intake during pregnancy and risk of fetal growth restriction: A large prospective observational study. *British Medical Journal, 337,* a2337.

Carey, S. (1999). Sources of conceptual change. In E. K. Scholnick, K. Nelson, S. A. Gelman, & P. H. Miller (Eds.), *Conceptual development: Piaget's legacy* (pp. 293–326). Mahwah, NJ: Erlbaum.

Carey, S., & Markman, E. M. (1999). Cognitive development. In B. M. Bly & D. E. Rumelhart (Eds.), *Cognitive science* (pp. 201–254). San Diego: Academic Press.

Carli, L. L., & Eagly, A. H. (2000). Gender effects on influence and emergent leadership. In G. N. Powell (Ed.), *Handbook of gender in organizations* (pp. 203–222). Newbury Park, CA: Sage.

Carlo, G., Koller, S. H., Eisenberg, N., Da Silva, M., & Frohlich, C. (1996). A cross-national study on the relations among prosocial moral reasoning, gender role orientations, and prosocial behaviors. *Developmental Psychology, 32,* 231–240.

Carlson, C., Uppal, S., & Prosser, E. (2000). Ethnic differences in processes contributing to the self-esteem of early adolescent girls. *Journal of Early Adolescence, 20,* 44–67.

Carlson, M., & Earls, F. (1997). Psychological and neuroendocrinological sequelae of early social deprivation in institutionalized children in Romania. *Annals of the New York Academy of Sciences, 807,* 419–428.

Carlson, S. M., Moses, L. J., & Claxton, S. J. (2004). Individual differences in executive functioning and theory of mind: An investigation of inhibitory control and planning ability. *Journal of Experimental Child Psychology, 87,* 299–319.

Carlson, V. J., & Harwood, R. L. (2003). Attachment, culture, and the caregiving system: The cultural patterning of everyday experiences among Anglo and Puerto Rican mother–infant pairs. *Infant Mental Health Journal, 24,* 53–73.

Carmichael, S. L., & Shaw, G. M. (2000). Maternal life stress and congenital abnormalities. *Epidemiology, 11,* 30–35.

Carnelley, K. B., Wortman, C. B., Bolger, N., & Burke, C. T. (2006). The time course of grief reactions to spousal loss: Evidence from a national probability sample. *Journal of Personality and Social Psychology, 91,* 476–492.

Carpendale, J. I. M. (2000). Kohlberg and Piaget on stages and moral reasoning. *Developmental Review, 20,* 181–205.

Carpenter, M., Akhtar, N., & Tomasello, M. (1998). Fourteen- through eighteen-month-old infants differentially imitate intentional and accidental actions. *Infant Behavior and Development, 21,* 315–330.

Carpenter, M., Nagell, K., & Tomasello, M. (1998). Social cognition, joint attention, and communicative competence. *Monographs of the Society for Research in Child Development, 63*(4, Serial No. 255).

Carr, D. (2003). A "good death" for whom? Quality of spouse's death and psychological distress among older widowed persons. *Journal of Health and Social Behavior, 44,* 215–232.

Carr, D. (2004). Psychological well-being across three cohorts: A response to shifting work–family opportunities and expectations? In O. G. Brim, C. D. Ryff, & R. C. Kessler (Eds.), *How healthy are we? A national study of well-being at midlife* (pp. 452–484). Chicago: University of Chicago Press.

Carr, D., House, J. S., Wortman, C., Nesse, R., & Kessler, R. C. (2001). Psychological adjustment to sudden and anticipated spousal loss among older widowed persons. *Journal of Gerontology, 56B,* S237–S248.

Carroll, D., Phillips, A. C., Hunt, K., & Der, G. (2007). Symptoms of depression and cardiovascular reactions to acute psychological stress: Evidence from a population study. *Biological Psychology, 75,* 68–74.

Carroll, J. B. (2005). The three-stratum theory of cognitive abilities. In D. P. Flanagan & P. L. Harrison (Eds.), *Contemporary intellectual assessment: Theories, tests, and issues* (2nd ed., pp. 69–76). New York: Guilford.

Carskadon, M. A., Acebo, C., & Jenni, O. G. (2004). Regulation of adolescent sleep: Implications for behavior. In R. E. Dahl & L. P. Spear (Eds.), *Adolescent brain development: Vulnerabilities and opportunities* (pp. 276–291). New York: New York Academy of Sciences.

Carskadon, M. A., Harvey, K., Duke, P., Anders, T. F., Litt, I. F., & Dement, W. C. (2002). Pubertal changes in daytime sleepiness. *Sleep, 25,* 525–605.

Carstensen, L. L., Fung, H. H., & Charles, S. T. (2003). Socioemotional selectivity theory and the regulation of emotion in the second half of life. *Motivation and Emotion, 27,* 103–123.

Carstensen, L. L., Gottman, J. M., & Levenson, R. W. (1995). Emotional behavior in long-term marriage. *Psychology and Aging, 10,* 140–149.

Carstensen, L. L., Isaacowitz, D. M., & Charles, S. T. (1999). Taking time seriously: A theory of socio-emotional selectivity. *American Psychologist, 54,* 165–181.

Carter, B., & McGoldrick, M. (2005). *The expanded family life cycle: Individual, family, and social perspectives* (3rd ed.). Boston: Allyn and Bacon.

Carter, C. S., Hofer, T., Seo, A. Y., & Leeuwenburgh, C. (2007). Molecular mechanisms of life- and health-span extension: Role of calorie restriction and exercise intervention. *Applied Physiology, Nutrition, and Metabolism, 32,* 954–966.

Carver, K., Joyner, K., & Udry, J. R. (2003). National estimates of adolescent romantic relationships. In P. Florsheim (Ed.), *Adolescent romantic relations and sexual behavior: Theory, research, and practical implications* (pp. 23–56). Mahwah, NJ: Erlbaum.

Carver, P. R., Egan, S. K., & Perry, D. G. (2004). Children who question their heterosexuality. *Developmental Psychology, 40,* 43–53.

Casasola, M., Cohen, L. B., & Chiarello, E. (2003). Six-month-old infants' categorization of containment spatial relations. *Child Development, 74,* 679–693.

Casavant, M. J., Blake, K., Griffith, J., Yates, A., & Copley, L. M. (2007). Consequences of use of anabolic androgenic steroids. *Pediatric Clinics of North America, 54,* 677–690.

Case, R. (1996). Introduction: Reconceptualizing the nature of children's conceptual structures and their development in middle childhood. In R. Case & Y. Okamoto (Eds.), The role of central conceptual structures in the development of children's thought. *Monographs of the Society for Research in Child Development, 246*(61, Serial No. 246), pp. 1–26.

Case, R. (1998). The development of central conceptual structures. In D. Kuhn & R. Siegler (Eds.), *Handbook of child psychology: Vol. 2. Cognition, perception, and language* (5th ed., pp. 745–800). New York: Wiley.

Case, R., & Okamoto, Y. (Eds.). (1996). The role of central conceptual structures in the development of children's thought. *Monographs of the Society for Research in Child Development, 61*(1–2, Serial No. 246).

Caserta, M. S., & Gillett, P. A. (1998). Older women's feelings about exercise and their adherence to an aerobic regimen over time. *Gerontologist, 38,* 602–609.

Caserta, M. S., Lund, D. A., & Obray, S. J. (2004). Promoting self-care and daily living skills among older widows and widowers: Evidence from the Pathfinders Demonstration Project. *Omega, 49,* 217–236.

Casey, B. J., Getz, S., & Galvan, A. (2008). The adolescent brain. *Developmental Review, 28,* 62–77.

Casper, L. M., & Smith, K. E. (2002). Dispelling the myths: Self-care, class, and race. *Journal of Family Issues, 23,* 716–727.

Caspi, A., Elder, G. H., Jr., & Bem, D. J. (1987). Moving against the world: Life-course patterns of explosive children. *Developmental Psychology, 23,* 308–313.

Caspi, A., Elder, G. H., Jr., & Bem, D. J. (1988). Moving away from the world: Life-course patterns of shy children. *Developmental Psychology, 24,* 824–831.

Caspi, A., Harrington, H., Milne, B., Amell, J. W., Theodore, R. F., & Moffitt, T. E. (2003). Children's behavioral styles at age 3 are linked to their adult personality traits at age 26. *Journal of Personality, 71,* 495–513.

Caspi, A., Lynam, D., Moffitt, T. E., & Silva, P. A. (1993). Unraveling girls' delinquency: Biological, dispositional, and contextual contributions to adolescent misbehavior. *Developmental Psychology, 29,* 19–30.

Caspi, A., Moffitt, T. E., Morgan, J., Rutter, M., Taylor, A., Kim-Cohen, J., & Polo-Tomas, M. (2004). Maternal expressed emotion predicts children's antisocial behavior problems: Using monozygotic-twin differences to identify environmental effects on behavioral development. *Developmental Psychology, 40,* 149–161.

Caspi, A., & Roberts, B. W. (2001). Personality development across the life course: The argument for change and continuity. *Psychological Inquiry, 12,* 49–66.

Caspi, A., & Shiner, R. L. (2006). Personality development. In N. Eisenberg (Ed.), *Handbook of child psychology: Vol. 3. Social, emotional, and personality development* (6th ed., pp. 300–365). Hoboken, NJ: Wiley.

Cassia, V. M., Turati, C., & Simion, F. (2004). Can a nonspecific bias toward top-heavy patterns explain newborns' face preference? *Psychological Science, 15,* 379–383.

Cassidy, J. (2001). Adult romantic attachments: A developmental perspective on individual differences. *Review of General Psychology, 4,* 111–131.

Cassidy, J., & Berlin, L. J. (1994). The insecure/ambivalent pattern of attachment: Theory and research. *Child Development, 65,* 971–991.

Castillo, E. M., & Comstock, R. D. (2007). Prevalence of use of performance-enhancing substances among United States adolescents. *Pediatric Clinics of North America, 54,* 663–675.

Caton, D., Corry, M. P., Frigoletto, F. D., Hokins, D. P., Liberman, E., & Mayberry, L. (2002). The nature and management of labor pain: Executive summary. *American Journal of Obstetrics and Gynecology, 186,* S1–S15.

Ceci, S. J. (1991). How much does schooling influence general intelligence and its cognitive components? A reassessment of the evidence. *Developmental Psychology, 27,* 703–722.

Ceci, S. J. (1999). Schooling and intelligence. In S. J. Ceci & W. M. Williams (Eds.), *The nature–nurture debate: The essential readings* (pp. 168–175). Oxford, UK: Blackwell.

Ceci, S. J., Rosenblum, T. B., & Kumpf, M. (1998). The shrinking gap between high- and low-scoring groups: Current trends and possible causes. In U. Neisser (Ed.), *The rising curve* (pp. 287–302). Washington, DC: American Psychological Association.

Ceci, S. J., & Williams, W. M. (1997). Schooling, intelligence, and income. *American Psychologist, 52,* 1051–1058.

Cecil, J. E., Watt, P., Murrie, I. S. L., Wrieden, W., Wallis, D. J., Hetherington, M. M., Bolton-Smith, C., & Palmer, C. N. A. (2005). Childhood obesity and socioeconomic status: A novel role for height growth limitation. *International Journal of Obesity, 29,* 1199–1203.

Center for Communication and Social Policy. (Ed.). (1998). *National Television Violence Study* (Vol. 2). Newbury Park, CA: Sage.

Center for Effective Discipline. (2005). *Worldwide bans on corporal punishment.* Retrieved from www.stophitting.com/disatschool/facts.php

Cerella, J. (1990). Aging and information processing rate. In J. E. Birren & K. W. Schaie (Eds.), *Handbook of the psychology of aging* (3rd ed.), (pp. 201–221). San Diego: Academic Press.

Cernoch, J. M., & Porter, R. H. (1985). Recognition of maternal axillary odors by infants. *Child Development 56*, 1593–1598.

Cevenini, E., Invidia, L., Lescai, F., Salvioli, S., Tieri, P., Castellani, G., & Franceschi, G. (2008). Human models of aging and longevity. *Expert Opinion on Biological Therapy, 8*, 1393–1405.

CFAH (Center for Advancement of Health). (2003). *Report on Phase 1 of the Grief Research Gaps, Needs and Actions Project.* Washington, DC: Author.

Chamberlain, P. (2003). Antisocial behavior and delinquency in girls. In P. Chamberlain (Ed.), *Treating chronic juvenile offenders* (pp. 109–127). Washington, DC: American Psychological Association.

Champion, T. B. (2003). *Understanding storytelling among African-American children: A journey from Africa to America.* Mahwah, NJ: Erlbaum.

Chan, L. K. S., & Moore, P. J. (2006). Development of attributional beliefs and strategic knowledge in years 5–9: A longitudinal analysis. *Educational Psychology, 26*, 161–185.

Chan, R. W., Raboy, B., & Patterson, C. J. (1998). Psychosocial adjustment among children conceived via donor insemination by lesbian and heterosexual mothers. *Child Development, 69*, 443–457.

Chandra, A., Martino, S. C., Collins, R. L., Elliott, M. N., Berry, S. H., Kanouse, D. E., & Miu, A. (2008). Does watching sex on television predict teen pregnancy? Findings from a national longitudinal survey of youth. *Pediatrics, 122*, 1047–1054.

Chandra, R. K. (2002a). Influence of multinutrient supplement on immune response and infection-related illness in 50–65 year old individuals. *Nursing Research, 22*, 5–11.

Chandra, R. K. (2002b). Nutrition and the immune system from birth to old age. *European Journal of Clinical Nutrition, 56*(Suppl. 3), S73–S76.

Chang, L., Schwartz, D., Dodge, D. A., & McBride-Chang, C. (2003). Harsh parenting in relation to child emotion regulation and aggression. *Journal of Family Psychology, 17*, 598–606.

Channon, S., Mockler, C., & Lee, P. (2005). Executive functioning and speed of processing in phenylketonuria. *Neuropsychology, 19*, 679–686.

Chao, R. K. (1994). Beyond parental control and authoritarian parenting style: Understanding Chinese parenting through the cultural notion of training. *Child Development, 65*, 1111–1119.

Chao, R. K., & Good, G. E. (2004). Nontraditional students' perspectives on college education: A qualitative study. *Journal of College Counseling, 7*, 5–12.

Chao, R. K., & Tseng, V. (2002). Parenting of Asians. In M. H. Bornstein (Ed.), *Handbook of parenting: Vol 4* (2nd ed., pp. 59–94). Mahwah, NJ: Erlbaum.

Chappell, N., Gee, E., McDonald, L., & Stones, M. (2003). *Aging in contemporary Canada.* Toronto: Pearson Education Canada.

Charman, T., Baron-Cohen, S., Swettenham, J., Baird, G., Cox, A., & Drew, A. (2001). Testing joint attention, imitation, and play as infancy precursors to language and theory of mind. *Cognitive Development, 15*, 481–49.

Charman, W. N. (2008). The eye in focus: Accommodation and presbyopia. *Optometry, 91*, 207–225.

Charpak, N., Ruiz-Peláez, J. G., & Figueroa, Z. (2005). Influence of feeding patterns and other factors on early somatic growth of healthy, preterm infants in home-based kangaroo mother care: A cohort study. *Journal of Pediatric Gastroenterology and Nutrition, 41*, 430–437.

Chase-Lansdale, P. L., Gordon, R., Brooks-Gunn, J., & Klebanov, P. K. (1997). Neighborhood and family influences on the intellectual and behavioral competence of preschool and early school-age children. In J. Brooks-Gunn, G. Duncan, & J. L. Aber (Eds.), *Neighborhood poverty: Context and consequences for development* (pp. 79–118). New York: Russell Sage Foundation.

Chassin, L., Hussong, A., Barrera, M., Jr., Molina, B. S. G., Trim, R., & Ritter, J. (2004). Adolescent substance use. In R. M. Lerner & L. Steinberg (Eds.), *Handbook of adolescent psychology* (2nd ed., pp. 665–696). Hoboken, NJ: Wiley.

Chauhan, G. S., Shastri, J., & Mohite, P. (2005). Development of gender constancy in preschoolers. *Psychological Studies, 50*, 62–71.

Chavajay, P., & Rogoff, B. (1999). Cultural variation in management of attention by children and their caregivers. *Developmental Psychology, 35*, 1079–1090.

Chavajay, P., & Rogoff, B. (2002). Schooling and traditional collaborative social organization of problem solving by Mayan mothers and children. *Developmental Psychology, 38*, 55–66.

Cheah, C. S. L., & Nelson, L. J. (2004). The role of acculturation in the emerging adulthood of aboriginal college students. *International Journal of Behavioral Development, 28*, 495–507.

Checkley, W., Epstein, L. D., Gilman, R. H., Cabrera, L., & Black, R. E. (2003). Effects of acute diarrhea on linear growth in Peruvian children. *American Journal of Epidemiology, 157*, 166–175.

Chen, J. J. (2005). Relation of academic support from parents, teachers, and peers to Hong Kong adolescents' academic achievement: The mediating role of academic engagement. *Genetic, Social, and General Psychology Monographs, 131*, 77–127.

Chen, M. (2003). Wombs for rent: An examination of prohibitory and regulatory approaches to governing preconception arrangements. *Health Law in Canada, 23*, 33–50.

Chen, X., Wu, H., Chen, H., Wang, L., & Cen, G. (2001). Parenting practices and aggressive behavior in Chinese children. *Parenting: Science and Practice, 1*, 159–184.

Chen, Y.-C., Yu, M.-L., Rogan, W., Gladen, B., & Hsu, C.-C. (1994). A 6-year follow-up of behavior and activity disorders in the Taiwan Yu-cheng children. *American Journal of Public Health, 84*, 415–421.

Chen, Y.-J., & Hsu, C.-C. (1994). Effects of prenatal exposure to PCBs on the neurological function of children: A neuropsychological and neurophysiological study. *Developmental Medicine and Child Neurology, 36*, 312–320.

Cherlin, E. J., Barry, C. L., Prigerson, H. G., Schulman-Green, D., Johnson-Hurzeler, R., Kasl, S. V., & Bradley, E. H. (2007). Bereavement services for family caregivers: How often used, why, and why not. *Journal of Palliative Medicine, 10*, 148–158.

Chesney, M. A., Ekman, P., Friesen, W. V., Black, G. W., & Hecker, M. H. L. (1997). Type A behavior pattern: Facial behavior and speech components. In P. Ekman & E. L. Rosenberg (Eds.), *What the face reveals* (pp. 453–468). New York: Oxford University Press.

Chesney-Lind, M. (2001). Girls, violence, and delinquency: Popular myths and persistent problems. In S. O. White (Ed.), *Handbook of youth and justice* (pp. 135–158). New York: Kluwer Academic.

Chess, S., & Thomas, A. (1984). *Origins and evolution of behavior disorders.* New York: Brunner/Mazel.

Chhin, C. S., Bleeker, M. M., & Jacobs, J. E. (2008). Gender-typed occupational choices: The long-term impact of parents' beliefs and expectations. In H. M. G. Watt & J. S. Eccles (Eds.), *Gender and occupational outcomes: Longitudinal assessments of individual, social, and cultural influences* (pp. 215–234). Washington, DC: American Psychological Association.

Chi, M. T. H. (2006). Laboratory methods for assessing experts' and novices' knowledge. In K. A. Erics-

son, N. Charness, P. J. Feltovich, & R. R. Hoffman (Eds.), *The Cambridge handbook of expertise and expert performance* (pp. 167–184). New York: Cambridge University Press.

Chi, M. T. H., Glaser, R., & Farr, M. J. (Eds.). (1988). *The nature of expertise.* Hillsdale, NJ: Erlbaum.

Child Trends. (2008). *Facts at a glance.* Retrieved from www.childtrends.org/docdisp_page.cfm?LID=D6F165A5-00B3-4D76ABACFD97F248817C

Children's Defense Fund. (2008). *Annual report 2007.* Washington, DC: Author.

Children's Defense Fund. (2009). *State of America's children: 2000.* Washington, DC: Author.

Chinn, C. A., & Malhotra, B. A. (2002). Children's responses to anomalous scientific data: How is conceptual change impeded? *Journal of Educational Psychology, 94*, 327–343.

Chochinov, H. M. (2006). Dying, dignity, and new horizons in palliative end-of-life care. *CA: A Cancer Journal for Clinicians, 56*, 84–103.

Choi, J., Fauce, S. R., & Effros, R. B. (2008). Reduced telomerase activity in human T lymphocytes exposed to cortisol. *Brain, Behavior, and Immunity, 22*, 600–605.

Choi, S., & Gopnik, A. (1995). Early acquisition of verbs in Korean: A cross-linguistic study. *Journal of Child Language, 22*, 497–529.

Chomsky, C. (1969). *The acquisition of syntax in children from five to ten.* Cambridge, MA: MIT Press.

Chomsky, N. (1957). *Syntactic structures.* The Hague: Mouton.

Chomtho, S., Wells, J. C., Williams, J. E., Davies, P. S., Lucas, A., & Fewtrell, M. S. (2008). Infant growth and later body composition: Evidence from the 4-component model. *American Journal of Clinical Nutrition, 87*, 1776–1784.

Chouinard, M. M., & Clark, E. V. (2003). Adult reformulations of child errors as negative evidence. *Journal of Child Language, 30*, 637–669.

Christ, G. H., Siegel, K., & Christ, A. E. (2002). "It never really hit me . . . until it actually happened." *Journal of the American Medical Association, 288*, 1269–1278.

Christ, S. E., Steiner, R. D., Grange, D. K., Abrams, R. A., & White, D. A. (2006). Inhibitory control in children with phenylketonuria. *Developmental Neuropsychology, 30*, 845–864.

Christensen, A.-D., & Larsen, J. E. (2008). Gender, class, and family: Men and gender equality in a Danish context. *Social Politics: International Studies in Gender, State and Society, 15*, 53–78.

Christensen, K. A., Stephens, M. A. P., & Townsend, A. L. (1998). Mastery in women's multiple roles and well-being: Adult daughters providing care to impaired parents. *Health Psychology, 17*, 163–171.

Christenson, S. L., & Thurlow, M. L. (2004). School dropouts: Prevention considerations, interventions, and challenges. *Current Directions in Psychological Science, 13*, 36–39.

Chu, J., Zhou, C. C., Lu, N., Zhang, X., & Dong, F. T. (2008). Genetic variants in three genes and smoking show strong associations with susceptibility to exudative age-related macular degeneration in a Chinese population. *Chinese Medical Journal, 121*, 2525–2533.

Chudley, A. E., Conry, J., Cook, J. L., Loock, C., Rosales, T., & LeBlanc, N. (2005). Fetal alcohol spectrum disorder: Canadian guidelines for diagnosis. *Canadian Medical Association Journal, 172*, S1–S21.

Chumlea, W. C., Schubert, C. M., Roche, A. F., Kulin, H. E., Lee, P. A., Himes, J. H., & Sun, S. S. (2003). Age at menarche and racial comparisons in U.S. girls. *Pediatrics, 111*, 110–113.

Church, E. (2004). *Understanding stepmothers: Women share their struggles, successes, and insights.* Toronto: HarperCollins.

Cicchetti, D. (2007). Intervention and policy implications of research on neurobiological functioning in maltreated children. In J. L. Aber, S. J. Bishop-Josef, S. M. Jones, K. T. McLearn, & D. A. Phillips (Eds.),

Child development and social policy (pp. 167–184). Washington, DC: American Psychological Association.

Cicchetti, D., & Toth, S. L. (2006). Developmental psychopathology and preventive intervention. In K. A. Renninger & I. E. Sigel (Eds.), *Handbook of child psychology: Vol. 4. Child psychology in practice* (6th ed., pp. 497–547). Hoboken, NJ: Wiley.

Cicirelli, V. G. (1989). Feelings of attachment to siblings and well-being in later life. *Psychology and Aging, 4,* 211–216.

Cicirelli, V. G. (1995). *Sibling relationships across the life span.* New York: Plenum.

Cicirelli, V. G. (1999). Personality and demographic factors in older adults' fear of death. *Gerontologist, 39,* 569–579.

Cicirelli, V. G. (2001). Personal meanings of death in older adults and young adults in relation to their fears of death. *Death Studies, 25,* 663–683.

Cicirelli, V. G. (2002). *Older adults' views on death.* New York: Springer.

Cillessen, A. H. N., & Bellmore, A. D. (2004). Social skills and interpersonal perception in early and middle childhood. In P. K. Smith & C. H. Hart (Eds.), *Blackwell handbook of childhood social development* (pp. 355–374). Malden, MA: Blackwell.

Cillessen, A. H. N., & Mayeux, L. (2004). From censure to reinforcement: Developmental changes in the association between aggression and social status. *Child Development, 75,* 147–163.

Cinamon, R. G., & Rich, Y. (2002). Gender differences in the importance of work and family roles: Implications for work–family conflict. *Sex Roles, 47,* 531–541.

Clark, K. E., & Ladd, G. W. (2000). Connectedness and autonomy support in parent–child relationships: Links to children's socio-emotional orientation and peer relationships. *Developmental Psychology, 36,* 485–498.

Clarke-Stewart, K. A., Althusen, V., & Goosens, F. (2001). Day care and the Strange Situation. In A. Göncu & E. L. Klein (Eds.), *Children in play, story, and school* (pp. 241–266). New York: Guilford.

Clarke-Stewart, K. A., & Brentano, C. (2006). *Divorce: Causes and consequences.* New Haven: Yale University Press.

Clarke-Stewart, K. A., & Hayward, C. (1996). Advantages of father custody and contact for the psychological well-being of school-age children. *Journal of Applied Developmental Psychology, 17,* 239–270.

Clarkson, T. W., Magos, L., & Myers, G. J. (2003). The toxicology of mercury—current exposures and clinical manifestations. *New England Journal of Medicine, 349,* 1731–1737.

Clausen, J. A. (1975). The social meaning of differential physical and sexual maturation. In S. E. Dragastin & G. H. Elder (Eds.), *Adolescence in the life cycle: Psychological change and the social context* (pp. 25–47). New York: Halsted.

Clearfield, M. W., & Nelson, N. M. (2006). Sex differences in mothers' speech and play behavior with 6-, 9-, and 14-month-old infants. *Sex Roles, 54,* 127–137.

Clearfield, M. W., Obsborn, C. N., & Mullen, M. (2008). Learning by looking: Infants' social looking behavior across the transition from crawling to walking. *Journal of Experimental Child Psychology, 100,* 297–307.

Cleary, J. P., Walsh, D. M., Hofmeister, J. J., Shankar, G. M., Kuskowski, M. A., Selkoe, D. J., & Ashe, K. H. (2005). Natural oligomers of the amyloid-beta protein specifically disrupt cognitive function. *Nature Neuroscience, 8,* 79–84.

Clements, D. H., & Sarama, J. (2003). Young children and technology: What does the research say? *Young Children, 58*(6), 34–40.

Clements, D. H., & Sarama, J. (2008). Experimental evaluation of the effects of a research-based preschool mathematics curriculum. *American Educational Research Journal, 45,* 443–494.

Cleveland, E. S., & Reese, E. (2005). Maternal structure and autonomy support in conversations about the past: Contributions to children's autobiographical memory. *Developmental Psychology, 41,* 376–388.

Clinchy, B. M. (2002). Revisiting women's ways of knowing. In B. K. Hofer & P. R. Pintrich (Eds.), *Personal epistemology: The psychological beliefs about knowledge and knowing* (pp. 63–87). Mahwah, NJ: Erlbaum.

Clingempeel, W. G., & Henggeler, S. W. (2003). Aggressive juvenile offenders transitioning into emerging adulthood: Factors discriminating persistors and desistors. *American Journal of Orthopsychiatry, 73,* 310–323.

Coatsworth, J. D., Sharp, E. H., Palen, L., Darling, N., Cumsille, P., & Marta, M. (2005). Exploring adolescent self-defining leisure activities and identity experiences across three countries. *International Journal of Behavioral Development, 29,* 361–370.

Coe, C. L., & Laudenslager, M. L. (2007). Psychosocial influences on immunity, including effects on immune maturation and senescence. *Brain, Behavior, and Immunity, 21,* 1000–1008.

Cohan, C. L., & Kleinbaum, S. (2002). Toward a greater understanding of the cohabitation effect: Premarital cohabitation and marital communication. *Journal of Marriage and Family, 64,* 180–192.

Cohen, L. B. (2003). Commentary on Part I: Unresolved issues in infant categorization. In D. H. Rakison & L. M. Oakes (Eds.), *Early category and concept development: Making sense of the blooming, buzzing confusion* (pp. 193–209). New York: Oxford University Press.

Cohen, L. B., & Cashon, C. H. (2006). Infant cognition. In D. Kuhn & R. Siegler (Eds.), *Handbook of child psychology: Vol. 2. Cognition, perception, and language* (6th ed., pp. 214–251). Hoboken, NJ: Wiley.

Cohen, P., Kasen, S., Chen, H., Hartmark, C., & Gordon, K. (2003). Variations in patterns of developmental transitions in the emerging adulthood period. *Developmental Psychology, 39,* 657–669.

Cohen-Bendahan, C. C. C., van de Beek, C., & Berenbaum, S. A. (2005). Prenatal sex hormones effects on child and adult sex-typed behavior: Methods and findings. *Neuroscience and Biobehavioral Reviews, 29,* 353–384.

Cohen-Shalev, A. (1986). Artistic creativity across the adult life span: An alternative approach. *Interchange, 17*(4), 1–16.

Cohler, B. J., & Hostetler, A. J. (2007). Gay lives in the Third Age: Possibilities and paradoxes. In J. B. James & P. Wink (Eds.), *Annual review of gerontology and geriatrics* (Vol. 26, pp. 193–209). New York: Springer.

Coholl, A., Kassotis, J., Parks, R., Vaughan, R., Bannister, H., & Northridge, M. (2001). Adolescents in the age of AIDS: Myths, misconceptions, and misunderstandings regarding sexually transmitted diseases. *Journal of the National Medical Association, 93,* 64–69.

Coie, J. D., Dodge, K. A., & Coppotelli, H. (1982). Dimensions and types of social status: A cross-age perspective. *Developmental Psychology, 18,* 557–570.

Coke, M. M. (1992). Correlates of life satisfaction among elderly African Americans. *Journal of Gerontology, 47,* P316–P320.

Coker, A. D. (2003). African American female adult learners: Motivations, challenges, and coping strategies. *Journal of Black Studies, 33,* 654–674.

Col, N. F., Weber, G., Stiggelbout, A., Chuo, J., D'Agostino, R., & Corso, P. (2004). Short-term menopausal hormone therapy for symptom relief. *Archives of Internal Medicine, 164,* 1634–1640.

Colapinto, J. (2001). *As nature made him: The boy who was raised as a girl.* New York: Perennial.

Colby, A., Kohlberg, L., Gibbs, J., & Lieberman, M. (1983). A longitudinal study of moral judgment. *Monographs of the Society for Research in Child Development, 48*(1–2, Serial No. 200).

Colcombe, S. J., Erickson, K. I., Raz, N., Webb, A. G., Cohen, N. J., & McAuley, E. (2003). Aerobic fitness reduces brain tissue loss in aging humans. *Journal of Gerontology, 58,* M176–M180.

Colcombe, S. J., Erickson, K. I., Scalf, P. E., Kim, J. S., Prakash, R., & McAuley, E. (2006). Aerobic exercise training increases brain volume in aging humans. *Journal of Gerontology, 61A,* 1166–1170.

Colcombe, S. J., Kramer, A. F., Erickson, K. I., Scalf, P., McAuley, E., & Cohen, N. J. (2004). Cardiovascular fitness, cortical plasticity, and aging. *Proceedings of the National Academy of Sciences, 101,* 3316–3321.

Cole, D. A., Martin, J. M., Peeke, L. A., Seroczynski, A. D., & Fier, J. (1999). Children's over- and under-estimation of academic competence: A longitudinal study of gender differences, depression, and anxiety. *Child Development, 70,* 459–473.

Cole, D. A., Maxwell, S. E., Martin, J. M., Peeke, L. G., Seroczynski, A. D., & Tram, J. M. (2001). The development of multiple domains of child and adolescent self-concept: A cohort sequential longitudinal design. *Child Development, 72,* 1723–1746.

Cole, E. R., & Stewart, A. J. (1996). Meanings of political participation among black and white women: Political identity and social responsibility. *Journal of Personality and Social Psychology, 71,* 130–140.

Cole, M. (1990). Cognitive development and formal schooling: The evidence from cross-cultural research. In L. C. Moll (Ed.), *Vygotsky and education* (pp. 89–110). New York: Cambridge University Press.

Coleman, M., Ganong, L., & Fine, M. (2000). Reinvestigating remarriage: Another decade of progress. *Journal of Marriage and Family, 62,* 1288–1307.

Coleman, M., Ganong, L., & Leon, K. (2006). Divorce and postdivorce relationships. In A. L. Vangelisti & D. Perlman (Eds.), *The Cambridge handbook of personal relationships* (pp. 157–173). New York: Cambridge University Press.

Coleman, P. G., Ivani-Chalian, C., & Robinson, M. (2004). Religious attitudes among British older people: Stability and change in a 20-year longitudinal study. *Ageing and Society, 24,* 167–188.

Coles, L. (2004). Demography of human supercentenarians. *Journal of Gerontology, 59A,* 579–586.

Coley, R. L. (1998). Children's socialization experiences and functioning in single-mother households: The importance of fathers and other men. *Child Development, 69,* 219–230.

Coley, R. L., Morris, J. E., & Hernandez, D. (2004). Out-of-school care and problem behavior trajectories among low-income adolescents: Individual, family, and neighborhood characteristics as added risks. *Child Development, 75,* 948–965.

Collings, P. (2001). "If you got everything, it's good enough": Perspectives on successful aging in a Canadian Inuit community. *Journal of Cross-Cultural Gerontology, 16,* 127–155.

Collins, N. L., Guichard, A. C., Ford, M. B., & Feeney, B. C. (2006). Responding to need in intimate relationships: Normative processes and individual differences. In M. Mikulincer & G. S. Goodman (Eds.), *Dynamics of romantic love* (pp. 149–189). New York: Guilford.

Collins, W. A. (2003). More than myth: The developmental significance of romantic relationships during adolescence. *Journal of Research on Adolescence, 13,* 1–24.

Collins, W. A., & Laursen, B. (2004). Parent–adolescent relationships and influences. In R. M. Lerner & L. Steinberg (Eds.), *Handbook of adolescent psychology* (2nd ed., pp. 331–361). New York: Wiley.

Collins, W. A., & Madsen, S. D. (2006). Personal relationships in adolescence and early adulthood. In A. L. Vangelisti & D. Perlman (Eds.), *The Cambridge handbook of personal relationships* (pp. 191–209). New York: Cambridge University Press.

Collins, W. A., Madsen, S. D., & Susman-Stillman, A. (2002). Parenting during middle childhood. In M. H. Bornstein (Ed.), *Handbook of parenting: Vol. 1* (2nd ed., pp. 73–101). Mahwah, NJ: Erlbaum.

Collins, W. A., & Russell, G. (1991). Mother–child and father–child interactions in middle childhood and adolescence. *Developmental Review, 11,* 99–136.

Collins, W. A., & van Dulmen, M. (2006a). "The course of true love(s) . . .": Origins and pathways in the development of romantic relationships. In A. Booth & A. Crouter (Eds.), *Romance and sex in adolescence and emerging adulthood: Risks and opportunities* (pp. 63–86). Mahwah, NJ: Erlbaum.

Collins, W. A., & van Dulmen, M. (2006b). Friendships and romance in emerging adulthood: Assessing distinctiveness in close relationships. In J. J. Arnett & J. L. Tanner (Eds.), *Emerging adults in America: Coming of age in the 21st century* (pp. 219–234). Washington, DC: American Psychological Association.

Collins, W. K., & Steinberg, L. (2006). Adolescent development in interpersonal context. In N. Eisenberg (Ed.), *Handbook of child psychology: Vol. 3. Social, emotional, and personality development* (6th ed., pp. 1003–1067). Hoboken, NJ: Wiley.

Colman, L. L., & Colman, A. D. (1991). *Pregnancy: The psychological experience.* New York: Noonday Press.

Colman, R .J., Anderson, R. M., Johnson, S. C., Kastman, E. K., Kosmatka, K. J., & Beasley, T. M., et al. (2009). Caloric restriction delays disease onset and mortality in rhesus monkeys. *Science, 325,* 201–204.

Colombo, J. (1995). On the neural mechanism underlying developmental and individual differences in visual fixation in infancy. *Developmental Review, 15,* 97–135.

Colombo, J. (2002). Infant attention grows up: The emergence of a developmental cognitive neuroscience perspective. *Current Directions in Psychological Science, 11,* 196–199.

Coltrane, S. (1996). *Family man.* New York: Oxford University Press.

Comijs, H. C., Jonker, C., van Tilberg, W., and Smit, J. H. (1999). Hostility and coping capacity as risk factors of elder mistreatment. *Social Psychiatry and Psychiatric Epidemiology, 34,* 48–52.

Commission on Adolescent Suicide Prevention. (2005). Targeted youth suicide prevention programs. In D. L. Evans, E. B. Foa, R. E. Gur, H. Hending, & C. P. O'Brien (Eds.), *Treating and preventing adolescent mental health disorders: What we know and what we don't know* (pp. 463–469). New York: Oxford University Press.

Commission on Children at Risk. (2008). Hardwired to connect: The new scientific case for authoritative communities. In K. K. Kline (Ed.), *Authoritative communities: The scientific case for nurturing the whole child* (pp. 3–68). New York: Springer.

Comstock, G., & Scharrer, E. (2006). Media and popular culture. In K. A. Renninger & I. E. Sigel (Eds.), *Handbook of child psychology: Vol. 4. Child psychology in practice* (6th ed., pp. 817–863). Hoboken, NJ: Wiley.

Comunian, A. L., & Gielen, U. P. (2000). Sociomoral reflection and prosocial and antisocial behavior: Two Italian studies. *Psychological Reports, 87,* 161–175.

Comunian, A. L., & Gielen, U. P. (2006). Promotion of moral judgment maturity through stimulation of social role-taking and social reflection: An Italian intervention study. *Journal of Moral Education, 35,* 51–69.

Conboy, B. T., & Thal, D. J. (2006). Ties between the lexicon and grammar: Cross-sectional and longitudinal studies of bilingual toddlers. *Child Development, 77,* 712–735.

Conger, R. D., & Conger, K. J. (2002). Resilience in Midwestern families: Selected findings from the first decade of a prospective, longitudinal study. *Journal of Marriage and Family, 64,* 361–373.

Conger, R. D., & Donnellan, M. B. (2007). An interactionist perspective on the socioeconomic context of human development. *Annual Review of Psychology, 58,* 175–199.

Conger, R. D., Wallace, L., Sun, Y., Simons, L., McLoyd, V., & Brody, G. (2002). Economic pressure in African American families: A replication and extension of the family stress model. *Developmental Psychology, 38,* 179–193.

Connell, M. W., Sheridan, K., & Gardner, H. (2003). On abilities and domains. In R. J. Sternberg & E. Grigorenko (Eds.), *Perspectives on the psychology of abilities, competencies, and expertise* (pp. 126–155). New York: Cambridge University Press.

Conner, D. B., & Cross, D. R. (2003). Longitudinal analysis of the presence, efficacy, and stability of maternal scaffolding during informal problem-solving interactions. *British Journal of Developmental Psychology, 21,* 315–334.

Connidis, I. A. (1994). Sibling support in older age. *Journal of Gerontology, 49,* S309–S317.

Connidis, I. A., & Campbell, L. D. (1995). Closeness, confiding, and contact among siblings in middle and late adulthood. *Journal of Family Issues, 16,* 722–745.

Connolly, J., Craig, W., Goldberg, A., & Pepler, D. (2004). Mixed-gender groups, dating, and romantic relationships in early adolescence. *Journal of Research on Adolescence, 14,* 185–207.

Connolly, J., & Goldberg, A. (1999). Romantic relationships in adolescence: The role of friends and peers in their emergence and development. In W. Furman, B. B. Brown, & C. Feiring (Eds.), *The development of romantic relationships in adolescence* (pp. 266–290). New York: Cambridge University Press.

Connolly, J. A., & Doyle, A. B. (1984). Relations of social fantasy play to social competence in preschoolers. *Developmental Psychology, 20,* 797–806.

Connor, L. T., Spiro, A., Obler, L. K., & Albert, M. L. (2004). Change in object naming ability during adulthood. *Journal of Gerontology, 59B,* P203–P209.

Conti, S., Farchi, G., Masocco, M., Minelli, G., Toccaceli, V., & Vichi, M. (2003). Gender differentials in life expectancy in Italy. *European Journal of Epidemiology, 18,* 107–112.

Conway, L. (2007, April 5). Drop the Barbie: Ken Zucker's reparatist treatment of gender-variant children. *Trans News Updates.* Retrieved from ai.eecs.umich.edu/people/conway/TS/News/Drop%20the%20Barbie.htm

Conwell, Y., & Duberstein, P. R. (2001). Suicide in elders. *Annals of the New York Academy of Sciences, 932,* 132–150.

Conwell, Y., Duberstein, P. R., & Caine, E. D. (2002). Risk factors for suicide in later life. *Biological Psychiatry, 52,* 193–204.

Conyers, C., Miltenberger, R., Maki, A., Barenz, R., Jurgens, M., Sailer, A., Haugen, M., & Kopp, B. (2004). A comparison of response cost and differential reinforcement of other behaviors to reduce disruptive behavior in a preschool classroom. *Journal of Applied Behavior Analysis, 37,* 411–415.

Cook, W. L. (2000). Understanding attachment security in family context. *Journal of Personality and Social Psychology, 78,* 285–294.

Cooney, T. M., & Mortimer, J. T. (1999). Family structure differences in the timing of leaving home: Exploring mediating factors. *Journal of Research on Adolescence, 9,* 367–393.

Cooper, C., Harvey, N., Cole, Z., Hanson, M., & Dennison, E. (2009). Developmental origins of osteoporosis: The role of maternal nutrition. In B. Koletzko, T. Decsi, D. Molnár, & A. de la Hunty (Eds.), *Early nutrition programming and health outcomes in later life: Obesity and beyond* (pp. 31–39). New York: Springer Science + Business Media.

Cooper, C., Sayer, A. A., & Dennison, E. M. (2006). The developmental environment: Clinical perspectives on effects on the musculoskeletal system. In P. Gluckman & M. Hanson (Eds.), *Developmental origins of health and disease* (pp. 392–405). Cambridge, UK: Cambridge University Press.

Cooper, C., Selwood, A., & Livingston, G. (2008). The prevalence of elder abuse and neglect: A systematic review. *Age and Ageing, 37,* 151–160.

Cooper, Z., & Fairburn, C. G. (2002). Cognitive-behavioral treatment of obesity. In T. A. Wadden & A. J. Stunkard (Eds.), *Handbook of obesity treatment* (3rd ed., pp. 465–479). New York: Guilford.

Coplan, R. J., Prakash, K., O'Neil, K., & Armer, M. (2004). Do you "want" to play? Distinguishing between conflicted shyness and social disinterest in early childhood. *Developmental Psychology, 40,* 244–258.

Copple, C., & Bredekamp, S. (2009). *Developmentally appropriate practice in early childhood programs* (3rd ed.). Washington, DC: National Association for the Education of Young Children.

Cornish, A. M., McMahon, C. A., Ungerer, J. A., Barnett, B., Kowalenko, N., & Tennant, C. (2005). Postnatal depression and infant cognitive and motor development in the second postnatal year: The impact of depression chronicity and infant gender. *Infant Behavior and Development, 28,* 407–417.

Cornwell, A. C., & Feigenbaum, P. (2006). Sleep biological rhythms in normal infants and those at high risk for SIDS. *Chronobiology International, 23,* 935–961.

Corr, C. A. (1993). Coping with dying: Lessons that we should and should not learn from the work of Elisabeth Kübler-Ross. *Death Studies, 17,* 69–83.

Corr, C. A. (2003). Loss, grief, and trauma in public tragedy. In M. Lattanzi-Licht & K. J. Doka (Eds.), *Living with grief: Coping with public tragedy* (pp. 63–76). New York: Brunner-Routledge.

Corr, C. A., & Corr, D. M. (2007). Historical and contemporary perspectives on loss, grief, and mourning. In C. A. Corr & D. M. Corr (Eds.), *Handbook of thanatology* (pp. 131–142). New York: Routledge.

Correa-Chávez, M., Rogoff, B., & Mejía-Arauz, R. (2005). Cultural patterns in attending to two events at once. *Child Development, 76,* 664–678.

Cortese, D. A., & Smith, H. C. (2003). *Mayo Clinic family health book* (3rd ed.). New York: Harper-Collins.

Cosden, M., Peerson, S., & Elliott, K. (1997). Effects of prenatal drug exposure on birth outcomes and early child development. *Journal of Drug Issues, 27,* 525–539.

Costos, D., Ackerman, R., & Paradis, L. (2002). Recollections of menarche: Communication between mothers and daughters regarding menstruation. *Sex Roles, 46,* 49–59.

Côté, J. E. (2006). Emerging adulthood as an institutionalized moratorium: Risks and benefits to identity formation. In J. J. Arnett (Ed.), *Emerging adults in America: Coming of age in the 21st century* (pp. 85–116). Washington, DC: American Psychological Association.

Côté, S. M., Vaillancourt, T., Barker, E. D., Nagin, D., & Tremblay, R. E. (2007). The joint development of physical and indirect aggression: Predictors of continuity and change during childhood. *Development and Psychopathology, 19,* 37–55.

Coulton, C. J., Crampton, D. S., Irwin, M., Spilsbury, J. C., & Korbin, J. E. (2007). How neighborhoods influence child maltreatment: A review of the literature and alternative pathways. *Child Abuse and Neglect, 31,* 1117–1142.

Courage, M. L., & Howe, M. L. (1998). The ebb and flow of infant attentional preferences: Evidence for long-term recognition memory in 3-month-olds. *Journal of Experimental Child Psychology, 18,* 98–106.

Courchesne, E., Carper, R., & Akshoomoff, N. (2003). Evidence of brain overgrowth in the first year of life in autism. *Journal of the American Medical Association, 290,* 337–344.

Couturier, J. L., & Lock, J. (2006). Denial and minimization in adolescents with anorexia nervosa. *International Journal of Eating Disorders, 39,* 212–216.

Covington, C. Y., Nordstrom-Klee, B., Ager, J., Sokol, R., & Delaney-Black, V. (2002). Birth to age 7 growth of children prenatally exposed to drugs: A prospective cohort study. *Neurotoxicology and Teratology, 24,* 489–496.

Cowan, C. P., & Cowan, P. A. (2000). *When partners become parents: The big life change for couples.* Mahwah, NJ: Erlbaum.

Cowan, P. A., & Cowan, C. P. (2002). Interventions as tests of family systems theories: Marital and family relationships in children's development and psychopathology. *Development and Psychopathology, 14,* 731–759.

Cowan, P. A., & Cowan, C. P. (2004). From family relationships to peer rejection to antisocial behavior in middle childhood. In J. B. Kupersmidt & K. A. Dodge (Eds.), *Children's peer relations: From development to intervention* (pp. 159–177). Washington, DC: American Psychological Association.

Cox, G. (2002). The Native American patient. In R. B. Gilbert (Ed.), *Health care and spirituality: Listening, assessing, caring* (pp. 107–127). Amityville, NY: Baywood.

Crago, M. B., Annahatak, B., & Ningiuruvik, L. (1993). Changing patterns of language socialization in Inuit homes. *Anthropology and Education Quarterly, 24,* 205–223.

Craig, C. M., & Lee, D. N. (1999). Neonatal control of sucking pressure: Evidence for an intrinsic tau-guide. *Experimental Brain Research, 124,* 371–382.

Crain, W. (2005). *Theories of development* (5th ed.). Upper Saddle River, NJ: Prentice-Hall.

Crair, M. C., Gillespie, D. C., & Stryker, M. P. (1998). The role of visual experience in the development of columns in cat visual cortex. *Science, 279,* 566–570.

Cramer, R. E., Schaefer, J. T., & Reid, S. (2003). Identifying the ideal mate: More evidence for male–female convergence. In N. J. Pallone (Ed.), *Love, romance, sexual interaction: Research perspectives from current psychology* (pp. 61–73). New Brunswick, NJ: Transaction Publishers.

Cratty, B. J. (1986). *Perceptual and motor development in infants and children* (3rd ed.), Englewood Cliffs, NJ: Prentice-Hall.

Crawford, J. (1997). *Best evidence: Research foundations of the bilingual education act.* Washington, DC: National Clearinghouse for Bilingual Education.

Crawford, N. (2003, September). Understanding children's atypical gender behavior. *APA Monitor,* p. 40.

Crawley, L., Payne, R., Bolden, J., Payne, T., Washington, P., & Williams, S. (2000). Palliative and end-of-life care in the African American community. *Journal of the American Medical Association, 284,* 2518–2521.

Creasey, G. L. (2002). Associations between working models of attachment and conflict management behavior in romantic couples. *Journal of Counseling Psychology, 49,* 365–375.

Creasey, G. L., Jarvis, P. A., & Berk, L. E. (1998). Play and social competence. In O. N. Saracho & B. Spodek (Eds.), *Multiple perspectives on play in early childhood education* (pp. 116–143). Albany: State University of New York Press.

Creasey, G. L., & Ladd, A. (2004). Negative mood regulation expectancies and conflict behaviors in late adolescent college student romantic relationships: The moderating role of generalized attachment representations. *Journal of Research on Adolescence, 14,* 235–255.

Crick, N. R., Casas, J. F., & Nelson, D. A. (2002). Toward a more comprehensive understanding of peer maltreatment: Studies of relational victimization. *Current Directions in Psychological Science, 11,* 98–101.

Crick, N. R., & Nelson, D. A. (2002). Relational and physical victimization within friendships: Nobody told me there'd be friends like these. *Journal of Abnormal Child Psychology, 30,* 599–607.

Crick, N. R., Ostrov, J. M., Appleyard, K., Jansen, E., & Casas, J. F. (2004). Relational aggression in early childhood: You can't come to my birthday party unless. . . . In M. Putallaz & K. Bierman (Eds.), *Aggression, antisocial behavior, and violence among girls: A developmental perspective* (pp. 71–89). New York: Guilford.

Crick, N. R., Ostrov, J. M., Burr, J. E., Cullerton-Sen, C., Jansen-Yeh, E., & Ralston, P. (2006). A longitudinal study of relational and physical aggression in preschool. *Journal of Applied Developmental Psychology, 27,* 254–268.

Crick, N. R., Ostrov, J. M., & Werner, N. E. (2006). A longitudinal study of relational aggression, physical aggression, and social-psychological adjustment. *Journal of Abnormal Child Psychology, 34,* 131–142.

Crockenberg, S., & Leerkes, E. (2003). Infant negative emotionality, caregiving, and family relationships. In A. C. Crouter & A. Booth (Eds.), *Children's influence on family dynamics* (pp. 57–78). Mahwah, NJ: Erlbaum.

Crockenberg, S., & Leerkes, E. (2004). Infant and maternal behaviors regulate infant reactivity to novelty at 6 months. *Developmental Psychology, 40,* 1123–1132.

Crockett, L. J., Raffaelli, M., & Shen, Y.-L. (2006). Linking self-regulation and risk proneness to risky sexual behavior: Pathways through peer pressure and early substance use. *Journal of Research on Adolescence, 16,* 503–525.

Crohan, S. E., & Antonucci, T. C. (1989). Friends as a source of social support in old age. In R. G. Adams & R. Blieszner (Eds.), *Older adult friendship* (pp. 129–146). Newbury Park, CA: Sage.

Croker, R. (2007). *The boomer century: 1946–2046: How America's most influential generation changed everything.* New York: Springboard Press.

Cross, S., & Markus, H. (1991). Possible selves across the life span. *Human Development, 34,* 230–255.

Crouch, J. L., Skowronski, J. J., Milner, J. S., & Harris, B. (2008). Parental responses to infant crying: The influence of child physical abuse risk and hostile priming. *Child Abuse and Neglect, 32,* 702–710.

Crouter, A. C., & Bumpus, M. F. (2001). Linking parents' work stress to children's and adolescents' psychological adjustment. *Current Directions in Psychological Science, 10,* 156–159.

Crouter, A. C., & Head, M. R. (2002). Parental monitoring and knowledge of children. In M. H. Bornstein (Ed.), *Handbook of parenting: Vol. 3. Being and becoming a parent* (2nd ed., pp. 461–483). Mahwah, NJ: Erlbaum.

Csikszentmihalyi, M., & Rathunde, K. (1990). The psychology of wisdom: An evolutionary interpretation. In R. J. Sternberg (Ed.), *Wisdom: Its nature, origins, and development* (pp. 25–51). New York: Cambridge University Press.

Cui, X., & Vaillant, G. E. (1996). Antecedents and consequences of negative life events in adulthood: A longitudinal study. *American Journal of Psychiatry, 153,* 21–26.

Cuijpers, P. (2002). Effective ingredients of school-based drug prevention programs: A systematic review. *Addictive Behaviors, 27,* 1009–1023.

Culbertson, F. M. (1997). Depression and gender: An international review. *American Psychologist, 52,* 25–51.

Cully, J. A., LaVoie, D., & Gfeller, J. D. (2001). Reminiscence, personality, and psychological functioning in older adults. *Gerontologist, 41,* 89–95.

Cumming, E., & Henry, W. E. (1961). *Growing old: The process of disengagement.* New York: Basic Books.

Cummings, E. M., & Davies, P. T. (1994). Maternal depression and child development. *Journal of Child Psychology and Psychiatry, 35,* 73–112.

Curlin, F. A., Nwodim, C., Vance, J. L., Chin, M. H., & Lantos, J. D. (2008). To die, to sleep: U.S. physicians' religious and other objections to physician-assisted suicide, terminal sedation, and withdrawal of life support. *American Journal of Hospice and Palliative Medicine, 25,* 112–120.

Curtiss, K., Hayslip, B., Jr., & Dolan, D. C. (2007). Motivational style, length of residence, voluntariness, and gender as influences on adjustment to long term care: A pilot study. *Journal of Human Behavior in the Social Environment, 15,* 13–34.

Cutler, L. J. (2007). Physical environments of assisted living: Research needs and challenges. *Gerontologist, 47*(Special Issue III), 68–82.

Cutler, R. G., & Mattson, M. P. (2006). Introduction: The adversities of aging. *Ageing Research Reviews, 5,* 221–238.

Cutler, S. J., & Hendricks, J. (2001). Emerging social trends. In R. H. Binstock & L. K. George (Eds.), *Handbook of aging and the social sciences* (5th ed., pp. 462–480). San Diego, CA: Academic Press.

Cutrona, C. E., Hessling, R. M., Bacon, P. L., & Russell, D. W. (1998). Predictors and correlates of continuing involvement with the baby's father among adolescent mothers. *Journal of Family Psychology, 12,* 369–387.

Cutter, W. J., Daly, E. M., Robertson, D. M. W., Chitnis, X. A., van Amelsvoort, T. A. M. J., & Simmons, A. (2006). Influence of X chromosome and hormones on human brain development: A magnetic resonance imaging and proton magnetic resonance spectroscopy study of Turner syndrome. *Biological Psychiatry, 59,* 273–283.

Cyr, M., McDuff, P., & Wright, J. (2006). Prevalence and predictors of dating violence among adolescent female victims of child sexual abuse. *Journal of Interpersonal Violence, 21,* 1000–1017.

D

Dabrowska, E. (2000). From formula to schema: The acquisition of English questions. *Cognitive Linguistics, 11,* 1–20.

Dahl, R. E., & Lewin, D. S. (2002). Pathways to adolescent healthy sleep regulation and behavior. *Journal of Adolescent Health, 31,* 175–184.

Dahlberg, L. L., & Simon, T. R. (2006). Predicting and preventing youth violence: Developmental pathways and risk. In L. L. Dahlberg & T. R. Simon (Eds.), *Preventing violence: Research and evidence-based intervention strategies* (pp. 97–124). Washington, DC: American Psychological Association.

Dal Santo, J. A., Goodman, R. M., Glik, D., & Jackson, K. (2004). Childhood unintentional injuries: Factors predicting injury risk among preschoolers. *Journal of Pediatric Psychology, 29,* 273–283.

Damjanovic, A. M., Yang, Y., Glaser, R., Kiecolt-Glaser, J. K., & Nguyen, H. (2007). Accelerated telomere erosion is associated with a declining immune function of caregivers of Alzheimer's disease patients. *Journal of Immunology, 179,* 4249–4254.

Damon, W. (1988a). *The moral child.* New York: Free Press.

Damon, W. (1988b). *Self-understanding in childhood and adolescence.* New York: Cambridge University Press.

Damon, W. (1990). Self-concept, adolescent. In R. M. Lerner, A. C. Petersen, & J. Brooks-Gunn (Eds.), *The encyclopedia of adolescence* (Vol. 2, pp. 87–91). New York: Garland.

Damon, W. (2004). *The moral advantage: How to succeed in business by doing the right thing.* San Francisco: Berrett-Koehler.

Damon, W., & Hart, D. (1988). *Self-understanding in childhood and adolescence.* New York: Cambridge University Press.

Daniels, D. H., Kalkman, D. L., & McCombs, B. L. (2001). Young children's perspectives on learning and teacher practices in different classroom contexts: Implications for motivation. *Early Education and Development, 12,* 253–273.

Daniels, E., & Leaper, C. (2006). A longitudinal investigation of sport participation, peer acceptance, and self-esteem among adolescent girls and boys. *Sex Roles, 55,* 875–880.

Dannemiller, J. L., & Stephens, B. R. (1988). A critical test of infant pattern preference models. *Child Development, 59,* 210–216.

Dansinger, M. L., Tatsioni, A., Wong, J. B., Chung, M., & Balk, E. M. (2007). Meta-analysis: The effect of dietary counseling for weight loss. *Annals of Internal Medicine, 147,* 41–50.

Darroch, J. E., Frost, J. J., & Singh, S. (2001). *Teenage sexual and reproductive behavior in developed countries: Can more progress be made?* New York: Alan Guttmacher Institute.

Darwin, C. (1936). *On the origin of species by means of natural selection.* New York: Modern Library. (Original work published 1859)

D'Augelli, A. R. (2002). Mental health problems among lesbian, gay, and bisexual youths ages 14 to 21. *Clinical Child Psychology and Psychiatry, 7,* 433–456.

D'Augelli, A. R. (2006). Developmental and contextual factors and mental health among lesbian, gay, and bisexual youths. In A. M. Omoto & H. S. Howard (Eds.), *Sexual orientation and mental health: Examining identity and development in lesbian, gay, and bisexual people* (pp. 37–53). Washington, DC: American Psychological Association.

D'Augelli, A. R., Grossman, A. H., Salter, N. P., Vasey, J. J., Starks, M. T., & Sinclair, K. O. (2005). Predicting the suicide attempts of lesbian, gay, and bisexual youth. *Suicide and Life-Threatening Behavior, 35,* 646–660.

Davidov, M., & Grusec, J. E. (2006). Untangling the links of parental responsiveness to distress and warmth to child outcomes. *Child Development, 77,* 44–58.

Davidson, R. J. (1994). Asymmetric brain function, affective style, and psychopathology: The role of early experience and plasticity. *Development and Psychopathology, 6,* 741–758.

Davies, P. A., & Lindsay, L. L. (2004). Everyday marital conflict and child aggression. *Journal of Abnormal Child Psychology, 32,* 191–202.

Davis, K. F., Parker, K. P., & Montgomery, G. L. (2004). Sleep in infants and young children. Part 1: Normal sleep. *Journal of Pediatric Health Care, 18,* 65–71.

Dawson, G., Ashman, S. B., Panagiotides, H., Hessl, D., Self, J., Yamada, E., & Embry, L. (2003). Preschool outcomes of children of depressed mothers: Role of maternal behavior, contextual risk, and children's brain activity. *Child Development, 74,* 1158–1175.

Dawson, T. L. (2002). New tools, new insights: Kohlberg's moral judgment stages revisited. *International Journal of Behavioral Development, 26,* 154–166.

Deák, G. O., Ray, S. D., & Brenneman, K. (2003). Children's perseverative appearance–reality errors are related to emerging language skills. *Child Development, 74,* 944–964.

Deary, I. J. (2001). *g* and cognitive elements of information progressing: An agnostic view. In R. J. Sternberg & E. L. Grigorenko (Eds.), *The general factor of intelligence: How general is it?* (pp. 447–479). Mahwah, NJ: Erlbaum.

Deary, I. J., & Der, G. (2005). Reaction time, age, and cognitive ability: Longitudinal findings from age 16 to 63 years in representative population samples. *Aging, Neuropsychology, and Cognition, 12,* 187–215.

Deary, I. J., Strand, S., Smith, P., & Fernandes, C. (2007). Intelligence and educational achievement. *Intelligence, 35,* 13–21.

Deater-Deckard, K., Lansford, J. E., Dodge, K. A., Pettit, G. S., & Bates, J. E. (2003). The development of attitudes about physical punishment: An 8-year longitudinal study. *Journal of Family Psychology, 17,* 351–360.

Deater-Deckard, K., Pike, A., Petrill, S. A., Cutting, A. L., Hughes, C., & O'Connor, T. G. (2001). Nonshared environmental processes in social-emotional development: An observational study of identical twin differences in the preschool period. *Developmental Science, 4,* F1–F6.

DeBerry, K. M., Scarr, S., & Weinberg, R. (1996). Family racial socialization and ecological competence: Longitudinal assessments of African-American transracial adoptees. *Child Development, 67,* 2375–2399.

DeBoer, T., Scott, L. S., & Nelson, C. A. (2007). Methods for acquiring and analyzing infant event-related potentials. In M. de Haan (Ed.), *Infant EEG and event-related potentials* (pp. 5–37). New York: Psychology Press.

de Bruyn, E. H. (2005). Role strain, engagement and academic achievement in early adolescence. *Educational Studies, 31,* 15–27.

de Grey, A. D. N. J. (2005). The unfortunate influence of the weather on the rate of ageing: Why human caloric restriction or its emulation may only extend life expectancy by 2–3 years. *Gerontology, 51,* 73–82.

de Haan, M., Bauer, P. J., Georgieff, M. K., & Nelson, C. A. (2000). Explicit memory in low-risk infants aged 19 months born between 27 and 42 weeks of gestation. *Developmental Medicine and Child Neurology, 42,* 304–312.

de Haan, M., & Johnson, M. H. (2003). Mechanisms and theories of brain development. In M. de Haan & M. H. Johnson (Eds.), *The cognitive neuroscience of development* (pp. 1–18). Hove, UK: Psychology Press.

Deissinger, T. (2007). "Making schools practical": Practice firms and their function in the full-time vocational school system in Germany. *Education + Training, 49,* 364–378.

deJong, A., & Franklin, B. A. (2004). Prescribing exercise for the elderly: Current research and recommendations. *Current Sports Medicine Reports, 3,* 337–343.

Dekker, M. C., Ferdinand, R. F., van Lang, D. J., Bongers, I. L., van der Ende, J., & Verhulst, F. C. (2007). Developmental trajectories of depressive symptoms from early childhood to late adolescence: Gender differences and adult outcome. *Journal of Child Psychology and Psychiatry, 48,* 657–666.

DeKosky, S. T., Williamson, J. D., Fitzpatrick, A. L., Kronmal, R. A., Ives, D. G., & Saxton, J. A. (2008). Ginkgo biloba for prevention of dementia: A randomized controlled trial. *Journal of the American Medical Association, 300,* 2253–2262.

Deković, M., & Buist, K. L. (2005). Multiple perspectives within the family: Family relationship patterns. *Journal of Family Issues, 26,* 467–490.

DeLamater, J., & Moorman, S. M. (2007). Sexual behavior in later life. *Journal of Aging and Health, 19,* 921–945.

Delgado-Gaitan, C. (1994). Socializing young children in Mexican-American families: An intergenerational perspective. In P. Greenfield & R. Cocking (Eds.), *Cross-cultural roots of minority child development* (p. 55–86). Hillsdale, NJ: Erlbaum.

De Lisi, R., & Gallagher, A. M. (1991). Understanding gender stability and constancy in Argentinean children. *Merrill-Palmer Quarterly, 37,* 483–502.

Dell, D. L. (2001). Adolescent pregnancy. In N. L. Stotland & D. E. Stewart (Eds.), *Psychological aspects of women's health care* (pp. 95–116). Washington, DC: American Psychiatric Association.

DeLoache, J. S. (1987). Rapid change in symbolic functioning of very young children. *Science, 238,* 1556–1557.

DeLoache, J. S. (2002). The symbol-mindedness of young children. In W. Hartup & R. A. Weinberg (Eds.), *Minnesota Symposia on Child Psychology* (Vol. 32, pp. 73–101). Mahwah, NJ: Erlbaum.

De Marco, A. C., & Berzin, S. C. (2008). The influence of family economic status on home-leaving patterns during emerging adulthood. *Families in Society, 89,* 208–218.

DeMarie, D., Miller, P. H., Ferron, J., & Cunningham, W. R. (2004). Path analysis tests of theoretical models of children's memory performance. *Journal of Cognition and Development, 5,* 461–492.

Demetriou, A., Christou, C., Spanoudis, G., & Platsidou, M. (2002). The development of mental processing: Efficiency, working memory, and thinking. *Monographs of the Society for Research in Child Development, 67*(1, Serial No. 268).

Dempster, F. N., & Corkill, A. J. (1999). Interference and inhibition in cognition and behavior: Unifying themes for educational psychology. *Educational Psychology Review, 11,* 1–88.

DeNavas-Walt, C., Proctor, B. D., & Smith, J. C. (2009). *Income, poverty, and health insurance coverage in the United States: 2008.* U.S. Census Bureau, Current Population Reports, P60–236. Washington, DC: U.S. Government Printing Office.

Denham, S. A., Blair, K., Schmidt, M., & DeMulder, E. (2002). Compromised emotional competence: Seeds of violence sown early? *American Journal of Orthopsychiatry, 72,* 70–82.

Denham, S. A., & Kochanoff, A. T. (2002). Parental contributions to preschoolers' understanding of emotion. *Marriage and Family Review, 34,* 311–343.

Denissen, J. J. A., Zarrett, N. R., & Eccles, J. S. (2007). I like to do it, I'm able, and I know I am: Longitudinal couplings between domain-specific achievement, self-concept, and interest. *Child Development, 78,* 430–447.

Denmark, F. L., & Klara, M. D. (2007). Empowerment: A prime time for women over 50. In V. Muhlbauer & J. C. Chrisler (Eds.), *Women over 50* (pp. 182–203). New York: Springer.

Dennerstein, L., Dudley, E., & Guthrie, J. (2002). Empty nest or revolving door? A prospective study of women's quality of life in midlife during the phase of children leaving and re-entering the home. *Psychological Medicine, 32,* 545–550.

Dennerstein, L., & Lehert, P. (2004). Modeling mid-aged women's sexual functioning: A prospective, population-based study. *Journal of Sex and Marriage Therapy, 30,* 173–183.

Denney, N. W. (1990). Adult age differences in traditional and practical problem solving. *Advances in Psychology, 72,* 329–349.

Denney, N. W., & Pearce, K A. (1989). A developmental study of practical problem solving in adults. *Psychology and Aging, 4,* 438–442.

Dennis, T., Bendersky, M., Ramsay, D., & Lewis, M. (2006). Reactivity and regulation in children prenatally exposed to cocaine. *Developmental Psychology, 42,* 688–697.

Dennison, B. A., Straus, J. H., Mellits, D., & Charney, E. (1998). Childhood physical fitness tests: Predictor of adult physical activity levels? *Pediatrics, 82,* 342–350.

Dent, A., & Stewart, A. (2004). *Sudden death in childhood: Support for the bereaved family.* London: Butterworth-Heinemann.

DePaulo, B. M., & Morris, W. L. (2005). Singles in society and in science. *Psychological Inquiry, 16,* 142–149.

DePaulo, B. M., & Morris, W. L. (2006). The unrecognized stereotyping and discrimination against singles. *Current Directions in Psychological Science, 15,* 251–254.

Der, G., Batty, G. D., & Deary, I. J. (2006). Effect of breastfeeding on intelligence in children: Prospective study, sibling pairs analysis, and meta-analysis. *British Medical Journal, 333,* 945.

Der, G., & Deary, I. J. (2006). Age and sex differences in reaction time in adulthood: Results from the United Kingdom Health and Lifestyle Survey. *Psychology and Aging, 21,* 62–73.

de Ribaupierre, A., & Lecerf, T. (2006). Relationships between working memory and intelligence from a developmental perspective: Convergent evidence from a neo-Piagetian and a psychometric approach. *European Journal of Cognitive Psychology, 18,* 109–137.

Derom, C., Thiery, E., Vlietinck, R., Loos, R., & Derom, R. (1996). Handedness in twins according to zygosity and chorion type: A preliminary report. *Behavior Genetics, 26,* 407–408.

DeRose, L. M., & Brooks-Gunn, J. (2006). Transition into adolescence: The role of pubertal processes. In L. Balter & C. S. Tamis-LeMonda (Eds.), *Child psychology: A handbook of contemporary issues* (2nd ed., pp. 385–414). New York: Psychology Press.

DeRosier, M. E. (2007). Peer-rejected and bullied children: A safe schools initiative for elementary school students. In J. E. Zins, M. J. Elias, & C. A. Maher (Eds.), *Bullying, victimization, and peer harassment* (pp. 257–276). New York: Haworth.

DeRosier, M. E., & Thomas, J. M. (2003). Strengthening sociometric prediction: Scientific advances in the assessment of children's peer relations. *Child Development, 75,* 1379–1392.

de Rosnay, M., & Hughes, C. (2006). Conversation and theory of mind: Do children talk their way to socio-cognitive understanding? *British Journal of Developmental Psychology, 24,* 7–37.

Derwinger, A., Neely, A. S., & Bäckman, L. (2005). Design your own memory strategies! Self-generated strategy training versus mnemonic training in old age: An 8-month follow-up. *Neuropsychological Rehabilitation, 15,* 37–54.

De Schipper, J. C., van IJzendoorn, M. H., & Tavecchio, L. W. C. (2004). Stability in center day care: Relations with children's well-being and problem behavior in day care. *Social Development, 13,* 531–550.

Deveson, A. (1994). *Coming of age: Twenty-one interviews about growing older.* Newham, Australia: Scribe.

de Villiers, J. G., & de Villiers, P. A. (1973). A cross-sectional study of the acquisition of grammatical morphemes in child speech. *Journal of Psycholinguistic Research, 2,* 267–278.

de Villiers, J. G., & de Villiers, P. A. (2000). Linguistic determinism and the understanding of false beliefs. In P. Mitchell & K. J. Riggs (Eds.), *Children's reasoning and the mind* (pp. 87–99). Hove, UK: Psychology Press.

De Vogli, R., Mistry, R., Gnesolto, R., & Cornia, G. A. (2005). Has the relation between income inequality and life expectancy disappeared? Evidence from Italy and top industrialized countries. *Journal of Epidemiology and Community Health, 59,* 158–162.

DeVries, R. (2001). Constructivist education in preschool and elementary school: The sociomoral atmosphere as the first educational goal. In S. L. Golbeck (Ed.), *Psychological perspectives on early childhood education* (pp. 153–180). Mahwah, NJ: Erlbaum.

de Waal, F. B. M. (1993). Sex differences in chimpanzee (and human) behavior: A matter of social values? In M. Hechter, L. Nadel, & R. E. Michod (Eds.), *The origin of values* (pp. 285–303). New York: Aldine de Gruyter.

de Waal, F. B. M. (2001). *Tree of origin.* Cambridge, MA: Harvard University Press.

de Weerd, A. W., & van den Bossche, A. S. (2003). The development of sleep during the first months of life. *Sleep Medicine Reviews, 7,* 179–191.

de Weerth, C., & Buitelaar, J. K. (2005). Physiological stress reactivity in human pregnancy—a review. *Neuroscience and Biobehavioral Reviews, 29,* 295–312.

De Wolff, M. S., & van IJzendoorn, M. H. (1997). Sensitivity and attachment: A meta-analysis on parental antecedents of infant attachment. *Child Development, 68,* 571–591.

Dey, J. G., & Hill, C. (2007). *Behind the pay gap.* Washington, DC: American Association of University Women.

Dey, S., Flather, M. D., Devlin, G. P., Brieger, D., Gurfinkle, D. P., & Steg, P. G. (2009). Sex-related differences in the presentation, treatment and outcomes among patients with acute coronary syndromes. *Heart, 95,* 20–26.

Diamond, A. (2004). Normal development of prefrontal cortex from birth to young adulthood: Cognitive functions, anatomy, and biochemistry. In D. T. Stuff & R. T. Knight (Eds.), *Principles of frontal lobe function* (pp. 466–503). New York: Oxford University Press.

Diamond, L. M. (1998). Development of sexual orientation among adolescent and young adult women. *Developmental Psychology, 34,* 1085–1095.

Diamond, L. M. (2003). Love matters: Romantic relationships among sexual-minority adolescents. In P. Florsheim (Ed.), *Adolescent romantic relations and sexual behavior* (pp. 85–108). Mahwah, NJ: Erlbaum.

Diamond, L. M. (2006). The intimate same-sex relationships of sexual minorities. In A. L. Vangelisti & D. Perlman (Eds.), *The Cambridge handbook of personal relationships* (pp. 293–312). New York: Cambridge University Press.

Diamond, L. M., & Lucas, S. (2004). Sexual minority and heterosexual youths' peer relationships: Experiences, expectations, and implications for well-being. *Journal of Research on Adolescence, 14,* 313–340.

Diamond, M., & Sigmundson, H. K. (1999). Sex reassignment at birth. In S. J. Ceci & W. M. Williams (Eds.), *The nature–nurture debate* (pp. 55–75). Malden, MA: Blackwell.

Dias, M. G., & Harris, P. L. (1988). The effect of make-believe play on deductive reasoning. *British Journal of Developmental Psychology, 6,* 207–221.

Dias, M. G., & Harris, P. L. (1990). The influence of the imagination on reasoning by young children. *British Journal of Developmental Psychology, 8,* 305–318.

Dick, D. M., Rose, R. J., Viken, R. J., & Kaprio, J. (2000). Pubertal timing and substance use: Associations between and within families across late adolescence. *Developmental Psychology, 36,* 180–189.

Dickens, W. T., & Flynn, J. R. (2006). Black Americans reduce the racial IQ gap: Evidence from standardization samples. *Psychological Science, 17,* 913–920.

Dickinson, D. K., & McCabe, A. (2001). Bringing it all together: The multiple origins, skills, and environmental supports of early literacy. *Learning Disabilities Research and Practice, 16,* 186–202.

Dickinson, D. K., McCabe, A., Anastasopoulos, L., Peisner-Feinberg, E. S., & Poe, M. D. (2003). The comprehensive language approach to early literacy: The interrelationships among vocabulary, phonological sensitivity, and print knowledge among preschool-age children. *Journal of Educational Psychology, 95,* 465–481.

Dick-Read, G. (1959). *Childbirth without fear.* New York: Harper & Row.

Dickstein, M. (1992). After utopia: The 1960s today. In B. L. Tischler (Ed.), *Sights on the sixties* (pp. 13–24). New Brunswick, NJ: Rutgers University Press.

Diehl, M., & Berg, K. M. (2007). Personality and involvement in leisure activities during the Third Age: Findings from the Ohio Longitudinal Study. In J. B. James & P. Wink (Eds.), *Annual review of gerontology and geriatrics* (Vol. 26, pp. 211–226). New York: Springer.

Diehl, M., Coyle, N., & Labouvie-Vief, G. (1996). Age and sex differences in strategies of coping and defense across the life span. *Psychology and Aging, 11,* 127–139.

Diener, E., Gohm, C. L., Suh, E., & Oishi, S. (2000). Similarity of the relations between marital status and subjective well-being across cultures. *Journal of Cross-Cultural Psychology, 31,* 419–436.

Dildy, G. A., Jackson, G. M., Fowers, G. K., Oshiro, B. T., Varner, M. W., & Clark, S. L. (1996). Very advanced maternal age. Pregnancy after age 45. *American Journal of Obstetrics and Gynecology, 175,* 668–674.

Dillaway, H., & Broman, C. (2001). Race, class, and gender differences in marital satisfaction and divisions of household labor among dual-earner couples. *Journal of Family Issues, 22,* 309–327.

Dillon, M., & Wink, P. (2004). American religion, generativity, and the therapeutic culture. In E. de St. Aubin & D. P. McAdams (Eds.), *The generative society: Caring for future generations* (pp. 15–31). Washington, DC: American Psychological Association.

Dilworth-Anderson, P., Goodwin, P. Y., & Williams, S. W. (2004). Can culture help explain the physical health effects of caregiving over time among African American caregivers? *Journal of Gerontology, 59B,* S138–S145.

Ding, Q., Bruce-Keller, A. J., Chen, Q., & Keller, J. N. (2004). Analysis of gene expression in neural cells subject to chronic proteasome inhibition. *Free Radical Biology and Medicine, 36,* 445–455.

DiPietro, J. A., Bornstein, M. H., Costigan, K. A., Pressman, E. K., Hahn, C.-S., & Painter, K. (2002). What does fetal movement predict about behavior during the first two years of life? *Developmental Psychobiology, 40,* 358–371.

DiPietro, J. A., Caulfield, L. E., Irizarry, R. A., Chen, P., Merialdi, M., & Zavaleta, N. (2006). Prenatal development of intrafetal and maternal–fetal synchrony. *Behavioral Neuroscience, 120,* 687–701.

DiPietro, J. A., Hodgson, D. M., Costigan, K. A., & Hilton, S. C. (1996). Fetal neurobehavioral development. *Child Development, 67,* 2553–2567.

Dirks, J. (1982). The effect of a commercial game on children's Block Design scores on the WISC-R test. *Intelligence, 6,* 109–123.

DiTommaso, E., Brannen, C., & Burgess, M. (2005). The universality of relationship characteristics: A cross-cultural comparison of different types of attachment and loneliness in Canadian and visiting Chinese students. *Social Behavior and Personality, 33,* 57–68.

Dixon, L., & Browne, K. (2003). The heterogeneity of spouse abuse: A review. *Aggression and Violent Behavior, 8,* 107–130.

Dixon, R. A. (2003). Themes in the aging of intelligence: Robust decline with intriguing possibilities. In R. J. Sternberg, J. Lautrey, & T. I. Lubart (Eds.), *Models of intelligence: International perspectives* (pp. 151–167). Washington, DC: American Psychological Association.

Djahanbakhch, O., Ezzati, M., & Zosmer, A. (2007). Reproductive ageing in women. *Journal of Pathology, 211,* 219–231.

Dodd, V. L. (2005). Implications of kangaroo care for growth and development in preterm infants. *JOGNN, 34,* 218–232.

Dodge, K. A., Coie, J. D., & Lynam, D. (2006). Aggression and antisocial behavior in youth. In N. Eisenberg (Ed.), *Handbook of child psychology: Vol. 3. Social, emotional, and personality development* (6th ed., pp. 719–788). New York: Wiley.

Dodge, K. A., McLoyd, V. C., & Lansford, J. E. (2006). The cultural context of physically disciplining children. In V. C. McLoyd, N. E. Hill, & K. A. Dodge (Eds.), *African-American family life: Ecological and cultural diversity* (pp. 245–263). New York: Guilford.

Dodson, T. A., & Borders, L. D. (2006). Men in traditional and nontraditional careers: Gender role attitudes, gender role conflict, and job satisfaction. *Career Development Quarterly, 54,* 283–296.

Dohnt, H., & Tiggemann, M. (2006). The contribution of peer and media influences to the development of body satisfaction and self-esteem in young girls: A prospective study. *Developmental Psychology, 42,* 929–936.

Dolbin-MacNab, M. L. (2006). Just like raising your own? Grandmothers' perceptions of parenting a second time around. *Family Relations, 55,* 564–575.

Dombrowski, S. C., Noonan, K., & Martin, R. P. (2007). Low birth weight and cognitive outcomes: Evidence for a gradient relationship in an urban, poor, African American birth cohort. *School Psychology Quarterly, 22,* 26–43.

Donahue, M. J., & Benson, P. L. (1995). Religion and the well-being of adolescents. *Journal of Social Issues, 51,* 145–160.

Donatelle, R. J. (2009). *Health: The basics* (8th ed.). San Francisco: Benjamin Cummings.

Dondi, M., Simion, F., & Caltran, G. (1999). Can newborns discriminate between their own cry and the cry of another newborn infant? *Developmental Psychology, 35,* 418–426.

Done, D. J., & Thomas, J. A. (2001). Training in communication skills for informal carers of people suffering from dementia: A cluster randomized clinic trial comparing a therapist led workshop and booklet. *International Journal of Geriatric Psychiatry, 16,* 816–821.

Donnellan, M. B., Larsen-Rife, D., & Conger, R. D. (2005). Personality, family history, and competence in early adult romantic relationships. *Journal of Personality and Social Psychology, 88,* 562–576.

Donnellan, M. B., Trzesniewski, K. H., Robins, R. W., Moffitt, T. E., & Caspi, A. (2005). Low self-esteem is related to aggression, antisocial behavior, and delinquency. *Psychological Science, 16,* 328–335.

D'Onofrio, B. M., Turkheimer, E., Emery, R. E., Slutske, W. S., Heath, A. C., Madden, P. A., & Martin, N. G. (2006). A genetically informed study of the processes underlying the association between parental marital instability and offspring adjustment. *Developmental Psychology, 42,* 486–499.

Dorris, M. (1989). *The broken cord.* New York: Harper & Row.

Dowdney, L. (2000). Annotation: Childhood bereavement following parental death. *Journal of Child Psychology and Psychiatry and Allied Disciplines, 41,* 819–830.

Dowling, E. M., Gestsdottir, S., Anderson, P. M., von Eye, A., Almerigi, J., & Lerner, R. M. (2004). Structural relations among spirituality, religiosity, and thriving in adolescence. *Applied Developmental Psychology, 8,* 7–16.

Downs, A. C., & Fuller, M. J. (1991). Recollections of spermarche: An exploratory investigation. *Current Psychology: Research and Reviews, 10,* 93–102.

Drela, N., Kozdron, E., & Szczypiorski, P. (2004). Moderate exercise may attenuate some aspects of immunosenescence. *BMC Geriatrics, 4,* 8.

Drewett, R. F., Corbett, S. S., & Wright, C. M. (2006). Physical and emotional development, appetite and body image in adolescents who failed to thrive as infants. *Journal of Child Psychology and Psychiatry, 47,* 524–531.

Drewnowski, A., & Shultz, J. M. (2001). Impact of aging on eating behaviors, food choices, nutrition, and health status. *Journal of Nutrition, Health, and Aging, 5,* 75–79.

Driscoll, M. C. (2007). Sickle cell disease. *Pediatrics in Review, 28,* 259–268.

Drotar, D., Pallotta, J., & Eckerle, D. (1994). A prospective study of family environments of children hospitalized for nonorganic failure-to-thrive. *Developmental and Behavioral Pediatrics, 15,* 78–85.

Drotar, D., Witherspoon, D. O., Zebracki, K., & Peterson, C. C. (2006). *Psychological interventions in childhood chronic illness.* Washington, DC: American Psychological Association.

Dubé, E. M., Savin-Williams, R. C., & Diamond, L. M. (2001). Intimacy development, gender, and ethnicity among sexual-minority youths. In A. R. D'Augelli & C. J. Patterson (Eds.), *Lesbian, gay, and bisexual identities and youth* (pp. 129–152). New York: Oxford University Press.

DuBois, D. L., Burk-Braxton, C., Swenson, L. P., Tevendale, H. D., Lockerd, E. M., & Moran, B. L. (2002). Getting by with a little help from self and others: Self-esteem and social support as resources during early adolescence. *Developmental Psychology, 38,* 822–939.

DuBois, D. L., Felner, R. D., Brand, S., & George, G. R. (1999). Profiles of self-esteem in early adolescence: Identification and investigation of adaptive correlates. *American Journal of Community Psychology, 27,* 899–932.

Duckworth, A. L., & Seligman, M. E. P. (2005). Self-discipline outdoes IQ in predicting academic performance of adolescents. *Psychological Science, 12,* 939–944.

Duggan, A., McFarlane, E., Fuddy, L., Burrell, L., Higman, S. M., Windham, A., & Sia, C. (2004). Randomized trial of a statewide home visiting program: Impact in preventing child abuse and neglect. *Child Abuse and Neglect, 28,* 597–622.

Dumas, J. A., & Hartman, M. (2003). Age differences in temporal and item memory. *Psychology and Aging, 18,* 573–586.

Duncan, G. J., Dowsett, C. J., Claessens, A., Magnuson, K., Huston, A. C., Klebanov, P., et al. (2007). School readiness and later achievement. *Developmental Psychology, 43,* 1428–1446.

Duncan, G. J., & Magnuson, K. A. (2003). Off with Hollingshead: Socioeconomic resources, parenting, and child development. In M. H. Bornstein & R. H. Bradley (Eds.), *Socioeconomic status, parenting, and child development* (pp. 83–106). Mahwah, NJ: Erlbaum.

Duniz, M., Scheer, P. J., Trojovsky, A., Kaschnitz, W., Kvas, E., & Macari, S. (1996). Changes in psychopathology of parents of NOFT (nonorganic failure to thrive) infants during treatment. *European Child and Adolescent Psychiatry, 5,* 93–100.

Dunlosky, J., & Hertzog, C. (2001). Measuring strategy production during associative learning: The relative utility of concurrent versus retrospective reports. *Memory and Cognition, 29,* 247–253.

Dunn, J. (1989). Siblings and the development of social understanding in early childhood. In P. G. Zukow (Ed.), *Sibling interaction across cultures* (pp. 106–116). New York: Springer-Verlag.

Dunn, J. (1994). Temperament, siblings, and the development of relationships. In W. B. Carey & S. C. McDevitt (Eds.), *Prevention and early intervention* (pp. 50–58). New York: Brunner/Mazel.

Dunn, J. (2002). The adjustment of children in stepfamilies: Lessons from community studies. *Child and Adolescent Mental Health, 7,* 154–161.

Dunn, J. (2004). Sibling relationships. In P. K. Smith & C. H. Hart (Eds.), *Handbook of childhood social development* (pp. 223–237). Malden, MA: Blackwell.

Dunn, J. (2005). Moral development in early childhood and social interaction in the family. In M. Killen & J. G. Smetana (Eds.), *Handbook of moral development* (pp. 331–350). Mahwah, NJ: Erlbaum.

Dunn, J., Cheng, H., O'Connor, T. G., & Bridges, L. (2004). Children's perspectives on their relationships with their nonresident fathers: Influences, outcomes and implications. *Journal of Child Psychology and Psychiatry, 45,* 553–566.

Dunne, E. J., & Dunne-Maxim, K. (2004). Working with families in the aftermath of suicide. In F. Walsh & M. McGoldrick (Eds.), *Living beyond loss: Death in the family* (2nd ed., pp. 272–284). New York: Norton.

Durbin, D. L., Darling, N., Steinberg, L., & Brown, B. B. (1993). Parenting style and peer group membership among European-American adolescents. *Journal of Research on Adolescence, 3,* 87–100.

Durlak, J. A., & Riesenberg, L. A. (1991). The impact of death education. *Death Studies, 15,* 39–58.

Durlak, J. A., & Weissberg, R. P. (2007). *The impact of after-school programs that promote personal and social skills.* Chicago: Collaborative for Academic, Social, and Emotional Learning.

Durston, S., Pol, H. E. H., Schnack, H. G., Buitelaar, J. K., Steenhuis, M. P., & Minderaa, R. B. (2004). Magnetic resonance imaging of boys with attention-deficit/hyperactivity disorder and their unaffected siblings. *Journal of the American Academy of Child and Adolescent Psychiatry, 43,* 332–340.

Dusek, J. B. (1987). Sex roles and adjustment. In D. B. Carter (Ed.), *Current conceptions of sex roles and sex typing* (pp. 211–222). New York: Praeger.

Dutton, D. G. (2007). *The abusive personality: Violence and control in intimate relationships* (2nd ed.). New York: Guilford.

Dutton, D. G., & Nicholls, T. L. (2005). The gender paradigm in domestic violence research and theory: Part 1. The conflict of theory and data. *Aggression and Violent Behavior, 10,* 680–714.

Dutton, D. G., Nicholls, T. L., & Spidel, A. (2005). Female perpetrators of intimate abuse. In F. P. Buttell & M. M. Carney (Eds.), *Women who perpetrate relationship violence: Moving beyond political correctness* (pp. 1–31). New York: Haworth Press.

Dweck, C. S. (2002). Messages that motivate: How praise molds students' beliefs, motivation, and performance (in surprising ways). In J. Aronson (Ed.), *Improving academic achievement: Impact of psychological factors on education* (pp. 37–60). San Diego, CA: Academic Press.

Dykman, R., Casey, P. H., Ackerman, P. T., & McPherson, W. B. (2001). Behavioral and cognitive status in school-aged children with a history of failure to thrive during early childhood. *Clinical Pediatrics, 40,* 63–70.

Dykstra, P. A. (2006). Off the beaten track: Childlessness and social integration in late life. *Research on Aging, 28,* 749–767.

Dykstra, P. A., & Hagestad, G. O. (2007). Roads less taken: Developing a nuanced view of older adults without children. *Journal of Family Issues, 28,* 1275–1310.

Dzurova, D., & Pikhart, H. (2005). Down syndrome, paternal age and education: Comparison of California and the Czech Republic. *BMC Public Health, 5,* 69.

E

Eagly, A. H., & Karau, S. J. (2002). Role congruity theory of prejudice toward female leaders. *Psychological Review, 109,* 573–598.

Eagly, A. H., & Wood, W. (1999). The origins of sex differences in human behavior: Evolved dispositions versus social roles. *American Psychologist, 54,* 408–423.

Eaker, E.D., Sullivan. L. M., Kelly-Hayes, M., D'Agostino, R. B., & Benjamin, E. J. (2004). Anger and hostility predict the development of atrial fibrillation in men in the Framingham Offspring Study. *Circulation, 109,* 1267–1271.

Eaton, D. K., Davis, K. S., Barrios, L., Brener, N. D., & Noonan, R. K. (2007). Associations of dating violence victimization with lifetime participation, co-occurrence, and early initiation of risk behaviors among U.S. high school students. *Journal of Interpersonal Violence, 22,* 585–602.

Eaves, L., Silberg, J., Foley, D., Bulik, C., Maes, H., & Erkanli, A. (2004). Genetic and environmental influences on the relative timing of pubertal change. *Twin Research, 7,* 471–481.

Eberhart-Phillips, J. E., Frederick, P. D., & Baron, R. C. (1993). Measles in pregnancy: A descriptive study of 58 cases. *Obstetrics and Gynecology, 82,* 797–801.

Ebner, N. C., Freund, A. M., & Baltes, P. B. (2006). Developmental changes in personal goal orientation from young to late adulthood: From striving for gains to maintenance and prevention of losses. *Psychology and Aging, 21,* 664–678.

Eccles, J. S. (2004). Schools, academic motivation, and stage–environment fit. In R. M. Lerner & L. Steinberg (Eds.), *Handbook of Adolescent Psychology* (2nd ed., pp. 125–154). Hoboken, N. J.: Wiley.

Eccles, J. S., & Gootman, J. (Eds.). (2002). *Community programs to promote youth development*. Washington, DC: National Academy Press.

Eccles, J. S., Jacobs, J. E., & Harold, R. D. (1990). Gender-role stereotypes, expectancy effects, and parents' role in the socialization of gender differences in self-perceptions and skill acquisition. *Journal of Social Issues, 46*, 183–201.

Eccles, J. S., Templeton, J., Barber, B., & Stone, M. (2003). Adolescence and emerging adulthood: The critical passageways to adulthood. In M. H. Bornstein, L. Davidson, C. L. M., Keyes, K. A. Moore, & the Center for Child Well-Being (Eds.), *Well-being: Positive development across the life course* (pp. 383–406). Mahwah, NJ: Erlbaum.

Eder, R. A., & Mangelsdorf, S. C. (1997). The emotional basis of early personality development: Implications for the emergent self-concept. In R. Hogan, J. Johnson, & S. Briggs (Eds.), *Handbook of personality psychology* (pp. 209–240). San Diego, CA: Academic Press.

Edwards, J. N., & Booth, A. (1994). Sexuality, marriage, and well-being: The middle years. In A. S. Rossi (Ed.), *Sexuality across the life course* (pp. 233–259). Chicago: University of Chicago Press.

Edwards, O. W., & Oakland, T. D. (2006). Factorial invariance of Woodcock-Johnson III scores for African Americans and Caucasian Americans. *Journal of Psychoeducational Assessment, 24*, 358–366.

Egan, S. K., & Perry, D. G. (2001). Gender identity: A multidimensional analysis with implications for psychosocial adjustment. *Developmental Psychology, 37*, 451–463.

Egeland, B., Jacobvitz, D., & Sroufe, L. A. (1988). Breaking the cycle of abuse. *Child Development, 59*, 1080–1088.

Eggebeen, D. J., & Sturgeon, S. (2006). Demography of the baby boomers. In S. K. Whitbourne & S. L. Willis (Eds.), *The baby boomers grow up: Contemporary perspectives on midlife* (pp. 3–21). Mahwah, NJ: Erlbaum.

Ehrensaft, M. K., Cohen, P., & Johnson, J. G. (2006). Development of personality disorder symptoms and the risk for partner violence. *Journal of Abnormal Psychology, 115*, 474–483.

Ehrensaft, M. K., Moffitt, T. E., & Caspi, A. (2004). Clinically abusive relationships in an unselected birth cohort: Men's and women's participation and developmental antecedents. *Journal of Abnormal Psychology, 113*, 258–270.

Einstein, G. O., McDaniel, M. A., Manzi, M., Cochran, B., & Baker, M. (2000). Prospective memory and aging: Forgetting intentions over short delays. *Psychology and Aging, 15*, 671–683.

Eisenberg, N. (2003). Prosocial behavior, empathy, and sympathy. In M. H. Bornstein & L. Davidson (Eds.), *Well-being: Positive development across the life course* (pp. 253–265). Mahwah, NJ: Erlbaum.

Eisenberg, N., Fabes, R. A., Shepard, S. A., Murphy, B. C., Jones, S., & Guthrie, I. K. (1998). Contemporaneous and longitudinal prediction of children's sympathy from dispositional regulation and emotionality. *Developmental Psychology, 34*, 910–924.

Eisenberg, N., Fabes, R. A., & Spinrad, T. L. (2006). Prosocial development. In N. Eisenberg (Ed.), *Handbook of child psychology: Vol. 3. Social, emotional, and personality development* (6th ed., pp. 646–718). Hoboken, NJ: Wiley.

Eisenberg, N., Gershoff, E. T., Fabes, R. A., Shepard, S. A., Cumberland, A. J., & Losoya, S. H. (2001). Mothers' emotional expressivity and children's behavior problems and social competence: Mediation through children's regulation. *Developmental Psychology, 37*, 475–490.

Eisenberg, N., Smith, C. L., Sadovsky, A., & Spinrad, T. L. (2004). Effortful control: Relations with emotion regulation, adjustment, and socialization in childhood. In R. Baumeister & K. D. Vohs (Eds.), *Handbook of self-regulation: Research, theory, and applications* (pp. 259–282). New York: Guilford.

Eisenberg, N., Zhou, Q., Spinrad, T. L., Valiente, C., Fabes, R. A., & Liew, J. (2005). Relations among positive parenting, children's effortful control, and externalizing problems: A three-wave longitudinal study. *Child Development, 76*, 1055–1071.

Elavsky, S., & McAuley, E. (2007). Physical activity and mental health outcomes during menopause: A randomized controlled trial. *Annals of Behavioral Medicine, 33*, 132–142.

Elder, G. H., Jr., & Conger, R. (2000). *Children of the land: Adversity and success in rural America*. Chicago: University of Chicago Press.

Elder, G. H., Jr., Nguyen, T. V., & Caspi, A. (1985). Linking family hardship to children's lives. *Child Development, 56*, 361–375.

Elfenbein, D. S., & Felice, M. E. (2003). Adolescent pregnancy. *Pediatric Clinics of North America, 50*, 781–800.

Elias, C. L., & Berk, L. E. (2002). Self-regulation in young children: Is there a role for sociodramatic play? *Early Childhood Research Quarterly, 17*, 1–17.

Elkind, D. (1994). *A sympathetic understanding of the child: Birth to sixteen* (3rd ed.). Boston: Allyn and Bacon.

Elkind, D., & Bowen, R. (1979). Imaginary audience behavior in children and adolescents. *Developmental Psychology, 15*, 33–44.

Ellickson, P. L., D'Amico, E. J., Collins, R. L., & Klein, D. J. (2005). Marijuana use and later problems: When frequency of recent use explains age of initiation effects. *Substance Use and Misuse, 40*, 343–359.

Elliott, J. G. (1999). School refusal: Issues of conceptualization, assessment, and treatment. *Journal of Child Psychology and Psychiatry and Allied Disciplines, 40*, 1001–1012.

Ellis, B. J. (2004). Timing of pubertal maturation in girls: An integrated life history approach. *Psychological Bulletin, 130*, 920–958.

Ellis, B. J., & Essex, M. J. (2007). Family environments, adrenarche, and sexual maturation: A longitudinal test of a life history model. *Child Development, 78*, 1799–1817.

Ellis, L., & Bonin, S. L. (2003). Genetics and occupation-related preferences: Evidence from adoptive and non-adoptive families. *Personality and Individual Differences, 35*, 929–937.

Ellis, W. E., & Zarbatany, L. (2007). Explaining friendship formation and friendship stability: The role of children's and friends' aggression and victimization. *Merrill-Palmer Quarterly, 53*, 79–104.

Elman, J. L. (2001). Connectionism and language acquisition. In M. Tomasello & E. Bates (Eds.), *Language development* (pp. 295–306). Oxford, UK: Blackwell.

Else-Quest, N. M., Hyde, J. S., Goldsmith, H. H., & Van Hulle, C. A. (2006). Gender differences in temperament: A meta-analysis. *Psychological Bulletin, 132*, 33–72.

El-Sheikh, M., Cummings, E. M., & Reiter, S. (1996). Preschoolers' responses to ongoing interadult conflict: The role of prior exposure to resolved versus unresolved arguments. *Journal of Abnormal Child Psychology, 24*, 665–679.

Eltzschig, H. K., Lieberman, E. S., & Camann, W. R. (2003). Regional anesthesia and analgesia for labor and delivery. *New England Journal of Medicine, 384*, 319–332.

Elwert, F., & Christakis, N. A. (2006). Widowhood and race. *American Sociological Review, 71*, 16–41.

Emanuel, E. J., Fairclough, D. L., & Emanuel, L. L. (2000). Attitudes and desires related to euthanasia and physician-assisted suicide among terminally ill patients and their caregivers. *Journal of the American Medical Association, 284*, 2460–2468.

Emery, R. E., & Laumann-Billings, L. (1998). An overview of the nature, causes, and consequences of abusive family relationships: Toward differentiating maltreatment and violence. *American Psychologist, 53*, 121–135.

Emery, R. E., Sbarra, D., & Grover, T. (2005). Divorce mediation: Research and reflections. *Family Court Review, 43*, 22–37.

Englund, M. E., Egeland, B., & Collins, W. A. (2008). Exceptions to high school dropout predictions in a low-income sample: Do adults make a difference? *Journal of Social Issues, 64*, 77–93.

Ennemoser, M., & Schneider, W. (2007). Relations of television viewing and reading: Findings from a 4-year longitudinal study. *Journal of Educational Psychology, 99*, 349–368.

Entwisle, D. R., Alexander, K. L., & Olson, L. S. (2005). First grade and educational attainment by age 22: A new story. *American Journal of Sociology, 110*, 1458–1502.

Epel, E. S., Blackburn, E., Lin, J., Dhabhar, F., Adler, N., & Morrow, J. D. (2004). Accelerated telomere shortening in response to exposure to life stress. *Proceedings of the National Academy of Sciences, 101*, 17312–17315.

Epel, E. S., Linn, J., Wilhelm, F., Mendes, W., Adler, N., & Dolbier, C. (2006). Cell aging in relation to stress arousal and cardiovascular disease risk factors. *Psychoneuroendocrinology, 31*, 277–287.

Epel, E. S., Merkin, S. S., Cawthon, R., Blackburn, E. H., Adler, N. E., Pletcher, M. J., & Seeman, T. S. (2009). The rate of leukocyte telomere shortening predicts mortality from cardiovascular disease in elderly men: A novel demonstration. *Aging, 1*, 81–88.

Epstein, L. H., Roemmich, J. N., & Raynor, H. A. (2001). Behavioral therapy in the treatment of pediatric obesity. *Pediatric Clinics of North America, 48*, 981–983.

Erath, S. A., Bierman, K. L., & the Conduct Problems Prevention Research Group. (2006). Aggressive marital conflict, maternal harsh punishment, and child aggressive-disruptive behavior: Evidence for direct and mediate relations. *Journal of Family Psychology, 20*, 217–226.

Erden, F., & Wolfgang, C. H. (2004). An exploration of the differences in prekindergarten, kindergarten, and first-grade teachers' beliefs related to discipline when dealing with male and female students. *Early Child Development and Care, 174*, 3–11.

Erickson, K. L., Colcombe, S. J., Wadhwa, R., Bherer, L., Peterson, M. S., & Scalf, P. E. (2007). Training-induced plasticity in older adults: Effects of training on hemispheric asymmetry. *Neurobiology of Aging, 28*, 272–283.

Erikson, E. H. (1950). *Childhood and society*. New York: Norton.

Erikson, E. H. (1968). *Identity, youth, and crisis*. New York: Norton.

Erikson, E. H. (1998). *The life cycle completed. Extended version with new chapters on the ninth stage by Joan M. Erikson*. New York: Norton.

Ertekin-Tanner, N. (2007). Genetics of Alzheimer's disease: A centennial review. *Neurologic Clinics, 25*, 611–667.

Espy, K. A., Molfese, V. J., & DiLalla, L. F. (2001). Effects of environmental measures on intelligence in young children: Growth curve modeling of longitudinal data. *Merrill-Palmer Quarterly, 47*, 42–73.

Esterberg, K. G., Moen, P., & Dempster-McClain, D. (1994). Transition to divorce: A life-course approach to women's marital duration and dissolution. *Sociological Quarterly, 35*, 289–307.

Estourgie-van Burk, G. F., Bartels, M., van Beijsterveldt, T. C., Delemarre-van de Waal, H. A., & Boomsma, D. I. (2006). Body size in five-year-old twins: Heritability and comparison to singleton standards. *Twin Research and Human Genetics, 9*, 646–655.

Ethier, K. A., Kershaw, T., Niccolai, L., Lewis, J. B., & Ickovics, J. R. (2003). Adolescent women underestimate their susceptibility to sexually transmitted infections. *Sexually Transmitted Infections, 79*, 408–411.

Evans, A. M., & Scutter, S. D. (2004). How common are "growing pains" in young children? *Journal of Pediatrics, 145,* 255–258.

Evans, E., Hawton, K., & Rodham, K. (2004). Factors associated with suicidal phenomena in adolescents: A systematic review of population-based studies. *Clinical Psychology Review, 24,* 957–979.

Evans, G. W. (2006). Child development and the physical environment. *Annual Review of Psychology, 57,* 424–451.

Evans, G. W., & Kantrowitz, E. (2002). Socioeconomic status and health: The potential role of environmental risk exposure. *Annual Review of Public Health, 23,* 303–331.

Evans, J. (2008). Antioxidant supplements to prevent or slow down the progression of AMD: A systematic review and meta-analysis. *Eye, 22,* 751–760.

Everman, D. B., & Cassidy, S. B. (2000). Genetics of childhood disorders: XII. Genomic imprinting: Breaking the rules. *Journal of the American Academy of Child and Adolescent Psychiatry, 38,* 386–389.

F

Fabes, R. A., Eisenberg, N., Hanish, L. D., & Spinrad, T. L. (2001). Preschoolers' spontaneous emotion vocabulary: Relations to likeability. *Early Education and Development, 12,* 11–27.

Fabes, R. A., Eisenberg, N., McCormick, S. E., & Wilson, M. S. (1988). Preschoolers' attributions of the situational determinants of others' naturally occurring emotions. *Developmental Psychology, 24,* 376–385.

Fabes, R. A., Martin, C. L., & Hanish, L. D. (2003). Young children's play qualities in same-, other-, and mixed-sex peer groups. *Child Development, 74,* 921–932.

Facio, A., & Micocci, F. (2003). Emerging adulthood in Argentina. *New Directions for Child and Adolescent Development, 100,* 21–31.

Fagan, J. F., Holland, C. R., & Wheeler, K. (2007). The prediction, from infancy, of adult IQ and achievement. *Intelligence, 35,* 225–231.

Fagard, J., & Pezé, A. (1997). Age changes in interlimb coupling and the development of bimanual coordination. *Journal of Motor Behavior, 29,* 199–208.

Fagot, B. I. (1984). The child's expectations of differences in adult male and female interactions. *Sex Roles, 11,* 593–600.

Fagot, B. I. (1985). Changes in thinking about early sex role development. *Developmental Review, 5,* 83–98.

Fagot, B. I., & Hagan, R. I. (1991). Observations of parent reactions to sex-stereotyped behaviors: Age and sex effects. *Child Development, 62,* 617–628.

Fagot, B. I., & Leinbach, M. D. (1989). The young child's gender schema: Environmental input, internal organization. *Child Development, 60,* 663–672.

Fahrmeier, E. D. (1978). The development of concrete operations among the Hausa. *Journal of Cross-Cultural Psychology, 9,* 23–44.

Fairburn, C. G. (2005). Evidence-based treatment of anorexia nervosa. *International Journal of Eating Disorders, 37,* S26–S30.

Fairburn, C. G., & Harrison, P. J. (2003). Eating disorders. *Lancet, 361,* 407–416.

Faircloth, B. S., & Hamm, J. V. (2005). Sense of belonging among high school students representing four ethnic groups. *Journal of Youth and Adolescence, 34,* 293–309.

Fajardo, M., & Di Cesare, P. E. (2005). Disease-modifying therapies for osteoarthritis. *Drugs and Aging, 22,* 141–161.

Falbo, T. (1992). Social norms and the one-child family: Clinical and policy implications. In F. Boer & J. Dunn (Eds.), *Children's sibling relationships* (pp. 71–82). Hillsdale, NJ: Erlbaum.

Falbo, T., & Poston, D. L., Jr. (1993). The academic, personality, and physical outcomes of only children in China. *Child Development, 64,* 18–35.

Falbo, T., Poston, D. L., Jr., Triscari, R. S., & Zhang, X. (1997). Self-enhancing illusions among Chinese schoolchildren. *Journal of Cross-Cultural Psychology, 28,* 172–191.

Falck-Ytter, T., Gredebäck, G., & von Hofsten, C. (2006). Infants predict other people's action goals. *Nature Neuroscience, 9,* 878–879.

Family Caregiver Alliance. (2005). *Fact sheet: Selected caregiver statistics.* Retrieved from www.caregiver.org/factsheets/selected_caregiver_statisticsC.html

Family Caregiver Alliance. (2009). *Fact sheet: Selected caregiver statistics.* Retrieved from www.caregiver.org/caregiver/jsp/content_node.jsp?nodeid=439

Fanslow, C. A. (1981). Death: A natural facet of the life continuum. In D. Krieger (Ed.), *Foundations for holistic health nursing practices: The renaissance nurse* (pp. 249–272). Philadelphia: Lippincott.

Fantz, R. L. (1961, May). The origin of form perception. *Scientific American, 204* (5), 66–72.

Farrant, K., & Reese, E. (2000). Maternal style and children's participation in reminiscing: Stepping stones in children's autobiological memory development. *Journal of Cognition and Development, 1,* 193–225.

Farrington, D. P. (2004). Conduct disorder, aggression, and delinquency. In R. M. Lerner & L. Steinberg (Eds.), *Handbook of adolescent psychology* (2nd ed., pp. 627–664). New York: Wiley.

Farver, J. M., & Branstetter, W. H. (1994). Preschoolers' prosocial responses to their peers' distress. *Developmental Psychology, 30,* 334–341.

Farver, J. M., Kim, Y. K., & Lee, Y. (1995). Cultural differences in Korean- and Anglo-American preschoolers' social interaction and play behaviors. *Child Development, 66,* 1088–1099.

Fashola, O. S., & Slavin, R. E. (1998). Effective dropout prevention and college attendance programs for students placed at risk. *Journal of Education for Students Placed at Risk, 3,* 159–183.

Fasig, L. G. (2000). Toddlers' understanding of ownership: Implications for self-concept development. *Social Development, 9,* 370–382.

Fattibene, P., Mazzei, F., Nuccetelli, C., & Risica, S. (1999). Prenatal exposure to ionizing radiation: Sources, effects, and regulatory aspects. *Acta Paediatrica, 88,* 693–702.

Federal Interagency Forum on Child and Family Statistics. (2008). *America's children: Key national indicators of well-being, 2008.* Retrieved from www.childstats.gov/americaschildren/tables.asp

Federenko, I. S., & Wadhwa, P. D. (2004). Women's mental health during pregnancy influences fetal and infant developmental and health outcomes. *CNS Spectrums, 9,* 198–206.

Federico, M. J., & Liu, A. H. (2003). Overcoming childhood asthma disparities of the inner-city poor. *Pediatric Clinics of North America, 50,* 655–675.

Feeney, J. A. (1999). Adult romantic attachment and couple relationships. In J. Cassidy & P. R. Shaver (Eds.), *Handbook of attachment* (pp. 355–377). New York: Guilford.

Feeney, J. A., Hohaus, L., Noller, P., & Alexander, R. P. (2001). *Becoming parents: Exploring the bonds between mothers, fathers, and their infants.* New York: Cambridge University Press.

Fehr, B. (1994). Prototype based assessment of laypeoples' views of love. *Personal Relationships, 1,* 309–331.

Feinberg, M. E., McHale, S. M., Crouter, A. C., & Cumsille, P. (2003). Sibling differentiation: Sibling and parent relationship trajectories in adolescence. *Child Development, 74,* 1261–1274.

Feinsilver, S. H. (2003). Sleep in the elderly: What is normal? *Clinical Geriatric Medicine, 19,* 177–188.

Feiring, C., Taska, L., & Lewis, M. (1999). Age and gender differences in children's and adolescents' adaptation to sexual abuse. *Child Abuse and Neglect, 23,* 115–128.

Feldman, A. F., & Matjasko, J. L. (2007). Profiles and portfolios of adolescent school-based extracurricular activity participation. *Journal of Adolescence, 30,* 313–332.

Feldman, P. J., & Steptoe, A. (2004). How neighborhoods and physical functioning are related: The roles of neighborhood socioeconomic status, perceived neighborhood strain, and individual health risk factors. *Annals of Behavioral Medicine, 27,* 91–99.

Feldman, R. (2003). Infant–mother and infant–father synchrony: The coregulation of positive arousal. *Infant Mental Health Journal, 24,* 1–23.

Feldman, R. (2006). From biological rhythms to social rhythms: Physiological precursors of mother–infant synchrony. *Developmental Psychology, 42,* 175–188.

Feldman, R. (2007). Maternal versus child risk and the development of parent–child and family relationships in five high-risk populations. *Development and Psychopathology, 19,* 293–312.

Feldman, R., & Eidelman, A. I. (2003). Skin-to-skin contact (kangaroo care) accelerates autonomic and neurobehavioral maturation in preterm infants. *Developmental Medicine and Child Neurology, 45,* 274–281.

Feldman, R., Eidelman, A. I., & Rotenberg, N. (2004). Parenting stress, infant emotion regulation, maternal sensitivity, and the cognitive development of triplets: A model for parent and child influences in a unique ecology. *Child Development, 75,* 1774–1791.

Feldman, R., Eidelman, A. I., Sirota, L., & Weller, A. (2002). Comparison of skin-to-skin (kangaroo) and traditional care: Parenting outcomes and preterm infant development. *Pediatrics, 110,* 16–26.

Feldman, R., Greenbaum, C. W., & Yirmiya, N. (1999). Mother–infant affect synchrony as an antecedent of the emergence of self-control. *Developmental Psychology, 35,* 223–231.

Feldman, R., & Klein, P. S. (2003). Toddlers' self-regulated compliance to mothers, caregivers, and fathers: Implications for theories of socialization. *Developmental Psychology, 39,* 680–692.

Feldman, R., Sussman, A. L., & Zigler, E. (2004). Parental leave and work adaptation at the transition to parenthood: Individual, marital, and social correlates. *Applied Developmental Psychology, 25,* 459–479.

Feldman, R., Weller, A., Sirota, L., & Eidelman, A. I. (2003). Testing a family intervention hypothesis: The contribution of mother–infant skin-to-skin contact (kangaroo care) to family interaction, proximity, and touch. *Journal of Family Psychology, 17,* 94–107.

Felner, R. D., Favazza, A., Shim, M., Brand, S., Gu, K., & Noonan, N. (2002). Whole school improvement and restructuring as prevention and promotion: Lessons from STEP and the Project on High Performance Learning Communities. *Journal of School Psychology, 39,* 177–202.

Felsman, D. E., & Blustein, D. L. (1999). The role of peer relatedness in late adolescent career development. *Journal of Vocational Behavior, 54,* 279–295.

Feng, Q. (2005). Postnatal consequences of prenatal cocaine exposure and myocardial apoptosis: Does cocaine in utero imperil the adult heart? *British Journal of Pharmacology, 144,* 887–888.

Fenson, L., Dale, P. S., Reznick, J. S., Bates, E., Thal, D. J., & Pethick, S. J. (1994). Variability in early communicative development. *Monographs of the Society for Research in Child Development, 59*(5, Serial No. 242).

Feret, A., Steinweg, S., Griffin, H. C., & Glover, S. (2007). Macular degeneration: Types, causes, and possible interventions. *Geriatric Nursing, 28,* 387–392.

Fergusson, D. M., & Horwood, J. (2003). Resilience to childhood adversity: Results of a 21-year study. In S. S. Luthar (Ed.), *Resilience and vulnerability* (pp. 130–155). New York: Cambridge University Press.

Fergusson, D. M., & Woodward, L. J. (1999). Breast-feeding and later psychosocial adjustment. *Paediatric and Perinatal Epidemiology, 13,* 144–157.

Fernald, A., & Hurtado, N. (2006). Names in frames: Infants interpret words in sentence frames faster than words in isolation. *Developmental Science, 9,* F33–F40.

Fernald, A., & Morikawa, H. (1993). Common themes and cultural variations in Japanese and American mothers' speech to infants. *Child Development, 64,* 637–656.

Fernald, A., Perfors, A., & Marchman, V. A. (2006). Picking up speed in understanding: Speech processing efficiency and vocabulary growth across the 2nd year. *Developmental Psychology, 42,* 98–116.

Fernald, A., Taeschner, T., Dunn, J., Papousek, M., Boyssen-Bardies, B., & Fukui, I. (1989). A cross-language study of prosodic modifications in mothers' and fathers' speech to preverbal infants. *Journal of Child Language, 16,* 477–502.

Fernald, L. C., & Grantham-McGregor, S. M. (1998). Stress response in school-age children who have been growth-retarded since early childhood. *American Journal of Clinical Nutrition, 68,* 691–698.

Fernyhough, C., & Fradley, E. (2005). Private speech on an executive task: Relations with task difficulty and task performance. *Cognitive Development, 20,* 103–120.

Ferrell, B. A. (1995). Pain evaluation and management in the nursing home. *Annals of Internal Medicine, 123,* 681–687.

Ficca, G., Fagioli, I., Giganti, F., & Salzarulo, P. (1999). Spontaneous awakenings from sleep in the first year of life. *Early Human Development, 55,* 219–228.

Field, D. (1997). "Looking back, what period of your life brought you the most satisfaction?" *International Journal of Aging and Human Development, 45,* 169–194.

Field, D. (1999). Stability of older women's friendships: A commentary on Roberto. *International Journal of Aging and Human Development, 48,* 81–83.

Field, D., & Millsap, R. E. (1991). Personality in advanced old age: Continuity or change? *Journal of Gerontology, 46,* 299–308.

Field, T. (2001). Massage therapy facilitates weight gain in preterm infants. *Current Directions in Psychological Science, 10,* 51–54.

Field, T., Diego, M., Hernandez-Reif, M., Figueiredo, B., Schanberg, S., & Kuhn, C. (2007). Sleep disturbances in depressed pregnant women and their newborns. *Infant Behavior and Development, 30,* 127–133.

Field, T., Hernandez-Reif, M., Feijo, L., & Freedman, J. (2006). Prenatal, perinatal and neonatal stimulation: A survey of neonatal nurseries. *Infant Behavior and Development, 29,* 24–31.

Field, T., Hernandez-Reif, M., & Freedman, J. (2004). Stimulation programs for preterm infants. *Social Policy Report of the Society for Research in Child Development, 18*(1).

Field, T. M., Woodson, R., Greenberg, R., & Cohen, D. (1982). Discrimination and imitation of facial expressions by neonates. *Science, 218,* 179–181.

Fiese, B. H., & Schwartz, M. (2008). Reclaiming the family table: Mealtimes and child health and well-being. *Social Policy Report of the Society for Research in Child Development, 22*(4), 3–18.

Finchum, T., & Weber, J. A. (2000). Applying continuity theory to elder adult friendships. *Journal of Aging and Identity, 5,* 159–168.

Fingerman, K. L. (2000). "We had a nice little chat": Age and generational differences in mothers' and daughters' descriptions of enjoyable visits. *Journal of Gerontology, 55B,* P95–P106.

Fingerman, K. L. (2001a). A distant closeness: Intimacy between parents and their children in later life. *Generations, 25,* 26–33.

Fingerman, K. L. (2001b). *Aging mothers and their adult daughters: A study in mixed emotions.* New York: Springer.

Fingerman, K. L. (2004). The role of offspring and in-laws in grandparents' ties to their grandchildren. *Journal of Family Issues, 25,* 1026–1049.

Fingerman, K. L., & Birditt, K. S. (2003). Do we get better at picking our battles? Age group differences in descriptions of behavioral reactions to interpersonal tensions. *Journal of Gerontology, 60B,* P121–P128.

Fingerman, K. L., Hay, E. L., Dush, C. M. K., Cichy, K. E., & Hosterman, S. J. (2007). Parents' and offspring's perceptions of change and continuity when parents experience the transition to old age. *Advances in Life Course Research, 12,* 275–305.

Finkel, D., Reynolds, C. A., McArdle, J. J., & Pedersen, N. L. (2007). Age changes in processing speed as a leading indicator of cognitive aging. *Psychology and Aging, 22,* 558–568.

Finucane, M. L., Mertz, C. K., Slovic, P., & Schmidt, E. S. (2005). Task complexity and older adults' decision-making competence. *Psychology and Aging, 20,* 71–84.

Fiori, K. L., Smith, J., & Antonucci, T. C. (2007). Social network types among older adults: A multidimensional approach. *Journal of Gerontology, 62B,* P322–P330.

Firestone, R. W. (1994). Psychological defenses against death anxiety. In R. A. Neimeyer (Ed.), *Death anxiety handbook* (pp. 217–241). Washington, DC: Taylor & Francis.

Fisch, H., Hyun, G., Golden, R., Hensle, T. W., Olsson, C. A., & Liberson, G. L. (2003). The influence of paternal age on Down syndrome. *Journal of Urology, 169,* 2275–2278.

Fischer, K. W., & Bidell, T. R. (1991). Constraining nativist inferences about cognitive capacities. In S. Carey & R. Gelman (Eds.), *The epigenesis of mind: Essays on biology and cognition* (pp. 199–235). Hillsdale, NJ: Erlbaum.

Fischer, K. W., & Bidell, T. R. (2006). Dynamic development of action and thought. In R. M. Lerner (Ed.), *Handbook of child psychology: Vol. 1. Theoretical models of human development* (6th ed., pp. 313–399). Hoboken, NJ: Wiley.

Fischman, M. G., Moore, J. B., & Steele, K. H. (1992). Children's one-hand catching as a function of age, gender, and ball location. *Research Quarterly for Exercise and Sport, 63,* 349–355.

Fish, M. (2004). Attachment in infancy and preschool in low socioeconomic status rural Appalachian children: Stability and change and relations to preschool and kindergarten competence. *Development and Psychopathology, 16,* 293–312.

Fisher, C. B. (1993, Winter). Integrating science and ethics in research with high-risk children and youth. *Social Policy Report of the Society for Research in Child Development, 4*(4).

Fisher, C. B. (2005). Deception research involving children: Ethical practices and paradoxes. *Ethics and Behavior, 15,* 271–287.

Fisher, S. K., Easterly, S., & Lazear, K. J. (2008). Lesbian, gay, bisexual and transgender families and their children. In T. P. Gullotta & G. M. Blau (Eds.), *Family influences on child behavior and development: Evidence-based prevention and treatment approaches* (pp. 187–208). New York: Routledge.

Fishman, S. B. (2004). *Double or nothing? Jewish families and mixed marriage.* Waltham, MA: Brandeis University Press.

FitzGerald, D. P., & White, K. J. (2003). Linking children's social worlds: Perspective-taking in parent–child and peer contexts. *Social Behavior and Personality, 31,* 509–522.

Fitzgibbons, P. J., & Gordon-Salant, S. (1998). Auditory temporal order perception in younger and older adults. *Journal of Speech, Language, and Hearing Research, 41,* 1052–1060.

Fitzpatrick, J., & Sollie, D. L. (1999). Influence of individual and interpersonal factors on satisfaction and stability in romantic relationships. *Personal Relationships, 6,* 337–350.

Fivush, R. (2001). Owning experience: Developing subjective perspective in autobiographical narratives. In C. Moore & K. Lemmon (Eds.), *The self in time: Developmental perspectives* (pp. 35–52). Mahwah, NJ: Erlbaum.

Flake, A. W. (2003). Surgery in the human fetus: The future. *Journal of Physiology, 547,* 45–51.

Flaks, D. K., Ficher, I., Masterpasqua, F., & Joseph, G. (1995). Lesbians choosing motherhood: A comparative study of lesbian and heterosexual parents and their children. *Developmental Psychology, 31,* 105–114.

Flanagan, C. A., Stout, M., & Gallay, L. S. (2008). It's my body and none of your business: Developmental changes in adolescents' perceptions of rights concerning health. *Journal of Social Issues, 64,* 815–834.

Flannery, D. J., Hussey, D. L., Biebelhausen, L., & Wester, K. L. (2003). Crime, delinquency, and youth gangs. In G. R. Adams & M. D. Berzonsky (Eds.), *Blackwell handbook of adolescence* (pp. 502–522). Malden, MA: Blackwell.

Flannery, K. A., & Liederman, J. (1995). Is there really a syndrome involving the co-occurrence of neuro-developmental disorder, talent, non–right handedness and immune disorder among children? *Cortex, 31,* 503–515.

Flavell, J. H., Flavell, E. R., & Green, F. L. (2001). Development of children's understanding of connections between thinking and feeling. *Psychological Science, 12,* 430–432.

Flavell, J. H., Green, F. L., & Flavell, E. R. (1993). Children's understanding of the stream of consciousness. *Child Development, 64,* 387–398.

Flavell, J. H., Green, F. L., & Flavell, E. R. (1995). Young children's knowledge about thinking. *Monographs of the Society for Research in Child Development, 60*(1, Serial No. 243).

Flavell, J. H., Green, F. L., & Flavell, E. R. (2000). Development of children's awareness of their own thoughts. *Journal of Cognition and Development, 1,* 97–112.

Fleischman, D. A., Wilson, R. S., Gabrieli, J. D. E., Bienias, J. L., & Bennett, D. A. (2004). A longitudinal study of implicit and explicit memory in old persons. *Psychology and Aging, 19,* 617–625.

Fleming, V. M., & Alexander, J. M. (2001). The benefits of peer collaboration: A replication with a delayed posttest. *Contemporary Educational Psychology, 26,* 588–601.

Fletcher, A. C., Nickerson, P., & Wright, K. L. (2003). Structured leisure activities in middle childhood: Links to well-being. *Journal of Community Psychology, 31,* 641–659.

Flom, R., & Pick, A. D. (2003). Verbal encouragement and joint attention in 18-month-old infants. *Infant Behavior and Development, 26,* 121–134.

Flood, D. G., & Coleman, P. D. (1988). Cell type heterogeneity of changes in dendritic extent in the hippocampal region of the human brain in normal aging and in Alzheimer's disease. In T. L. Petit & G. O. Ivy (Ed.), *Neural plasticity: A lifespan approach* (pp. 265–281). New York: Alan R. Liss.

Florian, V., & Mikulincer, M. (1998). Symbolic immortality and the management of the terror of death: The moderating role of attachment style. *Journal of Personality and Social Psychology, 74,* 725–734.

Florsheim, P., & Smith, A. (2005). Expectant adolescent couples' relations and subsequent parenting behavior. *Infant Mental Health Journal, 26,* 533–548.

Flynn, E. (2006). A microgenetic investigation of stability and continuity in theory of mind development. *British Journal of Developmental Psychology, 24,* 631–654.

Fomon, S. J., & Nelson, S. E. (2002). Body composition of the male and female reference infants. *Annual Review of Nutrition, 22,* 1–17.

Fonda, S. J., Clipp, E. C., & Maddox, G. L. (2002). Patterns in functioning among residents of an affordable assisted living housing facility. *Gerontologist, 42,* 178–187.

Fong, T. G., Tulebaev, S. R., & Inouye, S. K. (2009). Delirium in elderly adults: Diagnosis, prevention and treatment. *Nature Reviews Neurology, 5,* 210–220.

Fontana, L. (2008). Calorie restriction and cardiometabolic health. *European Journal of Cardiovascular Prevention and Rehabilitation, 15,* 3–9.

Fontana, L. (2009). The scientific basis of caloric restriction leading to longer life. *Current Opinion in Gastroenterology, 25,* 144–150.

Fontana, L., Weiss, E., Villareal, D. T., Klein, S., & Holloszy, J. O. (2009). IGF-1, nutrition and aging: The big picture. *Aging Cell, 8,* 215.

Forman, D. R., Aksan, N., & Kochanska, G. (2004). Toddlers' responsive imitation predicts preschool-age conscience. *Psychological Science, 15,* 699–704.

Forman, D. R., O'Hara, M. W., Stuart, S., Gorman, L. L., Larsen, K. E., & Coy, K. C. (2007). Effective treatment for postpartum depression is not sufficient to improve the developing mother–child relationship. *Development and Psychopathology, 19,* 585–602.

Forry, N. D., Leslie, L. A., & Letiecq, B. L. (2007). Marital quality in interracial relationships: The role of sex role ideology and perceived fairness. *Journal of Family Issues, 28,* 1538–1552.

Forste, R., & Heaton, T. B. (2004). The divorce generation: Well-being, family attitudes, and socioeconomic consequences of marital disruption. *Journal of Divorce and Remarriage, 42,* 95–114.

Foster, M. A., Lambert, R., Abbott-Shim, M., McCarty, F., & Franze, S. (2005). A model of home learning environment and social risk factors in relation to children's emergent literacy and social outcomes. *Early Childhood Research Quarterly, 20,* 13–36.

Foster, W. A., & Miller, M. (2007). Development of the literacy achievement gap: A longitudinal study of kindergarten through third grade. *Language, Speech, and Hearing Services in Schools, 38,* 173–181.

Fowden, A. L., Giussani, D. A., & Forhead, A. J. (2005). Endocrine and metabolic programming during intrauterine development. *Early Human Development, 81,* 723–734.

Fowler, J. W. (1981). *Stages of faith.* San Francisco: Harper & Row.

Fox, C. L., & Boulton, M. J. (2006). Friendship as a moderator of the relationship between social skills problems and peer victimization. *Aggressive Behavior, 32,* 110–121.

Fox, N. A. (1991). If it's not left, it's right: Electroencephalograph asymmetry and the development of emotion. *American Psychologist, 46,* 863–872.

Fox, N. A., & Davidson, R. J. (1986). Taste-elicited changes in facial signs of emotion and the asymmetry of brain electrical activity in newborn infants. *Neuropsychologia, 24,* 417–422.

Foy, J. G., & Mann, V. (2003). Home literacy environment and phonological awareness in preschool children: Differential effects for rhyme and phoneme awareness. *Applied Psycholinguistics, 24,* 59–88.

Fozard, J. L., & Gordon-Salant, S. (2001). Changes in vision and hearing with aging. In J. E. Birren & K. W. Schaie (Eds.), *Handbook of the psychology of aging* (pp. 241–266). San Diego: Academic Press.

Franco, P., Chabanski, S., Szliwowski, H., Dramaix, M., & Kahn, A. (2000). Influence of maternal smoking on autonomic nervous system in healthy infants. *Pediatric Research, 47,* 215–220.

Frank, D. A., Rose-Jacobs, R., Beeghly, M., Wilbur, M., Bellinger, D., & Cabral, H. (2005). Level of prenatal cocaine exposure and 48-month IQ: Importance of preschool enrichment. *Neurotoxicology and Teratology, 27,* 15–28.

Franklin, M. (1995). The effects of differential college environments on academic learning and student

perceptions of cognitive development. *Research in Higher Education, 36,* 127–153.

Franz, M. J., VanWormer, J. J., Crain, A. L., Boucher, J. L., Histon, T., Caplan, W., Bowman, J. D., & Pronk, N. P. (2007). Weight-loss outcomes: A systematic review and meta-analysis of weight-loss clinical trials with a minimum 1-year follow-up. *Journal of the American Dietetic Association, 107,* 1755–1767.

Frazier, L. D. (2002). Perceptions of control over health: Implications for sense of self in healthy and ill older adults. In S. P. Shohov (Ed.), *Advances in psychology research* (Vol. 10, pp. 145–163). Huntington, NY: Nova Science Publishers.

Frazier, L. D., & Hooker, K. (2006). Possible selves in adult development: Linking theory and research. In C. Dunkel & J. Kerpelman (Eds.), *Possible selves: Theory, research and applications* (pp. 41–59). Hauppauge, NY: Nova Science.

Frederickson, B. L., & Carstensen, L. L. (1990). Relationship classification using grade of membership analysis: A typology of sibling relationships in later life. *Journal of Gerontology, 45,* S43–S51.

Fredricks, J. A., & Eccles, J. S. (2002). Children's competence and value beliefs from childhood through adolescence: Growth trajectories in two male-sex-typed domains. *Developmental Psychology, 38,* 519–533.

Fredricks, J. A., & Eccles, J. S. (2005). Developmental benefits of extracurricular involvement: Do peer characteristics mediate the link between activities and youth outcomes? *Journal of Youth and Adolescence, 34,* 507–520.

Fredricks, J. A., & Eccles, J. S. (2006). Is extracurricular participation associated with beneficial outcomes? Concurrent and longitudinal relations. *Developmental Psychology, 42,* 698–713.

Freedman, M. (1999). *Prime time: How baby boomers will revolutionize retirement and transform America.* New York: Public Affairs.

Freedman-Doan, C., Wigfield, A., Eccles, J. S., Blumenfeld, P., Arbreton, A., & Harold, R. D. (2000). What am I best at? Grade and gender differences in children's beliefs about ability improvement. *Journal of Applied Developmental Psychology, 21,* 379–402.

Freeman, D. (1983). *Margaret Mead and Samoa: The making and unmaking of an anthropological myth.* Cambridge, MA: Harvard University Press.

Freeman, L., Caserta, M., Lund, D., Rossa, S., Dowdy, A., & Partenheimer, A. (2006). Music thanatology: Prescriptive harp music as palliative care for the dying patient. *American Journal of Hospice and Palliative Care, 23,* 100–104.

Freiman, A., Bird, G., Metelitsa, A. I., Barankin, B., & Lauzon, G. J. (2004). Cutaneous effects of smoking. *Journal of Cutaneous Medicine and Surgery, 8,* 415–423.

French, S. A., Story, M., & Jeffrey, R. W. (2001). Environmental influences on eating and physical activity. *Annual Review of Public Health, 22,* 309–335.

Freud, A. (1969). Adolescence as a developmental disturbance. In G. Caplan & S. Lebovici (Eds.), *Adolescence* (pp. 5–10). New York: Basic Books.

Freud, S. (1973). *An outline of psychoanalysis.* London: Hogarth. (Original work published 1938)

Freud, S. (1974). *The ego and the id.* London: Hogarth. (Original work published 1923)

Freund, A. M., & Baltes, P. B. (1998). Selection, optimization, and compensation as strategies of life management: Correlations with subjective indicators of successful aging. *Psychology and Aging, 13,* 531–543.

Freund, A. M., & Baltes, P. B. (2000). The orchestration of selection, optimization and compensation: An action-theoretical conceptualization of a theory of developmental regulation. In W. J. Perrig & A. Grob (Eds.), *Control of human behavior, mental processes, and consciousness* (pp. 35–58). Mahwah, NJ: Erlbaum.

Freund, A. M., & Ebner, N. C. (2005). The aging self: Shifting from promoting gains to balancing losses.

In W. Greve, K. Rothermund, & D. Wentura (Eds.), *The adaptive self: Personal continuity and intentional self-development* (pp. 185–202). New York: Hogrefe.

Freund, A. M., & Smith, J. (1999). Content and function of the self-definition in old and very old age. *Journal of Gerontology, 54B,* P55–P67.

Frey, A., Ruchkin, V., Martin, A., & Schwab-Stone, M. (2009). Adolescents in transition: School and family characteristics in the development of violent behaviors entering high school. *Child Psychiatry and Human Development, 40,* 1–13.

Fried, P. A., Watkinson, B., & Gray, R. (2003). Differential effects on cognitive functioning in 13- to 16-year-olds prenatally exposed to cigarettes and marijuana. *Neurotoxicology and Teratology, 25,* 427–436.

Friedman, D. S. (2006, January). Understanding who is at high risk of having glaucoma. *Gleams,* pp. 1–2. Retrieved from www.umm.edu/patiented/articles/who_gets_glaucoma_000025_5.htm

Friedman, E. M., & Lawrence, D. A. (2002). Environmental stress mediates changes in neuroimmunological interactions. *Toxicological Sciences, 67,* 4–10.

Friedman, J. M. (2006). *The effects of drugs on the fetus and nursing infant: A handbook for health care professionals.* Baltimore: Johns Hopkins University Press.

Friedman, S. L., & Scholnick, E. K. (1997). An evolving "blueprint" for planning: Psychological requirements, task characteristics, and social–cultural influences. In S. L. Friedman & E. K. Scholnick (Eds.), *The developmental psychology of planning: Why, how, and when do we plan?* (pp. 3–22). Mahwah, NJ: Erlbaum.

Fries, J. F. (2003). Measuring and monitoring success in compressing morbidity. *Annals of Internal Medicine, 139,* 455–459.

Frith, U. (2003). *Autism: Explaining the enigma* (2nd ed.). Malden, MA: Blackwell.

Fry, C. L. (1985). Culture, behavior, and aging in the comparative perspective. In J. E. Birren & K. W. Schaie (Eds.), *Handbook of the psychology of aging* (2nd ed., pp. 216–244). New York: Van Nostrand Reinhold.

Fry, P. S. (2001). Predictors of health-related quality of life perspectives, self-esteem, and life satisfactions of older adults following spousal loss: An 18-month follow-up study of widows and widowers. *Gerontologist, 41,* 787–798.

Fry, P. S. (2003). Perceived self-efficacy domains as predictors of fear of the unknown and fear of dying among older adults. *Psychology and Aging, 18,* 474–486.

Fry, P. S., & Debats, D. L. (2006). Sources of life strengths as predictors of late-life mortality and survivorship. *International Journal of Aging and Human Development, 62,* 303–334.

Fuchs, D., Fuchs, L. S., Mathes, P. G., & Martinez, E. A. (2002a). Preliminary evidence on the standing of students with learning disabilities in PALS and no-PALS classrooms. *Learning Disabilities Research and Practice, 17,* 205–215.

Fuchs, L. S., Fuchs, D., Yazkian, L., & Powell, S. R. (2002b). Enhancing first-grade children's mathematical development with peer-assisted learning strategies. *School Psychology Review, 31,* 569–583.

Fukunaga, A., Uematsu, H., & Sugimoto, K. (2005). Influences of aging on taste perception and oral somatic sensation. *Journal of Gerontology, 60A,* 109–113.

Fuligni, A. J. (1998). The adjustment of children from immigrant families. *Current Directions in Psychological Science, 7,* 99–103.

Fuligni, A. J. (2004). The adaptation and acculturation of children from immigrant families. In U. P. Gielen & J. Roopnarine (Eds.), *Childhood and adolescence: Cross-cultural perspectives* (pp. 297–318). Westport, CT: Praeger.

Fuligni, A. J., Yip, T., & Tseng, V. (2002). The impact of family obligation on the daily activities and psychological well-being of Chinese-American adolescents. *Child Development, 73,* 302–314.

Fuligni, A. J., & Yoshikawa, H. (2003). Socioeconomic resources, parenting, and child development among immigrant families. In M. H. Bornstein & R. H. Bradley (Eds.), *Socioeconomic status, parenting, and child development* (pp. 107–124). Mahwah, NJ: Erlbaum.

Fuligni, A. S., Han, W.-J., & Brooks-Gunn, J. (2004). The Infant-Toddler HOME in the 2nd and 3rd years of life. *Parenting: Science and Practice, 4,* 139–159.

Fuller, C., Keller, L., Olson, J., Plymale, A., & Gottesman, M. (2005). Helping preschoolers become healthy eaters. *Journal of Pediatric Health Care, 19,* 178–182.

Fuller-Thomson, E., & Minkler, M. (2000). The mental and physical health of grandmothers who are raising their grandchildren. *Journal of Mental Health and Aging, 6,* 311–323.

Fuller-Thomson, E., & Minkler, M. (2005). Native American grandparents raising grandchildren: Findings from the Census 2000 Supplementary Survey and implications for social work practice. *Social Work, 50,* 131–139.

Fuller-Thomson, E., & Minkler, M. (2007). Mexican American grandparents raising grandchildren: Findings from the Census 2000 American Community Survey. *Families in Society, 88,* 567–574.

Fullerton, J. T., Navarro, A. M., & Young, S. H. (2007). Outcomes of planned home birth: An integrative review. *Journal of Midwifery and Women's Health, 52,* 323–333.

Fulmer, T. (2008). Screening for mistreatment of older adults. *American Journal of Nursing, 108,* 52–56.

Fung, H. H., & Carstensen, L. L. (2004). Motivational changes in response to blocked goals and foreshortened time: Testing alternatives to socioemotional selectivity theory. *Psychology and Aging, 19,* 68–78.

Fung, H. H., Carstensen, L. L., & Lang, F. R. (2001). Age-related patterns in social networks among European Americans and African Americans: Implications for socioemotional selectivity across the life span. *International Journal of Aging and Human Development, 52,* 185–206.

Furchtgott-Roth, D. (2009). *Testimony on the gender pay gap* (testimony before the Joint Economic Committee, U.S. House of Representatives). Washington, DC: Hudson Institute.

Furman, W., & Shaffer, L. (2003). The role of romantic relationships in adolescent development. In P. Florsheim (Ed.), *Adolescent romantic relations and sexual behavior* (pp. 3–22). Mahwah, NJ: Erlbaum.

Furstenberg, F. F., Jr., & Harris, K. M. (1993). When and why fathers matter: Impact of father involvement on children of adolescent mothers. In R. I. Lerman & T. J. Ooms (Eds.), *Young unwed fathers* (pp. 117–138). Philadelphia: Temple University Press.

Fuson, K. C., & Burghard, B. H. (2003). Multidigit addition and subtraction methods invented in small groups and teacher support of problem solving and reflection. In J. J. Baroody & A. Dowker (Eds.), *The development of arithmetic concepts and skills* (pp. 267–304). Mahwah, NJ: Erlbaum.

Fussell, E., & Furstenberg, F. F., Jr. (2005). The transition to adulthood during the twentieth century. In R. A. Settersten, Jr., F. F. Furstenberg, Jr., & R. G. Rumbaut (Eds.), *On the frontier of adulthood* (pp. 29–75). Chicago: University of Chicago Press.

Fuster, J. J., & Andres, V. (2006). Telomere biology and cardiovascular disease. *Circulation Research, 99,* 1167–1180.

Fyfe, M. (2006, April). Music and love help defy the doctors. Retrieved from www.theage.com.au/news/national/music-and-love-help-dying-defy-the-doctors/2006/03/31/1143441339517.html

G

Gabbay, S. G., & Wahler, J. J. (2002). Lesbian aging: Review of a growing literature. *Journal of Gay and Lesbian Social Services, 14,* 1–21.

Gabrel, C. S. (2000). *Advance data from Vital and Health Statistics of the Centers for Disease Control and Prevention.* Washington, DC: U.S. Department of Health and Human Services.

Gabriel, Z., & Bowling, A. (2004). Quality of life from the perspectives of older people. *Ageing and Society, 24,* 675–691.

Gailliot, M. T., Schmeichel, B. J., & Baumeister, R. F. (2006). Self regulatory processes defend against the threat of death: Effects of self-control depletion and trait self-control on thoughts and fears of dying. *Journal of Personality and Social Psychology, 91,* 49–62.

Galambos, N. L., Almeida, D. M., & Petersen, A. C. (1990). Masculinity, femininity, and sex role attitudes in early adolescence: Exploring gender intensification. *Child Development, 61,* 1905–1914.

Galambos, N. L., Barker, E. T., & Krahn, H. J. (2006). Depression, anger, and self-esteem in emerging adulthood: Seven-year trajectories. *Developmental Psychology, 42,* 350–365.

Galambos, N. L., & Maggs, J. L. (1991). Children in self-care: Figures, facts, and fiction. In J. V. Lerner & N. L. Galambos (Eds.), *Employed mothers and their children* (pp. 131–157). New York: Garland.

Gallardo, G., Schlüter, O. M., & Südhof, T. C. (2008). A molecular pathway of neurodegeneration linking alpha-synuclein to ApoE and Abeta pepites. *Nature Neurosicence, 11,* 301–308.

Galler, J. R., Ramsey, C. F., Morley, D. S., Archer, E., & Salt, P. (1990). The long-term effects of early kwashiorkor compared with marasmus. IV. Performance on the National High School Entrance Examination. *Pediatric Research, 28,* 235–239.

Galloway, J., & Thelen, E. (2004). Feet first: Object exploration in young infants. *Infant Behavior and Development, 27,* 107–112.

Gallup News Service. (2006). *Religion most important to blacks, women, and older Americans.* Retrieved from www.gallup.com/poll/25585/Religion-Most-Important-Blacks-Women-Older-Americans.aspx?version=print

Ganger, J., & Brent, M. R. (2004). Reexamining the vocabulary spurt. *Developmental Psychology, 40,* 621–632.

Ganong, L. H., & Coleman, M. (1994). *Remarried family relationships.* Thousand Oaks, CA: Sage.

Ganong, L. H., & Coleman, M. (2004). *Stepfamily relationships: Development, dynamics, and interventions.* New York: Kluwer/Plenum.

Ganong, L. H., Coleman, M., Fine, M., & Martin, P. (1999). Stepparents' affinity-seeking and affinity-maintaining strategies with stepchildren. *Journal of Family Issues, 20,* 299–327.

Gans, D., & Silverstein, M. (2006). Norms of filial responsibility for aging parents across time and generations. *Journal of Marriage and Family, 68,* 961–976.

Garces, E., Thomas, D., & Currie, J. (2002). Longer-term effects of Head Start. *American Economic Review, 92,* 999–1012.

Garcia, M. M., Shaw, D. S., Winslow, E. B., & Yaggi, K. E. (2000). Destructive sibling conflict and the development of conduct problems in young boys. *Developmental Psychology, 36,* 44–53.

Garcia-Bournissen, F., Tsur, L., Goldstein, L. H., Staroselsky, A., Avner, M., & Asrar, H. J. (2008). Fetal exposure to isotretinoin—an international problem. *Reproductive Toxicology, 25,* 124–128.

García Coll, C., & Magnuson, K. (1997). The psychological experience of immigration: A developmental perspective. In A. Booth, A. C. Crouter, & N. Landale (Eds.), *Immigration and the family* (pp. 91–131). Mahwah, NJ: Erlbaum.

Gardner, H. (1983). *Frames of mind: The theory of multiple intelligences.* New York: Basic Books.

Gardner, H. (1993). *Multiple intelligences: The theory in practice.* New York: Basic Books.

Gardner, H. (1998a). Are there additional intelligences? The case of the naturalist, spiritual, and existential intelligences. In J. Kane (Ed.), *Educational information and transformation.* Upper Saddle River, NJ: Prentice-Hall.

Gardner, H. (1998b). Extraordinary cognitive achievements (ECA): A symbol systems approach. In R. M. Lerner (Ed.), *Handbook of child psychology: Vol. 1. Theoretical models of human development* (5th ed., pp. 415–466). New York: Wiley.

Gardner, H. (2000). *Intelligence reframed: Multiple intelligences for the twenty-first century.* New York: Basic Books.

Gardner, J. P., Li, S., Srinivasan, S. R., Chen, W., Kimura, M., & Lu, X. (2005). Rise in insulin resistance is associated with escalated telomere attrition. *Circulation, 111,* 2171–2177.

Garmezy, N. (1993). Children in poverty: Resilience despite risk. *Psychiatry, 56,* 127–136.

Garner, P. W. (2003). Child and family correlates of toddlers' emotional and behavioral responses to a mishap. *Infant Mental Health Journal, 24,* 580–596.

Gartstein, M. A., & Rothbart, M. K. (2003). Studying infant temperament via the revised infant behavior questionnaire. *Infant Behavior and Development, 26,* 64–86.

Gasden, V. (1999). Black families in intergenerational and cultural perspective. In M. E. Lamb (Ed.), *Parenting and child development in "nontraditional" families* (pp. 221–246). Mahwah, NJ: Erlbaum.

Gaskins, S. (1999). Children's daily lives in a Mayan village: A case study of culturally constructed roles and activities. In R. Göncü (Ed.), *Children's engagement in the world: Sociocultural perspectives* (pp. 25–61). Cambridge, UK: Cambridge University Press.

Gaskins, S. (2000). Children's daily activities in a Mayan village: A culturally grounded description. *Cross-Cultural Research, 34,* 375–389.

Gaskins, S., Haight, W., & Lancy, D. F. (2007). The cultural construction of play. In A. Göncü & S. Gaskins (Eds.), *Play and development: Evolutionary, sociocultural, and functional perspectives* (pp. 179–202). Mahwah, NJ: Erlbaum.

Gathercole, S. E., Adams, A.-M., & Hitch, G. (1994). Do young children rehearse? An individual-differences analysis. *Memory and Cognition, 22,* 201–207.

Gathercole, V., Sebastián, E., & Soto, P. (1999). The early acquisition of Spanish verb morphology: Across-the-board or piecemeal knowledge? *International Journal of Bilingualism, 3,* 133–182.

Gatz, M., Bengtson, V. L., & Blum, M. J. (1990). Caregiving families. In J. E. Birren & K. W. Schaie (Eds.), *Handbook of the psychology of aging* (3rd ed., pp. 404–426). San Diego, CA: Academic Press.

Gatz, M., Kasl-Godley, J. E., & Karel, M. J. (1996). Aging and mental disorders. In J. E. Birren & K. W. Schaie (Eds.), *Handbook of the psychology of aging* (pp. 365–382). Sand Diego: Academic Press.

Gauvain, M. (2004). Bringing culture into relief: Cultural contributions to the development of children's planning skills. In R. V. Kail (Ed.), *Advances in child development and behavior* (pp. 39–71). San Diego, CA: Elsevier.

Gauvain, M., de la Ossa, J. L., & Hurtado-Ortiz, M. T. (2001). Parental guidance as children learn to use cultural tools: The case of pictorial plans. *Cognitive Development, 16,* 551–575.

Gauvain, M., & Rogoff, B. (1989). Ways of speaking about space: The development of children's skill in communicating spatial knowledge. *Cognitive Development, 4,* 295–307.

Gavin, J., Scott, A., & Duffield, J. (2005). *Internet dating more successful than thought.* Retrieved from www.sciencedaily.com/releases/2005/02/050218125144.htm

Gayle, B. M., Preiss, R. W., & Allen, M. (2002). A meta-analytic interpretation of nonintimate interpersonal conflict. In M. Allen & R. W. Preiss (Eds.), *Interpersonal communication research: Advances through meta-analysis* (pp. 345–368). Mahwah, NJ: Erlbaum.

Gazelle, H., & Rudolph, K. D. (2004). Moving toward and away from the world: Social approach and avoidance trajectories in anxious and solitary youth. *Child Development, 75,* 829–849.

Gazzaley, A., Cooney, J. W., Rissman, J., & D'Esposito, M. (2005). Top-down suppression deficit underlies working memory impairment in normal aging. *Nature Neuroscience, 8,* 1298–1300.

Ge, X., Brody, G. H., Conger, R. D., Simons, R. L., & Murry, V. (2002). Contextual amplification of the effects of pubertal transition on African American children's deviant peer affiliation and externalized behavioral problems. *Developmental Psychology, 38,* 42–54.

Ge, X., Conger, R. D., & Elder, G. H., Jr. (1996). Coming of age too early: Pubertal influences on girls' vulnerability to psychological distress. *Child Development, 67,* 3386–3400.

Ge, X., Conger, R. D., & Elder, G. H., Jr. (2001). The relation between puberty and psychological distress in adolescent boys. *Journal of Research on Adolescence, 11,* 49–70.

Ge, X., Jin, R., Natsuaki, M. N., Frederick, X., Brody, G. H., Cutrona, C. E., & Simons, R. L. (2006). Pubertal maturation and early substance use risks among African American children. *Psychology of Addictive Behaviors, 20,* 404–414.

Geary, D. C. (1999). Evolution and developmental sex differences. *Current Directions in Psychological Science, 8,* 115–120.

Geary, D. C. (2006a). Development of mathematical understanding. In D. Kuhn & R. Siegler (Eds.), *Handbook of child psychology: Vol. 2. Cognition, perception, and language* (pp. 777–810). Hoboken, NJ: Wiley.

Geary, D. C. (2006b). Evolutionary developmental psychology: Current status and future directions. *Developmental Review, 26,* 113–119.

Gee, C. B., & Rhodes, J. E. (2003). Adolescent mothers' relationship with their children's biological fathers: Social support, social strain, and relationship continuity. *Journal of Family Psychology, 17,* 370–383.

Geiger, H. J. (2007). Health disparities: What do we know? What should we do? In A. J. Schulz & L. Mullings (Eds.), *Gender, race, class, and health: Intersectional approaches* (pp. 3–17). San Francisco: Jossey-Bass.

Gelman, R. (1972). Logical capacity of very young children: Number invariance rules. *Child Development, 43,* 75–90.

Gelman, S. A. (2003). *The essential child.* New York: Oxford University Press.

Gelman, S. A., Coley, J. D., Rosengren, K. S., Hartman, E., & Pappas, A. (1998). Beyond labeling: The role of maternal input in the acquisition of richly structured categories. *Monographs of the Society for Research in Child Development, 63*(1, Serial No. 253).

Gelman, S. A., & Kalish, C. W. (2006). Conceptual development. In D. Kuhn & R. Siegler (Eds.), *Handbook of child psychology: Vol. 2. Cognition, perception, and language* (6th ed., pp. 687–733). Hoboken, NJ: Wiley.

Gelman, S. A., & Koenig, M. A. (2003). Theory-based categorization in early childhood. In D. H. Rakison & L. M. Oakes (Eds.), *Early category and concept development* (pp. 330–359). New York: Oxford University Press.

Gelman, S. A., & Opfer, J. E. (2002). Development of the animate–inanimate distinction. In U. Goswami (Ed.), *Blackwell handbook of childhood cognitive development* (pp. 151–166). Malden, MA: Blackwell.

Gelman, S. A., Taylor, M. G., & Nguyen, S. P. (2004). Mother–child conversations about gender. *Monographs of the Society for Research in Child Development, 69*(1, Serial No. 275), pp. 1–127.

Gennari, L., & Bilezikian, J. P. (2007). Osteoporosis in men: Pathophysiology and treatment. *Current Rheumatology Reports, 9,* 71–77.

Gerard, J. M., Krishnakumar, A., & Buehler, C. (2006). Marital conflict, parent–child relations, and youth maladjustment: A longitudinal investigation of spillover effects. *Journal of Family Issues, 27,* 951–975.

Gergely, G., & Watson, J. (1996). The social biofeedback theory of parental affect-mirroring: The development of emotional self-awareness and self-control in infancy. *International Journal of Psychoanalysis, 77,* 1181–1212.

Gergely, G., & Watson, J. (1999). Early socioemotional development: Contingency perception and the social-biofeedback model. In P. Rochat (Ed.), *Early social cognition: Understanding others in the first months of life* (pp. 101–136). Mahwah, NJ: Erlbaum.

Gergen, M., & Gergen, K. J. (2003). Positive aging. In J. F. Gubrim & J. A. Holstein (Eds.), *Ways of aging* (pp. 203–224). Malden: Blackwell Publishers Ltd.

Germino, B. B. (2003). Dying at home. In I. Corless, B. B. Germino, & M. A. Pittman (Eds.), *Dying, death, and bereavement: A challenge for the living* (pp. 105–116). New York: Springer.

Gershoff, E. T. (2002a). Corporal punishment by parents and associated child behaviors and experiences: A meta-analytic and theoretical review. *Psychological Bulletin, 128,* 539–579.

Gershoff, E. T. (2002b). Corporal punishment, physical abuse, and the burden of proof: Reply to Baumrind, Larzelere, and Cowan (2002), Holden (2002), and Parke (2002). *Psychological Bulletin, 128,* 602–611.

Gershoff, E. T., & Aber, J. L. (2006). Neighborhoods and schools: Contexts and consequences for the mental health and risk behaviors of children and youth. In L. Balter & C. S. Tamis-LeMonda (Eds.), *Child psychology: A handbook of contemporary issues* (2nd ed., pp. 611–645). New York: Psychology Press.

Gerstorf, D., Ram, N., Estabrook, R., Schupp, J., Wagner, G. G., & Lindenberger, U. (2008). Life satisfaction shows terminal decline in old age: Longitudinal evidence from the German socioeconomic panel study. *Developmental Psychology, 44,* 1148–1159.

Gertner, S., Greenbaum, C. W., Sadeh, A., Dolfin, Z., Sirota, L., & Ben-Nun, Y. (2002). Sleep-wake patterns in preterm infants and 6 month's home environment: Implications for early cognitive development. *Early Human Development, 68,* 93–102.

Gesell, A. (1933). Maturation and patterning of behavior. In C. Murchison (Ed.), *A handbook of child psychology.* Worcester, MA: Clark University Press.

Gest, S. D., Domitrovich, C. E., & Welsh, J. A. (2005). Peer academic reputation in elementary school: Associations with changes in self-concept and academic skills. *Journal of Educational Psychology, 97,* 337–346.

Geurts, H. M., Verte, S., Oosterlaan, J., Roeyers, H., & Sergeant, J. A. (2004). How specific are executive functioning deficits in attention-deficit hyperactivity disorder and autism? *Journal of Child Psychology and Psychiatry, 45,* 836–854.

Gibbs, J. C. (1991). Toward an integration of Kohlberg's and Hoffman's theories of morality. In W. M. Kurtines & J. L. Gewirtz (Eds.), *Handbook of moral behavior and development* (Vol. 1, pp. 183–222). Hillsdale, NJ: Erlbaum.

Gibbs, J. C. (2006). Should Kohlberg's cognitive developmental approach to morality be replaced with a more pragmatic approach? Comment on Krebs and Denton (2005). *Psychological Review, 113,* 666–671.

Gibbs, J. C. (2010). *Moral development and reality: Beyond the theories of Kohlberg and Hoffman* (2nd ed.). Boston: Pearson Allyn & Bacon.

Gibbs, J. C., Basinger, K. S., Grime, R. L., & Snarey, J. R. (2007). Moral judgment development across cultures: Revisiting Kohlberg's universality claims. *Developmental Review, 24,* 443–500.

Gibbs, J. C., Moshman, D., Berkowitz, M. W., Basinger, K. S., & Grime, R. L. (2009). Taking development seriously: Critique of the 2008 *JME* special issue on moral functioning. *Journal of Moral Education, 38,* 271–282.

Gibson, E. J. (1970). The development of perception as an adaptive process. *American Scientist, 58,* 98–107.

Gibson, E. J. (2000). Perceptual learning in development: Some basic concepts. *Ecological Psychology, 12,* 295–302.

Gibson, E. J. (2003). The world is so full of a number of things: On specification and perceptual learning. *Ecological Psychology, 15,* 283–287.

Gibson, E. J., & Walk, R. D. (1960). The "visual cliff." *Scientific American, 202,* 64–71.

Gibson, J. J. (1979). *The ecological approach to visual perception.* Boston: Houghton Mifflin.

Gibson, P. A. (2005). Intergenerational parenting from the perspective of American grandmothers. *Family Relations, 54,* 280–297.

Giles, J. W., & Heyman, G. D. (2005). Young children's beliefs about the relationship between gender and aggressive behavior. *Child Development, 76,* 107–121.

Gillies, R. M. (2000). The maintenance of cooperative and helping behaviours in cooperative groups. *British Journal of Educational Psychology, 70,* 97–111.

Gillies, R. M. (2003). The behaviors, interactions, and perceptions of junior high school students during small-group learning. *Journal of Educational Psychology, 95,* 137–147.

Gilligan, C. F. (1982). *In a different voice.* Cambridge, MA: Harvard University Press.

Gilliom, M., Shaw, D. S., Beck, J. E., Schonberg, M. A., & Lukon, J. L. (2002). Anger regulation in disadvantaged preschool boys: Strategies, antecedents, and the development of self-control. *Developmental Psychology, 38,* 222–235.

Ginsburg, H. P. (1997). *Entering the child's mind: The clinical interview in psychological research and practice.* New York: Cambridge University Press.

Ginsburg, H. P., Lee, J. S., & Boyd, J. S. (2008). Mathematics education for young children: What it is and how to promote it. *Social Policy Report of the Society for Research in Child Development, 12*(1).

Ginsburg-Block, M. D., Rohrbeck, C. A., & Fantuzzo, J. W. (2006). A meta-analytic review of social, self-concept, and behavioral outcomes of peer-assisted learning. *Journal of Educational Psychology, 98,* 732–749.

Gitlin, L. N., Belle, S. H., Burgio, L. D., Szaja, S. J., Mahoney, D., & Gallagher-Thompson, D. (2003). Effect of multicomponent interventions on caregiver burden and depression: the REACH multisite initiative at 6-month follow-up. *Psychology and Aging, 18,* 361–374.

Gladstone, I. M., & Katz, V. L. (2004). The morbidity of the 34- to 35-week gestation: Should we reexamine the paradigm? *American Journal of Perinatology, 21,* 9–13.

Glasgow, K. L., Dornbusch, S. M., Troyer, L., Steinberg, L., & Ritter, P. L. (1997). Parenting styles, adolescents' attributions, and educational outcomes in nine heterogeneous high schools. *Child Development, 68,* 507–523.

Gleitman, L. R., Cassidy, K., Nappa, R., Papfragou, A., & Trueswell, J. C. (2005). Hard words. *Language Learning and Development, 1,* 23–64.

Gleitman, L. R., & Newport, E. (1996). *The invention of language by children.* Cambridge, MA: MIT Press.

Glowinski, A. L., Madden, P. A. F., Bucholz, K. K., Lynskey, M. T., & Heath, A. C. (2003). Genetic epidemiology of self-reported lifetime DSM-IV major depressive disorder in a population-based twin sample of female adolescents. *Journal of Child Psychology and Psychiatry and Allied Disciplines, 44,* 988–996.

Gluckman, P. D., Sizonenko, S. V., & Bassett, N. S. (1999). The transition from fetus to neonate—an endocrine perspective. *Acta Paediatrica Supplement, 88*(428), 7–11.

Godkin, M., Krant, M., & Doster, N. (1984). The impact of hospice care on families. *International Journal of Psychiatry in Medicine, 13,* 153–165.

Goering, J. (Ed.). (2003). *Choosing a better life? How public housing tenants selected a HUD experiment to improve their lives and those of their children: The Moving to Opportunity Demonstration Program.* Washington, DC: Urban Institute Press.

Gold, D. T. (1996). Continuities and discontinuities in sibling relationships across the life span. In V. L. Bengtson (Ed.), *Adulthood and aging: Research on continuities and discontinuities* (pp. 228–243). New York: Springer.

Goldberg, A. P., Dengel, D. R., & Hagberg, J. M. (1996). Exercise physiology and aging. In E. L. Schneider & J. W. Rowe (Eds.), *Handbook of the biology of aging* (pp. 331–354). San Diego: Academic Press.

Goldberg, M. C., Maurer, D., & Lewis, T. L. (2001). Developmental changes in attention: The effects of endogenous cueing and of distracters. *Developmental Science, 4,* 209–219.

Goldberg, S., Benoit, D., Blokland, K., & Madigan, S. (2003). Atypical maternal behavior, maternal representations, and infant disorganized attachment. *Development and Psychopathology, 15,* 239–257.

Goldenberg, C., Gallimore, R., Reese, L., & Garnier, H. (2001). Cause or effect? Immigrant Latino parents' aspirations and expectations, and their children's school performance. *American Educational Research Journal, 38,* 547–582.

Goldfield, B. A. (1987). The contributions of child and caregiver to referential and expressive language. *Applied Psycholinguistics, 8,* 267–280.

Goldman, N., & Takahashi, S. (1996). Old-age mortality in Japan: Demographic and epidemiological perspectives. In G. Caselli & A. D. Lopez (Eds.), *Health and mortality among elderly populations* (pp. 157–181). New York: Oxford University Press.

Goldscheider, F., & Goldscheider, C. (1999). *The changing transition to adulthood: Leaving and returning home.* Thousand Oaks, CA: Sage.

Goldschmidt, L., Richardson, G. A., Cornelius, M. D., & Day, N. L. (2004). Prenatal marijuana and alcohol exposure and academic achievement at age 10. *Neurotoxicology and Teratology, 26,* 521–532.

Goldsmith, H. H., Pollak, S. D., & Davidson, R. J. (2008). Developmental neuroscience perspectives on emotion regulation. *Child Development Perspectives, 2,* 132–140.

Goldsmith, L. T. (2000). Tracking trajectories of talent: Child prodigies growing up. In R. C. Friedman & B. M. Shore (Eds.), *Talents unfolding: Cognition and development* (pp. 89–122). Washington, DC: American Psychological Association.

Goldsteen, M., Houtepen, R., Proot, I. M., Abu-Saad, H. H., Spreeuwenberg, C., & Widdershoven, G. (2006). What is a good death? Terminally ill patients dealing with normative expectations around death and dying. *Patient Education and Counseling, 64,* 378–386.

Goldstein, S. E., Davis-Kean, P. E., & Eccles, J. S. (2005). Parents, peers, and problem behavior: A longitudinal investigation of the impact of relationship perceptions and characteristics on the development of adolescent problem behavior. *Developmental Psychology, 41,* 401–413.

Golinkoff, R. M., & Hirsh-Pasek, K. (2006). Baby wordsmith: From associationist to social sophisticate. *Current Directions in Psychological Science, 15,* 30–33.

Golomb, C. (2004). *The child's creation of a pictorial world* (2nd ed.). Mahwah, NJ: Erlbaum.

Golombok, S., Perry, B., Burston, A., Murray, C., Mooney-Somers, J., Stevens, M., & Golding, J. (2003). Children with lesbian parents: A community study. *Developmental Psychology, 39,* 20–33.

Golombok, S., Rust, J., Zervoulis, K., Croudace, T., Golding, J., & Hines, M. (2008). Developmental trajectories of sex-typed behavior in boys and girls: A longitudinal general population study of children aged 2.5–8 years. *Child Development, 79,* 1583–1593.

Golombok, S., & Tasker, F. L. (1996). Do parents influence the sexual orientation of their children? Findings from a longitudinal study of lesbian families. *Developmental Psychology, 32,* 3–11.

Gomez-Perez, E., & Ostrosky-Solis, F. (2006). Attention and memory evaluation across the life span: Heterogeneous effects of age and education. *Journal of Clinical and Experimental Neuropsychology, 28,* 477–494.

Göncü, A. (1993). Development of intersubjectivity in the dyadic play of preschoolers. *Early Childhood Research Quarterly, 8,* 99–116.

Göncü, A., Patt, M. B., & Kouba E. (2004). Understanding young children's pretend play in context. In P. K. Smith & C. H. Hart (Eds.), *Blackwell handbook of childhood social development* (pp. 418–437). Malden, MA: Blackwell.

Gonzalez, A.-L., & Wolters, C. A. (2006). The relation between perceived parenting practices and achievement motivation in mathematics. *Journal of Research in Childhood Education, 21,* 203–217.

Good, T. L., & Brophy, J. (2003). *Looking in classrooms* (9th ed.). Boston: Allyn and Bacon.

Goode, V., & Goode, J. D. (2007). De facto zero tolerance: An exploratory study of race and safe school violations. In J. L. Kincheloe & K. Hayes (Eds.), *Teaching city kids: Understanding and appreciating them* (pp. 85–96). New York: Peter Lang.

Goodwin, R., & Pillay, U. (2006). Relationships, culture, and social change. In A. L. Vangelisti & D. Perlman (Eds.), *The Cambridge handbook of personal relationships* (pp. 760–779). New York: Cambridge University Press.

Gootman, E. (2005, January 16). New York City: The politics of promotion. *New York Times.* Retrieved from www.nytimes.com/2005/01/16/education/edlife/EDGOOT.html

Gopnik, A., & Nazzi, T. (2003). Words, kinds, and causal powers: A theory theory perspective on early naming and categorization. In D. H. Rakison & L. M. Oakes (Eds.), *Early category and concept development* (p. 303–329). New York: Oxford University Press.

Gordon, L. H., Temple, R. R., & Adams, D. W. (2005). Premarital counseling from the PAIRS perspective. In M. Harway (Ed.), *Handbook of couples therapy* (pp. 7–27). Hoboken, NJ: Wiley.

Gormally, S., Barr, R G., Wertheim, L., Alkawaf, R., Calinoiu, N., & Young, S. N. (2001). Contact and nutrient caregiving effects on newborn infant pain responses. *Developmental Medicine and Child Neurology, 43,* 28–38.

Gorman, T. E., Ahern, S. P., Wiseman, J., & Skrobik, Y. (2005). Residents' end-of-life decision making with adult hospitalized patients: A review of the literature. *Academic Medicine, 80,* 622–633.

Goswami, U. (1996). Analogical reasoning and cognitive development. In H. Reese (Ed.), *Advances in child development and behavior* (Vol. 26, pp. 91–138). New York: Academic Press.

Gott, M., & Hinchliff, S. (2003). How important is sex in later life? The views of older people. *Social Science and Medicine, 56,* 1617–1628.

Gott, M., Seymour, J., Bellamy, G., Clark, D., & Ahmedzai, S. (2004). Older people's views about home as a place of care at the end of life. *Palliative Medicine, 18,* 460–467.

Gottesman, I. I. (1963). Genetic aspects of intelligent behavior. In N. Ellis (Ed.), *Handbook of mental deficiency* (pp. 253–296). New York: McGraw-Hill.

Gottfredson, G. D., & Duffy, R. D. (2008). Using a theory of vocational personalities and work environments to explore subjective well-being. *Journal of Career Assessment, 16,* 44–59.

Gottfredson, L. S. (2005). Applying Gottfredson's theory of circumscription and compromise in career guidance and counseling. In S. D. Brown & R. W. Lent (Eds.), *Career development and counseling* (pp. 71–100). Hoboken, NJ: Wiley.

Gottfried, A. E., Gottfried, A. W., & Bathurst, K. (2002). Maternal and dual-earner employment status and parenting. In M. H. Bornstein (Ed.), *Handbook of parenting. Vol. 2: Biology and ecology of parenting* (2nd ed., pp. 207–229). Mahwah, NJ: Erlbaum.

Gottlieb, B., Beitel, L. K., & Trifiro, M. A. (2001). Somatic mosaicism and variable expressivity. *Trends in Genetics, 11,* 70–82.

Gottlieb, G. (1998). Normally occurring environmental and behavioral influences on gene activity: From central dogma to probabilistic epigenesis. *Psychological Review, 105,* 792–802.

Gottlieb, G. (2000). Environmental and behavioral influences on gene activity. *Current Directions in Psychological Science, 9,* 93–97.

Gottlieb, G. (2003). On making behavioral genetics truly developmental. *Human Development, 46,* 337–355.

Gottlieb, G. (2007). Probabilistic epigenesis. *Developmental Science, 10,* 1–11.

Gottlieb, G., Wahlsten, D., & Lickliter, R. (2006). The significance of biology for human development: A developmental psychobiological systems view. In R. M. Lerner (Ed.), *Handbook of child psychology: Vol. 1. Theoretical models of human development* (6th ed., pp. 210–257). Hoboken, NJ: Wiley.

Gottman, J. M., Katz, L. F., & Hooven, C. (1997). *Meta-emotion: How families communicate emotionally.* Mahwah, NJ: Erlbaum.

Gottman, J. M., & Levenson, R. W. (2000). The timing of divorce: Predicting when a couple will divorce over a 14-year period. *Journal of Marriage and Family, 62,* 737–745.

Gould, E. (2007). How widespread is adult neurogenesis in mammals? *Nature Reviews: Neuroscience, 8,* 481–488.

Gould, E., Reeves, A. J., Graziano, M. S. A., & Gross, C. G. (1999). Neurogenesis in the neocortex of adult primates. *Science, 286,* 548–552. Gould, J. L., & Keeton, W. T. (1996). *Biological science* (6th ed.). New York: Norton.

Gould, M., Jamieson, P., & Romer, D. (2003). Media contagion and suicide among the young. *American Behavioral Scientist, 46,* 1269–1284.

Graber, J. A. (2003). Puberty in context. In C. Hayward (Ed.), *Gender differences at puberty* (pp. 307–325). New York: Cambridge University Press.

Graber, J. A. (2004). Internalizing problems during adolescence. In R. M. Lerner & L. Steinberg (Eds.), *Handbook of adolescent psychology* (2nd ed., pp. 587–626). Hoboken, NJ: Wiley.

Graber, J. A., Brooks-Gunn, J., & Warren, M. P. (2006). Pubertal effects on adjustment in girls: Moving from demonstrating effects to identifying pathways. *Journal of Youth and Adolescence, 35,* 413–423.

Graber, J. A., Lewinsohn, P. M., Seeley, J. R., & Brooks-Gunn, J. (1997). Is psychopathology associated with timing of pubertal development? *Journal of the American Academy of Child and Adolescent Psychiatry, 36,* 1768–1776.

Graber, J. A., Nichols, T., Lynne, S. D., Brooks-Gunn, J., & Botwin, G. J. (2006). A longitudinal examination of family, friend, and media influences on competent versus problem behaviors among urban minority youth. *Applied Developmental Science, 10,* 75–85.

Graber, J. A., Seeley, J. R., Brooks-Gunn, J., & Lewinsohn, P. M. (2004). Is pubertal timing associated with psychopathology in young adulthood? *Journal of the American Academy of Child and Adolescent Psychiatry, 43,* 718–726.

Gralinski, J. H., & Kopp, C. B. (1993). Everyday rules for behavior: Mothers' requests to young children. *Developmental Psychology, 29,* 573–584.

Granger, R. C. (2008). After-school programs and academics: Implications for policy, practice, and research. *Social Policy Report of the Society for Research in Child Development, 22*(2), 3–11.

Granier-Deferre, C., Bassereau, S., Ribeiro, A., Jacquet, A.-Y., & Lecanuet, J.-P. (2003). *Cardiac "orienting" response in fetuses and babies following in utero melody-learning.* Paper presented at the 11th European Conference on Developmental Psychology, Milan, Italy.

Granillo, T., Jones-Rodriguez, G., & Carvajal, S. C. (2005). Prevalence of eating disorders in Latina adolescents: Associations with substance use and other correlates. *Journal of Adolescent Health, 36,* 214–220.

Granot, T. (2005). *Without you: Children and young people growing up with loss and its effects.* London: Jessica Kingsley.

Grantham-McGregor, S., Powell, C., Walker, S., Chang, S., & Fletcher, P. (1994). The long-term follow-up of severely malnourished children who participated in an intervention program. *Child Development, 65,* 428–439.

Grantham-McGregor, S., Schofield, W., & Powell, C. (1987). Development of severely malnourished children who received psychosocial stimulation: Six-year follow-up. *Pediatrics, 79,* 247–254.

Grantham-McGregor, S., Walker, S. P., & Chang, S. (2000). Nutritional deficiencies and later behavioral development. *Proceedings of the Nutrition Society, 59,* 47–54.

Gratton, M. A., & Vásquez, A. E. (2003). Age-related hearing loss: Current research. *Current Opinion in Otolaryngology—Head and Neck Surgery, 11,* 367–371.

Gray, K. A., Day, N. L., Leech, S., & Richardson, G. A. (2005). Prenatal marijuana exposure: Effect on child depressive symptoms at ten years of age. *Neurotoxicology and Teratology, 27,* 439–448.

Gray, M. R., & Steinberg, L. (1999). Unpacking authoritative parenting: Reassessing a multidimensional construct. *Journal of Marriage and the Family, 61,* 574–587.

Gray-Little, B., & Carels, R. (1997). The effects of racial and socioeconomic consonance on self-esteem and achievement in elementary, junior high, and high school students. *Journal of Research on Adolescence, 7,* 109–131.

Gray-Little, B., & Hafdahl, A. R. (2000). Factors influencing racial comparisons of self-esteem: A quantitative review. *Psychological Bulletin, 126,* 26–54.

Green, G. E., Irwin, J. R., & Gustafson, G. E. (2000). Acoustic cry analysis, neonatal status and long-term developmental outcomes. In R. G. Barr, B. Hopkins, & J. A. Green (Eds.), *Crying as a sign, a symptom, and a signal* (pp. 137–156). Cambridge, UK: Cambridge University Press.

Greenberg, S. A. (2007). *A profile of older Americans: 2007.* Washington, DC: National Institute on Aging.

Greenberger, E., Chen, C., Tally, S. R., & Dong, Q. (2000). Family, peer, and individual correlates of depressive symptomatology among U.S. and Chinese adolescents. *Journal of Counseling and Clinical Psychology, 68,* 209–219.

Greenberger, E., O'Neil, R., & Nagel, S. K. (1994). Linking workplace and homeplace: Relations between the nature of adults' work and their parenting behavior. *Developmental Psychology, 30,* 990–1002.

Greendorfer, S. L., Lewko, J. H., & Rosengren, K. S. (1996). Family and gender-based socialization of children and adolescents. In F. L. Smoll & R. E. Smith (Eds.), *Children and youth in sport: A biopsychological perspective* (pp. 89–111). Dubuque, IA: Brown & Benchmark.

Greene, M. L., Way, N., & Pahl, K. (2006). Trajectories of perceived adult and peer discrimination among black, Latino, and Asian American adolescents: Patterns and psychological correlates. *Developmental Psychology, 42,* 218–238.

Greene, S. M., Anderson, E., Hetherington, E. M., Forgath, M. S., & DeGarmo, D. S. (2003). Risk and resilience after divorce. In R. Walsh (Ed.), *Normal family processes* (pp. 96–120). New York: Guilford.

Greenfield, P. (1992, June). *Notes and references for developmental psychology.* Conference on Making Basic Texts in Psychology More Culture-Inclusive and Culture Sensitive, Western Washington University, Bellingham, WA.

Greenfield, P. M. (2004). *Weaving generations together: Evolving creativity in the Maya of Chiapas.* Santa Fe, NM: School of American Research.

Greenfield, P. M., Keller, H., Fuligni, A., & Maynard, A. (2003). Cultural pathways through universal development. *Annual Review of Psychology, 54,* 461–490.

Greenfield, P. M., Suzuki, L. K., & Rothstein-Fish, C. (2006). Cultural pathways through human development. In K. A. Renninger & I. E. Sigel (Eds.), *Handbook of child psychology: Vol. 4. Child psychology in practice* (6th ed., pp. 655–699). Hoboken, NJ: Wiley.

Greenhill, L. L., Halperin, J. M., & Abikoff, H. (1999). Stimulant medications. *Journal of the American Academy of Child and Adolescent Psychiatry, 38,* 503–512.

Greenough, W. T., & Black, J. E. (1992). Induction of brain structure by experience: Substrates for cognitive development. In M. R. Gunnar & C. A. Nelson (Eds.), *Minnesota Symposia on Child Psychology* (pp. 155–200). Hillsdale, NJ: Erlbaum.

Greenspan, S. I., & Shanker, S. G. (2004). *The first idea: how symbols, language, and intelligence evolved from our primate ancestors to modern humans.* Cambridge, MA: Da Capo Press.

Gregg, V., Gibbs, J. C., & Fuller, D. (1994). Patterns of developmental delay in moral judgment by male and female delinquents. *Merrill-Palmer Quarterly, 40,* 538–553.

Gregory, A., & Weinstein, R. S. (2004). Connection and regulation at home and in school: Predicting growth in achievement for adolescents. *Journal of Adolescent Research, 19,* 405–427.

Griffin, Z. M., & Spieler, D. H. (2006). Observing the what and when of language production for different age groups by monitoring speakers' eye movements. *Brain and Language, 99,* 272–288.

Grigorenko, E. L. (2000). Heritability and intelligence. In R. J. Sternberg (Ed.), *Handbook of intelligence* (pp. 53–91). Cambridge, UK: Cambridge University Press.

Grob, A., & Flammer, A. (1999). Macrosocial context and adolescents' perceived control. In F. D. Alsaker & A. Flammer (Eds.), *The adolescent experience* (pp. 99–114). Mahwah, NJ: Erlbaum.

Grob, A., Krings, F., & Bangerter, A. (2001). Life markers in biographical narratives of people from three cohorts: A life span perspective in its historical context. *Human Development, 44,* 171–190.

Grolnick, W. S., Kurowski, C. O., Dunlap, K. G., & Hevey, C. (2000). Parental resources and the transition to junior high. *Journal of Research on Adolescence, 10,* 466–488.

Grossbaum, M. F., & Bates, G. W. (2002). Correlates of psychological well-being at midlife: The role of generativity, agency and communion, and narrative themes. *International Journal of Behavioral Development, 26,* 120–127.

Grossman, A. H., D'Augelli, A. R., & Hershberger, S. L. (2000). Social support networks of lesbian, gay, and bisexual adults 60 years of age and older. *Journal of Gerontology, 55B,* P171–179.

Grossmann, K., Grossmann, K. E., Spangler, G., Suess, G., & Unzner, L. (1985). Maternal sensitivity and newborns' orientation responses as related to quality of attachment in Northern Germany. In I. Bretherton & E. Waters (Eds.), Growing points of

attachment theory and research. *Monographs of the Society for Research in Child Development, 50*(1–2, Serial No. 209).

Grotevant, H. D. (1998). Adolescent development in family contexts. In N. Eisenberg (Ed.), *Handbook of child psychology: Vol. 3. Social, emotional, and personality development* (5th ed., pp. 1097–1149). New York: Wiley.

Grow-Maienza, J., Hahn, D.-D., & Joo, C.-A. (2001). Mathematics instruction in Korean primary schools: Structure, processes, and a linguistic analysis of questioning. *Journal of Educational Psychology, 93,* 363–376.

Gruendel J., & Aber, J. L. (2007). Bridging the gap between research and child policy change: The role of strategic communications in policy advocacy. In J. L. Aber, S. J. Bishop-Josef, S. M. Jones, K. T. McLearn, & D. Phillips (Eds.), *Child development and social policy: Knowledge for action* (pp. 43–58). Washington, DC: American Psychological Association.

Gruenewald, D. A., & White, E. J. (2006). The illness experience of older adults near the end of life: A systematic review. *Anesthesiology Clinics of North America, 24,* 163–180.

Grunau, R. E., Whitfield, M. F., & Fay, T. B. (2004). Psychosocial and academic characteristics of extremely low birth weight (<or=800g) adolescents who are free of major impairment compared with term-born control subjects. *Pediatrics, 114,* E725–E732.

Grundy, E. (2005). Reciprocity in relationships: Socioeconomic and health influences on intergenerational exchanges between Third Age parents and their adult children in Great Britain. *British Journal of Sociology, 56,* 233–255.

Grusec, J. E. (1988). *Social development: History, theory, and research.* New York: Springer.

Grusec, J. E. (2006). The development of moral behavior and conscience from a socialization perspective. In M. Killen & J. Smetana (Eds.), *Handbook of moral development* (pp. 243–265). Philadelphia: Erlbaum.

Grusec, J. E., & Goodnow, J. J. (1994). Impact of parental discipline methods on the child's internalization of values: A reconceptualization of current points of view. *Developmental Psychology, 30,* 4–19.

Grzywacz, J. G., & Marks, N. F. (2001). Social inequalities and exercise during adulthood: Toward an ecological perspective. *Journal of Health and Social Behavior, 42,* 202–220.

Guay, F., Marsh, H. W., & Boivin, M. (2003). Academic self-concept and academic achievement: Developmental perspectives on their causal ordering. *Journal of Educational Psychology, 95,* 124–136.

Guignard, J.-H., & Lubart, T. (2006). Is it reasonable to be creative? In J. C. Kaufman & J. Baer (Eds.), *Creativity and reason in cognitive development* (pp. 269–281). New York: Cambridge University Press.

Guildner, S. H., Loeb, S., Morris, D., Penrod, J., Bramlett, M., Johnston, L., & Schlotzhauer, P. (2001). A comparison of life satisfaction and mood in nursing home residents and community-dwelling elders. *Archives of Psychiatric Nursing, 15,* 232–240.

Guilford, J. P. (1985). The structure-of-intellect model. In B. B. Wolman (Ed.), *Handbook of intelligence* (pp. 225–266). New York: Wiley.

Gullone, E. (2000). The development of normal fear: A century of research. *Clinical Psychology Review, 20,* 429–451.

Gulotta, T. P. (2008). How theory influences treatment and prevention practice within the family. In T. P. Gulotta (Ed.), *Family influences on child behavior and development: Evidence-based prevention and treatment approaches* (pp. 1–20). New York: Routledge.

Gunnar, M. R., & Cheatham, C. L. (2003). Brain and behavior interfaces: Stress and the developing brain. *Infant Mental Health Journal, 24,* 195–211.

Gunnar, M. R., Morison, S. J., Chisholm, K., & Schuder, M. (2001). Salivary cortisol levels in children adopted from Romanian orphanages. *Development and Psychopathology, 13,* 611–628.

Gunnar, M. R., & Quevedo, K. (2007). The neurobiology of stress and development. *Annual Review of Psychology, 58,* 145–173.

Gunnar, M. R., & Vasquez, D. M. (2001). Low cortisol and a flattening of expected day-time rhythm: Potential indices of risk in human development. *Development and Psychopathology, 13,* 515–538.

Gunnoe, M. L., & Mariner, C. L. (1997). Toward a developmental-contextual model of the effects of parental spanking on children's aggression. *Archives of Pediatrics and Adolescent Medicine, 151,* 768–775.

Gure, A., Ucanok, Z., & Sayil, M. (2006). The associations among perceived pubertal timing, parental relations and self-perception in Turkish adolescents. *Journal of Youth and Adolescence, 35,* 541–550.

Gureje, O., Ogunniyi, A., Baiyewu, O., Price, B., Unverzagt, F. W., & Evans, R. M. (2006). APOE epsilon4 is not associated with Alzheimer's disease in elderly Nigerians. *Annals of Neurology, 59,* 182–185.

Gurucharri, C., & Selman, R. L. (1982). The development of interpersonal understanding during childhood, preadolescence, and adolescence: A longitudinal follow-up study. *Child Development, 53,* 924–927.

Gustafson, G. E., Wood, R. M., & Green, J. A. (2000). Can we hear the causes of infants' crying? In R. G. Barr & B. Hopkins (Eds.), *Crying as a sign, a symptom, and a signal: Clinical, emotional, and developmental aspects of infant and toddler crying* (pp. 8–22). New York: Cambridge University Press.

Gutman, L. M. (2006). How student and parent goal orientations and classroom goal structures influence the math achievement of African Americans during the high school transition. *Contemporary Educational Psychology, 31,* 44–63.

Gutman, L. M., & Midgley, C. (2000). The role of protective factors in supporting the academic achievement of poor African-American students during the middle school transition. *Journal of Youth and Adolescence, 29,* 223–248.

Gutman, L. M., Sameroff, A. J., & Cole, R. (2003). Academic growth curve trajectories from 1st grade to 12th grade: Effects of multiple social risk factors and preschool child factors. *Developmental Psychology, 39,* 777–790.

Gutmann, D. (1977). The cross-cultural perspective: Notes toward a comparative psychology of aging. In J. E. Birren & K. W. Schaie (Eds.), *Handbook of the psychology of aging* (pp. 302–326). New York: Van Nostrand Reinhold.

Gutmann, D. L., & Huyck, M. H. (1994). Development and pathology in post-parental men: A community study. In E. Thompson, Jr. (Ed.), *Older men's lives* (pp. 65–84). Thousand Oaks, CA: Sage.

Gutteling, B. M., de Weerth, C., Zandbelt, N., Mulder, E. J. H., Visser, G. H. A., & Buitelaar, J. K. (2006). Does maternal prenatal stress adversely affect the child's learning and memory at age six? *Journal of Abnormal Child Psychology, 34,* 789–798.

Guyuron, B., Rose, D. J., Weinfeld, A. B., Eshraghi, Y., Fathi, A., & Iamphongsai, S. (2009). Factors contributing to the facial aging of identical twins. *Plastic and Reconstructive Surgery, 123,* 1321–1331.

Gwiazda, J., & Birch, E. E. (2001). Perceptual development: Vision. In E. B. Goldstein (Ed.), *Blackwell handbook of perception* (pp. 636–668). Oxford, UK: Blackwell.

H

Hack, M., & Klein, N. (2006). Young adult attainments of preterm infants. *Journal of the American Medical Association, 295,* 695–696.

Hagberg, B., Alfredson, B. B., Poon, L. W., & Homma, A. (2001). Cognitive functioning in centenarians: A coordinated analysis of results from three countries. *Journal of Gerontology, 56B,* P141–P151.

Hagekull, B., Bohlin, G., & Rydell, A. (1997). Maternal sensitivity, infant temperament, and the development of early feeding problems. *Infant Mental Health Journal, 18,* 92–106.

Haidt, J. (2001). The emotional dog and its rational tail: A social intuitionist approach to moral judgment. *Psychological Review, 108,* 814–834.

Haight, W. L., & Miller, P. J. (1993). *Pretending at home: Early development in a sociocultural context.* Albany, NY: State University of New York Press.

Hainline, L. (1998). The development of basic visual abilities. In A. Slater (Ed.), *Perceptual development: Visual, auditory, and speech perception in infancy* (pp. 5–50). Hove, UK: Psychology Press.

Hajjar, R. R., & Kamel, H. K. (2004). Sexuality in the nursing home, Part 1: Attitudes and barriers to sexual expression. *Journal of the American Medical Directors Association, 5,* S43–S47.

Hakuta, K., Bialystok, E., & Wiley, E. (2003). Critical evidence: A test of the critical-period hypothesis for second-language acquisitions. *Psychological Science, 14,* 31–38.

Halbreich, U. (2004). The diagnosis of premenstrual syndromes and premenstrual dysphoric disorder—clinical procedures and research perspectives. *Gynecological Endocrinology, 19,* 320–334.

Hale, C. M., & Tager-Flusberg, H. (2003). The influence of language on theory of mind: A training study. *Developmental Science, 6,* 346–359.

Hales, C. N., & Ozanne, S. E. (2003). The dangerous road of catch-up growth. *Journal of Physiology, 547,* 5–10.

Halfon, N., & McLearn, K. T. (2002). Families with children under 3: What we know and implications for results and policy. In N. Halfon & K. T. McLearn (Eds.), *Child rearing in America: Challenges facing parents with young children* (pp. 367–412). New York: Cambridge University Press.

Halford, G. S. (2002). Information-processing models of cognitive development. In U. Goswami (Ed.), *Blackwell handbook of childhood cognitive development* (pp. 555–574). Malden, MA: Blackwell.

Halford, G. S. (2005). Development of thinking. In K. J. Holyoak & R. G. Morrison (Eds.), *The Cambridge handbook of thinking and reasoning* (pp. 529–558). New York: Cambridge University Press.

Halford, G. S., & Andrews, G. (2006). Reasoning and problem solving. In D. Kuhn & R. Siegler (Eds.), *Handbook of child psychology: Vol. 2. Cognition, perception, and language* (6th ed., pp. 557–608). Hoboken, NJ: Wiley.

Hall, C. B., Derby, C., LeValley, A., Katz, M. J., Verghese, J., & Lipton, R. B. (2007). Education delays accelerated decline on a memory test in persons who develop dementia. *Neurology, 69,* 1657–1664.

Hall, D. G., & Graham, S. A. (1999). Lexical form class information guides word-to-object mapping in preschoolers. *Child Development, 70,* 78–91.

Hall, G. S. (1904). *Adolescence.* New York: Appleton.

Hall, J. G. (2003). Twinning. *The Lancet, 362,* 735–743.

Hall, K., Murrell, J., Ogunniyi, A., Deeg, M., Baiyewu, O., & Gao, S. (2006). Cholesterol, APOE genotype, and Alzheimer disease: An epidemiologic study of Nigerian Yoruba. *Neurology, 66,* 223–227.

Halle, T. G. (2003). Emotional development and well-being. In M. H. Bornstein, L. Davidson, C. L. M. Keyes, K. A. Moore, & the Center for Child Well-Being (Eds.), *Well-being: Positive development across the life course* (pp. 125–138). Mahwah, NJ: Erlbaum.

Hallenbeck, J. (2006). Palliative care training for the generalist: A luxury or a necessity? *Journal of General Internal Medicine, 21,* 1005–1006.

Haller, J. (2005). Vitamins and brain function. In H. R. Lieberman, R. B. Kanarek, & C. Prasad (2005). *Nutritional neuroscience* (pp. 207–233). Philadelphia: Taylor & Francis.

Halliday, J. L., Watson, L. F., Lumley, J., Danks, D. M., & Sheffield, L. S. (1995). New estimates of Down syndrome risks of chorionic villus sampling, amniocentesis, and live birth in women of advanced maternal age from a uniquely defined population. *Prenatal Diagnosis, 15,* 455–465.

Hallinan, M. T., & Kubitschek, W. N. (1999). Curriculum differentiation and high school achievement. *Social Psychology of Education, 3,* 41–62.

Halpern, C. T., Udry, J. R., & Suchindran, C. (1997). Testosterone predicts initiation of coitus in adolescent females. *Psychosomatic Medicine, 59,* 161–171.

Halpern, D. F. (2000). *Sex differences in cognitive abilities* (3rd ed.). Mahwah, NJ: Erlbaum.

Halpern, D. F. (2005a). How time-flexible work policies can reduce stress, improve health, and save money. *Stress and Health, 21,* 157–168.

Halpern, D. F. (2005b). Psychology at the intersection of work and family: Recommendations for employers, working families, and policymakers. *American Psychologist, 60,* 397–409.

Halpern, D. F., Benbow, C. P., Geary, D. C., Gur, R. C., Hyde, J. S., & Gernsbacher, M. A. (2007). The science of sex differences in science and mathematics. *Psychological Science in the Public Interest, 8,* 1–51.

Halpern, D. F., Wai, J., & Saw, A. (2005). A psychobiological model: Why females are sometimes greater than and sometimes less than males in math achievement. In D. F. Halpern, J. Wai, & A. Saw (Eds.), *Gender differences in mathematics: An integrative psychological approach* (pp. 48–72). New York: Cambridge University Press.

Halpern-Felsher, B. L., & Cauffman, E. (2001). Costs and benefits of a decision: Decision-making competence in adolescents and adults. *Journal of Applied Developmental Psychology, 22,* 257–273.

Haltzman, S., Holstein, N., & Moss, S. B. (2007). Men, marriage, and divorce. In J. E. Grant & M. N. Potenza (Eds.), *Textbook of men's mental health* (pp. 283–305). Washington, DC: American Psychiatric Publishing.

Hamer, D. H., Hu, S., Magnuson, V. L., Hu, N., & Pattatucci, A. M. L. (1993). A linkage between DNA markers on the X chromosome and male sexual orientation. *Science, 261,* 321–327.

Hamer, M., Wolvers, D., & Albers, R. (2004). Using stress models to evaluate immuno-modulating effects of nutritional intervention in healthy individuals. *Journal of the American College of Nutrition, 23,* 637–646.

Hamilton, S. F., & Hamilton, M. A. (2000). Research, intervention, and social change: Improving adolescents' career opportunities. In L. J. Crockett & R. K. Silbereisen (Eds.), *Negotiating adolescence in times of social change* (pp. 267–283). New York: Cambridge University Press.

Hammes, B., & Laitman, C. J. (2003). Diethylstilbestrol (DES) update: Recommendations for the identification and management of DES-exposed individuals. *Journal of Midwifery and Women's Health, 48,* 19–29.

Hammond, C. J., Snieder, H., Spector, T. D., & Gilbert, C. E. (2000). Genetic and environmental factors in age-related nuclear cataracts in monozygotic and dizygotic twins. *New England Journal of Medicine, 342,* 1786–1790.

Han, S. K., & Moen, P. (1999). Clocking out: Temporal patterning of retirement. *American Journal of Sociology, 105,* 191–236.

Han, W.-J., & Waldfogel, J. (2003). Parental leave: The impact of recent legislation on parents' leave taking. *Demography, 40,* 191–200.

Hanke, W., Sobala, W., & Kalinka, J. (2004). Environmental tobacco smoke exposure among pregnant women: Impact on fetal biometry at 20–24 weeks of gestation and newborn child's birth weight. *International Archives of Occupational and Environmental Health, 77,* 47–52.

Hankin, B. L., & Abela, J. R. Z. (2005). Depression from childhood through adolescence and adulthood: A developmental vulnerability and stress perspective. In B. L. Hankin & J. R. Z. Abela (Eds.), *Development of psychopathology: A vulnerability-stress perspective* (pp. 245–288). Thousand Oaks, CA: Sage.

Hannon, E. E., & Johnson, S. P. (2004). Infants use meter to categorize rhythms and melodies: Implications for musical structure learning. *Cognitive Psychology, 50,* 354–377.

Hannon, E. E., & Trehub, S. E. (2005a). Metrical categories in infancy and adulthood. *Psychological Science, 16,* 48–55.

Hannon, E. E., & Trehub, S. E. (2005b). Tuning in to musical rhythms: Infants learn more readily than adults. *Proceedings of the National Academy of Sciences, 102,* 12639–12643.

Hannon, T. S., Rao, G., & Arslanian, S. A. (2005). Childhood obesity and type 2 diabetes mellitus. *Pediatrics, 116,* 473–480.

Hansen, M., Janssen, I., Schiff, A., Zee, P. C., & Dubocovich, M. L. (2005). The impact of school daily schedule on adolescent sleep. *Pediatrics, 115,* 1555–1561.

Hansson, R. O., & Stroebe, M. S. (2007). The dual process model of coping with bereavement and development of an integrative risk factor framework. In R. O. Hansson & M. S. Stroebe (Eds.), *Bereavement in late life: Coping, adaptation, and developmental influences* (pp. 41–60). Washington, DC: American Psychological Association.

Harachi, T. W., Fleming, C. B., White, H. R., Ensminger, M. E., Abbott, R. D., Catalano, R. F., & Haggerty, K. P. (2006). Aggressive behavior among girls and boys during middle childhood: Predictors and sequelae of trajectory group membership. *Aggressive Behavior, 32,* 279–293.

Hardre, P. L., & Reeve, J. (2003). A motivational model of rural students' intentions to persist in, versus drop out of, high school. *Journal of Educational Psychology, 95,* 347–356.

Hardy, J. B., Astone, N. M., Brooks-Gunn, J., Shapiro, S., & Miller, T. L. (1998). Like mother, like child: Intergenerational patterns of age at first birth and associations with childhood and adolescent characteristics and adult outcomes in the second generation. *Developmental Psychology, 34,* 1220–1232.

Hardy, S. A., & Carlo, G. (2005). Religiosity and prosocial behaviours in adolescence: The mediating role of prosocial values. *Journal of Moral Education, 34,* 231–249.

Harley, B., & Jean, G. (1999). Vocabulary skills of French immersion students in their second language. *Zeitschrift für Interkulturellen Fremdsprachenunterricht, 4*(2). Retrieved from http://www.ualberta.ca

Harley, K., & Reese, E. (1999). Origins of autobiographical memory. *Developmental Psychology, 35,* 1338–1348.

Harlow, H. F., & Zimmerman, R. (1959). Affectional responses in the infant monkey. *Science, 130,* 421–432.

Harman, D. (2002). Aging: Overview. *Annals of the New York Academy of Sciences, 959,* 1–21.

Harman, S. M., & Blackman, M. R. (2004). Use of growth hormone for prevention or treatment of effects of aging. *Journal of Gerontology, 59,* 652–658.

Harold, G. T., Shelton, K. H., Goeke-Morey, M. C., & Cummings, E. M. (2004). Marital conflict, child emotional security about family relationships, and child adjustment. *Social Development, 13,* 350–376.

Harris, J. R. (1998). *The nurture assumption: Why children turn out the way they do.* New York: Free Press.

Harris, P. B. (1998). Listening to caregiving sons: Misunderstood realities. *Gerontologist, 38,* 342–352.

Harris, R. L., Ellicott, A. M., & Holmes, D. S. (1986). The timing of psychosocial transitions and changes in women's lives: An examination of women aged 45 to 60. *Journal of Personality and Social Psychology, 51,* 409–416.

Harris, Y. R., & Graham, J. A. (2007). *The African American child: Development and challenges.* New York: Springer.

Harrison, A. O., Wilson, M. N., Pine, C. J., Chan, S. Q., & Buriel, R. (1994). Family ecologies of ethnic minority children. In G. Handel & G. G. Whitchurch (Eds.), *The psychosocial interior of the family* (pp. 187–210). New York: Aldine de Gruyter.

Harrist, A. W., Zaia, A. F., Bates, J. E., Dodge, K. A., & Pettit, G. S. (1997). Subtypes of social withdrawal in early childhood: Sociometric status and social–cognitive differences across four years. *Child Development, 68,* 278–294.

Hart, B. (2004). What toddlers talk about. *First Language, 24,* 91–106.

Hart, B., & Risley, T. R. (1995). *Meaningful differences in the everyday experience of young American children.* Baltimore: Paul H. Brookes.

Hart, C. H., Burts, D. C., Durland, M. A., Charlesworth, R., DeWolf, M., & Fleege, P. O. (1998). Stress behaviors and activity type participation of preschoolers in more and less developmentally appropriate classrooms: SES and sex differences. *Journal of Research in Childhood Education, 13,* 176–196.

Hart, C. H., Newell, L. D., & Olsen, S. F. (2003). Parenting skills and social–communicative competence in childhood. In J. O. Greene & B. R. Burleson (Eds.), *Handbook of communication and social interaction skills* (pp. 753–797). Mahwah, NJ: Erlbaum.

Hart, C. H., Yang, C., Nelson, L. J., Robinson, C. C., Olsen, J. A., Nelson, D. A., Porter, C. L., Jin, S., Olsen, S. F., & Wu, P. (2000). Peer acceptance in early childhood and subtypes of socially withdrawn behavior in China, Russia, and the United States. *International Journal of Behavioral Development, 24,* 73–81.

Hart, D., & Fegley, S. (1995). Prosocial behavior and caring in adolescence: Relations to self-understanding and social judgment. *Child Development, 66,* 1346–1359.

Hart, H. M., McAdams, D. P., Hirsch, B. J., & Bauer, J. J. (2001). Generativity and social involvement among African Americans and white adults. *Journal of Research in Personality, 35,* 208–230.

Harter, S. (1998). The development of self-representations. In N. Eisenberg (Ed.), *Handbook of child psychology: Vol. 3. Social, emotional, and personality development* (5th ed., pp. 553–618). New York: Wiley.

Harter, S. (1999). *The construction of self: A developmental perspective.* New York: Guilford.

Harter, S. (2003). The development of self-representations during childhood and adolescence. In M. R. Leary & J. P. Tangney (Eds.), *Handbook of self and identity* (pp. 610–642). New York: Guilford.

Harter, S. (2006). The self. In N. Eisenberg (Ed.), *Handbook of child psychology: Vol. 3. Social, emotional, and personality development* (6th ed., pp. 505–570). Hoboken, NJ: Wiley.

Harter, S., & Whitesell, N. (1989). Developmental changes in children's understanding of simple, multiple, and blended emotion concepts. In C. Saarni & P. Harris (Eds.), *Children's understanding of emotion* (pp. 81–116). Cambridge, UK: Cambridge University Press.

Hartley, A. (2006). Changing role of the speed of processing construct. In J. E. Birren & K. W. Schaie (Eds.), *Handbook of the psychology of aging* (6th ed., pp. 183–207). Burlington, MA: Academic Press.

Hartman, J., & Warren, L. H. (2005). Explaining age differences in temporal working memory. *Psychology and Aging, 20,* 645–656.

Hartup, W. W. (2006). Relationships in early and middle childhood. In A. L. Vangelisti & D. Perlman (Eds.), *Cambridge handbook of personal relationships* (pp. 177–190). New York: Cambridge University Press.

Hartup, W. W., & Abecassis, M. (2004). Friends and enemies. In P. K. Smith & C. H. Hart (Eds.), *Blackwell handbook of childhood social development* (pp. 285–306). Malden, MA: Blackwell.

Hartup, W. W., & Stevens, N. (1999). Friendships and adaptation across the life span. *Current Directions in Psychological Science, 8,* 76–79.

Harvey, M. W. (2001). Vocational-technical education: A logical approach to dropout prevention for secondary special education. *Preventing School Failure, 45,* 108–113.

Harwood, M. D., & Farrar, M. J. (2006). Conflicting emotions: The connection between affective perspective taking and theory of mind. *British Journal of Developmental Psychology, 24,* 401–418.

Harwood, R., Leyendecker, B., Carlson, V., Asencio, M., & Miller, A. (2002). Parenting among Latino families in the U.S. In M. H. Bornstein (Ed.), *Handbook of parenting: Vol. 4. Social conditions and applied parenting* (4th ed., pp. 21–46). Mahwah, NJ: Erlbaum.

Hasher, L., Zacks, R. T., & May, C. P. (1999). Inhibitory control, circadian arousal, and age. In D. Gopher & A. Koriat (Eds.), *Attention and performance* (Vol. 17, pp. 653–675). Cambridge, MA: MIT Press.

Hasler, P., & Zouali, M. (2005). Immune receptor signaling, aging, and autoimmunity. *Cellular Immunology, 233,* 102–108.

Hassing, L. B., Johansson, B., Berg, S., Nilsson, S. E., Pedersen, N. L., Hofer, S. M., & McClearn, G. (2002). Terminal decline and markers of cerebro- and cardiovascular disease: Findings from a longitudinal study of the oldest old. *Journal of Gerontology, 57B,* P268–P276.

Hastrup, B. (2007). Healthy aging in Denmark? In M. Robinson, W. Novelli, C. Pearson, & L. Norris (Eds.), *Global health and global aging* (pp. 71–84). San Francisco: Jossey-Bass.

Hatch, L. R., & Bulcroft, K. (2004). Does long-term marriage bring less frequent disagreements? *Journal of Family Issues, 25,* 465–495.

Hatfield, E., Rapson, R. L, & Martel, L. D. (2007). Passionate love and sexual desire. In S. Kitayama & D. Cohen (Eds.), *Handbook of cultural psychology* (pp. 760–779). New York: Guilford.

Hauck, F. R., Herman, S. M., Donovan, M., Iyasu, S., Moore, C. M., & Donoghue, E. (2003). Sleep environment and the risk of sudden infant death syndrome in an urban population: The Chicago Infant Mortality Study. *Pediatrics, 111,* 1207–1214.

Hauf, P., Aschersleben, G., & Prinz, W. (2007). Baby do–baby see! How action production influences action perception in infants. *Cognitive Development, 22,* 16–32.

Hausfather, A., Toharia, A., LaRoche, C., & Engelsmann, F. (1997). Effects of age of entry, day-care quality, and family characteristics on preschool behavior. *Journal of Child Psychology and Psychiatry, 38,* 441–448.

Hawes, C., & Phillips, C. D. (2007). Defining quality in assisted living: Comparing apples, oranges, and broccoli. *Gerontologist, 47*(Special Issue III), 40–50.

Hawkins, J. D., Catalano, R. F., & Miller, J. Y. (1992). Risk and protective factors for alcohol and other drug problems in adolescence and early adulthood: Implications for substance abuse prevention. *Psychological Bulletin, 112,* 64–105.

Hawkins, J. N. (1994). Issues of motivation in Asian education. In H. F. O'Neil, Jr., & M. Drillings (Eds.), *Motivation: Theory and research* (pp. 101–115). Hillsdale, NJ: Erlbaum.

Hawkley, L. C., & Cacioppo, J. T. (2004). Stress and the aging immune system. *Brain, Behavior and Immunity, 18,* 114–119.

Hay, P., & Bacaltchuk, J. (2004). Bulimia nervosa. *Clinical Evidence, 12,* 1326–1347.

Hayflick, L. (1994). *How and why we age.* New York: Ballantine.

Hayflick, L. (1998). How and why we age. *Experimental Gerontology, 33,* 639–653.

Hayne, H. (2002). Thoughts from the crib: Meltzoff and Moore (1994) alter our views of mental representation during infancy. *Infant Behavior and Development, 25,* 62–64.

Hayne, H. (2004). Infant memory development: Implications for childhood amnesia. *Developmental Review, 24,* 33–73.

Hayne, H., Boniface, J., & Barr, R. (2000). The development of declarative memory in human infants: Age-related changes in deferred imitation. *Behavioral Neuroscience, 114,* 77–83.

Hayne, H., Rovee-Collier, C., & Perris, E. E. (1987). Categorization and memory retrieval by three month olds. *Child Development, 58,* 750–767.

Hays, J. C., & George, L. K. (2002). The life-course trajectory toward living alone: Racial differences. *Research on Aging, 24,* 283–307.

Hayslip, B., Jr., Emick, M. A., Handerson, C. E., & Elias, K. (2002). Temporal variations in the experience of custodial grandparenting: A short-term longitudinal study. *Journal of Applied Gerontology, 21,* 139–156.

Hayslip, B., Jr., & Kaminski, P. L. (2005). Grandparents raising their grandchildren. *Marriage and Family Review, 37,* 147–169.

Haywood, K. M., & Getchell, N. (2005). *Life span motor development* (4th ed.). Champaign, IL: Human Kinetics.

Hazell, L. V. (2001). Multicultural aftercare issues. In O. D. Weeks & C. Johnson (Eds.), *When all the friends have gone: Guide for aftercare providers* (pp. 57–71). Amityville, NY: Baywood.

Head Start Bureau. (2008). *Head Start fact sheet.* Retrieved from www.acf.hhs.gov/programs/ohs/about/fy2008.html

Health and Disability Research Institute. (2006). *Fear of falling: A matter of balance.* Boston: Author.

Health Canada. (2006). *Sexually transmitted infections surveillance and epidemiology.* Retrieved from www.phac-aspc.gc.ca/sti-its-surv-epi/surveillance_e.html

Heath, S. B. (1990). The children of Trackton's children: Spoken and written in social change. In J. Stigler, G. Herdt, & R. A. Shweder (Eds.), *Cultural psychology: Essays on comparative human development* (pp. 496–519). New York: Cambridge University Press.

Heaton, T. B. (2002). Factors contributing to increasing marital stability in the United States. *Journal of Family Issues, 23,* 392–409.

Hebert, M., & Tourigny, M. (2004). Child sexual abuse prevention: A review of evaluative studies and recommendations for program development. In S. P. Serge (Ed.), *Advances in psychology research* (Vol. 29, pp. 123–155). Hauppauge, NY: Nova Science Publishers.

Heckman, J. J., & Masterov, D. V. (2004). *The productivity argument for investing in young children.* Working Paper 5, Invest in Kids Working Group, Committee for Economic Development. Retrieved from jenni.uchicago.edu/Invest

Hedberg, K., Hopkins, D., & Kohn, M. (2003). Five years of legal physician-assisted suicide in Oregon. *New England Journal of Medicine, 348,* 961–964.

Hedge, J. W., Borman, W. C., & Lammlein, S. E. (2006). *The aging workforce: Realities, myths, and implications for organizations.* Washington, DC: American Psychological Association.

Hedges, L. V., & Nowell, A. (1998). Black–white test score convergence since 1995. In C. Jencks & M. Phillips (Eds.), *The black–white test score gap* (pp. 149–181). Washington, DC: Brookings Institution.

Hediger, M. L., Overpeck, M. D., Ruan, W. J., & Troendle, J. F. (2002). Birthweight and gestational age effects on motor and social development. *Paediatric and Perinatal Epidemiology, 16,* 33–46.

Heilbronn, L. K., & Ravussin, E. (2003). Calorie restriction and aging: Review of the literature and implications for studies in humans. *American Journal of Clinical Nutrition, 78,* 361–369.

Heinz, W. R. (1999). Job entry patterns in life-course perspective. In W. R. Heinz (Ed.), *From education to work: Cross-national perspectives* (pp. 214–231). New York: Cambridge University Press.

Helm, H. M., Hays, J. C., Flint, E. P., Koenig, H. G., & Blazer, D. G. (2000). Does private religious activity prolong survival? A six-year follow-up study of 3,851 older adults. *Journal of Gerontology, 55A,* M400–M405.

Helson, R. (1992). Women's difficult times and the rewriting of the life story. *Psychology of Women Quarterly, 16,* 331–347.

Helson, R. (1997). The self in middle age. In M. E. Lachman & J. B. James (Eds.), *Multiple paths of midlife development* (pp. 21–43). Chicago: University of Chicago Press.

Helson, R., & Cate, R. A. (2007). Late middle age: Transition to the Third Age. In J. B. James & P. Wink (Eds.), Annual review of gerontology and geriatrics (Vol. 26, pp. 83–101). New York: Springer.

Helson, R., Jones, C. J., & Kwan, V. S. Y. (2002). Personality change over 40 years of adulthood: Hierarchical linear modeling analyses of two longitudinal samples. *Journal of Personality and Social Psychology, 83,* 752–766.

Helson, R., Mitchell, V., & Moane, G. (1984). Personality and patterns of adherence and nonadherence to the social clock. *Journal of Personality and Social Psychology, 46,* 1079–1096.

Helson, R., & Picano, J. (1990). Is the traditional role bad for women? *Journal of Personality and Social Psychology, 59,* 311–320.

Helson, R., Soto, C. J., & Cate, R. A. (2006). From young adulthood through the middle ages. In D. K. Mroczek & T. D. Little (Eds.), *Handbook of personality development* (pp. 337–352). Mahwah, NJ: Erlbaum.

Helson, R., & Wink, P. (1992). Personality change in women from the early 40s to the early 50s. *Psychology and Aging, 7,* 46–55.

Heltzner, E. P., Cauley, J. A., Pratt, S. R., Wisniewski, S. R., Zmuda, J. M., & Talbott, E. O. (2005). Race and sex differences in age-related hearing loss: The health, aging and body composition study. *Journal of the American Geriatrics Society, 53,* 2119–2127.

Helwig, C. C. (1995). Adolescents' and young adults' conceptions of civil liberties: Freedom of speech and religion. *Child Development, 66,* 152–166.

Helwig, C. C. (2006). Rights, civil liberties, and democracy across cultures. In M. Killen & J. G. Smetana (Eds.), *Handbook of moral development* (pp. 185–210). Philadelphia: Erlbaum.

Helwig, C. C., & Jasiobedzka, U. (2001). The relation between law and morality: Children's reasoning about socially beneficial and unjust laws. *Child Development, 72,* 1382–1393.

Helwig, C. C., & Prencipe, A. (1999). Children's judgments of flags and flag-burning. *Child Development, 70,* 132–143.

Helwig, C. C., & Turiel, E. (2004). Children's social and moral reasoning. In P. K. Smith & C. H. Hart (Eds.), *Blackwell handbook of childhood social development* (pp. 476–490). Malden, MA: Blackwell.

Henderson, D., Buchanan, J. A., & Fisher, J. E. (2002). Violence and the elderly population: Issues for prevention. In P. A. Schewe (Ed.), *Preventing violence in relationships: Interventions across the life span* (pp. 223–245). Washington, DC: American Psychological Association.

Henderson, H. A., Marshall, P. J., Fox, N. A., & Rubin, K. H. (2004). Psychophysiological and behavioral evidence for varying forms and functions of nonsocial behavior in preschoolers. *Child Development, 75,* 251–263.

Henderson, V. W. (2009). Estrogens, episodic memory, and Alzheimer's disease: A critical update. *Seminars in Reproductive Medicine, 27,* 283–293.

Hendrick, S. S., & Hendrick, C. (1993). Lovers as friends. *Journal of Social and Personal Relationships, 10,* 459–466.

Hendrick, S. S., & Hendrick, C. (2002). Love. In C. R. Snyder & S. J. Lopez (Eds.), *Handbook of positive psychology* (pp. 472–484). New York: Oxford University Press.

Hendricks, J., & Cutler, S. J. (2004). Volunteerism and socioemotional selectivity in later life. *Journal of Gerontology, 59B,* S251–S257.

Hendrie, H. H. (2001). Exploration of environmental and genetic risk factors for Alzheimer's disease: The value of cross-cultural studies. *Current Directions in Psychological Science, 10,* 98–101.

Hendry, L. B., & Kloep, M. (2007). Conceptualizing emerging adulthood: Inspecting the emperor's new clothes? *Child Development Perspectives, 1,* 74–79.

Henggeler, S., Sheidow, A. J., & Lee, T. (2007). Multisystemic treatment of serious clinical problems in youths and their families. In D. W. Springer & A. R. Roberts (Eds.), *Handbook of forensic mental health with victims and offenders* (pp. 315–345). New York: Springer.

Henning, K., Jones, A. R., & Holdford, R. (2005). Attributions of blame among male and female domestic violence offenders. *Journal of Family Violence, 20,* 131–139.

Henrich, C. C., Brookmeyer, K. A., Shrier, L. A., & Shahar, G. (2006). Supportive relationships and sexual risk behavior in adolescence: An ecological–transactional approach. *Journal of Pediatric Psychology, 31,* 286–297.

Henrich, C. C., Kuperminc, G. P., Sack, A., Blatt, S. J., & Leadbeater, B. J. (2000). Characteristics and homogeneity of early adolescent friendship groups: A comparison of male and female clique and nonclique members. *Applied Developmental Science, 4,* 15–26.

Henricsson, L., & Rydell, A. M. (2004). Elementary school children with behavior problems: Teacher–child relations and self-perception. A prospective study. *Merrill-Palmer Quarterly, 50,* 111–138.

Henry, J. D., MacLeod, M. S., Phillips, L. H., & Crawford, J. R. (2004). A meta-analytic review of prospective memory and aging. *Psychology and Aging, 19,* 27–39.

Herbst, J. H., McCrae, R. R., Costa, P. T., Jr., Feaganes, J. R., & Siegler, I. C. (2000). Self-perceptions of stability and change in personality at midlife: The UNC Alumni Heart Study. *Assessment, 7,* 379–388.

Herman, M. (2004). Forced to choose: Some determinants of racial identification in multiracial adolescents. *Child Development, 75,* 730–748.

Herman-Giddens, M. E. (2006). Recent data on pubertal milestones in United States children: The secular trend toward earlier development. *International Journal of Andrology, 29,* 241–246.

Hermann, M., Untergasser, G., Rumpold, H., & Berger, P. (2000). Aging of the male reproductive system. *Experimental Gerontology, 35,* 1267–1279.

Hernandez, M., & Newcomer, R. (2007). Assisted living and special populations: What do we know about differences in use and potential access barriers? *Gerontologist, 47*(Special Issue III), 110–117.

Herrera, E., Reissland, N., & Shepherd, J. (2004). Maternal touch and maternal child-directed speech: Effects of depressed mood in the postnatal period. *Journal of Affective Disorders, 81,* 29–39.

Herrnstein, R. J., & Murray, C. (1994). *The bell curve.* New York: Free Press.

Hershey, D. A., Jacobs-Lawson, J. M., McArdle, J. J., & Hamagami, F. (2007). Psychological foundations of financial planning for retirement. *Journal of Adult Development, 14,* 26–36.

Hershey, D. A., Walsh, D. A., Brougham, R., & Carter, S. (1998). Challenges of training pre-retirees to make sound financial planning decisions. *Educational Gerontology, 24,* 447–470.

Herz, B. K. (2004). *What works in girls' education: Evidence and policies from the developing world.* New York: Council on Foreign Relations.

Herzog, D. B., Eddy, K. T., & Beresin, E. V. (2006). Anorexia and bulimia nervosa. In M. K. Dulcan &

J. M. Wiener (Eds.), *Essentials of child and adolescent psychiatry* (pp. 527–560). Washington, DC: American Psychiatric Publishing.

Hesketh, K., Ball, K., Crawford, D., Campbell, K., & Salmon, J. (2007). Mediators of the relationship between maternal education and children's TV viewing. *American Journal of Preventive Medicine, 33,* 41–47.

Hespos, S. J., & Baillargeon, R. (2001). Reasoning about containment events in very young infants. *Cognition, 78,* 207–245.

Hess, T. M., & Hinson, J. T. (2006). Age-related variation in the influences of aging stereotypes on memory in adulthood. *Psychology and Aging, 21,* 621–625.

Hess, T. M., Hinson, J. T., & Statham, J. A. (2004). Explicit and implicit stereotype activation effects on memory: Do age and awareness moderate the impact of priming? *Psychology and Aging, 19,* 495–505.

Hesse, E., & Main, M. (2000). Disorganized infant, child, and adult attachment: Collapse in behavioral and attentional strategies. *Journal of the American Psychoanalytic Association, 48,* 1097–1127.

Hessler, R. M., Eriksson, B. G., Dey, D., Steen, G., Sundh, V., & Steen, B. (2003). The compression of morbidity debate in aging: An empirical test using the gerontological and geriatric population studies in Göteborg, Sweden. *Archives of Gerontology and Geriatrics, 37,* 213–222.

Hetherington, E. M. (1999). Should we stay together for the sake of the children? In E. M. Hetherington (Ed.), *Coping with divorce, single-parenting, and remarriage: A risk and resiliency perspective* (pp. 93–116). Hillsdale, NJ: Erlbaum.

Hetherington, E. M. (2003). Social support and the adjustment of children in divorced and remarried families. *Childhood, 10,* 237–254

Hetherington, E. M., Henderson, S. H., & Reiss, D. (1999). Adolescent siblings in stepfamilies: Family functioning and adolescent adjustment. *Monographs of the Society for Research in Child Development, 64*(4, Serial No. 259).

Hetherington, E. M., & Jodl, K. M. (1994). Stepfamilies as settings for child development. In A. Booth & J. Dunn (Eds.), *Stepfamilies: Who benefits? Who does not?* (pp. 55–79). Hillsdale, NJ: Erlbaum.

Hetherington, E. M., & Kelly, J. (2002). *For better or for worse: Divorce reconsidered.* New York: Norton.

Hetherington, E. M., & Stanley-Hagan, M. (2000). Diversity among stepfamilies. In D. H. Demo, K. R. Allen, & M. A. Fine (Eds.), *Handbook of family diversity* (pp. 173–196). New York: Oxford University Press.

Hewlett, B. S. (2004). Fathers in forager, farmer, and pastoral cultures. In M. E. Lamb (Ed.), *The role of the father in child development* (4th ed., pp. 182–195). Hoboken, NJ: Wiley.

Hewlett, S. (2003). *Creating a life.* New York: Miramax.

Heyman, G. D., & Dweck, C. S. (1998). Children's thinking about traits: Implications for judgments of the self and others. *Child Development, 69,* 391–403.

Heyman, G. D., & Legare, C. H. (2004). Children's beliefs about gender differences in the academic and social domains. *Sex Roles, 50,* 227–239.

Hickling, A. K., & Wellman, H. M. (2001). The emergence of children's causal explanations and theories: Evidence from everyday conversation. *Developmental Psychology, 37,* 668–683.

Hietanen, A., Era, P., Sorri, M., & Heikkinen, E. (2004). Changes in hearing in 80-year-old people: A 10-year follow-up study. *International Journal of Audiology, 43,* 126–135.

Higginbottom, G. M. A. (2006). 'Pressure of life': Ethnicity as a mediating factor in mid-life and older peoples' experience of high blood pressure. *Sociology of Health and Illness, 28,* 583–610.

High, P. C., LaGasse, L., Becker, S., Ahlgren, I., & Gardner, A. (2000). Literacy promotion in primary care pediatrics: Can we make a difference? *Pediatrics, 105,* 927–934.

Hildreth, K., & Rovee-Collier, C. (2002). Forgetting functions of reactivated memories over the first year of life. *Developmental Psychobiology, 41,* 277–288.

Hildreth, K., Sweeney, B., & Rovee-Collier, C. (2003). Differential memory-preserving effects of reminders at 6 months. *Journal of Experimental Child Psychology, 84,* 41–62.

Hilgers, K. K., Akridge, M., Scheetz, J. P., & Kinance, D. E. (2006). Childhood obesity and dental development. *Pediatric Dentistry, 28,* 18–22.

Hill, D. (2003). *Europe: When dying seems better than living.* New York: Radio Free Europe. Retrieved from http://www.rferl.org/nca/features/2003/01/22012003154227.as

Hill, E. J., Mead, N. T., Dean, L. R., Hafen, D. M., Gadd, R., & Palmer, A. A. (2006). Researching the 60-hour dual-earner workweek. *American Behavioral Scientist, 49,* 1184–1203.

Hill, J. L., Brooks-Gunn, J., & Waldfogel, J. (2003). Sustained effects of high participation in an early intervention for low-birth-weight premature infants. *Developmental Psychology, 39,* 730–744.

Hill, N. E., & Taylor, L. C. (2004). Parental school involvement and children's academic achievement: Pragmatics and issues. *Current Directions in Psychological Science, 13,* 161–164.

Hill, N. M., & Schneider, W. (2006). Brain changes in the development of expertise: Neuroanatomical and neurophysiological evidence about skill-based adaptations. In K. A. Ericsson, N. Charness, P. J. Feltovich, & R. R. Hoffman (Eds.), *The Cambridge handbook of expertise and expert performance* (pp. 653–682). New York: Cambridge University Press.

Hillis, S. D., Anda, R. F., Dube, S. R., Felitti, V. J., Marchbanks, P. A., & Marks, J. S. (2004). The association between adverse childhood experiences and adolescent pregnancy, long-term psychosocial consequences, and fetal death. *Pediatrics, 113,* 320–327.

Hillman, C. H., Erickson, K. I., & Kramer, A. F. (2008). Be smart, exercise your heart: Exercise effects on brain and cognition. *Nature Reviews Neuroscience, 9,* 58–65.

Hillman, J. L. (2000). *Clinical perspectives on elderly sexuality.* New York: Kluwer Academic.

Hillman, J. L., & Stricker, G. (1994). A linkage of knowledge and attitudes toward elderly sexuality: Not necessarily a uniform relationship. *Gerontologist, 34,* 256–260.

Hilt, L. M. (2004). Attribution retaining for therapeutic change: Theory, practice, and future directions. *Imagination, Cognition, and Personality, 23,* 289–307.

Hinojosa, T., Sheu, C.-F., & Michael, G. F. (2003). Infant hand-use preference for grasping objects contributes to the development of a hand-use preference for manipulating objects. *Developmental Psychobiology, 43,* 328–334.

Hirsch, C. (1996). Understanding the influence of gender role identity on the assumption of family caregiving roles by men. *International Journal of Aging and Human Development, 42,* 103–121.

Hirsh-Pasek, K., & Golinkoff, R. M. (2003). *Einstein never used flash cards.* New York: Rodale.

Hirsh-Pasek, K., Golinkoff, R. M., Berk, L. E., & Singer, D. G. (2009). *A mandate for playful learning in preschool: Presenting the evidence.* New York: Oxford University Press.

Hoch-Espada, A., Ryan, E., & Deblinger, E. (2006). Child sexual abuse. In J. E. Fisher & W. T. O'Donohue (Eds.), *Practitioner's guide to evidence-based psychotherapy* (pp. 177–188). New York: Springer.

Hochwarter, W. A., Ferris, G. R., Perrewe, P. L., Witt, L. A., & Kiewitz, C. (2001). A note on the nonlinearity of the age–job satisfaction relationship. *Journal of Applied Social Psychology, 31,* 1223–1237.

Hodges, J., & Tizard, B. (1989). Social and family relationships of ex-institutional adolescents. *Journal of Child Psychology and Psychiatry, 30,* 77–97.

Hodges, R. M., & French, L. A. (1988). The effect of class and collection labels on cardinality, class-inclusion, and number conservation tasks. *Child Development, 59,* 1387–1396.

Hoenig, H., Taylor, D. H., Jr., & Sloan, F. A. (2003). Does assistive technology substitute for personal assistance among the disabled elderly? *American Journal of Public Health, 93,* 330–337.

Hoff, B. (2001). *Full report of the prevalence, incidence, and consequences of violence against women.* Washington, DC: U.S. Department of Justice.

Hoff, E. (2003). The specificity of environmental influence: Socioeconomic status affects early vocabulary development via maternal speech. *Child Development, 74,* 1368–1378.

Hoff, E. (2004). The specificity of environmental influence: Socioeconomic status affects early vocabulary development via maternal speech. *Child Development, 74,* 1368–1378.

Hoff, E., Laursen, B., & Tardif, T. (2002). Socioeconomic status and parenting. In M. H. Bornstein (Ed.), *Handbook of parenting* (pp. 231–252). Mahwah, NJ: Erlbaum.

Hofferth, S. L., & Anderson, K. G. (2003). Are all dads equal? Biology versus marriage as a basis for paternal investment. *Journal of Marriage and Family, 65,* 213–232.

Hoffman, L. W. (2000). Maternal employment: Effects of social context. In R. D. Taylor & M. C. Wang (Eds.), *Resilience across contexts: Family, work, culture, and community* (pp. 147–176). Mahwah, NJ: Erlbaum.

Hoffman, M. L. (2000). *Empathy and moral development.* New York: Cambridge University Press.

Hoffman, S., & Hatch, M. C. (1996). Stress, social support and pregnancy outcome: A reassessment based on research. *Paediatric and Perinatal Epidemiology, 10,* 380–405.

Hoffmann, W. (2001). Fallout from the Chernobyl nuclear disaster and congenital malformations in Europe. *Archives of Environmental Health, 56,* 478–483.

Hogan, B. E., & Linden, W. (2004). Anger response styles and blood pressure: At least don't ruminate about it! *Annals of Behavioral Medicine, 27,* 38–49.

Hogan, D. B., MacKnight, C., & Bergman, H. (2003). Models, definitions, and criteria of frailty. *Aging Clinical and Experimental Research, 15*(Suppl. to No. 3), 3–29.

Hoglund, W. L., & Leadbeater, B. J. (2007). Managing threat: Do social-cognitive processes mediate the link between peer victimization and adjustment problems in early adolescence? *Journal of Research on Adolescence, 17,* 525–540.

Hokoda, A., & Fincham, F. D. (1995). Origins of children's helpless and mastery achievement patterns in the family. *Journal of Educational Psychology, 87,* 375–385.

Holditch-Davis, D., Belyea, M., & Edwards, L. J. (2005). Prediction of 3-year developmental outcomes from sleep development over the preterm period. *Infant Behavior and Development, 79,* 49–58.

Holland, J. L. (1985). *Making vocational choices: A theory of vocational personalities and work environments.* Englewood Cliffs, NJ: Prentice-Hall.

Holland, J. L. (1997). *Making vocational choices: A theory of vocational personalities and work environments* (3rd ed.). Odessa, FL: Psychological Assessment Resources.

Hollich, G. J., Hirsh-Pasek, K., & Golinkoff, R. M. (2000). Breaking the language barrier: An emergentist coalition model for the origins of word learning. *Monographs of the Society for Research in Child Development, 65*(3, Serial No. 262).

Holmes-Rovner, M., Rovner, D. R., Padonu, G., Talarczyk, G., Kroll, J., Rothert, M., & Breer, L. (1996). African-American women's attitudes and expectations of menopause. *American Journal of Preventive Medicine, 12,* 420–423.

Holobow, N., Genesee, F., & Lambert, W. (1991). The effectiveness of a foreign language immersion program for children from different ethnic and social class backgrounds: Report 2. *Applied Psycholinguistics, 12,* 179–198.

Holowka, S., Brosseau-Lapré, F., & Petitto, L. A. (2002). Semantic and conceptual knowledge underlying bilingual babies' first signs and words. *Language Learning, 52,* 205–262.

Honein, M. A., Paulozzi, L. J., & Erickson, J. D. (2001). Continued occurrence of Accutane-exposed pregnancies. *Teratology, 64,* 142–147

Hong, Z.-R., Veach, P. M., & Lawrenz, F. (2003). An investigation of the gender stereotyped thinking of Taiwanese secondary school boys and girls. *Sex Roles, 48,* 495–504.

Hood, B. M. (2004). Is looking good enough or does it beggar belief? *Developmental Science, 7,* 415–417.

Hooker, K. (1992). Possible selves and perceived health in older adults and college students. *Journal of Gerontology, 47,* P85–P89.

Hooyman, N. R., & Kiyak, H. A. (2008). *Social gerontology: A multidisciplinary perspective* (8th ed.). Boston: Allyn and Bacon.

Hopper, S. V. (1993). The influence of ethnicity on the health of older women. *Clinics in Geriatric Medicine, 9,* 231–259.

Hoppmann, C. A., Gerstorf, D., Smith, J., & Klumb, P. L. (2007). Linking possible selves and behavior: Do domain-specific hopes and fears translate into daily activities in very old age? *Journal of Gerontology, 62B,* P104–P111.

Horgan, D. (1978). The development of the full passive. *Journal of Child Language, 5,* 65–80.

Horn, J. L., Donaldson, G., & Engstrom, R. (1981). Apprehension, memory, and fluid intelligence decline through the "vital years" of adulthood. *Research on Aging, 3,* 33–84.

Horn, J. L., & Noll, J. (1997). Human cognitive capabilities: Gf–Gc theory. In D. P. Flanagan, J. L. Genshaft, & P. L. Harrison (Eds.), *Beyond traditional intellectual assessment* (pp. 53–91). New York: Guilford.

Horner, S. L., & Gaither, S. M. (2004). Attribution retraining instruction with a second-grade class. *Early Childhood Education Journal, 31,* 165–170.

Horner, T. M. (1980). Two methods of studying stranger reactivity in infants: A review. *Journal of Child Psychology and Psychiatry, 21,* 203–219.

Hospice Foundation of America. (2005). *The dying process: A guide for caregivers.* Washington, DC: Author.

Hospice Foundation of America. (2009). *Hospice services and expenses.* Retrieved from www.hospicefoundation.org/hospiceInfo/services.asp

Houlihan, J., Kropp. T., Wiles, R., Gray, S., & Campbell, C. (2005). *Body burden: The pollution in newborns.* Washington, DC: Environmental Working Group.

House, J. S., Lantz, P. M., & Herd, P. (2005). Continuity and change in the social stratification of aging and health over the life course: Evidence from a nationally representative longitudinal study from 1986 to 2001/2002 (Americans' Changing Lives Study). *Journal of Gerontology, 60B*(Special Issue II), 15–26.

Houts, R. M., Barnett-Walker, K. C., Paley, B., & Cox, M. J. (2008). Patterns of couple interaction during the transition to parenthood. *Personal Relationships, 15,* 103–122.

Howard, A. W. (2002). Automobile restraints for children: A review for clinicians. *Canadian Medical Association Journal, 167,* 769–773.

Howard, B. V., Manson, J. E., Stefanick, M. L., Beresford, S. A., Frank, G., & Jones, B. (2006). Low-fat dietary pattern and weight change over 7 years: The Women's Health Initiative Dietary Modification Trial. *Journal of the American Medical Association, 295,* 39–49.

Howe, N., Aquan-Assee, J., & Bukowski, W. M. (2001). Predicting sibling relations over time: Synchrony between maternal management styles and sibling relationship quality. *Merrill-Palmer Quarterly, 47,* 121–141.

Howell, L. C., & Beth, A. (2002). Midlife myths and realities: Women reflect on their experiences. *Journal of Women and Aging, 14,* 189–204.

Hoyer, W. J., & Verhaeghen, P. (2006). Memory aging. In J. E. Birren & K. W. Schaie (Eds.), *Handbook of the psychology of aging* (6th ed., pp. 209–232). Burlington, MA: Elsevier Academic Press.

HSBC & Oxford Institute of Ageing. (2007). *The future of retirement.* London: HSBC Insurance.

Hu, F. B., & Manson, J. E. (2001). Diet, lifestyle, and the risk of type 2 diabetes mellitus in women. *New England Journal of Medicine, 345,* 790–797.

Hu, Y., Wood, J. F., Smith, V., & Westbrook, N. (2004). Friendships through IM: Examining the relationship between instant messaging and intimacy. *Journal of Computer-Mediated Communication, 10*(1). Retrieved from jcmc.indiana.edu/vol10/issue1

Huang, H. Y., Caballero, B., Chang, S., Alberg, A., Semba, R., & Schneyer, C. (2006, May). Multivitamin/mineral supplements and prevention of chronic disease. *Evidence Report/Techology Assessment, 139,* 1–117.

Huang, Q., & Sverke, M. (2007). Women's occupational career patterns over 27 years: Relations to family of origin, life careers, and wellness. *Journal of Vocational Behavior, 70,* 369–397.

Hubbs-Tait, L., Nation, J. R., Krebs, N. F., & Bellinger, D. C. (2005). Neurotoxicants, micronutrients, and social environments: Individual and combined effects on children's development. *Psychological Science in the Public Interest, 6,* 57–121.

Hubert, H. B., Bloch, D. A., Oehlert, J. W., & Fries, J. F. (2002). Lifestyle habits and compression of morbidity. *Journal of Gerontology, 57A,* M347–351.

Huddleston, J., & Ge, X. (2003). Boys at puberty: Psychosocial implications. In C. Hayward (Ed.), *Gender differences at puberty* (pp. 113–134). New York: Cambridge University Press.

Hudson, J. A., Fivush, R., & Kuebli, J. (1992). Scripts and episodes: The development of event memory. *Applied Cognitive Psychology, 6,* 483–505.

Hudson, J. A., Sosa, B. B., & Shapiro, L. R. (1997). Scripts and plans: The development of preschool children's event knowledge and event planning. In S. L. Friedman & E. K. Scholnick (Eds.), *The developmental psychology of planning* (pp. 77–102). Mahwah, NJ: Erlbaum.

Hudson, J. M. (2008). Automatic memory processes in normal ageing and Alzheimer's disease. *Cortex, 44,* 345–349.

Huesmann, L. R. (1986). Psychological processes promoting the relation between exposure to media violence and aggressive behavior by the viewer. *Journal of Social Issues, 42,* 125–139.

Huesmann, L. R., Moise-Titus, J., Podolski, C., & Eron, L. D. (2003). Longitudinal relations between children's exposure to TV violence and their aggressive and violent behavior in young adulthood: 1977–1992. *Developmental Psychology, 39,* 201–221.

Hughes, C., & Dunn, J. (1998). Understanding mind and emotion: Longitudinal associations with mental-state talk between young friends. *Developmental Psychology, 34,* 1026–1037.

Hughes, D., Rodriguez, J., Smith, E. P., Johnson, D. J., Stevenson, H. C., & Spicer, P. (2006). Parents' ethnic-racial socialization practices: A review of research and directions for future study. *Developmental Psychology, 42,* 747–770.

Hughes, J. N., Cavell, T. A., & Grossman, P. B. (1997). A positive view of self: Risk or protection for aggressive children? *Development and Psychopathology, 9,* 75–94.

Hughes, J. N., & Kwok, O. (2006). Classroom engagement mediates the effect of teacher–student support on elementary students' peer acceptance. *Journal of School Psychology, 43,* 465–480.

Hughes, J. N., & Kwok, O. (2007). Influence of student–teacher and parent–teacher relationships on lower achieving readers' engagement and achievement in the primary grades. *Journal of Educational Psychology, 99,* 39–51.

Hughes, J. N., Zhang, D., & Hill, C. R. (2006). Peer assessments of normative and individual teacher–student support predict social acceptance and engagement among low-achieving children. *Journal of School Psychology, 43,* 447–463.

Hughes, T. F., Andel, R., Small, B. J., Borenstein, A. R., & Mortimer, J. A. (2008). The association between social resources and cognitive change in older adults: Evidence from the Charlotte County Healthy Aging Study. *Journal of Gerontology, 63B,* P241–P244.

Huijbregts, S. C. J., Séguin, J. R., Zelazo, P. D., Parent, S., Japel, C., & Tremblay, R. E. (2006). Interrelations between maternal smoking during pregnancy, birth weight and sociodemographic factors in the prediction of early cognitive abilities. *Infant and Child Development, 15,* 593–607.

Huizink, A. C., & Mulder, E. J. (2006). Maternal smoking, drinking or cannabis use during pregnancy and neurobehavioral and cognitive functioning in human offspring. *Neuroscience and Biobehavioral Reviews, 30,* 24–41.

Hultman, C. M., Torrang, A., Tuvblad, C., Cnattingius, S., Larsson, J.-O., & Lichtenstein, P. (2007). Birth weight and attention-deficit/hyperactivity symptoms in childhood and early adolescence: A prospective Swedish twin study. *Journal of the American Academy of Child and Adolescent Psychiatry, 46,* 370–377.

Hultsch, D. F., Hertzog, C., Dixon, R. A., & Small, B. J. (1998). *Memory change in the aged.* New York: Cambridge University Press.

Hultsch, D. F., MacDonald, S. W. S., & Dixon, R. A. (2002). Variability in reaction time performance of younger and older adults. *Journal of Gerontology, 57B,* P101–P115.

Humphrey, T. (1978). Function of the nervous system during prenatal life. In U. Stave (Ed.), *Perinatal physiology* (pp. 651–683). New York: Plenum.

Hungerford, T. L. (2003). Is there an American way of aging? Income dynamics of the elderly in the United States and Germany. *Research on Aging, 25,* 435–455.

Hunnius, S., & Geuze, R. H. (2004a). Developmental changes in visual scanning of dynamic faces and abstract stimuli in infants: A longitudinal study. *Infancy, 6,* 231–255.

Hunnius, S., & Geuze, R. H. (2004b). Gaze shifting in infancy: A longitudinal study using dynamic faces and abstract stimuli. *Infant Behavior and Development, 27,* 397–416.

Hunt, C. E., & Hauck, F. R. (2006). Sudden infant death syndrome. *Canadian Medical Association Journal, 174,* 1861–1869.

Huotilainen, M., Kujala, A., Hotakainen, M., Parkkonen, L., Taulu, S., & Simola, J. (2005). Short-term memory functions of the human fetus recorded with magneto-encephalography. *NeuroReport, 16,* 81–84.

Hursh, D. (2007). Assessing No Child Left Behind and the rise of neoliberal education policies. *American Educational Research Journal, 44,* 493–518.

Hursti, U. K. (1999). Factors influencing children's food choice. *Annals of Medicine, 31,* 26–32.

Hurt, H., Brodsky, N. L., Roth, H., Malmud, E., & Giannetta, J. M. (2005). School performance of children with gestational cocaine exposure. *Neurotoxicology and Teratology, 27,* 203–211.

Husaini, B. A., Blasi, A. J., & Miller, O. (1999). Does public and private religiosity have a moderating effect on depression? A bi-racial study of elders in the American south. *International Journal of Aging and Human Development, 48,* 63–72.

Huston, A. C., & Alvarez, M. M. (1990). The socialization of gender role development in early adolescence. In R. Montemayor, G. R. Adams, & T. P. Gullotta (Eds.), *From childhood to adolescence: A transitional period?* (pp. 156–179). Newbury Park, CA: Sage.

Huttenlocher, P. R. (2002). *Neural plasticity: The effects of environment on the development of the cerebral cortex.* Cambridge, MA: Harvard University Press.

Huyck, M. H. (1990). Gender differences in aging. In J. E. Birren & K. W. Schaie (Eds.), *Handbook of the psychology of aging* (3rd ed., pp. 124–134). New York: Academic Press.

Huyck, M. H. (1995). Marriage and close relationships of the marital kind. In R. Blieszner & V. H. Bedford (Eds.), *Handbook of aging and the family* (pp. 181–200). Westport, CT: Greenwood Press.

Huyck, M. H. (1996). Continuities and discontinuities in gender identity in midlife. In V. L. Bengtson (Ed.), *Adulthood and aging* (pp. 98–121). New York: Springer-Verlag.

Huyck, M. H. (1998). Gender roles and gender identity in midlife. In S. L. Willis & J. D. Reid (Eds.), *Life in the middle* (pp. 209–232). San Diego: Academic Press.

Hyde, J. S., Essex, M. J., Clark, R., & Klein, M. H. (2001). Maternity leave, women's employment, and marital incompatibility. *Journal of Family Psychology, 15,* 476–491.

Hyde, T. B., Kruszon-Moran, D., McQuillan, G. M., Cossen, C., Forghani, B., & Reef, S. E. (2006). Rubella immunity levels in the United States population: Has the threshold of viral elimination been reached? *Clinical Infectious Diseases, 43*(Suppl. 3), S146-S150.

I

Iglowstein, I., Jenni, O. G., Molinari, L., & Largo, R. H. (2003). Sleep duration from infancy to adolescence: Reference values and generational trends. *Pediatrics, 111,* 302–307.

Ihinger-Tallman, M., & Pasley, K. (1997). Stepfamilies in 1984 and today—A scholarly perspective. *Marriage and Family Review, 26,* 19–40.

Illeris, K. (2004). *Adult education and adult learning.* Melbourne, FL: Krieger Publishing.

Imai, M., & Haryu, E. (2004). The nature of word-learning biases and their roles for lexical development: From a cross-linguistic perspective. In D. G. Hall & S. R. Waxman (Eds.), *Weaving a lexicon* (pp. 411–444). Cambridge, MA: MIT Press.

Indusekhar, R., Usman, S. B., & O'Brien, S. (2007). Psychological aspects of premenstrual syndrome. *Best Practice and Research Clinical Obstetrics and Gynecology, 21,* 207–210.

Ingram, D. K., Roth, G. S., Lane, M. A., Ottinger, M. A., Zou, S., de Cabo, R., & Mattison, J. A. (2006). The potential for dietary restriction to increase longevity in humans: Extrapolation from monkey studies. *Biogerontology, 7,* 143–148.

Inhelder, B., & Piaget, J. (1958). *The growth of logical thinking from childhood to adolescence: An essay on the construction of formal operational structures.* New York: Basic Books. (Original work published 1955)

Institute for Social Research. (2002). U.S. husbands do more housework. Ann Arbor: Author. Retrieved from: http://www.newswise.com/articles/2002/3/timeuse.umi.html

International Human Genome Sequencing Consortium. (2004). Finishing the euchromatic sequence of the human genome. *Nature, 21,* 931–945.

Iocaboni, M., Molnar-Szakacs, I., Gallese, V., Buccino, G., & Mazziotta, J. C. (2005). Grasping the intentions of others with one's own mirror neuron system. *Public Library of Science: Biology, 3*(3), e79.

Irvine, A. B., Ary, D. V., & Bourgeois, M. S. (2003). An interactive multimedia program to train professional caregivers. *Journal of Applied Gerontology, 22,* 269–288.

Isabella, R. (1993). Origins of attachment: Maternal interactive behavior across the first year. *Child Development, 64,* 605–621.

Isabella, R., & Belsky, J. (1991). Interactional synchrony and the origins of infant–mother attachment: A replication study. *Child Development, 62,* 373–384.

Ishihara, K., Warita, K., Tanida, T., Sugawara, T., Kitagawa, H., & Hoshi, N. (2007). Does paternal exposure to 2, 3, 7, 8-tetrachlorodibenzo-p-dioxin (TCDD) affect the sex ratio of offspring? *Journal of Veterinary Medical Science, 69,* 347–352.

Israel, M., Johnson, C., & Brooks, P. J. (2000). From states to events: The acquisition of English passive participles. *Cognitive Linguistics, 11,* 103–129.

Issa, A. M., Mojica, W. A., Morton, S. C., Traina, S., Newberry, S. J., Hilton, L. G., Garland, R. H., & MacLean, C. H. (2006). The efficacy of omega-3 fatty acids on cognitive function in aging and dementia: A systematic review. *Dementia and Geriatric Cognitive Disorders, 21,* 88–96.

Itti, E., Gaw, G. I. T., Pawlikowska-Haddal, A., Boone, K. B., Mlikotic, A., & Itti, L. (2006). The structural brain correlates of cognitive deficits in adults with Klinefelter's syndrome. *Journal of Clinical Endocrinology and Metabolism, 91,* 1423–1427.

Izard, C. E., & Ackerman, B. P. (2000). Motivational, organizational, and regulatory functions of discrete emotions. In M. Lewis & J. M. Haviland-Jones (Eds.), *Handbook of emotions* (2nd ed., pp. 253–264). New York: Guilford.

Izard, C. E., Hembree, E. A., & Huebner, R. R. (1987). Infants' emotional expressions to acute pain. *Developmental Psychology, 23,* 105–113.

Izard, C. E., Trentacosta, C. J., King, K. A., & Mostow, A. J. (2004). An emotion-based prevention program for Head Start children. *Early Education and Development, 15,* 407–422.

J

Jaakkola, J. J., & Gissler, M. (2004). Maternal smoking in pregnancy, fetal development, and childhood asthma. *American Journal of Public Health, 94,* 136–140.

Jaccard, J., Dodge, T., & Dittus, P. (2002). Parent–adolescent communication about sex and birth control: A conceptual framework. In S. S. Feldman & D. A. Rosenthal (Eds.), *Talking sexuality: Parent–adolescent communication* (pp. 9–41). San Francisco: Jossey-Bass.

Jaccard, J., Dodge, T., & Dittus, P. (2003). Maternal discussions about pregnancy and adolescents' attitudes toward pregnancy. *Journal of Adolescent Health, 33,* 84–87.

Jackson, G. R., & Owsley, C. (2000). Scotopic sensitivity during adulthood. *Vision Research, 40,* 2467–2473.

Jackson, R. A., Gibson, K. A., & Wu, Y. W. (2004). Perinatal outcomes in singletons following in vitro fertilization: A meta-analysis. *Obstetrics and Gynecology, 103,* 551–563.

Jackson, T., Fritch, A., Nagaska, T., & Gunderson, J. (2002). Towards explaining the association between shyness and loneliness: A path analysis with American college students. *Social Behavior and Personality, 30,* 263–270.

Jackson, V. A., Sullivan, A. M., Gadmer, N. M., Seltzer, D., Mitchell, A. M., & Lakoma, M. D. (2005). "It was haunting . . .": Physicians' descriptions of emotionally powerful patient deaths. *Academic Medicine, 80,* 648–656.

Jacobs, J. A., & King, R. B. (2002). Age and college completion: A life-history analysis of women aged 15–44. *Sociology of Education, 75,* 211–230.

Jacobs, J. E., & Klaczynski, P. A. (2002). The development of judgment and decision making during childhood and adolescence. *Current Directions in Psychological Science, 11,* 145–149.

Jacobs, J. E., Lanza, S., Osgood, D. W., Eccles, J. S., & Wigfield, A. (2002). Changes in children's self-competence and values: Gender and domain differ-ences across grades one through twelve. *Child Development, 73,* 509–527.

Jacobs, J. E., & Weisz, V. (1994). Gender stereotypes: Implications for gifted education. *Roeper Review, 16,* 152–155.

Jacobs, J. N., & Kelley, M. L. (2006). Predictors of paternal involvement in childcare in dual-earner families with young children. *Fathering, 4,* 23–47.

Jacobs-Lawson, J. M., Hershey, D. A., & Neukam, K. A. (2004). Gender differences in factors that influence time spent planning for retirement. *Journal of Women and Aging, 16,* 55–69

Jacobson, J. L., & Jacobson, S. W. (2003). Prenatal exposure to polychlorinated biphenyls and attention at school age. *Journal of Pediatrics, 143,* 780–788.

Jacobson, K. C., & Crockett, L. J. (2000). Parental monitoring and adolescent adjustment: An ecological perspective. *Journal of Research on Adolescence, 10,* 65–97.

Jacobson, S. W., Jacobson, J. L., Sokol, R. J., Chiodo, L. M., & Corobana, R. (2004). Maternal age, alcohol abuse history, and quality of parenting as moderators of the effects of prenatal alcohol exposure on 7.5-year intellectual function. *Alcoholism: Clinical and Experimental Research, 28,* 1732–1745.

Jadack, R. A., Hyde, J. S., Moore, C. F., & Keller, M. L. (1995). Moral reasoning about sexually transmitted diseases. *Child Development, 66,* 167–177.

Jaffee, S. R., Caspi, A., Moffitt, T. E., Belsky, J., & Silva, P. (2001). Why are children born to teen mothers at risk for adverse outcomes in young adulthood? Results of a 20-year longitudinal study. *Development and Psychopathology, 13,* 377–397.

Jaffee, S. R., & Hyde, J. S. (2000). Gender differences in moral orientation: A meta-analysis. *Psychological Bulletin, 126,* 703–706.

Jaffee, S. R., Moffitt, T. E., Caspi, A., & Taylor, A. (2003). Life with (or without) father: The benefits of living with two biological parents depend on the father's antisocial behavior. *Child Development, 74,* 109–126.

Jambunathan, S., Burts, D. C., & Pierce, S. (2000). Comparisons of parenting attitudes among five ethnic groups in the United States. *Journal of Comparative Family Studies, 31,* 395–406.

James, J. B., Lewkowicz, C., Libhaber, J., & Lachman, M. (1995). Rethinking the gender identity crossover hypothesis: A test of a new model. *Sex Roles, 32,* 185–207.

James, J. B., & Wink, P. (2007). The Third Age: A rationale for research. In J. B. James & P. Wink (Eds.), *Annual review of gerontology and geriatrics* (Vol. 26, pp. xix–xxxii). New York: Springer.

James, J. B., & Zarrett, N. (2007). Ego integrity in the lives of older women. *Journal of Adult Development, 13,* 61–75.

Jang, Y., Bergman, E., Schonfeld, L., & Molinari, V. (2007). The mediating role of health perceptions in the relation between physical and mental health: A study of older residents in assisted living facilities. *Journal of Aging and Health, 19,* 439–452.

Janosz, M., Le Blanc, M., Boulerice, B., & Tremblay, R. E. (2000). Predicting different types of school dropouts: A typological approach with two longitudinal samples. *Journal of Educational Psychology, 92,* 171–190.

Jansen, A., Theunissen, N., Slechten, K., Nederkoorn, C., Boon, B., Mulkens, S., & Roefs, A. (2003). Overweight children overeat after exposure to food cues. *Eating Behaviors, 4,* 197–209.

Janssens, J. M. A. M., & Deković, M. (1997). Child rearing, prosocial moral reasoning, and prosocial behaviour. *International Journal of Behavioral Development, 20,* 509–527.

Jarvis, J. F., & van Heerden, H. G. (1967). The acuity of hearing in the Kalahari Bushman: A pilot study. *Journal of Laryngology and Otology, 81,* 63–68.

Jayakody, R., & Cabrera, N. (2002). What are the choices for low-income families? Cohabitation, marriage, and remaining single. In A. Booth &

A. C. Crouter (Eds.), *Just living together* (pp. 85–96). Mahwah, NJ: Erlbaum.

Jayakody, R., & Kalil, A. (2002). Social fathering in low-income, African-American families with preschool children. *Journal of Marriage and Family, 64,* 504–516.

Jellinger, K. A. (2008). Morphologic diagnosis of "vascular dementia"—a critical update. *Journal of the Neurological Sciences, 270,* 1–12.

Jemal, A., Siegel, R., Ward, E., Hao, Y., Xu, J., Murray, T., & Thun, M. J. (2008). Cancer statistics, 2008. *CA: Cancer Journal for Clinicians, 58,* 71–96.

Jenkins, J. M., Rasbash, J., & O'Connor, T. G. (2003). The role of the shared family context in differential parenting. *Developmental Psychology, 39,* 99–113.

Jenkins, J. M., Turrell, S. L., Kogushi, Y., Lollis, S., & Ross, H. S. (2003). A longitudinal investigation of the dynamics of mental state talk in families. *Child Development, 74,* 905–920.

Jenkins, K. R., Pienta, A. M., & Horgas, A. L. (2002). Activity and health-related quality of life in continuing care retirement communities. *Research on Aging, 24,* 124–149.

Jennings, B. J., Ozanne, S. E., Dorling, M. W., & Hales, C. N. (1999). Early growth determines longevity in male rats and may be related to telomere shortening in the kidney. *FEBS Letters, 448,* 4–8.

Jensen, A. R. (1969). How much can we boost IQ and scholastic achievement? *Harvard Educational Review, 39,* 1–123.

Jensen, A. R. (1998). *The g factor: The science of mental ability.* New York: Praeger.

Jensen, A. R. (2001). Spearman's hypothesis. In J. M. Collis & S. Messick (Eds.), *Intelligence and personality: Bridging the gap in theory and measurement* (pp. 3–24). Mahwah, NJ: Erlbaum.

Jeon, Y.-H., Brodaty, H., & Chesterson, J. (2005). Respite care for caregivers and people with severe mental illness: Literature review. *Journal of Advanced Nursing, 49,* 297–306.

Jeynes, W. H. (2005). A meta-analysis of the relation of parental involvement to urban elementary school student academic achievement. *Urban Education, 40,* 237–269.

Jiao, S., Ji, G., & Jing, Q. (1996). Cognitive development of Chinese urban only children and children with siblings. *Child Development, 67,* 387–395.

Jneid, H., Fonarow, G. C., Cannon, C. P., Hernandez, A. F., Palacios, I. F., & Maree, A. O. (2008). Sex differences in medical care and early death after acute myocardial infarction. *Circulation, 118,* 2803–2810.

Joh, A. S., & Adolph, K. E. (2006). Learning from falling. *Child Development, 77,* 89–102.

John, U., Meyer, C., Rumpf, H. J., & Hapke, U. (2003). Probabilities of alcohol high-risk drinking, abuse or dependence estimating on grounds of tobacco smoking and nicotine dependence. *Addiction, 98,* 805–814.

Johnson, C. L. (1998). Effects of adult children's divorce on grandparenthood. In M. E. Szinovacz (Ed.), *Handbook on grandparenthood* (pp. 87–96). Westport, CT: Greenwood Press.

Johnson, C. L., & Troll, L. E. (1994). Constraints and facilitators to friendships in late life. *Gerontologist, 34,* 79–87.

Johnson, D. E. (2000). Medical and developmental sequelae of early childhood institutionalization in Eastern European adoptees. In C. A. Nelson (Ed.), *Minnesota symposia on child psychology* (Vol. 31, pp. 113–162). Mahwah, NJ: Erlbaum.

Johnson, D. E. (2002). Adoption and the effect on children's development. *Early Human Development, 68,* 39–54.

Johnson, J. G., Cohen, P., Smailes, E. M., Kasen, S., & Brook, J. S. (2002). Television viewing and aggressive behavior during adolescence and adulthood. *Science, 295,* 2468–2471.

Johnson, K. C., & Daviss, B.-A. (2005). Outcomes of planned home births with certified professional midwives: Large prospective study in North America. *British Medical Journal, 330,* 1416.

Johnson, K. S., Elbert-Avila, K. I., & Tulsky, J. A. (2005). The influence of spiritual beliefs and practices on the treatment preferences of African Americans: A review of the literature. *Journal of the American Geriatrics Society, 53,* 711–719.

Johnson, K. S., Juchibhatla, M., Tanis, D., & Tulsky, J. A. (2008). Racial differences in hospice revocation to pursue aggressive care. *Archives of Internal Medicine, 168,* 218–224.

Johnson, M. D., Cohan, C. L., Davilla, J., Lawrence, E., Rogge, R. D., Karney, B. R., Sullivan, K. T., & Bradbury, T. N. (2005). Problem-solving skills and affective expressions as predictors of change in marital satisfaction. *Journal of Consulting and Clinical Psychology, 73,* 15–27.

Johnson, M. H. (1999). Ontogenetic constraints on neural and behavioral plasticity: Evidence from imprinting and face processing. *Canadian Journal of Experimental Psychology, 55,* 77–90.

Johnson, M. H. (2001). The development and neural basis of face recognition: Comment and speculation. *Infant and Child Development, 10,* 31–33.

Johnson, M. H. (2005). Developmental neuroscience, psychophysiology, and genetics. In M. H. Bornstein & M. E. Lamb (Eds.), *Developmental science: An advanced textbook* (5th ed., pp. 187–222). Mahwah, NJ: Erlbaum.

Johnson, S. P., Slemmer, J. A., & Amso, D. (2004). Where infants look determines how they see: Eye movements and object perception performance in 3-month-olds. *Infancy, 6,* 185–201.

Johnson, W., & Krueger, R. F. (2007). The psychological benefits of vigorous exercise: A study of discordant MZ twin pairs. *Twin Research and Human Genetics, 10,* 275–283.

Johnston, L. D., O'Malley, P. M., Bachman, J. G., & Schulenberg, J. E. (2008). *Monitoring the future: National results on adolescent drug use.* Bethesda: MD: U.S. Department of Health and Human Services.

Johnston, M. V., Nishimura, A., Harum, K., Pekar, J., & Blue, M. E. (2001). Sculpting the developing brain. *Advances in Pediatrics, 48,* 1–38.

Jome, L. M., Surething, N. A., & Taylor, K. K. (2005). Relationally oriented masculinity, gender nontraditional interests, and occupational traditionality of employed men. *Journal of Career Development, 32,* 183–197.

Jones, F. (2003). *Religious commitment in Canada, 1997 and 2000. Religious Commitment Monograph No. 3.* Ottawa: Christian Commitment Research Institute.

Jones, J., Lopez, A., & Wilson, M. (2003). Congenital toxoplasmosis. *American Family Physician, 67,* 2131–2137.

Jones, K. M., Whitbourne, S. K., & Skultety, K. M. (2006). Identity processes and the transition to midlife among the baby boomers. In S. K. Whitbourne & S. L. Willis (Eds.), *The baby boomers grow up: Contemporary perspectives on midlife* (pp. 149–164). Mahwah, NJ: Erlbaum.

Jones, M. C., & Mussen, P. H. (1958). Self-conceptions, motivations, and interpersonal attitudes of early- and late-maturing girls. *Child Development, 29,* 491–501.

Jones, N. A., Field, T., & Davalos, M. (2000). Right frontal EEG asymmetry and lack of empathy in preschool children of depressed mothers. *Child Psychiatry and Human Development, 30,* 189–204.

Jones, R. K., Purcell, A., Singh, S., & Finer, L. B. (2005). Adolescents' reports of parental knowledge of adolescents' use of sexual health services and their reactions to mandated parental notification for prescription contraceptives. *Journal of the American Medical Association, 293,* 340–348.

Jones, S. S. (2006). Exploration or imitation? The effect of music on 4-week-old infants' tongue protrusions. *Infant Behavior and Development, 29,* 126–130.

Jopp, D., & Rott, C. (2006). Adaptation in very old age: Exploring the role of resources, beliefs, and attitudes for centenarians' happiness. *Psychology and Aging, 21,* 266–280.

Jordan, B. (1993). *Birth in four cultures.* Prospect Heights, IL: Waveland.

Jordan, J., & Neimeyer, R. (2003). Does grief counseling work? *Death Studies, 27,* 765–786.

Jose, P., Huntsinger, C., Huntsinger, P., & Liaw, F.-R. (2000). Parental values and practices relevant to young children's social development in Taiwan and the United States. *Journal of Cross-Cultural Psychology, 31,* 677–702.

Joseph, R. M., & Tager-Flusberg, H. (2004). The relationship of theory of mind and executive functions to symptom type and severity in children with autism. *Development and Psychopathology, 16,* 137–155.

Joyner, M. H., & Kurtz-Costes, B. (1997). Metamemory development. In W. Schneider & F. E. Weinert (Eds.), *Memory performance and competencies: Issues in growth and development* (pp. 275–300). Hillsdale, NJ: Erlbaum.

Julkunen, J. (1996). Suppressing your anger: Good manners, bad health? In C. D. Spielberger & I. G. Sarason (Eds.), *Stress and emotion: Anxiety, anger, and curiosity* (Vol. 16, pp. 227–240). Washington, DC: Taylor & Francis.

Julkunen, J., & Ahlström, R. (2006). Hostility, anger, and sense of coherence as predictors of health-related quality of life. Results of an ASCOT substudy. *Journal of Psychosomatic Research, 61,* 33–39.

Jusczyk, P. W. (2001). In the beginning, was the word. . . . In F. Lacerda & C. von Hofsten (Eds.), *Emerging cognitive abilities in early infancy* (pp. 173–192). Mahwah, NJ: Erlbaum.

Jusczyk, P. W. (2002). Some critical developments in acquiring native language sound organization. *Annals of Otology, Rhinology and Laryngology, 189,* 11–15.

Jusczyk, P. W., & Hohne, E. A. (1997). Infants' memory for spoken words. *Science, 277,* 1984–1986.

K

Kagan, J. (2003). Behavioral inhibition as a temperamental category. In R. J. Davidson, K. R. Scherer, & H. H. Goldsmith (Eds.), *Handbook of affective science* (pp. 320–331). New York: Oxford University Press.

Kagan, J. (2008). In defense of qualitative changes in development. *Child Development, 79,* 1606–1624.

Kagan, J., Arcus, D., Snidman, N., Feng, W. Y., Hendler, J., & Greene, S. (1994). Reactivity in infants: A cross-national comparison. *Developmental Psychology, 30,* 342–345.

Kagan, J., & Fox, N. A. (2006). Biology, culture, and temperamental biases. In N. Eisenberg (Ed.), *Handbook of child psychology: Vol. 3. Social, emotional, and personality development* (6th ed., pp. 167–225). Hoboken, NJ: Wiley.

Kagan, J., & Saudino, K. J. (2001). Behavioral inhibition and related temperaments. In R. N. Emde & J. K. Hewitt (Eds.), *Infancy to early childhood: Genetic and environmental influences on developmental change* (pp. 111–119). New York: Oxford University Press.

Kagan, J., Snidman, N., Kahn, V., & Towsley, S. (2007). The preservation of two infant temperaments into adolescence. *Monographs of the Society for Research in Child Development, 72*(2, Serial No. 287).

Kagan, J., Snidman, N., Zentner, M., & Peterson, E. (1999). Infant temperament and anxious symptoms in school-age children. *Development and Psychopathology, 11,* 209–224.

Kagawa, Y. (1978). Impact of westernization on the nutrition of Japanese: Changes in physique, cancer, longevity, and centenarians. *Preventive Medicine, 7,* 205–217.

Kahana, E., King, C., Kahana, B., Menne, H., Webster, N. J., & Dan, A. (2005). Successful aging in the face of chronic disease. In M. L. Wykle, P. J. Whitehouse, & D. L. Morris (Eds.), *Successful aging through the life span* (pp. 101–126). New York: Springer.

Kahn, P. H., Jr. (1992). Children's obligatory and discretionary moral judgments. *Child Development, 63,* 416–430.

Kail, R. V. (2003). Information processing and memory. In M. H. Bornstein, L. Davidson, C. L. M. Keyes, K. A. Moore, and the Center for Child Well-Being (Eds.), *Well-being: Positive development across the life course* (pp. 269–280). Mahwah, NJ: Erlbaum.

Kail, R. V., & Park, Y. (1992). Global developmental change in processing time. *Merrill-Palmer Quarterly, 38,* 525–541.

Kail, R. V., & Park, Y. (1994). Processing time, articulation time, and memory span. *Journal of Experimental Child Psychology, 57,* 281–291.

Kaisa, A., Stattin, H., & Nurmi, J. (2000). Parenting styles and adolescents' achievement strategies. *Journal of Adolescence, 23,* 205–222.

Kalache, A., Aboderin, I., & Hoskins, I. (2002). Compression of morbidity and active ageing: Key priorities for public health policy in the 21st century. *Bulletin of the World Health Organization, 80,* 243–244.

Kalil, A., Levine, J. A., & Ziol-Guest, K. M. (2005). Following in their parents' footsteps: How characteristics of parental work predict adolescents' interest in parents' working jobs. In B. Schneider & L. J. Waite (Eds.), *Being together, working apart: Dual-career families and the work–life balance* (pp. 422–442). New York: Cambridge University Press.

Kalof, L. (2000). Ethnic differences in female sexual victimization. *Sexuality and Culture, 2,* 75–97.

Kamo, Y. (1998). Asian grandparents. In M. E. Szinovacz (Ed.), *Handbook on grandparenthood* (pp. 97–112). Westport, CT: Greenwood Press.

Kane, P., & Garber, J. (2004). The relations among depression in fathers, children's psychopathology, and father–child conflict: A meta-analysis. *Clinical Psychology Review, 24,* 339–360.

Kane, R. A., Lum, T. Y., Cutler, L. J., Degenholtz, H. B., & Yu, T.-C. (2007). Resident outcomes in small-house nursing homes: A longitudinal evaluation of the initial Green House program. *Journal of the American Geriatrics Society, 55,* 836–839.

Kaplan, D. L., & Keys, C. B. (1997). Sex and relationship variables as predictors of sexual attraction in cross-sex platonic friendships between young heterosexual adults. *Journal of Social and Personal Relationships, 14,* 191–206.

Kaplowitz, P. (2006). Pubertal development in girls: Secular trends. *Current Opinion in Obstetrics and Gynecology, 18,* 487–491.

Karger, H., & Stoesz, D. (2008). *American social welfare policy: A pluralist approach.* Boston: Allyn & Bacon.

Karpati, A. M., Rubin, C. H., Kieszak, S. M., Marcus, M., & Troiano, R. P. (2002). Stature and pubertal stage assessment in American boys: The 1988–1994 Third National Health and Nutrition Examination Survey. *Journal of Adolescent Health, 30,* 205–212.

Kasmauski, K., & Jaret, P. (2003). *Impact: On the frontlines of global health.* Washington, DC: National Geographic.

Kassel, J. D., Weinstein, S., Skitch, S. A., Veilleux, J., & Mermelstein, R. (2005). The development of substance abuse in adolescence: Correlates, causes, and consequences. In J. D. Kassel, S. Weinstein, S. A. Skitch, J. Veilleux, & R. Mermelstein (Eds.), *Development of psychopathology: A vulnerability-stress perspective* (pp. 355–384). Thousand Oaks, CA: Sage.

Kastenbaum, R. J. (2009). *Death, society, and human experience* (10th ed.). Boston: Allyn and Bacon.

Kato, I., Franco, P., Groswasser, J., Scaillet, S., Kelmanson, I., Togari, H., & Kahn, A. (2003). Incomplete arousal processes in infants who were victims of sudden death. *American Journal of Respiratory and Critical Care, 168,* 1298–1303.

Katz, L. F., & Windecker-Nelson, B. (2004). Parental meta-emotion philosophy in families with conduct-problem children: Links with peer relations. *Journal of Abnormal Child Psychology, 32,* 385–398.

Katzman, D. K. (2005). Medical complications in adolescents with anorexia nervosa: A review of the literature. *International Journal of Eating Disorders, 37,* S52–S59.

Kaufman, A. S. (2001). WAIS-III IQs, Horn's theory, and generational changes from young adulthood to old age. *Intelligence, 29,* 131–167.

Kaufman, A. S., & Horn, J. L. (1996). Age changes on tests of fluid and crystallized intelligence for females and males on the Kaufman Adolescent and Adult Intelligence Test (KAIT) at ages 17 to 94 years. *Archives of Clinical Neuropsychology, 11,* 97–121.

Kaufman, J., Csibra, G., & Johnson, M. H. (2005). Oscillatory activity in the infant brain reflects object maintenance. *Proceedings of the National Academy of Sciences, 102,* 15271–15274.

Kausler, D. H. (1994). *Learning and memory in normal aging.* San Diego: Academic Press.

Kavanaugh, R. D. (2006). Pretend play. In B. Spodek & O. N. Saracho (Eds.), *Handbook of research on the education of young children* (2nd ed., pp. 269–278). Mahwah, NJ: Erlbaum.

Kavsek, M. (2004). Predicting later IQ from infant visual habituation and dishabituation: A meta-analysis. *Journal of Applied Developmental Psychology, 25,* 369–393.

Kaye, W. (2008). Neurobiology of anorexia and bulimia nervosa. *Physiology and Behavior, 94,* 121–135.

Kazdin, A. E. (2003). Problem-solving skills training and parent management training for conduct disorder. In A. E. Kazdin & J. R. Weisz (Eds.), *Evidence-based psychotherapies for children and adolescents* (pp. 241–262). New York: Guilford.

Kazdin, A. E., & Whitley, M. E. (2003). Treatment of parental stress to enhance therapeutic change among children referred for aggressive and antisocial behavior. *Journal of Consulting and Clinical Psychology, 71,* 504–515.

Keating, D. P. (1979). Adolescent thinking. In J. Adelson (Ed.), *Handbook of adolescent psychology* (pp. 211–246). New York: Wiley.

Keating, D. P. (2004). Cognitive and brain development. In R. M. Lerner & L. Steinberg (Eds.), *Handbook of adolescent psychology* (2nd ed., pp. 45–84). Hoboken, NJ: Wiley.

Keil, F. C. (1986). Conceptual domains and the acquisition of metaphor. *Cognitive Development, 1,* 73–96.

Keil, F. C., & Lockhart, K. L. (1999). Explanatory understanding in conceptual development. In E. K. Scholnick, K. Nelson, S. A. Gelman, & P. H. Miller (Eds.), *Conceptual development: Piaget's legacy* (pp. 103–130). Mahwah, NJ: Erlbaum.

Keith, P. M., & Schafer, R. B. (1991). *Relationships and well-being over the life stages.* New York: Praeger.

Keith, T. Z., Keith, P. B., Quirk, K. J., Sperduto, J., Santillo, S., & Killings, S. (1998). Longitudinal effects of parent involvement on high school grades: Similarities and differences across gender and ethnic groups. *Journal of School Psychology, 36,* 335–363.

Keller, H., Borke, Y. J., Kärtner, J., Jensen, H., & Papaligoura, Z. (2004). Developmental consequences of early parenting experiences: Self-recognition and self-regulation in three cultural communities. *Child Development, 75,* 1745–1760.

Keller, H., Kärtner, J., Borke, J., Yovsi, R., & Kleis, A. (2005). Parenting styles and the development of the categorical self: A longitudinal study on mirror self-recognition in Cameroonian Nso and German families. *International Journal of Behavioral Development, 29,* 496–504.

Kelley, S. A., Brownell, C. A., & Campbell, S. B. (2000). Mastery motivation and self-evaluative affect in toddlers: Longitudinal relations with maternal behavior. *Child Development, 71,* 1061–1071.

Kelley, S. S., Borawski, E. A., Flocke, S. A., & Keen, K. J. (2003). The role of sequential and concurrent sexual relationships in the risk of sexually transmitted diseases among adolescents. *Journal of Adolescent Health, 32,* 296–305.

Kellman, P. J., & Arterberry, M. E. (2006). Infant visual perception. In D. Kuhn & R. Siegler (Eds.), *Handbook of child psychology: Vol. 2. Cognition, perception, and language* (6th ed., pp. 109–160). Hoboken, NJ: Wiley.

Kelly, D. J., Liu, S., Ge, L., Quinn, P. C., Slater, A. M., Lee, K., Liu, Q., & Pascalis, O. (2007). Cross-race preferences for same-race faces extend beyond the African versus Caucasian contrast in 3-month-old infants. *Infancy, 11,* 87–95.

Kelly, N., & Norwich, B. (2004). Pupils' perceptions of self and of labels: Moderate learning difficulties in mainstream and special schools. *British Journal of Educational Psychology, 74,* 411–435.

Kemkes-Grottenhaler, A. (2003). Postponing or rejecting parenthood? Results of a survey among female academic professionals. *Journal of Biosocial Science, 35,* 213–226.

Kemp, E. A., & Kemp, J. E. (2002). *Older couples: New romances.* Berkeley, CA: Celestial Arts.

Kemper, S., Kynette, D., & Norman, S. (1992). Age differences in spoken language. In R. L. West & J. D. Sinnott (Eds.), *Everyday memory and aging* (pp. 138–152). New York: Springer-Verlag.

Kemper, S., Thompson, M., & Marquis, J. (2001). Longitudinal change in language production: Effects of aging and dementia on grammatical complexity and prepositional content. *Psychology and Aging, 16,* 600–614.

Kendig, H., Dykstra, P. A., van Gaalen, R. I., & Melkas, T. (2007). Health of aging parents and childless individuals. *Journal of Family Issues, 28,* 1457–1486.

Kendler, K. S., Thornton, L. M., Gilman, S. E., & Kessler, R. C. (2000). Sexual orientation in a U.S. national sample of twin and non-twin sibling pairs. *American Journal of Psychiatry, 157,* 1843–1846.

Kennedy, A. M., & Gust, D. A. (2008). Measles outbreak associated with a church congregation: A study of immunization attitudes of congregation members. *Public Health Reports, 123,* 126–134.

Kennedy, G. E., & Kennedy, C. E. (1993). Grandparents: A special resource for children in stepfamilies. *Journal of Divorce and Remarriage, 19,* 45–68.

Kennell, J., Klaus, M., McGrath, S., Robertson, S., & Hinkley, C. (1991). Continuous emotional support during labor in a U.S. hospital. *Journal of the American Medical Association, 265,* 2197–2201.

Kerber, R. A., O'Brien, E., Smith, K. R., & Cawthon, R. M. (2001). Familial excess longevity in Utah genealogies. *Journals of Gerontology, 567,* B130–B139.

Kerckhoff, A. C. (2002). The transition from school to work. In J. T. Mortimer & R. Larson (Eds.), *The changing adolescent experience* (pp. 52–87). New York: Cambridge University Press.

Keren, M., Feldman, R., Namdari-Weinbaum, I., Spitzer, S., & Tyano, S. (2005). Relations between parents' interactive style in dyadic and triadic play and toddlers' symbolic capacity. *American Journal of Orthopsychiatry, 75,* 599–607.

Kerestes, M., & Youniss, J. E. (2003). Rediscovering the importance of religion in adolescent development. In R. M. Lerner, F. Jacobs, & D. Wertlieb (Eds.), *Handbook of applied developmental science* (Vol. 1, pp. 165–184). Thousand Oaks, CA: Sage.

Kerestes, M., Youniss, J., & Metz, E. (2004). Longitudinal patterns of religious perspective and civic integration. *Applied Developmental Science, 8,* 39–46.

Kernis, M. H. (2002). Self-esteem as a multifaceted construct. In T. M. Brinthaupt & R. P. Lipka (Eds.), *Understanding early adolescent self and identity* (pp. 57–88). Albany, NY: State University of New York Press.

Kernohan, W. G., Hasson, F., Hutchison, P., & Cochrane, B. (2006). Patient satisfaction with hospice day care. *Supportive Care in Cancer, 14,* 462–468.

Kerr, D. C. R., Lopez, N. L., Olson, S. L., & Sameroff, A. J. (2004). Parental discipline and externalizing behavior problems in early childhood: The roles of moral regulation and child gender. *Journal of Abnormal Child Psychology, 32,* 369–383.

Kesler, S. R. (2007). Turner syndrome. *Child and Adolescent Psychiatric Clinics of North America, 16,* 709–722.

Kessler, R. C., Adler, L. A., Barkley R., Biederman, J., Conners, C. K., & Demler, O. (2006). The prevalence and correlates of adult ADHD in the United States: Results from the National Comorbidity Survey Replication. *American Journal of Psychiatry, 163,* 716–723.

Kessler, R. C., Adler, L. A., Barkley, R., Biederman, J., Conners, C. K., & Faraone, S. V. (2005). Patterns and predictors of attention-deficit/hyperactivity disorder persistence into adulthood: Results from the National Comorbidity Survey Replication. *Biological Psychiatry, 57,* 1442–1451.

Kettl, P. (1998). Alaska Native suicide: Lessons for elder suicide. *International Psychogeriatrics, 10,* 205–211.

Kettunen, J. A., & Kujala, U. M. (2004). Exercise therapy for people with rheumatoid arthritis and osteoarthritis. *Scandinavian Journal of Medicine and Science in Sports, 14,* 138–142.

Keyes, C. L. M., & Ryff, C. D. (1998). Generativity and adult lives: Social structural contours and quality of life consequences. In D. P. McAdams & E. de St. Aubin (Eds.), *Generativity and adult development: How and why we care for the next generation* (pp. 227–263). Washington, DC: American Psychological Association.

Keyes, C. L. M., Shmotkin, D., & Ryff, C. D. (2002). Optimizing well-being: The empirical encounter of two traditions. *Journal of Personality and Social Psychology, 82,* 1007–1022.

Kiebzak, G. M., Beinart, G. A., Perser, K., Ambrose, C. G., Siff, S. J., & Heggeness, M. H. (2002). Undertreatment of osteoporosis in men with hip fracture. *Archives of Internal Medicine, 162,* 2217–2222.

Killen, M., Crystal, D., & Watanabe, H. (2002). The individual and the group: Japanese and American children's evaluations of peer exclusion, tolerance of difference, and prescriptions for conformity. *Child Development, 73,* 1788–1802.

Killen, M., Lee-Kim, J., McGlothlin, H., & Stangor, C. (2002). How children and adolescents evaluate gender and racial exclusion. *Monographs of the Society for Research in Child Development, 67*(4, Serial No. 271).

Killen, M., Margie, N. G., & Sinno, S. (2006). Morality in the context of intergroup relationships. In M. Killen & J. G. Smetana (Eds.), *Handbook of moral development* (pp. 155–183). Mahwah, NJ: Erlbaum.

Killen, M., & Nucci, L. P. (1995). Morality, autonomy, and social conflict. In M. Killen & D. Hart (Eds.), *Morality in everyday life: Developmental perspectives* (pp. 52–86). Cambridge, UK: Cambridge University Press.

Killian, T., Turner, J., & Cain, R. (2005). Depressive symptoms of caregiving women in midlife: The role of physical health. *Journal of Women and Aging, 17,* 115–127.

Kilpatrick, S. W., & Sanders, D. M. (1978). Body image stereotypes: A developmental comparison. *Journal of Genetic Psychology, 132,* 87–95.

Kim, A., & Merriam, S. B. (2004). Motivations for learning among older adults in a learning retirement institute. *Educational Gerontology, 30,* 441–455.

Kim, J. E., & Moen, P. (2002a). Is retirement good or bad for subjective well-being? *Current Directions in Psychological Science, 10,* 83–86.

Kim, J. E., & Moen, P. (2002b). Moving into retirement: Preparation and transitions in late midlife. In M. E. Lachman (Ed.), *Handbook of midlife development* (pp. 487–527). New York: Wiley.

Kim, J. E., & Moen, P. (2002c). Retirement transitions, gender, and psychological well-being: A life-course, ecological model. *Journal of Gerontology, 57B,* P212–P222.

Kim, J. M. (1998). Korean children's concepts of adult and peer authority and moral reasoning. *Developmental Psychology, 34,* 947–955.

Kim, J. M., & Turiel, E. (1996). Korean children's concepts of adult and peer authority. *Social Development, 5,* 310–329.

Kim, J.-Y., McHale, S. M., Crouter, A. C., & Osgood, D. W. (2007). Longitudinal linkages between sibling relationships and adjustment from middle childhood through adolescence. *Developmental Psychology, 43,* 960–973.

Kim, J.-Y., McHale, S. M., Osgood, D. W., & Crouter, A. C. (2006). Longitudinal course and family correlates of sibling relationships from childhood through adolescence. *Child Development, 77,* 1746–1761.

Kim, M., McGregor, K. K., & Thompson, C. K. (2000). Early lexical development in English- and Korean-speaking children: Language general and language-specific patterns. *Journal of Child Language, 27,* 225–254.

Kim, S. Y. H., Appelbaum, P. S. J., Olin, D. V., & Jason, T. (2004). Proxy and surrogate consent in geriatric neuropsychiatric research: Update and recommendations. *American Journal of Psychiatry, 161,* 797–806.

Kim, S., & Hasher, L. (2005). The attraction effect in decision making: Superior performance by older adults. *Quarterly Journal of Experimental Psychology, 58A,* 120–133.

Kimbro, R. T. (2006). On-the-job moms: Work and breastfeeding initiation and duration for a sample of low-income women. *Maternal and Child Health Journal, 10,* 19–26.

King, A. C. (2001). Interventions to promote physical activity by older adults. *Journal of Gerontology, 56A,* 36A–46A.

King, A. C., Castro, C., Wilcox, S., Eyler, A. A., Sallis, J. F., & Brownson, R. C. (2000). Personal and environmental factors associated with physical inactivity among different racial–ethnic groups of U.S. middle-aged and older-aged women. *Health Psychology, 19,* 354–364.

King, A. C., Kiernan, M., Oman, R. F., Kraemer, H., Hull, M., & Ahn, D. (1997). Can we identify who will adhere to long-term physical activity? Signal detection methodology as a potential aid to clinical decision making. *Health Psychology, 16,* 380–389.

King, E. M., & Mason, A. D. (2001). *Engendering development: Through gender equality in rights, resources, and voice.* Washington, DC: UNICEF.

King, L. A., & Hicks, J. A. (2007). Whatever happened to "What might have been"? *American Psychologist, 62,* 625–636.

King, P. E., & Furrow, J. L. (2004). Religion as a resource for positive youth development: Religion, social capital, and moral outcomes. *Developmental Psychology, 40,* 703–713.

King, P. M., & Kitchener, K. S. (1994). *Developing reflective judgment: Understanding and promoting intellectual growth and critical thinking in adolescents and adults.* San Francisco: Jossey-Bass.

King, P. M., & Kitchener, K. S. (2002). The reflective judgment model: Twenty years of research on epistemic cognition. In B. K. Hofer & P. R. Pintrich (Eds.), *Personal epistemology: The psychological beliefs about knowledge and knowing* (pp. 37–61). Mahwah, NJ: Erlbaum.

King, V., & Scott, M. E. (2005). A comparison of cohabiting relationships among older and younger adults. *Journal of Marriage and Family, 67,* 271–285.

Kingsberg, S. A. (2002). The impact of aging on sexual function in women and their partners. *Archives of Sexual Behavior, 31,* 431–437.

Kinney, D. (1999). From "headbangers" to "hippies": Delineating adolescents' active attempts to form an alternative peer culture. In J. A. McLellan & M. J. V. Pugh (Eds.), *The role of peer groups in adolescent social identity: Exploring the importance of stability and change* (pp. 21–35). San Francisco: Jossey-Bass.

Kinser, K., & Deitchman, J. (2007). Tenacious persisters: Returning adult students in higher education. *Journal of College Student Retention, 9,* 75–94.

Kirby, D. (2002a). Antecedents of adolescent initiation of sex, contraceptive use, and pregnancy. *American Journal of Health Behavior, 26,* 473–485.

Kirby, D. (2002b). Effective approaches to reducing adolescent unprotected sex, pregnancy, and childbearing. *Journal of Sex Research, 39,* 51–57.

Kirchner, G. (2000). *Children's games from around the world.* Boston: Allyn and Bacon.

Kirk, K. M., Bailey, J. M., Dunne, M. P., & Martin, N. G. (2000). Measurement models for sexual orientation in a community twin sample. *Behavior Genetics, 30,* 345–356.

Kirkham, N. Z., Cruess, L., & Diamond, A. (2003). Helping children apply their knowledge to their behavior on a dimension-switching task. *Developmental Science, 6,* 449–476.

Kirkham, N. Z., Slemmer, J. A., & Johnson, S. P. (2002). Visual statistical learning in infancy: Evidence for a domain general learning mechanism. *Cognition, 83,* B35–B42.

Kisilevsky, B. S., Hains, S. M. J., Lee, K., Xie, X., Huang, H., Ye, H. H., Zhang, K., & Wang, Z. (2003). Effects of experience on fetal voice recognition. *Psychological Science, 14,* 220–224.

Kite, M. E., & Whitley, B. E., Jr. (2003). Do heterosexual women and men differ in their attitudes toward homosexuality? A conceptual and methodological analysis. In L. D. Garnets & D. C. Kimmel (Eds.), *Psychological perspectives on lesbian, gay, and bisexual experiences* (2nd ed., pp. 165–187). New York: Columbia University Press.

Kite, M. E., Stockdale, G. D., Whitley, B. E., Jr., & Johnson, B. T. (2005). Attitudes toward younger and older adults: An updated meta-analytic review. *Journal of Social Issues, 61,* 241–266.

Kito, M. (2005). Self-disclosure in romantic relationships and friendships among American and Japanese college students. *Journal of Social Psychology, 145,* 127–145.

Kitzmann, K. M., Cohen, R., & Lockwood, R. L. (2002). Are only children missing out? Comparison of the peer-related social competence of only children and siblings. *Journal of Social and Personal Relationships, 19,* 299–316.

Kivipelto, M., Rovio, S., Ngandu, T., Karenhold, I., Eskelinen, M., & Winblad, B. (2008). Apolipoprotein E epsilon4 magnifies lifestyle risks for dementia: A population-based study. *Journal of Cellular and Molecular Medicine, 12,* 2762–2771.

Klaczynski, P. A. (2001). Framing effects on adolescent task representations, analytic and heuristic processing, and decision making: Implications for the normative/descriptive gap. *Applied Developmental Psychology, 22,* 289–309.

Klaczynski, P. A., & Narasimham, G. (1998). Development of scientific reasoning biases: Cognitive versus ego-protective explanations. *Developmental Psychology, 34,* 175–187.

Klaczynski, P. A., Schuneman, M. J., & Daniel, D. B. (2004). Theories of conditional reasoning: A developmental examination of competing hypotheses. *Developmental Psychology, 40,* 559–571.

Klareskog, L., Padyukov, L., Rönnelid, J., & Alfredsson, L. (2006). Genes, environment and immunity in the development of rheumatoid arthritis. *Current Opinion in Immunology, 18,* 650–655.

Klass, D. (2004). The inner representation of the dead child in the psychic and social narratives of bereaved parents. In R. A. Neimeyer (Ed.), *Meaning reconstruction and the experience of loss* (pp. 77–94). Washington, DC: American Psychological Association.

Klaw, E. L., Rhodes, J. E., & Fitzgerald, L. F. (2003). Natural mentors in the lives of African-American adolescent mothers: Tracking relationships over time. *Journal of Youth and Adolescence, 32,* 223–232.

Klebanov, P. K., Brooks-Gunn, J., McCarton, C., & McCormick, M. C. (1998). The contribution of neighborhood and family income to developmental test scores over the first three years of life. *Child Development, 69,* 1420–1436.

Kleespies, P. M. (2004). Concluding thoughts on suffering, dying and choice. In P. M. Kleespies (Ed.), *Life and death decisions: Psychological and ethical considerations in end-of-life care* (pp. 163–167). Washington, DC: American Psychological Association.

Klein, B. E., Klein, R., Lee, K. E., & Meuer, S. M. (2003). Socioeconomic and lifestyle factors and the 10-year incidence of age-related cataracts. *American Journal of Ophthalmology, 136,* 506–512.

Klein, M. C. (2006). Does epidural analgesia increase rate of cesarean section? *Canadian Family Physician, 52,* 419–421.

Klein, P. J., & Meltzoff, A. N. (1999). Long-term memory, forgetting, and deferred imitation in 12-month-old infants. *Developmental Science, 2,* 102–113.

Kleinspehn-Ammerlahn, A., Kotter-Grühn, D., & Smith, J. (2008). Self-perceptions of aging: Do subjective age and satisfaction with aging change during old age? *The Journals of Gerontology Series B: Psychological Sciences and Social Sciences, 63,* 377–385.

Klenberg, L., Korkman, M., & Lahti-Nuuttila, P. (2001). Differential development of attention and executive functions in 3- to 12-year-old Finnish children. *Developmental Neuropsychology, 20,* 407–428.

Klesges, L. M., Johnson, K. C., Ward, K. D., & Barnard, M. (2001). Smoking cessation in pregnant women. *Obstetrics and Gynecology Clinics of North America, 28,* 269–282.

Kliegel, M., Jäger, T., & Phillips, L. H. (2008). Adult age differences in event-based prospective memory: A meta-analysis on the role of focal versus nonfocal cues. *Psychology and Aging, 23,* 203–208.

Kliewer, W., Fearnow, M. D., & Miller, P. A. (1996). Coping socialization in middle childhood: Tests of maternal and paternal influences. *Child Development, 67,* 2339–2357.

Kline, G. H., Stanley, S. M., Markman, H. J., Olmos-Gallo, P. A., St. Peters, M., Whitton, S. W., & Prado, L. M. (2004). Timing is everything: Pre-engagement cohabitation and increased risk for poor marital outcomes. *Journal of Family Psychology, 18,* 311–318.

Klingman, A. (2006). Children and war trauma. In K. A. Renninger & I. E. Sigel (Eds.), *Handbook of child psychology: Vol. 4. Child psychology in practice* (6th ed., pp. 619–652). Hoboken, NJ: Wiley.

Klingner, J. K., Vaughn, S., Hughes, M. T., Schumm, J. S., & Elbaum, B. (1998). Outcomes for students with and without learning disabilities in inclusive classrooms. *Learning Disabilities Research and Practice, 13,* 153–161.

Kloep, M., & Hendry, L. B. (2007). Retirement: A new beginning? *The Psychologist, 20,* 742–745.

Klomsten, A. T., Skaalvik, E. M., & Espnes, G. A. (2004). Physical self-concept and sports: Do gender differences exist? *Sex Roles, 50,* 119–127.

Klump, K. L., Kaye, W. H., & Strober, M. (2001). The evolving foundations of eating disorders. *Psychiatric Clinics of North America, 24,* 215–225.

Kluwer, E. S., & Johnson, M. D. (2007). Conflict frequency and relationship quality across the transition to parenthood. *Journal of Marriage and Family, 69,* 1089–1106.

Knafo, A., & Plomin, R. (2006). Parental discipline and affection and children's prosocial behavior: Genetic and environmental links. *Journal of Personality and Social Psychology, 90,* 147–164.

Knight, B. G., Kaskie, B., Robinson, G., & Dave, J. (2006). Improving the mental health of older adults. In J. E. Birren & K. Warner Schaie (Eds.),

Handbook of the psychology of aging (6th ed., pp. 407–424). Burlington, MA: Elsevier Academic Press.

Knoester, C., & Eggebeen, D. J. (2006). The effects of the transition to parenthood and subsequent children on men's well-being and social participation. *Journal of Family Issues, 27,* 152–1560.

Knopf, M., Kraus, U., & Kressley-Mba, R. A. (2006). Relational information processing of novel unrelated actions by infants. *Infant Behavior and Development, 29,* 44–53.

Knopman, D. S. (2006). Dementia and cerebrovascular disease. *Mayo Clinics Proceedings, 81,* 223–230.

Ko, K. J., Berg, C. A., Butner, J., Uchino, B. N., & Smith, T. W. (2007). Profiles of successful aging in middle-age and older adult married couples. *Psychology and Aging, 22,* 705–718.

Kobayashi, T., Hiraki, K., & Hasegawa, T. (2005). Auditory-visual intermodal matching of small numerosities in 6-month-old infants. *Developmental Science, 8,* 409–419.

Kobayashi, T., Kazuo, H., Ryoko, M., & Hasegawa, T. (2004). Baby arithmetic: One object plus one tone. *Cognition, 91,* B23–B34.

Kobayashi, Y. (1994). Conceptual acquisition and change through social interaction. *Human Development, 37,* 233–241.

Kochanska, G. (1991). Socialization and temperament in the development of guilt and conscience. *Child Development, 62,* 1379–1392.

Kochanska, G., & Aksan, N. (2006). Children's conscience and self-regulation. *Journal of Personality, 74,* 1587–1617.

Kochanska, G., Aksan, N., & Carlson, J. J. (2005). Temperament, relationships, and young children's receptive cooperation with their parents. *Developmental Psychology, 41*(4), 648–660.

Kochanska, G., Aksan, N., & Joy, M. E. (2007). Children's fearfulness as a moderator of parenting in early socialization: Two longitudinal studies. *Developmental Psychology, 43,* 222–237.

Kochanska, G., Aksan, N., & Nichols, K. E. (2003). Maternal power assertion in discipline and moral discourse contexts: Commonalities, differences, and implications for children's moral conduct and cognition. *Developmental Psychology, 39,* 949–963.

Kochanska, G., Aksan, N., Prisco, T. R., & Adams, E. E. (2008). Mother–child and father–child mutually responsive orientation in the first 2 years and children's outcomes at preschool age: Mechanisms of influence. *Child Development, 79,* 30–44.

Kochanska, G., Casey, R. J., & Fukumoto, A. (1995). Toddlers' sensitivity to standard violations. *Child Development, 66,* 643–656.

Kochanska, G., Forman, D. R., Aksan, N., & Dunbar, S. B. (2005). Pathways to conscience: Early mother–child mutually responsive orientation and children's moral emotion, conduct, and cognition. *Journal of Child Psychology and Psychiatry, 46,* 19–34.

Kochanska, G., Gross, J. N., Lin, M.-H., & Nichols, K. E. (2002). Guilt in young children: Development, determinants, and relations with broader system standards. *Child Development, 73,* 461–482.

Kochanska, G., & Knaack, A. (2003). Effortful control as a personality characteristic of young children: Antecedents, correlates, and consequences. *Journal of Personality, 71,* 1087–1112.

Kochanska, G., Murray, K. T., & Harlan, E. T. (2000). Effortful control in early childhood: Continuity and change, antecedents, and implications for social development. *Developmental Psychology, 36,* 220–232.

Koelsch, S., Gunter, T., von Cramon, D., Zysset, S., Lohmann, G., & Friederici, A. (2002). Bach speaks: A cortical "language network" serves the processing of music. *NeuroImage, 17,* 956–966.

Koestner, R., Franz, C., & Weinberger, J. (1990). The family origins of empathic concern: A 26-year longitudinal study. *Journal of Personality and Social Psychology, 58,* 709–717.

Kogan, N., & Mills, M. (1992). Gender influences on age cognitions and preferences: Sociocultural or sociobiological? *Psychology and Aging, 7,* 98–106.

Kohen, D. E., Brooks-Gunn, J., Leventhal, T., & Hertzman, C. (2002). Neighborhood income and physical and social disorder in Canada: Associations with young children's competencies. *Child Development, 73,* 1844–1860.

Kohlberg, L. (1966). A cognitive-developmental analysis of children's sex-role concepts and attitudes. In E. E. Maccoby (Ed.), *The development of sex differences* (pp. 82–173). Stanford, CA: Stanford University Press.

Kohlberg, L. (1969). Stage and sequence: The cognitive-developmental approach to socialization. In D. A. Goslin (Ed.), *Handbook of socialization theory and research* (pp. 347–480). Chicago: Rand McNally.

Kohlberg, L., Levine, C., & Hewer, A. (1983). *Moral stages: A current formulation and a response to critics.* Basel, Switzerland: Karger.

Kohn, M. L. (2006). *Change and stability: A cross-national analysis of social structure and personality.* Greenbrae, CA: Paradigm Press.

Kohn, M. L., Naoi, A., Schoenbach, C., Schooler, C., & Slomczynski, K. M. (1990). Position in the class structure and psychological functioning in the United States, Japan, and Poland. *American Journal of Sociology, 95,* 964–1008.

Kohn, M. L., & Schooler, C. (1978). The reciprocal effects of the substantive complexity of work and intellectual flexibility: A longitudinal assessment. *American Journal of Sociology, 84,* 24–52.

Kohn, M. L., & Slomczynski, K. M. (1990). *Social structure and self-direction: A comparative analysis of the United States and Poland.* Cambridge, MA: Blackwell.

Kohn, M. L., Zaborowski, W., Janicka, K., Mach, B. W., Khmelko, V., Slomczynski, K. M., Heyman, C., & Podobnik, B. (2000). Complexity of activities and personality under conditions of radical social change: A comparative analysis of Poland and Ukraine. *Social Psychology Quarterly, 63,* 187–207.

Kolomer, S. R., & McCallion, P. (2005). Depression and caregiver mastery in grandfathers caring for their grandchildren. *International Journal of Aging and Human Development, 60,* 283–294.

Komp, D. M. (1996). The changing face of death in children. In H. M. Spiro, M. G. M. Curnen, & L. P. Wandel (Eds.), *Facing death: Where culture, religion, and medicine meet* (pp. 66–76). New Haven: Yale University Press.

Komsi, N., Räikkönen, K., Pesonen, A.-K., Heinonen, K., Keskivaara, P., Järvenpää, A.-L., & Strandberg, T. E. (2006). Continuity of temperament from infancy to middle childhood. *Infant Behavior and Development, 29,* 494–508.

Kono, S. (2004). Secular trend of colon cancer incidence and mortality in relation to fat and meat intake in Japan. *European Journal of Cancer Prevention, 13,* 127–132.

Konold, T. R., & Pianta, R. C. (2005). Empirically-derived, person-oriented patterns of school readiness in typically developing children: Description and prediction to first-grade achievement. *Applied Developmental Science, 9,* 174–187.

Kopp, C. B., & Neufeld, S. J. (2003). Emotional development during infancy. In R. Davidson, K. R. Scherer, & H. H. Goldsmith (Eds.), *Handbook of affective sciences* (pp. 347–374). Oxford, UK: Oxford University Press.

Kornhaber, M. L. (2004). Using multiple intelligences to overcome cultural barriers to identification for gifted education. In D. Boothe & J. C. Stanley (Eds.), *In the eyes of the beholder: Critical issues for diversity in gifted education* (pp. 215–225). Waco, TX: Prufrock Press.

Kotchoubey, B., Lang, S., Mezger, G., Schmalohr, D., Schneck, M., & Semmler, A. (2005). Information processing in severe disorders of consciousness:

Vegetative state and minimally conscious state. *Clinical Neurophysiology, 116*, 2441–2453.

Kotre, J. (1999). *Make it count: How to generate a legacy that gives meaning to your life.* New York: Free Press.

Kozer, E., Costei, A. M., Boskovic, R., Nulman, I., Nikfar, S., & Koren, G. (2003). Effects of aspirin consumption during pregnancy on pregnancy outcomes: Meta-analysis. *Birth Defects Research, Part B, Developmental and Reproductive Toxicology, 68,* 70–84.

Kozulin, A. (Ed.). (2003). *Vygotsky's educational theory in cultural context.* Cambridge, U.K.: Cambridge University Press.

Kraaij, V., Arensman, E., & Spinhoven, P. (2002). Negative life events and depression in elderly persons: A meta-analysis. *Journal of Gerontology, 57B,* P87–P94.

Kraaij, V., Pruymboom, E., & Garnefski, N. (2002). Cognitive coping and depressive symptoms in the elderly: A longitudinal study. *Aging and Mental Health, 6,* 275–281.

Krafft, K., & Berk, L. E. (1998). Private speech in two preschools: Significance of open-ended activities and make-believe play for verbal self-regulation. *Early Childhood Research Quarterly, 13,* 637–658.

Kraft, J. M., & Werner, J. S. (1999). Aging and the saturation of colors. 2. Scaling of color appearance. *Journal of the Optical Society of America, 16,* 231–235.

Kramer, A. F., Fabiani, M., & Colcombe, S. J. (2006). Contributions of cognitive neuroscience to the understanding of behavior and aging. In J. E. Birren & K. W. Schaie (Eds.), *Handbook of the psychology of aging* (6th ed., pp. 57–83). Burlington, MA: Elsevier Academic Press.

Kramer, A. F., Hahn, S., & Gopher, D. (1998). Task coordination and aging: Explorations of executive control processes in the task switching paradigm. *Acta Psychologica, 101,* 339–378.

Kramer, A. F., & Kray, J. (2006). Aging and attention. In E. Bialystok & F. I. M. Fergus (Eds.), *Lifespan cognition: Mechanisms of change* (pp. 57–69). New York: Oxford University Press.

Kramer, A. F., & Madden, D. J. (2008). Attention. In F. I. M. Craik & T. A. Salthouse (Eds.), *Handbook of aging and cognition* (pp. 189–249). New York: Psychology Press.

Kramer, D. A. (2003). The ontogeny of wisdom in its variations. In J. Demick & C. Andreoletti (Eds.), *Handbook of adult development* (pp. 131–151). New York: Springer.

Kramer, M. S., Guo, T., Platt, R. W., Sevkowskaya, Z., Dzikovich, I., & Collet, J. P. (2003). Infant growth and health outcomes associated with 3 compared with 6 mo. of exclusive breastfeeding. *American Journal of Clinical Nutrition, 78,* 291–295.

Kramer, S. E., Kapteyn, T. S., Kuik, D. J., & Deeg, D. J. (2002). The association of hearing impairment and chronic diseases with psychosocial health status in older age. *Journal of Aging and Health, 14,* 122–137.

Krampe, R. T., & Charness, N. (2007). Aging and expertise. In K. A. Ericsson, N. Charness, P. J. Feltovich, & R. R. Hoffman (Eds.), *Cambridge handbook of expertise and expert performance* (pp. 723–742). New York: Cambridge University Press.

Krause, N. (1990). Perceived health problems, formal/informal support, and life satisfaction among older adults. *Journal of Gerontology, 45,* S193–S205.

Krause, N. (2001). Social support. In R. H. Binstock & L. K. George (Eds.), *Handbook of aging and the social sciences* (5th ed., pp. 272–294). San Diego, CA: Academic Press.

Krause, N. (2005). God-mediated control and psychological well-being in late life. *Research on Aging, 27,* 136–164.

Krebs, D., & Denton, K. (2005). Toward a more pragmatic approach to morality: A critical evaluation of Kohlberg's model. *Psychological Review, 112,* 629–649.

Kreppner, J. M., Rutter, M., Beckett, C., Castle, J., Colvert, E., Groothues, C., Hawkins, A., & O'Connor, T. G. (2007). Normality and impairment following profound early institutional deprivation: A longitudinal follow-up into early adolescence. *Developmental Psychology, 43,* 931–946.

Krettenauer, T. (2005). The role of epistemic cognition in adolescent identity formation: Further evidence. *Journal of Youth and Adolescence, 34,* 185–198.

Krevans, J., & Gibbs, J. C. (1996). Parents' use of inductive discipline: Relations to children's empathy and prosocial behavior. *Child Development, 67,* 3263–3277.

Krishnamoorthy, J. S., Hart, C., & Jelalian, E. (2006). The epidemic of childhood obesity: Review of research and implications for public policy. *Social Policy Report of the Society for Research in Child Development, 9*(2).

Kroger, J. (2001). What transits in an identity status transition: A rejoinder to commentaries. *Identity, 3,* 291–304.

Kroger, J. (2005). *Identity in adolescence: The balance between self and other.* New York: Routledge.

Kroger, J. (2007). *Identity development: Adolescence through adulthood* (2nd ed.). Thousand Oaks, CA: Sage.

Kroneman, L., Loeber, R., & Hipwell, A. E. (2004). Is neighborhood context differently related to externalizing problems and delinquency for girls compared with boys? *Clinical Child and Family Psychology Review, 7,* 109–122.

Kropf, N. P., & Pugh, K. L. (1995). Beyond life expectancy: Social work with centenarians. *Journal of Gerontological Social Work, 23,* 121–137.

Krumhansl, C. L., & Jusczyk, P. W. (1990). Infants' perception of phrase structure in music. *Psychological Science, 1,* 70–73.

Kubik, M. Y., Lytle, L. A., Hannan, P. J., Perry, C. L., & Story, M. (2003). The association of the school food environment with dietary behaviors of young adolescents. *American Journal of Public Health, 93,* 1168–1173.

Kübler-Ross, E. (1969). *On death and dying.* New York: Macmillan.

Kubotera, T. (2004). Japanese religion in changing society: The spirits of the dead. In J. D. Morgan & P. Laungani (Eds.), *Death and bereavement around the world: Vol. 4. Asia, Australia, and New Zealand* (pp. 95–99). Amityville, NY: Baywood Publishing Company.

Kubzansky, L. D., Wright, R. J., Cohen, S., Weiss, S., Rosner, B., & Sparrow, D. (2002). Breathing easy: A prospective study of optimism and pulmonary function in the Normative Aging Study. *Annals of Behavioral Medicine, 24,* 345–353.

Kuczynski, L. (1984). Socialization goals and mother–child interaction: Strategies for long-term and short-term compliance. *Developmental Psychology, 20,* 1061–1073.

Kuczynski, L. (2003). Beyond bidirectionality. In L. Kuczynski (Ed.), *Handbook of dynamics in parent–child relations* (pp. 3–24). Thousand Oaks, CA: Sage.

Kuczynski, L., & Lollis, S. (2002). Four foundations for a dynamic model of parenting. In J. R. M. Gerris (Ed.), *Dynamics of parenting.* Hillsdale, NJ: Erlbaum.

Kuebli, J., Butler, S., & Fivush, R. (1995). Mother–child talk about past emotions: Relations of maternal language and child gender over time. *Cognition and Emotion, 9,* 265–283.

Kugelmass, J., & Ainscow, M. (2004). Leadership for inclusion: A comparison of international practices. *Journal of Research in Special Educational Needs, 4,* 133–141.

Kuhl, P. K., Tsao, F.-M., & Liu, H.-M. (2003). Foreign-language experience in infancy: Effects of short-term exposure and social interaction on phonetic learning. *Proceedings of the National Academy of Sciences, 100,* 9096–9101.

Kuhn, D. (1999). Metacognitive development. *Current Directions in Psychological Science, 9,* 178–181.

Kuhn, D. (2000). Theory of mind, metacognition, and reasoning: A life-span perspective. In P. Mitchell & K. J. Riggs (Eds.), *Children's reasoning and the mind* (pp. 301–326). Hove, UK: Psychology Press.

Kuhn, D. (2002). What is scientific thinking, and how does it develop? In U. Goswami (Ed.), *Blackwell handbook of childhood cognitive development* (pp. 371–393). Malden, MA: Blackwell.

Kuhn, D., Amsel, E., & O'Loughlin, M. (1988). *The development of scientific thinking skills.* Orlando, FL: Academic Press.

Kuhn, D., & Dean, D. (2004). Connecting scientific reasoning and causal inference. *Journal of Cognition and Development, 5,* 261–288.

Kuhn, D., & Franklin, S. (2006). The second decade: What develops (and how)? In D. Kuhn & R. S. Siegler (Eds.), *Handbook of child psychology: Vol. 2. Cognition, perception, and language* (6th ed.). Hoboken, NJ: Wiley.

Kuklinski, M. R., & Weinstein, R. S. (2001). Classroom and developmental differences in a path model of teacher expectancy effects. *Child Development, 72,* 1554–1578.

Kulik, K. (2001). Marital relationships in late adulthood: Synchronous versus asynchronous couples. *International Journal of Aging and Human Development, 52,* 323–339.

Kumar, S., & O'Brien, A. (2004). Recent developments in fetal medicine. *British Medical Journal, 328,* 1002–1006.

Kunemund, H., Motel-Klingebiel, A., & Kohli, M. (2005). Do intergenerational transfers from elderly parents increase social inequality among their middle-aged children? Evidence from the German Aging Survey. *Journal of Gerontology, 60B,* S30–S36.

Kunisaki, S. M., & Jennings, R. W. (2008). Fetal surgery. *Journal of Intensive Care Medicine, 23,* 33–51.

Kunnen, E. S., & Bosma, H. A. (2003). Fischer's skill theory applied to identity development: A response to Kroger. *Identity, 3,* 247–270.

Kunzinger, E. L., III. (1985). A short-term longitudinal study of memorial development during early grade school. *Developmental Psychology, 21,* 642–646.

Kunzmann, U., Little, T., & Smith, J. (2002). Perceiving control: A double-edged sword in old age. *Journal of Gerontology, 57B,* P484–P491.

Kurdek, L. A. (1998). Relationship outcomes and their predictors: Longitudinal evidence from heterosexual married, gay cohabiting, and lesbian cohabiting couples. *Journal of Marriage and the Family, 60,* 553–568.

Kurdek, L. A. (2005). Gender and marital satisfaction early in marriage: A growth curve approach. *Journal of Marriage and Family, 67,* 68–84.

Kurdek, L. A. (2006). Differences between partners from heterosexual, gay, and lesbian cohabiting couples. *Journal of Marriage and Family, 68,* 509–528.

Kurdek, L. A., & Fine, M. A. (1994). Family acceptance and family control as predictors of adjustment in young adolescents: Linear, curvilinear, or interactive effects? *Child Development, 65,* 1137–1146.

Kwon, Y. H., Fingert, J. H., Kuehn, M. H., & Alward, W. L. (2009). Primary open-angle glaucoma. *New England Journal of Medicine, 360,* 1113–1124.

L

Labouvie-Vief, G. (1980). Beyond formal operations: Uses and limits of pure logic in life-span development. *Human Development, 23,* 141–160.

Labouvie-Vief, G. (1985). Logic and self-regulation from youth to maturity: A model. In M. Commons, F. Richards, & C. Armon (Eds.), *Beyond formal operations: Late adolescent and adult cognitive development* (pp. 158–180). New York: Praeger.

Labouvie-Vief, G. (2003). Dynamic integration: Affect, cognition, and the self in adulthood.

Current Directions in Psychological Science, 12, 201–206.

Labouvie-Vief, G. (2005). Self-with-other representations and the organization of the self. *Journal of Research in Personality, 39,* 185–205.

Labouvie-Vief, G. (2006). Emerging structures of adult thought. In J. J. Arnett & J. L. Tanner (Eds.), *Emerging adults in America: Coming of age in the 21st century* (pp. 59–84). Washington, DC: American Psychological Association.

Labouvie-Vief, G. (2008). When differentiation and negative affect lead to integration and growth. *American Psychologist, 63,* 564–565.

Labouvie-Vief, G., Chiodo, L. M., Goguen, L. A., Diehl, M., & Orwoll, L. (1995). Representations of self across the life span. *Psychology and Aging, 10,* 404–415.

Labouvie-Vief, G., DeVoe, M., & Bulka, D. (1989). Speaking about feelings: Conceptions of emotion across the life span. *Psychology and Aging, 4,* 425–437.

Labouvie-Vief, G., & Diehl, M. (1999). Self and personality development. In J. C. Kavanaugh & S. K. Whitbourne (Eds.), *Gerontology: An interdisciplinary perspective* (pp. 238–268). New York: Oxford University Press.

Labouvie-Vief, G., & Diehl, M. (2000). Cognitive complexity and cognitive-affective integration: Related or separate domains of adult development? *Psychology and Aging, 15,* 490–504.

Labouvie-Vief, G., Diehl, M., Jain, E., & Zhang, F. (2007). Six-year change in affect optimization and affect complexity across the adult life span: A further examination. *Psychology and Aging, 22,* 738–751.

Labouvie-Vief, G., & Gonzalez, M. M. (2004). Dynamic integration: Affect optimization and differentiation in development. In D. Y. Dai & R. J. Sternberg (Eds.), *Motivation, emotion, and cognition: Integrative perspectives on intellectual functioning and development* (pp. 237–272). Mahwah, NJ: Erlbaum.

Labouvie-Vief, G., & Medler, M. (2002). Affect optimization and affect complexity: Modes and styles of regulation in adulthood. *Psychology and Aging, 17,* 571–588.

Lachman, M. E. (2004). Development in midlife. *Annual Review of Psychology, 55,* 305–331.

Lachman, M. E., & Bertrand, R. M. (2002). Personality and self in midlife. In M. E. Lachman (Ed.), *Handbook of midlife development* (pp. 279–309). New York: Wiley.

Lachman, M. E., & Firth, K. M. P. (2004). The adaptive value of feeling in control during midlife. In O. G. Brim, C. D. Ryff, & R. C. Kessler (Eds.), *How healthy are we? A national study of well-being at midlife* (pp. 320–349). Chicago: University of Chicago Press.

Lacor, P. N., Buniel, M. C., Furlow, P. W., Clemente, A. S., Velasco, P. T., & Wood, M. (2007). Abeta oligomer-induced aberrations in synapse composition, shape, and density provide a molecular basis for loss of connectivity in Alzheimer's disease. *Journal of Neuroscience, 27,* 796–807.

Lacourse, E., Nagin, D., Tremblay, R. E., Vitaro, F., & Claes, M. (2003). Developmental trajectories of boys' delinquent group membership and facilitation of violent behaviors during adolescence. *Development and Psychopathology, 15,* 183–197.

Ladd, G. W., Birch, S. H., & Buhs, E. S. (1999). Children's social and scholastic lives in kindergarten: Related spheres of influence? *Child Development, 70,* 1373–1400.

Ladd, G. W., Buhs, E. S., & Seid, M. (2000). Children's initial sentiments about kindergarten: Is school liking an antecedent of early classroom participation and achievement? *Merrill-Palmer Quarterly, 46,* 255–279.

Ladd, G. W., & Burgess, K. B. (1999). Charting the relationship trajectories of aggressive, withdrawn, and aggressive/withdrawn children during early grade school. *Child Development, 70,* 910–929.

Ladd, G. W., Herald, S. L., & Kochel, K. P. (2006). School readiness: Are there social prerequisites? *Early Education and Development, 17,* 115–150.

Ladd, G. W., LeSieur, K., & Profilet, S. M. (1993). Direct parental influences on young children's peer relations. In S. Duck (Ed.), *Learning about relationships* (Vol. 2, pp. 152–183). London: Sage.

Ladd, G. W., & Pettit, G. S. (2002). Parenting and the development of children's peer relationships. In M. Bornstein (Ed.), *Handbook of parenting* (2nd ed.). Mahwah, NJ: Erlbaum.

Ladd, G. W., & Troop-Gordon, W. (2003). The role of chronic peer difficulties in the development of children's psychological adjustment problems. *Child Development, 74,* 1344–1367.

LaFontana, K. M., & Cillessen, A. H. N. (1999). Children's interpersonal perceptions as a function of sociometric and peer perceived popularity. *Journal of Genetic Psychology, 160,* 225–242.

Lagattuta, K. H., Wellman, H. M., & Flavell, J. H. (1997). Preschoolers' understanding of the link between thinking and feeling: Cognitive cuing and emotional change. *Child Development, 68,* 1081–1104.

Lagercrantz, H., & Slotkin, T. A. (1986). The "stress" of being born. *Scientific American, 254,* 100–107.

Lagnado, L. (2001, November 2). Kids confront Trade Center trauma. *Wall Street Journal,* pp. B1, B6.

Laible, D. (2007). Attachment with parents and peers in late adolescence: Links with emotional competence and social behavior. *Personality and Individual Differences, 43,* 1185–1197.

Laible, D., & Song, J. (2006). Constructing emotional and relational understanding: The role of affect and mother–child discourse. *Merrill-Palmer Quarterly, 52,* 44–69.

Laible, D., & Thompson, R. A. (2002). Mother–child conflict in the toddler years: Lessons in emotion, morality, and relationships. *Child Development, 73,* 1187–1203.

Laird, R. D., Jordan, K. Y., Dodge, K. A., Pettit, G. S., & Bates, J. E. (2001). Peer rejection in childhood, involvement with antisocial peers in early adolescence, and the development of externalizing behavior problems. *Development and Psychopathology, 13,* 337–354.

Laird, R. D., Pettit, G. S., Dodge, K. A., & Bates, J. E. (2005). Peer relationship antecedents of delinquent behavior in late adolescence: Is there evidence of demographic group differences in developmental processes? *Development and Psychopathology, 17,* 127–144.

Lamarche, V., Brendgen, M., Boivin, M., Vitaro, F., Perusse, D., & Dionne, G. (2006). Do friendships and sibling relationships provide protection against peer victimization in a similar way? *Social Development, 15,* 373–393.

Lamaze, F. (1958). *Painless childbirth.* London: Burke.

Lamb, M. E., & Ahnert, L. (2006). Nonparental child care: Context, concepts, correlates, and consequences. In K. A. Renninger & I. E. Sigel (Eds.), *Handbook of child psychology: Vol. 4. Child psychology in practice* (6th ed., pp. 700–778). Hoboken, NJ: Wiley.

Lamb, M. E., & Lewis, C. (2004). The development and significance of father–child relationships in two-parent families. In M. E. Lamb (Ed.), *The role of the father in child development* (4th ed., pp. 272–306). Hoboken, NJ: Wiley.

Lamb, M. E., Thompson, R. A., Gardner, W., Charnov, E. L., & Connell, J. P. (1985). Infant–mother attachment: The origins and developmental significance of individual differences in the Strange Situation: Its study and biological interpretation. *Behavioral and Brain Sciences, 7,* 127–147.

Lamberg, L. (2007). Menopause not always to blame for sleep problems in midlife women. *Journal of the American Medical Association, 297,* 1865–1866.

Lambert, S. M., Masson, P., & Fisch, H. (2006). The male biological clock. *World Journal of Urology, 24,* 611–617.

Lanctot, K. L., Herrmann, N., Eryavec, G., van Reekum, R., Reed, K., & Naranjo, C. A. (2002). Central serotonergic activity is related to the aggressive behaviors of Alzheimer's disease. *Neuropsychopharmacology, 27,* 646–654.

Landau, M. (2007). Exogenous factors in skin aging. *Current Problems in Dermatology, 35,* 1–13.

Landman, J., Vandewater, E. A., Stewart, A. J., & Malley, J. E. (1995). Missed opportunities: Psychological ramifications of counterfactual thought in midlife women. *Journal of Adult Development, 2,* 87–97.

Lang, F. R., & Baltes, M. M. (1997). Being with people and being alone in later life: Costs and benefits for everyday functioning. *International Journal of Behavioral Development, 21,* 729–749.

Lang, F. R., Staudinger, U. M., & Carstensen, L. L. (1998). Perspectives on socioemotional selectivity in late life: How personality and social context do (and do not) make a difference. *Journal of Gerontology, 53B,* P21–P30.

Langer, G. (2004). *ABC News Prime Time Live Poll: The American Sex Survey.* Retrieved from abcnews.go.com/Primetime/News/story?id=174461&page=1

Langer, J., Gillette, P., & Arriaga, R. I. (2003). Toddlers' cognition of adding and subtracting objects in action and in perception. *Cognitive Development, 18,* 233–246.

Lansford, J. E., Antonucci, T. C., Akiyama, H., & Takahashi, K. (2005). A quantitative and qualitative approach to social relationships and well-being in the United States and Japan. *Journal of Comparative Family Studies, 36,* 1–22.

Lansford, J. E., Criss, M. M., Pettit, G. S., Dodge, K. A., & Bates, J. E. (2003). Friendship quality, peer group affiliation, and peer antisocial behavior as moderators of the link between negative parenting and adolescent externalizing behavior. *Journal of Research on Adolescence, 13,* 161–184.

Lansford, J. E., Deater-Deckard, K., Dodge, K. A., Bates, J. E., & Pettit, G. S. (2004). Ethnic differences in the link between physical discipline and later adolescent externalizing behaviors. *Journal of Child Psychology and Psychiatry, 45,* 801–812.

Lansford, J. E., Malone, P. S., Castellino, D. R., Dodge, K. A., Pettit, G., & Bates, J. E. (2006). Trajectories of internalizing, externalizing, and grades for children who have and have not experienced their parents' divorce or separation. *Journal of Family Psychology, 20,* 292–301.

Lantz, P. M., House, J. S., Lepkowski, J. M., Williams, D. R., Mero, R. P., & Chen, J. (1998). Socioeconomic factors, health behaviors, and mortality. *Journal of the American Medical Association, 279,* 1703–1708.

Lantz, P. M., Lynch, J. W., House, J. S., Lepkowski, J. M., Mero, R. P., & Musick, M. (2001). Socioeconomic disparities in health change in a longitudinal study of U.S. adults: The role of health risk behaviors. *Social Science and Medicine, 53,* 29–40.

Larbi, A., Franceschi, C., Mazzatti, D., Solana, R., Wikby, A., & Pawelec, G. (2008). Aging of the immune system as a prognostic factor for human longevity. *Physiology, 23,* 64–74.

Larsen, J. A., & Nippold, M. A. (2007). Morphological analysis in school-age children: Dynamic assessment of a word learning strategy. *Language, Speech, and Hearing Services in Schools, 38,* 201–212.

Larson, D. G., & Hoyt, W. T. (2007). What has become of grief counseling? An evaluation of the empirical foundations of the new pessimism. *Professional Psychology: Research and Practice, 38,* 347–355.

Larson, E. B., Shadlen, M. F., Wang, L., McCormick, W. C., Bowen, J. D., Teri, L., & Kukull, W. A. (2004). Survival after initial diagnosis of Alzheimer disease. *Annals of Internal Medicine, 140,* 501–509.

Larson, E. B., Wang, L., Bowen, J. D., McCormick, W. C., & Teri, L. (2006). Exercise is associated with reduced risk for incident dementia among persons 65 years of age and older. *Annals of Internal Medicine, 144,* 73–81.

Larson, R. W. (2001). How U.S. children and adolescents spend time: What it does (and doesn't) tell us about their development. *Current Directions in Psychological Science, 10,* 160–164.

Larson, R. W., & Ham, M. (1993). Stress and "storm and stress" in early adolescence: The relationship of negative events with dysphoric affect. *Developmental Psychology, 29,* 130–140.

Larson, R. W., & Lampman-Petraitis, C. (1989). Daily emotional states as reported by children and adolescents. *Child Development, 60,* 1250–1260.

Larson, R. W., Mannell, R., & Zuzanek, J. (1986). Daily well-being of older adults with friends and family. *Psychology and Aging, 1,* 117–126.

Larson, R. W., Moneta, G., Richards, M. H., & Wilson, S. (2002). Continuity, stability, and change in daily emotional experience across adolescence. *Child Development, 73,* 1151–1165.

Larson, R. W., & Richards, M. (1998). Waiting for the weekend: Friday and Saturday night as the emotional climax of the week. In A. C. Crouter & R. Larson (Eds.), *Temporal rhythms in adolescence: Clocks, calendars, and the coordination of daily life* (pp. 37–51). San Francisco: Jossey-Bass.

Larsson, M., & Bäckman, L. (1998). Modality memory across the adult life span: Evidence for selective age-related olfactory deficits. *Experimental Aging Research, 24,* 63–82.

Larsson, M., Öberg, C., & Bäckman, L. (2005). Odor identification in old age: Demographic, sensory and cognitive correlates. *Aging, Neuropsychology, and Cognition, 12,* 231–244.

Larzelere, R. E., Schneider, W. N., Larson, D. B., & Pike, P. L. (1996). The effects of discipline responses in delaying toddler misbehavior recurrences. *Child and Family Behavior Therapy, 18,* 35–57.

Lashley, F. R. (2007). Essentials of clinical genetics in nursing practice. New York: Springer.

Lattanzi-Licht, M., & Doka, K. J. (Eds.). (2003). *Living with grief: Coping with public tragedy.* New York: Brunner-Routledge.

Latz, S., Wolf, A. W., & Lozoff, B. (1999). Sleep practices and problems in young children in Japan and the United States. *Archives of Pediatric and Adolescent Medicine, 153,* 339–346.

Lauer, P. A., Akiba, M., Wilkerson, S. B., Apthorp, H. S., Snow, D., & Martin-Glenn, M. (2006). Out-of-school time programs: A meta-analysis of effects for at-risk students. *Review of Educational Research, 76,* 275–313.

Laumann, E. O., Gagnon, J. H., Michael, R. T., & Michaels, S. (1994). *The social organization of sexuality.* Chicago: University of Chicago Press.

Laumann, E. O., Paik, A., & Rosen, R. C. (1999). Sexual dysfunction in the United States: Prevalence and predictors. *Journal of the American Medical Association, 281,* 537–544.

Laureys, S., & Boly, M. (2007). What is it like to be vegetative or minimally conscious? *Current Opinion in Neurology, 20,* 609–613.

Laursen, B., Coy, K., & Collins, W. A. (1998). Reconsidering changes in parent–child conflict across adolescence: A meta-analysis. *Child Development, 69,* 817–832.

Lavelli, M., & Fogel, A. (2005). Developmental changes in the relationship between the infant's attention and emotion during early face-to-face communication: The 2-month transition. *Developmental Psychology, 41,* 265–280.

Law, K. L., Stroud, L. R., Niaura, R., LaGasse, L. L., Giu, L., & Lester, B. M. (2003). Smoking during pregnancy and newborn neurobehavior. *Pediatrics, 111,* 1318–1323.

Lawrence, A. R., & Schigelone, A. R. S. (2002). Reciprocity beyond dyadic relationships: Aging-related communal coping. *Research on Aging, 24,* 684–704.

Lawrence, K., Kuntsi, J., Coleman, M., Campbell, R., & Skuse, D. (2003). Face and emotion recognition deficits in Turner syndrome: A possible role for X-linked genes in amygdala development. *Neuropsychology, 17,* 39–49.

Lawson, K. R., & Ruff, H. A. (2004). Early attention and negative emotionality predict later cognitive and behavioral function. *International Journal of Behavioral Development, 28,* 157–165.

Lawton, M. P. (2001). Emotion in later life. *Current Directions in Psychological Science, 10,* 120–123.

Lazar, I., & Darlington, R. (1982). Lasting effects of early education: A report from the Consortium for Longitudinal Studies. *Monographs of the Society for Research in Child Development, 47*(2–3, Serial No. 195).

Lazarus, R. S. (1999). *Stress and emotion: A new synthesis.* New York: Springer.

Lazarus, R. S., & Lazarus, B. N. (1994). *Passion and reason.* New York: Oxford University Press.

Leadbeater, B., & Hoglund, W. (2006). Changing the social texts of peer victimization. *Journal of the Canadian Academy of Child and Adolescent Psychiatry, 15,* 21–26.

Leaper, C. (1994). Exploring the correlates and consequences of gender segregation: Social relationships in childhood, adolescence, and adulthood. In C. Leaper (Ed.), *New directions for child development* (No. 65, pp. 67–86). San Francisco: Jossey-Bass.

Leaper, C., Anderson, K. J., & Sanders, P. (1998). Moderators of gender effects on parents' talk to their children: A meta-analysis. *Developmental Psychology, 34,* 3–27.

Leaper, C., & Friedman, C. K. (2007). The socialization of gender. In J. E. Grusec & P. D. Hastings (Eds.), *Handbook of socialization: Theory and research* (pp. 561–587). New York: Guilford.

Leaper, C., Leve, L., Strasser, T., & Schwartz, R. (1995). Mother–child communication sequences: Play activity, child gender, and marital status effects. *Merrill-Palmer Quarterly, 41,* 307–327.

Leaper, C., Tenenbaum, H. R., & Shaffer, T. G. (1999). Communication patterns of African-American girls and boys from low-income, urban backgrounds. *Child Development, 70,* 1489–1503.

Lease, S. H. (2003). Testing a model of men's nontraditional occupational choices. *Career Development Quarterly, 51,* 244–258.

LeBlanc, L. A., Goldsmith, T., & Patel, D. R. (2003). Behavioral aspects of chronic illness in children and adolescents. *Pediatric Clinics of North America, 50,* 859–878.

Lecanuet, J.-P., Granier-Deferre, C., Jacquet, A.-Y., Capponi, I., & Ledru, L. (1993). Prenatal discrimination of a male and female voice uttering the same sentence. *Early Development and Parenting, 2,* 217–228.

Lechner, V., & Neal, M. (1999). *Working and caring for the elderly: International perspectives.* New York: Routledge.

Lecuyer, E., & Houck, G. M. (2006). Maternal limit-setting in toddlerhood: Socialization strategies for the development of self-regulation. *Infant Mental Health Journal, 27,* 344–370.

Lee, C.-Y. S., & Doherty, W. J. (2007). Marital satisfaction and father involvement during the transition to parenthood. *Fathering, 5,* 75–96.

Lee, D. J., & Markides, K. S. (1990). Activity and morality among aged persons over an eight-year period. *Journal of Gerontology, 45,* S39–S42.

Lee, E. E., & Farran, C. J. (2004). Depression among Korean, Korean American, and Caucasian American family caregivers. *Journal of Transcultural Nursing, 15,* 18–25.

Lee, E. O. (2007). Religion and spirituality as predictors of well-being among Chinese American and Korean American older adults. *Journal of Religion, Spirituality and Aging, 19,* 77–100.

Lee, E. O., & Sharpe, T. (2007). Understanding religious/spiritual coping and support resources among African American older adults: A mixed method approach. *Journal of Religion, Spirituality and Aging, 19,* 55–75.

Lee, G. R., DeMaris, A., Bavin, S., & Sullivan, R. (2001). Gender differences in the depressive effect of widowhood in later life. *Journal of Gerontology, 56B,* S56–S61.

Lee, J. M., Appulgiese, D., Kaciroti, N., Corwyn, R. F., Bradley, R. H., & Lumeng, J. C. (2007). Weight status in young girls and the onset of puberty. *Pediatrics, 119,* e624–e630.

Lee, S. J., Ralston, H. J., Partridge, J. C., & Rosen, M. A. (2005). Fetal pain: A systematic multidisciplinary review of the evidence. *Journal of the American Medical Association, 294,* 947–954.

Lee, S. M., Burgeson, C. R., Fulton, J. E., & Spain, C. G. (2007). Physical education and physical activity: Results from the School Health Policies and Programs Study, 2006. *Journal of School Health, 77,* 435–463.

Lee, V. E., & Burkam, D. T. (2002). *Inequality at the starting gate.* Washington, DC: Economic Policy Institute.

Lee, V. E., & Burkam, D. T. (2003). Dropping out of high school: The role of school organization and structure. *American Educational Research Journal, 40,* 353–393.

Lefebvre, F., Mazurier, E., & Tessier, R. (2005). Cognitive and educational outcomes in early adulthood for infants weighing 1000 grams or less at birth. *Acta Paediatrica, 94,* 733–740.

Legacy Project. (2009). *Fast facts on grandparenting and intergenerational mentoring.* Retrieved from www.legacyproject.org/specialreports/fastfacts.html

Lehman, D., Ellard, J., & Wortman, C. (1986). Social support for the bereaved: Recipients' and providers' perspectives on what is helpful. *Journal of Consulting and Clinical Psychology, 54,* 438–446.

Lehman, D. R., & Nisbett, R. E. (1990). A longitudinal study of the effects of undergraduate training on reasoning. *Developmental Psychology, 26,* 952–960.

Lehr, V. T., Zeskind, P. S., Ofenstein, J. P., Cepeda, E., Warrier, I., & Aranda, J. V. (2007). Neonatal facial coding system scores and spectral characteristics of infant crying during newborn circumcision. *Clinical Journal of Pain, 23,* 417–424.

Leman, P. J. (2005). Authority and moral reasons: Parenting style and children's perceptions of adult rule justifications. *International Journal of Behavioral Development, 29,* 265–270.

Lemche, E., Lennertz, I., Orthmann, C., Ari, A., Grote, K., Hafker, J., & Klann-Delius, G. (2003). Emotion-regulatory process in evoked play narratives: Their relation with mental representations and family interactions. *Praxis der Kinderpsychologie und Kinderpsychiatrie, 52,* 156–171.

Lemme, B. H. (2006). *Development in adulthood* (4th ed.). Boston: Allyn & Bacon.

Lempert, H. (1990). Acquisition of passives: The role of patient animacy, salience, and lexical accessibility. *Journal of Child Language, 17,* 677–696.

Lenroot, R. K., & Giedd, J. N. (2006). Brain development in children and adolescents: Insights from anatomical magnetic resonance imaging. *Neuroscience and Biobehavioral Reviews, 30,* 718–729.

Lent, R. W., & Brown, S. D. (2002). Social cognitive career theory and adult career development. In R. W. Lent & S. D. Brown (Eds.), *Adult career development: Concepts, issues, and practices* (3rd ed., pp. 76–97). Columbus, OH: National Career Development Association.

Leon, K. (2003). Risk and protective factors in young children's adjustment to parental divorce: A review of the research. *Family Relations, 52,* 258–270.

Lepage, J.-F., & Théoret, H. (2007). The mirror neuron system: Grasping others' actions from birth? *Developmental Science, 10,* 513–523.

Lerner, R. M. (2006). Developmental science, developmental systems, and contemporary theories of human development. In R. M. Lerner (Ed.), *Handbook of child psychology: Vol. 1. Theoretical models of human development* (6th ed., pp. 1–17). Hoboken, NJ: Wiley.

Lerner, R. M., Rothbaum, F., Boulos, S., & Castellino, D. R. (2002). Developmental systems perspective on parenting. In M. H. Bornstein (Ed.), *Handbook of parenting: Vol. 2* (2nd ed., pp. 315–344). Mahwah, NJ: Erlbaum.

Lerner, R. M., Theokas, C., & Bobek, D. L. (2005). Concepts and theories of human development: Historical and contemporary dimensions. In M. H. Bornstein & M. E. Lamb (Eds.), *Developmental science: An advanced textbook* (pp. 3–43). Mahwah, NJ: Erlbaum.

Leslie, A. M. (2004). Who's for learning? *Developmental Science, 7,* 417–419.

Lester, B. M., LaGasse, L., Seifer, R., Tronick, E. Z., Bauer, C., & Shankaran, S. (2003). The maternal lifestyle study (MLS): Effects of prenatal cocaine and/or opiate exposure on auditory brain response at one month. *Journal of Pediatrics, 142,* 279–285.

Lester, B. M., Masten, A. S., & McEwen, B. (Eds.). (2006). *Resilience in children.* New York: Annals of the New York Academy of Sciences.

Letherby, G. (2002). Childless and bereft? Stereotypes and realities in relation to "voluntary" and "involuntary" childlessness and womanhood. *Sociological Inquiry, 72,* 7–20.

Leung, M. C. M., Zhang, J., & Zhang, J. (2004). An economic analysis of life expectancy by gender with application to the United States. *Journal of Health Economics, 23,* 737–759.

LeVay, S. (1993). *The sexual brain.* Cambridge, MA: MIT Press.

Levenson, R. W., Carstensen, L. L., & Gottman, J. M. (1993). Long-term marriage: Age, gender, and satisfaction. *Psychology and Aging, 8,* 301–313.

Leventhal, E. A., Leventhal, H., Schaefer, P. M., & Easterling, D. (1993). Conservation of energy, uncertainty reduction, and swift utilization of medical care among the elderly. *Journal of Gerontology, 48,* P78–P86.

Leventhal, T., & Brooks-Gunn, J. (2003). Children and youth in neighborhood contexts. *Current Directions in Psychological Science, 12,* 27–31.

Levin, I., & Bus, A. G. (2003). How is emergent writing based on drawing? Analyses of children's products and their sorting by children and mothers. *Developmental Psychology, 39,* 891–905.

Levin, J. S., Taylor, R. J., & Chatters, L. M. (1994). Race and gender differences in religiosity among older adults: Findings from four national surveys. *Journal of Gerontology, 49,* S137–S145.

Levine, L. E. (1983). Mine: Self-definition in 2-year-old boys. *Developmental Psychology, 19,* 544–549.

Levine, L. J. (1995). Young children's understanding of the causes of anger and sadness. *Child Development, 66,* 697–709.

Levine, M. (2005). *Ready or not, here life comes.* New York: Simon & Schuster.

LeVine, R. A., Dixon, S., LeVine, S., Richman, A., Leiderman, P. H., Keefer, C. H., & Brazelton, T. B. (1994). *Child care and culture: Lessons from Africa.* New York: Cambridge University Press.

LeVine, R. A., LeVine, S. E., Richman, A., Tapia Uribe, M. R., Suderland Correa, C., & Miller, P. M. (1991). Women's schooling and child care in the demographic transition: A Mexican case study. *Population and Development Review, 17,* 459–496.

LeVine, R. A., LeVine, S. E., Rowe, M. L., & Schnell-Anzola, B. (2004). Maternal literacy and health behavior: A Nepalese case study. *Social Science and Medicine, 58,* 863–877.

LeVine, R. A., LeVine, S. E., & Schnell, B. (2001). "Improve the women": Mass schooling, female literacy, and worldwide social change. *Harvard Educational Review, 71,* 1–50.

Levinson, D. J. (1978). *The seasons of a man's life.* New York: Knopf.

Levinson, D. J. (1986). A conception of adult development. *American Psychologist, 41,* 3–13.

Levinson, D. J. (1996). *The seasons of a woman's life.* New York: Knopf.

Levitt, T., Fugelsang, J., & Crossley, M. (2006). Processing speed, attentional capacity, and age-related memory change. *Experimental Aging Research, 32,* 263–295.

Levy, B. R. (2003). Mind matters: Cognitive and physical effects of aging self-stereotypes. *Journal of Gerontology, 58B,* P203–P211.

Levy, B. R., & Banaji, M. R. (2002). Implicit ageism. In T. D. Nelson (Ed.), *Ageism: Stereotyping and prejudice against older persons* (pp. 49–75). Cambridge, MA: MIT Press.

Levy, B. R., Hausdorff, J., Hencke, R., & Wei, J. Y. (2000). Reducing cardiovascular stress with positive self-stereotypes of aging. *Journal of Gerontology, 55B,* P205–P213.

Levy, B. R., Slade, M. D., Kunkel, S. R., & Kasl, S. V. (2002). Longevity increased by positive self-perceptions of aging. *Journal of Personality and Social Psychology, 83,* 261–270.

Lewis, M. (1992). *Shame: The exposed self.* New York: Free Press.

Lewis, M. (1997). *Altering fate: Why the past does not predict the future.* New York: Guilford.

Lewis, M. (1998). Emotional competence and development. In D. Pushkar, W. M. Bukowski, A. E. Schwartzman, E. M. Stack, & D. R. White (Eds.), *Improving competence across the lifespan* (pp. 27–36). New York: Plenum.

Lewis, M., & Brooks-Gunn, J. (1979). *Social cognition and the acquisition of self.* New York: Plenum.

Lewis, M., Ramsay, D. S., & Kawakami, K. (1993). Differences between Japanese infants and Caucasian American infants in behavioral and cortisol response to inoculation. *Child Development, 64,* 1722–1731.

Lewis, M., Sullivan, M. W., Stanger, C., & Weiss, M. (1989). Self development and self-conscious emotions. *Child Development, 60,* 146–156.

Li, D.-K., Willinger, M., Petitti, D. B., Odouli, R., Liu, L., & Hoffman, H. J. (2006). Use of a dummy (pacifier) during sleep and risk of sudden infant death syndrome (SIDS): Population based case-control study. *British Medical Journal, 332,* 18–21.

Li, Q. (2006). Cyberbullying in schools: A research of gender differences. *School Psychology International, 27,* 157–170.

Li, S.-C., Lindenberger, U., Hommel, B., Aschersleben, G., Prinz, W., & Baltes, P. B. (2004). Transformation in the couplings among intellectual abilities and constituent cognitive processes across the life span. *Psychological Science, 15,* 155–163.

Liang, J., Bennett, J. M., Krause, N. M., Chang, M., Lin, S., Chuang, Y. L., & Wo, S. (1999). Stress, social relationships, and old age mortality in Taiwan. *Journal of Clinical Epidemiology, 52,* 983–995.

Liang, J., Bennett, J., Krause, N., Kobayashi, E., Kim, H., Brown, J. W., Akiyama, H., Sugiawa, H., & Jain, A. (2002). Old age mortality in Japan: Does the socioeconomic gradient interact with gender and age? *Journal of Gerontology, 57,* S294–S307.

Liang, J., Krause, N. M., & Bennett, J. M. (2001). Social exchange and well-being: Is giving better than receiving? *Psychology and Aging, 16,* 511–523.

Liben, L. S. (1999). Developing an understanding of external spatial representations. In I. E. Sigel (Ed.), *Development of mental representation* (pp. 297–321). Mahwah, NJ: Erlbaum.

Liben, L. S. (2006). Education for spatial thinking. In K. A. Renninger & I. E. Sigel (Eds.), *Handbook of child psychology: Vol. 4. Child psychology in practice* (6th ed., pp. 197–247). Hoboken, NJ: Wiley.

Liben, L. S., & Bigler, R. S. (2002). The developmental course of gender differentiation: Conceptualizing, measuring, and evaluating constructs and pathways. *Monographs of the Society for Research in Child Development, 6*(4, Serial No. 271).

Liben, L. S., Bigler, R. S., & Krogh, H. R. (2001). Pink and blue collar jobs: Children's judgments of job status and job aspirations in relation to sex of worker. *Journal of Experimental Child Psychology, 79,* 346–363.

Liben, L. S., & Downs, R. M. (1993). Understanding person–space–map relations: Cartographic and developmental perspectives. *Developmental Psychology, 29,* 739–752.

Liben, L. S., & Signorella, M. L. (1993). Gender-schematic processing in children: The role of initial interpretations of stimuli. *Developmental Psychology, 29,* 141–149.

Lickliter, R., & Bahrick, L. E. (2000). The development of infant intersensory perception: Advantages of a comparative convergent-operations approach. *Psychological Bulletin, 126,* 260–280.

Lidz, C. S. (2001). Multicultural issues and dynamic assessment. In L. A. Suzuki & J. G. Ponterotto (Eds.), *Handbook of multicultural assessment: Clinical, psychological, and educational applications* (2nd ed., pp. 523–539). San Francisco: Jossey-Bass.

Lidz, J. (2007). The abstract nature of syntactic representations. In E. Hoff & M. Shatz (Eds.), *Blackwell handbook of language development* (pp. 277–303). Malden, MA: Blackwell.

Lieven, E., Pine, J., & Baldwin, G. (1997). Lexically based learning and early grammatical development. *Journal of Child Language, 24,* 187–220.

Li-Grining, C. P. (2007). Effortful control among low-income preschoolers in three cities: Stability, change, and individual differences. *Developmental Psychology, 43,* 208–221.

Lillard, A. (2003). Pretend play and cognitive development. In U. Goswami (Ed.), *Blackwell handbook of childhood cognitive development* (pp. 189–205). Malden, MA: Blackwell.

Lillard, A. (2007). *Montessori: The science behind the genius.* New York: Oxford University Press.

Lillard, A., & Else-Quest, N. (2006). Evaluating Montessori education. *Science, 313,* 1893–1894.

Lim, V. K. G. (2002). Gender differences and attitudes toward homosexuality. *Journal of Homosexuality, 43,* 85–97.

Linares, T. J., Singer, L. T., Kirchner, H., Lester, H., Short, E. J., & Min, M. O. (2006). Mental health outcomes of cocaine-exposed children at 6 years of age. *Journal of Pediatric Psychology, 31,* 85–97.

Lindau, S. T., Schumm, L. P., Laumann, E. O., Levinson, W., O'Muircheartaigh, C. A., & Waite, L. J. (2007). A study of sexuality and health among older adults in the United States. *New England Journal of Medicine, 357,* 762–774.

Lindley, L. D. (2005). Perceived barriers to career development in the context of social-cognitive career theory. *Journal of Career Assessment, 13,* 271–287.

Lindsay, C., Almey, M., & Normand, J. (2002). *Youth in Canada.* Retrieved from http://www.statcan.ca/english/IPS/Data/85-511-XPE.htm

Lindsay-Hartz, J., de Rivera, J., & Mascolo, M. F. (1995). Differentiating guilt and shame and their effects on motivation. In J. P. Tangney & K. W. Fischer (Eds.), *Self-conscious emotions* (pp. 274–300). New York: Guilford.

Lindsey, E. W., & Mize, J. (2000). Parent–child physical and pretense play: Links to children's social competence. *Merrill-Palmer Quarterly, 46,* 565–591.

Linebarger, D. L., Kosanic, A. Z., Greenwood, C. R., & Doku, N. S. (2004). Effects of viewing the television program *Between the Lions* on the emergent literacy skills of young children. *Journal of Educational Psychology, 96,* 297–308.

Linley, P. A. (2003). Positive adaptation to trauma: Wisdom as both process and outcome. *Journal of Traumatic Stress, 16,* 601–610.

Linscheid, T. R., Budd, K. S., & Rasnake, L. K. (2005). Pediatric feeding problems. In M. C. Roberts (Ed.),

Handbook of pediatric psychology and psychiatry (3rd ed., pp. 481–488). New York: Guilford.

Linver, M. R., Martin, A., & Brooks-Gunn, J. (2004). Measuring infants' home environment: The ITHOME for infants between birth and 12 months in four national data sets. *Parenting: Science and Practice, 4,* 115–137.

Lipsitt, L. P. (2003). Crib death: A biobehavioral phenomenon? *Psychological Science, 12,* 164–170.

Liszkowski, U., Carpenter, M., Henning, A., Striano, T., & Tomasello, M. (2004). Twelve-month-olds point to share attention and interest. *Developmental Science, 7,* 297–307.

Little, C., & Carter, A. S. (2005). Negative emotional reactivity and regulation in 12-month-olds following emotional challenge: Contributions of maternal–infant emotional availability in a low-income sample, *Infant Mental Health Journal, 26,* 354–368.

Liu, J., Raine, A., Venables, P. H., Dalais, C., & Mednick, S. A. (2003). Malnutrition at age 3 years and lower cognitive ability at age 11 years. *Archives of Paediatric and Adolescent Medicine, 157,* 593–600.

Liu, X. Z., & Yan, D. (2007). Ageing and hearing loss. *Journal of Pathology, 211,* 188–197.

Lloyd, C. B. (2005). *Growing up global: The changing transitions to adulthood in developing countries.* Washington, DC: National Academy Press.

Lloyd-Jones, D., Adams, R., Carnethon, M., De Simone, G., Ferguson, B., & Flegal, K. (2009). Heart disease and stroke statistics—2009 update. *Circulation, 119,* e21–e181.

Lochman, J. E., & Dodge K. A. (1998). Distorted perceptions in dyadic interactions of aggressive and nonaggressive boys: Effects of prior expectations, context, and boys' age. *Development and Psychopathology, 10,* 495–512.

Lock, J., & Kirz, N. (2008). Eating disorders: Anorexia nervosa. In W. E. Craighead, D. J. Miklowitz, & L. W. Craighead (Eds.), *Psychopathology: History, diagnosis, and empirical foundations* (pp. 467–494). Hoboken, NJ: Wiley.

Lockhart, R. S., & Craik, F. I. M. (1990). Levels of processing: A retrospective commentary on a framework for memory research. *Canadian Journal of Psychology, 44,* 87–112.

Loeb, S., Fuller, B., Kagan, S. L., & Carrol, B. (2004). Child care in poor communities: Early learning effects of type, quality, and stability. *Child Development, 75,* 47–65.

Loehlin, J. C., Horn, J. M., & Willerman, L. (1997). Heredity, environment, and IQ in the Texas Adoption Project. In R. J. Sternberg & E. L. Grigorenko (Eds.), *Intelligence, heredity, and environment* (pp. 105–125). New York: Cambridge University Press.

Loehlin, J. C., Jonsson, E. G., Gustavsson, J. P., Stallings, M. C., Gillespie, N. A., Wright, M. J., & Martin, N. G. (2005). Psychological masculinity–femininity via the gender diagnosticity approach: Heritability and consistency across ages and populations. *Journal of Personality, 73,* 1295–1319.

Loehlin, J. C., & Martin, N. G. (2001). Age changes in personality traits and their heritabilities during the adult years: Evidence from Australian twin registry samples. *Personality and Individual Differences, 30,* 1147–1160.

Loewy, E. H. (2004). Euthanasia, physician assisted suicide and other methods of helping along death. *Health Care Analysis, 12,* 181–191.

Loganovskaja, T. K., & Loganovsky, K. N. (1999). EEG, cognitive and psychopathological abnormalities in children irradiated in utero. *International Journal of Psychophysiology, 34,* 211–224.

Loganovsky, K. N., Loganovskaja, T. K., Nechayev, S. Y., Antipchuk, Y. Y., & Bomko, M. A. (2008). Disrupted development of the dominant hemisphere following prenatal irradiation. *Journal of Neuropsychiatry and Clinical Neurosciences, 20,* 274–291.

Logroscino, G., Kang, J. H., & Grodstein, F. (2004). Prospective study of type 2 diabetes and cognitive decline in women aged 70–81 years. *British Medical Journal, 328,* 548.

Lohman, D. F. (2000). Measures of intelligence: Cognitive theories. In A. E. Kazdin (Ed.), *Encyclopedia of psychology: Vol. 5* (pp. 147–150). Washington, DC: American Psychological Association.

Long, D. D. (1985). A cross-cultural examination of fears of death among Saudi Arabians. *Omega, 16,* 43–50.

Loock, C., Conry, J., Cook, J. L., Chudley, A. E., & Rosales, T. (2005). Identifying fetal alcohol spectrum disorder in primary care. *Canadian Medical Association Journal, 172,* 628–630.

Lopata, H. Z. (1996). *Current widowhood: Myths and realities.* Thousand Oaks, CA: Sage.

Lorenz, K. (1952). *King Solomon's ring.* New York: Crowell.

Louie, V. (2001). Parents' aspirations and investment: The role of social class in the educational experiences of 1.5- and second generation Chinese Americans. *Harvard Educational Review, 71,* 438–474.

Louis, J., Cannard, C., Bastuji, H., & Challemel, M. J. (1997). Sleep ontogenesis revisited: A longitudinal 24-hour home polygraphic study on 15 normal infants during the first two years of life. *Sleep, 20,* 323–333.

Lourenco, O. (2003). Making sense of Turiel's dispute with Kohlberg: The case of the child's moral competence. *New Ideas in Psychology, 21,* 43–68.

Lövdén, M., Bergman, L., Adolfsson, R., Lindenberger, U., & Nilsson, L.-G. (2005). Studying individual aging in an interindividual context: Typical paths of age-related, dementia-related, and mortality-related cognitive development in old age. *Psychology and Aging, 20,* 303–316.

Love, J. M., Chazan-Cohen, R., & Raikes, H. (2007). Forty years of research knowledge and use: From Head Start to Early Head Start and beyond. In J. L. Aber, S. J. Bishop-Josef, S. M. Jones, K. T. McLearn, & D. Phillips (Eds.), *Child development and social policy: Knowledge for action* (pp. 79–95). Washington, DC: American Psychological Association.

Love, J. M., Harrison, L., Sagi-Schwartz, A., van IJzendoorn, M. H., Ross, C., & Ungerer, J. A. (2003). Child care quality matters: How conclusions may vary with context. *Child Development, 74,* 1021–1033.

Love, J. M., Kisker, E. E., Ross, C., Raikes, H., Constantine, J., Boller, K., & Brooks-Gunn, J. (2005). The effectiveness of early Head Start for 3-year-old children and their parents: Lessons for policy and programs. *Developmental Psychology, 41,* 885–901.

Love, J. M., Tarullo, L. B., Raikes, H., & Chazan-Cohen, R. (2006). Head Start: What do we know about its effectiveness? What do we need to know? In K. McCartney & D. Phillips (Eds.), *Blackwell handbook of early childhood development* (pp. 550–575). Malden, MA: Blackwell.

Lowenstein, A., Katz, R., & Gur-Yaish, N. (2007). Reciprocity in parent–child exchange and life satisfaction among the elderly: A cross-national perspective. *Journal of Social Issues, 63,* 865–883.

Lubart, T. I. (2003). In search of creative intelligence. In R. J. Sternberg, J. Lautrey, & T. I. Lubart (Eds.), *Models of intelligence: International perspectives* (pp. 279–292). Washington, DC: American Psychological Association.

Lubart, T. I., & Sternberg, R. J. (1998). Life span creativity: An investment theory approach. In C. E. Adams-Price (Ed.), *Creativity and successful aging.* New York: Springer.

Lucas, R. E., Clark, A. E., Georgellis, Y., & Diener, E. (2003). Reexamining adaptation and the set point model of happiness: Reactions to changes in marital status. *Journal of Personality and Social Psychology, 84,* 803–805.

Lucas, S. R., & Behrends, M. (2002). Sociodemographic diversity, correlated achievement, and de facto tracking. *Sociology of Education, 75,* 328–348.

Lucas, T. W., Wendorf, C. A., Imamoglu, E. O., Shen, J., Parkhill, M. R., Weisfeld, C. C. & Weisfeld, G. E. (2004). Marital satisfaction in four cultures as a function of homogamy, male dominance, and female attractiveness. *Sexualities, Evolution and Gender, 6,* 97–130.

Lucas-Thompson, R., & Clarke-Stewart, K. A. (2007). Forecasting friendship: How marital quality, maternal mood, and attachment security are linked to children's peer relationships. *Journal of Applied Developmental Psychology, 28,* 499–514.

Ludemann, P. M. (1991). Generalized discrimination of positive facial expressions by seven- and ten-month-old infants. *Child Development, 62,* 55–67.

Ludvig, J., Miner, B., & Eisenberg, M. J. (2005). Smoking cessation in patients with coronary artery disease. *American Heart Journal, 149,* 565–572.

Luecken, L. J. (2008). Long-term consequences of parental death in childhood: Psychological and physiological manifestations. In M. S. Stroebe, R. O. Hansson, H. Schut, & W. Stroebe (Eds.), *Handbook of bereavement research and practice* (pp. 397–416). Washington, DC: American Psychological Association.

Lukas, C., & Seiden, H. M. (2007). *Silent grief: Living in the wake of suicide* (rev. ed.). London, U.K.: Jessica Kingsley.

Luke, A., Cooper, R. S., Prewitt, T. E., Adeyemo, A. A., & Forrester, T. E. (2001). Nutritional consequences of the African diaspora. *Annual Review of Nutrition, 21,* 47–71.

Luna, B., Garver, K. E., Urban, T. A., Lazar, N. A., & Sweeney, J. A. (2004). Maturation of cognitive processes from late childhood to adulthood. *Child Development, 75,* 1357–1372.

Luna, B., Thulborn, K. R., Monoz, D. P., Merriam, E. P., Garver, K. E., Minshew, N. J., Keshavan, M. S., Genovese, C. R., Eddy, W. F., & Sweeney, J. A. (2001). Maturation of widely distributed brain function subserves cognitive development. *NeuroImage, 13,* 786–793.

Lund, D. A. (1993). Widowhood: The coping response. In R. Kastenbaum (Ed.), *Encyclopedia of adult development* (pp. 537–541). Phoenix, AZ: Oryx Press.

Lund, D. A. (1996). Bereavement and loss. In J. E. Birren (Ed.), *Encyclopedia of gerontology* (pp. 173–183). San Diego: Academic Press.

Lund, D. A. (1998). Statements and perspectives from leaders in the field of aging in Utah. In *Utah sourcebook on aging.* Salt Lake City: Empire Publishing.

Lund, D. A. (2005). *My journey* [Sue's letter]. Unpublished document. Salt Lake City, UT: University of Utah.

Lund, D. A., & Caserta, M. S. (2001). When the unexpected happens: Husbands coping with the deaths of their wives. In D. Lund (Ed.), *Men coping with grief* (pp. 147–166). Amityville, NY: Baywood.

Lund, D. A., & Caserta, M. S. (2004a). Facing life alone: Loss of a significant other in later life. In D. Doda (Ed), *Living with grief: Loss in later life* (pp. 207–223). Washington, DC: Hospice Foundation of America.

Lund, D. A., & Caserta, M. S. (2004b). Older men coping with widowhood. *Geriatrics and Aging, 7*(6), 29–33.

Lund, D. A., Caserta, M. S., de Vries, B., & Wright, S. (2004). Restoration after bereavement. *Generations Review, 14,* 9–15.

Lund, D. A., Wright, S. D., & Caserta, M. S. (2005). Respite services: Enhancing the quality of daily life for caregivers and persons with dementia. *Geriatrics and Aging, 8,* 60–65.

Luo, L., & Craik, F. I. M. (2008). Aging and memory: A cognitive approach. *Canadian Journal of Psychiatry, 53,* 346–353.

Luo, Y., & Baillargeon, R. (2005). When the ordinary seems unexpected: Evidence for incremental physical knowledge in young infants. *Cognition, 95,* 297–328.

Lusardi, A., & Mitchell, O. S. (2007). Baby boomer retirement security: The roles of planning, financial literacy, and housing wealth. *Journal of Monetary Economics, 54,* 205–224.

Luster, T., & Haddow, J. L. (2005). Adolescent mothers and their children: An ecological perspective. In T. Luster & J. L. Haddow (Eds.), *Parenting: An ecological perspective* (2nd ed., pp. 73–101). Mahwah, NJ: Erlbaum.

Luthar, S. S. (2006). Resilience in development: A synthesis of research across five decades. In D. Cicchetti & D. J. Cohen (Eds.), *Developmental psychopathology: Vol. 3. Risk, disorder, and adaptation* (2nd ed., pp. 739–795). Hoboken, NJ: Wiley.

Luthar, S. S., & Becker, B. E. (2002). Privileged but pressured: A study of affluent youth. *Child Development, 73,* 1593–1610.

Luthar, S. S., & Latendresse, S. J. (2005). Children of the affluent: Challenges to well-being. *Current Directions in Psychological Science, 14,* 49–53.

Luxembourg Income Study. (2008). *LIS key figures.* Retrieved from www.lisproject.org/php/kf/kf.php

Luyckx, K., Goossens, L., & Soenens, B. (2006). A developmental contextual perspective on identity construction in emerging adulthood: Change dynamics in commitment formation and commitment evaluation. *Developmental Psychology, 42,* 366–380.

Luyckx, K., Goossens, L., Soenens, B., & Beyers, W. (2006). Unpacking commitment and exploration: Preliminary validation of an integrative model of late adolescent identity formation. *Journal of Adolescence, 29,* 361–378.

Luzzo, D. A. (1999). Identifying the career decision-making needs of nontraditional college students. *Journal of Counseling and Development, 77,* 135–140.

Lynch, S. K., Turkheimer, E., D'Onofrio, B. M., Mendle, J., Emery, R. E., Slutske, W. S., & Martin, N. G. (2006). A genetically informed study of the association between harsh punishment and offspring behavioral problems. *Journal of Family Psychology, 20,* 190–198.

Lyness, K. S., & Heilman, M. E. (2006). When fit is fundamental: Performance evaluations and promotions of upper-level female and male managers. *Journal of Applied Psychology, 90,* 777–785.

Lyness, K. S., & Thompson, D. (1997). Above the glass ceiling? A comparison of matched samples of female and male executives. *Journal of Applied Psychology, 82,* 359–375.

Lyon, T. D., & Flavell, J. H. (1994). Young children's understanding of "remember" and "forget." *Child Development, 65,* 1357–1371.

Lyons-Ruth, K., Yellin, C., Melnick, S., & Atwood, G. (2005). Expanding the concept of unresolved mental states: Hostile/helpless states of mind on the Adult Attachment Interview are associated with disrupted mother–infant communication and infant disorganization. *Development and Psychopathology, 27,* 1–23.

Lytton, H., & Gallagher, L. (2002). Parenting twins and the genetics of parenting. In M. H. Bornstein (Ed.), *Handbook of parenting* (Vol. 1, pp. 227–253). Mahwah, NJ: Erlbaum.

M

Maas, F. K. (2008). Children's understanding of promising, lying, and false belief. *Journal of General Psychology, 13,* 301–321.

Maas, F. K., & Abbeduto, L. J. (2001). Children's judgments about intentionally and unintentionally broken promises. *Journal of Child Language, 28,* 517–529.

Macaluso, A., & De Vito, G. (2004). Muscle strength, power and adaptations to resistance training in older people. *European Journal of Applied Physiology, 91,* 450–472.

Maccoby, E. E. (1984). Socialization and developmental change. *Child Development, 55,* 317–328.

Maccoby, E. E. (1998). *The two sexes: Growing up apart, coming together.* Cambridge, MA: Belknap.

Maccoby, E. E. (2002). Gender and group process: A developmental perspective. *Current Directions in Psychological Science, 11,* 54–58.

MacDonald, W. L., & DeMaris, A. (1996). The effects of stepparent's gender and new biological children. *Journal of Family Issues, 17,* 5–25.

Macek, P., Bejček, J., & Vaníčková, J. (2007). Contemporary Czech emerging adults: Generation growing up in the period of social changes. *Journal of Adolescent Research, 22,* 444–475.

Machin, G. A. (2005). Multiple birth. In H. W. Taeusch, R. A. Ballard, & C. A. Gleason (Eds.), *Avery's diseases of the newborn* (8th ed., pp. 57–62). Philadelphia: Saunders.

Mackenbach, J. P. (2002). Income inequality and population health. *British Medical Journal, 324,* 1–2.

Mackey, K., Arnold, M. K., & Pratt, M. W. (2001). Adolescents' stories of decision making in more and less authoritative families: Representing the voices of parents in narrative. *Journal of Adolescent Research, 16,* 243–268.

Mackie, S., Show, P., Lenroot, R., Pierson, R., Greenstein, D. K., & Nugent, T. F., III. (2007). Cerebellar development and clinical outcome in attention deficit hyperactivity disorder. *American Journal of Psychiatry, 164,* 647–655.

MacWhinney, B. (2005). Language development. In M. H. Bornstein & M. E. Lamb (Eds.), *Developmental science: An advanced textbook* (5th ed., pp. 359–387). Mahwah, NJ: Erlbaum.

Maddi, S. R. (1999). The personality construct of hardiness: I. Effects on experiencing, coping, and strain. *Consulting Psychology Journal: Practice and Research, 51,* 83–94.

Maddi, S. R. (2005). On hardiness and other pathways to resilience. *American Psychologist, 60,* 261–262.

Maddi, S. R. (2006). Hardiness: The courage to be resilient. In J. C. Thomas, D. L. Segal, & M. Hersen (Eds.), *Comprehensive handbook of personality and psychopathology: Vol. 1. Personality and everyday functioning* (pp. 306–321). Hoboken, NJ: Wiley.

Maddi, S. R. (2007). The story of hardiness: Twenty years of theorizing, research, and practice. In A. Monat, R. S. Lazarus, & G. Reevy (Eds.), *Praeger handbook on stress and coping* (Vol. 2, pp. 327–340). Wastport, CT: Praeger.

Maddi, S. R., & Hightower, M. (1999). Hardiness and optimism as expressed in coping patterns. *Consulting Psychology Journal: Practice and Research, 51,* 95–105.

Maddox, G. L. (1963). Activity and morale: A longitudinal study of selected elderly subjects. *Social Forces, 42,* 195–204.

Madigan, S., Moran, G., & Pederson, D. R. (2006). Unresolved states of mind, disorganized attachment relationships, and disrupted interactions of adolescent mothers and their infants. *Developmental Psychology, 42,* 293–304.

Madnawat, A. V. S., & Kachhawa, P. S. (2007). Age, gender, and living circumstances: Discriminating older adults on death anxiety. *Death Studies, 31,* 763–769.

Madon, S., Jussim, L., & Eccles, J. (1997). In search of the powerful self-fulfilling prophecy. *Journal of Personality and Social Psychology, 72,* 791–809.

Madsen, S. A., & Juhl, T. (2007). Paternal depression in the postnatal period assessed with traditional and male depression scales. *Journal of Men's Health and Gender, 4,* 26–31.

Maglio, C. J., & Robinson, S. E. (1994). The effects of death education on death anxiety: A meta-analysis. *Omega, 29,* 319–335.

Magnusson, D. (1999). Holistic interactionism: A perspective for research on personality development. In L. A. Pervin & O. P. John (Eds.), *Handbook of personality: Theory and research* (2nd ed., pp. 219–247). New York: Guilford.

Magolda, M. B. B. (2002). Epistemological reflection: The evolution of epistemological assumptions from age 18 to 30. In B. K. Hofer & P. R. Pintrich (Eds.), *Personal epistemology* (pp. 89–102). Mahwah, NJ: Erlbaum.

Mahanran, L. G., Bauman, P. A., Kalman, D., Skolnik, H., & Pele, S. M. (1999). Master athletes: Factors affecting performance. *Sports Medicine, 28,* 273–285.

Mahoney, J. L. (2000). Participation in school extracurricular activities as a moderator in the development of antisocial patterns. *Child Development, 71,* 502–516.

Maier, D. M., & Newman, M. J. (1995). Legal and psychological considerations in the development of a euthanasia statute for adults in the United States. *Behavioral Sciences and the Law, 13,* 3–25.

Main, M., & Goldwyn, R. (1998). *Adult attachment classification system.* London: University College.

Main, M., & Solomon, J. (1990). Procedures for identifying infants as disorganized/disoriented during the Ainsworth Strange Situation. In M. Greenberg, D. Cicchetti, & M. Cummings (Eds.), *Attachment in the preschool years: Theory, research, and intervention* (pp. 121–160). Chicago: University of Chicago Press.

Mains, D. S., Nowels, C. T., Cavender, T. A., Etschmaier, M., & Steiner, J. F. (2005). A qualitative study of work and work return in cancer survivors. *Psycho-Oncology, 14,* 992–1004.

Majdandžić, M., & van den Boom, D. C. (2007). Multimethod longitudinal assessment of temperament in early childhood. *Journal of Personality, 75,* 12.

Majnemer, A., & Barr, R. G. (2005). Influence of supine sleep positioning on early motor milestone acquisition. *Developmental Medicine and Child Neurology, 47,* 370–376.

Major, B., Spencer, S., Schmader, T., Wolfe, C., & Crocker, J. (1998). Coping with negative stereotypes about intellectual performance: The role of psychological disengagement. *Personality and Social Psychology Bulletin, 24,* 34–50.

Makin, J., Fried, P. A., & Watkinson, B. (1991). A comparison of active and passive smoking during pregnancy: Long-term effects. *Neurotoxicology and Teratology, 13,* 5–12.

Makishita, H., & Matsunaga, K. (2008). Differences of drivers' reaction times according to age and mental workload. *Accident Analysis Prevention, 40,* 567–575.

Makrantonaki, E., & Xouboulis, C. C. (2007). Molecular mechanisms of skin aging: State of the art. *Annals of the New York Academy of Sciences, 1119,* 40–50.

Malaguarnera, L., Ferlito, L., Imbesi, R. M., Gulizia, G. S., Di Mauro, S., Maugeri, D., Malaguarnera, M., & Messina, A. (2001). Immunosenescence: A review. *Archives of Gerontology and Geriatrics, 32,* 1–14.

Malatesta, C. Z., Grigoryev, P., Lamb, C., Albin, M., & Culver, C. (1986). Emotion socialization and expressive development in preterm and full-term infants. *Child Development, 57,* 316–330.

Malina, R. M., & Bouchard, C. (1991). *Growth, maturation, and physical activity.* Champaign, IL: Human Kinetics.

Malone, M. M. (1982). Consciousness of dying and projective fantasy of young children with malignant disease. *Developmental and Behavioral Pediatrics, 3,* 55–60.

Mandler, J. M. (2004). Thought before language. *Trends in Cognitive Sciences, 8,* 508–513.

Mandler, J. M., & McDonough, L. (1998). On developing a knowledge base in infancy. *Developmental Psychology, 34,* 1274–1288.

Mangelsdorf, S. C., Schoppe, S. J., & Buur, H. (2000). The meaning of parental reports: A contextual approach to the study of temperament and behavior problems. In V. J. Molfese & D. L. Molfese (Eds.), *Temperament and personality across the life span* (pp. 121–140). Mahwah, NJ: Erlbaum.

Mani, T. M., Bedwell, J. S., & Miller, L. S. (2005). Age-related decrements in performance on a brief continuous performance task. *Archives of Clinical Neuropsychology, 20*, 575–586.

Manlove, J. S. (1997). Early motherhood in an intergenerational perspective: The experiences of a British cohort. *Journal of Marriage and the Family, 59*, 263–279.

Manlove, J. S., Terry-Humen, E., Ikramullah, E. N., & Moore, K. A. (2006). The role of parent religiosity in teens' transitions to sex and contraception. *Journal of Adolescent Health, 39*, 578–587.

Mannell, R. C. (1999). Older adults, leisure, and wellness. *Journal of Leisurability, 26*(2), 3–10.

Manole, M. D., & Hickey, R. W. (2006). Preterminal gasping and effects on the cardiac function. *Critical Care Medicine, 34*(Suppl.), S438–S441.

Manton, K. C., Gu, X. L., & Ukraintseva, S. V. (2005). Declining prevalence of dementia in the U.S. elderly population. *Advances in Gerontology, 16*, 30–37.

Maratsos, M. (1998). The acquisition of grammar. In D. Kuhn & R. S. Siegler (Eds.), *Handbook of child psychology: Vol. 2. Cognition, perception, and language* (5th ed., pp. 421–466). New York: Wiley.

Maratsos, M. (2000). More overregularizations after all: New data and discussion on Marcus, Pinker, Ullman, Hollander, Rosen, & Xu. *Journal of Child Language, 27*, 183–212.

Marcia, J. E. (1980). Identity in adolescence. In J. Adelson (Ed.), *Handbook of adolescent psychology* (pp. 159–187). New York: Wiley.

Marcon, R. A. (1999a). Differential impact of preschool models on development and early learning of inner-city children: A three-cohort study. *Developmental Psychology, 35*, 358–375.

Marcon, R. A. (1999b). Positive relationships between parent–school involvement and public school inner-city preschoolers' development and academic performance. *School Psychology Review, 28*, 395–412.

Marcus, G. F. (1995). Children's overregularization of English plurals: A quantitative analysis. *Journal of Child Language, 22*, 447–459.

Marcus-Newhall, A., Thompson, S., & Thomas, C. (2001). Examining a gender stereotype: Menopausal women. *Journal of Applied Social Psychology, 31*, 698–719.

Mariano, K. A., & Harton, H. C. (2005). Similarities in aggression, inattention/hyperactivity, depression, and anxiety in middle childhood friendships. *Journal of Social and Clinical Psychology, 24*, 471–496.

Markman, E. M. (1992). Constraints on word learning: Speculations about their nature, origins, and domain specificity. In M. R. Gunnar & M. P. Maratsos (Eds.), *Minnesota Symposia on Child Psychology* (Vol. 25, pp. 59–101). Hillsdale, NJ: Erlbaum.

Markova, G., & Legerstee, M. (2006). Contingency, imitation, and affect sharing: Foundations of infants' social awareness. *Developmental Psychology, 42*, 132–141.

Markovits, H., Benenson, J., & Dolensky, E. (2001). Evidence that children and adolescents have internal models of peer interactions that are gender differentiated. *Child Development, 72*, 879–886.

Marks, G. N., Cresswell, J., & Ainley, J. (2006). Explaining socioeconomic inequalities in student achievement: The role of home and school factors. *Educational Research and Evaluation, 12*, 105–128.

Marks, N. F. (1996). Caregiving across the lifespan: National prevalence and predictors. *Family Relations, 45*, 27–36.

Marks, N. F., Bumpass, L. L., & Jun, H. (2004). Family roles and well-being during the middle life course. In O. G. Brim, C. D. Ryff, & R.C. Kessler (Eds.), *How healthy are we? A national study of well-being at midlife* (pp. 514–549). Chicago: University of Chicago Press.

Marks, N. F., & Lambert, J. D. (1998). Marital status continuity and change among young and midlife adults. *Journal of Family Issues, 19*, 652–686.

Markstrom, C. A., & Kalmanir, H. M. (2001). Linkages between the psychosocial stages of identity and intimacy and the ego strengths of fidelity and love. *Identity, 1*, 179–196.

Markstrom, C. A., Sabino, V., Turner, B., & Berman, R. (1997). The Psychosocial Inventory of Ego Strengths: Development and validation of a new Eriksonian measure. *Journal of Youth and Adolescence, 26*, 705–732.

Markus, H. R., & Herzog, A. R. (1992). The role of self-concept in aging. In K. W. Schaie & M. P. Lawton (Eds.), *Annual review of gerontology and geriatrics* (pp. 110–143). New York: Springer.

Marlier, L., & Schaal, B. (2005). Human newborns prefer human milk: Conspecific milk odor is attractive without postnatal exposure. *Child Development, 76*, 155–168.

Marra, R., & Palmer, B. (2004). Encouraging intellectual growth: Senior college student profiles. *Journal of Adult Development, 11*, 111–122.

Marsh, H. W. (1990). The structure of academic self-concept: The Marsh/Shavelson model. *Journal of Educational Psychology, 82*, 623–636.

Marsh, H. W., & Ayotte, V. (2003). Do multiple dimensions of self-concept become more differentiated with age? The differential distinctiveness hypothesis. *Journal of Educational Psychology, 95*, 687–706.

Marsh, H. W., Craven, R., & Debus, R. (1998). Structure, stability, and development of young children's self-concepts: A multicohort–multioccasion study. *Child Development, 69*, 1030–1053.

Marsh, H. W., Ellis, L. A., & Craven, R. G. (2002). How do preschool children feel about themselves? Unraveling measurement and multidimensional self-concept structure. *Developmental Psychology, 38*, 376–393.

Marsh, H. W., Gerlach, E., Trautwein, U., Lüdtke, O., & Brettschneider, W.-D. (2007). Longitudinal study of preadolescent sport self-concept and performance: Reciprocal effects and causal ordering. *Child Development, 78*, 1640–1656.

Marshall-Baker, A., Lickliter, R. & Cooper, R. P. (1998). Prolonged exposure to a visual pattern may promote behavioral organization in preterm infants. *Journal of Perinatal and Neonatal Nursing, 12*, 50–62.

Martin, C. L., & Fabes, R. A. (2001). The stability and consequences of young children's same-sex peer interactions. *Developmental Psychology, 37*, 431–446.

Martin, C. L., & Halverson, C. F. (1987). The role of cognition in sex role acquisition. In D. B. Carter (Ed.), *Current conceptions of sex roles and sex typing: Theory and research* (pp. 123–137). New York: Praeger.

Martin, C. L., & Ruble, D. (2004). Children's search for gender cues: Cognitive perspectives on gender development. *Current Directions in Psychological Science, 13*, 67–70.

Martin, C. L., Ruble, D. N., & Szkrybalo, J. (2002). Cognitive theories of early gender development. *Psychological Bulletin, 128*, 903–933.

Martin, G. L., & Pear, J. (2007). *Behavior modification: What it is and how to do it* (8th ed.). Upper Saddle River, NJ: Prentice-Hall.

Martin, K. A. (1996). *Puberty, sexuality and the self: Girls and boys at adolescence.* New York: Routledge.

Martin, P., Long, M. V., & Poon, L. W. (2002). Age changes and differences in personality traits and states of the old and very old. *Journal of Gerontology, 57B*, P144–P152.

Martínez-Frías, M. L., Bermejo, E., Rodríguez-Pinilla, E., & Frías, J. L. (2004). Risk for congenital anomalies associated with different sporadic and daily doses of alcohol consumption during pregnancy: A case-control study. *Birth Defects Research, Part A, Clinical and Molecular Teratology, 70*, 194–200.

Martins, P. A., Hoffman, D. J., Fernandes, M. T., Nascimento, C. R., Roberts, S. B., Sesso, R., & Sawaya, A. L. (2004). Stunted children gain less lean body mass and more fat mass than their non-stunted counterparts: A prospective study. *British Journal of Nutrition, 92*, 819–825.

Martinson, I. M., Davies, E., & McClowry, S. G. (1987). The long-term effect of sibling death on self-concept. *Journal of Pediatric Nursing, 2*, 227–235.

Marzolf, D. P., & DeLoache, J. S. (1994). Transfer in young children's understanding of spatial representations. *Child Development, 65*, 1–15.

Masataka, N. (1996). Perception of motherese in a signed language by 6-month-old deaf infants. *Developmental Psychology, 32*, 874–879.

Mascolo, M. F., & Fischer, K. W. (2007). The codevelopment of self and sociomoral emotions during the toddler years. In C. A. Brownell & C. B. Kopp (Eds.), *Socioemotional development in the toddler years: Transitions and transformations* (pp. 66–99). New York: Guilford.

Mashburn, A. J. (2008). Quality of social and physical environments in preschools and children's development of academic, language, and literacy skills. *Applied Developmental Science, 12*, 113–127.

Maslach, C., Schaufeli, W. B., & Leiter, M. P. (2001). Job burnout. *Annual Review of Psychology, 52*, 397–422.

Mason, M. G., & Gibbs, J. C. (1993a). Role-taking opportunities and the transition to advanced moral judgment. *Moral Education Forum, 18*, 1–12.

Mason, M. G., & Gibbs, J. C. (1993b). Social perspective taking and moral judgment among college students. *Journal of Adolescent Research, 8*, 109–123.

Masten, A. S. (2001). Ordinary magic: Resilience processes in development. *American Psychologist, 56*, 227–238.

Masten, A. S., Coatsworth, J. D., Neemann, J., Gest, S. D., Tellegen, A., & Garmezy, N. (1995). The structure and coherence of competence from childhood through adolescence. *Child Development, 66*, 1635–1659.

Masten, A. S., & Gewirtz, A. H. (2006). Vulnerability and resilience in early child development. In K. McCartney & D. Phillips (Eds.), *Blackwell handbook of early childhood development* (pp. 22–43). Malden, MA: Blackwell.

Masten, A. S., & Powell, J. L. (2003). A resilience framework for research, policy, and practice. In S. S. Luthar (Ed.), *Resilience and vulnerability* (pp. 1–25). New York: Cambridge University Press.

Masten, A. S., & Reed, M. J. (2002). Resilience in development. In C. R. Snyder & S. J. Lopez (Eds.), *Handbook of positive psychology* (pp. 74–88). New York: Oxford University Press.

Masten, A. S., & Shaffer, A. (2006). How families matter in child development: Reflections from research on risk and resilience. In A. S. Masten & A. Shaffer (Eds.), *Families count: Effects on child and adolescent development* (pp. 5–25). New York: Cambridge University Press.

Mastropieri, D., & Turkewitz, G. (1999). Prenatal experience and neonatal responsiveness to vocal expression of emotion. *Developmental Psychobiology, 35*, 204–214.

Masur, E. F., & Rodemaker, J. E. (1999). Mothers' and infants' spontaneous vocal, verbal, and action imitation during the second year. *Merrill-Palmer Quarterly, 45*, 392–412.

Mathews, T. J., & MacDorman, M. F. (2008). Infant mortality statistics from the 2005 period linked birth/infant death data set. *National Vital Statistics Reports, 57*(2), 1–32.

Mathiesen, K. S., & Prior, M. (2006). The impact of temperament factors and family functioning on resilience processes from infancy to school age. *European Journal of Developmental Psychology, 3*, 357–387.

Matthews, F., & Brayne, C. (2005). The incidence of dementia in England and Wales: Findings from the five identical sites of the MRC CFA Study. *PLoS Medicine, 2,* e193

Matthews, K. A., Gump, B. B., Harris, K. F., Haney, T. L., & Barefoot, J. C. (2004). Hostile behaviors predict cardiovascular mortality among men enrolled in the Multiple Risk Factor Intervention Trial. *Circulation, 109,* 66–70.

Mattson, S. N., Calarco, K. E., & Lang, A. R. (2006). Focused and shifting attention in children with heavy prenatal alcohol exposure. *Neuropsychology, 20,* 361–369.

Maume, D. J., Jr. (2004). Is the glass ceiling a unique form of inequality? *Work and Occupations, 31,* 250–274.

Maurer, T. J. (2001). Career-relevant learning and development, worker age, and beliefs about self-efficacy for development. *Journal of Management, 27,* 123–140.

Maurer, T. J. (2007). Employee development and training issues related to the aging workforce. In K. S. Shultz & G. A. Adams (Eds.), *Aging and work in the 21st century* (pp. 163–178). Mahwah, NJ: Erlbaum.

Maurer, T. J., Wrenn, K. A., & Weiss, E. M. (2003). Toward understanding and managing stereotypical beliefs about older workers' ability and desire for learning and development. In J. J. Martocchio & G. R. Ferris (Eds.), *Research in personnel and human resources management* (Vol. 22, pp. 253–285). Stamford, CT: JAI Press.

Mayberry, R. I. (1994). The importance of childhood to language acquisition: Evidence from American Sign Language. In J. C. Goodman & H. C. Nusbaum (Eds.), *The development of speech perception: The transition from speech sounds to spoken words* (pp. 57–90). Cambridge, MA: MIT Press.

Mayes, L. C. (1999). Reconsidering the concept of vulnerability in children using the model of prenatal cocaine exposure. In T. B. Cohen & E. M. Hossein (Eds.), *The vulnerable child* (Vol. 3, pp. 35–54). Madison, CT: International Universities Press.

Mayeux, L., & Cillessen, A. H. N. (2003). Development of social problem solving in early childhood: Stability, change, and associations with social competence. *Journal of Genetic Psychology, 164,* 153–173.

Maynard, A. E. (2002). Cultural teaching: The development of teaching skills in Maya sibling interactions. *Child Development, 73,* 969–982.

Maynard, A. E., & Greenfield, P. M. (2003). Implicit cognitive development in cultural tools and children: Lessons from Maya Mexico. *Cognitive Development, 18,* 489–510.

Maynard, A. E., Subrahmanyam, K., & Greenfield, P. M. (2005). Technology and the development of intelligence: From the loom to the computer. In R. J. Sternberg & D. D. Preiss (Eds.), *Intelligence and technology: The impact of tools in the nature and development of human abilities* (pp. 29–53). Mahwah, NJ: Erlbaum.

Maynard, C. K. (2003). Differentiate depression from dementia. *Nurse Practitioner, 28*(3), 27–29.

Mayseless, O., & Sharf, M. (2003). What does it mean to be an adult? The Israeli experience. *New Directions for Child and Adolescent Development, 100,* 33–49.

Mazzarella, S. R. (2007). Cyberdating success stories and the mythic narrative of living "happily-ever-after with the one." In M.-L. Galician & D. L. Merskin (Eds.), *Critical thinking about sex, love, and romance in the mass media* (pp. 23–37). Mahwah, NJ: Erlbaum.

McAdams, D. P. (2006). The redemptive self: Generativity and the stories Americans live by. *Research in Human Development, 3,* 81–100.

McAdams, D. P. (2008). Generativity, the redemptive self, and the problem of a noisy ego in American life. In H. A. Wayment & J. J. Bauer (Eds.), *Transcending self-interest: Psychological explorations of the quiet ego* (pp. 235–242). Washington, DC: American Psychological Association.

McAdams, D. P., & de St. Aubin, E. (1992). A theory of generativity and its assessment through self-report, behavioral acts, and narrative themes in autobiography. *Journal of Personality and Social Psychology, 62,* 1003–1015.

McAdams, D. P., Hart, H. M., & Maruna, S. (1998). The anatomy of generativity. In D. P. McAdams & E. de St. Aubin (Eds.), *Generativity and adult development* (pp. 7–43). Washington, DC: American Psychological Association.

McAdams, D. P., & Logan, R. L. (2004). What is generativity? In E. de St. Aubin & D. P. McAdams (Eds.), *The generative society: Caring for future generations* (pp. 15–31). Washington, DC: American Psychological Association.

McAlister, A., & Peterson, C. C. (2006). Mental playmates: Siblings, executive functioning and theory of mind. *British Journal of Developmental Psychology, 24,* 733–751.

McAlister, A., & Peterson, C. C. (2007). A longitudinal study of child siblings and theory of mind development. *Cognitive Development, 22,* 258–270.

McAuley, E., & Elavsky, S. (2008). Self-efficacy, physical activity, and cognitive function. In W. W. Spirduso, L. W. Poon, & W. Chodzko-Zajko (Eds.). *Exercise and its mediating effects on cognition* (pp. 69–84). Champaign, IL: Human Kinetics.

McAuley, E., Mihalko, S. L., & Bane, S. M. (1997). Exercise and self-esteem in middle-aged adults: Multidimensional relationships and physical fitness and self-efficacy influences. *Journal of Behavioral Medicine, 20,* 67–83.

McBee, M. T. (2006). A descriptive analysis of referral sources for gifted identification screening by race and socioeconomic status. *Journal of Secondary Gifted Education, 17,* 103–111.

McBride-Chang, C., & Kail, R. V. (2002). Cross-cultural similarities in the predictors of reading acquisition. *Child Development, 73,* 1392–1407.

McCabe, A. (1997). Developmental and cross-cultural aspects of children's narration. In M. Bamberg (Ed.), *Narrative development: Six approaches* (pp. 137–174). Mahwah, NJ: Erlbaum.

McCall, R. B., & Carriger, M. S. (1993). A meta-analysis of infant habituation and recognition memory performance as predictors of later IQ. *Child Development, 64,* 57–79.

McCartney, K., Dearing, E.,Taylor, B., & Bub, K. (2007). Quality child care supports the achievement of low-income children: Direct and indirect pathways through caregiving and the home environment. *Journal of Applied Developmental Psychology, 28,* 411–426.

McCartney, K., Harris, M. J., & Bernieri, F. (1990). Growing up and growing apart: A developmental meta-analysis of twin studies. *Psychological Bulletin, 107,* 226–237.

McCartney, K., Owen, M., Booth, C., Clarke-Stewart, A., & Vandell, D. (2004). Testing a maternal attachment model of behavior problems in early childhood. *Journal of Child Psychology and Psychiatry, 45,* 765–778.

McCarton, C. (1998). Behavioral outcomes in low birth weight infants. *Pediatrics, 102,* 1293–1297.

McCarty, M. E., & Ashmead, D. H. (1999). Visual control of reaching and grasping in infants. *Developmental Psychology, 35,* 620–631.

McCarty, M. E., & Keen, R. (2005). Facilitating problem-solving performance among 9- and 12-month-old infants. *Journal of Cognition and Development, 6,* 209–228.

McClearn, G. E., Johansson, B., Berg, S., & Pedersen, N. L. (1997). Substantial genetic influence on cognitive abilities in twins 80 or more years old. *Science, 276,* 1560–1563.

McColgan, K. L., & McCormack, T. (2008). Searching and planning: Young children's reasoning about past and future event sequences. *Child Development, 79,* 1477–1479.

McCrae, R., & Costa, P. T., Jr. (2006). Cross-cultural perspectives on adult personality trait develop-ment. In D. K. Mroczek & T. D. Little (Eds.), *Handbook of personality development* (pp. 129–146). Mahwah, NJ: Erlbaum.

McCune, L. (1993). The development of play as the development of consciousness. In M. H. Bornstein & A. O'Reilly (Eds.), *New directions for child development* (No. 59, pp. 67–79). San Francisco: Jossey-Bass.

McCurry, S. M., Logsdon, R. G., Teri, L., & Vitello, M. V. (2007). Evidence-based psychological treatments for insomnia in older adults. *Psychology and Aging, 22,* 18–27,

McDaniel, J., Purcell, D., & D'Augelli, A. R. (2001). The relationship between sexual orientation and risk for suicide: Research findings and future directions for research and prevention. *Suicide and Life-Threatening Behavior, 31,* 84–105.

McDaniel, M. A., Einstein, G. O., & Rendell, P. G. (2007). The puzzle of inconsistent age-related declines in prospective memory: A multiprocess explanation. In M. Kliegel, M. A. McDaniel, & G. O. Einstein (Eds.), *Prospective memory: Cognitive, neuroscience, developmental, and applied perspectives* (pp. 141–160). Mahwah, NJ: Erlbaum.

McDill, T., Hall, S. K., & Turell, S. C. (2006). Aging and creating families: Never-married heterosexual women over forty. *Journal of Women and Aging, 18,* 37–50.

McDonagh, M. S., Osterweil, P., & Guise, J. M. (2005). The benefits and risks of inducing labour in patients with prior cesarean delivery: A systematic review. *BJOG, 112,* 1007–1015.

McDonald, L., & Robb, A. L. (2004). The economic legacy of divorce and separation for women in old age. *Canadian Journal on Aging, 23*(Suppl. 1), S83–S97.

McDonald, S. W. S., Hultsch, D. F., & Dixon, R. A. (2003). Performance variability is related to change in cognition: Evidence from the Victoria Longitudinal Study. *Psychology and Aging, 18,* 510–523.

McDonough, L. (1999). Early declarative memory for location. *British Journal of Developmental Psychology, 17,* 381–402.

McElhaney, K. B., & Allen, J. P. (2001). Autonomy and adolescent social functioning: The moderating effect of risk. *Child Development, 72,* 220–235.

McElwain, N. L., & Booth-LaForce, C. (2006). Maternal sensitivity to infant distress and nondistress as predictors of infant–mother attachment security. *Journal of Family Psychology, 20,* 247–255.

McEwen, B. S. (2007). Physiology and neurobiology of stress an adaptation: Central role of the brain. *Physiological Reviews, 87,* 873–904.

McFadden, S. H. (1996). Religion, spirituality, and aging. In J. E. Birren & K. W. Schaie (Eds.), *Handbook of the psychology of aging* (pp. 182–177). San Diego: Academic Press.

McFarlane, J., Malecha, A., Watson, K., Gist, J., Batten, E., Hall, I., & Smith, S. (2005). Intimate partner assault against women: Frequency, health consequences, and treatment outcomes. *Obstetrics and Gynecology, 105,* 99–108.

McGee, G. (1997). Legislating gestation. *Human Reproduction, 12,* 407–408.

McGee, L. M., & Richgels, D. J. (2008). *Literacy's beginnings: Supporting young readers and writers* (5th ed.). Boston: Allyn and Bacon.

McGoldrick, M. (2004). Echoes from the past: Helping families deal with their ghosts. In F. Walsh & M. McGoldrick (Eds.), *Living beyond loss* (pp. 99–118). New York: Norton.

McGoldrick, M., Schlesinger, J. M., Lee, E., Hines, P. M., Chan, J., & Almeida, R. (2004). Mourning in different cultures. In F. Walsh & M. McGoldrick (Eds.), *Living beyond loss* (pp. 119–160). New York: Norton.

McGue, M., & Christensen, K. (2002). The heritability of level and rate-of-change in cognitive functioning in Danish twins aged 70 years and older. *Experimental Aging Research, 28,* 435–451.

McHale, J. P., Kazali, C., Rotman, T., Talbot, J., Carleton, M., & Lieberson, R. (2004). The transition to coparenthood: Parents' prebirth expectations and early coparental adjustment at 3 months postpartum. *Development and Psychopathology, 16,* 711–733.

McHale, J. P., Khazan, I., Erera, P., Rotman, T., DeCourcey, W., & McConnell, M. (2002a). Coparenting in diverse family systems. In M. H. Bornstein (Ed.), *Handbook of parenting: Vol. 3* (2nd ed., pp. 75–107). Mahwah, NJ: Erlbaum.

McHale, J. P., Kuersten-Hogan, R., & Rao, N. (2004). Growing points for coparenting theory and research. *Journal of Adult Development, 11,* 221–234.

McHale, J. P., Lauretti, A., Talbot, J., & Pouquette, C. (2002b). Retrospect and prospect in the psychological study of coparenting and family group process. In J. P. McHale & W. S. Grolnick (Eds.), *Retrospect and prospect in the psychological study of families* (pp. 127–165). Mahwah, NJ: Erlbaum.

McHale, J. P., & Rotman, T. (2007). Is seeing believing? Expectant parents' outlooks on coparenting and later coparenting solidarity. *Infant Behavior and Development, 30,* 63–81.

McHale, J. P., Vinden, P. G., Bush, L., Richer, D., Shaw, D., & Smith, B. (2005). Patterns of personal and social adjustment among sport-involved and non-involved urban middle-school children. *Sociology of Sport Journal, 22,* 119–136.

McHale, S. M., Crouter, A. C., Kim, J.-Y., Burton, L. M., Davis, K. D., Dotterer, A. M., & Swanson, D. P. (2006). Mothers' and fathers' racial socialization in African-American families: Implications for youth. *Child Development, 77,* 1387–1402.

McIntosh, H., Metz, E., & Youniss, J. (2005). Community service and identity formation in adolescents. In J. S. Mahoney, R. W. Larson, & J. S. Eccles (Eds.), *Organized activities as contexts of development: Extracurricular activities, after-school and community programs* (pp. 331–351). Mahwah, NJ: Erlbaum.

McKenna, J. J. (2001). Why we never ask "Is it safe for infants to sleep alone?" *Academy of Breast Feeding Medicine News and Views, 7*(4), 32, 38.

McKenna, J. J. (2002, September/October). Breastfeeding and bedsharing still useful (and important) after all these years. *Mothering, 114.* Retrieved from www.mothering.com/articles/new_baby/sleep/mckenna.html

McKenna, J. J., & McDade, T. (2005). Why babies should never sleep alone: A review of the co-sleeping controversy in relation to SIDS, bed-sharing, and breastfeeding. *Paediatric Respiratory Reviews, 6,* 134–152.

McKenna, J. J., & Volpe, L. E. (2007). Sleeping with baby: An Internet-based sampling of parental experiences, choices, perceptions, and interpretations in a Western industrialized context. *Infant and Child Development, 16,* 359–385.

McKim, W. A. (2002). *Drugs and behavior* (5th ed.). Upper Saddle River, NJ: Prentice-Hall.

McKinney, C., Donnelly, R., & Renk, K. (2008). Perceived parenting, positive and negative perceptions of parents, and late adolescent emotional adjustment. *Child and Adolescent Mental Health, 13,* 66–73.

McKown, C., & Weinstein, R. S. (2002). Modeling the role of child ethnicity and gender in children's differential response to teacher expectations. *Journal of Applied Social Psychology, 32,* 159–184.

McKown, C., & Weinstein, R. S. (2003). The development and consequences of stereotype consciousness in middle childhood. *Child Development, 74,* 498–515.

McKusick, V. A. (2007). *Online Mendelian inheritance in man.* Retrieved from www.ncbi.nlm.nih.gov/sites/entrez?db=omim

McLanahan, S. (1999). Father absence and the welfare of children. In E. M. Hetherington (Ed.), *Coping with divorce, single parenting, and remarriage: A risk and resiliency perspective* (pp. 117–145). Mahwah, NJ: Erlbaum.

McLean, K. C. (2008). Stories of the young and the old: Personal continuity and narrative identity. *Developmental Psychology, 44,* 254–264.

McLoyd, V. C., Aikens, N. L., & Burton, L. M. (2006). Child poverty, policy, and practice. In K. A. Renninger & I. E. Sigel (Eds.), *Handbook of child psychology: Vol. 4. Child psychology in practice* (6th ed., pp. 700–778). Hoboken, NJ: Wiley.

McLoyd, V. C., Kaplan, R., Hardaway, C. R., & Wood, D. (2007). Does endorsement of physical discipline matter? Assessing moderating influences on the maternal and child psychological correlates of physical discipline in African-American families. *Journal of Family Psychology, 21,* 165–175.

McMahon, C. A., Barnett, B., Kowalenko, N. M., & Tennant, C. C. (2006). Maternal attachment state of mind moderates the impact of postnatal depression on infant attachment. *Journal of Child Psychology and Psychiatry, 47,* 660–669.

MCR Vitamin Study Research Group. (1991). Prevention of neural tube defects: Results of the Medical Research Council Vitamin Study. *Lancet, 338,* 131–137.

Mead, M. (1928). *Coming of age in Samoa.* Ann Arbor, MI: Morrow

Medina, J., & Puntillo, K. A. (2006). *Palliative care and end-of-life issues in critical care.* New York: Jones & Bartlett.

Meegan, S. P., & Berg, C. A. (2002). Contexts, functions, forms, and processes of collaborative everyday problem solving in older adulthood. *International Journal of Behavioral Development, 26,* 6–15.

Meek, J. (2002). Basic principles of optical imaging and application to the study of infant development. *Developmental Science, 5,* 371–380.

Meeus, W. (1996). Studies on identity development in adolescence: An overview of research and some new data. *Journal of Youth and Adolescence, 25,* 569–598.

Meeus, W., Oosterwegel, A., & Vollebergh, W. (2002). Parental and peer attachment and identity development in adolescence. *Journal of Adolescence, 25,* 93–106.

Meeus, W. H. J., Branje, S. J. T., van der Valk, I., & de Wied, M. (2007). Relationships with intimate partner, best friend, and parents in adolescence and early adulthood: A study of the saliency of the intimate partnership. *International Journal of Behavioral Development, 31,* 569–580.

Mehlmadrona, L., & Madrona, M. M. (1997). Physician- and midwife-attended home births—effects of breech, twin, and post-dates outcome data on mortality rates. *Journal of Nurse-Midwifery, 42,* 91–98.

Mehlson, M., Platz, M., & Fromholt, P. (2003). Life satisfaction across the life course: Evaluations of the most and least satisfying decades of life. *International Journal of Aging and Human Development, 57,* 217–236.

Meins, E., Fernyhough, C., Russell, J., & Clark-Carter, D. (1998). Security of attachment as a predictor of symbolic and mentalizing abilities: A longitudinal study. *Social Development, 7,* 1–24.

Meins, E., Fernyhough, C., Wainwright, R., Clark-Carter, D., Gupta, M. D., Fradley, E., & Tucker, M. (2003). Pathways to understanding mind: Construct validity and predictive validity of maternal mind-mindedness. *Child Development, 74,* 1194–1211.

Melby, M. K., Lock, M., & Kaufert, P. (2005). Culture and symptom reporting at menopause. *Human Reproduction Update, 11,* 495–512.

Meltzoff, A. N. (1995). Understanding the intentions of others: Re-enactment of intended acts by 18-month-old children. *Developmental Psychology, 31,* 838–850.

Meltzoff, A. N. (2007). 'Like me': A foundation for social cognition. *Developmental Science, 10,* 126–134.

Meltzoff, A. N., & Kuhl, P. K. (1994). Faces and speech: Intermodal processing of biologically relevant signals in infants and adults. In D. J. Lewkowicz & R. Lickliter (Eds.), *The development of intersensory perception* (pp. 335–369). Hillsdale, NJ: Erlbaum.

Meltzoff, A. N., & Moore, M. K. (1977). Imitation of facial and manual gestures by human neonates. *Science, 198,* 75–78.

Meltzoff, A. N., & Moore, M. K. (1994). Imitation, memory, and the representation of persons. *Infant Behavior and Development, 17,* 83–99.

Meltzoff, A. N., & Moore, M. K. (1999). Persons and representations: Why infant imitation is important for theories of human development. In J. Nadel & G. Butterworth (Eds.), *Imitation in infancy* (pp. 9–35). Cambridge, UK: Cambridge University Press.

Melzi, G., & Ely, R. (2009). Language development in the school years. In J. B. Gleason & N. B. Ratner (Eds.), *The development of language* (7th ed., pp. 391–435). Boston: Allyn and Bacon.

Mendle, J., Turkheimer, E., & Emery, R. E. (2007). Detrimental psychological outcomes associated with early pubertal timing in adolescent girls. *Developmental Review, 27,* 151–171.

Meneilly, G. S. (2006). Diabetes in the elderly. *Medical Clinics of North America, 90,* 909–923.

Mennella, J. A., & Beauchamp, G. K. (1998). Early flavor experiences: Research update. *Nutrition Reviews, 56,* 205–211.

Menon, U. (2001). Middle adulthood in cultural perspective: The imagined and the experienced in three cultures. In M. E. Lachman (Ed.), *Handbook of midlife development* (pp. 40–74). New York: Wiley.

Ment, L. R., Vohr, B., Allan, W., Katz, K. H., Schneider, K. C., Westerveld, M., Duncan, C. C., & Makuch, R. W. (2003). Change in cognitive function over time in very low-birth-weight infants. *Journal of the American Medical Association, 289,* 705–711.

Mercer, C. H., Bailey, J. V., Johnson, A. M., Erens, B., Wellings, K., Fenton, K., & Copas, A. J. (2007). Women who report having sex with women: British national probability data on prevalence, sexual behaviors, and health outcomes. *Research and Practice, 97,* 1126–1133.

Mergenhagen, P. (1996). Her own boss. *American Demographics, 18,* 36–41.

Merrill, D. M. (1997). *Caring for elderly parents.* Westport, CT: Auburn House.

Mervis, C. B., Pani, J. R., & Pani, A. M. (2003). Transaction of child cognitive-linguistic abilities and adult input in the acquisition of lexical categories at the basic and subordinate levels. In D. H. Rakison & L. M. Oakes (Eds.), *Early category and concept development* (pp. 242–274). New York: Oxford University Press.

Messman, S. J., Canary, D. J., & Hause, K. S. (2000). Motives to remain platonic, equity, and the use of maintenance strategies in opposite-sex friendships. *Journal of Social and Personal Relationships, 17,* 67–94.

Metcalf, B. S., Voss, L. D., Hosking, J., Jeffery, A. N., & Wilkin, T. J. (2008). Physical activity at the government-recommended level and obesity-related health outcomes: A longitudinal study. *Archives of Disease in Childhood, 93,* 772–777.

Meyer, B. J. F., Russo, C., & Talbot, A. (1995). Discourse comprehension and problem solving: Decisions about the treatment of breast cancer by women across the lifespan. *Psychology and Aging, 10,* 84–103.

Meyer, B. J. F., Talbot, A. P., & Ranalli, C. (2007). Why older adults make more immediate treatment decisions about cancer than younger adults. *Psychology and Aging, 22,* 505–524.

Meyer, I. H. (2003). Prejudice, social stress, and mental health in lesbian, gay, and bisexual populations:

Conceptual issues and research evidence. *Psychological Bulletin, 129,* 674–697.

Meyer-Bahlburg, H. F. L., Ehrhardt, A. A., Rosen, L. R., Gruen, R. S., Veridiano, N. P., Vann, F. H., & Neuwalder, H. F. (1995). Prenatal estrogens and the development of homosexual orientation. *Developmental Psychology, 31,* 12–21.

Meyers, C., Adam, R., Dungan, J., & Prenger, V. (1997). Aneuploidy in twin gestations: When is maternal age advanced? *Obstetrics and Gynecology, 89,* 248–251.

Mezulis, A. H., Hyde, J. S., & Clark, R. (2004). Father involvement moderates the effect of maternal depression during a child's infancy on child behavior problems in kindergarten. *Journal of Family Psychology, 18,* 575–588.

Miceli, P. J., Whitman, T. L., Borkowski, J. G., Braungart-Riekder, J., & Mitchell, D. W. (1998). Individual differences in infant information processing: The role of temperamental and maternal factors. *Infant Behavior and Development, 21,* 119–136.

Michael, R. T., Gagnon, J. H., Laumann, E. O., & Kolata, G. (1994). *Sex in America.* Boston: Little, Brown.

Michaels, G. Y. (1988). Motivational factors in the decision and timing of pregnancy. In G. Y. Michaels & W. A. Goldberg (Eds.), *The transition to parenthood: Current theory and research* (pp. 23–61). New York: Cambridge University Press.

Michalik, N. M., Eisenberg, N., Spinrad, T. L., Ladd, B., Thompson, M., & Valiente, C. (2007). Longitudinal relations among parental emotional expressivity and sympathy and prosocial behavior in adolescence. *Social Development, 16,* 286–309.

Mikulincer, M., Florian, V., & Hirschberger, G. (2003). The existential function of close relationships: Introducing death into the science of love. *Personality and Social Psychology Review, 7,* 20–40.

Milberger, S., Biederman, J., Faraone, S. V., Guite, J., & Tsuang, M. T. (1997). Pregnancy, delivery and infancy complications and attention deficit hyperactivity disorder: Issues of gene–environment interaction. *Biological Psychiatry, 41,* 65–75.

Milbury, P. E., & Richer, A. C. (2008). *Understanding the antioxidant controversy.* Westport, CT: Praeger.

Milevsky, A., Schlechter, M., Netter, S., & Keehn, D. (2007). Maternal and paternal parenting styles in adolescents: Associations with self-esteem, depression, and life satisfaction. *Journal of Child and Family Studies, 16,* 39–47.

Milkie, M. A., Bierman, A., & Schieman, S. (2008). How adult children influence older parents' mental health: Integrating stress-process and life-course perspectives. *Social Psychology Quarterly, 71,* 86–105.

Miller, J., Slomczynski, K. M., & Kohn, M. L. (1985). Continuity of learning-generalization: The effect of job on men's intellective process in the United States and Poland. *American Journal of Sociology, 91,* 593–615.

Miller, J. G. (2006). Insights into moral development from cultural psychology. In M. Killen & J. Smetana (Eds.), *Handbook of moral development* (pp. 375–398). Philadelphia: Erlbaum.

Miller, J. G., & Bersoff, D. M. (1995). Development in the context of everyday family relationships: Culture, interpersonal morality, and adaptation. In M. Killen & D. Hart (Eds.), *Morality in everyday life: Developmental perspectives* (pp. 259–282). Cambridge: Cambridge University Press.

Miller, K. S., Forehand, R., & Kotchick, B. (1999). Adolescent sexual behavior in two ethnic minority samples: The role of family variables. *Journal of Marriage and the Family, 61,* 85–98.

Miller, L. T., & Vernon, P. A. (1992). The general factor in short-term memory, intelligence, and reaction time. *Intelligence, 16,* 5–29.

Miller, P. H. (2001). *Theories of developmental psychology* (4th ed.). New York: Worth.

Miller, P. H., & Bigi, L. (1979). The development of children's understanding of attention. *Merrill-Palmer Quarterly, 25,* 235–250.

Miller, P. J., Hengst, J. A., & Wang, S. (2003). Ethnographic methods: Applications from developmental cultural psychology. In P. M. Carnic & J. E. Rhodes (Eds.), *Qualitative research in psychology* (pp. 219–242). Washington, DC: American Psychological Association.

Miller, P. J., Wang, S., Sandel, T., & Cho, G. E. (2002). Self-esteem as folk theory: A comparison of European American and Taiwanese mothers' beliefs. *Parenting: Science and Practice, 2,* 209–239.

Miller, P. J., Wiley, A. R., Fung, H., & Liang, C. H. (1997). Personal storytelling as a medium of socialization in Chinese and American families. *Child Development, 68,* 557–568.

Miller, R. B. (2000). Do children make a marriage unhappy? *Family Science Review, 13,* 60–73.

Miller, R. B., Hemesath, K., & Nelson, B. (1997). Marriage in middle and later life. In T. D. Hargrave & S. M. Hanna (Eds.), *The aging family* (pp. 178–198). New York: Brunner/Mazel.

Miller, S. A., Hardin, C. A., & Montgomery, D. E. (2003). Young children's understanding of the conditions for knowledge acquisition. *Journal of Cognition and Development, 4,* 325–356.

Miller, S. C., Mor, V., Wu, N., Gozalo, P., & Papane, K. (2002). Does receipt of hospice care in nursing homes improve the management of pain at the end of life? *Journal of the American Geriatrics Society, 50,* 507–515.

Miller, S. S., & Cavanaugh, J. C. (1990). The meaning of grandparenthood and its relationship to demographic, relationship, and social participation variables. *Journal of Gerontology, 45,* P244–P246.

Milligan, K., Astington, J. W., & Dack, L. A. (2007). Language and theory of mind: Meta-analysis of the relation between language ability and false-belief understanding. *Child Development, 78,* 622–646.

Mills, D., Plunkett, K., Prat, C., & Schafer, G. (2005). Watching the infant brain learn words: Effects of language and experience. *Cognitive Development, 20,* 19–31.

Mills, R. S. L. (2005). Taking stock of the developmental literature on shame. *Developmental Review, 25,* 26–63.

Mills, R., & Grusec, J. (1989). Cognitive, affective, and behavioral consequences of praising altruism. *Merrill-Palmer Quarterly, 35,* 299–326.

Mills, T. L., Gomez-Smith, Z., & De Leon, J. M. (2005). Skipped generation families: Sources of psychological distress among grandmothers of grandchildren who live in homes where neither parent is present. *Marriage and Family Review, 37,* 191–212.

Miner-Rubino, K., Winter, D. G., & Stewart, A. J. (2004). Gender, social class, and the subjective experience of aging: Self-perceived personality change from early adulthood to late midlife. *Personality and Social Psychology Bulletin, 30,* 1599–1610.

Minkler, M., & Fuller-Thomson, E. (2005). African American grandparents raising grandchildren: A national study using the Census 2000 American Community Survey. *Journal of Gerontology, 60B,* S82–S92.

Mintzer, J. E. (2001). Underlying mechanisms of psychosis and aggression in patients with Alzheimer's disease. *Journal of Clinical Psychiatry, 62*(Suppl. 21), 23–25.

Misailidi, P. (2006). Young children's display rule knowledge: Understanding the distinction between apparent and real emotions and the motives underlying the use of display rules. *Social Behavior and Personality, 34,* 1285–1296.

Mishra, G., & Kuh, D. (2006). Perceived change in quality of life during the menopause. *Social Science and Medicine, 62,* 93–102.

Mitchell, B. D., Hsueh, W. C., King, T. M., Pollin, T. I., Sorkin, J., Agarwala, R., Schäffer, A. A., &

Shuldiner, A. R. (2001). Heritability of life span in the Old Order Amish. *American Journal of Medical Genetics, 102,* 346–352.

Mitchell, V., & Helson, R. (1990). Women's prime of life. *Psychology of Women Quarterly, 14,* 451–470.

Miura, I. T., & Okamoto, Y. (2003). Language supports for mathematics understanding and performance. In A. J. Baroody & A. Dowker (Eds.), *The development of arithmetic concepts and skills* (pp. 229–242). Mahwah, NJ: Erlbaum.

Mizushima, S., & Yapori, Y. (1992). Nutritional improvement, cardiovascular diseases and longevity in Japan. *Nutrition and Health, 8,* 97–105.

Moen, P. (2003). *It's about time: Couples and careers.* Ithaca, NY: Cornell University Press.

Moen, P., & Altobelli, J. (2007). Strategic selection as a retirement project: Will Americans develop hybrid arrangements? In J. B. James & P. Wink (Eds.), *Annual review of gerontology and geriatrics* (Vol. 26, pp. 61–82). New York: Springer.

Moen, P., & Roehling, P. V. (2005). *The career mystique.* Bolder, CO: Rowman & Littlefield.

Moens, E., Braet, C., & Soetens, B. (2007). Observation of family functioning at mealtime: A comparison between families of children with and without overweight. *Journal of Pediatric Psychology, 32,* 52–63.

Moerk, E. L. (2000). *The guided acquisition of first language skills.* Westport, CT: Ablex.

Moffitt, T. E. (2006). A review of research on the taxonomy of life-course persistent versus adolescence-limited antisocial behavior. In F. T. Cullen, J. P. Wright, & K . Blevins (Eds.), *Taking stock: The status of criminological theory* (pp. 277–311). New Brunswick, NJ: Transaction Publishers.

Mojet, J., Christ-Hazelhof, E., & Heidema, J. (2001). Taste perception with age: Generic or specific losses in threshold sensitivity to the five basic tastes? *Chemical Senses, 26,* 845–860.

Moll, H., & Tomasello, M. (2006). Level I perspective-taking at 24 months of age. *British Journal of Developmental Psychology, 24,* 603–613.

Moll, I. (1994). Reclaiming the natural line in Vygotsky's theory of cognitive development. *Human Development, 37,* 333–342.

Moller, K., Hwang, C. P., & Wickberg, B. (2008). Couple relationship and transition to parenthood: Does workload at home matter? *Journal of Reproductive and Infant Psychology, 26,* 57–68.

Mondloch, C. J., Lewis, T., Budreau, D. R., Maurer, D., Dannemillier, J. L., Stephens, B. R., & Kleiner-Gathercoal, K. A. (1999). Face perception during early infancy. *Psychological Science, 10,* 419–422.

Monk, C., Fifer, W. P., Myers, M. M., Sloan, R. P., Trien, L., & Hurtado, A. (2000). Maternal stress responses and anxiety during pregnancy: Effects on fetal heart rate. *Developmental Psychobiology, 36,* 67–77.

Monk, C., Myers, M. M., Sloan, R. P., Ellman, L. M., & Fifer, W. P. (2003). Effects of women's stress-elicited physiological activity and chronic anxiety on fetal heart rate. *Journal of Developmental and Behavioral Pediatrics, 24,* 32–38.

Monk, C., Sloan, R., Myers, M. M., Ellman, L., Werner, E., Jeon, J., Tager, F., & Fifer, W. P. (2004). Fetal heart rate reactivity differs by women's psychiatric status: An early marker for developmental risk? *Journal of the American Academy of Child and Adolescent Psychiatry, 43,* 283–290.

Monsour, M. (2002). *Women and men as friends.* Mahwah, NJ: Erlbaum.

Montemayor, R., & Eisen, M. (1977). The development of self-conceptions from childhood to adolescence. *Developmental Psychology, 37,* 826–838.

Montepare, J. M. (2006). Body consciousness across the adult years: Variations with actual and subjective age. *Journal of Adult Development, 13,* 102–107.

Montgomery, M. J. (2005). Psychosocial intimacy and identity: From early adolescence to emerging adulthood. *Journal of Adolescent Research, 20*, 346–374.

Montgomery, M. J., & Côté, J. E. (2003). College as a transition to adulthood. In G. R. Adams & M. D. Berzonsky (Eds.), *Blackwell handbook of adolescence* (pp. 149–172). Malden, MA: Blackwell.

Montorsi, F. (2005). Assessment, diagnosis, and investigation of erectile dysfunction. *Clinical Cornerstone, 7*, 29–35.

Montoya, A. G., Sorrentino, R., Lukas, S. E., & Price, B. H. (2002). Long-term neuropsychiatric consequences of "ecstasy" (MDMA): A review. *Harvard Review of Psychiatry, 10*, 212–220.

Moon, C., Cooper, R. P., & Fifer, W. P. (1993). Two-day-old infants prefer their native language. *Infant Behavior and Development, 16*, 495–500.

Moon, S. M., & Feldhusen, J. F. (1994). The Program for Academic and Creative Enrichment (PACE): A follow-up study ten years later. In R. F. Subotnik & K. D. Arnold (Eds.), *Beyond Terman: Contemporary longitudinal studies of giftedness and talent* (pp. 375–400). Norwood, NJ: Ablex.

Moore, A., & Stratton, D. C. (2002). *Resilient widowers*. New York: Springer.

Moore, D. R., & Florsheim, P. (2001). Interpersonal processes and psychopathology among expectant and nonexpectant adolescent couples. *Journal of Consulting and Clinical Psychology, 69*, 101–113.

Moore, E. G. J. (1986). Family socialization and the IQ test performance of traditionally and transracially adopted black children. *Developmental Psychology, 22*, 317–326.

Moore, K. L., & Persaud, T. V. N. (2008). *Before we are born* (7th ed.). Philadelphia: Saunders.

Moore, M. K., & Meltzoff, A. N. (2004). Object permanence after a 24-hr delay and leaving the locale of disappearance: The role of memory, space, and identity. *Developmental Psychology, 40*, 606–620.

Moore, M. R., & Brooks-Gunn, J. (2002). Adolescent parenthood. In M. H. Bornstein (Ed.), *Handbook of parenting: Vol. 3* (2nd ed., pp. 173–214). Mahwah, NJ: Erlbaum.

Moore, W. S. (2002). Understanding learning in a postmodern world: Reconsidering the Perry scheme of ethical and intellectual development. In B. K. Hofer & P. R. Pintrich (Eds.), *Personal epistemology* (pp. 17–36). Mahwah, NJ: Erlbaum.

Moran, S., & Gardner, H. (2006). Extraordinary achievements: A developmental and systems analysis. In D. Kuhn & R. Siegler (Eds.), *Handbook of child psychology: Vol. 2. Cognition, perception, and language* (6th ed., pp. 905–949). Hoboken, NJ: Wiley.

Morelli, G., Rogoff, B., Oppenheim, D., & Goldsmith, D. (1992). Cultural variation in infants' sleeping arrangements: Questions of independence. *Developmental Psychology, 28*, 604–613.

Morelli, G. A., Rogoff, B., & Angelillo, C. (2003). Cultural variation in young children's access to work or involvement in specialized child-focused activities. *International Journal of Behavioral Development, 27*, 264–274.

Morgan, J. D., & Laungani, P. (2005). General introduction. In J. D. Morgan & P. Laungani (Eds.), *Death and bereavement around the world* (pp. 1–4). Amityville, NY: Baywood.

Morgane, P. J., Austin-LaFrance, R., Bronzino, J., Tonkiss, J., Diaz-Cintra, S., Cintra, L., Kemper, T., & Galler, J. R. (1993). Prenatal malnutrition and development of the brain. *Neuroscience and Biobehavioral Reviews, 17*, 91–128.

Morley, J. E. (2001). Decreased food intake with aging. *Journal of Gerontology, 56A*, 81–88.

Morris, G., & Baker-Ward, L. (2007). Fragile but real: Children's capacity to use newly acquired words to convey preverbal memories. *Child Development, 78*, 448–458.

Morris, M. C., Evans, D. A., Schneider, J. A., Tangney, C. C., Bienias, J. L., & Aggarwal, N. T. (2006). Dietary folate and vitamins B-12 and B-6 not asso-

ciated with incident Alzheimer's disease. *Journal of Alzheimer's Disease, 9*, 435–443.

Morris, M. C., Evans, D. A., Tangney, C. C., Bienias, J. L., & Wilson, R. S. (2005). Fish consumption and cognitive decline with age in a large community study. *Archives of Neurology, 62*, 1849–1853.

Morrison, V. (2008). Ageing and physical health. In B. Woods & L. Clare (Eds.), *Handbook of the clinical psychology of ageing* (2nd ed., pp. 57–74). Chichester, UK: Wiley.

Morrongiello, B. A., Fenwick, K. D., & Chance, G. (1998). Crossmodal learning in newborn infants: Inferences about properties of auditory-visual events. *Infant Behavior and Development, 21*, 543–554.

Morrongiello, B. A., Midgett, C., & Shields, R. (2001). Don't run with scissors: Young children's knowledge of home safety rules. *Journal of Pediatric Psychology, 26*, 105–115.

Morrongiello, B. A., Ondejko, L., & Littlejohn, A. (2004). Understanding toddlers' in-home injuries: I. Context, correlates, and determinants. *Journal of Pediatric Psychology, 29*, 415–431.

Morrow, D. F. (2006). Gay, lesbian, and transgender adolescents. In D. F. Morrow & L. Messinger (Eds.), *Sexual orientation and gender expression in social work practice* (pp. 177–195). New York: Columbia University Press.

Mosby, L., Rawls, A. W., Meehan, A. J., Mays, E., & Pettinari, C. J. (1999). Troubles in interracial talk about discipline: An examination of African American child rearing narratives. *Journal of Comparative Family Studies, 30*, 489–521.

Mosca, L., Mochari, H., Christian, A., Berra, K., Taubert, K., & Mills, T. (2005). National study of women's awareness, preventive action and barriers to cardiovascular health. *Circulation, 113*, 525–534.

Mosconi L., Brys, M., Glodzik-Sobanska, L., De Santi, S., Rusinek, H., & de Leon, M. J. (2007). Early detection of Alzheimer's disease using neuroimaging. *Experimental Gerontology, 42*, 129–138.

Moses, L. J., Baldwin, D. A., Rosicky, J. G., & Tidball, G. (2001). Evidence for referential understanding in the emotions domain at twelve and eighteen months. *Child Development, 72*, 718–735.

Mosher, W. D., Chandra, A., & Jones, J. (2005). *Sexual behavior and selected health measures: Men and women 15–44 years of age, United States 2002*, Vol. 362. Atlanta: U.S. Centers for Disease Control and Prevention.

Moshman, D. (1998). Identity as a theory of oneself. *Genetic Epistemologist, 26*(3), 1–9.

Moshman, D. (1999). *Adolescent psychological development: Rationality, morality, and identity*. Mahwah, NJ: Erlbaum.

Moshman, D. (2003). Developmental change in adulthood. In J. Demick & C. Andreoletti (Eds.), *Handbook of adult development* (pp. 43–61). New York: Plenum.

Moshman, D. (2005). *Adolescent psychological development: Rationality, morality, and identity* (2nd ed.). Mahwah, NJ: Erlbaum.

Moshman, D., & Franks, B. A. (1986). Development of the concept of inferential validity. *Child Development, 57*, 153–165.

Moshman, D., & Geil, M. (1998). Collaborative reasoning: Evidence for collective rationality. *Thinking and Reasoning, 4*, 231–248.

Moss, E., Cyr, C., Bureau, J.-F., Tarabulsy, G. M., & Dubois-Comtois, K. (2005). Stability of attachment during the preschool period. *Developmental Psychology, 41*, 773–783.

Mottus, R., Indus, K., & Allik, J. (2008). Accuracy of only children stereotype. *Journal of Research in Personality, 42*, 1047–1052.

Mounts, N. S., Valentiner, D. P., Anderson, K. L., & Boswell, M. K. (2006). Shyness, sociability, and parental support for the college transition: Relation to adolescents' adjustment. *Journal of Youth and Adolescence, 35*, 71–80.

Moxley, D. P., Najor-Durack, A., & Dumbrigue, C. (2001). *Keeping students in higher education*. London: Kogan Page.

Moyer, M. S. (1992). Sibling relationships among older adults. *Generations, 16*(3), 55–58.

Mroczek, D. K., & Kolarz, C. M. (1998). The effect of age on positive and negative affect: A developmental perspective on happiness. *Journal of Personality and Social Psychology, 75*, 1333–1349.

Mroczek, D. K., & Spiro, A., III. (2005). Change in life satisfaction during adulthood: Findings from the Veterans Affairs Normative Aging Study. *Journal of Personality and Social Psychology, 88*, 189–202.

Mroczek, D. K., & Spiro, A., III. (2007). Personality change influences mortality in older men. *Psychological Science, 18*, 371–376.

Mrug, S., Hoza, B., & Gerdes, A. C. (2001). Children with attention-deficit/hyperactivity disorder: Peer relationships and peer-oriented interventions. In D. W. Nangle & C. A. Erdley (Eds.), *The role of friendship in psychological adjustment* (pp. 51–77). San Francisco: Jossey-Bass.

Mueller, C. M., & Dweck, C. S. (1998). Intelligence praise can undermine motivation and performance. *Journal of Personality and Social Psychology, 75*, 33–52.

Muenchow, S., & Marsland, K. W. (2007). Beyond baby steps: Promoting the growth and development of U.S. child-care policy. In J. L. Aber, S. J. Bishop-Josef, S. M. Jones, K. T. McLearn, & D. Phillips (Eds.), *Child development and social policy: Knowledge for action* (pp. 97–112). Washington, DC: American Psychological Association.

Mulder, E. J. H., Robles de Medina, P. G., Huizink, A. C., Van den Bergh, B. R. H., Buitelaar, J. K., & Visser, G. H. A. (2002). Prenatal maternal stress: Effects on pregnancy and the (unborn) child. *Early Human Development, 70*, 3–14.

Müller, O., & Krawinkel, M. (2005). Malnutrition and health in developing countries. *Canadian Medical Association Journal, 173*, 279–286.

Müller, U., Overton, W. F., & Reese, K. (2001). Development of conditional reasoning: A longitudinal study. *Journal of Cognition and Development, 2*, 27–49.

Mulvaney, M. K., McCartney, K., Bub, K. L., & Marshall, N. L. (2006). Determinants of dyadic scaffolding and cognitive outcomes in first graders. *Parenting: Science and Practice, 6*, 297–310.

Mulvaney, M. K., & Mebert, C. J. (2007). Parental corporal punishment predicts behavior problems in early childhood. *Journal of Family Psychology, 21*, 389–397.

Mumme, D. L., Bushnell, E. W., DiCorcia, J. A., & Lariviere, L. A. (2007). Infants' use of gaze cues to interpret others' actions and emotional reactions. In R. Flom, K. Lee, & D. Muir (Eds.), *Gaze-following: Its development and significance* (pp. 143–170). Mahwah, NJ: Erlbaum.

Munakata, Y. (2001). Task-dependency in infant behavior: Toward an understanding of the processes underlying cognitive development. In F. Lacerda, C. von Hofsten, & M. Heimann (Eds.), *Emerging cognitive abilities in early infancy* (pp. 29–52). Mahwah, NJ: Erlbaum.

Munakata, Y. (2006). Information processing approaches to development. In D. Kuhn & R. S. Siegler (Eds.), *Handbook of child psychology: Vol. 3. Cognition, perception, and language* (6th ed., pp. 426–463). Hoboken, NJ: Wiley.

Munakata, Y., Casey, B. J., & Diamond, A. (2004). Developmental cognitive neuroscience: Progress and potential. *Trends in Cognitive Sciences, 8*, 122–128.

Mundy, P. (2003). The neural basis of social impairments in autism: The role of the dorsal medial-frontal cortex and anterior cingulate system. *Journal of Child Psychology and Psychiatry and Allied Disciplines, 44*, 793–809.

Mundy, P., & Stella, J. (2000). Joint attention, social orienting, and nonverbal communication in autism. In A. M. Wetherby & B. M. Prizant (Eds.), *Autism spectrum disorders* (Vol. 9, pp. 55–77). Baltimore, MD: Paul H. Brookes.

Munroe, R. L., & Romney, A. K. (2006). Gender and age differences in same-sex aggregation and social behavior. *Journal of Cross-Cultural Psychology, 37,* 3–19.

Muris, P., Merckelbach, H., Gadet, B., & Moulaert, V. (2000). Fears, worries, and scary dreams in 4- to 12-year-old children: Their content, developmental pattern, and origins. *Journal of Clinical Child Psychology, 29,* 43–52.

Muris, P., Merckelbach, H., Ollendick, T. H., King, N. J., & Bogie, N. (2001). Children's nighttime fears: Parent–child ratings of frequency, content, origins, coping behaviors, and severity. *Behaviour Research and Therapy, 39,* 13–28.

Murphy, S. A. (2008). The loss of a child: Sudden death and extended illness perspectives. In M. S. Stroebe, R. O. Hansson, H. Schut, & W. Stroebe (Eds.), *Handbook of bereavement research and practice* (pp. 375–396). Washington, DC: American Psychological Association.

Murtagh, K. N., & Hubert, H. B. (2004). Gender differences in physical disability among an elderly cohort. *American Journal of Public Health, 94,* 1406–1411.

Mussen, P., & Eisenberg-Berg, N. (1977). *Roots of caring, sharing, and helping.* San Francisco: Freeman.

Mustanski, B. S., Viken, R. J., Kaprio, J., Pulkkinen, L., & Rose, R. J. (2004). Genetic and environmental influences on pubertal development: Longitudinal data from Finnish twins at ages 11 and 14. *Developmental Psychology, 40,* 1188–1198.

Mustillo, S., Worthman, C., Erkanli, A., Keeler, G., Angold, A., & Costello, E. J. (2003). Obesity and psychiatric disorder: Developmental trajectories. *Pediatrics, 111,* 851–859.

Mutchler, J. E., Burr, J. A., & Caro, F. G. (2003). From paid worker to volunteer: Leaving the paid workforce and volunteering in later life. *Social Forces, 81,* 1267–1293.

Mutran, E. J., Danis, M., Bratton, K. A., Sudha, S., & Hanson, L. (1997). Attitudes of the critically ill toward prolonging life: The role of social support. *Gerontologist, 37,* 192–199.

Myers, D. G. (2000). The funds, friends, and faith of happy people. *American Psychologist, 55,* 56–67.

Myers, M. G., Brown, S. A., Tate, S., Abrantes, A., & Tomlinson, K. (2001). *Adolescents, alcohol, and substance abuse* (pp. 275–296). New York: Guilford.

Myerson, J., Hale, S., Wagstaff, D., Poon, L. W., & Smith, G. A. (1990). The information-loss model: A mathematical theory of age-related cognitive slowing. *Psychological Review, 97,* 475–487.

Myowa-Yamakoshi, M., Tomonaga, M., Tanaka, M., & Matsuzawa, T. (2004). Imitation in neonatal chimpanzees *(Pan troglodytes). Developmental Science, 7,* 437–442.

N

Nadel, J., Prepin, K., & Okanda, M. (2005). Experiencing contingency and agency: First step toward self-understanding in making a mind? *Interaction Studies, 6,* 447–462.

Nader, K. (2002). Treating children after violence in schools and communities. In N. B. Webb (Ed.), *Helping bereaved children: A handbook for practitioners* (pp. 214–244). New York: Guilford.

Nader, K., Dubrow, N., & Stamm, B. H. (1999). *Honoring differences: Cultural issues in the treatment of trauma and loss.* Washington, DC: Taylor & Francis.

Nader, P. R., Bradley, R. H., Houts, R. M., McRitchie, S. L., & O'Brien, M. (2008). Moderate-to-vigorous physical activity from ages 9 to 15 years. *Journal of the American Medical Association, 16,* 295–305.

Nagy, E., Compagne, H., Orvos, H., Pal, A., Molnar, P., & Janszky, I. (2005). Index finger movement imitation by human neonates: Motivation, learning, and

left-hand preference. *Pediatric Research, 58,* 749–753.

Nagy, W. E., & Scott, J. A. (2000). Vocabulary processes. In M. L. Kamil & P. B. Mosenthal (Eds.), *Handbook of reading research* (Vol. 3, pp. 269–284). Mahwah, NJ: Erlbaum.

Naigles, L. R., & Swenson, L. D. (2007). Syntactic supports for word learning. In E. Hoff & M. Shatz (Eds.), *Blackwell handbook of language development* (pp. 212–231). Malden, MA: Blackwell.

Naito, M., & Seki, Y. (2009). The relationship between second-order false belief and display rules reasoning: Integration of cognitive and affective social understanding. *Developmental Science, 12,* 150–164.

Nakamura, J., & Csikszentmihalyi, M. (2002). The concept of flow. In C. R. Snyder & S. J. Lopez (Eds.), *Handbook of positive psychology* (pp. 89–105). New York: Oxford University Press.

Nánez, J., Sr., & Yonas, A. (1994). Effects of luminance and texture motion on infant defensive reactions to optical collision. *Infant Behavior and Development, 17,* 165–174.

Narayan, C. (2008). Is there a double standard of aging? Older men and women and ageism. *Educational Gerontology, 34,* 782–787.

Nastasi, B. K., & Clements, D. H. (1994). Effectance motivation, perceived scholastic competence, and higher-order thinking in two cooperative computer environments. *Journal of Educational Computing Research, 10,* 249–275.

Natale, R., & Dodman, N. (2003). Birth can be a hazardous journey: Electronic fetal monitoring does not help. *JOGC, 25,* 1007–1009.

National Council of Youth Sports. (2008). *Report on trends and participation in organized youth sports.* Stuart, FL: Author.

National Institute on Aging. (2005). *Progress report on Alzheimer's disease 2004–2005: New discoveries, new insights.* Bethesda, MD: Author.

National Institute on Aging, U. S. Department of Health and Human Services. (2008). 2007 Progress report on Alzheimer's disease. Retrieved from www.nia.nih.gov/Alzheimers/Publications/ADProgress2007

National Institutes of Health. (2008). *Genes and disease.* Retrieved from www.ncbi.nlm.nih.gov/books/bv.fcgi?rid=gnd.TOC&depth=2

National Osteoporosis Foundation. (2008). *Fast facts.* Retrieved from www.nof.org/professionals/Fast_Facts_Osteoporosis.pdf

National Safe Kids Campaign. (2005). *Report to the nation: Trends in unintentional childhood injury mortality: 1987–2000.* Washington, DC: Author.

National Women's Law Center. (2007). *When girls don't graduate we all fail.* Washington, DC: Author.

Naveh-Benjamin, M. (2000). Adult age differences in memory performance: Tests of an associative deficit hypothesis. *Journal of Experimental Psychology: Learning, Memory, and Cognition, 26,* 1170–1187.

Naveh-Benjamin, M., Brav, T. K., & Levy, D. (2007). The associative memory deficit of older adults: The role of strategy utilization. *Psychology and Aging, 22,* 202–208.

Naveh-Benjamin, M., Craik, F. I. M., Guez, J., & Kreuger, S. (2005). Divided attention in younger and older adults: Effects of strategy and relatedness on memory performance and secondary task costs. *Journal of Experimental Psychology: Learning, Memory, and Cognition, 31,* 520–537.

Naveh-Benjamin, M., Hussain, Z., Guez, J., & Bar-On, M. (2003). Adult age differences in episodic memory: Further support for an associative-deficit hypothesis. *Journal of Experimental Psychology: Learning, Memory, and Cognition, 29,* 826–837.

Neal, M. B., & Hammer, L. B. (2007). *Working couples caring for children and aging parents.* Mahwah, NJ: Erlbaum.

Neff, K. D., & Helwig, C. C. (2002). A constructivist approach to understanding the development of

reasoning about rights and authority within cultural contexts. *Cognitive Development, 17,* 1429–1450.

Neimeyer, R. A. (Ed.). (1994). *Death anxiety handbook.* Washington, DC: Taylor & Francis.

Neimeyer, R. A. (2001a). Meaning reconstruction and loss. In R. A. Neimeyer (Ed.), *Meaning reconstruction and the experience of loss* (pp. 1–9). Washington, DC: American Psychological Association.

Neimeyer, R. A. (2001b). The language of loss: Grief therapy as a process of meaning reconstruction. In R. A. Neimeyer (Ed.), *Meaning reconstruction and the experience of loss* (pp. 261–292). Washington, DC: American Psychological Association.

Neimeyer, R. A., & Van Brunt, D. (1995). Death anxiety. In H. Waas & R. A. Neimeyer (Eds.), *Dying: Facing the facts* (3rd ed., pp. 49–88). Washington, DC: Taylor & Francis.

Neitzel, C., & Stright, A. D. (2003). Mothers' scaffolding of children's problem solving: Establishing a foundation of academic self-regulatory competence. *Journal of Family Psychology, 17,* 147–159.

Nelson, C. A. (2001). The development and neural bases of face recognition. *Infant and Child Development, 10,* 3–18.

Nelson, C. A. (2002). Neural development and lifelong plasticity. In R. M. Lerner, F. Jacobs, & D. Wertlieb (Eds.), *Handbook of applied developmental science* (Vol. 1, pp. 31–60). Thousand Oaks, CA: Sage.

Nelson, C. A., & Bosquet, M. (2000). Neurobiology of fetal and infant development: Implications for infant mental health. In C. H. Zeanah, Jr. (Ed.), *Handbook of infant mental health* (2nd ed., pp. 37–59). New York: Guilford.

Nelson, C. A., Thomas, K. M., & de Haan, M. (2006). Neural bases of cognitive development. In D. Kuhn & R. Siegler (Eds.), *Handbook of child psychology: Vol. 2. Cognition, perception, and language* (6th ed., pp. 3–57). Hoboken, NJ: Wiley.

Nelson, D. A., Nelson, L. J., Hart, C. H., Yang, C., & Jin, S. (2005). Parenting and peer-group behavior in cultural context. In X. Chen, B. Schneider, & D. French (Eds.), *Peer relations in cultural context.* New York Cambridge University Press.

Nelson, D. A., Hart, C. H., Yang, C., Olsen, J. A., & Jin, S. (2006a). Aversive parenting in China: Associations with child physical and relational aggression. *Child Development, 77,* 554–572.

Nelson, D. A., Nelson, L. J., Hart, C. H., Yang, C., & Jin, S. (2006b). Parenting and peer-group behavior in cultural context. In X. Chen, D. French, & B. Schneider (Eds.), *Peer relations in cultural context* (pp. 213–246). New York: Cambridge University Press.

Nelson, D. A., Robinson, C. C., & Hart, C. H. (2005). Relational and physical aggression of preschool-age children: Peer status linkages across informants. *Early Education and Development, 16,* 115–139.

Nelson, H. D. (2008). Menopause. *Lancet, 371,* 760–770.

Nelson, H. D., Humphrey, L. L., Nygren, P., Teutsch, S. M., & Allan, J. D. (2002). Postmenopausal hormone replacement therapy: Scientific review. *Journal of the American Medical Association, 288,* 872–881.

Nelson, K. (1973). Structure and strategy in learning to talk. *Monographs of the Society for Research in Child Development, 38*(1–2, Serial No. 149).

Nelson, L. J., & Chen, X. (2007). Emerging adulthood in China: The role of social and cultural factors. *Child Development Perspectives, 1,* 86–91.

Nelson, L. J., Padilla-Walker, L. M., Carroll, J. S., Madsen, S. D., Barry, C. M., & Badger, S. (2007). "If you want me to treat you like an adult, start acting like one!" Comparing the criteria that emerging adults and their parents have for adulthood. *Journal of Family Psychology, 21,* 665–674.

Nemet, D., Barkan, S., Epstein, Y., Friedland, O., Kowen, G., & Eliakim, A. (2005). Short- and long-term beneficial effects of a combined dietary–behavioral–physical activity intervention for the treatment of childhood obesity. *Pediatrics, 115,* e443–e449.

Netz, Y., Wu, M.-J., Becker, B. J., & Tenenbaum, G. (2005). Physical activity and psychological well-being in advanced age: A meta-analysis of intervention studies. *Psychology and Aging, 20,* 272–284.

Neugarten, B. L. (1968a). Adult personality: Toward a psychology of the life cycle. In B. Neugarten (Ed.), *Middle age and aging* (pp. 137–147). Chicago: University of Chicago Press.

Neugarten, B. L. (1968b). The awareness of middle aging. In B. L. Neugarten (Ed.), *Middle age and aging* (pp. 93–98). Chicago: University of Chicago Press.

Neugarten, B. L. (1979). Time, age, and the life cycle. *American Journal of Psychiatry, 136,* 887–894.

Neugarten, B. L., & Neugarten, D. A. (1987, May). The changing meanings of age. *Psychology Today, 21*(5), 29–33.

Neuhouser, M. L., Wasserthel-Smoller, S., Thomson, C., Aragaki, A., Anderson, G. L., & Manson, J. E. (2009). Multivitamin use and risk of cancer and cardiovascular disease in the Women's Health Initiative cohorts. *Archives of Internal Medicine, 169,* 294–304.

Neuman, S. B. (1999). Books make a difference: A study of access to literacy. *Reading Research Quarterly, 34,* 286–311.

Neumann, K. F., Rojo, L., Navarrete, L. P., Farias, G., Reyes, P., & Maccioni, R. B. (2008). Insulin resistance and Alzheimer's disease: Molecular links and clinical implications. *Current Alzheimer Research, 5,* 438–447.

Neumark-Sztainer, D., Hannan, P. J., Story, M., Croll, J., & Perry, C. (2003). Family meal patterns: Associations with sociodemographic characteristics and improved dietary intake among adolescents. *Journal of the American Dietetic Association, 103,* 317–322.

Neville, H. A., & Heppner, M. J. (2002). Prevention and treatment of violence against women: An examination of sexual assault. In C. L. Juntunen & D. R. Atkinson (Eds.), *Counseling across the life span: Prevention and treatment* (pp. 261–277). Thousand Oaks, CA: Sage.

Neville, H. J., & Bavelier, D. (2002). Human brain plasticity: Evidence from sensory deprivation and altered language experience. In M. A. Hofman, G. J. Boer, A. J. G. D. Holtmaat, E. J. W. van Someren, J. Berhaagen, & D. F. Swaab (Eds.), *Plasticity in the adult brain: From genes to neurotherapy* (pp. 177–188). Amsterdam: Elsevier Science.

Nevin, R. (2000). How lead exposure relates to temporal changes in IQ, violent crime, and unwed pregnancy. *Environmental Research, 83,* 1–22.

Newcomb, A. F., Bukowski, W. M., & Pattee, L. (1993). Children's peer relations: A meta-analytic review of popular, rejected, neglected, controversial, and average sociometric status. *Psychological Bulletin, 113,* 99–128.

Newcomb, M. D., Abbott, R. D., Catalano, R. F., Hawkins, J. D., Battin-Pearson, S., & Hill, K. (2002). Mediational and deviance theories of late high school failure: Process roles of structural strains, academic competence, and general versus specific problem behavior. *Journal of Counseling Psychology, 49,* 172–186.

Newcombe, N. S., & Huttenlocher, J. (1992). Children's early ability to solve perspective-taking problems. *Developmental Psychology, 28,* 635–643.

Newport, E. L. (1991). Contrasting conceptions of the critical period for language. In S. Cary & R. Gelman (Eds.), *The epigenesis of mind: Essays on biology and cognition* (pp. 111–130). Hillsdale, NJ: Erlbaum.

Newport, E. L., & Aslin, R. N. (2000). Innately constrained learning: Blending old and new approaches to language acquisition. In S. C. Howell, S. A. Fish, & T. Keith-Lucas (Eds.), *Proceedings of the 24th Annual Boston University Conference on*

Language Development (pp. 1–21). Somerville, MA: Cascadilla Press.

Newsom, J. T. (1999). Another side to caregiving: Negative reactions to being helped. *Current Directions in Psychological Science, 8,* 183–187.

Newsom, J. T., & Schulz, R. (1996). Social support as a mediator in the relation between functional status and quality of life in older adults. *Psychology and Aging, 11,* 34–44.

Ng, F. F., Pomerantz, E. M., & Lam, S. (2007). European American and Chinese parents' responses to children's success and failure: Implications for children's responses. *Developmental Psychology, 43,* 1239–1255.

Ngata, P. (2004). Death, dying, and grief: A Maori perspective. In J. D. Morgan & P. Laungani (Eds.), *Death and bereavement around the world: Vol. 4. Asia, Australia, and New Zealand* (pp. 95–99). Amityville, NY: Baywood.

Ngo-Metzger, Q., Phillips, R. S., & McCarthy, E. P. (2007). Ethnic disparities in hospice use among Asian-American and Pacific Islander patients dying with cancer. *Journal of the American Geriatric Society, 56,* 139–144.

NHPCO (National Hospice and Palliative Care Organization). (2005). 83% of Americans want to die at home. Retrieved from www.nhpco.org/templates/1/homepage.cfm

NHPCO (National Hospice and Palliative Care Organization). (2008). *NHPCO facts and figures: Hospice care in America.* Alexandria, VA: Author.

Ni, Y. (1998). Cognitive structure, content knowledge, and classificatory reasoning. *Journal of Genetic Psychology, 159,* 280–296.

NICHD (National Institute of Child Health and Human Development) Early Child Care Research Network. (1997). The effects of infant child care on infant–mother attachment security: Results of the NICHD Study of Early Child Care. *Child Development, 68,* 860–879.

NICHD (National Institute of Child Health and Human Development) Early Child Care Research Network. (1999). Child care and mother–child interaction in the first 3 years of life. *Developmental Psychology, 35,* 1399–1413.

NICHD (National Institute of Child Health and Human Development) Early Child Care Research Network. (2000a). Characteristics and quality of child care for toddlers and preschoolers. *Applied Developmental Science, 4,* 116–135.

NICHD (National Institute of Child Health and Human Development) Early Child Care Research Network. (2000b). The relation of child care to cognitive and language development. *Child Development, 71,* 960–980.

NICHD (National Institute of Child Health and Human Development) Early Child Care Research Network. (2001). Before Head Start: Income and ethnicity, family characteristics, child care experiences, and child development. *Early Education and Development, 12,* 545–575.

NICHD (National Institute of Child Health and Human Development) Early Child Care Research Network. (2002a). Child-care structure → process → outcome: Direct and indirect effects of childcare quality on young children's development. *Psychological Science, 13,* 199–206.

NICHD (National Institute of Child Health and Human Development) Early Child Care Research Network. (2002b). The interaction of child care and family risk in relation to child development at 24 and 36 months. *Applied Developmental Science, 6,* 144–156.

NICHD (National Institute of Child Health and Human Development) Early Child Care Research Network. (2003). Does quality of child care affect child outcomes at age 4½? *Developmental Psychology, 39,* 451–469.

NICHD (National Institute of Child Health and Human Development) Early Child Care Research Network. (2004). Trajectories of physical aggres-

sion from toddlerhood to middle childhood. *Monographs of the Society for Research in Child Development, 69*(4, Serial No. 278).

NICHD (National Institute of Child Health and Human Development) Early Child Care Research Network. (2006). Child-care effect sizes for the NICHD Study of Early Child Care and Youth Development. *American Psychologist, 61,* 99–116.

Nichols, S. L., & Berliner, D. C. (2007). The pressure to cheat in a high-stakes testing environment. In E. M. Anderman & T. B. Murdock (Eds.), *Psychology of academic cheating* (pp. 289–311). San Francisco: Jossey-Bass.

Nichols, W. C., & Pace-Nichols, M. A. (2000). Childless married couples. In W. C. Nichols, M. A. Pace-Nichols, D. S. Becvar, & A. Y. Napier (Eds.), *Handbook of family development and intervention* (pp. 171–188). New York: Wiley.

Nickman, S. L., Rosenfeld, A. A., Fine, P., MacIntyre, J. C., Pilowsky, D. J., & Howe, R. A. (2005). Children in adoptive families: Overview and update. *Journal of the American Academy of Child and Adolescent Psychiatry, 44,* 987–995.

Niehaus, M. D., Moore, S. R., Patrick, P. D., Derr, L. L., Lorntz, B., Lima, A. A., & Gurerrant, R. L. (2002). Early childhood diarrhea is associated with diminished cognitive function 4 to 7 years later in children in a northeast Brazilian shanty-town. *American Journal of Tropical Medicine and Hygiene, 66,* 590–593.

Niemeyer, D. (2006). *Eighth annual report on Oregon's Death with Dignity Act.* Portland: Oregon Department of Human Services.

Nigg, J. T., & Breslau, N. (2007). Prenatal smoking exposure, low birth weight, and disruptive behavior disorders. *Journal of the American Academy of Child and Adolescent Psychiatry, 46,* 362–369.

Nippold, M. A., Taylor, C. L., & Baker, J. M. (1996). Idiom understanding in Australian youth: A cross-cultural comparison. *Journal of Speech and Hearing Research, 39,* 442–447.

Noland, J. S., Singer, L. T., Short, E. J., Minnes, S., Arendt, R. E., & Krichner, H. L. (2005). Prenatal drug exposure and selective attention in preschoolers. *Neurotoxicology and Teratology, 27,* 429–438.

Nolen-Hoeksema, S. (2002). Gender differences in depression. In I. H. Gotlib & C. L. Hammen (Eds.), *Handbook of depression* (pp. 492–509). New York: Guilford.

Nolen-Hoeksema, S. (2006). The etiology of gender differences in depression. In C. M. Mazure & G. Puryear (Eds.), *Understanding depression in women: Applying empirical research to practice and policy* (pp. 9–43). Washington, DC: American Psychological Association.

Nomaguchi, K. M., & Milkie, M. A. (2003). Costs and rewards of children: The effects of becoming a parent on adults' lives. *Journal of Marriage and Family, 65,* 356–374.

Nordhus, I. H. (2008). Manifestations of depression and anxiety in older adults. In B. Woods & L. Clare (Eds.), *Handbook of the clinical psychology of ageing* (pp. 97–110). Hoboken, NJ: Wiley-Interscience.

Noterdaeme, M., Mildenberger, K., Minow, F., & Amorosa, H. (2002). Evaluation of neuromotor deficits in children with autism and children with a specific speech and language disorder. *European Child and Adolescent Psychiatry, 11,* 219–225.

Nucci, L. P. (1996). Morality and the personal sphere of action. In E. Reed, E. Turiel, & T. Brown (Eds.), *Values and knowledge* (pp. 41–60). Hillsdale, NJ: Erlbaum.

Nucci, L. P. (2001). *Education in the moral domain.* New York: Cambridge University Press.

Nucci, L. P. (2002). The development of moral reasoning. In U. Goswami (Ed.), *Blackwell handbook of childhood cognitive development* (pp. 303–325). Malden, MA: Blackwell.

Nucci, L. P. (2005). Culture, context, and the psychological sources of human rights concepts. In W. Edelstein & G. Nunner-Winkler (Eds.), *Morality in context* (pp. 365–394). Amsterdam, Netherlands: Elsevier.

Nuland, S. B. (1993). *How we die.* New York: Random House.

Nussbaum, J. F. (1994). Friendship in older adulthood. In M. L. Hummer, J. M. Wiemann, & J. F. Nussbaum (Eds.), *Interpersonal communication in older adulthood* (pp. 209–225). Thousand Oaks, CA: Sage.

O

Oakes, L. M., & Madole, K. L. (2003). Principles of developmental change in infants' category formation. In D. H. Rakison & L. M. Oakes (Eds.), *Early category and concept development: Making sense of the blooming, buzzing confusion* (pp. 132–158). New York: Oxford University Press.

Oakes, L. M., Coppage, D. J., & Dingel, A. (1997). By land or by sea: The role of perceptual similarity in infants' categorization of animals. *Developmental Psychology, 33,* 396–407.

Oberecker, R., & Friederici, A. D. (2006). Syntactic event-related potential components in 24-month-olds' sentence comprehension. *NeuroReport, 17,* 1017–1021.

Oberecker, R., Friedrich, M., & Friederici, A. D. (2005). Neural correlates of syntactic processing in two-year-olds. *Journal of Cognitive Neuroscience, 17,* 1667–1678.

Oberlander, T. F., Warburton, W., Misri, S., Jaafar, A., & Hertzman, C. (2006). Neonatal outcomes after prenatal exposure to selective serotonin reuptake inhibitor antidepressants and maternal depression using population-based linked health data. *Archives of General Psychiatry, 63,* 898–906.

Obermeyer, C. M. (2000). Menopause across cultures: A review of the evidence. *Menopause, 7,* 184–192.

Obradović, J., & Masten, A. S. (2007). Developmental antecedents of young adult civic engagement. *Applied Developmental Science, 11,* 2–19.

O'Connor, C. (1997). Dispositions toward (collective) struggle and educational resilience in the inner city: A case analysis of six African-American high school students. *American Educational Research Journal, 34,* 593–629.

O'Connor, M. G., & Kaplan, E. F. (2003). Age-related changes in memory. In J. Demick & C. Andreoletti (Eds.), *Handbook of adult development* (pp. 121–130). New York: Springer.

O'Connor, P. (2003). Dying in the hospital. In I. Corless, B. B. Germino, & M. A. Pitman (Eds.), *Dying, death, and bereavement: A challenge for the living* (2nd ed., pp. 87–103). New York: Springer.

O'Connor, T. G., Marvin, R. S., Rutter, M., Olrich, J. T., Britner, P. A., & the English and Romanian Adoptees Study Team. (2003). Child–parent attachment following early institutional deprivation. *Development and Psychopathology, 15,* 19–38.

O'Connor, T. G., Rutter, M., Beckett, C., Keaveney, L., Dreppner, J. M., & the English and Romanian Adoptees Study Team. (2000). The effects of global severe privation on cognitive competence: Extension and longitudinal follow-up. *Child Development, 71,* 376–390.

Oden, M. H., & Terman, L. M. (1968). The fulfillment of promise—40-year follow-up of the Terman gifted group. *Genetic Psychology Monographs, 77,* 3–93.

OECD (Organisation for Economic Cooperation and Development). (2006). *Starting strong II: Early childhood education and care.* Paris: OECD Publishing. Retrieved from www.sourceoecd.org/education/9264035451

OECD (Organisation for Economic Cooperation and Development). (2008a). *Education at a glance 2008: OECD indicators.* Paris: Author.

OECD (Organisation for Economic Cooperation and Development). (2008b). *OECD Health data: 2008.* Retrieved from secure.cihi.ca/cihiweb/dispPage.jsp?cw_page=media_26jun2008_e

Ogawa, J. R., Sroufe, L. A., Weinfield, N. S., Carlson, E. A., & Egeland, B. (1997). Development and the fragmented self: Longitudinal study of dissociative symptomatology in a nonclinical sample. *Development and Psychopathology, 9,* 855–879.

Ogbu, J. U. (2003). *Black American students in an affluent suburb: A study of academic disengagement.* Mahwah, NJ: Erlbaum.

Ogden, C. L., Carroll, M. D., & Flegal, K. M. (2008). High body mass index for age among U.S. children and adolescents, 2003–2006. *Journal of the American Medical Association, 299,* 2401–2405.

Ogden, C. L., Carroll, M. D., McDowell, M., Tabak, C. J., & Flegal, K. M. (2006). Prevalence of overweight and obesity in the United States, 1999–2004. *Journal of the American Medical Association, 295,* 1549–1555.

O'Halloran, C. M., & Altmaier, E. M. (1996). Awareness of death among children: Does a life-threatening illness alter the process of discovery? *Journal of Counseling and Development, 74,* 259–262.

Okagaki, L., Hammond, K. A., & Seamon, L. (1999). Socialization of religious beliefs. *Journal of Applied Developmental Psychology, 20,* 273–294.

Okagaki, L., & Sternberg, R. J. (1993). Parental beliefs and children's school performance. *Child Development, 64,* 36–56.

Okami, P., Weisner, T., & Olmstead, R. (2002). Outcome correlates of parent–child bedsharing: An eighteen-year longitudinal study. *Developmental and Behavioral Pediatrics, 23,* 244–253.

O'Keefe, M. J., O'Callaghan, M., Williams, G. M., Najman, J., & Bor, W. (2003). Learning, cognitive, and attentional problems in adolescents born small for gestational age. *Pediatrics, 112,* 301–307.

Olafson, E., & Boat, B. W. (2000). Long-term management of the sexually abused child: Considerations and challenges. In R. M. Reece (Ed.), *Treatment of child abuse: Common ground for mental health, medical, and legal practitioners* (pp. 14–35). Baltimore: Johns Hopkins University Press.

O'Laughlin, E. M., & Anderson, V. N. (2001). Perceptions of parenthood among young adults: Implications for career and family planning. *American Journal of Family Therapy, 29,* 95–108.

Old, S. R., & Naveh-Benjamin, M. (2008a). Age-related changes in memory: Experimental approaches. In S. M. Hofer & D. F. Alwin (Eds.), *Handbook of cognitive aging: Interdisciplinary perspectives* (pp. 151–167). Thousand Oaks, CA: Sage.

Old, S. R., & Naveh-Benjamin, M. (2008b). Differential effects of age on item and associative measures of memory: A meta-analysis. *Psychology and Aging, 23,* 104–118.

Ollendick, T. H., King, N. J., & Muris, P. (2002). Fears and phobias in children: Phenomenology, epidemiology, and aetiology. *Child and Adolescent Mental Health, 7,* 98–106.

Oller, D. K. (2000). *The emergence of the speech capacity.* Mahwah, NJ: Erlbaum.

Olshansky, S. J., Hayflick, L., & Perls, T. T. (2004). Antiaging medicine: The hype and the reality— Part II. *Journal of Gerontology, 59A,* 649–651.

Olson, R. E. (2000). Is it wise to restrict fat in the diets of children? *Journal of the American Dietetic Association, 100,* 28–32.

Olson, S. L., Bates, J. E., Sandy, J. M., & Lantheir, R. (2000). Early development precursors of externalizing behavior in middle childhood and adolescence. *Journal of Abnormal Child Psychology, 28,* 119–133.

Omar, H., McElderry, D., & Zakharia, R. (2003). Educating adolescents about puberty: What are we missing? *International Journal of Adolescent Medicine and Health, 15,* 79–83.

Ondrusek, N., Abramovitch, R., Pencharz, P., & Koren, G. (1998). Empirical examination of the ability of children to consent to clinical research. *Journal of Medical Ethics, 24,* 158–165.

O'Neill, M., Bard, K. A., Kinnell, M., & Fluck, M. (2005). Maternal gestures with 20-month-old

infants in two contexts. *Developmental Science, 8,* 352–359.

Ong, A. D., & Allaire, J. C. (2005). Cardiovascular intraindividual variability in later life: The influence of social connectedness and positive emotions. *Psychology and Aging, 20,* 476–485.

Ong, A. D., Edwards, L. M., & Bergeman, C. S. (2006). Hope as a source of resilience in later adulthood. *Personality and Individual Differences, 41,* 1263–1273.

Oosterwegel, A., & Oppenheimer, L. (1993). *The self-system: Developmental changes between and within self-concepts.* Hillsdale, NJ: Erlbaum.

O'Rahilly, R., & Müller, F. (2001). *Human embryology and teratology.* New York: Wiley-Liss.

Orbio de Castro, B., Veerman, J. W., Koops, W., Bosch, J. D., & Monshouwer, H. J. (2002). Hostile attribution of intent and aggressive behavior: A meta-analysis. *Child Development, 73,* 916–934.

Ordonana, J. R., Caspi, A., & Moffitt, T. E. (2008). Unintentional injuries in a twin study of preschool children: Environmental, not genetic risk factors. *Journal of Pediatric Psychology, 33,* 185–194.

Ornish, D., Lin, J., Daubenmier, J., Weidner, G., Epel, E. S., & Kemp, C. (2008). Increased telomerase activity and comprehensive lifestyle changes: A pilot study. *Lancet Oncology, 9,* 1048–1057.

Orzano, A. J., & Scott, J. G. (2004). Diagnosis and treatment of obesity in adults: An applied evidence-based review. *Journal of the American Board of Family Practice, 17,* 359–369.

Osborne, J. (1994). Academics, self-esteem, and race: A look at the underlying assumption of the disidentification hypothesis. *Personality and Social Psychology Bulletin, 21,* 449–455.

Osherson, D. N., & Markman, E. M. (1975). Language and the ability to evaluate contradictions and tautologies. *Cognition, 2,* 213–226.

Ostrov, J. M., Crick, N. R., & Stauffacher, K. (2006). Relational aggression in sibling and peer relationships during early childhood. *Applied Developmental Psychology, 27,* 241–253.

Ostrov, J. M., Gentile, D. A., & Crick, N. R. (2006). Media exposure, aggression, and prosocial behavior during early childhood: A longitudinal study. *Social Development, 15,* 612–627.

Otis, N., Grouzet, F. M. E., & Pelletier, L. G. (2005). Latent motivational change in an academic setting: A three-year longitudinal study. *Journal of Educational Psychology, 97,* 170–183.

Ovando, C. J., & Collier, V. P. (1998). *Bilingual and ESL classrooms: Teaching in multicultural contexts.* Boston: McGraw-Hill.

Owens, R. E. (2005). *Language development: An introduction.* Boston: Allyn and Bacon.

Owsley, C., Ball, K., McGwin, G., Jr., Sloane, M. E., Roenker, D. L., White, M. F., & Overley, E. T. (1998). Visual processing impairment and risk of motor vehicle crash among older adults. *Journal of the American Medical Association, 279,* 1083–1088.

Özçaliskan, S. (2005). On learning to draw the distinction between physical and metaphorical motion: Is metaphor an early emerging cognitive and linguistic capacity? *Journal of Child Language, 32,* 291–318.

Özçaliskan, S., & Goldin-Meadow, S. (2005). Gesture is at the cutting edge of early language development. *Cognition, 96,* B101–B113.

P

Padula, M. A., & Miller, D. L. (1999). Understanding graduate women's reentry experiences. *Psychology of Women Quarterly, 23,* 327–343.

Pagani, L. S., Japel, C., Vitaro, F., Tremblay, R. E., Larose, S., & McDuff, P. (2008). When predictions fail: The case of unexpected pathways toward high school dropout. *Journal of Social Issues, 64,* 175–193.

Pager, D., & Shepherd, H. (2008). The sociology of discrimination: Racial discrimination in employment, housing, credit, and consumer markets. *Annual Review of Sociology, 34*, 181–209.

Palacio-Quintin, E. (2000). Les services de garde et le développement de l'enfant [The impact of day care on child development]. *ISUMA: Canadian Journal of Policy Research, 1*(2), 25–30.

Palincsar, A. S. (2003). Advancing a theoretical model of learning and instruction. In B. J. Zimmerman (Ed.), *Educational psychology: A century of contributions* (pp. 459–475). Mahwah, NJ: Erlbaum.

Palmer, J. R., Hatch, E. E., Rao, R. S., Kaufman, R. H., Herbst, A. L., & Noller, K. L. (2001). Infertility among women exposed prenatally to diethylstilbestrol. *American Journal of Epidemiology, 154*, 316–321.

Palop, J. J., Chin, J., Roberson, E. D., Wang, J., Thwin, M. T., & Bien-Ly, N. (2007). Aberrant excitatory neuronal activity and compensatory remodeling of inhibitory hippocampal circuits in mouse models of Alzheimer's disease. *Neuron, 55*, 697–711.

Pan, B. A., & Snow, C. E. (1999). The development of conversation and discourse skills. In M. Barrett (Ed.), *The development of language* (pp. 229–249). Hove, UK: Psychology Press.

Pan, H. W. (1994). Children's play in Taiwan. In J. L. Roopnarine, J. E. Johnson, & F. H. Hooper (Eds.), *Children's play in diverse cultures* (pp. 31–50). Albany, NY: SUNY Press.

Panish, J. B., & Stricker, G. (2002). Perceptions of childhood and adult sibling relationships. *NYS Psychologist, 14*, 33–36.

Papadakis, A. A., Prince, R. P., Jones, N. P., & Strauman, T. J. (2006). Self-regulation, rumination, and vulnerability to depression in adolescent girls. *Development and Psychopathology, 18*, 815–829.

Paquette, D. (2004). Theorizing the father–child relationship: Mechanisms and developmental outcomes. *Human Development, 47*, 193–219.

Paradis, J. (2007). Second language acquisition in childhood. In E. Hoff & M. Shatz (Eds.), *Blackwell handbook of language development* (pp. 387–405). Malden, MA: Blackwell.

Pardum, C. J., L'Engle, K. L., & Brown, J. D. (2005). Linking exposure to outcomes: Early adolescents' consumption of sexual content in six media. *Mass Communication and Society, 87*, 75–91.

Parent, A., Teilmann, G., Juul, A., Skakkebaek, N. E., Toppari, J., & Bourguignon, J. (2003). The timing of normal puberty and the age limits of sexual precocity: Variations around the world, secular trends, and changes after migration. *Endocrine Reviews, 24*, 668–693.

Paris, S. G., & Paris, A. H. (2006). Assessments of early reading. In K. A. Renninger & I. E. Sigel (Eds.), *Handbook of child psychology: Vol. 4. Child psychology in practice* (6th ed., pp. 48–74). Hoboken, NJ: Wiley.

Park, D. C., Lautenschlager, G., Hedden, T., Davidson, N. S., Smith, A. D., & Smith, P. K. (2002). Models of visuospatial and verbal memory across the adult life span. *Psychology and Aging, 17*, 299–320.

Park, D. C., & Payer, D. (2006). Working memory across the adult lifespan. In E. Bialystok & F. I. M. Craik (Eds.), *Lifespan cognition: Mechanisms of change* (pp. 128–142). New York: Oxford University Press.

Parke, R. D. (2002). Fathers and families. In M. H. Bornstein (Ed.), *Handbook of parenting: Vol. 3* (2nd ed., pp. 27–73). Mahwah, NJ: Erlbaum.

Parke, R. D., & Buriel, R. (2006). Socialization in the family: Ethnic and ecological perspectives. In N. Eisenberg (Ed.), *Handbook of child psychology: Vol. 3. Social, emotional, and personality development* (6th ed., pp. 429–504). Hoboken, NJ: Wiley.

Parke, R. D., Coltrane, S., Fabricius, W., Powers, J., & Adams, M. (2004a). Assessing father involvement in Mexican-American families. In R. Day & M. E. Lamb (Eds.), *Conceptualizing and measuring paternal involvement* (pp. 17–38). Mahwah, NJ: Erlbaum.

Parke, R. D., Simpkins, S. D., McDowell, D. J., Kim, M., Killian, C., Dennis, J., Flyr, M. L., Wild, M., & Rah, Y. (2004b). Relative contributions of families and peers to children's social development. In P. K. Smith & C. H. Hart (Eds.), *Blackwell handbook of childhood social development* (pp. 156–177). Malden, MA: Blackwell.

Parker, F. L., Boak, A. Y., Griffin, K. W., Ripple, C., & Peay, L. (1999). Parent–child relationship, home learning environment, and school readiness. *School Psychology Review, 28*, 413–425.

Parker, J. G., Low, C. M., Walker, A. R., & Gamm, B. K. (2005). Friendship jealousy in young adolescents: Individual differences and links to sex, self esteem, aggression, and social adjustment. *Developmental Psychology, 41*, 235–250.

Parker, S. W., Nelson, C. A., & the Bucharest Early Intervention Project Core Group. (2005). The impact of early institutional rearing on the ability to discriminate facial expressions of emotion: An event-related potential study. *Child Development, 76*, 54–72.

Parmelee, P. A., & Lawton, M. P. (1990). The design of special environments for the aged. In J. E. Birren & K. W. Schaie (Eds.), *Handbook of the psychology of aging* (3rd ed., pp. 464–488). San Diego, CA: Academic Press.

Parten, M. (1932). Social participation among preschool children. *Journal of Abnormal and Social Psychology, 27*, 243–269.

Pascalis, O., de Haan, M., & Nelson, C. A. (2002). Is face processing species-specific during the first year of life? *Science, 296*, 1321–1323.

Pascarella, E. T., & Terenzini, P. T. (1991). *How college affects students.* San Francisco: Jossey-Bass.

Pasinetti, G. M., & Eberstein, J. A. (2008). Metabolic syndrome and the role of dietary lifestyles in Alzheimer's disease. *Journal of Neurochemistry, 106*, 1503–1514.

Pasterski, V. L., Geffner, M. E., Brain, C., Hindmarsh, P., & Brook, C. (2005). Prenatal hormones and postnatal socialization by parents as determinants of male-typical toy play in girls with congenital adrenal hyperplasia. *Child Development, 76*, 264–278.

Paterson, D. S., Trachtenberg, F. L., Thompson, E. G., Belliveau, R. A., Beggs, A. H., & Darnall, R. (2006). Multiple serotonergic brainstem abnormalities in sudden infant death syndrome. *Journal of the American Medical Association, 296*, 2124–2132.

Pattenden, S., Antova, T., Neuberger, M., Nikiforov, B., De Sario, M., Grize, L., & Heinrich, J. (2006). Parental smoking and children's respiratory health: Independent effects of prenatal and postnatal exposure. *Tobacco Control, 15*, 294–301.

Patterson, C. J. (2002). Lesbian and gay parenthood. In M. H. Bornstein (Ed.), *Handbook of parenting* (Vol. 3, pp. 317–338). Mahwah, NJ: Erlbaum.

Patterson, G. R., & Fisher, P. A. (2002). Recent developments in our understanding of parenting: Bidirectional effects, causal models, and the search for parsimony. In M. H. Bornstein (Ed.), *Handbook of parenting* (Vol. 5, pp. 59–88). Mahwah, NJ: Erlbaum.

Patterson, G. R., & Yoerger, K. (2002). A developmental model for early- and late-onset delinquency. In J. B. Reid & G. R. Patterson (Eds.), *Antisocial behavior in children and adolescents* (pp. 147–172). Washington, DC: American Psychological Association.

Patterson, M. L., & Werker, J. F. (2002). Infants' ability to match dynamic phonetic and gender information in the face and voice. *Journal of Experimental Child Psychology, 81*, 93–115.

Paul, J. J., & Cillessen, A. H. N. (2003). Dynamics of peer victimization in early adolescence: Results from a four-year longitudinal study. *Journal of Applied School Psychology, 19*, 25–43.

Paulussen-Hoogeboom, M. C., Stams, G. J. J. M., Hermanns, J. M. A., & Peetsma, T. T. D. (2007). Child negative emotionality and parenting from infancy

to preschool: A meta-analytic review. *Developmental Psychology, 43*, 438–453.

Pawelec, G., Wagner, W., Adibzadeh, M., & Engel, A. (1999). T cell immunosenescence in vitro and in vivo. *Experimental Gerontology, 34*, 419–429.

Payne, B. K., & Fletcher, L. B. (2005). Elder abuse in nursing homes: Prevention and resolution strategies and barriers. *Journal of Criminal Justice, 33*, 119–125.

PCA America. (2009). *Healthy Families America FAQ.* Retrieved from www.healthyfamiliesamerica.org/about_us/findex.shtml

Peake, A., & Harris, K. L. (2002). Young adults' attitudes toward multiple role planning: The influence of gender, career traditionality, and marriage plans. *Journal of Vocational Behavior, 60*, 405–421.

Pearlman, D. N., Zierler, S., Meersman, S., Kim, H. K., Viner-Brown, S. I., & Caron, C. (2006). Race disparities in childhood asthma: Does where you live matter? *Journal of the National Medical Association, 98*, 239–247.

Peck, R. C. (1968). Psychological developments in the second half of life. In B. L. Neugarten (Ed.), *Middle age and aging* (pp. 88–92). Chicago: University of Chicago Press.

Pedersen, W. C., Miller, L. C., Putcha-Bhagavatula, A. D., & Yang, Y. (2002). Evolved sex differences in the number of partners desired? The long and the short of it. *Psychological Science, 13*, 157–161.

Pederson, D. R., & Moran, G. (1996). Expressions of the attachment relationship outside of the Strange Situation. *Child Development, 67*, 915–927.

Peisner-Feinberg, E. S., Burchinal, M. R., Clifford, R. M., Culkin, M. L., Howes, C., Kagan, S. L., & Yazijian, N. (2001). The relation of preschool child-care quality to children's cognitive and social developmental trajectories through second grade. *Child Development, 72*, 1534–1553.

Pellegrini, A. D. (1992). Kindergarten children's social cognitive status as a predictor of first grade success. *Early Childhood Research Quarterly, 7*, 565–577.

Pellegrini, A. D. (2003). Perceptions and functions of play and real fighting in early adolescence. *Child Development, 74*, 1522–1533.

Pellegrini, A. D. (2004). Rough-and-tumble play from childhood through adolescence: Development and possible functions. In P. K. Smith & C. H. Hart (Eds.), *Blackwell handbook of childhood social development* (pp. 438–453). Malden, MA: Blackwell.

Pellegrini, A. D. (2005). *Recess: Its role in development and education.* Mahwah, NJ: Erlbaum.

Pellegrini, A. D., & Holmes, R. M. (2006). The role of recess in primary school. In D. G. Singer, R. M. Golinkoff, & K. Hirsh-Pasek (Eds.), *Play = learning* (pp. 36–53). New York: Oxford University Press.

Pellegrini, A. D., Huberty, P. D., & Jones, I. (1995). The effects of recess timing on children's playground and classroom behaviors. *American Educational Research Journal, 32*, 845–864.

Pellegrini, A. D., Kato, K., Blatchford, P., & Baines, E. (2002). A short-term longitudinal study of children's playground games across the first year of school: Implications for social competence and adjustment to school. *American Educational Research Journal, 39*, 991–1015.

Pellegrini, A. D., & Smith, P. K. (1998). Physical activity play: The nature and function of a neglected aspect of play. *Child Development, 69*, 577–598.

Peña, R., Wall, S., & Person, L. (2000). The effect of poverty, social inequality, and maternal education on infant mortality in Nicaragua, 1988–1993. *American Journal of Public Health, 90*, 64–69.

Penedo, F. J., & Dahn, J. R. (2005). Exercise and well-being: A review of mental and physical health benefits associated with physical activity. *Current Opinion in Psychiatry, 18*, 189–193.

Penny, H., & Haddock, G. (2007). Anti-fat prejudice among children: The 'mere proximity' effect in 5–10 year olds. *Journal of Experimental Social Psychology, 43*, 678–683.

Peralta de Mendoza, O. A., & Salsa, A. M. (2003). Instruction in early comprehension and use of a symbol–referent relation. *Cognitive Development, 18,* 269–284.

Perkins, H. W. (1991). Religious commitment, yuppie values, and well-being in post-collegiate life. *Review of Religious Research, 32,* 244–251.

Perlmutter, M. (1984). Continuities and discontinuities in early human memory: Paradigms, processes, and performances. In R. V. Kail, Jr., & N. R. Spear (Eds.), *Comparative perspectives on the development of memory* (pp. 253–287). Hillsdale, NJ: Erlbaum.

Perlmutter, M., Kaplan, M., & Nyquist, L. (1990). Development of adaptive competence in adulthood. *Human Development, 33,* 185–197.

Perls, T., Levenson, R., Regan, M., & Puca, A. (2002). What does it take to live to 100? *Mechanisms of Ageing and Development, 123,* 231–242.

Perls, T., & Terry, D. (2003). Understanding the determinants of exceptional longevity. *Annals of Internal Medicine, 139,* 445–449.

Perone, S., Madole, K. L., Ross-Sheehy, S., Carey, M., & Oakes, L. M. (2008). The relation between infants' activity with objects and attention to object appearance. *Developmental Psychology, 44,* 1242–1248.

Perry, W. G., Jr. (1981). Cognitive and ethical growth. In A. Chickering (Ed.), *The modern American college* (pp. 76–116). San Francisco: Jossey-Bass.

Perry, W. G., Jr. (1998). *Forms of intellectual and ethical development in the college years: A scheme.* San Francisco: Jossey-Bass. (Originally published 1970)

Perry-Jenkins, M., Repetti, R. L., & Crouter, A. C. (2000). Work and family in the 1990s. *Journal of Marriage and the Family, 62,* 981–998.

Peshkin, A. (1997). *Places of memory: Whiteman's schools and Native American communities.* Mahwah, NJ: Erlbaum.

Peters, R. D. (2005). A community-based approach to promoting resilience in young children, their families, and their neighborhoods. In R. D. Paters, B. Leadbeater, & R. J. McMahon (Eds.), *Resilience in children, families, and communities: Linking context to practice and policy* (pp. 157–176). New York: Kluwer Academic.

Peters, R. D., Petrunka, K., & Arnold, R. (2003). The Better Beginnings, Better Futures Project: A universal, comprehensive, community-based prevention approach for primary school children and their families. *Journal of Clinical Child and Adolescent Psychology, 32,* 215–227.

Petersen, N., & Gonzales, R. C. (1999). *Career counseling models for diverse populations.* Belmont, CA: Wadsworth.

Peterson, B. E. (2002). Longitudinal analysis of midlife generativity, intergenerational roles, and caregiving. *Psychology and Aging, 17,* 161–168.

Peterson, B. E., & Duncan, L. E. (2007). Midlife women's generativity and authoritarianism: Marriage, motherhood, and 10 years of aging. *Psychology and Aging, 22,* 411–419.

Peterson, B. E., Smirles, K. A., & Wentworth, P. A. (1997). Generativity and authoritarianism: Implications for personality, political involvement, and parenting. *Journal of Personality and Social Psychology, 72,* 1202–1216.

Peterson, C., & Seligman, M. E. (2004). *Character strengths and virtues.* New York: Oxford University Press.

Petitto, L. A., Holowka, S., Sergio, L. E., Levy, B., & Ostry, D. J. (2004). Baby hands that move to the rhythm of language: Hearing babies acquiring sign languages babble silently on the hands. *Cognition, 93,* 43–73.

Petitto, L. A., Holowka, S., Sergio, L. E., & Ostry, D. (2001, September 6). Language rhythms in babies' hand movements. *Nature, 413,* 35–36.

Petitto, L. A., & Marentette, P. F. (1991). Babbling in the manual mode: Evidence for the ontogeny of language. *Science, 251,* 1493–1496.

Pettit, G. S. (2004). Violent children in developmental perspective. *Current Directions in Psychological Science, 13,* 194–197.

Pew Research Center. (2006). *Strong public support for right to die.* Retrieved from http://people-press.org/reports

Pfeffer, C. R. (2006). Suicide and suicidality. In M. K. Dulcan & J. M. Wiener (Eds.), *Essentials of child and adolescent psychiatry* (pp. 621–632). Washington, DC: American Psychiatric Publishing.

Phillips, M. (1997). What makes schools effective? A comparison of the relationships of communitarian climate and academic climate to mathematics achievement and attendance during middle school. *American Educational Research Journal, 34,* 633–662.

Phillipsen, L. C. (1999). Associations between age, gender, and group acceptance and three components of friendship quality. *Journal of Early Adolescence, 19,* 438–464.

Phinney, J. S. (2007). Ethnic identity exploration in emerging adulthood. In J. J. Arnett & J. L. Tanner (Eds.), *Emerging adults in America: Coming of age in the 21st century* (pp. 117–134). Washington, DC: American Psychological Association.

Phinney, J. S., & Chavira, V. (1995). Parental ethnic socialization and adolescent outcomes in ethnic minority families. *Journal of Research on Adolescence, 5,* 31–53.

Phinney, J. S., Horenczyk, G., Liebkind, K., & Vedder, P. (2001). Ethnic identity, immigration, and well-being: An interactional perspective. *Journal of Social Issues, 57,* 493–510.

Phinney, J. S., Ong, A., & Madden, T. (2000). Cultural values and intergenerational value discrepancies in immigrant and non-immigrant families. *Child Development, 71,* 528–539.

Piaget, J. (1926). *The language and thought of the child.* New York: Harcourt, Brace, & World. (Original work published 1923)

Piaget, J. (1930). *The child's conception of the world.* New York: Harcourt, Brace, & World. (Original work published 1926)

Piaget, J. (1951). *Play, dreams, and imitation in childhood.* New York: Norton. (Original work published 1945)

Piaget, J. (1952). *The origins of intelligence in children.* New York: International Universities Press. (Original work published 1936)

Piaget, J. (1967). *Six psychological studies.* New York: Vintage.

Piaget, J. (1971). *Biology and knowledge.* Chicago: University of Chicago Press.

Pianta, R., Egeland, B., & Erickson, M. F. (1989). The antecedents of maltreatment: Results of the Mother–Child Interaction Research Project. In D. Cicchetti & V. Carlson (Eds.), *Child maltreatment* (pp. 203–253). New York: Cambridge University Press.

Pianta, R. C., Hamre, B., & Stuhlman, M. (2003). Relationships between teachers and children. In W. M. Reynolds & G. E. Miller (Eds.), *Handbook of psychology: Educational psychology* (Vol. 7, pp. 199–234). New York: Wiley.

Pickrell, T. M. (2006, July). Driver alchohol involvement in fatal crashes by age group and vehicle type. *Traffic Safety Facts.* Washington, DC: U.S. Department of Transportation.

Pietz, J., Peter, J., Graf, R., Rauterberg, R. I., Rupp, A., & Sontheimer, D. (2004). Physical growth and neurodevelopmental outcome of nonhandicapped low-risk children born preterm. *Early Human Development, 79,* 131–143.

Pillemer, K. A., Mueller-Johnson, K. U., Mock, S. E., Suitor, J. J., & Lachs, M. S. (2007). Interventions to prevent elder mistreatment. In L. S. Doll, S. Bonzo, J. A. Mercy, & D. A. Sleet (Eds.), *Handbook of injury and violence prevention* (pp. 241–254). New York: Springer Science + Business Media.

Pillemer, K., & Suitor, J. (2002). Explaining mothers' ambivalence toward their adult children. *Journal of Marriage and the Family, 64,* 602–613.

Pillow, B. (2002). Children's and adults' evaluation of the certainty of deductive inferences, inductive inferences, and guesses. *Child Development, 73,* 779–792.

Pinderhughes, E. E., Dodge, K. A., Bates, J. E., Pettit, G. S., & Zelli, A. (2000). Discipline responses: Influences of parents' socioeconomic status, ethnicity, beliefs about parenting, stress, and cognitive-emotional processes. *Journal of Family Psychology, 14,* 380–400.

Pinderhughes, E. E., Nix, R., Foster, E. M., Jones, D., & the Conduct Problems Prevention Research Group. (2001). Parenting in context: Impact of neighborhood poverty, residential stability, public services, social networks, and danger on parental behaviors. *Journal of Marriage and Family, 63,* 941–953.

Pinquart, M. (2003). Loneliness in married, widowed, divorced, and never-married older adults. *Journal of Social and Personal Relationships, 20,* 31–53.

Pinquart, M., & Sörensen, S. (2001). Gender differences in self-concept and psychological well-being in old age: A meta-analysis. *Journal of Gerontology, 56B,* P195–P213.

Pinquart, M., & Sörensen, S. (2006). Gender differences in caregiver stressor, social resources, and health: An updated meta-analysis. *Journal of Gerontology, 61B,* P33–P45.

Pipp, S., Easterbrooks, M. A., & Harmon, R. J. (1992). The relation between attachment and knowledge of self and mother in one-year-old infants to three-year-old infants. *Child Development, 63,* 738–750.

Pizarro, D. A., & Bloom, P. (2003). The intelligence of the moral intuitions: Comment on Haidt (2001). *Psychological Review, 110,* 193–196.

Plassmana, B. L., Langa, K. M., Fisher, G. G., Heeringa, S. G., Weir, D. R., Ofstedal, M. B., Burke, J. R., Hurd M. D., Potter, G. G., Rodgers, W. L., Steffens, D. C., Willis, R. J., & Wallace, R. B. (2007). Prevalence of dementia in the United States: The aging, demographics, and memory study. *Neuroepidemiology, 29,* 125–132.

Pleck, J. H., & Masciadrelli, B. P. (2004). Paternal involvement by U.S. residential fathers: Levels, sources, and consequences. In M. E. Lamb (Ed.), *The role of the father in child development* (4th ed., pp. 222–271). Hoboken, NJ: Wiley.

Plomin, R. (1994). *Genetics and experience: The interplay between nature and nurture.* Thousand Oaks, CA: Sage.

Plomin, R. (2003). General cognitive ability. In R. Plomin & J. C. DeFries (Eds.), *Behavioral genetics in the postgenomic era* (pp. 183–201). Washington, DC: American Psychological Association.

Plomin, R. (2005). *Finding genes in child psychology and psychiatry: When are we going to be there?* Unpublished manuscript. London: King's College.

Plomin, R., DeFries, J. C., Craig, I. W., & McGuffin, P. (2003). Behavioral genomics. In R. Plomin, J. C. DeFries, I. W. Craig, & P. McGuffin (Eds.), *Behavioral genetics in the postgenomic era* (pp. 531–540). Washington, DC: American Psychological Association.

Plomin, R., DeFries, J. C., McClearn, G. E., & McGuffin, P. (2001). *Behavioral genetics* (4th ed.). New York: Worth.

Plomin, R., & Spinath, F. M. (2004). Intelligence: Genetics, genes, and genomics. *Journal of Personality and Social Psychology, 86,* 112–129.

Podewils, L. J., Guallar, E., Kuller, L. H., Fried, L. P., Lopez, O. L., Carlson, M., & Lyketsos, C. G. (2005). Physical activity, APOE genotype, and dementia risk: Findings from the Cardiovascular Health Cognition Study. *American Journal of Epidemiology, 161,* 639–651.

Pogarsky, G., Thornberry, T. P., & Lizotte, A. J. (2006). Developmental outcomes for children of young mothers. *Journal of Marriage and Family, 68,* 332–344.

Pohl, R. (2002). *Poverty in Canada.* Ottawa, ON: Innercity Ministries.

Polka, L., & Werker, J. F. (1994). Developmental changes in perception of non-native vowel contrasts. *Journal of Experimental Psychology: Human Perception and Performance, 20,* 421–435.

Pomerantz, E. M., & Eaton, M. M. (2000). Developmental differences in children's conceptions of parental control: "They love me, but they make me feel incompetent." *Merrill-Palmer Quarterly, 46,* 140–167.

Pomerantz, E. M., & Ruble, D. N. (1998). The multidimensional nature of control: Implications for the development of sex differences in self-evaluation. In J. Heckhausen & C. S. Dweck (Eds.), *Motivation and self-regulation across the lifespan* (pp. 159–184). New York: Cambridge University Press.

Pomerantz, E. M., & Saxon, J. L. (2001). Conceptions of ability as stable and self-evaluative processes: A longitudinal examination. *Child Development, 72,* 152–173.

Pomerleau, A., Scuccimarri, C., & Malcuit, G. (2003). Mother–infant behavioral interactions in teenage and adult mothers during the first six months postpartum: Relations with infant development. *Infant Mental Health Journal, 24,* 495–509.

Pons, F., Lawson, J., Harris, P. L., & de Rosnay, M. (2003). Individual differences in children's emotion understanding: Effects of age and language. *Scandinavian Journal of Psychology, 44,* 347–353.

Popenoe, D. (2006). *Debunking divorce myths.* Retrieved from health.discovery.com/centers/loverelationships/articles/divorce.html

Portes, A., & Rumbaut, R. G. (2005), Introduction: The second generation and the Children of Immigrants Longitudinal Study. *Ethnic and Racial Studies, 28,* 983–999.

Posada, G., Carbonell, O. A., Alzate, G., & Plata, S. J. (2004). Through Colombian lenses: Ethnographic and conventional analyses of maternal care and their associations with secure base behavior. *Developmental Psychology, 40,* 508–518.

Posner, M. I., & Rothbart, M. K. (2007). *Educating the human brain.* Washington, DC: American Psychological Association.

Pothiwala, P., Evans, E. M., & Chapman-Novakofski, K. M. (2006). Ethnic variation in risk for osteoporosis among women: A review of biological and behavioral factors. *Journal of Women's Health, 15,* 709–719.

Poulin-Dubois, D., Serbin, L. A., Eichstedt, J. A., Sen, M. G., & Beissel, C. F. (2002). Men don't put on make-up: Toddlers' knowledge of the gender stereotyping of household activities. *Social Development, 11,* 166–181.

Powlishta, K. K., Serbin, L. A., & Moller, L. C. (1993). The stability of individual differences in gender typing: Implications for understanding gender segregation. *Sex Roles, 29,* 723–737.

Prager, K. J., & Bailey, J. M. (1985). Androgyny, ego development, and psychological crisis resolution. *Sex Roles, 13,* 525–535.

Pratt, M. W., Norris, J. E., Hebblethwaite, S., & Arnold, M. L. (2008). Intergenerational transmission of values: Family generativity and adolescents' narratives of parent and grandparent value teaching. *Journal of Personality, 76,* 171–198.

Pratt, M. W., Skoe, E. E., & Arnold, M. L. (2004). Care reasoning development and family socialization patterns in later adolescence: A longitudinal analysis. *International Journal of Behavioral Development, 28,* 139–147.

Preece, J., & Findsen, B. (2007). Keeping people active: Continuing education programs that work. In M. Robinson, W. Novelli, C. Pearson, & L. Norris (Eds.), *Global health and global aging* (pp. 313–322). San Francisco: Jossey-Bass.

Preissler, M. A., & Carey, S. (2004). Do both pictures and words function as symbols for 18- and 24-month-old children? *Journal of Cognition and Development, 5,* 185–212.

Prentice, R. L., Chlebowski, R. T., Stefanik, M. L., Mason, J. E., Pettinger, M., & Hendrix, S. L. (2008). Estrogen plus progestin therapy and breast cancer in recently postmenopausal women. *American Journal of Epidemiology, 167,* 1207–1216.

Pressley, M., & Hilden, D. (2006). Cognitive strategies. In D. Kuhn & R. Siegler (Eds.), *Handbook of child psychology: Vol. 2. Cognition, perception, and language* (6th ed., pp. 511–556). Hoboken, NJ: Wiley.

Pressley, M., Wharton-McDonald, R., Raphael, L. M., Bogner, K., & Roehrig, A. (2002). Exemplary first-grade teaching. In B. M. Taylor & P. D. Pearson (Eds.), *Teaching reading: Effective schools, accomplished teachers* (pp. 73–88). Mahwah, NJ: Erlbaum.

Prevatt, F. (2003). Dropping out of school: A review of intervention programs. *Journal of School Psychology, 41,* 377–399.

Previc, F. H. (1991). A general theory concerning the prenatal origins of cerebral lateralization. *Psychological Review, 98,* 299–334.

Priddy, K. D. (2004). Is there logic behind fetal monitoring? *Journal of Obstetric, Gynecologic, and Neonatal Nursing, 33,* 550–553.

Princeton Religion Research Center. (1999). *Religious Practices in the United States.* Princeton, NJ: Author.

Prinstein, M. J., Boergers, J., & Spirito, A. (2001). Adolescents' and their friends' health-risk behavior: Factors that alter or add to peer influences. *Journal of Pediatric Psychology, 26,* 287–298.

Prinstein, M. J., Boergers, J., & Vernberg, E.M. (2001). Overt and relational aggression in adolescents: Social–psychological adjustment of aggressors and victims. *Journal of Clinical Child Psychology, 30,* 479–491.

Prinstein, M. J., & La Greca, A. M. (2002). Peer crowd affiliation and internalizing distress in childhood and adolescence: A longitudinal follow-back study. *Journal of Research on Adolescence, 12,* 325–351.

Prinstein, M. J., Meade, C. S., & Cohen, G. L. (2003). Adolescent oral sex, peer popularity, and perceptions of best friends' sexual behavior. *Journal of Pediatric Psychology, 28,* 243–249.

Proctor, M. H., Moore, L. L., Gao, D., Cupples, L. A., Bradlee, M. L., Hood, M. Y., & Ellison, R. C. (2003). Television viewing and change in body fat from preschool to early adolescence: The Framingham Children's Study. *International Journal of Obesity, 27,* 827–833.

Programme for International Student Assessment. (2003). *Learning for tomorrow's world: First results from Programme for International Student Assessment 2003.* Retrieved from www.pisa.oecd.org

Programme for International Student Assessment. (2005). *School factors related to quality and equity.* Retrieved from www.pisa.oecd.org

Programme for International Student Assessment. (2006). *PISA 2006: Science competencies for tomorrow's world.* Retrieved from www.oecd.org

Pronczuk, J., & Surdu, S. (2008). Children's environmental health in the twenty-first century. *Annals of the New York Academy of Sciences, 1140,* 143–154.

Proulx, K., & Jacelon, C. (2004). Dying with dignity: The good patient versus the good death. *American Journal of Hospice and Palliative Care, 21,* 116–120.

Provins, K. A. (1997). Handedness and speech: A critical reappraisal of the role of genetic and environmental factors in the cerebral lateralization of function. *Psychological Review, 104,* 554–571.

Pruchno, R., & McKenney, D. (2000). The effects of custodial and coresident households on the mental health of grandmothers. *Journal of Mental Health and Aging, 6,* 291–310.

Pruden, S. M., Hirsh-Pasek, K., Golinkoff, R. M., & Hennon, E. A. (2006). The birth of words: Ten-month-olds learn words through perceptual salience. *Child Development, 77,* 266–280.

Pryor, J., & Rodgers, B. (2001). *Children in changing families: Life after parental separation.* Oxford, UK: Blackwell.

Prysak, M., Lorenz, R. P., & Kisly, A. (1995). Pregnancy outcome in nulliparous women 35 years and older. *Obstetrics and Gynecology, 85,* 65–70.

Puhl, R., & Brownell, K. D. (2006). Confronting and coping with weight stigma: An investigation of overweight and obese individuals. *Obesity, 14,* 1802–1815.

Pujol, J., Soriano-Mas, C., Ortiz, H., Sebastián-Gallés, N., Losilla, J. M., & Deus, J. (2006). Myelination of language-related areas in the developing brain. *Neurology, 66,* 339–343.

Putallaz, M., Grimes, C. L., Foster, K. J., Kupersmidt, J. B., Coie, J. D., & Dearing, K. (2007). Overt and relational aggression and victimization: Multiple perspectives within the school setting. *Journal of School Psychology, 45,* 523–547.

Putnam, F. W. (2003). Ten-year research update review: Child sexual abuse. *Journal of the American Academy of Child and Adolescent Psychiatry, 42,* 269–278.

Pyka, G., Lindenberger, E., Charette, S., & Marcus, R. (1994). Muscle strength and fiber adaptations to a year-long resistance training program in elderly men and women. *Journal of Gerontology, 49,* M22–27.

Pyszczynski, T., Greenberg, J., Solomon, S., Arndt, J., & Schimel, J. (2004). Why do people need self-esteem? A theoretical and empirical view. *Psychological Bulletin, 130,* 435–468.

Q

Qiu, C., Bäckman, L., Winblad, B., Agüero-Torres, H., & Fratiglioni, L. (2001). The influence of education on clinically diagnosed dementia incidence and mortality data from the Kungsholmen Project. *Archives of Neurology, 58,* 2034–2039.

Quick, H. E., & Moen, P. (1998). Gender, employment, and retirement quality: A life course approach to the differential experiences of men and women. *Journal of Occupational Health Psychology, 3,* 44–64.

Quill, T. E. (1991). Death and dignity: A case of individualized decision making. *New England Journal of Medicine, 324,* 691–694.

Quine, S., Wells, Y., de Vaus, D., & Kendig, H. (2007). When choice in retirement decisions is missing: Qualitative and quantitative findings of impact on well-being. *Australasian Journal on Ageing, 26,* 173–179.

Quinn, P. C. (2008). In defense of core competencies, quantitative change, and continuity. *Child Development, 79,* 1633–1638.

Quinn, T. C., & Overbaugh, J. (2005). HIV/AIDS in women: An expanding epidemic. *Science, 308,* 1582–1583.

Quist, J. F., & Kennedy, J. L. (2001). Genetics of childhood disorders: XXIII. ADHD, part 7: The serotonin system. *Journal of the American Academy of Child and Adolescent Psychiatry, 40,* 253–256.

R

Raaijmakers, Q. A. W., Engels, R. C. M. E., & Van Hoof, A. (2005). Delinquency and moral reasoning in adolescence and young adulthood. *International Journal of Behavioral Development, 29,* 247–258.

Rabbitt, P., Lunn, M., & Wong, D. (2008). Death, dropout, and longitudinal measurements of cognitive change in old age. *Journal of Gerontology, 63B,* P271–P278.

Rabig, J., Thomas, W., Kane, R., Cutler, L. J., & McAlilly, S. (2006). Radical redesign of nursing homes: Applying the Green House concept in Tupelo, Mississippi. *Gerontologist, 46,* 533–539.

Rabiner, D. J., O'Keeffe, J., & Brown, D. (2004). A conceptual framework of financial exploitation of older persons. *Journal of Elder Abuse and Neglect, 16,* 53–73.

Radvansky, G. A., Zacks, R. T., & Hasher, L. (2005). Age and inhibition: The retrieval of situation models. *Journal of Gerontology, 60B,* P276–P278.

Ragow-O'Brien, D., Hayslip, B., Jr., & Guarnaccia, C. A. (2000). The impact of hospice on attitudes toward funerals and subsequent bereavement adjustment. *Omega, 41,* 291–305.

Rahman, Q., & Wilson, G. D. (2003). Born gay? The psychobiology of human sexual orientation. *Personality and Individual Differences, 34,* 1337–1382.

Raikes, H. A., Robinson, J. L., Bradley, R. H., Raikes, H. H., & Ayoub, C. C. (2007). Developmental trends in self-regulation among low-income toddlers. *Social Development, 16,* 128–149.

Raikes, H. A., & Thompson, R. A. (2006). Family emotional climate, attachment security, and young children's emotion knowledge in a high-risk sample. *British Journal of Developmental Psychology, 24,* 89–104.

Rakison, D. H. (2005). Developing knowledge of objects' motion properties in infancy. *Cognition, 96,* 183–214.

Rakison, D. H. (2006). Make the first move: How infants learn about self-propelled objects. *Developmental Psychology, 42,* 900–912.

Rakoczy, H., Tomasello, M., & Striano, T. (2004). Young children know that trying is not pretending: A test of the "behaving-as-if" construal of children's early concept of pretense. *Developmental Psychology, 40,* 388–399.

Ramaswami, A., & Dreher, G. F. (2007). The benefits associated with workplace mentoring relationships. In T. D. Allen & L. T. Eby (Eds.), *Blackwell handbook of mentoring: A multiple perspectives approach* (pp. 211–231). Malden, MA: Blackwell.

Ramchandani, P., Stein, A., Evans, J., O'Connor, T. G., & the ALSPAC Study Team. (2005). Paternal depression in the postnatal period and child development: A prospective population study. *Lancet, 365,* 2201–2205.

Ramey, C. T., Ramey, S. L., & Lanzi, R. G. (2006). Children's health and education. In K. A. Renninger & I. E. Sigel (Eds.), *Handbook of child psychology: Vol. 4. Child psychology in practice* (6th ed., pp. 864–892). Hoboken, NJ: Wiley.

Ramey, S. L., & Ramey, C. T. (1999). Early experience and early intervention for children "at risk" for developmental delay and mental retardation. *Mental Retardation and Developmental Disabilities, 5,* 1–10.

Ramos, E., Frontera, W. R., Llorpart, A., & Feliciano, D. (1998). Muscle strength and hormonal levels in adolescents: Gender related differences. *International Journal of Sports Medicine, 19,* 526–531.

Ramos, M. C., Guerin, D. W., Gottfried, A. W., Bathurst, K., & Oliver, P. H. (2005). Family conflict and children's behavior problems: The moderating role of child temperament. *Structural Equation Modeling, 12,* 278–298.

Rando, T. A. (1995). Grief and mourning: Accommodating to loss. In H. Wass & R. A. Neimeyer (Eds.), *Dying: Facing the facts* (3rd ed., pp. 211–241). Washington, DC: Taylor & Francis.

Rangel, M. C., Gavin, L., Reed, C., Fowler, M. G., & Lee, L. M. (2006). Epidemiology of HIV and AIDS among adolescents and young adults in the United States. *Journal of Adolescent Health, 39,* 156–163.

Rapp, S. R., Espeland, M. A., Shumaker, S. A., Henderson, V. W., Brunner, R. L., & Manson, J. E. (2003). Effect of estrogen plus progestin on global cognitive function in postmenopausal women: The Women's Health Initiative Memory Study: A randomized controlled trial. *Journal of the American Medical Association, 289,* 2663–2672.

Raqib, R., Alam, D. S., Sarker, P., Ahmad, S. M., Ara, G., & Yunus, M. (2007). Low birth weight is associated with altered immune function in rural Bangladeshi children: A birth cohort study. *American Journal of Clinical Nutrition, 85,* 845–852.

Rasch, E. K., Hirsch, R., Paulose-Ram, R., & Hochberg, M. C. (2003). Prevalence of rheumatoid arthritis in persons 60 years of age and older in the United States: Effect of different methods of classification. *Arthritis and Rheumatism, 48,* 917–926.

Rasmussen, C., Ho, E., & Bisanz, J. (2003). Use of the mathematical principle of inversion in young children. *Journal of Experimental Child Psychology, 85,* 89–102.

Rasmussen, C. H., & Johnson, M. E. (1994). Spirituality and religiosity: Relative relationships to death anxiety. *Omega, 29,* 313–318.

Rasmussen, E. R., Neuman, R. J., Heath, A. C., Levy, F., Hay, D. A., & Todd, R. D. (2004). Familial clustering of latent class and DSM-IV defined attention-deficit hyperactivity disorder (ADHD) subtypes. *Journal of Child Psychology and Psychiatry, 45,* 589–598.

Rathunde, K., & Csikszentmihalyi, M. (2005). The social context of middle school: Teachers, friends, and activities in Montessori and traditional school environments. *Elementary School Journal, 106,* 59–79.

Rauber, M. (2006, May 18). Parents aren't sitting still as recess disappears. *Parents in Action.* Retrieved from http://healthyschoolscampaign.org/news/media/food/2006-05_recess_disappears.php

Raver, C. C. (2003). Does work pay psychologically as well as economically? The role of employment in predicting depressive symptoms and parenting among low-income families. *Child Development, 74,* 1720–1736.

Ravid, D., & Tolchinsky, L. (2002). Developing linguistic literacy: A comprehensive model. *Journal of Child Language, 29,* 417–447.

Rawlins, W. K. (2004). Friendships in later life. In J. F. Nussbaum & J. Coupland (Eds.), *Handbook of communication and aging research* (2nd ed., pp. 273–299). Mahwah, NJ: Erlbaum.

Ray, V., & Gregory, R. (2001). School experiences of the children of lesbian and gay parents. *Family Matters, 59,* 28–35.

Rayner, K., & Pollatsek, A. (1989). *The psychology of reading.* Englewood Cliffs, NJ: Prentice-Hall.

Rayner, K., Pollatsek, A., & Starr, M. S. (2003). Reading. In A. F. Healy & R. W. Proctor (Eds.), *Handbook of psychology: Experimental psychology* (Vol. 4, pp. 549–574). New York: Wiley.

Raz, N. (2005). The aging brain observed in vivo: Differential changes and their modifiers. In R. Cabeza, L. Nyberg, & D. Park (Eds.), *Cognitive neuroscience of aging: Linking cognitive and cerebral aging* (pp. 19–57). New York: Oxford University Press.

Reay, A. C., & Browne, K. D. (2008). Elder abuse and neglect. In B. Woods & L. Clare (Eds.), *Handbook of the clinical psychology of ageing* (pp. 311–322). Chichester, UK: Wiley.

Reday-Mulvey, G. (2000). Gradual retirement in Europe. *Journal of Aging and Social Policy, 11,* 49–60.

Reddin, J. (1997). High-achieving women: Career development patterns. In H. S. Farmer (Ed.), *Diversity and women's career development* (pp. 95–126). Thousand Oaks, CA: Sage.

Redman, L. M., Martin, C. K., Williamson, D. A., & Ravussin, E. (2008). Effect of caloric restriction in non-obese humans on physiological, psychological and behavioral outcomes. *Physiology and Behavior, 94,* 643–648.

Reginster, J. Y., & Burlet, N. (2006). Osteoporosis: A still increasing prevalence. *Bone, 38,* 4–9.

Reid, H. M., & Fine, A. (1992). Self-disclosure in men's friendships: Variations associated with intimate relations. In P. M. Nardi (Ed.), *Men's friendships* (pp. 153–171). Newbury Park, CA: Sage.

Reis, O., & Youniss, J. (2004). Patterns in identity change and development in relationships with mothers and friends. *Journal of Adolescent Research, 19,* 31–44.

Reis, S. M. (2004). We can't change what we don't recognize: Understanding the special needs of gifted females. In S. Baum (Ed.), *Twice-exceptional and special populations of gifted students* (pp. 67–80). Thousand Oaks, CA: Corwin Press.

Reiss, A. L., & Dant, C. C. (2003). The behavioral neurogenetics of fragile X syndrome: Analyzing gene–brain–behavior relationships in child developmental psychopathologies. *Development and Psychopathology, 15,* 927–968.

Reiss, D. (2003). Child effects on family systems: Behavioral genetic strategies. In A. C. Crouter & A. Booth (Eds.), *Children's influence on family dynamics: The neglected side of family relationships* (pp. 3–36). Mahwah, NJ: Erlbaum.

Reiss, N. S., & Tishler, C. L. (2008). Suicidality in nursing home residents: Part II. Prevalence, risk factors, methods, assessment, and management. *Professional Psychology: Research and Practice, 39,* 271–275.

Reitzes, D. C., & Mutran, E. J. (2002). Self-concept as the organization of roles: Importance, centrality, and balance. *Sociological Quarterly, 43,* 647–667.

Renninger, K. A. (1998). Developmental psychology and instruction: Issues from and for practice. In I. Sigel & K. A. Renninger (Eds.), *Handbook of child psychology: Vol. 4. Child psychology and practice* (pp. 211–274). New York: Wiley.

Repacholi, B. M. (1998). Infants' use of attentional cues to identify the referent of another person's emotional expression. *Developmental Psychology, 33,* 12–21.

Repacholi, B. M., & Gopnik, A. (1997). Early reasoning about desires: Evidence from 14- and 18-month-olds. *Developmental Psychology, 33,* 12–21.

Repacholi, B. M., & Trapolini, T. (2004). Attachment and preschool children's understanding of maternal versus non-maternal psychological states. *British Journal of Developmental Psychology, 22,* 395–415.

Resnick, M., & Silverman, B. (2005). *Some reflections on designing construction kits for kids.* Proceedings of the Conference on Interaction Design and Children, Boulder, CO.

Resnick, M. B., Gueorguieva, R. V., Carter, R. L., Ariet, M., Sun, Y., Roth, J., Bucciarelli, R. L., Curran, J. S., & Mahan, C. S. (1999). The impact of low birth weight, perinatal conditions, and sociodemographic factors on educational outcome in kindergarten. *Pediatrics, 104,* e74.

Resnick, S. M., Pham, D. L., Kraut, M. A., Zonderman, A. B., & Davatzikos, C. (2003). Longitudinal magnetic resonance imaging studies of older adults: A shrinking brain. *Journal of Neuroscience, 23,* 3295–3301.

Rest, J. R. (1979). *Development in judging moral issues.* Minneapolis: University of Minnesota Press.

Resta, R., Biesecker, B. B., Bennett, R. L., Blum, S., Hahn, S. E., Strecker, M. N., & Williams, J. L. (2006). A new definition of genetic counseling: National Society of Genetic Counselors' Task Force Report. *Journal of Genetic Counseling, 15,* 77–83.

RESULTS. (2006). *The abolition of public school fees.* Retrieved from www.results.org/website/article.asp?id=1718

Reuter-Lorenz, P. A., & Cappell, K. A. (2008). Neurocognitive aging and the compensation hypothesis. *Current Directions in Psychological Science, 17,* 177–182.

Reuter-Lorenz, P. A., & Mikels, J. A. (2005). The aging mind and brain: Implictions of enduring plasticity for behavioral and cultural change. In P. Baltes, P. A. Reuter-Lorenz, & F. Roesler (Eds.), *Lifespan development and the brain: The perspective of biocultural co-constructivism.* London: Cambridge University Press.

Reyes-Ortiz, C. A., Kuo, Y.-F., DiNuzzo, A. R., Ray, L. A., Raji, M. A., & Markides, K. S. (2005). Near vision impairment predicts cognitive decline: Data from the Hispanic established populations for epidemiologic studies of the elderly. *Journal of the American Geriatric Society, 53,* 681–686.

Reyna, V. F., & Farley, F. (2006). Risk and rationality in adolescent decision making: Implications for theory, practice, and public policy. *Psychological Science in the Public Interest, 7,* 1–44.

Reynolds, C. R., & Kaiser, S. M. (1990). Test bias in psychological assessment. In T. B. Gutkin & C. R. Reynolds (Eds.), *The handbook of school psychology* (pp. 487–525). New York: Wiley.

Reynolds, K., Henderson, M., Schulman, A., & Hanson, L. C. (2002). Needs of the dying in nursing homes. *Journal of Palliative Medicine, 5,* 895–901.

Rhein, J. von (1997, January 19). Ardis Krainik, Lyric Opera's life force, dies. *Chicago Tribune,* pp. 1, 16.

Rhoades, G. K., Stanley, S. M., & Markman, H. J. (2006). Pre engagement cohabitation and gender asymmetry in marital commitment. *Journal of Family Psychology, 20,* 553–560.

Rhone, M., & Basu, A. (2008). Phytochemicals and age-related eye diseases. *Nutrition Reviews, 66,* 465–472.

Richards, M. (2004). Assisted reproduction, genetic technologies, and family life. In J. Scott, J. Treas, & M. Richards (Eds.), *The Blackwell companion to the sociology of families* (pp. 478–498). Malden, MA: Blackwell.

Richardson, V. E. (2007). A dual process model of grief counseling: Findings from the changing lives of older couples (CLOC) study. *Journal of Gerontological Social Work, 48,* 311–329.

Richie, B. S., Fassinger, R. E., Linn, S. G., Johnson, J., Prosser, J., & Robinson, S. (1997). Persistence, connection, and passion: A qualitative study of the career development of highly achieving African American–black and white women. *Journal of Counseling Psychology, 44,* 133–148.

Richler, J., Luyster, R., Risi, S., Hsu, W.-L., Dawson, G., & Bernier, R. (2006). Is there a 'regressive phenotype' of autism spectrum disorder associated with the measles-mumps-rubella vaccine? A CPEA study. *Journal of Autism and Developmental Disorders, 36,* 299–316.

Richmond, L. J. (2004). When spirituality goes awry: Students in cults. *Professional School Counseling, 7,* 367–375.

Rideout, V., & Hamel, E. (2006). *The media family: Electronic media in the lives of infants, toddlers, preschoolers and their parents.* Menlo Park, CA: Henry J. Kaiser Family Foundation.

Riediger, M., Li, S.-C., & Lindenberger, U. (2006). Selection, optimization, and compensation as developmental mechanisms of adaptive resource allocation: Review and preview. In J. E. Birren & K. W., Schaire (Eds.), *Handbook of the psychology of aging* (6th ed.) (pp. 289–313). Burlington, MA: Academic Press.

Rigby, K. (2004). Bullying in childhood. In P. K. Smith & C. H. Hart (Eds.), *Blackwell handbook of childhood social development* (pp. 549–568). Malden, MA: Blackwell.

Riley, E. P., McGee, C. L., & Sowell, E. R. (2004). Teratogenic effects of alcohol: A decade of brain imaging. *American Journal of Medical Genetics: Part C, Seminars in Medical Genetics, 127,* 35–41.

Riley, L. D., & Bowen, C. P. (2005). The sandwich generation: Challenges and coping strategies of multigenerational families. *Counseling and Therapy for Couples and Families, 13,* 52–58.

Ripperger, T., Gadzicki, D., Meindl, A. & Schlegelberger, B. (2009). Breast cancer susceptibility: Current knowledge and implications for genetic counseling. *European Journal of Human Genetics, 17,* 722–731.

Ripple, C. H., & Zigler, E. (2003). Research, policy, and the federal role in prevention initiatives for children. *American Psychologist, 58,* 482–490.

Ritchey, L. H., Ritchey, P. N., & Dietz, B. E. (2001). Clarifying the measurement of activity. *Activities, Adaptation, and Aging, 26,* 1–21.

Rittman, M., Kuzmeskus, L. B., & Flum, M. A. (2000). A synthesis of current knowledge on minority elder abuse. In T. Tatara (Ed.), *Understanding elder abuse in minority populations* (pp. 221–238). Philadelphia: Brunner/Mazel.

Riva, D., & Giorgi, C. (2000). The cerebellum contributes to higher functions during development: Evidence from a series of children surgically treated for posterior fossa tumours. *Brain, 123,* 1051–1061.

Rivkees, S. A. (2003). Developing circadian rhythmicity in infants. *Pediatrics, 112,* 373–381.

Rivlin, R. S. (2007). Keeping the young–elderly healthy: Is it too late to improve our health through nutrition? *American Journal of Clinical Nutrition, 86*(Suppl.), 1572S–1576S.

Rizzolatti, G., & Craighero, L. (2004). The mirror-neuron system. *Annual Review of Neuroscience, 27,* 169 192.

Robb, A. S., & Dadson, M. J. (2002). Eating disorders in males. *Child and Adolescent Psychiatric Clinics of North America, 11,* 399–418.

Roberson, E. D., Scearce-Livie, K., Palop, J. J., Yan, F., Cheng, I. H., & Wu, T. (2007). Reducing endogenous tau ameliorates amyloid beta-induced deficits in an Alzheimer's disease mouse model. *Science, 316,* 750–754.

Roberts, B. W., & DelVecchio, W. E. (2000). The rank-order consistency of personality traits from childhood to old age: A quantitative review of longitudinal studies. *Psychological Bulletin, 126,* 3–25.

Roberts, B. W., Kuncel, N., Shiner, R., Caspi, A., & Goldberg, L. R. (2007). The power of personality: A comparative analysis of the predictive validity of personality traits, SES, and IQ. *Perspectives on Psychological Science, 2,* 313–345.

Roberts, B. W., & Mroczek, D. (2008). Personality and trait change in adulthood. *Current Directions in Psychological Science, 17,* 31–35.

Roberts, B. W., Robins, R. W., Caspi, A., & Trzesniewski, K. H. (2003). Personality trait development in adulthood. In J. L. Mortimer & M. Shanahan (Eds.), *Handbook of the life course* (pp. 579–598). New York: Plenum.

Roberts, B. W., Walton, K. E., & Viechtbauer, W. (2006). Patterns of mean-level change in personality traits across the life course: A meta-analysis of longitudinal studies. *Psychological Bulletin, 132,* 3–25.

Roberts, D. F., Foehr, U. G., & Rideout, V. (2005). *Generation M: Media in the lives of 8–18 year olds.* Menlo Park, CA: Henry J. Kaiser Family Foundation.

Roberts, D. F., Henriksen, L., & Foehr, U. G. (2004). Adolescents and media. In R. M. Lerner & L. Steinberg (Eds.), *Handbook of adolescent psychology* (2nd ed., pp. 627–664). Hoboken, NJ: Wiley.

Roberts, J. E., Burchinal, M. R., & Durham, M. (1999). Parents' report of vocabulary and grammatical development of American preschoolers: Child and environment associations. *Child Development, 70,* 92–106.

Roberts, J. M., & Masten, A. S. (2004). Resilience in context. In R. D. Peters, R. McMahon, & B. Leadbeater (Eds.), *Resilience in children, families, and communities: Linking context to practice and policy* (pp. 13–25). New York: Kluwer Academic.

Roberts, P. (2006). From my space to our space: The functions of Web memorials in bereavement. *The Forum, 32,* 1–4.

Roberts, P., & Newton, P. M. (1987). Levinsonian studies of women's adult development. *Psychology and Aging, 2,* 154–163.

Roberts, P., & Vidal, L. A. (1999–2000). Perpetual care in cyberspace: A portrait of memorials on the Web. *Omega, 40,* 521–545.

Roberts, R. E., Attkisson, C. C., & Rosenblatt, A. (1998). Prevalence of psychopathology among children and adolescents. *American Journal of Psychiatry, 155,* 715–725.

Robinson, C. C., Anderson, G. T., Porter, C. L., Hart, C. H., & Wouden-Miller, M. (2003). Sequential transition patterns of preschoolers' social interactions during child-initiated play: Is parallel-aware play a bi-directional bridge to other play states? *Early Childhood Research Quarterly, 18,* 3–21.

Robinson, J. L., Lee, B. E., Preiksaitis, J. K., Plitt, S., & Tipplies, G. A. (2006). Prevention of congenital rubella syndrome What makes sense in 2006? *Epidemiologic Reviews, 28,* 81–87.

Robles, T. F., & Kiecolt-Glaser, J. K. (2003). The physiology of marriage: Pathways to health. *Physiology and Behavior, 79,* 409–416.

Rochat, P. (1989). Object manipulation and exploration in 2- to 5-month-old infants. *Developmental Psychology, 25,* 871–884.

Rochat, P. (1998). Self-perception and action in infancy. *Experimental Brain Research, 123,* 102–109.

Rochat, P. (2001). *The infant's world.* Cambridge, MA: Harvard University Press.

Rochat, P. (2003). Five levels of self-awareness as they unfold early in life. *Consciousness and Cognition, 12,* 717–731.

Rochat, P., & Goubet, N. (1995). Development of sitting and reaching in 5- to 6-month-old infants. *Infant Behavior and Development, 18,* 53–68.

Rochat, P., & Hespos, S. J. (1997). Differential rooting responses by neonates: Evidence for an early sense of self. *Early Development and Parenting, 6,* 105–112.

Rochat, P., & Striano, T. (2002). Who's in the mirror? Self–other discrimination in specular images by four- and nine-month-old infants. *Infant and Child Development, 11,* 289–303.

Rochat, P., Striano, T., & Blatt, L. (2002). Differential effects of happy, neutral, and sad still-faces on 2-, 4-, and 6-month-old infants. *Infant and Child Development, 11,* 289–303.

Rodkin, P. C., Farmer, T. W., Pearl, R., & Van Acker, R. (2006). They're cool: Social status and peer group supports for aggressive boys and girls. *Social Development, 15,* 175–204.

Roelfsema, N. M., Hop, W. C., Boito, S. M., & Wladimiroff, J. W. (2004). Three-dimensional sonographic measurement of normal fetal brain volume during the second half of pregnancy. *American Journal of Obstetrics and Gynecology, 190,* 275–280.

Roeser, R. W., Eccles, J. S., & Freedman-Doan, C. (1999). Academic functioning and mental health in adolescence: Patterns, progressions, and routes from childhood. *Journal of Adolescent Research, 14,* 135–174.

Roeser, R. W., Eccles, J. S., & Sameroff, A. J. (2000). School as a context of early adolescents' academic and social-emotional development: A summary of research findings. *Elementary School Journal, 100,* 443–471.

Rogers, L. J. (2000). Evolution of hemispheric specialization: Advantages and disadvantages. *Brain and Language, 73,* 236–253.

Rogoff, B. (1998). Cognition as a collaborative process. In D. Kuhn & R. S. Siegler (Eds.), *Handbook of child psychology: Vol. 2. Cognition, perception, and language* (5th ed., pp. 679–744). New York: Wiley.

Rogoff, B. (2003). *The cultural nature of human development.* New York: Oxford University Press.

Rogoff, B., & Chavajay, P. (1995). What's become of research on the cultural basis of cognitive development? *American Psychologist, 50,* 859–877.

Rogoff, B., Malkin, C., & Gilbride, K. (1984). Interaction with babies as guidance in development. In B. Rogoff & J. V. Wertsch (Eds.), *Children's learning in the "zone of proximal development"* (New directions for child development, No. 23, pp. 31–44). San Francisco: Jossey-Bass.

Rogoff, B., Paradise, R., Arauz, R. M., Correa-Chávez, M., & Angelillo, C. (2003). Firsthand learning through intent participation. *Annual Review of Psychology, 54,* 175–203.

Rogoff, B., & Waddell, K. J. (1982). Memory for information organized in a scene by children from two cultures. *Child Development, 53,* 1224–1228.

Rogol, A. D., Roemmich, J. N., & Clark, P. A. (2002). Growth at puberty. *Journal of Adolescent Health, 31*, 192–200.

Rohner, R. P., & Veneziano, R. A. (2001). The importance of father love: History and contemporary evidence. *Review of General Psychology, 5*, 382–405.

Roid, G. (2003). *The Stanford-Binet Intelligence Scales, Fifth Edition, interpretive manual.* Itasca, IL: Riverside Publishing.

Roisman, G. I., Madsen, S. D., Hennighausen, K. H., Sroufe, L. A., & Collins, W. A. (2001). The coherence of dyadic behavior across parent–child and romantic relationships as mediated by the internalized representation of experience. *Attachment and Human Development, 3*, 156–172.

Roisman, G. I., Padron, E., Sroufe, L. A., & Egeland, B. (2002). Earned-secure attachment status in retrospect and prospect. *Child Development, 73*, 1204–1219.

Roizen, N. J., & Patterson, D. (2003). Down's syndrome. *Lancet, 361*, 1281–1289.

Rokach, A. (2001). Perceived causes of loneliness in adulthood. *Journal of Social Behavior and Personality, 15*, 67–84.

Rokach, A. (2003). Strategies of coping with loneliness throughout the lifespan. In N. J. Pallone (Ed.), *Love, romance, sexual interaction: Research perspectives from current psychology* (pp. 225–344). New Brunswick, NJ: Transaction.

Rokach, A., & Neto, F. (2006). Age, culture, and coping with loneliness. *Psychology and Education, 43*, 1–21.

Rokach, R., Cohen, O., & Dreman, S. (2004). Who pulls the trigger? Who initiates divorce among over 45-year-olds. *Journal of Divorce and Remarriage, 42*, 61–83.

Román, G. C. (2003). Vascular dementia: Distinguishing characteristics, treatment, and prevention. *Journal of the American Geriatrics Society, 51*, S296–S304.

Rome-Flanders, T., & Cronk, C. (1995). A longitudinal study of infant vocalizations during mother–infant games. *Journal of Child Language, 22*, 259–274.

Romero, A. J., & Roberts, R. E. (2003). The impact of multiple dimensions of ethnic identity on discrimination and adolescents' self-esteem. *Journal of Applied Social Psychology, 33*, 2288–2305.

Rönnqvist, L., & Domellöf, E. (2006). Quantitative assessment of right and left reaching movements in infants: A longitudinal study from 6 to 36 months. *Developmental Psychobiology, 48*, 444–459.

Roopnarine, J. L., & Evans, M. E. (2007). Family structural organization, mother–child and father–child relationships and psychological outcomes in English-speaking African Caribbean and Indo Caribbean families. In M. Sutherland (Ed.), *Psychology of development in the Caribbean.* Kingston, Jamaica: Ian Randle.

Roopnarine, J. L., Hossain, Z., Gill, P., & Brophy, H. (1994). Play in the East Indian context. In J. L. Roopnarine, J. E. Johnson, & F. H. Hooper (Eds.), *Children's play in diverse cultures* (pp. 9–30). Albany: State University of New York Press.

Roopnarine, J. L., Krishnakumar, A., Metindogan, A., & Evans, M. (2006). Links between parenting styles, parent–child academic interaction, parent–school interaction, and early academic skills and social behaviors in young children of English-speaking Caribbean immigrants. *Early Childhood Research Quarterly, 21*, 238–252.

Roopnarine, J. L., Talukder, E., Jain, D., Joshi, P., & Srivastav, P. (1990). Characteristics of holding, patterns of play, and social behaviors between parents and infants in New Delhi, India. *Developmental Psychology, 26*, 667–673.

Rosander, K., & von Hofsten, C. (2004). Infants' emerging ability to represent occluded object motion. *Cognition, 91*, 1–22.

Rose, A. J., & Asher, S. R. (1999). Children's goals and strategies in response to conflicts within a friendship. *Developmental Psychology, 35*, 69–79.

Rose, A. J., Carlson, W., & Waller, E. M. (2007). Prospective associations of co-rumination with friendship and emotional adjustment: Considering the socioemotional trade-offs of co-rumination. *Developmental Psychology, 43*, 1019–1031.

Rose, A. J., Swenson, L. P., & Waller, E. M. (2004). Overt and relational aggression and perceived popularity: Developmental differences in concurrent and prospective relations. *Developmental Psychology, 40*, 378–387.

Rose, S. A., & Feldman, J. F. (1997). Memory and speed: Their role in the relation of infant information processing to later IQ. *Child Development, 68*, 610–620.

Rose, S. A., Feldman, J. F., & Janowski, J. J. (2001). Attention and recognition memory in the 1st year of life: A longitudinal study of preterm and full-term infants. *Developmental Psychology, 37*, 135–151.

Rose, S. A., Jankowski, J. J., & Senior, G. J. (1997). Infants' recognition of contour-deleted figures. *Journal of Experimental Psychology: Human Perception and Performance, 23*, 1206–1216.

Roseboom, T., de Rooij, S., & Painter, R. (2006). The Dutch famine and its long-term consequences for adult health. *Early Human Development, 82*, 485–491.

Rosen, A. B., & Rozin, P. (1993). Now you see it, now you don't: The preschool child's conception of invisible particles in the context of dissolving. *Developmental Psychology, 29*, 300–311.

Rosen, D. (2003). Eating disorders in children and young adolescents: Etiology, classification, clinical features, and treatment. *Adolescent Medicine: State of the Art Reviews, 14*, 49–59.

Rosen, P. J., Milich, R., & Harris, M. J. (2007). Victims of their own cognitions: Implicit social cognitions, emotional distress, and peer victimization. *Journal of Applied Developmental Psychology, 28*, 211–226.

Rosen, S., Bergman, M., & Plester, D. (1962). Presbycusis study of a relatively noise-free population in the Sudan. *Transactions of the American Otological Society, 50*, 135–152.

Rosenblatt, P. C. (1993). Cross-cultural variation in the experience, expression, and understanding of grief. In D. P. Irish, K. F. Lundquist, & V. J. Nelsen (Eds.), *Ethnic variations in dying, death, and grief* (pp. 13–19). Washington, DC: Taylor & Francis.

Rosenblatt, P. C. (2008). Grief across cultures: A review and research agenda. In M. S. Stroebe, R. O. Hansson, H. Schut, & W. Stroebe (Eds.), *Handbook of bereavement research and practice* (pp. 207–222). Washington, DC: American Psychological Association.

Rosengren, K. S., & Hickling, A. K. (2000). The development of children's thinking about possible events and plausible mechanisms. In K. S. Rosengren, C. N. Johnson, & P. L. Harris (Eds.), *Imagining the impossible* (pp. 75–98). Cambridge, UK: Cambridge University Press.

Rosenman, R. H., Brand, R. J., Jenkins, C. D., Friedman, M., Strauss, R., & Wurm, M. (1975). Coronary heart disease in the Western Collaborative Group Study: Final follow-up experience of 8½ years. *Journal of the American Medical Association, 223*, 872–877.

Roseth, C. J., Pellegrini, A. D., Bohn, C. M., van Ryzin, M., & Vance, N. (2007). Preschoolers' aggression, affiliation, and social dominance relationships: An observational, longitudinal study. *Journal of School Psychology, 45*, 479–497.

Rossi, A. S. (2001). (Ed.). *Caring and doing for others: Social responsibility in the domains of family, work, and community.* Chicago: University of Chicago Press.

Rossi, A. S. (2004). Social responsibility to family and community. In O. G. Brim, C. D. Ryff, & R. C. Kessler (Eds.), *How healthy are we? A national study of well-being at midlife* (pp. 550–585). Chicago: University of Chicago Press.

Rossi, A. S. (2005). The menopausal transition and aging processes. In O. G. Brim, C. D. Ryff, & R. C. Kessler (Eds.), *How healthy are we? A national study of well-being at midlife* (pp. 153–201). Chicago: University of Chicago Press.

Rossi, A. S., & Rossi, P. H. (1990). *Of human bonding: Parent–child relations across the life course.* New York: Aldine de Gruyter.

Rossouw, J. E. (2007). Postmenopausal hormone therapy for disease prevention: Have we learned any lessons from the past? *Clinical Pharmacology and Therapeutics, 83*, 14–16.

Rothbart, M. K. (2003). Temperament and the pursuit of an integrated developmental psychology. *Merrill-Palmer Quarterly, 50*, 492–505.

Rothbart, M. K., Ahadi, S. A., & Evans, D. E. (2000). Temperament and personality: Origins and outcome. *Journal of Personality and Social Psychology, 78*, 122–135.

Rothbart, M. K., & Bates, J. E. (2006). Temperament. In N. Eisenberg (Ed.), *Handbook of child psychology: Vol. 3. Social, emotional, and personality development* (6th ed., pp. 99–166). Hoboken, NJ: Wiley.

Rothbart, M. K., & Mauro, J. A. (1990). Questionnaire approaches to the study of infant temperament. In J. W. Fagen & J. Colombo (Eds.), *Individual differences in infancy: Reliability, stability and prediction* (pp. 411–429). Hillsdale, NJ: Erlbaum.

Rothbart, M. K., Posner, M. I., & Kieras, J. (2006). Temperament, attention, and the development of self-regulation. In K. McCartney & D. Phillips (Eds.), *Blackwell handbook of early childhood development* (pp. 338–357). Malden, MA: Blackwell.

Rothbaum, F., Pott, M., Azuma, H., Miyake, K., & Weisz, J. (2000a). The development of close relationships in Japan and the United States: Paths of symbiotic harmony and generative tension. *Child Development, 71*, 1121–1142.

Rothbaum, F., Weisz, J., Pott, M., Miyake, K., & Morelli, G. (2000b). Attachment and culture: Security in the United States and Japan. *American Psychologist, 55*, 1093–1104.

Rovee-Collier, C. K. (1999). The development of infant memory. *Current Directions in Psychological Science, 8*, 80–85.

Rovee-Collier, C. K., & Barr, R. (2001). Infant learning and memory. In G. Bremner & A. Fogel (Eds.), *Blackwell handbook of infant development* (pp. 139–168). Oxford, UK: Blackwell.

Rovee-Collier, C. K., & Bhatt, R. S. (1993). Evidence of long-term memory in infancy. *Annals of Child Development, 9*, 1–45.

Rowe, D. C. (1994). *The limits of family influence: Genes, experience, and behavior.* New York: Guilford.

Rowe, S., & Wertsch, J. V. (2002). Vygotsky's model of cognitive development. In G. Bremner & A. Fogel (Eds.), *Blackwell handbook of infant development* (pp. 538–554). Oxford, UK: Blackwell.

Rowland, C. F. (2007). Explaining errors in children's questions. *Cognition, 104*, 106–134.

Rowland, C. F., & Pine, J. M. (2000). Subject-auxiliary inversion errors and wh-question acquisition: "What children do know?" *Journal of Child Language, 27*, 157–181.

Rowland, D. T. (2007). Historical trends in childlessness. *Journal of Family Issues, 28*, 1311–1337.

Roy, K. M., & Lucas, K. (2006). Generativity as second chance: Low-income fathers and transformation of the difficult past. *Research in Human Development, 3*, 139–159.

Rubenstein, L. Z., Stevens, J. A., & Scott, V. (2008). Interventions to prevent falls among older adults. In L. S. Doll, S. E. Bonzo, D. A. Sleet, J. A. Mercy, & E. N. Haas (Eds.), *Handbook of injury and violence prevention* (pp. 37–53). New York: Springer.

Rubin, D. C. (2002). Autobiographical memory across the lifespan. In P. Graf & N. Ohta (Eds.), *Lifespan development of human memory* (pp. 159–184). Cambridge, MA: MIT Press.

Rubin, D. C., & Berntsen, D. (2006). People over forty feel 20% younger than their age: Subjective age across the lifespan. *Psychonomic Bulletin and Review, 13*, 776–780.

Rubin, D. C., Rahhal, T. A., & Poon, L. W. (1998). Things learned in early adulthood are remembered best. *Memory and Cognition, 26*, 3–19.

Rubin, D. C., & Schulkind, M. D. (1997). Distribution of important and word-cued autobiographical memories in 20-, 35-, and 70-year-old adults. *Psychology and Aging, 12*, 524–535.

Rubin, K. H., Bukowski, W. M., & Parker, J. G. (2006). Peer interactions, relationships, and groups. In N. Eisenberg (Ed.), *Handbook of child psychology: Vol. 3. Social, emotional, and personality development* (6th ed., pp. 571–645). Hoboken, NJ: Wiley.

Rubin, K. H., Burgess, K. B., & Coplan, R. (2002). Social withdrawal and shyness. In P. K. Smith & C. H. Hart (Eds.), *Blackwell handbook of child social development* (pp. 329–352). Oxford, UK: Blackwell.

Rubin, K. H., Burgess, K. B., & Hastings, P. D. (2002). Stability and social-behavioral consequences of toddlers' inhibited temperament and parenting behaviors. *Child Development, 73*, 483–495.

Rubin, K. H., & Coplan, R. J. (1998). Social and nonsocial play in childhood: An individual differences perspective. In O. N. Saracho & B. Spodek (Eds.), *Multiple perspectives on play in early childhood education* (pp. 144–170). Albany: State University of New York Press.

Rubin, K. H., Coplan, J., Chen, X., Buskirk, A. A., & Wojslawowicz, J. C. (2005). Peer relationships in childhood. In M. H. Bornstein & M. E. Lamb (Eds.), *Developmental science: An advanced textbook* (pp. 469–512). Mahwah, NJ: Erlbaum.

Rubin, K. H., Fein, G. G., & Vandenberg, B. (1983). Play. In E. M. Hetherington (Ed.), *Handbook of child psychology: Vol. 4. Socialization, personality, and social development* (4th ed., pp. 693–744). New York: Wiley.

Rubin, K. H., Hastings, P. D., Stewart, S. L., Henderson, H. A., & Chen, X. (1997). The consistency and concomitants of inhibition: Some of the children, all of the time. *Child Development, 68*, 467–483.

Rubin, K. H., Watson, K. S., & Jambor, T. W. (1978). Free-play behaviors in preschool and kindergarten children. *Child Development, 49*, 539–536.

Rubinstein, R. L., Alexander, B. B., Goodman, M., & Luborsky, M. (1991). Key relationships of never married, childless older women: A cultural analysis. *Journal of Gerontology, 46*, S270–S277.

Ruble, D. N., Alvarez, J., Bachman, M., Cameron, J., Fuligni, A., García Coll, C., & Rhee, E. (2004). The development of a sense of "we": The emergence and implications of children's collective identity. In M. Bennett & F. Sani (Eds.), *The development of the social self* (pp. 29–76). Hove, UK: Psychology Press.

Ruble, D. N., Martin, C. L., & Berenbaum, S. A. (2006). Gender development. In N. Eisenberg (Ed.), *Handbook of child psychology: Vol. 3. Social, emotional, and personality development* (6th ed., pp. 226–299). Hoboken, NJ: Wiley.

Ruble, D. N., Taylor, L. J., Cyphers, L., Greulich, F. K., Lurye, L. E., & Shrout, P. E. (2007). The role of gender constancy in early gender development. *Child Development, 78*, 1121–1136.

Rudolph, K. D., Lambert, S. F., Clark, A. G., & Kurlakowsky, K. D. (2001). Negotiating the transition to middle school: The role of self-regulatory processes. *Child Development, 72*, 929–946.

Rudy, D., & Grusec, J. E. (2006). Authoritarian parenting in individualist and collectivist groups: Associations with maternal emotion and cognition and children's self-esteem. *Journal of Family Psychology, 20*, 68–78.

Ruff, H. A., & Capozzoli, M. C. (2003). Development of attention and distractibility in the first 4 years of life. *Developmental Psychology, 39*, 877–890.

Ruff, H. A., & Rothbart, M. K. (1996). *Attention in early development.* New York: Oxford University Press.

Ruffman, T. (1999). Children's understanding of logical inconsistency. *Child Development, 70*, 887–895.

Ruffman, T., & Langman, L. (2002). Infants' reaching in a multi-well A not B task. *Infant Behavior and Development, 25*, 237–246.

Ruffman, T., Perner, J., Olson, D. R., & Doherty, M. (1993). Reflecting on scientific thinking: Children's understanding of the hypothesis–evidence relation. *Child Development, 64*, 1617–1636.

Ruffman, T., Slade, L., Devitt, K., & Crowe, E. (2006). What mothers say and what they do: The relation between parenting, theory of mind, language, and conflict/cooperation. *British Journal of Developmental Psychology, 24*, 105–124.

Ruhm, C. J. (1996). Gender differences in employment behavior during late middle age. *Journal of Gerontology, 51B*, S11–S17.

Runco, M. A. (1992). Children's divergent thinking and creative ideation. *Developmental Review, 12*, 233–264.

Rurup, M. L., Muller, M. T., Onwuteaka-Philipsen, B. D., van der Heide, A., van der Wal, G., & van der Maas, P. J. (2005). Requests for euthanasia or physician-assisted suicide from older persons who do not have a severe disease: An interview study. *Psychological Medicine, 35*, 665–671.

Rusbult, C. E., Coolsen, M. K., Kirchner, J. L., & Clarke, J. A. (2006). Commitment. In A. L. Vangelisti & D. Perlman (Eds.), *The Cambridge handbook of personal relationships* (pp. 615–635). New York: Cambridge University Press.

Rusconi, A. (2004). Different pathways out of the parental home: A comparison of West Germany and Italy. *Journal of Comparative Family Studies, 35*, 627–649.

Rushton, J. L., Forcier, M., & Schectman, R. M. (2002). Epidemiology of depressive symptoms in the National Longitudinal Study of Adolescent Health. *Journal of the American Academy of Child and Adolescent Psychiatry, 41*, 199–205.

Rushton, J. P., & Bons, T. A. (2005). Mate choice and friendship in twins. *Psychological Science, 16*, 555–559.

Rushton, J. P., & Jensen, A. R. (2005). Thirty years of research on race differences in cognitive ability. *Psychology, Public Policy, and Law, 11*, 235–294.

Rushton, J. P., & Jensen, A. R. (2006). The totality of available evidence shows the race IQ gap still remains. *Psychological Science, 17*, 921–924.

Russac, R. J., Gatliff, C., Reece, M., & Spottswood, D. (2007). Death anxiety across the adult years: An examination of age and gender effects. *Death Studies, 31*, 549–561.

Russell, A., Mize, J., & Bissaker, K. (2004). Parent–child relationships. In P. K. Smith & C. H. Hart (Eds.), *Blackwell handbook of childhood social development* (pp. 204–222). Malden, MA: Blackwell.

Russell, J. A. (1990). The preschooler's understanding of the causes and consequences of emotion. *Child Development, 61*, 1872–1881.

Russell, J. A., Douglas, A. J., & Ingram, C. D. (2001). Brain preparations for maternity—adaptive changes in behavioral and neuroendocrine systems during pregnancy and lactation. *Progress in Brain Research, 133*, 1–38.

Russell, R. B., Petrini, J. R., Damus, K., Mattison, D. R., & Schwarz, R. H. (2003). The changing epidemiology of multiple births in the United States. *Obstetrics and Gynecology, 101*, 129–135.

Rutter, M. (2002). Nature, nurture, and development: From evangelism through science toward policy and practice. *Child Development, 73*, 1–21.

Rutter, M. (2006). *Genes and behavior: Nature–nurture interplay explained.* Malden, MA: Blackwell.

Rutter, M. (2007). Gene–environment interdependence. *Developmental Science, 10*, 12–18.

Rutter, M., Colvert, E., Kreppner, J., Beckett, C., Castle, J., & Groothues, C. (2007). Early adolescent outcomes for institutionally deprived and non-deprived adoptees. I: Disinhibited attachment. *Journal of Child Psychology and Psychiatry, 48*, 17–30.

Rutter, M., & the English and Romanian Adoptees Study Team. (1998). Developmental catch-up, and deficit, following adoption after severe global early privation. *Journal of Child Psychology and Psychiatry, 39*, 465–476.

Rutter, M., O'Connor, T. G., and the English and Romanian Adoptees Study Team. (2004). Are there biological programming effects for psychological development? Findings from a study of Romanian adoptees. *Developmental Psychology, 40*, 81–94.

Rutter, M., Pickles, A., Murray, R., & Eaves, L. (2001). Testing hypotheses on specific environmental causal effects on behavior. *Psychological Bulletin, 127*, 291–324.

Ryan, E. B., Jin, Y., Anas, A. P., & Luh, J. J. (2004). Communication beliefs about youth and old age in Asia and Canada. *Journal of Cross-Cultural Gerontology, 19*, 343–360.

Ryan, R. M., Fauth, R. C., & Brooks-Gunn, J. (2006). Childhood poverty: Implications for school readiness and early childhood education. In B. Spodek & O. N. Saracho (Eds.), *Handbook of research on the education of young children* (2nd ed., pp. 323–346). Mahwah, NJ: Erlbaum.

Rybash, J. M., & Hrubi-Bopp, K. L. (2000). Isolating the neural mechanisms of age-related changes in human working memory. *Nature Neuroscience, 3*, 509–515.

Ryff, C. D. (1989). In the eye of the beholder: Views of psychological well-being among middle-aged and older adults. *Psychology and Aging, 4*, 195–210.

Ryff, C. D. (1991). Possible selves in adulthood and old age: A tale of shifting horizons. *Psychology and Aging, 6*, 286–295.

Ryff, C. D. (1995). Psychological well-being in adult life. *Current Directions in Psychological Science, 4*, 99–104.

Ryff, C. D., & Singer, B. H. (2005). Social environments and the genetics of aging: Advancing knowledge of protective health mechanisms. *Journal of Gerontology, 60B*, 12–23.

Ryff, C. D., Singer, B. H., & Seltzer, M. M. (2002). Pathways through challenge: Implications for well-being and health. In L. Pulkkinen & A. Caspi (Eds.), *Paths to successful development* (pp. 302–328). Cambridge, UK: Cambridge University Press.

S

Saarni, C. (2000). Emotional competence: A developmental perspective. In R. Bar-On & J. D. A. Parker (Eds.), *Handbook of emotional intelligence* (pp. 68–91). San Francisco: Jossey-Bass.

Saarni, C., Campos, J. J., Camras, L. A., & Witherinton, D. (2006). Emotional development: Action, communication, and understanding. In N. Eisenberg (Ed.), *Handbook of child psychology: Vol. 3. Social, emotional, and personality development* (6th ed., pp. 226–299). Hoboken, NJ: Wiley.

Sabbagh, M. A., Xu, F., Carlson, S. M., Moses, L. J., & Lee, K. (2006). The development of executive functioning and theory of mind: A comparison of Chinese and U.S. preschoolers. *Psychological Science, 17*, 74–81.

Sachdev, P. S., Brodaty, H., & Looi, J. C. L. (1999). Vascular dementia: Diagnosis, management, and possible prevention. *Medical Journal of Australia, 170*, 81–85.

Sacks, P. (2005). "No child left": What are schools for in a democratic society? In S. Olfman (Ed.), *Childhood lost: How American culture is failing our kids* (pp. 185–202). Westport, CT: Praeger.

Sadeh, A. (1997). Sleep and melatonin in infants: A preliminary study. *Sleep, 20*, 185–191.

Sadler, T. W. (2006). *Langman's medical embryology* (10th ed.). Baltimore: Williams and Wilkins.

Saenger, P. (2003). Dose effects of growth hormone during puberty. *Hormone Research, 60*(Suppl. 1), 52–57.

Saffran, J. R., Aslin, R. N., & Newport, E. L. (1996). Statistical learning by 8-month-old infants. *Science, 27,* 1926–1928.

Saffran, J. R., & Thiessen, E. D. (2003). Pattern induction by infant language learners. *Developmental Psychology, 39,* 484–494.

Saffran, J. R., & Thiessen, E. D. (2007). Domain-general learning capacities. In E. Hoff & M. Shatz (Eds.), *Blackwell handbook of language development* (pp. 68–86). Malden, MA: Blackwell.

Saffran, J. R., Werker, J. F., & Werner, L. A. (2006). The infant's auditory world: Hearing, speech, and the beginnings of language. In D. Kuhn & R. Siegler (Eds.), *Handbook of child psychology: Vol. 2. Cognition, perception, and language* (6th ed., pp. 58–108). Hoboken, NJ: Wiley.

Safren, S. A., & Pantalone, D. W. (2006). Social anxiety and barriers to resilience among lesbian, gay, and bisexual adolescents. In A. M. Omoto & H. S. Kurtzman (Eds.), *Sexual orientation and mental health: Examining identity and development in lesbian, gay, and bisexual young people* (pp. 55–71). Washington, DC: American Psychological Association.

Saginak, K. A., & Saginak, M. A. (2005). Balancing work and family: Equity, gender, and marital satisfaction. *Counseling and Therapy for Couples and Families, 13,* 162–166.

Saha, C., Riner, M. E., & Liu, G. (2005). Individual and neighborhood-level factors in predicting asthma. *Archives of Pediatrics and Adolescent Medicine, 159,* 759–763.

Saigal, S., Stoskopf, B., Streiner, D., Boyle, M., Pinelli, J., & Paneth, N. (2006). Transition of extremely low-birth-weight infants from adolescence to young adulthood. *Journal of the American Medical Association, 295,* 667–675.

Saitta, S. C., & Zackai, E. H. (2005). Specific chromosome disorders in newborns. In H. W. Taeusch, R. A. Ballard, & C. A. Gleason (Eds.), *Avery's diseases of the newborn* (8th ed., pp. 204–215). Philadelphia: Saunders.

Salbe, A. D., Weyer, C., Lindsay, R. S., Ravussin, E., & Tataranni, P. A. (2002). Assessing risk factors for obesity between childhood and adolescence: I. Birth weight, childhood adiposity, parental obesity, insulin, and leptin. *Pediatrics, 110,* 299–306.

Salerno, M., Micillo, M., Di Maio, S., Capalbo, D., Ferri, P., & Lettiero, T. (2001). Longitudinal growth, sexual maturation and final height in patients with congenital hypothyroidism detected by neonatal screening. *European Journal of Endocrinology, 145,* 377–383.

Salihu, H. M., Shumpert, M. N., Slay, M., Kirby, R. S., & Alexander, G. R. (2003). Childbearing beyond maternal age 50 and fetal outcomes in the United States. *Obstetrics and Gynecology, 102,* 1006–1014.

Salley, B. J., & Dixon, W. E., Jr. (2007). Temperamental and joint attentional predictors of language development. *Merrill-Palmer Quarterly, 53,* 131–154.

Salmela-Aro, K., Nurmi, J.-E., Saisto, T., & Halmesmaki, E. (2001). Goal reconstruction and depressive symptoms during the transition to motherhood: Evidence from two cross-lagged longitudinal studies. *Journal of Personality and Social Psychology, 81,* 1144–1159.

Salmivalli, C., & Voeten, M. (2004). Connections between attitudes, group norms, and behaviour in bullying situations. *International Journal of Behavioral Development, 28,* 246–258.

Salter, D., McMillan, D., Richards, M., Talbot, T., Hodges, J., Bentovim, A., & Hastings, R. (2003). Development of sexually abusive behavior in sexually victimized males: A longitudinal study. *Lancet, 361,* 471–476.

Salthouse, T. A. (1996). Constraints on theories of cognitive aging. *Psychonomic Bulletin and Review, 3,* 287–299.

Salthouse, T. A. (2005). Relations between cognitive abilities and measures of executive functioning. *Neuropsychology, 19,* 532–545.

Salthouse, T. A. (2006). Aging of thought. In E. Bialystok & F. I. M. Craik (Eds.), *Lifespan cognition: Mechanisms of change* (pp. 274–284). New York: Oxford University Press.

Salthouse, T. A., & Caja, S. J. (2000). Structural constraints on process explanations in cognitive aging. *Psychology and Aging, 15,* 44–55.

Salthouse, T. A., Fristoe, N., & Rhee, S. H. (1996). How localized are age-related effects on neuropsychological measures? *Neuropsychology, 10,* 272–285.

Salvioli, S., Capri, M., Santoro, A., Raule, N., Sevini, F., & Lukas, S. (2008). The impact of mitochondrial DNA on human lifespan: A view from studies on centenarians. *Biotechnology Journal, 3,* 740–749.

Samarel, N. (1991). *Caring for life and death.* Washington, DC: Hemisphere.

Samarel, N. (1995). The dying process. In H. Wass & R. A. Neimeyer (Eds.), *Dying: Facing the facts* (3rd ed., pp. 89–116). Washington, DC: Taylor & Francis.

Sameroff, A. (2006). Identifying risk and protective factors for healthy child development. In A. Clarke-Stewart & J. Dunn (Eds.), *Families count: Effects on child and adolescent development* (pp. 53–76). New York: Cambridge University Press.

Sampselle, C. M., Harris, V., Harlow, S. D., & Sowers, M. (2002). Midlife development and menopause in African-American and Caucasian women. *Health Care for Women International, 23,* 351–363.

Samuels, M. (2003). Viruses and sudden infant death. *Paediatric Respiratory Reviews, 4,* 178–183.

Samuelsson, S. M., Alfredson, B. B., Hagberg, B., Anonymous, Nordbeck, B., Brun, A., Gustafson, L., & Risberg, J. (1997). The Swedish Centenarian Study: A multidisciplinary study of five consecutive cohorts at the age of 100. *International Journal of Aging and Human Development, 45,* 223–253.

Sandberg, J. F., & Hofferth, S. L. (2001). Changes in children's time with parents: United States, 1981–1997. *Demography, 38,* 423–436.

Sanders, C. M. (1999). *Grief: The mourning after* (2nd ed.). New York: Wiley.

Sanders, O. (2006). *Evaluating the Keeping Ourselves Safe Programme.* Wellington, NZ: Youth Education Service, New Zealand Police. Retrieved from www.nzfvc.org.nz/accan/papers-presentations/abstract11v.shtml

Sann, C., & Streri, A. (2007). Perception of object shape and texture in human newborns: Evidence from cross-modal transfer tasks. *Developmental Science, 10,* 399–410.

Sansavini, A., Bertoncini, J., & Giovanelli, G. (1997). Newborns discriminate the rhythm of multisyllabic stressed words. *Developmental Psychology, 33,* 3–11.

Santtila, P., Wager, I., Witting, K., Harlaar, N., Jern, P., Johansson, A., Varjonen, M., & Sandnabba, K. (2008). Discrepancies between sexual desire and sexual activity: Gender differences and associations with relationship satisfaction. *Journal of Sex and Marital Therapy, 34,* 31–44.

Sanz, A., Pamplona, R., & Barja, G. (2006). Is the mitochondrial free radical theory of aging intact? *Antioxidants and Redox Signaling, 8,* 582–599.

Sapp, F., Lee, K., & Muir, D. (2000). Three-year-olds' difficulty with the appearance–reality distinction: Is it real or is it apparent? *Developmental Psychology, 36,* 547–560.

Sarason, S. B. (1977). *Work, aging, and social change.* New York: Free Press.

Sarnecka, B. W., & Gelman, S. A. (2004). Six does not just mean a lot: Preschoolers see number words as specific. *Cognition, 92,* 329–352.

Sasser-Coen, J. A. (1993). Qualitative changes in creativity in the second half of life: A life-span developmental perspective. *Journal of Creative Behavior, 27,* 18–27.

Sato, T., Matsumoto, T., Kawano, H., Watanabe, T., Uematsu, Y., & Semine, K. (2004). Brain masculinization requires androgen receptor function.

Proceedings of the National Academy of Sciences, 101, 1673–1678.

Saucier, J. F., Sylvestre, R., Doucet, H., Lambert, J., Frappier, J. Y., Charbonneau, L., & Malus, M. (2002). Cultural identity and adaptation to adolescence in Montreal. In F. J. C. Azima & N. Grizenko (Eds.), *Immigrant and refugee children and their families: Clinical, research, and training issues* (pp. 133–154). Madison, WI: International Universities Press.

Saudino, K. J. (2003). Parent ratings of infant temperament: Lessons from twin studies. *Infant Behavior and Development, 26,* 100–107.

Saudino, K. J., & Plomin, R. (1997). Cognitive and temperamental mediators of genetic contributions to the home environment during infancy. *Merrill-Palmer Quarterly, 43,* 1–23.

Sauls, D. J. (2002). Effects of labor support on mothers, babies, and birth outcomes. *Journal of Obstetric, Gynecologic, and Neonatal Nursing, 31,* 733–741.

Savin-Williams, R. C. (2001). A critique of research on sexual-minority youths. *Journal of Adolescence, 24,* 5–13.

Savin-Williams, R. C. (2003). Lesbian, gay, and bisexual youths' relationships with their parents. In L. D. Garnets & D. C. Kimmel (Eds.), *Psychological perspectives on lesbian, gay, and bisexual experiences* (2nd ed., pp. 299–326). New York: Columbia University Press.

Savin-Williams, R. C., & Diamond, L. M. (2004). Sex. In R. M. Lerner & L. Steinberg (Eds.), *Handbook of adolescent development* (2nd ed., pp. 189–231). Hoboken, NJ: Wiley.

Savin-Williams, R. C., & Ream, G. L. (2003). Sex variations in the disclosure to parents of same-sex attractions. *Journal of Family Psychology, 17,* 429–438.

Saygin, A. P., Wilson, S. M., Dronkers, N. F., & Bates, E. (2004). Action comprehension in aphasia: Linguistic and non-linguistic deficits and their lesion correlates. *Neuropsychologia, 42,* 1788–1804.

Saylor, M. M., Baldwin, D. A., & Sabbagh, M. A. (2005). Word learning: A complex product. In G. Hall & S. Waxman (Eds.), *Weaving a lexicon.* Cambridge, MA: MIT Press.

Saylor, M. M., & Troseth, G. L. (2006). Preschoolers use information about speakers' desires to learn new words. *Cognitive Development, 21,* 214–231.

Scarmeas, N., Luchsinger, J. A., Mayeux, R., & Stern, Y. (2007). Mediterranean diet and Alzheimer disease mortality. *Neurology, 69,* 1084–1093.

Scarr, S., & McCartney, K. (1983). How people make their own environments: A theory of genotype environment effects. *Child Development, 54,* 424–435.

Scarr, S., & Weinberg, R. A. (1983). The Minnesota Adoption Studies: Genetic differences and malleability. *Child Development, 54,* 260–267.

Schaal, B., Marlier, L., & Soussignan, R. (2000). Human fetuses learn odours from their pregnant mother's diet. *Chemical Senses, 25,* 729–737.

Schafer, R. (1999). *Determinants of living arrangements of the elderly.* Boston: Joint Center for Housing Studies, Harvard University.

Schaie, K. W. (1994). The course of adult intellectual development. *American Psychologist, 49,* 304–313.

Schaie, K. W. (1996). *Intellectual development in adulthood: The Seattle Longitudinal Study.* New York: Cambridge University Press.

Schaie, K. W. (1998). The Seattle Longitudinal Studies of Adult Intelligence. In M. P. Lawton & T. A. Salthouse (Eds.), *Essential papers on the psychology of aging* (pp. 263–271). New York: New York University Press.

Schaie, K. W. (2005). *Developmental influences on adult intelligence: The Seattle Longitudinal Study.* New York: Oxford University Press.

Schalet, A. (2007). Adolescent sexuality viewed through two different cultural lenses. In M. S. Tepper & A. F. Owens (Eds.), *Sexual health: Vol. 3.*

Moral and cultural foundations (pp. 365–387). Westport, CT: Praeger.

Scharrer, E., & Comstock, G. (2003). Entertainment televisual media: Content patterns and themes. In E. L. Palmer & B. M. Young (Eds.), *The faces of televisual media: Teaching, violence, selling to children* (pp. 161–193). Mahwah, NJ: Erlbaum.

Scherer, J. M., & Simon, R. J. (1999). *Euthanasia and the right to die: A comparative view.* Lanham, MD: Rowman & Littlefield.

Schewe, P. A. (2007). Interventions to prevent sexual violence. In L. S. Doll, S. E. Bonzo, D. A. Sleet, & J. A. Mercy (Eds.), *Handbook of injury and violence prevention* (pp. 223–240). New York: Springer Science + Business Media.

Schieber, R. A., & Sacks, J. J. (2001). Measuring community bicycle helmet use among children. *Public Health Reports, 116,* 113–121.

Schieman, S., Van Gundy, K., & Taylor, J. (2001). Status, role, and resource explanations for age patterns in psychological distress. *Journal of Health and Social Behavior, 42,* 80–96.

Schieman, S., & Plickert, G. (2007). Functional limitations and changes in levels of depression among older adults: A multiple-hierarchy stratification perspective. *Journal of Gerontology, 62B,* S36–S42.

Schilling, O., & Wahl, H.-W. (2002). Family networks and life satisfaction of older adults in rural and urban regions. *Kolner Zeitschrift fur Soziologie und Sozialpsychologie, 54,* 304–317.

Schlegel, A., & Barry, H., III. (1991). *Adolescence: An anthropological inquiry.* New York: Free Press.

Schlossberg, N. (2004). *Retire smart, retire happy: Finding your true path in life.* Washington, DC: American Psychological Association.

Schmidt, K.-H., Neubach, B., & Heuer, H. (2007). Self-control demands, cognitive control deficits, and burnout. *Work and Stress, 21,* 142–154.

Schmidt, L. A., Fox, N. A., Rubin, K. H., Sternberg, E. M., Gold, P. W., & Smith, C. C. (1997). Behavioral and neuroendocrine correlates in shy children. *Developmental Psychobiology, 35,* 119–135.

Schmidt, L. A., Fox, N. A., Schulkin, J., & Gold, P. W. (1999). Behavioral and psychophysiological correlates of self-presentation in temperamentally shy children. *Developmental Psychobiology, 30,* 127–140.

Schmidt, L. A., Santesso, D. L., Schulkin, J., & Segalowitz, S. J. (2007). Shyness is a necessary but not sufficient condition for high salivary cortisol in typically developing 10-year-old children. *Personality and Individual Differences, 43,* 1541–1551.

Schmitz, S., Fulker, D. W., Plomin, R., Zahn-Waxler, C., Emde, R. N., & DeFries, J. C. (1999). Temperament and problem behaviour during early childhood. *International Journal of Behavioural Development, 23,* 333–355.

Schneewind, K. A., & Gerhard, A. (2002). Relationship personality, conflict resolution, and marital satisfaction in the first 5 years of marriage. *Family Relations, 51,* 63–71.

Schneider, B. A., Daneman, M., Murphy, D. R., & See, S. K. (2000). Listening to discourse in distracting settings: The effects of aging. *Psychology and Aging, 15,* 110–125.

Schneider, B. H., Atkinson, L., & Tardif, C. (2001). Child–parent attachment and children's peer relations: A quantitative review. *Developmental Psychology, 37,* 87–100.

Schneider, E. L. (1992). Biological theories of aging. *Generations, 16*(4), 7–10.

Schneider, W. (2002). Memory development in childhood. In U. Goswami (Ed.), *Blackwell handbook of childhood cognitive development* (pp. 236–256). Malden, MA: Blackwell.

Schneider, W., & Bjorklund, D. F. (1992). Expertise, aptitude, and strategic remembering. *Child Development, 63,* 461–473.

Schneider, W., & Bjorklund, D. F. (1998). Memory. In D. Kuhn & R. S. Siegler (Eds.), *Handbook of child*

psychology: Vol. 2. Cognition, perception, and language (5th ed., pp. 467–521). New York: Wiley.

Schneider, W., & Pressley, M. (1997). *Memory development between two and twenty* (2nd ed.). Mahwah, NJ: Erlbaum.

Schneller, D. P., & Arditti, J.A. (2004). After the breakup: Interpreting divorce and rethinking intimacy. *Journal of Divorce and Remarriage, 42,* 1–37.

Schnohr, P., Nyboe, J., Lange, P., & Jensen, G. (1998). Longevity and gray hair, baldness, facial wrinkles, and arcus senilis in 13,000 men and women: The Copenhagen City Heart Study. *Journal of Gerontology, 53,* M347–350.

Scholl, B. J., & Leslie, A. M. (2000). Minds, modules, and meta-analysis. *Child Development, 72,* 696–701.

Scholl, T. O., Heidiger, M. L., & Belsky, D. H. (1996). Prenatal care and maternal health during adolescent pregnancy: A review and meta-analysis. *Journal of Adolescent Health, 15,* 444–456.

Scholnick, E. K. (1995, Fall). Knowing and constructing plans. *SRCD Newsletter,* pp. 1–2, 17.

Schooler, C., Mulatu, M. S., & Oates, G. (1999). The continuing effects of substantively complex work on the intellectual functioning of older workers. *Psychology and Aging, 14,* 483–506.

Schoon, L., & Parsons, S. (2002). Teenage aspirations for future careers and occupational outcomes. *Journal of Vocational Behavior, 60,* 262–288.

Schoppe-Sullivan, S. J., Brown, G. L., Cannon, E. A., Mangelsdorf, S. C., & Sokolowski, M. S. (2008). Maternal gatekeeping, coparenting quality, and fathering behavior in families with infants. *Journal of Family Psychology, 22,* 389–398.

Schoppe-Sullivan, S. J., Mangelsdorf, S. C., Frosch, C. A., & McHale, J. (2004). Associations between coparenting and marital behavior from infancy to the preschool years. *Journal of Family Psychology, 18,* 194–207.

Schott, J. M., & Rossor, M. N. (2003). The grasp and other primitive reflexes. *Journal of Neurological and Neurosurgical Psychiatry, 74,* 558–560.

Schroots, J. J. F., van Dijkum, C., & Assink, M. H. J. (2004). Autobiographical memory from a life span perspective. *International Journal of Aging and Human Development, 58,* 69–85.

Schuetze, P., & Eiden, R. D. (2006). The association between maternal cocaine use during pregnancy and physiological regulation in 4- to 8-week-old infants: An examination of possible mediators and moderators. *Journal of Pediatric Psychology, 31,* 15–26,

Schull, W. J. (2003). The children of atomic bomb survivors: A synopsis. *Journal of Radiological Protection, 23,* 369–394.

Schulman, K. A., Berlin, J. A., Harless, W., Kerner, J. F., Sistrunk, S., & Gersh, B. J. (1999). The effect of race and sex on physicians' recommendations for cardiac catheterization. *New England Journal of Medicine, 340,* 618–626.

Schulte-Ruther, M., Markowitsch, H. J., Fink, G. R., & Piefke, M. (2007). Mirror neuron and theory of mind mechanisms involved in face-to-face interactions: A functional magnetic resonance imaging approach to empathy. *Journal of Cognitive Neuroscience, 19,* 1354–1372.

Schultz, R., & Beach, S. (1999). Caregiving as a risk factor for mortality: The caregiver health effects study. *Journal of the American Medical Association, 282,* 2215–2219.

Schultz, R., Burgio, L., Burns, R., Eisdorfer, C., Gallagher-Thompson, D., Gitlin, L. N., & Mahoney, D. F. (2003). Resources for enhancing Alzheimer's caregiver health (REACH): Overview, site-specific outcomes, and future directions. *Gerontologist, 43,* 514–520.

Schulz, R., & Curnow, C. (1988). Peak performance and age among superathletes: Track and field, swimming, baseball, tennis, and golf. *Journal of Gerontology, 43,* P113–P120.

Schumacher, B., Garinis, G. A., & Hoeijmakers, J. H. J. (2007). Age to survive: DNA damage and aging. *Trends in Genetics, 24,* 77–85.

Schunk, D. H., & Pajares, F. (2005). Competence perceptions and academic functioning. In A. J. Andrew & C. S. Dweck (Eds.), *Handbook of competence and motivation* (pp. 85–104). New York: Guilford.

Schwanenflugel, P. J., Henderson, R. L., & Fabricius, W. V. (1998). Developing organization of mental verbs and theory of mind in middle childhood: Evidence from extensions. *Developmental Psychology, 34,* 512–524.

Schwartz, B. L., & Frazier, L. D. (2005). Tip-of-the-tongue states and aging: Contrasting psycholinguistic and metacognitive perspectives. *Journal of General Psychology, 132,* 377–391.

Schwartz, J. P., & Waldo, M. (2004). Group work with men who have committed partner abuse. In J. L. DeLucia-Waack, D. A. Gerrity, C. R. Kalodner, & M. T. Riva (Eds.), *Handbook of group counseling and psychotherapy* (pp. 576–592). Thousand Oaks, CA: Sage.

Schwartz, S. J., Côté, J. E., & Arnett, J. J. (2005). Identity and agency in emerging adulthood: Two developmental routes in the individualization process. *Youth and Society, 37,* 201–229.

Schwartz, S. J., Pantin, H., Prado, G., Sullivan, S., & Szapocznik, J. (2005). Family functioning, identity, and problem behavior: Immigrant early adolescents. *Journal of Early Adolescence, 25,* 392–420.

Schwebel, D. C., & Brezausek, C. M. (2007). Father transitions in the household and young children's injury risk. *Psychology of Men and Masculinity, 8,* 173–184.

Schwebel, D. C., & Gaines, J. (2007). Pediatric unintentional injury: Behavioral risk factors and implications for prevention. *Journal of Developmental and Behavioral Pediatrics, 28,* 245–254.

Schweiger, W. K., & O'Brien, M. (2005). Special needs adoption: An ecological systems approach. *Family Relations, 54,* 512–522.

Schweinhart, L. J., Montie, J., Xiang, Z., Barnett, W. S., Belfield, C. R., & Nores, M. (2005). *Lifetime effects: The High/Scope Perry Preschool Study through age 40.* Ypsilanti, MI: High/Scope Press.

Schweizer, K., Moosbrugger, H., & Goldhammer, F. (2006). The structure of the relationship between attention and intelligence. *Intelligence, 33,* 589–611.

Schwier, C., van Maanen, C., Carpenter, M., & Tomasello, M. (2006). Rational imitation in 12-month-old infants. *Infancy, 10,* 303–311.

Schwimmer, J. B., Burwinkle, T. M., & Varni, J. W. (2003). Health-related quality of life of severely obese children and adolescents. *Journal of the American Medical Association, 289,* 1813–1819.

Scott, C. S., Arthur, D., Owen, R., & Panizo, M. I. (1989). Black adolescents' emotional response to menarche. *Journal of the National Medical Association, 81,* 285–290.

Scott, L. D. (2003). The relation of racial identity and racial socialization to coping with discrimination among African Americans. *Journal of Black Studies, 20,* 520–538.

Scully, D., & Marolla, J. (1998). "Riding the bull at Gilley's": Convicted rapists describe the rewards of rape. In M. E. Odem & J. Clay-Warner (Eds.), *Confronting rape and sexual assault* (pp. 181–198). Wilmington, DE: Scholarly Resources.

Seaton, E. K., Scottham, K. M., & Sellers, R. M. (2006). The status model of racial identity development in African American adolescents: Evidence of structure, trajectories, and well-being. *Child Development, 77,* 1416–1426.

Seeman, E. (2002). Pathogenesis of bone fragility in women and men. *Lancet, 359,* 1841–1850.

Seeman, E. (2008). Structural basis of growth-related gain and age-related loss of bone strength. *Rheumatology, 47,* iv2–iv8.

Seeman, T. E., Huang, M.-H., Bretsky, P., Crimmins, E., Launer, L., & Guralnik, J. M. (2005). Education and APOE-e4 in longitudinal cognitive decline:

MacArthur Studies of Successful Aging. *Journal of Gerontology, 60B*, P74–P83.

Seiberling, K. A., & Conley, D. B. (2004). Aging and olfactory and taste function. *Otolaryngologic Clinics of North America, 37*, 1209–1228.

Seidman, E., Aber, J. L., & French, S. E. (2004). Assessing the transitions to middle and high school. *Journal of Adolescent Research, 19*, 3–30.

Seidman, E., Lambert, L. E., Allen, L., & Aber, J. L. (2003). Urban adolescents' transition to junior high school and protective family transactions. *Journal of Early Adolescence, 23*, 166–193.

Seifer, R., & Schiller, M. (1995). The role of parenting sensitivity, infant temperament, and dyadic interaction in attachment theory and assessment. In E. Waters, B. E. Vaughn, G. Posada, & K. Kondo-Ikemura (Eds.), Caregiving, cultural, and cognitive perspectives on secure-base behavior and working models: New growing points of attachment theory and research. *Monographs of the Society for Research in Child Development, 60*(2–3, Serial No. 244).

Seitz, V., & Apfel, N. H. (2005). Creating effective school-based interventions for pregnant teenagers. In R. DeV. Peters, B. Leadbeater, & R. J. McMahon (Eds.), *Resilience in children, families, and communities: Linking context to practice and policy* (pp. 65–82). New York: Kluwer Academic.

Selman, R. L. (1976). Social-cognitive understanding: A guide to educational and clinical practice. In T. Lickona (Ed.), *Moral development and behavior: Theory, research, and social issues* (pp. 299–316). New York: Holt, Rinehart and Winston.

Selman, R. L. (1980). *The growth of interpersonal understanding.* New York: Academic Press.

Selman, R. L., & Byrne, D. F. (1974). A structural-developmental analysis of levels of role taking in middle childhood. *Child Development, 45*, 803–806.

Selwood, A., Johnston, K., Katona, C., Lyketsos, C., & Livingston, G. (2007). Systematic review of the effect of psychological interventions on family caregivers of people with dementia. *Journal of Affective Disorders, 101*, 75–89.

Selwyn, P. A. (1996). Before their time: A clinician's reflections on death and AIDS. In H. M. Spiro, M. G. M. Curnen, & L. P. Wandel (Eds.), *Facing death: Where culture, religion, and medicine meet* (pp. 33–37). New Haven, CT: Yale University Press.

Sen, M. G., Yonas, A., & Knill, D. C. (2001). Development of infants' sensitivity to surface contour information for spatial layout. *Perception, 30*, 167–176.

Senchina, D. S., & Kohut, M. L. (2007). Immunological outcomes of exercise in older adults. *Clinical Interventions in Aging, 2*, 3–16.

Serafini, T. E., & Adams, G. R. (2002). Functions of identity: Scale construction and validation. *Identity: An International Journal of Theory and Research, 2*, 361–389.

Serbin, L. A., Powlishta, K. K., & Gulko, J. (1993). The development of sex typing in middle childhood. *Monographs of the Society for Research in Child Development, 58*(2, Serial No. 232).

Sergeant, J. F., Ekerdt, D. J., & Chapin, R. (2008). Measurement of late-life residential relocation: Why are rates for such a manifest event so varied? *Journal of Gerontology, 63B*, S92–S98.

Sermon, K., Van Steirteghem, A., & Liebaers, I. (2004). Preimplantation genetic diagnosis. *Lancet, 363*, 1633–1641.

Service Canada. (2009). *Guide to Canada Pension Plan disability benefits.* Retrieved from www.service-canada.gc.ca/eng/isp/pub/cpp/disability/guide/sectionb.shtml

Sesame Workshop. (2008). *Sesame Street season 37 press kit.* Retrieved from www.sesameworkshop.org/aboutus/pressroom/presskits/season37/sesame_street.php

Settles, I. H., Cortina, L. M., Malley, J., & Stewart, A. J. (2006). The climate for women in academic science: The good, the bad, and the changeable. *Psychology of Women Quarterly, 30*, 47–58.

Sewall, G., & Burns, L. H. (2006). Involuntary childlessness. In S. N. Covington & L. H. Burns (Eds.), *Infertility counseling: A comprehensive handbook for clinicians* (2nd ed., pp. 411–427). New York: Cambridge University Press.

Seymour, S. C. (1999). *Women, family, and child care in India.* Cambridge, UK: Cambridge University Press.

Shah, T., Sullivan, K., & Carter, J. (2006). Sudden infant death syndrome and reported maternal smoking during pregnancy. *American Journal of Public Health, 96*, 1757–1759.

Shainess, N. (1961). A re-evaluation of some aspects of femininity through a study of menstruation: A preliminary report. *Comparative Psychiatry, 2*, 20–26.

Shanahan, L., McHale, S. M., Crouter, A. C., & Osgood, D. W. (2007). Warmth with mothers and fathers from middle childhood to late adolescence: Within- and between-families comparisons. *Developmental Psychology, 43*, 551–563.

Shanahan, M. J., Mortimer, J. T., & Krüger, H. (2002). Adolescence and adult work in the twenty-first century. *Journal of Research on Adolescence, 12*, 99–120.

Shapiro, A. E., Gottman, J. M., & Carrere, S. (2000). The baby and the marriage: Identifying factors that buffer against decline in marital satisfaction after the first baby arrives. *Journal of Family Psychology, 14*, 59–70.

Shapka, J. D., & Keating, D. P. (2005). Structure and change in self-concept during adolescence. *Canadian Journal of Behavioural Science, 37*, 83–96.

Shatz, M. (2007). On the development of the field. In E. Hoff & M. Shatz (Eds.), *Blackwell handbook of language development* (pp. 1–20). Malden, MA: Blackwell.

Shaver, P., Furman, W., & Buhrmester, D. (1985). Transition to college: Network changes, social skills, and loneliness. In S. Duck & D. Perlman (Eds.), *Understanding personal relationships: An interdisciplinary approach* (pp. 193–219). London: Sage.

Shaw, B. A. (2005). Anticipated support from neighbors and physical functioning during later life. *Research on Aging, 27*, 503–525.

Shaw, D. S., Gilliom, M., Ingoldsby, E. M., & Nagin, D. S. (2003). Trajectories leading to school-age conduct problems. *Developmental Psychology, 39*, 189–200.

Shaw, P., Eckstrand, K., Sharp, W., Blumenthal, J., Lerch, J. P., & Greenstein, D. (2007, November 16). Attention-deficit/hyperactivity disorder is characterized by a delay in cortical maturation. *Proceedings of the National Academy of Sciences Online.* Retrieved from www.pnas.org/cgi/content/abstract/0707741104v1

Shea, J. L. (2006). Cross-cultural comparison of women's midlife symptom-reporting: A China study. *Culture, Medicine, and Psychiatry, 30*, 331–362.

Shedler, J., & Block, J. (1990). Adolescent drug use and psychological health: A longitudinal inquiry. *American Psychologist, 45*, 612–630.

Sheehy, A., Gasser, T., Molinari, L., & Largo, R. H. (1999). An analysis of variance of the pubertal and midgrowth spurts for length and width. *Annals of Human Biology, 26*, 309–331.

Shenkin, J. D., Broffitt, B., Levy, S. M., & Warren, J. J. (2004). The association between environmental tobacco smoke and primary tooth caries. *Journal of Public Health Dentistry, 64*, 184–186.

Sherman, A. M., de Vries, B., & Lansford, J. E. (2000). Friendship in childhood and adulthood: Lessons across the life span. *International Journal of Aging and Human Development, 51*, 31–51.

Sherman, A. M., Lansford, J. E., & Volling, B. L. (2006). Sibling relationships and best friendships in young adulthood: Warmth, conflict, and well-being. *Personal Relationships, 13*, 151–165.

Sherman, C. W., Rosenblatt, D. E., & Antonucci, T. C. (2008). Elder abuse and mistreatment: A life span and cultural context. *Indian Journal of Gerontology, 22.*

Sherman, S. L., Freeman, S. B., Allen, E. G., & Lamb, N. E. (2005). Risk factors for nondisjunction of trisomy 21. *Cytogenetic Genome Research, 111*, 273–280.

Sherrod, L. R., & Spiewak, G. S. (2008). Possible interrelationships between civic engagement, positive youth development, and spirituality/religiosity. In R. M. Lerner, R. W. Roeser, & E. Phelps (Eds.), *Positive youth development and spirituality: From theory to research* (pp. 322–338). West Conshohocken, PA: Templeton Foundation Press.

Sherry, B., McDivitt, J., Brich, L. L., Cook, F. H., Sanders, S., Prish, J. L., Francis, L. A., & Scanlon, K. S. (2004). Attitudes, practices, and concerns about child feeding and child weight status among socioeconomically diverse white, Hispanic, and African-American mothers. *Journal of the American Dietetic Association, 104*, 215–221.

Shields, G., King, W., Fulks, S., & Fallon, L. F. (2002). Determinants of perceived safety among the elderly: An exploratory study. *Journal of Gerontological Social Work, 38*, 73–83.

Shields, M. (2005). *Overweight Canadian children and adolescents.* Nutrition: Findings from the Canadian Community Health Survey. Statistics Canada Catalogue No. 82-620-MWE2005001. Retrieved from www.statcan.ca/english/research/82-620MIE/2005001/pdf/cobesity.pdf

Shimizu, H. (2001). Japanese adolescent boys' senses of empathy (omoiyari) and Carol Gilligan's perspectives on the morality of care: A phenomenological approach. *Culture and Psychology, 7*, 453–475.

Shin, J. S., Hong, A., Solomon, M. J., & Lee, C. S. (2006). The role of telomeres and telomerase in the pathology of human cancer and aging. *Pathology, 38*, 103–113.

Shipman, H. L., Brickhouse, N. W., Dagher, Z., & Letts, W. J., IV. (2002). Changes in student views of religion and science in a college astronomy course. *Science Education, 86*, 526–547.

Shock, N. W. (1977). Biological theories of aging. In J. E. Birren & K. W. Schaie (Eds.), *Handbook of the psychology of aging* (pp. 103–115). New York: Van Nostrand Reinhold.

Shonk, S. M., & Cicchetti, D. (2001). Maltreatment, competency deficits, and risk for academic and behavioral maladjustment. *Developmental Psychology, 37*, 3–17.

Shonkoff, J., & Phillips, D. (Eds.). (2001). *Neurons to neighborhoods: The science of early childhood development.* Washington, DC: National Academy Press.

Shuey, K., & Hardy, M. A. (2003). Assistance to aging parents and parents-in-law: Does lineage affect family allocation decisions? *Journal of Marriage and Family, 65*, 418–431.

Shultz, K. S., & Wang, M. (2007). The influence of specific physical health conditions on retirement decisions. *International Journal of Aging and Human Development, 65*, 149–161.

Shumaker, S. A., Legault, C., Thal, L., Wallace, R. B., Ockene, J. K., & Hendrix, S. L. (2003). Estrogen plus progestin and the incidence of dementia and mild cognitive impairment in postmenopausal women: The Women's Health Initiative Memory Study: A randomized controlled trial. *Journal of the American Medical Association, 289*, 2651–2662.

Shure, M. B., & Aberson, B. (2005). Enhancing the process of resilience through effective thinking. In S. Goldstein & R. B. Brooks (Eds.), *Handbook of resilience in children* (pp. 373–394). New York: Kluwer Academic.

Shwalb, D. W., Nakawaza, J., Yamamoto, T., & Hyun, J.-H. (2004). Fathering in Japanese, Chinese, and Korean cultures: A review of the research literature.

In M. E. Lamb (Ed.), *The role of the father in child development* (4th ed., pp. 146–181). Hoboken, NJ: Wiley.

Shweder, R. A., Goodnow, J. J., Hatano, G., LeVine, R. A., Markus, H. R., & Miller, P. J. (2006). The cultural psychology of development: One mind, many mentalities. In R. M. Lerner (Ed.), *Handbook of child psychology: Vol. 1. Theoretical models of human development* (6th ed., pp. 716–792). Hoboken, NJ: Wiley.

Sidebotham, P., Heron, J., & the ALSPAC Study Team. (2003). Child maltreatment in the "children of the nineties:" The role of the child. *Child Abuse and Neglect, 27,* 337–352.

Siebenbruner, J., Zimmer-Gembeck, M. J., & Egeland, B. (2007). Sexual partners and contraceptive use: A 16-year prospective study predicting abstinence and risk behavior. *Journal of Research on Adolescence, 17,* 179–206.

Siegler, R. S. (1996). *Emerging minds: The process of change in children's thinking.* New York: Oxford University Press.

Siegler, R. S. (2007). Cognitive variability. *Developmental Science, 10,* 104–109.

Siegler, R. S., & Alibali, M. W. (2005). *Children's thinking* (4th ed.). Upper Saddle River, NJ: Prentice-Hall.

Siegler, R. S., & Mu, Y. (2008). Chinese children excel on novel mathematics problems even before elementary school. *Psychological Science, 19,* 759–763.

Siegler, R. S., & Svetina, M. (2006). What leads children to adopt new strategies? A microgenetic/cross-sectional study of class inclusion. *Child Development, 77,* 997–1015.

Siegrist, J., Wahrendorf, M., von dem Knesebeck, O., Jurges, H., & Borsch-Supan, A. (2007). Quality of work, well-being, and intended early retirement of older employees—Baseline results from the SHARE study. *European Journal of Public Health, 17,* 62–68.

Siervogel, R. M., Maynard, L. M., Wisemandle, W. A., Roche, A. F., Guo, S. S., Chumlea, W. C., & Towne, B. (2000). Annual changes in total body fat and fat-free mass in children from 8 to 18 years in relation to changes in body mass index: The Fels Longitudinal Study. *Annals of the New York Academy of Sciences, 904,* 420–423.

Sigman, M. (1995). Nutrition and child development: More food for thought. *Current Directions in Psychological Science, 4,* 52–55.

Silk, J. S., Morris, A. S., Kanaya, T., & Steinberg, L. (2003). Psychological control and autonomy granting: Opposite ends of a continuum or distinct constructs? *Journal of Research on Adolescence, 13,* 113–128.

Silvén, M. (2001). Attention in very young infants predicts learning of first words. *Infant Behavior and Development, 24,* 229–237.

Silver, E. J., & Bauman, L. J. (2006). The association of sexual experience with attitudes, beliefs, and risk behaviors of inner-city adolescents. *Journal of Research on Adolescence, 16,* 29–45.

Silver, M. H., & Perls, T. T. (2000). Is dementia the price of a long life? An optimistic report from centenarians. *Journal of Geriatric Psychiatry, 33,* 71–79.

Silverman, P. R. (2004). Dying and bereavement in historical perspective. In J. Berzoff & P. R. Silverman (Eds.), *Living with dying: A handbook for end-of-life healthcare practitioners* (pp. 128–149). New York: Columbia University Press.

Silverman, P. R., & Nickman, S. L. (1996). Children's construction of their dead parents. In D. Klass, P. R. Silverman, & S. L. Nickman (Eds.), *Continuing bonds: New understandings of grief* (pp. 73–86). Washington, DC: Taylor & Francis.

Silverman, W. K., & Pina, A. A. (2008). Psychosocial treatments for phobic and anxiety disorders in youth. In R. G. Steele, T. D. Elkin, & M. Roberts (Eds.), *Handbook of evidence-based therapies for children and adolescents: Bridging science and practice* (pp. 65–82). New York: Springer.

Silverstein, M., & Bengtson, V. L. (1991). Do close parent–child relations reduce the mortality risk of older parents? *Journal of Health and Social Behavior, 32,* 382–395.

Silverstein, M., Conroy, S., Wang, H., Giarrusso, R., & Bengtson, V. L. (2002). Reciprocity in parent–child relations over the adult life course. *Journal of Gerontology, 57B,* S3–S13.

Silverstein, M., & Marenco, A. (2001). How Americans enact the grandparent role across the family life course. *Journal of Family Issues, 22,* 493–522.

Silvi, J. (2004). Deaths from motor vehicle traffic accidents in selected countries of the Americas, 1985–2001. *Epidemiological Bulletin, 25,* 2–5.

Simcock, G., & DeLoache, J. (2006). Get the picture? The effects of iconicity on toddlers' reenactment from picture books. *Developmental Psychology, 42,* 1352–1357.

Simcock, G., & Hayne, H. (2002). Breaking the barrier? Children fail to translate their preverbal memories into language. *Psychological Science, 13,* 225–231.

Simcock, G., & Hayne, H. (2003). Age-related changes in verbal and nonverbal memory during early childhood. *Developmental Psychology, 39,* 805–814.

Simmons, R. G., & Blyth, D. A. (1987). *Moving into adolescence.* New York: Aldine De Gruyter.

Simon, N. M., Smoller, J. W., McNamara, K. L., Maser, R. S., Zlata, A. K., & Pollack, M. H. (2006). Telomere shortening and mood disorders: Preliminary support for a chronic stress model of accelerated aging. *Biological Psychiatry, 60,* 432–435.

Simoneau, M., & Markovits, H. (2003). Reasoning with premises that are not empirically true: Evidence for the role of inhibition and retrieval. *Developmental Psychology, 39,* 964–975.

Simons, J. S., Dodson, C. S., Bell, D., & Schachter, D. L. (2004). Specific- and partial-source memory: Effects of aging. *Psychology and Aging, 19,* 689–694.

Simons-Morton, B. G., & Haynie, D. L. (2003). Growing up drug free: A developmental challenge. In M. H. Bornstein, L. Davidson, C. L. M. Keyes, K. A. Moore, & the Center for Child Well-Being (Eds.), *Well-being: Positive development across the life course* (pp. 109–122). Mahwah, NJ: Erlbaum.

Simonton, D. K. (1991). Creative productivity through the adult years. *Generations, 15*(2), 13–16.

Simonton, D. K. (2000). Creativity: Cognitive, personal, developmental, and social aspects. *American Psychologist, 55,* 151–158.

Simonton, D. K. (2006). Historiometric methods. In K. A. Ericsson, N. Charness, P. J. Feltovich, & R. R. Hoffman (Eds.), *The Cambridge handbook of expertise and expert performance* (pp. 319–335). New York: Cambridge University Press.

Simpson, J. A., & Harris, B. A. (1994). Interpersonal attraction. In A. L. Weber & J. H. Harvey (Eds.), *Perspectives on close relationships* (pp. 45–66). Boston: Allyn and Bacon.

Simpson, J. A., Rholes, W. S., Campbell, L., Tran, S., & Wilson, C. L. (2003). Adult attachment, the transition to parenthood, and depressive symptoms. *Journal of Personality and Social Psychology, 84,* 1172–1187.

Simpson, J. L., de la Cruz, F., Swerdloff, R. S., Samango-Sprouse, C., Skakkebaek, N. E., & Graham, J. M., Jr. (2003). Klinefelter syndrome: Expanding the phenotype and identifying new research directions. *Genetic Medicine, 5,* 460–468.

Simpson, J. M. (2001). Infant stress and sleep deprivation as an aetiological basis for the sudden infant death syndrome. *Early Human Development, 61,* 1–43.

Simpson, R. (2004). Masculinity at work: The experiences of men in female dominated occupations. *Work, Employment and Society, 18,* 349–368.

Simpson, R. (2005). Men in non-traditional occupations: Career entry, career orientation and experience of role strain. *Gender, Work and Organization, 12,* 363–380.

Singer, D. G., & Singer, J. L. (2005). *Imagination and play in the electronic age.* Cambridge, MA: Harvard University Press.

Singer, L. T., Minnes, S., Short, E., Arendt, R., Farkas, K., Lewis, B., & Klein, N. (2004). Cognitive outcomes of preschool children with prenatal cocaine exposure. *Journal of the American Medical Association, 291,* 2448–2456.

Singer, Y., Bachner, Y. G., Shvartzman, P., & Carmel, S. (2005). Home death—the caregivers' experiences. *Journal of Pain and Symptom Management, 30,* 70–74.

Singleton, J. L., & Newport, E. L. (2004). When learners surpass their models: The acquisition of American Sign Language from inconsistent input. *Cognitive Psychology, 49,* 370–407.

Sinkkonen, J., Anttila, R., & Siimes, M. A. (1998). Pubertal maturation and changes in self-image in early adolescent Finnish boys. *Journal of Youth and Adolescence, 27,* 209–218.

Sinnott, J. D. (2003). Postformal thought and adult development: Living in balance. In J. Demick & C. Andreoletti (Eds.), *Handbook of adult development* (pp. 221–238). New York: Kluwer Academic.

Skiba, R. J., & Rausch, M. K. (2006). Zero tolerance, suspension, and expulsion: Questions of equity and effectiveness. In C. M. Evertson & C. S. Weinstein (Eds.), *Handbook of classroom management: Research, practice, and contemporary issues* (pp. 1063–1089). Mahwah, NJ: Erlbaum.

Skinner, B. F. (1957). *Verbal behavior.* New York: Appleton-Century-Crofts.

Slade, A., Belsky, J., Aber, J. L., & Phelps, J. L. (1999). Mothers' representations of their relationships with their toddlers: Links to adult attachment and observed mothering. *Developmental Psychology, 35,* 611–619.

Slater, A. (2001). Visual perception. In G. Bremner & A. Fogel (Eds.), *Blackwell handbook of infant development* (pp. 5–34). Malden, MA: Blackwell.

Slater, A., Brown, E., Mattock, A., & Bornstein, M. H. (1996). Continuity and change in habituation in the first 4 months from birth. *Journal of Reproductive and Infant Psychology, 14,* 187–194.

Slater, A., & Quinn, P. C. (2001). Face recognition in the newborn infant. *Infant and Child Development, 10,* 21–24.

Sloter, E., Schmid, T. E., Marchetti, F., Eskenazi, B., & Nath, J. (2006). Quantitative effects of male age on sperm motion. *Human Reproduction, 21,* 2868–2875.

Slutske, W. S., Hunt-Carter, E. E., Nabors-Oberg, R. E., Sher, K. J., Bucholz, K. K., & Madden, P. A. F. (2004). Do college students drink more than their non-college-attending peers? Evidence from a population-based longitudinal female twin study. *Journal of Abnormal Psychology, 113,* 530–540.

Slyper, A. H. (2006). The pubertal timing controversy in the USA, and a review of possible causative factors for the advance in timing of onset of puberty. *Clinical Endocrinology, 65,* 1–8.

Small, M. (1998). *Our babies, ourselves.* New York: Anchor.

Smart, J., & Hiscock, H. (2007). Early infant crying and sleeping problems: A pilot study of impact on parental well-being and parent-endorsed strategies for management. *Journal of Paediatrics and Child Health, 43,* 284–290.

Smetana, J. G. (2002). Culture, autonomy, and personal jurisdiction in adolescent–parent relationships. In R. V. Kail & H. W. Reese (Eds.), *Advances in child development and behavior* (Vol. 29, pp. 51–87). San Diego, CA: Academic Press.

Smetana, J. G. (2006). Social-cognitive domain theory: Consistencies and variations in children's moral and social judgments. In M. Killen & J. G. Smetana (Eds.), *Handbook of moral development* (pp. 119–154). Mahwah, NJ: Erlbaum.

Smetana, J. G., Metzger, A., & Campione-Barr, N. (2004). African-American late adolescents' relationships with parents: Developmental transitions and longitudinal patterns. *Child Development, 75,* 932–947.

Smith, B. H., Barkley, R. A., & Shapiro, C. J. (2006). Attention-deficit/hyperactivity disorder. In E. J. Mash & R. A. Barkley (Eds.), *Treatment of childhood disorders* (3rd ed., pp. 65–136). New York: Guilford.

Smith, C., Perou, R., & Lesesne, C. (2002). Parent education. M. H. Bornstein (Ed.), *Handbook of parenting* (Vol. 4, pp. 389–410). Mahwah, NJ: Erlbaum.

Smith, C. D., Chebrolu, H., Wekstein, D. R., Schmitt, F. A., & Markesbery, W. R. (2007). Age and gender effects on human brain anatomy: A voxel-based morphometric study in healthy elderly. *Neurobiology of Aging, 28,* 1075–1087.

Smith, C. L., Calkins, S. D., Keane, S. P., Anastopoulos, A. D., & Shelton, T. L. (2004). Predicting stability and change in toddler behavior problems: Contributions of maternal behavior and child gender. *Developmental Psychology, 40,* 29–42.

Smith, C. M., & Cotter, V. T. (2008). Age-related changes in health. In E. Capezuti, D. Zwicker, M. Mezey, T. T. Fulmer, & D. Gray-Miceli (Eds.), *Evidence-based geritric nursing protocols for best practice* (3rd ed., pp. 431–458). New York: Springer.

Smith, G. C., Kohn, S. J., Savage-Stevens, S. E., Finch, J. J., Ingate, R., & Lim, Y. (2000). The effects of interpersonal and personal agency on perceived control and psychological well-being in adulthood. *Gerontologist, 40,* 458–468.

Smith, J., & Baltes, P. B. (1999). Life-span perspectives on development. In M. H. Bornstein & M. E. Lamb (Eds.), *Developmental psychology: An advanced textbook* (4th ed., pp. 275–311). Mahwah, NJ: Erlbaum.

Smith, J., Duncan, G. J., & Lee, K. (2003). The black–white test score gap in young children: Contributions of test and family characteristics. *Applied Developmental Science, 7,* 239–252.

Smith, J., & Freund, A. M. (2002). The dynamics of possible selves in old age. *Journal of Gerontology, 57B,* P492–P500.

Smith, J., & Ross, H. (2007). Training parents to mediate sibling disputes affects children's negotiation and conflict understanding. *Child Development, 78,* 790–805.

Smith, L. B., Jones, S. S., Gershkoff-Stowe, L., & Samuelson, L. (2002). Object name learning provides on-the-job training for attention. *Psychological Science, 13,* 13–19.

Smith, N., Young, A., & Lee, C. (2004). Optimism, health-related hardiness and well-being among older Australian women. *Journal of Health Psychology, 9,* 741–752.

Smith, P., Perrin, S., Yule, W., & Rabe-Hesketh, S. (2001). War exposure and maternal reactions in the psychological adjustment of children from Bosnia-Hercegovina. *Journal of Child Psychology and Psychiatry and Allied Disciplines, 42,* 395–404.

Smith, P. K., Ananiadou, K., & Cowie, H. (2003). Interventions to reduce school bullying. *Canadian Journal of Psychiatry, 48,* 591–599.

Smith, T. W., Glazer, K., Ruiz, J. M., & Gallo, L. C. (2004). Hostility, anger, aggressiveness, and coronary heart disease: An interpersonal perspective on personality, emotion, and health. *Journal of Personality, 72,* 1217–1270.

Smock, P. J., & Gupta, S. (2002). *Cohabitation in contemporary North America.* In A. Booth & A. C. Crouter (Eds.), *Just living together* (pp. 53–84). Mahwah, NJ: Erlbaum.

Snarey, J., Son, L., Kuehne, V. S., Hauser, S., & Vaillant, G. (1987). The role of parenting in men's psychosocial development: A longitudinal study of early adulthood infertility and midlife generativity. *Developmental Psychology, 23,* 593–603.

Sneed, J. R., & Whitbourne, S. K. (2001). Identity processing styles and the need for self-esteem in middle-aged and older adults. *International*

Journal of Aging and Human Development, 52, 311–321.

Sneed, J. R., & Whitbourne, S. K. (2003). Identity processing and self-consciousness in middle and later adulthood. *Journal of Gerontology, 58B,* P313–P319.

Sneed, J. R., Whitbourne, S. K., & Culang, M. E. (2006). Trust, identity, and ego integrity: Modeling Erikson's core stages over 34 years. *Journal of Adult Development, 13,* 148–157.

Snell, E. K., Adam, E. K., & Duncan, G. J. (2007). Sleep and the body mass index and overweight status of children and adolescents. *Child Development, 78,* 309–323.

Snidman, N., Kagan, J., Riordan, L., & Shannon, D. C. (1995). Cardiac function and behavioral reactivity. *Psychophysiology, 32,* 199–207.

Snow, C. E., & Beals, D. E. (2006). Mealtime talk that supports literacy development. In R. W. Larson, A. R. Wiley, & K. R. Branscomb (Eds.), *Family mealtime as a context of development and socialization* (pp. 51–66). San Francisco: Jossey-Bass.

Snow, C. E., & Kang, J. Y. (2006). Becoming bilingual, biliterate, and bicultural. In K. A. Renninger & I. E. Sigel (Eds.), *Handbook of child psychology: Vol. 4. Child psychology in practice* (6th ed., pp. 75–102). Hoboken, NJ: Wiley.

Snyder, J., Brooker, M., Patrick, M. R., Snyder, A., Schrepferman, L., & Stoolmiller, M. (2003). Observed peer victimization during early elementary school: Continuity, growth, and relation to risk for child antisocial and depressive behavior. *Child Development, 74,* 1881–1898.

Soares, C. N. (2007). Menopausal transition and depression: Who is at risk and how to treat it? *Expert Review of Neurotherapeutics, 7,* 1285–1293.

Sobel, D. M. (2006). How fantasy benefits young children's understanding of pretense. *Developmental Science, 9,* 63–75.

Social Security and Medicare Board of Trustees. (2009). *Status of the Social Security and Medicare program.* Retrieved from www.ssa.gov/OACT/TR

Society for Research in Child Development. (2007). *SRCD ethical standards for research with children.* Retrieved from www.srcd.org/index.php?option= com_content&task=view&id=68&Itemid=110

Society of Obstetricians and Gynaecologists. (2008). *Record high caesarean rate rasing concerns among Canada's obstetricians.* Retrieved from www.sogc .org/media/pdf/articles/artcaesareanrate080625.pdf

Soderstrom, M., Dolbier, C., Leiferman, J., & Steinhardt, M. (2000). The relationship of hardiness, coping strategies, and perceived stress to symptoms of illness. *Journal of Behavioral Medicine, 23,* 311–328.

Soderstrom, M., Seidl, A., Nelson, D. G. K., & Jusczyk, P. W. (2003). The prosodic bootstrapping of phrases: Evidence from prelinguistic infants. *Journal of Memory and Language, 49,* 249–267.

Sofi, F., Cesari, F., Abbate, R., Gensini, G, F., & Casini, A. (2008). Adherence to Mediterranean diet and health status: Meta-analysis. *British Medical Journal, 337,* a1344.

Solomon, J. C., & Marx, J. (1995). "To grandmother's house we go": Health and school adjustment of children raised solely by grandparents. *Gerontologist, 35,* 386–394.

Somary, K., & Stricker, G. (1998). Becoming a grandparent: A longitudinal study of expectations and early experiences as a function of sex and lineage. *Gerontologist, 38,* 53–61.

Sondergaard, C., Henriksen, T. B., Obel, C., & Wisborg, K. (2002). Smoking during pregnancy and infantile colic. *Journal of the American Academy of Child and Adolescent Psychiatry, 41,* 147.

Sörensen, S., & Pinquart, M. (2005). Racial and ethnic differences in the relationship of caregiving stressors, resources, and sociodemographic variables to caregiver depression and perceived physical health. *Aging and Mental Health, 9,* 482–495.

Sørensen, T. I., Holst, C., & Stunkard, A. J. (1998). Adoption study of environmental modifications of the genetic influences on obesity. *International Journal of Obesity and Related Metabolic Disorders, 22,* 73–81.

Sosa, R., Kennell, J., Klaus, M., Robertson, S., & Urrutia, J. (1980). The effect of a supportive companion on perinatal problems, length of labor, and mother–infant interaction. *New England Journal of Medicine, 303,* 597–600.

Sowell, E. R., Thompson, P. M., Welcome, S. E., Henkenius, A. L., Toga, A. W., & Peterson, B. S. (2003). Cortical abnormalities in children and adolescents with attention-deficit hyperactivity disorder. *Lancet, 362,* 1699–1707.

Sowell, E. R., Trauner, D. A., Gamst, A., & Jernigan, T. (2002). Development of cortical and subcortical brain structures in childhood and adolescence: A structural MRI study. *Developmental Medicine and Child Neurology, 44,* 4–16.

Sowers, M. F., Zheng, H., Tomey, K., Karvonen-Gutierrez, M. J., Li, X., Matheos, Y., & Symons, J. (2007). Changes in body composition in women over six years at midlife: Ovarian and chronological aging. *Journal of Clinical Endocrinology and Metabolism, 92,* 895–901.

Spadoni, A. D., McGee, C. L., Frayer, S. L., & Riley, E. P. (2007). Neuroimaging and fetal alcohol spectrum disorders. *Neuroscience and Biobehavioral Reviews, 31,* 239–245.

Spear, L. P. (2004). Adolescent brain development and animal models. In R. E. Dahl & L. P. Spear (Eds.), *Adolescent brain development: Vulnerabilities and opportunities* (pp. 23–26). New York: New York Academy of Sciences.

Spear, L. P. (2008). The psychobiology of adolescence. In K. K. Kline (Ed.), *Authoritative communities: The scientific case for nurturing the whole child* (pp. 263–280). New York: Springer Science + Business Media.

Spector, A. Z. (2006). Fatherhood and depression: A review of risks, effects, and clinical application. *Issues in Mental Health Nursing, 27,* 867–883.

Speece, D. L., Ritchey, K. D., Cooper, D. H., Roth, F. P., & Schatschneider, C. (2004). Growth in early reading skills from kindergarten to third grade. *Contemporary Educational Psychology, 29,* 312–332.

Speece, M. W., & Brent, S. B. (1996). The development of children's understanding of death. In C. A. Corr & D. M. Corr (Eds.), *Handbook of childhood death and bereavement* (pp. 29–50). New York: Springer.

Spelke, E. S. (2000). Core knowledge. *American Psychologist, 55,* 1233–1242.

Spelke, E. S. (2004). Core knowledge. In N. Kanwisher & J. Duncan (Eds.), *Attention and performance* (Vol. 20, pp. 29–56). Oxford, UK: Oxford University Press.

Spelke, E. S., & Kinzler, K. D. (2007). Core knowledge. *Developmental Science, 10,* 89–96.

Spence, M. J., & DeCasper, A. J. (1987). Prenatal experience with low-frequency maternal voice sounds influences neonatal perception of maternal voice samples. *Infant Behavior and Development, 10,* 133–142.

Spencer, J. P., & Perone, S. (2008). Defending qualitative change: The view from dynamical systems theory. *Child Development, 79,* 1639–1647.

Spencer, J. P., Verejiken, B., Diedrich, F. J., & Thelen, E. (2000). Posture and the emergence of manual skills. *Developmental Science, 3,* 216–233.

Spera, C. (2005). A review of the relationship among parenting practices, parenting styles, and adolescent school achievement. *Educational Psychology Review, 17,* 125–146.

Spere, K. A., Schmidt, L. A., Theall-Honey, L. A., & Martin-Chang, S. (2004). Expressive and receptive language skills of temperamentally shy preschoolers. *Infant and Child Development, 13,* 123–133.

Spira, A. (1992). *Les comportements sexuels en France.* Paris: La Documentation Française.

Spirito, A., Valeri, S., Boergers, J., & Donaldson, D. (2003). Predictors of continued suicidal behavior in adolescents following a suicide attempt. *Journal of Clinical Child and Adolescent Psychology, 32,* 284–289.

Spitze, G., & Gallant, M. P. (2004). "The bitter with the sweet": Older adults' strategies for handling ambivalence in relations with their adult children. *Research on Aging, 26,* 387–412.

Spock, B., & Needlman, R. (2004). *Dr. Spock's baby and child care* (8th ed.). New York: Pocket.

Spokane, A. R., & Cruza-Guet, M. C. (2005). Holland's theory of vocational personalities in work environments. In S. D. Brown & R. W. Lent (Eds.), *Career development and counseling* (pp. 24–41). Hoboken, NJ: Wiley.

Sprecher, S. (1999). "I love you more today than yesterday": Romantic partners' perceptions of changes in love and related affect over time. *Journal of Personality and Social Psychology, 76,* 46–53.

Sridhar, D., & Vaughn, S. (2001). Social functioning of students with learning disabilities. In D. P. Hallahan & B. K. Keogh (Eds.), *Research and global perspectives in learning disabilities* (pp. 65–91). Mahwah, NJ: Erlbaum.

Srivastava, S., John, O. P., Gosling, S. D., & Potter, J. (2003). Development of personality in early and middle adulthood: Set like plaster or persistent change? *Journal of Personality and Social Psychology, 84,* 1041–1053.

Sroufe, L. A. (2005). Attachment and development: A prospective, longitudinal study from birth to adulthood. *Attachment and Human Development, 7,* 349–367.

Sroufe, L. A., & Waters, E. (1976). The ontogenesis of smiling and laughter: A perspective on the organization of development in infancy. *Psychological Review, 83,* 173–189.

Sroufe, L. A., & Wunsch, J. P. (1972). The development of laughter in the first year of life. *Child Development, 43,* 1324–1344.

St James-Roberts, I. (2007). Helping parents to manage infant crying and sleeping: A review of the evidence and its implications for services. *Child Abuse Review, 16,* 47–69.

St James-Roberts, I., Goodwin, J., Peter, B., Adams, D., & Hunt, S. (2003). Individual differences in responsivity to a neurobehavioural examination predict crying patterns of 1-week-old infants at home. *Developmental Medicine and Child Neurology, 45,* 400–407.

St. Louis, G. R., & Liem, J. H. (2005). Ego identity, ethnic identity, and the psychosocial well-being of ethnic minority and majority college students. *Identity, 5,* 227–246.

Stackert, R. A., & Bursik, K. (2003). Why am I unsatisfied? Adult attachment style, gendered irrational relationship beliefs, and young adult romantic relationship satisfaction. *Personality and Individual Differences, 34,* 1419–1429.

Stahl, S. A., & Miller, P. D. (2006). Whole language and language experience approaches for beginning reading: A quantitative research synthesis. In K. A. Dougherty Stahl & M. C. McKenna (Eds.), *Reading research at work: Foundations of effective practice* (pp. 9–35). New York: Guilford.

Stams, G. J. M., Brugman, D., Deković, M., van Rosmalen, L., van der Laan, P., & Gibbs, J. C. (2006). The moral judgment of juvenile delinquents: A meta-analysis. *Journal of Abnormal Child Psychology, 34,* 697–713.

Stams, G. J. M., Juffer, F., & van IJzendoorn, M. H. (2002). Maternal sensitivity, infant attachment, and temperament in early childhood predict adjustment in middle childhood: The case of adopted children and their biologically unrelated parents. *Developmental Psychology, 38,* 806–821.

Standley, J. M. (1998). The effect of music and multimodal stimulation on responses of premature infants in neonatal intensive care. *Pediatric Nursing, 24,* 532–538.

Stanley, C., Murray, L., & Stein, A. (2004). The effect of postnatal depression on mother–infant interaction, infant response to the still-face perturbation, and performance on an instrumental learning task. *Development and Psychopathology, 16,* 1–18.

Stanovich, K. E. (2007). *How to think straight about psychology* (8th ed.). Boston: Allyn and Bacon.

Starr, J. M., Deary, I. J., Fox, H. C., & Whalley, L. J. (2007). Smoking and cognitive change from age 11 to 66: A confirmatory investigation. *Addictive Behaviors, 32,* 63–68.

Starr, R. J. (1999). Music therapy in hospice care. *American Journal of Hospice and Palliative Care, 16,* 739–742.

Statistics Canada. (2006). *Hours spent doing unpaid housework for the population 15 years and over of Canada, 2006 Census—20% sample data.* Retrieved from www12.statcan.ca/english/census06/data/topics/

Stattin, H., & Magnusson, D. (1990). *Pubertal maturation in female development.* Hillsdale, NJ: Erlbaum.

Stattin, H., & Magnusson, D. (1996). Leaving home at an early age among females. In J. A. Graber & J. S. Dubas (Eds.), *New directions for child development* (No. 71, pp. 53–69). San Francisco: Jossey-Bass.

Staudinger, U. M. (1996). Wisdom and the social-interactive foundation of the mind. In P. B. Baltes & U. M. Staudinger (Eds.), *Interactive minds: Lifespan perspectives on the social foundation of cognition* (pp. 276–315). New York: Cambridge University Press.

Staudinger, U. M., Dörner, J., & Mickler, C. (2005). Wisdom and personality. In R. J. Sternberg & J. Jordan (Eds.), *A handbook of wisdom: Psychological perspectives* (pp 191–219). New York: Cambridge University Press.

Staudinger, U. M., Fleeson, W., & Baltes, P. B. (1999). Predictors of subjective physical health and global well-being: Similarities and differences between the United States and Germany. *Journal of Personality and Social Psychology, 76,* 305–319.

Staudinger, U. M., & Lindenberger, U. (2003). Understanding human development takes a metatheory and multiple disciplines. In U. M. Staudinger & U. Lindenberger (Eds.), *Understanding human development: Dialogues with life span psychology* (pp. 1–13). Norwell, MA: Kluwer.

Staudinger, U. M., Smith, J., & Baltes, P. B. (1992). Wisdom-related knowledge in a life-review task: Age differences and the role of professional specialization. *Psychology and Aging, 7,* 271–281.

Steele, C. M. (1997). A threat in the air: How stereotypes shape intellectual identity and performance. *American Psychologist, 52,* 613–629.

Steele, S., Joseph, R. M., & Tager-Flusberg, H. (2003). Developmental change in theory of mind abilities in children with autism. *Journal of Autism and Developmental Disorders, 33,* 461–467.

Stehr-Green, P., Tull, P., Stellfeld, M., Mortenson, P. B., & Simpson, D. (2003). Autism and thimerosal-containing vaccines: Lack of consistent evidence for an association. *American Journal of Preventive Medicine, 25,* 101–106.

Stein, J. H., & Reiser, L. W. (1994). A study of white middle-class adolescent boys' responses to "semenarche" (the first ejaculation). *Journal of Youth and Adolescence, 23,* 373–384.

Stein, M. B., Lang, A. J., Laffaye, C., Satz, L. E., Lenox, R. J., & Dresselhaus, T. R. (2004). Relationship of sexual assault history to somatic symptoms and health anxiety in women. *General Hospital Psychiatry, 26,* 178–183.

Stein, N., & Levine, L. J. (1999). The early emergence of emotional understanding and appraisal: Implications for theories of development. In T. Dalgleish & M. J. Power (Eds.), *Handbook of cognition and emotion* (pp. 383–408). Chichester, UK: Wiley.

Steinberg, L., Blatt-Eisengart, I., & Cauffman, E. (2006). Patterns of competence and adjustment among adolescents from authoritative, authoritarian, indulgent, and neglectful homes: A replication in a sample of serious juvenile offenders. *Journal of Research on Adolescence, 16,* 47–58.

Steinberg, L. D., Darling, N. E., & Fletcher, A. C. (1995). Authoritative parenting and adolescent development: An ecological journey. In P. Moen, G. H. Elder, Jr., & K. Luscher (Eds.), *Examining lives in context* (pp. 423–466). Washington, DC: American Psychological Association.

Steinberg, L. D., & Morris, A. S. (2001). Adolescent development. *Annual Review of Psychology, 52,* 83–110.

Steinberg, L. D., & Silk, J. S. (2002). Parenting adolescents. In M. H. Bornstein (Ed.), *Handbook of parenting* (Vol. 1, pp. 103–134). Mahwah, NJ: Erlbaum.

Steiner, H. A., & Miller, J. M. (2008). Disparity in utilization of implantable cardioverter-defibrillators in treatment of heart failure based on sex and race. *Women's Health, 4,* 23–25.

Steiner, J. E. (1979). Human facial expression in response to taste and smell stimulation. In H. W. Reese & L. P. Lipsitt (Eds.), *Advances in child development and behavior* (Vol. 13, pp. 257–295). New York: Academic Press.

Steiner, J. E., Glaser, D., Hawilo, M. E., & Berridge, D. C. (2001). Comparative expression of hedonic impact: Affective reactions to taste by human infants and other primates. *Neuroscience and Biobehavioral Review, 25,* 53–74.

Steinhausen, C. (2006). Eating disorders: Anorexia nervosa and bulimia nervosa. In C. Gillberg, R. Harrington, & H. Steinhausen (Eds.), *A clinician's handbook of child and adolescent psychiatry* (pp. 272–303). New York: Cambridge University Press.

Steinlein, O. K. (2004). Genes and mutations in human idiopathic epilepsy. *Brain Development, 26,* 213–218.

Stenberg, C. (2003). Effects of maternal inattentiveness on infant social referencing. *Infant and Child Development, 12,* 399–419.

Stenberg, C., & Campos, J. (1990). The development of anger expressions in infancy. In N. Stein, B. Leventhal, & T. Trabasso (Eds.), *Psychological and biological approaches to emotion* (pp. 247–282). Hillsdale, NJ: Erlbaum.

Stern, D. (1985). *The interpersonal world of the infant.* New York: Basic Books.

Stern, M., & Karraker, K. H. (1989). Sex stereotyping of infants: A review of gender labeling studies. *Sex Roles, 20,* 501–522.

Sternberg, R. J. (2001). Why schools should teach for wisdom: The balance theory of wisdom in educational settings. *Educational Psychologist, 36,* 227–245.

Sternberg, R. J. (2002). Intelligence is not just inside the head: The theory of successful intelligence. In J. Aronson (Ed.), *Improving academic achievement* (pp. 227–244). San Diego, CA: Academic Press.

Sternberg, R. J. (2003). The development of creativity as a decision-making process. In R. K. Sawyer, V. John-Steiner, S. Moran, R. J. Sternberg, D. H. Feldman, J. Nakamura, & M. Csikszentmihalyi (Eds.), *Creativity and development* (pp. 91–138). New York: Oxford University Press.

Sternberg, R. J. (2005). The triarchic theory of successful intelligence. In D. P. Flanagan & P. L. Harrison (Eds.), *Contemporary intellectual assessment: Theories, tests, and issues* (pp. 103–119). New York: Guilford.

Sternberg, R. J., Forsythe, G. B., Hedlund, J., Horvath, J. A., Wagner, R. K., Williams, W. M., Snook, S. A., & Grigorenko, E. L. (2000). *Practical intelligence in everyday life.* Cambridge, UK: Cambridge University Press.

Sternberg, R. J., & Grigorenko, E. L. (2002). *Dynamic testing.* New York: Cambridge University Press.

Sternberg, R. J., & Lubart, T. I. (1996). Investing in creativity. *American Psychologist, 51,* 677–688.

Sternberg, R. J., & Lubart, T. I. (2001). Wisdom and creativity. In J. E. Birren & K. W. Schaie (Eds.),

Handbook of the psychology of aging (pp. 500–522). San Diego: Academic Press.

Stevens, J. C., & Cruz, L. A. (1996). Spatial acuity of touch: Ubiquitous decline with aging revealed by repeated threshold testing. *Somatosensory and Motor Research, 13,* 1–10.

Stevenson, H. W., Lee, S., & Mu, X. (2000). Successful achievement in mathematics: China and the United States. In C. F. M. van Lieshout & P. G. Heymans (Eds.), *Developing talent across the life span* (pp. 167–183). Philadelphia: Psychology Press.

Stevenson, R., & Pollitt, C. (1987). The acquisition of temporal terms. *Journal of Child Language, 14,* 533–545.

Steward, D. K. (2001). Behavioral characteristics of infants with nonorganic failure to thrive during a play interaction. *American Journal of Maternal Child Nursing, 26,* 79–85.

Stewart, A. J., & Lavaque-Manty, D. (2008). Advancing women faculty in science and engineering: An effort in institutional transformation. In H. M. G. Watt & J. S. Eccles (Eds.), *Gender and occupational outcomes* (pp. 299–322). Washington, DC: American Psychological Association.

Stewart, A. J., & Malley, J. E. (2004). Women of the greatest generation. In C. Daiute & C. Lightfoot (Eds.), *Narrative analysis: Studying the development of individuals in society* (pp. 223–244). Thousand Oaks, CA: Sage.

Stewart, A. J., & Ostrove, J. M. (1998). Women's personality in middle age: Gender, history and midcourse correction. *American Psychologist, 53,* 1185–1194.

Stewart, A. J., Ostrove, J. M., & Helson, R. (2001). Middle aging in women: Patterns of personality change from the 30s to the 50s. *Journal of Adult Development, 8,* 23–37.

Stewart, A. J., & Vandewater, E. A. (1999). "If I had to do over again . . .": Midlife review, midcourse corrections, and women's well-being in midlife. *Journal of Personality and Social Psychology, 76,* 270–283.

Stewart, A. L., Verboncoeur, C. J., McLellan, B. Y., Gillis, D. E., Rush, S., & Mills, K. M. (2001). Physical activity outcomes of CHAMPS II: A physical activity promotion program for older adults. *Journal of Gerontology, 56A,* M465–M470.

Stewart, P., Reihman, J., Lonky, E., Darvill, T., & Pagano, J. (2000). Prenatal PCB exposure and Neonatal Behavioral Assessment Scale (NBAS) performance. *Neurotoxicology and Teratology, 22,* 21–29.

Stewart, R. B., Jr. (1990). *The second child: Family transition and adjustment.* Newbury Park, CA: Sage.

Stewart, R. B., Jr., Kozak, A. L., Tingley, L. M., Goddard, J. M., Blake, E. M., & Cassel, W. A. (2001). Adult sibling relationships: Validation of a typology. *Personal Relationships, 8,* 299–324.

Stewart, S., Stinnett, H., & Rosenfeld, L. B. (2000). Sex differences in desired characteristics of short-term and long-term relationship partners. *Journal of Social and Personal Relationships, 17,* 843–853.

Stice, E. (2003). Puberty and body image. In C. Hayward (Ed.), *Gender differences at puberty* (pp. 61–76). New York: Cambridge University Press.

Stice, E., Presnell, K., & Bearman, S. K. (2001). Relation of early menarche to depression, eating disorders, substance abuse, and comorbid psychopathology among adolescent girls. *Developmental Psychology, 37,* 608–619.

Stifter, C. A., Coulehan, C. M., & Fish, M. (1993). Linking employment to attachment: The mediating effects of maternal separation anxiety and interactive behavior. *Child Development, 64,* 1451–1460.

Stiles, J. (2001). Neural plasticity in cognitive development. *Developmental Neuropsychology, 18,* 237–272.

Stiles, J., Reilly, J., Paul, B., & Moses, P. (2005). Cognitive development following early brain injury: Evidence for neural adaptation. *Trends in Cognitive Sciences, 9,* 136–143.

Stilson, S. R., & Harding, C. G. (1997). Early social context as it relates to symbolic play: A longitudinal investigation. *Merrill-Palmer Quarterly, 43,* 682–693.

Stinchcomb, J. B., Bazemore, G., & Riestenberg, N. (2006). Beyond zero tolerance: Restoring justice in secondary schools. *Youth Violence and Juvenile Justice, 4,* 123–147.

Stine-Morrow, E. A. L., Soederberg Miller, L.M., Gagne, D. D., & Hertzog, C. (2008). Self-regulated reading in adulthood. *Psychology and Aging, 23,* 131–153.

Stipek, D. J. (1995). The development of pride and shame in toddlers. In J. P. Tangney & K. W. Fischer (Eds.), *Self-conscious emotions* (pp. 237–252). New York: Guilford.

Stipek, D. J., Feiler, R., Daniels, D., & Milburn, S. (1995). Effects of different instructional approaches on young children's achievement and motivation. *Child Development, 66,* 209–223.

Stipek, D. J., Gralinski, J. H., & Kopp, C. B. (1990). Self-concept development in the toddler years. *Developmental Psychology, 26,* 972–977.

Stoch, M. B., Smythe, P. M., Moodie, A. D., & Bradshaw, D. (1982). Psychosocial outcome and CT findings after growth undernourishment during infancy: A 20-year developmental study. *Developmental Medicine and Child Neurology, 24,* 419–436.

Stockman, N. K. A., Schenkel, T. C., Brown, J. N., & Duncan, A. M. (2005). Comparison of energy and nutrient intakes among meals and snacks of adolescent males. *Preventive Medicine, 41,* 203–210.

Stone, M. R., & Brown, B. B. (1999). Identity claims and projections: Descriptions of self and crowds in secondary school. In J. A. McLellan & M. J. V. Pugh (Eds.), *The role of peer groups in adolescent social identity: Exploring the importance of stability and change* (pp. 7–20). San Francisco: Jossey-Bass.

Stone, R. I., & Reinhard, S. C. (2007). The place of assisted living in long-term care and related service systems. *Gerontologist, 47,* 23–32.

Storey, A. E., Walsh, C. J., Quinton, R. L., & Wynn-Edwards, K. E. (2000). Hormonal correlates of paternal responsiveness in new and expectant fathers. *Evolution and Human Behavior, 21,* 79–95.

Stormshak, E. A., Bierman, K. L., McMahon, R. J., Lengua, L. J., & the Conduct Problems Prevention Research Group. (2000). Parenting practices and child disruptive behavior problems in early elementary school. *Journal of Clinical Child Psychology, 29,* 17–29.

Stouthamer-Loeber, M., Wei, E., Loeber, R., & Masten, A. S. (2004). Desistance from persistent serious delinquency in the transition to adulthood. *Development and Psychopathology, 16,* 897–918.

Strapp, C. M., & Federico, A. (2000). Imitations and repetitions: What do children say following recasts? *First Language, 20,* 273–290.

Straus, M. A., & Stewart, J. H. (1999). Corporal punishment by American parents: National data on prevalence, chronicity, severity, and duration, in relation to child and family characteristics. *Clinical Child and Family Psychology Review, 2,* 55–70.

Strawbridge, W. J., Shema, S. J., Cohen, R. D., & Kaplan, G. A. (2001). Religious attendance increases survival by improving and maintaining good health behaviors. *Annals of Behavioral Medicine, 23,* 68–74.

Strazdins, L., Clements, M. S., Korda, R. J., Broom, D. H., & D'Souza, R. M. (2006). Unsociable work? Nonstandard work schedules, family relationships, and children's well-being. *Journal of Marriage and the Family, 68,* 394–410.

Streissguth, A. P., Bookstein, F. L., Barr, H. M., Sampson, P. D., O'Malley, K., & Young, J. K. (2004). Risk factors for adverse life outcomes in fetal alcohol syndrome and fetal alcohol effects. *Journal of Developmental and Behavioral Pediatrics, 25,* 228–238.

Streissguth, A. P., Treder, R., Barr, H. M., Shepard, T., Bleyer, W. A., Sampson, P. D., & Martin, D. (1987). Aspirin and acetaminophen use by pregnant women and subsequent child IQ and attention decrements. *Teratology, 35,* 211–219.

Streri, A. (2005). Touching for knowing in infancy: The development of manual abilities in very young infants. *European Journal of Developmental Psychology, 2,* 325–343.

Striano, T., & Rochat, P. (2000). Emergence of selective social referencing in infancy. *Infancy, 1,* 253–264.

Striano, T., Tomasello, M., & Rochat, P. (2001). Social and object support for early symbolic play. *Developmental Science, 4,* 442–455.

Striegel-Moore, R. H., & Franko, D. L. (2006). Adolescent eating disorders. In R. H. Striegel-Moore & D. L. Franko (Eds.), *Child and adolescent psychopathology: Theoretical and clinical implications* (pp. 160–183). New York: Routledge.

Stright, A. D., Neitzel, C., Sears, K. G., & Hoke-Sinex, L. (2002). Instruction begins in the home: Relations between parental instruction and children's self-regulation in the classroom. *Journal of Educational Psychology, 93,* 456–466.

Stroebe, M. S., & Schut, H. (1999). The dual process model of coping with bereavement: Rationale and description. *Death Studies, 23,* 197–224.

Stroebe, M. S., van der Houwen, K., & Schut, H. (2008). Bereavement support, intervention, and research on the Internet: A critical review. In M. S. Stroebe, R. O. Hansson, H. Schut, & W. Stroebe (Eds.), *Handbook of bereavement research and practice* (pp. 551–574). Washington, DC: American Psychological Association.

Stroebe, W., Stroebe, M., Abakoumkin, G., & Schut, H. (1996). The role of loneliness and social support in adjustment to loss: A test of attachment versus stress theory. *Journal of Personality and Social Psychology, 70,* 1241–1249.

Strohschein, L. (2005). Parental divorce and child mental health trajectories. *Journal of Marriage and Family, 67,* 1286–1300.

Stromquist, N. P. (2007). Gender equity education globally. In S. S. Klein, B. Richardson, D. A. Grayson, L. H. Fox, & C. Kramarae (Eds.), *Handbook for achieving gender equity through education* (2nd ed., pp. 33–42). Mahwah, NJ: Erlbaum.

Strough, J., Hicks, P. J., Swenson, L. M., Cheng, S., & Barnes, K. A. (2003). Collaborative everyday problem solving: Interpersonal relationships and problem dimensions. *International Journal of Aging and Human Development, 56,* 43–66.

Strough, J., Leszczynski, J. P., Neely, T. L., Flinn, J. A., & Margrett, J. (2007). From adolescence to later adulthood: Femininity, masculinity, and androgyny in six age groups. *Sex Roles, 57,* 385–396.

Strouse, D. L. (1999). Adolescent crowd orientations: A social and temporal analysis. In J. A. McLellan & M. J. V. Pugh (Eds.), *The role of peer groups in adolescent social identity: Exploring the importance of stability and change* (pp. 37–54). San Francisco: Jossey-Bass.

Stuart, G. L., Moore, T. M., Gordon, K. C., Ramsey, S. E., & Kahler, C. W. (2006). Psychopathology in women arrested for domestic violence. *Journal of Interpersonal Violence, 21,* 376–389.

Stuart, M., & Weinrich, M. (2001). Home- and community-based long-term care: Lessons from Denmark. *Gerontologist, 41,* 474–480.

Studelska, J. V. (2006, Spring). At home in birth. *Midwifery Today,* pp. 32–33.

Stull, D., & Scarisbrick-Hauser, A. (1989). Never-married elderly. *Research on Aging, 11,* 124–139.

Styne, D. M. (2003). The regulation of pubertal growth. *Hormone Research, 60*(Suppl. 1), 22–26.

Suarez-Orozco, C., Todorova, I., & Qin, D. B. (2006). The well-being of immigrant adolescents: A longitudinal perspective on risk and protective factors. In F. A. Villarruel & T. Luster (Eds.), *The crisis in youth mental health: Critical issues and effective programs: Vol. 2. Disorders in adolescence* (pp. 53–83). Westport, CT: Praeger.

Subbotsky, E. (2004). Magical thinking in judgments of causation: Can anomalous phenomena affect ontological causal beliefs in children and adults? *British Journal of Developmental Psychology, 22,* 123–152.

Subrahmanyam, K., Smahel, D., & Greenfield, P. (2006). Connecting developmental constructions to the Internet: Identity presentation and sexual exploration in online teen chat rooms. *Developmental Psychology, 42,* 395–406.

Sullivan, M. A. (1995). May the circle be unbroken: The African-American experience of death, dying, and spirituality. In J. K. Parry & A. S. Ryan (Eds.), *A cross-cultural look at death, dying, and religion* (pp. 160–171). Chicago: Nelson-Hall.

Sullivan, M. W., & Lewis, M. (2003). Contextual determinants of anger and other negative expressions in young infants. *Developmental Psychology, 39,* 693–705.

Summers, R. W., & Hoffman, A. M. (Eds.). (2006). *Elder abuse: A public health perspective.* Washington, DC: American Public Health Association.

Super, C. M. (1981). Behavioral development in infancy. In R. H. Monroe, R. L. Monroe, & B. B. Whiting (Eds.), *Handbook of cross-cultural human development* (pp. 181–270). New York: Garland.

Super, D. E. (1990). A life span, life space approach to career development. In D. Brown & L. Brooks (Eds.), *Career choice and development* (2nd ed., pp. 197–261). San Francisco: Jossey-Bass.

Super, D. E. (1994). A life span, life space perspective on convergence. In M. L. Savikas & R. W. Lent (Eds.), *Convergence in career development theories* (pp. 62–71). Palo Alto, CA: Consulting Psychologists Press.

Susman, E. J., & Rogol, A. (2004). Puberty and psychological development. In R. M. Lerner & L. Steinberg (Eds.), *Handbook of adolescent psychology* (2nd ed., pp. 15–44). Hoboken, NJ: Wiley.

Sutton, M. J., Brown, J. D., Wilson, K. M., & Klein, J. D. (2002). Shaking the tree of forbidden fruit: Where adolescents learn about sexuality and contraception. In J. D. Brown, J. R. Steele, & K. Walsh-Childers (Eds.), *Sexual teens, sexual media* (pp. 25–55). Mahwah, NJ: Erlbaum.

Sveen, C.-A., & Walby, F. A. (2008). Suicide survivors' mental health and grief reactions: A systematic review of controlled studies. *Suicide and Life-Threatening Behavior, 38,* 13–29.

Swanson, J. L., & Fouad, N. A. (1999). Applying theories of person-environment fit to the transition from school to work. *Career Development Quarterly, 47,* 337–347.

Sweet, S., & Moen, P. (2007). Integrating educational careers in work and family. *Community, Work and Family, 10,* 231–250.

Symons, D. K. (2001). A dyad-oriented approach to distress and mother–child relationship outcomes in the first 24 months. *Parenting: Science and Practice, 1,* 101–122.

Szaflarski, J. P., Binder, J. R., Possing, E. T., McKiernan, K. A., Ward, B. D., & Hammeke, T. A. (2002). Language lateralization in left-handed and ambidextrous people: fMRI data. *Neurology, 59,* 238–244.

Szlemko, W. J., Wood, J. W., & Thurman, P. J. (2006). Native Americans and alcohol: Past, present, and future. *Journal of General Psychology, 133,* 435–451.

T

Tabibi, Z., & Pfeffer, K. (2007). Finding a safe place to cross the road: The effect of distractors and the role of attention in children's identification of safe and dangerous road-crossing sites. *Infant and Child Development, 16,* 193–206.

Taga, G., Asakawa, K., Maki, A., Konishi, Y., & Koizumi, H. (2003). Brain imaging in awake infants by near-infrared optical topography. *Proceedings of the National Academy of Sciences, 100,* 10722–10727.

Tager-Flusberg, H., & Zukowski, A. (2009). Putting words together: Morphology and syntax in the preschool years. In J. B. Gleason & B. Ratner (Ed.), *The development of language* (7th ed., pp. 139–191). Boston: Allyn and Bacon.

Tahir, L., & Gruber, H. E. (2003). Developmental trajectories and creative work in late life. In J. Demick & C. Andreoletti (Eds.), *Handbook of adult development* (pp. 239–255). New York: Springer.

Takagi, E., Silverstein, M., & Crimmins, E. (2007). Intergenerational coresidence of older adults in Japan: Conditions for cultural plasticity. *Journal of Gerontology, 62B,* S330–S339.

Takahashi, K. (1990). Are the key assumptions of the "Strange Situation" procedure universal? A view from Japanese research. *Human Development, 33,* 23–30.

Takamura, J., & Williams, B. (2002). *Informal caregiving: Compassion in action.* Arlington, TX: Arc of the United States.

Tamis-LeMonda, C. S., & Bornstein, M. H. (1989). Habituation and maternal encouragement of attention in infancy as predictors of toddler language, play, and representational competence. *Child Development, 60,* 738–751.

Tamis-LeMonda, C. S., Shannon, J. D., Cabrera, N. J., & Lamb, M. E. (2004). Fathers and mothers at play with their 2- and 3-year-olds: Contributions to language and cognitive development. *Child Development, 75,* 1806–1820.

Tamis-LeMonda, C. S., Way, N., Hughes, D., Yoshikawa, H., Kalman, R. K., & Niwa, E. Y. (2008). Parents' goals for children: The dynamic coexistence of individualism and collectivism in cultures and individuals. *Social Development, 17,* 183–209.

Tammelin, T., Näyhä, S., Hills, A. P., & Järvelin, M. (2003). Adolescent participation in sports and adult physical activity. *American Journal of Preventive Medicine, 24,* 22–28.

Tamrouti-Makkink, I. D., Dubas, J. S., Gerris, J. R. M., & van Aken, A. G. (2004). The relation between the absolute level of parenting and differential parental treatment with adolescent siblings' adjustment. *Journal of Child Psychology and Psychiatry, 45,* 1397–1406.

Tanaka, H., & Higuchi, M. (1998). Age, exercise performance, and physiological functional capacities. *Advances in Exercise Sports Physiology, 4,* 51–56.

Tanaka, H., & Seals, D. R. (1997). Age and gender interactions in physiological functional capacity: Insight from swimming performance. *Journal of Applied Physiology, 82,* 846–851.

Tanaka, H., & Seals, D. R. (2003). Dynamic exercise performance in master athletes: Insight into the effects of primary human aging on physiological functional capacity. *Journal of Applied Physiology, 95,* 2152–2162.

Tangney, J. P. (2001). Constructive and destructive aspects of shame and guilt. In A. C. Bohart & D. J. Stipek (Eds.), *Constructive and destructive behavior* (pp. 127–145). Washington, DC: American Psychological Association.

Tangri, S. S., & Jenkins, S. R. (1997). Why expecting conflict is good. *Sex Roles, 36,* 725–746.

Tanne, J. H. (1992). "Granny dumping" in the U.S. *British Medical Journal, 304,* 333–334.

Tanner, J. M., Healy, M., & Cameron, N. (2001). *Assessment of skeletal maturity and prediction of adult height* (3rd ed.). Philadelphia: Saunders.

Tardif, T. (2006). But are they really verbs? Chinese words for action. In K. Hirsh-Pasek & R. M. Golinkoff (Eds.), *Action meets word: How children learn verbs* (pp. 477–498). New York: Oxford University Press.

Tardif, T., Gelman, S. A., & Xu, F. (1999). Putting the "noun bias" in context: A comparison of English and Mandarin. *Child Development, 70,* 620–635.

Tardif, T., Wellman, H. M., & Cheung, K. M. (2004). False belief understanding in Cantonese-speaking children. *Journal of Child Language, 31,* 779–800.

Tardon, A., Lee, W. J., Delgado-Rodriguez, M., Dosemeci, M., Albanese, D., Hoover, R., & Blair, A. (2005). Leisure-time physical activity and lung cancer: A meta-analysis. *Cancer Causes and Control, 16,* 389–397.

Tarry-Adkins, J. L., Martin-Gronert, M. S., Chen, J. H., Cripps, R. L., & Ozanne, S. E. (2008). Maternal diet influences DNA damage, aortic telomere length, oxidative stress, and antioxidant defense capacity in rats. *FASEB Journal, 22,* 2037–2044.

Tarullo, A. R., & Gunnar, M. R. (2006). Child maltreatment and the developing HPA axis. *Hormones and Behavior, 50,* 632–639.

Tasker, F. (2005). Lesbian mothers, gay fathers, and their children: A review. *Developmental and Behavioral Pediatrics, 26,* 224–240.

Taumoepeau, M., & Ruffman, T. (2006). Mother and infant talk about mental states relates to desire language and emotion understanding. *Child Development, 77,* 465–481.

Taylor, M. (1996). The development of children's beliefs about the social and biological aspects of gender differences. *Child Development, 67,* 1555–1571.

Taylor, M. C., & Hall, J. A. (1982). Psychological androgyny: Theories, methods, and conclusions. *Psychological Bulletin, 92,* 347–366.

Taylor, M. G., & Lynch, S. M. (2004). Trajectories of impairment, social support, and depressive symptoms in later life. *Journal of Gerontology, 59B,* S238–S246.

Taylor, R. J., Lincoln, K. D., & Chatters, L. M. (2005). Supportive relationships with church members among African Americans. *Family Relations, 54,* 501–511.

Taylor, W. C., Sallis, J. F., Lees, E., Hepworth, J. T., Feliz, K., Volding, D. C., Cassels, A., & Tobin, J. N. (2007). Changing social and built environments to promote physical activity: Recommendations from low-income, urban women. *Journal of Physical Activity and Health, 4,* 54–65.

Teicher, M. H., Dumont, N. L., Ito, Y., Vaituzis, C., Giedd, J., & Andersen, S. L. (2004). Childhood neglect is associated with reduced corpus callosum area. *Biological Psychiatry, 56,* 80–85.

Tellings, A. (1999). Psychoanalytical and genetic-structuralistic approaches to moral development: Incompatible views? *Psychoanalytic Review, 86,* 903–914.

Temkin-Greener, H., Bajorska, A., Peterson, D. R., Kunitz, S. J., Gross, D., & Williams, T. F. (2004). Social support and risk-adjusted mortality in a frail older population. *Medical Care, 42,* 779–788.

Temple, J. A., & Reynolds, A. J. (2006). Economic returns of investments in preschool education. In E. Zigler & S. Jones (Eds.), *A vision for universal prekindergarten* (pp. 37–68). New York: Cambridge University Press.

Temple, J. L., Giacomelli, A. M., Roemmich, J. N., & Epstein, L. H. (2007). Overweight children habituate slower than non-overweight children to food. *Physiology and Behavior, 9,* 250–254.

Tenenbaum, H. R., & Leaper, C. (2002). Are parents' gender schemas related to their children's gender-related cognitions? A meta-analysis. *Developmental Psychology, 38,* 615–630.

Tenenbaum, H. R., & Leaper, C. (2003). Parent–child conversations about science: The socialization of gender inequities? *Developmental Psychology, 39,* 34–47.

Tenenbaum, H. R., Snow, C. E., Roach, K. A., & Kurland, B. (2005). Talking and reading science: Longitudinal data on sex differences in mother–child conversations in low-income families. *Journal of Applied Developmental Psychology, 26,* 1–19.

ten Tusscher, G. W., & Koppe, J. G. (2004). Perinatal dioxin exposure and later effects—a review. *Chemosphere, 54,* 1329–1336.

Terenzini, P. T., Pascarella, E. T., & Blimling, G. S. (1999). Students' out-of-class experiences and their influence on learning and cognitive development: A literature review. *Journal of College Student Development, 40,* 610–623.

Terwel, J., Gillies, R. M., van den Eeden, P., & Hoek, D. (2001). Cooperative learning processes of students: A longitudinal multilevel perspective. *British Journal of Educational Psychology, 71,* 619–645.

Tessier, R., Cristo, M., Velez, S., Giron, M., Nadeau, L., & Figueroa de Calume, Z. (2003). Kangaroo mother care: A method of protecting high-risk premature infants against developmental delay. *Infant Behavior and Development, 26,* 384–397.

Testa, M., Livingston, J. A., Vanzile-Tamsen, C., & Frone, M. R. (2003). The role of women's substance use in vulnerability to forcible and incapacitated rape. *Journal of Studies in Alcohol, 64,* 756–764.

Teti, D. M., Saken, J. W., Kucera, E., & Corns, K. M. (1996). And baby makes four: Predictors of attachment security among preschool-age firstborns during the transition to siblinghood. *Child Development, 67,* 579–596.

Teyber, E. (2001). *Helping children cope with divorce* (rev. ed.). San Francisco: Jossey-Bass.

Thacker, S. B., & Stroup, D. F. (2003). Revisiting the use of the electronic fetal monitor. *Lancet, 361,* 445–446.

Thapar, A., Fowler, T., Rice, F., Scourfield, J., van den Bree, M., Thomas, H., Harold, G., & Hay, D. (2003). Maternal smoking during pregnancy and attention deficit hyperactivity disorder symptoms in offspring. *American Journal of Psychiatry, 160,* 1985–1989.

Thatcher, R. W., Lyon, G. R., Rumsey, J., & Krasnegor, J. (1996). *Developmental neuroimaging.* San Diego, CA: Academic Press.

Thatcher, R. W., Walker, R. A., & Giudice, S. (1987). Human cerebral hemispheres develop at different rates and ages. *Science, 236,* 1110–1113.

Theisen, S. C., Mansfield, P. K., Seery, B. L., & Voda, A. (1995). Predictors of midlife women's attitudes toward menopause. *Health Values, 19,* 22–31.

Thelen, E. (1989). The (re)discovery of motor development: Learning new things from an old field. *Developmental Psychology, 25,* 946–949.

Thelen, E., Schöner, G., Scheier, C., & Smith, L. B. (2001). The dynamics of embodiment: A field theory of infant perseverative reaching. *Behavioral and Brain Sciences, 24,* 1–34.

Thelen, E., & Smith, L. B. (2006). Dynamic systems theories. In R. M. Lerner (Ed.), *Handbook of child psychology: Vol. 1. Theoretical models of human development* (6th ed., pp. 258–312). Hoboken, NJ: Wiley.

Théoret, E., Halligan, M., Kobayashi, F., Fregni, H., Tager-Flusberg, H., & Pascual-Leone, A. (2005). Impaired motor facilitation during action observation in individuals with autism spectrum disorder, *Current Biology, 15,* R84–R85.

Thomas, A., & Chess, S. (1977). *Temperament and development.* New York: Brunner/Mazel.

Thomas, A., Chess, S., & Birch, H. G. (1968). *Temperament and behavior disorders in children.* New York: New York University Press.

Thomas, C. L., & Dimitrov, D. M. (2007). Effects of a teen pregnancy prevention program on teens' attitudes toward sexuality: A latent trait modeling approach. *Developmental Psychology, 43,* 173–185.

Thomas, K. A., & Tessler, R. C. (2007). Bicultural socialization among adoptive families: Where there is a will, there is a way. *Journal of Family Issues, 28,* 1189–1219.

Thomas, R. M. (2005). *Comparing theories of child development* (6th ed.). Belmont, CA: Wadsworth.

Thompson, A., Hollis, C., & Richards, D. (2003). Authoritarian parenting attitudes as a risk for conduct problems: Results of a British national cohort study. *European Child and Adolescent Psychiatry, 12,* 84–91.

Thompson, P. M., Giedd, J. N., Woods, R. P., MacDonald, D., Evans, A. C., & Toga, A. W. (2000). Growth patterns in the developing brain detected by using continuum mechanical tensor maps. *Nature, 404,* 190–192.

Thompson, R. A. (2000). The legacy of early attachments. *Child Development, 71,* 145–152.

Thompson, R. A. (2006). The development of the person: Social understanding, relationships, conscience, self. In N. Eisenberg (Ed.), *Handbook of child psychology: Vol. 3. Social, emotional, and personality development* (6th ed., pp. 24–98). Hoboken, NJ: Wiley.

Thompson, R. A., Easterbrooks, M. A., & Padilla-Walker, L. M. (2003). Social and emotional development in infancy. In R. M. Lerner & M. A. Easterbrooks (Eds.), *Social and emotional development in infancy* (pp. 91–112). New York: Wiley.

Thompson, R. A., & Goodvin, R. (2007). Taming the tempest in the teapot. In C. A. Brownell & C. B. Kopp (Eds.), *Socioemotional development in the toddler years: Transitions and transformations* (pp. 320–341). New York: Guilford.

Thompson, R. A., & Leger, D. W. (1999). From squalls to calls: The cry as a developing socioemotional signal. In B. Lester, J. Newman, & F. Pedersen (Eds.), *Biological and social aspects of infant crying.* New York: Plenum.

Thompson, R. A., & Limber, S. (1991). "Social anxiety" in infancy: Stranger wariness and separation distress. In H. Leitenberg (Ed.), *Handbook of social and evaluation anxiety* (pp. 85–137). New York: Plenum.

Thompson, R. A., Meyer, S., & McGinley, M. (2006). Understanding values in relationships: The development of conscience. In M. Killen & J. G. Smetana (Eds.), *Handbook of moral development* (pp. 267–298). Mahwah, NJ: Erlbaum.

Thompson, R. A., & Nelson C. A. (2001). Developmental science and the media. *American Psychologist, 56,* 5–15.

Thompson, R. A., & Raikes, H. A. (2007). The social and emotional foundations of school readiness. In D. F. Perry, R. K. Kaufmann, & J. Knitzer (Eds.), *Social and emotional health in early childhood: Building bridges between services and systems* (pp. 13–35). Baltimore, MD: Paul H. Brookes.

Thornton, J., Edwards, R., Mitchell, P., Harrison, R. A., Buchan, I., & Kelly, S. P. (2005). Smoking and age-related macular degeneration: A review of association. *Eye, 19,* 935–944.

Thornton, R., & Light, L. L. (2006). Language comprehension and production in normal aging. In J. E. Birren & K. Warner Schaie (Eds.), *Handbook of the psychology of aging* (6th ed., pp. 261–287). Burlington, MA: Elsevier Academic Press.

Thornton, S. (1999). Creating conditions for cognitive change: The interaction between task structures and specific strategies. *Child Development, 70,* 588–603.

Tienari, P., Wahlberg, K. E., & Wynne, L. C. (2006). Finnish adoption study of schizophrenia: Implications for family interventions. *Families, Systems, and Health, 24,* 442–451.

Tienari, P., Wynne, L. C., Lasky, K., Moring, J., Nieminen, P., & Sorri, A. (2003). Genetic boundaries of the schizophrenia spectrum: Evidence from the Finnish adoptive family study of schizophrenia. *American Journal of Psychiatry, 160,* 1587–1594.

Tiggemann, M., & Anesbury, T. (2000). Negative stereotyping of obesity in children: The role of controllability beliefs. *Journal of Applied Social Psychology, 30,* 1977–1993.

Tincoff, R., & Jusczyk, P. W. (1999). Some beginnings of word comprehension in 6-month-olds. *Psychological Science, 10,* 172–175.

Tizard, B., & Rees, J. (1975). The effect of early institutional rearing on the behaviour problems and affectional relationships of four-year-old children. *Journal of Child Psychology and Psychiatry, 16,* 61–73.

Tjepkema, M. (2005). Insomnia. *Health Reports, 17,* 9–25.

Tofler, I. R., Knapp, P. K., & Drell, M. J. (1998). The achievement by proxy spectrum in youth sports: Historical perspective and clinical approach to pressured and high-achieving children and adolescents. *Child and Adolescent Psychiatric Clinics of North America, 7,* 803–820.

Tomasello, M. (1992). *First verbs: A case study of early grammatical development.* New York: Cambridge University Press.

Tomasello, M. (1999). Having intentions, understanding intentions, and understanding communicative intentions. In P. D. Zelazo, J. W. Astington, & J. Wilde (Eds.), *Developing theories of intention: Social understanding and self-control* (pp. 63–75). Mahwah, NJ: Erlbaum.

Tomasello, M. (2003). *Constructing a language: A usage-based theory of language acquisition.* Cambridge, MA: Harvard University Press.

Tomasello, M. (2005). Beyond formalities: The case of language acquisition. *Linguistic Review, 22,* 183–197.

Tomasello, M. (2006). Acquiring linguistic constructions. In D. Kuhn & R. Siegler (Eds.), *Handbook of child psychology: Vol. 2: Cognition, perception, and language* (6th ed., pp. 255–298). Hoboken, NJ: Wiley.

Tomasello, M., & Akhtar, N. (1995). Two-year-olds use pragmatic cues to differentiate reference to objects and actions. *Cognitive Development, 10,* 201–224.

Tomasello, M., & Rakoczy, H. (2003). What makes human cognition unique? From individual to shared to collective intentionality. *Mind and Language, 18,* 121–147.

Tomasello, M., Striano, T., & Rochat, P. (1999). Do young children use objects as symbols? *British Journal of Developmental Psychology, 17,* 563–584.

Tomer, A., Eliason, G., & Smith, J. (2000). Beliefs about the self, life, and death: Testing aspects of a comprehensive model of death anxiety and death attitudes. *Death attitudes and the older adult: Theories, concepts, and applications* (pp. 109–122). Philadelphia: Taylor & Francis.

Toomela, A. (2002). Drawing as a verbally mediated activity: A study of relationships between verbal, motor, visuospatial skills and drawing in children. *International Journal of Behavioral Development, 26,* 234–247.

Torges, C. M., Stewart, A. J., & Miner-Rubino, K. (2005). Personality after the prime of life: Men and women coming to terms with regrets. *Journal of Research in Personality, 39,* 148–165.

Tornstam, L. (1997). Gero-transcendence: A reformulation of disengagement theory. *Aging, 1,* 55–63.

Tornstam, L. (2000). Transcendence in later life. *Generations, 23*(10), 10–14.

Toro-Morn, M., & Sprecher, S. (2003). A cross-cultural comparison of mate preferences among university students: The United States vs. the People's Republic of China (PRC). *Journal of Comparative Family Studies, 34,* 151–170.

Torrance, E. P. (1988). The nature of creativity as manifest in its testing. In R. J. Sternberg (Ed.), *The nature of creativity: Contemporary psychological perspectives* (pp. 43–75). New York: Cambridge University Press.

Torrey, B. B., & Haub, C. (2004). A comparison of U.S. and Canadian mortality in 1998. *Population and Development Review, 30,* No. 3.

Tracy, J. L., Robins, R. W., & Lagattuta, K. H. (2005). Can children recognize pride? *Emotion, 5,* 251–257.

Trafford, A. (2004). *My time: Making the most of the rest of your life.* New York: Basic Books.

Trahms, C. M., & Pipes, P. L. (1997). *Nutrition in infancy and childhood* (6th ed.). New York: McGraw-Hill.

Trappe, S. (2007). Marathon runners: How do they age? *Sports Medicine, 37,* 302–305.

Trautner, H. M., Gervai, J., & Nemeth, R. (2003). Appearance–reality distinction and development of gender constancy understanding in children. *International Journal of Behavioral Development, 27,* 275–283.

Trautner, H. M., Ruble, D. N., Cyphers, L., Kirsten, B., Behrendt, R., & Hartmann, P. (2005). Rigidity and flexibility of gender stereotypes in childhood: Developmental or differential? *Infant and Child Development, 14,* 365–381.

Treasure, J., & Schmidt, U. (2005). Anorexia nervosa. *Clinical Evidence, 13,* 1148–1157.

Trehub, S. E. (2001). Musical predispositions in infancy. *Annals of the New York Academy of Sciences, 930,* 1–16.

Treloar, S. A., Heath, A. C., & Martin, N. G. (2002). Genetic and environmental influences on premenstrual symptoms in an Australian twin sample. *Psychological Medicine, 32,* 25–38.

Tremblay, L., & Frigon, J.-Y. (2005). Precocious puberty in adolescent girls: A biomarker of later psychosocial adjustment problems. *Child Psychiatry and Human Development, 36,* 73–94.

Tremblay, R. E. (2000). The development of aggressive behaviour during childhood: What have we learned in the past century? *International Journal of Behavioral Development, 24,* 129–141.

Tremblay, R. E. (2004). Decade of behavior distinguished lecture: Development of physical aggression during infancy. *Infant Mental Health Journal, 25,* 399–407.

Tremblay, R. E., Japel, C., Perusse, D., Voivin, M., Zoccolillo, M., Montplaisir, J., & McDuff, P. (1999). The search for the age of "onset" of physical aggression: Rousseau and Bandura revisited. *Criminal Behavior and Mental Health, 9,* 8–23.

Triandis, H. C. (1995). *Individualism and collectivism.* Boulder, CO: Westview Press.

Triandis, H. C. (2005). Issues in individualism and collectivism research. In R. M. Sorrentino, D. Cohen, J. M. Olson, & M. P. Zanna (Eds.), *Culture and social behavior: The Ontario Symposium* (Vol. 10, pp. 207–225). Mahwah, NJ: Erlbaum.

Triandis, H. C. (2007). Culture and psychology: A history of the study of their relationship. In S. Kitayama & D. Cohen (Eds.), *Handbook of cultural psychology* (pp. 59–76). New York: Guilford.

Trickett, P. K., & Putnam, F. W. (1998). Developmental consequences of child sexual abuse. In P. K. Trickett & C. J. Schellenbach (Eds.), *Violence against children in the family and community* (pp. 39–56). Washington, DC: American Psychological Association.

Trocomé, N., & Wolfe, D. (2002). *Child maltreatment in Canada: The Canadian Incidence Study of Reported Child Abuse and Neglect.* Retrieved from www.hc-sc.gc.ca/pphb-dgspsp/cm-vee

Tronick, E., Morelli, G., & Ivey, P. (1992). The Efe forager infant and toddler's pattern of social relationships: Multiple and simultaneous. *Developmental Psychology, 28,* 568–577.

Tronick, E. Z., Thomas, R. B., & Daltabuit, M. (1994). The Quechua manta pouch: A caretaking practice for buffering the Peruvian infant against the multiple stressors of high altitude. *Child Development, 65,* 1005–1013.

Troop-Gordon, W., & Asher, S. R. (2005). Modifications in children's goals when encountering obstacles to conflict resolution. *Child Development, 76,* 568–582.

Troyer, A. K., Häfliger, A., Cadieux, M. J., & Craik, F. I. M. (2006). Name and face learning in older adults: Effects of level of processing, self-generation, and intention to learn. *Journal of Gerontology, 61B,* P67–P74.

Trudel, G., Villeneuve, V., Anderson, A., & Pilon, G. (2008). Sexual and marital aspects of old age: An update. *Sexual and Relationship Therapy, 23,* 161–169.

True, M. M., Pisani, L., & Oumar, F. (2001). Infant–mother attachment among the Dogon of Mali. *Child Development, 72,* 1451–1466.

Trusty, J. (1999). Effects of eighth-grade parental involvement on late adolescents' educational expectations. *Journal of Research and Development in Education, 32,* 224–233.

Trzesniewski, K. H., Donnellan, M. B., & Robins, R. W. (2003). Stability of self-esteem across the life span. *Journal of Personality and Social Psychology, 84,* 205–220.

Tsai, A. G., & Wadden, T. A. (2005). Systematic review: An evaluation of major commercial weight loss programs in the United States. *Annals of Internal Medicine, 142,* 56–66.

Tsang, P. S., & Shaner, T. L. (1998). Age, attention, expertise, and time-sharing performance. *Psychology and Aging, 13,* 323–347.

Tsuang, M. T., Bar, J. L., Harley, R. M., & Lyons, M. J. (2001). The Harvard Twin Study of Substance Abuse: What we have learned. *Harvard Review of Psychiatry, 9,* 267–279.

Tucker, C. J., McHale, S. M., & Crouter, A. C. (2001). Conditions of sibling support in adolescence. *Journal of Family Psychology, 15,* 254–271.

Tudge, J. R. H. (1992). Processes and consequences of peer collaboration: A Vygotskian analysis. *Child Development, 63,* 1364–1397.

Tunmer, W. E., & Chapman, J. W. (2002). The relation of beginning readers' reported word identification strategies to reading achievement, reading-related skills, and academic self-perceptions. *Reading and Writing, 15,* 341–358.

Turati, C. (2004). Why faces are not special to newborns: An account of the face preference. *Current Directions in Psychological Science, 13,* 5–8.

Turesson, C., & Matteson, E. L. (2006). Genetics of rheumatoid arthritis. *Mayo Clinic Proceedings, 81,* 94–101.

Turiel, E. (2006). The development of morality. In N. Eisenberg (Ed.), *Handbook of child psychology: Vol. 3. Social, emotional, and personality development* (6th ed., pp. 789–857). Hoboken, NJ: Wiley.

Turkheimer, E., Haley, A., Waldron, M., D'Onofrio, B., & Gottesman, I. I. (2003). Socioeconomic status modifies heritability of IQ in young children. *Psychological Science, 14,* 623–628.

Turnbull, M., Hart, D., & Lapkin, S. (2003). Grade 6 French immersion students' performance on large-scale reading, writing, and mathematics tests: Building explanations. *Alberta Journal of Educational Research, 49,* 6–23.

Turner, B. F. (1982). Sex-related differences in aging. In B. B. Wolman (Ed.), *Handbook of developmental psychology* (pp. 912–936). Englewood Cliffs, NJ: Prentice-Hall.

Turner, P. J., & Gervai, J. (1995). A multidimensional study of gender typing in preschool children and their parents: Personality, attitudes, preferences, behavior, and cultural differences. *British Journal of Developmental Psychology, 11,* 323–342.

Turner, R. N., Hewstone, M., & Voci, A. (2007). Reducing explicit and implicit outgroup prejudice via direct and extended contact: The mediating role of self-disclosure and intergroup anxiety. *Journal of Personality and Social Psychology, 93,* 369–388.

Tuyen, J. M., & Bisgard, K. (2003). Community setting: Pertussis outbreak. Atlanta, GA: U.S. Centers for Disease Control and Prevention. Retrieved from www.cdc.gov/nip/publications/pertussis/chapter10.pdf

Twenge, J. M. (1997). Changes in masculine and feminine traits over time: A meta-analysis. *Sex Roles, 36,* 305–325.

Twenge, J. M. (2001). Changes in women's assertiveness in response to status and roles: A cross-temporal meta-analysis, 1931–1993. *Journal of Personality and Social Psychology, 81,* 133–145.

Twenge, J. M., & Campbell, W. K. (2001). Age and birth cohort differences in self-esteem: A cross-temporal meta-analysis. *Personality and Social Psychology Review, 5,* 321–344.

Twenge, J. M., & Crocker, J. (2002). Race and self-esteem: Meta-analyses comparing whites, blacks, Hispanics, Asians, and America Indians and comment on Gray-Little and Hafdahl (2000). *Psychological Bulletin, 128,* 371–408.

Tynes, B., Reynolds, L., & Greenfield, P. M. (2004). Adolescence, race and ethnicity on the Internet: A comparison of discourse in monitored vs. unmonitored chat rooms. *Journal of Applied Developmental Psychology, 25,* 667–684.

Tyrka, A. R., Graber, J. A., & Brooks-Gunn, J. (2000). The development of disordered eating: Correlates and predictors of eating problems in the context of adolescence. In A. J. Sameroff & M. Lewis (Eds.), *Handbook of developmental psychopathology* (2nd ed., pp. 607–624). New York: Kluwer.

U

Uhlenberg, P., & Hammill, B. G. (1998). Frequency of grandparent contact with grandchild sets: Six factors that make a difference. *Gerontologist, 38,* 276–285.

Ukrainetz, T. A., Justice, L. M., Kaderavek, J. N., Eisenberg, S. L., Gillam, R., & Harm, H. M. (2005). The development of expressive elaboration in fictional narratives. *Journal of Speech, Language, and Hearing Research, 48,* 1363–1377.

Umana-Taylor, A. J., & Alfaro, E. C. (2006). Ethnic identity among U.S. Latino adolescents: Measurement and implications for well-being. In F. A. Villarruel & T. Luster (Eds.), *The crisis in youth mental health: Critical issues and effective programs: Vol. 2. Disorders in adolescence* (pp. 195–211). Westport, CT: Praeger.

Umana-Taylor, A. J., & Updegraff, K. A. (2007). Latino adolescents' mental health: Exploring the interrelations among discrimination, ethnic identity, cultural orientation, self-esteem, and depressive symptoms. *Journal of Adolescence, 30,* 549–567.

Underhill, K., Montgomery, P., & Operario, D. (2007). Sexual abstinence only programmes to prevent HIV infection in high-income countries: Systematic review. *British Medical Journal, 335,* 248.

Underwood, M. K. (2003). *Social aggression among girls.* New York: Guilford.

UNICEF (United Nations Children's Fund). (2005). *Child poverty in rich countries: 2005.* Report Card No. 6. Florence, Italy: UNICEF Innocenti Research Centre.

UNICEF (United Nations Children's Fund). (2006). *Immunization Summary 2006.* Geneva, Switzerland: World Health Organization.

UNICEF (United Nations Children's Fund). (2008). *Immunization summary: A statistical reference containing data through 2006.* Geneva, Switzerland: World Health Organization.

UNICEF (United Nations Children's Fund). (2009). *State of the world's children.* New York: Author.

United Nations. (2002). *Human development report 2001.* New York: Author.

United Nations. (2006a). *Preventing HIV in women and infants.* Retrieved from www.unfpa.org/hiv/transmission.htm

United Nations. (2006b). *World population prospects: The 2006 revision. Population database.* Retrieved from esa.un.org/unpp/index.asp?panel=2

U.S. Administration on Aging, National Center on Elder Abuse. (2009). *Frequently asked questions about elder abuse.* Retrieved from www.ncea.aoa.gov/ncearoot/Main_Site/FAQ/Questions.aspx

U.S. Census Bureau. (2008). Food insecurity: Percentage of children ages 0–17 in food-insecure households by severity of food insecurity and selected characteristics. Retrieved from www.childstats.gov/americaschildren/tables/econ3a.asp

U.S. Census Bureau. (2009a). *International data base.* Retrieved from www.census.gov/ipc/www/idb

U.S. Census Bureau. (2009b). *Statistical abstract of the United States* (128th ed.). Washington, DC: U.S. Government Printing Office.

U.S. Centers for Disease Control and Prevention. (2005). *Preventing lead poisoning in young children.* Atlanta: Author.

U.S. Centers for Disease Control and Prevention. (2007). *Sexually transmitted disease surveillance: 2006.* Retrieved from www.cdc.gov/std/stats

U.S. Department of Agriculture. (2007). *Expenditures on children by families.* Miscellaneous Publication No. 1528-2007. Washington, DC: U.S. Government Printing Office.

U.S. Department of Education. (2003). The Nation's Report Card: National Assessment of Educational Progress: 2003 results. Retrieved from nces.ed.gov/nationsreportcard/mathematics

U.S. Department of Education. (2005). *Trial urban district report cards in reading and mathematics, 2005.* Retrieved from nces.ed.gov/nationsreportcard/nrc/tuda_reading_mathematics_2005

U.S. Department of Education. (2007a). *Comparative indicators of education in the United States and other G-8 countries: 2006.* Washington, DC: National Center for Education Statistics.

U.S. Department of Education. (2007b). *The Nation's Report Card: Mathematics 2007.* Retrieved from nces.ed.gov/pubsearch/pubsinfo.asp?pubid=2007494

U.S. Department of Education. (2007c). *The Nation's Report Card: Reading 2007.* Retrieved from nces.ed.gov/pubSearch/pubsinfo.asp?pubid=2007496

U.S. Department of Education. (2007d). *The Nation's Report Card: Writing 2007.* Retrieved from nces.ed.gov/pubsearch/pubsinfo.asp?pubid=2008468

U.S. Department of Education. (2008). *The condition of education.* Retrieved from nces.ed.gov/programs/coe/list/i4.asp

U.S. Department of Education. (2009). *Digest of education statistics, 2008.* Washington, DC. U.S. Government Printing Office.

U.S. Department of Health and Human Services. (2002). Cohabitation, marriage, divorce, and remarriage in the United States. *Vital and Health Statistics,* Series Report 23, Number 22. Washington, DC: U.S. Government Printing Office.

U.S. Department of Health and Human Services. (2004). *National nursing home survey* (NNHS). Retrieved from www.cdc.gov/nchs/nnhs.htm

U.S. Department of Health and Human Services. (2007a). Abortion surveillance—United States, 2004. *Morbidity and Mortality Weekly Report, 56*(SS09), 1–33. Retrieved from www.cdc.gov/mmwr/preview/mmwrhtml/ss5609a1.htm

U.S. Department of Health and Human Services. (2007b). *Births: Preliminary data for 2005.* Retrieved from www.cdc.gov/nchs/products/pubs/pubd/hestats/prelimbirths05/prelimbirths05.htm

U.S. Department of Health and Human Services. (2007c). National, state, and local area vaccination coverage among children aged 19–35 months—United States, 2006. *Morbidity and Mortality Weekly Report, 56*(34), 880–885.

U.S. Department of Health and Human Services. (2007d). *Prenatal care.* Retrieved from www.cdc.gov/nchs/fastats/prenatal.htm

U.S. Department of Health and Human Services. (2007e, April). Trends in oral health status: United States, 1988–1994 and 1999–2004. *Vital and Health Statistics, 11*(No. 248).

U.S. Department of Health and Human Services. (2008a). Annual smoking-attributable mortality, years of potential life lost, and productivity losses—United States, 2000–2004. *Morbidity and Mortality Weekly Report, 57,* 1226–1228.

U.S. Department of Health and Human Services. (2008b). Births: Final data for 2006. *National Vital Statistics Report, 56.* Retrieved from www.cdc.gov/nchs/data/nvsr/nvsr56/nvsr56_07.pdf

U.S. Department of Health and Human Services. (2008c). Breastfeeding among U.S. children born 1999–2005, CDC National Immunization Survey. Retrieved from www.cdc.gov/breastfeeding/data/NIS_data/index.htm

U.S. Department of Health and Human Services. (2008d). *Child maltreatment, 2006.* Retrieved from www.acf.hhs.gov/programs/cb/pubs/cm06/index.htm

U.S. Department of Health and Human Services. (2008e). *Deaths by place of death, age, race, and sex: United States, 1999–2004.* Retrieved from www.cdc.gov/nchs/datawh/statab/unpubd/mortabs/gmwk309_10.htm

U.S. Department of Health and Human Services. (2008f). *FASTATS: Births—methods of delivery.* Retrieved from www.cdc.gov/nchs/fastats/delivery.htm

U.S. Department of Health and Human Services, Centers for Medicare and Medicaid Services. (2008g). *National health expenditure data.* Retrieved from www.cms.hhs.gov/NationalHealthExpendData/02_NationalHealthAccountsHistorical.asp#TopOfPage

U.S. Department of Health and Human Services. (2008h). *Profile of older Americans 2008.* Retrieved from www.aoa.gov/AoARoot/Aging_Statistics/Profile/2008/docs/2008profile.pdf

U.S. Department of Health and Human Services. (2008i). *Your Medicare coverage.* Retrieved from www.medicare.gov/coverage/Home.asp

U.S. Department of Health and Human Services. (2008j). Youth Risk Behavior Surveillance—United States, 2007. *Morbidity and Mortality Weekly Report, 57*(No. SS-4), Retrieved from www.cdc.gov/HealthyYouth/yrbs

U.S. Department of Health and Human Services. (2009a). *Health, United States, with chartbook on trends in the health of Americans.* Hyattsville, MD: National Center for Health Statistics.

U.S. Department of Health and Human Services. (2009b). *National Survey on Drug Use and Health.* Retrieved from www.drugabusestatistics.samhsa.gov/nhsda.htm

U.S. Department of Health and Human Services. (2009c). *Obesity and American Indians/Alaska Natives.* Retrieved from www.omhrc.gov/templates/content.aspx?lvl=3&lvlID=537&ID=6457

U.S. Department of Health and Human Services. (2009d). *Physical activity for everyone: Recommendations.* Retrieved from www.cdc.gov/nccdphp/dnpa/physical/recommendations/index.htm

U.S. Department of Justice. (2008). *Crime in the United States, 2007.* Retrieved from www.fbi.gov/ucr/cius2007/index.html

U.S. Department of Labor. (2004, August 25). Number of jobs held, labor market activity, and earnings growth among younger baby boomers: Recent results from a longitudinal survey. *News* USDL041678. Washington DC: Bureau of Labor Statistics.

U.S. Department of Labor, Bureau of Labor Statistics. (2008). *Consumer expenditure survey: 2007.* Retrieved from www.bls.gov/cex/csxstnd.htm

U.S. Living Will Registry. (2005). *Advance directive forms.* Retrieved from www.uslivingwillregistry.com/forms.shtm

Ursano, R. J., & Shaw, J. A. (2007). Children of war and opportunities for peace. *Journal of the American Medical Association, 298,* 567.

Utz, R. L., Carr, D., Nesse, R., & Wortman, C. B. (2002). The effect of widowhood on older adults' social participation: An evaluation of activity, disengagement, and continuity theories. *Gerontologist, 42,* 522–533.

V

Vaillancourt, T., Hymel, S., & McDougall, P. (2003). Bullying is power: Implications for school-based intervention strategies. *Journal of Applied Social Psychology, 19,* 157–176.

Vaillkyt, G. E. (1977). *Adaptation to life.* Boston: Little, Brown.

Vaillant, G. E. (1993). *The wisdom of the ego.* Cambridge, MA: Harvard University Press.

Vaillant, G. E. (1994). "Successful aging" and psychosocial well-being. In E. H. Thompson, Jr. (Ed.), *Older men's lives* (pp. 22–41). Thousand Oaks, CA: Sage.

Vaillant, G. E. (2002). *Aging well.* Boston: Little, Brown.

Vaillant, G. E., & Koury, S. H. (1994). Late midlife development. In G. H. Pollock & S. I. Greenspan (Eds.), *The course of life* (pp. 1–22). Madison, CT: International Universities Press.

Vaillant, G. E., & Mukamal, K. (2001). Successful aging. *American Journal of Psychiatry, 158,* 839–847.

Vaillant, G. E., & Vaillant, C. O. (1990). Determinants and consequences of creativity in a cohort of gifted women. *Psychology of Women Quarterly, 14,* 607–616.

Valdés, G. (1998). The world outside and inside schools: Language and immigrant children. *Educational Researcher, 27*(6), 4–18.

Valentine, J. C., DuBois, D. L., & Cooper, H. (2004). The relation between self-beliefs and academic achievement: A meta-analytic review. *Educational Psychologist, 39,* 111–133.

Valian, V. (1999). Input and language acquisition. In W. C. Ritchie & T. K. Bhatia (Eds.), *Handbook of child language acquisition* (pp. 497–530). San Diego: Academic Press.

Valkenburg, P. M., & Peter, J. (2007a). Internet communication and its relation to well-being: Identifying some underlying mechanisms. *Media Psychology, 9,* 43–58.

Valkenburg, P. M., & Peter, J. (2007b). Preadolescents' and adolescents' online communication and their closeness to friends. *Developmental Psychology, 43,* 267–277.

van Asselt, D. (2006). Advance directives: Prerequisites and usefulness. *Zeitschrift für Gerontologie und Geriatrie, 39,* 371–375.

van Baarsen, B. (2002). Theories on coping with loss: The impact of social support and self-esteem on adjustment to emotional and social loneliness following a partner's death in later life. *Journal of Gerontology, 57B,* S33–S42.

Vandell, D. L., & Posner, J. K. (1999). Conceptualization and measurement of children's after-school environments. In S. L. Friedman & T. D. Wachs (Eds.), *Measuring environment across the life span* (pp. 167–196). Washington, DC: American Psychological Association.

Vandell, D. L., Reisner, E. R., Pierce, K. M., Brown, B. B., Lee, D., Bolt, D., & Pechman, E. M. (2006). *The study of promising after-school programs: Examination of longer term outcomes after two years of program experiences.* Madison, WI: University of Wisconsin. Retrieved from www.wcer.wisc.edu/childcare/statements.html

Vandell, D. L., & Shumow, L. (1999). After-school child care programs. *Future of Children, 9*(2), 64–80.

Van den Bergh, B. R. H. (2004). High antenatal maternal anxiety is related to ADHD symptoms, externalizing problems, and anxiety in 8- and 9-year-olds. *Child Development, 75,* 1085–1097.

Van den Bergh, B. R. H., & De Rycke, L. (2003). Measuring the multidimensional self-concept and global self-worth of 6- to 8-year-olds. *Journal of Genetic Psychology, 164,* 201–225.

Vandewater, E. A., & Stewart, A. J. (1997). Women's career commitment patterns and personality development. In M. E. Lachman & J. B. James (Eds.), *Multiple paths of midlife development* (pp. 375–410). Chicago: University of Chicago Press.

Van Eyken, E., Van Camp, G., & Van Laer, L. (2007). The complexity of age-related hearing impairment:

Contributing environmental and genetic factors. *Audiology and Neurotology, 12,* 345–358.

van IJzendoorn, M. H. (1995). Adult attachment representations, parental responsiveness, and infant attachment: A meta-analysis on the predictive validity of the Adult Attachment Interview. *Psychological Bulletin, 117,* 387–403.

van IJzendoorn, M. H., Juffer, F., & Poelhuis, C. W. K. (2005). Adoption and cognitive development: A meta-analytic comparison of adopted and non-adopted children's IQ and school performance. *Psychological Bulletin, 131,* 301–316.

van IJzendoorn, M. H., & Kroonenberg, P. M. (1988). Cross-cultural patterns of attachment: A meta-analysis of the Strange Situation. *Child Development, 59,* 147–156.

van IJzendoorn, M. H., & Sagi, A. (1999). Cross-cultural patterns of attachment. In J. Cassidy & P. R. Shaver (Eds.), *Handbook of attachment: Theory, research, and clinical applications* (pp. 713–734). New York: Guilford.

van IJzendoorn, M. H., Schuengel, C., & Bakermans-Kranenburg, M. J. (1999). Disorganized attachment in early childhood: Meta-analysis of precursors, concomitants, and sequelae. *Development and Psychopathology, 11,* 225–249.

van IJzendoorn, M. H., Vereijken, C. M. J. L., Bakermans-Kranenburg, M. J., & Riksen-Walraven, J. M. (2004). Assessing attachment security with the Attachment Q Sort: Meta-analytic evidence for the validity of the Observer AQS. *Child Development, 75,* 1188–1213.

Van Keer, H. (2004). Fostering reading comprehension in fifth grade by explicit instruction in reading strategies and peer tutoring. *British Journal of Educational Psychology, 74,* 37–70.

van Solinge, H., & Henkens, K. (2008). Adjustment to and satisfaction with retirement: Two of a kind? *Psychology and Aging, 23,* 422–434.

Van Volkom, M. (2006). Sibling relationships in middle and older adulthood: A review of the literature. *Marriage and Family Review, 40,* 151–170.

Varendi, H., & Porter, R. H. (2001). Breast odour as the only maternal stimulus elicits crawling toward the odour source. *Acta Paediactrica, 90,* 372–375.

Varnhagen, C. (2007). Children and the Internet. In J. Gackenbach (Ed.), *Psychology and the Internet* (2nd ed., pp, 37–54). Amsterdam: Elsevier.

Vartanian, L. R., & Powlishta, K. K. (1996). A longitudinal examination of the social-cognitive foundations of adolescent egocentrism. *Journal of Early Adolescence, 16,* 157–178.

Vaughn, B. E., Kopp, C. B., & Krakow, J. B. (1984). The emergence and consolidation of self-control from eighteen to thirty months of age: Normative trends and individual differences. *Child Development, 55,* 990–1004.

Vazsonyi, A. T., Hibbert, J. R., & Snider, J. B. (2003). Exotic enterprise no more? Adolescent reports of family and parenting processes from youth in four countries. *Journal of Research on Adolescence, 13,* 129–160.

Velkoff, V. (2000, January–March). Centenarians in the United States, 1990 and beyond. *Statistical Bulletin, U.S. Bureau of the Census.* Washington, DC: U.S. Government Printing Office.

Velleman, R. D. B., Templeton, L. J., & Copello, A. G. (2005). The role of the family in preventing and intervening with substance use and misuse: A comprehensive review of family interventions, with a focus on young people. *Drug and Alcohol Review, 24,* 93–109.

Venet, M., & Markovits, H. (2001). Understanding uncertainty with abstract conditional premises. *Merrill-Palmer Quarterly, 47,* 74–99.

Venezia, M., Messinger, D. S., Thorp, D., & Mundy, P. (2004). The development of anticipatory smiling. *Infancy, 6,* 397–406.

Veneziano, R. A. (2003). The importance of paternal warmth. *Cross-Cultural Research, 37,* 265–281.

Veniegas, R., & Peplau, L. A. (1997). Power and the quality of same-sex friendships. *Psychology of Women Quarterly, 21,* 279–297.

Verghese, J., Lipston, R. B., Katz, M. J., Hall, C. B., Derby, C. A., & Kuslansky, G. (2003). Leisure activities and the risk of dementia in the elderly. *New England Journal of Medicine, 348,* 2508–2516.

Veríssimo, M., & Salvaterra, F. (2006). Maternal secure-base scripts and children's attachment security in an adopted sample. *Attachment and Human Development, 8,* 261–273.

Vesco, K. K., Haney, E. M., Humphrey, L., Fu, R., & Nelson, H. D. (2007). Influence of menopause on mood: A systematic review of cohort studies. *Climacteric, 10,* 448–465.

Victor, C., Scambler, S., Bond, J., & Bowling, A. (2000). Being alone in later life: Loneliness, social isolation, and living alone. *Reviews in Clinical Gerontology, 10,* 407–417.

Vidaeff, A. C., Carroll, M. A., & Ramin, S. M. (2005). Acute hypertensive emergencies in pregnancy. *Critical Care Medicine, 33,* S307–S312.

Vinden, P. G. (1996). Junín Quechua children's understanding of mind. *Child Development, 67,* 1707–1716.

Vinden, P. G. (2002). Understanding minds and evidence for belief: A study of Mofu children in Cameroon. *International Journal of Behavioral Development, 26,* 445–452.

Vinters, H. V. (2001). Aging and the human nervous system. In J. E. Birren & K. W. Schaie (Eds.), *Handbook of the psychology of aging* (pp. 135–160). San Diego: Academic Press.

Visher, E. B., Visher, J. S., & Pasley, K. (2003). Remarriage, families and stepparenting. In F. Walsh (Ed.), *Normal family processes* (pp. 153–175). New York: Guilford.

Vita, A. J., Terry, R. B., Hubert, H. B., & Fries, J. F. (1998). Aging, health risks, and cumulative disability. *New England Journal of Medicine, 338,* 1035–1041.

Vitali, P., Migliaccio, R., Agosta, F., Rosen, H. J., & Geschwind, M. D. (2008). Neuroimaging in dementia. *Seminars in Neurology, 28,* 467–483.

Vivanti, G., Nadig, A., Ozonoff, S., & Rogers, S. J. (2008). What do children with autism attend to during imitation tasks? *Journal of Experimental Psychology, 101,* 186–205.

Vogel, D. A., Lake, M. A., Evans, S., & Karraker, H. (1991). Children's and adults' sex-stereotyped perceptions of infants. *Sex Roles, 24,* 605–616.

Vogels, N., Diepvens, K., & Westerterp-Plantenga, M. S. (2005). Predictors of long-term weight maintenance. *Obesity Research, 13,* 2162–2168.

Volling, B. L. (2001). Early attachment relationships as predictors of preschool children's emotion regulation with a distressed sibling. *Early Education and Development, 12,* 185–207.

Volling, B. L., & Belsky, J. (1992). Contribution of mother–child and father–child relationships to the quality of sibling interaction: A longitudinal study. *Child Development, 63,* 1209–1222.

Volling, B. L., McElwain, N. L., & Miller, A. L. (2002). Emotion regulation in context: The jealousy complex between young siblings and its relations with child and family characteristics. *Child Development, 73,* 581–600.

Volling, B. L., McElwain, N. L., Notaro, P. C., & Herrera, C. (2002). Parents' emotional availability and infant emotional competence: Predictors of parent–infant attachment and emerging self-regulation. *Journal of Family Psychology, 16,* 447–465.

Volpicelli, J. R. (2001). Alcohol abuse and alcoholism. *Journal of Clinical Psychiatry, 62*(Suppl. 20), 4–10.

Vondra, J. I., Hommerding, K. D., & Shaw, D. S. (1999). Stability and change in infant attachment in a low-income sample. In J. I. Vondra & D. Barnett (Eds.), *Atypical attachment in infancy and early childhood among children at developmental risk. Monographs of the Society for Research in Child Development, 64*(3, Serial No. 258), 119–144.

Vondra, J. I., Shaw, D. S., Searingen, L., Cohen, M., & Owens, E. B. (2001). Attachment stability and emotional and behavioral regulation from infancy to preschool age. *Development and Psychopathology, 13,* 13–33.

von Hofsten, C. (2004). An action perspective on motor development. *Trends in Cognitive Sciences, 8,* 266–272.

Vouloumanos, A., & Werker, J. F. (2004). Tuned to the signal: The privileged status of speech for young infants. *Developmental Science, 7,* 270–276.

Vygotsky, L. S. (1978). *Mind in society: The development of higher mental processes.* Cambridge, MA: Harvard University Press. (Original works published 1930, 1933, and 1935)

Vygotsky, L. S. (1987). Thinking and speech. In R. W. Rieber, & A. S. Carton (Eds.), & N. Minick (Trans.), *The collected works of L. S. Vygotsky: Vol. 1. Problems of general psychology* (pp. 37–285). New York: Plenum. (Original work published 1934)

W

Wachs, T. D., & Bates, J. E. (2001). Temperament. In G. Bremner & A. Fogel (Eds.), *Blackwell handbook of infant development* (pp. 465–501). Oxford, UK: Blackwell.

Wadden, T. A., & Foster, G. D. (2000). Behavioral treatment of obesity. *Medical Clinics of North America, 84,* 441–461.

Wade, T. J., & Cairney, J. (1997). Age and depression in a nationally representative sample of Canadians: A preliminary look at the National Population Health Survey. *Canadian Journal of Public Health, 88,* 297–302.

Wadhwa, P. D., Sandman, C. A., & Garite, T. J. (2001). The neurobiology of stress in human pregnancy: Implications for prematurity and development of the fetal central nervous system. *Progress in Brain Research, 133,* 131–142.

Wagner, R. K. (2000). Practical intelligence. In R. J. Sternberg (Ed.), *Handbook of intelligence* (pp. 380–395). New York: Cambridge University Press.

Wahlsten, D. (1994). The intelligence of heritability. *Canadian Psychology, 35,* 244–259.

Wainryb, C. (1997). The mismeasure of diversity: Reflections on the study of cross-cultural differences. In H. D. Saltzstein (Ed.), *New directions for child development* (No. 76, pp. 51–65). San Francisco: Jossey-Bass.

Waite, L. J. (1999, July). *Debunking the marriage myth: It works for women, too.* Paper presented at the annual Smart Marriages Conference, Washington, DC.

Wakeley, A., Rivera, S., & Langer, J. (2000). Can young infants add and subtract? *Child Development, 71,* 1477–1720.

Walberg, H. J. (1986). Synthesis of research on teaching. In M. C. Wittrock (Ed.), *Handbook of research on teaching* (3rd ed., pp. 214–229). New York: Macmillan.

Waldfogel, J. (2001). International policies toward parental leave and child care. *Future of Children 11,* 52–61.

Waldinger, R. J., Schulz, M. S., Hauser, S. T., Allen, J. P., & Crowell, J. A. (2004). Reading others' emotions: The role of intuitive judgments in predicting marital satisfaction, quality, and stability. *Journal of Family Psychology, 18,* 58–71.

Waldron, H. B., Turner, C. W., & Ozechowski, T. J. (2005). Profiles of change in behavioral and family interventions for adolescent substance abuse and dependence. In H. A. Liddle & C. L. Rowe (Eds.), *Adolescent substance abuse: Research and clinical advances* (pp. 357–374). Cambridge, UK: Cambridge University Press.

Waldrop, D. P., & Weber, J. A. (2001). From grandparent to caregiver: The stress and satisfaction of raising grandchildren. *Families in Society, 82,* 461–472.

Walenski, M., Tager-Flusberg, H., & Ullman, M. T. (2006). Language in autism. In S. O. Moldin &

J. L. R. Rubenstein (Eds.), *Understanding autism: From basic neuroscience to treatment* (pp. 175–203). Boca Raton, FL: CRC Press.

Walker, A., Rosenberg, M., & Balaban-Gil, K. (1999). Neurodevelopmental and neurobehavioral sequelae of selected substances of abuse and psychiatric medications in utero. *Neurological Disorders: Developmental and Behavioral Sequelae, 8,* 845–867.

Walker, L. J. (1995). Sexism in Kohlberg's moral psychology? In W. M. Kurtines & J. L. Gewirtz (Eds.), *Moral development: An introduction* (pp. 83–107). Boston: Allyn and Bacon.

Walker, L. J. (2004). Progress and prospects in the psychology of moral development. *Merrill-Palmer Quarterly, 50,* 546–557.

Walker, L. J. (2006). Gender and morality. In M. Killen & J. G. Smetana (Eds.), *Handbook of moral development* (pp. 93–118). Philadelphia: Erlbaum.

Walker, L. J., & Taylor, J. H. (1991a). Family interactions and the development of moral reasoning. *Child Development, 62,* 264–283.

Walker, L. J., & Taylor, J. H. (1991b). Stage transitions in moral reasoning: A longitudinal study of developmental processes. *Developmental Psychology, 27,* 330–337.

Walker-Andrews, A. (1997). Infants' perception of expressive behaviors: Differentiation of multimodal information. *Psychological Bulletin, 121,* 437–456.

Walkowiak, J., Wiener, J., Fastabend, A., Heinzow, B., Krämer, U., & Schmidt, E. (2001). Environmental exposure to polychlorinated biphenyls and quality of the home environment: Effects on psychodevelopment in early childhood. *Lancet, 358,* 1602–1607.

Wall, M., & Côté, J. (2007). Developmental activities that lead to dropout and investment in sport. *Physical Education and Sport Pedagogy, 12,* 77–87.

Wallace, J. M., Jr., Bachman, J. G., O'Malley, P. M., Schulenberg, J. E., Cooper, S. M., & Johnston, L. D. (2003). Gender and ethnic differences in smoking, drinking, and illicit drug use among American 8th, 10th, and 12th grade students, 1976–2000. *Addiction, 98,* 225–234.

Walls, C. T., & Zarit, S. H. (1991). Informal support from black churches and the well-being of elderly blacks. *Gerontologist, 31,* 490–495.

Walsh, C. A., Ploeg, J., Lohfeld, L., Horne, J., MacMillan, H., & Lai, D. (2007). Violence across the lifespan: Interconnections among forms of abuse as described by marginalized Canadian elders and their caregivers. *British Journal of Social Work, 37,* 491–514.

Walsh, F., & McGoldrick, M. (2004). Loss and the family: A systemic perspective. In F. Walsh & M. McGoldrick (Eds.), *Living beyond loss: Death in the family* (2nd ed., pp. 3–26). New York: Norton.

Walsh, K. E., & Berman, J. R. (2004). Sexual dysfunction in the older woman: An overview of the current understanding and management. *Therapy in Practice, 21,* 655–675.

Walston, J., Hadley, E. C., Ferrucci, L., Guralnik, J. M., Newman, A. B., Studenski, S. A., Ershler, W. B., Harris, T., & Fried, L. P. (2006). Research agenda for frailty in older adults: Toward a better understanding of physiology and etiology: Summary from the American Geriatrics Society/National Institute on Aging Research Conference on Frailty in Older Adults. *Journal of the American Geriatrics Society, 54,* 991–1001.

Wang, H., & Amato, P. R. (2000). Predictors of divorce adjustment: Stressors, resources, and definitions. *Journal of Marriage and Family, 62,* 655–668.

Wang, Q. (2004). The emergence of cultural self-construct: Autobiographical memory and self-description in American and Chinese children. *Developmental Psychology, 40,* 3–15.

Wang, Q. (2006). Relations of maternal style and child self-concept to autobiographical memories in Chinese, Chinese immigrant, and European American 3-year-olds. *Child Development, 77,* 1794–1809.

Wang, Q., Pomerantz, E. M., & Chen, H. (2007). The role of parents' control in early adolescents' psychological functioning: A longitudinal investigation in the United States and China. *Child Development, 78,* 1592–1610.

Wang, S., Baillargeon, R., & Paterson, S. (2005). Detecting continuity violations in infancy: A new account and new evidence from covering and tube events. *Cognition, 95,* 129–173.

Wannamethee, G., Shaper, A. G., & Macfarlane, P. W. (1993). Heart rate, physical activity, and mortality from cancer and other noncardiovascular diseases. *American Journal of Epidemiology, 137,* 735–748.

Ward, R. A., & Spitze, G. D. (2007). Nestleaving and coresidence by young adult children: The role of family relations. *Research on Aging, 29,* 257–277.

Wark, G. R., & Krebs, D. L. (1996). Gender and dilemma differences in real-life moral judgment. *Developmental Psychology, 32,* 220–230.

Warnock, F., & Sandrin, D. (2004). Comprehensive description of newborn distress behavior in response to acute pain (newborn male circumcision). *Pain, 107,* 242–255.

Warr, P. B. (1994). Age and employment. In M. D. Dunnette, L. Hough, & H. Triandis (Eds.), *Handbook of industrial and organizational psychology* (pp. 485–550). Palo Alto, CA: Consulting Psychologists Press.

Warr, P. (2001). Age and work behavior: Physical attributes, cognitive abilities, knowledge, personality traits, and motives. *International Review of Industrial and Organizational Psychology, 16,* 1–36.

Warr, P., Butcher, V., Robertson, I., & Callinan, M. (2004). Older people's well-being as a function of employment, retirement, environmental characteristics, and role preference. *British Journal of Psychology, 95,* 297–324.

Warren, A. R., & Tate, C. S. (1992). Egocentrism in children's telephone conversations. In R. M. Diaz & L. E. Berk (Eds.), *Private speech: From social interaction to self-regulation* (pp. 245–264). Hillsdale, NJ: Erlbaum.

Warren, S. L., & Simmens, S. J. (2005). Predicting toddler anxiety/depressive symptoms: Effects of caregiver sensitivity of temperamentally vulnerable children. *Infant Mental Health Journal, 26,* 40–55.

Wasik, B. A., & Bond, M. A. (2001). Beyond the pages of a book: Interactive book reading and language development in preschool classrooms. *Journal of Educational Psychology, 93,* 243–250.

Wass, H. (2004). A perspective on the current state of death education. *Death Studies, 28,* 289–308.

Wasserman, E. A., & Rovee-Collier, C. (2001). Pick the flowers and mind your As and 2s! Categorization by pigeons and infants. In M. E. Carroll & J. B. Overmier (Eds.), *Animal research and human health: Advancing human welfare through behavioral science* (pp. 263–279). Washington, DC: American Psychological Association.

Waterman, A. S., & Whitbourne, S. K. (1982). Androgyny and psychosocial development among college students and adults. *Journal of Personality, 50,* 121–133.

Waters, E., & Cummings, E. M. (2000). A secure base from which to explore close relationships. *Child Development, 71,* 164–172.

Waters, E., Merrick, S., Treboux, D., Crowell, J., & Albersheim, L. (2000). Attachment security in infancy and early adulthood: A twenty-year longitudinal study. *Child Development, 71,* 684–689.

Waters, E., Vaughn, B. E., Posada, G., & Kondo-Ikemura, K. (Eds.). (1995). Caregiving, cultural, and cognitive perspectives on secure-base behavior and working models: New growing points of attachment theory and research. *Monographs of the Society for Research in Child Development, 60*(2–3, Serial No. 244).

Watkins, W. E., & Pollitt, E. (1998). Iron deficiency and cognition among school-age children. In S. G. McGregor (Ed.), *Recent advances in research on the effects of health and nutrition on children's development and school achievement in the Third World.* Washington, DC: Pan American Health Organization.

Watson, A. C., Nixon, C. L., Wilson, A., & Capage, L. (1999). Social interaction skills and theory of mind in young children. *Developmental Psychology, 35,* 386–391.

Watson, D. J. (1989). Defining and describing whole language. *Elementary School Journal, 90,* 129–141.

Watson, J. B., & Raynor, R. (1920). Conditioned emotional reactions. *Journal of Experimental Psychology, 3,* 1–14.

Watson, M. (1990). Aspects of self development as reflected in children's role playing. In D. Cicchetti & M. Beeghly (Eds.), *The self in transition: Infancy to childhood* (pp. 281–307). Chicago: University of Chicago Press.

Watt, L. M., & Cappeliez, P. (2000). Integrative and instrumental reminiscence therapies for depression in older adults: Intervention strategies and treatment effectiveness. *Aging and Mental Health, 4,* 166–177.

Watts-English, T., Fortson, B. L., Gibler, N., Hooper, S. R., & De Bellis, M. D. (2006). The psychobiology of maltreatment in childhood. *Journal of Social Issues, 62,* 717–736.

Waxman, S. R., & Senghas, A. (1992). Relations among word meanings in early lexical development. *Developmental Psychology, 28,* 862–873.

Webb, N. B. (2002). September 11, 2001. In N. B. Webb (Ed.), *Helping bereaved children: A handbook for practitioners* (pp. 365–384). New York: Guilford.

Weber, C., Hahne, A., Friedrich, M., & Friederici, A. (2004). Discrimination of word stress in early infant perception: Electrophysiological evidence. *Cognitive Brain Research, 18,* 149–161.

Weber, J. A., & Waldrop, D. P. (2000). Grandparents raising grandchildren: Families in transition. *Journal of Gerontological Social Work, 33,* 27–46.

Wechsler, D. (2002). *WPPSI-III: Wechsler Preschool and Primary Scale of Intelligence* (3rd ed.). San Antonio, TX: Psychological Corporation.

Wechsler, D. (2003). *WISC-IV: Wechsler Intelligence Scale for Children* (4th ed.). San Antonio, TX: Psychological Corporation.

Weems, C. F., & Costa, N. M. (2005). Developmental differences in the expression of childhood anxiety symptoms and fears. *Journal of the American Academy of Child and Adolescent Psychiatry, 44,* 656–663.

Wegesin, D. J., Jacobs, D. M., Zubin, N. R., & Ventura, P. R. (2000). Source memory and encoding strategy in normal aging. *Journal of Clinical and Experimental Neuropsychology, 22,* 455–464.

Wehren, A., De Lisi, R., & Arnold, M. (1981). The development of noun definition. *Journal of Child Language, 8,* 165–175.

Weikart, D. P. (1998). Changing early childhood development through educational intervention. *Preventive Medicine, 27,* 233–237.

Weimer, B. L., Kerns, K. A., & Oldenburg, C. M. (2004). Adolescents' interactions with a best friend: Associations with attachment style. *Journal of Experimental Child Psychology, 88,* 102–120.

Weinberg, M. K., & Tronick, E. Z. (1994). Beyond the face: An empirical study of infant affective configurations of facial, vocal, gestural, and regulatory behaviors. *Child Development, 65,* 1503–1515.

Weindruch, R., Keenan, K. P., Carney, J. M., Fernandes, G., Feuers, R. J., & Floyd, R. A. (2001). Caloric restriction mimetics: Metabolic interventions. *Journal of Gerontology, 56A,* 20–33.

Weiner, J., & Tardif, C. (2004). Social and emotional functioning of children with learning disabilities: Does special education placement make a difference? *Learning Disabilities Research and Practice, 19,* 20–32.

Weinfield, N. S., Sroufe, L. A., & Egeland, B. (2000). Attachment from infancy to early adulthood in a high-risk sample: Continuity, discontinuity, and their correlates. *Child Development, 71,* 695–702.

Weinfield, N. S., Whaley, G. J. L., & Egeland, B. (2004). Continuity, discontinuity, and coherence in attachment from infancy to late adolescence: Sequelae of organization and disorganization. *Attachment and Human Development, 6*, 73–97.

Weingarten, H. R. (1988). Late life divorce and the life review. *Journal of Gerontological Social Work, 12*(3–4), 83–97.

Weingarten, H. R. (1989). The impact of late life divorce: A conceptual and empirical study. *Journal of Divorce, 12*, 21–38.

Weinstein, R. S. (2002). *Reaching higher: The power of expectations in schooling.* Cambridge, MA: Harvard University Press.

Weisfield, G. E. (1997). Puberty rites as clues to the nature of human adolescence. *Cross-Cultural Research, 31*, 27–54.

Weiss, A., Costa, P. T., Jr., Karuza, J., Duberstein, P. R., Friedman, B., & McCrae, R. M. (2005). Cross-sectional age differences in personality among Medicare patients aged 65 to 100. *Psychology and Aging, 20*, 182–185.

Weiss, K. M. (2005). Cryptic causation of human disease: Reading between the germ lines. *Trends in Genetics, 21*, 82–88.

Weissberg, R. W. (2006). Modes of expertise in creative thinking: Evidence from case studies. In K. A. Ericsson, N. Charness, P. J. Feltovich, & R. R. Hoffman (Eds.), *The Cambridge handbook of expertise and expert performance* (pp. 761–787). New York: Cambridge University Press.

Weisz, A. N., & Black, B. M. (2002). Gender and moral reasoning: African American youths respond to dating dilemmas. *Journal of Human Behavior in the Social Environment, 6*, 17–34.

Weizman, Z. O., & Snow, C. E. (2001). Lexical output as related to children's vocabulary acquisition: Effects of sophisticated exposure and support for meaning. *Developmental Psychology, 37*, 265–279.

Wekerle, C., Wall, A.-M., Leung, E., & Trocmé, N. (2007). Cumulative stress and substantiated maltreatment: The importance of caregiver vulnerability and adult partner violence. *Child Abuse and Neglect, 31*, 427–443.

Wekerle, C., & Wolfe, D. A. (2003). Child maltreatment. In E. J. Mash & R. A. Barkley (Eds.), *Child psychopathology* (2nd ed., pp. 632–684). New York: Guilford.

Wellman, H. M. (2002). Understanding the psychological world: Developing a theory of mind. In U. Goswami (Ed.), *Blackwell handbook of child cognitive development* (pp. 167–187). Malden, MA: Blackwell.

Wellman, H. M., & Hickling, A. K. (1994). The mind's "I": Children's conception of the mind as an active agent. *Child Development, 65*, 1564–1580.

Weng, N. (2008). Aging of the immune system: How much can the adaptive immune system adapt? *Immunity, 24*, 495–499.

Weng, X., Odouli, R., & Li, D.-K. (2008). Maternal caffeine consumption during pregnancy and the risk of miscarriage: A prospective cohort study. *American Journal of Obstetrics and Gynecology, 198*, 279e1–279e8.

Wentworth, N., Benson, J. B., & Haith, M. M. (2000). The development of infants' reaches for stationary and moving targets. *Child Development, 71*, 576–601.

Wentzel, K. R., Barry, C. M., & Caldwell, K. A. (2004). Friendships in middle school: Influences on motivation and school adjustment. *Journal of Educational Psychology, 96*, 195–203.

Werner, E. E. (1989, April). Children of the garden island. *Scientific American, 260*(4), 106–111.

Werner, E. E. (1991). Grandparent–grandchild relationships amongst U.S. ethnic groups. In P. K. Smith (Ed.), *The psychology of grandparenthood: An international perspective* (pp. 68–82). London: Routledge.

Werner, E. E. (2001). *Journeys from childhood to midlife: Risk, resilience, and recovery.* Ithaca, NY: Cornell University Press.

Werner, E. E., & Smith, R. S. (1982). *Vulnerable but invincible.* New York: McGraw-Hill.

Werner, E. E., & Smith, R. S. (1992). *Overcoming the odds: High-risk children from birth to adulthood.* Ithaca, NY: Cornell University Press.

Werner, E. E., & Smith, R. S. (2001). *Journeys from childhood to midlife: Risk, resilience, and recovery.* Ithaca, NY: Cornell University Press.

Werner, N. E., & Crick, N. R. (2004). Maladaptive peer relationships and the development of relational and physical aggression during middle childhood. *Social Development, 13*, 495–514.

West, R. L., & Craik, F. I. M. (1999). Age-related decline in prospective memory: The roles of cue accessibility and cue sensitivity. *Psychology and Aging, 14*, 264–272.

Westerhof, G. J., Bohlmeijer, E., & Valenkamp, M. W. (2004). In search of meaning: A reminiscence program for older persons. *Educational Gerontology, 30*, 751–766.

Westermann, G., Mareschal, D., Johnson, M. H., Sirois, S., Spratling, M. W., & Thomas, M. S. C. (2007). Neuroconstructivism. *Developmental Science, 10*, 75–83.

Westermeyer, J. F. (1998). Predictors and characteristics of mental health among men at midlife: A 32-year longitudinal study. *American Journal of Orthopsychiatry, 68*, 265–273.

Westermeyer, J. F. (2004). Predictors and characteristics of Erikson's life cycle model among men: A 32-year longitudinal study. *International Journal of Aging and Human Development, 58*, 29–48.

Wethington, E. (2000). Expecting stress: Americans and the "midlife crisis." *Motivation and Emotion, 24*, 85–103.

Wethington, E., Kessler, R. C., & Pixley, J.E. (2005). Turning points in adulthood. In O. G. Brim, C. D. Ryff, & R. C. Kessler (Eds.), *How healthy are we? A national study of well-being at midlife* (pp. 586–613). Chicago: University of Chicago Press.

Wexler, I. D., Branski, D., & Kerem, E. (2006). War and children. *Journal of the American Medical Association, 296*, 579–581.

Weyermann, M., Rothenbacher, D., & Brenner, H. (2006). Duration of breast-feeding and risk of overweight in childhood: A prospective birth cohort study from Germany. *International Journal of Obesity, 30*, 1281–1287.

Whalley, L. (2001). *The aging brain.* London: Weidenfeld & Nicolson.

Wheeler, I. (2001). Parental bereavement: The crisis of meaning. *Death Studies, 25*, 51–66.

Whipple, E. E. (2006). Child abuse and neglect: Consequences of physical, sexual, and emotional abuse of children. In H. E. Fitzgerald, B. M. Lester, & B. Zuckerman (Eds.), *The crisis in youth mental health: Critical issues and effective programs: Vol. 1. Childhood disorders* (pp. 205–229). Westport, CT: Praeger.

Whisman, M. A., Uebelacker, L. A., Tolejko, N., Chatav, Y., & McKelvie, M. (2006). Marital discord and well-being in older adults: Is the association confounded by personality? *Psychology and Aging, 21*, 626–631.

Whitaker, D. J., Baker, C. K., & Arias, I. (2007). Interventions to prevent intimate partner violence. In L. S. Doll, S. E., Bonzo, D. A. Sleet, & J. A. Mercy (Eds.), *Handbook of injury and violence prevention* (pp. 203–221). New York: Springer Science + Business Media.

Whitbeck, L., Hoyt, D. R., & Huck, S. M. (1994). Early family relationships, intergenerational solidarity, and support provided to parents by their adult children. *Journal of Gerontology, 49*, 585–594.

Whitbourne, S. K. (1996). *The aging individual: Physical and psychological perspectives.* New York: Springer.

Whitbourne, S. K. (2001). The physical aging process in midlife: Interactions with psychological and sociocultural factors. In M. E. Lachman (Ed.), *Handbook of midlife development* (pp. 109–155). New York: Wiley.

Whitbourne, S. K. (2002). *The aging individual: Physical and psychological perspectives.* New York: Springer.

Whitbourne, S. K., & Willis, S. L. (2006). Preface. In S. K. Whitbourne & S. L. Willis (Eds.), *The baby boomers grow up* (pp. vii–ix). Mahwah, NJ: Erlbaum.

Whitbourne, S. K., Zuschlag, M. K., Elliot, L. B., & Waterman, A. S. (1992). Psychosocial development in adulthood: A 22-year sequential study. *Journal of Personality and Social Psychology, 63*, 260–271.

White, L. (2001). Sibling relationships over the life course: A panel analysis. *Journal of Marriage and Family, 63*, 555–568.

White, L. K. (1994). Coresidence and leaving home: Young adults and their parents. *Annual Review of Sociology, 20*, 81–102.

Whiteman, S. D., & Loken, E. (2006). Comparing analytic techniques to classify dyadic relationships: An example using siblings. *Journal of Marriage and Family, 68*, 1370–1382.

Whitesell, N. R., Mitchell, C. M., Spicer, P., and the Voices of Indian Teens Project Team. (2009). A longitudinal study of self-esteem, cultural identity, and academic success among American Indian adolescents. *Cultural Diversity and Ethnic Minority Psychology, 15*, 38–50.

Whiteside, M. F. (2006). Remarried systems. In L. Combrinck-Graham (Ed.), *Children in family contexts: Perspectives on treatment* (pp. 163–189). New York: Guilford.

Whiteside-Mansell, L., Bradley, R. H., Owen, M. T., Randolph, S. M., & Cauce, A. M. (2003). Parenting and children's behavior at 36 months: Equivalence between African-American and European-American mother–child dyads. *Parenting: Science and Practice, 3*, 197–234.

Whitlock, J. L., Powers, J. L., & Eckenrode, J. (2006). The virtual cutting edge: The Internet and adolescent self-injury. *Developmental Psychology, 42*, 407–417.

Whitmer, R. A., Gunderson, E. P., Quesenberry, C. P., Jr., Zhou, J., & Yaffe, K. (2007). Body mass index in midlife and risk of Alzheimer disease and vascular dementia. *Current Alzheimer Research, 4*, 103–109.

Wichmann, C., Coplan, R. J., & Daniels, T. (2004). The social cognitions of socially withdrawn children. *Social Development, 13*, 377–392.

Wichstrøm, L. (2006). Sexual orientation as a risk factor for bulimic symptoms. *International Journal of Eating Disorders, 39*, 448–453.

Wickens, A. P. (2001). Aging and the free radical theory. *Respiration Physiology, 128*, 379–391.

Wideen, M. F., O'Shea, T., Pye, I., & Ivany, G. (1997). High-stakes testing and the teaching of science. *Canadian Journal of Education, 22*, 428–444.

Wigfield, A., Battle, A., Keller, L. B., & Eccles, J. S. (2002). Sex differences in motivation, self-concept, career aspiration, and career choice: Implications for cognitive development. In A. McGillicuddy-De Lisi & R. De Lisi (Eds.), *Biology, society, and behavior: The development of sex differences in cognition* (pp. 93–124). Westport, CT: Ablex.

Wigfield, A., & Eccles, J. S. (1994). Children's competence beliefs, achievement values, and general self-esteem change across elementary and middle school. *Journal of Early Adolescence, 14*, 107–138.

Wigfield, A., Eccles, J. S., Schiefele, U., Roeser, R. W., & Davis-Kean, P. (2006). Development of achievement motivation. In N. Eisenberg (Ed.), *Handbook of child psychology: Vol. 3. Social, emotional, and personality development* (6th ed., pp. 933–1002). Hoboken, NJ: Wiley.

Wigfield, A., Eccles, J. S., Yoon, K. S., Harold, R. D., Arbreton, A. J., Freedman-Doan, C., & Blumenfeld, P. C. (1997). Changes in children's competence beliefs and subjective task values across the elementary school years: A three-year study. *Journal of Educational Psychology, 89,* 451–469.

Wilber, K. H., & McNeilly, D. P. (2001). Elder abuse and victimization. In J. E. Birren (Ed.), *Handbook of the psychology of aging* (pp. 569–591). San Diego: Academic Press.

Wilbur, J., Chandler, P. J., Dancy, B., & Lee, H. (2003). Correlates of physical activity in urban Midwestern African-American women. *American Journal of Preventive Medicine, 25,* 45–52.

Wilbur, J., Vassalo, A., Chandler, P., McDevitt, J., & Miller, A. M. (2005). Midlife women's adherence to home-based walking during maintenance. *Nursing Research, 54,* 33–40.

Wilcox, A. J., Weinberg, C. R., & Baird, D. D. (1995). Timing of sexual intercourse in relation to ovulation: Effects on the probability of conception, survival of the pregnancy, and sex of the baby. *New England Journal of Medicine, 333,* 1517–1519.

Wilke, C. J., & Thompson, C. A. (1993). First-year reentry women's perceptions of their classroom experiences. *Journal of the Freshman Year Experience, 5,* 69–90.

Wilkinson, K., Ross, E., & Diamond, A. (2003). Fast mapping of multiple words: Insights into when "the information provided" does and does not equal "the information perceived." *Applied Developmental Psychology, 24,* 739–762.

Wilkinson, R. B. (2004). The role of parental and peer attachment in the psychological health and self-esteem of adolescents. *Journal of Youth and Adolescence, 33,* 479–493.

Willatts, P. (1999). Development of means–end behavior in young infants: Pulling a support to retrieve a distant object. *Developmental Psychology, 35,* 651–667.

Wille, M. C., Weitz, B., Kerper, P., & Frazier, S. (2004). Advances in preconception genetic counseling. *Journal of Perinatal and Neonatal Nursing, 18,* 28–40.

Williams, C. (2006). Dilemmas in fetal medicine: Premature application of technology or responding to women's choice? *Sociology of Health and Illness, 28,* 1–20.

Williams, F. M. K., & Spector, T. D. (2006). Recent advances in the genetics of osteoporosis. *Musculoskeletal and Neuronal Interactions, 6,* 27–35.

Williams, J. M., & Currie, C. (2000). Self-esteem and physical development in early adolescence: Pubertal timing and body image. *Journal of Early Adolescence, 20,* 129–149.

Williams, K. (2003). Has the future of marriage arrived? A contemporary examination of gender, marriage, and psychological well-being. *Journal of Health and Social Relationships, 44,* 470–487.

Williams, K., & Dunne-Bryant, A. (2006). Divorce and adult psychological well-being: Clarifying the role of gender and age. *Journal of Marriage and Family, 68,* 1178–1196.

Williams, N., & Torrez, D. J. (1998). Grandparenthood among Hispanics. In M. E. Szinovacz (Ed.), *Handbook on grandparenthood* (pp. 87–96). Westport, CT: Greenwood Press.

Williams, P. E., Weis, L. G., & Rolfhus, E. (2003). *WISC-IV: Theoretical model and test blueprint.* San Antonio, TX: Psychological Corporation.

Williams, S., & Dale, J. (2006). The effectiveness of treatment for depression/depressive symptoms in adults with cancer: A systematic review. *British Journal of Cancer, 94,* 372–390.

Williamson, J., Softas-Nall, B., & Miller, J. (2003). Grandmothers raising grandchildren: An exploration of their experiences and emotions. *Counseling and Therapy for Couples with Families, 11,* 23–32.

Willinger, M., Ko, C.-W., Hoffman, H. J., Kessler, R. C., & Corwin, M. J. (2003). Trends in infant bed sharing in the United States. *Archives of Pediatrics and Adolescent Medicine, 157,* 43–49.

Willis, S. L., & Schaie, K. W. (1999). Intellectual functioning in midlife. In S. L. Willis & J. D. Reid (Eds.),

Life in the middle (pp. 105–146). San Diego: Academic Press.

Willis, S. L., Tennstedt, S. L., Marsiske, M., Ball, K., Elias, J., & Koepke, K. M. (2006). Long-term effects of cognitive training on everyday functional outcomes in older adults. *Journal of the American Medical Association, 296,* 2805–2814.

Willoughby, J., Kupersmidt, J. B., & Bryant, D. (2001). Overt and covert dimensions of antisocial behavior. *Journal of Abnormal Child Psychology, 29,* 177–187.

Wilmoth, J. M. (2001). Living arrangements among older immigrants in the United States. *Gerontologist, 41,* 228–238.

Wilson, D. K., Kirtland, K. A., Ainsworth, B. E., & Addy, C. L. (2004). Socioeconomic status and perceptions of access and safety for physical activity. *Annals of Behavioral Medicine, 28,* 20–28.

Wilson, R. S., Arnold, S. E., Schneider, J. A., Kelley, J. F., Tang, Y., & Bennett, D. A. (2006). Chronic psychological distress and risk of Alzheimer's disease in old age. *Neuroepidemiology, 27,* 143–153.

Wilson, R. S., Beckett, L. A., Evans, D. A., & Bennett, D. A. (2003). Terminal decline in cognitive function. *Neurology, 60,* 1782–1787.

Windsor, T. D., Anstey, K. J., & Rodgers, B. (2008). Volunteering and psychological well-being among young–old adults: How much is too much? *Gerontologist, 48,* 59–70.

Wingfield, A., & Stine-Morrow, E. A. L. (2000). Language and speech. In F. I. M. Craik & T. A. Salthouse (Eds.), *Handbook of aging and cognition* (2nd ed., pp. 359–416). Mahwah, NJ: Erlbaum.

Wink, P. (2006). Who is afraid of death? Religiousness, spirituality, and death anxiety in late adulthood. *Journal of Religion, Spirituality and Aging, 18,* 93–110.

Wink, P. (2007). Everyday life in the Third Age. In J. B. James & P. Wink (Eds.), *Annual review of gerontology and geriatrics* (Vol. 26, pp. 243–261). New York: Springer.

Wink, P., & Dillon, M. (2002). Spiritual development across the adult life course: Findings from a longitudinal study. *Journal of Adult Development, 9,* 79–94.

Wink, P., & Dillon, M. (2003). Religiousness, spirituality, and psychosocial functioning in late adulthood: Findings from a longitudinal study. *Psychology and Aging, 18,* 916–924.

Wink, P., & Helson, R. (1993). Personality change in women and their partners. *Journal of Personality and Social Psychology, 65,* 597–605.

Wink, P., & James, J. B. (2007). Is the Third Age the crown of life? In J. B. James & P. Wink (Eds.), *Annual review of gerontology and geriatrics* (Vol. 26, pp. 305–325). New York: Springer.

Wink, P., & Schiff, B. (2002). To review or not to review? The role of personality and life events in life review and adaptation to older age. In J. D. Webster & B. K. Haight (Eds.), *Critical advances in reminiscence work* (pp. 44–75). New York: Springer.

Wink, P., & Scott, J. (2005). Does religiousness buffer against the fear of death and dying in late adulthood? Findings from a longitudinal study. *Journal of Gerontology, 60B,* P207–P214.

Winn, R., & Newton, N. (1982). Sexual activity in aging: A study of 106 cultures. *Archives of Sexual Behavior, 11,* 283–298.

Winner, E. (1986, August). Where pelicans kiss seals. *Psychology Today, 20*(8), 25–35.

Winner, E. (1988). *The point of words: Children's understanding of metaphor and irony.* Cambridge, MA: Harvard University Press.

Winner, E. (1996). *Gifted children: Myths and realities.* New York: Basic Books.

Winner, E. (2000). The origins and ends of giftedness. *American Psychologist, 55,* 159–169.

Winner, E. (2003). Creativity and talent. In M. H. Bornstein, L. Davidson, C. L. M. Keyes, K. A. Moore, & the Center for Child Well-Being (Eds.),

Well-being: Positive development across the life course (pp. 371–380). Mahwah, NJ: Erlbaum.

Winsler, A. (2009). Still talking to ourselves after all these years: A review of current research on private speech. In A. Winsler, C. Fernyhough, & I. Montero (Eds.), *Private speech, executive functioning, and the development of self-regulation.* New York: Cambridge University Press.

Winsler, A., Fernyhough, C., & Montero, I. (2009). *Private speech, executive functioning, and the development of verbal self-regulation.* New York: Cambridge University Press.

Winsler, A., Naglieri, J., & Manfra, L. (2006). Children's search strategies and accompanying verbal and motor strategic behavior: Developmental trends and relations with task performance among children age 5 to 17. *Cognitive Development, 21,* 232–248.

Winslow, R. D., Mehta, D., & Fuster, V. (2005). Sudden cardiac death: Mechanisms, therapies and challenges. *Cardiovascular Medicine, 2,* 352–360.

Winter, D. G., Torges, C. M., Stewart, A. J., Henderson-King, D., & Henderson-King, E. (2007). Pathways toward the Third Age: Studying a cohort from the "golden age." In J. B. James & P. Wink (Eds.), *The crown of life: Dynamics of the early postretirement period* (pp. 103–130). New York: Springer.

Wintergest, E. S., Maggini, S., & Hornig, D. H. (2007). Contribution of selected vitamins and trace elements to immune function. *Annals of Nutrition and Metabolism, 51,* 301–323.

Wissink, I. B., Deković, M., & Meijer, A. M. (2006). Parenting behavior, quality of the parent–adolescent relationship, and adolescent functioning in four ethnic groups. *Journal of Early Adolescence, 26,* 133–159.

Witherington, D. C. (2005). The development of prospective grasping control between 5 and 7 months: A longitudinal study. *Infancy, 7,* 143–161.

Wojciechowski, W. C. (1998). Issues in caring for older lesbians. *Journal of Gerontological Nursing, 24,* 28–33.

Wolak, J., Finkelhor, D., Mitchell, K. J., & Ybarra, M. L. (2008). Online "predators" and their victims: Myths, realities, and implications for prevention and treatment. *American Psychologist, 63,* 111–128.

Wolak, J., Mitchell, K. J., & Finkelhor, D. (2003). Escaping or connecting? Characteristics of youth who form close online relationships. *Journal of Adolescence, 26,* 105–119.

Wolak, J., Mitchell, K., & Finkelhor, D. (2007). Unwanted and wanted exposure to online pornography in a national sample of youth Internet users. *Pediatrics, 119,* 247–257.

Wolchik, S. A., Wilcox, K. L., Tein, J.-Y., & Sandler, I. N. (2000). Maternal acceptance and consistency of discipline as buffers of divorce stressors on children's psychological adjustment problems. *Journal of Abnormal Child Psychology, 28,* 87–102.

Wolfe, D. A., Scott, K., Wekerle, C., & Pittman, A. (2001). Child maltreatment: Risk of adjustment problems and dating violence in adolescence. *Journal of the American Academy of Child and Adolescent Psychiatry, 40,* 282–289.

Wolfe, V. V. (2006). Child sexual abuse. In E. J. Mash & R. A. Barkley (Eds.), *Treatment of childhood disorders* (3rd ed., pp. 647–727). New York: Guilford.

Wolff, P. H. (1966). The causes, controls and organization of behavior in the neonate. *Psychological Issues, 5*(1, Serial No. 17).

Wolff, P. H., & Fesseha, G. (1999). The orphans of Eritrea: A five-year follow-up study. *Journal of Child Psychology and Psychiatry and Allied Disciplines, 40,* 1231–1237.

Wolfinger, N. H. (2000). Beyond the intergenerational transmission of divorce: Do people replicate the patterns of marital instability they grew up with? *Journal of Family Issues, 21,* 1061–1086.

Wolfinger, N. H. (2005). *Understanding the divorce cycle.* New York: Cambridge University Press.

Wolinsky, F. D., Unverzagt, F. W., Smith, D. M., Jones R., Stoddard, A., & Tennstedt, S. L. (2006). The ACTIVE cognitive training trail and health-related quality of life: Protection that lasts for 5 years. *Journal of Gerontology, 61A,* 1324–1329.

Wolkove, N., Elkholy, O., Baltzan, M., & Palaycw, M. (2007). Sleep and aging: 1. Sleep disorders commonly found in older people. *Canadian Medical Association Journal, 17,* 1299–1304.

Women's Health Initiative. (2002). Risks and benefits of estrogen plus progestin in healthy post-menopausal women: Principal results from the Women's Health Initiative randomized control trial. *Journal of the American Medical Association, 288,* 321–333.

Women's Health Initiative. (2004). Effects of conjugated equine estrogen in postmenopausal women with hysterectomy: The Women's Health Initiative Randomized Controlled Trial. *Journal of the American Medical Association, 291,* 1701–1712.

Wong, C. A., Eccles, J. S., & Sameroff, A. (2003). The influence of ethnic discrimination and ethnic identification on African American adolescents' school and socioemotional adjustment. *Journal of Personality, 71,* 1197–1232.

Wong, M. M., Nigg, J. T., Zucker, R. A., Puttler, L. I., Fitzgerald, H. E., Jester, J. M., Glass, J. M., & Adams, K. (2006). Behavioral control and resiliency in the onset of alcohol and illicit drug use: A prospective study from preschool to adolescence. *Child Development, 77,* 1016–1033.

Wood, E., Desmarais, S., & Gugula, S. (2002). The impact of parenting experience on gender stereotyped toy play of children. *Sex Roles, 47,* 39–49.

Wood, J. J., Emmerson, N. A., & Cowan, P. A. (2004). Is early attachment security carried forward into relationships with preschool peers? *British Journal of Developmental Psychology, 22,* 245–253.

Wood, J. M. (2002). Aging, driving and vision. *Clinical and Experimental Optometry, 85,* 214–220.

Wood, W., & Eagly, A. H. (2000). Once again, the origins of sex differences. *American Psychologist, 55,* 1062–1063.

Woods, B. (2008). Suicide and attempted suicide in later life. In B. Woods & L. Clare (Eds.), *Handbook of the clinical psychology of ageing* (2nd ed., pp. 111–119). Chichester, UK: Wiley.

Woodward, J., & Ono, Y. (2004). Mathematics and academic diversity in Japan. *Journal of Learning Disabilities, 37,* 74–82.

Woolf, L. M. (2001). Gay and lesbian aging. *SIECUS Report, 30,* 16–21.

Woolley, J. D. (1997). Thinking about fantasy: Are children fundamentally different thinkers and believers from adults? *Child Development, 68,* 991–1011.

Worden, J. W. (2000). Toward an appropriate death. In T. A. Rando (Ed.), *Clinical dimensions of anticipatory mourning* (pp. 267–277). Champaign, IL: Research Press.

Worden, J. W. (2009). *Grief counseling and grief therapy* (4th ed.). New York: Springer.

World Cancer Research Fund/American Institute for Cancer Research. (2007). *Food, nutrition, physical activity, and the prevention of cancer: A global perspective.* Washington, DC: American Institute for Cancer Research.

World Education Services. (2007). *World education database.* Retrieved from www.wes.org

World Federation of Right to Die Societies. (2006). Public opinion. Retrieved from www.worldrtd.net

World Health Organization. (2000). Violence against women information pack. Retrieved from http://www.who.int/frh-whd/VAW/infopack/English

World Health Organization. (2002). *World report on violence and health.* Geneva: Author.

World Health Organization. (2005). *WHO Multi-Country Study on Women's Health and Domestic Violence Against Women.* Geneva: Author.

World Health Organization. (2008a). *The global burden of disease: 2004.* Geneva, Switzerland: Author.

World Health Organization. (2008b). The World Health Organization's Infant Feeding Recommendation. Retrieved from www.who.int/nutrition/topics/infantfeeding_recommendation/en/index.html

World Health Organization. (2008c). *World report on child injury prevention.* Geneva, Switzerland: Author.

World Health Organization. (2009). *Estimated healthy life expectancy (HALE) at birth and age 60, by sex, WHO member states, 2002.* Retrieved from www.who.int/whosis/indicators/2007HALE0/en

World Press Review. (2004). Obesity: A worldwide issue. Retrieved from www.worldpress.org/Africa/1961.cfm

Worrell, F. C., & Gardner-Kitt, D. L. (2006). The relationship between racial and ethnic identity in black adolescents: The cross-racial identity scale and the multigroup ethnic identity measure. *Identity, 6,* 293–315.

Wray, L. A., Alwin, D. F., & McCammon, R. J. (2005). Social status and risky health behaviors: Results from the health and retirement study. *Journal of Gerontology, 60B,* S85–S92.

Wray, S. (2007). Health, exercise, and well-being: The experiences of midlife women from diverse ethnic backgrounds. *Social Theory and Health, 5,* 126–144.

Wright, B. C. (2006). On the emergence of the discriminative mode for transitive inference. *European Journal of Cognitive Psychology, 18,* 776–800.

Wright, J. C., Huston, A. C., Murphy, K. C., St. Peters, M., Pinon, M., Scantlin, R., & Kotler, J. (2001). The relations of early television viewing to school readiness and vocabulary of children from low-income families: The Early Window Project. *Child Development, 72,* 1347–1366.

Wright, K. (2003). Relationships with death: The terminally ill talk about dying. *Journal of Marital and Family Therapy, 29,* 439–454.

Wright, M., Wood, J., Lynch, T., & Clark, D. (2008). Mapping levels of palliative care development: A global view. *Journal of Pain and Symptom Management, 35,* 469–485.

Wright, M. O., & Masten, A. S. (2005). Resilience processes in development. In S. Goldstein & R. B. Brooks (Eds.), *Handbook of resilience in children* (pp. 17–37). New York: Springer.

Wright, V. C., Chang, J., Jeng, G., & Macaluso, M. (2008). Assisted reproductive technology surveillance—United States, 2005. *Morbidity and Mortality Weekly Report, 57*(5), 1–23.

Wright, W. E., & Shay, J. W. (2005). Telomere biology in aging and cancer. *Journal of the American Geriatric Society, 53,* S292–S294.

Wrotniak, B. H., Epstein, L. H., Raluch, R. A., & Roemmich, J. N. (2004). Parent weight change as a predictor of child weight change in family-based behavioral obesity treatment. *Archives of Pediatric and Adolescent Medicine, 158,* 342–347.

Wu, A. M. S., Tang, C. S. K., & Kwok, T. C. Y. (2002). Death anxiety among Chinese elderly people in Hong Kong. *Journal of Aging and Health, 14,* 42–56.

Wu, L. L., Bumpass, L. L., & Musick, K. (2001). Historical and life course trajectories of nonmarital childbearing. In L. L. Wu & B. Wolfe (Eds.), *Out of wedlock: Causes and consequences of nonmarital fertility* (pp. 3–48). New York: Russell Sage Foundation.

Wu, T., Mendola, P., & Buck, G. M. (2002). Ethnic differences in the presence of secondary sex characteristics and menarche among U.S. girls: The Third National Health and Nutrition Examination Survey, 1988–1994. *Pediatrics, 110,* 752–757.

Wu, W., Brickman, A. M., Luchsinger, J., Ferrazzano, P., Pichiule, P., Yoshita, M., & Brown, T. (2008). The brain in the age of old: The hippocampal formation is targeted differentially by diseases of late life. *Annals of Neurology, 64,* 698–706.

Wu, Y. (2006). Overweight and obesity in China. *British Medical Journal, 333,* 362–363.

Wyatt, J. M., & Carlo, G. (2002). What will my parents think? Relations among adolescents' expected parental reactions, prosocial moral reasoning, and prosocial and antisocial behaviors. *Journal of Adolescent Research, 16,* 646–666.

Wynn, K., Bloom, P., & Chiang, W.-C. (2002). Enumeration of collective entities by 5-month-old infants. *Cognition, 83,* B55–B62.

Wynne-Edwards, K. E. (2001). Hormonal changes in mammalian fathers. *Hormones and Behavior, 40,* 139–145.

Wysong, A., Lee, P. P., & Sloan, F. A. (2009). Longitudinal incidence of adverse outcomes of age-related macular degeneration. *Archives of Ophthalmology, 127,* 320–327.

X

Xu, X., & Lai, S.-C. (2004). Gender ideologies, marital roles, and marital quality in Taiwan. *Journal of Family Issues, 25,* 318–355.

Xue, Y., & Meisels, S. J. (2004). Early literacy instruction and learning in kindergarten: Evidence from the early childhood longitudinal study—kindergarten classes of 1998–1999. *American Educational Research Journal, 41,* 191–229.

Y

Yaari, R., & Corey-Bloom, J. (2007). Alzheimer's disease. *Seminars in Neurology, 27,* 32–41.

Yaffe, K., Blackwell, T., Kanaya, A. M., Davidowitz, N., Barrett-Connor, E., & Krueger, K. (2004). Diabetes, impaired fasting glucose, and development of cognitive impairment in older women. *Neurology, 63,* 658–663.

Yaffe, K., Fox, P., Newcomer, R., Sands, L., Lindquist, K., Dane, K., & Covinsky, K. E. (2002). Patient and caregiver characteristics and nursing home placement in patients with dementia. *Journal of the American Medical Association, 287,* 2090–2097.

Yale, M. E., Messinger, D. S., Cobo-Lewis, A. B., Oller, D. K., & Eilers, R. E. (1999). An event-based analysis of the coordination of early infant vocalizations and facial actions. *Developmental Psychology, 35,* 505–513.

Yamamoto, K. (2004). The care of the dying and the grieving in Japan. In J. D. Morgan & P. Laungani (Eds.), *Death and bereavement around the world: Vol. 4. Death and bereavement in Asia, Australia, and New Zealand* (pp. 101–107). Amityville, NY: Baywood Publishing Company.

Yang, C. (2008, April). *The influence of one-child policy on child rearing, family, and society in post-Mao China.* Invited address, Illinois State University.

Yang, C.-K., & Hahn, H.-M. (2002). Cosleeping in young Korean children. *Developmental and Behavioral Pediatrics, 23,* 151–157.

Yao, L., & Robert, S. A. (2008). The contributions of race, individual socioeconomic status, and neighborhood socioeconomic context to the self-rated health trajectories and mortality of older adults. *Research on Aging, 30,* 251–273.

Yap, M. B. H., Allen, N. B., & Ladouceur, C. D. (2008). Maternal socialization of positive affect: The impact of invalidation on adolescent emotion regulation and depressive symptomatology. *Child Development, 79,* 1415–1431.

Yates, L. B., Djousée, L., Kurth, T., Buring, J. E., & Gaziano, J. M. (2008). Exceptional longevity in men: Modifiable factors associated with survival and function to age 90 years. *Archives of Internal Medicine, 168,* 284–290.

Yates, T. M., Egeland, B., & Sroufe, L. A. (2003). Rethinking resilience: A developmental process perspective. In S. S. Luthar (Ed.), *Resilience and vulnerability: Adaptation in the context of childhood adversities* (pp. 243–266). New York: Cambridge University Press.

Yeh, C. J., Kim, A. B., Pituc, S. T., & Atkins, M. (2008). Poverty, loss, and resilience: The story of Chinese immigrant youth. *Journal of Counseling Psychology, 55,* 34–48.

Yehuda, R., Engel, S. M., Brand, S. R., Seckl, J., Marcus, S. M., & Berkowitz, G. S. (2005). Transgenerational effects of posttraumatic stress disorder in babies of mothers exposed to the World Trade Center attacks during pregnancy. *Journal of Clinical Endocrinology and Metabolism, 90,* 4115–4118.

Yeung, D. Y., Fung, H. H., & Lang, F. R. (2008). Self-construal moderates age differences in social network characteristics. *Psychology and Aging, 23,* 222–226.

Yeung, W. (1996). Buddhism, death, and dying. In J. K. Parry & A. S. Ryan (Eds.), *A cross-cultural look at death, dying, and religion* (pp. 74–83). Chicago: Nelson-Hall.

Yip, R., Scanlon, K., & Trowbridge, F. (1993). Trends and patterns in height and weight status of low-income U.S. children. *Critical Reviews in Food Science and Nutrition, 33,* 409–421.

Yirmiya, N., Erel, O., Shaked, M., & Solomonica-Levi, D. (1998). Meta-analyses comparing theory of mind abilities of individuals with autism, individuals with mental retardation, and normally developing individuals. *Psychological Bulletin, 124,* 283–307.

Yonas, A., Elieff, C., & Arterberry, M. E. (2002). Emergence of sensitivity to pictorial depth cues: Charting development in individual infants. *Infant Behavior and Development, 25,* 295–314.

Yoshida, H., & Smith, L. B. (2003). Known and novel noun extensions: Attention at two levels of abstraction. *Child Development, 74,* 564–577.

Youn, G., Knight, B. G., Jeon, H., & Benton, D. (1999). Differences in familism values and caregiving outcomes among Korean, Korean American, and White American dementia caregivers. *Psychology and Aging, 14,* 355–364.

Young, H. M. (1998). Moving to congregate housing: The last chosen home. *Journal of Aging Studies, 12,* 149–165.

Young, J. F., & Mroczek, D. K. (2003). Predicting intraindividual self-concept trajectories during adolescence. *Journal of Adolescence, 26,* 589–603.

Young, T., Rabago, D., Zgierska, A., Austin, D., & Finn, L. (2002). Objective and subjective sleep quality in premenopausal, perimenopausal, and post-menopausal women in the Wisconsin Sleep Cohort Study. *Epidemiology, 26,* 667–672.

Youngblade, L. M., & Dunn, J. (1995). Individual differences in young children's pretend play with mother and sibling: Links to relationships and understanding of other people's feelings and beliefs. *Child Development, 66,* 1472–1492.

Young-Hyman, D., Tanofsky-Kraff, M., Yanovski, S. Z., Keil, M., Cohen, M. L., & Peyrot, M. (2006). Psychological status and weight-related distress in overweight or at-risk-for-overweight children. *Obesity, 14,* 2249–2258.

Yu, B. P. (2006). Why calorie restriction would work for human longevity. *Biogerontology, 7,* 179–182.

Yu, S., Yarnell, J. W. G., Sweetnam, P. M., & Murray, L. (2003). What level of physical activity protects against premature cardiovascular death? The Caerphilly Study. *Heart, 89,* 502–506.

Yuan, A. S. V., & Hamilton, H. A. (2006). Stepfather involvement and adolescent well-being: Do mothers and nonresidential fathers matter? *Journal of Family Issues, 27,* 1191–1213.

Yunger, J. L., Carver, P. R., & Perry, D. G. (2004). Does gender identity influence children's psychological well-being? *Developmental Psychology, 40,* 572–582.

Z

Zacks, R. T., & Hasher, L. (2006) Aging and long-term memory: Deficits are not inevitable. In E. Bialystok & F. I. M. Craik (Eds.), *Lifespan cognition: Mechanisms of change* (pp. 162–177). New York: Oxford University Press.

Zahn-Waxler, C., Radke-Yarrow, M., & King, R. M. (1979). Child-rearing and children's prosocial initiations toward victims of distress. *Child Development, 50,* 319–330.

Zahn-Waxler, C., & Robinson, J. (1995). Empathy and guilt: Early origins of feelings of responsibility. In J. P. Tangney & K. W. Fischer (Eds.), *Self-conscious emotions* (pp. 143–173). New York: Guilford.

Zahn-Waxler, C., Schiro, K., Robinson, J. L., Emde, R. N., & Schmitz, S. (2001). Empathy and prosocial patterns in young MZ and DZ twins: Development and genetic and environmental influences. In R. N. Emde & J. K. Hewitt (Eds.), *Infancy to early childhood: Genetic and environmental influences on developmental change* (pp. 141–162). New York: Oxford University Press.

Zakowski, S. G., Hall, M. H., Klein, L. C., & Baum, A. (2001). Appraised control, coping, and stress in a community sample: A test of the goodness-of-fit hypothesis. *Annals of Behavioral Medicine, 23,* 158–165.

Zane, N., & Yeh, M. (2002). The use of culturally based variables in assessment: Studies on loss of face. In K. Kurasaki, S. Okazaki, & S. Sue (Eds.), *Asian American mental health: Assessment theories and methods* (pp. 123–138). Dordrecht, Netherlands: Kluwer Academic.

Zapf, D., Seifert, C., Schmutte, B., Mertini, H., & Hotz, M. (2001). Emotion work and job stressors and their effects on burnout. *Psychology and Health, 16,* 527–545.

Zaretsky, M. D. (2003). Communication between identical twins: Health behavior and social factors are associated with longevity that is greater among identical than fraternal U.S. World War II veteran twins. *Journal of Gerontology, 58,* 566–572.

Zarit, S. H., & Eggebeen, D. J. (2002). Parent–child relationships in adulthood and later years. In M. H. Bornstein (Ed.), *Handbook of parenting, Vol. 1* (2nd ed., pp. 135–161). Mahwah, NJ: Erlbaum.

Zaslow, M. J., Weinfield, N. S., Gallagher, M., Hair, E. C., Ogawa, J. R., Egeland, B., Tabors, P. O., & De Temple, J. M. (2006). Longitudinal prediction of child outcomes from differing measures of parenting in a low-income sample. *Developmental Psychology, 42,* 27–37.

Zelazo, N. A., Zelazo, P. R., Cohen, K. M., & Zelazo, P. D. (1993). Specificity of practice effects on elementary neuromotor patterns. *Developmental Psychology, 29,* 686–691.

Zelazo, P. D., Frye, D., & Rapus, T. (1996). An age-related dissociation between knowing rules and using them. *Cognitive Development, 11,* 37–63.

Zelazo, P. D., Muller, U., Frye, D., & Marcovitch, S. (2003). The development of executive function: Cognitive complexity and control—revised. *Monographs of the Society for Research in Child Development, 68*(3), 93–119.

Zeldin, A. L., & Pajares, F. (2000). Against the odds: Self-efficacy beliefs of women in mathematical, scientific, and technological careers. *American Educational Research Journal, 37,* 215–246.

Zeman, J., Shipman, K., & Suveg, C. (2002). Anger and sadness regulation: Predictions to internalizing and externalizing symptoms in children. *Journal of Clinical Child and Adolescent Psychology, 31,* 393–398.

Zenger, T., & Lawrence, B. (1989). Organizational demography: The differential effects of age and tenure distributions on technical communication. *Academy of Management Journal, 32,* 353–376.

Zeskind, P. S., & Barr, R. G. (1997). Acoustic characteristics of naturally occurring cries of infants with "colic." *Child Development, 68,* 394–403.

Zeskind, P. S., & Lester, B. M. (2001). Analysis of infant crying. In L. T. Singer & P. S. Zeskind (Eds.), *Biobehavioral assessment of the infant* (pp. 149–166). New York: Guilford.

Zhan, H. J., & Montgomery, R. J. V. (2003). Gender and elder care in China: The influence of filial piety and structural constraints. *Gender and Society, 17,* 209–229.

Zhang, Q. F. (2004). Economic transition and new patterns of parent–adult child coresidence in urban China. *Journal of Marriage and Family, 66,* 1231–1245.

Zhou, M., & Bankston, C. L. (1998). *Growing up American: How Vietnamese children adapt to life in the United States.* New York: Russell Sage Foundation.

Zhou, M., & Xiong, S. (2005). The multifaceted American experiences of the children of Asian immigrants: Lessons for segmented assimilation. *Ethnic and Racial Studies, 28,* 1119–1152.

Zhou, X., Huang, J., Wang, Z., Wang, B., Zhao, Z., Yang, L., & Zheng-zheng, Y. (2006). Parent–child interaction and children's number learning. *Early Child Development and Care, 176,* 763–775.

Zielinski, D. S., & Bradshaw, C. P. (2006). Ecological influences on the sequelae of child maltreatment: A review of the literature. *Child Maltreatment, 11,* 49–62.

Zimmer-Gembeck, M. J., Siebenbruner, J., & Collins, W. A. (2001). Diverse aspects of dating: Associations with psychosocial functioning from early to middle adolescence. *Journal of Adolescence, 24,* 313–336.

Zimmerman, C. (2005). *The development of scientific reasoning skills: What psychologists contribute to an understanding of elementary science learning.* Report to the National Research Council, Committee on Science Learning Kindergarten through Eighth Grade. Normal, IL: Illinois State University.

Zimmerman, C. (2007). The development of scientific thinking skills in elementary and middle school. *Developmental Review, 27,* 172–223.

Zimmerman, F. J., Christakis, D. A., & Meltzoff, A. N. (2007). Television and DVD/video viewing in children younger than 2 years. *Archives of Pediatrics and Adolescent Medicine, 161,* 473–479.

Zimmerman, L. K., & Stansbury, K. (2004). The influence of emotion regulation, level of shyness, and habituation on the neuroendocrine response of three-year-old children. *Psychoneuroendocrinology, 29,* 973–982.

Zimmerman, P., & Becker-Stoll, F. (2002). Stability of attachment representations during adolescence: The influence of ego-identity status. *Journal of Adolescence, 25,* 107–124.

Zubenko, G. S., Zubenko, W. N., McPherson, S., Spoor, E., Marin, D. B., & Farlow, M. R. (2003). A collaborative study of the emergence and clinical features of the major depressive syndrome of Alzheimer's disease. *American Journal of Psychiatry, 160,* 857–866.

Zucker, A. N., Ostrove, J. M., & Stewart, A. J. (2002). College-educated women's personality development in adulthood: Perceptions and age differences. *Psychology and Aging, 17,* 236–244.

Zucker, K. J. (2006). "I'm half-boy, half-girl": Play psychotherapy and parent counseling for gender identity disorder. In R. L. Spitzer, M. B. First, J. B. W. Williams, & M. Gibbon (Eds.), *DSM-IV-TR Casebook: Vol. 2. Experts tell how they treated their own patients* (pp. 322–334). Washington, DC: American Psychiatric Publishing.

Zukow-Goldring, P. (2002). Sibling caregiving. In M. H. Bornstein (Ed.), *Handbook of parenting: Vol. 3* (2nd ed., pp. 253–286). Hillsdale, NJ: Erlbaum.

Zwart, M. (2007). The Dutch system of perinatal care. *Midwifery Today with International Midwife, 81*(Spring), 46.

Name Index

Italic n following page number indicates source for an illustration or figure.

Subject Index

Alphabetization is letter-by-letter (e.g., "Genes" precedes "Gene therapy").